HAMPTON YACHT GROUP

Endurance 750
LONG RANGE CRUISER
4 STATEROOMS | 6 HEADS

Unsurpassed
QUALITY. FINISH. FIT. EXPERIENCE.

Endurance 658L
LONG RANGE CRUISER

4 STATEROOMS | 4 HEADS

Endurance 590
NEW MODEL

3 STATEROOMS | 2 HEADS

HAMPTON 650
LUXURY MOTORYACHT

3 STATEROOMS | 3 HEADS

901 FAIRVIEW AVE N #A150 | SEATTLE, WA 98109
SEATTLE@HAMPTONYACHTGROUP.COM | 206.623.5200 | WWW.HAMPTONYACHTGROUP.COM

Waggoner Guide Region Map

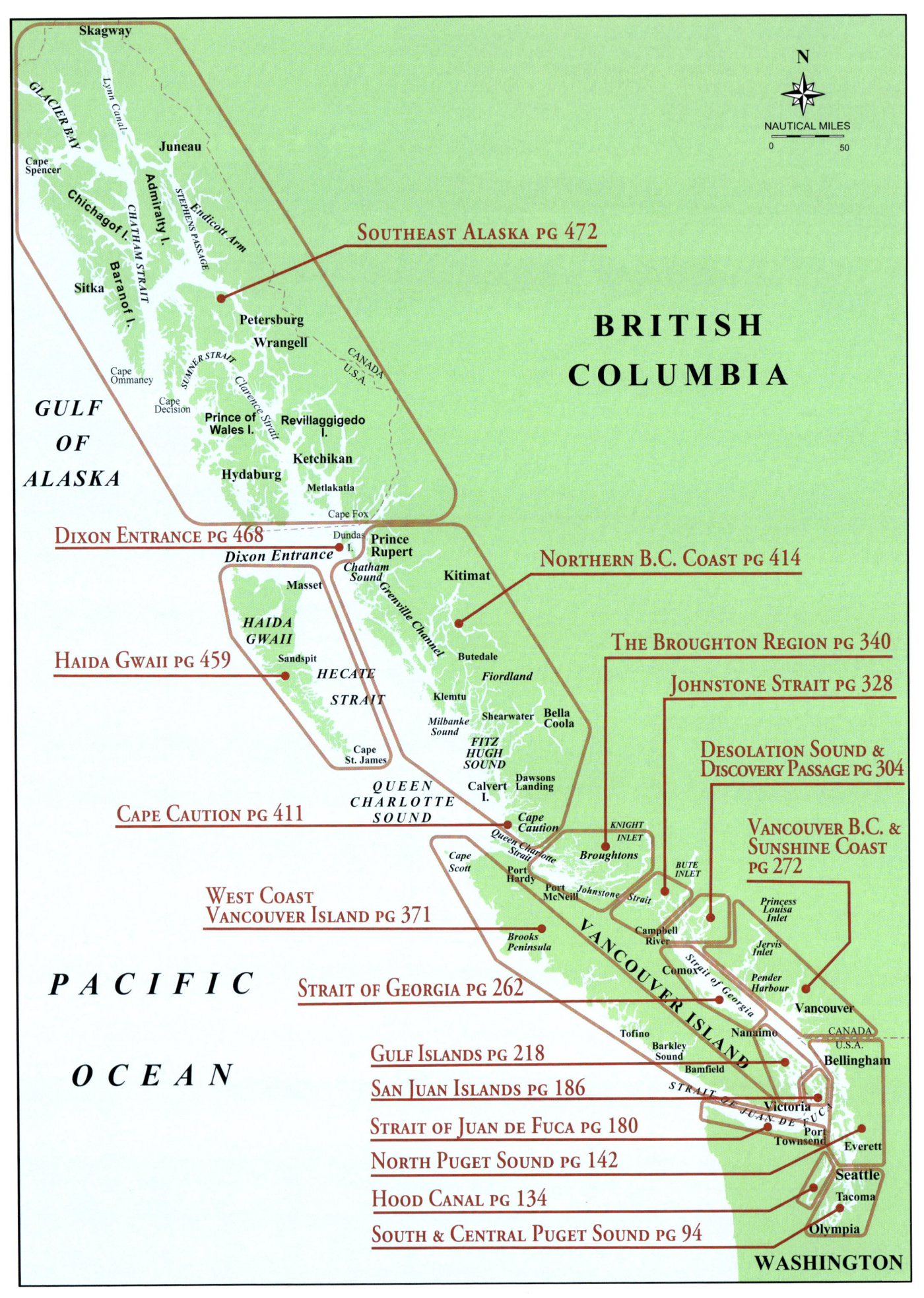

BRITISH COLUMBIA

GULF OF ALASKA

PACIFIC OCEAN

WASHINGTON

- Southeast Alaska pg 472
- Dixon Entrance pg 468
- Northern B.C. Coast pg 414
- Haida Gwaii pg 459
- The Broughton Region pg 340
- Johnstone Strait pg 328
- Desolation Sound & Discovery Passage pg 304
- Cape Caution pg 411
- Vancouver B.C. & Sunshine Coast pg 272
- West Coast Vancouver Island pg 371
- Strait of Georgia pg 262
- Gulf Islands pg 218
- San Juan Islands pg 186
- Strait of Juan de Fuca pg 180
- North Puget Sound pg 142
- Hood Canal pg 134
- South & Central Puget Sound pg 94

2 www.WaggonerGuide.com

Our cover photo features a sailboat passing historic Fisgard Lighthouse at Esquimalt Harbour on Vancouver Island. The harbour is home to Canada's Pacific Coast naval base. The lighthouse is on Fisgard Island which is part of the Fort Rodd Hill National Historic Site open to the public.
Cover Photo by Lorena Landon
Cover design by graphic artist Mariah Wakeling.

2023 WAGGONER CRUISING GUIDE

TABLE OF CONTENTS

5	Messages from the Editors
6	Field Correspondents
7	What's New In The 2023 Waggoner
8	Waggoner and The Waggoner Cruising Guide
10	How To Cruise the Pacific Northwest
18	U.S. and Canadian Customs Information
24	Marine Weather
33	VHF Radio Procedures & Channels
36, 37	Tides, Currents and Tidal Rapids
39	State and Provincial Parks and Public Wharfs
40, 43	About Anchoring and Rafting Protocol
44, 47	Chartering and Flotilla Cruising
49	Cellular, Internet & Satellite Communications
55	Charts and Chartplotters
59	Rules of the Road
60	Buoys, Beacons and Ranges
62	Underway In Low Visibility
64	Vessel Traffic Service
66	Traditional Territories In B.C.
71	Viewing Whales and Marine Mammals
72	Fishing and Shellfish Collecting
74	Floatplane Travel
76	Emergencies, Contingencies, & Security
80	2023 Theme - *Dream Itineraries*
94 - 472	Cruising Areas
512	Reference Pages
516	Index to Places
527	Advertiser Index

CRUISING AREAS

94	South and Central Puget Sound
134	Hood Canal
142	North Puget Sound
180	Strait of Juan de Fuca
186	San Juan Islands
218	Gulf Islands
262	Strait of Georgia
272	Vancouver B.C. and Sunshine Coast
304	Desolation Sound and Discovery Passage
328	Johnstone Strait
340	The Broughton Region
371	West Coast of Vancouver Island
411	Cape Caution
414	Northern B.C. Coast
459	Haida Gwaii
468	Dixon Entrance
472	Southeast Alaska

Scan This QR code for the latest.

tinyurl.com/WG22xCh01

We want to hear from you!

Your comments, suggestions and corrections are welcomed. We appreciate hearing from you, our valued readers of this publication.

You are invited to provide suggestions for inclusion in the Waggoner of your favorite anchorages and unique discoveries. Our readers are interested in your experiences and tips, which may serve as an article of interest or important news item. Send us your suggestions, questions, or experiences to **info@waggonerguide.com**

CAUTION

This book was designed to provide experienced skippers with cruising information about the waters covered. While great effort has been taken to make the Waggoner Cruising Guide complete and accurate, it is possible that oversights, differences of interpretation, and factual errors will be found. Thus none of the information contained in the book is warranted to be accurate or appropriate for any specific need. Furthermore, variations in weather and sea conditions, a mariner's skills and experience, and the presence of luck (good or bad) can dictate a mariner's proper course of action.

The Waggoner Cruising Guide should be viewed as a reference only and not a substitute for official government charts, tide and current tables, coast pilots, sailing directions, and local notices to mariners. The Waggoner Cruising Guide assumes the user to be law-abiding and of good will. The suggestions offered are not all-inclusive, but are meant to help avoid unpleasantness or needless delay. Maps are not for navigation. Maps do not show all navigation marks, obstacles, hazards, and structures. Maps are for reference only.

The publisher, editors, and authors assume no liability for errors or omissions, or for any loss or damages incurred from using this publication.

Copyright © 2023 by Waggoner Media Group
Published by Fine Edge Nautical & Recreational Publishing

All rights reserved. Except for use in a review, no part of this book may be reproduced or utilized in any form or by any means, electronic or mechanical, including photocopying, recording, or by any information storage or retrieval system without written permission of the publisher.

Printed in Canada
ISBN: 978-1-7341312-7-7

Library of Congress information available upon request.

Book Sales U.S.
Fine Edge Nautical & Recreational Publishing
Store: 902 - 8th Street
             Anacortes, WA 98221
Mailing: PO Box 726
             Anacortes, WA 98221
Phone (360) 299-8500
Fax (360) 299-0535
Email: orders@FineEdge.com
www.WaggonerGuideBooks.com

Like us on Facebook
Waggoner Cruising Guide
WaggonerGuide.com

Direct advertising inquiries to:
Waggoner Media Group
PO Box 726
Anacortes, WA 98221 USA
Phone (360) 299-8500
Fax (360) 299-0535
Email: advertising@waggonerguide.com
www.WaggonerGuide.com

Book Sales Canada
Chyna Sea Ventures, Ltd.
Store: Unit 4, 147 Fern Rd. E
             Qualicum Beach, BC, V9K 1T2
Mailing: PO Box 284
             Qualicum Beach, BC, V9K 1S8
Phone: (250) 594-1184
Fax: (250) 594-1185
Email: orders@ChynaSea.com
www.ChynaSea.com

Twitter
@TheWaggoner

WAGGONER CRUISING GUIDE

Founding Editor
Robert Hale

Editor/Publisher
Mark Bunzel

Managing Editors
Lorena Landon
Leonard Landon

Art & Technical Production
Leonard Landon, Mariah Wakeling

Advertising Sales
Sue Peterson, Karla Locke, Mark Bunzel

Advertising Production
Melanie Haage

Field Correspondents
Dale & Cathleen Blackburn,
Beth & Toni Carpenter,
Sandy & Will Dupleich,
Melissa Gervais,
Toni & Steve Jefferies,
Dan & Karin Leach,
Janine & Nick Mott,
Jim Norris & Anita Fraser,
Bob & Shino Posey,
John Shepard

Correspondents/Contributors
Bruce & Margaret Evertz, Annie Feyereisen, Gil & Karen Flanagan, Gill Graham, Robert & Marilynn Hale, Jennifer & James Hamilton, Steve & Elsie Hulsizer, Tom Kincaid, John & Lorraine Littlewood, Doug Miller, Kevin Monahan, Hira Reid

Proofreading
Dale Blackburn, Janine & Nick Mott, Jim Norris, Sue Peterson, Bob Posey, John Shepard

Reference Maps
Leonard Landon, Melanie Haage

Photography
Dale Blackburn, Peter Brown, Mark Bunzel, John & Ivy Cruz, Eric Deitz, Sandy Dupleich, Deane Hislop, Lorena Landon, Steve Jefferies, Janine Mott, Dale Miller, Doug Miller, Jim Norris, Don Odegard, John Shepard, Chuck Wengenroth

Drone Photography
Leonard Landon

Office
Karen Lane; Ian Kelsey

Reference Sources
BC Parks, BC Marine Parks Forever Society, Canada Customs, U.S. Customs, First Nations, National Weather Service, Northwest Marine Trade Association (NMTA), WA Dept. of Fish & Wildlife, BC and WA Parks, WA Dept. of Ecology, WA Dept. of Natural Resources (DNR), Peter Puget Project, Puget Sound Pilots, Recreational Boaters Association of Washington (RBAW), Whale Wise

ARE ROUGH WATERS IN OUR WAKE?

Well, some could say one of the biggest hindrances to boating – the pandemic – is behind us. Well not really.

Yes, Canada has dropped all pandemic related restrictions, and US boaters are now able to freely pass over the border in both directions via normal customs clearance procedures. While this is a relief to US boaters, non-US travelers seeking to enter US waters are still required to be fully vaccinated and provide proof of vaccinations upon request; however, this policy may be eliminated in the near future. As I write this, we are still hearing of new novel virus strains that seem to be announced every week. Our friends and associates are still experiencing covid symptoms. For me, I will still be carrying Covid test kits on my boat for my guests and myself, just in case.

Covid did have a benefit for the boating world. Boat sales reached a peak during the pandemic as many saw the benefits of vacationing isolated on a boat, enjoying the beautiful scenery of the Inside Passage. More boats on the water contributed to crowded moorages, and reservations were harder to get. Likewise, space for permanent moorage was hard to find.

The pandemic also meant that the labor markets were challenged. Restaurants found they could not always be open on the days scheduled due to a lack of staff. Repair yards did not have enough staff to meet their backlog of repair and maintenance work, and supply chain issues delayed repairs and new boat deliveries. It may take more time for all of these challenges to get ironed out. For 2023, be ready with a backup plan; it's still the best way to move forward. Make reservations where you can, and be prepared because things might change.

What has not changed is that we have one of the best cruising grounds in the world with plenty of wildlife, beautiful scenery, and warm and friendly people in the towns and villages along the way. Use this guidebook to plan your route and destinations; get out there and explore. Be safe on the water and enjoy time with your family and friends.

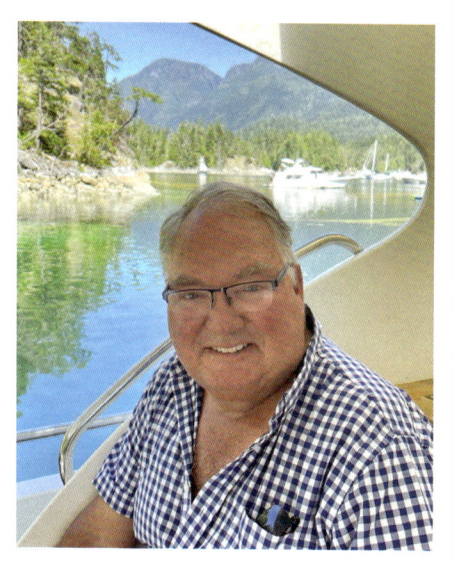

Mark Bunzel, Editor & Publisher

HAS ANYTHING CHANGED?

The Landon's and *Waggoner* Field Correspondents spent the cruising season collecting the many changes found each year at marinas, and testing new anchorages for the *Waggoner Guide*. With the first season open after two years of U.S./Canada border closures, it comes as no surprise that there are numerous updates and important changes documented for the waters of British Columbia, as well as changes for destinations in Washington and Southeast Alaska.

Many of the marinas and resorts used the Covid years to make substantial dock improvements, and municipalities and cities began construction on new breakwaters and slip allocations, or started the permitting process for improvements. While some of the smaller facilities have come and gone, others are creating much-needed additional moorage capacity. The trend to use permanent tenant slips for seasonal guest moorage continues. Likewise, technology is moving forward at a fast pace, with more apps for boaters and more options for connectivity while cruising. You will find all these updates and more in the *2023 Waggoner Cruising Guide*.

Our theme for 2023 is "Dream Itineraries." The most frequently asked questions we get are: "where do you suggest we go?" and "how long does it take to get there?" and "what can we do when we get there?" For experienced boaters as well as for boaters new to the area, you will find a dozen suggested itineraries for various cruising waters of the Pacific Northwest. These itineraries are found at the end of Chapter 1, the Compendium. Chapter 1 also includes helpful information about how to go cruising in the Pacific Northwest.

Our boating advocacy work is a year-round effort, working with organizations on both sides of the border to ensure the future of sustainable and responsible recreational boating. We are passionate about boating, and literally work day and night to ensure that we all, and those of the next generations, can experience this unique boating lifestyle

We continue to add more maps in the Waggoner Guide, a total of 285 maps in the 2023 edition, 34 of which are new dock diagrams or area maps. You will also find drawings for trails and information regarding new watchmen programs for wildlife viewing. To answer your question, has anything changed? see "What's New in the 2023 Waggoner" on page 7.

Leonard & Lorena Landon, Managing Editors

MEET OUR FIELD CORRESPONDENTS

Dale and Cathleen Blackburn have lived in Washington for nearly 30 years. They have five adult children and a two dogs. Shortly before Dale retired in 2013, they purchased *Fiddler,* a 46-foot DeFever Pilothouse trawler, and have recorded their boating adventures from Olympia to Juneau at MVFiddler.com. Dale also volunteers as a Marine Park Host at Blake Island Marine State Park. Cathleen is an avid gardener, transitioning most of their lawn into a bird and pollinator friendly habitat. They are active members of Meydenbauer Bay Yacht Club and Port Ludlow Yacht Club. Dale and Cathleen enjoy meeting other boaters and visiting new locations.

Capt. Beth and Toni Carpenter are an adventurous and active marine cruising pair. They spend weekends cruising the San Juan Islands, greater Salish Sea and beyond in their power catamaran TacocaT. Beth grew up aboard commercial and recreational vessels in Anacortes and comes from a family with a long maritime history. She has been piloting power boats for over 30 years and a graduate of US Maritime Academy, earning her USCG 100 Ton Master license and Commercial Towing Endorsement. Toni is also a local to the Pacific NW, she's been a First Mate and deckhand on hundreds of cruises including the self-delivery of TacocaT from San Francisco Bay to Everett. This 14-day Pacific Ocean cruise included the daily navigation of crossing coastal river bars into various ports. Beth and Toni both work in local government as Cartographers, building maps and applications.

Sandy and Will Dupleich have been boaters since 2000 and love to spend time on the water. They are members of the Bellevue Yacht Club, with Will having served as Commodore. They started their boating adventures with their 3 children and the family dog on a 12-foot folding boat and now own a 50-foot trawler named Sea Bear. They have cruised all around the Puget Sound region and the San Juan and Gulf Islands, as well as Desolation Sound and the Sunshine Coast in British Columbia. One day soon, they hope to cruise to Southeast Alaska. You can follow the Sea Bear crew on their blog site at MVSeaBear.com, where they share stories about their cruises as well as tips and tricks learned over 20+ years of boating. Whenever possible, they love to spend time exploring new anchorages and marinas, or enjoying a quiet weekend at their home port, Elliott Bay Marina.

Melissa (Missy) Gervais has been boating on the West Coast her whole life and is a member of the Royal Vancouver Yacht Club. She enjoys anchoring out in marine parks and taking photos of the many scenic destinations in British Columbia. She boats with two Irish Setters, Jonathan and Pip, aboard her 58-foot power boat, As You Wish II. Melissa enjoys cruising the Gulf Islands and Sunshine Coast during vacation time from her active career with Pacific Yacht Systems. In her spare time, she hosts a fun website, missygoesboating.com, featuring everything cool for women who boat. She also writes articles for Northwest Yachting Magazine.

Toni and Steve Jefferies are retired teachers and live full time on Hat Island. After 15 wonderful years sailing a Catalina 30, they now enjoy cruising in a Beneteau 423 aptly named "Readership." In 2021 they spent 4-months enjoying their first cruise to Southeast Alaska. In 2022, cruising took them to the West Coast of Vancouver Island to visit and explore the communities and islands of Barkley Sound. Toni and Steve are both avid skiers, snowboarders, kayakers, and hikers. They are headed to Nepal for the fall season of 2022 to hike to Everest Base Camp. On Hat Island they serve as Volunteer Fire Fighters and are both nationally certified EMTs.

Dan and Karin Leach are retired and live aboard their Passport 40 in Anacortes. Dan started sailing when he was a kid. His high school graduation gift from his dad was a 15 foot sailboat and a copy of Joshua Slocom's *Sailing Alone Around the World*. Karin started sailing in 2004 when Dan said, "Hey, we should get back into sailing…only on bigger boats." She took lessons so that if he got hit by the boom, she could get back home. They've been cruising the waters between Washington and Alaska ever since. Karin is perfecting her small oven bread recipes. Dan just wants to keep everything on the boat in working order and keep Karin happy. According to Dan, "Girls stay if the heater and the head work." Dan and Karin cruise the NW waters from spring to fall and land cruise in their RV from fall to spring.

Janine and Nick Mott cruise the Salish Sea aboard Touch of Gray, an American Tug 362. Tacoma residents, they appreciate South Sound cruising in the shoulder seasons and spend much of the summer in the San Juan and Gulf Islands. The Motts have been to Desolation Sound twice and look forward to future trips to the Broughtons and Alaska. They enjoy island hiking, exploring by dinghy, and kayaking. They also carry electric bikes aboard for seeing the sights ashore. When not boating, Janine and Nick travel and spend time with family, including two young grandsons. More about their adventures at https://jmcmott.wixsite.com/touchofgrayat362-01

MEET OUR FIELD CORRESPONDENTS

Anita Fraser and Jim Norris have been boating nearly their entire lives, having been engaged in commercial fishing, marine research, and more recently as active recreational boaters. They are Great Loop veterans, completing "The Loop" in 2008 on a 32-foot Grand Banks. Since 2010 they have cruised extensively between their home port of Port Townsend and Glacier Bay, Alaska on their 42-foot Krogen, *Spirit Quest*. Their northern trips have included the west side of Vancouver Island and Haida Gwaii. They have also cruised as far south as San Diego, spending a winter in Oxnard, California. Each year they explore their favorite destinations and personal secret places in Northern B.C. and Southeast Alaska.

Bob and Shino Posey owned a PT 38 Trawler for many years in which they explored the Pacific Northwest and BC's lower mainland. Bob started boating with runabouts in the 60's. They currently own a 24-foot Sea Sport Explorer, based in Anacortes, which provides flexibility in planning a variety of cruising destinations. They spend most summers cruising the San Juan and Gulf Islands and enjoy visiting Chatterbox Falls in Princess Louisa Inlet and other iconic locations. Bob and Shino trailered their boat to Prince Rupert BC and cruised the Inside Passage to Southeast Alaska, where they rendezvoused with family and friends at Port Alexander on Baranof Island.

John Shepard started sailing, racing, and instructing as a teenager in San Diego. As a Naval junior, John had free use of boats that provided recreational opportunities for servicemen, and he took full advantage sailing and racing in the waters of Southern California. John first started cruising the Pacific Northwest with a trailerable boat, exploring rivers, lakes and bays. Inspired by reading Jonathan Raban's book, *Passage to Juneau*, John purchased a Cal 35 Cruiser sloop, named *Hadley*. John undertook refurbishing *s/v Hadley*, making extensive repairs and refits. With projects nearly complete, a fast-moving boat appeared out of the fog near Double Bluff on Whidbey Island and clipped his starboard stern. Thankfully the stern quarter and transom were mostly fiberglass repairs; a quick maneuver had helped avoid a more serious collision. *Hadley* was repaired and happy to be once again weaving through island passages in all sorts of weather and crossing the straits that make up our water playground of the Pacific Northwest.

WHAT'S NEW IN THE 2023 WAGGONER

Much has changed in the boating community since the Covid years. Marinas have come and gone, others have completely rebuilt their docks, added amenities, or changed booking procedures. Some marinas have changed ownership and have creative ideas for the future. Others have installed Starlink for better connectivity.

Each year the Waggoner Editors and Waggoner Field Correspondents spend the summer months gathering all the changes at marinas and anchorages that are so important for boaters to have at their fingertips. The U.S./Canada border having been closed for two years, it's not surprising that there are numerous updates documented in the 2023 Waggoner Guide for both sides of the border. Hundreds of updates are gathered each year, and that's especially true for the 2023 edition of the Waggoner Cruising Guide.

Here are a few of the exciting new additions to the 2023 Waggoner:

2023 Theme - Dream Itineraries 
- 12 Custom Itineraries for trips ranging from nearby local waters to the coveted destination of Southeast Alaska
- Located at the end of the Compendium - Chapter 1

Making the Guidebook Easier to Use 
- Side tabs on each page have been expanded to include the Chapter's title along with the page number to make it easier to find the page you are looking for.
- Broughton Region Chapter now combines the marinas & anchorages for the related areas of Broughtons and North Vancouver Island into a single chapter.

Destinations & Places to Go
- New write ups have been added for sights to see, places to visit, and anchorages.
- Some of your favorite destinations have changed and you will find the needed updated information.

New Charter & Rewritten Floatplane Sections 
- The list of floatplane operators is up-to-date and we have added traveler tips for this fun transportation experience.
- Styled after the Floatplane section, we have added information about the various types of on-the-water charter operations along with three lists of PNW operators.

Maps & Dock Diagrams
- 34 New Maps/Dock Diagrams
- 285 Maps in Total for 2023
- New Mapping for Penrose I. Marine Park
- New Map of Harmony Islands with stern tie pin locations
- New Map with all the Gwaii Haanas Watchmen Sites 
- Full-page map of Vancouver B.C.'s False Creek area, complete with dock diagrams, and anchoring locations
- Hiking trails added to maps

Updates throughout each chapter
- Marina reservation procedures, contact information, amenities & services, and where to find your assigned moorage space are all kept current and up-to-date
- VHF Radio Stations, new easy to read diagram and reference table
- DAA - Designated Anchoring Areas within the Port of Vancouver B.C. governance area, including Deep Cove, Port Moody and Steveston
- How to Anchor Your Dinghy
- Liability insurance requirements for guest moorage
- 100's of Updates for the waters of Washington, British Columbia, and Southeast Alaska

New Sidebars to help you get the most from your boating
- Fiordland Conservancy
- Let's Talk Trash
- Anchoring Using Your Fishfinder

2023 WAGGONER CRUISING GUIDE

WAGGONER AND THE WAGGONER CRUISING GUIDE

WAGGONER NAME

In 1584 the Dutch pilot Lucas Janszoon Waghenaer published a volume of navigation principles, tables, charts, and sailing directions, which served as a guide for other such books for the next 200 years. These "*Waggoners,*" as they came to be known, were very popular; and in 1588, an English translation of the original book was made. During the next 30 years, 24 editions of the book were published in Dutch, German, Latin, and English. Other authors followed the example set by Waghenaer. Soon, American, British, and French navigators had Waggoners for most of the waters they sailed.

Today's Waggoner (pronounced wag-on-er), in honor of the Dutch pilot, is proud to carry on the respected tradition of providing first-hand knowledge, reference maps, and information to help mariners get the most out of their recreational boating adventures in the Pacific Northwest.

Lucas was not only an expert cartographer, he was also an experienced pilot. He sailed the seas as a chief officer between 1550 and 1579. His years of sailing experience and contacts with harbour officials and seamen, provided the impetus for his chart making. The Dutch were the foremost European hydrographers and cartographers of the day. Lucas Waghenaer played a major role in the early development of Dutch nautical chart-making and was one of the founding fathers of the North Holland School. After his seafaring adventures, he worked in the port of Enkhuizen as collector of maritime dues; it was here that he passed away in 1606.

Waghenaer's published text was based on traditional navigation, but his charts added an important component, which created the world's first published pilot guide. His charts showed coastal panoramas and land profiles as viewed from the sea. Compass intersections were used to plot prominent coastal features. Although some of these features were exaggerated, his charts were primarily intended for approaches to important harbours.

Waghenaer's first publication, Spieghel der zeevaerdt (Mariner's Mirror), appeared in 1584, which was a combination of nautical charts, sailing directions, and instruction for navigation on the western and north-western coastal waters of Europe; it was the first of its kind in the history of nautical cartography. A second part was published the next year and reprinted several times and translated into several languages. In 1592, his second pilot book, Thresoor der zeevaert (Treasure of Navigation) was published. His third and last publication, the Enkhuizen Sea Chart Book, was published in 1598.

Waghenaer's publications have withstood the test of time as a model for marine guidebooks with instructions, chartletts, and piloting tips. We hope you enjoy the annually updated Waggoner Cruising Guide, published by Fine Edge Nautical Publishing based in Anacortes, Washington.

It is inconclusive or unknown if any of Waghenaer's publications included advertising to defray his costs of printing and publication. It is noted that he died in apparent poverty, and that the municipal authorities extended his pension a year longer for his widow.

WAGGONER ADVOCACY

Boaters in the Northwest associate the name Waggoner with its must-have printed Waggoner Cruising Guide that has served boaters for nearly 30 years. Boaters identify the Waggoner Cruising Guide as their authoritative source of how to cruise the Inside Passage. From its start in the early 1990's, the guidebook has been the source for detailed information to help boaters navigate the challenges of boating. Challenges in the early days included navigating without GPS, Internet, electronic charts, chartplotters, moving-map displays, digital radar, sufficient bottom sonar, and satellite communication. Dealing with the elements and maintaining situational awareness were the constant ongoing tasks.

Over the course of the past decades, recreational boating has changed. Many of the challenges from yesteryears have been conquered by technology and more sophisticated reliable boats. However, today's boaters have new and different challenges. The challenges today are more about where you can and can't go – restrictions, environmental concerns, ecological issues, and territorial restrictions mandate boater behavior. These restrictions, laws, and regulations are constantly changing. Navigation and environmental changes are documented and communicated by the Coast Guard through "Local Notice to Mariners," however, today's regulations, limitations, and restrictions are not as well documented, and often communicated through a variety of different sources. Not all restrictions may be widely documented since some rules tend to be local knowledge only. The net effect of all of this, unfortunately, puts limits on where and what recreational boaters can do today.

Waggoner has engaged in advocating for boaters and for the environment in such a way that recreational boaters can still enjoy the unique aspects of being out on open waters to enjoy the natural environment and discover different cultures and life styles. We are actively partnering with such organizations as RBAW (Recreational Boaters Association of Washington), BC Marine Parks Forever Society, NMTA (Northwest Marine Trade Association), Department of Natural Resources (DNR), SeaKeepers, Washington Sea Grant, Washington Clean Vessel Act, and Whale Wise. Our work with these organizations is twofold 1) through our connections we help to communicate the concerns and needs of the boating community; and 2) we want to help formulate forward looking policies in such a way that the needs of both boaters and the environment are met.

One of our first undertakings, which started 4 years ago, addressed the eelgrass topic. Eelgrass protection groups wanted to close known eelgrass areas for anchorage. Waggoner's approach was to include detailed mapping and descriptions of eelgrass areas in the Waggoner Guide to help boaters voluntarily anchor outside of eelgrass areas. Our next agenda item is focused on expanding opportunities for boater destinations. Initial ideas include more mooring buoys and stern-tie pins to protect not only the environment but to also address boating capacity issues. The Waggoner name goes well beyond the production of a quality guidebook and includes seasonal webcasts covering various boating issues, class training through Boat Show University and Cruisers College, semi-monthly eNews publications, timely notices on Waggoner Facebook, and Webinar presentations.

WAGGONER AND THE WAGGONER CRUISING GUIDE

Waggoner Guide (pronounced [wagənər] not [wagənir]) has been guiding boaters to the spectacular Northwest destinations since 1994. It provides the reader with information about marinas, anchorages, passages, and attractions from Olympia, Washington to Skagway, Alaska, including the marine waters of British Columbia. *The Waggoner is The Most Trusted Source for Northwest Boating Information*, and many of our readers refer to it as their bible for northwest cruising. This all-inclusive guidebook is updated annually.

Waggoner Guide strives to be the most up-to-date cruising guidebook, with accurate, verified information. The writing style is intended to be as concise, factual, and informative as possible.

How the Book is Organized. The first section of the book, referred to as the *Compendium*, contains valuable information that helps boaters plan and execute a successful trip. This *Compendium* chapter has instructional material regarding customs, weather, anchoring, communications, and other pertinent how-to information.

The body of the book is divided into chapters by geographic cruising regions for Washington State, British Columbia, and Southeast Alaska. Keeping with the south to north organization, material within each chapter generally progresses northward. Each chapter begins with an overview of the area followed by detailed information for each marina, along with passages and designated anchorages. Ports, harbors, and cities with multiple boating facilities also begin with an overview description to help the reader become familiar with the local cruising area.

Reference maps for the chapter's coverage area are located at the beginning of the chapter with additional reference maps found throughout the chapter. A Legend of symbols used on Waggoner Guide reference maps can be found in this section. Area reference maps indicate destinations with numbers, which correspond to the numbered text for marinas and significant anchorages. Reference maps are not for navigation and do not show all navigation aids, beacons, marks, lights, and hazards. Maps are not to scale and are for reference purposes only. Boaters should carry up-to-date electronic charts and/or paper charts.

You will also find "Local Knowledge" and Sidebars (short articles) within many of the chapters. Local Knowledge provides helpful tips and warnings regarding shoals, rocks, tides and current for specific locations, which may not be depicted on navigational charts. Sidebars relate personal experiences or informative nautical topics that are helpful to the reader. Sidebars also provide historical background for a number of destinations, enlightening the imagination and purpose of why we go there in the first place.

The Year's Theme. Some of the Sidebars in the Waggoner Guide focus on a chosen theme for the year, with articles highlighting a nautical topic of interest.

How the Book is Made. The Waggoner Guide Team of Northwest boaters cruise the waters of the Pacific Northwest, including the Inside Passage to Alaska each year, gathering updates for marinas, anchorages, and waterways found in the Waggoner Guide. The Waggoner Team, along with experienced Field Correspondents and knowledgeable contributors, provide the many hundreds of updates included in each year's edition of the Waggoner Cruising Guide. While it is not possible to physically go to every anchorage or marina each year, every effort is made to get the latest information directly from marinas by phone or other means.

Editorial work begins in September to incorporate these changes and updates, including new reference maps and photos. Editors, proof readers, and designers of maps, ads, and page layout spend untold hours preparing copy for final proofs, while meeting our print deadline. The much-anticipated announcement of the current edition of the Waggoner Guide is provided in our eNews. Copies of the *Waggoner Cruising Guide* are made available at the Seattle Boat Show, where boaters enthusiastically purchase the new edition and begin making plans for their next adventure. Copies are also available at retailers throughout the PNW, at www.waggonerguidebooks.com, and at Amazon.

How to send us Comments and Feedback. The Waggoner Team invites your comments, suggestions and corrections. We appreciate hearing from our readers regarding ways we can improve our publication. Your ideas for future editions are always welcome along with your experiences and tips, which inform and help other boaters. Contact us through our website, www.WaggonerGuide.com, or by telephone (360) 299-8500; you can also find us on Facebook. We invite you to contact us at **info@waggonerguide.com**

WaggonerGuide.com and eNews. At WaggonerGuide.com, we have a dedicated team of experienced boaters and travel experts who share a variety of articles each month about boating in Washington, British Columbia, and Southeast Alaska. Some of the topics include maintenance tips, cruising destinations, boat reviews, and on-the-water reporting. You'll also find boating seminar announcements, guidebook updates, access to free downloads, and our collection of boating and nautical-theme books in the Waggoner Store.

A great way to stay tuned into WaggonerGuide.com is to subscribe to Waggoner eNews. This newsletter is sent out twice a month and contains our latest boating related articles. All of our content is geared toward you, our reader, who lives and breathes boating in the Pacific Northwest.

To enroll in Waggoner eNews, visit WaggonerGuide.com. You'll find the subscribe button on the right column. Or, visit our Facebook page at https://www.facebook.com/WaggonerCruisingGuide and in the left-hand column, you'll find the Subscribe to eNews tab. There is no cost to subscribe.

Advertisers. Advertising helps provide the best cruising information at the best price to you, the cruising public; advertisements often provide more extensive information about the facility that is not part of the mission of the Waggoner Guide. Advertising helps us keep in touch with the marinas and service providers, who provide information about what is coming for the next cruising season. This symbiotic relationship helps the Waggoner Team stay in communication with the Marine Trade Industry and provide guidance regarding cruisers' needs.

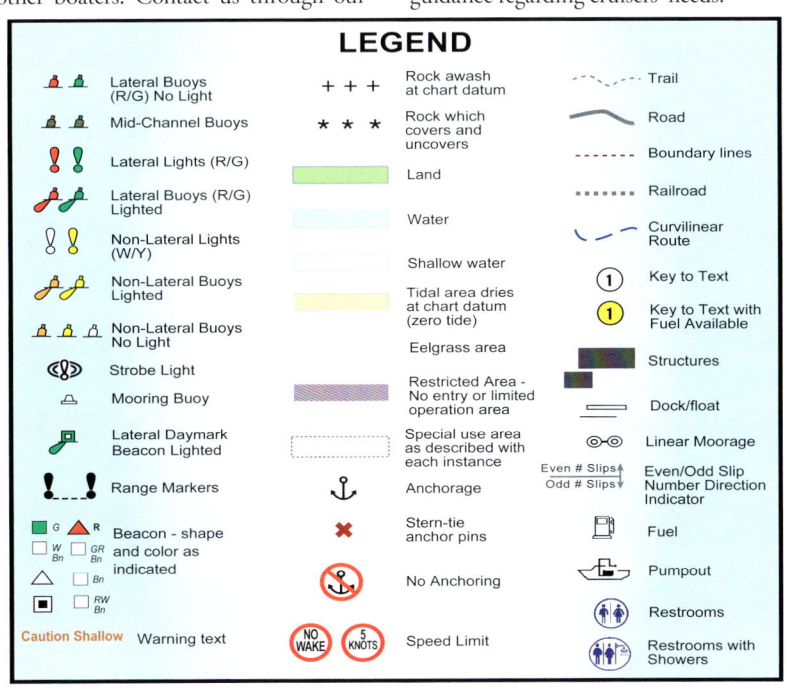

LEGEND

Symbol	Description	Symbol	Description	Symbol	Description
	Lateral Buoys (R/G) No Light	+++	Rock awash at chart datum		Trail
	Mid-Channel Buoys	***	Rock which covers and uncovers		Road
	Lateral Lights (R/G)		Land		Boundary lines
	Lateral Buoys (R/G) Lighted		Water		Railroad
	Non-Lateral Lights (W/Y)		Shallow water		Curvilinear Route
	Non-Lateral Buoys Lighted		Tidal area dries at chart datum (zero tide)	1	Key to Text
	Non-Lateral Buoys No Light		Eelgrass area	1	Key to Text with Fuel Available
	Strobe Light		Restricted Area - No entry or limited operation area		Structures
	Mooring Buoy				Dock/float
	Lateral Daymark Beacon Lighted		Special use area as described with each instance		Linear Moorage
	Range Markers	⚓	Anchorage	Even # Slips↑ Odd # Slips↓	Even/Odd Slip Number Direction Indicator
G R W Bn GR Bn	Beacon - shape and color as indicated	✗	Stern-tie anchor pins		Fuel
△ Bn		🚫	No Anchoring		Pumpout
■ RW Bn		NO WAKE / 5 KNOTS	Speed Limit		Restrooms
Caution Shallow	Warning text				Restrooms with Showers

HOW TO CRUISE THE PACIFIC NORTHWEST

Developing an Itinerary. Planning an itinerary for you and your crew generates enthusiasm for the trip and establishes team effort. For many, trip planning is part of the fun, starting months before the actual trip. It's fun to dream about what your cruise will be like, what you want to see and do.

Start by involving the crew with pre-trip research, or create the first draft as Captain. Look through the many cruising guides available (we stock most in the WaggonerGuide.com store). You can look through past issues of magazines that cover the Northwest such as *Pacific Yachting, Northwest Yachting, 48 Degrees North,* and *SEA Magazine* to name a few. Start that short list of places you want to visit for the first time, re-visit, or see from a different point of view. You may have specific destinations in mind that you want to share with guests who have never seen this beautiful area.

Prioritize activities and destinations based on everyone's interests and work together to finalize the itinerary. Depending on how much time you have for the trip and understanding the distances involved, you can create an itinerary with reasonable expectations. Time should be factored in for provisioning, fuel stops, weather delays, and transiting time-dependent passages such as rapids along your route. Consider time for relaxing too. Those on a tight schedule might move to a different destination every day to see as much as possible. Others plan for a day or two, or plan short cruising legs to allow plenty of time to fully enjoy each destination.

Asking a few basic questions will help you develop an itinerary. Many boaters have preconceived ideas about their anticipated cruise, or expect to see and do certain things they have in mind. A pre-planned itinerary, with some specifics, helps set the expectations for a pleasant and rewarding cruise.

How much time do you have, including the trip back?

What speed do you expect to cruise at?

What do you want to see? This list could include wildlife, quaint villages, cannery ruins, museums, or simply relax at remote anchorages.

What activities do you want to do? Perhaps go fishing, swimming, or kayaking. Or you may prefer attending happy hours at the smaller marinas, or souvenir shopping when in town. Walking the beaches and hiking the trails found on many of the islands is always a favorite. You may have a crew that is split, where some will want to see the local museum, while others rummage through the shops in town. There are many locations that fit this criteria.

Are friends and family flying in to meet you? Options may include commercial airports, smaller community airports, or perhaps arriving by floatplane at more remote areas. You may want to factor in extra time for missed connections if you have guests arriving by plane.

Are you planning a 1-week or 2-week bareboat charter? There are so many places to go and enjoy both near and far. Most people who are new to the area start by cruising among the San Juan Islands on a 1-week to 2-week itinerary, leaving from the charter bases in Anacortes or Bellingham. If you want to focus on the islands of British Columbia, there are bareboat charter companies in Sidney, Nanaimo and Vancouver. If you really just want to cruise Desolation Sound and the Broughton Islands, there is a reputable charter company in Comox, BC where you can save a day or two by starting your cruise much closer to these areas.

With the basic information collected, create an itinerary in a spreadsheet, or on a pad of paper. Start laying out a day on each line with a few notes. There may be some special events in which you want to participate. Your schedule may shift, so remain flexible. A 90-mile day of cruising may be too much, or a passage may miss slack at one of the tidal rapids.

At Waggoner, we like to start our itinerary with the "knowns" in place. For example, if we were planning a trip north to Desolation Sound, the Broughtons or Southeast Alaska and leaving from Anacortes, we know to plan for clearing Canadian Customs. We have three basic choices for clearance heading north: Sidney, Bedwell Harbour, or Victoria.

CRUISING THE PNW - TOPICS
Developing an Itinerary
"Gates" and Their Effect
Anchoring vs. Marinas
Marinas
Marina Dockhand Help
Moorage Reservations
State & Provincial Parks
Mooring Buoys
Shore Power
Trailering a Boat
Waste Discharge
Be Self-reliant
VHF Radio
Provisioning
Potable Water

Nexus, i68 and Canpass holders will have many more options to clear Customs if the entire crew is registered in the programs.

Typically we cross over to the Canadian Gulf Islands and work our way north through the protected waters of the islands. We then look at the times of slack water for Dodd Narrows, near Nanaimo, to determine the approximate time and point of departure.

When leaving from Seattle, you may need to allow a day to reach the Anacortes area or the San Juan Islands. Stopping in historic Roche Harbor or Friday Harbor may be a crew member's request. However, it may make more sense to save this stop for the return trip from Canada, since both locations are a U.S. Customs Port of Entry.

"Gates" and Their Effect. The Pacific Northwest is a series of cruising areas separated by what we call "gates"— significant bodies of water that must be crossed. Although gates define our experience and abilities, they also serve as natural stopping points. Some cruisers stay in Puget Sound because the Strait of Juan de Fuca and San Juan Channel is a gate. Some stay in the Gulf Islands because the Strait of Georgia and Dodd Narrows crossing is a gate bringing concerns about the sea state conditions. Some go no farther than Desolation Sound because Johnstone Strait and the reversing tidal rapids north of Desolation Sound are gates. And some stay south of Cape Caution because the ocean swells of Queen Charlotte Sound can be looked at as a gate. Gates exist all the way up the coast, all the way to Alaska.

Once beyond a gate and in a given cruising area, the waters are protected. Fortunately, summer weather usually is agreeable. With a study of the tide and current books, a close eye on the winds, an understanding of the weather, and a properly-equipped boat, the gates can be negotiated in safety, and often in comfort. The farther you want to explore, the more time is needed. For the dedicated summertime cruiser, time is often the principal element limiting cruising choices.

For more about about gates, see the *Tides and Currents* section later in this chapter.

Tidal current rapids are one of the important "gates" along the Inside Passage that require careful timing for safe and comfortable passage.

HOW TO CRUISE THE PACIFIC NORTHWEST

CRUISING THE PNW - TOPICS
- Best Months
- Charts and Chartplotters
- Publications
- It Takes A Team
- About The Boat
- Use FRS Radios
- Carry Tools and Spares
- Use Scoot-Gard
- Insurance
- Clothing
- Update Credit Cards
- Pets
- Assisting Others
- Don't Be Cheap
- Boat Cards

Anchoring vs. Marinas. Compared with the waters farther north, Puget Sound has fewer anchorages. Most Puget Sound cruising is from marina to marina, or hanging off state park buoys. The San Juan Islands and Canadian Gulf Islands have many marinas and many anchorages. Desolation Sound is mostly anchorages with a few marinas. State and provincial marine parks dot the waterways from Puget Sound to Desolation Sound, many but not all, with mooring buoys. The Broughtons have many, many anchorages, a few family-run marinas, and dock facilities at Native villages. West Coast Vancouver Island and the waters north of Cape Caution have a few marinas but mostly anchorages. It is possible to cruise the Inside Passage all the way to the top of Vancouver Island and stay only in a marina. For more information regarding anchoring, see *About Anchoring* in this chapter.

Marinas. Cruising with the correct expectations makes for a pleasant experience and a happy crew. Marinas in the Pacific Northwest vary from upscale resorts to makeshift docks and everything in-between. A person who expects 5-star facilities and service at every stop will be disappointed. Especially in the remote areas, where the docks and other facilities can be rather on the rough side. Service at Native villages up the coast, for example, is provided on their terms, in their way, and that's different from the city approach most Waggoner readers are accustomed to. When we're out cruising, we have found it helpful to relax and take things as they come.

It's the wide variety of experiences that makes for interesting cruising in this part of the world. The one topic we have less patience with is cleanliness. We think public washrooms, showers, and laundry areas should be clean and in good condition, always.

Marinas vary in size, service, and amenities. Most marinas include all the necessary services like power, water, restroom facilities and laundry, while other guest docks may not have water or laundry available. Power is usually included in the moorage rate at all-inclusive resorts.

Marinas in the Pacific Northwest are run by a variety of entities, including municipalities, tribal First Nations, and regional corporations, to privately owned family operated marinas.

Guest moorage space is sometimes first-come, first-served, but many offer advance reservations. Depending on the marina, guest moorage may be side-tie, or it may be in an assigned slip. Some marinas have dedicated guest moorage areas and/or use tenanted unoccupied slips for guest moorage, called "hot berthing."

Marina Dockhand Help. Many of the larger destination marinas with ample guest moorage will routinely have dockhands that can help you upon arrival. A few of the resort-style marinas will have dockhands that personally welcome you to the facility and help orient you with the marina features and services.

Dockhand help at the resorts is usually seasonal help and any gratiuity for their docking and dockline assistance is welcomed but not required. If you need help at any of the marina facilities with line-handling, make a request; most marinas are happy to assist.

Moorage Reservations. Many marinas accept advance reservations for transient moorage. Reserving moorage in advance is always a good idea and highly recommended during the busy summer season. A telephone call is the most universally accepted means for making reservations. Increasingly, marinas have online reservation services available on their website and a few accept email requests. Some marinas require a credit card to confirm a slip reservation, while others do not. Ask about their policy for charging your credit card and about their cancelation policy in case weather or unexpected delays cause a change in plans. Some marinas charge for no-shows. Ask about your slip assignment; a few marinas assign a slip at the time of reservation. Others request that you contact them by VHF radio or cell phone upon arrival.

It's best to contact the marina directly for slip reservations. However, there are third-party online marina slip reservation providers where you can review marinas, check moorage rates, and request a reservation. These third-party providers are growing in popularity in the Northwest, including Dockwa and SwiftHarbour. It is best to check the marina's website first before contacting any third-party booking provider; the marina website provides the link to their booking service.

State & Provincial Parks. Marine parks can be found throughout Washington State and British Columbia. Some offer moorage docks for short term and overnight stays and many have mooring buoys for small to mid-sized boats. Southeast Alaska has a few state mooring docks and mooring buoys. For more about these parks, see the *State and Provincial Parks and Public Wharves* section in this chapter.

Mooring Buoys. It's often easier to pick up a mooring buoy from the stern or mid-ships, not the bow. If the bow of the boat is very high off the water it may be impossible to loop a line through a mooring buoy ring. Carry a line aft to a low point of the hull (it may be the swim step), loop it through the ring on the buoy, then carry the line back to the bow. You may want to cleat or tie off one end of the line amidships to keep control of it throughout the process.

Mooring buoys are often limited to small or medium sized boats. State and provincial park buoys are generally limited to boats 45 feet and under. Maximum boat size on some mooring buoys depends upon wind speeds. Rafting on mooring buoys is usually not allowed.

Shore Power. Marinas typically have alternating current shore power service available for guest boaters to plug into during their stay. Marina shore power connections are in sizes ranging from 15 amperage (amp) to 200 amp and a select few at 400 amp. The most common is 30 and 50 amp. Each amperage service has different sockets and its corresponding plug style. All 30 amp service

Moorage reservations are available at most marinas and are important during prime season. Contact the marina directly or use third-party booking services.

HOW TO CRUISE THE PACIFIC NORTHWEST

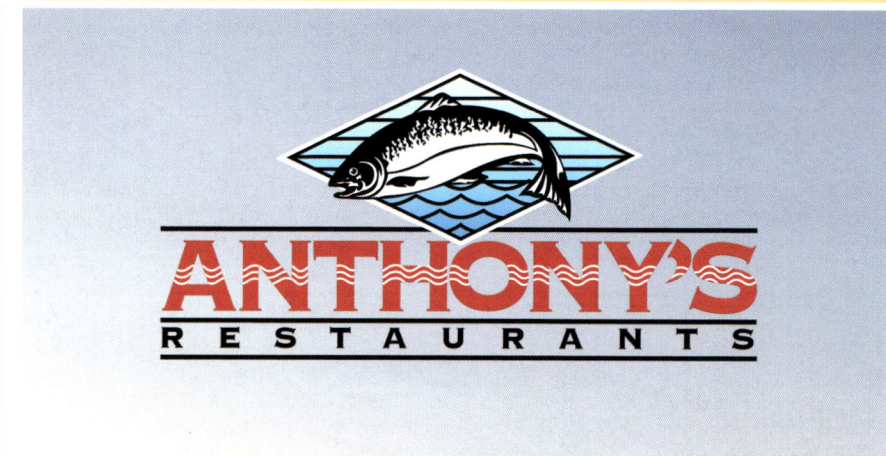

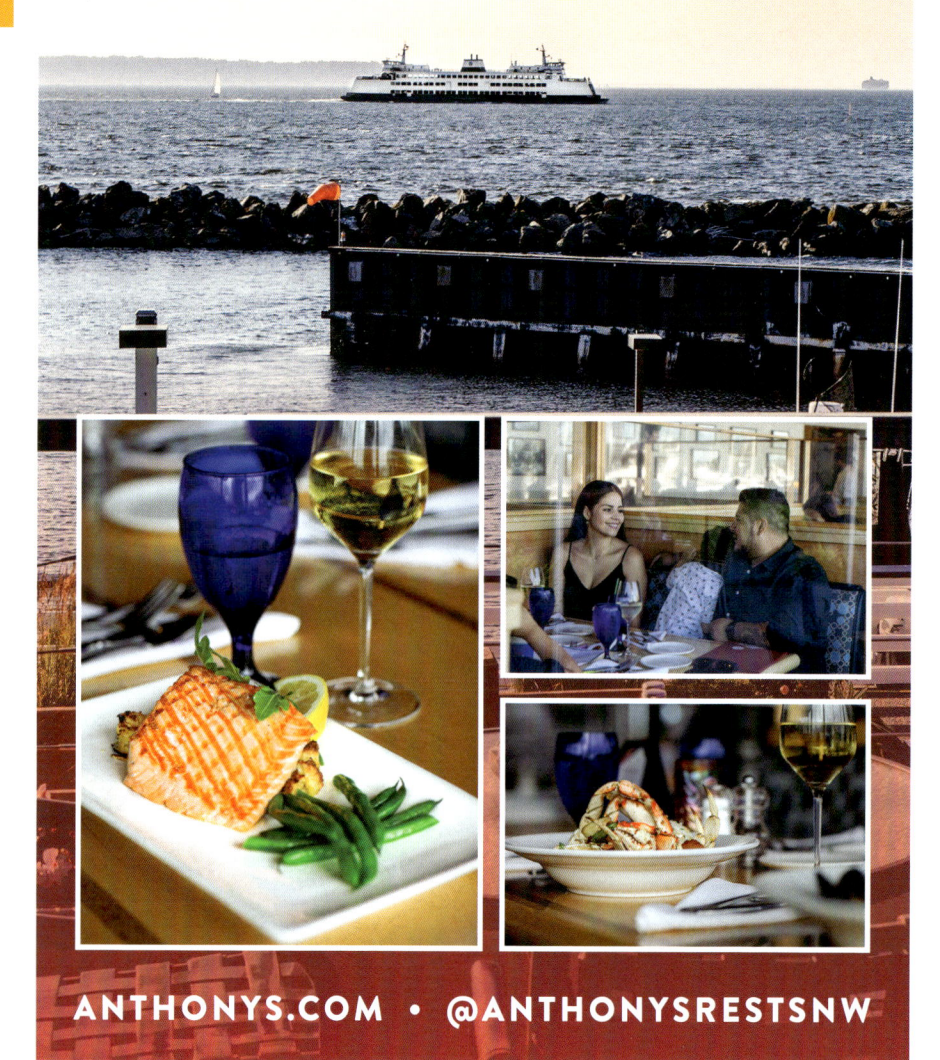

uses the same socket/plug. 50 amp service is available in both 125 and 125/250 volt and each has a different socket/plug style. 20 amp service has its own socket/plug style and 100 amp has its own socket/plug. Adapters are available to convert differing plug types. 15, 20, and 30 amp are 125 Volts.

Since not all docks have breakers to turn off individual outlets, we turn the boat's 125-volt switch to OFF before we hook up or unplug shore power. If the dock power has its own breaker, we turn it to OFF, too. When everything is hooked up, we turn the dock switch to ON, and then the boat switch.

Around 2015, building code in Washington and Alaska required marinas installing new shore power to equip the service with Equipment Leakage Circuit Interrupter (ELCI) protection (similar to GFCI protection in your household kitchen and bathroom circuits). Many Southeast Alaska marinas, Washington State marinas, and a few B.C. marinas have adopted ELCI protection.

Over the past few years, new marinas and rebuilt marinas have installed ELCI devices. Shore power at these marinas have fault protection that will "trip" the shore power breaker and turn off power to your boat if the device detects current leakage.

Faulty boat wiring or appliances can cause current to "leak" and find a path other than the Hot and Neutral wires. The Ground wire is the safety net that is designed to safely carry this leaking current to a grounding point. On a boat, the Ground wire has several connections, one goes to the shore power connection and another goes to the boat's bonding system that electrically connects the boat's metal parts in the sea water. This bonding connection can allow faulty leaking current to energize the water around the boat, causing an unsafe situation should someone fall in the water.

ELCI is the device that, when installed on the shore power pedestal and/or on your boat, will protect against electrocution by detecting current leakage and turn off the AC shore power connection. On the marina shore power side of the connection, building code requires ELCI devices on all newly installed shore power service.

On the boat, American Boat & Yacht Council (ABYC) standards call for an ELCI device; so if your boat was built after 2015, you most likely have ELCI protection. For older boats, an ELCI device can be added that will not only make your boat safer, it will ensure that you don't have problems when you plug into shore power at marinas with ELCI-protected shore power.

The ELCI Breaker may trip if:
- Reverse Y-splitters are used that are not designed for ELCI
- Marine battery chargers (try turning off or lower the amperage setting)
- Self-testing galvanic isolators (replace with a newer isolator or disable)
- Home-store (non-marine) appliances
- Inverters that are not designed for marine use

HOW TO CRUISE THE PACIFIC NORTHWEST

If you are still having problems, it's probably time to call in a qualified ABYC technician.

ELCI, RCD, GFCI, and GFI are all devices that perform the same function of detecting amperage leakage by sensing an amperage imbalance on the Hot and Neutral wires. The difference is in the level of imbalance, or leaking amperage that trips the breaker.

Trailering a Boat. Trailering is faster and more affordable than running a boat on its own bottom, and it avoids difficult passages across open water—the "gates" described earlier. Trailer boats can be towed to all the cruising grounds from Puget Sound to the far end of Vancouver Island. Even the sounds and inlets of the west coast of Vancouver Island can be seen easily and safely. Some people trailer all the way up Vancouver Island, launch at Port Hardy, and—watching the weather carefully—cruise north past Cape Caution to Rivers Inlet and beyond.

Many boats are trailered from the B.C. Interior to launch at Bella Coola or Prince Rupert. It's a long drive, but the waters they get to are some of the finest in the world. From Prince Rupert, you can cruise north into Southeast Alaska, which is not accessible by road. Another option is to tow the boat and trailer onto the ferry. Although expensive, both the BC Ferries and the Alaska Marine Highway ferries allow trailered boats.

Be Self-reliant. Don't venture out with the idea that if things go wrong, you can always call the Coast Guard. An important part of good seamanship is being able to handle whatever's thrown at you. Calling the Coast Guard is for true emergencies.

VHF Radio. Nearly all boats are equipped with VHF Marine Radios. These radios are an important part of safe and efficient cruising. It is important to operate the radio correctly and know how to use it in an emergency. Which channel (frequency) to use, and not use, along with the protocol for communication, is described in the *VHF Radio Procedures* section of this chapter. A table of marine VHF Channels and their use can be found in the *Reference Pages* at the back of this book.

Provisioning. Quality food on board is a big part of the cruising experience. Having that perfect meal surrounded by magnificent scenery is part of what makes our boating lifestyle so special. It is a fine balance between meals that are fun to prepare and keeping life and chores on board simple.

Looking at an itinerary, roughly how many nights will you be dining on board versus eating at the good restaurants along the way? Do you have anyone on your crew who has special food needs, is a vegetarian, needs gluten-free or likes milk in their coffee? Fat-free milk or whole milk? Does anyone on the crew have any allergies, or food items they need every day? If you are doing the cooking - how much work are you prepared to do?

Pancakes in the morning or frozen waffles? It begs the question - do you have maple syrup on board? Or, do you like to sleep in and leave breakfast items out for crew and guests to help themselves. Are you headed to Canada, or from Canada into the U.S.? Will you need to purchase items once you cross the border, due to border restrictions?

Where will the food be stored? Do you have a refrigerator, freezer, or are you working from a cooler with ice? Your menu planning will change based on what foods you can store safely.

If you will be joining others for potluck, be prepared to have your favorite dish to share for Happy Hours. You will want to have a few recipes that are quick and easy to prepare. Stock what you need, being mindful of the border crossing limits.

One of our instructors and an excellent cook, Lynette Brower, pre-prepares foods and places them into plastic bags for a complete meal. She keeps freezer bags filled with chicken or steaks broken down into portions for dinners. When she has guests, out come two bags. Often she will store the spices inside the bag along with the food item. By planning ahead with pre-packaged meals, time is saved and entertaining becomes more enjoyable.

Prepare a list, indicate whether you should buy items in Canada or the U.S. depending on which direction you are headed across the border. Chocolate, candy, and liquor are generally more expensive in Canada due to the taxes imposed. The selection of wines at retail is better in the U.S. and maybe you should just pay the duty of 90% of the value for a selection of good wines for your vacation cruise – that's right - almost double. Luckily many customs agents will average the value of your wine low when calculating the duty. Let them come up with a value. Have a list of what is on board; but in reality, it is very hard to value liquor coming into the country.

Do not try to sneak extra alcohol into either country. We have seen too many bottles of very good liquor confiscated because the boater was not honest. Agents seem to be looking for liquor more than anything else. The irony is that laws go back to the thinking that one might be smuggling liquor into the country for profit, denying a country of duty and tax.

Don't forget the incidentals. A charcoal grill needs charcoal and lighter fluid. Is your grill gas? Do you need a supply of propane tanks?

If your boat has limited storage space, remove food from boxes and bulky packaging. Mark the inner bag with a Sharpie. Cut the cooking directions from the box and tape it to the inner bag. This also reduces the refuse disposal underway. Once north of Desolation Sound, getting rid of trash is a challenge and an expense. Many resorts charge by the bag or the pound to take your trash. Sometimes the trash needs to be stored for several days in the lazerette before it can be responsibly disposed.

Store dry food items in plastic bins sized to fit the galley cabinets or storage spaces. Bins keep canned goods from sliding around in rough seas and can be safely stowed.

Unless you happen to be cruising on a mega-yacht, mealtime cleanup will be without a garbage disposal and dishwasher. Paper plates are a great option to reduce the dishwashing chore and reduce fresh water use (often a limited resource). You will likely be using more paper towels than at home. Paper towels make cleanup a breeze. It's best to wipe out greasy pots and pans rather than send oil and grease down the drain and into the sea water around your boat. Paper goods tend to be more expensive the farther north you go. Remember, everything has to be barged or flown in to the more remote locations.

Some people over stock their boats with food. There are places to purchase food items on the Inside Passage. Smaller stores are often found near the marinas and will have needed staple items. Fresh produce is sometimes harder to find especially the farther north you go.

Potable Water. *"Is your water potable?"* That's often one of the first questions boaters ask marinas when cruising the Northern BC Coast, the Broughton Archipelago and sometimes even in the Gulf Islands. Boaters often find a 'boil water' notice or 'not-potable' sign at water spigots and hose-bibs on the docks.

These notices indicate that the marina's private water system has not been certified by the Health Department as a public water system. Establishing a water system as a certified public water supply is an extensive and costly process, often not justifiable at remote, small marinas. Sometimes it requires a process for purification and exposure to UV light to kill certain bacteria. Sometimes the water is good and just needs to be tested regularly and sent in for certification. Water from private water systems may or may not be tested regularly but is used routinely, and may have been used for years with no ill effects.

When in doubt, filter water

2023 WAGGONER CRUISING GUIDE

HOW TO CRUISE THE PACIFIC NORTHWEST

If other than owners are using or consuming water from a non-certified water system, the Government requires that a non-potable or boil notice be posted. The sign doesn't mean that the water is bad, but rather serves to inform guest users of the water source and allow the guest user to make a choice or further inquiries.

As boaters, what do we do with this information? Depending on your comfort level, there are several options:

- Simply don't use the marina water, use only the water from your onboard tank.
- Do your own checking – ask locals if they regularly use the water for household needs and then make your choice.
- Carry and use a 3-stage water filter (the third stage needs to be a ceramic filter) and use this to filter the marina water.
- If you have a watermaker onboard, you may wish to make your own water.
- Another option is to sanitize the marina water put in your tank with a chemical additive. You will need to research and purchase these additives before your trip.
- Lastly, adding filters and a UV light sanitizing system to your onboard water system will help ensure you have safe water no matter where you fill your tank.

A few water sources on Northern BC Coast and in the Broughtons have a slight tannin or brown color to the water. While the water may be potable and not harmful, it certainly can be unappealing. Nature has its own filtration system that sometimes picks up coloring from cedar roots, resulting in the weak tea appearance to the water. This is an isolated issue, and most of the marinas and water sources in the area have clear water.

Small outlying marinas provide a surprising number of amenities for boaters, including acceptable sources of water. During their short business season, it's amazing what they can and do provide for the boating community. We encourage boaters to let them know how much we appreciate their facilities.

Best Months. The prime cruising months begin in April and end by October, with July-August the most popular. Boats are used year-round in Puget Sound. On winter weekends Puget Sound's popular ports are surprisingly busy. Cabin heat is a must in the fall and winter.

North of Puget Sound, pleasure boating is best done between early May and late September. Really dependable summer weather (little rain, long days of glorious sunshine) normally doesn't arrive in the Northwest until July. September can be an outstanding cruising month. The crowds are gone and the weather can be perfect.

Use caution when cruising during the winter months. Storms lash the British Columbia coast. Some, with flexible schedules, cruise year round. It takes a good understanding of the weather, and a warm, dry boat. There are many resources available to understand the weather and help keep you from an unexpected surprise. See the *Marine Weather* section of this chapter for our approach and suggestions for understanding the weather.

Charts and Chartplotters. To keep this book informative and up-to-date, we have stuck our nose into many ports, bays, and coves along the coast. In the process we have become unyielding advocates of chartplotters, up-to-date charts, and navigation publications. Properly used, charts not only keep a boat out of trouble, they allow one to enter areas you wouldn't want to try without the chart.

Chartplotters and electronic charts are now the standard. Most mariners no longer carry paper charts and instead carry multiple devices and copies of electronic charts.

Tablets and smartphones, with built-in GPS receiver systems and robust batteries, provide excellent redundancy. Low cost, highly effective chartplotting software is available for most tablet platforms. Many of these Apps make updating charts easy. If relying on a tablet or smartphone as a backup, consider carrying an extra battery pack.

When using electronic charts, be aware that hazards can disappear at certain zoom levels. We always examine our route at several zoom levels to ensure that it is free of hazards.

Whatever form of charts you decide to carry, keep them updated. While rocks haven't changed location, navigation aids do

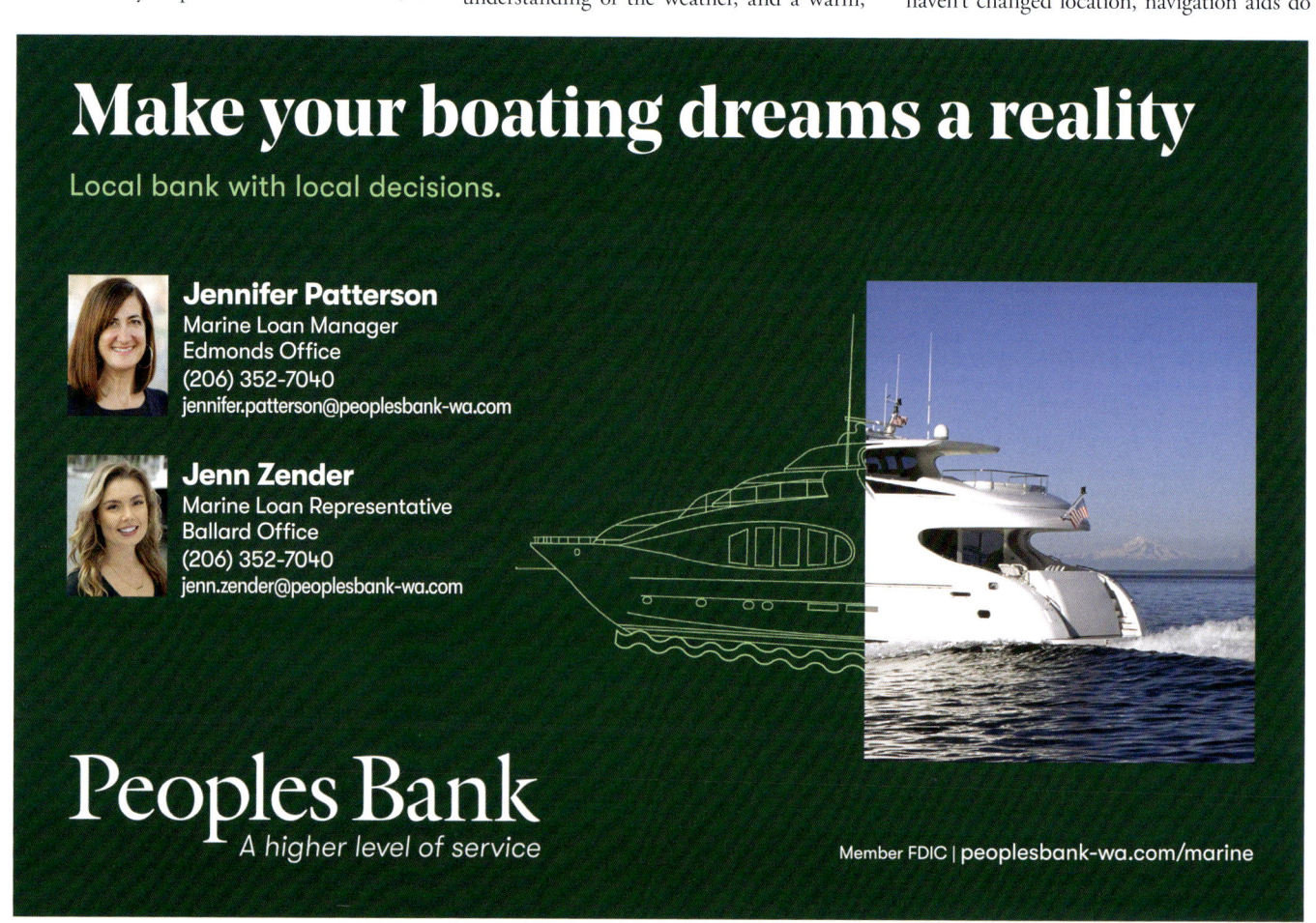

Make your boating dreams a reality
Local bank with local decisions.

Jennifer Patterson
Marine Loan Manager
Edmonds Office
(206) 352-7040
jennifer.patterson@peoplesbank-wa.com

Jenn Zender
Marine Loan Representative
Ballard Office
(206) 352-7040
jenn.zender@peoplesbank-wa.com

Peoples Bank
A higher level of service

Member FDIC | peoplesbank-wa.com/marine

HOW TO CRUISE THE PACIFIC NORTHWEST

change. New charts reflect the change on electronic updates. A five year old (or older) chartplotter may have very old charts and not reflect navigational updates.

For more information about charts and chartplotters, see the *Charts and Chartplotters* section later in this chapter.

Publications. Many cruising guides cover the Inside Passage and each offers a different point of view. We carry as many as we can fit, and keep several open at the helm. The U.S. Coast Pilot and Canadian Sailing Directions are good resources to have aboard, but they are focused on large commercial craft navigation.

Accurate tide and current tables are essential. Many electronic charting packages include tide and current data. Note: Both U.S. and Canadian government tide tables are not corrected for Daylight Saving Time, so you'll have to make the corrections manually. Capt'n Jack's, covering Puget Sound, and Ports and Passes, covering Olympia to Prince Rupert and Southeast Alaska, are excellent and are corrected for Daylight Savings Time. Ports and Passes is updated each year with official government data.

U.S. Coast Guard Local Notices to Mariners, Canadian Notices to Shipping, and Canadian Notices to Mariners provide updated information on navaids and regulatory changes. U.S. and Canadian light lists are useful, too. Both of these can be found online, search on "local notice to mariners."

Don't hold back on purchasing charts and other navigation information. *Remember:* the rocks, tides, and weather are indifferent to how much the boat costs. They treat all boats equally; invest wisely in charts and an up-to-date guidebook.

It Takes a Team. Like many boating couples, we work together as a team, checking and doublechecking routes, depths, and charted hazards along a chosen course. If we question or doubt our path, we come to a stop until the safest course can be verified before continuing on. This is not the time for wounded pride or "I told you so's," it's a matter of successfully accomplishing the task at hand, and the opportunity to learn and grow as a team.

Everything looks different on the water, so it's easy to mistake land marks and aids to navigation. The more experienced you are as a team, the better off you will be when the going gets tough, or when you are faced with a true emergency. Both partners should know how to use the radio, handle the helm, navigate, and manage sea conditions for a safe arrival into port. Docking and line-handling should be shared responsibilities. It's a good idea to schedule time for practice as well as a shake-down cruise for boat maintenance checks. The more comfortable you become with your own skills and know what your boat can handle, the more fun you will have.

On a power vessel, it is imperative to conduct engine room checks, requiring a confident partner to take over the helm. Extended excursions or overnight passages for

Farmers markets are a fun and rewarding part of provisioning during the cruise

both power and sail, require taking turns at the helm so your partner can get some rest. The more you learn, the more opportunities you will have for new adventures farther afield. Share the experience.

About the Boat. Northwest cruising is coastal cruising in generally protected waters, so blue-water ocean voyaging vessels are not required. But the waters can get rough. Whether power or sail, good Northwest cruising boats are strongly built and seaworthy. Lightweight pontoon boats or open ski boats that are so popular on inland lakes are not well suited to these waters.

The weather can be cool and often wet. Northwest cruising powerboats tend to have large cabins and ample window area. Northwest cruising sailboats tend to have dodgers across the fronts of the cockpits or even full cockpit enclosures. Winds often are light and on the nose—"noserlies"—so sailboats should have good power.

Most Northwest cruising boats are equipped with cabin heat. It could be heat generated while the engine is running, a diesel heater or diesel furnace, or electric space heaters on the dock's shore power. Heat can add comfort when it is raining, on a cool night, or when cruising in the off-season.

GPS and chartplotters are standard equipment on Northwest cruising boats. A chartplotter, whether a dedicated marine unit, computer software on a PC or pad/tablet, or app software on your smartphone makes it easy to always know your position.

AIS (Automatic Identification System) is increasingly popular and common-place on Northwest boats. AIS receivers display vessel name, course, speed, and closest point of approach for nearby boats equipped with an AIS transponder, which broadcasts the vessel's boat information, course, and speed. Large commercial and pleasure craft, ferries, cruise ships, and freighters, all broadcast AIS signals. Increasingly, pleasure boats of all sizes are equipped with AIS transponders as well.

Radar has grown better and prices are trending down. Newer digital radar systems require less power, are lighter and often plug right into a chartplotter. Most important, the new digital radar units are very sensitive and provide a better resolution and presentation in color. Since fog and rain clouds can lower visibility to near-zero any time of the year, cruising boats in the Northwest often end up with radar. Autopilots take the uncertainty out of steering in fog and make long passages less tiring. They too are quickly added.

Dinghies and tenders and convenient dinghy launching/recovery systems are important. When anchored or tied to a mooring buoy, the dinghy will be used to travel to shore. Some cruisers use their dinghies extensively for exploring and fishing.

Substantial anchoring systems are important. See the *About Anchoring* section of this chapter for more information.

The minimum size for a cruising boat probably is in the 18- to 20-foot range, and that's pretty minimum. Most mom-and-pop cruising boats fall into the 25- to 50-foot size range, with the majority in the 32- to 50-foot range—large enough to be comfortable, small enough to be handled by two people.

Waste Discharge. There are three types of discharge from a boat that are regulated in both U.S. and BC waters: black water or sewage; gray water from sinks and showers; and bilge water from the vessel's bilge areas. Details of the regulations vary by jurisdiction but the objective is the same, to keep potentially damaging discharge from entering the sea.

Today, most boats with marine toilets are equipped with a Type III Marine Sanitation Device (MSD) or holding tank that stores black water for later disposal at a shore side pumpout facility. Some vessels are equipped with Type I or Type II MSDs where black water is treated before being discharged overboard. No Discharge Zones (NDZ) are areas where discharge of untreated, and in the case of Washington State waters, treated black water, may not be discharged overboard. All

2023 WAGGONER CRUISING GUIDE

HOW TO CRUISE THE PACIFIC NORTHWEST

of Puget Sound waters up to the Canadian border are a NDZ, where no black water (treated and untreated) may be discharged. Free pumpout stations are located at marinas, fuel docks, and public docks throughout Washington's inside waters.

In B.C. waters, there are 14 NDZs located in confined waters such as small bays and harbors where the exchange of sea water is limited. Pumpout facilities can be found on BC's inside waters up to Campbell River and Desolation Sound areas. From Campbell River north to Prince Rupert, pumpout facilities are few and far between. West Coast Vancouver Island has very few. Some pumpouts in BC are free while some charge for their use.

Gray water discharge from onboard sinks and showers is generally not restricted or regulated, and it is okay to discharge overboard. Most boats have no facility for holding gray water. Fortunately, there are only three known locations where it is requested that gray water not be discharged. Longbranch and Eagle Harbor in Washington State, and Pirates Cove in BC, request "no gray water discharge." As a practical matter, most people understand that few boats have facilities for holding gray water and simply ask for voluntary measures to limit the amount of gray water discharge — detergents, soaps, shampoo, and other potentially damaging liquids.

Bilge water containing oils, antifreeze, and other hazardous liquids may not be discharged overboard. Some used motor oil disposal locations also accept bilge water. Improved bilge pumps are now available that detect oil in the bilge and protect against accidental discharge of oil and oily bilge water.

Use FRS (Family Radio Service) Radios. Inexpensive, handy, no license required. If cruising with other boats, they keep needless chatter off VHF channels. Headsets improve communication between skipper, first mate and crew, and reduce the need for shouting when docking. Couples credit headsets with saving a relationship by avoiding yelling.

Carry Tools and Spares. Our tool box is in the main cabin, available for immediate access. It seems like we are in that box at least once a day, usually for something minor, but it has to be fixed. Carry all owner's manuals, extra engine oil, transmission fluid, hydraulic fluid, coolant, and distilled water (for the batteries), spare V-belts, ignition parts, impellers and filters. Carry a spare raw water pump. The list of tools and spares has no end. You can't prepare for everything, but you can prepare for likely problems. Self-amalgamating tape is useful to repair a leaking high pressure fuel line, or to repair a broken oven door handle. This stretchy tape works like magic.

Use Scoot-Gard. This is the bumpy, rubbery material carried on big rolls at the marine store. It keeps things from sliding around. We use it for drawer and shelf liners, food trays and cups while underway, and beneath the laptop computer with our charting and navigation program.

Emergencies & Contingencies. The unexpected can happen, everything from mechanical failures to medical emergencies. If you have a mechanical failure that is urgent but does not pose an immediate danger to anyone's life or to the vessel itself, you can have the Coast Guard send out a PAN-PAN call regarding your situation and location, so that vessels nearby can provide assistance as needed.

In medical emergencies, the Coast Guard can provide locations for the nearest clinic or hospital; and for life-threatening medical emergencies, provide air-lift services. The Coast Guard may also have an on-duty flight surgeon to talk with. If you are known to have health issues, it may be wise to invest in emergency travel insurance. We carry DAN travel insurance, designed for boaters. In Canada, you can dial 811 for free medical information. In the U.S., medical insurance plans often have a free advice nurse line to call for helpful information.

Insurance. Purchasing and maintaining insurance for your vessel, including liability coverage, is a necessary part of boat ownership. When you consider the costs involved in the loss of a vessel, recovery costs, cleanup to the environment, and injury or loss of life, not having insurance can spell financial ruin.

Start here, start now!

FLAGSHIP MARITIME

U.S. Coast Guard Captain's License Training

OUPV / 6-Pack • Upgrade OUPV to Master 100 Tons
Commercial Assistance Towing • Auxiliary Sail Endorsement
FCC Marine Radio Operator Permit • License Renewals
Maritime Licensing and Consulting Services

Experience the Flagship difference for yourself!
Enroll today!
(253) 905-5972
www.flagshipmaritimellc.com

HOW TO CRUISE THE PACIFIC NORTHWEST

Some marinas require evidence of Liability coverage for overnight guest moorage stays.

It is important to choose an insurance agent or agency that specializes in marine insurance and understands all the aspects of recreational boating. The cost of boat insurance varies widely based on a number of factors regarding both the vessel and the owner's experience. The best insurance policy is the one that is appropriate for your vessel, your experience, and where you plan to do your boating. The list below includes a number of the variables that influence cost.

The Vessel
- Year, make, and model
- Purchase price
- Construction – fiberglass, wood, steel
- Power – inboard, outboard; power or sail
- Speed – maximum speed

Vessel Owner
- Training
- Experience
- Loss history
- Navigation area

Insurance companies usually require a boat survey after a number of years of operation. Be sure to check your policy and schedule a boat survey ahead of time. The survey may result in some needed repairs to maintain the current cost of your boat insurance.

The area in which you will be navigating also plays a role in the cost of insurance. Navigating in more remote areas like West Coast Vancouver Island and Southeast Alaska carries additional risks than boating in well-charted, protected inside waters. The time of year you are out boating also is a factor. Be sure you know your limits of navigation per the policy. If going beyond the policy's defined navigation area, you should get a special "trip permit" for a specified period of time to cruise the area; the cost of the trip permit will depend on your experience and may or may not be granted. Navigation limits used by some insurers for PNW waters are:

- Inland Waters of Puget Sound and British Columbia – includes everything inside a 25-mile radius of Cape Flattery, not west of Hope Island, and south of 51 Degrees North.
- Inside Passage to Southeast Alaska – the Inside Waters plus the waters of Gulf of Alaska not west of Cape Spencer; you need to be south of 51 Degrees North between September 16 through May 14.
- Coast Wise & Inland Waters – allows travel in Southeast Alaska and coastal cruising but not west of Cape Spenser nor south of Acapulco.

Clothing. Except for some areas of Desolation Sound in the summer, most of the waters of the Northwest are cold. Even during warm weather you may welcome a sweater or jacket. Layering clothing works well. Rain gear is essential on sailboats and when hiking ashore. Rubber boots are a must. Shoreside and restaurant attire can be as nice as you want; most people do fine with comfortable sports clothes.

Update Credit Cards. Credit and debit cards seem to be the preferred form of payment on both sides of the border. Even the remote areas have some means of accepting credit or debit cards. Some credit card companies have a very favorable exchange rate. Before traveling out of the country, call your credit card companies to tell them where you will be and the dates of your trip. Otherwise they will refuse a charge, usually at the most awkward moment.

Assisting Others. When helping arriving boats, follow the skipper's instructions. When we take a line we hold it loosely, awaiting instructions. Most skippers have a plan that will stop the boat and lay it alongside the dock. A bow line pulled tight at the wrong time can ruin the plan: the bow swings toward the dock and the stern swings away. Obviously, if the landing plan has failed and the boat is being swept off, the dock crew goes into action. Even then it's a good idea to confirm with the skipper rather than acting on one's own.

Don't Be Cheap. It's bad form to come in by dinghy and use a private marina's facilities and not pay for the privilege. Even if a direct charge is not made, usually something can be purchased. Offering to pay for temporary moorage is appreciated. Boaters should be pleased to do their part in providing financial support for marinas; we want these facilities to be there in the future.

Boat Cards. Consider making a boat card. One of the joys of cruising is the people you meet along the way. Boat cards are like business cards for your boat, and make it easy to stay in touch with people you meet.

Pets. Keep pets on leash, and clean up after them. Many people cruise with pets. Some marinas are more pet-friendly than others. Use the designated pet-walking areas. Don't let the dog lift his leg against the water faucet or power box. Carry plastic bags and clean up if the pet doesn't make it to the potty area. Some designated wildlife areas do not permit dogs ashore.

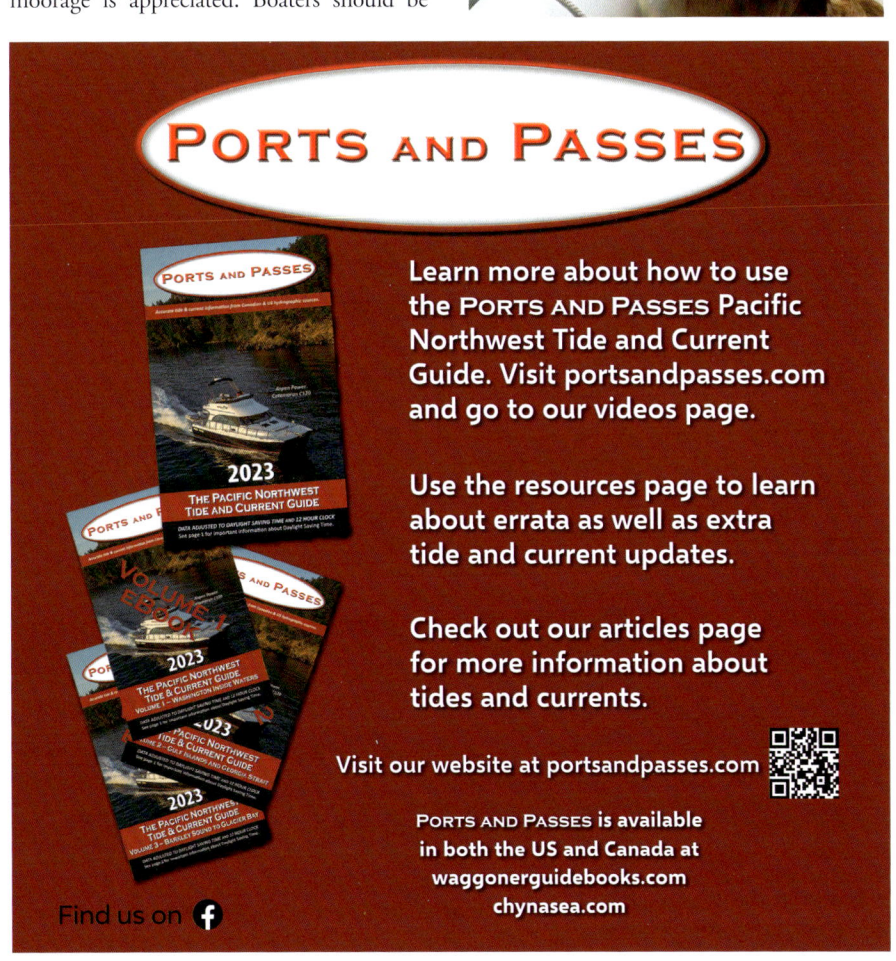

PORTS AND PASSES

Learn more about how to use the PORTS AND PASSES Pacific Northwest Tide and Current Guide. Visit portsandpasses.com and go to our videos page.

Use the resources page to learn about errata as well as extra tide and current updates.

Check out our articles page for more information about tides and currents.

Visit our website at portsandpasses.com

PORTS AND PASSES is available in both the US and Canada at
waggonerguidebooks.com
chynasea.com

Find us on [f]

2023 WAGGONER CRUISING GUIDE

U.S. AND CANADIAN CUSTOMS INFORMATION

U.S. Customs – CBP ROAM App & CBP One App

U.S. Customs and Border Protection (CBP) ROAM App can be used when entering at state of Washington and Alaska Ports of Entry. The App can make your arrival reporting with U.S. Customs a lot easier. **R**eporting **O**ffsite **A**rrival – **M**obile, **ROAM** App, can be used at Washington pleasure craft Port of Entry locations including Anacortes, Point Roberts, Friday Harbor, Roche Harbor, and Port Angeles. In Alaska the App can be used at Ketchikan and Wrangell Ports of Entry. This official CBP App will support Apple iOS and Google Android phones and tablet mobile devices. Travelers entering U.S. waters can check-in using the App, and CBP officers can initiate a video chat for information verification, or an interview if required. If approved for entry, boaters do not have to report in-person at a Port of Entry.

Overview ROAM App, input your biographic, vessel, and trip details into the App. Then submit your arrival for CBP Officer review by pressing the App's **Report Arrival** selection on your mobile device. A CBP Officer may initiate a video chat to further interview travelers. Once the CBP Officer reviews the information, you will receive a notification and email with your clearance status and next steps, if applicable. The App needs to have cellular data connection or Wi-Fi service to report and process your arrival. The App works best with 4G, LTE, or better cell service. However, boaters are successfully using it on 3G as well.

Who Can Use the ROAM App? U.S. and foreign travelers can use the App to report arrival. You don't need to be part of a trusted traveler program to use ROAM. Reporting arrival in-person at one of the Port of Entry locations is still available. Cruising Licenses can be requested with the ROAM App and the License is usually emailed to you. Travelers who must pay duties will need to report in-person to CBP at the nearest Port of Entry. Travelers with I-68 or Nexus may still report by calling the CBP Small Boat Reporting Office; however, this option may be replaced by ROAM at some future date.

To Install and Prepare the App, you will need an iOS or Android phone or tablet with camera. You will also need an email address. The App is free and available from the Apple App Store and the Google Play Store. To get started:

- Download and install the App.
- Setup a Login.gov account (if you don't already have one). Login.gov is a U.S. General Services Administration website and service, providing a single sign-in account to multiple participating government programs. If you are enrolled in Nexus you probably already have a Login.gov account. You can create an account from the ROAM App.
- After opening the App and logging-in, add information about your boat (make, year, registration number, length). You can add and save information for more than one boat.
- Add information about the travelers who will be on your boat when reporting in with ROAM. The App will scan each person's travel documents such as Passport, Nexus, Enhanced U.S. Drivers License, Global Entry, Birth Certificate (kids 15 and under), and Permanent Resident Card.

To Report Arrival with ROAM App:

- Report Arrival as soon as you enter U.S. waters. Report Arrival requests made outside of U.S. waters will be rejected; except CBP in Ketchikan may allow arrival reports with ROAM in Prince Rupert, where cell coverage is better.
- Ensure that you have a good cell signal and that you will be able to maintain cell coverage.
- Open and sign-in to the ROAM App.
- Press the **Report Arrival** selection, then select the mode of transportation (boat) and select travelers from saved profile information and designate one of the selected travelers as the vessel master.
- Answer all questions with further details and items to declare.
- Press the **Submit** selection - you will get a tracking number - this is NOT your clearance number.
- The app goes into pending status while CBP officers on the other end process the information. Be patient, this may take a while (5, 10, 15 minutes or more) before receiving a response.
- You will next get a response from the App with a clearance number, or instructions for further processing, which may include going to the nearest CBP Port of Entry for in-person processing.
- Your clearance number will show on the App and in a message to the email address on your Login.gov account profile.

CBP One App

CBP plans to replace CBP ROAM with added functionality to their existing CBP One App. CBP One is a free official CBP App that is currently available for download on Android and iOS devices. CBP One has been in use since late 2020 for I-94 travelers and other commercial border crossings. CBP plans on moving the CBP ROAM App function to the CBP One umbrella. CBP One will become a border crossing App with many features and services. Once the pleasure boat reporting functionality is available on CBP One, the ROAM App will be withdrawn.

CBP One functionality to report arrival and for foreign-flagged vessels to request a Cruising License is expected to be equivalent or better than the existing CBP ROAM App. One already has a number of border related functions and appears to be targeted as the umbrella CBP App for a wide array of border related functions.

It is not clear how the ROAM to One App transition will happen and if ROAM will continue to be available for an overlap period.

For more about CBP ROAM and CBP One, see the CBP website www.cbp.gov.

[Leonard Landon]

U.S. AND CANADIAN CUSTOMS INFORMATION

U.S. / CANADA BORDER CROSSING

Customs must be cleared whenever the U.S.-Canada border is crossed in either direction. Generally, the process is quick and straightforward; but if the skipper isn't prepared with the proper information, it can be time consuming. It is extremely important to follow all the rules and be polite. While customs officers are trained in courtesy and usually are cordial, they have at their disposal regulations that can ruin your day. Take border crossing seriously, failure to follow the rules can have onerous consequences. Prepare ahead of time by inventorying items on board that need to be declared. Declare everything that must be reported, have a written list, don't trust your memory. Follow all the rules and report to customs as soon as possible after crossing the border. We know of an instance where a pleasure boater had their vessel seized by customs officials for failure to report their arrival in a timely manner. Their boat was finally returned, but only after paying a fine of $1,000. Another boater neglected to sign their new passport, which caused some significant delays and anxiety for family members. Be prepared and follow the rules so border crossings are non-events.

All vessels are required to clear with Customs when arriving in either the U.S. or Canada from a foreign port. Canadian and U.S. vessels do not need to clear out when leaving Canada. U.S. vessels do not need to clear out when leaving the U.S., except if the vessel is being exported. Canadian vessels with a U.S. Cruising License do not need to clear out when leaving U.S. waters. All non-U.S. flagged vessels (including Canadian) without a U.S. Cruising License are required to check-out when leaving U.S. waters.

Customs hours, rules, and requirements can and do change with short notice throughout the year. We urge readers to check the U.S. Customs and Border Protection (CBP) website www.cbp.gov and Canada Border Services Agency (CBSA) website www.cbsa-asfc.gc.ca for the latest. Check the Waggoner Guide website www.WaggonerGuide.com for border crossing updates.

Passports. If you don't have passports, we encourage you to get them. Lacking a passport, carry proof of citizenship such as an enhanced driver's license, enhanced identification, birth certificate, certificate of citizenship or naturalization, and photo ID. Standard (non-enhanced) drivers licenses are not proof of citizenship and are not accepted for border crossing. Citizens of some countries need visas as well. Carry birth certificates for all minors aboard — you may be asked for them.

Trusted Traveler Programs. Canada and U.S. have a number of Trusted Traveler Programs that expedite border crossings for boaters when all on board the vessel are enrolled in one of these programs. Nexus is a joint Canada and U.S. program that is recognized on both sides of the border and can expedite customs clearance going either direction. Most other programs are singular to one side of the border or the other.

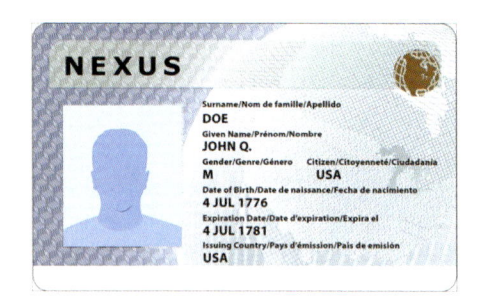

Nexus. With Nexus, each person applies online and then is contacted to set an appointment for an interview by both Canadian and U.S. customs agents at the Vancouver, B.C., Blaine, WA or Seattle, WA CBP offices. The card is good for 5 years, and the cost is $50 U.S. or CDN per person. From start to finish, the entire process takes several months. If you cross the border by car along with your card, you'll have the additional benefit of using the Nexus lanes at the border. For general information or to begin the application process, U.S. citizens can go to www.cbp.gov, and Canadians go to www.cbsa-asfc.gc.ca.

Clearance Numbers. A clearance number will be issued to you when you have successfully completed reporting to the respective U.S. or Canadian customs agency. Keep a record of your clearance number, along with the date, time and location of clearance. You may be asked for this number later. Canada requires that foreign flagged vessels post their clearance number on a dock side viewable window while in Canadian waters. Keep a record of interactions with border officers. If you have received permissions or instructions from a customs officer via telephone, record the date and time of the conversation along with name or badge number.

Contact Customs or Coast Guard. If unforeseen circumstances don't allow you to report to customs authorities as soon as possible after crossing the border, telephone customs authorities and report your circumstances. If you don't have cellular coverage, hail the Coast Guard on VHF and report your situation. This applies to crossing the border in either direction and with both Coast Guard agencies.

Don't Cross Border with Marijuana. Even though recreational marijuana may be legal in both British Columbia and the State of Washington, it is illegal to transport marijuana in any quantity across the Canada-U.S. border in either direction.

Be sure to have your passports ready when clearing customs.

Scan This QR code for the latest.

tinyurl.com/WG22xCh01

2023 WAGGONER CRUISING GUIDE

CANADIAN CUSTOMS INFORMATION

CANADA BORDER SERVICES AGENCY (CBSA) Proof of citizenship and identification, such as Canadian or U.S. passport, U.S. Passport card, Trusted Traveler Program cards (Nexus and Sentri), State or Provincial issued enhanced driver's license, is required of all on board when entering Canada. If you are bringing a child other than your own into Canada, carry a notarized statement authorizing you to take the child into Canada and proof that the person signing the statement has custody of the child. The letter should include parents' or guardians' addresses and phone numbers. Canada Border Services Agency website has a sample letter.

Reporting to Canada Customs. All vessels arriving in Canada from a foreign country must clear Border Services immediately after the vessel comes to rest. The master, or the master's designated representative, must report to Border Services in-person or by telephone from a Border Services direct land line phone, or by calling (888) 226-7277. No one else may leave the vessel, and no baggage or merchandise may be removed from the vessel.

You must report at a designated port of entry, see the list below. At some locations, Border Services officers will be present; at many other locations you will report by telephone. Even if you report by telephone, your boat may be subject to inspection. To avoid delays, have the following information ready when you report:

- Vessel name, length, and Coast Guard documentation number or state/province registration number
- Number of people on board
- Names, addresses, citizenship, birth dates and passport numbers of all passengers
- Purpose of the trip
- Number of pets on board – proof of vaccination needed
- Declare if you have cash over $10,000
- Length of absence from Canada (Canadian boats); Length and purpose of stay in Canada (U.S. boats)
- Quantity and type of alcoholic beverages
- Declare all goods being imported, including firearms

Once cleared, either by phone or by an officer, you will be given a clearance number. Post your clearance number in both side windows. Log this number with the date, time, and place of clearance. Vessels are subject to re-inspection while in Canadian waters, usually by RCMP officers when their patrol boat reaches a marina. The officers are well trained and polite, but be sure you don't have anything on board you shouldn't have.

ArriveCAN App. Established in 2020 as part of the Covid-19 process for entering or returning to Canada. Use of the ArriveCAN App was discontinued in October 2022 and is no longer required. The App is still available and can be used when flying into one of three major airports to save time by completing an Advance CBSA Declaration.

Nexus. If all passengers aboard a boat have a Nexus permit, a vessel can clear Canada Border Services Agency by calling, toll-free, (866) 996-3987 at least 30 minutes and up to 4 hours before arriving at a designated CBSA or Nexus reporting station. The vessel must physically check in at a designated CBSA or Nexus reporting station/dock.

At the time of Nexus call-in, the Border Services officer will ask for the vessel's identification number, vessel's intended reporting station, estimated time of arrival (ETA), purpose of the trip, and length of stay. You must appear at the appointed reporting station before your declared ETA and wait at the station until the ETA. If no officer is present at the reporting station before the ETA, you may continue on your way, without further action.

A good practice is to take a photo, with date and time stamp, of yourselves and your boat at the reporting station – just in case. In the accompanying list of designated reporting stations, note that some are for Nexus/Canpass vessels only and can only be used by vessels where all on board have Nexus or Canpass.

Canpass-Private Boats. Canpass-Private Boats program was discontinued in 2018. New applications for the program are no longer being accepted. Those with valid and unexpired Canpass cards can continue to use them until the expiration date.

Firearms Restrictions. You may not bring switchblades, most handguns, automatic weapons, anti-personnel pepper spray or mace into Canada. Under certain circumstances, some long guns are allowed. Bear spray, if labeled as such, is permitted if declared. A Non-Resident Firearm Declaration Form is needed to bring firearms into Canada. Call the Canadian Firearms Centre at (800) 731-4000 for a copy of the form, or download one from www.cfc-cafc.gc.ca. The cost is $25 CDN, and it is good for 60 days. All weapons and firearms must be declared to CBSA.

Liquor & Tobacco Restrictions. Not more than 1.14 liters (38.5 oz.) of hard liquor, or 1.5 liters of wine, or a total of 1.14 liters of wine and liquor, or 24 12-ounce bottles of beer or ale per person of legal drinking age (19 years old in B.C.). Not more than 1 carton of cigarettes and 2 cans (200 grams) of tobacco and 50 cigars or cigarillos, and 200 tobacco sticks per person 19 or older without paying duty and taxes on the excess amount.

Food Restrictions. Food restrictions are subject to change without notice. Check the CBSA website at **www.cbsa-asfc.gc.ca** for updates. Canadian customs has an interactive website where you enter the food item you are planning to bring into Canada, and after selecting options regarding the item's origin and planned use, you will get an Approved or Not Approved determination. See the CBSA website for a link to this Automated Import Reference System (AIRS) website.

Other than restricted foods, you can carry quantities of food appropriate for your stay. Be aware of the following restrictions and limitations:

- No houseplants (including potted herbs)
- No apples, no pitted fruit (apricots, plums, peaches) Cherries are sometimes okay
- Potatoes from US are allowed – 1 bag per person of US #1 commercially packaged
- All firewood is prohibited

If in doubt, call (204) 983-3500 for inspection.

CBSA officers routinely come to your boat when clearing customs into Canada

CANADIAN CUSTOMS INFORMATION

CBSA Points of Entry locations have a direct connect landline phone for contacting CBSA, or you can use your cell phone.

Duty-free Limits. Canadian residents returning to Canada may be eligible for a personal exemption on duty for goods brought into Canada. An exemption on goods up to $200 CDN is allowed for out-of-country stays of more than 24 hours. The exemption for stays of 48 hours or more is $800 CDN and may include alcohol and tobacco items. See the CBSA website for full details.

Declare All Items. If in doubt, declare it to CBSA. This is especially true for food items. If you are not sure, simply declare it and let the CBSA officer make the decision. It is always best to inform CBSA agents of items that you have on board. Failure to declare items can result in fines and penalties.

Pets. Owners of dogs and cats must bring a certificate issued by a licensed U.S. or Canadian veterinarian clearly identifying the pet and certifying that it has been vaccinated against rabies during the previous 36 months.

Cannabis. Even though recreational cannabis is legal in both Washington State and British Columbia, transporting cannabis across the border in any form without a permit or exemption remains a serious criminal offence. The prohibition applies regardless of whether you hold a medical document authorizing the use of cannabis for medical purposes and regardless of traveling from an area that has decriminalized cannabis.

Currency. Cash or other monetary instruments in excess of $10,000 CDN must be reported.

For current rules and regulations, check out the CBSA website at www.cbsa-asfc.gc.ca.

B.C. POINTS OF ENTRY

Designated B.C. Points of Entry for Pleasure Craft Reporting
All locations contact Canada Border Services Agency
Toll-free (888) 226-7277 (7 days a week, 24 hours a day)

Bedwell Harbour: May 1 to Thursday before Victoria Day
  9:00 a.m. to 5:00 p.m.
  Friday before Victoria Day to Labour Day
  8:00 a.m. to 8:00 p.m.
  Tuesday after Labour Day to Sept. 30
  9:00 a.m. to 5:00 p.m.

Cabbage Island: (Canpass/Nexus only)

Campbell River: Coast Marina;
  Discovery Harbour Marina

Galiano Island: Montague Harbour Marina
  (Canpass/Nexus only)

Mayne Island: Horton Bay (Canpass/Nexus only)
  Miners Bay (Canpass/Nexus only)

Nanaimo: Nanaimo Port Authority Basin–E Dock

North Pender Is.: Port Browning Marina (Canpass/Nexus only)

Prince Rupert: Cow Bay Marina
  Fairview Govt. Dock
  Prince Rupert Rowing and Yacht Club
  Rushbrooke Government Dock

Saltspring Is.: Ganges Harbour–Seaplane Dock
  First floating breakwater (Canpass/Nexus only)
  Royal Victoria YC Outst.(Canpass/Nexus only)

Sidney: Canoe Cove Marina
  Port Sidney Marina
  Royal Victoria YC Outstation
  Tsehum Harbour Public Wharf
  Van Isle Marina

Ucluelet: 52 Steps Dock–seasonal only in the past;
  Closed during Covid and Closed in 2022
  Contact CBSA for current status

Vancouver: False Creek Fisherman's Wharf
  Steveston Harbour Authority (Canpass/Nexus)
  Royal Vancouver Yacht Club–Coal Harbour
  Harbour Green Dock

Victoria: Oak Bay Marina
  Royal Victoria YC (Cadboro Bay)
  Raymur Point CBSA Dock
  Cdn Forces Sailing Assoc. (Esquimalt Hrbr)

White Rock: White Rock Government Dock
  Crescent Beach Marina

U.S. CUSTOMS INFORMATION

U.S. CUSTOMS AND BORDER PROTECTION (CBP) requires approved identification, such as a U.S. or Canadian passport, U.S. Passport card, Trusted Traveler Program cards (Nexus and Sentri), I-68, State or Provincial issued enhanced driver's license for entry to the U.S. We recommend that everyone aboard have a passport.

Reporting to U.S. Customs. The boat's captain must report arrival in U.S. waters and obtain clearance from CBP at a designated port of entry; OR by using the CBP ROAM/CBP One smartphone App; OR if all on board are enrolled in Nexus, I-68, or Global Entry, clearance may be conducted by calling (800) 562-5943. Whether in-person, by ROAM/One App, or by voice call, have the following information at-hand in order to avoid delays:

- Name, date of birth and citizenship of all persons on board (including passport number or citizenship identification)
- Name of the boat and vessel registration or documentation number
- Nexus BR Number
- Vessel homeport and current location
- CBP user fee decal number (30 feet in length and over), or Cruising License Number for foreign flagged vessels (including Canadian vessels).
- Canadian customs clearance number for U.S. flagged boats.
- Estimated length of stay in U.S. for Canadian vessels and other foreign flagged vessels.
- For U.S. vessels, date you departed U.S. and how long you were in Canada

Designated Washington U.S. Ports of Entry. Arrivals requiring an in-person report may be made at any of the following Ports of Entry: Friday Harbor, Roche Harbor, Port Angeles, Point Roberts, and Anacortes. All other ports require appointments to be made in advance for in-person inspections (during regular business hours only). Don't assume that if you call for an appointment you will get one. To save time and avoid problems, clear U.S. Customs at one of the five designated Ports of Entry. If you arrive after normal business hours, call (800) 562-5943 for further instructions. Local customs office numbers are listed later in this section. I-68s are available at all locations listed.

Entering Alaska. All vessels entering Southeast Alaska from a foreign country must clear U.S. Customs. Vessels may clear customs by reporting in-person in Ketchikan; OR with CBP ROAM/One App; OR by telephone if all on board are enrolled in Nexus, I-68 or Global Entry. For detailed instructions on clearing U.S. Customs in Alaska, see the *Southeast Alaska Chapter*.

CBP ROAM/One APP. CBP ROAM and CBP One are official smartphone Apps that can make your arrival reporting within U.S. waters easier and may expedite your U.S. customs clearance. Boaters can check-in with CBP using the App as soon as they enter U.S. waters and have cell phone coverage. CBP officers access your boat and traveler information with the App and can open a video chat to obtain and verify information if needed. CBP will then either clear you for entry with a clearance number, or direct you to a designated U.S. Port of Entry for further processing. Those approved for entry do not need to report in-person at a Port of Entry. The App is available for clearance 24/7. Check with CBP to confirm hours of operation.

Membership in a Trusted Traveler program is not required in order to use the App; it can be used by U.S. and foreign travelers. The App can be used when entering at Washington and Alaska Ports of Entry for pleasure craft. The App supports iOS and Android phones and tablet mobile devices. The App works best with 4G, 5G or LTE service and is reported to also work with 3G service. Boaters needing a Cruising License can request a Cruising License via the App; and if granted, it can be emailed. Those who must pay duty will need to report in-person to a Port of Entry. For more about the App and its use, see the www.cbp.gov website.

Clearing by Telephone. Boaters with nothing to declare normally can clear U.S. Customs by telephone, if all on board have Nexus, I-68s or Global Entry. With Nexus, I-68 or Global Entry, you can call the Small Boat Reporting Office after entering U.S. waters, at (800) 562-5943 to report arrival and request clearance. When calling underway, call from an area with good reception. While you report, slow to idle speed to reduce background noise and remain in the good reception area. The Small Boat Reporting Office operates from 7:00 a.m. to 10:00 p.m. from May through September, and from 7:00 a.m. to 8:00 p.m. the balance of the year. If you enter the U.S. outside these hours, you must remain aboard your boat until you can clear.

I-68. The I-68 Permit is valid for 1 year from the date of issue. U.S. citizens, Lawful Permanent Residents, Canadian citizens and Landed Immigrants of Canada who are nationals of Visa Waiver Program countries are eligible to apply. The cost is $16 per person, $32 for families. Apply at CBP offices within the Puget Sound area. Bring proof of citizenship, such as a passport, certified copy of your birth certificate, photo ID, and vessel information. Each person applying must appear. Children under 14 can be listed on parents' I-68.

Small Vessel Reporting System (SVRS). The Small Vessel Reporting System program was replaced in 2018 with the CBP ROAM App. SVRS program is no longer available.

U.S. Customs and Border Protection
www.cbp.gov
(877) 227-5511

CBP ROAM App is planned to be replaced with CBP One App. CBP One is planned to functionally replace CBP ROAM.

Processing Fee (CBP Decal). Pleasure vessels 30 feet in length or more must pay an annual processing (user) fee for the CBP Decal to enter or re-enter the United States. Vessels less than 30 feet are not subject to the fee, provided they have nothing to declare. Payment is required at or before the vessel's first arrival each calendar year. If you report by telephone, they charge your credit card. A non-transferable decal will be issued upon payment. Renewal notices for the next year's decal are mailed or emailed in the autumn. Vessels with a valid Cruising License do not have to pay this fee and do not require a CBP Decal. Order your sticker before you need to enter the U.S. Even if you have Nexus, I-68 or Global Entry preclearance, lack of a current-year sticker may direct you to a designated port of entry for inspection. User Fee stickers are not sold at CBP offices, but can be ordered online at https://dtops.cbp.dhs.gov, or by phone (317) 298-1245, or email decals@cbp.dhs.gov, or through the ROAM/One App.

Cruising License. A Cruising License (sometimes referred to as a Cruising Permit) is available to Canadian and most foreign flagged vessels. A Cruising License saves time and money for foreign flagged vessels frequenting U.S. waters. Foreign vessels without a Cruising License must complete form CBP-1300 and pay a Navigation Fee upon entering U.S. waters, and each subsequent movement between U.S. ports, and upon exiting U.S. waters. With a Cruising License, you only need to complete form CBP-1300 upon the vessel's initial reporting and clearance with CBP. There is no fee for the Cruising License or form CBP-1300.

To get a Cruising License, foreign vessels upon entering U.S. waters can request a Cruising License at a Port of Entry; OR when reporting arrival with CBP ROAM/One App upon their initial entry. There is no charge for the Cruising License, and vessels with a Cruising License do not need the CBP Decal. Cruising Licenses are good for one year or upon surrendering to CBP when leaving U.S. waters. Cruising Licenses cannot be extended and are available only when the vessel reports arrival at Port of Entry or via CBP ROAM/One.

Foreign flagged vessels made outside of the U.S. must wait 15 days after expiration of their Cruising License before requesting a new one. During this 15-day period, the vessel may enter and depart U.S. waters by submitting a CBP-1300 and paying the Navigation Fee upon entry, exit, and movement. Vessels made in U.S. are exempt from this 15-day waiting period.

U.S. CUSTOMS INFORMATION

Cruising Licenses do not affect customs reporting requirements. Foreign vessels with a Cruising License are required to report arrival upon entering U.S. waters at a Port of Entry or by CBP ROAM/One app and provide their Cruising License Number. Vessels with a Cruising License are required to report movement from one port to another within U.S. waters. All of Washington's inside waters ports (Ports of Puget Sound), except for Blaine and Pt. Roberts, are treated by CBP as one port, and reporting port to port movement is not required within Ports of Puget Sound locations. In Southeast Alaska, vessels with a Cruising License are required to Report Arrival with CBP upon movement between ports after their initial entry into U.S. waters. Port to port reporting can be done with CBP ROAM/One app or by contacting the nearest CBP office.

Food Restrictions. Food restrictions are subject to change without notice. See www.WaggonerGuide.com/Updates for the latest information about border crossing. For specific food related questions, contact an Agricultural Specialist at (360) 332-8661 or (360) 988-2971. As a general guideline, any food you bring into the U.S. must be made or grown in Canada or the U.S., and labeled as such. Potatoes should be kept in original commercial packaging. Don't bring fresh tropical fruits or vegetables in, even if you bought them in the U.S. CBP recommends declaring all meat and produce when entering the U.S. If declared, prohibited goods will be seized but no fine will be levied. Subject to change without notice, use the following list to minimize problems:

- No sheep, lamb or goat in any form; this includes pet food
- Beef, pork, chicken, turkey and meat products from Canada are allowed
- Keep pet food in original packaging
- No fresh citrus, regardless of where you bought it
- No fresh produce (vegetables or fruit) grown outside the U.S. and Canada
- Canned fruits and vegetables, however, are unrestricted regardless of origin; leave labels/stickers on cans
- No tomatoes
- No garlic, chives, green onions, leeks, and other green Allium vegetables from Canada
- No cut flowers or potted plants (they are subject to so many restrictions that it's better to leave them in Canada and avoid the hassle)
- Seafood is okay
- Dairy products are okay
- Eggs are usually okay
- All firewood is prohibited; boaters with firewood may be required to return to Canada to dispose of it

Pets. Dogs and cats must be healthy. The requirement for evidence of rabies vaccination for dogs coming from certain countries was removed in 2018. Birds are subject to USDA Veterinarian inspection to enter or re-enter. It is usually not advisable to bring birds across the border.

Currency. Cash or other monetary instruments in excess of $10,000 U.S. per boat must be reported.

Duty-free Limits. U.S. residents outside of the U.S. less than 48 hours can import merchandise up to $200 in value per person without duty. If the stay is more than 48 hours, the limit is $800 per person.

For ease and simplicity, try to restrict what you bring back home to products made or grown in Canada (sometimes even that isn't sufficient). For the latest customs information, go to the U.S. Customs and Border Protection website pages for pleasure boats at www.cbp.gov.

Declare All Items. If in doubt, declare the item to CBP. This is especially true for food products. If you are not sure, simply declare it and let the CBP officer make the decision. It is always best to inform CBP agents of items that you have on board. Failure to declare items can result in fines and penalties.

Pilotage Exemption for Foreign Flagged Vessels. Foreign flagged vessels (other than Canadian) in Washington waters are required by Washington State law to have an exemption in order to operate without a professional Pilot. To request an exemption, download and submit an application from the www.pilotage.wa.gov website or call the Washington Board of Pilotage Commissioners at (206) 215-3904.

Aquatic Invasive Species (AIS) Prevention Permit. Most boats operating in Washington State waters that do not have a Washington State registration sticker need to purchase and carry an AIS Prevention Permit. Dinghies are exempt. Permits can be purchased online at fishhunt.dfw.wa.gov/#/catalog/products on the "Other" tab, or at any Washington State Department of Fish and Wildlife license retailer. The permit is good for one year.

U.S. POINTS OF ENTRY

Anacortes (360) 293-2331
 Office at Cap Sante Marina
 8:00 a.m. to 8:00 p.m. Summer
 8:00 a.m. to 5:00 p.m. Off-season
 closed 1 ½ hours mid-afternoon)

Friday Harbor (360) 378-2080
 Customs booth at the dock with phone
 Office at Spring & First Streets
 8:00 a.m. to 8:00 p.m. Summer
 8:00 a.m. to 5:00 p.m. Off-season

Point Roberts (360) 945-5211
 or (360) 945-2314
 Customs Dock near Fuel Dock
 8:00 a.m. to 8:00 p.m. Summer
 8:00 a.m. to 5:00 p.m. Off-season

Port Angeles (360) 457-4311
 Office Boat Haven
 8:00 a.m. to 9:00 p.m. Summer
 8:00 a.m. to 5:30 p.m. Off-season

Roche Harbor (360) 378-2080
 Customs dock at Roche Harbor Marina
 8:00 a.m. to 8:00 p.m. Summer
 8:00 a.m. to 5:00 p.m. Off-season

Ketchikan (907) 225-2254
 Call and wait for agent at assigned slip
 6:00 a.m. to 6:00 p.m. Year-round
 Available 7/24 by phone

Other Customs Offices
(by appointment only, call 24 hours ahead for availability and instructions):

Bellingham (360) 734-5463
Blaine (360) 332-6318
Everett (425) 259-0246
Port Townsend (360) 385-3777

Clearing customs at Roche Harbor on San Juan Island

MARINE WEATHER - COLLECTING AND EVALUATING

MARINE WEATHER - TOPICS

Step by Step Process for Collecting and Evaluating Weather
Go-NoGo Worksheet
Go-NoGo Checklists
Where To Get Weather Information
Interpreting Forecast Charts & Reports
VHF Marine Broadcast Sequence
Lightstation Report Formats
Weather Buoy Information
Weather Station Maps

Weather is one of the biggest fears of many boat crews. There is a lot of information available when you know how to get it, know how to understand it and evaluate it in order to make an effective go, or no-go decision.

Go-NoGo Worksheet. A worksheet to facilitate collecting and organizing forecast and observed conditions information is available as a free download at the Waggoner Guide Store. A sample follows, see *Passage Go-NoGo Worksheet* on this page.

Internet, Cell Phone and VHF WX. At Waggoner, we have developed a means of using all of the weather information available to avoid getting into an uncomfortable situation. Many boaters do not realize how you can use the internet to gather a good picture of the weather. No internet available? If you have cell phone coverage, you can call for weather and buoy reports. Out in a very remote area? If you have VHF WX coverage, you can gather the right information you need over the radio. In remote areas of Haida Gwaii and Northern B.C., you can use satellite based systems such as Garmin InReach, Iridium Go, and Globalstar Sat-Fi to access weather information. There is a description of this system in the *Cellular, Internet and Satellite Communications* section of this chapter.

STEP 1 - Weather Overview. First, start by using the internet to view weather information days before your intended departure. Use the NOAA Ocean Prediction Center, Pacific Region, Current Surface Analysis and then the 24, 48, 72, and 96 hour forecasts to look at the weather patterns as they develop and cross the Pacific Ocean.

We look at the High and Low pressure systems (see Figures 1, 2, & 3 on the following pages) and how they are forecast to move; typically from west to east. While this is offshore weather, it provides an indication of the weather systems that will pass over Puget Sound and the Inside Passage. Often in July and early August, a large high pressure system will sit offshore resulting in good weather for an extended period of time. This is called the Pacific High and typically offers favorable conditions.

STEP 2 - Isobar Lines. Next we look at the isobar lines over the coastal areas where we will be cruising. The isobar lines show the change in barometric pressure over a distance (see Figures 1, 2, & 3). Tighter isobar patterns show areas of wind and its counterclockwise direction around a low. We look for areas of big lazy (widely separated) isobars around a high indicating limited wind. Looking at the weather charts gives us a visual overview of the weather and the systems that will be affecting our route over the next couple of days. To add to the overview, we look at one of the visual services on the internet, www.windy.com. This website puts the weather prediction models into motion, where you can see the wind patterns circulating and how they flow across the Pacific. You can also see a visual of the offshore wind and sea conditions. Another popular weather App for mariners is PredictWind. It too presents a lot of visual information when an internet connection is available.

STEP 3 - The Forecast. We then look at the NOAA Marine Forecasts for US waters, and when traveling north into British Columbia, we look at the Environment Canada Marine Pacific reports and forecasts. We compare the forecast in text format with the NOAA Surface Analysis charts. They should coincide (see Figures 4, 5, & 6).

STEP 4 - Weather Reporting Stations. Using the three *Weather Reporting Stations* reference maps in the following pages, enter the weather reporting station names that are along your day's planned route onto the worksheet. Then gather the current observed weather reports for these stations from either the internet, by calling the recorded weather telephone number(s) noted on the following page, or by listening on the WX VHF. The Go-NoGo worksheet list of weather reporting stations keeps us focused on the stations we care to record from the continuous audio format. When listening to the WX channels, listen for the station names along the route. Figures 7 and 8 on the following pages have outlines of the Continuous Marine Broadcasts for both U.S. NWS and Environment Canada. They are different. The outline will help you determine where you are in the sequence of a WX broadcast.

Passage GO-NoGO Worksheet

Day's Passage:

Date: _10/21/22_   From: _Nanaimo_   To: _Pender Hbr._
Sunrise: _7:45 am_   Sunset: _6:13 pm_   Lunar Cycle Stage _Waning_

Location	Time	Heading	Tidal Current Flood/Ebb
Nanaimo	9 am	329 m	
check status of WG restricted area			
Pender Harbour			

Weather Forecast Synopsis Notes:

Strait of Georgia Today, Tonight, and Saturday
At 10:30 am PDT today departing low 1008mb located over
Southern Explorer; a ridge west of offshore waters.

Forecast by Reporting Station in Direction of Day's Passage:

1. _Strait of Georgia N._ _Strong wind warning in effect. Winds NW 10-15 knots evening; NW 15-25 overnight; 15-20 am_
2. _____
3. _Strait of Georgia S._ _Wind W 5-15 knots am and evening; 15-20 overnight; visibility 1 mile rain._

Lightstation and Buoy Reports:

1. _46146 Halibut_ Wind Dir & Speed _SSW 8 gust 9_ Sea Condition _0.3 m 2.8 sec_
2. _Entrance Island_ Wind Dir & Speed _S 6_ Sea Condition _____
3. _Entrance Lightstation_ Wind Dir & Speed _S 10 E_ Sea Condition _1 ft. CHP_

---

www.WaggonerGuide.com

MARINE WEATHER - COLLECTING AND EVALUATING

COLLECTING WEATHER FORECASTS AND OBSERVED WEATHER INFORMATION

Via Internet
Environment Canada — weather.gc.ca/marine/
NOAA National Weather Svc. — www.weather.gov/sew
National Data Buoy Center — www.ndbc.noaa.gov
Ocean Prediction Center — ocean.weather.gov

Via Telephone
Seattle — 206-526-6087
Vancouver — 604-666-3655
Victoria — 250-363-6880
 — 250-363-6492
Comox — 250-339-0748
Alert Bay — 250-974-5305
Prince Rupert — 250-624-9009
Tofino — 250-726-3415

Via VHF Radio Continuous Broadcasts
See the following pages for a list of Continuous Broadcast VHF weather channels, including maps of forecast area names and transmitting stations.

Collecting Weather Buoy Information
Via Internet
U.S. NOAA National Weather Svc. www.weather.gov/sew
National Data Buoy Center www.ndbc.noaa.gov

Via Telephone
(Have Buoy numbers from maps on following pages)
Dial-A-Buoy 888-701-8992 or 301-713-9620

Start with the synopsis for the area, then record the relevant station reports and lighthouse and buoy reports, with particular attention to the reported wind direction, speed, and sea condition.

STEP 5 - Check the Tides and Currents. Look up in a Tide and Current Guide to determine whether you will be cruising with a Flood or an Ebb current, and the time of slack. This will be useful in understanding the sea state as the day progresses. Avoid wind opposing current situations. This information is not included in a weather forecast and must be understood by the mariner using a tide and current guide or software to understand the sea state. It may be best to delay a departure for a couple of hours for a more favorable current situation. Look up the phase of the moon in the Tide and Current guide. A full moon or a new moon means tides and currents will be at their strongest, and slack will be very short for tidal rapids.

Once all this information is gathered, you can develop a picture of the weather for your departure and route for the day. You will understand where the weather systems are and the resulting conditions for your route.

You and Your Boat's Tolerances. You should compare forecast conditions and observations with tolerances for your vessel and especially for your crew. You can minimize surprises while underway by gathering and evaluating as much information as possible from as many sources as possible. Gather the information described above so there aren't too many surprises while underway, though Mother Nature is known to shift plans.

It's always a good idea to have fail-safe contingency plans or duck-in points if things change. For crossing the Strait of Georgia or Cape Caution, you can look to see if you have an opposing, beam-to, or following sea. This may change your go or no-go tolerances or the direction on your route.

Go-NoGo Checklists. Checklists to aid in evaluating conditions for a Go or NoGo decision are located in four chapters describing the passages: Strait of Juan de Fuca; Strait of Georgia; Cape Caution; and Dixon Entrance. These checklists summarize the more important conditions to consult before making that all important decision to proceed. The lists include specifics for the area including weather forecasts, names and numbers for weather buoys, and names of lighthouse and weather station locations to consult when evaluating conditions. The checklists are intended to be summarized lists.

Checklist items are grouped into these topic areas: Tides & Currents; Weather System Predictions; Weather & Seas Forecasts; Observations & Present Conditions; Go-NoGo Decision; Fail-Safe Contingency Plans. The heading line for each category includes a brief notation (Internet; Phone; Satellite; VHF) listing the sources for current information.

Monitor and Log Actual Conditions. At regular intervals along your planned route, make log entries noting the wind and sea conditions you encounter. Record how your boat handled the different seas. Your actual conditions may be significantly different from forecast conditions. Make note of wind speeds and the dominant wave period interval.

Planned vs Actual. After arriving at your destination, review your log of actual conditions encountered along your route, to help develop experience with the forecasting tools. This will help develop experientially based interpretation of forecast weather for future trips and make the next go or no-go decision easier.

For a better understanding of weather. Consider learning more and taking a weather course. Waggoner and our Seattle Boat Show University or Cruisers College programs offer courses with weather experts, from 3-hour seminars to multi-day courses. Understanding the weather is a fascinating part of boating. The rewards when you get it right are substantial for you and your crew.

NORTHWEST RIGGING
Rig Locally - Sail Globally

Standing Rigging • Lifelines • Cable Railings • Swaging
Running Rigging • Custom Rope Work • Splicing
Furler Sales & Installation • Hardware

360.293.1154 • www.nwrigging.com • info@nwrigging.com • 620 30th Street, Anacortes

2023 WAGGONER CRUISING GUIDE

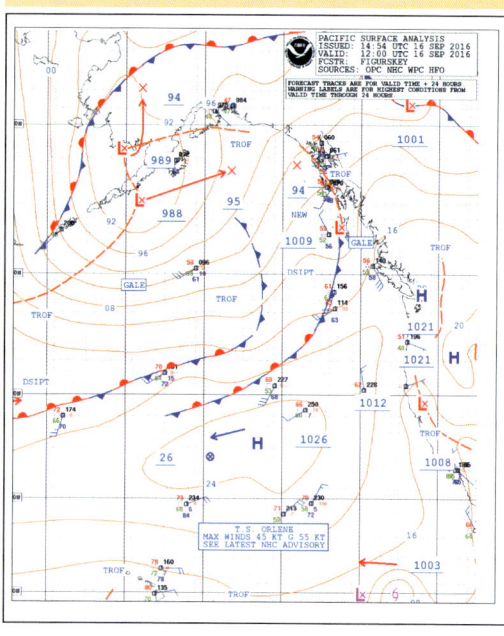

MARINE WEATHER - FORECAST CHARTS & REPORTS

Current Surface Analysis Chart

The Current Surface Analysis Chart for September 16, 2016 shows High Pressure over the area from Seattle up through the Strait of Georgia.

Big lazy isobar lines indicate light wind.

Note how this is consistent with both the U.S. National Weather Service (NWS) and Canadian Environment Canada text forecasts on the the right.

Figure 1

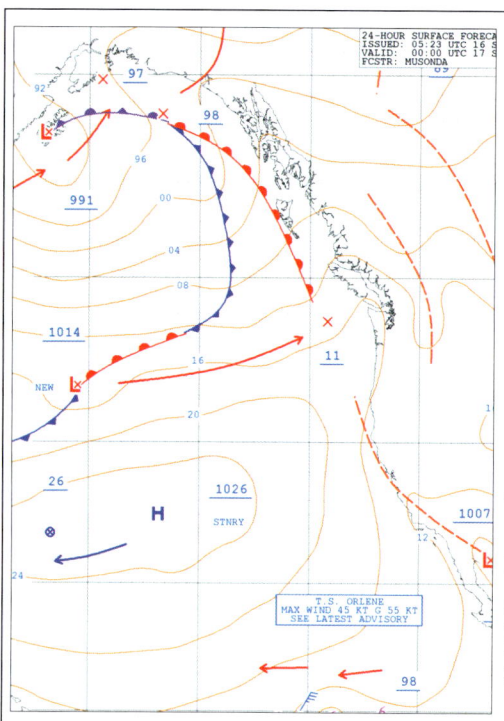

24-Hour Surface Analysis Chart

On this 24-Hour Surface Forecast we can see the Low pressure system moving in from offshore and the isobars bunching up tighter.

The text forecasts show the wind and waves picking up as the Low comes ashore on Saturday through Saturday night. You can use this information to make a go or no-go decision.

From this you can see that it would be best to go north on Friday. If you cannot leave then you should most likely wait until Sunday.

Figure 2

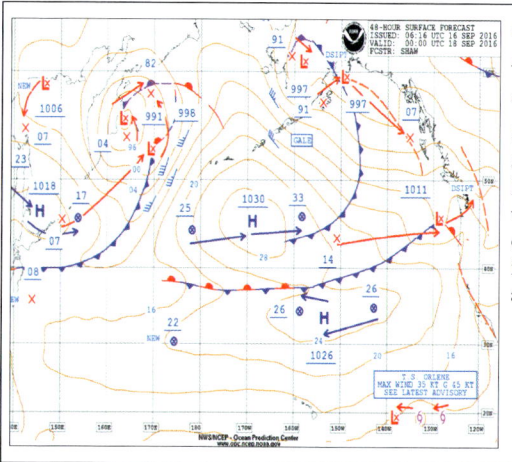

48-Hour Surface Analysis Chart

This 48-Hour Surface Forecast shows that another low is approaching with forecast seas of 2 feet. Tuesday's forecast returns to about 1 foot seas.

Figure 3

```
National Weather Service Marine Forecast FZUS56 KSEW

FZUS56 KSEW 160957
CWFSEW

COASTAL WATERS FORECAST FOR WASHINGTON
NATIONAL WEATHER SERVICE SEATTLE WA
300 AM PDT FRI SEP 16 2016

INLAND WATERS OF WESTERN WASHINGTON AND THE NORTHERN AND CENTRAL
WASHINGTON COASTAL WATERS INCLUDING THE OLYMPIC COAST NATIONAL
MARINE SANCTUARY

PZZ100-161615-
300 AM PDT FRI SEP 16 2016

.SYNOPSIS FOR THE NORTHERN AND CENTRAL WASHINGTON COASTAL AND INLAND
WATERS...LIGHT ONSHORE FLOW CONTINUING TODAY. A COLD FRONT WILL
APPROACH THE WASHINGTON COASTAL WATERS FROM THE NW TONIGHT AND MOVE
THROUGH THE AREA DURING THE DAY SATURDAY FOR INCREASED ONSHORE FLOW.
A SURFACE TROUGH WILL MOVE ACROSS THE AREA ON SUNDAY. WEAK ONSHORE
FLOW WILL DEVELOP ON MONDAY AND CONTINUE INTO TUESDAY.

PZZ150-161615-
COASTAL WATERS FROM CAPE FLATTERY TO JAMES ISLAND OUT 10 NM-
300 AM PDT FRI SEP 16 2016

TODAY
N WIND TO 10 KT...BECOMING SW IN THE AFTERNOON. WIND WAVES
1 FT. W SWELL 3 FT AT 10 SECONDS.
TONIGHT
SW WIND 5 TO 15 KT...BECOMING S 10 TO 20 KT AFTER
MIDNIGHT. WIND WAVES 1 TO 3 FT. W SWELL 4 FT AT 9 SECONDS. RAIN
LIKELY IN THE EVENING...THEN RAIN AFTER MIDNIGHT.
SAT
S WIND 15 TO 25 KT...BECOMING SW 5 TO 15 KT IN THE
AFTERNOON. WIND WAVES 2 TO 4 FT. W SWELL 5 FT AT 8 SECONDS. RAIN
LIKELY IN THE MORNING...THEN A CHANCE OF RAIN IN THE AFTERNOON.
```

Figure 4   **NWS Synopsis for Coastal Waters**

```
PZZ133-161615-
NORTHERN INLAND WATERS INCLUDING THE SAN JUAN ISLANDS-
300 AM PDT FRI SEP 16 2016

TODAY
LIGHT WIND...BECOMING S TO 10 KT IN THE AFTERNOON. WIND
WAVES 1 FT OR LESS.
TONIGHT
S WIND 5 TO 15 KT. WIND WAVES 2 FT OR LESS. A CHANCE OF
RAIN IN THE EVENING...THEN RAIN AFTER MIDNIGHT.
SAT
SE WIND 10 TO 20 KT...RISING TO 15 TO 25 KT IN THE
AFTERNOON. WIND WAVES 2 TO 4 FT. RAIN IN THE MORNING...THEN RAIN
LIKELY IN THE AFTERNOON.
SAT NIGHT
S WIND 5 TO 15 KT. WIND WAVES 2 FT OR LESS.
SUN
SW WIND TO 10 KT. WIND WAVES 1 FT OR LESS.
SUN NIGHT
SW WIND 5 TO 15 KT...BECOMING S AFTER MIDNIGHT. WIND
WAVES 2 FT OR LESS.
MON
SE WIND 5 TO 15 KT...BECOMING SW. WIND WAVES 2 FT OR LESS.
TUE
SW WIND TO 10 KT. WIND WAVES 1 FT OR LESS.
```

Figure 5   **NWS Forecast for Northern Waters**

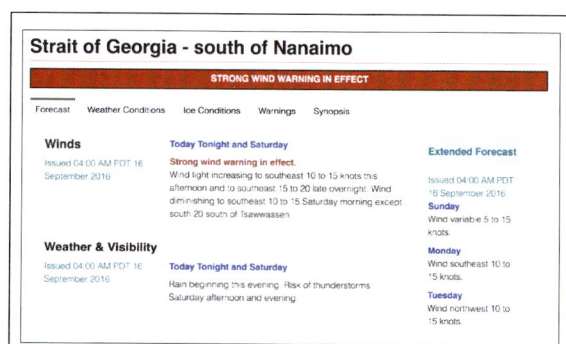

Strait of Georgia - south of Nanaimo

STRONG WIND WARNING IN EFFECT

Forecast | Weather Conditions | Ice Conditions | Warnings | Synopsis

Winds
Issued 04:00 AM PDT 16 September 2016

Today Tonight and Saturday
Strong wind warning in effect.
Wind light increasing to southeast 10 to 15 knots this afternoon and to southeast 15 to 20 late overnight. Wind diminishing to southeast 10 to 15 Saturday morning except south 20 south of Tsawwassen.

Extended Forecast
Issued 04:00 AM PDT 16 September 2016
Sunday
Wind variable 5 to 15 knots.
Monday
Wind southeast 10 to 15 knots.
Tuesday
Wind northwest 10 to 15 knots.

Weather & Visibility
Issued 04:00 AM PDT 16 September 2016

Today Tonight and Saturday
Rain beginning this evening. Risk of thunderstorms Saturday afternoon and evening.

Figure 6   **Environment Canada Forecast Strait of Georgia - South of Nanaimo**

MARINE WEATHER - VHF CONTINUOUS BROADCASTS

U.S. Coast Guard and Canadian Coast Guard provide weather forecast and current condition observations as a continuous loop recording throughout the day on various VHF weather radio frequencies, commonly referred to as WX1 through WX8.

These continuous marine broadcast recordings contain the latest National Weather Service or Environment Canada forecasts and observed conditions. Canadian forecasts are updated four times per day at 04:00, 10:30, 16:00, and 21:30. U.S. forecasts are updated at 04:00 and 16:00 with updates as needed 09:00 - 11:00 and 20:00 - 23:00. The recorded broadcast is reset to the latest forecast at these times.

The broadcast loop cycles through the named forecast areas as shown on the three regional maps on the following pages. Listen carefully for your desired area forecast, otherwise you will have to wait through the entire loop. Recording the broadcast on your smart phone allows you to quickly replay desired portions.

The two frames on this page list the sequence of information presented on the U.S. and Canadian continuous broadcast loops. The lists will help to know where you are in the recorded sequence of the VHF broadcasts. When listening to WX channels, listen for the station names along the route.

For a complete listing of WX channel numbers and their transmitter locations, see the three *Marine Weather - Reporting Stations* maps on the following pages. The maps also show weather buoy locations and buoy numbers.

U.S. NOAA National Weather Service
The following numbered list is the order of information presented on NWS VHF continuous broadcasts.

1. Introduction
- Date and time the forecast was prepared
- Name of forecast area
 - For a complete listing of forecast area names and their locations, see the *Marine Weather - Reporting Stations* maps on the following pages.

2. Marine Synopsis
- An overview for an area, delivered by day

3. Hourly Observations Roundup
- Weather conditions including wind speed (in knots), wind direction and barometric pressure (in millibars)
 - For a complete listing of observed conditions names and locations, see the *Marine Weather - Reporting Stations* maps on the following pages.

4. Marine Observations and Buoy Reports
- Wind and sea conditions
 - For a listing of observation locations and buoys, see the *Marine Weather - Reporting Stations* maps on the following pages.

5. Regional Weather Forecasts
- Forecast weather for communities in the area

6. Marine Forecast by Area
- Forecast winds, seas, and sky conditions for current and next three days
- Special advisories such as Small Craft and Gale Warnings

7. Marine Forecast Issued by Environment Canada
- For areas near the Canada border, such as the Strait of Juan de Fuca, Environment Canada forecast information will be broadcast

8. Pressure Reports
- Barometric pressure observations

9. Special Advisories

Figure 7

Environment Canada
The following lists the order of information presented on VHF weather channels in Canadian waters.

1. Introduction
- Date and time the forecast was prepared
- Warnings
- Name of forecast area
 - Juan de Fuca Strait – East Entrance
 - Juan de Fuca Strait – Central
 - Haro Strait
 - Strait of Georgia – South of Nanaimo
 - Strait of Georgia – North of Nanaimo
 - Howe Sound
 - Johnstone Strait

2. Weather Summary by Area
- Summary by named area - see the list above or the three *Marine Weather - Reporting Stations* maps on the following pages for a listing of area names.

3. Marine Weather Forecast Statement
- Forecast winds, seas, and sky conditions for Today, Tonight, and Tomorrow
- Special advisories such as Small Craft and Gale Warnings

4. Technical Marine Synopsis
- Weather systems summary and position
- Forecast weather systems 24 hour movement

5. Extended Marine Forecast for Pacific Water
- Forecast conditions for 2 – 5 days
- Delivered by area
 - Juan de Fuca Strait – East Entrance
 - Juan de Fuca Strait – Central
 - Haro Strait
 - Strait of Georgia – South of Nanaimo
 - Strait of Georgia – North of Nanaimo
 - Howe Sound
 - Johnstone Strait

6. Automated Reports - Weather conditions from automatic reporting stations.

7. Ocean Buoy Reports
- Wind direction, speed, combined seas, and barometric pressure from buoys.

8. Lighthouse Weather Reports
- Wind and sea conditions updated hourly by lighthouse operators
 - See *Marine Weather - Light Station and Buoy Reports* on the following pages for a description of these reports and decoding tips.

9. Local Marine Weather Reports

10. Special Reports
- Special notices - such as status of Military exercise areas like - Whiskey Golf (WG)

Figure 8

2023 WAGGONER CRUISING GUIDE

MARINE WEATHER - REPORTING STATIONS NORTH

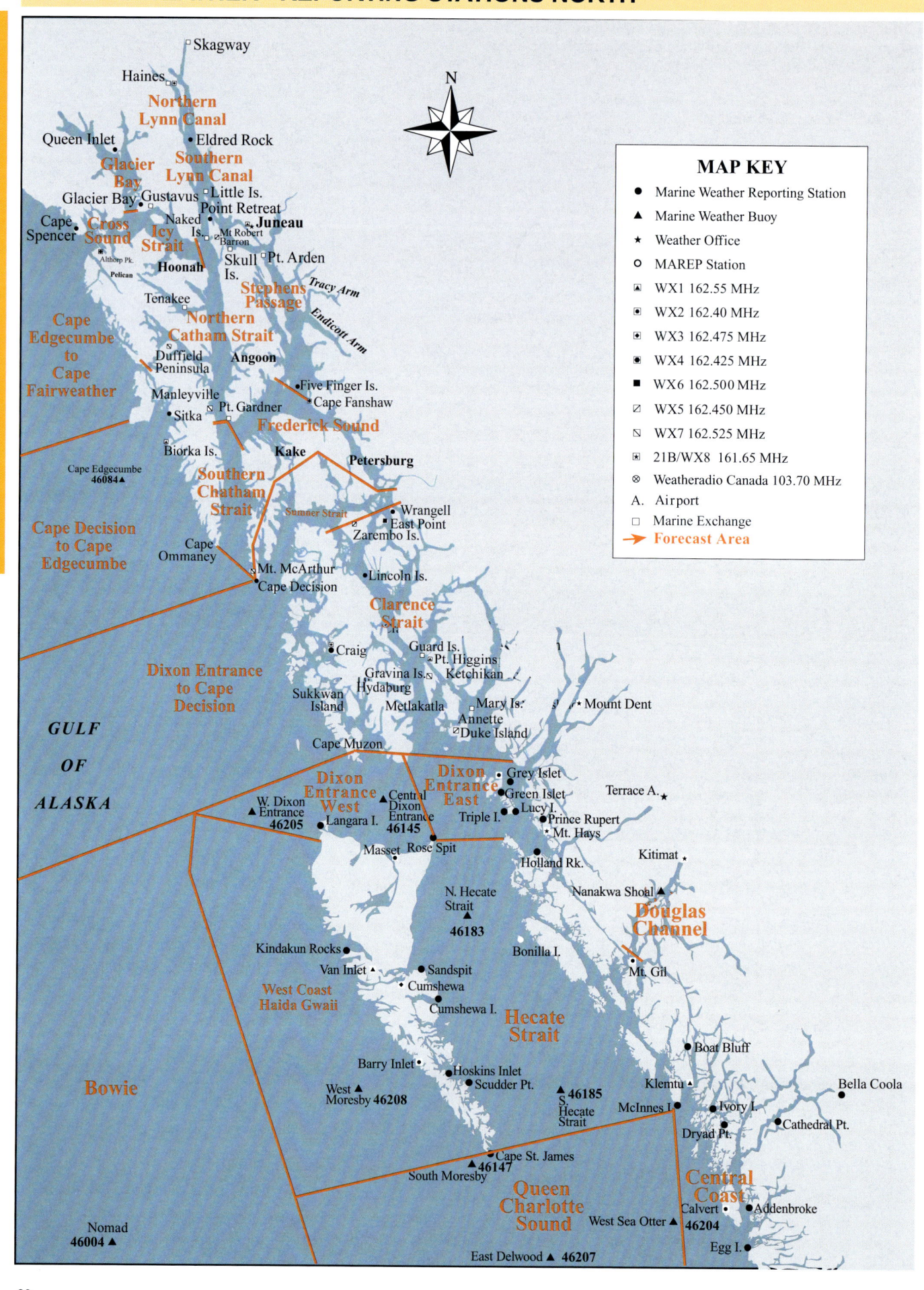

MAP KEY

- ● Marine Weather Reporting Station
- ▲ Marine Weather Buoy
- ★ Weather Office
- ○ MAREP Station
- ◰ WX1 162.55 MHz
- ◉ WX2 162.40 MHz
- ◑ WX3 162.475 MHz
- ◕ WX4 162.425 MHz
- ■ WX6 162.500 MHz
- ◨ WX5 162.450 MHz
- ◩ WX7 162.525 MHz
- ◧ 21B/WX8 161.65 MHz
- ⊗ Weatheradio Canada 103.70 MHz
- A. Airport
- □ Marine Exchange
- → Forecast Area

MARINE WEATHER - REPORTING STATIONS SOUTH

MAP KEY
- ● Marine Weather Reporting Station
- ▲ Marine Weather Buoy
- ★ Weather Office
- ○ MAREP Station
- WX1 162.55 MHz
- WX2 162.40 MHz
- WX3 162.475 MHz
- WX4 162.425 MHz
- WX6 162.500 MHz
- WX5 162.450 MHz
- WX7 162.525 MHz
- 21B/WX8 161.65 MHz
- ⊗ Weatheradio Canada 103.70 MHz
- A. Airport
- ☐ Marine Exchange
- → Forecast Area

MARINE RESEARCH

UNITED NATIONS RECOGNIZES THE TULA FOUNDATION

Boaters who have plied the waters of Northern British Columbia are undoubtedly familiar with the beautiful beaches and hiking trails at Pruth Bay. Most importantly, Pruth Bay is home to the Hakai Institute ecological observatory. Boaters are permitted to use the Institute's dinghy dock to hike the trails at Pruth Bay, which lead to several lovely beaches. Boaters also appreciate the Wi-Fi service that is accessible while anchored in the bay to get important weather updates. What boaters might not know is the extensive research conducted by the Hakai Institute under the umbrella of the Tula Foundation as well as research done at their sister location on Quadra Island at Heriot Bay.

The fact that the United Nations Ocean Decade (2021-2030) has designated the Tula Foundation as the "Northeast Pacific Regional Collaborative Center" of Ocean Science for sustainability is testament to the excellent work conducted by the Hakai Institute. The Institute works in conjunction with Canadian and U.S. universities and government agencies on both sides of the border. This Regional collaborative effort covers the Pacific Coast from Baja California to the Aleutian Islands.

The Hakai Institute conducts long-term scientific research, including ocean temperature data collection, DNA bar coding of many ocean species, spawning events, understanding kelp and seagrass habitats, geospatial mapping, disease resistant studies, and much more. For example, in 2021 scientists mapped the extensive seagrass meadows on the northern end of Calvert Island to figure out why it was thriving in this unlikely spot known for rough waters and strong currents, conditions that are not normally associated as good sites for seagrass.

Eric Peterson, Director of the Tula Foundation, joined the Waggoner Team on May 26th as special guest on "Waggoner Webcasts Live." You can watch the recorded program to learn more about the fascinating studies conducted by the Hakai Institute and the important significance of the Tula Foundation having been named by the United Nations as the Ocean Decade Collaborative Center for the Northeast Pacific Ocean, and learn how to get involved. To watch the program, go to: https://waggonerguide.com/waggoner-webcasts/

All are encouraged to learn more about the Ocean Decade and Tula's Regional Collaborative Center at https://oceandecadenortheastpacific.org; to learn more about the Hakai Institute see https://www.hakai.org.

[Lorena Landon]

MARINE WEATHER - LIGHT STATION & BUOY REPORTS

COLLECTING LIGHTSTATION REPORTS

Hourly reports originate from observations provided by Canadian Coast Guard staffed lightstations. Reports are normally taken during daylight hours. The "Issued at" field at the top of the report indicates the Universal Time Coordinated (UTC) and date of the observation. (subtract 8 hours, or 7 hours during daylight savings, for local time)

Via Internet: Environment Canada   weather.gc.ca/marine/

Format and Order of Lighstation Report:

Name|Sky|Visibility|Weather|Wind Direction|Wind Speed|SeaState|Swell|Remarks

Sample Reports:
CARMANAH   OVC 15 RW E 22G30 2FT CHP
MCINNES   CLDY 15 CLM 1FT CHP LO SW
BOAT BLUFF PC 15 NW04 RPLD

Name: Station Identification Name
Sky: Sky Conditions – CLR (clear); CLDY (cloudy); PT CLDY (party cloudy); X (obscured); -X (partially obscured
Visibility: Visibility measured in miles
Weather: Weather Elements – R (rain); RW (rain showers); S (snow); SW (snow showers); -L (drizzle); F (fog); T (thunder); A (hail);
Wind Direction: 8 compass points–N, S, E, W, NE, NW, SE, SW
Wind Speed: wind speed and gusts in knots; or CLM for calm.
Sea State: Wave height in feet and sea state - SMTH (smooth); RPLD (ripped); CHP (chop); MOD (moderate); RUF (rough)
Swell: Direction and state of swell – LO (0 to 2 meters); MOD (2 to 4 meters); and HVY (greater than 4 meters)
Remarks: Abbreviations such as (OCNL RW- for occasional light rain shower)

COLLECTING WEATHER BUOY REPORTS

Weather reporting buoys and remote observation stations are deployed throughout. These buoys transmit weather and sea condition information which is collected and made available to the public by the National Data Buoy Center (NDBC), a part of the National Weather Service. NDBC reporting stations are identified by number for locating information for a specific location. Buoys are also named for nearby geographic locations. NDBC current data and historical data is available via internet and telephone.

Via Internet
U.S. NOAA National Weather Svc. www.weather.gov/sew
National Data Buoy Center www.ndbc.noaa.gov

Via Telephone
(Have Buoy numbers from maps on following pages)
Dial-A-Buoy 888-701-8992 or 301-713-9620/

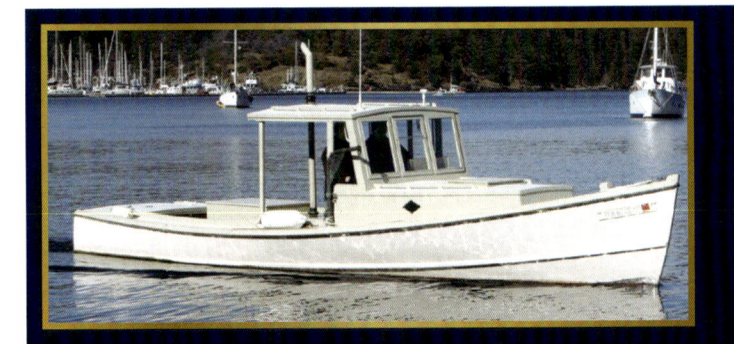

Social Separation...of the Finest Kind!

www.devlinboat.com

2023 WAGGONER CRUISING GUIDE   31

Fisheries Supply
Marine Supplies Since 1928

VHF Reimagined

Vesper Cortex VHF | AIS | Monitor

A REVOLUTION IN MARINE COMMUNICATION that will change your VHF experience forever. Be alerted to potential collision threats, see critical information about their position, speed and time until impact. Tap the vessel on the intuitive wet and glove capable touchscreen to initiate a DSC call immediately. Monitor and control on-board systems both on and off the boat via smartphone app. And that is just the beginning. VHF will never be the same again.

vesper
A Garmin Brand

For more innovative Vesper navigation products please visit
fisheriessupply.com/vesper

Call us 800.426.6930 | FisheriesSupply.com | 1900 N. Northlake Way, Seattle

VHF RADIO PROCEDURES

VHF RADIO TOPICS

Station Licenses, U.S. Vessels
Station Licenses, Canadian Vessels
Operator's Permit, U.S.
Operator's Permit, Canada
How to use the VHF radio
The Low Power Switch
When Not to Call on Channel 16
DSC & GMDSS
Mayday Hoaxes
Contacting the Coast Guard by Cell
Automatic Identification System (AIS)
VHF Texting (VDSMS)
Phonetic Alphabet & Distress
VHF Radio Channels

The VHF radio is an important piece of safety equipment, and VHF 16 should be monitored when the boat is underway. While monitoring, you will hear weather and safety warnings, and be aware of what's happening around you. A boat close by, for example, may be having problems and call for help. By monitoring your radio, you can respond.

Station Licenses, U.S. Vessels. Until 1996, U.S. pleasure craft were required to have station licenses for their marine VHF radios. In 1996, however, the requirement was dropped for pleasure craft under 20 meters (65 feet), operating inside the U.S. only. All U.S. vessels operating in foreign waters, including Canada, still need a U.S. station license. With the 1999 dropping of station licenses in Canada (see below), it was hoped that pleasure craft exempted from station licenses in the U.S. no longer would need a station license to travel in Canadian waters. It now appears that it would require an act of Congress—literally!—to exempt U.S. pleasure craft from needing a station license for Canadian travel, and that's not likely. As a practical matter, Canadian authorities do not enforce U.S. radio license laws, and U.S. authorities are not going to follow a boat into Canada. In other words, there's no enforcement. We have our station license, however, and would not be without it, enforcement or no enforcement.

RADIO CHECK

U.S. and Canadian Coast Guard ask that VHF Radio Check requests be made on a working channel; avoid using Channel 16. In U.S. waters, Channel 9 is an alternate Hailing channel; in B.C. try channel 83A

We recommend that our readers do the same. Apply for your station license at the same time you register for your Maritime Mobile Service Identity (MMSI) number. You will need this number to use the Digital Selective Calling (DSC) and emergency calling features all VHF radios have. You can register online at www.fcc.gov, using the Universal Licensing System (ULS). The online process is cumbersome, but the processing time is short. The forms are also available from the FCC at (888) 225-5322 (Monday through Friday), if you apply by mail. If you call, choose menu option 2, Licensing. The person who took our call was well-informed and helpful. A station license serves the entire vessel, regardless of the number of VHF radios the vessel has.

The station license also covers the use of a tender's VHF radio (such as a handheld model) as long as the radio is used in tender service, and as long as it is not used on land. It's all right for two or more radios from the same vessel with the same call sign to talk to each other via handheld VHF radio. U.S. pleasure craft longer than 20 meters, and all U.S. commercial vessels, are required to have an FCC station licenses.

Station Licenses, Canadian Vessels. Beginning in March 1999, station licenses no longer were issued to Canadian vessels so long as 1) the vessel is not operated in the sovereign waters of a country other than Canada or the U.S.; 2) the radio equipment on board the vessel is capable of operating only on frequencies that are allocated for maritime mobile communications or marine radio navigation. Canadian vessels not meeting those two requirements must have station licenses.

Operator's Permit, U.S. The U.S. does not require operator's permits for VHF radio use within the U.S. For foreign travel, however, a Restricted Radio Operator's permit is required. The U.S. individual permit is issued for life, and costs $60. If you are from the U.S. and take a boat to Canada, you will need a Restricted Radio Operator permit. Use Schedule E of FCC Form 605 to apply, and Form 159 to remit payment. If you are applying for both a station license and a Restricted Radio Operator permit you will need a separate Form 159 for each application. The forms can be downloaded from www.fcc.gov, or you can apply electronically on the FCC website.

Operator's Permit, Canada. Canada requires each person operating a VHF radio to have a Restricted Operator's Certificate. For Canadian residents a test must be passed, but the certificate is free and issued for life. Training for the test and the issuing of certificates is handled by the Canadian Power and Sail Squadrons.

COMPENDIUM

OCENS

Reliable voice, email and **messaging** communications for the **Inside Passage** to Alaska and beyond.

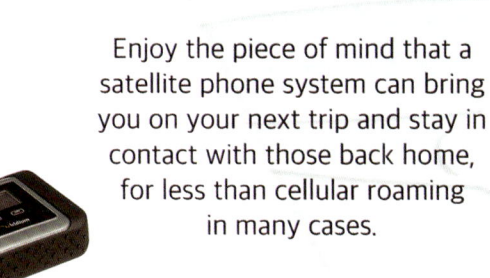

Enjoy the piece of mind that a satellite phone system can bring you on your next trip and stay in contact with those back home, for less than cellular roaming in many cases.

Satellite Communications Sales, Support, & Rentals

206.878.8270
www.ocens.com

Iridium Handhelds / Iridium Broadband / Iridium GO
Inmarsat FleetOne / Zoleo / BivyStick
*** Weather & Email Solutions ***

2023 WAGGONER CRUISING GUIDE   33

VHF RADIO PROCEDURES

How to Use the VHF Radio. The easiest way to get a general sense of radio use is to monitor VHF 16, the hailing and distress channel; VHF 22A, the U.S. Coast Guard channel; VHF 83A, the Canadian Coast Guard channel, and the working channels. The VTS (Vessel Traffic Service) channels are good, too, because you'll be listening to professional mariners at work. VTS transmissions are brief and often informal, but you'll be listening to experienced people in action. On VHF 16 and the ship-to-ship working channels, you'll also hear inexperienced people. The difference will be obvious. To use the radio, call on the calling channel, VHF 16. When communication is established, switch to a working channel for your conversation. Except in instances of distress, you may not have a conversation on VHF 16. VHF 09 may be used for conversations; but because it is an alternate calling channel in the U.S., the conversations should be brief.

The Low Power Switch. VHF radios can transmit at 25 watts, their highest power rating, or at 1 watt, the low power mode. Handheld VHF radios usually have a maximum power of 5 watts and low power of 1 watt. Whenever practical, use the low-power mode. Other vessels a few miles away can then use the same channel without interference from you. The difference between high power and low power affects transmission distance only. Reception ability is unaffected. Handheld radios should use low power whenever possible. The battery lasts longer. When making a securite call, such as transiting Dodd Narrows or Malibu Rapids, be sure to have your VHF radio set on **LOW POWER** (1 watt). A securite call is for traffic safety purposes only and is not a call for right-of-way. Vessels traveling with the current are the 'stand-on' and vessels traveling against the current flow are the 'give-way.'

When Not to Call on Channel 16. Large vessels in the VTS traffic lanes usually do not monitor VHF 16. They monitor the VTS channel for their area. In Puget Sound waters covered by Seattle VTS Traffic, large vessels also must monitor VHF 13, the bridge-to-bridge communications channel. Seattle Traffic covers all U.S. waters and the entire Strait of Juan de Fuca, including the Canadian side. If you are disabled in a traffic lane and a large vessel is bearing down on you, call the vessel on the appropriate VTS channel (see VHF Channels Map and VTS Radio Channels table in the *Vessel Traffic Service* section in this chapter). If you are still unsure about what to do, call the Coast Guard on VHF 16 and ask them to contact the vessel for you, or to provide you with the correct channel.

DSC & GMDSS. DSC stands for Digital Selective Calling, and is part of the Global Maritime Distress and Safety System (GMDSS). Basically, if you have a DSC radio with a valid MMSI (Maritime Mobile Service Identity) number in its memory and push the covered red button, the radio will send an automatic digital distress message on VHF 70. This message contains the MMSI number, which is linked to a database that includes your name, vessel information, emergency contacts, and other information. If the vessel's GPS is connected to the VHF, or the radio is equipped with a GPS receiver, the radio also transmits GPS coordinates. For this to work, the radio must have the vessel's MMSI number stored in its memory. MMSI numbers are issued in the United States by the FCC or BoatUS, and in Canada by Transport Canada and Industry Canada. Important for U.S. vessels traveling to Canada: Officially, MMSI numbers issued by BoatUS are only for use in the United States. However, a BoatUS MMSI number will work in Canada, but the database information may not be available to Canadian authorities. The distress signal and your location, if your radio is connected to a GPS signal, will be transmitted to authorities and other DSC equipped vessels to alert other boats.

Brief your crew before heading out on a passage on how to summon help using the red DISTRESS button on your VHF radio. Consider preparing a check-list for emergencies for your crew that includes summoning help on the VHF radio and even the location of your safety equipment. For more information on this critical topic, see WaggonerGuide.com and search for the article on "Prepare Your Vessel for an Emergency." The article has many useful tips on how to prepare an emergency manual for use by your crew in case of an emergency.

Mayday Hoaxes. Each year, hoax Mayday calls cost the U.S. and Canadian Coast Guards millions of dollars ($2 million in Seattle alone) and in some cases put lives at risk. Sometimes the hoax is Junior playing with Grandpa's radio, sometimes it is the result of things getting too festive, sometimes the caller has a mental problem. Now that direction-finding equipment can locate the sources of radio calls, arrests can be made and penalties assessed. Radios are not toys, and hoax Mayday calls are not jokes. Large fines and even jail terms are the penalties.

To Reach the Coast Guard by Cell or Smartphone App

U.S. Coast Guard Rescue Center Seattle 911 or (206) 220-7001

U.S. Coast Guard Rescue Center Juneau (for all of southeast Alaska) 911 or (907) 463-2000

Canadian Coast Guard 911 or *16 or (250) 413-8933

PHONETIC ALPHABET & VHF DISTRESS TERMS

Letter	Word	Pronunciation
A	Alpha	al-fah
B	Bravo	brah-voh
C	Charlie	char-lee
D	Delta	dell-tah
E	Echo	eck-oh
F	Foxtrot	foks-trot
G	Golf	golf
H	Hotel	hoh-tel
I	India	in-dee-ah
J	Juliet	jew-lee-ett
K	Kilo	key-loh
L	Lima	lee-mah
M	Mike	mike

Letter	Word	Pronunciation
N	November	no-vem-ber
O	Oscar	oss-cah
P	Papa	pah-pah
Q	Quebec	keh-beck
R	Romeo	row-me-oh
S	Sierra	see-air-rah
T	Tango	tang-go
U	Uniform	yoo-nee-form
V	Victor	vik-tah
W	Whiskey	wiss-key
X	XRay	ecks-ray
Y	Yankee	yang-key
Z	Zulu	zoo-loo

MAYDAY	Vessel threatened by grave and imminent danger and requests immediate assistance.
PAN PAN	Urgent message concerning safety of vessel or person on board or in sight.
SECURITÉ	Message concerning safety of navigation or meteorological warning.
SEELONCE MAYDAY	Mayday in progress, do not transmit normal communications.
SEELONCE FEENE	Resume normal communications.

VHF RADIO PROCEDURES

Android and iOS smartphones can access and hail U.S. Coast Guard with their free official USCG App. The App has an emergency button as well as access to other helpful information.

Scolding on the Radio. When a fellow boater does something that is dangerous or inconsiderate, proper VHF radio protocol does not allow the injured party to start yelling at "the boat that just went by" without identifying themselves – especially not on high power. If it's necessary to talk to the other boater – first switch to LOW POWER – then try to hail the boat by name and switch to a working channel.

Most people don't realize they're doing something wrong, so start by explaining the situation. Make sure it's a conversation and not a lecture. Explain the situation and listen to the response. A civil conversation is more likely to get results than an angry lecture. Make sure you are on a working channel and on low power.

Automatic Identification System (AIS). AIS is a VHF-based radio tracking system for commercial and recreational vessels. Vessels equipped with AIS transponders transmit their name, course, speed, MMSI number, vessel size, and destination. Vessels equipped with AIS receivers display information from surrounding vessels and warn of potential conflicts. Large commercial vessels are required to have Class-A transponders while recreational vessels optionally have Class-B transponders. In the past, the high cost limited AIS transponders to only larger recreational vessels and AIS receivers to some recreational boats. The cost to equip your boat with both transmit and receive continues to get more affordable all the time. AIS transmit is particularly valuable in low visibility situations and when operating near large commercial traffic. Vessel name and MMSI AIS information makes it much easier to call a nearby vessel regarding potential conflicts. The price to equip your vessel with an AIS receiver is very affordable and well worth the expense.

New AIS applications show up each season. Small AIS man-overboard devices that attach to life jackets are available; when activated, show a MOB alert on all AIS equipped vessels nearby. AIS system design provides for a number of different message types that include virtual navigation aids, observed weather information, and local harbor/port information.

VHF Texting (VDSMS). With a VDSMS enabled VHF Radio, you can now exchange SMS text messages with another VDSMS equipped VHF Radio. FCC approved this new VHF DSC feature in 2016. There is only one VHF radio equipped to use this feature.

The Uniden MHS335B and the West Marine equivalent DSC/GPS/VHF handheld radios are capable of text messaging from one VHF radio to another. It's a convenient way to keep in touch with a buddy boat without hailing them. Fishermen who don't want to give away the location of a great fishing hole can still keep in touch with their fishing buddies. These new radios are light weight and float and come with a hefty box of accessories. To use the VDSMS texting feature, you will need to enter your MMSI number into the phone.

To text message a buddy, you will need to have them in your DSC contact list. Key in your message (up to 150 characters) and select a VDSMS channel, and send. A Bluetooth connection and associated smartphone App is recommended to easily type the message. These new radios with the texting feature can be a little overwhelming at first, and they still have a few bugs to be worked out.

Avoid stepping on other conversations by listening before transmitting.

VHF Channels. Official government agencies manage the different VHF Radio frequencies (channels) and designate the purpose or usage for these channels. Channels are assigned or defined for hailing (calling another radio), commercial and recreational purposes.

You will find a table of these channels in the *Reference Pages* in the back of this book. Most boaters use a small subset of the many designated channels. Below is a diagram to help you find the common channels and their usages in Pacific Northwest waters. Vessels are required to monitor Channel 16 when not communicating on another channel.

VHF Channel Common Usage In Pacific Northwest Waters

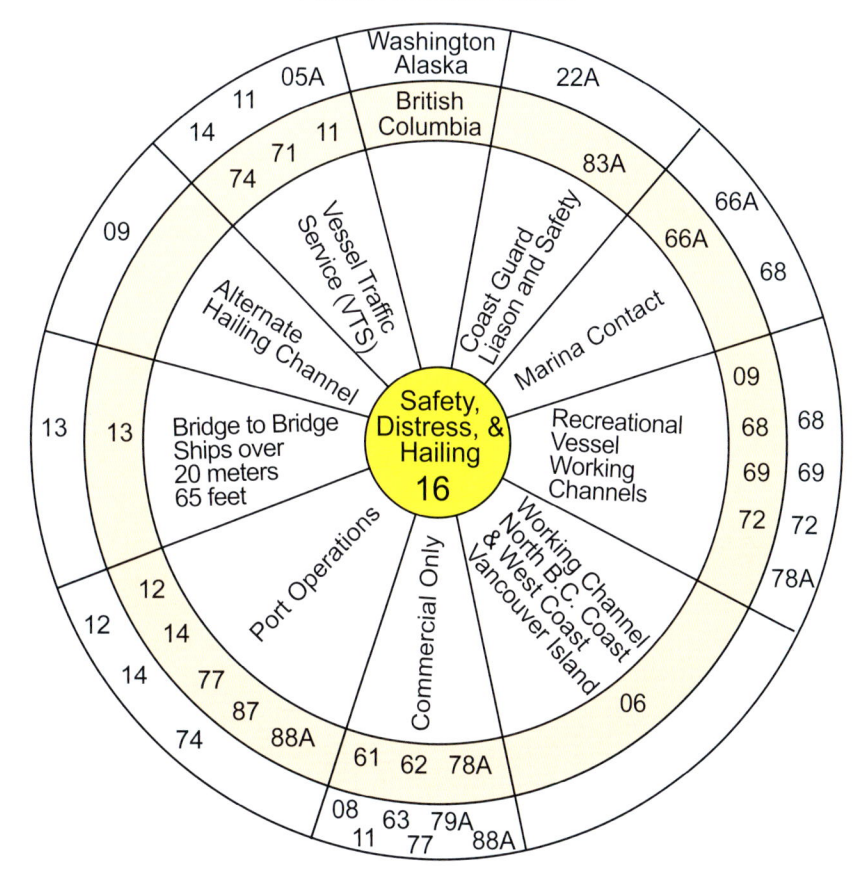

Segment	Channels
Washington / Alaska	05A, 11
British Columbia	11, 71
Vessel Traffic Service (VTS)	14, 74
Alternate Hailing Channel	09
Bridge to Bridge Ships over 20 meters 65 feet	13, 13
Port Operations	12, 14, 77, 87, 74, 88A
Commercial Only	12, 61, 62, 78A, 08, 11, 63, 77, 79A, 88A
Working Channel North B.C. Coast & West Coast Vancouver Island	06
Recreational Vessel Working Channels	09, 68, 69, 72, 78A, 68, 69, 72
Marina Contact	66A
Coast Guard Liaison and Safety	83A, 66A
(Center)	**Safety, Distress, & Hailing — 16**
	22A

2023 WAGGONER CRUISING GUIDE

TIDES AND CURRENTS

Tides are the periodic rise and fall of the water caused by the gravitational attraction of the moon and sun pulling on the oceans of the earth. The moon's gravitational pull (tidal force) causes both the earth and its water to bulge out – on the side closest to the moon, and on the side farthest from the moon – these bulges of water are high tides.

Tidal level or the height of tide is the vertical distance between the surface of the water and tidal or chart datum. Tidal datum is the reference plane from which tide levels are measured.

In the Pacific Northwest, there are two high tides and two low tides in a 24-hour and 50 minute period. Some areas on earth have only one high and one low each day, such as the Gulf of Mexico. Boaters visiting the Pacific Northwest may be surprised to discover the wide tidal range for this area. The tidal range (the difference between high and low) can be as much as 24 feet depending on the location and time of the month. Tides are highest during a new or full moon, when the gravity from the moon and sun are pulling together on the earth.

Tidal level prediction information comes from government sources – NOAA (National Oceanic and Atmospheric Administration) in the U.S., and in Canada, the Canadian Hydrographic Services (CHS). Commercial publications and apps get their prediction information from these two government sources. Commercial publications are normally more user friendly, are organized in a practical manner, and make adjustments for daylight savings. The commercial publication Ports and Passes covers tides and currents for Washington inside waters, British Columbia, and Southeast Alaska. Captain Jack's Tide Guide and Almanac covers tides and currents for Puget Sound, Strait of Juan de Fuca, Hood Canal, and the San Juan Islands.

Tidal Reference Stations are locations where tide level information has been studied and collected and daily tide height prediction tables have been prepared by NOAA and CHS. Secondary Stations are those where tide level information has been studied for a relatively shorter period of time and for which NOAA and CHS do not prepare daily tables but rather prepare correction factors to be applied to a data for a Tidal Reference Station.

Tidal height predictions are not an exact science and actual tide levels can be influenced by such things as atmospheric pressure, strong prolonged winds, and variations in fresh water discharge from rivers.

Tide height can be approximated by the rule of twelfths – take the difference in height between the high tide and low tide on that day, and divide that into 12 equal chunks.

Tide levels are typically given relative to a low-water tidal datum. In the U.S., tidal datum is the average of the lower of the two low tides or mean lower low water (MLLW). In Canada, it is given relative to Lower Low Water, Large Tide (LLWLT) and titled on charts as Lowest Normal Tide (LNT). Tidal datum between U.S. and Canada differ by as much as 5 feet. Because the U.S. tidal datum is higher, there are more U.S. minus tides than Canada.

For safe navigation and anchoring, boaters need to know what the vertical change will be over a certain period of time (see the *About Anchoring* topic in this chapter). Since the movements of the solar system that influence tides are predictable, changes in tide height and time are predictable. Boaters will want to carry the tide and current tables for the year in which they are cruising.

Vertical clearance under bridges and power lines should also be assessed for safe passage. Canadian charts generally give clearances or heights above Higher High Water, Large Tide, which means that the clearance will seldom be less than that shown on the Canadian chart. Charts in the U.S. use Mean High Water with half of the high waters rising above the mean high water level.

Currents. Water moving horizontally at various speeds are called currents. Winds, water density, and tides drive currents. Land features and sea floor features also influence the direction and speed of currents. A fast-moving body of water going through a narrow passageway intensifies, creating dangerous conditions.

While tides rise and fall, currents move horizontally from location to location and change direction. The rotation of the earth is a big influence on direction. In the Northern Hemisphere, the "trade winds" blow from east to west and pull surface water with them, creating currents. As these currents flow westward, the force of the Earth's rotation deflects them and the currents bend to the right heading north. In the Southern Hemisphere, the surface currents are bent to the left.

On the Inside Passage and Pacific Northwest waters, tidal currents are the result of water inflow and outflow between open ocean and inside waters. Bays, harbors, inlets, and tidal rivers and lagoons are all subject to current flow. A flood current is that which is flowing inland. In a flood tidal phase, the water is rising or moving into the shoreline. An ebb current is that which is flowing seaward. In an ebb tidal phase, the water level is falling or receding from the shoreline.

The movement of tidal current water through a narrow passage can create hazardous sea conditions in the form of eddies, whirlpools, rips, and overfalls. Eddies, whirlpools, and rips are circular water movement areas that can alter the boat's heading and reduce steerage. Rips and whirlpools can cause listing and rolling motion. Overfalls occur where large volumes of water are moving through a passage or over an underwater ridge.

Northwest waters and the Inside Passage have passages with some of the fastest flowing currents. Heavily traveled Seymour Narrows has flood currents that can reach 16 knots; lesser traveled Sechelt Rapids tops that with 16.5 knots.

Slack water is the usually short period when the tidal body of water is unstressed and occurs just before the current reverses its flow from ebb to flood, or flood to ebb. The time and duration of slack water varies and is related to the height of the tide at a given location. Although there may be no flow in either direction, eddies may still be present since the tide may still be rising. Upwellings may also be present – water below the surface rises to replace surface waters that have been transported away by strong winds. Boaters will want to consult their electronic charts and tide and current publications in order to safely transient certain passages at slack to avoid rapids and unsafe conditions

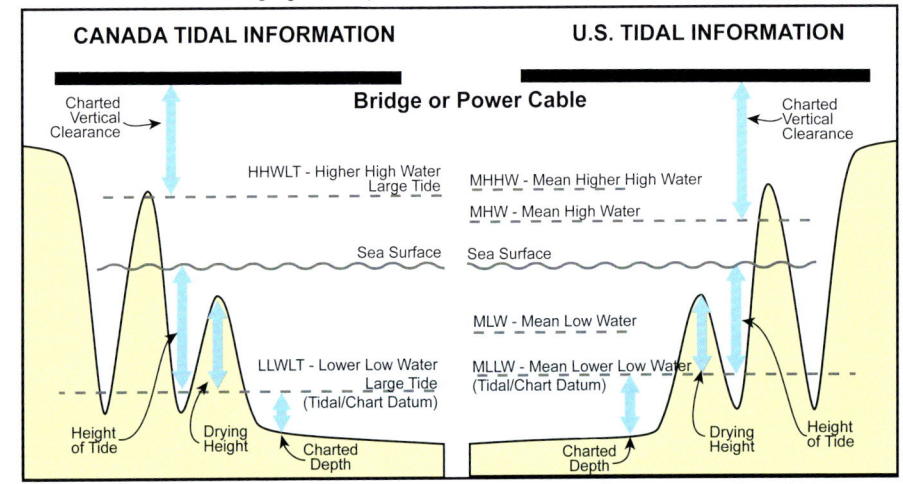

Tide level terminology, chart datum, and vertical clearance vary between Canada and U.S.

TIDAL RAPIDS

Transiting Tidal Rapids. The cautious advice—the first rule of thumb—for transiting tidal current rapids is to wait for slack water and go through then. This rule of thumb is fine but imperfect. There you sit, watching other boats go through before slack and after slack.

A second rule of thumb is a corollary of the first. It says that boats should arrive at a rapids an hour before predicted slack, so they're ready to go through as soon as the rapids grow quiet. Like most rules of thumb, this one doesn't always work either. Sometimes it appears as if the rapids would be safe much longer than an hour before or after. Sometimes one look tells you it's smarter to wait. With a little study, however, it's possible to predict when the window of opportunity will be wider or narrower.

Before going further, two definitions:

1- Slack Water is the time when rapids cease flowing one direction but haven't begun flowing the opposite direction. Another word for slack is turn, meaning the time when the water's flow turns from one direction to the other.

2 - Window of Opportunity. For purposes of this article, Window means a time when most boats can transit a rapids safely, without too much excitement.

This article gelled with me in Malibu Rapids at the mouth of Princess Louisa Inlet. It has its origins in the successful running of the Pacific Northwest's tidal current rapids over a span of nearly four decades.

Understand that my wife and I are the original cautious and conservative boaters when it comes to rapids. Several years ago we hiked from Big Bay, on B.C.'s Stuart Island, to Arran Rapids, one of the most deadly rapids on the coast. We arrived in what must have been the middle of a large tide exchange, with its frightening whitewater overfalls, upwellings and whirlpools that no sensible boat could be expected to survive. White water is full of air, and less buoyant than green water. Boats float lower, with less freeboard. Rudders lose effectiveness and propellers lose their bite. We got the message: Rapids are not to be trifled with.

With experience, we have developed a loose sense of when a rapids could be run at times other than slack. Until our transits of Malibu Rapids, however, this sense was not refined to any kind of structure.

For what it's worth, here's our thinking. But first,

Caution: Every rapids has its own personality and characteristics. What follows is general in nature, and may not apply to any given rapids. It is a way of looking at things, an approach to the problem. It is not a guarantee.

The determining factors are:
1) high water slack vs. low water slack;
2) neap tides vs. spring tides;
3) size of the exchange on each side of slack.

High water slack vs. low water slack. We entered Princess Louisa Inlet through Malibu Rapids without drama nearly two hours before high water slack. When we departed two days later we found definite swirls, overfalls and whirlpools only 20 minutes before low water slack. The two transits were entirely different.

Our entry to Princess Louisa Inlet was at high water, when the narrow, shallow channel was full. Our departure was at low water, when the channel was much less full and much narrower. The less water in the channel, the faster the current must run.

General Rule: The window of opportunity is wider at high water slack. The narrower and shallower the channel, the more this is true.

Neap tides vs. spring tides. Neap tides are small tides that occur around the times of half moon. Neaps often show only a small dip from one high water to the next. The widest windows of opportunity occur on that small dip.

Spring tides occur around the times of full moon or no moon. Low tides can be very low and high tides very high. On springs even the dip between two high tides can be significant. The windows of opportunity are narrower on spring tides than on neap tides.

Since it takes only a week to go from neap tide to spring tide (and another week to go from spring tide to neap tide), the experience from just a few days earlier has no bearing on the day you're going through. Each day, each transit, must be evaluated on its own.

Spring Tides

Narrow / Narrow / Narrow

Expect **Narrow Windows** at all slack periods with large changes between highs and lows.

Neap Tides

Narrow / Wide / Narrow / Wider

Expect **Narrow Windows** on large exchanges
Expect **Wider Windows** on small exchanges.

Size of the exchange. Imagine this exercise. Using a garden hose, fill a five-gallon container in a minute. Then fill a one-gallon container in a minute. You had to turn the flow of water way down for the one-gallon can.

Our neap tide entry through Malibu Rapids was near the top of a fairly small rise from lower low water to high water. The smaller the rise or fall, the less the current.

CONCLUSIONS:

1. The window is narrowest at lower low water slack. The tide has dropped a long way and will be rising a long way. The farther the tide has dropped and the farther it is to rise, the narrower the window. Also, the shallower and narrower the rapids, the narrower the window at lower low water. At lower low water, plan to go through fairly close to slack.

2. The window at high water slack is wider on neap tides than on spring tides. The window is widest in the "dip" between the two high waters on neap tides.

3. At high water slack, the window is narrower on the rise from lower low water. The window is wider between the next two high waters.

Disclaimer. Skippers are responsible for the welfare and safety of their vessels and passengers. The purpose of this article is to provide tools for evaluating situations. It is not the purpose of this article to tell a skipper when to transit a rapids. When in doubt, the safest course is to transit at slack water, regardless of what other boats are doing.

[Robert Hale]

EASY DOES IT!

HIDE-A-DAVIT SYSTEMS

The Hide-A-Davit cradles your tender securely when in the raised position, yet leaves the swim platform completely clear of hardware in the lowered position.

- Simple and robust design
- Easily removable cradle arms for storage when tender is not in use
- Compatible with inboard, outdrive and pod type propulsion

La Conner MARITIME SERVICE

www.laconnermaritime.com

Fisheries Supply
Marine Supplies Since 1928

FUSION APOLLO SERIES
The First Marine Stereos With Apple AirPlay® 2

MS-SRX400

MS-RA670

MS-RA770

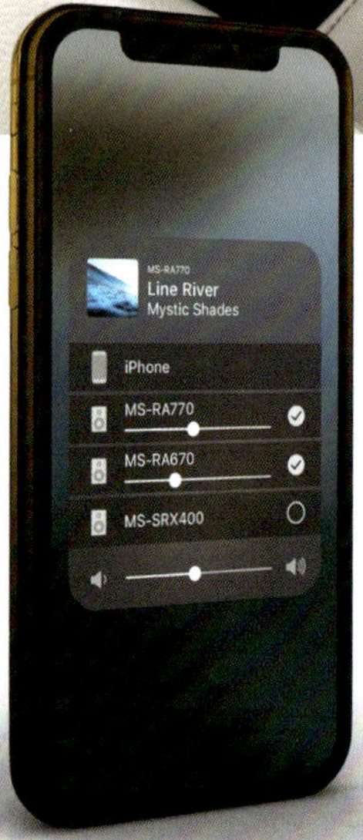

The world's first marine stereos to bring you seamless high-quality audio streaming over Apple AirPlay® 2

Enjoy seamless, high-quality audio streaming from an app via AirPlay 2 over Wi-Fi from a compatible Apple device to the Apollo Series stereos. With Apple AirPlay 2, you will be able to stream the same audio to every compatible stereo unit connected to the same network, and enjoy volume control individually or globally.

FUSION®
A Garmin Brand

For the complete line of innovative Fusion marine audio products please visit
fisheriessupply.com/fusion-electronics

Call us 800.426.6930 | FisheriesSupply.com | 1900 N. Northlake Way, Seattle

STATE AND PROVINCIAL PARKS AND PUBLIC WHARVES

The waters from Puget Sound through B.C. and Southeast Alaska are dotted with more than 200 state, provincial, and national parks, and in B.C., more than 220 public wharves.

Washington Parks & DNR. At the state level, parks are administered by the Washington State Parks and Recreation Commission and by the Department of Natural Resources (DNR). Usually, DNR sites are on the primitive side. State parks, which tend to be more developed, charge for moorage at buoys and docks. At State Marine Park docks and floats, expect to pay $.70 per foot, $15 minimum. State Park mooring buoys are $15 per night. The dock or buoy fee applies after 1:00 p.m., payable for even a stop-and-go visit, such as walking the dog. *Unless otherwise marked, buoys are for boats 45 feet and less; boats longer than 45 feet are not allowed on the buoys; rafting to another boat on a park buoy is not permitted.*

State Park moorage facilities, including docks, buoys, and linear moorage, have a maximum stay of 3-consecutive nights.

State parks charge moorage fees year-round. Annual moorage permits are available and valid from January 1 to December 31, $5 per foot, $60 minimum. Contact Washington State Parks Information, (360) 902-8844 (Monday through Friday), or infocent@parks.wa.gov. Or check their informative website at parks.state.wa.us/435/Boating. There is no registration or charge for anchoring.

Payment for staying at a park dock or mooring on a buoy is made at a self-registration payment box found at Washington State Parks. Some parks offer payment by phone (voice communication) as posted, via credit card with an additional fee for this service.

Campsite fees are paid in addition to dock or mooring buoy fees. Self-register ashore for campsites.

A few DNR public lands offer mooring buoys, which are designed for boats up to 50 feet. There is no charge to use a DNR mooring buoy.

Reservations. Moorage is unreserved. Leaving a dinghy or other personal property at a buoy or dock does not reserve moorage. Rafting is permitted on docks, but not mandatory. Reservations (for campsites only) in all state parks are accepted. Call toll-free (888) 226-7688.

Boat launch sites. State parks with boat launches charge fees of $7. The launch fee includes the daily parking fee. Annual launch permits cost $80 and are valid for a year from date of purchase. Contact Washington State Parks, (360) 902-8844, or from parks.state.wa.us/435/Boating.

Washington Boater Education Card. All operators of boats with motors of 15 horsepower or more born after January 1, 1955 are required to have their Washington State Boater Education Card. Washington State Parks administers this program. See their website at http://boat.wa.gov/ or call (360) 902-8555.

If you are boating in Canadian waters for longer than 44 days a Canadian Operator Card, or the equivalent issued by a state in the U.S. is required. The Washington Boater Education Card qualifies for cruising more than 44 days, as do U.S. Coast Guard licenses such as Captain's or Mate's license.

Canadian Boater Pleasure Craft Operator Card (PCOC). Canada has a similar program for its boaters, requiring boater education and certification. In B.C., several firms offer classes and testing services to prove competency. A special program called "Rental Boating Safety Checklist" is for power-driven rental boats and bareboat charter boats. Consult your Canadian charter company for more information and requirements.

B.C. Parks, Including Gulf Islands National Park Reserve Parks. Most B.C. marine parks have safe, all-weather anchorages, and some parks have floats or mooring buoys. Marine parks are open year-round. Some have no on-shore facilities, others have day-use facilities, picnic areas, and developed campsites. Most parks have drinking water. Overnight moorage fees ($12 for a buoy; $2/meter for dock moorage) are charged at a number of the more developed parks. No rafting is permitted on mooring buoys. No charge for anchoring, even with a stern-tie to shore. Tent sites are extra. Contact B.C. Parks General Information at www.env.gov.bc.ca/bcparks. For more information on the Gulf Islands National Park Reserve, contact (866) 944-1744, or see their website at www.pc.gc.ca. On the homepage select "Find a National Park" and select "Gulf Islands National Park Reserve."

Take your own paper to public toilets. Especially outhouses at parks and campgrounds. We speak from experience.

Public Wharves. In British Columbia, public wharves provide moorage for commercial vessels (primarily the fishing fleet) and pleasure craft. Especially in the off-season, public wharves are filled with fish boats, leaving little or no moorage for pleasure craft. Facilities vary, from a dock only, to fully-serviced marinas. Most of the public wharves now are operated by local harbor authorities or their equivalents. Locally-run public wharves charge market rates, and may reserve space for pleasure craft. Moorage fees vary. Those still operated by the province are easily identified by the red-painted railings on the access ramps.

Public docks provide access to parks and islands.

NO DISCHARGE ZONES (NDZ) - B.C. WATERS

BRITISH COLUMBIA - discharge of black water is not allowed in the following areas. Approved holding tanks are required in these areas. Macerator treatment systems, even if approved, do not qualify. Unless otherwise noted, Gray water is not included in the regulations.

- Pirates Cove (no gray)
- Prideaux Haven
- Roscoe Bay
- Smuggler Cove
- Squirrel Cove
- Tod Inlet
- Victoria Harbour
- Carrington Bay
- Cortes Bay
- Gorge Harbour
- Ladysmith Harbour
- Mansons Landing
- Montague Harbour
- Pilot Bay
- Burrard Inlet/False Creek

2023 WAGGONER CRUISING GUIDE

ABOUT ANCHORING

One of the unique features of boating is the freedom of movement and independence to make any protected body of water home for a quick lunch stop or an overnight. Some people look forward to dropping anchor in an unfamiliar cove or bay. Many people do not share this enthusiasm. There are a few general principles that will help everyone anchor successfully. Cruising from dock to dock is fun, and no one can fault the conveniences. But a world of possibilities opens to those who have good anchoring gear and know how to use it.

Use good gear. Big, strong anchors work; small, cheap anchors don't. The most experienced cruisers seem to carry the biggest anchors. Well-equipped, wide-ranging boats carry all of the common designs: Bruce, CQR (plow), Danforth, Delta, Northhill, Rocna, Manson Supreme, and Ultra. Make sure your anchor is made of high quality steel. If it's wedged in a rock, you don't want it to bend. While Danforth style anchors are easiest to bend, within the limits of their design, they can be made strong and expensive, or weak and cheap. There are no strong, cheap Danforth style anchors. Read the sizing charts carefully, and size your anchor for storm conditions. Some sizing charts are written for 20-knot winds. Others are written for 30 knots. The Bruce chart is written for 42 knots and Rocna sizing is based upon 50 knots. When the wind comes on to blow hard at 3:00 a.m., you don't want a 20-knot anchor out there.

Pick your spot. Unless you're setting out a stern anchor or running a stern-tie ashore, plan on your boat swinging through an entire 360-degree circle. You don't want to bump up against a rock, a dock or another boat. Be sure to account for tidal changes. We've seen anchored boats aground at low tide because they didn't allow for drying flats or a sand bar in their swing circle. Other anchored boats will tend to swing as your boat swings, but not always. One night at Jones Island in the San Juans, swirling tidal currents had anchored boats swooping toward one another in a "dance of death."

Carry ample rode. For an anchor to bury and hold properly, you should pay out anchor rode at least five times the water depth. In 20 feet of water you would want 100 feet of rode out. In 60 feet of water you would want 300 feet out. Often, especially in crowded anchorages during high summer season, it will not be possible to anchor on 5:1 scope (five times the depth of the water). That is understood. In fact, the norm for most Northwest anchorages seems to be 3:1. But I've watched people put out 30 feet of rode in 20 feet of water, and wonder why the anchor wouldn't bite. For the deep waters of the Pacific Northwest, carry at least 300 feet of anchor rode, whether all-chain or combination chain and rope. Opinions vary about how much chain a combination rode should include, but no one would criticize you for having at least a foot of chain for every foot of boat length. Mark your rode well with something that is easily seen and clearly indicates the length. We have seen people with all chain that have no markers and therefore no way to know how much rode is out.

Rope or chain? For years we used a combination anchor rode—a length of chain backed up with 300 feet of top-quality nylon rope—and we anchored successfully. On a smaller boat with no anchor windlass, a combination rode is the way to go. When we moved to the 37-footer we found a new religion: all-chain. With all-chain, if we let out 100 feet of chain in 30 feet of water, 70 feet of chain will be lying on the bottom after the anchor is set. At a pound a foot, that's 70 pounds of chain that must be lifted off the bottom before we get to the anchor. During settled conditions we now get by with less scope, and our swinging circle is smaller. In storm conditions, of course, we're back to 5:1, or as close to 5:1 as we can manage.

Pay out all-chain rode as you move astern, not in a pile on top of the anchor. If your windlass is freefall, use the clutch to allow the chain to pay out as you back-down. Initially, allow enough chain out to place the anchor on the bottom, then use movement astern to lay the chain along the bottom. Then secure the windlass clutch and begin to set the anchor.

Read the tide tables. If the overnight low tide isn't very low, a shallow anchorage can be just right. On the other hand, if the moon is either new or full (the two times during the month when the tidal range is the greatest) the shallow anchorage might go dry at low tide. You also want to know the maximum height of the tide during your stay. Set your scope for four to five times the water depth at high tide, or if you can't get five times, as much as you can get away with.

Set the anchor well. To get the best bury in the bottom, you want the angle between the anchor and the boat to be as flat as possible. After lowering the anchor, back well down before you set the hook. As you set, the rode should seem to stretch almost straight out from the bow. If the rode angles downward very much, you don't have enough scope out. When the anchor is set, you can shorten up to avoid swinging into other boats or onto a sandbar. You'll know, by the way, when the anchor is set. The anchor rode pulls straight and the boat stops. If you have any doubt as to whether the anchor is set, then it probably isn't. Weeds can foul an anchor, especially a Danforth style anchor, and many bottoms have weeds.

Once the anchor is set, you don't have to pour on all 600 horsepower to prove your point. Anchors gain holding power through pulling and relaxing over time, a process called soaking. An anchor put down for lunch might be recovered with little effort. Left overnight it might feel as if it had headed for China.

Look at your chart. For happy anchoring you want a good holding bottom, appropriate depths, and protection. The nautical chart can help with all these needs. If the chart says Foul, don't anchor there. If the chart shows submerged pilings at the head of the bay, avoid the head of the bay. If the chart shows 200-foot depths right up to the shoreline, that's a bad spot. If it shows the bay open to the full sweep of the prevailing wind and seas, find another bay or you could be in for a rough night. I find the easiest anchorages to be in 20 to 50 feet of water, with a decided preference for the 20- to 30-foot depths. Approach slowly, take a turn around the entire area to check the depths, and decide where you want the boat to lie after the anchor is set. Then go out to a spot that will give you sufficient scope and lower the anchor. Back way down, set the hook, and shorten up to the desired location.

Anchor in the right place. Don't anchor in cable crossing areas, or near charted underwater pipeline areas, or traveled channels.

Keep Your Distance. It is both safe and courteous to anchor a fair distance from other boats to allow for swinging room. Never drop your anchor on top of another's anchor; remember that a boat's anchor is deployed a distance out in front of the boat. The spot where another boat is anchored is NOT the place for your anchor!

Avoid Eelgrass Areas. Eelgrass and other sea grasses are an important part of the ecosystem. Eelgrass beds provide important habitat for fish species, filter pollutants, and store huge amounts of atmosphere-warming carbon. Eelgrass meadows can take years to recover, affecting marine life such as spawning herring and juvenile Chinook salmon that make eelgrass their home. These fish, among other species, are important food sources for marine mammals like Orca. The ability to purge pathogens from the ocean is another important attribute of eelgrass.

Eelgrass beds are normally close to shore and are completely submerged, with roots

Anchoring away from eelgrass avoids fouling your anchor and more importantly, saves ecologically important eelgrass.

ABOUT ANCHORING

anchored in sandy, muddy bottoms. An anchor can easily pull out the roots and eventually destroy these bedding areas. With the cooperation and support of the State of Washington DNR eelgrass mapping information, we are including the location of eelgrass in reported locations, more specifically in the San Juan Islands. This includes outlining eelgrass areas on large scale detailed maps. In select areas where boaters frequently anchor that are not mapped, we have added text noting the existence of eelgrass and the deepest DNR noted depth of the eelgrass. With this information, boaters can anchor in deeper water to avoid and protect eelgrass.

Use an anchor watch. There are a number of GPS based anchor watch systems that monitor your boat's position and signal an alarm if the boat moves outside of a predetermined boundary circle. There are a number of Android and iOS smartphone Apps available with anchor watch features. Some chartplotters and chartplotter PC software have boundary circle features. For these anchor watch systems to work well, place the center of the boundary circle at the spot where you drop the anchor. This may mean taking the anchor watch system to the bow when you center the circle. After centering the boundary circle, set the radius of the circle equal to the scope, plus the distance from the bow roller to the place on the boat where the anchor watch will rest while anchored, plus an appropriate GPS error factor, plus any significant tidal exchange that increases your swing. Anchor watch systems monitor the boat's current location and sound an alarm if outside of the boundary circle. Some smartphone apps can also SMS text or email an alarm to another phone that goes ashore with you.

How to use a trip line. If there is any indication that your planned anchoring area is prone to fouling or snagging your anchor, use a trip line to help recover your anchor. Anchors prepared for trip lines have a small hole at the nose of the anchor, somewhere near the top and far forward. Before deploying the anchor, attach a length of line that is longer than the maximum tidal water depth at your intended anchoring location. To the other end of the line attach a small float or buoy. Later when you go to weigh anchor and it is snagged on something, use the trip line to help free the fouled anchor. The float or buoy also alerts other boaters of your anchor's location.

Bridles and Snubbers. Anchor bridles and snubbers are lengths of nylon line attached to a chain hook. When the hook is attached to a deployed anchor chain and the nylon lines are attached to cleats on the boat, the bridle acts as a shock absorber to keep the anchor from breaking loose and to reduce chafe on the bow roller. As the wind and waves raise the boat, flex in the nylon lines absorb shock loads to avoid pulling the anchor free. Attached aft of the bow, bridles help reduce the boat's wind sailing and reduce yawing. To be effective the snubber lines need to be at least 30 feet long and should allow the chain attachment point, when deployed, to be below the waterline. Several pre-made bridles are available at marine suppliers or make your own.

Carry a Stern-tie. In some anchoring locations, where swing room is limited, you will set the anchor offshore, back toward shore

Anchor bridle snubber lines should be long enough and secured aft of the bow sprit.

to set, and take the dinghy in with a line from a stern cleat to a securing point on shore such as a rock, dead tree, or stern-tie pin. In many small bays, with limited swing room, it's the only way you can anchor. Sometimes you'll find a little niche for just your boat. We carry 600 feet of inexpensive polypropylene rope (because it floats) for stern ties. Some popular anchorages necessitating stern-tie have metal pins embedded in rock with rings or a length of chain, through which you can pass your stern-tie line. After passing the end through the ring, bring the end back to the boat. That way, when you are ready to depart, you can release and recover the stern-tie line without leaving the boat. When there are no stern-tie anchor pins, find something secure on shore to anchor your stern-tie line. Carry a disposable short length of rope, about 5 feet long, that can be looped around something solid on shore like a rock outcropping. As a last resort loop your stern-tie around a dead tree. Many parks in BC and Washington frown on using live trees.

Up-slope anchoring. Up-slope anchoring is used when the only convenient anchoring depths are near to shore. Up-slope anchoring involves dropping the anchor on the upsloping sea bottom as it shallows. Once the anchor is set, back-down toward the nearby shore and stern-tie to shore. The stern-tie holds the boat in a position where it is always pulling the main anchor up the slope and keeps the anchor set.

Secure the anchor rode to the boat. We have all heard stories about boaters losing their all chain anchor, when they discover that the end, buried under hundreds of pounds of rode in the chain locker, was not attached to the boat. Be sure the end of your anchor chain is attached to the boat – but not hard attached. The anchor should be attached to a length of nylon rope that is secured to the boat. Instead of leaving this nylon rope buried under a pile of chain in our chain locker, we coil the line and keep it high and dry attached to the side of the anchor locker. In the event the anchor is stuck or if you need to get away from the anchor quickly, the rope can be cut. Secure a floating buoy to the end of the nylon rope so that you can retrieve the anchor and chain later.

A custom-made Stern-tie reel mounted on rails looks great and works well.

An off-the-shelf plastic hose reel serves well for Stern-tie line on the back of a powerboat.

After securing the stern-tie line shoreside, bring the bitter-end of line back to the boat for easy release when it's time to depart.

ABOUT ANCHORING

ANCHORING USING YOUR FISHFINDER

How do you use your boat's fishfinder to help locate a good spot for anchoring and avoid dropping the anchor over rocks, kelp and eelgrass? When anchoring for the first time in a bay or cove, it's sometimes hit-and-miss to find the right spot. Charts are very general and not granular when it comes to bottom characteristics. Discover another valuable use for your fishfinder:

Overview. When anchoring in an unfamiliar location, it is helpful to know more about the bottom than is available from navigation charts and a depth sounder. Charts show general seabed characteristics (e.g., S = sand; M = mud; R = rocky; K = kelp; Grs = grass) and known rock locations. But they don't show the exact edges of grass or kelp beds and don't identify subtidal rocks and hard spots located within an otherwise soft seabed. A fishfinder (sometimes called an echosounder) helps provide this information.

Fishfinder vs Depth Sounder. A depth sounder typically gives only a digital reading of the depth under the boat. Some navigation programs track recent history of depths that helps understand the topography. A fishfinder not only gives the recent depth history, but, more importantly, also gives information about the strength of the returning acoustic signal. Every object has a unique "acoustic signature" and every fishfinder has a unique way of presenting that signature (usually in the form of a color scheme). Generally speaking, setting the frequency higher, say from 50 KHz to 200 KHz, is usually better.

Seabed Hardness. The harder the seabed the more acoustic energy it reflects back to the transducer. If the seabed is hard enough, the returning energy bounces off the boat, back to the seabed, and back to the boat creating a second echo. Second echoes are weaker and twice the depth of primary echoes. Fig. 1 shows soft seabed in Roche Harbor that does not create a second echo. Fig. 2 shows a harder seabed in Montague Harbor (note the second echo at twice the depth). The harder the bottom, more echoes will show up between the first and second echoes.

Rocks. The seabed is not always uniform. Fig. 3 from Gowland Harbour shows a hard or rocky section of an otherwise soft seabed. Note the second echoes under the hard spots. This information will help you avoid putting the anchor down on a hard spot.

Eelgrass. As noted in the main Waggoner text, cruisers should avoid anchoring in eelgrass. Fig. 4 shows the eelgrass at the west end of Roche Harbor. Note that the eelgrass gives a weaker echo than the seabed and that the reported digital depth is 12.8 ft (the top of the eelgrass) when the true depth to the seabed is 15 ft. Reporting depth to the top of thick vegetation is a characteristic of most depth sounders and fishfinders. Here the fishfinder helps to see the true depth.

Kelp. Fig. 5 shows understory kelp on a hard substrate (note the weak second echo) at Point Partridge. You don't want to anchor here. The bottom shown in Fig. 5 is the thick deep brown/rust colored line. The kelp is the same color as the seabed but has a yellow/green edge to it seen easiest on the right half of the photo/image. The short tails sticking down from the seabed indicate the hardest part of the seabed and are most likely rocks that the kelp is attached to. The blue/yellow targets in the water column above the seabed are most likely the bulbs of the young bull kelp. The second echo is the mostly yellow fine line at the bottom of the screen.

[Field Correspondent Jim Norris]

Figure 1 Soft Bottom Roche Harbor

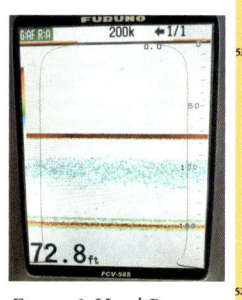

Figure 2 Hard Bottom Montague Harbour

Figure 3 Hard Spots in soft seabed Gowlland Harbour

Figure 4 Eelgrass Roche Harbor

Figure 5 Kelp Partridge Point

Anchoring the Dinghy. Due to the large tidal changes in Pacific Northwest waters, boaters leaving the dinghy at a beach landing for more than a few minutes will need to anchor the dinghy off shore, especially a dinghy that is too heavy to lift and carry any reasonable distance ashore.

One technique to anchor the dinghy requires equipping the dinghy with a long line (100 feet or more) attached to the bow and an elastic line (brand name Anchor Buddy), attached to the stern of the dinghy and a grapnel anchor. We have a short piece of chain connected between the anchor and the elastic line. To anchor the dinghy:

- Drop your passenger(s) on shore and have them hold the end of the long line attached to the bow
- Maneuver the dinghy off shore to water deep enough that the dinghy will remain afloat for the duration of your shoreside stay.
- Drop the anchor attached to the elastic line and secured to the stern of the dinghy.
- Motor forward to shore, or have your person on shore pull the dinghy in using the long bow line. Disembark while the person on shore holds the dinghy in position - the elastic line will be pulling away from shore.
- Once you and all your needed gear are off the dinghy, allow the elastic cord to pull the dinghy out to the anchor position. The elastic Anchor Buddy line stretches to about 20 feet; you may need more than one Anchor Buddy for an extended shallow beach area.
- Tie the bitter end of the long bow line to a solid object on shore.

Another Option to Anchor the Dinghy. Field Correspondent Jim Norris shares his method of anchoring a dinghy off the mud flats. Carry a mushroom anchor, 125 feet of leaded line, and a metal stake to use on the tide flat.

Tie the top of the anchor onto the skiff's stern with a short line (the length of the depth of water) and the base of the mushroom to one end of the 125-foot long line. Tie the other end of the 125 foot line to something on the beach.

If there is nothing to tie to on the beach, use the stake. Balance the anchor on the aft end of the dinghy tube and push the skiff offshore as far as possible. When the skiff stops floating away, pull the base of the anchor with the attached 125-foot line, causing the anchor to fall into the water and anchor the skiff.

When you return from exploring ashore, pull in the anchor and drag the skiff with it using the 125 foot long line. This is easily done if the tide is rising. The trick is to make sure to account for the tidal change.

RAFTING PROTOCOL

Tying next to another boat at the dock, on a mooring buoy, or at anchor, often saves space for other boaters at marinas that may have limited space, or in coves that cannot accommodate a large number of boats.

At Docks and Marinas
Waggoner Cruising Guide includes rafting information for marinas where rafting is needed. Some marinas may have signage that says "rafting is required" or "rafting is encouraged." Rafting is much more common at docks and marinas in Northern BC and Southeast Alaska where space is often limited. When tying-up at a marina where rafting is required, you are expected to allow another boat to tie next to you. At facilities where rafting is encouraged, it is courteous practice to allow other boats of similar size to tie-up next to you. Where the Waggoner Cruising Guide and the marina are silent on the subject, it is assumed that rafting is not commonly used at the facility, and that you are not expected to have other boats raft-up to you.

At facilities where rafting is required or encouraged, you should message your readiness for another boat to raft to you by fendering the outside of your boat. Approaching vessels should look for fenders on the outside of moored vessels, signaling that it's ok to raft up to your boat.

Many boaters enjoy tying up with those from the same yacht club or from other yacht clubs; fly your burgeee as a friendly invite. Boats should be of similar size or smaller when rafting together. Avoid rafting larger vessels to smaller vessels and watch for fairway intrusion.

As a courtesy, ask first if the vessel captain/crew is onboard and available to assist and to provide permission. If no one is onboard and there are no fenders on the outside, wait for the captain/crew to return or find another mooring location. Use extra caution when proceeding to raft-up to another vessel. Rafting is generally limited to three deep, with the preferred being 2-deep for pleasure boats. Fish boats often raft together when the fleet is in port; it is not uncommon to see 4 or more fish boats rafted together.

Vessel Separation Considerations
As with any alongside berth, have your fenders at the right height; approach slowly with a bow and stern line and preferably a back spring line ready to prevent the tide or wind setting your yacht astern.

Fender well at all points of contact and potential contact caused by large waves and wakes from passing boats. Check the superstructure for possible contact and fender the above superstructure that may make contact.

Sailboats should not have masts lined up in case you go rolling, causing spreaders to tangle. Move sailboats forward and backwards to ensure there is a decent gap between masts to allow for rolling.

Don't forget to check for conflicting or potentially damaging discharge from generator exhaust, furnace exhaust, and bilge discharge. The best practice is to avoid all generator operation; however, if you must, run the generator only at a reasonable time, and ask the neighboring boat if it possesses any problems; let them know how long it will be running.

Accessing the Dock from Boat to Boat
Ask the captain/crew of the inner vessel about the preferred path across their boat to access the dock; some boaters may prefer that you cross through their cockpit, while others may prefer you cross over their bow. Be mindful of the number of trips across other boats and keep it to a minimum.

Departing the Raft
Rafted boat operators should communicate with each other their plans for departure, to include time, day, and agreed-upon plan to allow inner boats to depart. When tying-off to another boat, it is helpful to bring the ends of your lines back to your boat; it makes it easier for you to leave without disturbing the other boaters.

Rafting on Mooring Buoys
As of 2021, rafting with other boats on a Washington State Marine Park mooring buoy is not allowed. While some marine park buoys may have old signage regarding rafting, Waggoner has been told by Washington Parks, that rafting on park mooring buoys is no longer allowed. DNR (Department of Natural Resources) mooring buoys may allow rafting, but boaters should use good judgement regarding boat size, weight, and wind conditions. Rafting to a boat on a mooring buoy has additional challenges due to swing action – have bow, stern, and spring lines and lots of fenders at the ready. Check with rules and regulations that may be posted on DNR buoys and/or onshore. There is no charge for the use of Washington State DNR buoys, which are designed for boats up to 50 feet.

Marine Park buoys in British Columbia allow 1 boat per buoy up to 50 feet, unless winds exceed 30 knots; and vessels up to 40 feet unless winds exceed 37 knots.

Most mooring buoys in Southeast Alaska are of substantial size and weight, which may allow for rafting if needed. Be sure to ask permission before rafting-up and approach the moored boat upwind. Wind conditions and boat size and weight should be taken into consideration.

CHARTERING

Those who don't yet own a boat or want to "test the waters" to discover the possibilities of the boating life style often find that chartering a boat is the perfect solution. Waggoner publisher Mark Bunzel and editors Leonard and Lorena Landon began their boating careers by first chartering boats as did many of today's experienced boaters. Chartering or renting a boat is a great option for those who live far from Pacific Northwest waters and don't want the expense and hassle of transporting their boat to the region. Then there are those who don't want the expense of owning and maintaining a boat and appreciate being able to return the chartered boat to port, knowing that it will be cleaned and maintained by the charter company. Insurance is normally included in the cost of chartering a boat, but those chartering are encouraged to purchase travel insurance for protection against cancellation penalties and/or unforeseeable circumstances.

The most popular charter boat waters run from the San Juan Islands to Desolation Sound, a distance of approximately 160 miles. These waters include the San Juan Islands, the Canadian Gulf Islands, the cities of Victoria and Vancouver, Howe Sound, Princess Louisa Inlet and the ever popular Desolation Sound. Most charters are for a week or two. It would take years of careful planning and repeat visits for a regular charter cruiser to see all there is to see in this area.

There is a wide variety of different types of chartering companies to suit the growing demand for on-the-water experiences. Many charter companies include the option to hire a skipper; or if qualified, act as your own skipper for your planned itinerary on the water. Some charterers even facilitate group flotillas. There are companies that rent smaller vessels for the day or half-day for fishing or sightseeing, while others cater to those who want to bring along family and friends on a larger yacht for an extended cruise. Other businesses provide the opportunity to be on the water for special occasions like weddings, anniversaries, or office parties aboard a vessel with captain, crew, and chef. Boat Clubs have grown in popularity and offer those with limited time the opportunity to choose from a selection of vessels to charter through a monthly membership.

Proof of Competency. To charter a boat in **Washington State**, a WA Boater's Education Card, which is required of individual boat owners/operators, is not required for those chartering a boat; however, those chartering a boat are required to sign and keep on board a copy of the Motor Vessel Rental Safety Checklist provided by the charter company.

In **British Columbia**, charter companies require proof of a Pleasure Craft Operator Card (PCOC) for residents of Canada, or a certificate from a Canadian boating safety course completed before April 1, 1999. For out of country visitors to Canada, an operator card that meets the requirements of his or her home state or country is accepted. Proof of competency is not required if a visitor to Canada is operating the boat in Canadian waters for less than 45 consecutive days.

There are no formal certifications required to operate a boat in **Alaska**, however, boat charters normally require a resume and proof of experience to meet insurance guidelines. Alaskans are encouraged to take a boating course and get an Alaska Boater Education Card.

Bareboat Charters. This chartering option refers to selecting from a pool of vessels maintained by the charter company that you can take out on your own for extended weeks of cruising. "Bareboat" normally refers to you acting as your own skipper and taking care of your own food provisioning. The chartering company will ask for a resume to confirm your boating experience and qualifications. An on-the-water demonstration of skills may also be required. Most bareboat charters, however, offer a skipper for hire if needed. The charter company will walk you through the boat so you can become familiar with the boat's systems and operation before departing on your journey. Many bareboat charters also provide classes with on-the-water training to help new boaters build experience for future chartering. Below is a sampling of bareboat charter companies:

Boat Clubs. Boat clubs have grown in popularity over the last few years, especially among young people with busy work

Bareboat Charters
Anacortes Yacht Charters
   Power and Sail
   anacortesyachtcharters.com
   360-293-4555;
Auke Bay Adventures (Juneau)
   Power (Nordic Tug & Cutwater)
   aukebayadventures.com
   208-631-3478
Desolation Sound Yacht Charters
   Power and Sail
   desolationsoundyachtcharters.com
   250-339-7222
Island Cruising
   Primarily Sail
   islandcruising.com
   250-656-7070
Nanaimo Yacht Charters
   Power and Sail
   nanaimoyachtcharters.com
   250-754-8601l
Northwest Explorations
   Power
   nwexplorations.com
   360-676-1248
San Juan Sailing & Yachting
   Power and Sail
   sanjuansailing.com
   360-671-4300

Boat Clubs
Carefree Boat Club
   Power, Sail, & Pontoon
   carefreeboats.com
   206-567-2628 Seattle
Club Yolo
   Power
   clubyolo.ca
   250-252-6549
   Mill Bay and Port Sidney
Freedom Boat Club
   Power and Pontoon
   freedomboatclub.com
   Seattle 206-707-2367
   Anacortes & Bellingham 360-797-9887
   North Vancouver B.C. 778-997-9106
   Sidney B.C. 250-800-3243
   see their website for other locations
   and phone numbers.
Funshare Boat Club (Seattle Boat Co.)
   Power - Cobalt and Malibu
   Watersport equipment included
   Seattle & Bellevue 206-589-8916
   Seattleboat.com/boat-club

Expedition Charters
Alaska Dream Cruises (Sitka)
   Large power yachts
   alaskadreamcruises.com
   907-747-8100
Expedition Broker Alaska Charter Yachts
   Power and Sail Yachts
   expeditionbroker.com
   877-267-2793
Maple Leaf Adventures
   B.C., Haida Gwaii,
   SE Alaska
   Power and Sail
   mapleleafadventures.com
   250-386-7245
Blackfish Marine
   Power yachts
   bluepacificcharters.ca
   604-669-8081

Event Charters
Seattle Yacht Charters
   Power Yachts
   seattleyachtchartersdaily.com
   888-526-2848;
Vancouver Yacht Charters
   vancouveryachtcharters.
   com; 604-779-9193

CHARTERING

schedules and limited time to enjoy family outings on the water.

An initial membership fee is charged to join the club, with monthly or annual fees thereafter. The initial membership fee can range from $4,000 to $6,000, with an average monthly fee of $275. Membership provides access to a range of different vessels. Services often include classroom and on-the-water training, valet dock staff, and ongoing maintenance, cleaning, and insurance for their fleet of boats. Members need to pay for their own fuel costs.

Other benefits also include social events and get-togethers. Some boat clubs have the option of using part of the initial membership fee as a down payment on the purchase of a boat from the fleet. Clubs may offer a variety of membership plans, depending on when and where you want to boat, especially if they have locations in several countries. In this case, reservations for a boat are made in advance, and members are required to complete a training course before they can start reserving boats.

Expedition Charters. For those who prefer not to be on a cruise ship with thousands of other guests, the smaller pocket cruise ships and expedition yachts are a nice alternative. These charters include a captain, crew, and chef with pre-built itineraries or custom itineraries. Expedition charters are typically booked for wildlife and glacier viewing, with shore excursions and evening programs. All meals are included. Access to special cultural sites and local scientists in the field are a benefit of expedition charters. Some charters have their own naturalist on board. These charters usually carry kayaks and provide fishing opportunities. Expedition charters are mostly sought by those wanting to see the remote regions of Southeast Alaska and Northern British Columbia.

Event Charters. While not everyone spends their vacation on the water, or has access to a boat, many folks seek opportunities to be on the water for special occasions such as weddings, anniversaries, retirement parties or office parties. These types of charters come with a captain, crew, and chef, or permit an outside caterer to provide food and drink. Fishing and sightseeing excursions can also be arranged.

Q&A Check List. When chartering a boat from a chartering company, be sure to do your homework and prepare a list of questions. There are many chartering companies to choose from and each may have specific requirements and/or limitations regarding cruising areas. Here are a few questions to ask and things to check:

- Ask about where you can and cannot take the boat – what region or boundary limits are there?
- Verify insurance coverage and any needed add-ons.
- Are dogs allowed on board?
- Ask about whale no-go zones, speed zones, and no-anchoring zones
- Ask about fuel capacity and fuel dock locations
- Verify the procedures and operation of the onboard VHF radio
- Check to see that electrical and mechanical systems are in order
- How do you operate the Head
- Is all required Coast Guard safety equipment on board such as life jackets, fire extinguishers, signaling devices, and other required equipment?
- Is all the appropriate, needed paperwork on board?
- Check the condition of the vessel inside and out; take photos for your records.

Chartering is a great way to try different styles of cruising. It's also an option for those who cruise their local waters and want to venture farther afield. You might want to participate in an organized charter flotilla guided by a professional that knows the area.

You don't have to miss out on a great experience at sea. You can plan and take your dream trip without the cost of owning a boat or the cost of transporting your boat from another part of the world.

With so many charter options, guidebooks, and available training, it's a great time to charter a boat and enjoy the beautiful waters of the Inside Passage with family and friends.

DESOLATION SOUND YACHT CHARTERS
Comox, British Columbia, Canada

YACHT CHARTERS, MANAGEMENT & TRAINING

Now Open at Comox Marina!
DESOLATION SOUND YACHT & MARINE SUPPLY STORE

YOUR PREMIER CHOICE FOR CHARTER AND MANAGEMENT

Tel: 250-339-4914 | Toll Free: 1-877-647-3815
charter@desolationsoundyachtcharters.com

New to Boating? Find a Pumpout Near You with the New Pumpout Nav App!

Pumpout Nav is a free interactive IOS and Android mobile app to help you empty the head and keep our waters healthy. Download the app today to find your nearest sewage pumpout or portable toilet waste stations in the app map! Learn more at PumpoutWashington.org

Pumpout Washington is a project of Washington Sea Grant in partnership with Washington State Parks Clean Vessel Act Program. Funding is provided by the U.S. Fish & Wildlife Service through the Sport Fish Restoration and Boating Trust Fund provided through your purchase of fishing equipment and motorboat fuels.

Save the waters you love

Pumpout Nav

Find the Nearest Pumpout, Dump Station or Floating Restroom

Powered by epical™

Not for navigation purposes

FLOTILLA CRUISING WITH NEW FRIENDS

There are many boaters who prefer cruising with other boats and crews as a group flotilla. For some, it is with a group of friends from a yacht club, a boat club, or with an organized commercial venture. They believe in safety in numbers, and often travel with one or more experienced crews to lead the group. Many use a flotilla trip as an opportunity to learn before they cruise on their own.

In the Northwest, there are several styles of flotilla cruises offered by different companies. They are all unique and have something different to offer. People who choose flotillas come in all ages, with varied boating experience. The common thread throughout is the opportunity for social interaction with other boaters, and the opportunity to gain a broader understanding of our Pacific Northwest waters.

Northwest Explorations in Bellingham, offers trips where customers charter a high-end yacht for multiple weeks with planned legs to Southeast Alaska, and planned legs for the return trip. Participants can purchase a chosen leg along the routes, depending on the amount of time you have to spend. Northwest Explorations supplies the boats, but you are captain and crew of your assigned vessel. Their fleet offers a variety of beautiful Grand Banks yachts and other brand yachts, including a DeFever and a Fleming 55. They call their flotilla trips "Mother Goose" flotillas, where most of the boats follow along together. A mother ship leads with crew, a naturalist, and a mechanic to support 5-8 boats. Activities are planned along the way. This format is ideal for those who live and boat in another area of the country or the world, or if you have limited time to take your boat up to Southeast Alaska. Northwest Explorations also offers flotilla trips to Desolation Sound

The Waggoner Cruising Guide has a flotilla program for the passage from Anacortes to Ketchikan in Southeast Alaska, and an additional flotilla from Anacortes to Desolation Sound. Boaters use their own vessels in this program. The group usually consists of 6-8 boats that vary in size and speed. Some boats stay clustered during each day's leg, while others choose to meet up at the end of the day at the designated rendezvous location. The complete trip is organized and planned around an itinerary with activities and education along the way, including weather and seamanship. This program offers seminar courses, conducted in the months prior to departure, to develop the skills needed for a confident passage home. Trip leaders prepare daily briefings and guide all the participants on the trip to help ensure a safe, pleasant passage. Friendships are made on the flotilla trips that last a lifetime.

Jim Rard and Crew from Marine Servicenter offer a 12-week "Sail Alaska" program for power and sailboats. Participants learn while cruising to Alaska. Once in Southeast Alaska, Jim reveals his favorite destinations through organized special events and wildlife viewing. Imagine building and firing up a stone pizza oven and having homemade pizza cooked on hot rocks at a remote island in Southeast Alaska.

Slowboat, led by former Waggoner Guide Managing Editor, Sam Landsman, and experienced cruisers Laura Domela and Kevin Morris, Slowboat specializes in adventure cruising. Their flotilla program takes boaters to unique, out of the way destinations. They offer flotilla cruises to and from Southeast Alaska, destinations within Southeast Alaska, and the West Coast of Vancouver Island for beginner and experienced cruisers traveling with their own boats. They too work with the participants to share their knowledge for the unique situations presented in remote locations.

All flotilla cruisers say they come back from these trips with new skills, confidence, and many new friends from their time on the water.

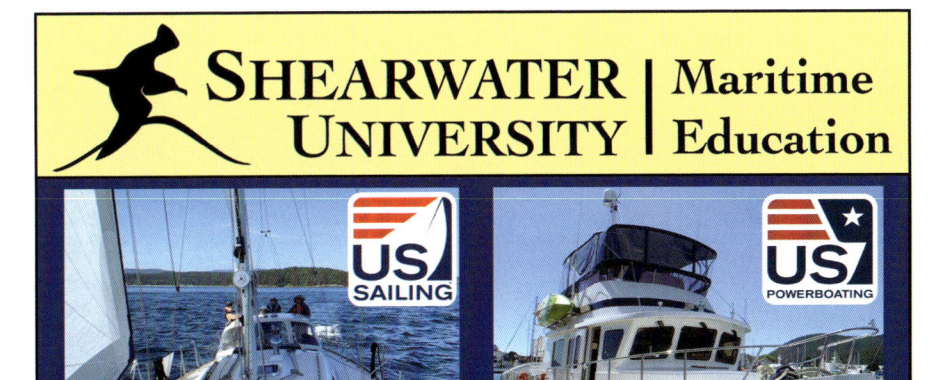

Shearwater University | Maritime Education

Best Practices in Maritime meets Best Practices in Education
Skills & knowledge for the Salish Sea, Inside Passage & Beyond

Train on Our Boats:
- Sail or power on top-quality yachts
- Community Sailing & Cruising - make friends & gain experience
- Sail/Cruise our boats as your own
- Certifications for world chartering

Train on Your Boat:
- Customized to your background, your goals, your sail or power boat
- Gain skills, safety & confidence
- Satisfy insurance requirements
- Certify to charter worldwide

ShearwaterUniversity.com

2023 WAGGONER CRUISING GUIDE

SEATTLE YACHTS
Sales & Service

NEW BOAT DEALER, PROFESSIONAL BROKERAGE SERVICES, & FULL SERVICE BOATYARD

Our full service boatyard and knowledgeable staff can provide:

- Haul outs (50 Ton Travel Lift)
- Inboard/outboard engine work
- Electronics, electrical repair & installation
- Painting, gelcoat repair and refinish
- Shaft, prop and strut repair
- Interior/exterior woodworking & brightwork
- Standard boat maintenance
- ...and more!

Sales - Anacortes & Seattle
844.692.2487 | info@seattleyachts.com

Service - Anacortes
360.293.3145 | Service@SeattleYachts.com

ALASKAN YACHTS | BULLFROG BOATS | Dehler | XCS Excess | Hanse | LEGACY | Moody
NIMBUS | Nordic Tugs | Northern Marine | NORTHWEST YACHTS | REGENCY | SCHAEFER | TARTAN

CELLULAR, INTERNET & SATELLITE COMMUNICATIONS

STAYING CONNECTED ONBOARD

The 2022 cruising season marked a huge breakthrough regarding onboard connectivity.

Over the last year, 5G cellular solutions and 5G cell towers in our favorite cruising grounds became widespread, offering a huge leap in data connection speeds and coverage.

The Starlink satellite-based system from SpaceX became a reality and cruisers now have a very viable option for staying connected in the most remote anchorages. Starlink is not only a breakthrough for individual boaters, but also indirectly makes remote marina Wi-Fi much more useable. In 2022, several outlying marinas in The Broughtons upgraded their earlier generation satellite-based internet with Starlink, dramatically increasing marina Wi-Fi useability.

While a lot of boaters love the idea of getting away from it all when they go cruising, most of us still want some level of connectivity with the rest of the world. In some cases, boaters want or need to work from the boat while they cruise. In other cases, having access to voice communications, email, web, social media, and streaming is highly desirable. Plus, with so many marine resources such as marina bookings, real time weather and wind forecasts available online, connectivity has become essential.

There are three main ways to stay connected while on the boat.

Wi-Fi - Many marinas and coastal towns offer Wi-Fi connectivity for boaters which allows you to connect to a shore-based hotspot to access the Internet. This solution may work ok, although there are many factors such as the equipment quality, bandwidth, and distance from the hotspot that may negatively impact getting a good connection. Vendors such as Wave Wi-Fi and MikroTik have solutions for providing a more functional Wi-Fi connectivity experience, but even these solutions cannot overcome a poorly implemented marina Wi-Fi infrastructure. Plus of course when you leave the marina, your Wi-Fi connection goes away.

5G/LTE Cellular - Virtually everyone owns a cell phone and while making phone calls is the primary use, using the phone for email, web, online apps, or setting it up to be a personal hotspot is very useful when you are on the water.

As you cruise to more remote areas, having a dedicated 4G or 5G cellular-based high-speed router coupled with high-gain antennas helps to bring in distant cell signals and provides an onboard Wi-Fi access point to keep all your devices connected. Companies such as Peplink have solutions specifically built for use on boats.

Another option is to install a cell booster from companies such as weBoost, which can amplify your cell phone signal and allow you to boost an unusable cell signal to enough bars to make a phone call. Many boaters in the past have installed both a cell booster for phones and a cellular router for data devices, but with Wi-Fi calling supported on all modern phones and carriers, a good router with a well-placed external antenna can provide coverage for both phone calls and data applications.

Cellular router devices require their own cell plan and SIM card. If you go this route, be sure to check with your cell carrier for compatibility with your device as well as things like areas of coverage, data limits, and roaming. Since these are cellular based, you typically need to be within 10-20 miles of a cell tower and not behind a mountain in order for this to work well. With good equipment, cellular connectivity is fairly reliable throughout the Salish Sea up to some parts of the Desolation Sound area. With fewer cell towers as you go north, or if you are in more isolated areas such as West Coast Vancouver Island, a cellular-based solution will not provide full-time connectivity.

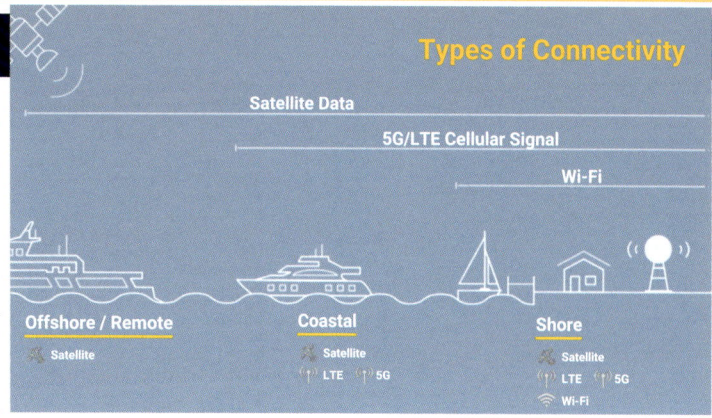

Satellite Connectivity - Marine satellite connectivity solutions from companies such as KVH have been available for years, but tend to be quite expensive for both the equipment and the data plans, and data connection speeds are slower than what we are used to. With fairly large dome antenna requirements, these solutions tend to be practical on larger power boats. These solutions communicate with satellites; they allow boaters to have some level of connectivity just about anywhere.

The 2022 cruising season marked a huge breakthrough in satellite-based connectivity with the introduction of Starlink from SpaceX. The Starlink solution consists of an external satellite antenna connected to a router with a Wi-Fi access point.

Starlink equipment and plans are reasonably priced, and allow boaters to be connected with high-speed, unlimited data throughout our Pacific Northwest cruising grounds and beyond. But Starlink is currently not designed to be used while moving and is not specifically built for use on recreational boats. The current Starlink satellite antenna is not marinized or ruggedized for use in extreme wind and sea conditions so it may need to be stowed while underway. There is no certified network of marine installers for Starlink, so boaters are on their own setting up the antenna and getting it all to work. The higher power draw of a satellite-based system is also a consideration for boaters. But despite those challenges, a lot of boaters deployed a Starlink system during the 2022 cruising season.

Based on reports from cruisers throughout the region, the overall experience has been mixed. Starlink is reported to have worked very well in remote areas of Canada where there was no cell coverage. Others reported that Starlink was not working well in crowded marinas due to obstructions and was sometimes slow in more congested, populated areas. Cellular on the other hand works very well in populated areas and allows boaters to be connected even in extreme conditions while underway. Given all that, a Peplink 5G cellular router plus a Starlink setup has become the go-to solution for a lot of boaters who need full time connectivity.

This is an exciting time with the pace of innovation and constant improvements. To keep informed see OnboardWireless.com, SeaBits.com, and the Mobile Internet Resource Center mobileinternetinfo.com.

[Doug Miller, President Onboard Wireless]

Starlink Antenna

Peplink Router

CELLULAR, INTERNET & SATELLITE COMMUNICATIONS

Voice and data communications remain one of the priorities when cruising. Lately, with a multitude of smart and connected devices onboard, data communications have become a top priority for cruisers. Email, social media, weather information, financial transactions, marina slip reservations, and web browsing have all become essential elements of today's cruising.

Cellular has been the most cost-effective solution for voice, messaging, and data communications in much of the Northwest cruising area. However, SpaceX's introduction of Starlink, with high-speed internet at affordable rates, gives boaters yet another option.

First generation Satellite service provides the best geographic coverage, but at a higher cost. Wi-Fi internet service is available from a number of different free and for-fee providers. In more remote areas, Wi-Fi service is not always available, or the service may be slow and unreliable. Wi-Fi at remote locations where the base station provider has Starlink, this Wi-Fi service has improved dramatically. Increased access to 5G cellular service is giving cellular data users a boost.

Cellular. In Washington, B.C. and SE Alaska waters, cruisers have a number of cellular providers to choose from, all with excellent voice, messaging, and data service. All of the Washington waters, except the western half of Strait of Juan de Fuca, have excellent cellular coverage.

Cellular providers have a range of plans at reasonable rates often with unlimited voice and data that include cross-border roaming. Today's cellular data speeds are good and service is very reliable. If you are on one of the newer rate plans, cellular is a cost effective way to handle your voice, messaging, and internet needs while cruising all of the Northwest waters. Be sure you have a voice, messaging, and data plan which includes roaming; if you don't, you may be shocked when you get the bill.

Three major cellular providers: Telus, Rogers, and Bell, operate in B.C. with voice, text messaging, and data coverage. Voice, messaging, and data coverage is complete from the U.S. border to Campbell River/Desolation Sound on the north. There is no coverage in Jervis Inlet and spotty in mountainous areas.

From Campbell River/Desolation Sound to Port McNeill, cellular coverage is fairly good with coverage on most of Johnstone Strait. There is spotty to no coverage in the passages and inlets off of the Strait. Coverage between Campbell River and Port McNeill on Johnstone Strait keeps getting better each season.

Cellular towers high atop mountains near Port McNeill and Port Hardy provide coverage in much of Queen Charlotte Strait, and the edge of the Broughtons. We have had cell coverage almost to Cape Caution, but don't expect to get coverage within the Broughtons.

Between Port Hardy and Prince Rupert, cell coverage is limited to the area around the towns of Bella Bella/Shearwater, Klemtu, Hartley Bay, Kitimat, and Bella Coola. The area around Prince Rupert has good cell coverage that continues north to the U.S. border in Dixon Entrance, where U.S. cell service begins.

Haida Gwaii has cell coverage in and around the cities of Daajing Giids (Queen Charlotte), Sandspit, and Masset.

The west coast of Vancouver Island has coverage from Hot Springs south to and including Barkley Sound. Alberni Inlet has coverage in some areas. There is coverage in Quatsino Sound in the north.

Southeast Alaska coverage begins in Dixon entrance near Cape Fox but is spotty until you pass the entrance to Behm Canal on your way to Ketchikan. Four major U.S. cellular carriers, AT&T, Verizon, T-Mobile, and GCI provide voice, data, and messaging coverage in and around populated areas in Southeast Alaska.

Check with your cellular provider for coverage in Southeast Alaska. For a map of cell tower locations, go to cellmapper.net.

Cellular Amplifiers. Cellular amplifiers are a good addition when cruising north of Campbell River and Desolation Sound. From Campbell River north, there are fewer cell towers, and the distances between them are much greater. Cellular signals emitting from the towers are powerful, but the return signals from your phone are relatively weak. A cell amplifier's main advantage is in boosting the signal from your phone so that the distant cell tower can "hear" your phone. The best amplifiers have an external antenna. Be sure and match the amplifier's frequencies to your phone, and the carriers for your planned cruising area.

Cruise ships have a predictable effect on cell service. In remote areas north of Campbell River and especially in southeast Alaska, cell phone service is noticeably degraded when a cruise ship or two are in the cell tower area. These remote systems, sized to limited cellular demand, are often swamped by the thousands of devices in the hands of cruise ship passengers.

Important: For emergency, distress, and rescue operations, cellular telephones are not a substitute for VHF radios. If you have a problem and need help, get on channel 16 and start calling. The Coast Guard and neighboring vessels will hear you and may be your closest and fastest aid.

Satellite Communications. Before SpaceX's Starlink satellite system, "satellite communications" generally referred to Iridium and Globalstar systems. These systems provide voice communication and data communications nearly everywhere. Prices for equipment have come down but airtime is still relatively expensive.

Messaging and data services were made much easier to use with the introduction of Iridium Go and Globalstar Sat-Fi devices. These devices bring satellite communications to your smartphone, tablet, and PC. Both Iridium Go and Sat-Fi connect your smartphone, or any Wi-Fi enabled device, to the respective satellite system for voice, data, and messaging. The devices are easy to use and allow multiple devices to connect to the satellite service. Data speeds are slow to very slow, with bandwidth for simple email and light browsing. Some weather information services are available. Both Iridium and Globalstar services and devices have data compression features that help internet browsing. Satellite device rentals are available.

Satellite coverage is different for each of the two providers, so check the coverage before buying devices. Both Iridium and Globalstar have coverage throughout the waters of the Inside Passage.

COMMUNICATIONS TOPICS
Cellular
Cellular Amplifiers
Satellite Communications
Satellite Messengers
Starlink
Wi-Fi Internet
Being a Good Wi-Fi Citizen
Wi-Fi Amplifiers
Smartphone Apps

Want to stay connected while cruising in the Pacific Northwest?

Find out how from the connectivity specialists at Onboard Wireless.

ONBOARD WIRELESS

OnboardWireless.com
206-486-0116

CELLULAR, INTERNET & SATELLITE COMMUNICATIONS

SpaceX Starlink. Starlink is the latest in Satellite internet service. Elon Musk's SpaceX company started providing high-speed low cost satellite based internet service to an initial customer base in 2021. Initially, customer dish antennas were in fixed locations. However, in early 2022, Starlink started offering smaller antennas and service plans for RVers. Starlink still prohibits using the service while underway. A number of boaters have the RV Starlink service and report service as far north as Ketchikan. Future Starlink plans call for service to mobile antennas for ship and airplane based stations.

Initial feedback from Starlink customers is good and is already showing itself as a game-changer for internet access to boaters in remote locations. Starlink is expected to deliver download speeds of about 100 Mbps. Starlink hasn't yet announced a schedule for mobile antennas. Starlink's low earth orbit architecture is unique and enables its faster data speeds.

Satellite Messengers. Satellite messengers like those from SPOT, Garmin, Zoleo, and Bivy Stick, offer an inexpensive way for cruisers to track and check in. Depending on the device and service plan selected, satellite messengers can send automated position reports, link to smartphones to send and receive text messages via satellite, or send a distress signal. Weather forecasts and marine weather forecasts are now available on some of these messaging devices. Satellite messengers rely on private satellite constellations, not the internationally organized Cospas-Sarsat network that EPIRBs and PLBs use. SOS messages go through a private emergency center that passes on the message to government emergency services. Satellite messengers are not EPIRBs and should not take the place of an EPIRB, but they can provide low-cost communications far beyond cell phone service. Satellite messengers offer the coverage of satellite service at a lower cost.

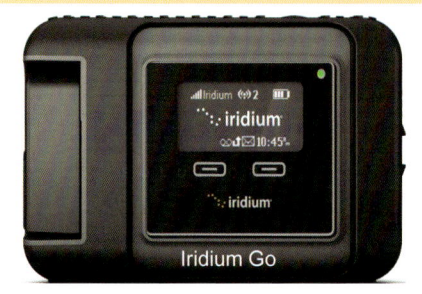

Wi-Fi Internet. Wi-Fi may be one of the most universal and inexpensive means of accessing the internet when cruising. However, availability, speed, and reliability are often problematic. Most marinas have Wi-Fi available for their guests. How the marina provides this Wi-Fi service varies from marina to marina. The larger, popular marinas have in-house installed commercial grade Wi-Fi systems that are accessible, and reliable with bandwidth for most internet needs. Other marinas have contracted with commercial Wi-Fi providers such as Shaw-Go for commercial grade Wi-Fi service. A few marinas with commercial grade Wi-Fi systems offer high bandwidth, for a fee, as an alternative to their lower bandwidth free Wi-Fi. Some marinas have in-house installed Wi-Fi, built from home-grade equipment connected to residential bandwidth internet service. In remote areas of B.C., where there are no landlines, marina Wi-Fi is via one of several satellite internet providers. In the past, most were limited bandwidth Dish Satellite Internet providers with much slower speeds and much higher cost than landline data service. Many of these remote marinas have switched to Starlink with much improved speed and lower cost. Marina operators provide this service to guests; and even with Starlink, it is best to be a thoughtful shared user of the marina's Wi-Fi system.

A decade ago, when a boat pulled into a marina moorage space, the boat might use one or possibly two Wi-Fi connection ports, and their usage consisted of simple emails and some limited bandwidth web browsing. But today, every person onboard has a smartphone that they want to connect to Wi-Fi, and they may have a tablet or PC. In addition, the boat has its own devices, including a chartplotter, wanting to connect. Young people onboard may have gaming devices as well. Then there's Fire TV that attempts to connect for streaming video or movies. Every piece of electronics today is Wi-Fi enabled. The demand for internet bandwidth has increased tenfold, putting an enormous strain on Wi-Fi systems.

Wi-Fi user expectations have changed dramatically; at home the average internet user has grown accustomed to large bandwidth internet connections with almost limitless amounts of data transfer. We all assume that any internet connection will be fast, available, and constant.

Marinas are challenged to keep up with this increasing demand. Remotely located marinas, where landline internet is not available, have nearly an impossible task trying to meet demand, some with very limited bandwidth satellite internet connections.

How to be a Good Wi-Fi citizen. Adjust your expectations and your internet usage for Wi-Fi. Be prepared for internet access to be slower than you might be accustomed to; allow extra time for the online task and have an alternate plan. Most importantly, adjust your internet usage to minimize data transfer.

- Turn off automatic updates. Not always as simple and straight-forward as it sounds.
- On smartphones, tablets, and PC's, turn off automatic photo backup to cloud storage. Do you really need all 200 images uploaded to the cloud right now?
- Smartphones – almost all of the apps on our smartphones are searching for app updates. This constant 'pinging' to check for updates is largely unnecessary internet traffic when we are out boating. So go through your apps one-by-one and turn off updates. Each app is different.
- Avoid apps like Facetime, Netflix, Amazon Video, and gaming apps.
- Limit your use: email without large attachments; Facebook, scrolling slowly and no video viewing; voice only Skype, no video; and limit smartphone usage when Wi-Fi is the only signal available.

Wi-Fi Amplifiers. When your assigned slip is far out on the end of the most distant dock, the marina's free Wi-Fi may not help you much if you don't have an amplifier onboard. Relatively inexpensive Wi-Fi amplifiers boost the often weak marina signal. Amplifiers allow you to reach otherwise unusable Wi-Fi signals from the surrounding area. These include Wi-Fi from providers like Shaw and Xfinity. Wi-Fi amplifiers connect to an onboard Wi-Fi router to bring the amplified signal throughout your boat. Wi-Fi amplifiers often allow boats at anchor to use nearby Wi-Fi.

CELLULAR, INTERNET & SATELLITE COMMUNICATIONS

There are literally any number of Apps for just about every topic imaginable. Android and iOS Smartphone Apps can help with so many boating related activities. But it's important to keep in mind that onboard dedicated marine systems should remain the primary systems. Apps are often free and easy to download and install. Free Apps can contain advertising. Occasionally, an enhanced version of the free App can be purchased for a small price. Apps can be very cost effective additions to onboard equipment and serve as excellent backup and augmentation to dedicated equipment like chartplotters, VHF radio, depth sounder, and radar. Increasingly, smartphone Apps are the human-interface through Wi-Fi to control and monitor equipment and devices on board; some good examples chartplotter and depth sounder information that can be shared with phones and tablets.

Before becoming too dependent upon the App's information, learn where the App came from and where it gets its information. Tides and currents information is a great example. There are a number of Apps that display tides and currents for various Northwest locations. But where is the information coming from and how accurate is it?

Here are some of the more popular boater related Apps.

U.S. Coast Guard – This official App is configurable and saves your information as well as details of one or more of the boats you use. Once configured, you can use the App to: request Emergency Assistance; geo-locate the nearest NOAA weather buoys and view the latest conditions; file a float plan; report a hazard to navigation; report a problem with a navigation aid; report pollution incidents; consult navigation rules; request a vessel safety check; and report suspicious activity. Good information resource and an Emergency Assistance function that sends your Lat/Lon information to the Coast Guard.

Barometer - There are a number of good barometer Apps for both Android and iOS that use the device's sensors to measure and, more importantly, track barometric pressure. Much better than tapping the glass face on the brass encased, wall mounted mechanical barometer.

U.S. Customs CBP ROAM/CBP One – These official Customs and Border Protection Apps support Android and iOS devices. Travelers entering the U.S. can check-in with CBP ROAM, and CBP officers can initiate a video chat for information verification, or an interview if required. If approved for entry, boaters do not have to report in-person at a Port of Entry. The App can be used at State of Washington and State of Alaska pleasure craft Port Of Entry locations. CBP plans to replace ROAM with CBP One sometime in the future.

Anchor Watch – Both the free and charge version of this anchoring App are feature rich. The App uses the iOS or Android device's GPS receiver to track the boat's position relative to the set anchor and sounds an alarm if the position exceeds a preset set distance from the anchor. There are other anchor watch Apps available, but this one has the added feature that will send an SMS message to another phone (on shore) in addition to sounding an alarm on the device left on the boat.

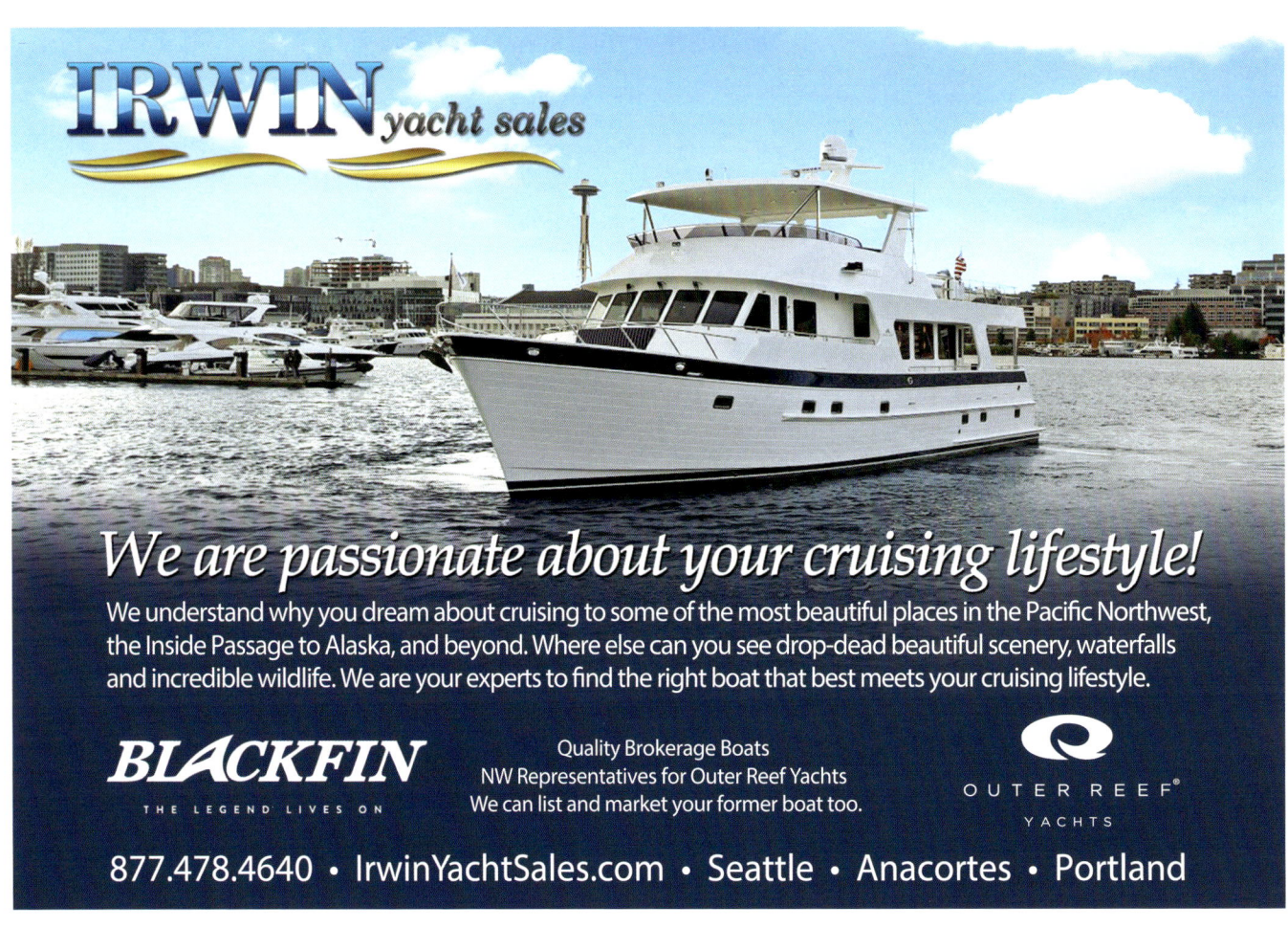

IRWIN yacht sales

We are passionate about your cruising lifestyle!

We understand why you dream about cruising to some of the most beautiful places in the Pacific Northwest, the Inside Passage to Alaska, and beyond. Where else can you see drop-dead beautiful scenery, waterfalls and incredible wildlife. We are your experts to find the right boat that best meets your cruising lifestyle.

BLACKFIN THE LEGEND LIVES ON

Quality Brokerage Boats
NW Representatives for Outer Reef Yachts
We can list and market your former boat too.

OUTER REEF YACHTS

877.478.4640 • IrwinYachtSales.com • Seattle • Anacortes • Portland

CELLULAR, INTERNET & SATELLITE COMMUNICATIONS

iNAVX – This very feature-rich iOS and Android App has many of the functions found on full-function chartplotters, including everything from real-time navigation on a full suite of downloadable nautical charts, to an anchor watch feature. Interfaces with Vesper's AIS Wi-Fi gateway and supports AIS transponders/receivers. Positioning, GRIB weather, routing, charting and tracking all combine to make this app a powerful navigation tool.

Marine Traffic - Provides up-to-date marine traffic information. It works well for monitoring ship traffic or monitoring friends. It can be used to monitor commercial vessel traffic, including ferries, if you don't have an onboard AIS.

Vessel Finder - Displays real time vessel positions and marine traffic from global AIS network. Map display of AIS information on vessels worldwide. With the pro version, you can build your own fleet of vessels you follow. Current and historical data. Android and iOS compatible.

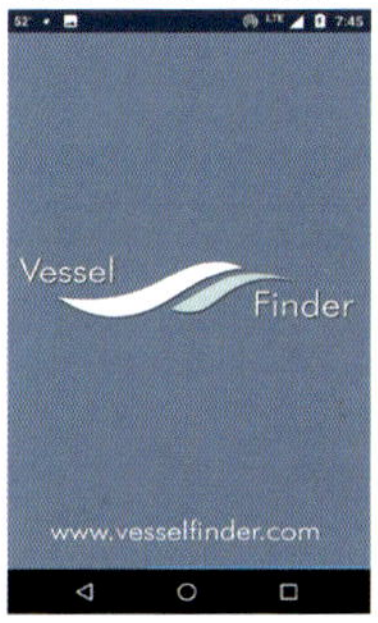

PredictWind – This Android and iOS App displays forecasts for wind speed, wind direction, sea state, wind waves, and swell, sky conditions and precipitation, and other information. One of the latest features includes predicting the affect of sea- state forecasts on your specific boat size and characteristics. You can zoom in on the forecast map to see micro area forecasts; which can be very helpful in route planning. Android, iOS and Web App.

SailFlow – Graphical indicator of current wind conditions and predicted wind. The App is location sensitive and presents a concise list of nearby stations with current conditions and hour-by-hour predicted winds for 7 days. Options include detailed and basic displays. Forecasts include sky conditions. Select from a number of prediction models. Android and iOS devices supported.

Navionics – This Android and iOS App is useful for boating, diving, and fishing, and comes with many features. You can view detailed nautical charts, sonar charts, and bathymetry charts, and NOAA charts. You can even change chart-overlay combinations to customize views. Content updates are provided on a regular basis. This is a popular App with an easy to use interface.

Pumpout Nav – This iOS and Android app provides boaters with a quick, easy way to look-up the location of pumpout facilities. The app uses the boater's location to suggest the nearest pumpout stations on a map or in the form of a list. Boaters can also report issues regarding a pumpout facility through the app; the app is interactive and easy to use. Users can specifically look for portable toilet dump stations only, and/or stationary pumpout facilities. The app includes pumpouts in Washington and parts of British Columbia. The app was created under the Clean Vessel Act Program.

Wunderground – Android and iOS, this is the Weather Underground App, an extensive weather forecasts and conditions service. This is a good full info weather resource with data from a network of stations providing area forecasts, weather radar, satellite maps, and severe weather warnings. Local weather stations with camera images provide helpful information about localized conditions. Use the camera images from a station on the other side of the fog bound strait to discover if it's clear on the other side. Select from "Forecast on Demand" or "NWS" for forecast information source.

Windy – This Android, iOS, and Web App is one of the best wind, wave, and weather forecasting tools available today. Forecast wind and wave conditions are put into motion on a map display that can be zoomed out to see coming weather patterns and zoomed in to see localized conditions. Professional weather forecast model options including ECMWF, NAM 5km and GFS 22km; allow comparison of models to improve your weather data interpretation. Forecast information is in data and graphical display format with color and movement. Ten-day forecasts show what's happening locally, regionally, and globally. Forecast conditions for ground level up to 13.5 kilometers let you see not only what is happening but what is steering the weather.

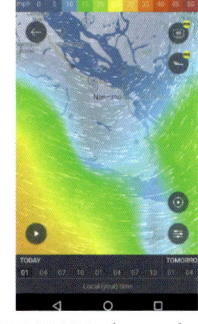

Marine Weather Forecast Pro – This iPad, iPhone, and Mac app provides NOAA marine weather forecasts, mainly from weather buoy data. A useful app to check wind speed and direction in specific areas of the ocean. This app gives 7-day marine weather forecasts and observed weather conditions by region selectable from a map view or from a table of stations.

Fish Washington – This free iOS and Android app provides up-to-date fishing regulations for lakes, rivers, and marine waters in Washington State. The app does not currently include information regarding shellfish. The app includes details on harvest limits, allowed gear, boat launches, and interactive mapping. Downloadable updates and offline support for use when not within cell service range.

WatchMate – This App is the display and controls for the Vesper AIS transponder receiver device. The App is only useful in conjunction with the Vesper. We list this here because the App, in conjunction with the Vesper unit, has some well-done AIS traffic alarms and an excellent anchor watch feature. Android and iOS compatible.

Savvy Navvy – This free app requires either a free account or an annual fee premium account. Free account functionality is very limited - U.S. charts only, 1-day weather, 1-day departure scheduling. Premium accounts include worldwide charts, tide information, route planning, fuel consumption planning, GPS position information, and satellite overlay.

A Garden for all Seasons

The Butchart Gardens
· OVER 100 YEARS IN BLOOM ·
NATIONAL HISTORIC SITE OF CANADA

Victoria, British Columbia
Canada

butchartgardens.com
866.652.4422 *(toll free)*

CHARTS AND CHARTPLOTTERS

Charts. In the not too distant past, large printed nautical charts filled drawers near the helm station on recreational boats. A cruising trip involved marking the planned route using pencil, parallel rules, and dividers. Over time, pencil marks recorded each trip with additional notes about discoveries along the way. For all but the rare exception, this has been replaced with electronic charts and GPS Multifunction Displays (MFD), also known as chartplotters.

In the U.S., National Oceanic and Atmospheric Administration (NOAA) is responsible for creating nautical charts; the Canadian Hydrographic Services (CHS), a department of Fisheries and Oceans, is the government agency that creates charts in Canada.

Electronic charts are available in two basic formats: Raster and Vector. Most MFDs use and display vector charts. Raster charts are digital images of paper charts. Paper charts are no longer available from the governmental agencies responsible for creating charts; however, they are available from third-party print-on-demand and specialty map and chart providers. Booklets with a set of regional printed charts (usually older versions of charts) are available at major marine supply retailers.

Electronic raster and vector charts are available as downloads directly from NOAA and CHS. NOAA makes downloadable charts available at no charge that are in an open format that may not be compatible with proprietary MFDs. All CHS charts are licensed and may be purchased directly from CHS or through retailers. Charts formatted for use in proprietary MFDs are available for purchase from one of several commercial chart providers, including Navionics, C-Map, and Garmin.

When using electronic charts, be aware that hazards can disappear at certain zoom levels. Always examine your route at several zoom levels to ensure that it is free of hazards.

Whatever form of charts you decide to carry, keep them updated. While rocks haven't changed location, navigation aids do change. Recently, for example, significant buoyage changes were made in Swinomish Channel. In British Columbia, some buoys were determined as unnecessary or redundant and were removed to meet budget goals. New charts reflect the change whether on paper or on new electronic updates. A five year old (or older) chartplotter may have very old charts and not reflect navigational updates.

In 2019, NOAA published their plan for phasing out and eliminating all NOAA Raster products by January 2025. This includes electronic versions of NOAA raster charts. The commonly referenced five-digit raster chart numbers will also be retired.

In the future, NOAA will be focusing on vector charts and over the course of five years will no longer update raster products. As part of the focus on vector products, NOAA is undertaking a multiyear program to re scheme vector charts into a standard rectangular, grid layout. The result will be a product suite of over 9,000 vector charts (also called cells). Many of these cells will be compiled at larger scale than the existing vector charts that they will replace, giving greater detail.

While raster charts are digital images of paper charts, vector charts are essentially databases used to prepare visual images. The database standards for current vector charts was created in 1993 and by today's standards is old and in need of updating. A new S-100 standard will allow newly created vector charts to bring new and better information to chartplotters and apps.

CHS in Canada will continue to update and produce raster products for Canadian waters. U.S. Army Corps of Engineers will continue to update and produce raster charts for U.S. navigable rivers.

Chart No. 1 cracks the code. Nautical charts are filled with important navigation information. Unfortunately, so much of the information is in the form of symbols, abbreviations and undefined terms that it can be confusing. Each country has published a book that shows each symbol and defines each term used on its charts. The U.S. book is titled *Chart No. 1*; and the Canadian book is titled *Chart 1*. The Canadian book is available from Canadian Hydrographic chart agencies. The U.S. book is produced by several private publishers. Copies are available at marine supply outlets.

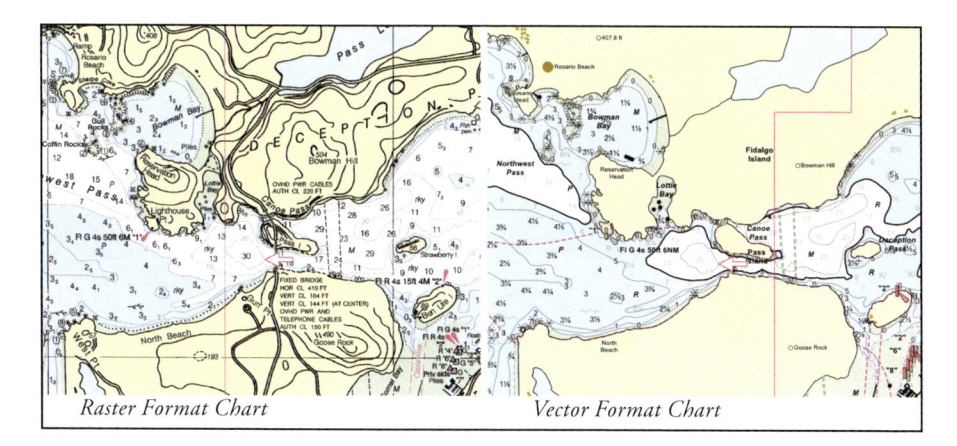

> **CHARTS AND CHARTPLOTTER TOPICS**
> Charts - Raster and Vector
> Chart No. 1 - the Key to Chart Symbols
> Large Scale, Small Scale Charts
> Differences Between U.S. & Canada Charts
> Waters Appear Deeper on U.S. Charts
> Clearances Appear Greater on U.S. Chart
> Canadian Charts Use More Symbols

The Canadian Coast Guard publication *The Canadian Aids to Navigation System* explains the Canadian buoyage and light system, and is highly recommended. A PDF version is available on the Canadian Coast Guard website. The cost for the print version is $7.50 (CDN) from Canadian Hydrographic chart agents, nautical bookstores and chandleries.

The introduction pages of both the U.S. and Canadian publications are filled with essential information. Don't overlook them.

Large scale, large detail, that's the easy way to remember the difference between small scale and large scale charts. A small scale chart shows a large part of the earth's surface, but in small detail. Conversely, a large scale chart shows a small part of the earth's surface, but of course in great detail. Yes, it's counter-intuitive and confusing, but that's how it is. In the Northwest, large scale harbor charts typically have scales of 1:6,000, 1:12,000, 1:24,000. Medium scale charts have a scale of 1:40,000. Small scale charts have scales of 1:73,000 or 1:80,000.

At a scale of 1:12,000, 1 inch on the chart equals 12,000 inches (1,000 feet) on the earth. At a scale of 1:80,000, 1 inch on the chart equals 80,000 inches (6,667 feet) on the earth. When you are looking for the rock or picking your way through a narrow channel, the larger the scale of your chart, the easier your task will be.

Differences between U.S. & Canada Charts. Canadian and U.S. charts, while similar in many ways, have important differences. U.S. charts are in fathoms and feet; most Canadian charts are metric. With all charts, read the chart title and margin information, or check the chartplotter settings, to see if the chart is metric, fathoms and feet, or feet. Two meters equals 6 feet 7 inches, or just over one fathom. The difference is significant. Don't confuse fathoms with meters or feet.

Waters appear to be deeper on U.S. charts. This difference is important wherever the water is shallow, and is the result of the two countries using different *tidal or chart datums*.

Depths on a chart are measured from the chart datum, also called the reference plane or **tidal datum**. On Canadian charts, the chart datum is either Lowest Normal Tides, or Lower Low Water, Large Tide. For that reason, you don't find many "minus tides" in Canadian tide tables.

On U.S. charts of Pacific Northwest waters,

Raster Format Chart *Vector Format Chart*

COMPENDIUM

Great experiences come in small islands

Relax and enjoy a weekend (or more!) on Fidalgo Island. With mild temperatures, lush forest lands to explore, and water that surrounds, staying here is a great way to spend your time away from home. Visit by car, ferry, plane or boat. Experience amazing restaurants, boutique shopping in historic downtown, nature viewing, multiple festivals across the year, live music, and so much more.

From Anchors to Zincs you can cover all of your boating needs in Anacortes! We have first class marinas and over 50 marine trades companies and professionals that are dedicated to providing quality parts and services. Let us help you buy, insure, store, moor, maintain, repair, and enjoy your boat, right here on beautiful Fidalgo island.

ANACORTES.ORG
360-293-3832

Download the app in Google Play or the Apple Store

GET IT ON Google Play

Download on the App Store

CHARTS AND CHARTPLOTTERS

however, the chart datum is Mean Lower Low Water. Mean Lower Low Water is the mean, or average, level of the lower of the two low tides each day. Since the U.S. chart datum has half the lower waters above it and half below it, U.S. tide books show minus tides.

It's not a question of whether the tide drops lower in Canada or the U.S. It's a question of where the depth is measured from. U.S. charts start their measurements from a point higher than Canadian charts. The difference can be as much as 1.5 meters, or almost 5 feet.

Example: Assume that you are in the U.S., skippering a sailboat. The sailboat's keel draws 5 feet, and you want to anchor overnight in a bay with a charted depth of one fathom (6 feet). According to the tide table, low tide will be minus 1.5 feet at 7:00 a.m. Knowing that your boat, with its 5 feet of draft, would be aground in 4.5 feet of water, you would look for a more suitable anchorage.

If this bay were in Canada, the chart would show a depth of perhaps just 1 meter (assuming a Lowest Normal Tide lower than the tide at 7:00 a.m.). The tide table would show a low tide at 7:00 a.m. of perhaps 0.4 meters. You would add the 1 meter depth from the chart to the 0.4 meter low tide from the tide table, and get 1.4 meters of water at 7:00 a.m. Since you draw more than 1.4 meters (55 inches), you would not anchor in the bay that night.

Important Exception: Both Canadian and U.S. charts show soundings in the other country's system when the charts cover both sides of the border. The U.S. chart would convert Canadian meters to U.S. fathoms, but would adopt the Canadian chart datum in Canadian waters. The Canadian metric chart would convert U.S. fathoms to meters, but would adopt the U.S. chart datum in U.S. waters. This is explained in the chart legends.

Clearances appear to be greater on U.S. charts. U.S. charts for Northwest waters measure clearances from Mean High Water. One-half the high waters are above the mean. Canadian charts measure clearances from Higher High Water, Large Tides. The same bridge, over the same waterway, would show less vertical clearance on a Canadian chart than on a U.S. chart. Metric Canadian charts show heights and depths in meters; Canadian charts in fathoms and feet show heights in feet and depths in fathoms. A Canadian metric chart might show a bridge clearance as "3," meaning 3 meters above Higher High Water, Large Tides. A U.S. chart would show a bridge clearance as "12" or more, meaning 12 feet or more above Mean High Water.

Canadian raster charts use more symbols to show buoys and tide rips. Canadian raster charts use symbols that approximate the shapes of buoys, with letters to indicate the buoy's characteristics. U.S. charts use a single diamond-shaped symbol for nearly all navigation buoys, with descriptive letters to indicate the buoy's characteristics.

CRUISING THE SHOULDERS

Prime cruising season in the Pacific Northwest is in July and August, that's when you find the largest number of boats out cruising. In the past, boating activity didn't get started until well after Memorial Day and dropped-off after Labor Day. More recently, boating activity starts earlier in the season and continues well into fall. There are several factors stretching the boating season into the shoulder months of spring and fall.

The Pacific Northwest and the Inside Passage have been discovered. More out-of-area boaters are enjoying the protected waters, mild climate, and the unique boater friendly destinations this area has to offer. Western Washington and specifically the Seattle metro area have seen an influx of people in recent years that are eager to enjoy the area's great boating. Add to this a vibrant economy, providing people with time and money to get out on the water, and you get a significant increase in boating activity seen over the last three to five years.

Spring and fall shoulder cruising seasons have much to offer the boater that has the flexibility to take advantage of these opportunities. Before Memorial Day and after Labor Day, there are so few recreational boaters out there that VHF channel 16 is almost silent. We sometimes switch to VHF weather channels to ensure the radio is working. There are far fewer boats during a shoulder season, easing competition for moorage, anchorage, and access to services. Yes, there are some trade-offs; marina staffing levels may be reduced, and hours and days of operation may be curtailed. In early spring, you may find marina facilities and staff that may not be completely ready for your visit. So, when cruising in shoulder season, be adaptable and flexible. You may need to leave a message and wait for a callback to your inquiry for moorage. You may have to arrive a little earlier and depart later to accommodate off-season office hours.

The rewards for cruising in the shoulder season are many. Prices are often reduced and availability is greater. Often people have more time to share insider information about places to visit or things to do. You may find other cruisers more eager to visit and share boating stories. You will get more use out of your annual state parks pass. You will have your choice of prime spots in popular anchorages.

For marina operators in the Broughtons and elsewhere, the boating season is unfortunately too short. Marinas welcome a longer season and tend to open earlier and stay open later if demand calls for it. Cruising the shoulder season can bring new friendships and new opportunities, and in the process, help to convince marinas to extend their season. Give it a try, get out there early and come back later in the season.

Which areas are best for shoulder season cruising? South, Central, and North Puget Sound are some areas that start the earliest and run much later in the season. These areas are effectively year-round boating destinations. Next, the San Juan Islands, Gulf Islands, Vancouver B.C. destinations are good early and late season areas. Desolation Sound, north to and including the Broughtons, tend to be later in the shoulder season with facilities ready for full operation around Memorial Day, and curtailing operations by mid-September. Because of resort fishing activity, West Coast Vancouver Island around Barkley Sound and Tofino get started earlier than Desolation Sound.

September and October can often be a surprisingly good time of the year to cruise the Pacific Northwest waters from Olympia to Desolation Sound. Despite the occasional early fall storms that will have you sheltered for a few days, there can be some excellent fall cruising with settled weather, gorgeous sunsets, and empty anchorages.

[Landons]

COMPENDIUM

2023 WAGGONER CRUISING GUIDE

"We go to places where nobody else can go."

— Victor & Anna Maria Larraguibel

Victor Larraguibel fell in love with sailing as a Lieutenant in the Chilean Navy. After many years, he and wife Anna Maria wanted to move on from sailing, but not from cruising, so they purchased a Nordhavn 64. It allows them to go exploring with their five children, seven grandchildren, and extended friend group in absolute comfort and safety. "I am very happy in this adventure we have together!" says Anna Maria. She especially loves the daily routine of waking up to a glorious view each morning while having the ability to change to a different fantastic view whenever they want.

Victor & Anna Maria Larraguibel aboard N64 GRANKITO

With a track record of more successful oceanic passages than all other motoryacht manufacturers combined, Nordhavn offers its owners comfortable, confident cruising. We are the go-to brand for anyone seeking adventure by sea.

Ready to start your search for the perfect passagemaking yacht? Visit the brokers at Nordhavn Northwest.

Nordhavn Yachts Northwest
1019 Q Ave, Suite G,
Anacortes, WA 98221
360.209.9780

Watch an interview with Victor and Anna Maria at www.nordhavn.com/Grankito

Discover the entire Nordhavn product line at www.nordhavn.com.
NORDHAVN WORLDWIDE USA | UK | AUSTRALIA | TURKEY info@nordhavn.com

NORDHAVN

RULES OF THE ROAD

Before heading out on the water for the season, we like to review the systems on our boat and handling procedures. Even experienced boaters run the risk of becoming complacent, and some boaters may simply not be aware of the nautical rules of the road. Understanding the terms "give-way" and "stand-on" is especially important for collision avoidance; the terminology is intended to ensure that everyone knows what to expect when boats encounter each other on the water.

A boat approaching your port side is the "Give-Way vessel." The Give-Way vessel is expected to change speed and/or heading to avoid a conflict and potential collision. The Give-Way vessel should change speed and direction early enough to make it obvious to the Stand-On vessel that evasive action is being taken to avoid a conflict. The "Stand-On-vessel" on the other hand is expected to remain on its course and speed.

Conversely, when a boat is approaching you from your starboard side, they are the "Stand-On vessel" and you become the "Give-Way vessel." You should alter heading and/or speed early and deliberately so that the Stand-On vessel can continue on their heading and speed.

The Give-Way/Stand-On rule of the road is intended to avoid the situation where both vessels alter speed and heading, creating greater confusion and danger. If the Give-Way vessel doesn't take early discernable action, the system won't work. Keep in mind that not all boaters are aware of the Give-Way, Stand-On rule. If the Give-Way vessel is not taking evasive action, you will need to adjust accordingly to avoid a collision.

Both vessels are required to take evasive action if a collision is imminent or possible.

The vessel's night-time navigation lights can help determine the vessel's Stand-On or Give-Way status. If you are seeing another vessel's Red navigation light, then you are the Give-Way and they are the Stand-On. If another vessel is seeing your Green navigation light, then you are the Give-Way. It all becomes easy when focusing on the Red and Green Navigation Lights on vessels.

What about overtaking another boat from behind? Boats approaching from behind are known as the "Burdened vessel" or "Give-Way vessel" which has the responsibility to slow down and give a wide berth for the boat they are passing. Boat wakes can cause uncomfortable rocking, possibly causing damage to items in the boat you're passing and even personal injury for which you are responsible; be sure to slow down and keep a wide berth. Keep in mind that a boat may be about to pass you, always look behind before making any sudden turns to avoid a potential collision; fast, smaller boats can be harder to see when behind you and may not have AIS.

The stand-on, give-way rule becomes less clear when a fast planing-hull boat is approaching the starboard side of a much slower displacement or semi-displacement-hull boat. Technically speaking, if the vessel approaching fron your starboard can see your green sidelight, they are deemed a crossing vessel and have the right of way (they are the stand-on vessel). If they can't see the green side light, they are an overtaking vessel and you have the right of way (you are the stand-on vessel). Unfortunately, many boaters mistakenly believe that they are automatically the stand-on vessel if they are approaching your starboard side. Fast boats on the plane tend to see slower trawler-style boats as fixed or stationary objects. A planing vessel has the speed and maneuverability when approaching at an angle to go around and behind the slower vessel, which is the safest/appropriate option, rather than crossing in front of another vessel's bow. The faster planing boat is implicitly the overtaking vessel and therefore the give-way vessel.

When passing a boat approaching head-on, boats normally pass port to port like cars. There may be hazards in the water, or other traffic concerns that require boats to pass starboard to starboard. It is best to make a deliberate, obvious turn ahead of time to tell the approaching boat on which side you plan to pass. If uncertain of the other captain's intentions, hail the boat in question on Ch 16 (on Low Power) to agree on which side you will be passing, port to port or starboard to starboard.

A review of the "rules of the road" and frequent self-reminders will help ensure a safe and pleasant boating experience for captain and crew.

Overtaking

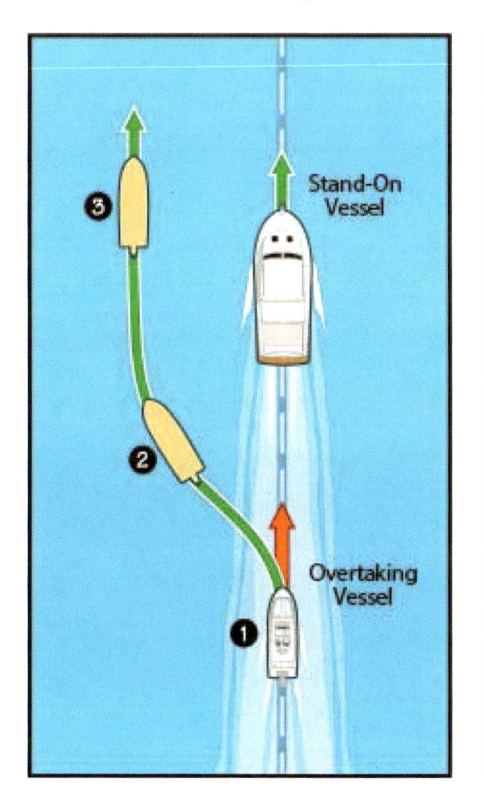

Head-On

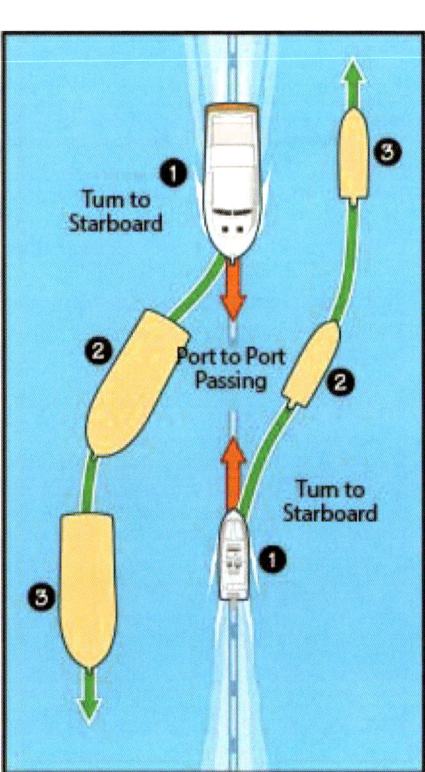

Crossing

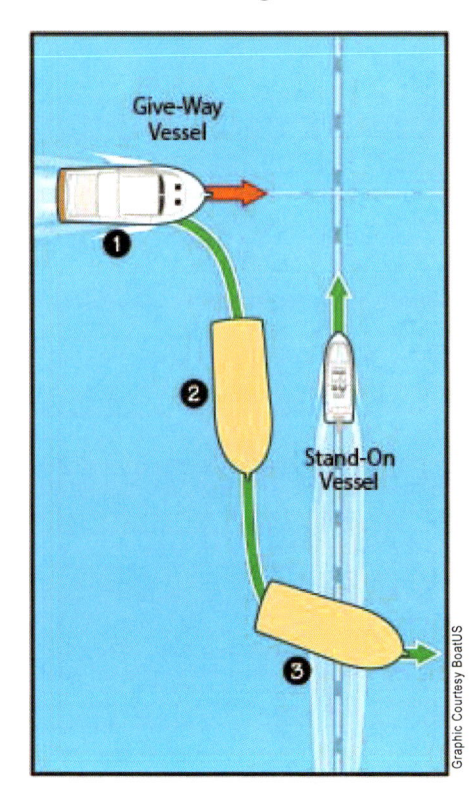

BUOYS, BEACONS AND RANGES

Aids to navigation help boaters safely navigate waters to avoid obstacles and hazards. While there are a number of different systems for marking channels, the Lateral System is the one most common throughout the Inside Passage and is summarized here. Some Canadian waters may be marked with the Cardinal System which uses yellow and black colored markers to indicate the safe passage waters. A description of the Cardinal System is in the Canadian Aids to Navigation System publication.

Red, Right, Returning means leave **Red** navigation aids off your **Right** hand when you're **Returning** from seaward. If the navigation mark is not red, leave it off your left hand when you're returning from seaward.

This is the general rule in U.S. and Canadian waters, with three subtle refinements:

• Safe water mark. A buoy with red and white vertical stripes that marks an approach or mid-channel. Unobstructed water surrounds this mark. Both inbound and outbound, it is good practice to leave this buoy to port.

• Preferred channel mark. A buoy or a beacon with red and green horizontal bands. This aid marks a channel junction or an obstruction. While the aid can be passed on either side, the color of the top band indicates the preferred or main channel.

• Isolated danger mark. An aid—either a buoy or a beacon—with black and red horizontal bands that marks an isolated danger (an example would be the Blakely Island Shoal Isolated Danger Buoy DS, west of Blakely Island in the San Juan Islands). These marks have navigable water all around, but should not be approached closely without caution.

Nuns. All red buoys marking channels are shaped as cones, and are called nuns. Most nun buoys are painted solid red. If the nun buoy has a green horizontal band painted on it, the buoy marks the meeting of two channels, with the left channel being the preferred, or main, channel. (If you leave the buoy to starboard, you will be in the left channel.) If lighted, the light will be red.

Cans. All green buoys marking channels are called cans. They are shaped like, well, cans. Most can buoys are painted solid green. If the can buoy has a horizontal red band painted on it, the buoy marks the meeting of two channels, with the right channel the preferred, or main channel. If lighted, the light will be green.

Beacons. Buoys float, and are held in place by heavy anchoring systems, but beacons are permanent navigation aids attached to the earth. Beacons can be located on land, installed on docks or breakwaters, or mounted on pilings. A lighthouse is a beacon. A beacon not on land will be placed in shallow water outside a channel. Do not pass a beacon close aboard. Give it considerable room.

An unlighted beacon is called a daybeacon. A lighted beacon is called a minor light. A minor light marking the right side of a channel will carry a red light (Red, Right, Returning). A minor light marking the left side of a channel will carry a green light. If a minor light marks the meeting of two channels, it will be red if the left channel is preferred; green if the right channel is preferred.

Daymarks are the colored panels mounted on beacons. Red panels are triangle shaped; green panels are square. A triangle shaped red panel with a green horizontal stripe indicates the meeting of two channels, with the left channel the preferred, or main channel. A square panel painted green with a red horizontal stripe indicates the meeting of two channels, with the right channel the preferred channel.

Whenever a navigation aid is marked with a horizontal stripe of contrasting color, the color at the top of the aid indicates the preferred, or main channel.

Approaching a channel from seaward, buoys and beacons are numbered, beginning with the marks to seaward. Red buoys, daybeacons, and minor lights carry even numbers, such as 2, 4, 6, and so on. Green buoys, daybeacons, and minor lights carry odd numbers, such as 1, 3, 5, and so on. Depending on the channel, it might be appropriate to skip some numbers, so that buoy 6 is roughly opposite buoy 5, even if no buoy 4 exists.

Ranges. Ranges are used to help a boat stay in the middle of a narrow channel.

Ranges are rectangular panels standing vertically, each with a wide stripe running from top to bottom down the middle of the panel. Ranges are attached to the earth and arranged in pairs, one behind the other. The rear range board stands taller than the front range board. To use a range, steer until the rear range board appears to be on top of the front board. You can steer toward a range, looking ahead (leading range), or away from a range, sighting astern (back range).

Buoys and beacons are not selected and placed at random. They follow a plan, although to a newcomer the plan may at times seem obscure.

Despite the complexity of the buoyage and light system, you will find that as you understand it better your enjoyment afloat will increase. At some point you will want a description of the entire system. For U.S. waters it is in the introduction to the Coast Guard Light List. For Canadian waters it is partly in the introduction to the Canadian Coast Guard List of Lights, Buoys and Fog Signals, and completely in the Canadian Coast Guard publication, The Canadian Aids to Navigation System. They are available at chart agencies, chandleries and online.

Red, Right Returning

RED, RIGHT, RETURNING from the sea means the conical red nun buoy marks the right side of the channel. Vessels returning from the sea upstream will leave red navigation aids to starboard. Red aids are assigned even numbers, beginning with No. 2 at the seaward end of the channel.

Nun Buoy

A GREEN CAN BUOY marks the left side of the channel. Vessels returning from the sea or upstream will leave green navigation aids to port. Green aids are assigned odd numbers, beginning with No. 1 at the seaward end of the channel. Buoys and beacons can be lighted or unlighted.

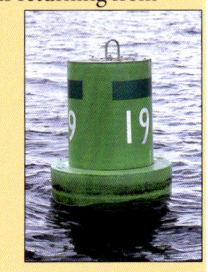

Can Buoy

A BEACON, such as this light at Webster Point in Lake Washington, is attached to the earth, and should be given a good offing. Port-hand beacons carry square green dayboards; starboard-hand beacons carry red triangular dayboards.

Lighted Beacon

CYLINDRICAL WHITE RESTRICTED OPERATIONS BUOYS, such as this one, mark speed zones, restricted anchoring areas, fish habitats and other important information.

Restricted Operation Buoy

RANGE MARKERS, such as this set in B.C.'s False Narrows are aligned when viewed from the established and marked channel. Ranges can be used when approaching and departing the markers.

Range Markers

BUOYS, BEACONS AND RANGES

The Lateral System of port and starboard buoys and beacons is the most common marking system in B.C. waters. Boaters will also find Cardinal System buoys and beacons. The Cardinal System indicates the direction of safe water around an obstacle. The system is based upon the cardinal compass points NESW. Safe water lies in the direction indicated by the buoy. These markers are spar or pillar shaped and colored yellow and black. The position of the colored bands and the shape of the topmark indicate the direction of the safest and deepest water.

A north Cardinal buoy indicates safe water is to the north of the buoy; south buoys indicate safe water is to the south, and so on.

The North Cardinal Buoy has two bands of equal size, with the black stripe located on the top, and the yellow stripe located on the bottom; top marks point up.

The East Cardinal Buoy has three equal bands, two black bands separated by yellow, and top marks pointing down.

The South Cardinal Buoy has two equal bands, with the black band placed on the bottom.

The West Cardinal Buoy has three equal sized bands, two yellow, separated by one black band.

If the buoys are lighted, the white light flashes at different Flash Group intervals to indicate the direction of safe water.

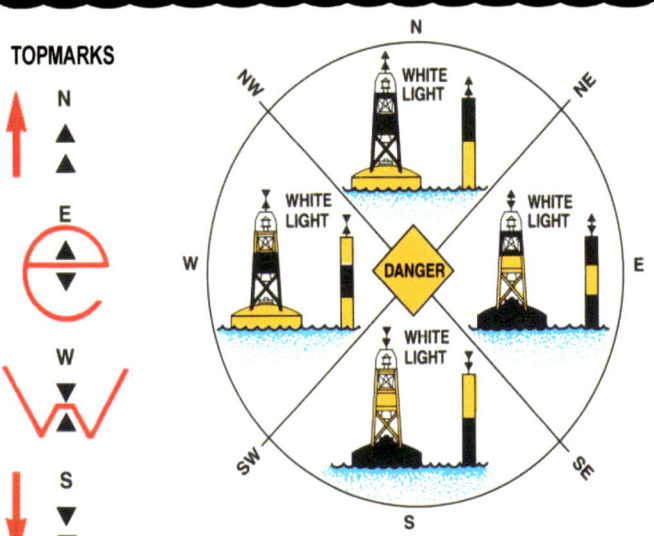

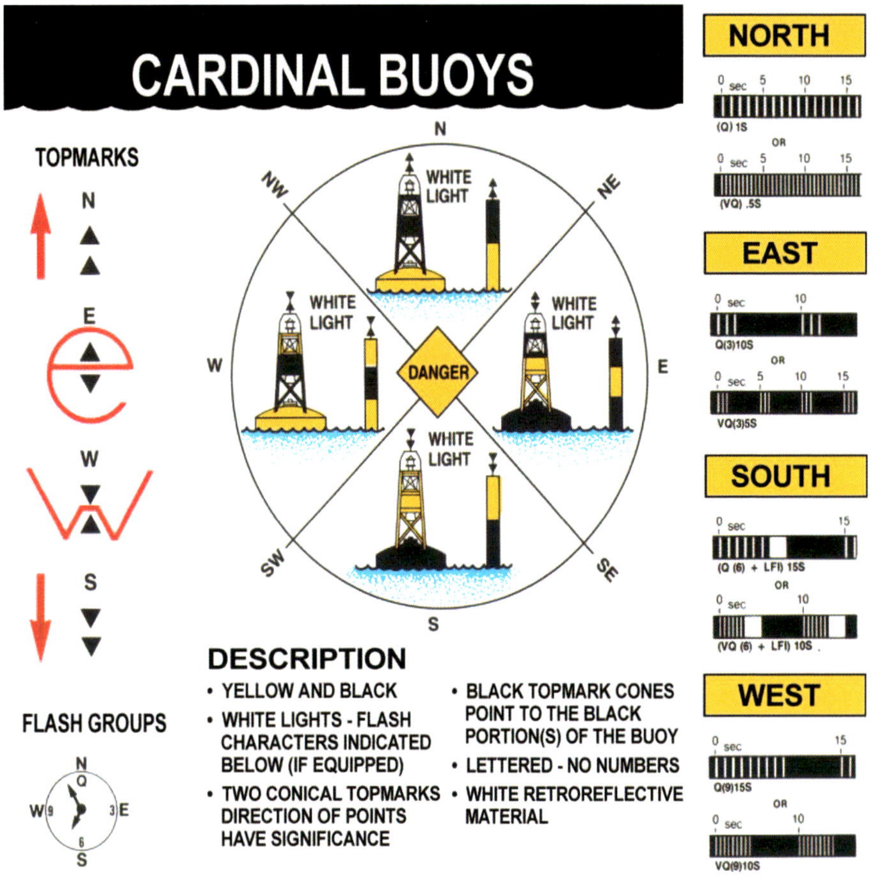

CARDINAL BUOYS

TOPMARKS

FLASH GROUPS

DESCRIPTION
- YELLOW AND BLACK
- WHITE LIGHTS - FLASH CHARACTERS INDICATED BELOW (IF EQUIPPED)
- TWO CONICAL TOPMARKS DIRECTION OF POINTS HAVE SIGNIFICANCE
- BLACK TOPMARK CONES POINT TO THE BLACK PORTION(S) OF THE BUOY
- LETTERED - NO NUMBERS
- WHITE RETROREFLECTIVE MATERIAL

NORTH — (Q) 1S OR (VQ) .5S
EAST — Q(3)10S OR VQ(3)5S
SOUTH — (Q (6) + LFl) 15S OR (VQ (6) + LFl) 10S
WEST — Q(9)15S OR VQ(9)10S

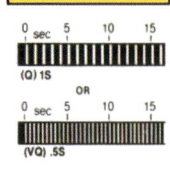

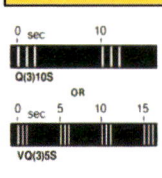

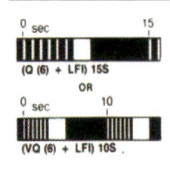

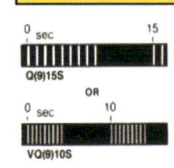

CRUISERS COLLEGE
INCREASE YOUR NAUTICAL KNOWLEDGE AND DIY CLASSES

WATCH FOR OUR SEMINAR COURSES ON:
- Hands-on Diesel Engine Troubleshooting
- Troubleshooting Electrical Problems on Your Boat
- Taking Care of the Fiberglass Boat
- Troubleshooting Outboard Motors
- Troubleshooting Vessel Systems
- Using New Technology for Navigation and Communications
- Cruising Essentials for Women
- Marine Weather

To see a schedule of our upcoming classes, go to www.WaggonerGuide.com/Seminars. For more information contact Michael Beemer at 360.766.6282 ext. 43515 or Mike.Beemer@skagit.edu

Cruisers College is brought to you by Center NW for Marine Manufacturing & Technology, Skagit Valley College, WAGGONER

2023 WAGGONER CRUISING GUIDE

UNDERWAY IN LOW VISIBILITY

UNDERWAY IN LOW VISIBILITY TOPICS
Running in Fog
Wildfire Smoke
Night Time Operation
Go or NoGo
Radar, AIS, Chartplotter, VHF
Listen & Look Carefully

Low Visibility. Fog, smoke, and darkness, all mean limited visibility for mariners and require special preparation and equipment. Fog is common during the summer months in Pacific Northwest Waters and the Inside Passage. Increasingly, smoke from wildfires obscures the skies and hampers visibility for days throughout the Inside Passage. Dusk and nighttime are some of the most challenging low visibility situations.

Fog is common from mid-July to early October in the Northwest and the Inside Passage. From Puget Sound northward through the San Juan Islands, Gulf Islands, Strait of Georgia and up Johnstone Strait morning fog can linger until noon time or later. Fog is an unavoidable part of cruising West Coast Vancouver Island. Fog can also be encountered along B.C.'s Central Coast and into Southeast Alaska in late summer. While fog often burns off by noon, it can linger for most of the day. Thick fog can impair visibility to something measured in feet, while other times it is only a mild interference. The marine weather forecast includes predicted fog, when fog is expected for a forecast region or area. However, localized fog is possible without a forecast.

Smoke. In the past few years, West Coast and Northwest wildfires in late summer and early fall have obscured skies and impaired visibility almost as much as fog. Unlike fog, smoke remains throughout the day and persists for a number of days until wind patterns change, or rainfall clears the air. Smoke usually affects a large area. Smoke may be part of a marine forecast but not as predictably as fog or other atmospheric conditions. The good news is that smoke is seldom as dense and as much of a visibility factor as fog. The bad news is that smoke takes some of the enjoyment from cruising.

Night Time. Recreational boaters in the PNW universally avoid travelling after dark. Underway boat movement after daylight hours is a hazardous undertaking and one that very few cruisers are willing to attempt. Charter operators routinely prohibit night-time underway operations of charter boats. Logs, limbs (big ones), root balls, and deadheads are a major concern for boat movement at night. Inside Passage waters are notorious for floating natural debris. Full and new moon high high-tide levels tend to float logs and other debris off of beaches, so there will predictably be more logs in the water after a higher high-tide. Hitting a log at cruise speed can cause significant damage and can easily create a sinking situation. Crab pot floats and lines are another hazard that is also very difficult to see and avoid at night. Entangling a crab pot line in the boat's prop will certainly cause problems. Seeing and avoiding navigation aids, mooring buoys, and other vessels are also night time hazards.

Go or NoGo? Should you set out in poor visibility in the first place? If you don't really have to go, don't. Running in low visibility situations is a stress-inducing business that can take the fun out of cruising. The wisest course may be to wait for improved visibility. Fog usually burns off later in the day and smoke will clear, given time.

In weighing a decision to run in low visibility, consider how well you know the waters you'll be navigating – a run through home water is a completely different challenge from transiting an area for the first time. Are the waters you'll navigate unobstructed – or encumbered with hazards that radar may not help you avoid? How much vessel traffic – big and small – might you encounter? High-traffic areas of Puget Sound, the Strait of Georgia, and the Inside Passage are subject to vessel traffic management systems. Do you know how to listen for VTS operators' instructions to mariners around you, and call them for guidance?

Make a Plan B. Where will you go if it becomes too risky to continue…or your nerves fail you? Is there a harbor along the route that is clear enough to enter safely even if you can't see a thing?

Underway in Low Visibility. As you spend more time cruising, you will probably have to run in low visibility someday. When circumstances are conducive, and you can do it safely, gain some experience underway using aids such as radar, AIS, depth sounder, VHF radio, and your ears. Learning to navigate and avoid hazards in low visibility is important. It can be a tremendous learning opportunity and confidence-booster. When you do, here are some tips:

Slow down. This sounds obvious – but some boaters have trouble doing this under any conditions. Reducing your speed increases the amount of time you have to spot obstacles, hazards, or vessels and take evasive action. If you hit something at reduced speed, it will do less damage, and you are more likely to avoid catastrophic damage.

Equipment. It goes without saying that you should have complete confidence in your navigation suite – plotter, depth-sounder, radar, AIS and VHF radio. You should know how to use them and know their limitations. Have reliable equipment and have backup for the critical ones. Have AIS transmit as well as receive, so that other vessels can see you on AIS. Digital radar will give you a better view than older analog radar. We rely on sight to orient ourselves in space and find our way. Deprive us of visual cues and we veer off course or ramble in circles, still convinced we're on course. Magnetic compasses have helped mariners for centuries, so trust yours. Better yet, the electronic compass built into your vessel's autopilot is even more accurate and enables your autopilot to steer a precise course for hours or days, freeing you to keep a closer watch.

Radar paints a clear picture of your surroundings, as long as you know how to read it and have correctly set the gain. It's a good habit to run with radar even in clear conditions so you can see how blips and images appear on screen in relation to vessels and objects around you while you can still see them.

AIS is an important piece of equipment for low-visibility operation. At a minimum, have AIS receive equipment, but at today's reasonable cost for transmit capability, why not let other AIS equipped vessels see you?

Fog can happen when warm moist air moves over cool waters.

Underway after sunset involves a number of visibility challenges and risks.

UNDERWAY IN LOW VISIBILITY

Your AIS display will show nearby vessels, their speed, direction of travel, and their VHF contact information. AIS is not a substitute for radar but an important complement. AIS information from nearby vessels can be delayed by several minutes; and therefore, AIS shows you where the vessel was located. Radar shows you where it is now.

The chartplotter, running reliable electronic charts, provides for safe accurate navigation in low visibility. Zoomed in at an appropriate level, a good plotter enables you to accurately pinpoint hazards. Remember, not all obstacles on all charts are depicted precisely, so a margin of error is prudent! Set your radar range to the same scale as your plotter – or overlay it on the plotter if you can – to match charted features with radar for a clearer picture of your surroundings. Three-dimensional charts that show bathymetric data are better still. Use your plotter's predicted track feature to point your way past hazards.

Finally, use your VHF radio. Commercial vessels routinely broadcast their approach to points or channels which may bring them close to other traffic, so monitor VTS channels as well as Channel 16. Follow their example and announce your intentions when you enter waters where you may meet other vessels; invite concerned craft to respond. If you spot a converging target on radar, call them to determine their intentions and discuss how to pass or cross safely.

Prepare the boat, crew, and electronics before entering the reduced visibility environment.

Listen and look carefully. There is still a place for our own sharpened senses when we think we can't see diddly. In steamship days, skippers and pilots blew a whistle and listened for the time it took for echoes to return in order to determine their distance from shore. It makes sense to throttle back from time to time. Step on deck and listen for whatever you might hear: a horn, voices, a nearby outboard, birds calling, the lap of waves against the shoreline, the low thrum of really big engines…or nothing at all.

In restricted visibility, Collision Regulations require you to sound a single prolonged (four to six seconds) horn blast every two minutes when you are under way, and two prolonged blasts if you are stopped. Sound carries well across still water and in fog, and sends a clear message to anyone around. Don't forget to use your nose, as well. Water smells different than land; the odor of guano may tip you off to a seabird colony on an isolated rock; a whiff of engine exhaust may warn you of vessels nearby.

Even when you're sure you can't see a thing, you often still can – if you look hard enough. Have your crew keep an intent bow watch for anything you may not see from the helm. Sometimes wearing sunglasses actually helps to see images in the fog. The white hull of that lone sport fisher rolling in the chop may appear faintly. Or the superstructure of a container ship or ferry may float serenely through the top layer of the mist…and, hopefully, it won't be too close.

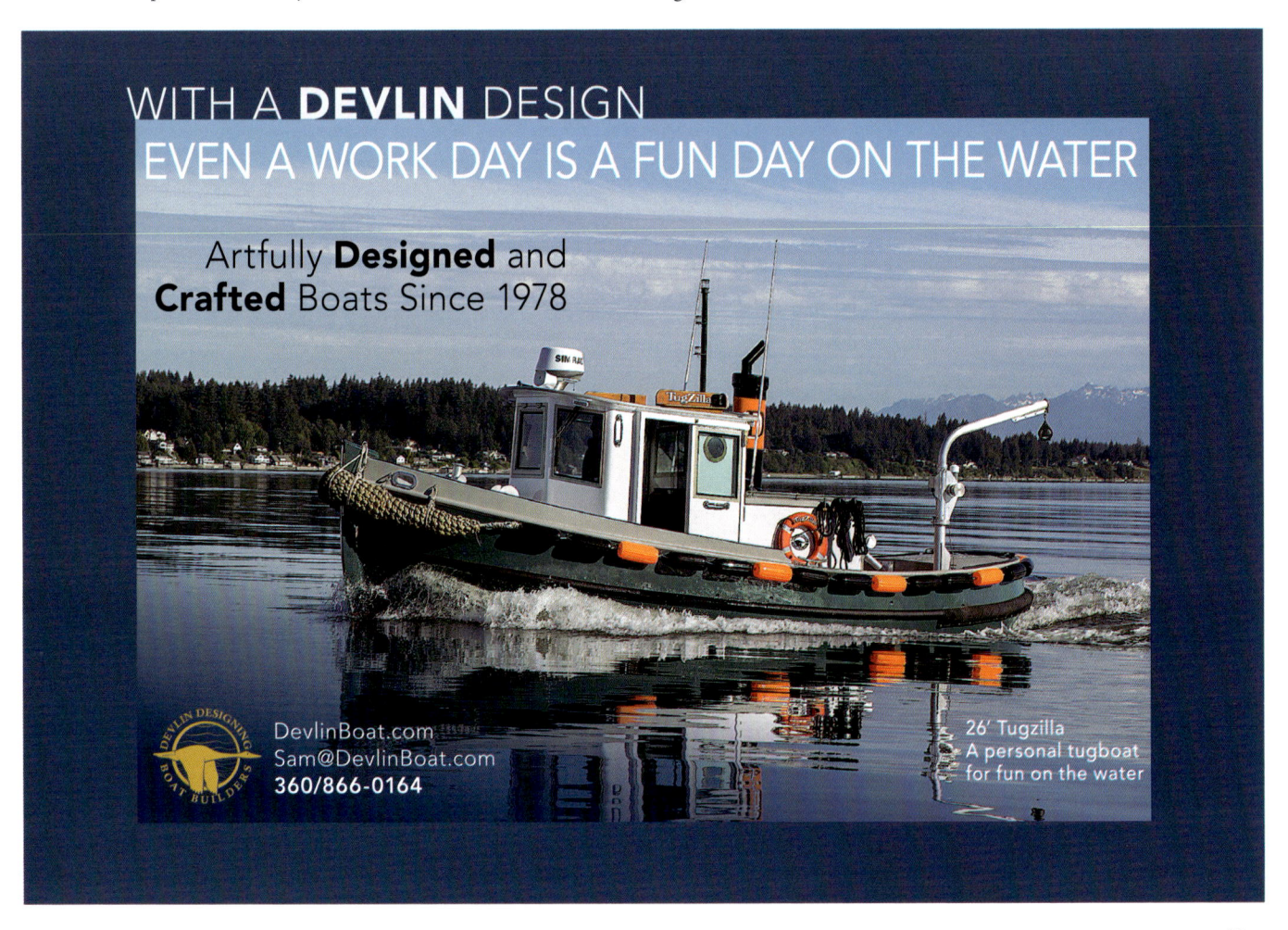

VESSEL TRAFFIC SERVICE - WHAT YOU NEED TO KNOW

VTS is primarily for commercial vessels, although all power driven vessels 40 meters (131 feet) or longer, commercial or recreational, must be active participants. Active VTS participants are required to maintain radio watch on the assigned VTS channel for the waters they are in, and to call in at designated points with their location, course, speed, and estimated time of arrival (ETA) at the next call-in point. The VTS centers keep track of all active participant vessels and advise of any traffic that might interfere.

All power driven vessels between 20 meters (66 feet) and 40 meters (131 feet) must be passive participants, meaning they must keep a radio watch on the appropriate VTS radio channels.

Pleasure craft should monitor VTS. Although recreational vessels shorter than 20 meters are exempt from being active or passive participants in VTS, they must know how to keep out of the way of large, slow-maneuvering vessels. We keep our radio set on the VTS channel for the area we are cruising to hear where the large commercial vessels are operating.

Turn Point Special Operating Area. Turn Point is the northwest corner of the San Juan Islands' Stuart Island, where Haro Strait joins Boundary Pass. Turn Point is a blind corner. A recreational vessel could be completely unaware of a fast approaching ship on the other side. Monitor channel 11.

Separation Zones. The VTS lanes in Puget Sound, the Strait of Juan de Fuca, and the approaches to Haro Strait and Rosario Strait are divided into inbound and outbound lanes, with a separation zone between the two. The separation zones vary in width and are shown in magenta on the charts.

With the following precautions, pleasure craft are free to operate in the Puget Sound VTS lanes:

Pleasure craft, even vessels under sail, do not have right-of-way over VTS participant vessels and must not impede them in any way.

Wherever practical, pleasure craft should stay out of the VTS lanes, or at least minimize the length of time spent in the lanes. Large commercial vessels are required to remain in the VTS lanes unless cleared to do otherwise. It makes no sense to compete for that space.

If inbound in the VTS lanes, run in the inbound lane; if outbound, run in the outbound lane. Keep a lookout astern for overtaking vessels.

If crossing the VTS lane(s), try to cross at right angles to minimize the time spent in the traffic lanes. This is not always possible or practical, but it should be the objective.

Do not loiter or fish in the VTS separation zones.

Be aware of what is going on—ahead, astern, and to the sides. In the jargon this is called "situational awareness." Give large vessels lots of room. Make early and substantial course adjustments. Show them some side, meaning the side of your boat. (This is good practice whenever two vessels meet, regardless of size.)

If there's any doubt at all, cross behind a large vessel, not in front of it. A container ship traveling at only 11 knots needs more than a mile to come to a complete stop. Many container ships travel at 20 knots or more, which lengthens their stopping distance.

If you see a tug, look for a tow. Never, ever, pass between a tug and its tow. Leave ample room when crossing behind a tow.

Radio communication. While active VTS participants (large vessels and tugs with tows) are required to maintain radio watch on the appropriate VTS radio channel, such as VHF 14 in Puget Sound south of Bush Point, they are not required to monitor VHF 16, and many do not. Participants in Seattle Traffic waters also are required to monitor VHF 13, the U.S. bridge-to-bridge channel. Canada does not use VHF 13.

To contact a large vessel in Seattle Traffic waters call on VHF 13. In Canada VTS waters call on the appropriate VTS channel, such as VHF 11 in southern Strait of Georgia waters.

We have made such calls a few times with excellent results. Twice in narrow channels, the large vessel voluntarily reduced speed to lower its wake. One time it was a cruise ship in northern B.C.; the other time it was a deadly-looking U.S. warship at the mouth of Admiralty Inlet.

Consolidation of Canadian Marine Communications and Traffic Services (MCTS) Centres:
- Vancouver Coast Guard Radio consolidated to Victoria Coast Guard Radio
- Comox Coast Guard Radio consolidated to Victoria Coast Guard Radio
- Tofino Coast Guard Radio consolidated to Prince Rupert Coast Guard Radio

Monitor VTS channels. This is called being a passive VTS participant. Many of the transmissions are extremely brief: a vessel calls in and is off the air almost before you realize it. But by monitoring you'll learn that a ferry is departing the dock, or that a large vessel is about to emerge from a channel just around the next point, or that a container ship is calling in from 5 miles behind you, traveling at 22 knots.

These are good things to know, even in clear weather. In thick weather, at night or in fog, the information is invaluable. We have even called the VTS center ourselves, such as prior to a fog-bound crossing of Puget Sound. We kept our transmission brief, and made sure we weren't a pest. Their response advised us of any potentially conflicting traffic and was always helpful, polite, and professional.

VESSEL TRAFFIC SERVICE PHONE NUMBERS

Washington:
Puget Sound Vessel Traffic Center (206) 217-6040

B.C.
Prince Rupert MCTS Centre (250) 627-3074 or (250) 627-3075
Victoria MCTS Centre (250) 363-6333

VTS RADIO CHANNELS

TRAFFIC AREA	AREA DESCRIPTION	VHF CHANNEL
Seattle Traffic	Puget Sound west of Whidbey Island and south of Bush Point.	14
Seattle Traffic	Strait of Juan de Fuca (including Canadian waters), and Puget Sound north of Bush Point on the west side of Whidbey Island, including the San Juan Islands and Rosario Strait. Also the entire east side of Whidbey Island.	05A
Prince Rupert Traffic – South	West Coast of Vancouver Island & approaches to the Strait of Juan de Fuca.	74
Victoria Traffic – Sector One	Southern Area, Race Rocks (Victoria) to Ballenas Island/ Merry Island. This includes Haro Strait, Boundary Pass, the Gulf Islands, and the southern part of the Strait of Georgia, except for Vancouver Harbour and the Fraser River.	11
Turn Point Special Operating Area	Haro Strait/Boundary Pass. See map and text.	11
Victoria Traffic – Sector Two	Fraser River, Sand Heads to Shoal Point, New Westminster.	74
Victoria Traffic – Sector Three	Vancouver Harbour and approaches.	12
Victoria Traffic – Sector Four	Ballenas Island/Merry Island north to Cape Caution. This includes the northern part of the Strait of Georgia and Inside Passage waters north to Cape Caution.	71
Prince Rupert Traffic – Sector One	Prince Rupert Harbour & approaches, including the north end of Grenville Channel, Chatham Sound, and all of Dixon Entrance to Langara Island.	71
Prince Rupert Traffic – Sector Two	Remainder of Zone. Hecate Strait, Cape Caution north to Alaska on the west side of Haida Gwaii.	11

VESSEL TRAFFIC SERVICE - VHF CHANNELS

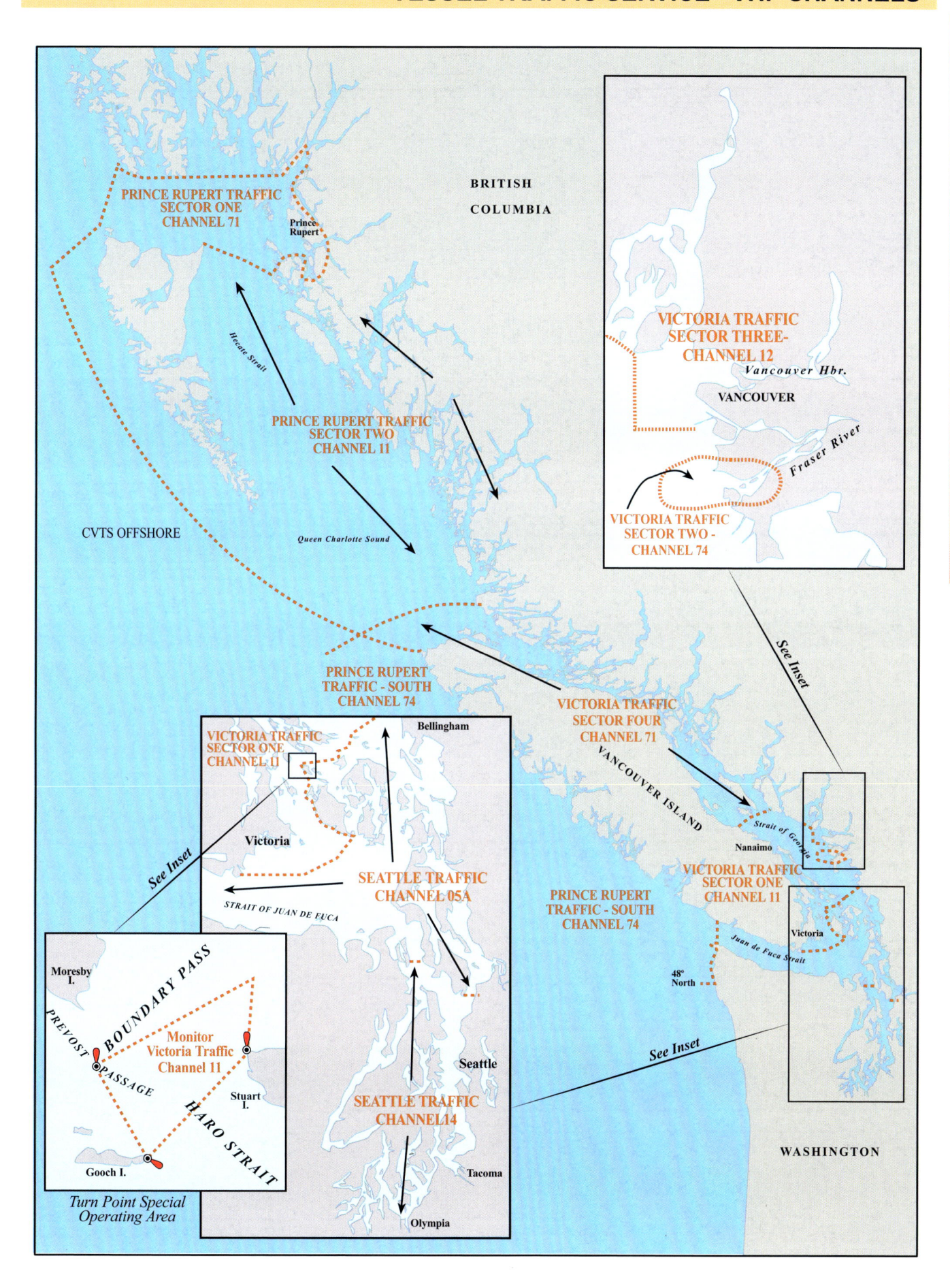

COMPENDIUM

- PRINCE RUPERT TRAFFIC SECTOR ONE — CHANNEL 71
- PRINCE RUPERT TRAFFIC SECTOR TWO — CHANNEL 11
- PRINCE RUPERT TRAFFIC - SOUTH — CHANNEL 74
- VICTORIA TRAFFIC SECTOR ONE — CHANNEL 11
- VICTORIA TRAFFIC SECTOR TWO — CHANNEL 74
- VICTORIA TRAFFIC SECTOR THREE — CHANNEL 12
- VICTORIA TRAFFIC SECTOR FOUR — CHANNEL 71
- SEATTLE TRAFFIC — CHANNEL 05A
- SEATTLE TRAFFIC — CHANNEL 14
- CVTS OFFSHORE
- Monitor Victoria Traffic Channel 11 — *Turn Point Special Operating Area*

BRITISH COLUMBIA — Prince Rupert, Hecate Strait, Queen Charlotte Sound, Vancouver Island, Vancouver Hbr., Vancouver, Fraser River, Strait of Georgia, Nanaimo, Juan de Fuca Strait, Victoria, 48° North

WASHINGTON — Bellingham, Seattle, Tacoma, Olympia, Strait of Juan de Fuca

Moresby I., Prevost Passage, Boundary Pass, Stuart I., Haro Strait, Gooch I.

2023 WAGGONER CRUISING GUIDE

UNDERSTANDING TRADITIONAL TERRITORIES IN B.C.

Traditional Territories of the First Nations. Boaters love visiting the waters, lands, and islands of British Columbia, but how many of us are aware of the numerous First Nations traditional territories and the names of the tribes and communities that we visit? Acknowledging native traditional lands is a way to show respect for the presence of Indigenous Peoples, both past and present. A long tradition among tribes of First Nations is to acknowledge the presence of the nation they are visiting.

Throughout history, Indigenous people did not use a system of land ownership, they saw themselves as part of the land, which is inseparable from their people. Today, "traditional territory" refers to a geographic area identified by a First Nation as the land they and/or their ancestors traditionally occupied and used. "Unceded" means that First Nations people never ceded or legally signed away their lands to the Crown or to Canada. While there is geographic overlap among the different territories, each nation has a unique language and culture.

There are more than 200 distinct First Nations in B.C., 30 different First Nation languages, and close to 60 dialects spoken in British Columbia. While Indigenous people represent only about 6 percent of the population in British Columbia, ninety-five percent of British Columbia, including Vancouver Island, is on unceded traditional First Nations territory. Indian Reserves cover just 0.4 percent of the B.C. land base.

There are many tribes within First Nations territories – a tribe refers to a number of bands that share a language, cultural aspects and beliefs. A band refers to a kinship-based group, and a clan refers to a group bound together by lineage. The term "Indian Band" comes from the 1876 Indian Act and refers to groups whose resources are managed by the federal government.

The Map below outlines the First Nations traditional territories of Vancouver Island and territories along the coast of Mainland British Columbia extending into Southeast Alaska.

West Vancouver Island (from south to north):
- Ditidaht Territory – the area around Port Renfrew and Ditidaht
- Nuu-Chah-Nulth Territory – inland and coastal areas of Barkley Sound, Clayoquot Sound, Nootka Sound, Esperanza, and Kyuquot Sound
- Kwakwaka'wakw – north end of Vancouver Island; Port Hardy and Port McNeill area; note this territory extends down the east side of Vancouver Island and across Queen Charlotte Strait to include lands on the mainland.

East Vancouver Island (from south to north):
- Lekwungen – greater Victoria area
- Quw'utsun – Cowichan area
- Sne-Nay-Muxw – Nanaimo area
- Qualicum – Qualicum Beach area
- K'omoks – Comox and Courtenay area

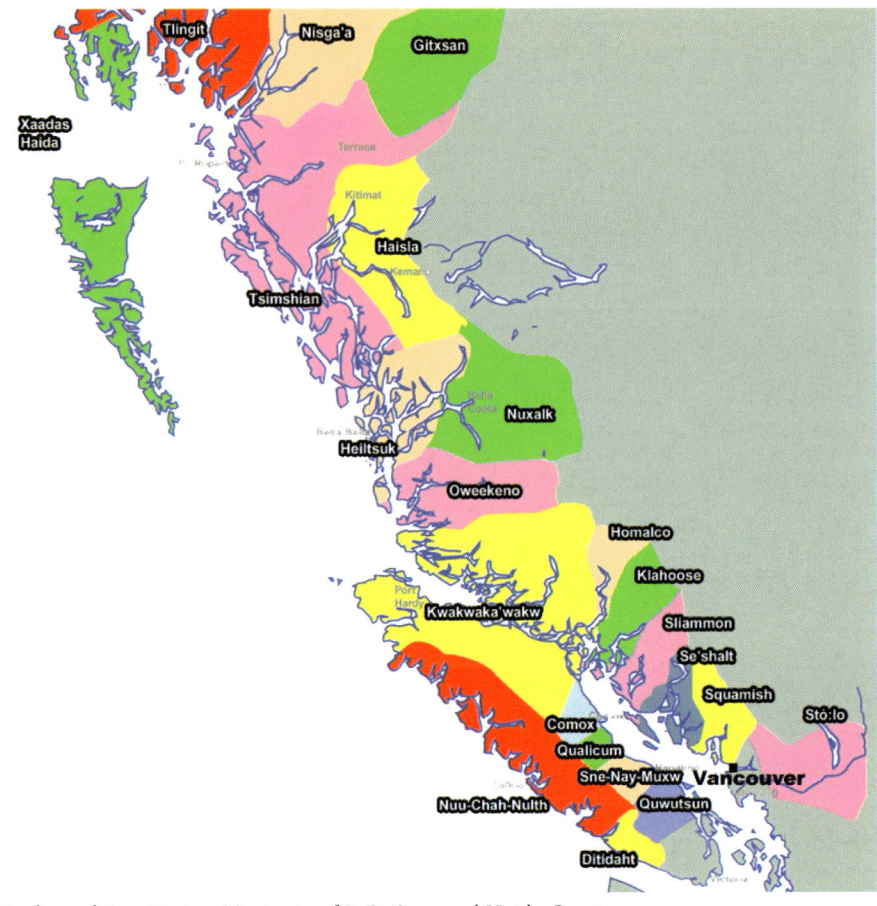

Traditional First Nations Territories of B.C. Coast and Haida Gwaii

- Kwakwaka'wakw – extends north of Comox to the tip of Vancouver Island, including Port McNeill, Port Hardy, and Campbell River, and across Queen Charlotte Strait to the mainland, including the Discovery Islands, and The Broughtons areas.

B.C. Mainland Coastal Territories (from south to north):
- Squamish – Howe Sound area
- Se'shalt – Jervis Inlet, Egmont, Sechelt area
- Sliammon – Powell River, Lund area
- Klahoose – Desolation Sound area, including Toba Inlet
- Homalco – Bute Inlet, Phillips Arm area
- Kwakwaka'wakw – Discovery Islands, and The Broughtons areas
- Oweekeno – Rivers Inlet, Fish Egg Inlet, and southern tip of Calvert Island
- Heiltsuk – Bella Bella, Shearwater, Ocean Falls, and Bella Coola areas
- Nuxalk – Bella Coola and Dean Channel areas
- Haisla – Kitimat and Kemano area
- Tsimshian – Extends from Milbank Sound along the coast to Prince Rupert and eastward up the Skeena River. The area includes familiar stops like Klemtu, Butedale, and Hartley Bay.
- Xaadas Haida – the islands of Haida Gwaii
- Nisga'a – the Nass River area
- Tlingit – the islands and coastal lands of Southeast Alaska - Cape Fox to Yakutat

Watchmen Programs. First Nations have a special connection with the land, animals, and the natural environment, which plays into their culture. Several First Nations in British Columbia serve as stewards or watchmen to protect sensitive areas like Grizzly bear habitat or historic native villages for visitations. These special sites are protected by limiting the number of visitors at any one time. In some cases, permits are required; in other cases, contacting the Watchmen by radio for further instructions is all that is required. These Watchmen programs are described in detail in the *Waggoner Guide*. Watchmen programs include the following:

1. Grizzly Bear Viewing in Glendale Cove, Knight Inlet (see Broughtons Chapter for details); contact "Glendale Cove Guardians" on VHF Ch 68

2. Visitations to historic village remains, Village Island (see Broughtons Chapter for details); contact Mamalilikulla First Nation for permission.

3. Tour of historic Kiixin Village, Bamfield (see West Coast Vancouver Island Chapter for details); access is by guided tour only.

Fisheries Supply
Marine Supplies Since 1928

Make Your Time on the Water More Enjoyable

VETUS and Maxwell systems make boating easy and carefree. They deliver a wide range of high-quality boat equipment to the top boat builders, boat yards and experienced boaters. All their equipment is backed by global expertise and support so you can spend more time focusing on what really matters.

VETUS | MAXWELL

For more innovative VETUS Maxwell marine products please visit **fisheriessupply.com/vetus-denouden**

Call us 800.426.6930 | FisheriesSupply.com | 1900 N. Northlake Way, Seattle

UNDERSTANDING TRADITIONAL TERRITORIES IN B.C.

Name	Territory	Pronunciation
Songhees First Nation	Greater Victoria	song-hees
Musqueam Indian Band	Greater Vancouver	muss-quee-um
Snuneymuxw First Nation	Nanaimo	snoo-NAI-muk
Stz'uminus First Nation	Chemainus/Ladysmith	sta-meen-us
Penelakut First Nations Tribe	Galiano & Penelakut Is.	pen-EL-ah-kut
Wei-Wai-Kai First Nation	Campbell River/Mudge	wee-way-kay
Shisha'lh First Nation	Queens Reach/Jervis	she-shaw
Tla'amin First Nation	Lund	ta-law-men
Tlowitsis Indian Band	Port Neville	toe-wit-sis
D'naxda'xw Awaetlala Nation	Broughtons	da-nuk-dah-a-wet-la
Kwikwasut'inuxw Haxwa'mis	Broughtons	quick-wah-sue-in-Hack-swah-mis
Mamalilikulla First Nation	Broughtons	mamma-leel-eh-quala
Gwa'sala 'Nakwaxda'xw Nations	Port Hardy	gwah-sah-la-nock-wock-da
Namgis First Nation	Alert Bay	nom-gees
Huu-Ay-Aht First Nation	Bamfield	hoo-EYE-at
Hesquiaht First Nation	Hot Springs Cove	HESS-kwee-at
Nuu-chah-nulth First Nation	Nootka Sound	new-cha-nulth
Wuikinuxv/Oweekeno Nation	Rivers Inlet	o-wik-en-o
Heiltsuk First Nation	Bella Bella	HAIL-suk
Nuxalk First Nation	Bella Coola	NOO-hulk
Kitasoo First Nation	Klemtu	kit-AH-soo
Gitga'at First Nation	Hartley Bay	GIT-gat
Metlakatla Indian Band	Prince Rupert area	met-la-kat-la

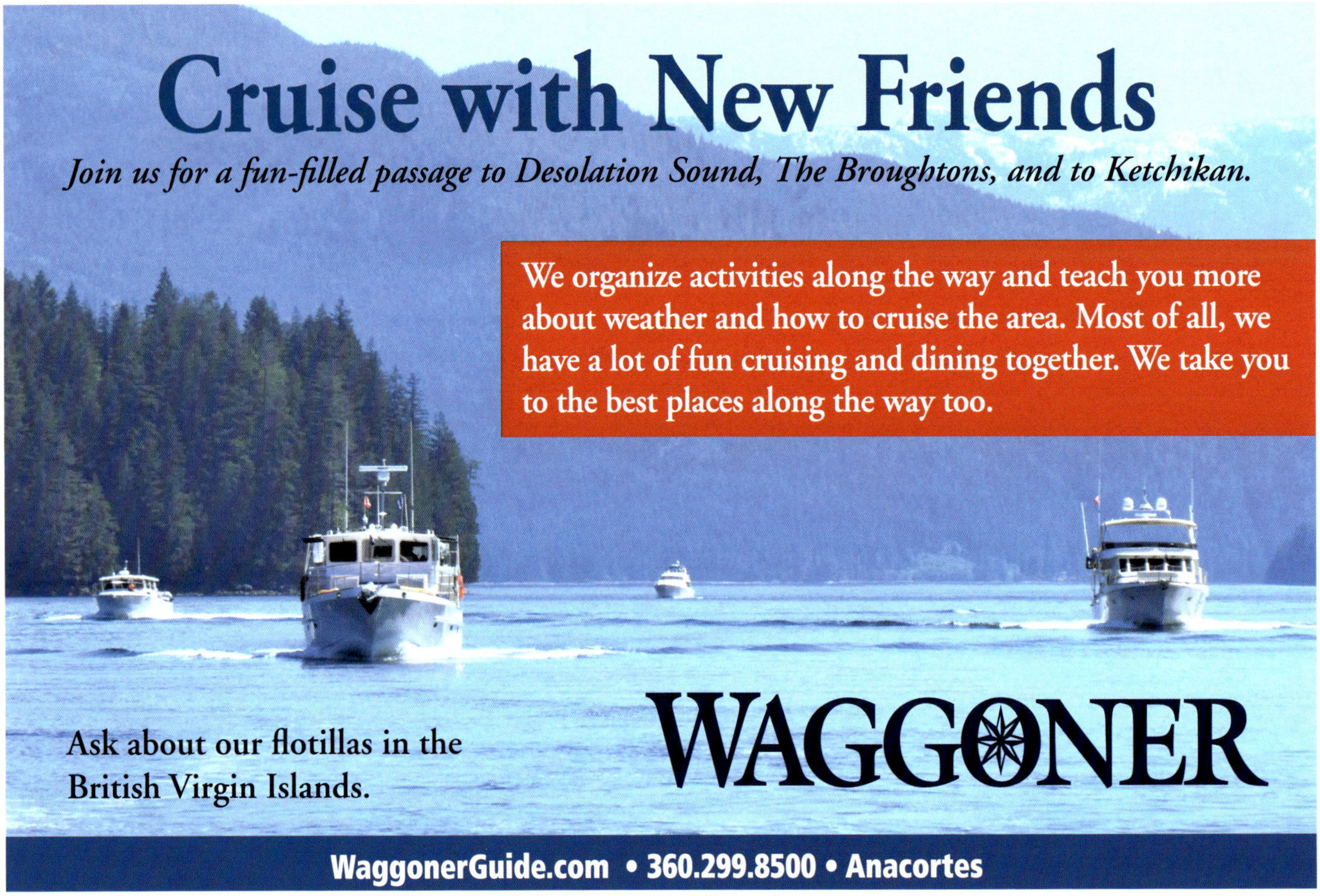

4. Grizzly Bear Viewing, Mussel Inlet estuary in Fiordland (see Northern B.C. Chapter for details); contact Kitasoo Guardians on VHF Ch 6.

5. Grizzly Bear Viewing, Khutze Inlet estuary in Fiordland (see Northern B.C. Chapter for details); Contact Kitasoo Guardians on VHF Ch 6.

6. Gwaii Haanas Village Watchmen Sites, Haida Gwaii (see Haida Gwaii chapter for details); a permit to visit these historic village sites is required; contact the Haida Heritage Centre.

First Nations Names and Pronunciations. There are many First Nations tribes or bands within each defined Traditional Territory. It's always good to learn the pronunciations of various peoples and places when we travel. Learning the pronunciations of First Nations is no exception. Some of the many First Nations names in B.C., along with the pronunciations, are listed in this table:

Cruise with New Friends

Join us for a fun-filled passage to Desolation Sound, The Broughtons, and to Ketchikan.

We organize activities along the way and teach you more about weather and how to cruise the area. Most of all, we have a lot of fun cruising and dining together. We take you to the best places along the way too.

Ask about our flotillas in the British Virgin Islands.

WAGGONER

WaggonerGuide.com • 360.299.8500 • Anacortes

www.WaggonerGuide.com

Explore. Dream. Discover.

NORTHWEST YACHT BROKERS ASSOCIATION

BOATS AFLOAT SHOW
EST. 1978

SOUTH LAKE UNION | SEATTLE

April 27-30 & September 14-17, 2023

BoatsAfloatShow.com

Fisheries Supply
Marine Supplies Since 1928

PLOT YOUR PARADISE
With Garmin GPSMAP X3 Series Chartplotters

GPSMAP® 7X3, 9X3, 12X3

Get a sharper view from your connected helm with the GPSMAP® x3 series chartplotters. These chartplotters feature higher-resolution displays in 7″, 9″ and 12″ sizes, and have 60% more pixels than previous-generation touchscreens. And with a compact footprint, vivid sonar color palette and nearly double the processing power of previous-generation GPSMAP devices, they seamlessly integrate into your Garmin marine system. GPSMAP x3 also features options for built-in Ultra High-Definition SideVü and ClearVü scanning sonars, supports Panoptix LiveScope™ sonar and 1 kW CHIRP traditional sonar as well as fully networkable radar and Auto Guidance[1] technology.

GARMIN™

For more innovative Garmin navigation products please visit
fisheriessupply.com/garmin

Call us 800.426.6930 | FisheriesSupply.com | 1900 N. Northlake Way, Seattle

WHALE WISE - VIEWING WHALES & MARINE MAMMALS

Observing marine life, including whales breaching, feeding or on the hunt, is always a thrill to see. The diversity and complexity of marine life in our coastal waters is truly extraordinary. It's one of the reasons boaters come to the waters of Washington State, British Columbia, and Alaska. Unfortunately, increased vessel traffic and noise threatens some of the whale population along with other factors like pollutants and lack of prey.

Laws and Guidelines. In WA and BC waters, marine mammals are protected by federal law that (in addition to other protections) requires vessels to remain a minimum distance of 100 yards and 200 yards if these mammals are resting or with young. These marine mammal protection laws have been in place for many years and govern boat and people proximity to marine wildlife.

Whale Warning Flag. While being good stewards of whale watching regulations, boaters can also help protect our whales by flying a 'Whale Warning Flag' when sighting whales. If you see this flag, slow to 7 knots or less, be prepared to adjust your course, and follow the whale watching regulations. If you see a whale, you are asked to fly the Whale Warning Flag to alert other boaters. If you would like one of these flags, contact Frances Robertson, Marine Program Coordinator for San Juan County, at francesr@sanjuanco.com. Don't forget to lower the flag once you or the whales have left the area.

Enforcement. Regulations are strictly enforced by various officials or agencies of Washington State, and the Province of British Columbia. Law enforcement personnel may board your vessel if you are in violation of whale watching regulations. In the U.S. that may be NOAA, Washington Department of Fish and Wildlife (WDFW), or the County Sheriff's Department. Canadian Fishery officers and BC Conservation officers provide enforcement in Canada.

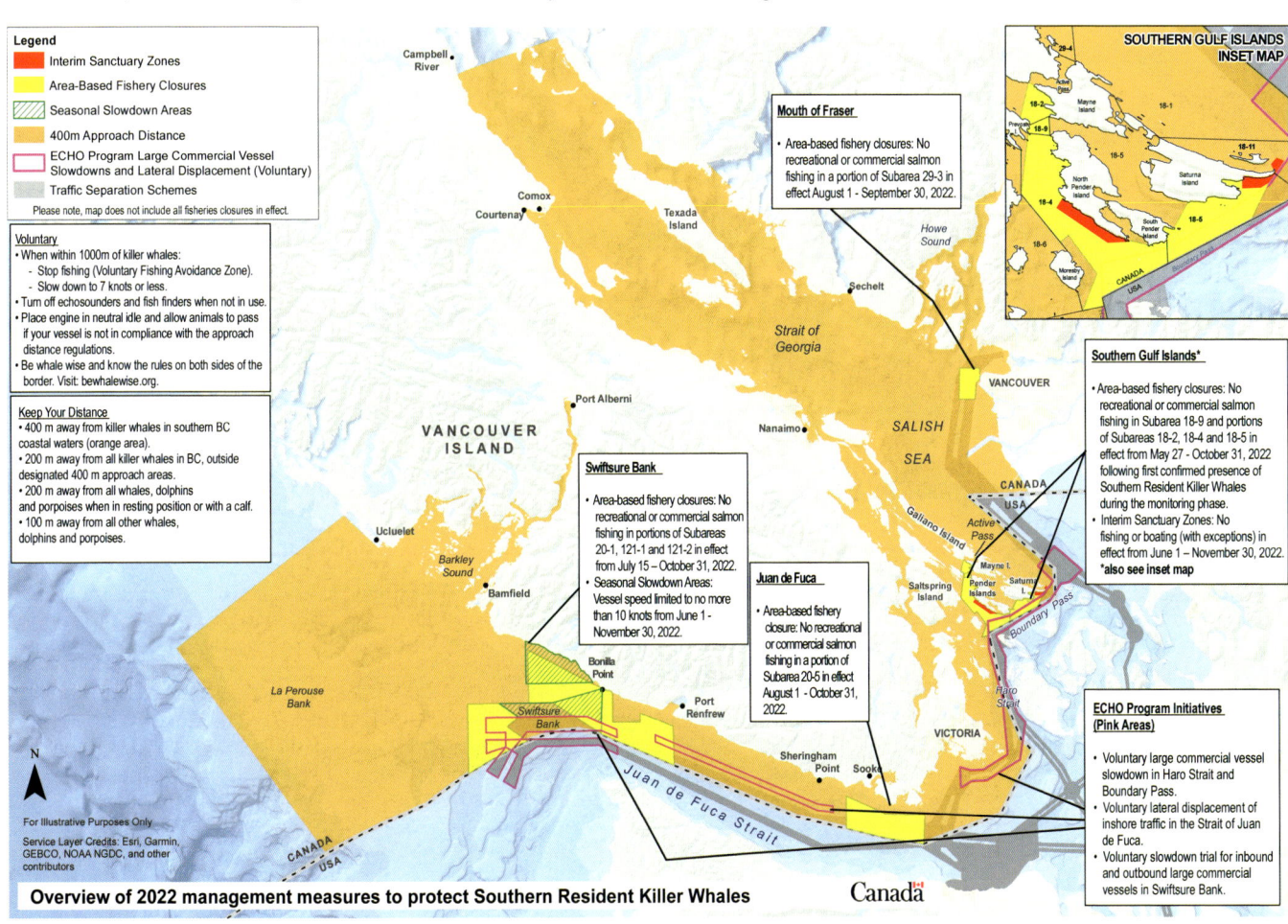

Quick Guide To Regulations for Marine Mammal Viewing

Canadian/BC Regulations

- 400 meters from killer whales in SRKW areas
- 200 meters from killer whales in BC waters other than SRKW areas
- Vessels are prohibited from entering any of 3 Sanctuary Zones June 1 to Nov. 30
  1. off East Pt. on Saturna Island
  2. southwest shore of North Pender I.
  3. Swiftsure Bank at the west entrance to Strait of Juan de Fuca
- 7 knots or less (voluntary) slow zone within 1000 meters of killer whales
- Turn off depth sounders (voluntary) when not in use
- Engine off or neutral idle (voluntary) near killer whales
- 100 meters from all marine mammals; 200 meters if resting or with young

U.S./Washington Regulations

- 400 yards from the path (behind and in front) of Southern Resident Orcas
- 300 yards from Southern Resident Orcas
- 7 knot speed limit within ½ mile of Southern Resident Orcas
- Disengage engine transmission if a Southern Resident Orca is within 300 yards
- 100 yards from non-killer whales, dolphins, porpoises, and other marine mammals; 200 yards if they are resting or with young
- Turn off echo / depth sounders (voluntary) when not in use
- Vessels are asked to avoid the Voluntary No-Go Zone on the west side of San Juan Island, extending ¼-mile offshore from Mitchell Bay to Cattle Point, and a ½-mile off Lime Kiln Lighthouse.

Overview of 2022 management measures to protect Southern Resident Killer Whales

2023 WAGGONER CRUISING GUIDE

FISHING & SHELLFISH COLLECTING

How To Catch Dinner. If you love to eat salmon, halibut, rockfish, crab or prawns - you are boating in the right place. Washington, Alaska, and British Columbia all require licenses to harvest virtually any type of seafood. Washington and Alaska licenses can be purchased at sporting goods stores and other retail outlets, or online with a credit card. British Columbia licenses can be purchased at Independent Access Providers (check their website for a list), or online with a credit card. If you purchase online, consider how you will print the license; unless you have a printer onboard, it may be best to do it at home ahead of time.

Investing in Gear. Crabbing is inexpensive and fun for even an inexperienced crew. Crabbing gear is relatively easy to purchase at a few hundred dollars, but the costs go up from there. Catching prawns can be more costly, especially if you purchase a pot puller to pull the weighted traps up from 250-350 feet deep. Many have outfitted their boats or dinghies to target salmon with all the best equipment, spending thousands of dollars for downriggers, trolling motors, special rods, reels, lures and a fishfinder. Some salmon fishing enthusiasts even tow a special boat set up to catch salmon. There is a lot of money invested, and we don't dare ask how much the investment totals compared to the cost of buying quality salmon at the market.

Charter Fishing. At the Waggoner Guide, we love to fish, or to put it more directly, we love to "catch" fish. Rather than investing a fortune "gearing up" to fish, we have gotten into the practice of hiring an expert with all the right equipment and going charter fishing for salmon or halibut once or twice a summer. Prices vary from reasonable to very expensive, ask before booking.

The experts know their local waters, where the fish are and how to fish. We nearly always fill our freezer with as much fish as we can handle and have a lot of fun. Your charter captain can conveniently issue fishing licenses for the charter, and has all the gear and fresh bait. Depending on the location, the charter captain also knows where to take the fish to be processed, flash frozen and stored in the freezer to be shipped home, where you can accept the shipment later.

Guests. We typically treat our guests to a fishing expedition in the Johnstone Strait areas, the Broughtons, Northern B.C. or in Southeast Alaska. A half-day charter will often do it; and with a good guide and good conditions, we limit out within the half-day charter and fill the freezer. We have also found it is best to ask the charter captain when to fish. Many start out the day early in the morning. We have also had excellent results when our charter captain suggested fishing on the evening change of tide.

Finding a Good Charter. Ask around at the marinas you will be visiting. They know the good local fishing guides. You may want to book a charter well in advance of your stay at a marina. When the bite is on, reservations with the best charter captains fill up quickly. The charter captains will often pick you up at your marina or even at your boat on the hook at an anchorage with a fast boat to quickly get you to the best fishing spots in the area. Most charter captains I have fished with take real pride in finding fish and helping you land them on the boat. They want you to catch fish, take them home, and tell your friends!

Catching Fish Without Fishing. There is another technique we have found to catch fish without even dropping a hook in the water. It all starts with being nice to people. Most fisherman catch more fish than they can use. We have seen some excellent techniques among pleasure boaters to catch fish with fresh baked bread, cookies and pies carried down a dock full of commercial fishing boats during the season, offering a trade. Many guys use the traditional technique of walking down the dock with a six pack of beer or a 20-dollar bill, which usually lands a catch. Keep in mind, however, that some commercial operators are not allowed to sell fish to individuals unless the operator holds a special license.

Avoiding Entanglement in Gillnets

Commercial gillnet fishing is common practice throughout SE Alaska, and recreational boaters need to keep a watchful eye to avoid entangling their props in gillnets. Gillnets are hung vertically in the water like curtains; the top edge of the gillnet is supported by floats, and the bottom edge is weighted to help form a wall in the water across the path of migrating salmon. Although hanging vertically, these nets extend behind the stern of the fish boat up to 900 to 1,800 feet in length. "Sternpickers" work their nets from the back of the boat and tend to be larger vessels operating in deeper waters, while "bowpickers" deploy the net from the bow and tend to be smaller boats operating in shallow river deltas. The size of the mesh determines the species and sex of the salmon to be caught.

Gillnetters can be recognized by the large drum or spool mounted on the stern or bow that sets and retrieves the net. Once it's decided to haul the net, it is slowly pulled in with the hydraulically powered drum. Fish caught in the net (usually by the gills) are shaken out, or hand-picked, and placed into the hold. The catch is rapidly cooled with ice or onboard refrigeration to preserve the quality of the fish, until the day's delivery can be made.

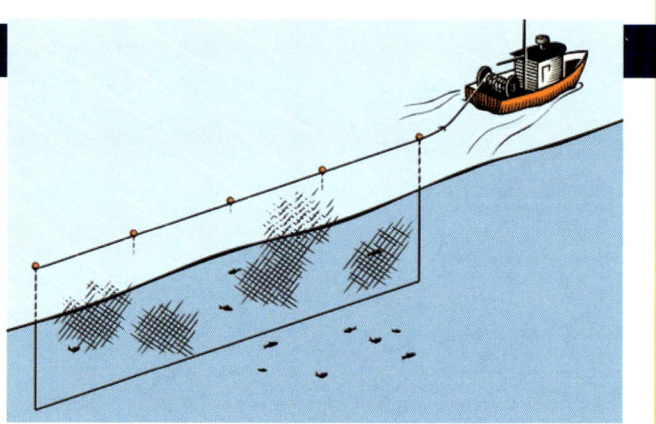

To avoid gillnets, a former gillnetter recommends that cruisers head toward the fish boat; it's the easiest thing to see. Once you get close enough to see the net's corkline, pass around the correct side of the fish boat. The corkline usually has a series of white floats. The end of the net is normally marked with a larger orange or yellow buoy. When numerous fish boats are operating in the same area, identifying where these nets begin and end can be a challenge. Locating the nets can also be a challenge when rough sea conditions hide some of the white buoys behind waves and chop. We have found that team work between captain and crew works best. Using binoculars, your crew member can spot and call-out the end of fish nets and identify a safe route. The helmsman can then navigate accordingly, often requiring a snake pattern around the commercial vessels and their long nets. Occasionally, the net is not attached to any fish boat and both ends of the net have an orange or yellow buoy. When you see commercial fish boats, remember to use caution, especially during gillnet season which normally runs from early July to mid-September.

FISHING & SHELLFISH COLLECTING

Freeze the Bounty. Crab meat can be frozen and keeps well up to a year. Pack in freezer bags or vacuum bags with clean seawater or milk. When you are ready, defrost and squeeze the excess liquid out of the meat. Freezing in milk or seawater also works well for uncooked prawns. It keeps the meat from breaking down and getting freezer burn. While much of your catch may end up frozen for later, fresh fish, prawns and crab, consumed just an hour or two after coming out of the water is about as good as it gets.

Fishing Regulations. Fishing and shellfish collection have become much more complicated and onerous over the years. Laws not only require fishing licenses for specific species, at specific times, and for specific locations, but also set possession limits and storage requirements for fish and shellfish identification purposes. Correspondent Deane Hislop, and professional fisherman Gill Graham, share additional information below, regarding fishing in the waters of British Columbia.

SPORT FISHING IN B.C.

Know Before You Go. British Columbia Sport Fishing regulations cover 47 different management areas and vary from area to area, and from year to year, so it is important that anyone planning to wet a line, drop a pot, pick oysters or dig clams in British Columbia tidal water obtain the latest copy of the Department of Fisheries and Oceans (DFO) Canada, British Columbia Sports Fishing Guide from an authorized license dealer. Guides and licenses are also available online at www.pac.dfo-mpo.gc.ca. Beware, regulations can change during the season, so it is wise to monitor the website for any in-season revisions.

If you are going fishing or harvesting shellfish in tidal waters, you need a Tidal Waters Sports Fishing License. If you're going fishing in fresh waters for salmon or any other species, you're required to have a Non-Tidal Angling License issued by the Province of B.C.

Before going fishing, make sure you can answer these five questions:

1. Can I fish at this time, at this location?
2. Is the gear, and the manner in which I plan to use it, legal for catching fish, crab, shrimp or prawns?
3. What can I catch and keep, and in what amount?
4. Do I have the correct license (and supplementary salmon stamp if needed), and do I need to record my catch on the license?
5. How many fish, crab, shrimp, clams, oysters can I possess, and how am I allowed to clean, package and transport them to my residence?

Certain coastal areas are designated Rockfish Conservation Areas (RCAs). Sport fishing is not allowed in RCAs. Gathering of invertebrates by hand picking or diving, or collecting crab, shrimp or prawn by trap, and smelt by gillnet may be allowed. Find out where B.C.'s RCAs are located at bcsportfishingguide.ca.

Reminders:

- Barbless hooks are required for all salmon and sea-run trout fishing. Treble barbless are acceptable in most areas.
- Know the size limit for the area fishing.
- In tidal waters, there's no limit to the number of fishing rods you can use.
- When filleting salmon, the tail must remain attached for the purpose of identification. The adipose fin or fin clip scar must also remain attached to determine if the fish is wild or hatchery.
- It's illegal to willfully snag hook a salmon. If you should foul hook a salmon, it must be released immediately.
- You must immediately record on your license all adult chinook you keep.
- Harvesting of northern abalone, an endangered species in B.C., is prohibited.

For more information on sport fishing in B.C., including seasons, limits, gear requirements and restrictions, go to bcsportfishingguide.ca.

Deane Hislop

Possession Limits. The number of fish or shellfish of any species that you are allowed to keep as your daily limit and in possession is determined by the area in which you are fishing. Knowing the number of the area you are in is imperative to staying within your limits and therefore legal.

The daily limits are what you are allowed to catch in one day, the in-possession limits are usually twice the daily limit. Once you have your possession limit you are done fishing, you must stop. The catch you eat, while still part of your daily limit, is not part of your possession limit. You may take or send your catch to your ordinary residence; once there, they are no longer part of your possession limit and you can fish again. However, the regulations are very clear on the explanation of your ordinary residence, and your boat is not included. The address on your driver's license is your ordinary residence.

Probably the most misunderstood, is the fact that if you are going to keep the crabs to take home, you cannot clean, cook and pick out the meat. The carapace, which is the shell on the top that you measure to determine his legality, has to be attached to the body. It is possible to lift it part way and clean out the innards, cook him, and then freeze him, however you cannot pick the meat from his shell. Technically, if you have frozen picked crab in your freezer, you committed an offence.

You can ship your catch to your ordinary residence, or someone else could take it home for you, however, there are certain criteria that have to be met to do this; check the regulations. Most importantly, remember the crabs have to have the carapace attached until they reach your residence. You cannot start catching more until your possession limit is in your ordinary residence.

Gill Graham

Rockfish Conservation Areas in B.C. Our coastal waters of British Columbia abound in wonderful delights from the sea. Rockfish species are one of these delicacies we can enjoy. Rockfish come in so many varieties, colors and shapes that a lot of people have no idea what they are catching. There are 37 varieties of Rockfish found on this coast. Yelloweye (red snapper) are rockfish. It is very important to know what species you are catching to stay within the regulations.

As man has learned over the ages, you just can't take and take and expect what you are taking to always be there. To protect our rockfish, Fisheries and Oceans Canada (DFO) designated protected areas for them in 2002. These areas are called Rockfish Conservation Areas or RCAs. There are more than 160 RCA locations along our coast, and you should know where they are. Before you go fishing, go to bcsportfishguide.ca and locate the area in which you will be fishing and take note of the RCA locations in that area. You might be surprised where some of these RCAs are located. Know before you go. Inside an RCA, you are not allowed to put a line in the water that is targeting any fin fish. You cannot troll for salmon in an RCA since rockfish will go after a lure; you cannot jig for lingcod since rockfish will go for your jig. You can handpick or dive for shellfish (invertebrates), you can fish for crab or prawns, you can catch smelt by gillnet, in the area. If your gear is attached to a fishing rod with a hook, jig, or lure, it cannot go in the water.

Many rockfish live to be over 100 years old; that 15-pound yelloweye you just brought up from 250 to 300 feet could be that old. Unlike salmon, rockfish don't survive well with catch and release. That is why there is no size limit for rockfish. If you catch a rockfish, DFO regulations state you have to keep that fish. If you are in an area that allows one (1) rockfish per day, you have your one limit no matter how big he is, or if you like him or not, he is yours.

Gill Graham

FLOATPLANE TRAVEL

For boaters who need to travel home during a cruise, need parts shipped to them, or want to have guests join them in remote areas, floatplane travel can be a good option.

Traveling by floatplane provides a new perspective for boaters. If you can, sit in the co-pilot seat. Take a map or use this guidebook and pick out the islands as you fly overhead. The view is unforgettable—especially on a sunny day when you can see for miles and the islands unfold before you. Sometimes whales are spotted, and the pilot may spend a few moments circling for a better view. On cloudy days you'll fly low—300 to 500 feet above the water.

Be prepared for a flight to have several stops along the route. If transiting from one country to the other, there may be a stop for customs clearance.

Floatplane operators are happy to accommodate boater's needs. We've seen floatplanes deliver parts as well as people to vessels in remote anchorages.

The cost to use a floatplane service may initially appear high, but the benefits of saving time and eliminating hassle are huge. After all, it's only a 3-hour flight from Port McNeill at the north end of Vancouver Island to reach Seattle, or Vancouver B.C.

Floatplane or Seaplane? The two terms are often interchangeably used. A floatplane is a type of seaplane but there is a technical difference. Both floatplanes and seaplanes can land and take off on water. Floatplanes are sometimes referred to as pontoon planes because the pontoons or floats attached to the plane touch the water. Seaplanes are often referred to as flying boats with wings because they are built around a hull. The hull or belly of the seaplane touches the water when landing and taking off. Throughout the guide, we refer to air travel via waterways as floatplane travel.

When travelling by air in the Northwest, you will most likely be traveling in a floatplane. Floatplanes, made by de Havilland Aircraft Company, are the most popular with floatplane operators and come in three sizes: Beaver, Otter, and Twin Otter. Wilderness Seaplanes is one of the few operators that flies seaplanes (Grumman Goose) on their Northern B.C. routes.

Frequent Traveller Tips.

- Baggage - there is limited baggage space and weight is a consideration. Most operators limit baggage size and weight, with a limit of 25 lbs (11 kg). Some may accept more baggage with an additional charge. Overall dimensions of baggage items may be limited.

- In-flight services & facilities - there are no in-flight services or facilities; you won't get offered beverages in-flight and you may not want it because there are no restroom facilities.

- Headsets or earplugs will be a welcome addition to help with a noisy environment.

- Pets can travel with you; there may be a charge for larger dogs and there may not be room for large dog kennels. Cats should be carried in softside carriers.

- Check-in Base Locations - is much easier and simpler than major airline travel. No long security lines and much more reasonable early arrival times. For domestic travel, most operators want travellers to arrive at least 30 mins before flight time and for international that usually increases to at least 1 hour.

- Check-in Remote Locations - many outlying locations are not staffed and the check-in happens when the floatplane arrives. Be sure and arrive at the remote check-in location well ahead of the scheduled time - the floatplane may be ahead of schedule and arrive early. Likewise, be patient; the floatplane may not arrive at the exact time.

- Documents - Photo id is required for all adults. Passport and visas are required for international travel.

NW SEAPLANES
(425) 277-1590
Seattle (Renton) to Desolation Sound, Port McNeill, Broughtons, Rivers Inlet and Charter Service

FRIDAY HARBOR SEAPLANES
(425) 277-1590
San Juan Islands to Seattle

KENMORE AIR
(866) 435-9524
Floatplanes & Land Planes
Seattle (Lake Union or Kenmore) to San Juans, Vancouver, and B.C. Inside Passage

WILDERNESS SEAPLANES
(800) 343-5963 or (250) 949-6353
Port Hardy to Broughtons, Northern B.C. Coast Destinations and Charters

HARBOUR AIR VANCOUVER
(800) 665-0212
Victoria, Vancouver, Gulf Island, Sunshine Coast, Tofino, and Charter Services

GULF ISLAND SEAPLANES
(250) 247-9992
Gabriola Island & Hornby Island to Vancouver Airport

INLAND AIR
(888) 624-2577
Prince Rupert, North B.C., Kitkatla, Hartley Bay, Haida Gwaii (Masset)

SEAIR SEAPLANES
(800) 447-3247 or (866) 692-6440
Vancouver to Gulf Islands and Nanaimo

TOFINO AIR
(866) 486-3249
Tofino to Nanaimo and Sunshine Coast, Tours and Charter Services

TAQUAN AIR
(907) 225-8800
Ketchikan based with Charter Services and Flightseeing

ALASKA SEAPLANES
(907) 789-3331
Juneau to most SE Alaska Communities Tours and Charter Services

WARD AIR
(907) 789-9150
Charter service based in Juneau flightseeing Tours,
flights to Lodges and USFS Cabins

FLOATPLANE TRAVEL

Aviation Buff Information: a floatplane ride can be particularly thrilling and knowing something about the equipment makes it even more interesting.

De Havilland Beaver - The venerable de Havilland DHC-2 Beaver is among the most widely used floatplanes in the northwest. Beaver production started in 1948 and nearly 1700 were built before production ended in 1967. Operators and enthusiasts alike still appreciate its unparalleled combination of short field performance, durability, and versatility. Pilots rave about flying them.

Originally powered with a 450 hp piston engine, many Beavers have been converted to turbine engines. Beavers can reach places other planes can't. They can carry things other planes can't, too. De Havilland engineers designed the Beaver with doors wide enough to accommodate a 45-gallon drum and the ability to carry 2100 pounds of payload. Piston Beavers cruise at about 100 knots burning about 23 gallons of fuel per hour—enviable economy compared to many powerboats. Turbine powered models have increased speed, payload capacity, and range.

De Havilland Otter - In 1952 de Havilland introduced the larger, more powerful version of the successful Beaver with the DHC-3 Otter. Crediting its larger carrying capacity, the Otter has been referred to as the "one-ton truck" compared to the "half-ton" Beaver. Originally powered with a 600 hp piston engine, most have been converted to turbine power. The Otter carries 9 to 11 passengers and the piston powered cruises at about 110 knots. 480 Otters were produced from 1952 to 1967.

De Havilland Twin Otter - The twin engine DHC-6 was produced by de Havilland from 1965 to 1988. Viking Air purchased the type certification and restarted production in 2008. Production stopped in 2019 and is planned to resume soon. Twin Otters are powered with twin turboprop engines and a cruise speed of about 160 knots. 270 Twin Otters have been built in three evolutionary models with increased speed, and payload capacity. Twin Otters normally carry about 20 passengers. Harbour Air operates several Twin Otters as part of its fleet.

NORTHWEST SEAPLANES

SCHEDULED AND CHARTER FLIGHTS
from Seattle to British Columbia's Inside Passage

Campbell River • Gorge Harbour • Desolation Sound • Refuge Cove • Toba Wilderness Marina
Cortes Bay • Big Bay • Dent Island • Blind Channel • Lagoon Cove • Kwatsi Bay • Echo Bay
Sullivan Bay • Port McNeill • Port Hardy • Rivers Inlet • Hakai Pass • Shearwater

FRIDAY HARBOR SEAPLANES

SCHEDULED AND CHARTER FLIGHTS
from Seattle to Roche Harbor and Friday Harbor

Convenient departures from South Lake Washington, just minutes from Seattle's Sea-Tac Airport and downtown Seattle. Quick 15 minute shuttle service to and from Sea-Tac.

For reservations and information call:

425-277-1590

U.S. and Canada 1-800-690-0086
or online at **www.nwseaplanes.com**
or at **www.fridayharborseaplanes.com**

2023 WAGGONER CRUISING GUIDE

EMERGENCIES & CONTINGENCIES

Accident Reporting. In U.S. waters, recreational boaters involved in an accident must remain at the scene of the accident and assist those injured or in danger, unless doing so would pose a danger to their vessel's crew or passengers. The operator or owner of the vessel is required to submit a written accident report when the accident results in: loss of life or disappearance from a vessel; an injury which requires medical treatment beyond first aid; property damage in excess of $2,000 ($500 in Alaska); or complete loss of the vessel. Federal law requires that in death, disappearance, and injury cases, reports are due within 48 hours; in other cases within 10 days.

In Washington State, report forms are available from Washington State Parks and Recreation at parks.state.wa.us/DocumentCenter/View/2213/ and are filed with the law enforcement agency where the accident occurred.

In Alaska, report forms are available from state DNR website http://dnr.alaska.gov/ and can be filed by email at officeofboatingsafety@alaska.gov.

In B.C. and all Canada waters, operators of recreational boats involved in a boating accident must report the accident to the local law enforcement, RCMP or police. If you are unsure, make an initial report with Canadian Coast Guard Marine Communications and Traffic Services (Coast Guard Radio). The accident must be reported as soon as possible.

Calling for Help - Signaling Distress. Boats nearby are often first to assist a fellow boater in distress. So, it is important to have an effective means of communicating a need for help to boaters and first responders such as Coast Guard and harbor patrol. Distress signaling methods vary depending upon your cruising grounds, from inland waters to coastal cruising. Check the coast guard's list of required distress signals for recreational craft. Consider carrying the following:
- International Orange Distress Signal Flag
- Orange hand-held smoke flares
- SOS signal lights and pyrotechnic aerial red flares
- VHF DSC Radio – both on board and handheld
- Emergency Position Indicating Radio Beacon (EPIRB) or Personal Location Beacon (PLB)
- InReach or Spot Satellite SOS devices

Contacting Coast Guard
- VHF Channel 16 – on DSC equipped radios press and hold the DISTRESS button
- Cell phone in WA and AK waters – 911
- Cell phone in B.C. waters - *16

Fire At Sea is one of the more serious emergencies. On land the primary response to fire is to move away. On board this is not always an option. Best preparation is to have adequate and appropriate fire extinguishing equipment, know how to use them, and have a plan for crew and guests. There are 6 types of extinguisher categorized by the extinguishing agent and the type of fire source. Both U.S. and Canada require varying types and number of fire extinguishers depending upon the boat size and equipment. It's best to carry more than the minimum required by regulation. Inspect extinguishers often. Some regulations require annual inspection. Rechargeable extinguishers should be recharged every 6 years and disposable extinguishers should be replaced at least every 10 to 12 years. Dry chemical extinguishers are inexpensive and popular, but very difficult to clean up when used. Clean-agent extinguishers are more expensive but as the name implies, they do not leave a mess when used.

Breakdowns. What to do when things get too quiet! The urgency and actions needed in case of a breakdown depend on sea conditions, wind, and weather. A cooling water pump failure once forced us to shutdown and address the problem. Luckily it happened at the head of Viner Sound in the Broughtons; no wind, no current, and no immediate risk of running aground. Fortune isn't always so good and you may be required to do one of the following:
- Anchor if you have no power and there is a risk of running aground – be ready to deploy the anchor if needed
- Reduce power and speed
- Ready any alternate or backup propulsion, such as Get-Home, sails, or single-engine in a multi-engine vessel - secure the non-operational engine, prop, & thru-hull
- Call for assistance; contact Coast Guard, towing service, or summon help from nearby vessels
- Use or exhibit signals to indicated distress and need of assistance if necessary.
- Research and isolate the problem

Flooding. Boating is all about water: adequate fresh water in the tank, not too much black water in the holding tank, and keeping sea water on the outside of the hull! When sea water is on the wrong side of the hull, it's important that you have the correct equipment, including an Emergency Repair Kit, and take corrective action.
- Locate the source of the leak; this may be difficult if there is oil, fuel, or debris clouding the accumulated water. Is it sea water? Look for clues as to the source.
- Stop or reduce the flooding using a Damage Repair Kit (see below)
- Remove accumulations of water using the boat's bilge pump(s), manual pumps, hand-held bailers. Carry a self-made "pump-in-a-bucket" consisting of a bilge pump wired with battery alligator clips and a length of discharge hose.
- Call for help – coast guard has portable pumps and nearby boats may have de-watering devices to assist
- Beaching – if sinking is inevitable, consider beaching the vessel on a soft muddy/sandy shallow beach area

Carry a Damage Repair Kit with tools and materials to temporarily stop or reduce flooding. Packaged kits are available on Amazon or make your own; it should include:
- Rubber, wooden, or Sta-Soft foam plugs of various sizes
- Pieces of wood and plywood
- Self-amalgamating tape & duct tape
- Hose clamps, Oakum, sealant, and caulk

Test bilge pumps at the beginning of each season to ensure that they are working; including discharging water overboard.

Running Aground. The best way to avoid running aground is to have reliable, current charts, know where you are at all times; and stop if unsure. If you do run aground, the following are steps to take:
- Assess whether you are taking on water
- Shutdown engine(s) to prevent fouling engine cooling systems with mud
- Contact Coast Guard to report your situation and request assistance
- Is tide level rising or falling; if rising it may be best to wait for higher water
- Discover which direction is deeper water
- If waiting through a tidal cycle, prepare the boat for heeling; close thru-hulls to prevent flooding as water rises.

MOB – Person Overboard. Be prepared when a crewmember falls in the water:
- Have a throwable floatation device – several types are available and may be coast guard required equipment, depending upon your boat size
- Have everyone on board wear a PFD when on deck, equipped with an attached MOB signaling device
- Alert all on board with "MAN OVERBOARD" announcement
- Mark the position on the chartplotter and/or note the Lat/Long position
- Maintain visual contact with the overboard person and turn toward them
- Use the throwable flotation and draw the in-water person to the boat
- Use a swim-ladder, sling, or lifting mechanism to bring the person back on board

Abandon Ship. The decision to abandon ship is very difficult. Once the decision is made:
- Wear all available waterproof clothing including gloves, hats, and life jacket
- Don survival suits if available
- Collect survival gear – hopefully a "ditch bag" is at the ready with necessary gear and survival basics
- Take all portable communications equipment: portable VHF, Satellite messenger, EPIRB, PLB, cell phones
- Note present Lat/Long position and issue a May Day call on VHF 16
- Launch and board a life raft or dinghy
- Remain clear of the sinking vessel

BOARDINGS

"Welcome Aboard" – may not be the first thing that comes to mind when someone in uniform steps aboard your vessel. However, if we are prepared, it's more likely that we will be ready to welcome these agents of safety and law enforcement when we are out cruising. There are a number of different agencies and agents that may board recreational vessels.

U.S. Agencies. On the U.S. side of the border, the Coast Guard (USCG) routinely boards vessels to check for compliance with required devices and safety equipment. If underway and approached by a USCG patrol vessel for boarding, the officer may want you to slow down, but continue underway. They will come alongside and board while underway; however, you may choose to come to a stop. An officer will board and conduct a standard safety inspection. Their inspection includes checking for proper vessel documentation, personal floatation devices, and vessel safety equipment. The inspection takes about 15 to 30 minutes and includes a 'results form' with any deficiencies noted on the signed form. Any deficiencies noted on the form must be addressed and acknowledged by the Coast Guard. If there are no deficiencies, you will receive the same signed form noting the successful inspection. Keep this form on the vessel as it serves to waive any subsequent inspection boarding within the next 12 months.

State police, county sheriff, city police, and port authorities have on-the-water patrol boats for safety, search and rescue, and law enforcement. Agents of these departments can and do board recreational vessels. Unlike the U.S. Coast Guard's once-a-year limit on vessel boarding, there is no limit for these other law enforcement agencies.

Retain the paperwork from a USCG boarding, it will save you from future boardings for one year.

Canada Agencies. On the Canadian side of the border, Canadian Coast Guard does not have maritime or law enforcement responsibilities and does not perform vessel inspections. Royal Canadian Mounted Police (RCMP) and city police have law enforcement responsibilities. RCMP does not routinely board vessels for marine safety inspections.

When cruising near the U.S. and Canada international border, you may be stopped and boarded by agents of the respective border patrol (U.S. Customs and Border Patrol, and Canadian Border Services Agency). They patrol the border crossings with their high-speed boats.

While fishing, crabbing, or prawning, agents from wildlife departments from Washington, Alaska, or British Columbia may board your vessel to check for compliance with seafood-collection rules and laws.

Preparation. While there are no guarantees, responsible cruisers can reduce their chances of boarding by keeping their boats clean, orderly, and in good condition; running the boat cautiously and competently, consistent with weather and sea conditions; doing nothing that would invite closer scrutiny. A current Coast Guard Auxiliary voluntary safety inspection sticker in the window might be a help. Consider doing your own inspection before the boating season to make sure you have all of your documentation, flares and approved life jackets or PFDs, placards and other items in order. For the complete list, you can search USCG Vessel Safety Checklist on the internet and find the same list used by the Coast Guard. Expect more checks by small boats. We watched armed USCG personnel in a mid-20-foot inflatable check the boats on moorings in Fossil Bay (Sucia Island) and board one of them.

Have all required boat documentation, licenses, and other paperwork ready in the event you are boarded. It is helpful to have a folder with the most current official documents. Keep a second folder for copies of original documents in the event you need to leave a copy with an official. Record each boarding event in your log, including the agent's name and authority. These agents help keep our cruising waters safe; thank them with a smile.

U.S. Coast Guard may want to board your vessel while remaining underway.

Extending our reach
Expanding our service

Alaska stores:
Anchorage
Cordova
Dillingham
Dutch Harbor
Homer
Kenai
Naknek
Sitka

Washington stores:
Bellingham
Seattle

LFS • **LFS MARINE SUPPLIES** • **Kachemak Gear Shed** A DIVISION OF LFS INC
LFS MARINE & OUTDOOR • **GO2MARINE**

800-426-8860 • info@lfsinc.com
www.Go2marine.com

U.S. HOMELAND SECURITY

Here are some do's and do-not's, drawn from material published by the U.S. Coast Guard and expanded upon by our own experiences.

Keep your distance from all military, cruise line or commercial shipping. For U.S. naval vessels, slow to minimum speed within 500 yards, and do not approach any U.S. naval vessel within 100 yards. Violation of the Naval Vessel Protection Zone is a felony offense. If you must pass within 100 yards of a U.S. naval vessel, you must contact the vessel or its Coast Guard escort vessel on VHF 16. The only exceptions to these requirements would be in a congested area, where there is no way to give this kind of room, or in a narrow channel, such as the mouth of the Snohomish River in Everett, which fronts on the Navy base there. In such cases, navigate slowly, predictably, and obey all instructions.

Observe and avoid all security zones. Also avoid commercial port operation areas, especially those that involve military, cruise line, or petroleum facilities. Observe and avoid other restricted areas near dams, power plants etc. Violators will face a quick, determined, and severe response. Translation: You risk being blown out of the water. The buoyed security zone protecting the Trident submarine base at Bangor, in Hood Canal, is a good example. The restricted area is patrolled by four high-speed small craft, at least two of them with impressive guns mounted on the decks. Although we give the security zone a wide berth as we go by, it is obvious that we are being watched. When we increase our speed from 8.5 knots to 16 knots one of the patrol craft will turn abruptly and run on a parallel course at our speed until we pass the far boundary. We thought about taking photos of the base with at least one of the patrol boats in view, but decided it would be prudent to motor along as predictably and innocently as possible.

Don't stop or anchor beneath bridges or in the channel. If you do, you can expect to be boarded by law enforcement officials.

Be alert for anything that looks peculiar or out of the ordinary. Report suspicious activities to local authorities, the Coast Guard, or port or marina security. Do not approach or challenge those acting in a suspicious manner. Suspicious behavior includes:

- Suspicious persons conducting unusual activities near bridges, refineries, or around high security areas on or near the water
- Individuals establishing roadside stands near marinas or other waterfront facilities
- Persons photographing or making diagrams of things, such as the underside of a bridge, the area around nuclear powerplants, and waterfront facilities near what might be high-risk vessels
- Unknown or suspicious persons loitering for long periods of time in waterfront areas
- Suspicious persons renting or attempting to procure or "borrow" watercraft
- Suspicious vendors attempting to sell or deliver merchandise or drop off packages in waterfront areas

Always secure and lock your boat when not on board. Do not leave your boat accessible to others. Always take the keys with you. When storing your boat, make sure it is secure and its engine is disabled. If the boat is on a trailer, make the trailer as immovable as possible.

Be Prepared for a Vessel Boarding. Expect to see U.S. Coast Guard surveillance and vessel boardings. The physical size and geographic complexity of Northwest waters make these waters difficult to patrol and quite "porous" for vessels doing illegal things. More "assets," as the military calls them, are being deployed here.

HARBOR PATROLS - WASHINGTON STATE

Emergency Contact:
Hail Coast Guard or Harbor Patrol on VHF Channel 16 or phone 911

Many counties and cities fund Marine Harbor Patrols, which work in conjunction with the U.S. Coast Guard, providing enforcement, search and rescue, and other services.

What Harbor Patrols Do:
- Provide marine law enforcement, rescue and assistance
- Investigate water-related accidents and collisions
- Ensure boater safety by removing debris and water hazards
- Perform boat safety inspections
- Provide marine fire response and suppression
- Manage marine special events, with large gatherings
- Participate in Homeland Security activities
- Provide service for disabled boats, boating accidents, and tows

Patrols and telephone numbers for non-emergency contact:
  Everett Police Marine Unit
    425-257-8400 Office
    425-407-3999 non-emergencies
  Gig Harbor Marine Unit
    253-851-8136 City
    253-853-2422 Chief of Police
  Jefferson County Marine Patrol
    360-385-9390 or 3831 Sheriff's Office
  Kitsap County Marine Unit
    360-337-7054 Sheriff's Office
  Mason County Marine Services
    360-427-9670x313 Sheriff's Office;
    360-426-4441 dispatch
  Mercer Island Marine Patrol
    206-275-7953 Office
  Olympia Police Harbor Patrol
    360-528-8049 Office
  San Juan County Marine Patrol
    360-378-4151 Sheriff's Office
  Seattle Harbor Patrol
    206-684-4071 General Inquiries
  Skagit County Sheriff
    360-416-1911 Business Office
  Tacoma Marine Services/Pierce Co.
    253-798-7530 Sheriff's Office
  Thurston County Sheriff
    360-786-5500 Office

Dream Itineraries

YOUR DREAM ITINERARY

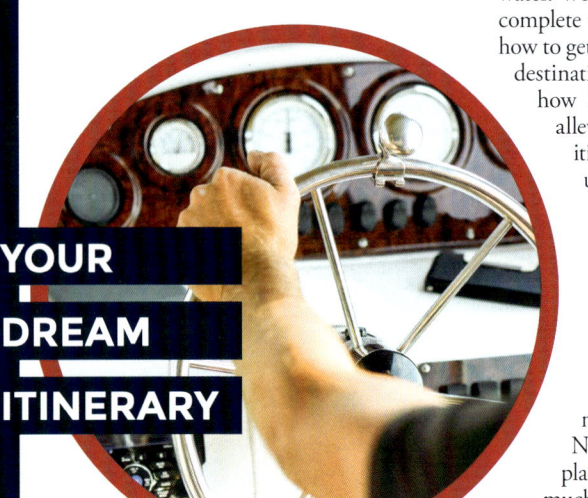

Most of us who began our boating life style started with the dream of being out on the water. We soon realized that the dream wasn't complete without knowing where to go and how to get there. Planning out a route to those destinations of interest, and understanding how long it takes to get there, helps alleviate pre-departure unknowns. An itinerary with arrival dates is most useful for making reservations at marinas, especially during the peak cruising season. Of course, you will need to allow extra time in case of delays due to weather.

Waggoner is often asked by first-time boaters, boaters new to the area, and boaters who have not grown up cruising the Pacific Northwest, our recommendations of places to go. Creating an itinerary has much to do with your particular interests: are you wanting to anchor out most of the time? See wildlife? Fish, catch crab, or hike trails? Or perhaps you enjoy fine dining and breweries, or metropolitan city life. Maybe you are seeking spectacular remote scenery that few others have the opportunity to visit. Perhaps you are a history buff that enjoys discovering ruins left behind from a previous era, or you are looking to experience a different culture and lifestyle. Other boaters may be looking for quality time with their family, including swimming, fishing, and playing at those beautiful parks and beaches.

No matter what, most of us want a unique experience that fits our dreams and expectations. Putting together an itinerary based on your interests has untold possibilities. The Waggoner Guide is a helpful tool for selecting a cruising area and your destinations of interest.

The Waggoner Theme this year is "Dream Itineraries." Included in this year's Waggoner Cruising Guide are a dozen sample itineraries to help you get the most from your cruising season. Most of the itineraries are written by our Field Correspondents, who are experienced Northwest boaters that help us put together the Waggoner with the latest updates and discoveries found in our local cruising grounds. You will find all of these itineraries in the following pages. What a unique opportunity we have to enjoy some of the best cruising grounds in the world.

Gulf Islands Highlights

This itinerary is for those who like to shop and walk well-groomed trails in a park-like setting. The cruise starts and ends in Anacortes. The longest day cruise is 38 nm; shortest is 7 nm. It's a perfect one week cruise for family or guests arriving from out of town.

Barkley Sound

This itinerary is an opportunity to experience the open waters of the Pacific. It takes two long days of cruising getting to Barkley Sound but then very short distances exploring the Broken Group Islands, small coves and inlets, and the two towns of Bamfield and Ucluelet in Barkley Sound.

GULF ISLANDS HIGHLIGHTS

We did this cruise with some friends from California, and they loved it. It's not for folks looking for a wilderness cruising experience. This is for those who like to shop and walk well-groomed trails in a park-like setting. The cruise starts and ends in Anacortes, which we have found to be the best place to pick up guests arriving from out of town. The longest day cruise is 38 nm; shortest is 7 nm. It's a perfect one week cruise for family or guests arriving from out of town, even those arriving by plane at SeaTac.

Day 1 Guests arrive in Anacortes and come aboard.
Things To Do
- Boat orientation (safety info, head instructions, ...)
- Last minute provisioning
- Dinner in town

Day 2 (38 nm to Victoria) Clear Customs, and moor at the Greater Victoria Harbour Authority, Causeway Floats in front of the Empress Hotel.
Things To Do
- Royal British Columbia Museum
- B.C. Maritime Museum.
- Afternoon Tea at the Empress Hotel
- B.C. Parliament Building
- Inner Harbour Street Performers
- Craigdarroch Castle
- Victoria Chinatown
- Victoria Bug Zoo
- Thunderbird Park
- Emily Carr House

Empress Hotel

Day 3. (25 nm to Sidney) Moor at Port Sidney Marina.
Things To Do
- Walk main street Beacon Ave. with interesting shops, art galleries, bakeries, and bookstores
- Stroll scenic waterfront promenade
- Visit Sidney Historical Museum
- Learn about the Salish Sea at Shaw Ocean Discovery Center
- Lunch, dinner, or drinks in one of many nearby restaurants

Day 4 (14 nm to Tod Inlet) Anchor or tie to one of Butchart Garden's four mooring buoys
Things To Do
- Dinghy ride to the Butchart Gardens' dock and feast upon the beautiful formal gardens
- Dinner in Butchart Gardens or Blues Bayou Cafe
- Enjoy Butchart Gardens' night time fireworks display

Day 5 (33 nm to Montague Harbour via Sansum Narrows) Anchor, or tie to a marine park buoy, or moor at Montague Marina
Things To Do
- Dinghy ride or kayak to Montague Harbour Marine Park and walk the easy trail around Gray Peninsula.
- Take the Hummingbird Pub bus to the Hummingbird Pub for dinner.

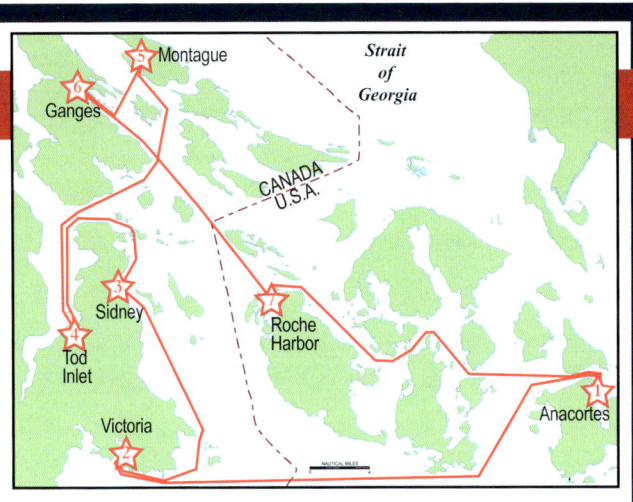

Day 6 (7 nm to Ganges). Since this is such a short cruise, this is a good time to have what we call "special" breakfast, or brunch, while at anchor in Montague Harbour before departure. We like waffles with fresh berries and whipped cream, sausage or bacon, and maybe Mimosas or Tequila Sunrises. At Ganges moor at first-come Kanaka public dock, or Ganges Marina, or Salt Spring Marina (reservations are an option).
Things To Do
- Join a guided tour of Art Gallery Studios
- Watch cheese making at Salt Spring Island Cheese Co.
- Sample locally produced wines
- Hastings House
- Get freshly baked goods at Embe Bakery & Barb's Buns
- Sample cool drinks at Salt Spring Wild Cider House.
- Enjoy food and entertainment at Tree House Café

Day 7 (25 nm to Roche Harbor) Clear US Customs and moor at Roche Harbor Marina or anchor in the bay.
Things To Do
- Swim in the pool
- Lunch, dinner, or cocktails at one of the restaurants
- Walk to the Afterglow Vista Mausoleum
- Dinghy ride to Westcott Bay Shellfish Company for fresh oysters
- Hike the trails around the quarries
- Visit the historic Hotel de Haro
- Visit the San Juan Islands Sculpture Park

Day 8 (30 nm to Anacortes) Guests depart.

[Itinerary By: Jim Norris]

Sidney Promenade

COMPENDIUM

2023 WAGGONER CRUISING GUIDE

SAN JUAN ISLANDS MARINAS & RESORTS

Those who appreciate a variety of amenities and activities at a single destination will surely love this itinerary. These resorts have swimming pools, cafes, and gift shops; there's something for the whole family to enjoy. Rent bicycles on Lopez and visit the country village, or enjoy an ice cream cone at Deer Harbor Marina. History buffs will not want to miss a tour of the historic Moran Mansion at Rosario, or the historic Inn, Mausoleum, and Lime Kilns at Roche Harbor. Discover the wonderful outdoor and indoor swimming pools, restaurants, hiking trails, and parks. Shoppers will love the boutiques at Friday Harbor and the many cafes and pubs. There is lots to see and do at these island marinas and resorts; be sure to make reservations at these popular destinations.

Day 1 (18 nm from Anacortes to Fisherman Bay, Lopez Island; 24 nm starting from Bellingham) Check the tide preditions to time your arrival at Fisherman Bay at mid- to high- tide slack ideally; the entrance channel is shallow. In the bay, Islands Marine Center or Lopez Islander Resort has moorage. Islander Resort has a restaurant, pool, and bike rentals. The delightful village of Lopez is a short walk or dinghy ride from the bay and has eateries, groceries, gift shops, and much more.

Things To Do
- Rent a bike and ride to the village for ice cream
- Shop the Saturday market 10 am to 2 pm May - Sept.

Day 2 (5 nm Fisherman Bay to Friday Harbor). The small full-service town of Friday Harbor has nearly everything you might want. Dining, museums, distilleries, breweries, scooter & ATV rentals, and upland tours and excursions. Whale watching tours and sport fishing charters.

Things To Do
- Visit the Whale Museum
- Shop the Palindaba Lavender store in town and visit the farm
- Visit the San Juan Historical museum
- San Juan Islands Museum of Art
- Enjoy an ice cream cone while watching the ferry come & go

Day 3 (11 nm Friday Harbor to Roche Harbor). Roche Harbor Resort is a first-class, full-service resort with dining options, swimming pool, historic lime kilns, trails, store, accommodations, airport, and upland excursions. This good sized marina has dedicated guest moorage slips that are full in prime summer months (make a reservation) but has open space in shoulder and off-season.

Things To Do
- Take the easy 1.0 mi walk to the McMillin mausoleum
- Walk the sculpture park and nearby off-leash dog park
- Dinghy to the nearby Westcott Bay Shellfish for fresh seafood
- Don't miss the "Colors Ceremony" at sunset May - September

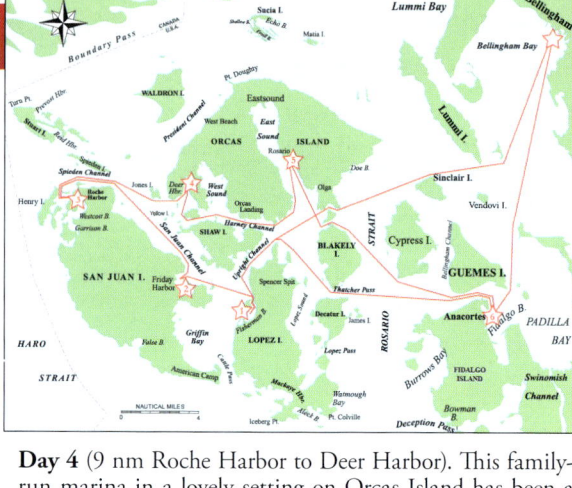

Day 4 (9 nm Roche Harbor to Deer Harbor). This family-run marina in a lovely setting on Orcas Island has been a notable destination for many decades. Moorage is popular, so make a reservation. There is a swimming pool, dining, hiking.

Things To Do
- Dinghy or paddle 2.1 nm to Yellow Island Nature Conservancy
- Dinghy or padddle 2 nm to Jones Island Marine Park
- Walk 1/2 mile to dine at Matthew's Smokehouse restaurant

Day 5 (11 nm Deer Harbor to Rosario Resort). The resort was formerly the Moran Mansion, built in 1906-1909. The resort offices, restaurant, gift shop, spa, and accommodations are housed in the mansion building. Some of the historic rooms and large pipe organ are open for viewing. The grounds are expansive and easy to walk and include a swimming pool. The small marina was recently rebuilt; reserve your slip or mooring buoy.

Things To Do
- Hike one of many trails in neighboring Moran State Park
- Enjoy a fine dining meal
- Hear and feel the music from the Organ's 1,972 pipes
- Turn Point Lighthouse from County dock 3.0 mi 250 ft

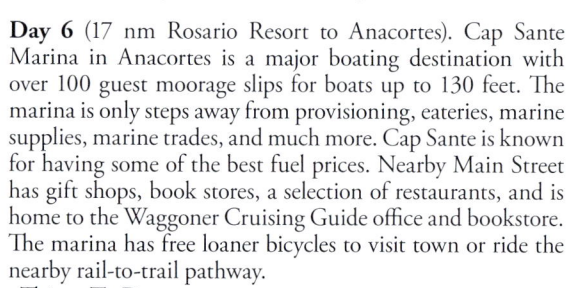

Day 6 (17 nm Rosario Resort to Anacortes). Cap Sante Marina in Anacortes is a major boating destination with over 100 guest moorage slips for boats up to 130 feet. The marina is only steps away from provisioning, eateries, marine supplies, marine trades, and much more. Cap Sante is known for having some of the best fuel prices. Nearby Main Street has gift shops, book stores, a selection of restaurants, and is home to the Waggoner Cruising Guide office and bookstore. The marina has free loaner bicycles to visit town or ride the nearby rail-to-trail pathway.

Things To Do
- Visit the Waggoner Cruising Guide office and bookstore
- Hike the 3/4 mile up to the Cap Sante Park viewpoint
- Enjoy fine dining overlooking the marina at Anthony's

Day 7 (15 nm Anacortes to Bellingham). Make the short trip to Bellingham for those who started there.

[Itinerary By: Leonard Landon]

SAN JUAN ISLANDS HIKING

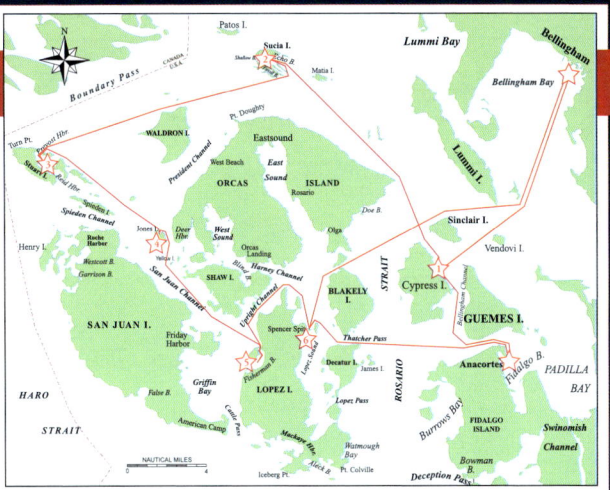

Overview. This itinerary is for people who like to hike. There is very little cruising time (the longest day is 19 nm) leaving maximum time for some serious hiking and eating. Consider a small flotilla (2-3 boats) and rotating special dinners between boats. We show an eight day itinerary starting and ending in Anacortes, but it can be shortened as desired. For detailed information about the trails mentioned here see the Washington Trails Association (www.wta.org). or AllTrails (www.alltrails.com).

Day 1 (12 nm Anacortes to Cypress Island via Vendovi Island). Vendovi Island is part of the San Juan Preservation Trust (www.sjpt.org). There is a 70-foot dock protected by a breakwater available for moorage on a first-come, first-served basis (time limit 3 hrs; no overnight mooring). The island is open for visitation May 1 - September 30 from 10 am- 6 pm. There are 3 miles of easy hiking trails. After exploring Vendovi Island cruise to Pelican Beach on Cypress Island (4 nm) and anchor or take a mooring buoy. The premier hike on Cypress Island is the Eagle Cliff Trail (2.4 miles round trip with a 730 ft elevation gain). This trail is closed from Feb 1 to Jul 15 to protect wildlife. For a complete review of this hike see https://waggonerguide.com/top-of-the-world-eagle-cliff. You can spend the night at Pelican Beach or continue south 1 nm to Eagle Harbor where you can take a mooring buoy or anchor.

Trails
- Eagle Cliff - 2.4 miles 730 ft elevation gain
- Vendovi Island - 3 miles of easy trails

Day 2 (10 nm Cypress Island to Rosario Resort). At Rosario Resort get a slip or take a mooring ball. There are over 30 miles of hiking trails in nearby Moran State Park. From the marina it is a 0.4 mile steep hike through the resort condos and a trail to reach the western end of the lagoon at Cascade Lake.

Trails
- Lagoon Loop - 0.7 mi
- Around Cascade Lake - 3.5 mi
- Cascade Creek to Cascade - Falls 3.1 mi RT

Day 3 (19 nm Rosario Resort to Sucia Island). Sucia Island trails are accessible from any of the anchorages. The three most popular trails are the Ewing Cove Trail, Lawson Bluff Trail, and the Sucia Island Loop Trail.

Trails
- Ewing Cove - 2.4 mi RT 150 ft elevation gain
- Lawson Bluff - 2.5 mi 167 ft elevation gain
- Sucia Loop Trail - 4.5 mi 456 ft elevation gain

Day 4 (Sucia Island and Matia Island). Spend a second day anchored at Sucia to hike more trails and to take the skiff over to Matia and hike the loop trail. Matia Island is part of the San Juan Islands Natural Wildlife Refuge (no dogs allowed on the trail).

Trails
- Matia Loop Trail - 1.6 mi 236 ft elevation gain

Day 5 (16 nm Sucia Island to Stuart Island). Anchor, tie to the dock, or take a mooring buoy in Reid or Prevost Harbors. Hike the loop trails north and south of the docks or hike the trail and roads to the Turn Point lighthouse from the State Park docks. If you are anchored or moored in Prevost Harbor, you can shorten the hike by taking the dinghy to the County public dock.

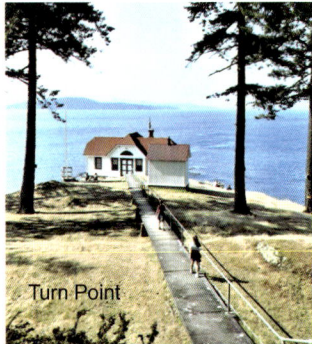

Trails
- Loop trail south of the marine park docks - about 1 mi
- Loop trail north of the marine park docks - about 1 mi
- Turn Point Lighthouse from park docks - 6.0 mi RT 280 ft
- Turn Point Lighthouse from County dock - 3.0 mi RT 250 ft

Day 6 (10 nm Stuart Island to Garrison Bay/Westcott Bay). Anchor in Garrison Bay or Westcott Bay and take the dinghy to the dock at English Camp in Garrison Bay. Hike to Young Hill and then around Bell Point. For a lunch break take the trail to Westcott Bay Shellfish for fresh oysters and more.

Trails
- Young Hill - 2.2 mi RT 587 ft
- Bell Point - 1.2 mi level
- Westcott Bay Shellfish - 1.0 mi RT level

Day 7 (10 nm Garrison Bay to Griffin Bay/American Camp). There is good anchorage along the south shore of Griffin Bay, but avoid the broad 2 fm shelf which is covered with eelgrass. There are several beach access points to the extensive trail system (see Waggoner map or park maps). The trails include ocean bluffs, beach tidepools, flowery meadows, pretty forests, a lighthouse, and wildlife sightings.

Trails
- Beach hikes and American Camp Trails

Day 8 (16 nm to Anacortes). Cruise back to Anacortes.

[Itinerary By: Jim Norris]

SAN JUAN ISLANDS
MARINE PARKS & ANCHORAGES

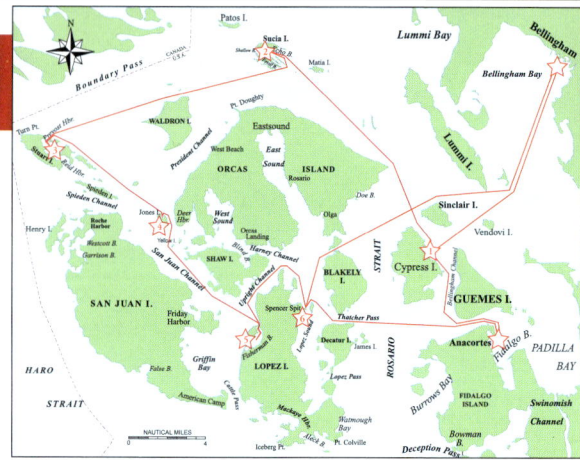

This 7-day itinerary is for those who love the adventure of anchoring out and hiking forest trails, sandy beaches, and country roads. You will likely see eagles, deer, and other wildlife. Sucia Island and Spencer Spit offer beach explorations, while Stuart Island and Fisherman Bay offer a taste of country island living. Discover the spectacular views atop Cypress Island and the expansive views from Turn Point Lighthouse on Stuart, or discover the old apple orchard and rope swing on Jones Island. Visit the unique shops, cafes, and bakery in the charming village of Fisherman Bay. The towns of Anacortes and Bellingham serve as beginning and ending points at nice marinas, with ample provisioning and summer events.

Day 1 (8 nm from Anacortes to Cypress Island; 14 nm starting from Bellingham) Nearly all of Cypress Island is public Dept. of Natural Resources land with 26 miles of hiking trails. Shoreside camping and exploring by kayak or dinghy. Mooring buoys and anchoring are available at 3 locations: Eagle Harbor, Cypress Head, and Pelican Beach.

Things To Do
- Hike the trail to Eagle Cliff (Closed Febrary 1 - July 15
- Hike the trail to the Old Airfield.
- Watch for wildlife

Day 2 (15 nm Cypress Island to Sucia Island). This boaters paradise is a Washington State Marine Park accessible only by boat. There are moorage docks, mooring buoys and anchorages in bays and coves around the island. The island has an excellent trail system, campsites, group campsites and restrooms. Although it is a popular destination, it can accommodate a large number of boats and boaters.

Things To Do
- Discover the history of the island including its US Prohibition role
- Hike the many trails
- Enjoy sunsets by a campfire
- Collect some crabs
- Explore area where stone was quarried for Seattle's street curbs

Fossil Bay, Sucia Island

Day 3 (17 nm Sucia Island to Stuart Island). Stuart Island has a small population of year-round and seasonal residents. There are no services or amenities on the island and it is not served by ferry. Stuart Island Marine Park faces to Prevost Harbor on the north and Reid Harbor on the south. There is a moorage dock, mooring buoys, and anchorage at both harbors. Come ashore to the park from either harbor where there are trails.

Things To Do
- Hike the trails and no-traffic dirt roads
- Visit the one-room schoolhouse
- Shop at the honor-system Treasure Chests in 2 locations
- Check out the 260 degree views of Haro Strait and Boundary Pass from Turn Point Lighthouse Park

Reid Harbor, Stuart Island

Day 4 (8 nm Stuart Island to Jones Island). All of Jones Island is a State Marine Park. The north bay has a mooring dock, mooring buoys and room for a few boats to anchor. Excellent hiking trails traverse the island with views, deer, and nature. South end has 3 mooring buoys that are somewhat exposed.

Things To Do
- Hike the center island trail to the homestead orchard
- Watch the deer feeding on apples from the orchard trees
- Enjoy the company of fellow boaters at the picnic tables

Day 5 (9 nm Jones Island to Fisherman Bay). Check the tide level and current predictions when entering Fisherman Bay. There is plenty of anchoring room in the well protected, shallow bay - don't anchor in the floatplane operations area. Explore the bay by dinghy or kayak. Beach land on the sandy beach at the entrance to the bay. Across the entrance channel from the sandy beach spit, there is a beach landing and stairway into the village of Lopez.

Things To Do
- Visit the stores, shops, and eateries in Lopez village
- Enjoy a sunset dinner on the boat or at the Lopez Islander Resort restaurant overlooking the bay.
- Rent bikes at the Lopez Ilander Resort and ride the lightly trafficed island roads.
- Checkout the seasonal Saturday Market in the village

Day 6 (9 nm Fisherman Bay to James Island). James Island is a State Marine Park with side tie moorage at a dock on the west side and mooring buoys on the east side. Its close proximity to Anacortes makes it a popular stop and an early arrival will help ensure space that you find space at the dock or on a mooring buoy. There are campsites at two locations on the island along with pit toilets. No water or power.

Things To Do
- Hike the trails that traverse the south half of the island, the north half of the island is a nature preserve area
- Circumnavigate the island by dinghy or kayak at low tide and check out the inter-tidal life on the rocky shores.
- Enjoy a summer evening sunset at one of the islands campsites. Take some marshmallows.

James Island

Day 7 (15 nm James Island to Anacortes). Pick your island departure time for the best current conditions crossing Rosario Strait and transiting Guemes Channel.

[Itinerary By: Leonard Landon]

Discover Hood Canal

Beginning in Seattle, this itinerary takes you to Port Ludlow at the entrance to Hood Canal and then south to the "bottom" of Hood Canal at fabulous Alderbrook Resort, with additional stops at Port Gamble, Pleasant Harbor, Dabob Bay, and Squamish Harbor. The approximate round trip distance is 166nm. The longest leg is 32nm.

Day 1 Seattle To Port Ludlow Marina (25nm). Make reservations online for moorage, or anchor off the docks, or at the inner harbor behind the two islets.
  Things To Do
  • Dine at the waterfront Port Ludlow Resort
  • Rent e-bikes from the resort to explore the area
  • Hike the many interesting trails
  • Take the shuttle to play the nearby Port Ludlow Golf Course

Day 2 Port Ludlow To Port Gamble Anchorage (8nm). Ample anchorage in 18-30 feet. Access to the village is via dinghy or kayak at a gravel beach below the General Store.
  Things To Do
  • Explore this historic charming town, with boutiques and cafes
  • Visit the Museum, covering company mill town history
  • Visit the historic General Store and special shell collection

Day 3 Port Gamble To Pleasant Harbor Marina (21nm). Check tide levels before transiting the narrow entrance (8 ft. at zero tide). Call or make reservations online, or anchor in the harbor (18-42 foot depths). A Marine State Park dock is also in the harbor.
  Things To Do
  • Have a cocktail on the rooftop patio
  • Eat at the pub
  • Relax in the heated pool or hot tub
  • Enjoy the local hikes (shuttle bus service)

Days 4 and 5 Pleasant Harbor To Alderbrook Resort (23nm). Call for reservations for 2 nights at the docks. Temporary free moorage while dining at the resort's restaurant.
  Things To Do
  • Fine dining in the resort restaurant
  • Rent a kayak or SUP
  • Hike an assortment of scenic nature trails
  • Play the PGA-class Alderbrook Golf Club
  • Take a sauna, hot tub soak, or a swim in the saltwater pool
  • Indulge yourself with a massage, body wrap, or facial (book well in advance)

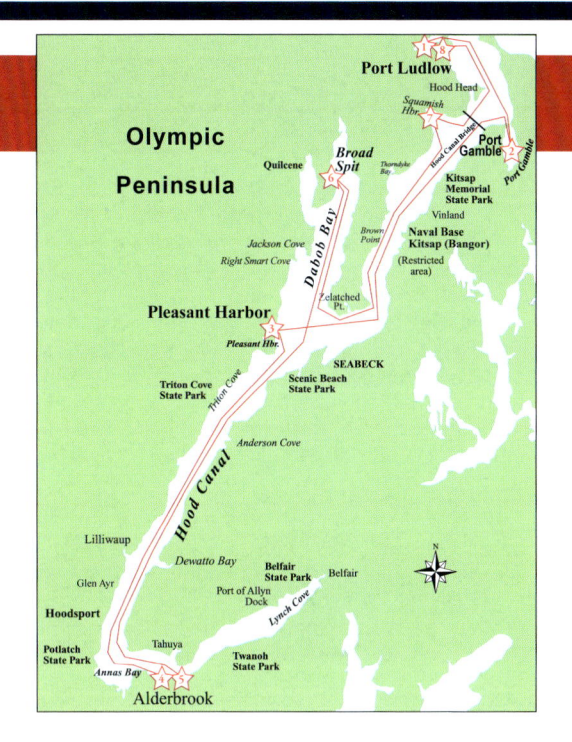

Day 6 Alderbrook To Broad Spit Anchorage, Dabob Bay (32nm). Located on the east side of Bolton Peninsula in Dabob Bay. Depending on the wind direction, you can anchor on either side of the spit, with easy access to shore.
  Things To Do
  • Dinghy or kayak to shore to enjoy some hikes

Day 7 Broad Spit Anchorage To Squamish Harbor Anchorage (22nm). Picturesque harbor located just south and west of Hood Canal Bridge with good anchoring depths and room for several boats. Avoid the charted reef in the harbor.
  • Explore the area by dinghy or kayak
  • Enjoy the picturesque country setting

Day 8 Squamish Harbor To Port Ludlow (10nm). A scenic trip back to Port Ludlow for fuel and pumpout facilities.

Anchor in the large bay or in the very protected back bay behind "the twins"
  Things To Do
  • Purchase convenience items at the marina store

Day 9 Return To Seattle (25nm)

[Itinerary By: Dale Blackburn]

Sailing Port Townsend to Barkley Sound

We wanted to explore part of Vancouver Island's West Coast but not circumnavigate the island. It's an opportunity to experience the open waters of the Pacific. We did this trip in mid-August to early September in our sailboat. As it turned out, there was very little wind for opportunities to sail, but instead calm waters, lots of warm sunny days, and wonderful empty anchorages. It takes two long days of cruising getting to Barkley Sound but then very short distances exploring the Broken Group Islands, small coves and inlets, and the two towns of Bamfield and Ucluelet in Barkley Sound.

Pre-trip Planning
- Reserve slip at Victoria Causeway Marina
- Make marina reservations in Port Renfrew, Bamfield, and Ucluelet if not planning to anchor, or if you will need to charge batteries on shore power.
- Download and configure CBP ROAM app

Day 1 Port Townsend Boat Haven. A great place to shop for last minute non-perishable provisions and top up fuel tanks before leaving US.
Things To Do
- Explore the town and enjoy lunch or dinner at one of the many eateries.

Day 2 To Victoria (35.2 nm). Clear Customs by phone at Raymur Point CBSA Boat Dock. Shop for perishable items (Red Barn Market, Thrifty Foods, and others)
Things To Do
- Take public bus (45 min ride) to Butchart Gardens in AM, reserve ahead for afternoon tea on deck or in the Dining Room
- Kayak or dinghy explore Gorge Waterway in Victoria Hrbr
- Walk natural and manicured trails in Beacon Hill Park to enjoy flowers and Juan de Fuca Straits views
- Fish & Chips at Red Fish Blue Fish on the waterfront; enjoy outdoor concerts, and market vendors

Day 3 To Port San Juan/Port Renfrew (52.3 nm). Moor at Pacific Gateway Marina or anchor outside the marina. Limited grocery supplies available from the General Store, half-mile to the east.
Things To Do
- Dinner at Bridgemans West Coast Eatery at marina or walk half mile to Port Renfrew Pub
- Ice Cream at Miss May's along the road to Port Renfrew

Day 4 To Bamfield (42.6 nm). Moor at East or West town docks or anchor in one of the inlets
Things To Do
- Dinghy to west side to walk the boardwalk to store/post office
- From the north end of the boardwalk, take a dirt road/trail to lovely Brady's Beach (about 30 mins) with views of the entrance to Barkley Sound and the Pacific.
- Make advance reservation for Kixiin Tour to former First Nation village site (bus transportation to tour site is provided)

Note: Over the next 5 days access to shore power is limited. Depending on your boat's power needs, you may need to return to Bamfield or continue directly to Ucluelet to charge batteries.

Day 5 To Port Alberni Yacht Club, Fleming Island (4.4 nm). Avoid the charted rocks when entering and exiting Robbers Passage. Guest moorage at the PAYC docks; power for yacht club members only.
Things to Do
- Hike the short YC trail on Fleming Island
- Take a warm dockside shower
- Explore Robbers Passage by kayak or dinghy

Day 6 To Effingham Bay (9.5 nm). Anchor in the bay.
Things to Do
- Explore the bay by kayak or dinghy
- Hike trail to site of former native village on island's east side. Old floats at the end of the inlet mark the trailhead. Trail requires some clambering over tree roots (15 minutes) to a beautiful rock/sand beach.
- Reportedly, there are wolves on the island. We made lots of noise and carried bear spray.

Day 7 To Turtle Bay (4 nm). Anchor in the bay north of Turtle Island.
Things to Do
- Relax and enjoy the solitude
- Explore the area by kayak or dinghy

Day 8 To Nettle Island (3.7 nm). Anchor in the bay northwest of the park ranger float
Things to Do
- Relax and enjoy the solitude
- Explore the area by kayak or dinghy

Day 9 To Pipestem Inlet (8.1 nm). Several anchorages are possible. We enjoy the small inlet between Bazett Is. and Vancouver Is. with stern tie (49.1.175'N 125.17.728'W) in 45-foot water depths.
Things to Do
- Kayak or dinghy up Lucky Creek on high tide to view waterfall (15 minutes). Scramble up the rocks for a spectacular view. Depart before the low tide leaves you stranded.
- Watch for bears foraging along the shore late day or early morning at low tides

Day 10 To Ucluelet Small Craft Harbor (13.8 nm). You may need to charge your batteries, refuel, and reprovision.
Things to Do
- Enjoy taste testing at Ucluelet Brewery
- Great coffee shops, bakeries, and restaurants
- Visit Pioneer Boat Works for any needed marine items
- Visit Manke Kayak museum and view community boatbuilding
- Hike Wild Pacific Trail to Amphritite Lighthouse

Day 11 & 12 Return to Port Townsend via Port Renfrew, Victoria, or extend into the Gulf or San Juan Islands.

[Itinerary By: Steve & Toni Jefferies]

SOUTH PUGET SOUND

Our local cruising ground includes wonderful locations in the South Puget Sound. We appreciate this area for many reasons: calmer sea conditions, a variety of great places to check out, beautiful scenery, and lots of wildlife. Plus…everyone else seems to go north! The destinations listed in this itinerary are just a few of our favorites; add a few if you want to extend your trip. Total cruising distance is approximately 85nm.

Day 1. Gig Harbor

Just north of The Narrows, this a lovely and logical spot to begin this tour. The location ticks all of our boxes: public dock/marina/anchoring options; restaurants and shops, small grocery markets, beautiful scenery, and great walking. One of our favorite things to do here is to grab sandwiches at the Harbor General Store and eat them with beers at 7 Seas Brewing.

Day 2. Penrose Point State Park (13nm from Gig Harbor)

Heading south under The Narrows bridges (check current!) and then around Fox Island through Hale Passage, you'll find this park located in Mayo Cove, in Carr Inlet. Lots of history here, and a fun place to visit. Boats can tie to a park mooring buoy or find a spot at the dock. We like to enjoy the 2.5 miles of hiking trails and the views of Mt. Rainier. This cove is also home to the Lakebay Marina and Resort.

Day 3. Jarrell Cove State Park (20nm from Penrose)

Continuing south from Mayo cove and through Pitt Passage (can be tricky!) you'll pass Filucy Bay and the Longbranch Improvement Club marina. (An additional destination if adding to this itinerary.) Continue through Drayton Passage and around Devil's Head (southern tip of the Key Peninsula) then head north into Case Inlet. Round the tip of Harstine Island, into Pickering Passage to find Jarrell Cove, a 67-acre marine camping park on the north end of the island. This secluded and picturesque little bay is perfect for some peace and quiet. Mooring buoys and dock space for boats, plus good anchorage. We like to paddle our kayaks and watch the wildlife. Jarrell's Cove Marina is also an option, located just across the cove from the park. Is it Harstine or Hartstene? You decide.

Day 4. Swantown Marina, Olympia (15nm from Jarrell)

For a little more action, we like to visit this marina (seventh largest in the state) to access the city of Olympia and its extraordinary year-round farmers market. Continue cruising south through Pickering Passage (31 ft. fixed bridge) along the west side of Squaxin Island and into Budd Inlet. This area is very pretty, reminding us of island cruising further north. If you have the time and inclination, stop at Hope Island Marine State Park, a 132-acre, watercraft-access only little gem, for a hike. (Dogs are not allowed.) Swantown Marina is on the west side of the port peninsula, with access to Percival Landing (another guest moorage option), the market, and all Olympia has to offer. We like to walk to Capital Lake and area parks.

For an additional stop, add Boston Harbor on your way in or out of Olympia.

5 Day. Oro Bay, Anderson Island (17nm from Swantown)

This is by far one of our favorite "nothin' to do but chill on the boat" anchorages! After heading north from Olympia through Dana Passage, and around into Nisqually Reach, you'll find Oro Bay at the southeast end of Anderson Island. What a spot! Quiet, calm, teaming with wildlife…and did I mention quiet? There are a few things going on here, but really…we like to hang out and enjoy the tranquility. The bay is home to a small craft marina and a couple of yacht club docks. Unless you have reciprocal privileges, the only way to get on shore is via the beach at Jacob's Point Park to take advantage of a 2.5-mile loop trail. One of our favorite things to do in Oro Bay is watch the derelict (and kinda spooky) ferry rise and fall with the tide.

Day 6. Tacoma (20nm from Oro Bay)

A great place to end this trip is back north through The Narrows and into Commencement Bay and the Foss Waterway. There are several moorage options and people we know usually stay at Dock Street Marina, located at the south end of the waterway. This area has restaurants, a wonderful waterfront walking path, and access up to Pacific Avenue and more of what Tacoma offers.

[Itinerary By: Janine & Nick Mott]

2023 WAGGONER CRUISING GUIDE

SOUTH SOUND
PETER PUGET HISTORY

On May 20, 1792 Captain George Vancouver and the HMS Discovery were anchored near Blake Island. Early that morning Captain Vancouver dispatched Lt. Peter Puget and a crew of 22 in two open launches to explore the waters to the south. Over the next week Lt Puget sailed and rowed throughout the many inlets of what we now call south Puget Sound. This itinerary follows their route, but does not overnight at all the same locations as Lt. Puget. As you cruise this route you can imagine the pristine shoreline that Lt.Puget and his crew enjoyed. To learn more about Lt. Puget's exploration check out the Lt. Peter Puget Memorial Project (pugetmemorial.blogspot.com). We show this loop itinerary starting and ending from Shilshole Marina.

Day 1 (23 nm) Cruise from Shilshole Marina to Gig Harbor. Lt. Puget started from Blake Island and stopped for breakfast at Olalla on the west side of Colvos Passage. He did not enter Gig Harbor, but this is a convenient stop for our itinerary and you can take advantage of all that Gig Harbor has to offer.

Jerisich Park, Gig Harbor

Day 2 (28 nm) Cruise from Gig Harbor to Penrose Point State Park with side trips into Wollochett Bay and to the head of Carr Inlet. After rowing through the Tacoma narrows, Lt. Puget stopped at Point Fosdick to wait for the tide change. He then explored Wollochett Bay and went north through Hale Pass. Be aware that the fixed bridge over Hale Pass has a vertical clearance of 31 ft and taller vessels will have to go around Fox Island. Lt. Puget proceeded to the head of Carr Inlet with stops near Arletta and Cutts Island and camped in Pitt Passage.

Day 3 (15 nm) Cruise from Penrose Point State Park to Oro Bay. Lt. Puget proceeded southwest through Balch Passage to Ketron Island and then a storm forced him to camp at Oro Bay. You can anchor in Oro Bay and hike the trails around Jacobs Point Park. Along the trail there is a plaque commemorating Lt. Puget's campsite.

Oro Bay, Anderson Island

Day 4 (24 nm) Cruise from Oro Bay to Jarrell Cove State Park with a side trip to the head of Case Inlet. From Oro Bay Lt. Puget went south to the Nisqually Delta and then north up Case Inlet, camping on Herron Island. You can proceed to the head of Case Inlet and maybe make a lunch stop at Grapeview before heading to Jarrell Cove State Park for the night.

Jarrell Cove Marine Park

Day 5 (24 nm) Cruise from Jarrell Cove State Park to Olympia with side trips up Totten and Eld Inlets. Lt. Puget camped in Pickering Passage and then continued south to explore Totten and Eld Inlets. If you arrive at Little Skookum Inlet (in Totten Inlet) at high tide, you can anchor and take the dinghy up the inlet. After exploring all of Eld Inlet Lt. Puget camped at Hunter Point. You can proceed up Budd Inlet to Olympia, or anchor or take a mooring buoy at Hope Island State Park and explore this beautiful park.

Day 6 (10 nm) Cruise from Olympia to Henderson Inlet. Lt. Puget did not visit Henderson Inlet, but you should. Anchor off Woodard Bay Wildlife Refuge and take the kayak or dinghy up the creeks at high tide.

Woodard Creek, Henderson Inlet

Day 7 (35 nm) Cruise from Henderson Inlet to Blake Island. After visiting Budd Inlet Lt. Puget decided that none of the inlets connected to a "Northwest Passage," and headed straight back to Blake Island to meet up with Captain Vancouver. But surprise … Captain Vancouver was not there as expected. Lt. Puget fires a cannon and Captain Vancouver returns a volley of fire. He was anchored at Restoration Point.

Blake Island

Day 8 (9 nm) Cruise from Blake Island State Park to Shilshole Bay Marina. Spend the morning hiking the many trails on Blake Island before heading back to Shilshole Bay Marina.

[Itinerary By: Jim Norris]

Lt. Peter Puget encampment on Puget Sound - Artist John Sykes

Lt. Peter Puget and exploration launches - Artist Steve Mayo

HMS Discovery at Restoration Point - Artist John Horton

LT. PETER PUGET'S 1792 EXPLORATION OF SOUTH SOUND

Lt. Peter Puget's Exploration of the Southern Waters Taking the Continental Shoreline to Starboard 20-27 May 1792

20 May - Depart at 0400 hrs in 2 launches from the HMS Discovery from Blake Island
- Breakfast at Olalla
- Await tide change at Pt. Fosdick and proceed to Indian Cove-Wollochet Bay
- Make camp at Shaw's Cove.
- Days run 16nm

21 May - Breakfast at Crow-Cutts Is.
- Alarm Cove- Hostile Indians
- Pitt Passage camp
- Day's run 20nm

22 May - Alter course to eastern shore Long-Ketron Is, disobeying Captain Vancouver's orders.
- Storm makes them find shelter in Oro Bay, Anderson Is.
- Day's run- 9nm

23 May - Depart and make way to Nisqually Reach, then head north to Case Inlet.
- Storm forces early camp on Wednesday- Herron Is.
- Day's run 15nm

24 May - Continue to explore Case Inlet and Pickering Passage
- Make camp on continental shore at 1800 hrs.
- Day's run 16nm

25 May - Explore Totten Inlet
- Make night camp at Hunter Point. Day's run 14nm

26 May - Begin exploring Eld Inlet and finds the friendliest Indians in a village south of Flapjack Point.
- Enter Budd inlet and Puget is convinced all southern waters end in mud flats and there is no Northwest Passage. He stops long enough for Whidbey to take his famous noon sight of 47 degrees, 03 minutes N. and sets the masts/sails and with the southerly wind and ebbing tide he sails non stop through the night, missing Captain Vancouver on Long-Ketron Is.

27 May - He arrives at Blake Island anchorage to find the HMS Discovery missing. He fires a canon and the ship's watch returns a volley of fire. 0200 hrs Lt Puget's party returns to the HMS Discovery which is anchored off Restoration Point.
- Day's run 64nm, Total nm- 162.

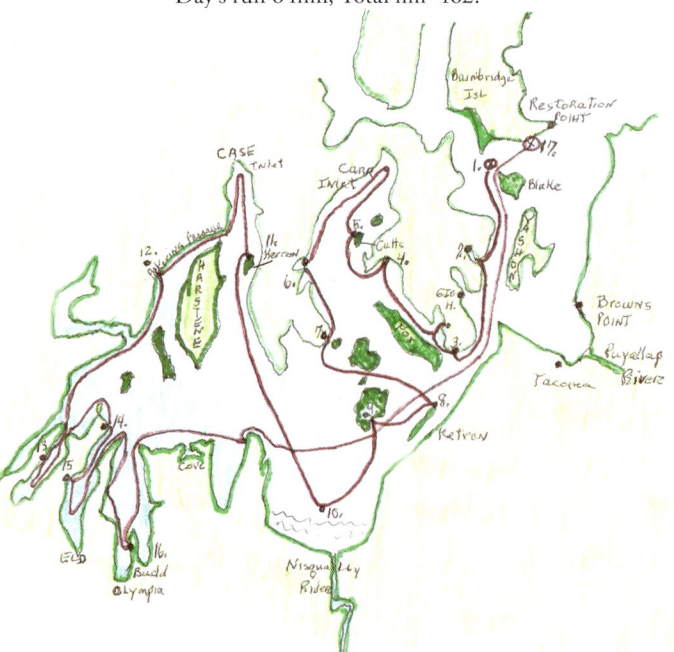

[Map & Daily Log - Hira Barbara Reid]
[The Peter Puget Memorial Project - pugetmemorial.blogspot.com]

ONE WEEK SOUTHEAST ALASKA

We think the area between Petersburg and Juneau has all the SE Alaska highlights: tide-water glaciers, icebergs, bears, whales, sea lions, fishing, kayaking, small-town Alaska, and big-town Alaska. This trip can be done in a week and in either direction. If possible, take more time to shorten the daily travel distances and allow for weather delays. The longest daily distance is 66 nm and the shortest is 21 nm. We describe the trip north to south.

Day 1 Rent a car the day before and provision. Guests arrive by plane in Juneau. Pick them up at the airport and then drive to the Mendenhall Glacier. We like to have lunch or dinner at the Red Dog Saloon. Yeah … its touristy and a bit corny, but the entertainers and the food are both good. And you get to feel the full cruise ship experience in this part of town. If you have more days, there are many other things to do (Museum, Tram ride, etc.)

Things To Do
- Ride the Mt. Roberts Tram for views of Juneau and hiking
- Don't miss the spectacular Alaska State Museum
- Ride the city bus 12 miles north to the Mendenhall Glacier

Day 2 (44 nm south Stephens Passage to Wood Spit) Anchor at Wood Spit near the entrance to Endicott Arm. Anchorage is exposed to the north; alternatively, anchor in Tracy Arm Cove which is protected from north winds. Nothing much to do in either anchorage except enjoy the scenery, keep icebergs from floating into the boat, and enjoy the sunset.

Things To Do
- In the evening watch for bear foraging in the grassy areas
- Follow the slow pace of icebergs floating down Tracy Arm

Day 3 (66 nm to Glacier Viewing and return) Cruise up Endicott Arm to visit Dawes Glacier. Spend as long as you want watching glacial calving activity. On the Endicott Arm return trip we do a bit of "ice fishing" - gathering floating glacial ice for drinks and the cooler. Ford's Terror can be a side trip or an overnight anchorage. The alternative to Endicott Arm and Dawes Glacier is Tracey Arm to view South Sawyer Glacier calving. The Tracey Arm trip is about 12 nm shorter, but has more commercial tour boat activity.

Things To Do
- Watch for wildlife using the icebergs as floats
- Take video of calving glaciers
- Get pictures of you and your boat in front of the glacier

Day 4 (44 nm Wood Spit to Windfall Harbor) Cruise across Stephens Passage and up Seymour Canal to Windfall Harbor. Seymour Canal has lots of whale activity, both humpback and orcas. Anchor in Windfall Harbor in preparation for the next day's visit to the Pack Creek Bear Observatory. You may see plenty of brown bears roaming the shoreline. On one trip we watched a sow with three cubs fishing at the very south end of the harbor. On another we anchored at the mouth of the creek just south of Pack Creek where a half dozen bears were fishing.

Things To Do
- Watch for Brown Bears along the shore
- Get your Permits ready for next day's Pack Creek entry

Day 5 (21 nm Windfall Harbor to Mole Harbor) Visit Pack Creek Bear Observatory and then cruise south to Mole Harbor. We typically spend the whole day at Pack Creek dividing time between the viewing spit at low tide and the viewing tower at high tide, with a lunch break back at the boat in between. You need to plan this trip well in advance because a permit is needed to enter the observatory and permits are limited to 24 per day. Half of the 24 are available for individuals and half go to commercial tour operators out of Juneau. We've had good luck halibut fishing at the entrance to Mole Harbor.

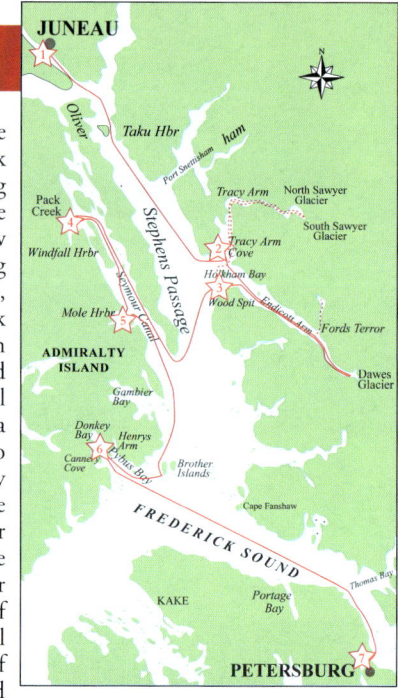

Things To Know About Pack Creek
- No pets on shore at anytime
- One permit needed per person
- All food and anything that smells like food brought on shore must be stored
- Dress in layers and be prepared for rain

Day 6 (37 nm Mole Harbor to Pybus Bay) For us, this cruise includes a salmon fishing stop along the east side of Gambier Island and a visit to the sea lion rookery located at the islet southwest of West Brother Island in Frederick Sound. If the weather is nice, we anchor between West Brother Island and the adjacent islets to the west and explore by kayak. The area around the Brothers has a lot of whale activity. About 7 nm west are several anchorages in Pybus Bay: Cannery Cove, Donkey Bay, and Henerys Arm. We haven't had much luck crabbing in Pybus Bay; better luck shrimping around the Midway Islands.

Things To Do
- Inquire at Pybus Bay Lodge in Cannery Cove about joining their fishing lodge guests for dinner. Ask early in the afternoon about availability.

Day 7 (54 nm Pybus Bay to Petersburg) In addition to the activities mentioned in Waggoner, there is the Clausen Museum and, our favorite, jigging for herring off the docks. A light rod with a herring jig rig (lots of little hooks closely spaced on a single line with a weight at the end). Don't reel in on the first tug; let the hooked herring shake the hooks enticing more to bite.

Things To Do
- Visit the Salty Pantry cafe for some delicious homemade foods; the menu varies and everything is good

Day 8 Guests depart from Petersburg airport. Time to provision and maybe go for a swim at the pool. At high tide take the dinghy up Petersburg Creek.

Things To Do
- Visit the Salty Pantry for breakfast on the way to the airport

[Itinerary By: Jim Norris]

SOUTHEAST ALASKA FOR TRAILERABLE BOATS

Boaters with trailerable vessels have the advantage of driving to a launch site in northern British Columbia, which shortens time on the water to reach Southeast Alaska. It's a great way to experience all that Southeast Alaska has to offer as well as providing the opportunity to sightsee in beautiful British Columbia along the way. We encourage owners of pocket cruisers to consider this three-week adventure, which we did in our 24-foot SeaSport Explorer. You will need to find a secure lot to park your vehicle and trailer like Four Seasons Maintenance & Storage (Les Palmer).

Getting There. Enjoy a scenic two-day 1000-mile drive north to Prince Rupert, B.C., where you can launch your boat at Cow Bay Marina. You may need to wait for a weather window to cross Dixon Entrance, the border between British Columbia and Alaska. With a boat that cruises 25 to 30 mph, you can reach Ketchikan, Alaska, 90 miles north of Prince Rupert, in about four hours.

Destination Ketchikan. The town of Ketchikan is your first main introduction to Southeast Alaska, where you can get provisions at grocery stores and marine supply shops. If needed, top off your boat's fuel tank at one of the two Petro Marine fuel docks. Ketchikan is a busy hub with several marina facilities for pleasure boats, fish boats, tour operators, and a cruise ship terminal. Alaska Airlines and Delta Airlines service Ketchikan so family and friends can join you for a tour of the area. Favorite sites in town include historic Creek Street, the Southeast Alaska Discovery Center Museum, and the Totem Heritage Center north of town. You can even take a floatplane tour of Misty Fjords for some stupendous views of Behm Canal located near Ketchikan.

Destination Port Alexander. From Ketchikan cruise north up Clarence Strait to make a fuel stop at Point Baker or Port Protection; these small villages are located at the north end of Prince of Wales Island. You will most likely see whales off Point Baker so keep a watchful eye. From here, head down Sumner Strait and around Cape Decision to head northwest, reaching Port Alexander near the southern tip of Baranof Island. The remote, charming village of Port Alexander is an opportunity to experience the self-sufficient life style that is found in many villages throughout Southeast Alaska. The port is protected by a natural breakwater of rock spires. You can anchor or find moorage at the docks.

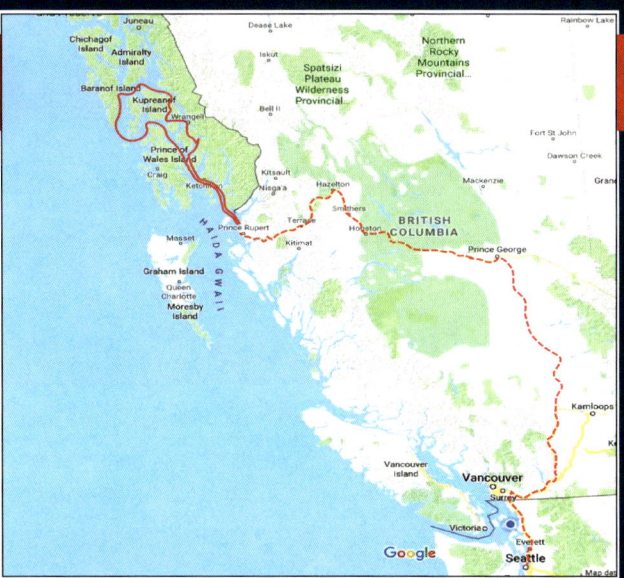

Baranof Warm Springs. From Port Alexander, cruise north up Chatham Strait for an overnight stay at Baranof Warm Springs. Hike the trail to the natural hot springs or opt to use one of the soaking tubs located above the docks. If the docks are full, you can anchor out and enjoy a fabulous view of the waterfall.

Destinations Petersburg and Wrangell. Heading westbound via Chatham Strait and Frederick Sound, circle around the top of Kupreanof Island to reach Petersburg. You may come across icebergs from nearby Le Conte Glacier drifting in Frederick Sound as you approach Petersburg. Backed by impressive mountain peaks, Petersburg offers a variety of hiking trails with scenic vistas. We recommend taking the small aluminum boat tour out of Petersburg to visit Le Conte Glacier, a must see. You can get provisions and fuel at either Petersburg or Wrangell. To visit Wrangell, head south through the 21 nm long Wrangell Narrows, with 60 plus channel markers and 5 ranges; watch out for tugs towing barges. While staying in Wrangell, visit Petroglyph Beach located northwest of town and/or take a tour to Anan Bay.

Bear Observatory, another must see. Both cities have multiple moorage facilities and scheduled airline flights for picking up or dropping off family members.

The Trip Back. Heading back down Clarence Strait from Wrangell, make a stop at Thorne Bay on Prince of Wales Island. This large bay has many nooks and crannies to explore. The friendly community of Thorne Bay has a grocery store and café. You can even rent a truck to explore other interesting sights on the island. Enjoy your cruise back to Ketchikan and then Prince Rupert for a couple nights of restful stay before driving back home. For more about this trip see waggonerguide.com/pocket-cruiser-discovering-se-alaska/

[Itinerary By: Bob Posey]

SOUTHEAST ALASKA EXPEDITED

In 2021 the only way to travel from Washington to Southeast Alaska through B.C. waters was by the most direct and expeditious route with no contact and limited fuel and provisions. Anchoring was allowed. Although there are so many excellent places to stop along the way in B.C., this unusual trip gave us the opportunity to discover a way to dedicate the most cruising time to SE Alaska waters. So if you are like us and have enjoyed many of the B.C. treasures and want to get to the SE Alaska gold mine of destinations, here is an itinerary to do just that.

Day 1 (25 nm from Anacortes to Roche Harbor) Roche Harbor Marina has excellent guest moorage, or you can anchor out for that early start the next morning. With the relatively short day's travel, there is plenty of time to enjoy a dinner at the restaurant and make final preparations.

Things To Note
- Top up fuel at the marina
- Buy any missing provisions that are allowed into Canada

Day 2 (62 nm Roche Harbor to Nanoose Harbour). Nanoose is a good anchoring spot, with ample protected space with favorable anchoring depths. There is a navy base in the NW corner of the harbour. All of the harbour is a military controlled access zone that requires contacting the Harbour Master (250) 213-3325 or Winchelsea Control (250) 363-7584 or VHF 10 when south of Maude Island.

Things To Note
- Clear Canadian Customs at one of the Sidney area Points of entry or Bedwell Harbour.
- Consider Gabriola Pass instead of Dodd Narrows.

Day 3 (73 nm Nanoose to Gowlland Harbour). With good weather, this straight shot up Strait of Georgia will be pleasant. Check the current at Cape Mudge. Gowlland Harbour has ample well-protected anchorage that is quiet and restful.

Things To Note
- Discovery Harbour in Campbell River has everything you might need: fuel, food, parts, & liquor.
- April Point Marina is a moorage option close by.

Day 4 (88 nm Gowlland to Port McNeill). This is a long day covering many miles; a favorable timing of Seymour Narrows and tide that is with you down Johnstone Strait helps. If winds are an issue in Johnstone Strait, use the back channels off the main Strait for protection until reaching York Island, then the Strait is the only option.

Things To Note
- Blind Channel Marina is a duck-in option; Forward Harbour, Port Neville, Port Harvey, Growler Cove, and Alert Bay are alternate or duck-in options.
- Anchor or find moorage at Port McNeill, with 2 marinas.
- Fuel, provisions, parts, and liquor are within walking distance.

Day 5 (30 nm Port McNeill to Port Alexander). Anchor here for an early next day push around Cape Caution. There is cell coverage for checking weather the night before and next day.

Things To Note
- If weather and endurance permits, it is possible to continue from Port McNeill around Cape Caution same day.

Day 6 (53 nm Port Alexander to Green Island Anchorage). Start the morning with a weather forecast; check West Sea Otter buoy conditions, and reports from Lightstations along the route around Cape Caution and into Fitz Hugh Sound. Know your boat's capabilities and handling in the forecast weather conditions. Review the Cape Caution chapter. Expect to have cell coverage until within a few miles of Cape Caution.

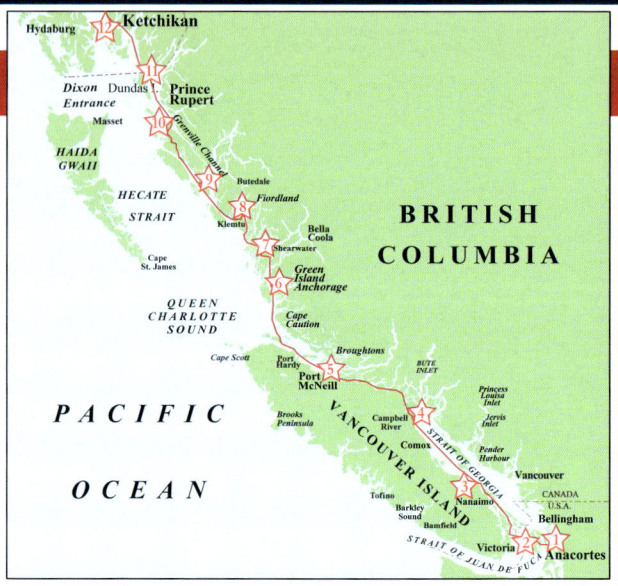

Things To Note
- Alternate destination options or duck-in places are Blunden Harbour, Millbrook Cove, Penrose Island Marine Park, and Pruth Bay.

Day 7 (43 nm Green Island Anchorage to Kliktsoatli Harbour, Shearwater). This shorter day leaves time to visit the store, restaurant, and recycle/garbage when mooring at the marina. Anchoring out is an option. Fuel is available.

Things To Note
- Cell is good in and near Shearwater/Bella Bella.

Day 8 (63 nm Kliktsoatli to Meyers Passage Anchorage). This outside route is more interesting with better anchoring options than the more protected Princess Royal Channel/Grenville Channel route. Distance is about the same.

Things To Note
- Timing current at Meyers Passage is important.

Day 9 (64 nm Meyers Psge. to Weinberg Inlet, Campania I). This scenic route has many anchoring options. Weinberg Inlet is a uniquely picturesque area with many anchorages.

Things To Note
- Parts of this outside route are open to Hecate Strait.

Day 10 (70 nm Weinberg to Lawson Harbour). Anchorage is good in Lawson Hrbr or in the unnamed larger bay on the west side of Lewis Island.

Things To Note
- Cell coverage from Prince Rupert is marginal but usable with data.

Day 11 (53 nm Lawson Hrbr to Brundige Inlet, Dundas I). Saving Prince Rupert for the mandatory customs clearance on the return trip saves some time.

Things To Note
- Cell cover is good until the approach to Dundas Is.
- Check weather for next day's Dixon Entrance crossing.

Day 12 (55 nm Dundas to Ketchikan). Dundas Island to Mary Is and Dixon Entrance requires a weather check. It's possible to cut one day off the itinerary by extending one of the shorter days.

Things To Note
- Cell coverage is spotty until past Mary Island.
- Use CBP ROAM app to clear customs.

[Itinerary By: Leonard Landon]

SOUTHEAST ALASKA GUEST CRUISE OUT OF KETCHIKAN

When visiting Southeast Alaska, you may want to have guests fly to Ketchikan and join you while enjoying this beautiful area. The airport is accessible by dinghy at a designated dinghy dock for pick up and drop off.

Our good friends flew in from the Midwest for 9 days and 8 nights. We decided to circumnavigate Revillagigedo Island, the island on which Ketchikan is located. Taking a counterclockwise route, we were awed by Misty Fjords National Monument, saw many bears, and enjoyed plentiful crabbing. The approximate distance of the loop is 140nm. The longest legs were on the first and last days of 40-45nm. The distance between anchorages ranges from 10-25nm.

Day 1 Guests Arrive in Ketchikan. There are three main marina facilities from which to choose, along with other moorage options. Mostly first-come, first-served; contact Ketchikan Harbors on VHF for slip assignment.

Things To Do
- Walk around town to see the sights, including historic Creek Street
- Take the tram to Cape Fox Lodge for lunch or a snack
- Dinner at one of the many restaurants

Day 2 Winstanley Island Anchorage
How & Why
- Cruise out Tongass Narrows, Revillagigedo Channel, and up the Eastern Part of Behm Canal to Winstanley Island and Shoalwater Pass, a distance of 41nm.
- Enter the anchorage from the north end of Winstanley Island through Shoalwater Pass and anchor in approximately 35 feet near the cabin onshore.
- Enjoy the serenity after a relatively long cruising day with a nice dinner onboard.

Day 3 Punchbowl Cove Buoy
How & Why
- Depart Winstanley anchorage the way you entered and proceed north.
- Circle around New Eddystone Rock, a 230 feet pillar of volcanic rock in the middle of the channel, it's impressive.
- Enter Rudyerd Bay and proceed to the head of Punchbowl Cove (10 nm) to see if the mooring buoy is available. If so, take it! Otherwise, you can anchor nearby.
- Look for bears; dinghy or kayak around the area and marvel at the beauty you have all to yourselves.
- If the buoy is taken, you may wish to proceed to Walker Cove, the next bay north.

Day 4 Walker Cove Buoy or Anchorage
How & Why
- Walker Cove is approximately 20nm from Punchbowl Cove.
- Tie to the one mooring buoy or anchor nearby.
- Explore the surroundings by dinghy or kayak and see the many waterfalls; bears are often seen in the area.

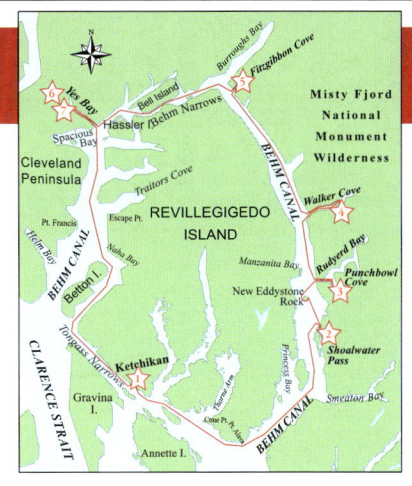

Day 5 Fitzgibbon Cove Anchorage
How & Why
- This cove is 25nm from Walker Cove
- Plentiful crabbing; enjoy those favorite crab recipes

Days 6 and 7 Yes Bay Anchorage
How & Why
- Cruise 24nm to the head of Yes Bay
- Visit Yes Bay Lodge for dinner (2-day advance notice)
- Kayak in the calm bay and look for bears on shore
- Plentiful crabbing; enjoy the restful location

Day 8 Cruise 45nm back to Ketchikan for more sightseeing opportunities.
Things To Do
- Check the status of Military Restricted Areas south of Escape Pt./Pt. Francis to Betton Island
- Visit the Totem Heritage Center and/or Saxman Village
- Learn about the land and people at the Southeast Alaska Discovery Center

Day 9 Guests depart Ketchikan; access the airport by taxi or dinghy.

[Itinerary By: Dale Blackburn]

South and Central Puget Sound

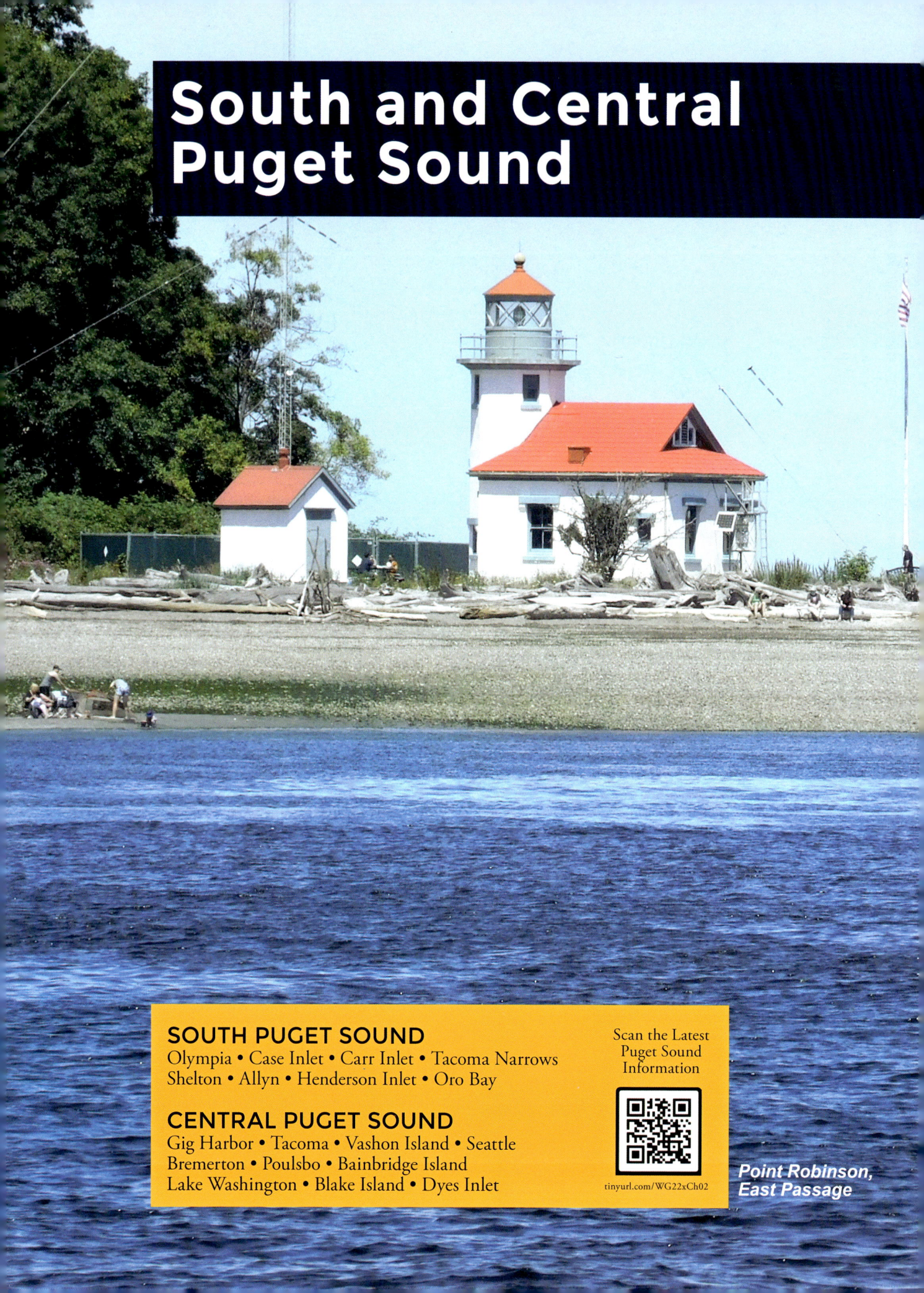

SOUTH PUGET SOUND
Olympia • Case Inlet • Carr Inlet • Tacoma Narrows
Shelton • Allyn • Henderson Inlet • Oro Bay

CENTRAL PUGET SOUND
Gig Harbor • Tacoma • Vashon Island • Seattle
Bremerton • Poulsbo • Bainbridge Island
Lake Washington • Blake Island • Dyes Inlet

Scan the Latest
Puget Sound
Information

tinyurl.com/WG22xCh02

Point Robinson, East Passage

SOUTH AND CENTRAL PUGET SOUND

South Puget Sound begins at Olympia and ends at Tacoma Narrows. For scenic quality, relatively calm seas and solitude, South Puget Sound is an excellent region to explore. For some reason, Seattle boats that voyage hundreds of miles north often do not consider venturing just a few miles south. Yet South Sound is dotted with marine parks and served by enough marinas to meet most needs. We like South Sound and recommend it.

The waters are generally flatter in South Sound, good for cruising year-round. The channels are relatively narrow and have enough bends to minimize fetch and prevent most wind from creating large seas. Tiderips, of course, still form where channels meet, and skippers must be aware of them.

Olympia is South Sound's only significant city. Getting away from civilization is easy, yet it is always close by. First-time visitors usually are surprised at the beauty of this area. Mt. Rainier, an inactive volcano 14,410 feet high, dominates many vistas. The islands and peninsulas tend to be either tree-covered or pastoral, with pockets of homes or commercial enterprise. Most marine parks have docks, buoys, and anchoring. The marinas are friendly and well-kept.

Case Inlet and Carr Inlet are the most scenic areas of South Sound, while Hammersly Inlet is the most challenging and adventuresome; the passage is narrow, depths are shallow, and currents can run to 8 knots.

From Tacoma northward is Central Puget Sound, offering attractive communities such as Winslow on Bainbridge Island, Poulsbo in Liberty Bay, and Kirkland on Lake Washington accessed via the Ballard Locks from Puget Sound. Extensive hiking trails are found at Dockton Park in Quartermaster Harbor on Vashon Island; and you won't want to miss the Blake Island Marine State Park with trails and lovely beaches. The traditional native dances and salmon bake dinners at Tillicum Village have been suspended until further notice. The city of Bremerton offers a look into Naval history. For those who love city life, Seattle offers numerous excellent restaurants, museums, and special events; the city is easily accessible by boat.

No Discharge Zone: All of the inside waters of Washington State from Puget Sound to the Canadian Border are a No Discharge Zone (NDZ). It is illegal to discharge any (treated and untreated) black water sewage. Gray water from showers and sinks is not covered by this restriction.

BUDD, ELD, TOTTEN INLETS

Budd Inlet. The mile-wide entrance to Budd Inlet is between Dofflemyer Point and Cooper Point. Approaching from the north, simply round Dofflemyer Point, where a white-painted light blinks every 4 seconds, and head for the Capitol dome.

Anchorage in Budd Inlet is along both shores in 10 to 20 feet, mud bottom, with Butler Cove and Tykle Cove preferred. For mobile pumpout service, contact Pelican Pump at (360) 402-8231, which serves the Olympia area.

Launch Ramps: Swantown Marina has a 2-lane launch ramp. Boston Harbor also has a launch ramp and parking.

Discover street art at Percival Landing in Olympia.

The City of Olympia's Squaxin Park (formerly Priest Point Park), on the east side of Budd Inlet, has one of the finest sand beaches in southern Puget Sound, accessible by kayak or dinghy. The park has trails, picnic tables, restrooms, and a playground.

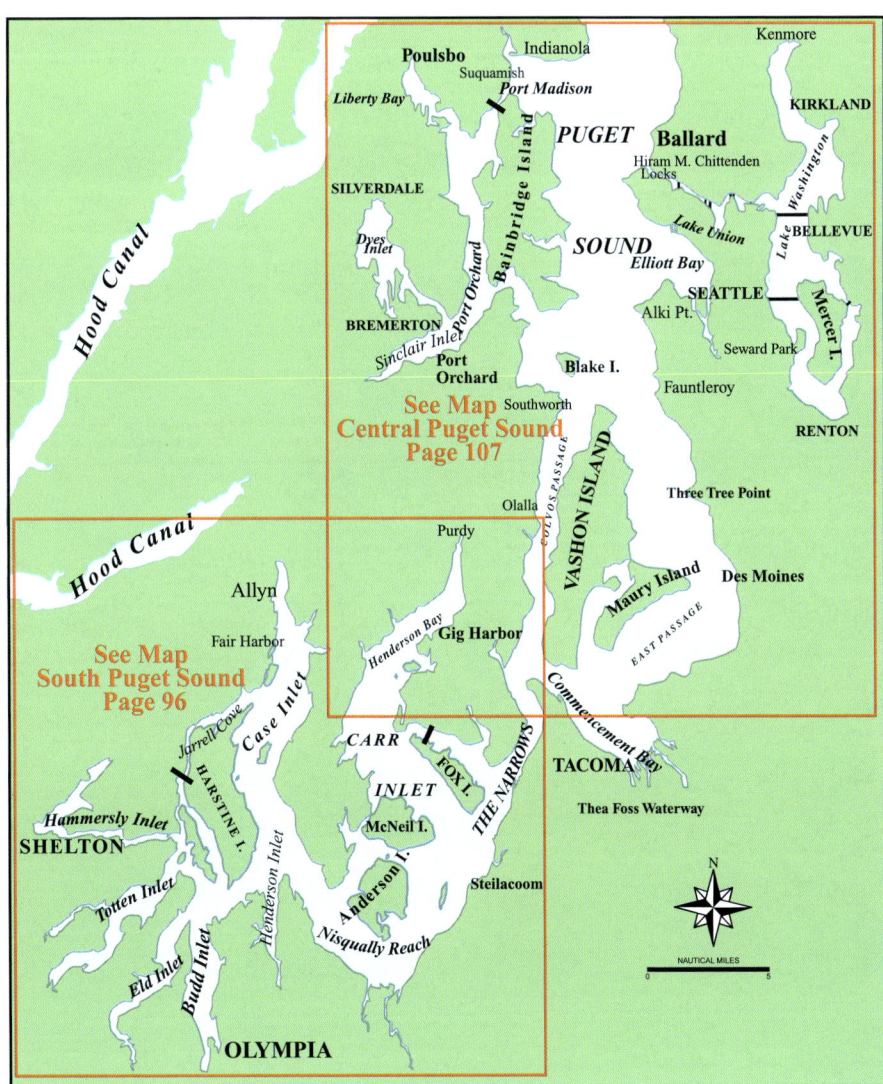

Puget Sound

SOUTH AND CENTRAL PUGET SOUND

Reference Only – Not for Navigation

Olympia. Olympia is one of the most charming stops in Puget Sound, the more so because so few boats from central and northern Puget Sound ever visit. Olympia is an undiscovered treat for many northern boaters.

Moorage in Olympia is at five marinas: NorthPoint Landing, Port Plaza Dock, Percival Landing, West Bay Marina, and Swantown Marina. Fuel is available at Swantown Marina, Zittel's Marina, and Boston Harbor.

To get to the marinas, continue past Olympia Shoal, marked by lighted beacons on the shoal's east and west sides. From Olympia Shoal, pick up the 28-foot-deep dredged and buoyed channel leading to the harbor. A spoils bank from channel dredging is east of the channel. The spoils area is quite shoal and parts of it dry. Stay in the channel.

The channel branches at a piling intersection marker east of the privately-owned West Bay Marina. The dayboard on the marker is green on top, red on the bottom. The green top-color marks the main channel. If you leave the marker to port you'll proceed down the western leg past the Port of Olympia large ship docks, to Percival Landing, and to the Olympia Yacht Club at the head of the inlet. If you leave the marker to starboard, you'll take the eastern leg to the Port of Olympia's Swantown Marina and Boatworks. On both sides of each channel the water shoals rapidly to drying flats. The Olympia harbor has a no-wake rule.

West Bay Marina has a few guest slips and a restaurant, but no fuel dock. The Olympia Yacht Club has guest moorage for members of reciprocal clubs only. In the western channel, Percival Landing and the Port Plaza dock have guest moorage. In the eastern channel, the Port of Olympia's Swantown Marina has guest moorage.

A beautifully landscaped walkway surrounds the Percival Landing area. It's a popular place for strolling, with an excellent view of harbor activities. Good restaurants, a supermarket, a fish market, several micro-breweries, and a wine shop are nearby. Some boaters find the number of people walking just above their boats disconcerting, although we have found nights to be quiet. Swantown Marina, in East Bay, does not have the crowds walking by the boats, but it's not as convenient for shopping and restaurant access.

Olympia is the state capital, and we urge a tour of the Capitol Campus and its buildings.

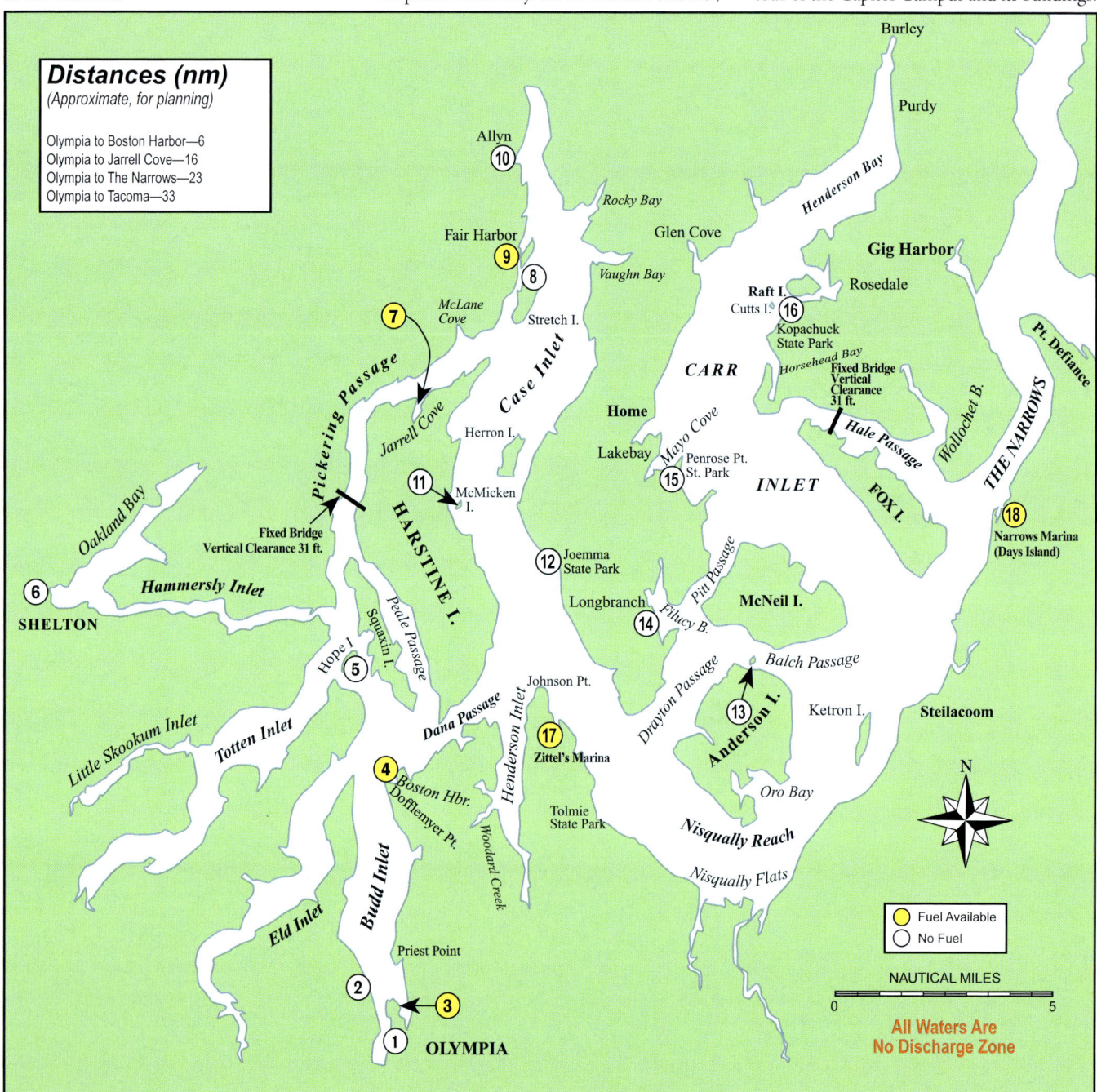

Distances (nm)
(Approximate, for planning)

Olympia to Boston Harbor—6
Olympia to Jarrell Cove—16
Olympia to The Narrows—23
Olympia to Tacoma—33

South Puget Sound

See Area Map Page 96 - Maps Not for Navigation

SOUTH AND CENTRAL PUGET SOUND

Besides housing the largest chandelier ever made by Louis Comfort Tiffany, the Capitol dome, at 287 feet tall, is one of the tallest masonry domes in North America. The grounds are beautiful and the buildings are magnificent. Informative tours are conducted on the hour, 10:00 a.m. to 3:00 p.m. on weekdays, 11:00 a.m. to 3:00 p.m. on weekends. No charge for these tours.

Downtown Olympia has its own charm. Parts of it got stuck in the '50s with old-style storefronts that you may recognize. The State Theater's art deco sign is not a bit out of place in Olympia's downtown. The Eastside Club Tavern, founded in 1942, has 42 taps for beer enthusiasts. Beers are rotated nearly everyday. The popular Olympia Oyster House has been a seafood venue since 1859.

Olympia hosts several festivals each year. For additional information visit: www.downtownolympia.com or www.visitolympia.com.

With all the services and shopping opportunities of a major city, combined with beauty and the friendliness of a small town, Olympia makes a truly pleasant destination for boaters exploring South Puget Sound. *Fuel.* Olympia has a fuel dock at Swantown Marina with marine gas and diesel.

THINGS TO DO

- **Washington State Capitol.** Take a short walk from the marinas for a free 60-minute tour of the architecturally magnificent legislative building.
- **Hands On Children's Museum.** This children's museum has exhibits and an outdoor discovery center. A must-see for kids. Adjacent to Swantown Marina, 414 Jefferson St. NE, hocm.org, (360) 956-0818.
- **Olympia Farmers Market.** One of the largest farmers markets in all of Puget Sound. It is open Thursday through Sunday, April to October, and limited days during the off-season. Located between Swantown Marina and Percival Landing.
- **Percival Landing Park.** See classic boats, sculptures, and views of the Capitol on this landscaped walkway around the harbor.
- **Antique and specialty shops.** More than 20 in the downtown area, a short walk from the waterfront.
- **Batdorf & Bronson Coffee Roasters.** Taste the difference and learn the finer points of coffee at Dancing Goats Coffee, 550 Capitol Way South, located across from the Farmers Market.

① **Percival Landing.** 217 Thurston Ave., Olympia, WA 98501; (360) 753-8380; www.olympiawa.gov. The park, with moorage, is adjacent to downtown Olympia near shopping, restaurants, and other facilities. Four-hour day moorage, no charge. Overnight stays with a maximum of 7 days in a 30-day period; first-come, first-served.

Olympia's Farmers Market features a nice selection of local produce and prepared foods.

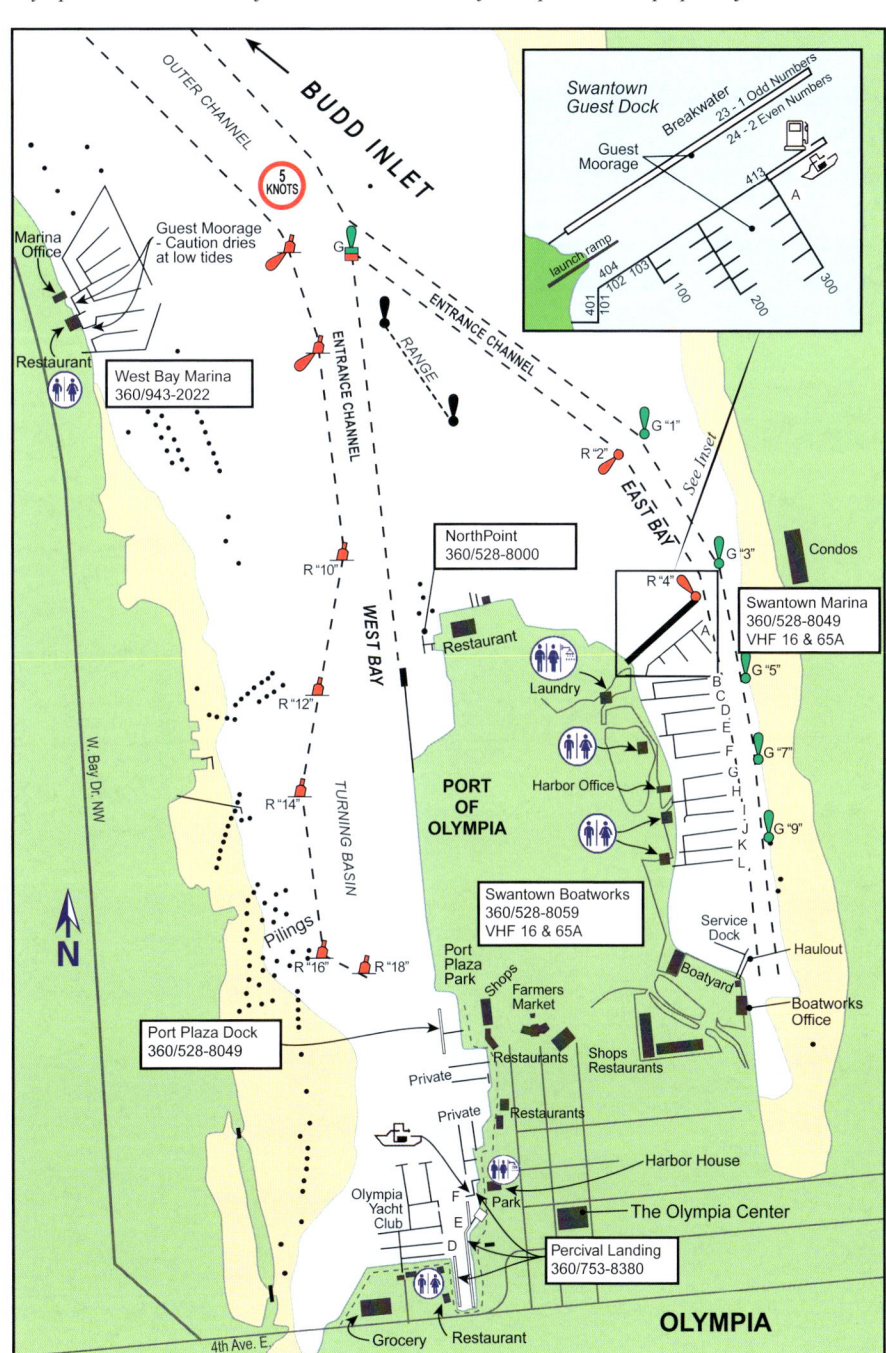

Port of Olympia

2023 waggoner CRUISING GUIDE 97

Guest moorage is along E float on the east side of the waterway. Water, 30 & 50 amp power are available on E float. Pumpout is on F float. D float, below the Olympia Oyster House restaurant on the west side, has limited space, no power or water. During business hours, register at the Olympia Center. After-hours, self-register at the station next to the parking lot; cash or checks only, no credit cards. Group reservations available from October 1 to April 30. Percival Landing restrooms and showers are located in Harbor House; public toilets upland from D float.

A seafood store and a well-stocked wine store are adjacent to Harbor House. Good grocery shopping at Bayview Thriftway, west of the yacht club. The Harbor House meeting center was built as part of the Percival Landing renovation and is available for group gatherings up to 30 people. Call (360) 753-8380. There are also two outdoor pavilions.

Limited guest moorage during the Wooden Boat Show in May and Harbor Days in early September, which includes tugboat races.

① **Port Plaza Dock.** 701 Columbia St. NW, Olympia, WA 98501; (360) 528-8049; marina@portolympia.com; www.swantownmarina.com. Monitors VHF 65A. This is a modern, all-concrete set of floats on the east side of the waterway leading to Percival Landing and Olympia Yacht Club. The docks are intended for day use but are available for overnight. Location is convenient to dining and shopping, 4 hours no charge. No water, no power. Self-register at the kiosk at the head of the ramp. Reservations accepted for a $5 non-refundable fee.

The Port Plaza itself is a work of art. The sculpted concrete work suggests waves. It's completely flat but very effective. Bronze shells, golf balls, drafting tools—all sorts of things are set into the cement. The more you look, the more you see.

ANTHONY'S HOMEPORT RESTAURANT
704 Columbia St. NW
(360) 357-9700

Hearthfire
1675 Marine Drive NE
(360) 705-3473

① **NorthPoint Landing.** 1675 Marine Drive NW, Olympia, WA 98501; (360) 528-8000; www.portolympia.com. Small dock operated by the Port of Olympia, at the north end of the waterway leading to Percival Landing and Olympia Yacht Club. Day use only. Max 4 hour stay. No power or water. 4 feet of depth at zero tide. Anthony's Hearthfire Grill is adjacent to the dock.

② **West Bay Marina.** 2100 Westbay Drive NW, Olympia, WA 98502; (360) 943-2022; westbaymarina@hotmail.com; www.westbay-marina.com. On the west side of Budd Inlet. Guest moorage to 40 feet; call ahead for availability. Facilities include 30 amp power, restrooms, showers, coin-operated laundry, pumpout. Use caution, docks are in disrepair and may be unsafe. Tugboat Annie's restaurant and pub, a longtime favorite, is on site.

③ **Swantown Marina, Port of Olympia.** 1022 Marine Drive NE, Olympia, WA 98501; (360) 528-8049; (360) 528-8031 fuel dock; marina@portolympia.com; www.swantownmarina.com. Certified Clean Marina. Monitors VHF 65A. This is the Port of Olympia small boat moorage. Open all year, 70+ guest moorage slips for vessels to 100 feet; call to reserve space. Fuel dock located on A Dock with diesel and ethanol-free gasoline.

Nice restrooms, showers and laundry. 20 dollar deposit for a key fob for access after-hours. Two pumpouts on the large fuel dock; portapotty dump, 30 & 50 amp power, garbage drop, waste oil dump, security patrols, well-tended grounds, free Wi-Fi. Reservations accepted for a nominal fee. Dry boat storage, 2-lane launch ramp. Ice is available at the fuel dock. Groceries are a 15-minute walk away. The Olympia Farmers Market and downtown attractions are within walking distance.

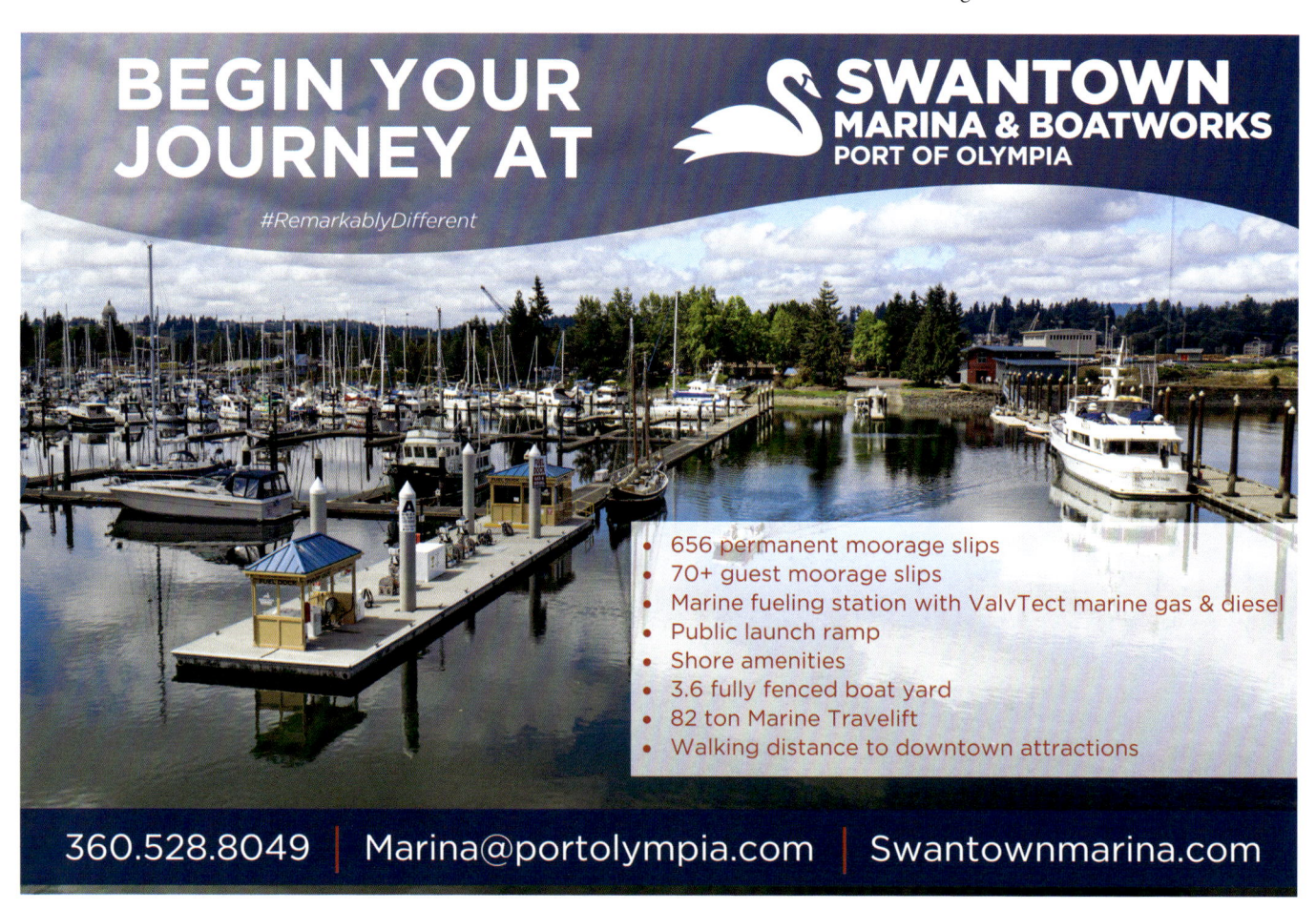

BEGIN YOUR JOURNEY AT SWANTOWN MARINA & BOATWORKS PORT OF OLYMPIA

#RemarkablyDifferent

- 656 permanent moorage slips
- 70+ guest moorage slips
- Marine fueling station with ValvTect marine gas & diesel
- Public launch ramp
- Shore amenities
- 3.6 fully fenced boat yard
- 82 ton Marine Travelift
- Walking distance to downtown attractions

360.528.8049 | Marina@portolympia.com | Swantownmarina.com

The marinas in Olympia are in the shadow of the Capitol building.

Percival Landing has ample side tie guest moorage.

The channel leading from the intersection beacon, with its green and red dayboard, can be confusing. If the weather is clear, you'll see a long, low 2-story condominium block on the eastern shore. Aim for those condominiums.

Guest moorage is on A-dock a short distance inside the entry next to the launch ramp. Register and pay moorage at the kiosk at the head of the ramp, or in the office at the head of I-Dock. Swantown Marina is parklike: clean, quiet, spacious and well-maintained.

Swantown Boatworks, (360) 528-8059, with 82-ton Travelift, is at the south end of the marina. Pettit Marine chandlery is located in the same building, offering marine repair services. Mechanics and marine personnel are located in adjacent offices.

Burfoot County Park. 6927 Boston Harbor Rd. NE, Olympia, WA 98506. Located a half-mile south of Dofflemyer Point. This is a 60-acre county park, open all year, day use only. Restrooms, picnic tables, trails, and play area. Anchoring or beaching only.

④ **Boston Harbor.** Boston Harbor is a half-moon shaped bay between Dofflemyer Point and Dover Point. Anchorage is limited but possible. Much of the bay is taken up by the Boston Harbor Marina.

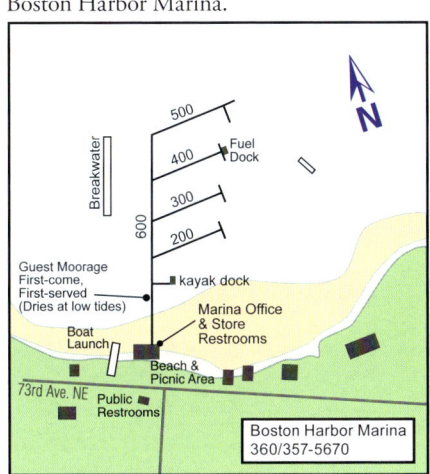

Boston Harbor Marina

④ **Boston Harbor Marina.** 312 - 73rd Ave. NE, Olympia, WA 98506; (360) 357-5670; www.bostonharbormarina.com. Phone ahead for slip assignment. Open all year with very limited guest moorage. Gas and diesel at the fuel dock. Best to call ahead regarding diesel. Guest moorage is located in front of the store on the west side of the 600 Dock and in unoccupied slips. Caution: the south end of the 600 Dock dries at low tide. The north docks, damaged by past storms, were replaced in 2019. 20 amp power, picnic area, beach access, free Wi-Fi, restrooms, but no showers. The launch ramp dries on minus tide. The store has groceries, ice, beer on tap, wine, and some marine supplies, gifts, clothing, and books. Sandwiches, soups, and soft-serve ice cream at the store. Breakfast menu offered daily. Rental kayaks available.

This is a real neighborhood place, a throwback to when small marinas up and down Puget Sound served surrounding communities. The marina has been the heart and soul of the Boston Harbor community since the 1920's. The quaint old store is built on pilings, and there's not a level floor to be found. The store and docks are gathering places for locals, and a cheery bunch they are. On Fridays, from Memorial Day to Labor Day, live music with beer tasting is held on the pier.

No-wake zone: Several white warning buoys off the mouth of Boston Harbor mark a no-wake zone. Please slow down. Wakes from passing craft play havoc with the moored boats.

Eld Inlet. Eld Inlet is immediately west of Budd Inlet, and extends about 5 miles south from Cooper Point before it becomes aptly-named Mud Bay. Hold to a mid-channel course past Cooper Point, which has an extensive drying shoal northward from the point.

Eld Inlet has no marinas, but anchorage is good, with a mud bottom along both shores. The entire shoreline is lined with houses. Located at the southern end of the inlet on the eastern shore is the waterfront activities center for The Evergreen State College. The center has a float and buildings to store canoes and other small craft used by students.

Frye Cove County Park. 4000 NW 61st Ave., Olympia, WA 98502. Just north of Flapjack Point in Eld Inlet. Open all year, day use only. Toilets, no other services. Anchoring or beaching only. Picnic shelters, barbecues, hiking trails.

⑤ **Hope Island Marine State Park.** (360) 426-9226. Junction of Totten Inlet and Pickering Passage. Boat access only. Trails crisscross the island leading through forest, meadows, and old orchards. Interpretive signs explain the island's history and ecology. Visitors rave about this park. The park currently has 1 mooring buoy on the west shore, with two more buoys to be added in the future. 1 mooring buoy is off the south shore and a second buoy for park staff. Decent anchorage in 30 feet or less is available on the east side. Currents can run strong on either side of Hope Island; be sure your anchor is set well. Stay west and south of the red nun buoy on the southeast corner of Hope Island, which marks a nasty, charted shoal. Campsites, pit toilets, no fires, no pets. Pack out all garbage.

Totten Inlet. Enter Totten Inlet past Steamboat Island, connected to the mainland by a causeway from Carlyon Beach. Homes line the shore along with a private marina. A beach, with shallow waters, is marked by a quick flashing light. All of Totten Inlet is less than 60 feet deep. The inlet shoals to drying mud flats toward its south end, called Oyster Bay.

The entrance to **Skookum Inlet** is on the west side of Totten Inlet, about 3 miles southwest of Steamboat Island. Skookum Inlet is called "Little Skookum" by locals, to differentiate it from nearby Hammersley Inlet, which they call "Big Skookum." Little Skookum is a pleasant exploration, but not navigable beyond Wildcat Harbor except by dinghy. Little Skookum is one of south Puget Sound's major oyster growing areas.

SOUTH AND CENTRAL PUGET SOUND

See Area Map Page 96 - Maps Not for Navigation

HAMMERSLEY INLET & SHELTON

Hammersley Inlet extends westward about 8 miles to Oakland Bay and the city of Shelton. Note the shoal area that blocks the entire south side of the entrance to Hammersley Inlet. Enter Hammersley Inlet on the north shore past Point Hungerford, marked by a beacon with a flashing red light. Depths range from 10 to 30 feet. Currents to 8 knots flood in and ebb out. The strongest currents occur around Cape Horn, a sharp, constricted bend just inside the entrance. Be mindful of tugs with tows. This scenic passage is lovely and is worth the side trip. Follow the chart and keep an eye on the depthfinder. It is best to plan a transit on a rising tide at mid-tide or higher. Moorage is at the Port of Shelton's Oakland Bay Marina, about a mile from Shelton.

Shelton. Shelton is the site of a major lumber mill, with rafted logs in storage in front of the town. Oakland Bay grows shallow north of Shelton, but is navigable at other than extreme low tide, and could offer anchorage on a mud bottom.

⑥ **Oakland Bay Marina**. 701 E Pine Street, Shelton, WA 98584; (360) 426-9476; syc@sheltonyachtclub.com; www.oaklandbaymarina.com. This marina is owned and operated by the Shelton Yacht Club. Open all year, 110 feet of first-come, first-served guest moorage; email or call to inquire about guest moorage availability. 30 amp power, water, pumpout and free Wi-Fi. Side-tie guest dock is located in the center between the boat houses; moorage available on both sides of the dock. Least depth 10 feet. No fuel. Marina Office and guest moorage payment box is located in a small shack on the main dock landing, open from 10:00 a.m. to 4:00 p.m. Monday-Friday. Marina restrooms are located on the connecting float to the south of the main dock. Home to the friendly Shelton Yacht Club. Reciprocal moorage on a space available basis. Groceries, restaurants, and services are in town, about a mile away.

A fixed bridge with vertical clearance of 31 feet connects Harstine Island with the Olympic Peninsula.

Plans are in the works to expand the marina, with the addition of a new breakwater and two dock extensions. Plans also include new restroom and laundry facilities.

PEALE AND PICKERING PASSAGES AND CASE INLET

Pickering Passage extends northward from Totten Inlet past the west sides of Squaxin Island and Harstine Island. A fixed bridge connects Harstine Island to the mainland with a mean high-water vertical clearance of 31 feet. A ferry service once crossed Pickering Passage between 1922 and 1969. The passage was named by Charles Wilkes during his 1838-1842 expedition in honor of the crew's Naturalist, Charles Pickering. The small marina located between Jarrell Cove and Dougall Point is private Indian Cove Marina.

Peale Passage runs along the east side of Squaxin Island. Shallow but passable depths. Squaxin Island is private. Protected anchorage can be found in the nooks off the eastern shore.

Jarrell Cove. Jarrell Cove is off Pickering Passage near the northwest corner of Harstine Island. Jarrell's Cove Marina and 43-acre Jarrell Cove State Marine Park occupy this pleasant, sheltered cove.

LOCAL KNOWLEDGE

SHALLOW AREA: A shallow spit at Jarrell Cove State Park extends from the point that protects the second park dock, the dock deeper in the cove. Boats sometimes cut the point too closely on low tides and go aground.

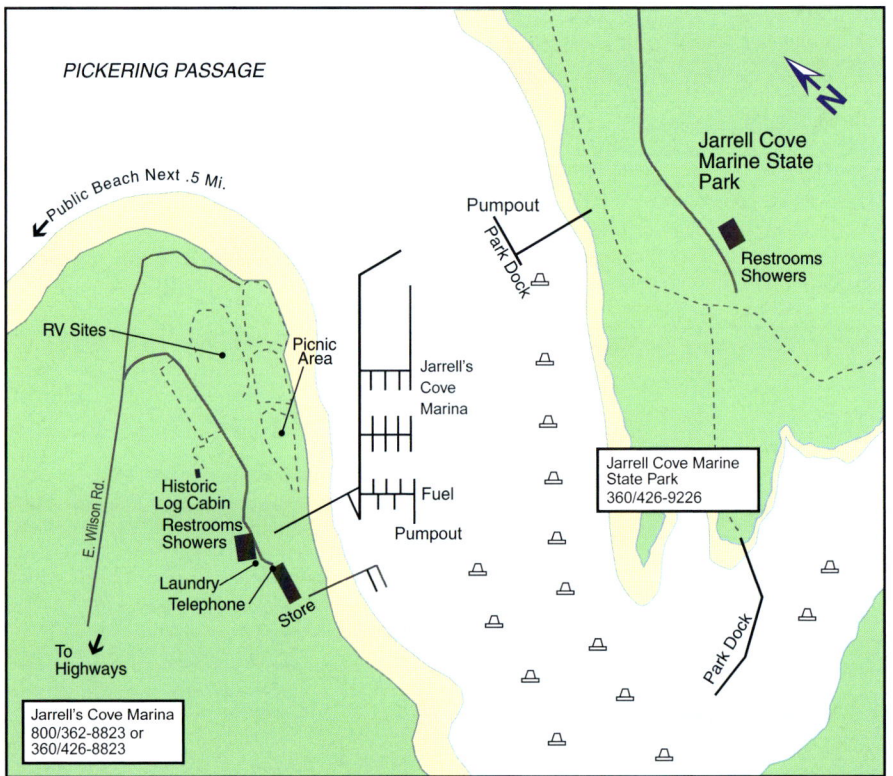

Oakland Bay Marina

Jarrell Cove

See Area Map Page 96 - Maps Not for Navigation

SOUTH AND CENTRAL PUGET SOUND

Beautiful Fair Harbor Marina on Case Inlet has guest moorage, store and gasoline at the fuel dock.

Reach Island. At the southern end of Reach Island is Fair Harbor, the location of Fair Harbor Marina. The bay has limited anchorage. The channel entrance to Fair Harbor Marina, as well as the waters off the marina, are not well charted. Zero-tide water depths at the channel entrance are approximately 18-20 feet, and approximately 12 feet around the marina floats. The channel north of the marina, under a bridge with a mean high water clearance of 16 feet, dries on a minus tide.

⑨ **Fair Harbor Marina.** 5050 E. Grapeview Loop Rd., P.O. Box 160, Grapeview, WA 98546; (360) 426-4028, or (253) 347-8235; fairharbormarina19@gmail.com; www.fairharbormarina.com. Open during the summer months with side-tie guest moorage on an 88-foot dock; reservations recommended. Year-round permanent moorage. Water, 20 & 30 amp power, garbage, and Wi-Fi. Restrooms, showers, and laundry. Fuel dock (gas only). Concrete launch ramp. Picnic areas. Susan and Vern Nelson retired and the marina was purchased by Kelly and Cindy Granger in early 2019. The store offers sundries, ice cream, and a nice selection of artisan gifts. A charming pavilion at the head of the dock is available for weddings and special events.

⑦ **Jarrell's Cove Marina.** 220 E. Wilson Rd., Shelton, WA 98584; (360) 426-8823. Open Memorial Day to Labor Day; 10:00 a.m. to 6:00 p.m. The fuel dock has diesel and gasoline. In the winter, the store is closed and fuel is by appointment. Facilities include 3 RV sites, 30 amp power, restrooms, showers, laundry, pumpout, limited guest moorage. Mostly permanent moorage with guest space in slips when available. The store has ice cream and convenience groceries, beer, ice, and some marine hardware. The piña colada shaved ice snow-cones are popular with adults; lots of other flavors available too. The store and fuel dock are open on weekends, plus Monday and Friday during the peak season.

⑦ **Jarrell Cove Marine State Park.** 391 E. Wingert Road, Shelton, WA 98584; (360) 426-9226. Northwest end of Harstine Island. Open all year. This is a large, attractive park, with 650 feet of dock space on two docks, 14 mooring buoys (boats 45 feet and under). 30 amp power on the park's southern dock. Clean and well-maintained restrooms and showers, picnic shelters, RV sites and standard campsites. Except for the single buoy between the inner dock and shore, mooring buoys have minimum 10 feet of water at all tides. The inner end of the outer dock can rest on mud bottom on minus tides. The inner dock has 6 feet of water on zero tide. The outer end has sufficient depths for most drafts on all tides. Fishing, clamming, hiking, and bird watching. This park is a wonderful off-season destination.

Moorage buoy fees can be paid by phone or at the shore-side station. To pay by phone, call the number on the buoy and provide the buoy's number and your credit card information. A nominal convenience fee is charged in addition to the moorage fee.

McLane Cove. Across Pickering Passage from Jarrell Cove. Protected, quiet, lined with forest. Anchorage in 10 to 20 feet.

⑧ **Stretch Island** has good anchorage in the bay south of the bridge to the mainland. The bridge has a mean high water clearance of 14 feet. The channel under the bridge dries at low tide.

⑧ **Stretch Point Marine State Park.** (360) 426-9226. On Stretch Island. Open all year, accessible only by boat. No power, no water, no restrooms or showers; no garbage drop, pack it in – pack it out. 5 overnight mooring buoys for boats 45 feet and under. Buoys arc close to shore because of a steep dropoff. Swimming and diving, oysters and mussels, and a smooth sand beach. The rustic shelters behind the beach are private property and not part of the park.

⑩ **Allyn Waterfront Park Marina (Port of Allyn).** P.O. Box 1, Allyn, WA 98524; (360) 275-2430; portofallyn@aol.com; www.portofallyn.com. Open all year, launch ramp, 250 feet of moorage for boats to 45 feet on a "T" shaped float at the end of a public pier. Restrooms on site; playground and picnic area nearby. The lovely gazebo is available to rent for special events. Potable water and power at the docks. The dock is exposed to winds. No fuel, but you can bring jerry cans to the gas station in town. Allyn is surrounded by shoal water, but can be approached by favoring the east side of the channel until opposite the wharf, then turning in. Depth at the mooring float is 5.25 feet at zero tide. Office hours are Monday through Friday, 11:00 a.m. to 4:30 p.m. Pay moorage at the office, or at the pay station. A waterfront park, 100-year-old

ON BEAUTIFUL HARSTINE ISLAND

Jarrell's Cove Marina

Gasoline, Diesel & Propane Fuel
Laundromat • Showers • Restrooms
Guest & Permanent Moorage
Pumpout
Hawaiian Shaved Ice
Store with Ice, Fishing Tackle,
Beer, Wine & Ice Cream

220 E. Wilson Road • Shelton, WA 98584
(360) 426-8823

Jarrell's Cove Marina is a popular stop with fuel, moorage, and store.

2023 waggoner CRUISING GUIDE   101

SOUTH AND CENTRAL PUGET SOUND

See Area Map Page 96 - Maps Not for Navigation

church, grocery and liquor store, post office, restaurants, wine tasting room, kayak rentals, and the George Kenny School of Chainsaw Carving are a short walk ashore.

If you're experiencing a craving for a manly, heart-stopping burger and shake, visit Big Bubba's Burgers, an Allyn landmark, across the road from Waterfront Park. Golfing available at nearby Lakeland Village Golf Course.

Rocky Bay. The best anchorage is behind a small sandspit extending from Windy Bluff. Enter with caution and round the little rocky islet off the end of the spit before circling in to anchor.

Vaughn Bay. For shallow draft vessels at high tide. Take a mid-channel course past the end of the spit, then turn to parallel the spit until safe anchoring depths are found near the head of the bay, or east of the spit. Jet skis and water skiers sometimes roar around during the day, but they quit at sundown and leave the bay peaceful at night. A launch ramp is on the north shore of the bay.

Herron Island. Privately owned.

⑪ **McMicken Island Marine State Park.** (360) 426-9226. On Case Inlet, off the east side of Harstine Island. Open all year. No overnight camping. Picnic and day-use facility. Toilets, and 5 overnight mooring buoys for boats 45 feet and under. Mooring buoys, are on the north and south sides of 11½-acre McMicken Island. The buoys on the north side are a little close to shore on minus tides. Self register and pay mooring buoy fee on shore. Anchorage is on either side of the island, good holding bottom.

A trail on McMicken Island leads to a nice view of the beach and surrounding waters. A sign says to watch for poison oak. An artificial reef is north of the island. Fishing, good clamming and oyster gathering, swimming. McMicken Island is accessible only by boat except on low tides, when it and Harstine Island are connected by a drying spit. The spit comes up quickly, and you could find yourself aground if you try to pass between the two islands. The park has no garbage drop and a "Pack it in–Pack it out" policy.

Harstine Island State Park. This park is across the bay from McMicken Island. Open all year, day use only. No power, water, or toilets. At low tide you can cross to McMicken Island State Park. Anchoring only. Clamming, beachcombing.

⑫ **Joemma Beach State Park.** (360) 902-8844 or (253) 884-1944 Formerly Robert F. Kennedy Recreational Area, southeast Case Inlet, just north of Whiteman Cove. Cascadia Marine Trail campsite, 500 feet of dock space in place from mid-May through mid-October, 4 mooring buoys (boats 45 feet and under), boat launch, vault toilets. No power, no showers. Garbage drop and recycling at the head of the ramp. Camping and picnic sites (including a covered shelter) on shore. This 122-acre marine camping park is named after Joe and Emma Smith, who lived on the premises from 1917 to 1932. Red Rock crabbing has occasionally been reported as excellent, right at the dock. The docks are exposed to southeast storms.

First-come guest moorage at Longbranch Improvement Club is side-tie in the yellow-painted areas.

DRAYTON PASSAGE, PITT PASSAGE, BALCH PASSAGE

Taylor Bay. Taylor Bay, on Anderson Island, offers limited anchorage near the entrance, but is exposed to southerlies.

Oro Bay has a shallow, well-marked entrance with good anchorage inside. Field Correspondent Jim Norris reported that the charted green buoy on the left side of the entrance was missing in 2022, in which case boaters should stay close to the two red buoys. Oro Bay has a tranquil, rural feeling about it. Entering, the first dock you come to is a Tacoma Yacht Club outstation. Next is Burwell's Landing, a Bremerton Yacht Club outstation. The Oro Bay Marina is home to Oro Bay Yacht Club, with some reciprocal moorage.

Two major parks, managed by the Anderson Island Park District, are the highlights of Oro Bay. Jacobs Point Park, the newer of the two, occupies most of the peninsula between inner and outer Oro Bay. Historically a pioneer farm, Jacobs Point Park provides 82 acres of trails, woodlands and beaches. Access is via a wooden staircase located north of the two red buoys. Stay on the trails, poison oak abounds. Andy's Park at the northeast corner of the bay provides 180 acres of wetlands, tidal estuary, and forest with a 2-mile nature trail loop. Access to Andy's Park is from Eckenstam Johnson Road, or through Jacobs Point Park.

Note: Dogs not permitted ashore.

In 1792, Lieutenant Peter Puget and his exploration party from the *HMS Discovery* took refuge in Oro Bay on Anderson Island to wait out a storm. Signage along the trail marks the spot where it is believed they camped.

Amsterdam Bay indents Anderson Island and is very shallow. Safe anchoring depths are right in the middle, when that spot is not already occupied by local residents' boats. The shores are rural and picturesque. If low tide isn't too low, it's a good place to spend the night. Observe a 5 mph or lower no-wake speed to prevent damage along the shoreline.

⑬ **Eagle Island Marine State Park.** (360) 426-9226. Ten-acre island on Balch Passage, off north side of Anderson Island. Open all year, day use only, 1 overnight mooring buoy on the east side, 2 overnight mooring buoys on the west side. Mooring buoys for boats 45 feet and under, self-register and pay mooring buoy fee on shore, or by phone as posted on the buoy. No toilets, power, or water. Boat access only. Avoid the reef, marked by a buoy, off the west side of the island. Fishing and clamming. Watch for poison oak. No fires, no garbage drop and a "Pack it in–Pack it out" policy, no camping.

Eagle Island is a lovely spot. Except for the current which can roar through, this is an excellent South Sound layover location. Lots of seals, a fine view of Mt. Rainier, and good anchoring on the east side. The island is covered with dense forest; trails are periodically maintained.

Filucy Bay. Filucy Bay is a fine anchorage. Anchor inside the spit to the south of the entrance, or in the north section, farther in. The north section is wooded, quiet, and protected with good holding over a mud bottom. The view of Mt.

Longbranch Marina

SOUTH AND CENTRAL PUGET SOUND

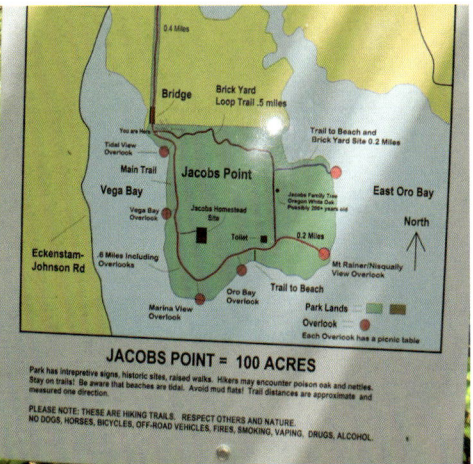

Jacobs Point Park on Anderson Island is a good reason to visit Oro Bay. Hike the 1.2 mile trail; dogs are not permitted ashore.

Rainier from the entrance of Filucy Bay is stunning. Longbranch Improvement Club Marina welcomes visiting boaters. Filucy Bay is designated as a no discharge zone. Homeowners around the bay shoot off impressive fireworks on the 4th of July, which can be seen from the Club Marina docks.

⑭ **Longbranch Improvement Club Marina.** 5213 Key Peninsula Hwy. S., Longbranch, WA 98351; (253) 202-2056, dockmaster; www.licweb.org. Longbranch is a good South Sound stopover, and popular as a destination for boating club cruises. Open all year, but hours vary in winter. The marina has 760 feet of side-tie dock space for guest moorage on a first-come, first-serve basis; 30 amp ELCI protected power, water, ice, Wi-Fi, and garbage drop. Toilets, no showers. No charge for 4-hour day moorage. Advance notification for groups is requested. Group cruises stack the boats in tightly, and raft several deep. Check their website for the schedule of group cruises. The guest moorage bull rails are painted yellow. The docks have a large covered area with roll-down canvas sides, lights, tables, chairs, heaters, barbecues, book exchange. This marina has a warm, friendly atmosphere.

If you've anchored out, the dinghy dock is on the west side of the main dock, next to the ramp. Dances are held Memorial Day and Labor Day at the historic Longbranch Improvement Club Hall, located about a half-mile away. The dances are popular and usually sell out.

Pitt Passage is a winding, shallow passage between McNeil Island and the mainland. Because the passage is shoal, many skippers avoid it. Safe transit, however, can be made by following the navigation aids between tiny Pitt Island and McNeil Island. The waters west of Pitt Island are shoal.

Red, Right, Returning assumes you are returning from the north. This means that from the north, run an S-shaped course to leave the green can Wyckoff Shoal Buoys 1 and 3 to port, then turn east across the north side of Pitt Island to leave the red Daybeacon 4 to starboard. Continue between Pitt Island and McNeil Island, to leave the red nun Buoy 6 to starboard. Study the chart carefully before making your first run through Pitt Passage. Note how Wyckoff Shoal extends westward from McNeill Island almost across the mouth of the passage.

McNeil Island was a federal prison, and later a state prison, which closed in 2011; it now serves as a Special Commitment Center. Boaters are to remain 100 yards off shore at all times; anchoring near the island is prohibited.

Correspondent Mary Campbell notes that local lore has it that during McNeil's time as a prison, escapees who made it to the other side of Pitt Passage found a warm bed and sandwiches at the home of a local grandma, who sent them on their way after they were rested and fed.

CARR INLET

Still Harbor. Located on the northeast side of McNeil Island. This bay may tempt boaters as an anchorage; however, the island is off limits to the public, and anchoring is not allowed in Still Harbor. McNeil Island is a Special Commitment Center for sexually violent predators. The island is closed to the public; no going ashore or anchoring. Boaters may circumnavigate the island, but must stay 100 yards from shore at all times.

McNEIL ISLAND - BOATERS BEWARE

McNeil Island, roughly 7 square miles, has been owned by the government for most of its modern history and has long been an island of intrigue and untold stories. The island lies just north of Anderson Island in Carr Inlet, off the Key Peninsula of South Puget Sound.

From 1875 to 1981, the island was a federal penitentiary, which housed some famous inmates like Robert Stroud, the "Birdman of Alcatraz" from 1909 to 1912; Alvin Karpis, kidnapper, bank robber, and the FBI's Public Enemy No. 1, captured in 1936; and the infamous Charles Manson held at McNeil during the 1960's.

In 1981 the federal government turned the island over to the Washington State Department of Corrections, and the prison was renamed to McNeil Island Corrections Center. A small passenger ferry ran from Steilacoom on the mainland to McNeil Island every two hours for registered visitors and supplies. In 2011, the prison closed due to the high cost of operating the prison, which once held over a thousand residents. At the time of closing, McNeil was the only prison left in North America that was accessible only by boat or air.

So why is McNeil Island still off limits to the general public and recreational vessels? The island now serves as the State's primary Special Commitment Center (SCC), where sexually violent predators are indefinitely committed for treatment. Most people are surprised to learn that even after offenders have served their time in prison, chronic offenders can be civilly committed and detained for the rest of their life; the Special Commitment Center on McNeil Island serves this purpose.

For public safety, boaters must stay off shore at least 100 yards from McNeil Island at all times. A harbor on the northwest side of the island, called Still Harbor, looks inviting as an anchorage, but it too is off limits; in fact, anchoring anywhere near the island is not permitted. Boaters may circumnavigate the island, but must maintain the 100-yard limit off shore as mandated by State law.

2023 WAGGONER CRUISING GUIDE

SOUTH AND CENTRAL PUGET SOUND

See Area Map Page 96 - Maps Not for Navigation

Anchor or moor on one of the Marine Park buoys at Cutts Island.

Watch for shallow waters when approaching Penrose Point Park dock.

Mayo Cove. The cove is pretty but is shallow, with drying shoals on either side. Waters are shallow approaching the marina and park docks. Charts may not accurately depict water depths. For exploring, take the dinghy part way up the inlet leading to Bay Lake.

Lakebay Marina & Resort. 15 Lorenz Road, Lakebay, WA 98349. Located across Mayo Cove from Penrose Point Marine State Park.

The Recreational Boating Association of Washington (RBAW) in conjunction with Washington State DNR (Dept. of Natural Resources) purchased the historic Lakebay Marina in December 2021. Funding for the purchase came from the RCO (Recreational Conservation Office) of Washington through grants and other funding sources. After developing the property, RBAW plans to hand over the marina to the State for a marine park. The Lakebay property and marina will be closed to visitors during the 2023 boating season as development continues.

The historic wharf, once used as a Mosquito Fleet landing, is on the Pierce County Historic Registry. Prior to becoming a marina, the Lakebay site was an egg and poultry co-op that operated from 1928 to 1958.

⑮ **Penrose Point Marine State Park.** (253) 884-2514. In Mayo Cove, west shore of Carr Inlet. Open for mooring and camping year-round. The 158-foot dock has 270 feet of side-tie space. Rafting permitted; 3-night maximum stay. The inner side of the dock grounds on lower tides. 7 mooring buoys for boats 45 feet and under – 4 buoys on the west side of Penrose Point in Mayo Cove, 3 buoys located on the east side of the Point. Self register and pay mooring fee on shore. Facilities include Cascadia Marine Trail campsite, picnic sites, restrooms, seasonal showers, pumpout (for boats up to 30 ft), portapotty dump. No power. Standard campsites, 2.5 miles of hiking and biking trails, clamming, oyster picking, swimming, fishing.

At low tide enter with care, giving the spit a wide berth; stay west of the line of mooring buoys in Mayo Cove.

Von Geldern Cove. Von Geldern Cove is a shallow bay exposed to northerly winds. Anchorage is possible near the entrance. Most of the shoreline is residential. The town of Home, with a launch ramp, has some supplies. Take the dinghy under the bridge at the head of the bay and explore the creek until it's too shallow.

The town has an interesting past. Home was founded in the late 1800's by three men and their families, who wanted to establish a community based on an anarchist philosophy. Land was provided to those who became members of the community's Association and agreed to the anarchist ideals. The community later divided into factions and eventually dissolved in 1919.

Glen Cove is protected by a spit, but is very shallow and not recommended for overnight anchorage.

Rosedale. Rosedale is a small community tucked in behind Raft Island. The shoreline around Rosedale is lined with homes and private docks. Weekends and good weather days in the summer will bring out a host of watercraft and water activity. In the off season, the area can be a bit more restful. Fair to good anchorage. Enter the bay to the north of Raft Island, since a causeway connects the island to the mainland across the very shoal south side. The small and quaint Island View Market, with groceries and liquor, has a dinghy dock.

Cutts Island Marine State Park. (253) 265-3606. Open all year, day use only, 7 overnight mooring buoys for boats 45 feet and under. Mooring buoys that went missing in 2020 were replaced in 2021. Self-register and pay mooring fee on shore, or by phone as posted on the buoy. The mooring fee can also be paid at Kopachuk Park. Accessible by boat only. No power, no water, no toilets, no camping or fires allowed. Easy row to Kopachuck Marine State Park. Cutts Island is connected to Raft Island by a drying shoal. Watch your depths if you try to cross between Cutts Island and Raft Island. We are told that in bygone days, Cutts Island was a Native American burial ground, and its local name is Dead Man's Island. Watch for poison oak when hiking.

⑯ **Kopachuck Marine State Park.** (253) 265-3606. Three miles north of Fox Island, just north of Horsehead Bay. Open all year for day use and mooring. 1-2 overnight mooring buoys for boats 45 feet and under. Self-register and pay mooring fee on shore, or by phone as posted on the buoy. Good bottom for anchoring, but unprotected. Underwater park with artificial reef for scuba diving. Kitchen shelters, picnic sites. Playground, trail, clamming, fishing. Swimming in shallow water off the beach area. The campgrounds are permanently closed due to hazardous trees.

Horsehead Bay. Horsehead Bay is an excellent anchorage, surrounded by fine homes. A launch ramp is near the harbor entrance. Good holding ground is a short distance inside the bay.

Hale Passage separates Fox Island from the Olympic Peninsula, and is crossed by a bridge with a mean high water clearance of 31 feet. A short distance east of the bridge, a green can buoy marks a drying, boulder-studded shoal. Pass to the north of the buoy. Currents run strongly through Hale Passage, with 1 to 2.5 knots common, flooding west and ebbing east. The ebb current is stronger than the flood.

Fox Island is connected to the mainland by a bridge with a mean high water clearance of 31 feet. Good anchorage can be found behind Tanglewood Island; The island is private, and residents are protective of their space, so it is a good idea to stay aboard unless invited ashore.

Penrose Point State Park & Lakebay Marina

Wollochet Bay. Wollochet Bay winds a couple of miles into the mainland off Hale Passage. The shores of the bay are lined with homes, many with mooring buoys, but good anchorage can be found. The mouth of the bay is open to southerly winds. Inside, the waters are protected. Tacoma Yacht Club has an outstation near the head of the bay. The bay can be active with youth sailing instruction in the summers. We've had good luck catching crab at the mouth of the bay.

A favorite pastime while visiting Wollochet Bay is launching the dinghy and exploring the saltwater marsh and estuary area at Wollochet Bay Estuary Park. The park, at the very head of the bay, has 854 linear feet of shoreline including the confluence of Artondale Creek.

Ketron Island. Privately owned.

HENDERSON INLET, NISQUALLY, STEILACOOM, TACOMA NARROWS

Henderson Inlet extends about 5 miles south from Itsami Ledge. The inlet has been the site of major logging operations over the years. A remaining log raft has become habitat for pupping seals, and the old train trestle now affords cover for bats that emerge at dusk. Anchorage is good along approximately half of the inlet before it becomes too shallow near the entrance to Woodard Creek. This area makes up the Woodard Bay Conservation Area. Seal pupping takes place mid-June to mid-August; stay 300 feet from seals on the raft near the old pilings. Hundreds of nesting Cormorants can be seen in Woodard Creek. Take the kayak or motor the dinghy slowly up the creek to enjoy the wildlife.

⑰ **Zittel's Marina Inc.** 9144 Gallea St. NE, Olympia, WA 98516; (360) 459-1950; www.zittelsmarina.com. Open all year, hours may vary in the winter. Ethanol-free gasoline and diesel at the fuel dock. Guest moorage in unoccupied slips and side-tie up to 65 feet when available (don't count on availability), 30 amp power, launch ramp, restrooms, portapotty dump, showers. Haulout and repairs, limited marine supplies, boat rentals, groceries, bait and tackle. Owned and operated by Mike and Kathi Zittel.

Tolmie Marine State Park. (360) 753-1519. Eight miles northeast of Olympia. This 105-acre park is open all year for day use and overnight moorage, except closed for day use Mondays and Tuesdays in winter. Restrooms and showers. 3 mooring buoys for boats 45 feet and under are well offshore; beach and shallows extend out some distance. It was reported in 2020 that a sunken buoy appears at low tide and is marked with a red marker buoy; the marker is not visible at high tide. Self-register and pay mooring fee on shore, or by phone as posted on the buoy. The underwater park for scuba diving includes sunken wooden barges. Hiking trails, picnic sites with barbecues, meeting room. Nice sandy beach. The park includes a small saltwater lagoon marsh area good for watching wildlife. No camping.

Anchorage in Henderson Inlet is good, with plenty of room and interesting exploring opportunities.

Nisqually Reach is the body of water south of Anderson Island, between the island and the mainland. The channel is marked by buoys along the extensive mudflats of the Nisqually River delta. The delta is a wildlife refuge, and is accessible by boat at half tide or better, by way of the Luhrs Beach launch ramp near Nisqually Head. Tom Kincaid has entered the river itself by dinghy, but from the water side the entrance is hard to spot. Opportunities for bird watching along the nature trail that skirts the wildlife refuge.

Steilacoom. Picnic area on a small pebble beach, launch ramp, and fishing pier adjacent to the ferry landing. A year-round 60-foot day-use dock available for hourly moorage, limited to boats 23 feet and under, adjacent to the ferry landing. Steilacoom, incorporated in 1854, is the oldest incorporated town in Washington. A museum, restaurants, and other services are nearby. Steilacoom Marina, at Gordon Point, is abandoned and dilapidated.

Chambers Creek Bridge. About 1 mile north of Chambers Bay is a possible settled weather, lunch-stop, day-anchoring spot in 30 to 40 feet of water offshore from a pedestrian bridge over the railroad tracks. Dinghy or kayak landing is just in front of the footbridge which will take walkers to a set of trails to wander through and around the world-class golf course.

LAKEBAY MARINA A SUCCESS STORY

After the successful purchase of historic Lakebay Marina through the cooperative efforts between DNR (State Department of Natural Resources) and RBAW (Recreational Boating Association of Washington), cleanup activity began at Lakebay Marina. The Purchase was made possible with funds from State grant monies via the Boating Facilities Grant program, along with donations from yacht clubs, individual boaters, and other organizations.

Work to-date includes the removal of derelict boats, along with docks deemed to be unsafe. The cleanup phase also included the removal of fuel tanks and remediation of environmental damage.

Phase II involves permitting and installation of new docks, expected to take 2-3 years. In the meantime, moorage at Lakebay Marina is closed. Future amenities at the marina include utilities, a new boat ramp, pumpout, and a new fuel dock. Picnic areas, public restrooms, and spaces for social gatherings are also planned.

Located adjacent to Penrose Point State Park in Mayo Cove on the Key Peninsula, Lakebay Marina and its 17.5 acres of uplands and tideland property surrounding the marina is a jewel that thankfully is being refurbished and preserved for continued public recreational access.

Funding for future development and construction at Lakebay Marina is ongoing and much needed to continue the rebuild in a timely manner. Applications for additional grants are being sought, and RBAW is offering naming rights to slips for $20,000 each. Would you like to have your yacht club's name on a slip? or perhaps your family name? – for this once in a lifetime opportunity, contact RBAW regarding making tax-deductible donations to their nonprofit 501(c)(3) Marine Parks Conservancy. RBAW welcomes all contributions large or small.

[Lorena Landon]

SOUTH AND CENTRAL PUGET SOUND

See Area Map Page 96 - Maps Not for Navigation

Currents run strong through the Tacoma Narrows, plan to time your passage appropriately.

Tacoma Narrows. All of the water in southern Puget Sound flows through Tacoma Narrows, with 4- to 6-knot currents or higher. Day Island Yacht Club, Narrows Marina, and Day Island Marina are on the east side of the south end of the Narrows.

The Tacoma Narrows bridges, more than a mile long and 180 feet above the water, are two of the world's longest suspension bridges. The original single span bridge opened in July of 1940 as the third longest suspension bridge in the world. Due to aerodynamic design issues and high winds, the original suspension span collapsed on November 7, 1940. A redesigned suspension span used the original towers. A second bridge was added in 2007 to accommodate increased traffic.

Back eddies form along the sides of the narrows, useful when transiting with an opposing current.

⑱ **Narrows Marina.** 9007 S. 19th St. Suite 100, Tacoma, WA 98466; (253) 564-3032; nmbt@narrowsmarina.com; www.narrowsmarina.com. Open all year except Christmas week, three days during Thanksgiving, and Easter Sunday. Ethanol-free gasoline and diesel at the fuel dock, restrooms, pumpout, guest moorage, long term parking, convenience store, tackle and live bait. Full service repairs on-site with a 9-ton lift.

Painted boards along the docks indicate where you can tie up. Green indicates free moorage for visits less than three hours. Blue indicates reserved guest moorage; call ahead for a slip assignment. The fuel dock is inside the breakwater in the northeast corner of the marina. Currents can run strongly at the docks.

Anthony's Boathouse 19 Restaurant and Narrows Brewing Company are on site. The top of the bar at Boathouse 19 is made from the old Day Island Bridge and the table tops are from Nalley Valley pickle barrels. Narrows Brewing Company has a tasting room where you can bring your own food and sample a variety of beers.

Titlow Park is a quarter-mile walk north of the marina with an historic lodge.

Boathouse 19
tacoma narrows marina
9001 S 19th St • (253) 565-1919

Days Island. If your destination is the Day Island Yacht Club at the back of the lagoon, run down the west side, close to Days Island and its boathouses. At lower tides this will be obvious, because a big drying shoal blocks the middle. Time your passage for mid-tide or higher. Least depth at zero tide is said to be 4 feet.

Titlow Park. Located on the Tacoma side, south of the Tacoma Narrows Bridge. Within walking distance of Narrows Marina. Open all year, park with tennis courts and 'Spray Ground' (splash park). In the park is the historic Titlow Lodge built in 1911. The Lodge was recently refurbished and is available to rent for special events. Titlow Park is a marine preserve with excellent diving.

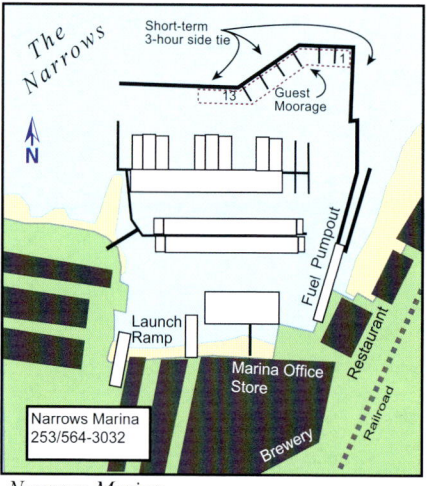

Narrows Marina

CENTRAL PUGET SOUND

⑲ **Gig Harbor.** www.gigharborguide.com. Gig Harbor is one of the most perfectly protected harbors in Puget Sound, and one of the most charming towns. The south shore is lined with moorages for the substantial commercial fish boat and pleasure boat fleets. The entrance to Gig Harbor is narrow, especially at low tide. Maintain a mid-channel course around the end of the spit. Boaters are requested to move in a counter clockwise direction in the harbor to avoid congestion.

Anchoring is allowed in Gig Harbor for up to 30 consecutive days. Depth is consistent throughout the harbor, averaging around 30 feet, but shallows quickly at the west and north ends. Holding ground is mostly mud. Stay away from the charted sewer outfall on the northwest center of the bay, and another that runs parallel to the south shore just off the end of the docks and piers.

Gig Harbor is home to a champion canoe and kayak racing team, and a junior sailing program.

Gig Harbor has overnight moorage, marine supplies, major repairs, and haulout. Mobile pumpout service is available through NW Mobile Pumpout (253-225-7660), and Terry & Sons Mobile Pumpout (206-437-6764).

The City of Gig Harbor maintains Jerisich Park (identifiable by the tall flagpole at its shoreward end) with a dinghy dock and a long moorage float.

We enjoy walking Gig Harbor's village-like commercial streets. The harbor is lined with shops, galleries, and specialty shops, including antiques. Building architecture is turn-of-the-20th-century. At least two shops in town serve enormous ice cream cones and have chairs out front, where you can enjoy your treat in the shade.

Several good restaurants, from casual to elegant. On the casual side, Tides Tavern (253-858-3982), a short distance inside the mouth of the bay, is a longtime favorite. If you are lucky, you'll find room to tie the boat at their private dock. Rafting is encouraged, 4-hour maximum stay. Tides Tavern personnel can come to your boat to take your order and deliver your meal dockside, a nice option for families. Anthony's, near the head of the bay, also has a dock. More likely, you'll take the dinghy or approach by land. The JW Trolley at the Gig Harbor Marina & Boatyard is a local Gig Harbor favorite for informal dining. Open 8:30 a.m. to dusk.

Finholm's Market and Deli, The Harbor General Store, and The Waterfront Natural Market offer some groceries within easy walking distance of the waterfront at the west end of the harbor. A waterfront Farmers Market is held on Thursday afternoons, starting in June at Skansie Brothers Park. Supermarkets are located uptown, best reached by bus or taxi. A trolley-themed bus service runs seven days a week between the waterfront and uptown during the summer months.

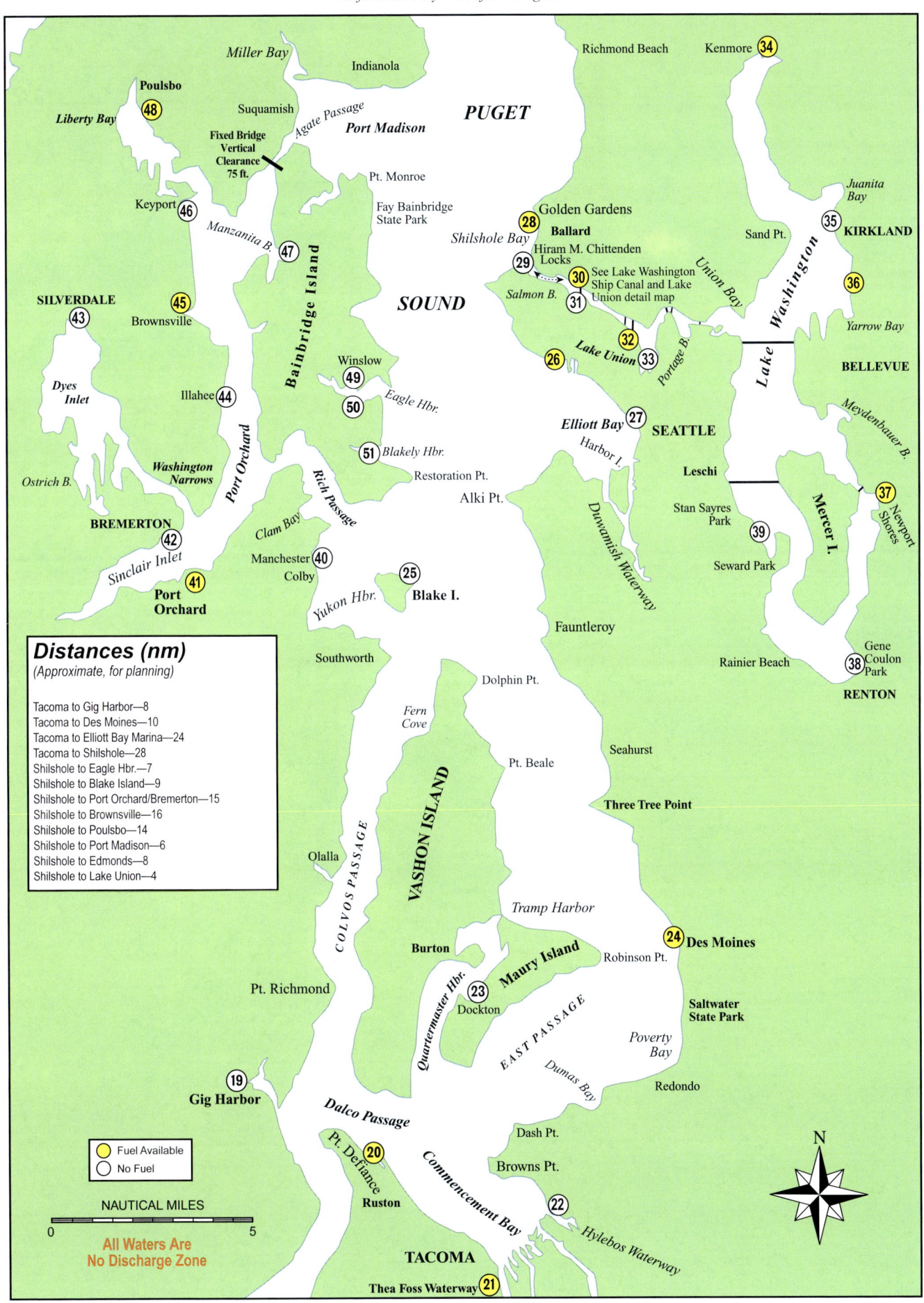

Reference Only – Not for Navigation   **SOUTH AND CENTRAL PUGET SOUND**

Distances (nm)
(Approximate, for planning)

Tacoma to Gig Harbor—8
Tacoma to Des Moines—10
Tacoma to Elliott Bay Marina—24
Tacoma to Shilshole—28
Shilshole to Eagle Hbr.—7
Shilshole to Blake Island—9
Shilshole to Port Orchard/Bremerton—15
Shilshole to Brownsville—16
Shilshole to Poulsbo—14
Shilshole to Port Madison—6
Shilshole to Edmonds—8
Shilshole to Lake Union—4

○ Fuel Available
○ No Fuel

NAUTICAL MILES
0 — 5

All Waters Are No Discharge Zone

Central Puget Sound

2023 WAGGONER CRUISING GUIDE   107

SOUTH AND CENTRAL PUGET SOUND

See Area Map Page 107 - Maps Not for Navigation

For a great view of Gig Harbor and Mt. Rainier, the local Lions Club built an observation area called the Finholm View Climb. The stairway is at the head of the bay, across the street from Anthony's Restaurant. Lee's SUP & Kayak rentals are located in front of Anthony's Restaurant.

For a romantic time with someone special, grab your favorite refreshment and take a gondola tour of the harbor (gigharborgondola.com). A small snack box of cheese, fruit and chocolates is provided.

For a beautiful view of the harbor entrance and the old ferry landing, visit the small park on the southeast end of Harborview Drive. The beautiful Gig Harbor History Museum (www.harborhistorymuseum.org) is superb, located at the west end of Harborview Drive.

Jerisich Dock in Gig Harbor has side-tie moorage on the dock and two mooring buoys for boats 32 feet and under.

ANTHONY'S AT GIG HARBOR
8827 Harborview Dr. N.
(253) 853-6353

⑲ **Gig Harbor Marina and Boatyard.** 3117 Harborview Drive, Gig Harbor, WA 98335; (253) 858-3535; www.gigharbormarina.com. Monitors VHF 69. Open all year with guest moorage in unoccupied slips as available and assigned. 30 amp power, water, garbage drop, and free Wi-Fi. Restrooms with showers. Reservations accepted. Full service boatyard with haulout to 50 tons. "The Club" building and classroom space are available for rendezvous and other events.

⑲ **Arabella's Landing.** 3323 Harborview Drive, Gig Harbor, WA 98335; (253) 851-1793; info@arabellaslanding.com; www.arabellaslanding.com. Open all year with permanent and guest moorage. Make reservations online; booking system shows available slips and slip sizes. Boats over 95 feet and yacht clubs should phone or email regarding needed space. 30 & 50 amp power, water, Wi-Fi, restrooms, showers, laundry, secured gate, and for fee pumpout. ADA accessible.

Stan and Judy Stearns developed this classy marina, located a short distance past the city dock close to shopping, restaurants, services, and groceries. Excellent concrete docks, beautiful grounds, and brick walkways. They have a well-trained crew to help with landings, make dinner reservations, or assist in finding someone to repair your boat if necessary. The moorage fee includes power, water, and showers. Group gatherings may make use of the clubhouse with lounge, fireplace, and coffee service.

Enjoy Netshed No. 9 restaurant at the top of the docks for breakfast and lunch, and make reservations for a 5-star dinner at Brix 25. Ship to Shore Marine Supply, on site, has an excellent stock of marine supplies and kayaks which you may try out in their infinity pool. Arabella's has two Airbnb suites for their guests that want to stay ashore. See GigHarborAirbnb for reservations for the "The Sail Loft" and "The Cove Suite."

Bayview Marina, just east of Arabella's Landing, is under the same ownership, with 250 feet of dock, 30 & 50 amp power and water on the dock.

⑲ **Jerisich Dock.** 3211 Harborview Drive, Gig Harbor, WA; (253) 851-6170, or (253) 851-8406; www.cityofgigharbor.net. Open all year, 420 feet of first-come, first-served dock space, 30 amp power, seasonal water, free seasonal pumpout. Rafting permitted on the east side of the dock. Two mooring buoys for vessels 32 feet and under (no charge), but required to register. This is an attractive and well-used public dock and park, located west of Tides Tavern on the downtown side of Gig Harbor. Maximum 3-night stay within a 10-day period. Pay overnight moorage fees at self-payment kiosk adjacent to the dock,

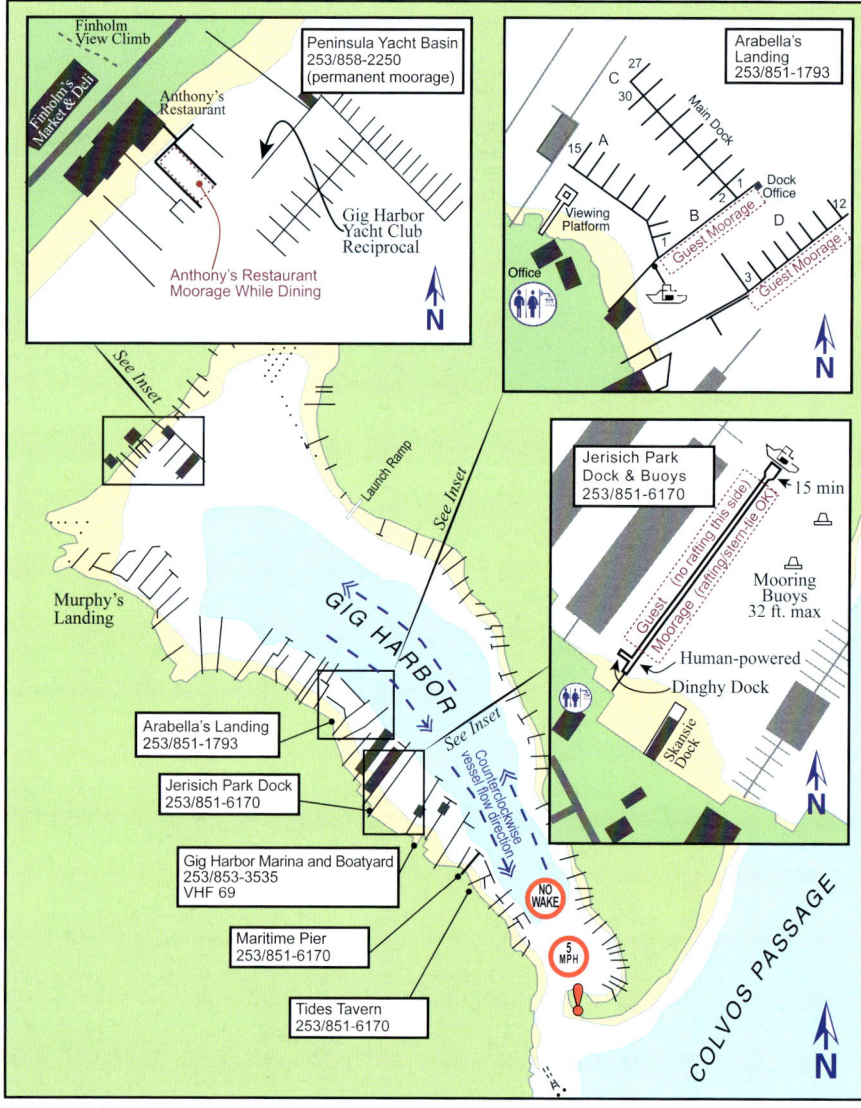

Gig Harbor

See Area Map Page 107 - Maps Not for Navigation

SOUTH AND CENTRAL PUGET SOUND

Breakwater Marina is within easy walking distance to restaurants at Point Ruston. The Tacoma Yacht Club reciprocal dock is equally close to Pt. Ruston.

credit and debit cards accepted. Dinghy dock is near shore on the west side; the east side is for human powered craft. Restaurants, groceries, and a seasonal trolley café are all within walking distance. Check your tide table; close to shore you could touch at low tide.

The Welcome Plaza is located upland from the Jerisich Dock in Skansie Brothers Park. Restrooms and showers for visiting boaters are located at the plaza. A viewing deck, with tables and chairs, is located above the restrooms.

Maritime Pier. 3003 Harborview Dr., Gig Harbor. A city public pier and 0.72 acre mini park with a 40-foot float for 15 min. load/unload; restrooms and year-round pumpout.

⑲ **Peninsula Yacht Basin.** 8913 N. Harborview Drive, Gig Harbor, WA 98332; (253) 858-2250; dockmaster@peninsulayachtbasin.com; peninsulayachtbasin.com. Open all year, no guest moorage, reciprocal privileges with Gig Harbor Yacht Club only. Maximum boat length 85 feet, 6-foot depth at zero tide, 20 & 30 amp power, restrooms, showers. Located on the north shore of Gig Harbor, next to Anthony's Restaurant.

TACOMA AREA

Commencement Bay. The southern shoreline of Commencement Bay is mostly parks, interspersed with buildings, housing, restaurants, and other facilities. At least two restaurants provide moorage for their patrons. Following this shoreline southeastward leads to the Thea Foss Waterway.

Tacoma's Commencement Bay is busy with commercial traffic. Most visiting boats choose to moor at one of several marinas in the Thea Foss Waterway. Museums, restaurants, and other attractions are a short walk from the docks.

Point Defiance. Point Defiance marks the northern end of Tacoma Narrows and is noted for swirling currents and excellent salmon fishing. The entire point is a major Tacoma park, complete with trails, a zoo, aquarium, gardens, sports facilities, and picnic areas.

Ruston. Point Defiance below the community of Ruston is the Tacoma terminus of the ferry to Vashon Island. The Point Defiance Marina (operated by Tacoma Parks) and Anthony's Restaurant at Point Defiance are west of the ferry dock. A large launch ramp, also operated by Tacoma Parks, is east of the ferry dock. Tow vehicle and trailer parking is available at the launch ramp. Breakwater Marina, with limited guest moorage, is located adjacent to the launch ramp. Tacoma Yacht Club has reciprocal moorage and is located in the same basin with Breakwater Marina.

The small town of Ruston was the site of a smelter for many years. The site and the surrounding Point Defiance area has recently been redeveloped. Dune Peninsula at Point Defiance Park is a unique, 11-acre waterfront attraction with pedestrian pathways, group gathering locations, and unparalleled bay viewing stops. The 600-foot-long, 50-foot-tall Wilson Way bridge is impressive and offers stairways with slides. You can use the bridge to access the Point Defiance Zoo.

A half-mile east, along a waterfront pathway, is the modern Point Ruston development with classy waterfront condos, shops, cafes, and a theater. A 'Splash Pad' play area overlooks the waterfront pathway. Point Ruston is definitely worth a visit.

⑳ **Breakwater Marina.** 5603 N. Waterfront Drive, Tacoma, WA 98407; (253) 752-6663 (office); (253) 752-6685 (service); www.breakwatermarina.com. Certified Clean Marina. Open all year, 15 & 30 amp power, restrooms, showers, laundry, portapotty dump, pumpout, propane, store. Limited guest moorage for boats up to 45 feet in unoccupied slips as assigned, call ahead or reserve online through Dockwa booking service. Repairs available. The Tacoma Yacht Club, located across from Breakwater Marina, offers reciprocal moorage for participating yacht clubs.

⑳ **Point Defiance Marina.** 5912 N. Waterfront Drive, Tacoma, WA 98407; (253) 591-5325; pointdefiancemarina.com. Certified Clean Marina and 5-Star EnviroStar rating, operated by the Tacoma Parks Department. Open 7 days a week all year except Thanksgiving and Christmas. Guest moorage is on the dock between the ferry landing and the 8-lane boat launch, 72 hour maximum stay. Pay at the boat launch kiosk. Ethanol-free gasoline, restrooms, free pumpout, some 30 amp power, dry storage for small boats, boat rentals. Bait, tackle, snacks, souvenirs and gift items at Point Defiance Boathouse Tackle Shop. Public fishing pier. Anthony's Restaurant is at the east end of the marina. The marina is within walking distance of the Point Defiance Zoo & Aquarium and Point Defiance Park. Bus service to greater Tacoma.

ANTHONY'S
AT · POINT · DEFIANCE
5910 N. Waterfront Drive
(253) 752-9700

Old Town Dock. Next to Jack Hyde Park (formerly Commencement Park). The docks are usable, but don't appear to get much traffic. Smaller boats only.

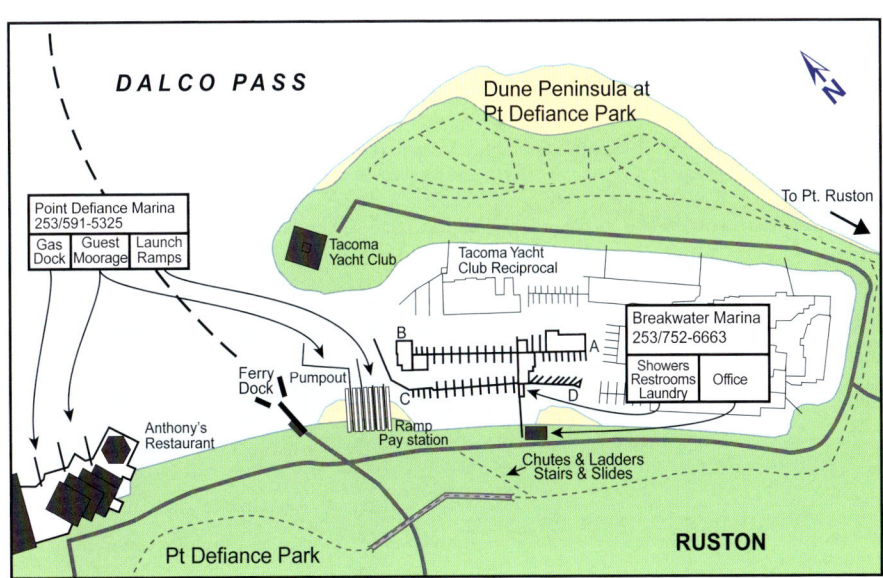

Point Defiance

2023 WAGGONER CRUISING GUIDE

TACOMA MUSEUMS

Tacoma Art Museum

The art museum supports and preserves the region's art history through its collections, changing exhibitions, and learning programs. The Northwest perspective alternates between historical and contemporary artists. Free events and programs for all ages. The Tacoma Art Museum (TAM) is located at 1701 Pacific Avenue; open Tuesdays through Sundays, free on Thursdays (253-272-4258).

Washington State History Museum

The museum maintains several permanent exhibits and features special exhibits relating to the history of the State of Washington. The Learning Center encourages visitors to discover more through interactive exhibits. The permanent Model Railroad, an 1,800 square-foot layout, has a *Washington in the 1950s* theme. This excellent State history museum is located in the old railroad Union Station at 1911 Pacific Avenue; open Tuesdays through Sundays (253-272-3500).

Museum of Glass

Visiting the Museum of Glass provides the opportunity to view craftsman at work, heating and shaping glass into sculptures, vases, and works of art at the Hot Shop. The Museum's galleries exhibit rotating and permanent glass art, including those of the world-famous artist, Dale Chihuly. Group tours and private events can be scheduled. The museum at 1801 Dock Street is within easy walking distance from the waterfront moorage; open Wednesdays through Sundays (253-284-4750).

America's Car Museum

This extensive car museum is one of the finest in the world, with exhibits displaying classic cars and rare cars from each period in time from the inception of the automobile. The stunning 165,000 square-foot facility houses hundreds of automobiles spanning over a 100 years of automotive history, plus exhibits on loan from private collectors. Meeting space, educational programs, and a café are available. This exceptional museum is located at 2702 East D Street, Tacoma; open daily (253-779-8490).

Foss Waterway Seaport

The museum at the Foss Waterway Seaport dock celebrates the area's rich maritime history and serves as a maritime education and event center. Exhibits cover maritime and boating history, commerce and trade, unique stories of Tacoma, and other boating related history. Special events are held as scheduled, a special treat for the entire family. Open Wednesdays through Sundays (253-272-2750).

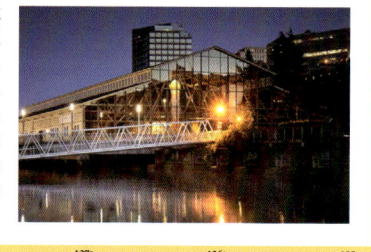

LOCAL KNOWLEDGE

STRONG CURRENTS: Currents, especially on large tides, can run stronger than expected in Thea Foss Waterway. Plan landings and departures accordingly.

Thea Foss Waterway. The Thea Foss Waterway (formerly City Waterway) has gone through a major renewal and revitalization.

Just inside the mouth of the waterway, Foss Waterway Seaport is a fascinating stop. It is housed in the century-old Balfour warehouse, once part of a mile-long row of wheat warehouses. The 300-foot-long by 150-foot-wide building is itself a museum exhibit. Displays inside include a lab, a working boat building shop, Willits canoe exhibit, marine biology exhibit, and an extensive display detailing Puget Sound's maritime history. Some 1200 feet of public floats make boat access easy.

Up on Pacific Avenue, the Union Railroad Station has been restored and rebuilt as the Federal Courthouse, and decorated with Dale Chihuly glass sculpture. The must-see Washington State History Museum, which shares the courthouse's beautiful architecture, is next door.

The Washington State History Museum is excellent. Allow at least two hours to see it; three or four hours is better. The museum is enjoyable for both children and adults.

At the head of the waterway, the Museum of Glass fronts on the waterway, immediately east of the courthouse and the Washington State History Museum.

The Chihuly Bridge of Glass connects the courthouse and history museum complex with the Museum of Glass. You can spend several hours there. The hot shop furnaces roar, and the crew may create a bowl, a vase, or candlestick holders before your eyes. Exhibits in the galleries rotate. The works on display are impressive.

The Tacoma Art Museum features regularly rotating exhibits, and the building itself is a work of architectural art.

America's Car Museum, across the road from the Tacoma Dome, draws large crowds. More than 350 cars, trucks and motorcycles are on display, dating from the beginning of motorized transport. Open 7 days a week, 10:00 a.m. to 5:00 p.m. Check website for weekly events. Highly recommended.

Downtown Tacoma is very different from other Puget Sound cities. Many of the old buildings are beautiful, and some are historic. One building has a plaque commemorating Russell G. O'Brien, who on October 18, 1893, originated the custom of standing during the playing of the Star Spangled Banner. We learn the most interesting things when we walk around.

Guest Moorage: Dock Street Marina, with guest moorage, is in front of the Museum of Glass. Guest moorage is also available at Foss

Harbor Marina. Side-tie guest moorage is available at Foss Waterway Seaport.

No Anchoring Zone: All of the Thea Foss Waterway is a no anchoring zone.

Breweries: Area breweries include McMenamins Elks Lodge on 565 Broadway; Odd Otter Brewing at 716 Pacific; Pacific Brewing & Malting at 610 Pacific Ave.; Dunagan Brewing Co. at 1126 Commerce St.; and 7 Seas Brewing at 2101 Jefferson Avenue.

Farmers Market: On Broadway between 9th and 11th Streets, a farmers market with 70 to 90 vendors. Thursdays, May through October from 10:00 a.m. to 3:00 p.m.

Light Rail: Light rail runs from the theater district at the north end of downtown Tacoma to a last stop, 2½ blocks from the Tacoma Dome and LeMay-America's Car Museum. At the museum district, the tracks are in the middle of Pacific Avenue, fronting the Washington State History Museum. The free trains are clean and safe. They run every 12 minutes from morning to evening.

Murray Morgan Bridge: Also known as the 11th Street Bridge, a vertical-lift bridge that spans the Thea Foss Waterway. Clearance at zero tide is 74 feet; clearance on an 11-foot high tide is 63 feet at the west side of the bridge. Clearance is 69 feet at zero tide on the east side of the bridge. A 2-hour advanced notice is required to have the bridge raised, call (253) 627-4655. Openings between 10:00 p.m. and 8:00 a.m. must be called in by 8:00 p.m. the night before.

The Foss Waterway and downtown Tacoma is a first class urban boating destination.

THINGS TO DO

- **America's Car Museum.** This museum is housed in a dramatic building, just up from the waterfront. See over 350 cars, trucks and motorcycles on display in the world's largest auto museum.
- **Museum of Glass.** With its iconic architecture near the waterfront and beautiful glasswork, this has become a key part of the Tacoma art scene.
- **Tacoma Art Museum.** Art in Tacoma continues with photography, paintings, and Chihuly glass.
- **Washington State History Museum.** Learn about Washington's past.
- **Tacoma Glassblowing Studio.** See how glass art is made.
- **Point Defiance Zoo & Aquarium.** See an Asian Forest Sanctuary, elephants and tigers. The large aquarium has octopi, sharks, and a beluga whale.
- **Children's Museum of Tacoma.** The museum serves young children and their parents through self-directed play; located on Pacific Avenue.
- **Daffodil Festival.** See the annual Daffodil street parade held in early April, followed by the parade of boats all decorated in daffodils, held mid-April.

㉑ **Foss Waterway Seaport.** 705 Dock St, Tacoma, WA 98402; (253) 272-2750; info@fosswaterwayseaport.org; www.fosswaterwayseaport.org. Located at the mouth of Foss Waterway. Visitor moorage along 1200 feet of floating dock. From the middle gangway to the south end, 30 & 50 amp power and water are available are available April 1 - November 1. Reservations accepted for groups. No power or water north of the middle gangway. No restrooms or garbage drop. For fee pumpout available April through September by reservation. Payment is made at the Seaport office, or drop box after hours, 4-hour free stay. A dock for floatplanes is attached to the northwest end of the Seaport Facility; watch for floatplane activity.

㉑ **Foss Harbor Marina.** 821 Dock Street, Tacoma, WA 98402; (253) 272-4404; info@fossharbor.com; www.fossharbormarina.com. Certified Clean Marina. Monitors VHF 71. Open all year. Reservations available online via Dockwa, or call ahead for space. Ethanol-free gasoline and diesel at the deep-water fuel dock, end of D dock. Visitor moorage to 95 feet in unoccupied slips as assigned. Additional 40-foot slips were added in 2021. Restrooms, showers, laundry, water, fixed and slip-side pumpout, portapotty dump. 30 & 50 amp power, Wi-Fi on the docks for a fee, kayak and SUP rentals. Store has a nice selection of wine, convenience groceries, ice, and marine supplies. An indoor lounge and outdoor patio are available for customers. Convenient walk to downtown restaurants and museums.

㉑ **Dock Street Marina.** 1817 Dock St., Tacoma, WA 98402; (253) 250-1906; info@dockstreetmarina.com; www.dockstreetmarina.com. Call ahead by phone for slip assignment. Certified Clean Marina. Concrete docks, security gates, 30, 50 & 100 amp power, water, slip-side pumpout, garbage, recycling drop, laundry, restrooms, free showers, free cable TV, some wheelchair access, kayak rentals. Complimentary bicycles for marina guests. This is the marina in front of the Museum of Glass. It is made up of two sets of docks—G and H docks are the southern, guest moorage docks. The permanent moorage 17th St. docks are immediately north.

The office, showers, and laundry are above the guest moorage docks, 30 slips 36-60 feet, with 127-foot pier ends. Concierge service. Pet-friendly. Moorage in the north docks is by assignment in unoccupied slips only. A 320-foot dock is in the north moorage.

Special events such as the Daffodil Marine Parade completely fill the marina. See their website for the complete list of special events. Rendezvous sometimes fill the marina, too. Reservations recommended, even in the off season.

Dock Street Marina is first-class, with an easy walk to many Tacoma restaurants and museums. Line assistance is available upon arrival.

㉑ **Dock Street North Pier.** (253) 272-4352; This is the long concrete float north of Dock Street Marina. No power, water, or garbage, reservations 24-hours in advance. Watch your depths at zero tide or lower.

㉑ **Delin Docks.** 1616 East D St., Tacoma, WA 98421; (253) 572-2524; info@delindocksmarina.com; www.delindocksmarina.com. Certified Clean Marina. Open all year, 30 & 50 amp power, water, restrooms, free showers, laundry, pumpout, portapotty dump. These are nice

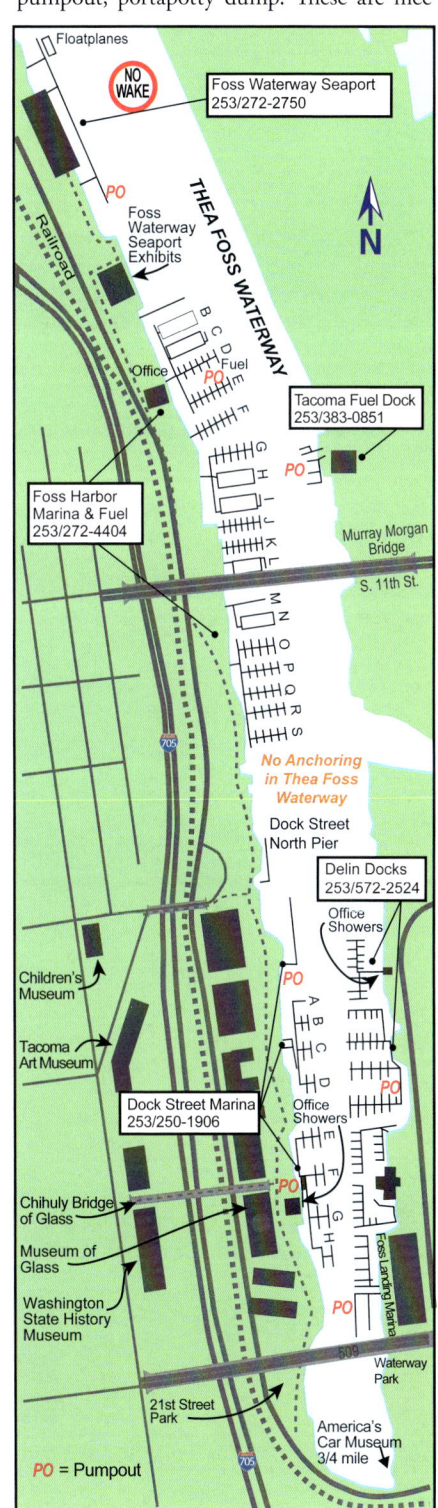

Thea Foss Waterway

docks with 30- to 60-foot slips, located immediately north of Johnny's Dock on the east side of Foss Waterway. They're primarily permanent moorage, although occasionally unoccupied slips might be used for guest moorage.

Note: Dock Street Marina and the Delin Docks are under the same management.

㉑ **Tacoma Fuel Dock.** 820 East D St., Tacoma, WA 98421; (253) 383-0851; (800) 868-3681, www.cbmsi.com. Fuel dock open all year except Thanksgiving, Christmas, and New Year's Day. Summer hours 8:00 a.m. to dusk, winter hours 8:00 a.m. to 4:30 p.m. Monitors VHF 69, summer only. Gasoline, diesel, ice, frozen herring, soft drinks, snacks. Located on the east side of Thea Foss Waterway; look for the large Tacoma Fuel Dock sign. The uplands house Commencement Bay Marine Services and the Tacoma Youth Marine Center, training young people in the skills needed for work on boats and along the waterfront. A portion of fuel sales supports the Sea Scouts and Tacoma Youth Marine Center.

Hylebos Waterway. The Hylebos Waterway follows the north shore of Commencement Bay and includes a number of moorages, boat builders, and boat service businesses. The shores are lined with heavy industry of many kinds, not all of it scenic. Still, an interesting exploration.

Guest moorage is at Chinook Landing Marina, a short distance up the waterway.

㉒ **Chinook Landing Marina.** 3702 Marine View Drive Suite 100, Tacoma, WA 98422; (253) 627-7676. Monitors VHF 79. Certified Clean Marina. Open all year, guest moorage available. Snacks and ice cream at the office. This is an excellent facility, 30 & 50 amp power, restrooms, showers, laundry, free Wi-Fi, pumpout, portapotty dump, 24-hour security. Larger boats should call ahead for availability. No shops or restaurants nearby. The well-stocked J&G Marine Supply chandlery is located about a mile away.

Tyee Marina. 5618 Marine View Dr. Tacoma WA 98422; (253) 383-5321. Permanent moorage only. Public pumpout station.

Browns Point Park. Open all year, day use only. Picnic tables and a swimming beach. The lighthouse is the focal point, with free tours of the light keepers cottage on Saturdays 1:00 p.m. to 4:00 p.m., May to October. For more information call the Points Northwest Historical Society (253) 927-2536.

Lavender Hill Farm, near Quartermaster Marina in Burton, sells lavender products seasonally.

VASHON ISLAND, COLVOS PASSAGE, EAST PASSAGE, DES MOINES, BLAKE ISLAND

Colvos Passage. The current always flows north in Colvos Passage, so heading north on a flood tide is a good choice. Colvos Passage offers little to entice a boater to stop, although you can anchor off Olalla and dinghy to the little store for a snack. Look for the replica of the Washington Monument high above the west shore between Anderson Pt. and Red Light "4".

Harper State Park. Located 1.5 miles west of the ferry landing at Southworth. Open all year, day use only. Anchoring only. The gravel launch ramp is usable at high tide only, but is the closest launch to Blake Island, 1 mile away.

Quartermaster Harbor. Quartermaster Harbor indents the south end of Vashon Island about 4 miles. It is protected on the east side by Maury Island, which connects to Vashon Island by a narrow spit of land. Dockton Park is a popular destination.

Anchorage is good throughout most of Quartermaster Harbor. Anchorage is also available on the east and on the south side of Burton Peninsula.

The Quartermaster Yacht Club (members of reciprocal clubs welcomed) is located in the inner harbor, as is the Quartermaster Marina. The village of Burton has a grocery, coffee shop, barber, and gift shop. Taxi service is available on Vashon Island (Vashon Taxi (206) 434-1121). A small DNR parcel on the south shore of Burton Peninsula (47° 23.28N 122° 27.97W) provides beach access to a short walk along Vashon Hwy SW into the village of Burton.

Jensen Park, on Burton Peninsula, has a launch ramp, beach, picnic tables and barbecues. Vashon Watersports rents kayaks, canoes, and stand-up paddleboards at the park.

㉓ **Dockton Park.** 9500 SW Dock Road, Dockton, WA 98070; (206) 477-6150, or (206) 463-3624. Operated by King County Parks. Moorage is first-come, first-served, with a maximum 3-day stay. No power, no water. Make payment at the debit/credit card station located on the south side of the pier restroom. Dockton is a popular 23-acre park on the west side of Maury Island in Quartermaster Harbor. The park has play equipment, nearby trails, fire pits, picnic shelters, picnic tables, barbecue areas, and restrooms.

Docks at Dockton Park were closed in May 2019 for planning and reconstruction. The inner docks and gangway were subsequently replaced in September 2021. The outside breakwater remains closed until repairs are completed. Breakwater construction to begin in 2023; in the meantime, the inner docks are available for guest moorage.

Dockton Forest, consisting of approximately 400 acres, offers 12 miles of hiking trails. The trailhead is located across the road from Dockton Park, look for the set of stairs behind the children's play area to find the crosswalk. Be sure to pick up a trail map from the box at the trailhead, as none of the trails have signage. It's about a mile to the vista that overlooks East Passage, which is also the location of an old quarry.

Anchoring Note: Holding can be fair to poor in the area north of the Dockton Park docks. If anchoring there, be sure of your set.

Quartermaster Marina. 23824 Vashon Highway SW, Vashon, WA 98070; (206) 463-3624. Open all year, guest moorage in unoccupied slips as assigned for vessels 25 to 50 feet. Call ahead for availability. Water, 30 & 50 amp power, restrooms, garbage drop, Wi-Fi, and pumpout by reservation. The marina is within steps of Burton village.

East Passage. Located between Vashon Island and the mainland. Large ships bound to or from Tacoma or Olympia use this route. Tidal currents flood south and ebb north, and normally are a little stronger in East Passage than in Colvos Passage on the west side of Vashon Island.

Dash Point State Park. 5700 SW Dash Point Rd., Federal Way, WA 98023; (253) 661-4955. Open all year, 398 acres, restrooms, showers, no power. Sandy beach, swimming, and primitive, partial utility, and full utility campsites.

See Area Map Page 107 - Maps Not for Navigation

SOUTH AND CENTRAL PUGET SOUND

Pedestrian friendly walkway to nearby park at Des Moines Marina

Redondo. A launch ramp, with 2 floats and a floating breakwater, is operated by the city of Des Moines. Fishing pier with coffee hut. Highline Community College operates the Marine Science and Technology Center (MaST), open to the public Saturdays 10:00 a.m. to 2:00 p.m. Anchor out and take the dinghy in.

Saltwater State Park. 25205 8th Place South #1, Des Moines, WA 98198; (253) 661-4956. Two miles south of Des Moines. Open all year, overnight camping. Two day-use-only mooring buoys. Restrooms, showers, no power. Artificial reef for scuba diving, and outside shower for scuba rinse-off. Sandy swimming beach. Vault toilets, primitive campsites, picnic tables and shelters, kitchen shelter, children's play equipment. Seasonal concession stand.

Maury Island Marine Park. 5405 SW 244th Street, Dockton, WA. This is a 300-acre park at the site of what once was a sand and gravel operation, 1.3 miles south of Point Robinson. Trails lead through the park. The anchorage, with fair holding, is protected in a northwesterly breeze. Popular with locals; anchorage is in about 100 feet of water, with shallower depths close to shore. On sunny days the winds are warmed as they cross Maury Island, making for good sunbathing. Operated by King County Parks.

Point Robinson. Point Robinson is surrounded by a 10-acre county park that can be approached by dinghy. The lighthouse is beautiful and the park has a nice beach, but no facilities for boaters. Sunday tours of the lighthouse are usually available mid-May through mid-September. Off-season tours can be scheduled by calling (206) 463-6672, or email captainjoe@centurytel.net. The gift shop (206-463-1323) is open seasonally on Saturdays and Sundays

Tramp Harbor, where Vashon Island joins Maury Island, has convenient anchoring depths, but only minimal protection from winds, particularly from the north. It is seldom used for overnight anchorage.

㉔ **Des Moines.** The City of Des Moines, between Tacoma and Seattle, is a good destination for clubs and groups. The Des Moines Marina has full services available.

Des Moines Beach Park is within easy walking distance of the marina and is where the 2-mile Des Moines Creek Trail begins. This woodland area is a Natural Preserve and ends at the Tyee Valley Golf Course. Both bicyclists and pedestrians may use the paved pathway.

ANTHONY'S
HOMEPORT RESTAURANT
421 South 227th St.
(206) 824-1947

㉔ **City of Des Moines Marina.** 22307 Dock Ave. S., Des Moines, WA 98188; (206) 824-5700; marinainfo@desmoineswa.gov; www.desmoinesmarina.com. The marina does not monitor VHF. Certified Clean Marina. Open all year. Gasoline, diesel, propane, 30 amp power, free Wi-Fi. Showers, no laundry. The marina and public pier has 1500 feet of guest moorage, much of it side-tie, for boats to 100 feet. Maximum boat length in permanent slips is 62 feet. Channel depth is 13 feet at zero tide. Stop at the fuel dock for directions to an empty berth. Free moorage up to 4 hours. Restrooms, free showers, 2 free pumpouts. Reservations accepted for boats 32 feet and larger, or groups of 5 or more boats, 1 day in advance. CSR Marine operates the repair yard, with a Travelift haulout to 25 tons.

The marina can assist yacht clubs or rendezvous with planning and special needs, including free shuttle service upon request.

Des Moines Marina is the closest marina

City of Des Moines Marina

SR3 - SEALIFE RESPONSE + REHAB + RESEARCH

SR3 is a marine animal rehabilitation center located at Des Moines Marina. This non-profit organization is dedicated to assisting entangled or injured marine animals and providing rehabilitation as needed. SR3 also conducts research through documentation and aerial images of whale pods and other marine animals.

Boaters can lend their support by keeping a lookout for whales that may be entangled in fishing gear. To learn more about SR3, or to make a financial donation, go to Sealifer3.org.

Report Entanglement Sightings to NOAA Fisheries Entanglement **Hotline at 877-767-9425**, or call the U.S. Coast Guard on VHF Ch 16. Keep the legal distance from whales, but do keep track of the whale's location until authorized responders and entanglement specialists arrive. Document the fishing gear or debris that has caused the entanglement and take photos. Boaters who want to learn more about how to assess, document, and report entangled marine animals can take a Level 1 U.S. Whale Entanglement Course online. To take the online course, go to: west-coast-training.whaledisentanglement.org.

[Lorena Landon]

2023 WAGGONER CRUISING GUIDE 113

SOUTH AND CENTRAL PUGET SOUND

to Sea-Tac Airport. The marina can provide shuttle service to and from the airport.

The guest area has a 25×100-foot concrete activity float with shelter, and concrete moorage floats. An 80-foot-long ADA-compliant ramp is available. The grounds are beautifully landscaped.

Services, including groceries, and several restaurants, are within walking distance of the marina. The 670-foot public fishing pier runs east-west. To enter the marina, leave the fishing pier to port and turn to starboard at the north end of the breakwater. At low tide the entrance is tight, especially with opposing traffic. At the south end of the marina, Des Moines Yacht Club has guest moorage for visiting members of reciprocal clubs.

Plans are in the works to redevelop the uplands to include a multi-purpose building, new restroom facilities, and attractive landscaping with stairs to access downtown.

The marina is home to SR3, a marine animal rehabilitation center dedicated to assisting entangled and injured marine animals.

Farmers market on Saturdays, June through September. July 4th "Fireworks over Des Moines."

Yukon Harbor offers good anchorage, well protected from the south but open to the northeast.

㉕ **Blake Island Marine State Park.** (360) 731-8330. Open all year, 475 acres with 1500 feet of dock space in the breakwater-protected marina. 24 mooring buoys for boats 45 feet and under ring the island. Two mooring buoys on the south end are restricted to vessels 36 feet and under. Pumpout, water, 30 amp power. No garbage drop and a "pack it in–pack it out" policy. Moorage is limited to 3 consecutive nights. Buoys on the east side are exposed to wakes from passing ships. Self-register and pay mooring buoy fee on shore, or by phone as posted on the buoy.

The marina is on the northeast shore of the island. To enter, follow the dredged channel marked by red and green beacons. Stay in the marked channel; the water is shoal on both sides of the beacons. Immediately inside the breakwater is a float for the State Parks boat. The northwest side of dock 1 is reserved for the park host and 30 minute load/unload. The rest of the floats are available on a first-come, first-serve basis. Expect to find them full during high season and on weekends year round. You can moor to the pilings, tied fore and aft (do not tie to the pumpout barge pilings); register and pay at the self-registration payment station. State Parks is developing plans for improvements at the marine park, including possible expansion of guest moorage space.

Blake Island has primitive campsites, including Cascadia Marine Trail campsites. An underwater reef is good for scuba diving. The park has picnic shelters, volleyball courts, nature trail, approximately 16 miles of hiking trails through dense forest, and 5 miles of shoreline to explore.

Tillicum Village is the site of a Native Longhouse replica, where salmon dinners were held in years past. The traditional Native Salmon BBQ & Dance performance have been suspended until Parks can obtain a new concessionaires partner. Argosy Cruises no longer provides excursions to the island. A snack window at the park is open July-September during various times of the day (usually 11:00 a.m., 3:00 p.m., and 6:00 p.m.).

Wildlife is abundant, including a high raccoon population not fearful of people. They roam the grounds and docks day or night looking for food. As in all state parks, there is a policy not to feed the animals. Park rangers recommend securing all garbage, pet food and ice chests; yes they can open an ice chest. Do not leave hatches open or you might find an unwelcomed surprise in your salon.

Blake Island is just a short hop from Elliott Bay Marina or Shilshole Bay Marina. The park is accessible only by boat and is one of the most popular stops on Puget Sound.

SEATTLE

Elliott Bay, the center of Seattle's shipping industry, is a busy ocean port. Keep a sharp watch for ferries coming and going from Colman Dock, for tugs with tows, and for commercial vessels of all kinds. Large vessels are slow to maneuver, and should always be given a wide berth. When there's any doubt at all, cross behind commercial vessels, not in front of them.

Piers 89, 90, and 91 in Smith Cove are heavily used by commercial ships. The Port of Seattle's grain terminal occupies part of the shoreline north of the regular commercial piers. Myrtle Edwards Park, including a fishing pier, stretches about a mile along the Elliott Bay waterfront. The piers on the central waterfront, too small for modern maritime commerce, have been converted to other uses, including a hotel, shops, museums, an aquarium, and places to sit and watch the harbor activity.

At Pier 36, south of the Colman ferry dock, the U.S. Coast Guard has its Seattle headquarters, including the Coast Guard Museum and Vessel Traffic Service.

Downtown Seattle is served by two excellent marinas: Elliott Bay Marina on the north shore below Magnolia Bluff, and Port of Seattle's Bell Harbor Marina at Pier 66. These two marinas make downtown Seattle easy to visit.

Seattle is often referred to as the "Boating Capital of America" and with little wonder. With abundant first-class visitor moorage, there is good reason to cruise to the Emerald City to find out what makes it so special.

Pumpout Service: Mobile pumpout service for the Seattle area is available through Pump MeOut (877-786-7631), and Pumpout Seattle (206-717-4997).

Taxi Service: Uber & Lyft; Farwest Taxi (206-622-1717); Orange Taxi (206-522-8800); STITA Taxi (206-246-9999); and Yellow Cab (206-622-6500).

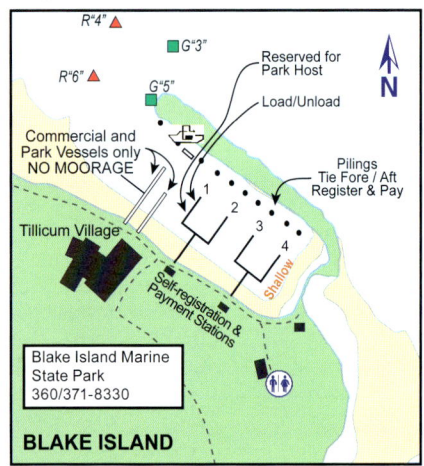

Longhouse on Blake Island

Blake Island Marine State Park

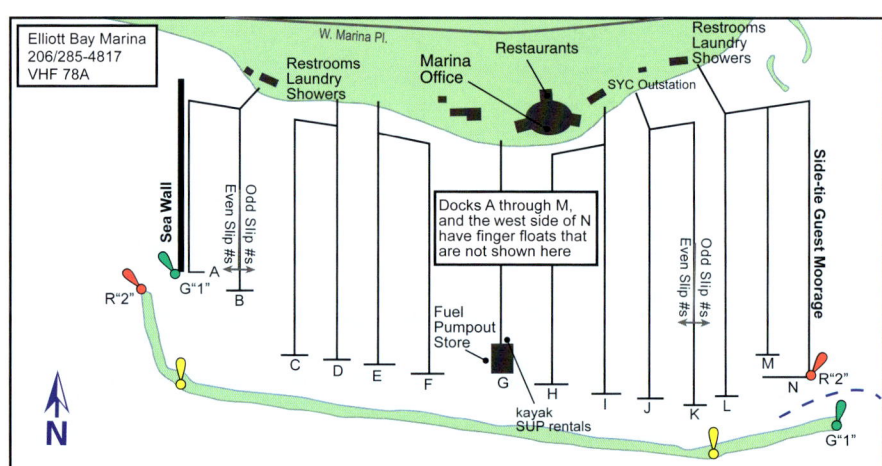

Elliott Bay Marina

See Area Map Page 107 - Maps Not for Navigation   **SOUTH AND CENTRAL PUGET SOUND**

Seattle's Great Wheel, a favorite attraction for tourists and locals

A day sail on Elliott Bay below Seattle's Space Needle

THINGS TO DO

- **Pike Place Market.** Unique shops with many specialty food items, even the first Starbucks. You can see cheese being made at Beechers. Watch out for flying salmon in the market. Don't miss the nearby Olympic Sculpture Park.
- **Seattle Aquarium.** See a coral reef, giant Pacific octopus, pinecone fish, and potbellied seahorses. Located at Pier 59, a few blocks south of Bell Harbor Marina.
- **Seattle Art Museum (SAM).** Locally curated exhibits and rotating exhibitions from the best art collections of the world.
- **Fremont Farmers Market.** Year-round on Sundays in this funky neighborhood. You never know what you might find.
- **Seattle Center.** Tour the Space Needle, or MoPop, the museum of pop culture formerly known as EMP—the Experience Music Project, and the Chihuly Garden and Glass Museum.
- **Pacific Science Center at Seattle Center.** Enjoy the IMAX Theater, the Planetarium or unique exhibits. Great for kids and adults.
- **Center for Wooden Boats**. Walk around the antique restored boats on South Lake Union. With membership and checkout, you can even rent a classic sailboat or powerboat for a cruise on the lake.
- **Museum of History and Industry (MOHAI).** Located in South Lake Union. Many exhibits on Seattle's heritage.
- **Museum of Flight.** A short taxi ride away is one of the nation's best flight museums. The Concorde, WWII aircraft, a Space Shuttle Simulator, a Boeing 707 and 787, and more.
- **Seattle Zoo**. An outstanding zoo for the day or an afternoon, just a cab ride away.
- **Seattle Children's Museum.** Over 22,000 sq. ft. of hands-on exhibits for kids, ages 10 months to 10 years, to explore, and daily educational programs.
- **Seattle Great Wheel.** Take a ride on one of Seattle's newest attractions. Great views day or night. Located at Pier 57.

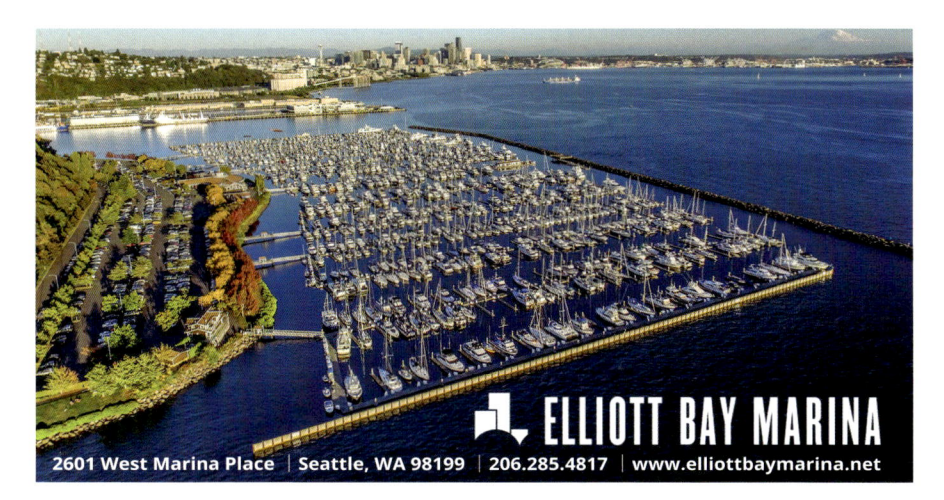

㉖ **Elliott Bay Marina.** 2601 W. Marina Place, Seattle, WA 98199; (206) 285-4817; info@elliottbaymarina.net; www.elliottbaymarina.net. Monitors VHF 78A. Certified Clean Marina. This is a beautiful marina, immaculately maintained, open all year. The fuel dock has gasoline, diesel, free pumpout, and a store with convenience groceries. Contact the office for waste oil disposal. Guest moorage available in unoccupied slips for most vessels on a first-come, first-serve basis. Reservations recommended for larger vessels 50 feet and up. Contact the marina regarding availability. Boaters can submit requests for reservations through Dockwa.com for any size boat. The marina has free cable TV, 30 & 50 amp power, up to 100 amp on outside moorage; some 200 amp available. Restrooms, laundry, pumpout, free showers, free use of kayaks, SUPs and bikes, and excellent 24-hour security. Enter through either end of the breakwater. The outside of N Dock accommodates superyachts up to 300 feet.

The marina office is on the ground level of the main building, near Maggie Bluffs Marina Grill. Elegant dining at the Palisade restaurant is located upstairs. It's 10 minutes by cab or Uber to downtown Seattle. There is easy access to the Seattle public transportation system within walking distance.

The marina is headquarters for the Downtown Sailing Series; 10 informal races Thursday evenings during the summer, with barbecue and awards afterward.

Whole Foods Market is about 1 mile away. A bike and walking path runs from the marina along scenic Myrtle Edwards waterfront park to the downtown waterfront. We took about an hour each way to walk between the marina and Pier 70. Seattle Yacht Club has an outstation (no reciprocal moorage) at the marina. Views of downtown, Mt. Rainier, Olympic Mountains.

ELLIOTT BAY MARINA
2601 West Marina Place | Seattle, WA 98199 | 206.285.4817 | www.elliottbaymarina.net

2023 **WAGGONER** CRUISING GUIDE   115

SOUTH AND CENTRAL PUGET SOUND

See Area Map Page 107 - Maps Not for Navigation

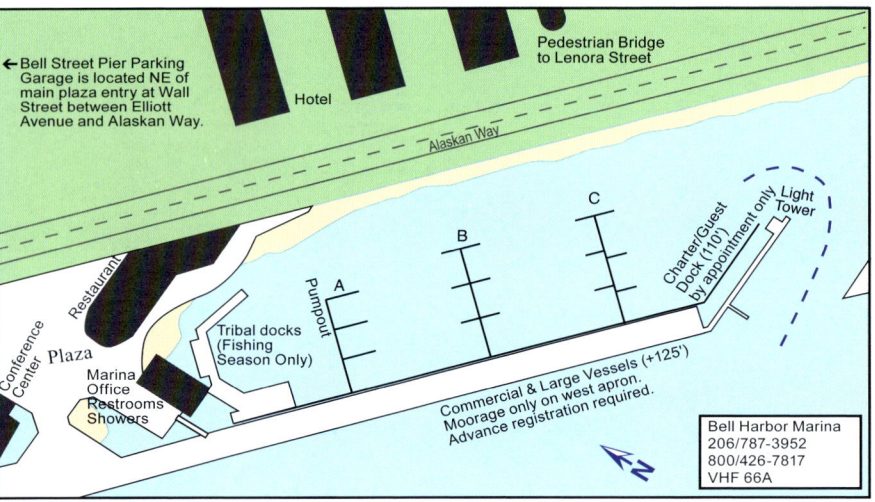

Bell Harbor Marina

㉗ **Bell Harbor Marina.** Pier 66, 2203 Alaskan Way, Seattle, WA 98121; (206) 787-3952; (206) 465-0554 after hours; bhm@portseattle.org; www.portseattle.org. Monitors VHF 66A. Certified Clean Marina. Open all year, 30, 50 & 100 amp power, water, restrooms, free showers, garbage/recycling drop, pumpout, 24-hour security. Entrance at 47°36.55'N/122°20.85'W—look for the distinctive spire as a landmark. Moorage reservations can be made by telephone or email.

The Port of Seattle's Bell Harbor Marina, with 37 slips, is part of Seattle's Central Waterfront Development, and is an easy cruising destination. Depending on the mix, the docks will hold as many as 70 visitor boats, 30 feet to 70 feet. The waterfront, with the Seattle Aquarium, a variety of shops, and the Seattle Great Wheel, is just outside the marina. It's a 2-block walk to the always interesting Pike Place Market.

Visitors can leave their boat at Bell Harbor and take in a game at T-Mobile Park for the Mariners or Lumen Field for the Seahawks or the Sounders. Three restaurants are just above the marina with many more restaurants and shops within walking distance.

Bell Harbor's facilities are top-notch, with excellent facilities, gated access, and an Anthony's restaurant on site. The staff is professional and alert.

Because of rough water in Elliott Bay, the breakwater entry is narrow. Boats larger than 70 feet will find the entry and turning basin a little tight. The Port of Seattle provides approximately 1900 feet of outside pier apron devoted to large vessels including superyachts and cruise ships.

Anthony's Pier 66 & Bell Street Diner
2201 Alaskan Way
(206) 448-6688

East Waterway. Both sides of East Waterway are lined with docks for commercial vessels, most of them loading or unloading containers. The waterway is navigable to Spokane Street, where a fixed bridge and foul ground block further navigation.

West Waterway. West Waterway and the connecting Duwamish River make a splendid sightseeing voyage.

Enter past busy Vigor Industrial shipyard (formerly Todd Shipyard) and the now-closed Lockheed Shipyard at the mouth, and motor along a fascinating variety of docks, ships, barges, small pleasure boats, mega-yachts, and abandoned hulks. Commercial buildings and the modest homes of South Park are on both sides.

You will go under the 1st Ave. S. Bridge,

BELL HARBOR MARINA — SEATTLE'S ONLY DOWNTOWN MARINA

CALL TO RESERVE GUEST MOORAGE
206-787-3952

See Area Map Page 107 - Maps Not for Navigation   **SOUTH AND CENTRAL PUGET SOUND**

vertical clearance 39 feet, and past the former site of the Boeing Company's Plant 2, to the 16th Ave. S. Bridge (renamed the South Park Bridge). The famed Delta Marine facility, builder of commercial fish boats and megayachts, is a short distance beyond the 16th Ave. S. (South Park) Bridge.

Transient moorage is available at Duwamish Yacht Club (206-767-9330) for reciprocal yacht club members; one 45-foot side-tie at the end of B dock. The yacht club is located one-half mile past the 16th Ave. S. Bridge; vessel clearance 34 feet. Past Delta Marine and the Duwamish Yacht Club, a low bridge blocks progress to all but small, open boats.

Don Armeni Park and Seacrest Park are located between Harbor Island and Duwamish Head. Don Armeni Park has a 4-lane launch ramp with floats. Seacrest Park has a fishing pier.

1st Avenue South Bridge. The Duwamish Bridge, officially known as the 1st Ave. South Bridge, spans the Duwamish Waterway, carrying vehicle traffic on State Hwy 99. The two bridge spans open for marine traffic from 9:30 a.m. to 2:30 p.m. daily, including federal holidays, except Columbus Day.

Bridge openings for marine traffic are not allowed Monday-Friday from 6:00 a.m. to 9:00 a.m. and 3:00 p.m. to 6:00 p.m. except for vessels of 5,000 gross tons or more.

To request an opening, call the bridge tender at (206) 764-4160, or call on VHF 13. Average opening time is 11 minutes; the far span is opened first. Vessel clearance, 39 feet.

Harbor Island Marina. 1001 Klickitat Way S.W., Seattle, WA 98134; (206) 787-3006; him@portofseattle.org; www.portofseattle.org. This Port of Seattle marina is located on the south end of Harbor Island and caters to long term tenants. No guest moorage. Pumpout station.

South Park Marina. 8604 Dallas Ave. S, Seattle, WA 98108; (206) 762-3880; info@southparkmarina.com; www.southparkmarina.com. Moorage and dry boat storage. Repair services on site, with a team of independent service providers. Haulouts to 45 feet. Boat owners may do work on their own boat. 30 amp power, water, restrooms, showers, and laundry.

SHILSHOLE BAY

Shilshole Bay indents the shoreline of Puget Sound north of West Point, and leads via a dredged channel to the Hiram M. Chittenden Locks (**Ballard Locks**) and the Lake Washington Ship Canal. Shilshole Bay Marina is north of the dredged channel, with entrances around the north and south ends of a long rock breakwater.

Lacking local knowledge, boats bound for the locks should follow the channel, marked by buoys, to the locks.

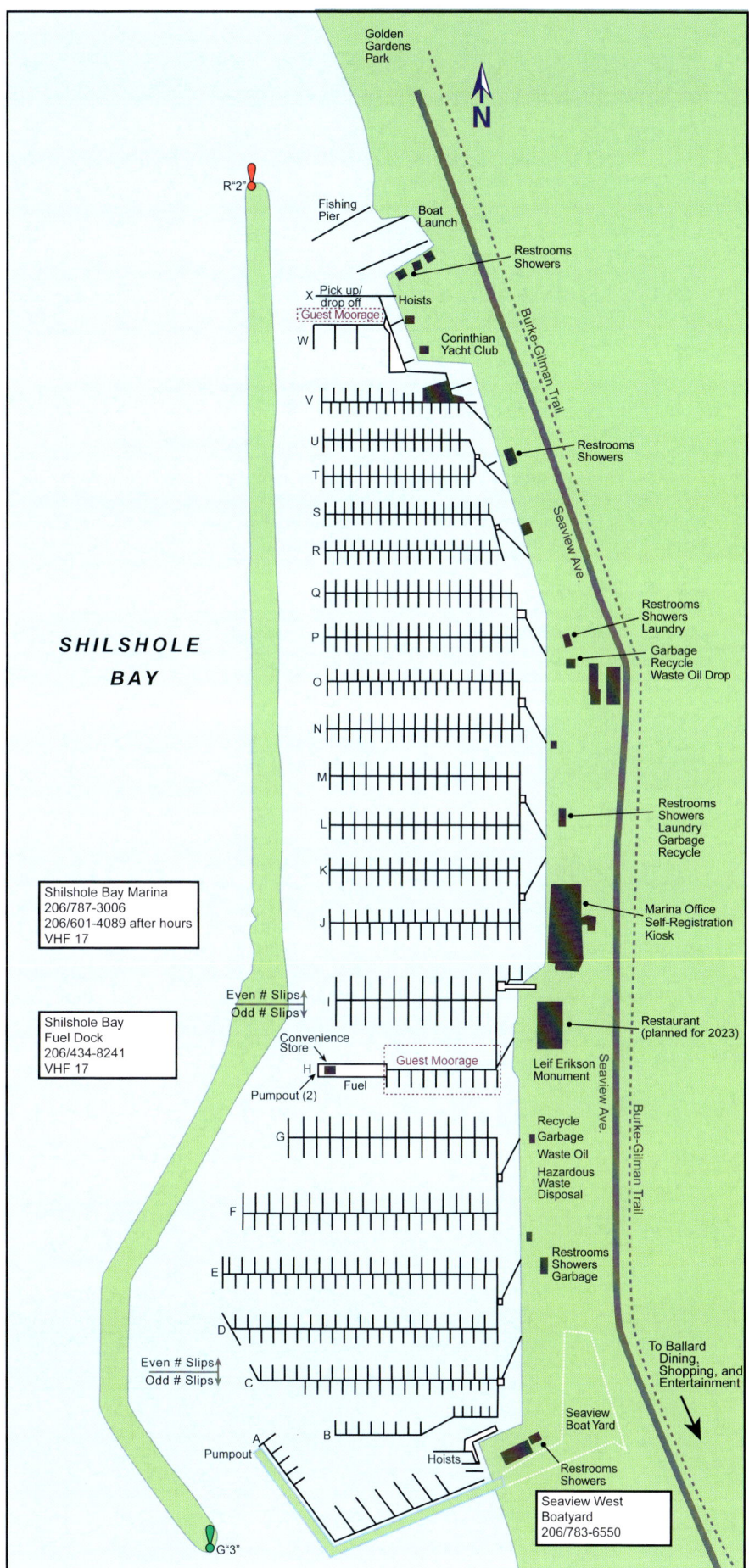

Shilshole Bay Marina

2023 waggoner CRUISING GUIDE   117

Hiram M. Chittenden Locks

The dredged, well-marked channel leading to the Hiram Chittenden Locks passes under the Burlington Northern bascule bridge. *Caution: Although Chart 18447 shows vertical clearance of this bridge to be 43 feet from mean high water, Local Notice to Mariners reports that the actual clearance may be closer to 41 feet. Clearance gauges have been installed at the draw.* The bridge is kept open unless a train is due. The opening signal is one long and one short blast, the same signal as for the Ballard, Fremont, University, and Montlake Bridges. Remember, though, if a train is due you will be ignored.

Your wait at the locks, in either direction, can be as short as zero or as long as several hours depending on the flow of commercial traffic. Emergency and commercial vessels have priority.

Approaching From Puget Sound: If you are approaching from Puget Sound, you'll starboard-side tie to the wall on the south side of the channel under the railroad bridge; use gloves to protect your hands from barnacles, creosote, and tar. If traffic is heavy, as it often is at the end of fair weather summer weekends, you may end up port-side tying to the wall west of the railroad bridge. Normally, only large commercial craft tie to that wall, but if the waiting area is crowded, you may be there too. The current always flows from the lake into the Sound. Approach carefully and be ready with extra fenders. Wait your turn and do not crowd ahead. Government vessels and commercial vessels have priority over pleasure craft, and will be directed into the locks ahead of pleasure craft.

Red and green lights on the large and small locks signal when you can enter. Red light means no; green light means yes. A loud hailer system also announces directions to the traffic waiting to transit.

Lock attendants do not respond to most radio calls from pleasure craft, but if you must communicate with them, call on VHF 13, using the 1-watt low-power mode, or phone (206) 783-7000; available 24 hours per day. If you need help, they will answer. If you're calling to complain, forget it.

There are two locks: a large lock 825 feet long and 80 feet wide, and a small lock 150 feet long and 30 feet wide. The large lock can handle vessels 700 feet long by 78 feet wide; the small lock can handle vessels up to 120 feet long by 26 feet wide. On a busy summer weekend, the large lock can take a half-hour or more to fill with vessels. Lock attendants will direct entering vessels to one lock or the other by light signals and the loud hailer. Each vessel should have bow and stern mooring lines at least 50 feet long with a 12-inch eye in one end. Fenders should be set out on both sides of the boat. You may be placed against the lock wall or rafted to another boat.

The lock attendants are conscientious, experienced, and helpful. They make eye contact with the helmsman of each vessel as it enters, and signal their intentions clearly. They are polite, but they give direct orders. Do exactly what they tell you to do. They have seen everything and know how to deal with problems.

If directed into the large lock, larger vessels will be brought in first and tied along the walls. Smaller vessels will raft off. Large vessel or small, be sure you have 50-foot mooring lines, bow and stern, in case you are put along the wall. The lock attendants will throw messenger lines to you. Tie your mooring lines to the messenger lines and they will take them to bollards on top of the lock wall.

There is usually some current in the locks, flowing from the lakes toward the Sound. Enter slowly but with enough speed for steerage. Once your lines are made fast, prepare to assist boats that lie alongside you. When the lock is closed and the water begins to rise, the vessels along the wall must keep a half-turn on their cleats and continuously take in slack. When the water has stopped rising, make all lines fast until you are told to leave.

If directed into the small lock, you will lie alongside a floating wall equipped with yellow-painted "buttons." Loop your bow and stern lines around the buttons, bring the lines back, and make them fast to cleats. The floating walls rise or fall with the water level, so you don't need to tend your lines during the transit. Caution: It is always possible that a floating wall could jam in its tracks. Stand by to slack your lines quickly if that happens.

When directed to do so, loosen your lines and move out of the locks slowly but with good steerage.

Approaching From The Lake: If you are westbound from the lake to the Sound, you still need 50-foot mooring lines, bow and stern, in case you lie along the wall of the large lock. However, you will be able to hand your lines to the attendant instead of tying them to messenger lines. Boats along the large lock wall will slack their lines as the water drops.

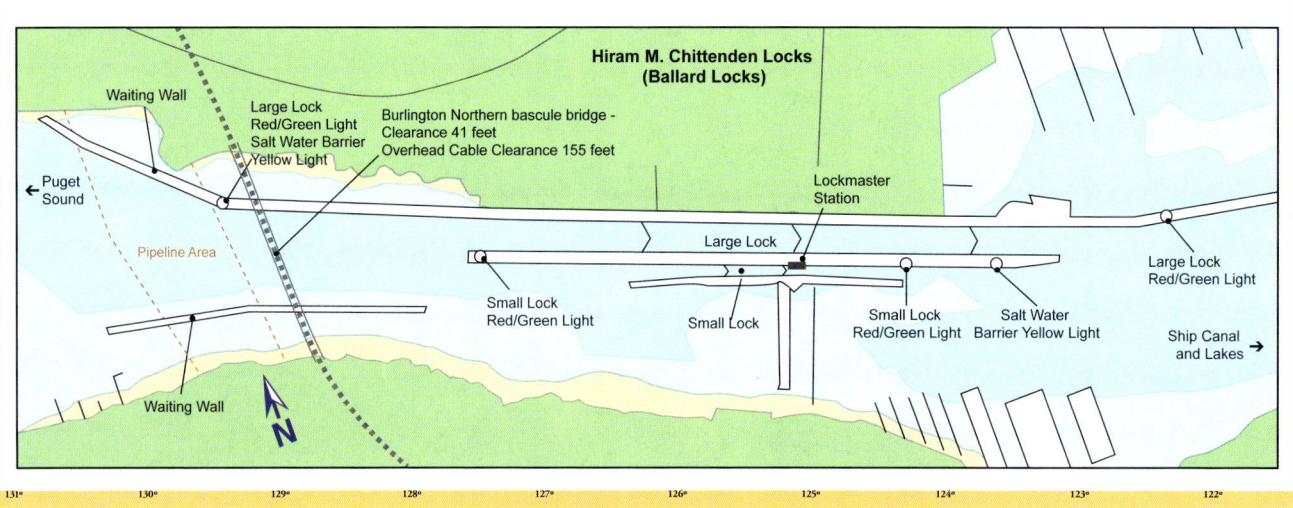

See Area Map Page 107 - Maps Not for Navigation

SOUTH AND CENTRAL PUGET SOUND

LOCAL KNOWLEDGE

Shallow Area: Do not stray south of the buoyed channel in Shilshole Bay. The water between the channel and Magnolia Bluff shoals rapidly.

㉘ **Shilshole Bay Marina.** 7001 Seaview Ave. NW, Suite 100, Seattle, WA 98117; (206) 787-3006; after hours call (206) 601-4089; sbm@portseattle.org; www.portseattle.org. Certified Clean Marina. Monitors VHF 17. Open all year, office hours 8:00 a.m. to 4:30 p.m., Monday through Saturday. This is a large, busy, well-equipped marina, operated by the Port of Seattle. The marina has guest moorage for more than 100 boats to 250 feet, 30, 50, & 100 amp power. Call for reservations.

Restrooms, showers and laundry facilities, with one building north of the office, and one building to the south. A third restroom without laundry is located on the far north end. Free cable TV on the guest docks, pumpout, portapotty dump. Waste oil disposal stations, recycling and garbage drop.

Walking distance to restaurants and a fast-food stand. Golden Gardens Park, with beach and picnic areas, is a short walk north of the marina. Take a short 1.7 mile bike ride or taxi to Ballard for shopping and a selection of dining options. Stop along the way and view the Ballard Locks.

The large Central Plaza, in front of the office building and adjacent to the guest docks, is nice for gatherings. Contact the office for event planning. Dukes Restaurant is coming to Shilshole in 2023.

Seaview West Boatyard (206-783-6550), with a 55-ton Travelift haulout, is at the south end of the marina. The boatyard has repair-yard supplies and propane. A wide launch ramp is at the north end of the marina.

㉘ **Shilshole Bay Fuel Dock**. 7029 Seaview Ave. NW, Seattle, WA 98117; (206) 783-7555. Open 7 days a week except Thanksgiving and Christmas. Ethanol-free gasoline, diesel, kerosene. At the end of H dock, the Port of Seattle operates a pumpout, bilge pumpout, and portapotty dump at the outer end of the dock. Convenience store carries ice, beverages, snacks, local guidebooks. Friendly people, clean and efficient operation.

LAKE WASHINGTON SHIP CANAL

The Lake Washington Ship Canal connects the Hiram Chittenden Locks with Lake Washington, a distance of approximately 5.5 miles. Except for a marked course in the middle of Lake Union, a 7-knot speed limit is enforced all the way to Webster Point, at the entrance to Lake Washington. Most boats travel about 6 knots.

If no bridge openings are needed, allow about 30 minutes between Lake Union and the locks, and about an hour between Lake Washington and the locks. The Lake Washington Ship Canal has fuel docks, ship repair yards, boatyards, and moorages. Keep an alert lookout for vessels pulling out or turning. This can be an active area.

LOCAL KNOWLEDGE

Sound Signals: For all of the bridges, the sound signal to request an opening is 1 long blast and 1 short. The bridge tender will answer with 1 long and 1 short blast if the bridge can be opened or 5 short blasts if it cannot.

Ship Canal Bridge Information. From west to east, the Lake Washington Ship Canal is crossed by the Ballard Bridge, vertical clearance 46 feet at the center; Fremont Bridge, vertical clearance 31 feet at the center; University Bridge, vertical clearance 45 feet at the center; and the Montlake Bridge, vertical clearance 48 feet at the center.

Rush Hour Restricted Openings: The Ballard, Fremont and University Bridges do not open for recreational vessel traffic weekdays from 7:00 a.m. to 9:00 a.m. and 4:00 p.m. to 6:00 p.m., except holidays.

Nighttime Bridge Openings: The Ballard, Fremont and University Bridges are untended at night between 11:00 p.m. and 7:00 a.m. One crew, based at the Fremont Bridge, stands by to open bridges for vessel traffic. For openings call one hour ahead on VHF 13, or by telephone (206) 386-4251.

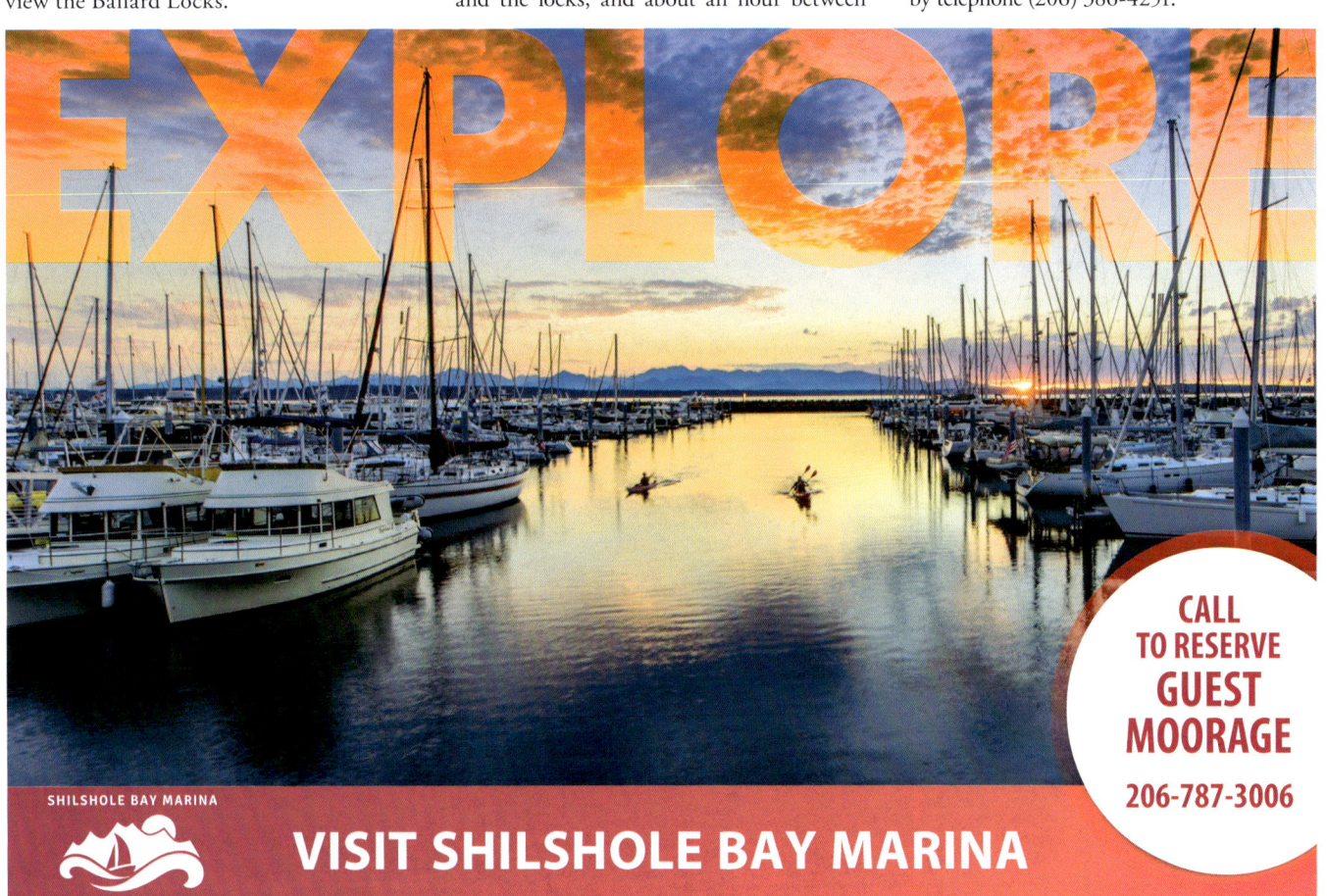

VISIT SHILSHOLE BAY MARINA

SHILSHOLE BAY MARINA
PORT OF SEATTLE

CALL TO RESERVE GUEST MOORAGE
206-787-3006

SOUTH AND CENTRAL PUGET SOUND   See Area Map Page 107 - Maps Not for Navigation

SHIP CANAL BRIDGE OPENINGS

BRIDGE	HEIGHT	RESTRICTED OPENING HOURS	
Burlington-Northern Railroad Bridge	43 feet MHW		
Ballard Bridge VHF 13	46 feet at center	Weekdays 0700-0900, 1600-1800 and Special Events	1-hour notice 2300-0700
Fremont Bridge VHF 13	31 feet at center	Weekdays 0700-0900, 1600-1800 and Special Events	1-hour notice 2300-0700
University Bridge VHF 13	45 feet at center	Weekdays 0700-0900, 1600-1800 and Special Events	1-hour notice 2300-0700
Montlake Bridge VHF 13	46 feet at center	May 1- Aug. 31: Weekdays 0700-0900, 1530-1830; Sept. 1-April 30: Weekdays 0700-1000, 1530-1900	May 1-Aug 31: 1230-1530 opens only on the hour and half hour

The Montlake Bridge is attended 24 hours a day, but between 11:00 p.m. and 7:00 a.m. vessels needing an opening must call ahead on VHF 13 or by telephone, (206) 720-3048.

㉚ **24th Avenue Landing.** At the foot of 24th Ave. NW on the north side of the Ship Canal, east of the locks. Open all year, day-use only up to 2 hours free of charge; no overnight stays. Dock has 300 feet of space, 40-foot maximum boat length. No power, water or showers. The Ballard business district is within walking distance.

㉚ **Ballard Oil Co.** 5300 26th Ave. NW, Seattle, WA 98107; (206) 783-0241; info@ballardoil.com; www.ballardoil.com. Open Monday through Saturday. Just east of the locks, on the north side of the Ship Canal. Diesel only. Set up to handle larger pleasure craft and commercial vessels.

㉛ **Salmon Bay.** The Port of Seattle's Fishermen's Terminal is located on the south side of the Lake Washington Ship Canal at Salmon Bay, a half-mile east of the locks. Although Fishermen's Terminal caters primarily to the large Seattle-based fishing fleet, guest and permanent moorage is available for pleasure craft.

A short term guest float is located along the inner bulkhead at the head of the west wall, often used by boaters while dining at Chinook's restaurant. Major repair facilities are nearby, as are stores offering a variety of marine services and supplies.

㉛ **Salmon Bay Marine Center.** 2284 W. Commodore Way #100, Seattle, WA 98199; (206) 450-9100; www.sbmc.com. On the south side of the Ship Canal, this facility has 18 slips to accommodate vessels from 60 to 240 feet. Most slips are sold or on long term lease. Short term moorage for large vessels may be available by reservation. Slips are 30 feet to 45 feet wide with a minimum depth of 12 feet. Power is single and 3-phase 240/480 and 208 volt–200 amp. A 50-cycle transformer is available. Black water connection at each slip with gray water pumpout. Free Wi-Fi, parking, and 4 electric utility cars for dock use. Marine repair companies and several large yacht brokerages are in the shoreside building.

㉛ **Salmon Bay Marina/Port of Seattle.** 2100 W. Commodore Way, Seattle, WA 98199; (206) 787-3395; salmonbay@portseattle.org; www.salmonbaymarina.com. Staff at Fishermen's Terminal respond to phone calls and email. Restrooms, showers, and laundry facilities, 30 & 50 amp power.

This marina was purchased by the Port of Seattle in June of 2018 and is for full time leased moorage only. Seattle Marine & Fishing Supply, a large chandlery, is across the street. Walking distance to restaurants and Fishermen's Terminal.

㉚ **Covich-Williams Chevron.** Dock Office, 5219 Shilshole Ave. NW, Seattle, WA 98107; (206) 784-0171; www.covichwilliams.com. On the north side of the Ship Canal, next to Salmon Bay Sand & Gravel. Open weekdays 8:00 a.m. to 5:00 p.m., Saturdays until noon; closed Sundays. Gasoline, diesel, kerosene. Carries filters, absorbent products, antifreeze, environmental products, fuel additives.

㉚ **Ballard Mill Marina.** 4733 Shilshole Ave. NW, Seattle, WA 98107; (206) 789-4777; ballardmillmarina@gmail.com; www.ballardmillmarina.com. Open all year, no guest moorage, 28 to 60 feet. Restrooms, pumpout, 20 & 30 amp power, showers. East of Covich-Williams Chevron fuel dock on the north side of the Ship Canal. Free pumpout on the east dock. Stores, restaurants, marine supplies, haulout and repairs nearby.

CHINOOK'S AT SALMON BAY
1900 W. Nickerson St.
(206) 283-4665

㉛ **Fishermen's Terminal/Port of Seattle.** 3919 18th Ave. W., Seattle, WA 98119; (206) 787-3395; (800) 426-7817; ft@portseattle.org; www.portseattle.org. Monitors VHF 17, 24 hours a day, 30, 50 & 100 amp power, water, restrooms & showers, security cameras, free pumpout (sewage and bilge), recycling, waste oil dump. Major repair and supply facilities nearby. Restaurants, fish sales, shops, small grocery store, chandlery, postal service on site. The marina is on the south side of the Ship Canal, immediately west of the Ballard Bridge. Guest moorage welcomed, first-come, first-served, call for slip assignment. Make payment at building No. C15 located at 3919 - 18th Ave. West.

Dining: Chinook's at Salmon Bay is good for sit-down dining. A takeout seafood window is on the east side of the building. Tables and chairs are on the deck or in a covered area. An excellent fish market is in the front of the building. The Highliner Pub and the Bay Café also offer dining. The side-tie guest mooring float is in front of the restaurant building; complimentary 4-hour moorage.

Fishermen's Terminal

See Area Map Page 107 - Maps Not for Navigation

SOUTH AND CENTRAL PUGET SOUND

LOCAL KNOWLEDGE

Floatplane Operations: A row of 5 lighted buoys in the center of Lake Union marks the take off and landing area for floatplanes. Pilots taking off and landing will trigger flashing lights to indicate air operations. Water craft need to stay 200 feet to either side of the line of buoys when lights are flashing.

Lake Union is lined with ship and boat moorages, houseboat moorages, and boating related businesses. It's the center of Seattle's boat sales industry. In the middle of the lake, a speed range marked by 4 buoys, is for sea trials. Other than the speed range, a 7-knot speed limit is enforced. A launch ramp is on the north shore, east of Gas Works Park. Gas Works Park is easily identifiable by the painted remnants of an industrial coal gas plant. Tyee Yacht Club and Puget Sound Yacht Club are located on Lake Union. The large Fisheries Supply marine store is located near Gas Works Park. Guest moorage is limited on Lake Union.

The south end of Lake Union is the home of Northwest Seaport. Next door is the Center for Wooden Boats and their Wagner Education Center housing classrooms, a sail loft, event space, and a boat shop. Lovely Lake Union Park, with the Museum of History and Industry (MOHAI), is adjacent. Kenmore Air's seaplane base is on the southwest shore, just across from the park.

A major ship repair yard, Lake Union Drydock, is on the eastern shore near the south end of the lake. Ivar's Salmon House, a popular waterfront restaurant, is at the north end of the lake under the I-5 freeway bridge, with temporary moorage for tenders and small boats while dining.

Pumpout Service: Mobile pumpout service for Lake Union and the Ship Canal is available through S.S. Head (206-228-9991). A public pumpout is available year-round at Gas Works Park Marina located on the east side of Gas Works Park on north Lake Union.

No Anchoring: Anchoring is not permitted in Lake Union except for specific authorized events such as the 4th of July fireworks in the evening.

㉜ **Morrison's North Star Marine.** 2732 Westlake Ave. N., Seattle, WA 98109; (206) 284-6600; www.morrisonsfueldock.com. Open all year, 7 days a week. Fuel dock with ethanol-free gasoline and diesel, no guest moorage. Restrooms, free pumpout, water. Handles oil changes; call for appointment. Limited marine hardware, local charts, groceries, beer, wine, ice. Friendly and well-run.

㉜ **Nautical Landing Marina.** 2500 Westlake Ave. N., Seattle, WA 98109; (206) 464-4614; info@nautical-landing.com; www.nautical-landing.com. Open all year for permanent and guest use for vessels from 60 to 300 feet. This facility is popular with superyachts and has services to match.

THE SEATTLE AQUARIUM

The Seattle Aquarium has long been a favorite tourist attraction and a draw for locals looking to spend time with family. As boaters out on the water, we have the opportunity to see marine mammals in the wild, including sea otters, seals, sea lions, and the playful Dall's porpoise; but unless we are scuba divers, we miss many of the creatures that mostly stay below the surface.

How often do we get to see the Giant Pacific Octopus, for example, which has adapted to our cold, oxygen-rich waters? The North Pacific Octopus is best seen at the Seattle Aquarium, where you can observe its graceful movements; its expanding arms, with two rows of suckers; and its ever-changing color, used for camouflage. The octopus is truly an impressive creature. The entire body of an octopus is compressible, so they can fit through surprisingly small openings. Other creatures best seen at the Aquarium include coral, unusual fish species, and a variety of sea anemones.

The Seattle Aquarium first opened in May of 1977 at Pier 59, after funds were allocated for a municipal aquarium. The Aquarium has seen modernization and expansion over the years, with more improvements to come. The recent removal of the Alaskan Way Viaduct, and reconstruction of the Seattle Seawall, has spurred on existing plans for a new Seattle waterfront park; the Aquarium will continue to be an important attraction, and play an integral part in the development of the new Seattle waterfront.

SOUTH AND CENTRAL PUGET SOUND

See Area Map Page 107 - Maps Not for Navigation

㉝ **MOHAI Docks** Center for Wooden Boats. Docks located in front of the Museum of History and Industry, on the south end of Lake Union, are managed by the Center for Wooden Boats (206-382-2628). The North Wall has 160 feet of side-tie moorage and one 60-foot slip. Overnight stays at $1.30 per foot; no power, no water. Reservations are available by phone (206-382-2628). Two-week maximum stay. The small concrete Art Float in front of the gazebo structure is for human-powered craft only.

The West Wall has 220 feet of side-tie moorage on a first-come, first-serve basis, no charge. Day-use only from sunrise to sundown. Overnight moorage on the West Wall is only for boats on display for special events.

㉝ **Lake Union Piers**. 901 Fairview Ave. N., Seattle, WA 98109; located at the southeast end of Lake Union; (206) 216-4199, a 24-hour phone number. Transient moorage at Lake Union Piers is managed by Chiles & Company. Transient moorage on a 160-foot dock on the west side of the plaza area; 3-hour maximum stay. An additional 70-foot dock running east and west between Daniels Broiler and the Center for Wooden Boats is also available for transient moorage; 3-hour maximum stay. Signage is located at these guest docks. Moorage is for free. No overnight stays. Usage of the docks is closely monitored.

Several restaurants are in the area. It's an easy walk to the Center for Wooden Boats and the Museum of History and Industry (MOHAI).

Buildings in the area have been re-purposed and modernized. "Lakeside at South Lake Union," an upscale restaurant with a five-course fixed-price meal, is located at Lake Union Piers. Waterway Cruises & Events, and Northwest Yacht Brokers are also tenants at the shoreside facilities.

㉝ **Marina Mart**. 1500 Westlake Ave. N., Seattle, WA 98109; (206) 268-3322; www.marinamart.com. Permanent moorage only, no guest moorage.

#MindTheZone

Be courteous, aware, and safe on Lake Union.

We all love Lake Union, and as the lake gets more use, we all need to be aware of other users of the lake.

From Memorial Day to Labor Day, five seaplane advisory buoys mark a landing and takeoff area running from the south end of the lake towards the north.

When the buoys' yellow lights are flashing:
- A seaplane is about to take off or land
- Move away from the advisory buoys, 200 feet east or west

At all times:
- If nearing or close to the buoys, be aware of where you are
- Consider moving through the buoy area quickly
- Never tie up to the buoys

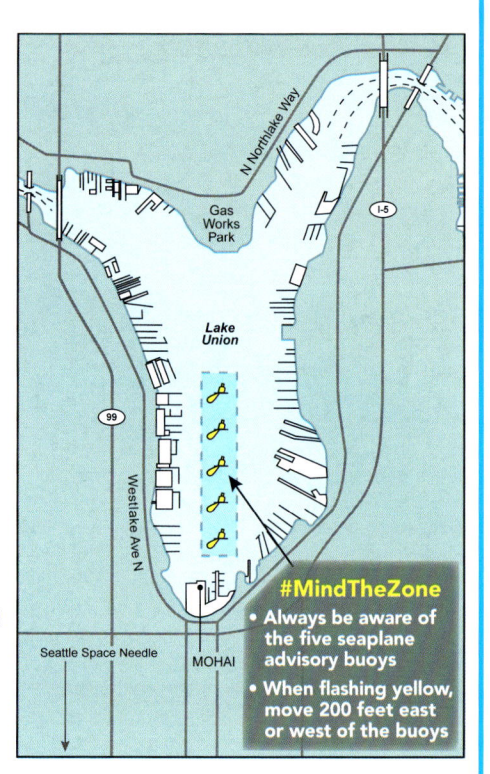

RECREATIONAL BOATING ASSOCIATION OF WASHINGTON

The voice of Northwest boating
rbaw.org/MindTheZone

#MindTheZone
- Always be aware of the five seaplane advisory buoys
- When flashing yellow, move 200 feet east or west of the buoys

Portage Bay. East of the University Bridge, vertical clearance 42 feet at the center, Portage Bay is the home of Seattle Yacht Club and Queen City Yacht Club. The University of Washington has several facilities along the north shore. The University Bridge opens to 1 long blast and 1 short.

Pumpout Service: A public pumpout station is located at Boat Street Marina in slip 79 and can accommodate vessels up to 55 feet. The private marina is located on the north shore of Portage Bay.

Montlake Cut. East of Portage Bay, the Montlake Cut connects to Union Bay and Lake Washington. The cut is narrow. When boat traffic is heavy, boat wakes can be turbulent as they bounce off the concrete side walls. Slow, steady speeds are called for. The Montlake Bridge, which crosses the cut, has a vertical clearance of 46 feet at the center. The bridge opens to 1 long blast and 1 short.

Union Bay. Union Bay is just east of the Montlake Cut and connects with Lake Washington. The dredged channel is well buoyed. The University of Washington's waterfront activities center is on the north shore, and the arboretum is on the south shore. Except for the dredged channel, the bay is shoal.

PACIFIC FIBERGLASS, INC.
Haulouts, Repair, Rejuvenation
(206) 789-4690

- Running gear
- Structural repair
- Major modifications
- Interior refinishing
- Bottom painting
- Blister repair
- Thruster installation
- The best LPU paint job

In Everett!
EVERETT YACHT SERVICE

Haulouts at Seattle's Canal Boatyard **and** Everett Marina!
pacificfiberglass.com
(206) 789 4690

I L♥VE LAKE UNION
#MindTheZone

See Area Map Page 107 - Maps Not for Navigation

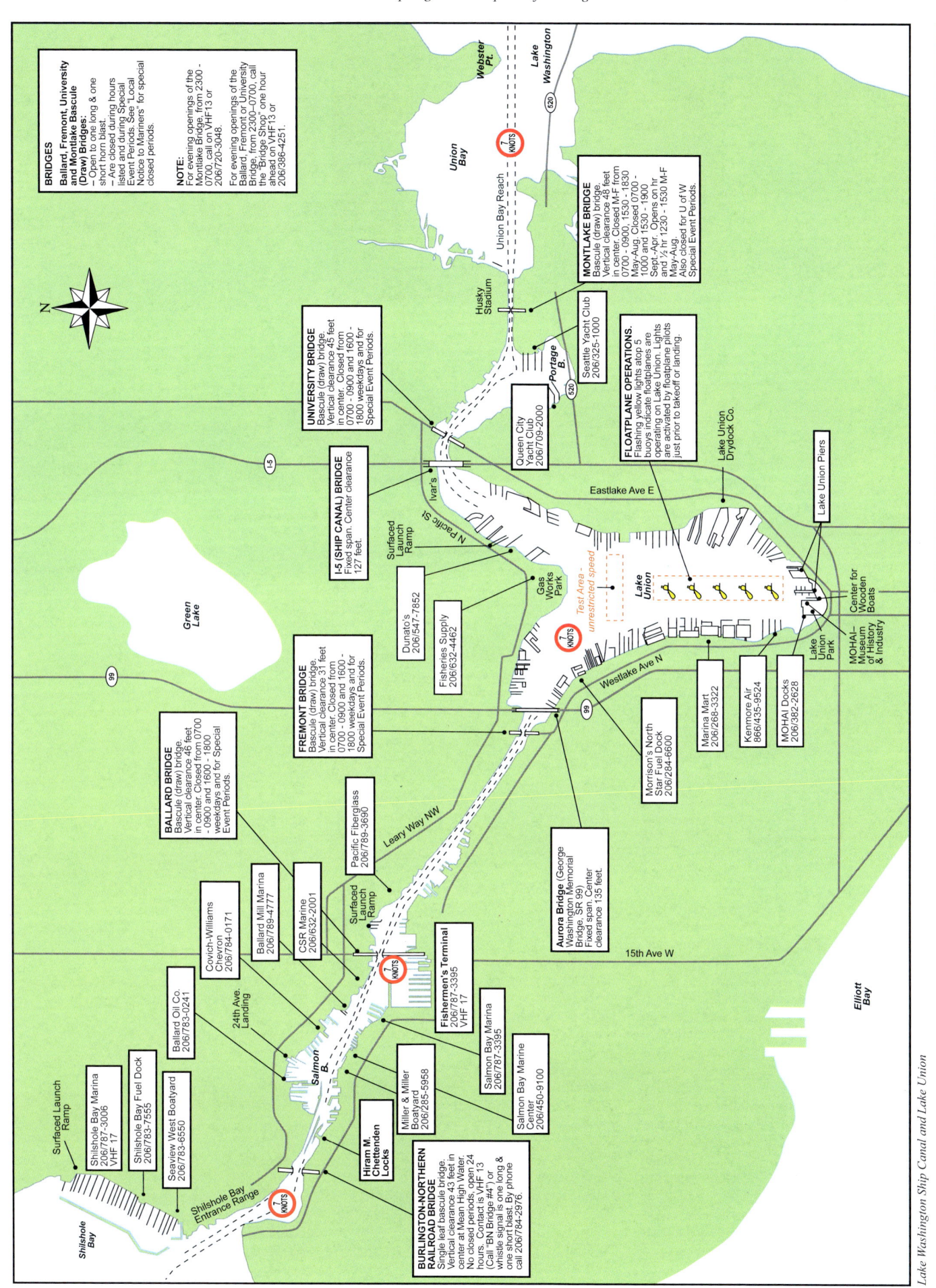

SOUTH AND CENTRAL PUGET SOUND

BRIDGES
Ballard, Fremont, University and Montlake Bascule (Draw) Bridges.
– Open to one long & one short horn blast.
– Are closed during hours listed and during Special Event Periods. See "Local Notice to Mariners" for special closed periods.

NOTE:
For evening openings of the Montlake Bridge, from 2300 - 0700, call on VHF 13 or 206/720-3048.

For evening openings of the Ballard, Fremont or University Bridge, from 2300–0700, call the "Bridge Shop" one hour ahead on VHF 13 or 206/386-4251.

MONTLAKE BRIDGE
Bascule (draw) bridge. Vertical clearance 48 feet in center. Closed M-F from 0700 - 0900, 1530 - 1830 May-Aug. Closed 0700 - 1000 and 1530 - 1900 Sept.-Apr. Opens on hr and ½ hr 1230 - 1530 M-F May-Aug. Also closed for U of W Special Event Periods.

UNIVERSITY BRIDGE
Bascule (draw) bridge. Vertical clearance 45 feet in center. Closed from 0700 - 0900 and 1600 - 1800 weekdays and for Special Event Periods.

I-5 (SHIP CANAL) BRIDGE
Fixed span. Center clearance 127 feet.

FLOATPLANE OPERATIONS.
Flashing yellow lights atop 5 buoys indicate floatplanes are operating on Lake Union. Lights are activated by floatplane pilots just prior to takeoff or landing.

FREMONT BRIDGE
Bascule (draw) bridge. Vertical clearance 31 feet in center. Closed from 0700 - 0900 and 1600 - 1800 weekdays and for Special Event Periods.

BALLARD BRIDGE
Bascule (draw) bridge. Vertical clearance 46 feet in center. Closed from 0700 - 0900 and 1600 - 1800 weekdays and for Special Event Periods.

AURORA BRIDGE (George Washington Memorial Bridge, SR 99). Fixed span. Center clearance 135 feet.

FISHERMEN'S TERMINAL
206/787-3395
VHF 17

BURLINGTON-NORTHERN RAILROAD BRIDGE
Single leaf bascule bridge. Vertical clearance 43 feet in center at Mean High Water. No closed periods, open 24 hours. Contact is VHF 13 (Call "BN Bridge #4") or whistle signal is one long & one short blast. By phone call 206/784-2976.

Shilshole Bay Marina 206/787-3006 VHF 17
Shilshole Bay Fuel Dock 206/783-7555
Seaview West Boatyard 206/783-6550
Ballard Oil Co. 206/783-0241
24th Ave. Landing
Covich-Williams Chevron 206/784-0171
Ballard Mill Marina 206/789-4777
CSR Marine 206/632-2001
Pacific Fiberglass 206/789-3690
Miller & Miller Boatyard 206/285-5958
Salmon Bay Marina 206/787-3395
Salmon Bay Marine Center 206/450-9100
Hiram M. Chittenden Locks
Dunato's 206/547-7852
Fisheries Supply 206/632-4462
Morrison's North Star Fuel Dock 206/284-6600
Marina Mart 206/268-3322
Kenmore Air 866/435-9524
MOHAI Docks 206/382-2628
Seattle Yacht Club 206/325-1000
Queen City Yacht Club 206/709-2000

Test Area - unrestricted speed

Lake Washington Ship Canal and Lake Union

Kirkland's Marina Park has a guest dock with slips for smaller boats, end tie and side tie.

LAKE WASHINGTON

Lake Washington, 16 miles long, defines the eastern border of Seattle, and washes the edges of Kenmore, Bothell, Kirkland, Medina, Bellevue, Mercer Island and Renton. Summer weekends will be busy. Watercraft of all types crisscross the lake and party-raft in the bays. Opening Day of Boating Season celebration in early May of each year fills the waters from Lake Washington to Portage Bay, with hundreds of decorated boats parading through the Montlake Cut. Seafair celebration weekend borders on madness.

The Lake Washington shoreline is filled from the waterline to the tops of the ridges with waterfront homes and mansions. Cruising the shores while admiring the elegant to modest homes is a perfect day-long experience. There is a 7-knot speed limit within 100 yards of shore, docks, and bridges throughout Lake Washington. Kirkland, Bellevue, Leschi, Madison Park, Juanita Bay, and Renton are some nice boater friendly day stops for lunch or dinner. Limited overnight guest moorage is available at marinas and public docks in Kirkland, Kenmore, Newport, and Renton. Restrictions on overnight anchoring on Lake Washington are enforced. Overnight anchoring is only allowed in Andrews Bay on the south end. At the north end of the lake, overnight anchoring is allowed in Juanita Bay; in Kenmore, off of Log Boom Park; and in fair weather, off St. Edwards Park.

Two floating bridges, I-90 and SR 520, cross Lake Washington and limit boater access to the south end of the lake with a maximum 70 feet of vertical clearance. Construction on the replacement SR 520 bridge floating span is complete. Work on the western connection to I-5 near Montlake continues. The replacement floating span does not have an opening section for boat traffic. Boat traffic passes under the fixed bridge at high-rises on either end along two navigation channels. Vertical clearance is 65 to 70 feet at the east high-rise and 42 to 49 feet at the west high-rise. Vertical clearances vary as the seasonal lake level is adjusted; higher water levels in spring and early summer, and lower levels in fall and winter. The I-90 floating bridge has a maximum vertical clearance of 34 feet at the west end and 37 feet at the east end. Least clearance at each end is 28 feet. The East Channel I-90 fixed bridge has a vertical clearance of 70 feet.

Sand Point. North from Webster Point, the first notable landmark is the former Naval Aviation base of Sand Point. Sand Point now includes Magnuson Park, which has a 2-lane launch ramp with floats. It is also the Northwest District headquarters for the National Oceanic and Atmospheric Administration (NOAA), which has a long piling pier along its north shore. Facilities west of NOAA are part of the park.

Kenmore. Kenmore offers two marinas: North Lake Marina, with permanent moorage slips, fuel dock, and repairs; and Harbour Village Marina with guest moorage. Kenmore is home to Kenmore Air, a major seaplane operation. Stay well clear of seaplane operating areas. Kenmore is at the mouth of the Sammamish River. Shoal water abounds. Find the buoys and stay in the dredged channel. The river is navigable by small, low, shallow-draft boats all the way to Lake Sammamish.

㉞ **Harbour Village Marina.** 6115 NE 175th St., Kenmore, WA 98028; (425) 485-7557; harbormaster@harbourvillage.net. Open all year with 400 feet of side-tie moorage on the outside of the breakwater. Office hours vary. 30 & 50 amp power, restrooms, and showers. Reservations online at www.dockwa.com. Caution for shallow water; follow the marked charted channel until abeam the marina.

㉞ **North Lake Marina.** 6201 NE 175th St., Kenmore, WA 98028; (425) 482-9465; susan@northlakemarina.com; www.northlakemarina.com. Open all year, closed weekends November through March. Ethanol-free gasoline at the fuel dock, no diesel. Permanent moorage only, no guest space. Parts, accessories, ice. Complete repairs available. Haulout to 20 tons.

Logboom Park. North shore of Lake Washington, Kenmore. Open all year, day use only moorage. Restrooms, no power, no showers. Trails, fishing pier, children's play equipment, picnic areas, and outdoor cooking facilities. The park is on the Burke-Gilman Trail, a walking and cycling trail that runs from Lake Union to the Sammamish River Trail. Note: Docks are in a state of disrepair and may be unsafe. Anchoring south of the park for up to 72 hours is allowed, watch for shallow water.

Saint Edward State Park. 14445 Juanita Drive NW, Kenmore, WA 98028; (425) 823-2992. Located on the northeast shore of Lake Washington, this 326-acre day-use park has trails and picnicking. Anchoring is possible off the park in fair weather for up to 72 hours. Beach landing only. A playground is located at the top of the bluff. A park pass can be purchased at the automated pay station. The historic brick building on the grounds served as a Catholic seminary in the 1930s, with hundreds of students in residence. The building was recently refurbished and offers luxury lodge accommodations, call (425) 470-6500 for reservations.

Juanita Bay. Anchorage for up to 72 hours is possible in Juanita Bay, which shoals gradually toward all shores. In nice summer weather, the bay is a crowded, popular, party-rafting destination. Off-season, the bay is quieter. The waterfront city park at the head of the bay provides a beach-landing opportunity. The waters adjacent to the park are a wildlife habitat area; all vessels are prohibited.

Kirkland. Kirkland is an outstanding cruising destination. The City of Kirkland's Marina Park visitor docks are well maintained, and connect directly with downtown. A good launch ramp is immediately north of the docks. If you enjoy tree-lined streets, superb dining, interesting boutiques and upscale galleries, you will not be disappointed. Kirkland is prosperous and it shows.

Next to Marina Park is the Kirkland Homeport Marina, which is primarily full-time, leased moorage; www.kirklandhomeportmarina.com.

A mile south of Marina Park is privately-owned Carillon Point Marina, with some guest moorage and access to restaurants and other businesses. Several restaurants in the area have their own docks for patrons.

ANTHONY'S
HOMEPORT RESTAURANT
135 Lake Street South
(425) 822-0225

㉟ **Marina Park.** 25 Lakeshore Plaza Drive, Kirkland, WA 98033; (425) 587-3300; www.kirklandwa.gov. Launch ramp adjacent. Open all year, 90 guest slips, restrooms, 30 amp power in some slips, Wi-Fi. No showers. This is a large and popular Lake Washington destination. Moorage is first-come, first-served and paid through electronic public pay stations located on the dock. Between 8:00 a.m. and

10:00 p.m. the first 3 hours free, ticket provided at pay station. Excellent access to downtown Kirkland. Nearby groceries, ice, and post office.

Use of the launch ramp can be purchased for a fee (each way) at the on-site pay station; a bollard in front of the ramp will lower upon payment. A key card for the season can be purchased from the city office at 123-Fifth Avenue. Use of the ramp is free from November 1st through March 31st. For additional information call (425) 587-3300.

Guest moorage can also be found along 150 feet of side-tie on the Second Avenue South Dock (Anthony's Restaurant), managed by the city. Check with Anthony's Restaurant for moorage while dining. The dock is located on the south side of a private marina. Make payment at the public pay station at the Marina Park.

㊱ **Carillon Point Marina.** 4100 Carillon Point, Kirkland, WA 98033; (425) 822-1700; www.carillon-point.com. Open all year, guest moorage, 30 & 50 amp power, Wi-Fi, restrooms, showers, pumpout, portapotty dump. The public pier on the north end of the marina has 150 to 200 feet of side-tie, 2-hour tie-ups at no charge. The inside of the pier is for boats 32 feet and under and the outside of the pier is for larger vessels. Overnight moorage in unoccupied slips as available. Reservations are available. This is a nice marina adjacent to a high-quality hotel with restaurants, spa, and shopping. Downtown Kirkland is 1.5 miles away by road.

㊱ **Yarrow Bay Marina.** 5207 Lake Washington Blvd. NE, Kirkland, WA 98033; (425) 822-6066; service@yarrowbaymarina.com; www.yarrowbaymarina.com. Open all year with ethanol-free gasoline and diesel, no guest moorage. Marine parts, restrooms, pumpout, haulout and repairs.

Cozy Cove and Fairweather Bay. Cozy Cove and Fairweather Bay are entirely residential, but anchorage is possible.

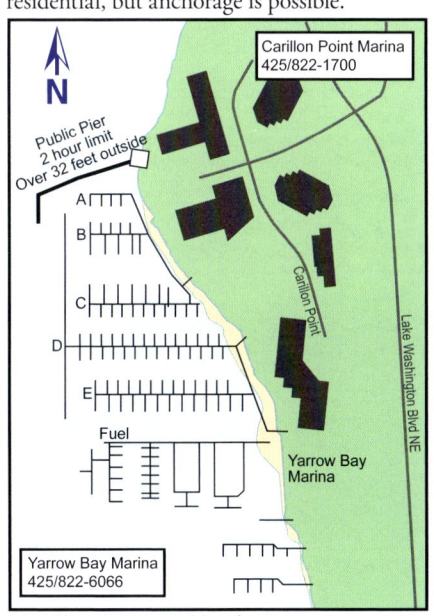

Carillon Point, Kirkland

See Area Map Page 107 - Maps Not for Navigation

SOUTH AND CENTRAL PUGET SOUND

Gene Coulon park, with launch ramps, dockside eateries, and day-use moorage

Meydenbauer Bay. Meydenbauer Bay is the home of Bellevue Marina and the Meydenbauer Bay Yacht Club, which has some moorage for reciprocal clubs. Meydenbauer Beach Park has a beautiful walkway over the water. Downtown Bellevue, with outstanding shopping, is nearby. Anchorage is possible in Meydenbauer Bay, although the water is deeper than most pleasure craft prefer. The marina off Beaux Arts Village, a short distance south of Meydenbauer Bay, is reserved for Beaux Arts residents.

Bellevue Marina. 99th Avenue NE, Bellevue, WA 98004; (425) 443-1090 Dock Master. Small boat visitor moorage between Pier 2 and Pier 3, day use only up to 4 hours between 8:00 a.m. and 9:00 p.m. daily. Seasonal portable toilets. City park Rangers monitor the facilities.

Luther Burbank Park. 2040 84th Avenue SE, Mercer Island, WA 98040; www.mercergov.org. Open all year, day use only, dock space for 30 or more boats. Restrooms, no power, no showers. No anchoring. Park has picnic areas, swimming areas, trails, tennis courts, amphitheater.

East Channel Bridge. The I-90 fixed bridge over the East Channel on the east side of Mercer Island, has a vertical clearance of 65 feet.

㊲ **Newport Shores.** 3911 Lake Washington Blvd. SE, Bellevue, WA 98006; (425) 641-2090; www.seattleboat.com. Newport Shores has a large private marina (Seattle Boat-Newport), with an adjacent public launch ramp and fuel dock. Open all year, call or visit website for hours. Fuel dock with gasoline and diesel, located just south of the I-90 East Channel Bridge at Newport Yacht Basin; snacks, beverages, and ice. Complete repairs available. Marine supplies and parts, boat sales, self-serve storage. Haulout to 35 tons.

㊳ **Gene Coulon Memorial Beach Park.** 1201 Lake Washington Blvd., Renton, WA 98055; (425) 430-6700; www.rentonwa.gov. Open all year, day use only. Slips for small boats and side-tie for larger vessels. Restrooms, showers, no power. Pay at the automated pay box. Showers in summer only, at the swim center. Ivar's and Kidd Valley restaurants in the park. Eight lanes for boat launching, very well organized, credit and debit cards only. No overnight parking in winter. This is a big, attractive, and much-used park with picnic shelters, playground equipment, tennis courts, horseshoe pits, volleyball courts, grassy areas and beaches. It has a fishing pier and a paved walkway along the water. Popular with everyone, especially families. Located on the southeast shore of Lake Washington, next to Boeing's Renton 737 complex.

Rainier Beach. Has a launch ramp and a private marina. It is the home of the Rainier Yacht Club. Limited guest moorage for visiting members of reciprocal clubs.

Andrews Bay. 5895 Lake Washington Blvd. S., Seattle, WA 98118; (206) 684-4396; www.seattle.gov. Andrews Bay is a popular anchoring spot, with room for many boats. Nestled in between Seward Park on Bailey Peninsula and the mainland, it is one of the few authorized pleasure boat anchorages in Lake Washington. Signs on the Seward Park shoreline mark the anchorage area, denoted by buoys marked with the letter "A". Put the hook down in 25 to 50 feet, excellent mud bottom, 72-hour maximum stay in a 7-day period. There is a 3 knot speed limit in Andrews Bay. A Seattle Parks swim area with bathhouse and lifeguards is at the head of the bay. A large grassy playfield is adjacent. Miles of trails lead through dense forest. Excellent stop, especially for families.

㊴ **Lakewood Moorage.** 4400 Lake Washington Blvd. S., Seattle, WA 98118; (206) 475-6559; www.seattle.gov. No guest moorage. Permanent moorage only.

Stan Sayers Memorial Park. www.seattle.gov. Open all year. Temporary, day use moorage only, not enough depth for larger boats. Restrooms, no power, no showers. Launch ramp with boarding floats. Tie up to the floats. This is the pit area for hydroplanes during the annual Seafair races.

2023 WAGGONER CRUISING GUIDE

SOUTH AND CENTRAL PUGET SOUND

See Area Map Page 107 - Maps Not for Navigation

RICH PASSAGE, PORT ORCHARD, BREMERTON, SILVERDALE

Rich Passage is winding but well-buoyed. From the west entrance, the city of Bremerton and the Naval Shipyard are clearly visible. For security reasons, stay well off the Naval facilities.

Currents run to 2 knots at the east entrance and 5.5 knots at the west entrance, flooding west and ebbing east.

LOCAL KNOWLEDGE

HEAVY TRAFFIC: Rich Passage is the ferry route between Seattle and Bremerton. Keep a sharp lookout ahead and astern and stay well clear of the ferries. Naval vessels also use Rich Passage to and from the Bremerton Naval Shipyard.

Manchester State Park. 7767 E. Hilldale, Port Orchard, WA 98366; (360) 902-8844; www.parks.wa.gov. Open 7 days a week year-round; 111 acres, day use and overnight camping. Restrooms, showers, no power. Anchoring only; a bit rough because of boat traffic in Rich Passage.

The park is in a shallow cove that is good for wading in summer and scuba diving offshore. There are picnic tables and shelters with fireplaces, campsites, nature and hiking trails. Old gun battery and emplacements are fun to explore.

㊵ **Port of Manchester.** P.O. Box 304, Manchester, WA 98353; (360) 871-0500; www.portofmanchester.com. Open all year, 400 feet of guest dock space, restroom, no overnight moorage. Dock can be dry on zero or minus tide. A launch ramp is adjacent to the dock. Overnight parking allowed. No power or other facilities at the dock. A restaurant and pub are a short walk away.

Port Orchard Marina

Fort Ward Park. 2241 Pleasant Beach, Bainbridge Island, WA 98110; (206) 842-2306; www.biparks.org. Open all year. Anchorage is exposed to wind and wakes from passing boat traffic. Toilets, launch ramp and hiking trails. Because of strong currents in Rich Passage, the underwater park is for expert scuba divers only. Bird watching from 2 bird blinds. Remains of historic fort emplacements to explore. No camping.

Port Orchard. The city of Port Orchard has long been a popular destination for Puget Sound boaters. It has a number of marinas that welcome visiting boats, including one, Port Orchard Marina, that is operated by the Port of Bremerton. Port Orchard Yacht Club, which welcomes visiting reciprocal yachts, is west of the Port Orchard Marina. Several other marinas have permanent moorage. Anchorage is in 50 to 60 feet, mud bottom. A passenger ferry runs between Port Orchard and Bremerton. Water Street boat launch has long term parking for tow vehicles and trailers.

Downtown Port Orchard has several antique and collectibles shops, and restaurants. Seasonal farmers market, 9:00 a.m. to 3:00 p.m. on Saturdays, mid-April through mid-October. The Port Orchard Public Market is open daily with a variety of local food and beverage vendors. Concerts by the Bay are held at Marina Waterfront Park June through September.

Besides a walkable waterfront featuring family friendly activities, playgrounds, parks and an array of excellent dining and shopping options, there are many events and festivals year round, www.exploreportorchard.com.

㊶ **Port Orchard Marina.** 707 Sidney Pkwy., Port Orchard, WA 98366; (360) 876-5535; kathyg@portofbremerton.org; www.portofbremerton.org. Certified Clean Marina. Monitors VHF 66A. Enter the marina around the west end of the breakwater. The entrance is marked with navigation lights. Open 7 days a week all year, except for fall/winter holidays. Gasoline and diesel at the fuel dock, guest moorage in 50 slips (40-foot), and side-tie moorage along 1500 feet of inside breakwater with another 1500 feet available on the outside. The aging 48-year old breakwater is scheduled to be replaced; construction is expected to begin some time in July 2023. The marina is well-managed, with clean restrooms and beautiful landscaping.

The marina has 30 amp power, water, restrooms, laundry, free showers, free pumpout, portapotty dump, and free Wi-Fi. An excellent children's play area is at the north end of the marina grounds. This is one of Puget Sound's popular destinations. Make reservations online or by phone. Four hours of day use free. It's one block to downtown Port Orchard. Repairs are nearby. Kayak rentals available through Kitsap Kayak & Recreation.

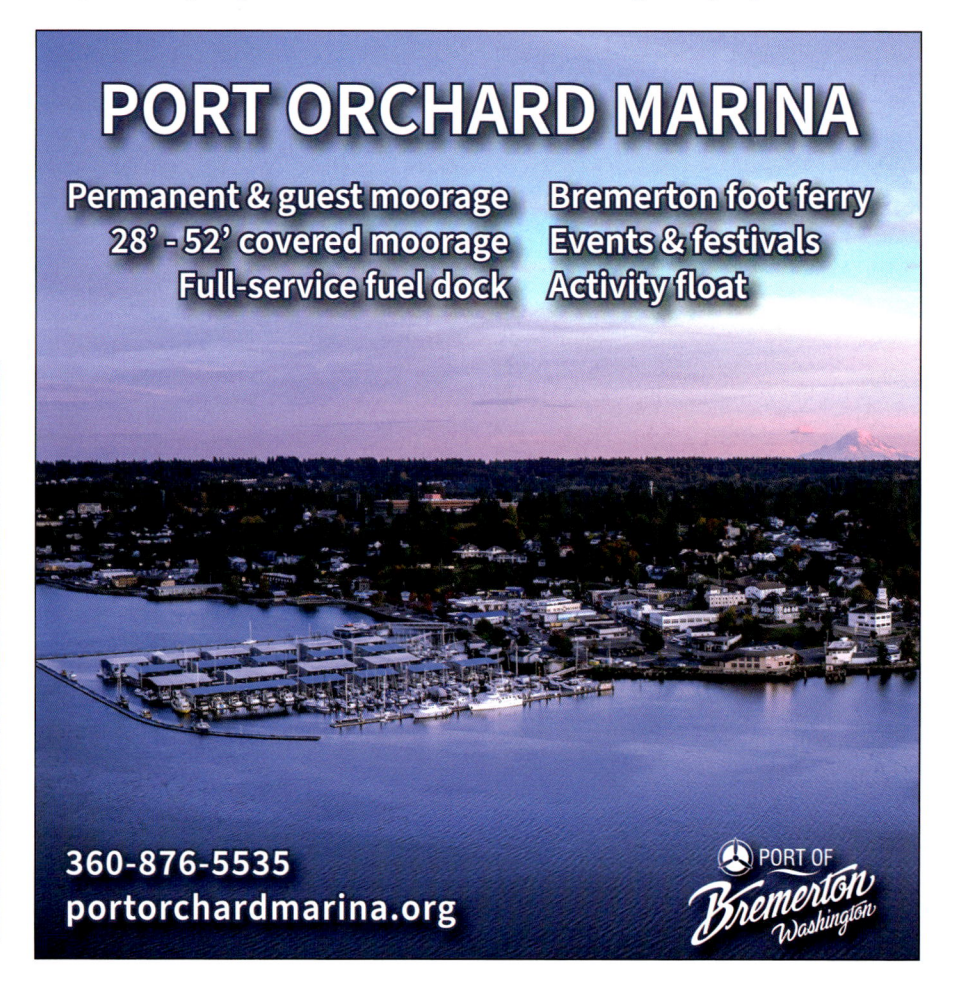

Bremerton. The redeveloped Bremerton waterfront offers excellent facilities and a lovely promenade. The Bremerton Harborside Kitsap Conference Center, with a Starbucks, Anthony's Restaurant, and Cold Stone Creamery, overlooks the marina. The Hampton Suites Hotel is next door. Bremerton is doing its best to shed a dowdy image and make a name for itself.

Points of interest include the Naval Museum, the historic destroyer USS Turner Joy, and the attractive city boardwalk. Many boaters take the passenger ferry for the 10- to 12-minute ride to Port Orchard, where the dining, the seasonal farmers market, antiques shopping, and boutiques are popular. Bremerton Marina is secured by a locked gate. Kitsap County buses in the adjacent transportation center can take you anywhere you wish to go, or take the ferry to downtown Seattle.

There is always something happening in Bremerton with its line-up of festivals and concerts. The Blackberry Festival is held Labor Day weekend, with booths ashore selling wonderful blackberry treats and more. We just happened to be there, and the festival was a hoot.

Located northeast of Bremerton, across Washington Narrows, is the popular Boat Shed restaurant (360-377-2600) adjacent to the Manette Bridge. The restaurant's 50-foot guest float is available while dining at the Boat Shed. Be prepared with fenders and lines. Current can run swiftly through Washington Narrows so plan accordingly.

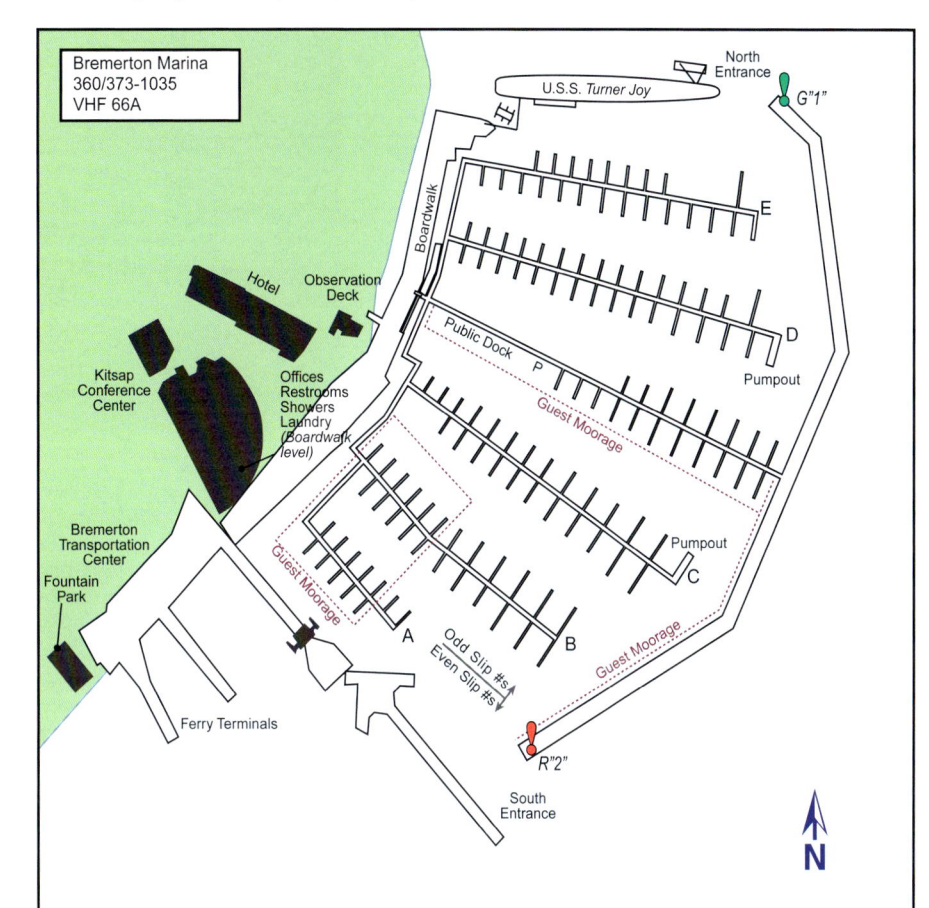

LOCAL KNOWLEDGE

STRONG CURRENTS: Tidal currents can make boat handling tricky in Bremerton Marina. It is best to time arrival and departure to coincide with slack water.

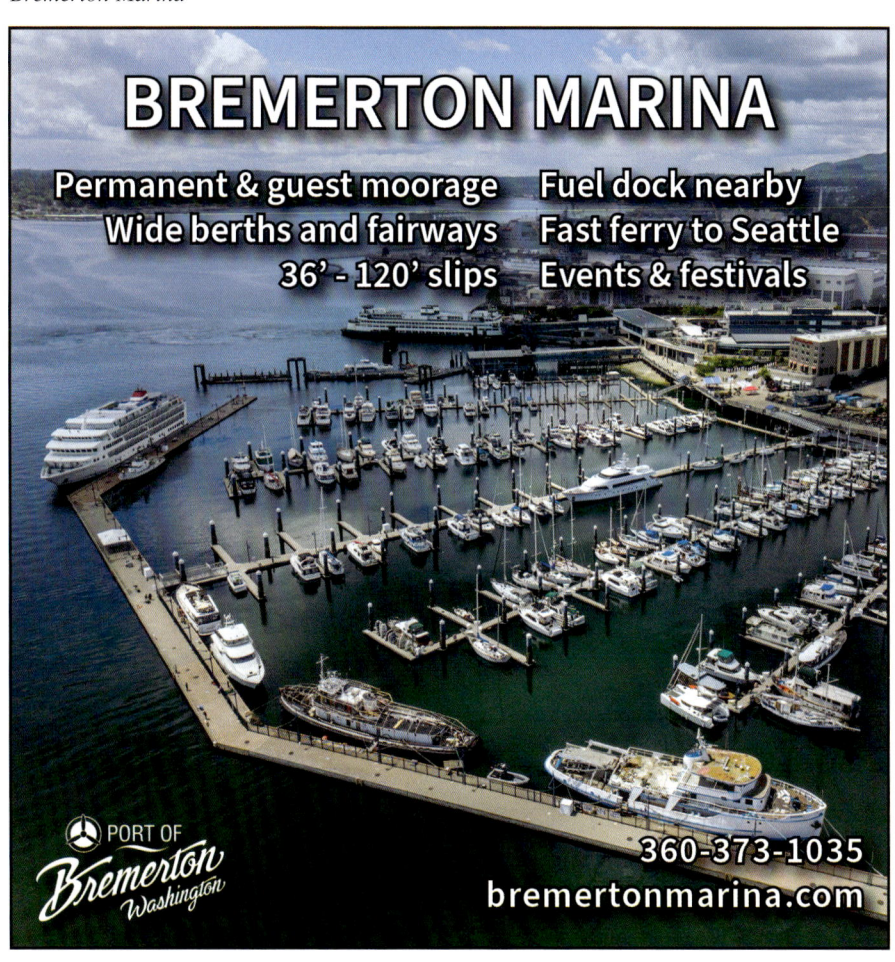

㊷ **Bremerton Marina.** 120 Washington Beach, Bremerton, WA 98367; (360) 373-1035; kathyg@portofbremerton.org. www.portofbremerton.org. Monitors VHF 66A. Certified Clean Marina. Located next to the ferry dock. Open all year, except for fall/winter holidays. Guest moorage in 80 to 100 slips and 990 feet inside of side-tie dock space, 30 & 50 amp power, water, garbage, including recycle bins. Restrooms, free showers, laundry, free Wi-Fi, 2 portapotty dumps. Shuttle service by appointment. No fuel is available. The nearest fuel dock is at Port Orchard. Reservations accepted online or by phone.

This quality marina has excellent docks and a breakwater to protect against ferry wakes. Fountain Park, a short walk to the other side of the ferry dock, is lovely. The dramatic fin-like sculptures are fountains meant to resemble the superstructure (called the sail) of a modern submarine.

Bremerton Marina

BREMERTON MARINA

Permanent & guest moorage
Wide berths and fairways
36' - 120' slips
Fuel dock nearby
Fast ferry to Seattle
Events & festivals

PORT OF Bremerton Washington

360-373-1035
bremertonmarina.com

SOUTH AND CENTRAL PUGET SOUND

See Area Map Page 107 - Maps Not for Navigation

ANTHONY'S AT SINCLAIR INLET
20 Washington Ave.
(360) 377-5004

The lovely park and dock at Old Silverdale are within steps of shops and a good bakery.

Washington Narrows connects Sinclair Inlet with Dyes Inlet. The narrows are crossed by two bridges with a minimum vertical clearance of 80 feet. Tidal currents, averaging over 2 knots, flood west and ebb east. Signs ask boaters to maintain minimum speed to reduce wake damage to the shore and to boats moored at the marina. A launch ramp with float and fishing pier is on the north side of the narrows about halfway along, part of the Lebo Street Recreation Area.

Bridgeview Marina. (360) 876-2522; Permanent moorage only, no transient space; pumpout is for moorage customers only.

Phinney Bay. Phinney Bay is the home of the Bremerton Yacht Club, with guest moorage for visiting reciprocal boats. Anchorage is good throughout the bay, which shoals toward each shore.

Ostrich Bay. Ostrich Bay offers good anchorage, with a mud bottom. The most popular anchorage is along the west side of the bay, facing dense forest, which is a designated marine park, with about 1400 feet of shoreline. This Bremerton City park has shore access trails, pathways, and benches. An old road that now serves as a trail leads up the hill past several concrete bunker-type structures. For some reason this entire area is overlooked. Even when the docks at Port Orchard and Bremerton are full on summer holiday weekends, Ostrich Bay has been almost empty.

Caution: Unexploded ordnance from years ago, when the Navy pier was used for loading munitions, has been found in the bay, especially in the vicinity of the pier.

Oyster Bay. A narrow but easily-run channel leads off Ostrich Bay into Oyster Bay, where perfectly protected anchorage is available toward the center of the bay. To enter, keep between the lines of mooring buoys and mooring floats on both sides of the channel. The channel shoals to about 6 feet at zero tide. Oyster Bay is surrounded by homes. The bay provides good protection from northerlies. Beware of the charted cable area and sewer line.

Dyes Inlet indents the Kitsap Peninsula northwest of Bremerton. Silverdale is on the north shore of Dyes Inlet and has a marina, waterfront park, boat ramp, and boardwalk. Dyes Inlet is connected to Sinclair Inlet via Port Washington Narrows.

㊸ **Silverdale Marina** (Port of Silverdale). P.O. Box 310, Silverdale, WA 98383; (360) 698-4918; portofsilverdale@wavecable.com; www.portofsilverdale.com. Open all year. Guest moorage along 1300 feet of wide, side-tie dock with a least depth of 10 feet at zero tide. No rafting. Moorage is on the honor system, but confirmed by personnel; use the payment drop box upland. Ten-night maximum stay. Group reservations accepted online for a $75 fee. Restrooms, 30 amp power; power is limited as not all power pedestals are currently operational. Seasonal potable water, pumpout, 2-lane concrete launch ramp. No long-term parking. The pumpout operates 8:00 a.m. to 10:00 p.m., weekends, May to October.

Future plans include moving the docks to deeper water for easier access and to eliminate regular dredging; power service would also be upgraded. Silverdale began the permitting process in 2022.

The marina is adjacent to county-run Silverdale Waterfront Park. The park has picnic tables, restrooms, fire pits, children's play area, pavilion and a Veterans Memorial. Interesting shops and dining are in adjacent Old Town Silverdale. Complete shopping is at the Kitsap Mall about a mile away. The Trails shopping center is about 1.5-miles away. The nearby Clear Creek Trail & Interpretive Center is a nice walk.

Whaling Days, a 3-day celebration the last weekend of July, draws big crowds, both from land and the water. Plan to anchor out. If you're on the dock, expect to be included in the carnival atmosphere. It's a big fair with live bands all weekend, activities for kids, outrigger canoe races, a fun run and more. See their website at www.whalingdays.com. Silverdale hosts the Kitsap Peninsula Water Trails Festival during the fourth weekend in June. Events include a 50K triathlon, kayak races, and waterfront activities.

BROWNSVILLE, POULSBO, NORTHERN PORT ORCHARD

Northern Port Orchard separates Bainbridge Island from the Kitsap Peninsula. Rich Passage and Sinclair Inlet are at the south end; Agate Passage is at the north. Brownsville and Poulsbo are the major marina destinations. The Agate Passage bridge has a vertical clearance of 75 feet. Currents in Agate Passage run to 6 knots on spring tides, flooding south and ebbing north.

㊹ **Illahee Marine State Park.** 3540 NE Bahia Vista Drive, Bremerton, WA 98310; (360) 478-6460. Located 3 miles northeast of Bremerton. Open all year, mooring and overnight camping. Guest moorage with 356 feet of side-tie dock space, 5 mooring buoys for boats 45 feet and under. Restrooms and showers, no power. The dock is protected by a floating concrete breakwater. Park has 3 kitchen shelters, picnic tables, campsites, horseshoe pits, ball field, hiking trails, and portable toilet. Popular for fishing and sunbathing. Most services are in the upland area, reached by a steep trail.

LOCAL KNOWLEDGE

ROCK: A nasty rock, almost awash at zero tide, is inshore from the mooring buoys at Illahee Park, approximately between the buoy nearest the dock and shore. Thanks to Correspondents Al & Becca Szymanski, S/V Halona, for the report.

㊺ **Port of Brownsville.** 9790 Ogle Rd. NE, Bremerton, WA 98311; (360) 692-5498; jerry@portofbrownsville.org; www.portofbrownsville.org. Certified Clean Marina. Monitors VHF 16, switch to 66A. First-come, first-served. Open all year, 7 days

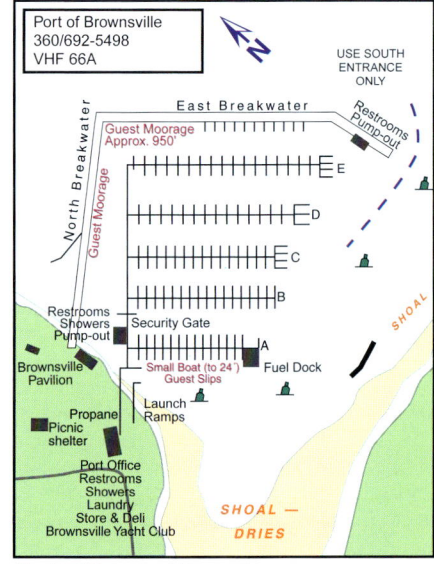

Port of Brownsville

Port of Keyport has 4 to 5 guest moorage spaces.

a week. Fuel dock has ethanol-free gasoline, diesel, and propane. Guest moorage in 25 24-foot slips, 20 40-foot slips, and 550 feet of side-tie moorage along the breakwater, 30 & limited 50 amp power, free Wi-Fi, restrooms, showers, laundry, book exchange, free pumpout, portapotty dump, in-slip pumpout service for a fee. Paved 2-lane launch ramp with ample parking.

Up on the wharf, a covered picnic/gathering pavilion, with tables, is inviting. Additional picnic tables are on the docks and in Burke Bay Overlook Park above the wharf, with barbecue. This is a popular destination for club cruises. Group reservations invited.

A breakwater marks the entrance to the marina. The channel and area around the fuel dock has been dredged to 9 feet at minus tide and well marked with green buoys to port on entrance, so you don't have to hug the south side of the dock. The Deli has snacks, beer, and wine selection. They make take-out food and can cater a gathering. This is a pleasant, friendly marina.

Groceries are available a short walk (city block) up the road at the Daily Stop.

Brownsville Appreciation Day: Fourth Saturday of September. Folksy and fun, small community at its best. Classic boats and cars, treasure hunt, unicycles, hot dogs and hamburgers. All proceeds (not just profits) divided among the local elementary schools.

Savory Treat: A short walk up the road from the marina, Sweeney's Country Meats has mouth-watering specialty meats. We tried a marinade jerky and some of the bacon. All were delicious and well worth a visit.

㊻ **Port of Keyport Marina.** P.O. Box 195, Keyport, WA 98345; (541) 760-0176; www.portofkeyport.com. Concrete docks with four to five 50-foot slips for guest moorage, first-come, first-served. Water, 30 amp power. No restrooms, portable toilet on site. Boat launch ramp. Three hours free; 3-day maximum overnight stays with moorage fee. Be mindful of the current when approaching the dock. The current nearly always flows west to east. Make payment at the self-registration payment box at the head of the dock. There are several restaurants in the area, and the must-see Naval Undersea Museum (360-396-4148). The Keyport Mercantile is located just upland from the docks.

A pedestrian gate, open 10:00 a.m. to 4:00 p.m., is about a quarter of a mile straight up Washington Street from the dock. The gate leads onto the Naval Base and the Naval Undersea Museum. You can view a simulation of a nuclear fast attack submarine, torpedoes and torpedo tubes, a Confederate mine from the Civil War, and learn the history of naval diving. The museum is open Wednesday through Monday. Admission is free.

Fletcher Bay. Fletcher Bay is shallow and not a good anchorage.

㊼ **Manzanita Bay.** Manzanita Bay is a good overnight sheltered anchorage for Seattle-area boats. The bay is all residential and has no public facilities, but the holding ground

CRUISING SHOULDER SEASONS

Prime cruising season in the Pacific Northwest is in July and August, that's when you find the largest number of boats out cruising. In the past, boating activity didn't get started until well after Memorial Day and dropped-off after Labor Day. More recently, boating activity starts earlier in the season and continues well into fall. There are several factors stretching the boating season into the shoulder months of spring and fall.

The Pacific Northwest and the Inside Passage have been discovered. More out-of-area boaters are enjoying the protected waters, mild climate, and the unique boater friendly destinations this area has to offer. Western Washington and specifically the Seattle metro area have seen an influx of people in recent years that are eager to enjoy the area's great boating.

Spring and fall shoulder cruising seasons have much to offer the boater. There are far fewer boats during a shoulder season, easing competition for moorage, anchorage, and access to services. Yes, there are some trade-offs; marina staffing levels may be reduced, and hours and days of operation may be curtailed. So, when cruising in the shoulder season, be adaptable and flexible. You may need to leave a message and wait for a callback to your inquiry for moorage. You may have to arrive a little earlier and depart later to accommodate off-season office hours.

The rewards for cruising in the shoulder season are many. Prices are often reduced and availability is greater. Often people have more time to share insider information about places to visit or things to do. You will get more use out of your annual State Parks Pass, and you will have your choice of prime spots in popular anchorages.

Which areas are best for shoulder season cruising? South, Central, and North Puget Sound are some areas that start the earliest and run much later in the season. These areas are effectively year-round boating destinations. Next, the San Juan Islands, Gulf Islands, Vancouver B.C. destinations are good early and late season areas. Desolation Sound, north to and including the Broughtons, tend to be later in the shoulder season with facilities ready for full operation around Memorial Day, and curtailing operations by mid-September. Because of resort fishing activity, West Coast Vancouver Island around Barkley Sound and Tofino get started earlier than Desolation Sound.

September and October can often be a surprisingly good time of the year to cruise the Pacific Northwest waters from Olympia to Desolation Sound. Despite the occasional early fall storms that will have you sheltered for a few days, there can be some excellent fall cruising with settled weather, gorgeous sunsets, and empty anchorages.

[Lorena Landon]

is excellent. Observe the 5-knot no-wake speed limit beginning halfway down the bay. Although the bay is lined with lovely homes, the surrounding hills give a feeling of seclusion. Field Correspondent, Jim Norris and Anita Fraser, report that you can paddle up the creek located at the north end of the bay at high tide; very secluded and scenic.

At the north end of the bay, Manzanita Landing, a former Mosquito Fleet landing, provides access to the trail system of Manzanita Park. From the landing take Manzanita Road NE to NE Day Road West. Walk east to the park, which is on the left (north) side of the street.

Liberty Bay. The entrance to Liberty Bay is past the Keyport Naval torpedo research and testing facility and around Lemolo Point. The Navy requests boats travel at no-wake speed past its facility. A power cable with 90-foot clearance crosses overhead. A sign on the beacon off Lemolo Point asks boaters to slow down in all of Liberty Bay; buoys post the speed limit. Much of Liberty Bay is covered by Wi-Fi. Three major marinas are along the north shore of Liberty Bay: a private marina; the Poulsbo Yacht Club; and the Port of Poulsbo Marina.

The private marina has no guest moorage. At the Poulsbo Yacht Club, reciprocal moorage is along the northwest perimeter of the floating breakwater. Some reciprocal moorage is still available on the inside of the older breakwater.

㊽ **Poulsbo.** Poulsbo, on Liberty Bay, is one of the most popular destinations on Puget Sound, partly because it is close to the major population centers, and partly because it is such a delightful place to visit. Settled originally by Scandinavians, the downtown business district still loudly (to say the least) maintains its Norwegian heritage. Everything most visitors need is available either near the water or at the malls located on the highway about a mile away.

The waterfront portions of Poulsbo make for a lovely walk. Victorian homes and gardens have been restored and preserved to perfection.

Restaurants, bakeries and many shops that specialize in gifts, collectibles and home accessories are a few steps away in downtown Poulsbo. Dining and shopping are popular. Sluys Poulsbo Bakery, Boehm's chocolates and Mora's Ice Creamery are favorites. Longship Marine (360-779-2378) is one of the few remaining second-hand marine stores offering marine supplies and woodworking materials. The store is located in a historic building on the lower level, with an entrance that faces the marina. The interior has been beautifully remodeled. The store's previous location, next door on Anderson Parkway, is now a housewares shop.

The nearby Poulsbo Marine Science Center is fun for families. Don't miss the Maritime Museum on Front Street, showcasing the rich maritime history of Poulsbo and the Mosquito Fleet that transported supplies, mail and people to and from the islands. Special events include the Saturday Farmers Market, May - October; Viking Fest, 3rd weekend in May; Scandinavian Midsommer Fest, June; 3rd of July Celebration; Traditional Street Dance, August; Yule Fest, December and the Chip Hanauer Winter Rendezvous held the second weekend in February.

Looking for a great day trip or a weekend getaway? Look no further, Poulsbo has it all.

㊽ **Poulsbo Marina / Port of Poulsbo.** 18809 Front St., P.O. Box 732, Poulsbo, WA 98370; (360) 779-9905; (360) 779-3505 ext. 1 (for reservations); office@portofpoulsbo.com; reservations@portofpoulsbo.com; www.portofpoulsbo.com. Monitors VHF 66A. Open 7 days a week, all year, except Christmas Day and New Year's Day. Register by 4:00 p.m. to get the combination for the showers and restrooms. The fuel dock has ethanol-free gasoline and diesel. The marina has 130 guest slips, 10-foot depths at low tide, and 30 amp ELCI-protected power on all docks. Guest slips on F and E docks. Side-tie on the end of E dock and F dock for larger vessels. The Port utilizes available permanent slips for guest moorage when available. Reservations accepted but may be limited during special events; phone or email for reservations. Short-term stays up to 4 hours for a nominal fee. Good restrooms and showers, laundry, pumpout, portapotty dump, launch ramp.

A new breakwater was constructed in late 2022 with (22) 50-foot slips, (25) 30-foot slips, and side-tie moorage on the outside of the breakwater for vessels up to 75 feet. The breakwater has 30 & 50 amp power and potable water.

A meeting room and activity float are available. Groceries, fine restaurants and shops within walking distance. If anchored out, dinghy tie-up is on the shore side of the dock closest to shore.

Agate Passage connects Port Orchard with Port Madison, and is crossed by a highway bridge with a vertical clearance of 75 feet. Currents in the pass run as high as 6 knots at spring tides, flooding south and ebbing north. The channel through the pass is well marked, but in general, a mid-channel course will serve.

For some reason, many craft go through Agate Passage too fast, creating havoc for slower craft. Agate Passage isn't very long. Keep the speed down, look astern to judge your wake, and give fellow boats a break.

PORT MADISON AND BAINBRIDGE ISLAND

Port Madison. Suitable anchorage can be found in the northwest corner of Port Madison, at the entrance to Miller Bay, in 40 to 60 feet of water; depths shallow quickly as you proceed north and west. Protected from westerly through northerly winds, it is subject to distant boat wakes transiting Agate Pass and ship wakes from Puget Sound traffic. Nearby Indianola

PUGET SOUND NO DISCHARGE ZONE

All of Puget Sound waters up to the Canadian border are a State of Washington designated No Discharge Zone (NDZ). It is illegal to discharge any (treated and untreated) black water sewage in this NDZ. In 2018, state law established the NDZ to improve area water quality and aid in the state's Shellfish Restoration initiative. Gray water is not included in the regulations and there is no change for gray water discharges from onboard sinks and showers.

The Vessel Sewage NDZ includes all Washington marine waters east of New Dungeness Light, at the east end of the Strait of Juan de Fuca, plus Lake Washington, Lake Union, and the waters that connect them to Puget Sound.

Compliance means using an approved marine sanitation holding tank, securing the overboard thru-hull in the closed position and using pumpout facilities. If you have a Type I or Type II Treatment Marine Sanitation Device, you will need to secure it in a manner which prevents discharge of treated or untreated sewage by closing the seacock and removing the handle, or using a wire-tie.

Washington State boaters already practice good stewardship of state waters. The vast majority of vessels have holding tanks for use at pumpout facilities. State enforcement agents are first emphasizing outreach and education.

See Area Map Page 107 - Maps Not for Navigation   **SOUTH AND CENTRAL PUGET SOUND**

dock and Suquamish community dock are nice landing locations with shore side access.

Miller Bay. Miller Bay indents the Northwest corner of Port Madison. It is very shallow and should be entered only at half tide or better, or with local knowledge. Like many bays on Puget Sound, Miller Bay has a drying shoal in the middle, so navigable water can be found only around the perimeter.

Mattson's Bay Marine. 20622 Miller Bay Rd. NE, Poulsbo, WA 98392; (360) 598-4900; mattsonsbaymarine@gmail.com. Open Tuesday through Saturday all year. Haulout to 30 feet, parts and complete repairs. Launch ramp, dry storage.

Suquamish. Suquamish is best known as the winter home of Chief Seattle and the former site of his Longhouse, the Old Man House village. With its restaurant and other cultural attractions, it makes a good day trip from Seattle.

The Suquamish community dock and float, just north of Agate Pass, provides short-term moorage for visiting boats. The east side of the float is exposed to chop from boat traffic and weather in outer Port Madison. If the protected space on the west side is not available, boaters can anchor and take the dinghy to the float. Good anchorage is northeast of the float. A boat ramp is south of the float; it's not usable at low tide.

Today, the town of Suquamish is the center of the Suquamish Indian Reservation. A community center across the street from the dock is patterned after the Old Man House. The Suquamish Museum is up the hill.

Sluys Bakery is the place to stop for your morning and afternoon sweet tooth treat. Nearby is Boehm's to satisfy the chocolate craving.

Visible above the community center is an impressive veterans memorial, with carved figures honoring Chief Kitsap, Chief Seattle, and Suquamish veterans.

From the veterans memorial, follow signs to Chief Seattle's grave in the Suquamish Tribal Cemetery behind the white church of St. Peter's Catholic Mission. The original gravestone placed by Seattle pioneers is still there, along with more recent Native carvings and inscriptions of Chief Seattle's words.

From Chief Seattle's grave, continue walking uphill to the Suquamish Museum. The museum is open 10:00 a.m. to 5:00 p.m., daily.

Since 1911, the Suquamish Tribe has been celebrating Chief Seattle Days on the third weekend of August. Activities include a traditional salmon bake, canoe races, baseball, drumming and dancing, and a memorial service honoring Chief Seattle.

Sully's Bistro & Bar is within easy walking distance of the dock. Agate Pass Cafe and Scratch Kitchen have closed.

Indianola. Indianola is distinguished by the long pier that served passengers and freight during Mosquito Fleet days. A float is installed during the summer to give access to the town, suited for dinghies, max stay 30 minutes while loading/unloading, or visiting the country store. The float grounds on low and minus tides. The Indianola Country Store, just upland from the pier, has been in business since the 1920s. It has a good selection of grocery items, beer and wine, and a popular deli.

Inner Port Madison. The inner, residential bay extends for about 1.5 miles into the north end of Bainbridge Island. This is where Port Madison Yacht Club and a large Seattle Yacht Club outstation (no reciprocals) are located. Anchorage is good throughout, with a wide bight about 0.75 mile inside the entrance. Shore access is possible from a dinghy dock at Hidden Cove Park just west of the SYC outstation. Farther in, Hidden Cove is a lovely spot. For Seattle area boats, this is an often-overlooked area to have a picnic lunch or a quiet night at anchor. The shores are private but the setting is idyllic.

Fay Bainbridge Park. www.biparks.org. South of Point Monroe on Bainbridge Island. Open all year; exposed, anchoring only. Restrooms, showers. The park has 3 kitchen shelters, fireplaces, fire rings, a beach area, launch ramp, utility and primitive campsites, children's play equipment, horseshoe pits, fishing, clamming, and a concession stand in summer.

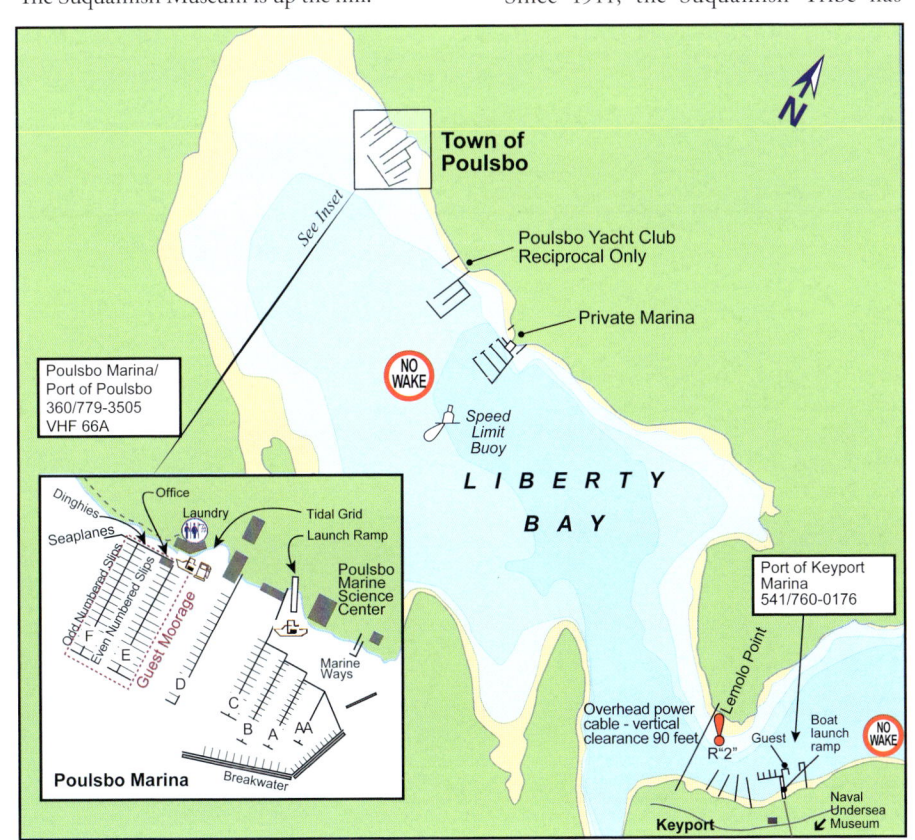

Liberty Bay

2023 WAGGONER CRUISING GUIDE   131

SOUTH AND CENTRAL PUGET SOUND

See Area Map Page 107 - Maps Not for Navigation

Eagle Harbor's City Dock has ample side-tie space to visit the charming City of Bainbridge Island.

Murden Cove. Murden Cove has convenient anchoring depths, but little protection from winds. It's a long row to shore, partly over drying flats. The residential community of Rolling Bay is at the head of the bay.

LOCAL KNOWLEDGE

NO ANCHOR ZONE: The bottom around the south entrance to Eagle Harbor has been capped with sand to prevent the spread of pollutants from a former creosote facility. Do not anchor in this area.

Eagle Harbor. Eagle Harbor is the location of the Winslow neighborhood of the City of Bainbridge Island. The entire island is considered the City of Bainbridge, which includes several neighborhood areas. Winslow is the western terminus of a ferry from downtown Seattle.

The neighborhood of Winslow has a guest dock and boat launch at the 5.5-acre Eagle Harbor Waterfront Park. Annual festivals and summer performances are held at the park. Anchorage in Eagle Harbor is available west of the Ferry Maintenance Yard, and at least 200 feet south of the marinas and east of the private tidelands. Anchorage up to 48 hours, no charge. Anchored boats must register at the Waterfront Park kiosk. An electronic self-registration payment kiosk for dock moorage and anchored boats is located at Eagle Harbor Waterfront Park.

Several marinas in the area provide guest moorage if a permanent tenant is away. All but one marina, Eagle Harbor Marina on the south shore, are on the town side of the harbor. Queen City Yacht Club, Meydenbauer Bay Yacht Club, and Seattle Yacht Club have outstations in Eagle Harbor. A pumpout station is located at Eagle Harbor Waterfront Park, and in-slip pumpouts are provided at Eagle Harbor Marina. At the west end of Eagle Harbor is the Dave Ullin Open Water Marina consisting of 16 private buoys, no public mooring.

We enjoy walking the streets of town, which offer boutiques, art shops, and a variety of good restaurants. The grocery store, within walking distance, has everything. The beautiful Bainbridge Island Museum of Art has a cafe. The Alehouse on Winslow, located next to the museum, has a nice selection of beer and cider on tap; patrons may bring in outside food. The grounds and gardens at Bloedel Reserve, on the north end of the island, are worth a visit. Kitsap Transit, at the ferry terminal, provides service during weekdays and Saturdays.

Eagle Harbor is entered through a marked channel past foul ground that extends south from Wing Point. Nun Buoy 2 is at the end of this foul ground, and the Tyee Shoal Beacon is a short distance south of Buoy 2. The ferries round Tyee Shoal Beacon, but other craft can use Buoy 2 safely, following the rule of Red, Right, Returning. Follow the markers all the way in. Shoal water extends out to the channel on both sides. Observe the 5-knot speed limit from Buoy 5. The far west end of the inner harbor is an Aquatic Conservancy area where power boats are not allowed.

No Discharge Zone. City requests no gray water discharge; use free showers ashore.

Pritchard Park, located along the south shore of the harbor, is a 50-acre park accessible by dinghy or kayak at a mile-long sandy beach.

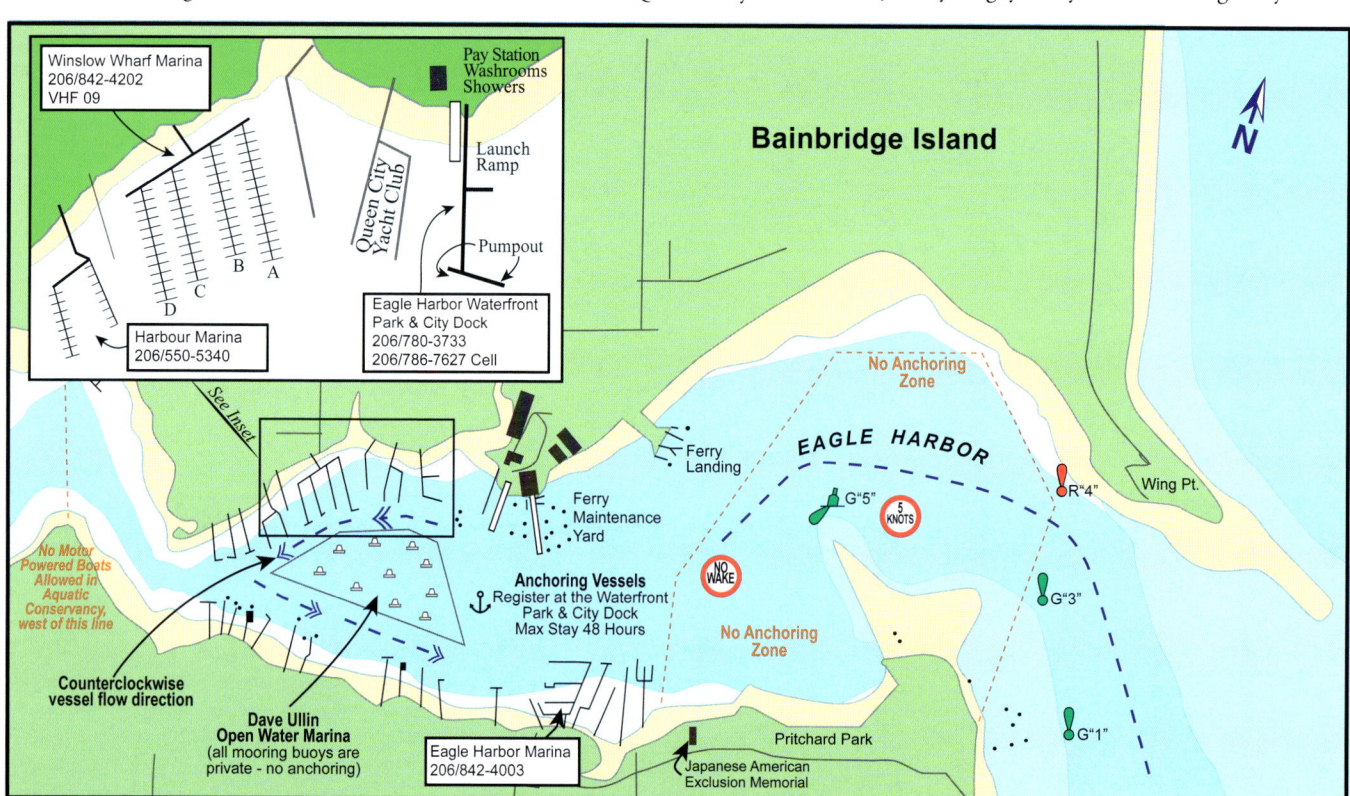

Eagle Harbor

Families once worked here in the mill town of Creosote. The park includes the Japanese American Exclusion Memorial; those of Japanese descent living on Bainbridge Island were the first in the Nation to experience internment orders during World War II.

㊾ **Eagle Harbor Waterfront Park & City Dock**. 280 Madison Ave. N., Bainbridge Island, WA 98110; (206) 780-3733 or (206) 786-7627 (cell), Tami Allen Harbormaster; www.ci.bainbridge-isl.wa.us. Open all year. 900 feet of guest side-tie moorage at the dock for vessels up to 70 feet. Walers marked in yellow are load/unload areas. Water, 30 & 50 amp ELCI-protected power, and pumpout. All moorage facilities are first-come, first-served. Washrooms, free showers, and garbage drop are located upland from the dock in the Waterfront Park. Rafting is required, no one is turned away; med-tie is an option. There is a nominal fee for stays up to 3 hours. Boat launch ramp is next to the dock. Payment for moorage is made at the electronic self-registration payment station located at the Park; shower code is shown on the receipt. Maximum 2-day stay in a seven-day period at the dock. The docks can be reserved for special group events, with a deposit and Dock Use Permit application. Community volunteer kiosk hosts greet boaters and help answer questions.

A short quarter-mile walk north from the Waterfront Park brings you to the center of town and the grocery store on Winslow Way. Half-mile long Winslow Way is lined on both sides with small shops, restaurants, pubs, and a bakery. One block north of Winslow Way on Ericksen Avenue is the Bainbridge Island Historical Museum.

㊾ **Winslow Wharf Marina.** P.O. Box 10297, 141 Parfitt Way SW, Bainbridge Island, WA 98110; (206) 842-4202; dave@winslowwharfmarina.com; www.winslowwharfmarina.com. Monitors VHF 09. Open Tuesday through Saturday, 9:00 a.m. to 5:00 p.m. Guest moorage in unoccupied slips as assigned. Maximum boat length 50 feet, 30 & 50 amp power, clean remodeled restrooms, free showers. Wi-Fi, laundry, book exchange. Pumpout and portapotty dump for tenants. Reservations required. Chandlery Marine, a well-stocked marine supply store, has a little bit of everything, (206) 842-7245. Seattle Yacht Club and Meydenbauer Bay Yacht Club have dock space reserved for their members. The spaces are clearly marked, and non-member boats may not use them.

㊾ **Harbour Marina.** 233 Parfitt Way SW, Bainbridge Island, WA 98110; (206) 550-5340; info@harbour-marina.com; www.harbour-marina.com. Open all year. Unoccupied slips used for guest boats, call ahead for availability. Facilities include 30 amp power, restrooms, free showers, laundry, pumpout. Located directly below Harbour Public House, an English-style pub with beer, wine, and food; families welcome. Moorage for visiting the pub and Pegasus Coffee House is clearly marked. Close to the Waterfront Trail and a short walk to downtown.

㊿ **Eagle Harbor Marina.** P.O. Box 11217, 5834 Ward Ave. NE, Bainbridge Island, WA 98110; (206) 842-4003; harbormaster@eagleharbormarina.com; www.eagleharbormarina.com. Open all year. Primarily permanent moorage with limited guest moorage, call ahead. Marina has 30, 50 & 100 amp ELCI-protected power. Restrooms, showers, laundry, pumpout, free Wi-Fi. Docks were recently replaced and upgraded, including monitored shore power, in-slip portable pumpout, year-round water, and security. This marina is on the south side of Eagle Harbor away from town; there are no restaurants or stores in the immediate area.

(51) **Blakely Harbor.** In the late 1800's Blakely Harbor was the site of ship building activities and the Port Blakely Mill, one of the world's largest sawmills. Now it is a quiet residential neighborhood. Some stub pilings remain from the old docks. The head of the bay, including the old mill pond and ruins of the concrete powerhouse, is now the 40-acre Port Blakely Park, with hiking trails; easy shore access by dinghy.

Good anchorage in 35 to 50 feet can be found far enough into the bay to be well protected, yet still have a view of the Seattle skyline. A few homes line the harbor shore. Sunset on a clear evening is beautiful. Blakely Rock is 0.5 mile off; give it a good offing. Enter Blakely Harbour in the middle of the mouth of the bay. A drying reef extends from the north shore, and shoals are along the south side.

Japanese American Exclusion Memorial

Eagle Harbor is the most visited harbor on Bainbridge Island, home to many nice marinas, a waterfront park and public boat dock, and easy walking access to many shops, restaurants, and museums. Cathleen and I have visited many times, but only recently discovered the Japanese American Exclusion Memorial.

Owned by the National Park Service and managed by the Bainbridge Island Japanese American Community, the memorial honors the 227 men, women, and children forcibly removed from their Bainbridge Island homes and sent to internment camps in California and Idaho during WWII, after the Japanese bombing of Pearl Harbor. Two-thirds of them were U.S. citizens. The Japanese Americans on Bainbridge Island were the first group of internees taken from their West Coast homes. Their friends and neighbors on Bainbridge Island defended them, stood beside them, and ultimately welcomed them back home after they were released.

The memorial wall, displaying the names and pictures of those taken, is built on the path walked by the internees on the way to the waiting ferries at the historic Eagledale ferry dock site. While the dock no longer exists, the memorial wall, and interpretive signs and photos vividly portray the solemn experiences that occurred there. The motto and mission of the memorial is Nidoto Nai Yoni, translated as "Let it Not Happen Again."

The memorial is open year-round and located on the south shore of Eagle Harbor, adjacent to Pritchard Park. To access the memorial from the water, land your dinghy or kayak on the sandy beach of Pritchard Park and take the short path to the memorial. It is free to visit.

For additional information on this memorial and other Bainbridge Island history, visit the Bainbridge Island Historical Museum, a short walk into town from the Waterfront Park and City Dock.

[Field Correspondents Dale & Cathleen Blackburn]

Hood Canal

HOOD CANAL
Port Gamble • Dabob Bay • Quilcene Bay
Pleasant Harbor • Hoodsport • Alderbrook

Scan the Latest
Hood Canal
Information

tinyurl.com/WG22xCh03

*Seabeck Bay,
Hood Canal*

HOOD CANAL

Hood Canal is a 65-mile-long glacier-carved fjord. Because the shorelines are fairly straight with few protected anchorages, Hood Canal is less used by pleasure craft than many other waterways. Most boaters don't realize that shrimping, oyster gathering, clamming and fishing can be outstanding. The shrimping season is short, usually in May, and on those days the boats are plentiful. In clear weather the views of the Olympic Mountains from Hood Canal are outstanding. Other than shrimpers and knowing fishermen, however, Hood Canal is largely undiscovered.

Several rivers flow from the Olympic Mountains into Hood Canal, and each has formed a mudflat off its mouth. Although the shoal off the Dosewallips River, a couple of miles south of Pulali Point, is marked, the shoals off the Duckabush, Fulton Creek, Hama Hama, and Lilliwaup rivers are not marked, nor is the extensive shoal off the Skokomish River at the Great Bend. Care must be taken to avoid running aground.

Pleasant Harbor and the Alderbrook Inn Resort can take larger boats, but many of the other marinas and parks on Hood Canal are aimed at trailerable boats. This has disappointed some people with larger boats.

No Discharge Zone: All of Hood Canal is a No Discharge Zone (NDZ). It is illegal to discharge any (treated and untreated) black water sewage. Gray water is okay.

Bywater Bay. Anchor in 6 to 12 feet, good holding on a soft mud bottom with room for several boats. The tombolo provides wave protection from north winds. A shallow draft boat can easily enter the lagoon at the northwest corner of the bay, which is part of the Wolfe Property State Park. The park encompasses the western half of the tombolo, the eastern half is private property.

The remaining western shore is that of Shine Tidelands State Park, adjoining the Wolfe property park. The Shine Tidelands is regularly seeded with clams and oysters; for closure dates and shellfish harvest dates, check the Washington Fish & Wildlife website. A few cabins and homes are set back from the shore.

① **Port Gamble.** Port Gamble is a fine anchorage, protected from wave action by a sandspit at the entrance. Anchorage in 18 to 30 feet is possible nearly anywhere; avoid the area just inside the spit where there may be former mill debris, and remain clear of the charted cable area. Currently no guest dock available at Port Gamble, but locals and visitors use the gravel beach below the General Store and old mill parking lot to land dinghies and kayaks.

Port Gamble is a historic, charming town. A museum, restaurants and small shops are on the tree-lined main street. Port Gamble began as a sawmill company-owned town, founded in 1853; the mill operated until 1995. The Port Gamble Historic Museum (360) 297-8078 covers the history of the mill and town; open daily, May through September.

Port Gamble has developed a Master Plan for the town's 16-acre waterfront property to be completed in phases. Continued environmental cleanup of the old mill site is ongoing. Field Correspondents Dale and Cathleen Blackburn report that a gate on the land side of the beach is closed from 5:00 p.m. to 8:00 a.m. and on Sundays and holidays, which is intended to deter car access. Boaters making use of the beach to visit by dinghy or kayak can still use the pedestrian gate passthrough.

LOCAL KNOWLEDGE

DANGEROUS ROCKS: Sisters, two substantial rocks about 200 yards apart, lie 0.4 mile south of the Hood Canal bridge on the west side. The rocks dry at half tide. The southern rock is marked by a large lighted beacon, yet from time to time an unwary boat manages to go up on these rocks. For safety, if you have passed under the western end of the bridge, turn eastward and run parallel until it is safe to turn south into Hood Canal.

Hood Canal Floating Bridge. The east end of the Hood Canal Floating Bridge has 50 feet of vertical clearance. Clearance on the west end is 33 feet. The bridge can be opened for larger vessels, but it is not manned. To arrange an opening call (360) 779-3233, which connects to a State Department of Transportation office in Tacoma. They will take your name, telephone number, name of your vessel, date and time of desired opening, and whether you are inbound or outbound. They also will ask what width opening you need (300 feet or 600 feet). One hour's notice is needed to get a crew to the bridge and prepare it for opening. No bridge openings between 3:00 p.m. and 6:15 p.m. daily, from Memorial Day to Labor Day.

Salsbury Point County Park. Just off the northeast end of the Hood Canal Bridge. Day use only, restrooms, no power. Anchoring only, 2 launch ramps. Picnic tables, fireplaces, children's play area. Nature trail. Sandy beach for experienced divers only because of strong currents.

Kitsap Memorial Marine State Park. (360) 779-3205; Four miles south of Hood Canal Bridge. Open all year, day use and overnight camping, 2 mooring buoys for boats 45 feet and under. Self-register and pay mooring buoy fee on shore, or by phone as posted on the buoy. Restrooms, showers, no power. Picnic sites, kitchen shelters, fireplaces. Standard

Hood Canal is backed by the picturesque Olympic Mountain Range.

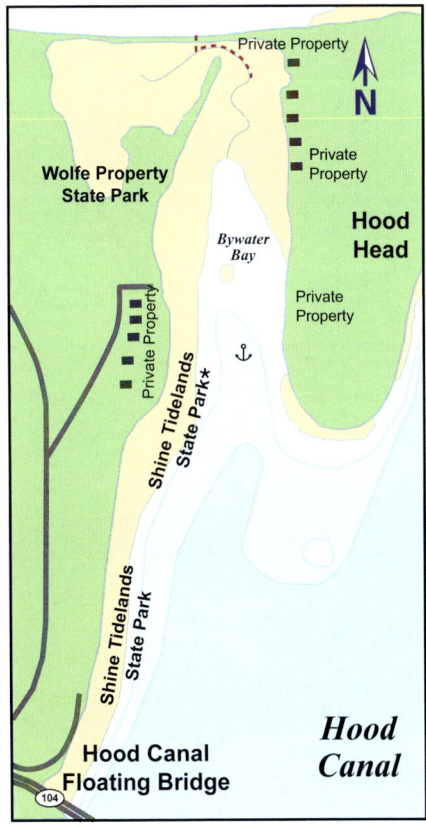

Bywater Bay

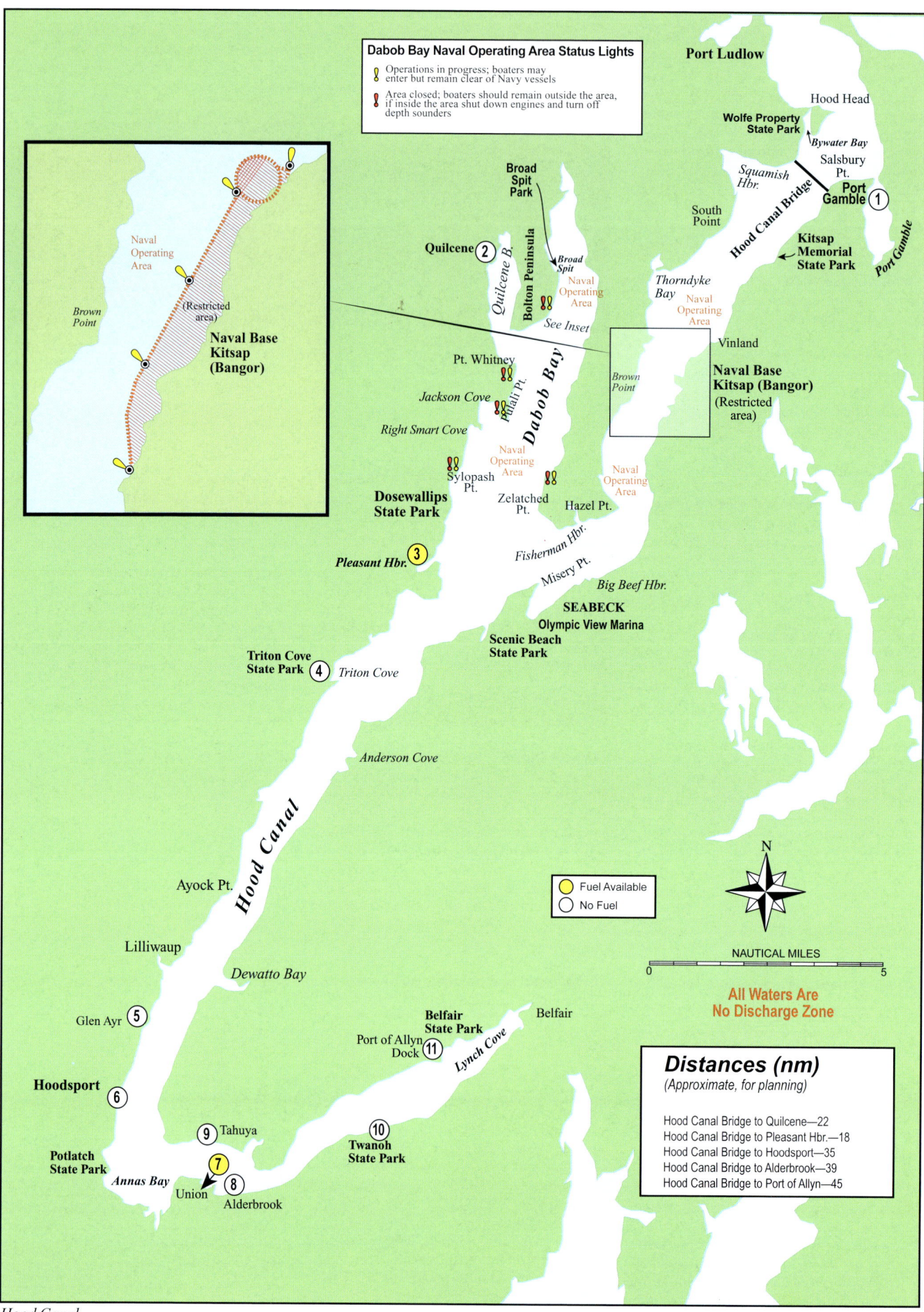

HOOD CANAL

Reference Only – Not for Navigation

Dabob Bay Naval Operating Area Status Lights
- Operations in progress; boaters may enter but remain clear of Navy vessels
- Area closed; boaters should remain outside the area, if inside the area shut down engines and turn off depth sounders

Port Ludlow
Hood Head
Wolfe Property State Park
Bywater Bay
Squamish Hbr.
Salsbury Pt.
Port Gamble ①
South Point
Hood Canal Bridge
Kitsap Memorial State Park
Port Gamble
Thorndyke Bay
Naval Operating Area
Vinland
Naval Base Kitsap (Bangor) (Restricted area)

Naval Operating Area
Brown Point
Naval Base Kitsap (Bangor) (Restricted area)

Broad Spit Park
Quilcene ②
Quilcene B.
Bolton Peninsula
Broad Spit
Naval Operating Area
See Inset
Brown Point

Pt. Whitney
Pulali Pt.
Jackson Cove
Dabob Bay
Right Smart Cove
Naval Operating Area
Sylopash Pt.
Zelatched Pt.
Hazel Pt.
Naval Operating Area

Dosewallips State Park
Fisherman Hbr.
Misery Pt.
Big Beef Hbr.
Pleasant Hbr. ③
SEABECK
Olympic View Marina
Scenic Beach State Park

Triton Cove State Park ④
Triton Cove

Anderson Cove

Hood Canal

Ayock Pt.

Lilliwaup
Dewatto Bay

Glen Ayr ⑤
Belfair State Park
Belfair
Port of Allyn Dock ⑪
Lynch Cove

Hoodsport ⑥
⑨ Tahuya
⑩ **Twanoh State Park**

Potlatch State Park
Annas Bay ⑦
⑧
Union
Alderbrook

⬤ Fuel Available
◯ No Fuel

NAUTICAL MILES
0   5

All Waters Are No Discharge Zone

Distances (nm)
(Approximate, for planning)

Hood Canal Bridge to Quilcene—22
Hood Canal Bridge to Pleasant Hbr.—18
Hood Canal Bridge to Hoodsport—35
Hood Canal Bridge to Alderbrook—39
Hood Canal Bridge to Port of Allyn—45

Hood Canal
136
www.WaggonerGuide.com

campsites, swimming beach, playground, horseshoe pits, volleyball courts, baseball field. Buoys are exposed to tidal currents and wind.

Squamish Harbor. Squamish Harbor has convenient anchoring depths throughout, with room for many boats. This is a large bay with several areas that offer protection from southwesterly through northerly winds. The bay is exposed to southerly through northeasterly winds. Avoid the charted, marked reef in the middle of the bay. The harbor is quite picturesque with open fields and country homes that dot the shoreline and hillsides. Views of the Hood Canal Bridge can be seen looking eastward from the harbor.

USS Henry M. Jackson returning to Bangor Naval Base on Hood Canal.

LOCAL KNOWLEDGE

RESTRICTED AREAS: Boaters should take great care not to enter the Restricted Area in front of the Bangor Naval Station on the east side of Hood Canal. The restricted area is 4 miles long, starting at Vinland in the north extending south to King Spit; the area is patrolled constantly to keep passing vessels well away. The patrol craft are fitted with guns and are authorized to shoot. Best practice is to stay west of mid-channel when transiting this area.

NAVAL OPERATING AREAS: Two adjoining Naval Operating areas cover a majority of Hood Canal, from South Point to Hazel Point. When transiting this area, boaters should monitor Channel 16. Look for Naval vessels flying a "Bravo" (red) flag during periods of Naval operations. A passage corridor outside the Operating Areas follows the west side of Hood Canal, hugging the eastern shoreline of Toandos Peninsula. Another Naval Operating & Exercise Area is in Dabob Bay, where flashing lights along the shoreline indicate the status of operations.

Naval Base Kitsap (Bangor). This is the location of Bangor Naval Station, homeport for a fleet of nuclear submarines. Several of these awesome machines often are visible to passing craft. Stay outside of the marked restricted area.

Seabeck Bay. Anchorage is possible behind Misery Point, with fair holding on a soft mud bottom and good protection from the south and west. The Seabeck General Store can be accessed by dinghy at the public beach northeast of the store. The store makes in-house sandwiches to order; A coffee stand and pizza shop are nearby. The adjacent Olympic View Marina is for permanent moorage only.

Scenic Beach State Park. South of Seabeck. Open for day use all year and overnight camping in summer only. Anchoring only. Standard and primitive campsites. Kitchen shelter, fireplaces, fire rings, horseshoe pits, volleyball areas. Scuba diving, swimming, hiking, shellfishing.

Fisherman Harbor. Fisherman Harbor can be entered only at high water, but once inside offers protected anchorage in 5 to 15 feet. Follow the natural channel into the bay, then turn south and follow the spit until anchoring depths are found. All the land around the bay is privately owned. Years ago, we tiptoed into Fisherman Harbor in a sailboat at something less than high tide. It was careful going, with a close watch from the bow and a bit of luck, but the boat got in without touching. Less foolish souls should wait for higher water. [Hale]

LOCAL KNOWLEDGE

NAVAL OPERATING AREA: Most of Dabob Bay is a Naval Operating & Exercise Area with 5 warning lights. Flashing amber lights indicate Naval operations are in progress; boaters may enter the area on an amber light but should keep well clear of Navy vessels. Flashing red lights indicate the area has been closed to navigation. If the lights turn red while you are inside the Operations Area, shut down engines and depth sounder until operations have ended. The 5 warning lights are located at Whitney Point, Pulali Point, and Sylopash Point on the west side of the bay; Zelatched Point on the east side of the bay; and at the north end of the bay on the southeast side of Bolton Peninsula. Some lights may not be operational or under repair. Boaters should look for other lights and look for Navy vessels. If in doubt, contact Dabob Range Control on Ch16 or call (360) 396-4108.

Dabob Bay. Popular and busy during a short shrimp season, Dabob otherwise is a quiet and out of the way cruising destination. Several coves offer anchorage for a few boats. Quilcene Bay has a large anchoring area and a small marina. There are some wonderful views of the Olympic Mountains from Quilcene Bay.

South of Pulali Point (western shore of Dabob Bay) is outside the Naval Operating Area and includes Jackson Cove and Right Smart Cove, where good anchorage can be found. Boaters should be aware of the Restricted Area just off Point Whitney, a charted no anchoring zone.

A State Department of Fish and Wildlife oyster research laboratory is at Whitney Point with a good launch ramp alongside.

Caution should be exercised when transiting Dabob Bay and Quilcene Bay to avoid the large number of shrimp pots during the season.

Broad Spit Park. On the east shore of Bolton Peninsula in Dabob Bay. Anchor on either side of the spit, depending on wind direction. Easy beach access, trails ashore. Lagoon that fills at high tide. Field Correspondent Jim Norris reports "We anchored two nights just north of Broad Spit in Dabob Bay. The wind was SE 20-25 all day. Given the full fetch of Hood Canal for waves to develop, I feared a nasty swell would bend around the spit and make life uncomfortable. Not so. The spit offered good protection from the waves, but not the wind. We swung around on the anchor, but no other motion in the boat."

Quilcene Bay. Anchor in 12 feet, good holding in mud along the east shore opposite

Access to the Seabeck store is via the public beach to the left of this picture.

HOOD CANAL

See Area Map Page 136- Maps Not for Navigation

Pleasant Harbor Marina is a popular destination, with heated swimming pool and hot tub.

the marina, with protection from moderate southerly winds. A breakwater-protected marina, Herb Beck Marina, is about a mile and a half south of the village of Quilcene.

② **Herb Beck Marina.** 1731 Linger Longer Rd., Quilcene, WA 98376; (360) 765-3131; www.portofpt.com/marinas/. Managed by the Port of Port Townsend. Monitors VHF 66A. Open Tuesday through Saturday, 8:00 a.m. - 4:30 p.m. in the summers; hours and days may vary during the off-season. Limited guest moorage to 40 feet, 20 & 30 amp power, water, showers, restrooms, pumpout, garbage drop. Call for reservations. This is a small, rustic marina. Swimming is great in the summer at a designated area just south of the marina, with water temperatures above 70 degrees.

Dosewallips State Park. (360) 796-4415; South of Brinnon. Park open all year for day use and overnight camping. Accessible by kayak or canoe. Restrooms, showers. Hiking trails, picnic areas, standard, utility, and primitive campsites.

Jackson Cove. Located on the west shore of Dabob Bay, Jackson Cove has good protection from all except southerly winds. The anchorage is semi-private with relatively few cabins along the shore. No beach access, as all properties are privately owned. Anchor over a U-shaped shelf of 40-50 feet.

Right Smart Cove. The unnamed cove just west of Wawa Pt. and south of Jackson Cove, Right Smart Cove is open to easterly through southerly winds. Anchorage for a few boats can be found in the middle of the cove, with fair to good holding on a mud bottom. A few cabins and homes dot the shore. Views of the Olympic Mountains.

Pleasant Harbor. Pleasant Harbor is a major stopping point on Hood Canal with a good destination resort marina and a state park dock. Enter through a narrow channel with least depth of 8 feet at zero tide. Inside, there's room to anchor, 18 to 42 feet, mud bottom.

Pleasant Harbor Marina has excellent facilities for visiting boaters. Home Port Marina of Pleasant Harbor in Brinnon is permanent moorage only, no guest moorage. A public boat launch ramp is located at the south end of the harbor and has toilet facilities.

Pleasant Harbor is full of boats in May, when the annual shrimping season is under way; at other times, it is a restful destination. For shrimping dates, go to www.wdfw.wa.gov.

③ **Pleasant Harbor Marina.** 308913 Hwy 101, Brinnon, WA 98320; (360) 796-4611; (800) 547-3479; reservations@phmresort.com; www.pleasantharbormarina.com. Monitors VHF 09 & 16. Open all year. Closed Thanksgiving and Christmas. Ethanol-free gasoline, diesel and propane at the fuel dock. The marina has approximately 60 guest slips and unoccupied slips as available; plans include adding guest moorage on J & K docks for summer 2023. 30 & 50 amp power. Side-tie moorage to 150 feet. Facilities include clean restrooms and free showers, laundry, free Wi-Fi, on-site security, and free pumpout at the fuel dock. A 2-hour tie-up near the fuel dock is available for store, restaurant, and pub customers.

The main building houses the marina office, restaurant, pub, and store. The store has a selection of gifts, clothing, some groceries, beer and wine. At the fuel dock you'll find ice cream, ice, crab and shrimp bait, and marine hardware.

A shuttle bus can take you to several local hikes that range in length from a 0.2 mile trail to a 130-foot-high waterfall, to a 3.5- mile loop of Dosewallips State Park.

This is a popular destination; call or reserve online, especially for weekends and holidays. Many of the permanent tenants spend considerable time at the marina, and life on the docks is quite friendly. Amenities include a barbecue and picnic area, swimming pool, hot tub, laser skeet range, and children's play area. Kayak, and SUP rentals. Live music May through September. Diane is the very capable manager.

③ **Pleasant Harbor Marine State Park.** (360) 796-4415. Open all year for day use and overnight mooring. No camping. Dock has 120 feet of space, 3-night maximum stay, first-come, first-served. This is the first dock on the right as you enter Pleasant Harbor.

Triton Head. A state park launch ramp is at Triton Head, and anchorage is possible off this little bight.

④ **Triton Cove State Park.** (360) 796-4415; West side of Hood Canal, south of the Dosewallips River. Open all year, day use only. Vault toilet, no power, no showers. Concrete launch ramp, picnic area.

⑤ **Glen Ayr Resort.** 25381 N U.S. Hwy 101, Hoodsport, WA 98548; (360) 877-9522; office@garesort.com; www.glenayr.

Pleasant Harbor

PLEASANT HARBOR
— MARINA & RECREATION COMMUNITY —

CALL NOW
360-796-4611

More Than Just A Marina...

YEAR ROUND MOORAGE

- 312 Slip Protected Marina • 30 & 50 Amp Power
- Non-Ethanol Gas & Diesel
- Vacuum Pump Out • Heated Pool & Hot Tub
- Permanent/Guest Moorage
- Groceries/Gift Shop

GALLEY & PUB

- Delicious Food
- Local Beers on Tap
- Local Wine Selection
- Roof Top Patio
- 3 Big Screen TVs

ACTIVITIES & ADVENTURES

For up-to-date activities and special events visit our website at pleasantharbormarina.com/marina

Play, Relax, Enjoy
www.pleasantharbormarina.com

CLEAN MARINA WASHINGTON

ENVIROSTARS CERTIFIED

HOOD CANAL

See Area Map Page 136 - Maps Not for Navigation

Alderbrook Resort and Spa has ample guest moorage for stays at this quality resort.

Guest moorage at Alderbrook Resort

com. Open all year. Nice docks and friendly staff. Moorage for boats up to 24 feet, motel and townhouse guests have priority. Space for transient boaters, except during shrimp season. Restrooms, guest showers, laundry. No power at the docks. Attractive location and popular diving destination.

⑥ **Hoodsport.** Hoodsport is popular with scuba divers as a place to view the giant Pacific octopus. Local marine preserves such as Octopus Hole and Sund Rock offer divers the chance to see octopus, wolf eels, rockfish, anemones and other marine life.

The town has a grocery store, hardware store, restaurants, an espresso shop, a beauty salon, and gift shops. The Washington Department of Fish and Wildlife operates a fish hatchery in town.

⑥ **Port of Hoodsport.** P.O. Box 429, Hoodsport, WA 98548; (360) 877-9350; portmail@hctc.com; www.portofhoodsport.us. Six guest moorage slips for boats up to 16 feet, one outside 40-foot slip subject to wave action. No power, no water. Garbage drop and picnic area. Self-register and pay at the head of the dock for stays over 12 hours. Grocery store across the highway; other businesses are within walking distance.

Sunrise Motel & Resort. 24520 Hwy 101, Hoodsport, WA 98548; (360) 877-5301; sunrise@hctc.com; myweb.hcc.net/sunrise. An older resort open all year, no power, no laundry. Restrooms and showers in motel rooms. Maximum boat length 20 feet. Moorage for those staying ashore. Underwater park, scuba air station, barbecue, hot tub.

Potlatch Marine State Park. (360) 877-5361. South of Hoodsport. Open all year, day use and overnight camping and mooring. Restrooms, showers, no power. Four mooring buoys (boats 45 feet and under) are offshore in deep water, except the second buoy as you approach from the north. We are told this buoy swings into 5-foot depths at zero tide. Self-register and pay mooring buoy fee on shore, or by phone as posted on the buoy. The park has a picnic area, an underwater park for scuba diving, hiking trails, campsites. Good wildlife-watching.

⑦ **Hood Canal Marina.** P.O. Box 305, 5101 E. Hwy 106, Union, WA 98592; (360) 898-2252; hoodcanalmarina@hctc.com; www.hood-canal-marina.com. Certified Clean Marina. Open all year. Fuel dock with ethanol-free gasoline and diesel, open daily 9:00 a.m. to 5:00 p.m., May through September, call ahead in off season. 30 amp power, free Wi-Fi, washrooms, and pumpout. Limited guest moorage, maximum 40-foot vessels.

Call ahead for moorage. Moorage fills quickly on specific days in May and June during shrimp season. The Union launch ramp is adjacent and has off-site secured parking. The Union City Market, at Hood Canal Marina, offers food items, crafts, books and clothing.

⑧ **Alderbrook Resort & Spa.** 10 E. Alderbrook Drive, Union, WA 98592; (360) 898-2200; (360) 898-2252; waterfront@alderbrookresort.com; www.alderbrookresort.com. Monitors VHF 16 & 68. Open all year, 1500 feet of guest moorage. Restrooms, showers, 30 & 50 amp power, water, swimming pool and whirlpool spa, free Wi-Fi. Pumpout available, check for availability in advance. Seaplane dock. Kayak, paddleboard, hydrobike and seacycle rentals. Their private yacht, *Lady Alderbrook*, is available for private parties. Contact sales@alderbrookresort.com for more details.

If you're looking for a quality resort experience, you'll find it here. The rooms are beautifully appointed, the grounds are immaculate, and the dining room is superb. Moorage is free while dining. They have an indoor pool, with a spa adjacent. Hiking trails surround the property. Everything you're looking for in a weekend getaway is here, including golf. Best to call ahead for reservations and prices. Special events include Oyster Month in April, Thunder on the Canal July 3rd, and Day After Thanksgiving Tree Lighting.

⑨ **Summertide Resort & Marina.** P.O. Box 450, 15781 NE Northshore Rd. Tahuya, WA 98588; (360) 275-9313; www.

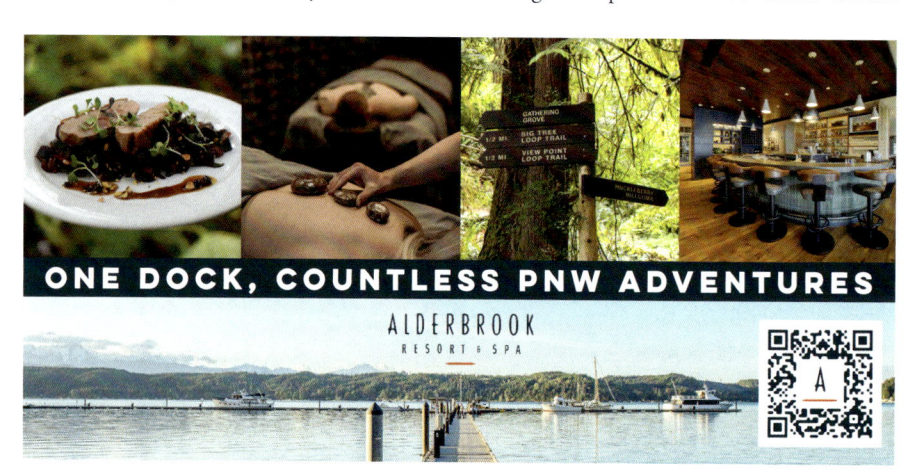

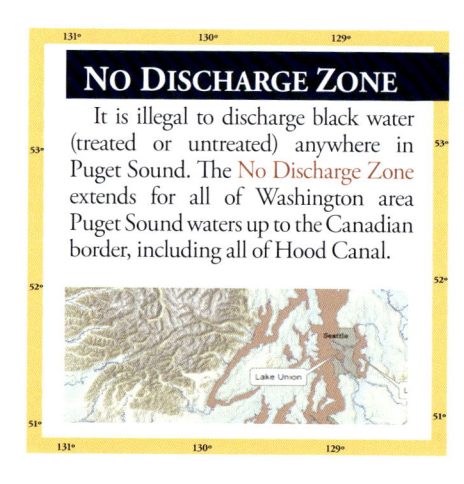

NO DISCHARGE ZONE

It is illegal to discharge black water (treated or untreated) anywhere in Puget Sound. The No Discharge Zone extends for all of Washington area Puget Sound waters up to the Canadian border, including all of Hood Canal.

Hood Canal Marina at the town of Union.

The view of Olympic Mountains and the Great Bend from Hood Canal Marina

summertideresort.com. Guest moorage, 20-foot maximum boat length. Reservations required. Restrooms, showers, Wi-Fi, no power. Launch ramp, RV spaces with hookups. Boat moorage is for those staying in one of the resort's rental cottages, or other upland accommodations; no overnighting aboard vessels at the dock. The store carries groceries, beer, wine, snacks, ice, bait, and tackle; boaters are welcome to stop for shopping at the store.

⑩ **Twanoh Marine State Park.** (360) 275-2222. Eight miles west of Belfair. Open all year, day use and overnight camping and mooring, except no camping in winter. Has 200 feet of overnight and day-use moorage dock, 6 mooring buoys for vessels 45 feet and under. Self-register and pay mooring fees on shore, or by phone as posted on the buoy. Restrooms, showers, pumpout, portapotty dump, power, no water. Be aware that water depth at the dock is only 3 feet at zero tide. This is a large and popular park, with launch ramp, playground, picnic areas, kitchen shelters, fireplaces. Launch ramp. Docks are removed from November through April. Standard, utility and primitive campsites, tennis courts, hiking trails.

Belfair State Park. (360) 275-0668. Three miles southwest of Belfair on the north shore of Hood Canal. Open all year for day use and overnight camping. Restrooms and showers. Anchor far offshore, if at all. Drying mudflats restrict approach to small, shallow-draft boats only. Popular park, camping reservations required in summer.

⑪ **Port of Allyn North Shore Dock.** P.O. Box 1, Allyn, WA 98524; (360) 275-2430; www.portofallyn.com. Open all year with 240 feet of side-tie dock space. Water, 30 amp power, portable toilets, seasonal pumpout and portapotty dump, no showers. Overnight moorage, maximum 45 feet, 14-day limit in the summer. Self-registration payment box on-site, or you can make reservations online. Launch ramp with credit, debit card payment, or pay on the website.

SHELL SHOCKED IN PORT GAMBLE

Tom Rice's great grandparents moved to Port Gamble in 1858, long before Washington became a state in 1889. They were one of the many families to move to the company town from East Machias, Maine to work for Puget Mill Company's sawmill in Port Gamble. When it permanently closed in 1995, it was the oldest continuously operating sawmill in the United States.

When Tom Rice was a child, he walked the local beaches with his grandmother; and as many of us do, he began collecting shells. His interest in shells grew as did his collection, and it became his lifelong passion as he traveled the world. Tom was a founding member of Conchologists of America and published 108 issues of the shell magazine Of Sea and Shore from 1970-2007. When Tom passed away in February 2022, he owned the largest private collection of shells in the world.

The second largest private shell collection is at the Sea and Shore Museum on the second floor of the Port Gamble General Store, which now oversees the collection. The museum was opened by Tom in 1973. It displays thousands of shells from his world travels, including a large section dedicated to local shells, such as the largest burrowing clam, the geoduck.

The 2023 Waggoner Cruising Guide describes the anchorage and town of Port Gamble. When you are out cruising, don't miss this historic and charming town. While you are there, it is well worth your time to walk up to the second floor of the General Store and witness the amazing shell collection of the legendary conchologist Tom Rice. It is free to visit.

[Dale Blackburn, Waggoner Field Correspondent]

North Puget Sound

NORTH PUGET SOUND
Kingston • Admiralty Inlet • Port Ludlow
Port Townsend • Edmonds • Everett
Langley • Saratoga Passage • Coupeville

SKAGIT BAY TO BELLINGHAM BAY
Oak Harbor • La Conner • Deception Pass
Anacortes • Bellingham

LUMMI BAY TO POINT ROBERTS
Semiahmoo Bay
Blaine • Point Roberts

Scan the Latest
North Puget Sound
Information

tinyurl.com/WG22xCh04

*Cone Islands,
Bellingham Channel*

NORTH PUGET SOUND

Reference Only – Not for Navigation

North Puget Sound. For the sake of organization and grouping, this chapter includes cruising grounds northward from Edmonds and Kingston to Point Roberts, the U.S. territory located at the southern end of the Strait of Georgia. At nearly 80 nautical miles from south to north, this is a large cruising area that includes a wide variety of micro climates along the mainland, several islands, and passages. North Puget Sound includes Edmonds and Kingston, northward to Whidbey Island.

At the south end of Whidbey Island, boaters can choose one of two routes to continue north. Westerly is the more direct route to the San Juan Islands and the waters of B.C., which takes you through Admiralty Inlet and on to Strait of Juan de Fuca. The more protected route takes you on sheltered waters along the east side of Whidbey Island to Deception Pass and Swinomish Channel, arriving at Anacortes, a major destination and jumping-off point for the San Juan Islands and Canadian waters. The Islands north of Anacortes and those near Bellingham are the less crowded versions of the San Juan Islands. Blaine and Point Roberts are the furthest north destinations on the U.S. side of the Canada/U.S. border.

The waters from Edmonds north to Deception Pass form what is meteorologically known as the "convergence zone," where weather and sea conditions can change. Whidbey Island, with Deception Pass, is one of the dominant features of North Puget Sound, along with smaller surrounding islands, including Cypress Island, Fidalgo Island, and Vendovi Island. Major community destinations include Kingston, Everett, Edmonds, Port Townsend, Port Ludlow, La Conner, Oak Harbor, Anacortes, Bellingham, and Blaine.

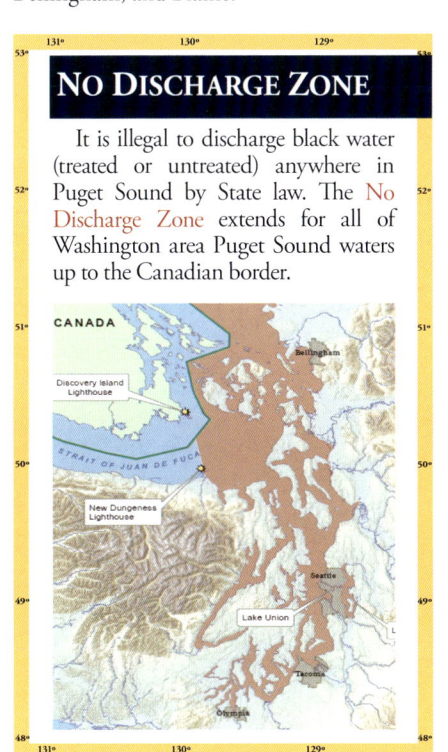

NO DISCHARGE ZONE

It is illegal to discharge black water (treated or untreated) anywhere in Puget Sound by State law. The No Discharge Zone extends for all of Washington area Puget Sound waters up to the Canadian border.

Distances (nm)
(Approximate, for planning)

Edmonds to Kingston—5
Edmonds to Port Ludlow—16
Edmonds to Port Hadlock—21
Edmonds to Port Townsend—25
Edmonds to Oak Harbor—33

See Map Lummi Bay to Point Roberts Page 175

See Map Skagit Bay to Bellingham Bay Page 159

See Map North Puget to Oak Harbor Page 144

North Puget Sound

2023 WAGGONER CRUISING GUIDE 143

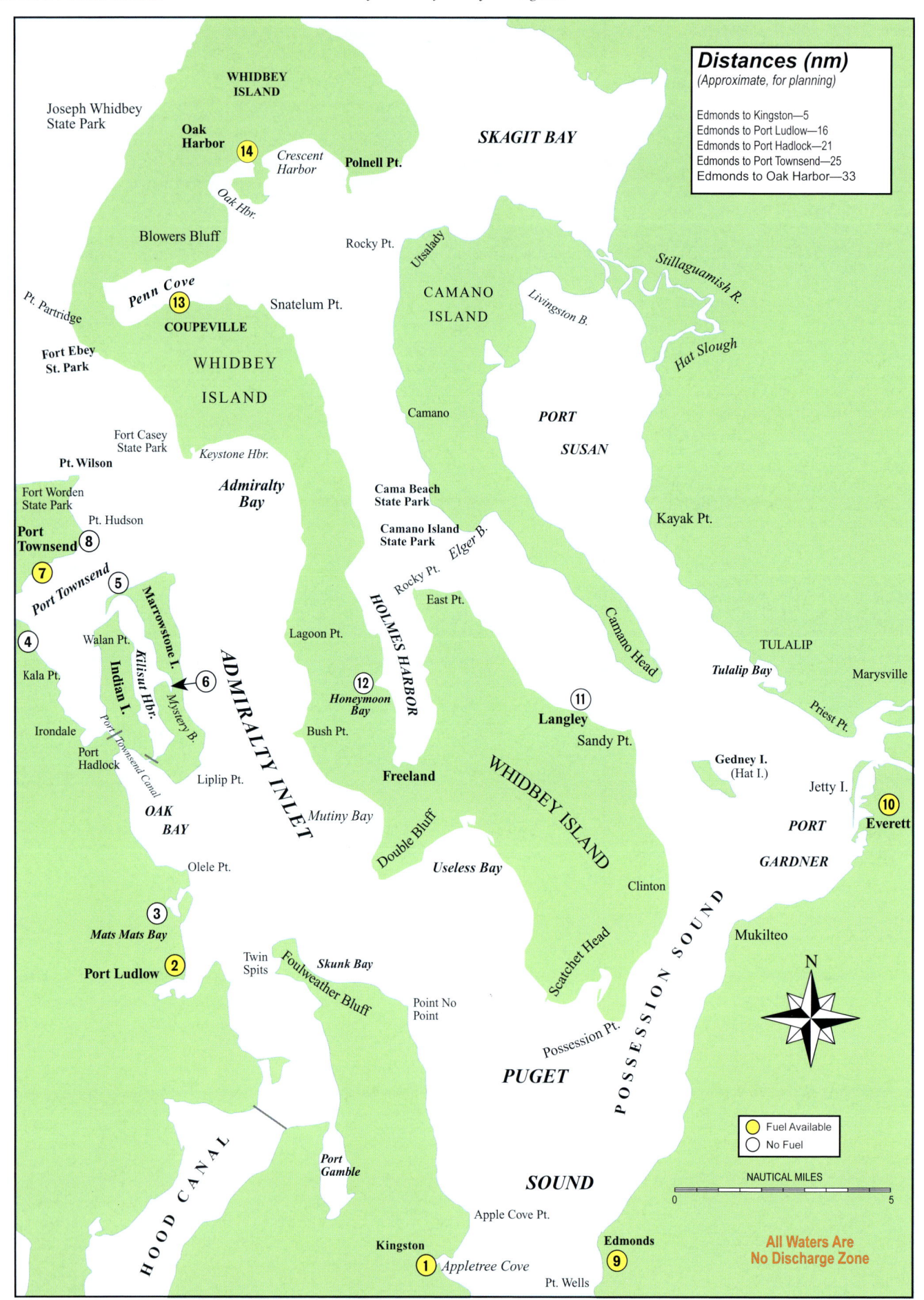

NORTH PUGET SOUND

Reference Only – Not for Navigation

Distances (nm)
(Approximate, for planning)

Edmonds to Kingston—5
Edmonds to Port Ludlow—16
Edmonds to Port Hadlock—21
Edmonds to Port Townsend—25
Edmonds to Oak Harbor—33

- Fuel Available
- No Fuel

All Waters Are No Discharge Zone

North Puget Sound to Oak Harbor

144 www.WaggonerGuide.com

See Area Map Page 144 - Maps Not for Navigation

NORTH PUGET SOUND

The cafes in Kingston are delightful and within easy walking distance.

Port of Kingston marina with breakwater protected guest moorage and fuel.

Kingston. Kingston, in Appletree Cove on the west side of Puget Sound, is the western terminus of the ferry run to Edmonds, and possibly the only city in Washington State where you can get an authentic French crepe at five o'clock in the morning while waiting for the ferry. A Port-owned marina, with a park, is located behind the breakwater. The park's meticulously maintained lawn and gardens are inviting. Kingston's tree shaded main street is lined with cafés with great food and colorful names, many with outdoor seating. Farther uptown is a grocery store and hardware store. On the north side of the ferry holding area a deck overlooks Puget Sound. A path leads to a Port-owned broad sandy beach filled with driftwood. It's a pleasant walk and great for families. On the park grounds next to the marina a farmers market, quite popular, is open 10:00 a.m. to 3:00 p.m. Sundays, May to mid-October. Concerts on the Cove, with a beer garden, are held Saturday evenings during July and August.

A pavilion on the park grounds, just up from the marina, is used for music concerts, gatherings, and weddings.

Anchoring is good south of the marina breakwater. Watch your depths. It gets shallow close to shore.

① **Port of Kingston.** P.O. Box 559, Kingston, WA 98346; (360) 297-3545; info@portofkingston.org; www.portofkingston.org. Monitors VHF 65A but prefers telephone calls. Open year-round, 47 guest slips to 50 feet, water and 30 & 50 amp power. At the deep water end of the guest dock, a float (with ELCI protected shore power) accommodates vessels up to 85 feet. The marina has restrooms, laundry, portapotty dump, free showers, free pumpout, in-berth pumpout on the guest dock, and free upgraded Wi-Fi throughout the marina. The fuel dock has ethanol-free gasoline, diesel and Delo lubricants. A dual-lane concrete launch ramp, with a float between the two lanes, is available. Parking (fee charged) for tow-vehicles and trailers. Two electric courtesy cars are available through the Port office for local trips to shopping several blocks away. They are fun to drive and popular; 30-minute usage recommended.

Four mooring buoys for boats to 40 feet are outside the breakwater north of the ferry dock. They are exposed to winds and wakes of passing boat traffic. Buoys are first-come, first-served at no charge. A small landing fee is charged if you dinghy in to the marina.

Moorage reservations are accepted with one day advance notice; call the Port office during business hours or see their website to make reservations online. Kingston is quite popular during the summer months, reservations are recommended. Slips marked "open" are first-come, first-served, and reserved slips are marked reserved.

Enter the marina around the end of the rock breakwater. Leave the two pilings that mark the edge of the dredged channel to port.

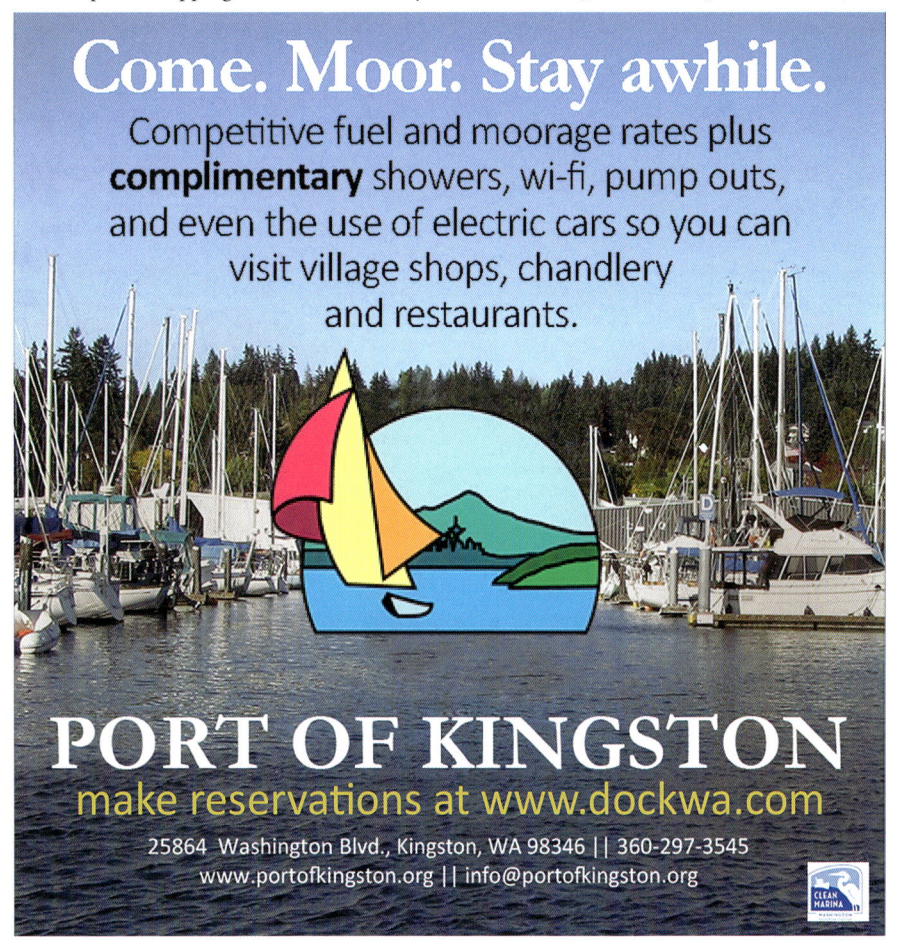

Kingston

Come. Moor. Stay awhile.

Competitive fuel and moorage rates plus **complimentary** showers, wi-fi, pump outs, and even the use of electric cars so you can visit village shops, chandlery and restaurants.

PORT OF KINGSTON
make reservations at www.dockwa.com

25864 Washington Blvd., Kingston, WA 98346 || 360-297-3545
www.portofkingston.org || info@portofkingston.org

2023 WAGGONER CRUISING GUIDE

NORTH PUGET SOUND

Leave the red buoy marking the end of the breakwater to starboard. Guest moorage is in slips extending from the dock that runs parallel to the breakwater, plus the side-tie float for larger boats at the outer end. The fuel float is at the shore end of the guest dock. Moor in any unreserved guest dock slip and register at the Port office. Gazebos, with picnic tables and power, are available for visiting boaters on a first-come, first-serve basis.

High-speed passenger ferry service to downtown Seattle. See the website for a schedule of music events and the weekend Farmer's Market. The nearby estuary is perfect for paddlers and bird watchers. The famous Christmas Lights, with over 150 sculptures and 500,000 lights, is a popular event during the shoulder season.

ADMIRALTY INLET

Admiralty Inlet begins at Point No Point in the south and ends at Point Wilson in the north. Admiralty Inlet is wide, deep, and straight, with no hazardous reefs or shoals. It makes up for this good design by often being the only patch of rough water for miles. Flood current or ebb, Admiralty Inlet waters swirl and lump up. If the wind is light, you'll see the swirls. If the wind is blowing, you'll be in the lump. Use the Bush Point current tables to predict the times of slack water, and the time and strength of maximum current.

If Admiralty Inlet is rough and you have to be there anyway, try to favor the eastern or western shores. The western shore is preferred. A suggested route is along Marrowstone Island, far enough off to avoid the rocks shown on the chart. Approach around Marrowstone Point inside the rough water just outside, and into Port Townsend Bay.

LOCAL KNOWLEDGE

CURRENT IN PORT TOWNSEND CANAL: If you are transiting Admiralty Inlet and deciding whether to take Port Townsend Canal or Admiralty Inlet to the east of Marrowstone Island, be aware that the current direction in Port Townsend Canal changes 2 to 3 hours before Admiralty Inlet off Bush Point. Check current predictions to avoid strong current against you in the canal. Port Townsend Canal currents are based on the Deception Pass current tables.

Point No Point. Point No Point, on the west side of Puget Sound (east of Hansville), is a popular salmon-fishing spot and a place where boats heading up-sound and down-sound tend to converge. Boat traffic can get heavy, especially when the salmon are running and the waters are literally covered with small sport fishing boats working along the tide-rip.

Watch out for this tide-rip. When a strong wind opposes a big tide, the waters off Point No Point can turn dangerous.

② **Port Ludlow.** Well-protected Port Ludlow indents the western shore of Puget Sound. It was once the site of a major Pope & Talbot sawmill, and now is a nice residential area, a destination resort and a marina. Anchorage is available in the main harbor, including west of the marina in depths of 40-55 feet. Note the charted cable area west of the marina and a 5-MPH no-wake speed limit in effect throughout that applies to all vessels, including dinghies.

Limited, but better protected anchorage, is in the landlocked inner harbor, reached by passing between two islets near the head of the bay with room for one or two shallow draft boats. The passage is shallow. Good anchorage, mud bottom, is in about 15 feet. Upscale homes are set well back and often screened by trees, providing some privacy and a lovely harbor charm.

A level, scenic one-mile pathway parallels Oak Bay Road, leading west from the marina to the Village Center which has a grocery, gift shop, and a pizza shop. Meydenbauer Bay Yacht Club has an outstation on the peninsula that forms the inner harbor.

② **Port Ludlow Resort and Marina.** 1 Gull Drive, Port Ludlow, WA 98365; (360) 437-0513; (877) 344-6725; marina@portludlowresort.com; www.portludlowresort.com. Monitors VHF 68. Certified Clean Marina. Open 7 days a week, all year. Ethanol-free gasoline and diesel at the fuel dock. Concrete docks, some of which are beginning to show their age. Guest

THE RESORT AT Port Ludlow

Play. Explore. Indulge. Relax.

Port Ludlow Marina is open year round and offers:

- Boat In and Golf Packages
- Golf Shuttle Available with Reservation
- Covered Pavilion and BBQ Fire Pit
- Fuel Dock and Pump Out
- Free WiFi
- Marina Gift Shop
- 30 Miles of Hiking Trails
- E-Bike Rentals
- Waterfront Dining at the Fireside Restaurant

ELITE FLEET 2021 | CLEAN MARINA WASHINGTON | VALVTECT MARINE FUEL

PORT LUDLOW golf. marina. inn. home.

www.PortLudlowResort.com • 360.437.0513

moorage in 50 slips and along 460 feet of dock, plus unoccupied slips as available, 30 & 50 amp power, water, restrooms, Wi-Fi, gazebo with barbecue, pumpout, portapotty dump, free showers. Pavilion tent for groups. Kayak, SUPs, and skiff rentals. Reservations available online.

A resort restaurant and lounge are within walking distance. Locals speak highly of the restaurant. Free shuttle for marina guests to the resort's 18-hole golf course. The marina store carries convenience items, a few groceries, propane and limited marine hardware. Shops, medical services, and a post office are located in the nearby Village Center. Marine mechanics from Port Townsend may be available. With its large grounds, pavilion tent, dining and golf, this is a popular destination for groups and rendezvous.

The marina often runs cruise-in specials that include moorage, golf, and restaurant credit. Check the marina website.

③ **Mats Mats Bay.** A course between Port Ludlow and Mats Mats Bay should avoid Snake Rock, close to shore, and Colvos Rocks and Klas Rocks, farther offshore. Colvos Rocks are marked by flashing lights at the north and south ends, and Klas Rocks by a diamond-shape dayboard with a flashing white light. Snake Rock is not marked.

Mats Mats Bay has a dogleg entrance with a least depth of 6 feet at zero tide. A lighted range shows the center of the outer channel. The channel is marked by lighted daymarks on pilings. Do not stray from the marked channel, especially at low water.

The entirety of Mats Mats Bay is private aquatic lands that are subject to the rules and regulations of the Mats Mats Bay Waterfront Owners Association. According to the Association's website (www.matsmatsbay.com), visitors are welcome and may anchor in the bay for up to 5 nights. The same website also suggests that visitors may require prior owner permission and may require proof of insurance. The area is monitored by neighboring waterfront homeowners who may approach visiting boaters.

Anchor in 9 to 15 feet in the middle or south part of the bay. The north end of the bay is shallow. The large number of boats on permanent moorings restricts anchoring options. Mats Mats Bay is well protected from almost any wind. A public launch ramp is at the south end of the bay.

Oak Bay. Oak Bay, with convenient anchoring depths, is at the southern approach to Port Townsend Canal. Oak Bay County Park is on the west side of the channel, approximately one mile south of the entrance to the canal.

Oak Bay County Park. Northwest shore of Oak Bay. Open all year, restrooms, launch ramp, campsites, picnic tables, no power, no water. Anchoring or beaching only. Marked by a rock jetty. Swimming, scuba diving, clamming, crabbing.

Port Townsend Canal. Port Townsend Canal (also known as Hadlock Canal) runs from Oak Bay to Port Townsend Bay through a relatively narrow dredged channel. The canal is well marked, easy to transit, and spanned by a bridge with 58-foot vertical clearance. Currents run to 3 knots. Port Townsend Canal is a secondary station under the Deception Pass reference station in the current tables.

Lateral mark beacons line the narrow entrance channel to Mats Mats Bay.

Port Hadlock and Irondale. The towns of Irondale and Port Hadlock are west of the northern entrance to Port Townsend Canal. A day-use dock is located at Irondale. The popular Ajax Cafe is located upland from the dock. Anchorage is good, sand bottom. Stay north of Skunk Island, due west from the marina. Permanent moorage at Port Hadlock Marina.

Port Hadlock Marina. 173 Hadlock Bay Rd., Port Hadlock, WA 98339; (360) 385-6368; www.porthadlockmarina.com. Permanent moorage marina.

Hadlock Public Dock. A Port of Port Townsend day-use dock, located at Irondale. 75 feet of side-tie guest moorage, with 4-hour maximum stay at no charge. The much loved Ajax Cafe, located upland, reopened for business after renovations; dinners served Tuesday-Sunday with scheduled live entertainment; call (360) 385-1965 for reservations. The adjacent **Northwest School of Wooden Boat Building** is worth a visit. Guided tours of the school are offered to the public on the first Friday of every month, starting at 3:00 p.m. The tour is approximately an hour and a half, covering boat building techniques and the school itself, which attracts students from around the world.

④ **Fort Townsend Marine State Park.** (360) 385-3595. Open summers only, 367 acres, approximately 2-3 mooring buoys for boats 45 feet or less; restrooms, showers, no power. Field Correspondent Jim Norris reports that the anchorage is rocky and that current tends to set the boat broadside to the swells coming in from the mouth of the bay. The park has campsites, swimming, playgrounds, hiking trails, picnic tables, fire rings, and kitchen shelters. Self-guided nature trail, clamming, fishing and scuba diving. Self-register and pay mooring buoy fee on shore, or by phone as posted on the buoy.

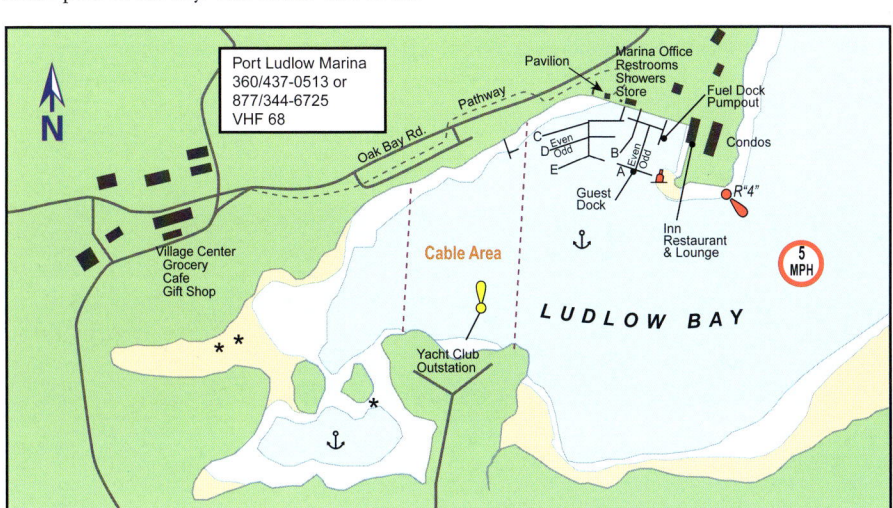

Port Ludlow

Stay informed at WaggonerGuide.com/Updates

NORTH PUGET SOUND

LOCAL KNOWLEDGE

RESTRICTED NO-ENTRY MILITARY AREA: Indian Island on the west shore of Kilisut Harbor is a Naval Ammunition Magazine Facility that is off-limits to all entry. Do not approach or go ashore anywhere on Indian Island. It is best to remain well offshore from the island.

Kilisut Harbor. Kilisut Harbor is entered through a channel between Walan Point and the spit protecting the harbor. When approaching the entrance, stay clear of the Navy restricted area off Walan Point. The channel is well marked though quite shallow, averaging about 11 feet; best to enter at high tide. Study the charts carefully, there are several sharp turns. Currents can run strongly. The channel swings past Fort Flagler State Park on the north shore, then continues through Kilisut Harbor to Mystery Bay. Mystery Bay State Park, on the north shore, has a long dock and mooring buoys. At the head of Mystery Bay is the village of Nordland.

Mystery Bay is a voluntary no anchoring zone to protect local shellfish and eelgrass, anchoring is not recommended. Ample anchorage can be found on the south end of Kilisut Harbor in Scow Bay.

In 2020, a bridge connecting Indian and Marrowstone Islands facilitated opening a channel between Scow Bay and Oak Bay for the first time in over 60 years.

⑤ **Fort Flagler Marine State Park.** (360) 385-1259. On Marrowstone Island. Open all year, 784 acres, day use, overnight mooring and camping. 256 feet of dock space with 6-foot depths at zero tide (docks removed in winter); watch for crab pots hanging from the dock. 4 to 6 mooring buoys for boats 45 feet or less, launch ramp. The current can run strongly through this area; allow for it when mooring. Restrooms, showers, portapotty dump, no power. Self-register and pay mooring fee on shore, or by phone as posted on the buoy.

Easy trails lead to old fortifications along the north shore of Marrowstone Island. Underwater park for divers. Snack and grocery concession. Boat rentals, fishing supplies. Standard, utility, and primitive campsites. Campsite reservations are a good idea in summer, call (800) 452-5687.

⑥ **Mystery Bay Marine State Park.** (360) 385-1259. In Kilisut Harbor on Marrowstone Island. Open all year, 10 acres, 683 feet dock space with 4.5-foot depth at zero tide, 6 to 8 mooring buoys for boats 45 feet or less. Pumpout, portapotty dump, toilets, launch ramp, no power, no showers. The park grounds are open for day use only, but overnight mooring is permitted at the dock and mooring buoys. Use the self-registration payment box at the bulletin board. The dock runs parallel to shore. Call Fort Flagler office for more information (360) 385-1259. The charming Nordland General Store at the shallow end of the bay (dinghy landing only) sustained extensive fire damage in November of 2020. The store is currently being rebuilt.

Port Townsend. Port Townsend has two Port-owned marinas, Point Hudson Marina and the Port of Port Townsend's Boat Haven. Boat Haven is closer to a supermarket, but Point Hudson is closer to downtown.

Port Townsend is a major boat building and repair center with craftsmen skilled in every nautical discipline. It is the home of the annual Wooden Boat Festival at Point Hudson Marina, held the weekend after Labor Day. Next to the Point Hudson Marina is the Northwest Maritime Center and the Wooden Boat Chandlery. Northwest Maritime Center often has boat building projects underway, visitors welcome. Wooden Boat Chandlery carries an array of nautical items. A Maritime Thrift Store for used gear is located in Boat Haven, 315 B Haines Place.

City Dock and Union Wharf, along Port Townsend's waterfront, are available April through September for guest moorage; first-come, first-serve basis; no power or water; often full during the peak season.

Port Townsend is a favorite destination. The commercial district is lined with imposing stone and brick buildings from before 1900. At that time, residents hoped Port Townsend would become the western terminus of the transcontinental railroad and the principal

NORTHWEST MARITIME CENTER
431 WATER ST, PORT TOWNSEND, WA
NWMARITIME.ORG

sailing classes & camps • navigation & seamanship classes • boat shop workshops • vocational training
school programs • adventure races • Wooden Boat Festival • 48° North magazine • and more!

city on Puget Sound. Victorian homes, many of them beautifully restored and cared for, are on the hill above the business district. Port Townsend's upper business district is at the top of a long flight of stairs from the lower district on Water Street. The town of Port Townsend is a haven for writers, craftspeople and artists of all kinds. Tourists overwhelm the town during the summer, but that shouldn't keep anybody away.

Whether you're a wooden boat fan, history buff or antique collector, Port Townsend has a little bit of everything. Even with limited time to spare, the town's distinctive charm and spectacular views of Admiralty Inlet are enough to make the trip worth it. The Port Townsend Passenger Ferry, Puget Sound Express, runs between Port Townsend and Friday Harbor, May to September, call (360) 385-5288 for details.

⑦ **Port of Port Townsend Boat Haven.** P.O. Box 1180, 2601 Washington Street, Port Townsend, WA 98368; (360) 385-2355; (800) 228-2803; info@portofpt.com; www.portofpt.com. Monitors VHF 66A. Open all year; first-come, first-served. Guest moorage along 900 feet of side-tie linear dock. 30 & 50 amp power, restrooms, showers, laundry, pumpout, portapotty dump, for-fee Wi-Fi, launch ramp. Garbage receptacles are locked. Make sure you get the code before carrying a load of garbage up the docks. Ethanol-free gasoline and diesel fuel at the fuel dock (The Fish 'N' Hole).

The marina is west of the ferry dock, and entered between a rock breakwater and a piling wavebreak. The first basin on the right has the Coast Guard float, home of the 87-foot Cutter *Osprey*, and slips for commercial vessels. The next basin is the recreational basin with combination fuel dock and registration dock, moorage slips, linear dock, launch ramps, and haulout facilities. Fuel/registration dock is on the right, after passing the Coast Guard float.

Call an hour ahead or check-in at the marina office for guest moorage availability and slip or side-tie assignment, which may be in the recreational basin or commercial basin. The moorage office, in combination with the yard office, is located upland from C-dock.

KILISUT BAY - OAK BAY CHANNEL

Water for the first time in decades now flows from Oak Bay into Kilisut Harbor's Scow Bay, between Marrowstone and Indian Islands. The channel has been blocked by a buildup of sediment since 1958, creating a land bridge.

In 2020 the land bridge was removed and replaced with a 440-foot concrete girder bridge. Water now flows again between these two bodies of water, re-establishing a historic migration route for salmon and eliminating stagnant water in Kilisut Harbor. Kayakers can now enjoy paddling through the newly dredged channel between Oak Bay and Scow Bay.

On a flood tide, the water flows north under the bridge as Kilisut Harbor fills slowly at its north entrance.

The project was completed under the WSDOT's Fish Passage Barrier Removal Program in partnership with the Washington Dept. of Fish & Wildlife.

Spaces may be available through the marina for reciprocal yacht club members with Port Townsend Yacht Club. After hours, empty slips are marked on a map board at the top of the launch ramp and fuel dock. Temporary tie-up is just past the fuel dock towards the launch ramps, 1-hour limit.

NOTICE: Boat Haven will most likely be busier than usual until mid-February 2023 due to the displacement of boats from Point Hudson during the North Jetty replacement project.

Customs clearance by appointment only during standard business hours 8:00 a.m. to 4:00 p.m.; call (360) 385-3777. There is only one CBP agent stationed in Port Townsend in an office at Point Hudson. Please plan accordingly.

A hardware store and a large Safeway supermarket are across the highway. The local co-op market is a few blocks closer to town. The Chamber of Commerce Visitor Information Center is just beyond Safeway.

Key City Fish, an excellent fish market, is in the boatyard area. Several good restaurants are nearby. More restaurants and a brew pub are in the Boat Haven area. The main part of the town, with more restaurants and shops, is a 5-7 block walk. The public bus runs along the main highway into town, about a 15 minute ride from Boat Haven.

A 300-ton Travelift and a smaller Travelift are available for haulout. Major boat building and repair facilities and a chandlery (Admiral Ship Supply) are at the Boat Haven, and a West Marine store is nearby.

⑦ **The Fish 'N' Hole**. (360) 385-7031. Ethanol-free gasoline and diesel fuel, open all year. Located inside the Boat Haven breakwater. Floating store carries soda, snacks, ice, bait, tackle.

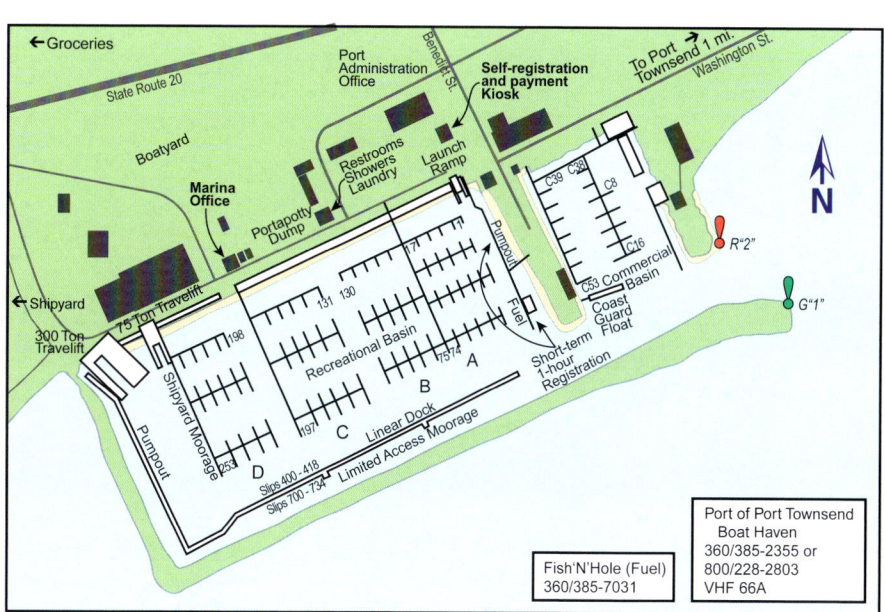

Port Townsend Boat Haven

2023 WAGGONER CRUISING GUIDE

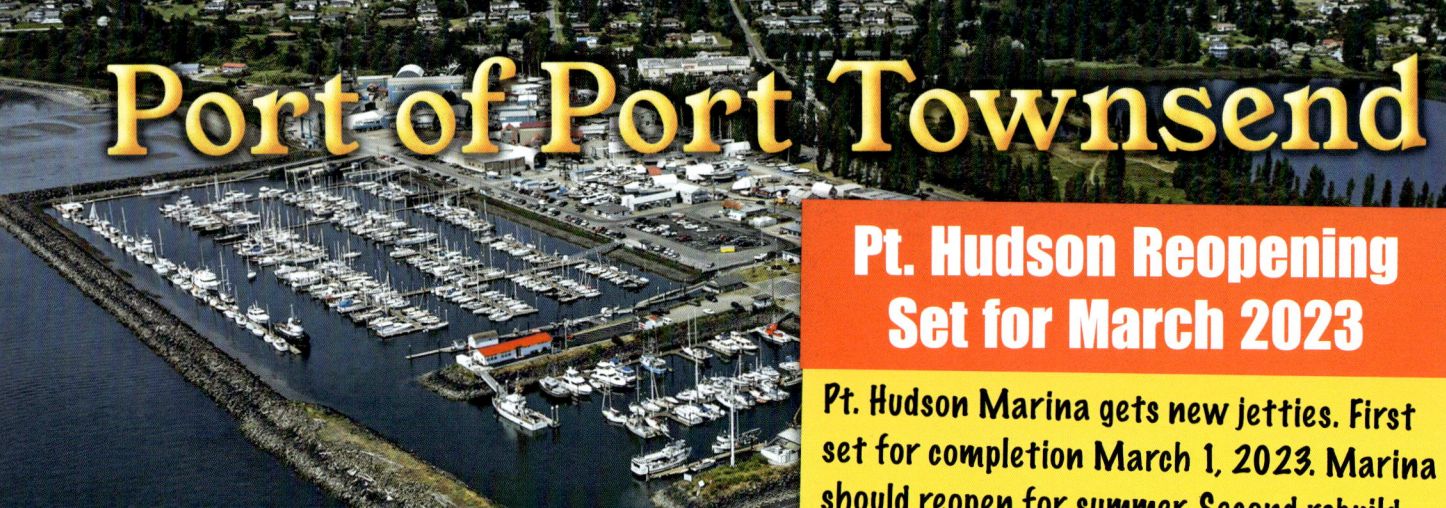

Port of Port Townsend

Pt. Hudson Reopening Set for March 2023

Pt. Hudson Marina gets new jetties. First set for completion March 1, 2023. Marina should reopen for summer. Second rebuild set for Sept. 2023 to March 2024. RV Park stays open. Check website for updates.

Small craft.
Large craft.
Tradecraft.

Four travel lifts and 400 marine trades serve the Boat Haven Marina.

A boatyard. A shipyard. Two marinas. Four haulouts. World's best marine trades. Northwest's coolest town.

✪ Boat Haven Marina has three lifts up to 300 tons & acres of yard space where you can do-it-yourself or hire the experts. Home to 400 of the world's best marine trades pros, also a chandlery, fuel, laundry, showers. Both marinas have power & water.

✪ Pt. Hudson rebuild: First jetty rebuild set to be done March 1, 2023. Marina should reopen from March to end of August. Second jetty rebuild scheduled for Sept. 2023 to March 2024. RV Park remains open. For updates, visit www.PortofPT.com. Moorage at Marina & spaces at RV Park can be made online via www.PortofPT.com; click on "Point Hudson."

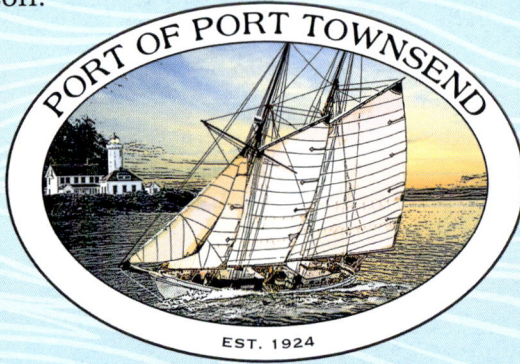

Pt. Hudson Marina is open late spring & summer 2023 with a new jetty.

400 marine trades pros ready to help

PORT OF PORT TOWNSEND
EST. 1924

Port Townsend
Point Hudson
Ferry

Boatyard: 360-385-6211   boatyard@portofpt.com
Boat Haven: 360-385-2355   boathaven@portofpt.com
Pt. Hudson: 360-385-2828   pointhudson@portofpt.com

Serving all of Jefferson County   www.PortofPT.com

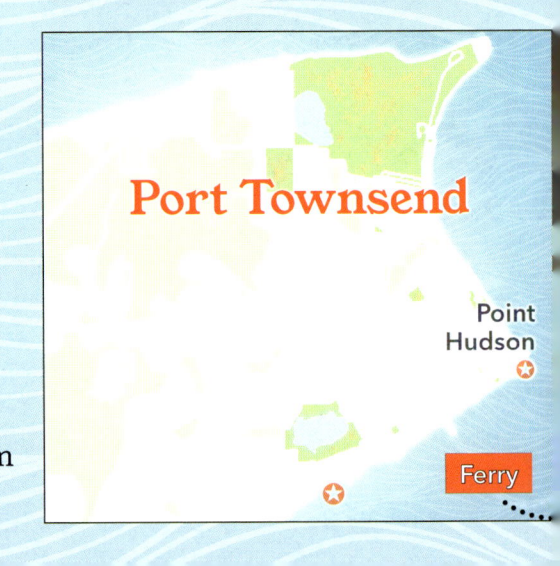

⑧ **Union Wharf**. Located at the end of Taylor Street, Port Townsend, WA 98368; (360) 385-2828; pthudson@portofpt.com; www.portofpt.com. 120 feet of side-tie; open April through September for first-come, first-served temporary and overnight stays. Self-registration and payment at the ramp; no power or water. Maximum 3-night stay. Vessels over 80 feet need advance notice, contact Pt. Hudson.

⑧ **City Dock**. Located at the end of Madison Street, Port Townsend, WA 98368; (360) 385-2828; pthudson@portofpt.com; www.portofpt.com. 70 feet of side-tie; open April through September for first-come, first-served temporary and overnight stays. Self-registration and payment at the ramp; no power or water. Maximum 3-night stay.

⑧ **Point Hudson Marina & RV Park**. P.O. Box 1180, Port Townsend, WA 98368; (360) 385-2828; (800) 228-2803; pthudson@portofpt.com; www.portofpt.com. Monitors VHF 09. Open all year, moorage slips to 70 feet. Water, 30 & 50 amp power, restrooms, showers, pumpout, laundry, for-fee Wi-Fi. Reservations are available online through the Molo Reservation system, which shows slip availability viewed on a marina map; a non-refundable registration fee is charged at the time of booking. Have all your paperwork ready when you start the online reservation process. An email is sent by the harbormaster for the moorage invoice.

Temporary tie-up is available for up to 4 hours, hail on VHF for space assignment. Ice, event facility, RV park and restaurants are on the property or nearby. The marina is within easy walking distance to town. The Jefferson County Transit Shuttle bus runs between Point Hudson and the Safeway located near Boat Haven.

Enter the marina between two piling breakwaters that force the channel into a distinct bend, directly into the prevailing northwesterly summer winds. The limitation on the size of boats is mainly due to the turns required to enter the breakwater. Replacement of the North Breakwater began in late 2022 for completion in March 2023. The marina office is in a white building on the north side.

The Sea Marine haulout and boatyard facility is at the west end of the basin. There's no grocery store nearby, so Sea Marine has ice, propane, and beer. Three restaurants are in the historic white buildings on the north side of the harbor. Other marine businesses at the harbor include Brion Toss Yacht Riggers, Best Coast Canvas, and The Artful Sailor located in the Sail Loft Building. The Wooden Boat Chandlery is located in the NW Maritime Center on the south side of the harbor entrance. The coffee shop at the Wooden Boat Chandlery has free Wi-Fi.

NOTICE: Point Hudson Marina will be closed to both permanent and guest moorage at the marina until mid-February 2023 to complete the replacement of the North Jetty. Visiting boats should be prepared to anchor out, weather permitting.

Customs clearance by appointment only during standard business hours 8:00 a.m. to 4:00 p.m.; call (360) 385-3777. There is only one CBP agent stationed in Port Townsend in an office at Point Hudson. Please plan accordingly.

Fort Worden Marine State Park. (360) 344-4400. North of Port Townsend. Open all year; approximately 6 mooring buoys. The float at the pier is out of service until further notice due to storm damage. Restrooms and showers. Best to use a buoy as this is not a good anchorage, although a friend found good sand bottom in about 18 feet. He also reported that the wakes from passing ship traffic rolled him out of his bunk all night, and he won't overnight there again. Others say they've had no trouble at all. Underwater park for scuba diving. Boat launch with two ramps. Tennis courts, picnic areas, snack bar concession near moorage area. Hiking trails, swimming, fishing. Utility and primitive campsites. Campsite reservations taken year-round. Call (800) 452-5687. Self-register and pay moorage fees on shore.

Upland, the old officers' quarters can be rented overnight. Fort buildings house the Marine Science Center and the Centrum Foundation, which conduct workshops and seminars on the arts each summer.

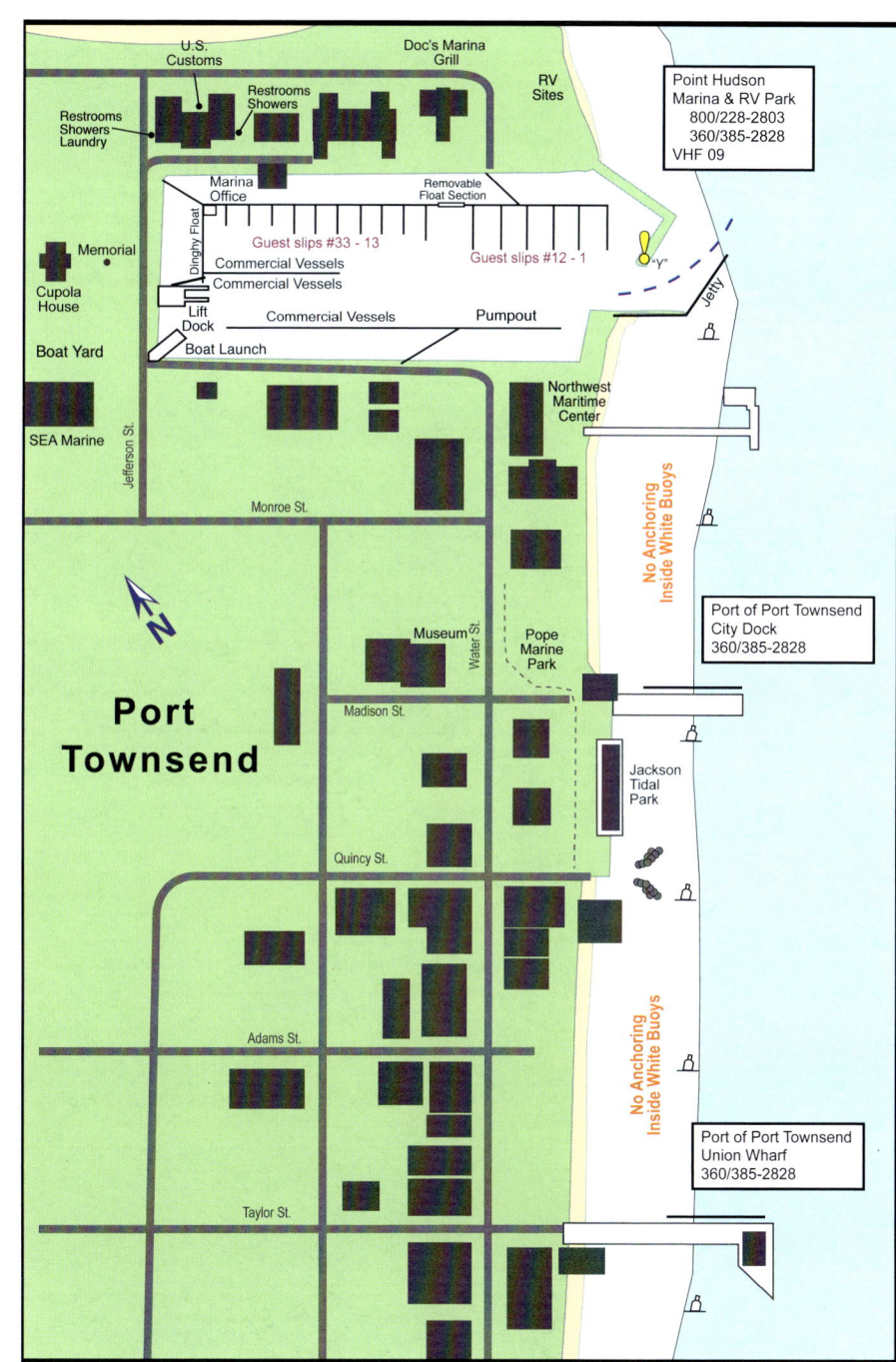

Port Townsend

NORTH PUGET SOUND

See Area Map Page 144 - Maps Not for Navigation

DON'T ROCK THE BOAT: SEASICKNESS PREVENTION

Motion Sickness of any kind is just terrible, but it is extra painful when interrupting your fun on a boat!

Unfortunately, the truth is, if you do not take preventative measures prior to leaving the dock, the catch up is nearly impossible.

It is important to first understand what motion sickness actually is. When you are on the boat, all of the cabinets, furniture and surroundings appear stable to your eyes because they are moving with you; you communicate to the brain that you are not moving, but your inner ear and muscles feel the boat's motion and acceleration and sends a conflicting message to your brain. We're moving, wait, no wait…no we're not! Your brain then reacts to the conflict by dumping the hormones epinephrine (adrenaline), norepinephrine and vasopressin into your system. It is best to keep your eyes fixed on the horizon, you will have a better chance of aligning your eyes perception with your inner ear's, thus minimizing the conflicting message to the brain. There is no way to predict who or when you may get seasick. Experienced Mariners can go years without experiencing this; and when the stars line up, there it is…Halley's Comet!

One way to prepare for potential seasickness is to take over-the-counter motion sickness medications such as Dramamine or Bonine. The active ingredient in these medications is called meclizine hydrochloride and is effective in preventing seasickness. The original formula of Dramamine contains dimenhydrinate, which is a mix of diphenhydramine (Benadryl) and another salt compound that I cannot enunciate, nor spell. The Diphenhydramine (Benadryl) can definitely cause drowsiness for many people, and who wants to sleep through a day on the water! There is a non-drowsy option and this is highly recommended. Bonine has artificial sweetener, and both Dramamine and Bonine contain lactose and come in chewable forms.

The most effective way to pre-medicate is to start taking these meds as prescribed, 1-2 days prior to leaving the shore so your body has adjusted to the medication and there is plenty in your system before you leave.

If you are highly prone to motion sickness, your doctor can prescribe the prescription strength of the oral medication Meclizine or a Scopolamine transdermal patch. The Scopolamine patch is a clear round medicated patch that is placed behind your ear and lasts up to 72 hours. The patch should be applied 4 hours prior to leaving land. The patch has some side effects, including a noticeably dry mouth and less commonly, dizziness. You should not use the patch if you have glaucoma or are pregnant. This is my personal favorite treatment method due to the ease of the treatment. One and done! The patch lasts for three full days. Very few things in my life are predictable for three straight days so this is a huge score!

Seabands™ are an option that is all natural. Seabands are an elastic cotton wristband that contains small plastic studs that apply acupressure to the wrist. This a natural remedy and there are no known side effects. The Nei kuan acupressure point on your wrist is the target and is located between the tendons directly under your index finger. To locate this point and ensure proper placement, place your middle three fingers on the inside of your wrist with your third finger on the crease of your wrist. The Nei kuan point is between the two central tendons just under your index finger. The button on the band should be positioned directly on this point. You need to wear a band on each wrist in order for it to be effective.

When or if you reach the need to throw up, just let it rip! You should experience immediate relief but don't be fooled, as usually there is more to come. Acceptance and deep breathing are a must right now. If it's safe, go outside to the mid-ship rail and please try to be downwind! Let it loose over the rail or into a designated bucket outside. Your fellow Mariners will understand. You are not the first, and certainly will not be the last!

There is unfortunately no tried and true cure for seasickness. You may feel the effects of this for a period of time, even after you are back on land. Remember the preventive measures prior to your next boating trip: hydrate, use medications, relax, look at the horizon.

Annie Feyereisen

LOCAL KNOWLEDGE

TIDE-RIP: The tide rip at Point Wilson can be dangerous to cruising boats. The bigger the ebb, the greater the chance for a tide-rip. A small ebb can produce no rip at all, particularly if the wind is light. Use the Bush Point current tables to predict the time of slack water and strength of maximum current. Those who think that a fast boat makes current tables unnecessary are wrong, and Point Wilson will prove them so.

Point Wilson. Point Wilson is the corner where Admiralty Inlet turns into the Strait of Juan de Fuca. On an ebb, a nasty tide-rip can build immediately north of Point Wilson, and stretch well across the mouth of Admiralty Inlet. If it's a big ebb and opposed by strong westerly winds, the seas in this area are not merely nasty, they are dangerous. They are high, steep and close together. They break. They are not long rollers; they are pyramid-shaped, and have no consistent pattern except for being ugly.

Since boats bound for the San Juan Islands or out the Strait of Juan de Fuca often schedule their passages to take advantage of the ebb, skippers must be aware of what can happen at Point Wilson, especially if a westerly is blowing. In such conditions, the wise approach is to favor the Whidbey Island side. The even wiser choice is to wait until slack water or the beginning of the flood. Better yet, wait for the wind to drop and then go at slack water.

For information on crossing the Strait of Juan de Fuca, see chapter titled, Strait of Juan de Fuca.

WEST WHIDBEY ISLAND

South Whidbey State Park. On Admiralty Inlet on the Whidbey Island side, just south of Lagoon Point. Open all year, day use only. Campground closed October 15 to March 15. Restrooms, showers, no power. Anchoring in calm conditions or beaching only. Picnic sites, hiking trail, underwater park for scuba diving.

Fort Casey State Park. (360) 678-4519. Admiralty Head, adjacent to Keystone Harbor on Admiralty Inlet. Open all year, day-use and overnight camping, restrooms, no power, no showers. Has a 2-lane launch ramp with boarding floats. Not a good anchorage; beachable boats are best. Underwater park with artificial reef for scuba divers. Picnic areas, standard and primitive campsites. Lighthouse and interpretive center. Historic displays and remains of the old fort to explore. Guided tours during summer.

Fort Ebey State Park. (360) 678-4636. Open all year for day use and overnight camping. The park has restrooms and

Port of Edmonds Marina with guest moorage has several restaurant options.

showers. Anchoring only, or small boats can be beached. Standard campsites, picnic sites. Interesting bunkers and gun batteries are in the old fort.

Joseph Whidbey State Park. (360) 678-4636. Northwest shore of Whidbey Island facing the Strait of Juan de Fuca. Open April through September, day use only. Toilets. Anchor or beach only. One mile of sandy beach on Puget Sound. Picnic sites.

NORTHEAST PUGET SOUND

⑨ **Edmonds**. Edmonds, a prosperous community with a small-town feel to it, is about 8 miles north of Shilshole Bay on the east side of Puget Sound. Edmonds has a major rock breakwater-protected marina (the Port of Edmonds Marina) with excellent facilities for visiting boats. At the marina and in the town a short distance away you'll find a number of very good restaurants, antique stores, a lively art scene, an historic 252-seat movie theater, art museum, performance theaters, and interesting shops and galleries. Edmonds "walks" well. This is an ideal destination for a weekend getaway, year-round. A courtesy van service to downtown Edmonds is provided for guests of the Port of Edmonds Marina. Don't miss Edmonds' many wonderful restaurants, including Chanterelle, The Cheesemonger's Table, and Daphnes Bar, among other fine dining establishments.

THINGS TO DO

- **Edmonds Waterfront Festival** (June)
- **Marina Concert Series:** Wednesday evenings and Sunday afternoons (June - mid-September).
- **Taste of Edmonds** (Around the second week of August.)
- **Edmonds Public Art Walking Tour**: 12 of 15 art pieces are in the city's central core.
- **Edmonds Historic Site Walking Tour**: This self guided tour takes you past 29 sites in a one-square-mile section of the city's historic center.
- **Scratch Distillery:** Learn about the distilling process for handcrafted vodkas and gin in a relaxed contemporary atmosphere. Tour & Tasting on Saturdays and Sundays.
- **Cascadia Art Museum** The museum showcases American regional art from the mid-19th to the mid-20th century.
- **Edmonds Center for the Arts** has theatre productions, comedy, film series, and live music.
- **Edmonds Segway Tours**: Learn about Edmond's history or take a sunset tour. Book online or call (206) 947-5439.

Anthony's Beach Cafe
456 Admiral Way
(425) 771-4400

ANTHONY'S HOMEPORT RESTAURANT
456 Admiral Way
(425) 771-4400

⑨ **Port of Edmonds**. 336 Admiral Way, Edmonds, WA 98020; (425) 775-4588; info@portofedmonds.org; www.portofedmonds.org. Monitors VHF 69. Certified Clean Marina and Certified Clean Boatyard. Open 7 days a week all year. The fuel dock has ethanol-free gasoline & diesel. The marina has 500 feet of guest side-tie dock space, plus unoccupied slips when available. They can accommodate boats to 100 feet. Reservations available online. The docks are served by 30 & 50 amp power, restrooms, showers, two pumpouts, a covered outdoor weather center, and public plaza. Used oil drop. Reservations accepted, with a fee.

Enter through the middle of the breakwater. Guest moorage and the fuel dock are immediately to the south. The marina has a large do-it-yourself work yard, a 10,000-pound public sling launch and a 50-ton Travelift. Close to two popular public beaches and a public fishing pier. An artificial reef for scuba diving (the first such site in the state) is next to the ferry dock just north of the marina. Fishing charters are available. It's a short walk to several restaurants. On Saturdays a market is set up near the downtown business district. The marina provides courtesy van service to downtown Edmonds. The marina personnel are friendly and helpful.

Possession Sound is on the southeast side of Whidbey Island between Possession Point and Mukilteo.

Mukilteo. (425) 263-8180. Mukilteo Lighthouse Park has a 4-lane launch ramp with floats available in the summer. The floats are exposed to ferry wakes, and waves generated by winds on Possession Sound and Port Gardner. A launch fee is charged. The ferry terminal is located one-half mile east of the old ferry landing previously adjacent to Ivar's Restaurant. The Mukilteo Lighthouse is open for visitors April through September.

Gedney Island. (425) 327-2607. Gedney Island, known locally as Hat Island, is privately owned. The marina on the north shore is for Gedney Island property owners and their guests, and members from reciprocal yacht clubs.

Tulalip Bay. Anchorage is possible, but Tulalip Bay is very shallow, with a reef guarding the entrance and drying shoals inside. Several private floats and mooring buoys owned by members of the Tulalip Tribes often occupy the bay.

LOCAL KNOWLEDGE

STRONG CURRENTS: Currents in the Snohomish River can be quite strong, particularly on an ebb tide. Allow for the current as you maneuver.

NIGHT LIGHTS: At night, lights ashore in Everett's Navy facilities make the entrance channel buoys very difficult to see and identify. A vessel approaching at night should be extremely cautious.

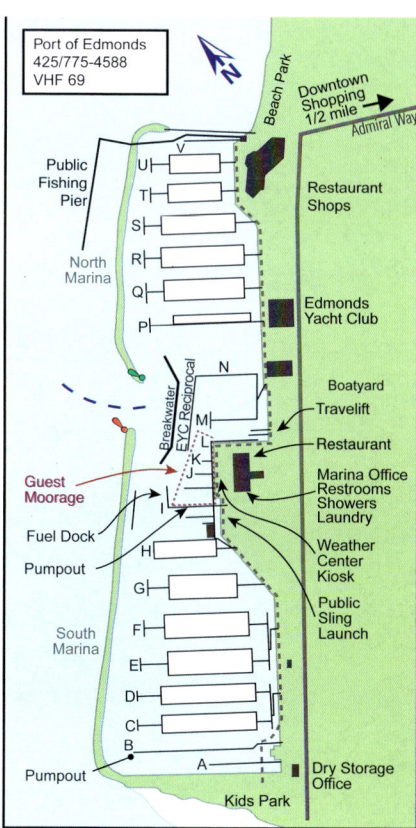

Port of Edmonds

NORTH PUGET SOUND

⑩ **Everett.** The Port of Everett Marina is home to a fishing fleet as well as private pleasure craft. Entry is about a mile upstream from the marked mouth of the Snohomish River. Information about moorage can be obtained from the fuel dock just inside the piling breakwater.

When you are in the river and approaching the marina entrance, watch for debris in the water and pay close attention to your navigation. Several aids to navigation, including one buoy marking a sunken ship, can be confusing. Although the channel can be entered between Lighted Buoy 3 and Light 5 off the south end of Jetty Island, the water between them is somewhat shoal. For complete safety we recommend entering by leaving Lighted Buoy 3 to port. The channel leads past the U.S. Navy homeport facilities.

The marina is a long hike from the central business district, but bus and taxi service are available.

Everett offers numerous activities of interest. The Port of Everett hosts a summertime waterfront concert series at Port Gardner Landing June through August, from 6:30 p.m. to 8:30 p.m. on Thursday and Saturday. The Angel of the Winds Arena at Everett (angelofthewindsarena.com) brings big-name entertainment. For professional sports with an intimate feeling, take in a minor league baseball game and cheer on the Aquasox. The July 4 fireworks show is Puget Sound's largest outside Seattle, and right in the laps of the Everett moorage.

Across the river from the marina is a Port-owned float at Jetty Island, which has what is probably the largest pure sand beach on Puget Sound. The Langus Waterfront Park, with a good launching facility, is on the north shore of the main river channel, a short distance up the river from the Port of Everett Marina. Mobile pumpout service is offered through Rose Head Service (425) 501-5242.

Farther up the Snohomish River, Dagmar's Landing is a large dry-land storage facility with a huge fork lift truck and a long float. A detailed chart or local knowledge are required before continuing beyond Dagmar's.

THINGS TO DO

- **Everett Farmers Market**. Produce, art, music, and food; Sundays, May-October located at Hewitt and Wetmore Avenues.
- **Schack Art Center.** Exhibits, events, classes; hot shop for glass blowing. Open Tue.-Sat., hours vary; call (425) 259-5050.
- **Evergreen Arboretum & Gardens**. 3.5 acres, with 10 themed gardens, walking paths, and sculptures. Holiday Lights in Dec.; open year round at 145 Alverson Blvd.
- **Music at the Marina**. Enjoy evening music concerts on Thursdays in August at Port Gardner Landing.
- **Angel of the Winds Arena.** International shows, sporting events and ice skating in this multi-purpose building at 2000 Hewitt Ave.; call (425) 322-2600.
- **Port Gardner Bay Winery.** A boutique winery with relaxed tastings. Classes in winemaking. 3006 Rucker Ave.; call (425) 339-0293 for hours.
- **Weyerhaeuser Building**. Visit the historic Gothic-style Weyerhaeuser building on the marina grounds. Future plans for the building include a coffee shop and a small museum.

ANTHONY'S HOMEPORT RESTAURANT
1726 West Marine View Dr.
(425) 252-3333

Anthony's Woodfire Grill
1722 West Marine View Dr.
(425) 258-4000

⑩ **Port of Everett Marina.** 1205 Craftsman Way, Suite 105, Everett, WA 98201; (425) 259-6001; (425) 388-0689 fuel dock; (425) 388-0672 security; marina@portofeverett.com; www.portofeverett.com. Monitors VHF 16. Certified Clean Marina. This is the largest public marina on the West Coast. Open all year; gasoline and diesel at the fuel dock. Over 5000 feet of guest moorage with depths 10 to 16 feet, unoccupied slips used when available. Guest moorage is first-come, first-served; self-pay stations are located throughout the marina; payment is by credit card. The designated first-come moorage areas are Dock 1 by Anthony's, the inside of Dock 5 by Hotel

Moor where there's more!

Port of EVERETT MARINA | **WATERFRONT PLACE @ PORT OF EVERETT**

The Port of Everett Marina offers 5,000 lineal feet of guest moorage for visiting boaters just steps away from world-class amenities, restaurants and outdoor activities at our transforming destination waterfront.

Book your stay today! Guest moorage reservations available via DockWA.com.

Call: 425.259.6001
Visit: portofeverett.com/marina

@portofeverett #portofeverett

Indigo, and Docks 7 & 8 by the boat launch; no power. Reservations are accepted for group rendezvous. Individual reservations available online via Dockwa. If staying less than six hours before 10 p.m., guest moorage is free. Water, 20, 30 & 50 amp power, restrooms, showers, laundry, multiple free pumpout stations, free portapotty dump, and for-fee Wi-Fi.

The Port of Everett is a large, complete marina complex, with hotels, restaurants, shops, boatyard, boat storage, full repair services, marine supplies, and chandleries. The Port of Everett has undergone substantial development of the uplands, including hotels, apartments, and a sky bridge connection to a community park with scenic vistas. Dock replacements are ongoing throughout the marina complex.

The half-square mile marina complex is made up of 3 in-water dock areas: South Docks, Central Docks, and North Docks. Uplands are in 5 named zones: Marina Village, Fisherman's Harbor, Craftsman District, Millwright District, and Jetty Landing.

The Port's Craftsman District has a Travelift haulout to 75 tons with yard storage, a boatyard for repairs and maintenance. The Travelift is at the east end of the moorage.

The Jetty Landing area to the north, has a 13-lane launch ramp (largest in the state).

The Port of Everett's North Docks offer a first-class 42-slip guest moorage facility. The concrete docks are wide, stable and heavily built. Power is 30 & 50 amp, with 100 amp at the end moorages. A pumpout line is built into the main docks with attachments at each slip. The basin has its own restrooms, showers, and laundry.

The Waterfront Center Building in the Craftsman District has an inside coffee area, a brew-pub restaurant and a distillery. The marina's office is located in the Waterfront Center Building. Harbor Marine, a complete marine supply store and chandlery, is on 10th Street in the Craftsman District. They have a snack bar and cafe with daily specials.

Marina Village has a selection of restaurants, shops, a hotel, and a West Marine store. On the east, between Marina Village and Fisherman's Harbor is the new pedestrian skybridge.

Fisherman's Harbor is the most recent development with multi-use apartments, restaurants, shops, and eateries. This area is located upland from Guest Dock 5 in the Central Docks basin.

Millwright District has yet to be redeveloped and currently has guest and tenant showers and laundry, along with storage yards.

Watch for strong currents when landing at the Guest Docks 1, 3, 7, and 8 on the Snohomish River. ADA accessible guest moorage available on South Guest Dock 2, east of Q-dock in the South Docks.

Note: Wind and current can make docking at Everett Marina challenging.

Pumpout Service: Rose Head Service (425-501-5242) provides pumpout mobile service one day per week for tenants and guests.

See Area Map Page 144 - Maps Not for Navigation

NORTH PUGET SOUND

EVERETT YACHT SERVICE

- Running gear
- Structural repair
- Interior refinishing
- Bottom painting
- Blister repair
- Thruster installation
- Diesel & gas mechanical systems service and repair

425-212-9923

Haulouts at the Everett Marina or with Pacific Fiberglass at Seattle's Canal Boatyard!

50' Sea Ray

pacificfiberglass.com [206] 789 4690

Jetty Island. (425) 257-8304; www.everettwa.org. Jetty Island is a lovely low sand island across the river from the Everett Marina. Jetty Island is open all year. Two large docks provide space for a number of boats. Boats can overnight at the dock. Jetty Island has toilets but no showers, no power, and no water for boats. The toilets are closed in winter. Pay station on shore.

River currents can make landing at the docks challenging. Before approaching the dock, be sure your boat is well-fendered, dock lines ready, and plans agreed upon.

Jetty Island is a wildlife preserve with great birdwatching. The Parks Department offers nature programs during the summer, and runs boats from the launch ramp to the island, no charge, July 4 through Labor Day.

Snohomish River Delta. The Snohomish River Delta has three main mouths—Steamboat Slough, Ebey Slough, and the main river—each of which is navigable for all or part of its length. All three River Delta channels have both fixed and opening bridges. Check charts for clearance and openings. Cautious boaters can cruise the delta.

Correspondent Tom Kincaid has cruised all of this area, some of it several times, in a 30-foot sailboat, a 36-foot powerboat, and an outboard-powered dinghy. The waters are subject to tidal action. Drying flats are off the river mouths. Enter only during the hours of highest tides. The Snohomish River Delta is a fascinating place with wildlife, calm anchorages, and quiet.

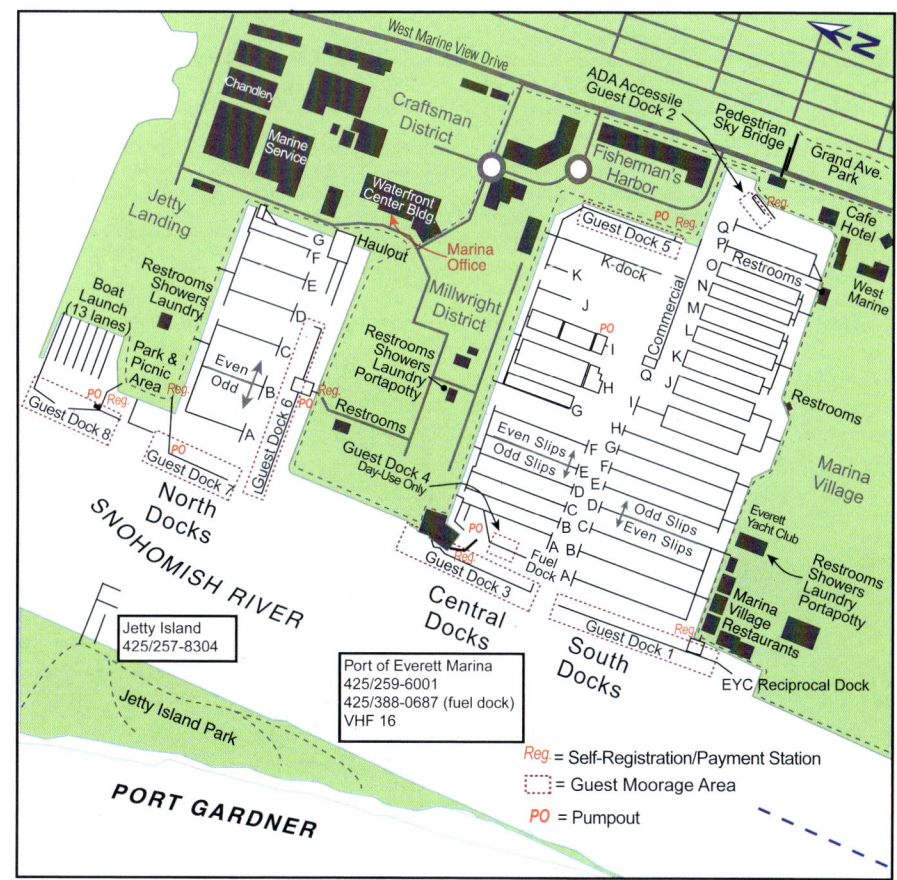

Port of Everett

2023 **Waggoner** CRUISING GUIDE

NORTH PUGET SOUND

See Area Map Page 144 - Maps Not for Navigation

Langus Waterfront Park. North shore of the Snohomish River. The park is open all year and has restrooms, but no guest moorage, power or showers. This is a City of Everett park with a 2-lane concrete launch ramp and boarding floats. A wide concrete float is for fishing and launching rowing shells.

Port Susan. Port Susan is surrounded by Camano Island to the west and the mainland to the east. A swampy waterway connects the northern end of Port Susan with Skagit Bay. Kayak Point in Port Susan is a Snohomish County Park. North of Kayak Point, Port Susan shoals to drying flats, through which meander the two mouths of the Stillaguamish River. At high tide it is possible to cross over these flats and enter South Pass to Stanwood, although the bridge just beyond Stanwood is very low.

Kayak Point County Park. 15610 Marine Drive, Stanwood, WA 98292; (360) 652-7992. Open all year, restrooms but no showers. Anchorage only close to shore. The anchorage is exposed to southerly winds. Launch ramp with boarding floats. Fishing pier, no overnight moorage at the pier.

Saratoga Passage. Saratoga Passage separates Camano Island from Whidbey Island. The waters are better protected and often smoother than Admiralty Inlet, and the current is less. Boats running between Seattle and the San Juan Islands often choose this inside route via Deception Pass or La Conner when the wind and seas are getting up in Admiralty Inlet.

This is not to say the waters are always smooth. One year, Bob and Marilynn Hale ran into uncomfortable seas while southbound in Saratoga Passage during a 25-knot southerly storm, and were forced to run back to Oak Harbor for shelter.

Saratoga Passage is relatively free of dangers, but it does have three tricks: Rocky Point(s) and Holmes Harbor. A study of the chart shows two Rocky Points in Saratoga Passage. One is on Whidbey Island at the entrance to Holmes Harbor; the other is at the north end of Camano Island.

Southbound boats may be tempted to go straight into Holmes Harbor instead of turning southeast past the Whidbey Island Rocky Point. If you're not watching your chart, the appeal is quite strong. Follow the Camano Island shoreline.

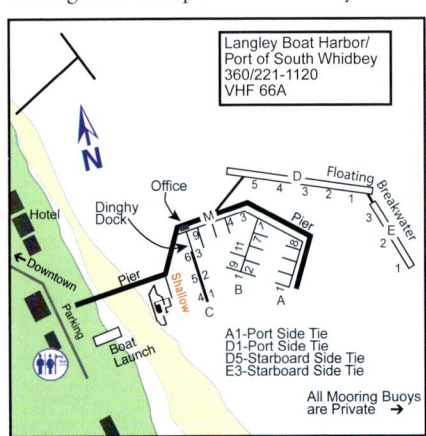

Cama Beach State Park. (360) 387-1550. Twelve miles southwest of Stanwood. Open all year, anchoring only. Restrooms, showers, small store, 15 miles of hiking and biking trails, 24 cabins, 7 deluxe cabins and 2 bungalows. The Center for Wooden Boats runs the boathouse and boat rental operation, first-come, first-served. Many classic rowboats and sailboats are available for hourly or daily rentals. The workshops on shore may have a boat building project or two underway. See the CWB website (www.cwb.org) for information on classes offered at Cama Beach and available boat rentals. Advance contact is recommended for hours and days of operation (360) 387-9361 or cama@cwb.org.

Elger Bay. Elger Bay is a good anchorage, mud bottom, with surprisingly good protection from northerly winds. Watch your depths close to the head of the bay.

Camano Island State Park. (360) 387-3031. Fourteen miles southwest of Stanwood. Open all year for day use and overnight camping, first-come, first-served. Restrooms, showers, no power. Anchoring only. Launch ramp. Underwater park for scuba diving. Cabins, standard and primitive campsites.

⑪ **Langley.** The Langley Boat Harbor serves the delightful village of Langley. If the boat harbor is crowded, as it usually is during the summer, anchorage is good south and east of the harbor, unless strong northerly winds make the area uncomfortable. There is a nominal dinghy landing fee.

The town of Langley itself has streets lined with historic buildings that house interesting shops, excellent galleries, fine restaurants, a whale museum, a craft brewery, and a vintage 250-seat movie theater. The Star Store is a well-stocked grocery, with fresh produce and a deli; an adjoining section carries kitchenware, gifts, and clothing. Langley is a good walking town. You'll find beautiful views of Saratoga Passage and a small park with stairs leading to the beach in town. A couple blocks from the cozy commercial district is where the farms begin.

⑪ **Port of South Whidbey/Langley.** P.O. Box 872, Freeland, WA 98249; (360) 221-1120; harbormaster@portofsouthwhidbey.

Guest moorage at Langley's Port of South Whidbey marina is on the inside of the breakwater.

Langley Boat Harbor

Langley's variety of shops and eateries are a major draw for boaters.

See Area Map Page 144 - Maps Not for Navigation

NORTH PUGET SOUND

Coupeville Wharf has a gift shop and a cafe with indoor & outdoor seating.

The Island County Historical Museum in Langley is worth a visit.

com; www.portofsouthwhidbey.com; Monitors VHF 66A. Guest moorage year-round. Approximately 1,100 feet of moorage. Gated docks D and E are located behind the outer breakwater; docks A, B, and C are behind the wall of the inner harbor and color coded. Depths shallow to approximately 8 feet at zero tide south of the breakwater. Check your depth. Restrooms and showers are located upland from the dock.

Reservations accepted online 48 hours in advance, highly recommended during the peak season. No rafting unless you are traveling with another boat or are having a group event. 20, 30, 50 & 100 amp power, launch ramp (higher tides only), pumpout barge, free Wi-Fi. Unique shops, boutiques, bakery, and grocery are up the hill in town. Free shuttle to town in season.

Holmes Harbor. Holmes Harbor indents the eastern shore of Whidbey Island for about 5 miles in a southerly direction. It is deep and relatively unprotected from strong northerlies. The harbor has a good launch ramp at the head and anchorage along either shore. Honeymoon Bay is a good anchorage. Holmes Harbor is subject to williwaws, the unusually strong gusts of wind that spill across the lower portion of Whidbey Island.

⑫ **Honeymoon Bay.** Honeymoon Bay is a favored anchorage on the west shore of Holmes Harbor. Private mooring buoys take up most of the good spots; but with a little diligence, satisfactory anchoring depths with adequate swinging room can be found. Honeymoon Bay is exposed to northerly winds.

Penn Cove. Penn Cove is about 10 miles north of Holmes Harbor. The cove extends nearly 4 miles west from Long Point, with the town of Coupeville on the southern shore. Anchorage is good along both shores and toward the head of the bay. A charted cable area runs through the center of cove to its head. But be aware that strong winds from the Strait of Juan de Fuca can blow across the low neck of Whidbey Island at the head of the cove. This is where the famous Penn Cove mussels come from. Watch for mussel-growing pens.

⑬ **Coupeville.** The town of Coupeville is served by the Coupeville Wharf, a 415-foot-long causeway on pilings extending over the beach to deep water. Coupeville is quaint, old, and friendly, with a variety of shops, galleries, and restaurants. A display of tribal canoes is 200 feet from the head of the wharf.

⑬ **Coupeville Wharf.** P.O. Box 128, Green Bank, WA 98253; (360) 678-6379. Call for fuel, water, or pumpout. Open all year, 480 feet of dock space, first-come, first-served. Make payment at the office located on the pier. Watch depths at low and minus tides. Depths are shallowest on the inside of the float, nearest the pier and becomes deeper on the outside east end. Gasoline and diesel at the fuel dock located on a float north of the pier. There is also room to anchor in front of town. All mooring buoys are private. Pumpout, restrooms and showers are on the wharf, no power or water on the float. Water is available from a hose located above the floats on the pier. A gift shop and a cafe are at the outer end of the wharf. The town's shops and restaurants are within easy walking distance. Island Transit, with stops nearby, offers free bus service to key points on Whidbey Island.

Captain Coupe Park. 602 NE Ninth St., Coupeville, WA 98239-0577; (360) 678-4461. Open all year with restrooms and nearby portapotty dump, no power, no showers. Anchoring only. A launch ramp with a float is installed in the summer. The park is one-quarter mile by water from Coupeville wharf. It's better to anchor closer to the wharf. Mud flats surround the launch area at low tide.

Watch the depth at Coupeville's moorage float. Easy access to shops, cafes, and museums.

Coupeville has some delightful shops.

2023 WAGGONER CRUISING GUIDE   157

NORTH PUGET SOUND

See Area Map Page 144 - Maps Not for Navigation

Oak Harbor Marina has guest moorage and picnic areas.

Oak Harbor's waterfront Windjammer Park is well-worth a visit.

SKAGIT BAY TO BELLINGHAM BAY

⑭ **Oak Harbor.** Oak Harbor is a shallow and well protected port with a major, city-owned marina. The entrance channel is marked by red and green buoys and beacons, beginning with Buoy 2, about 0.6 miles offshore from Maylor Point. From Buoy 2 the entry channel runs northward into Oak Harbor, and makes a 90-degree turn to the east for the final mile that leads to the marina. *Do not pass between Buoy 2 and Maylor Point.* The water there is shoal and littered with large boulders that have been known to tear stern drive units out of boats.

The only moorage is at the spacious Oak Harbor Marina. The marina has complete facilities and park grounds ashore for dog-walking, games, or strolling. It's a bit of a walk to town, and the nearest grocery store is 1½ miles away.

Anchorage can be found just outside the marina close to the entry channel. The bottom is soft; be sure your anchor is well set. A small float for dinghies is in front of the business district, about a 1-mile walk from the marina. The float dries at low tide.

The Windjammer Park (also known as City Beach) was completed in 2020 and offers expansive lawn areas, walkways, a lagoon, picnic tables, and play areas. Kitchen facilities located on each end of the park can be reserved for special gatherings, call (360) 279-4530. The park fronts the beautiful sandy beach of Oak Harbor.

Events: Holland Happening is the last weekend of April; the town's celebration of their Dutch heritage. Hydroplane races are held late July or early-August.

Festivals: Oak Harbor Music Festival is Labor Day weekend; free admission.

Taxi: (360) 682-6920 or (360) 279-9330.

LOCAL KNOWLEDGE

ENTRANCE CHANNEL: Shoals line each side of the channel all the way into Oak Harbor. You will go aground if you stray.

⑭ **Oak Harbor Marina.** 865 SE Barrington Dr., Oak Harbor, WA 98277; (360) 279-4575; csublet@ohmarina.org; www.ohmarina.org. Monitors VHF 16, switch to 68. Open all year (closed Sundays & holidays, October through March); twenty 40-foot slips on F-dock and side-tie along G-dock. Reservations accepted, with first night charged; non-refundable. Reservations can be made online. The fuel dock has mid-grade ethanol-free gasoline, diesel and propane. 20 & 30 amp power, water, restrooms, showers,

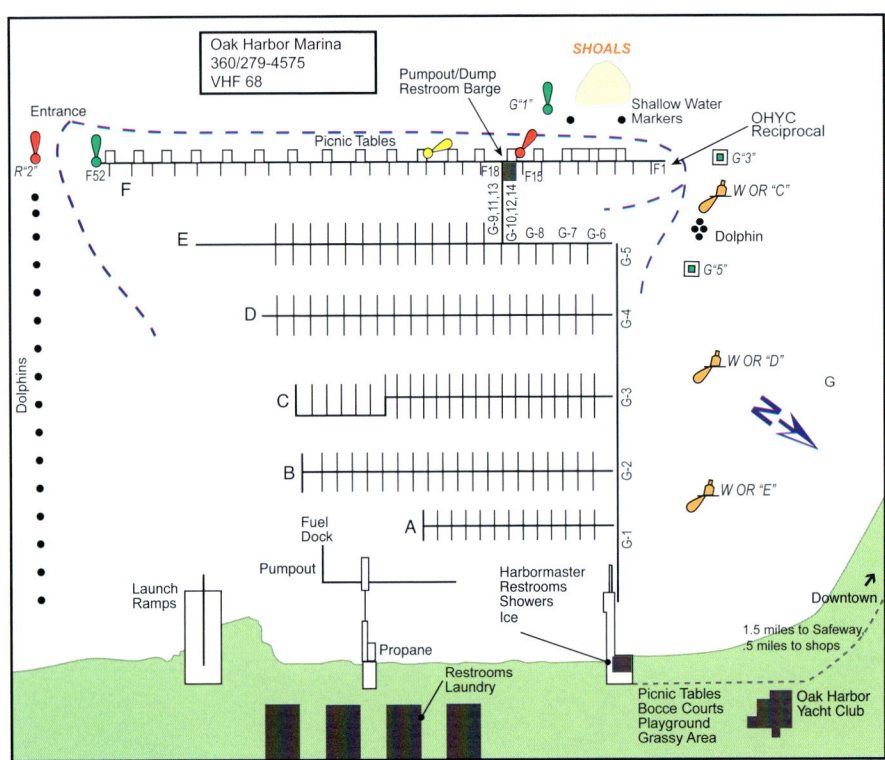

Oak Harbor Marina

Navy personnel memorial at Oak Harbor

laundry, pumpout, porta-potty dump, and free Wi-Fi.

One set of restrooms and showers is on the lower level of the administration building at the head of the docks. Additional restrooms, showers, and laundry are in buildings a short distance away. A floating restroom facility is on the guest moorage F-dock.

In the adjacent park, there are Bocce ball and Petanque courts. Free loaner bicycles at the marina.

Military and retired military (with DoD I.D.) can walk onto the Navy base area and use the Navy Exchange for shopping and provisioning. The Exchange is in one of the large buildings that formerly was a hangar. A seasonal convenience store is open in the summer.

A 100-foot-wide concrete launch ramp, built in 1942 to launch PBY Catalina patrol seaplanes, is at the south end of the marina. Extended parking for trailers and tow vehicles. Mariners Haven has repairs and a chandlery.

Oak Harbor Marina is protected by a floating concrete breakwater; guest moorage is in slips on the inside of this breakwater labeled F-dock, and along the float leading to shore, labeled G-dock. A dredged channel, 100 feet wide with a least depth of 12 feet at zero tide, leads along the west face of the breakwater and around the end, to side-tie moorage on G-dock. Water outside the channel is shoal. The safest approach to G-dock, north side moorage, is to head directly for the entrance light at the south end of the breakwater; then turn to port and proceed along the outside (west side) of the breakwater to the north moorage.

Crescent Harbor. Just east of Oak Harbor. The Navy facility along the western shore near the head of the bay has large old hangars that once housed PBY Catalina flying boat patrol aircraft. Crescent Harbor is exposed to southerly winds, but in northerlies or westerlies it's a good anchorage.

Rocky Point. Rocky Point is the area where the flood current coming in from Deception Pass to the north meets the flood current coming in from Saratoga Passage to the south.

Skagit Bay. Skagit Bay extends from Polnell Point and Rocky Point to Deception Pass. The bay becomes increasingly shoal toward the east due to Skagit River outflow. The navigable channel parallels the Whidbey Island shore, and is well marked by buoys. Use caution in this channel; buoys can be dragged out of position by tugs with tows.

The village of Utsalady, with a launch ramp, is on the Camano Island side of the channel. Anchorage there is not protected from northerly winds and waves, but correspondents James & Jennifer Hamilton report anchoring through a southeast gale without difficulty.

Reference Only – Not for Navigation

NORTH PUGET SOUND

Distances (nm)
(Approximate, for planning)

Edmonds to Anacortes—51
Rocky Pt. to Deception Pass—13
La Conner to Anacortes—10
Anacortes to Bellingham—16

○ Fuel Available
○ No Fuel

Skagit Bay to Bellingham Bay

2023 WAGGONER CRUISING GUIDE

NORTH PUGET SOUND

See Area Map Page 159 - Maps Not for Navigation

⑮ **Deception Pass Marine Park, Skagit Island, Hope Island.** Skagit Island and Hope Island are part of Deception Pass Marine State Park. Hope Island has 4 mooring buoys on the north side and good anchorage, particularly along the south shore. Check the depths before using the buoys. No power, water, restrooms or showers. Trails lead around and through the forested island. Self-register and pay mooring buoy fees on shore, or by phone as posted on the buoy.

Skagit Island, just to the north, has 2 mooring buoys along its north side. Self-register and pay mooring buoy fees on shore, or by phone as posted on the buoy.

Note: Pets are not permitted on shore at Hope Island, including the beaches.

Running with a flood current under Deception Pass Bridge on the way to Cornet Bay

Similk Bay. Similk Bay is shoal but navigable in shallow draft boats. Anchorage is possible almost anywhere.

⑮ **Deception Pass Marine Park, Kiket Island / Kukutali Preserve.** Located just east of Skagit Island. Kiket Island is part of the Deception Pass State Park and jointly managed with the Swinomish Tribal Community reservation. The Island is open to the public for day-use only from dawn to dusk. Although technically an island, Kiket is connected to Fidalgo Island by a thin tombolo. Kiket Island can only be accessed by non-motorized boats. Access to Flagstaff Point on the west end of Kiket Island is restricted. Trails, a viewing platform, and pit toilets can be found on Kiket Island.

Strawberry Island. This small, undeveloped island is part of the Deception Pass Marine State Park and is seldom visited. Strawberry Island (east of Deception Pass) should not be confused with the island of the same name located west of Cypress Island.

⑯ **Cornet Bay.** Cornet Bay, tucked in behind Ben Ure Island, indents the north shore of Whidbey Island just east of Deception Pass. A dredged channel marked by pilings leads to Deception Pass Marina and a state park, both of which offer visitor moorage, and serve as a place to hole up while waiting for the tidal change. The passage west of Ben Ure Island should not be attempted except at high tide, and then only by shallow draft boats. The channel to a county dock at the south end of the bay is very shallow and should only be attempted with local knowledge. Vessel Assist towing and emergency rescue office nearby.

⑯ **Deception Pass Marina.** 200 West Cornet Bay Road, Oak Harbor, WA 98277; (360) 675-5411. Open all year. Mostly permanent moorage, with space for visiting boats as available; contact by phone, no VHF. The docks have water and 30 amp power. Limited room for larger boats up to 65 feet. Ethanol-free gasoline, diesel, and propane at the fuel dock. The store carries convenience groceries, bait, tackle, charts, books, beer and wine. Restrooms, no showers (showers are available at the state park next door). Call ahead for availability of guest moorage. Nearby laundry and haulout.

⑯ **Deception Pass Marine State Park, Cornet Bay.** Open all year for day use and overnight moorage; first-come, first-served. Self-registration payment box on shore. New pier and floats were completed in 2022. The park has ample side-tie guest moorage on strings of 30-foot floats, 26 floats in all, accessed by a substantial new pier. Restrooms, showers, and pumpout; no power. A 5-lane launch ramp has boarding floats.

Hiking trails and picnic areas nearby. Convenience groceries, laundromat, and services are at Deception Pass Marina. On Ben Ure Island, a single cabin is available for rent. Reservations online or call (888) 226-7688.

LOCAL KNOWLEDGE

STRONG CURRENTS: Currents run to 8 knots in Deception Pass with strong eddies and overfalls. Dangerous waves can form when a big ebb current meets strong westerly winds. It is best to time an approach to enter the pass at or near slack water.

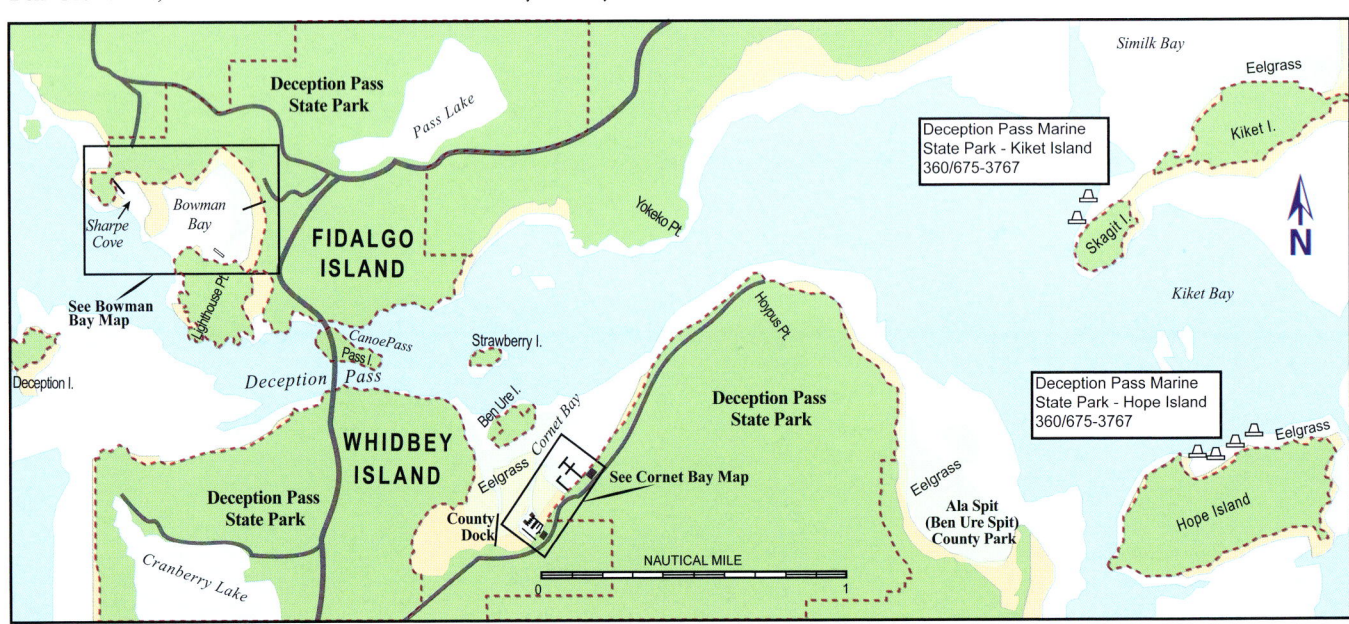

Deception Pass State Park

Deception Pass. Deception Pass narrows to 200 yards at Pass Island, one of the anchors for the spectacular 144-foot-high bridge that connects Whidbey Island and Fidalgo Island.

Tidal current predictions are shown under Deception Pass in the tide and current books. An even narrower pass, Canoe Pass, lies north of Pass Island. Kayaks use Canoe Pass, but lacking local knowledge we wouldn't run our boat through it.

From the west, the preferred route to Deception Pass is just to the south of Lighthouse Point and north of Deception Island.

North of Lighthouse Point, **Bowman Bay**, also known as Reservation Bay, is part of Deception Pass State Park.

⑰ **Deception Pass Marine State Park, Bowman Bay** (Reservation Bay). Open all year for day use and overnight camping and mooring. Restrooms with showers, no power. Bowman Bay has a gravel 1-lane launch ramp. Standard campsites are on the north shore. The park has picnic sites and outdoor kitchens. An underwater park for diving is near the mouth of Bowman Bay, near Rosario Head. When entering take care to avoid Coffin Rocks and Gull Rocks, which cover at high tide. Safe entry can be made by staying fairly close to the Reservation Head side of the entrance.

A mooring float, approximately 100 feet long and not connected to shore, is located behind Reservation Head. The park pier on the east side of the bay with a 40-foot float for dinghies, is closed indefinitely until repairs can be made. The small buoys next to the pier are used as a race course for remote-controlled miniature sailboats.

Anchorage is possible in the bay north of Rosario Head, but it is exposed to wave action from Rosario Strait.

⑰ **Deception Pass Marine State Park, Sharpe Cove.** Open all year for day use and overnight camping and mooring. The park has 160 feet of dock space, no power. Restrooms, showers, portapotty dump, picnic sites, kitchen. Campsites are east of Sharpe Cove. The onshore facility is the Walla Walla University Rosario Beach Marine Laboratory.

Shelter Bay Marina. 1000 Shoshone Drive, La Conner, WA 98257; (360) 466-3805; www.shelterbay.net; kemerson@shelterbay.net. Shelter Bay Marina is on the west side of Swinomish Channel just south of La Conner. Primarily permanent moorage, but some guest moorage space is available. Water, 30 & 50 amp power, pumpout, restrooms, showers, no laundry.

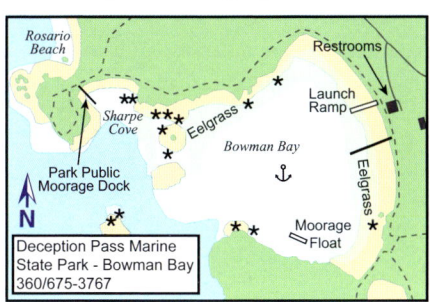

⑱ **La Conner.** The Port of Skagit's La Conner Marina, with two large moorage basins, is a short distance north of downtown La Conner. Both moorage basins have guest moorage and full facilities for visitors. Fuel is available adjacent to the marina at La Conner Landing. Propane is available through La Conner Marina, contact the marina office.

The town of La Conner has three public floats for guest moorage for boats up to 45 feet, with stays of 24 hours, located along the quarter-mile long waterfront boardwalk.

Current in Swinomish Channel can be strong and difficult to predict. Allow for current before landing anywhere along the channel.

The town of La Conner is thoroughly charming. It has excellent restaurants, galleries, museums, wine tasting rooms, and shops. During the summer, hordes of visitors arrive by car and tour bus. Even when crowded, the town is enjoyable. Free outdoor concert, parade, food vendors and fireworks on the 4th of July. On summer Sundays in Gilkey Square, live music from mid-June to August.

LOCAL KNOWLEDGE

STRONG CURRENTS: Strong current runs past the docks in La Conner on the Swinomish Channel. An arrow on the front of the fuel dock indicates the direction of flow.

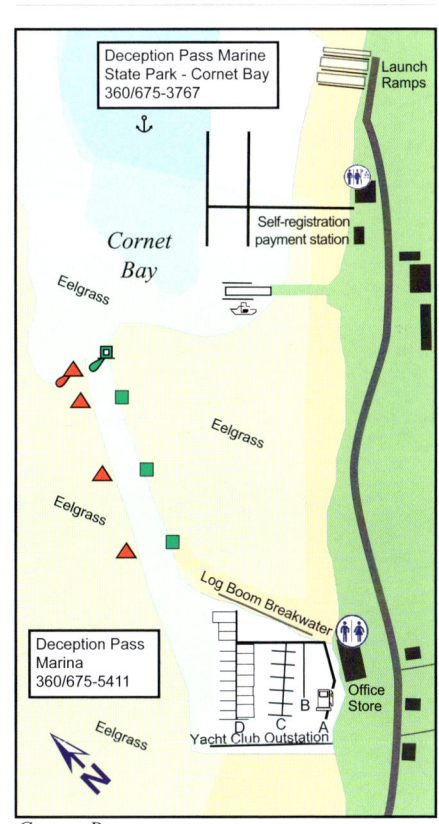

⑱ **La Conner Marina.** P.O. Box 1120, 613 N. 2nd St., La Conner, WA 98257; (360) 466-3118; www.portofskagit.com/la-conner-marina. Monitors VHF 66A. Open all year with 30 amp power on F-dock and 30 & 50 amp power on G-dock; water, free Wi-Fi, restrooms, showers, laundry, pumpout. Online reservations accepted two days in advance via Swift Harbor for G dock; F dock is first-come, first-served. A card-read pay station is available at the top of the ramp at both G dock and F dock. Access for the restrooms and showers is listed on the receipt. Haulout to 82 tons. Complete repairs available through La Conner Maritime.

F dock at the south basin has 1200 lineal feet of side-tie guest moorage. G dock at the north basin has another 1200 feet of side-tie moorage. E dock, near shore in the south basin, has 450 feet of guest moorage for the Swinomish Yacht Club. Unoccupied slips are used when available. If the moorage appears full, call anyway. They try to fit everybody in.

All shopping and services are within walking distance. A monorail launch can handle boats to 14,000 lbs. Trailers must be roller style, no bunks. A paved and lighted storage yard is available for trailers and tow vehicles.

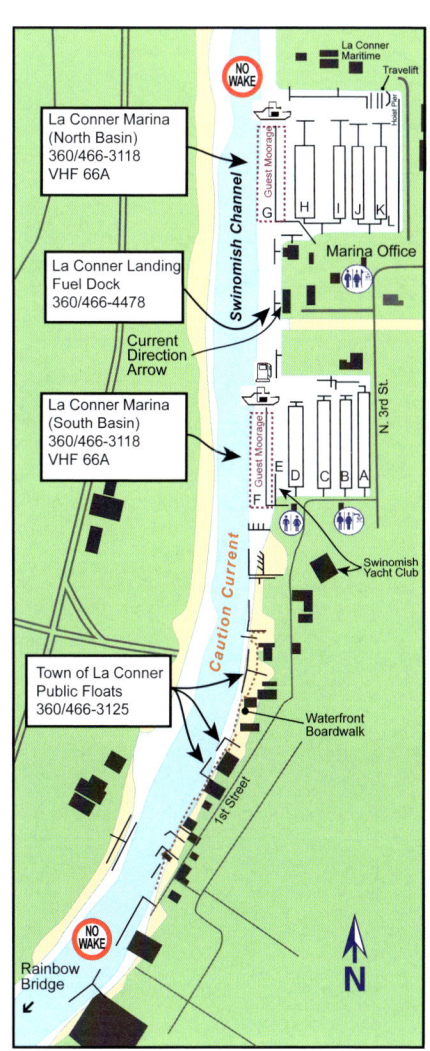

Bowman Bay

Cornet Bay

La Conner

SWINOMISH CHANNEL

The channel is well marked by buoys and a range, but follows a generally northerly direction past the town of La Conner with a fixed bridge that has a minimum vertical clearance of 75 feet, a fuel dock and marinas. To the north, it passes under fixed highway bridges and a swinging railroad bridge to enter Padilla Bay. The highway bridges have a vertical clearance of 75 feet. The railroad bridge is very low. Hundred-car-long crude oil trains headed to the local refinery can close the bridge for 20 minutes or more, holding up boat traffic. Overhead power and telephone cables cross at several charted locations, with a minimum vertical clearance of 72 feet. If you are there at the wrong time, consider dropping the anchor (watch for the marked pipeline crossing) until the train has passed.

From Hole in the Wall to the railroad swing bridge to the north, the channel is a no wake zone. Be particularly mindful of your wake when passing through La Conner.

Red, Right, Returning: The buoyage system for Swinomish Channel south of the town of La Conner assumes "return" is from the south. North of La Conner and in Padilla Bay, the dredged channel assumes "return" is from the north. Red navigation aids in Padilla Bay are on the west side.

The southern entrance to Swinomish Channel is just west of Goat Island. Do not turn into the channel until the range markers in Dugualla Bay, to the west, are in line. Between the entrance and Hole-in-the-Wall, current flows across the channel and can sweep a boat off course. Occasionally a deadhead log will imbed itself in the shallow bottom. Shelter Bay, with its private moorage, indents the western shore of Swinomish Channel just north of Hole in the Wall. Rainbow Bridge (actually faded orange) marks the south end of La Conner which lines the eastern shore of the channel for about a mile. Three city public floats, La Conner Marina, and several privately-owned floats serve restaurants and other businesses along the town waterfront. Across from La Conner the Swinomish Indian Reservation occupies most of the west side of the channel. Just after passing under two highway bridges 3.5 miles north of La Conner is the railroad swing bridge. The channel passes on the east side of the bridge's central support.

Swinomish Channel is dredged every four to six years, but it silts up between dredgings. Maintenance dredging of the channel was completed in November 2018. Keep in mind that the silting occurs at the same locations each time, so at low tide the wary boater can avoid them. Here are the troublesome shoaling areas and see the map:

1. West of Goat Island, the entrance to the channel is shoal. Especially on a low tide, swing wide and don't cut any of the entry buoys close. The channel leading past Goat Island is quite shoal. On very low tides deep draft vessels should wait for more water.
2. At Shelter Bay, a shoal extends from the west side of the channel, approximately from the southernmost house north to the entrance channel to Shelter Bay development. Favor the center of the channel.
3. Midway along the La Conner waterfront, a shoal extends from the west side of the channel, approximately between the middle of the restaurants on the La Conner side and a tall pole with antennas on the west side. Favor the east side of the channel.
4. Just south of the highway bridges, at the location marked "Pipeline Area," on the shore, sand accumulates on top of the pipeline.
5. Opposite Buoy 29, north of the railroad swing bridge. A troublesome shoal stretches across the entire channel.

Unless you plan to tie up at La Conner, the tidal water level is probably more important than the strength of the current flow. Best to transit on a rising tide.

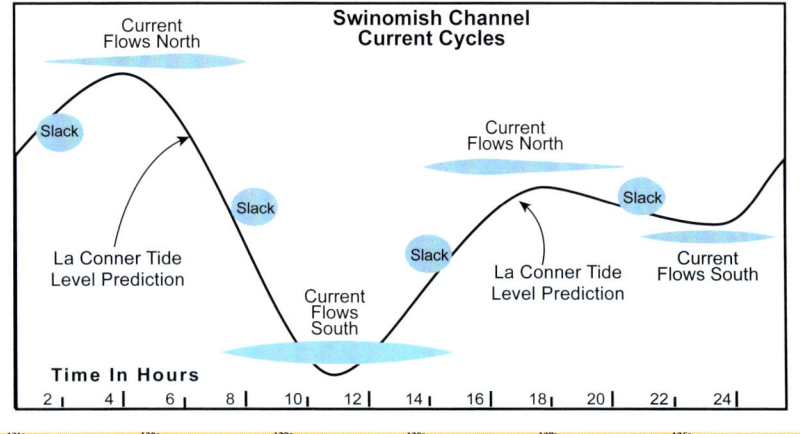

Swinomish Channel current predictions and slack water timing are dependent upon tidal high and low water level differences and river outflow. Therefore, time of slack water and current flow can only be estimated, based upon La Conner Tide level reference station.

- Slack water occurs at La Conner approximately half-way between high and low water.
- Current flows north from 2.5 to 4.0 hours before and after high tide.
- Current flows south from 2.5 to 4.0 hours before and after low tide.

At periods of minor tide change, current flow changes will be closer to 2.5 hours after predicted high or low; and during large tides, it will be closer to 4.0 hours. See Ports & Passes for more on Swinomish Channel currents.

La Conner Marina

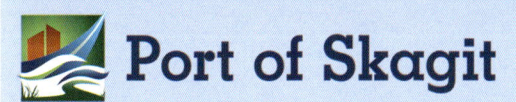

Port of Skagit

Walking distance to great dining and shopping.
Enjoy the guest docks at our friendly marina along the Swinomish Channel.

360-466-3118 | VHF 66A | www.portofskagit.com

Your Full-Service Repair and Refit Yard
In Destination La Conner

- Haul outs to 110 tons
- Providing solutions for safe and reliable boating for over 30 years

See the Hide-A-Davit in action on our website!!

Hull Paint & Repair

service@laconnermaritime.com

- Long & Short Term Storage
- Outboard & Diesel Repower Center
- Paint & Fiberglass Services
- Bow & Stern Thrusters
- Engine & Systems Service
- Electrical Systems

SEAKEEPER · ABYC · ALEXSEAL · VOLVO PENTA · SUZUKI MARINE · NORTHERN LIGHTS · NAIAD DYNAMICS

La Conner Maritime Service

Volvo Penta IPS Specialists

920 W. Pearle Jensen Way ▪ La Conner, WA 98257 (360) 466-3629 ▪ www.laconnermaritime.com

NORTH PUGET SOUND

See Area Map Page 159 - Maps Not for Navigation

⑱ **La Conner Landing Fuel Dock.** P.O. Box 1020, La Conner, WA 98257; (360) 466-4478. Open all year. Summer hours from 8:00 a.m. to 6:00 p.m. daily. Hours and days vary during the fall and winter, call ahead. Fuel dock with ethanol-free gasoline and diesel, pumpout. The store has tackle, bait, ice, marine items, and snacks.

Caution: Strong current flows past the dock. Look for the directional sign on the fuel shed labeled 'CURRENT' with an arrow indicating which way the current is running.

⑱ **Town of La Conner Public Floats.** (360) 466-3125. The town of La Conner has three floats with first-come, first-serve moorage for vessels 45 feet and under for stays up to 24 hours. The three separate floats are along the waterfront boardwalk that parallels the Swinomish Channel. The street-end floats are located at Benton, Calhoun and Washington Streets. Larger vessels may be accommodated at Benton float with prior approval by calling ahead. Self-registration and cash payment at payment drop boxes located at each of the floats. Call for stays longer than 24 hours. No water, no power; public restrooms are available in town and near the La Conner Marina.

Caution: Strong current flows past the floats, check the current before approaching.

Padilla Bay. The well-marked channel through Padilla Bay is about 3 miles long between drying flats. Don't take any shortcuts until north of Beacon 2, which marks the edge of Guemes Channel. Deeper draft boats, such as sailboats, should hold to a mid-channel course, especially at low tide. To the west of the channel are long docks serving ocean-going tankers calling at the two major oil refineries in Anacortes. Often tankers, barges, or tug boats lie at anchor in the bay awaiting room at the docks. Watch for crab pots in the bay and channel.

Saddlebag Island Marine State Park. Open all year for day use and overnight anchoring and camping. Boat access only. Anchorage is good off the north or south shore. Water depths are inconveniently deep on the west side, and inconveniently shallow on the east. Vault toilets, primitive campsites. Cascadia Marine Trail campsite. One-mile hiking trail. "Hot spot" for crabbing.

Take a stroll along La Conner's Waterfront Boardwalk to visit the many shops and eateries.

Huckleberry Island. North end of Padilla Bay, owned by the Samish Indian Nation. Open all year, day use only. No services. Undeveloped 10-acre island with anchoring or beaching only. No fires or camping. Pack out all garbage. Attractive to kayakers and scuba divers. Gravel beach on the southwest side of the island.

LOCAL KNOWLEDGE

SHALLOW: Fidalgo Bay is shallow; don't stray from the dredged, marked channels or you could find yourself aground. The anchorage area is open to strong southeast winds, causing anchors to drag.

INVASIVE EUROPEAN GREEN CRAB

European Green Crab is an invasive species that destroys and degrades eelgrass habitats by foraging and burrowing into the seabed, much more so than native crabs of the Pacific Northwest. Eelgrass is vitally important for fish that attach their eggs to eelgrass during spawning, which in turn provides food for other marine life. Green crabs feed on clams, oysters, mussels, and small crustaceans affecting the larger marine eco system and they also threaten aquaculture operations.

The transported invasive crab or larva may find its new environment favorable in which to live and even flourish; other times the environment may be unfavorable. The European Green Crab has been found in a few places in Washington State like Grays Harbor and Padilla Bay near Anacortes. The first Green Crab found in Washington inland waters was discovered in Westcott Bay on San Juan Island in 2016. This invasive crab seems more prevalent around the waters of Greater Vancouver, British Columbia and in Barkley Sound on West Vancouver Island.

How The Green Crab Got Here. The larva of Green Crabs is found in ballast water of commercial vessels. Commercial marine vessels take on and discharge millions of tons of water for ballast each day, which often contain aquatic intruders. Additionally, Green Crabs are sometimes found in seaweeds used as packing around shipments of lobsters and oysters. Recreational boaters can transport species in bait buckets, boat wells, or fouled hulls without realizing it. Inspecting and cleaning boat hulls can reduce the chances of unwanted stowaways. Government agencies have put into place a number of preventive measures, including required permits for movement of shellfish farms and equipment, both commercial and recreational.

How to Identify the Green Crab. While this invasive crab is predominantly green, it can morph into different colors – brownish, reddish, purplish, and yellowish. Its shell is serrated and pentagon-shaped, with five sharp spines or points on the side of each eye. The back legs are hairy and pointed, while the front claws are larger and each a different size.

Where to Report Sightings. As boaters, we can help by keeping our eye out for the European Green Crab. If you discover this invasive species, take a photo, record the location, leave it where you found it, and email the information to:
AISPACIFIC@dfo-mpo.gc.ca in Canada
crabteam@uw.edu in Washington State

It is illegal to possess a Green Crab.

Once the species has been confirmed at a site, aggressive trapping and removal can take place and will help reduce its numbers.

[Lorena Landon]

⑲ **Anacortes.** www.anacortes.org. Anacortes is a major boating center, with fishing and pleasure craft facilities in Fidalgo Bay, Guemes Channel, and Flounder Bay. The city's marine businesses can provide for a boater's every need, including food, fuel, and repairs. With seven haulout yards, Anacortes has the marine trades for any repair. For pumpout service, call Sanitation Offloading Solutions (SOS) (877) 767-6862.

Four marinas are located on the Fidalgo Bay side of town. Three additional marinas are located on the west end of Fidalgo Island. From north to south on Fidalgo Bay, the first is Cap Sante Marina, owned by the Port of Anacortes, with guest moorage, fuel, water, electricity, pumpout and haulout facilities.

The second, behind a prominent breakwater, is Anacortes Marina, where Northwest Marine Center has fuel, pumpout, 55 ton Travelift haulout, and repairs. Open seven days a week from 8:00 a.m. to 4:30 p.m. and 8:00 a.m. to 8:00 p.m. from Memorial Day weekend to Labor Day weekend. Permanent moorage only. Anacortes Yacht Charters and many bareboat charter boats are based in this marina. Follow the dredged channel to the marina entrance on the south side.

Next is the 360-foot-long dock and haulout ramp for Pacific Marine Center (360) 299-8820. Large vessels can be hauled out with their 200-ton Travelift and blocked in their extensive yard complex for maintenance and repairs. They also have multiple KMI Sea-lift machines for haulout on their ramp for vessels up to 65 feet. Limited moorage is available on their docks, typically reserved for repair or dry storage customers.

The fourth is Fidalgo Marina, where Cap Sante Marine has a 50 ton Travelift and the haulout ramp for North Harbor Diesel. The marina is protected by a piling breakwater, and is entered through the dredged channel marked by pilings extending from deeper water near Cap Sante.

Moving east to west along Guemes Channel, Dakota Creek Industries is a large shipyard with Syncrolift ship lift and drydock for vessels to 400 feet.

Next to the Guemes Ferry is Anchor Cove, a private marina with no transient moorage.

Next is Lovric's Sea-Craft with two marine ways for haulout, and a small dry dock.

Skyline Marina is in Flounder Bay on the southwest side of Fidalgo Island, 3 miles from downtown Anacortes. It has some guest moorage and a DIY yard with 55 ton Travelift haulout and a stationary lift accommodating 16,000 pounds.

U.S. Customs: Anacortes is a U.S. Customs port of entry with an office in the Cap Sante Marina harbormaster's building, Suite F. There is no designated customs dock, call Cap Sante marina office for a slip assignment, then call the Anacortes Customs Office at (360) 293-2331 for instructions. During the summer months between 1:00 p.m. and 3:00 p.m., agents are apt to be 4 miles away at the Washington State Ferry terminal clearing arrivals on the international ferry from Sidney, B.C. You may need to wait aboard your vessel until the agents return.

Events: Wine Festival, early April; Anacortes Waterfront Festival, early June at Cap Sante Marina; Shipwreck Day, July; Anacortes Arts Festival, early August; Summer Concert Series in July and August at Seafarers' Memorial Park. Oyster Run, late September; Bier on the Pier, early October. Check schedule at www.anacortes.org; info@anacortes.org; (360) 293-7911.

THINGS TO DO

- **Farmers Market.** Saturdays 9:00 a.m. to 2:00 p.m. next to the Depot Arts & Community Center; seasonal.
- **W. T. Preston**, an old snag boat, is part of the Anacortes History Museum. Located across from the north end of Cap Sante Marina.
- **Live music**. On Fridays and some Saturdays in July and August, the Port of Anacortes hosts free concerts at Seafarers' Memorial Park.
- **Skagit Cycle**. Rent a bike and ride the Tommy Thompson Trail, or just around town. Catch the Tommy Thompson Trail from R Avenue at Cap Sante Marina.
- **Rotary View Point Trail**. Walk to the top and view Mt. Baker and the marina from this scenic vantage point. Trail begins at the northeast end of Cap Sante Marina. Sunsets from here are particularly beautiful.
- **Stadium Trail**. From of the top of Rotary View Point Trail, continue onto Stadium Trail along the eastern ridge. Don't miss the outdoor stadium left over from the 1930's.
- **Seabear Smokehouse.** Learn the difference in taste between smoked pink, king and sockeye salmon at their smokehouse and factory store at 30th Street and T Ave.

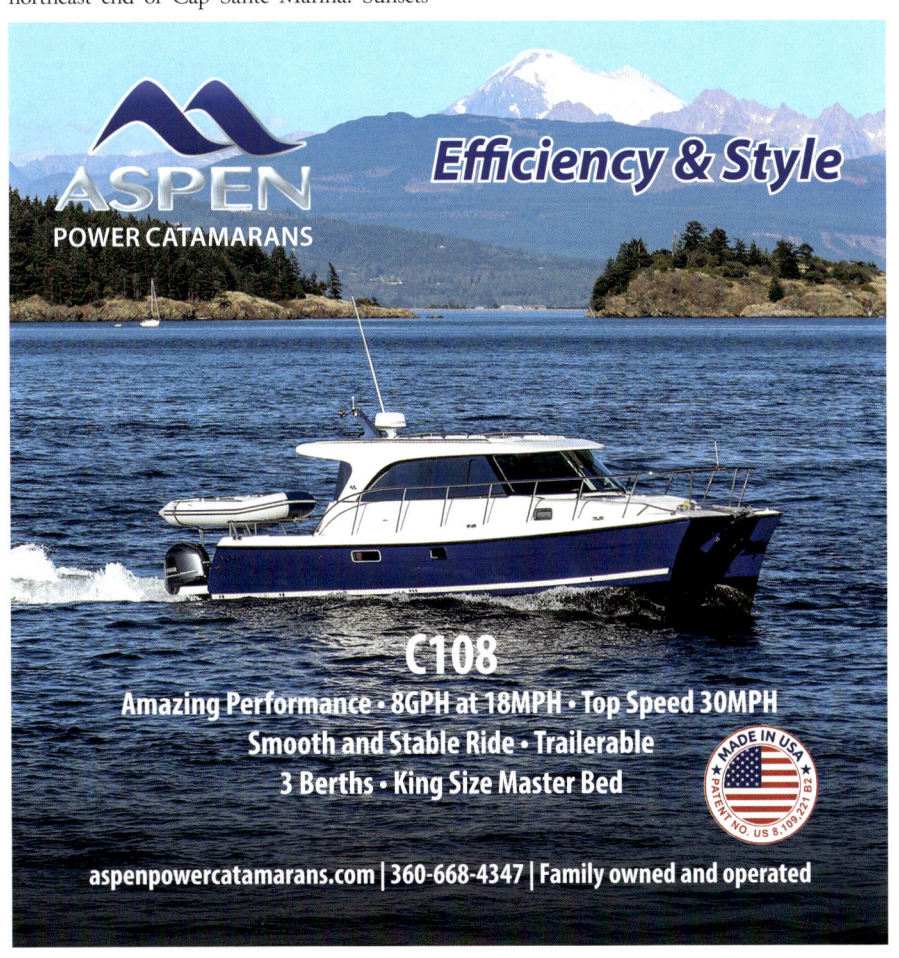

Cap Sante Marina

PORT OF ANACORTES — Est. 1926

Leading amenities, unrivaled views, and outstanding customer service make Cap Sante Marina in Anacortes your destination for year-round adventures in the Great Northwest. Centrally located between Victoria, B.C., and Seattle, Washington, Cap Sante offers more than 100 guest slips and accommodates vessels up to 130'. And our beautiful marina is within walking distance of restaurants, boutique shops, and local festivities and amenities in Anacortes' delightful downtown.

A Dock — *Boat lift* — *Captain Charlie* — *West Basin Esplanade* — *Summer concert Series*

Cap Sante Marina | Anacortes, Washington 98221 | 360-293-0694
VHF 66 US (66a) | portofanacortes.com | marina@portofanacortes.com

NORTH PUGET SOUND

⑲ **Cap Sante Marina/Port of Anacortes.** 100 Commercial Ave., 1019 Q Ave., Anacortes, WA 98221; (360) 293-0694; (360) 661-5000; marina@portofanacortes.com; www.portofanacortes.com. Monitors VHF 66A. Open all year with moorage to 120 feet. Call or radio ahead for slip assignment. There is a $5 fee for reservations. No fee for same-day reservations. The 18×120-foot fuel dock, with ethanol-free gasoline, and diesel is to port inside the breakwater. A high-volume fuel delivery hose is available. Propane near the boat launch lift. The marina has 20 & 30 amp power with some 50 & 100 amp power available, ELCI protected shore power on docks A & B. 5 pumpout carts (free), 2 portapotty dumps, restrooms, showers, and laundry. Guest boaters are given an access code to the laundry. A pumpout float is located just inside the harbor entrance. Used oil dump near the office. Free Wi-Fi throughout the marina. Loaner wheelchair available.

The Rotary Viewpoint Trail from Cap Sante in Anacortes, gets you to this great view of Padilla Bay.

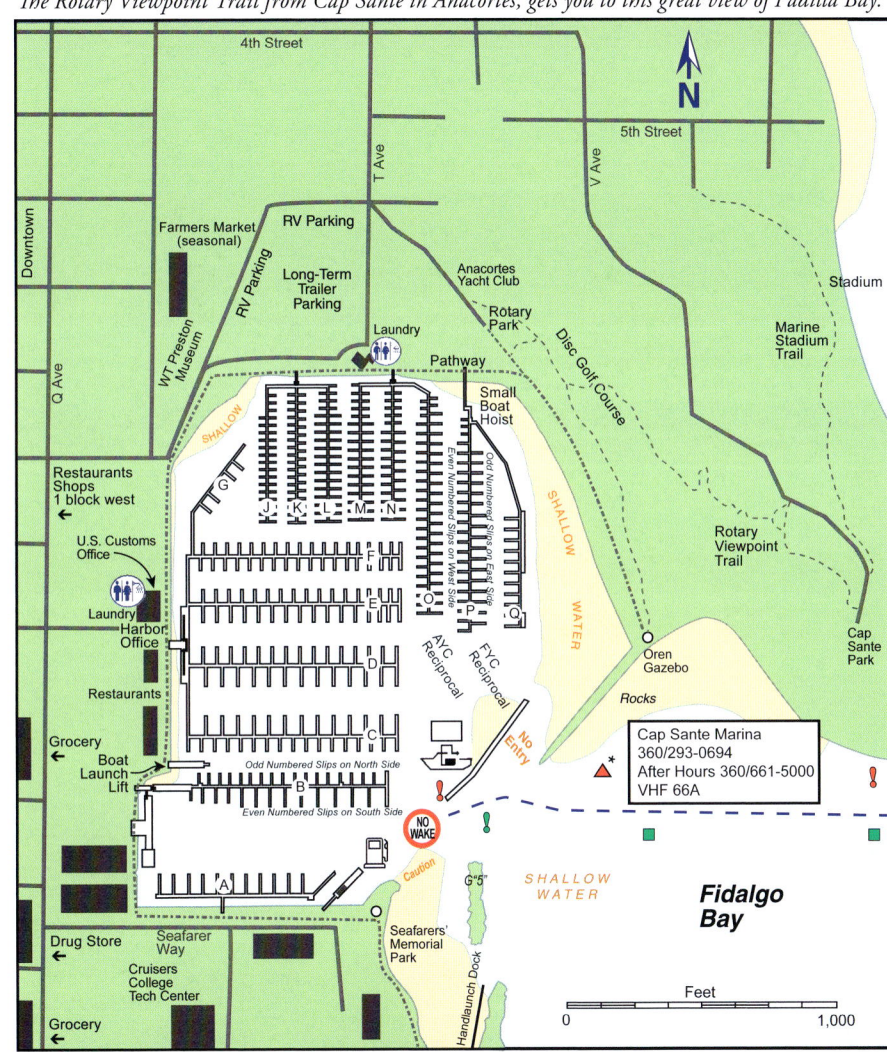

THE CABANA
1207 Q Avenue
(360) 588-0333

ANTHONY'S CAP SANTE MARINA
1207 Q Avenue
(360) 588-0333

Complimentary bicycles with baskets are available for marina guests. A monorail launch can handle boats to 25,000 pounds. A small hoist and dry storage yard for hand launching small boats is in the North Basin on P-Q dock. Call (360) 293-0694. Most of the guest area marina floats have been replaced by wide, stable concrete floats, with wide slips and wheelchair accessible ramps to shore. The floats are first-class in every way.

Follow the dredged and marked channel, and enter between the arms of a piling breakwater due east of Cap Sante. The area to port just inside the breakwater, towards Seafarers' Memorial Park, is shoal and should not be attempted. The harbormaster's office and U.S. Customs office are just north of C & D floats.

This is a clean and popular stop, located in the heart of downtown Anacortes. Complete facilities, including many good restaurants, large Safeway and Marketplace grocery stores, well-stocked Ace Hardware and Sebo's hardware stores, and two marine stores (West Marine, Marine Supply & Hardware) are within walking distance. An esplanade leads from the marina to the Seafarers' Memorial Park and building, and around the marina to Rotary Park. A dock for dinghies is behind a small breakwater at Seafarers' Memorial Park. The lawn and beach areas are used as a kayak launch.

Cap Sante Marina is considered the homeport of the San Juan Islands and is often used as a supply and provisioning point for cruises into the islands and further north.

Anacortes & Cap Sante Marina

NORTHWEST RIGGING
Rig Locally - Sail Globally

Standing Rigging • Lifelines • Cable Railings • Swaging
Running Rigging • Custom Rope Work • Splicing
Furler Sales & Installation • Hardware

360.293.1154 • www.nwrigging.com • info@nwrigging.com • 620 30th Street, Anacortes

2023 waggoner CRUISING GUIDE

NORTH HARBOR DIESEL
& Yacht Service Inc.

Service • Sales • Storage

AWARD WINNING YACHT SERVICE

- Complete diesel & gas Engine Services & Repowers
- Complete Interior Remodel & Design
- Custom Hull Modifications
- Fully Stocked Marine Store
- 22,000 Sq. Ft. Shop

Call 360-299-1920 patrick@northharbordiesel.com

SHORESIDE MARINA

- 5 Acres of dry outdoor storage
- Low monthly storage fees
- 4 Sea-Lifts - up to 65 Ft. & 45 Tons

For Shoreside Marina Information,
Call 360-299-1909 ed@northharbordiesel.com

INSIDE PASSAGE YACHT SALES

Now located at North Harbor Diesel
We match perfect boats to individual buyers. It is our passion! New boats from Lindell Yachts, Parker, and Sargo. Large inventory of used boats from center consoles to cruisers and pilot houses. It's not about the boat...it's about the lifestyle.

360.468.4997 • InsidePassageYachtSales.com

360-293-5551
Anacortes, WA
NorthHarborDiesel.com
service@northharbordiesel.com

MERCURY • YAMAHA • Sea Hawk PREMIUM YACHT FINISHES
Cummins Marine • VOLVO PENTA • NORTHERN LIGHTS • Hino • NORTHWEST MARINE TRADE ASSOCIATION • MEMBER ABYC Setting Standards for Safer Boating

NORTH PUGET SOUND

Cap Sante Marina in Anacortes is a very popular destination along the way to a larger and more distant cruise.

Anacortes is a popular destination in its own right, with hiking trails, cafes, and special events.

⑲ **Anacortes Marina**. 2415 T Avenue, Anacortes, WA 98221; (360) 293-4543. Primarily private moorage. Northwest Marine Center, with fuel dock, haulout, and repairs, is located there. Enter through the dredged channel to the south opening in the pilings. Exit the marina through the north opening in the breakwater. The fuel dock, pumpout and a 55 ton Travelift are straight ahead when you enter the marina.

⑲ **Seattle Yachts Service - South Yard** 2915 W Ave, Anacortes, WA 98221; (360) 293-3145; service@seattleyachts.com; www.seattleyachts.com. Open all year. Complete repair facilities with yard and haulout.

⑲ **Seattle Yachts Service - North Yard** 2417 T Avenue, Anacortes, WA 98221; (360) 293-8200; service@seattleyachts.com; www.seattleyachts.com. Open all year. Fuel dock with ethanol-free gasoline, diesel, propane, pumpout, portapotty dump, lubricants, engine oil. Complete repair facilities with yard and haulout to 55 tons.

⑲ **Fidalgo Marina.** 3101 V Place, Anacortes, WA 98221; (360) 299-0873. No guest overnight moorage, but a number of marine businesses are located there. Enter through the opening at the end of the dredged channel on the north side. First, to starboard, is the dock with a 50-ton Travelift for Cap Sante Marine, a full-service boatyard for repairs and refits (360) 293-3145.

Next are the staging docks with temporary moorage for the marine repair businesses. The city dock has marked temporary hourly moorage but no overnight. The ramp at the end of the small basin is for the 45-ton capacity KMI Sea-Lifts for North Harbor Diesel's repair yard and dry storage yards, and Banana Belt Boats brokerage storage yard.

Guemes Channel. On an ebb tide, waters in Guemes Channel can be very rough, especially west of the mouth of Bellingham Channel.

Watch for the Guemes ferry, a small car and passenger ferry that makes frequent crossings between Anacortes and Guemes Island.

Next to the ferry dock is Anchor Cove Marina, a private condo marina with covered and open slips.

Farther west is Lovric's Sea-Craft (360) 840-3271, a commercial shipyard and moorage with large marine ways for haulout.

Ship Harbor was once the primary harbor for Anacortes and offers some protection and reasonable anchorage. Watch for ferry traffic from the busy Washington State Ferries terminal in Ship Harbor. *Cross behind the ferries, not in front.*

Guemes Island. Guemes Island has no facilities specifically for boaters, although anchorage can be found along the north shore. Anchorage also can be found on the eastern shore in a tiny notch called Boat Harbor. A ferry connects Guemes Island to Anacortes.

Washington Park. www.cityofanacortes.org. West shore of Fidalgo Island on Guemes Channel. Open all year for day use and overnight camping. Restrooms, portapotty dump, showers. Anchoring or beaching only. Two-lane launch ramp, parking area, picnic tables, picnic shelters, fireplaces, campsites. Playground equipment. The loop road is 2.2 miles in length and is good for walking or jogging. The park has forested areas and viewpoints along the beaches overlooking Rosario Strait to Burrows Bay.

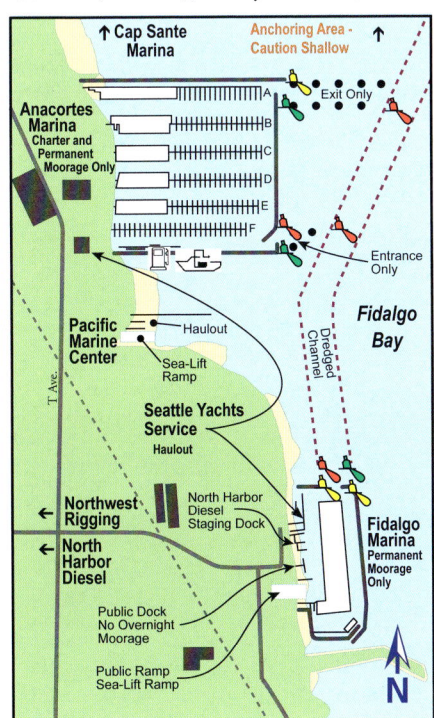

Anacortes South

Ship Harbor on Guemes Channel is near the Washington State Ferry terminal in Anacortes.

NORTH PUGET SOUND

Flounder Bay. Flounder Bay has been dredged to provide moorage for the Skyline real estate development. Skyline Marina and several charter companies are inside the spit. Also a small chandlery, Travelift, and other facilities, including a large dry storage building. Entry is from Burrows Bay along a dredged channel marked by lighted pilings.

⑳ **Skyline Marina.** 2011 Skyline Way, Anacortes, WA 98221; (360) 293-5134; info@skylinemarinecenter.com; www.skylinemarinecenter.com. Open all year, guest moorage, 30 amp power (ELCI-protected power on some docks), laundry, showers. Reservations can be made online. Fuel dock with ethanol-free gasoline, diesel and pumpout. A seaplane float is at the fuel dock. Propane at the marina office.

Complete boat repairs and services are available. There is a 16,000 pound stationary lift and a 55 ton Travelift. The yard has space for DIY repairs. Other marine services nearby. Secure inside and outside storage for boats, vehicles, and trailers.

A convenience store with grocery items is a block away. Water taxi to the San Juan Islands. The marina is 4 miles from downtown Anacortes. Fidalgo Yacht Club reciprocal space is located on the south side of the TDO dock, further in from the fuel dock area.

A building housing a kayak tour operator, a marine brokerage, bareboat charter and other marine related businesses are located upland. The nearby North Island Boat Company (360-293-2565) accepts used oil.

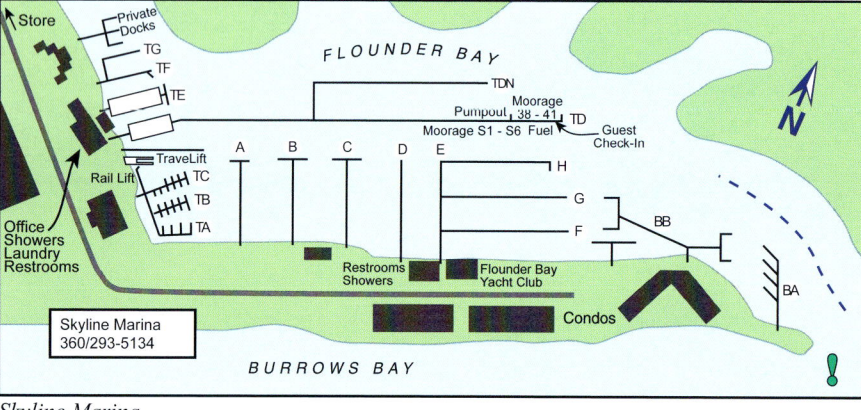

Skyline Marina

Everything a boater needs, all on one place!

* MOORAGE: GUEST & LONGTERM
* STORAGE: INDOOR & OUTDOOR
* LAUNCH & HAUL SERVICES
* FUEL DOCK: DIESEL & GASOLINE
* DO-IT-YOURSELF WORK YARD
* VALET LAUNCH AND STORAGE SERVICE

Skyline Marine Center
2011 SKYLINE WAY, ANACORTES WA 98221
360-293-5134
www.skylinemarinecenter.com

CALL FOR STORAGE & MOORAGE OPPORTUNITES

Burrows Island State Park, Alice Bight. The anchorage has room for two or three boats. A beach area provides good dinghy/kayak landing access to the upland two campsites, with a pit-toilet. Most of the island is part of the Burrows Island State Marine Park, an undeveloped 330-acre park. The campsites are part of the Washington Water Trails system. There are no trails on the island except for the short piece up to the campsites. Most of the shoreline is steep cliffs. The Burrows Island Lighthouse is on the west tip of the island. The bight is open to the southeast through the northeast. Anchoring is exposed to weather from the south and more so from the southeast. Holding is good on a mud bottom; anchorage is more steep-to than charts indicate.

Allan Island. Allan Island is privately owned; no public access.

Rosario Strait. One of the main north-south routes between Strait of Juan de Fuca and Strait of Georgia, and Bellingham Bay, used extensively by commercial ships, barges, and recreational vessels. Due to strong ebb currents and exposure to south winds, the strait develops choppy seas in gale or storm conditions. When crossing Rosario Strait, pleasure boats should be particularly watchful for commercial traffic.

Due to the narrow geography of the Strait, both north and south bound commercial traffic share one traffic lane. Pleasure craft should cross the traffic lane at right angles and monitor VTS on VHF 05A for advisories.

Cypress Island. Department of Natural Resources; paul.mcfarland@dnr.wa.gov. A park ranger told us he considers Cypress Island to be the "crown jewel" of the San Juan's, we agree. The island is nearly all public land, which is managed by the Washington State Department of Natural Resources. A network of trails leads through the Cypress Island Natural Resource Conservation Area and is one of the largest undeveloped island areas in the San Juan's. Approximately one-half mile of tidelands and marine bedlands that surround Cypress Island, Strawberry Island, and Cone Islands make up the Cypress Island Aquatic Reserve, overseen by DNR to conserve and minimize negative effects on aquatic habitats.

Best access is on the east side of the island at Cypress Head, Eagle Harbor, and Pelican Beach, where anchorage and approximately 25 DNR mooring buoys are located. Except for the Eagle Cliff Trail on the north end of the island. Island trails and moorage buoys are open year-round. DNR mooring buoys are not subject to the state park's boat size limitations and are open to all, no rafting. Beach access is permitted at all these locations. Pit toilets are available on shore, along with campsites and trailheads. No water on the island and no garbage service.

About a half-mile south of Pelican Beach, just past a small headland, two attractive little coves have room for one or two boats to anchor. Cascadia Marine Trail campsites are located at Pelican Beach and Cypress Head. Pets are allowed on leash, no bicycles.

Cypress Island has a fascinating history. Fishing villages once dotted the island, used seasonally by the Samish Tribe. In 1791, Spanish explorer Jose Narvaez arrived and named the island San Vincente. The name was changed to Cypress by Captain George Vancouver in 1792, when he mistook the island's juniper trees for cypress trees.

Pelican Beach. Located on the northeast side of Cypress Island, open all year. This DNR site has 6 mooring buoys, 5 campsites, compost toilets, a picnic shelter, fire pit, gravel beach, and interpretive signs. Numerous species of wildlife and birds can be observed. Public DNR beaches extend from the park around the north end of Cypress Island for 1.5 miles until just south of Foss Cove, where the north tip of the island is private property. The trailhead at Pelican Beach leads to the south and connects to year-round trails and the seasonal Eagle Cliff Trail. The Eagle Cliff Trail is closed from February 1 to July 15 to protect endangered wildlife.

Moorage is unprotected to the north. If anchored or moored to a buoy and the northerly wind comes in, you'll not want to stay. Current runs through the moorage and is subject to wakes from passing traffic.

Eagle Harbor. Located on the east side of Cypress Island towards the north end. Eagle Harbor is shallow, especially at low tide, but has 12 DNR mooring buoys designed for boats up to 50 feet. Use care in approaching all but the outermost of these buoys. The bay's shallow spots are truly shallow. Boaters should use caution and verify depths at lower tide levels. Convenient beach access to the island's trails can be found on the southwest shore of the harbor and the north shore. The trail at the beach landing at the head of the bay is muddy at low tide; bring boots. Trailheads and intersections are usually marked, but it's best to bring a trail map. No fires, no camping. If you have sufficient depth, Eagle Harbor provides good protection. Views of Mount Baker are breathtaking.

Cypress Head. Located on the east side of Cypress Island, open all year with 4 DNR mooring buoys and 9 campsites, picnic sites, compost toilets and trailhead that connects to the island's trails. Many species of birds and wildlife, good fishing. Tiderips at the south end of the island can cause wave action.

Deepwater Bay. Located on the southeast end of Cypress Island. Deepwater Bay is exposed to southerly winds, seas, and boat wakes. Fish Farm pens are no longer in Deepwater Bay. The last pen was removed in 2020. In 2017, strong currents collapsed one of the pens, releasing 300,000 Atlantic salmon.

About a dozen DNR mooring buoys at Cypress Island, Eagle Harbor

Secret Harbor. Located on the southeast end of Cypress Island, adjacent to Deepwater Bay. The head of Secret Harbor dries. DNR pit toilets and a kayak launch area are located at the head of the harbor, where you will find a trailhead to the island's network of trails. The dock located off the point on the southeast corner of the harbor is private.

Secret Harbor has a rich history. It was the home of a residential treatment facility for troubled youth that started in 1947. The isolated program on Cypress Island was successful at modifying the behaviors. The program and facility ran for more than 50 years at its island location; and except for supplies brought in by boat, it was self-sustaining. In 2005, the property was sold to the State of Washington and the program moved to the mainland where it provides best practices in the field of child welfare for boys and girls.

Strawberry Island. Strawberry Island, located west of Cypress Island in Rosario Strait, is an undeveloped public island that is managed by DNR. Strawberry Island is popular with kayakers. Strong currents and submerged rocks can make landing difficult; landings are best suited for kayaks rather than dinghies. An island with the same name located east of Deception Pass is part of Deception Pass State Park.

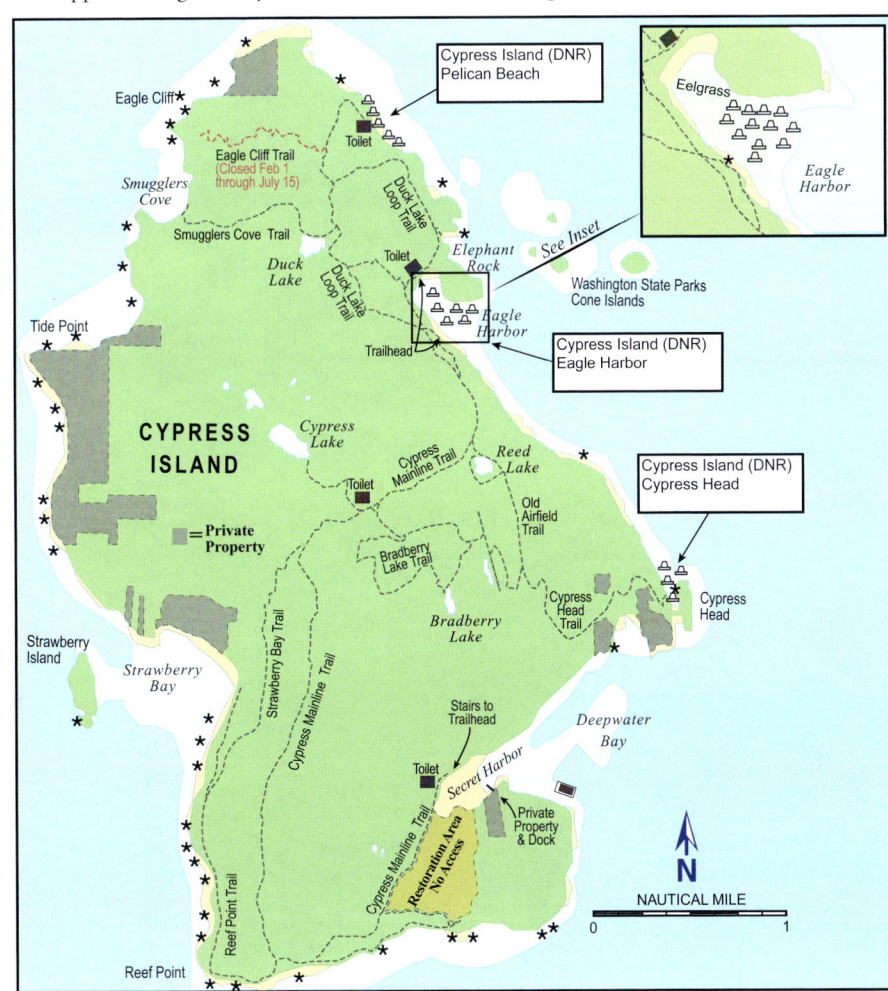

Cypress Island - Department of Natural Resources

NORTH PUGET SOUND

Vendovi Island. San Juan Preservation Trust, www.sjpt.org. Day use only, open April 1 through September 30, 10:00 a.m. to 6:00 p.m. Thursday through Monday. No anchoring. A 70-foot dock (3-hour max stay) behind a rock breakwater is on the north shore. All visitors must sign in and review visitor guidelines at the head of the dock upon arrival. A public restroom is in the building at the top of the hill.

Sinclair and Eliza Islands. A piling breakwater protects a loading and unloading dock on the south shore of Sinclair Island, but there are no facilities specifically for pleasure boaters. Eliza Island is privately owned, with a private dock and float on the north side. Anchorage is possible several places around the island. A maze of rocks and reefs extend nearly one mile north of Sinclair Island.

Larrabee State Park. (360) 676-2093. Seven miles south of Bellingham on Samish Bay. Open all year for day use and overnight camping. The park has restrooms and showers. This was Washington's first official state park, dedicated in 1923. It covers 2000 acres and is heavily used. Facilities include a launch ramp, kitchen shelters, picnic tables, standard, utility, and primitive campsites. Fishing, clamming, crabbing, scuba diving. Trails provide access to two freshwater lakes within the park. A 5.5-mile walking/bicycling trail connects with Bellingham.

Explore the previously private Vendovi Island from the day-use dock at this San Juan Trust Property.

Chuckanut Bay. Chuckanut Bay is a good anchorage with protection from prevailing winds in the north or south arms. Enter close to Governors Point to avoid extensive rocky shoals that partially block the entrance. The land around the bay is privately owned. The Hamiltons reported good holding and protection inside Governers Point. Field Correspondent Jim Norris noted sounds of the passing trains in the north anchorage area. Landons enjoyed exploring the bay and back cove by dinghy.

㉑ **Fairhaven Moorage.** (360) 714-8891; www.boatingcenter.org. Nine seasonal mooring buoys (for boats up to 35 feet), available May through October, a side-tie linear mooring system (max 3-day stay), and two boat launch ramps (for boats up to 38 feet) at Fairhaven are managed by the Community Boating Center. Launch ramps are tide-dependent and best suited to smaller boats. Pay moorage at the CBC office or pay box. Walk up to shops and restaurants in Fairhaven's lovely Victorian buildings. Just south of the business district you'll find a beautiful old park with mature plantings and great expanses of lawn. The Seaview Boatyard Dock (360) 676-8282 is located east of the Bellingham Cruise Terminal and guest linear moorage. The boatyard dock is used for staging in preparation for Travelift haulout.

LFS MARINE & OUTDOOR
Serving Northwest Washington Boaters For Over 50 Years.

Since 1967 LFS Marine & Outdoor has served the Pacific Northwest community. Now, with several stores in Western Washington and Alaska, LFS maintains its roots in Whatcom County with our flagship store and corporate office at Squalicum Harbor in Bellingham. The secret to our 50+ year success story has been dependable and reliable service through the most challenging times. We understand that our customers rely on us to help them navigate a successful boating and outdoor experience. That is why we're here for you, and that is why we're here to stay.

"They have so much stuff! It's a great place for any outdoors person or even DIY people. They have good prices too." —Google Review

851 Coho Way, Bellingham, WA • 360-734-3336 • 800-426-8860
www.Go2marine.com

NORTH PUGET SOUND

㉑ **Bellingham.** Bellingham is the largest city between Everett and the Canadian border, and has complete facilities for commercial and pleasure craft. Moorage, fuel, marine supplies, and repairs are available at the Port of Bellingham's Squalicum Harbor. Bellingham Yacht Club and Squalicum Yacht Club are nearby. BYC has moorage for members of reciprocal yacht clubs.

The charming Hotel Bellwether is near the mouth of the Squalicum Harbor south basin, adjacent to the Marina Restaurant and shops. The port runs a courtesy shuttle to downtown grocery stores, and the historic Fairhaven area shops and restaurants.

Mooring buoys and a linear moorage system are at Fairhaven, in the south part of Bellingham Bay. Fairhaven is a delightful stop with turn-of-the-20th-century Victorian buildings, boutiques, a large bookstore and other interesting shops. Fairhaven is also the southern terminus of the Alaska Marine Highway Ferry System, (360) 676-8445. As with Squalicum Harbor, you can take a bus or taxi to downtown Bellingham. Many shops, restaurants and a supermarket are within walking distance in this historic area. The Bellingham International Airport is convenient for arriving or departing guests.

Bellingham's scenic surroundings and its proximity to the San Juan Islands alone would be enough to draw many boaters. Bellingham is a college town with incredible shopping opportunities including provisioning for the galley. Squalicum Harbor has comfortable moorage and is a convenient base for cruising.

THINGS TO DO

- **Spark Museum of Electrical Invention.** Over 1,000 radios and many other electrical devices on display; electrical show.
- **Bellingham Railway Museum.** Model and actual trains, including a simulator.
- **Whatcom Museum.** Art, photography, and a family interactive gallery. Downtown.
- **Historic Fairhaven.** Good shopping and restaurants surrounded by period buildings. Peruse Village Books.
- **Bellingham Farmers Market.** Held in Depot Square, a glass and steel building modeled after a railroad station, with beams and arches salvaged from a local highway bridge. Wonderful local vendors every Saturday from 10:00 a.m. to 3:00 p.m. One of the largest markets in the state.
- **Boundary Bay Brewery & Bistro.** Across from the farmers market. Great beer garden and good food.
- **Mount Baker Theatre.** Enjoy a performance in this magnificently restored art deco theater built in 1927.
- **Mindport.** Not quite a science museum. Themes encourage creative play - 210 West Holly Street.
- **The Big Rock Garden.** More than 37 sculptures in this 2.5-acre park. Local and internationally acclaimed artists represented. Near Lake Whatcom, a cab ride away.
- **Marine Life Center.** See animal exhibits and touch pool - 1801 Roeder Ave in Harbor Park.

LOCAL KNOWLEDGE

SHALLOW AREA: A shoal habitat enhancement bench (4-foot depth at zero tide) is along the breakwater protecting the western basin of Squalicum Harbor. The bench extends approximately 200 feet out from the breakwater and runs approximately 400 feet along the breakwater. White cylindrical can buoys mark the outer corners. From its outer edge, the bench slopes another 100 feet into Bellingham Bay until it meets the sea floor. Give the buoys a good offing when running along the face of the breakwater.

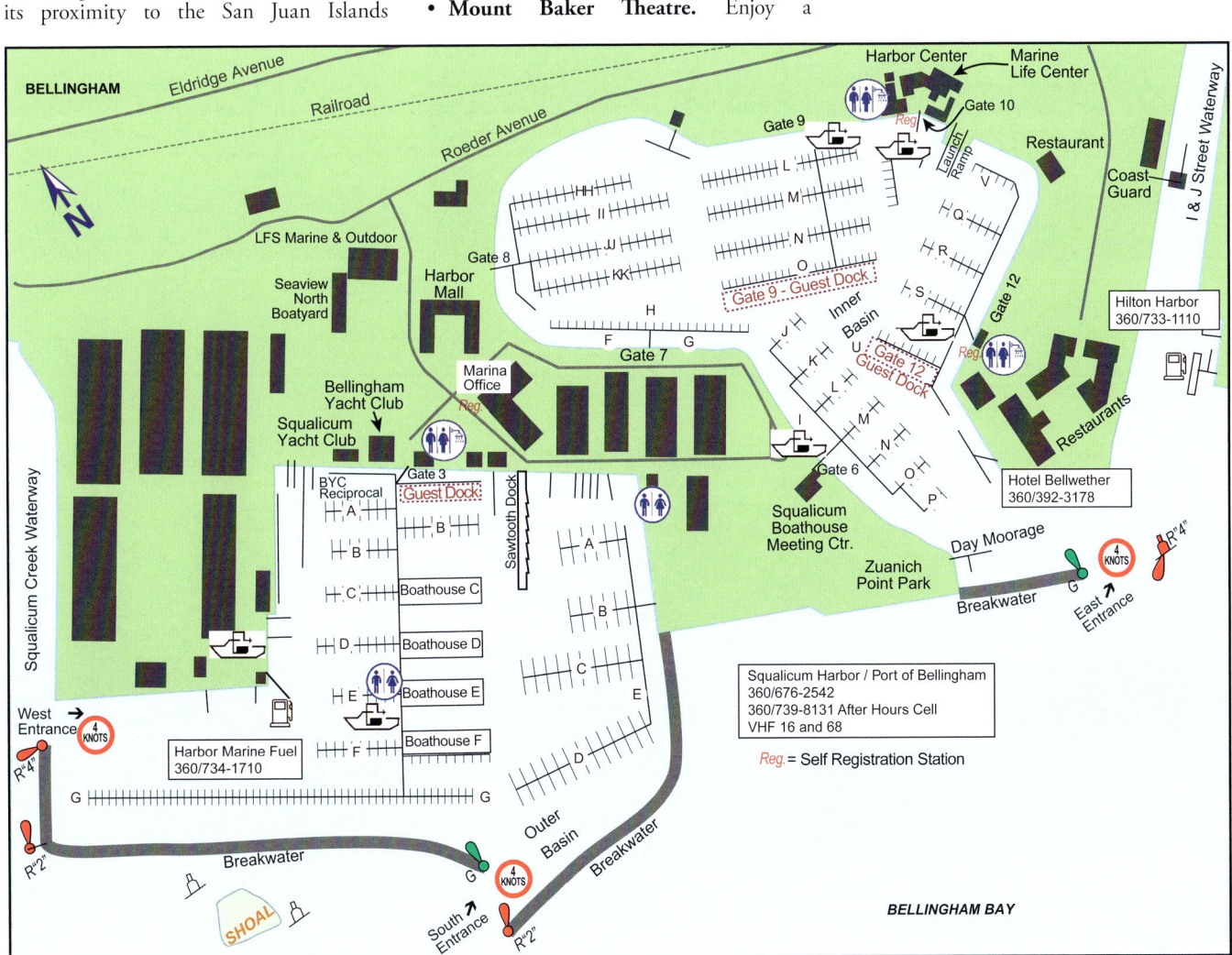

Port of Bellingham, Squalicum Harbor

NORTH PUGET SOUND

See Area Map Page 159 - Maps Not for Navigation

㉑ **Squalicum Harbor/Port of Bellingham.** 722 Coho Way, Bellingham, WA 98225; (360) 676-2542; (360) 739-8131 for after hours; squalicum@portofbellingham.com; www.portofbellingham.com. Certified Clean Marina. Monitors VHF 16, switch to 68. Open all year, guest moorage along 1000 feet of dock in two basins. Unoccupied slips are used when available, please call ahead. The marina has 20, 30 & 50 amp power (mostly 30 amp), restrooms, showers, laundry, pumpout, portapotty dump, and fee-based Ecco Wi-Fi. Three-day maximum stay in any 7-day period for visiting boats with longer stays subject to approval. The docks in both basins are gated for security. Restaurants nearby. Also chandleries and repair shops.

Seaview Boatyard runs the shipyard adjacent to the westernmost moorage basin. The yard has a 150-ton Travelift and a 35-ton Travelift.

Squalicum Harbor is divided into two moorage basins, each with its own entrance and guest moorage. The westernmost has restrooms located about halfway out the main pier, and onshore at the top of the dock ramp. Portable pumpout carts are kept at the restroom station.

In the eastern basin, guest moorage is just inside the breakwater entrance. Hotel Bellwether, with its dock, is located on the east side near the entrance. The hotel is part of a larger Port of Bellingham Bellwether development with park grounds, restaurants, boutiques, and a coffee shop.

Seasonally, you can buy fresh fish right off the boat. A marine life tank (great for kids) also is near the streetside parking lot. A 3-lane launch ramp, with extended-term parking for tow vehicles and trailers, is just east of the east basin.

ANTHONY'S AT SQUALICUM HARBOR
25 Bellwether Way
(360) 647-5588

Anthony's Hearthfire Grill
7 Bellwether Way
(360) 527-3473

Harbor Marine Fuel. (360) 734-1710. Open all year. Fuel dock with diesel and gasoline (containing ethanol). Store carries motor oils. Located in northern Squalicum Harbor, behind the breakwater.

㉑ **Hotel Bellwether.** 1 Bellwether Way, Bellingham, WA 98225; (360) 392-3178; reservations@hotelbellwether.com; www.hotelbellwether.com. Open all year, side-tie moorage along 220-foot concrete float, 30, 50 & 100 amp power. Larger boats tie outside, smaller boats tie inside. This is a classy small hotel, done to 5-star standards. Outstanding dining. Located just inside the mouth of the Squalicum Harbor east basin. Reservations required. Dog friendly.

Hilton Harbor Marina. 1000 Hilton Ave., Bellingham, WA 98225; (360) 733-1110; info@hiltonharbor.com. Fuel dock with gasoline only. Located at the south entrance to Squalicum Harbor at the foot of Hilton Avenue. Two 3 ton hoists, repairs. Oil disposal available.

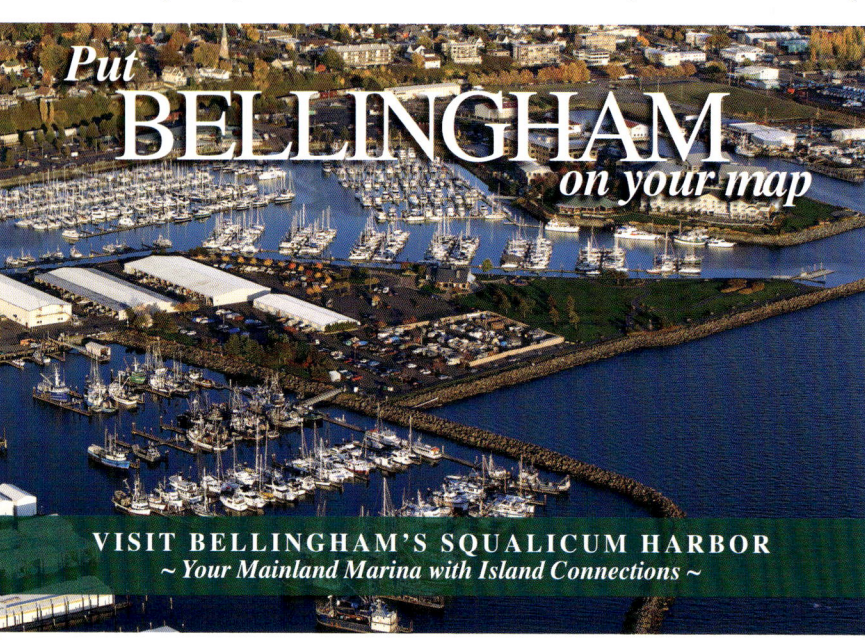

Put BELLINGHAM on your map

VISIT BELLINGHAM'S SQUALICUM HARBOR
~ Your Mainland Marina with Island Connections ~

A variety of restaurants, Hotel Bellwether, chandlery, trails and parks alongside our harbor and more than 1,000 feet of visitor dock space make Squalicum Harbor an ideal visitor destination.

- Friendly dockside service
- Several charter boat operations
- 3-lane boat launch open year-round
- Over-the-dock fuel service for bulk pricing
- Available Fuel Dock
- Diverse marine repair and supply services in the harbor
- Full Service Boatyard
- Restrooms, laundry and showers
- Holding tank pump-outs

- Closest U.S. port to Alaska
- Minutes away from the San Juan and Gulf Islands and midway between Seattle and Vancouver, B.C.
- An expanded Bellingham International Airport, providing more commercial flights to a growing number of destinations
- Outstanding visitor amenities:
  Vibrant downtown with entertainment, microbreweries, shopping, museum, seasonal farmers market
  Unsurpassed recreation opportunities – Mt Baker, golfing, bike trails

SQUALICUM HARBOR
Port of Bellingham

SQUALICUM HARBOR OFFICE: 722 Coho Way, Bellingham, WA 98225 • (360) 676-2542
squalicum@portofbellingham.com • www.portofbellingham.com

NORTH PUGET SOUND

LUMMI BAY TO PT. ROBERTS

Lummi Island. Lummi Island is high (1480 feet) and has no facilities specifically for visiting boaters. Anchorage is good in several places, including Inati Bay and along both shores of Hale Passage. A ferry connects Lummi Island to the mainland. Restaurants and other businesses are near this dock. The Lummi Nation's people haul their boats, including reef net boats, on the beach south of the ferry dock.

Inati Bay. Inati Bay is on the east side of Lummi Island, approximately 2 miles north of Carter Point. It is the best anchorage on Lummi Island, protected from all but northeasterly winds (rare in the summer) with good holding. There may be debris on the bottom left from the old Hood Canal caisson that was once moored here. A log boom chain is reported to lie on the north side of the bay near the rock wall. Member-only moorage at the Bellingham Yacht Club outstation property.

When entering Inati Bay, leave the white cautionary buoy well to starboard to avoid the rock that extends northward from the buoy. Stay close to the point of land on the south side of the entrance.

Lummi Island Recreation Site. Southeast shore of Lummi Island. Open all year, toilets, campsites.

Sandy Point. Sandy Point is a private real-estate development consisting of several canals with homes on them. No public facilities. Long docks serving a refinery and an aluminum plant extend from shore north of Sandy Point.

Birch Bay. Birch Bay at the southeastern end of Strait of Georgia is a large bay with excellent anchoring depths over a flat mud bottom. The bay is so large that it affords little protection from wind and waves. Open to the northwest, west, and southwest, Birch Bay is best used in calm conditions. Popular in the summer, you will find almost as many small craft as crab pot buoys. Large sections of the head of the bay are drying tidal areas. The cluster of buildings on the east shore marks the town of Birch Bay and the group of masts on the north shore marks the private Birch Bay Marina with no services for transient boaters.

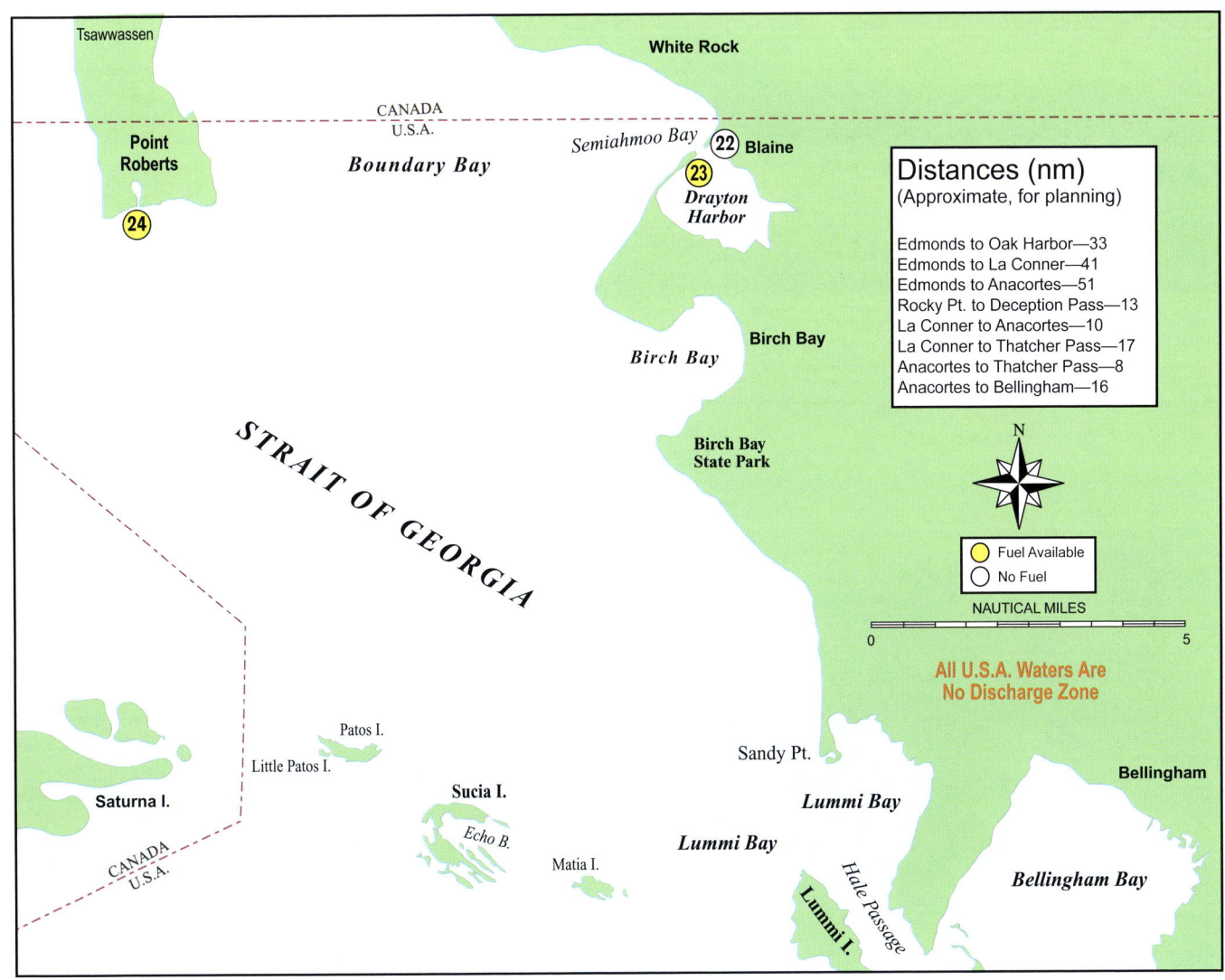

Distances (nm)
(Approximate, for planning)

Edmonds to Oak Harbor—33
Edmonds to La Conner—41
Edmonds to Anacortes—51
Rocky Pt. to Deception Pass—13
La Conner to Anacortes—10
La Conner to Thatcher Pass—17
Anacortes to Thatcher Pass—8
Anacortes to Bellingham—16

All U.S.A. Waters Are No Discharge Zone

Lummi Bay to Point Roberts

2023 WAGGONER CRUISING GUIDE   175

NORTH PUGET SOUND

See Area Map Page 175 - Maps Not for Navigation

Stroll the fine beach overlooking Semiahmoo Bay.

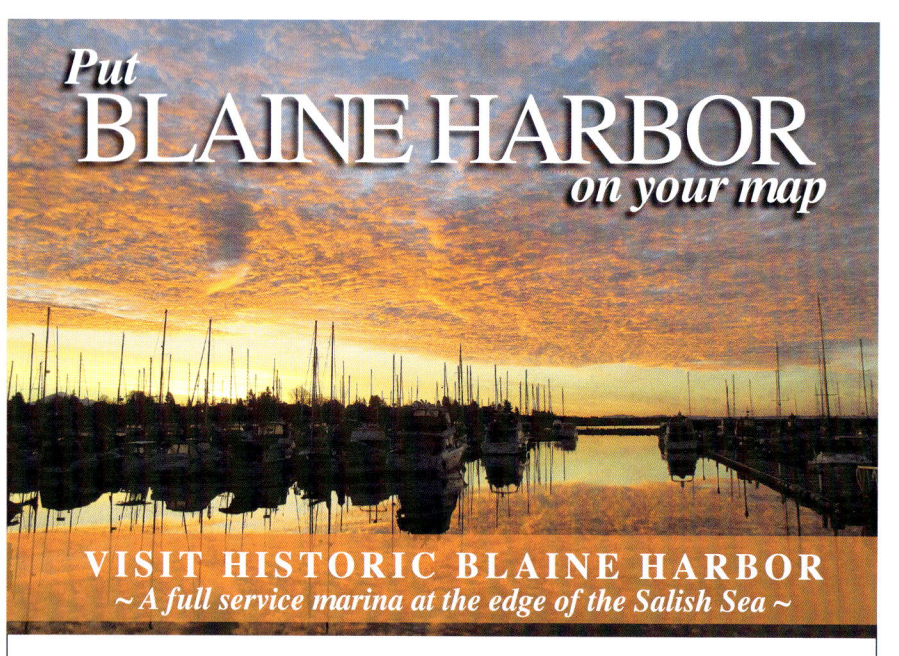

Put BLAINE HARBOR on your map

VISIT HISTORIC BLAINE HARBOR
~ *A full service marina at the edge of the Salish Sea* ~

Relax and re-provision on your Inside Passage Adventure Strategically located on the US - Canadian Border, 1 minute to Interstate 5!

- Over 800 feet of visitor moorage
- No reservations required
- Post office & marine supplies
- Provisions & liquor store,
- 30 minute drive to Bellingham & Vancouver BC
- Friendly dockside service
- 70 person Meeting Room for your group events
- Restrooms, laundry & showers
- New Children's Playground
- 2 lane boat launch with ample parking
- Boatyards & Marine Trades Services

Blaine Harbor promenade.

BLAINE HARBOR *Port of Bellingham*

BLAINE HARBOR OFFICE • 235 Marine Drive Blaine, WA 98230
360-647-6176 • www.portofbellingham.com • blaineharbor@portofbellingham.com

---

LOCAL KNOWLEDGE

Shoal Entry: The approach to Blaine through Semiahmoo Bay is shoal at all stages but high tide. Pay close attention to the buoys along the drying bank on the south side of the bay, and turn into the entrance channel before getting too close to the eastern shore.

㉒ **Blaine.** Blaine has two moorages in Drayton Harbor. One is owned by the Port of Bellingham; the other, Semiahmoo, is privately owned and has both permanent and guest moorage at this nice resort.

The Blaine Marina is on the east (port) side, with entry through an opening in the piling breakwater. Follow the signs to the guest moorage in the middle of the harbor.

The Semiahmoo Marina is on the west side of the entrance channel and has fuel. Both marinas have water, power, and other facilities ashore. The Port's marina gives access to the town of Blaine and a number of boating-related businesses and a good selection of restaurants. Semiahmoo Marina has access to two world-class golf courses. In the summer, Friday through Sunday, the classic foot ferry, *Plover,* operates between the two marinas or you can dinghy between the two.

With all that Blaine has to offer, no lack of things to do and fantastic sunsets, it makes a nice cruising destination. Don't miss "Blaine's Market by the Sea" held every Saturday from 9:00 a.m. to 2:00 p.m. at G Street Plaza during the summer months. Be sure to visit Blaine Marine Park and enjoy the waterfront trail.

Drayton Harbor is a sensitive shellfish harvesting area.

No Discharge Zone. Gray water okay.

㉒ **Blaine Harbor/Port of Bellingham**. P.O. Box 1245, 235 Marine Drive, Blaine, WA 98230; (360) 647-6176; blaineharbor@portofbellingham.com; www.portofbellingham.com. Monitors VHF 16, switch to 68. Certified Clean Marina. Side-tie guest moorage along 800 feet of wide dock, unoccupied slips up to 120' used when available. Services include 30 & 50 amp power, water, restrooms, showers, laundry, pumpout carts, portapotty dump, and fee-based Ecco Wi-Fi. Repairs, haulout, supplies available. Waste oil disposal. Two blocks to town. Concrete launch ramp with parking. Restaurants nearby. Courtesy shuttle to grocery store in town.

The side-tie guest (visitor) dock is served by a wide fairway for easy maneuvering. The shoreside facilities are built to a turn of the 20th century theme. The marina office is in the Boating Center building. A 65-person public meeting room, with kitchen, is also in this building at Gate 2. An attractive park with a children's playground and beach access is across the road on the north side of the spit. Walking distance to the Peace Arch at the border.

See Area Map Page 175 - Maps Not for Navigation

NORTH PUGET SOUND

Historic remains from a bygone era at Semiahmoo Resort grounds.

Rent bikes and ride the pathways at Drayton Harbor.

㉓ **Semiahmoo Marina.** 9540 Semiahmoo Parkway, Blaine, WA 98230; (360) 371-0440; moorageoffice@semiahmoomarina.com; www.semiahmoomarina.com. Monitors VHF 68. Open all year. Ethanol-free gasoline and diesel at the Semiahmoo Marina fuel dock; propane. Guest moorage in unoccupied slips when available. One 50-foot slip is reserved for reciprocal yacht clubs. Swift current may make docking difficult, best done at slack. Call before 5:00 p.m. regarding availability for all guest moorage; reservations can be made online. Services include 30 & 50 amp power, water, restrooms, free showers, laundry, pumpout, portapotty dump, and Wi-Fi. Marina store with gifts, clothing, beer, wine, and marine items. Marina Cafe serves breakfast and lunch.

The Semiahmoo Resort has a hotel, spa with pool, restaurants and kayak, SUP, and bicycle rentals. It is a full resort with all the amenities. If you have bicycles on board or have rented a bike, you can ride the 1.2-mile scenic pathway to the Alaska Packers Association Cannery & Fishing Museum, located at 9261 Semiahmoo Parkway. Museum displays, housed in an original cannery building, include machinery and historic photos. Open weekends 1:00 p.m. to 5:00 p.m., Memorial Day through September.

The par 72 Semiahmoo course is outstanding. Day passes available for marina guests. Telephone (360) 371-7015.

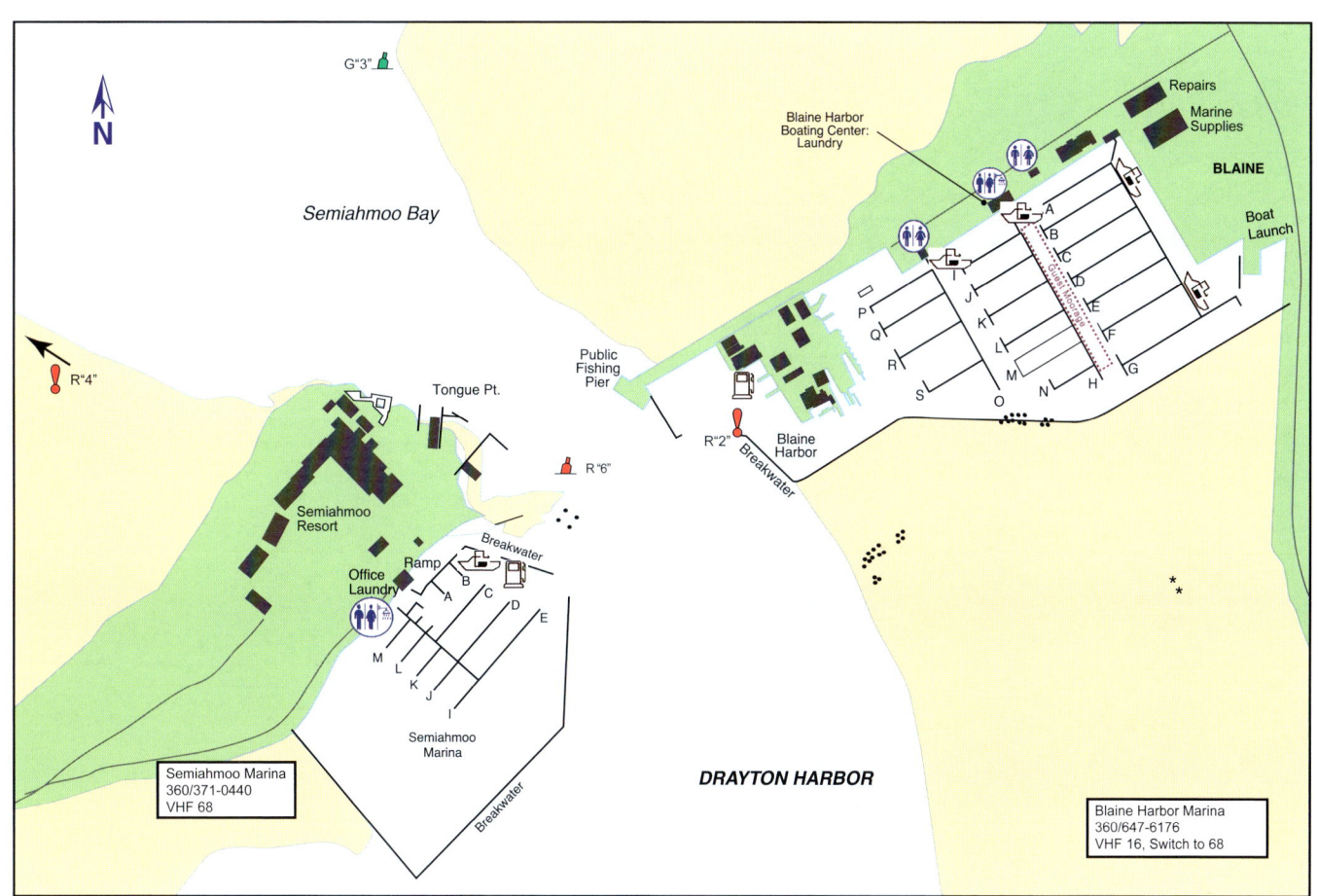

Drayton Harbor

NORTH PUGET SOUND

See Area Map Page 175 - Maps Not for Navigation

㉔ **Point Roberts.** Point Roberts is a low spit of land extending south from Canada into U.S. waters. Although physically separated from the U.S., Point Roberts is U.S. territory and part of the state of Washington. The Point Roberts Marina is on the south shore. Enter via a dredged channel skirted by drying flats. The channel was last dredged in the fall of 2017. Four ocean-front parks, one located at each corner of 4.9 square mile Point Roberts, can be reached by bicycle.

㉔ **Point Roberts Marina Resort.** 713 Simundson Drive, Point Roberts, WA 98281; (360) 945-2255; prmarina@pointrobertsmarina.com; www.pointrobertsmarina.com. Monitors VHF 66A. Open all year. Fuel dock with mid-grade gasoline, diesel, propane, ice, beer & wine, fishing licenses, tackle, convenience items. The fuel dock is open daily during the summer season until 5:00 p.m., Sunday through Thursday; and until 8:00 p.m. on Friday and Saturday. Guest moorage in unoccupied slips. Phone ahead for slip assignment, reservations required, call or use the registration form online. Services include 30 & 50 amp power, (ELCI-protected power on some docks), water, restrooms, showers, laundry, garbage drop, free pumpouts. No Wi-Fi and weak cell signal. Used oil drop.

The Breakwaters Bar & Grill at the marina is delightful, reservations recommended for large groups; (360) 945-2628. Other restaurants, golf and groceries are nearby. Haulout to 35 tons. Westwind Marine Services, with repairs and a chandlery, is in the main building and has seasonal hours.

Point Roberts is a U.S. Customs port of entry. The first dock to starboard has a direct-dial telephone to customs hanging outside the white shack. Agents typically drive over from the Point Roberts border office. Summer hours 8:00 a.m. to 8:00 p.m., winter hours 8:00 a.m. to 5:00 p.m. Consider calling ahead at (360) 945-5211.

Lighthouse Marine County Park. (360) 945-4911; lthouse@pointroberts.net; www.whatcomcounty.us. Open for day use and overnight camping in summer, day use only in winter. On the southwest corner of Point Roberts. Anchor north of the park and row in, or moor at Point Roberts Marina and walk or ride a bike over. Facilities include boat launch ramp with seasonal staging float, campsites, picnic shelters, fire pits, barbecues, restrooms, showers, sand and gravel beach. Also a whale exhibit, playground, boardwalk, and picnic shelters. Whales can sometimes be seen from the park. A small public airstrip is along the eastern perimeter of the park.

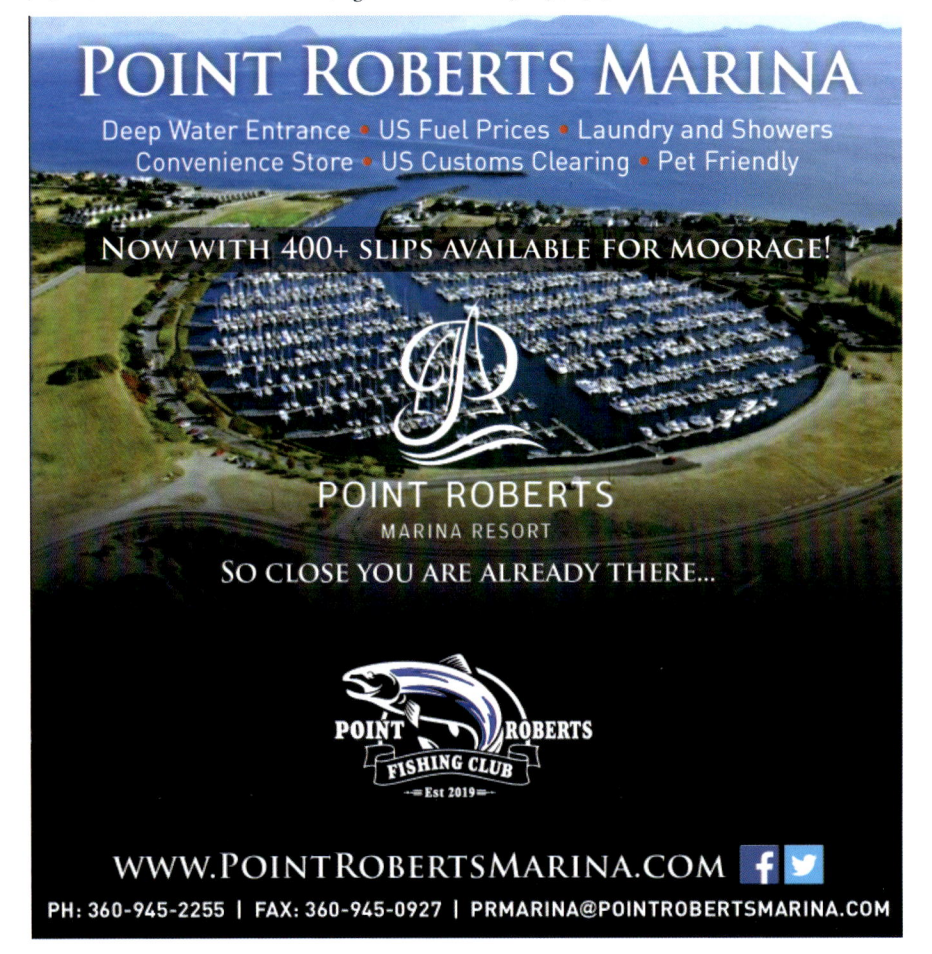

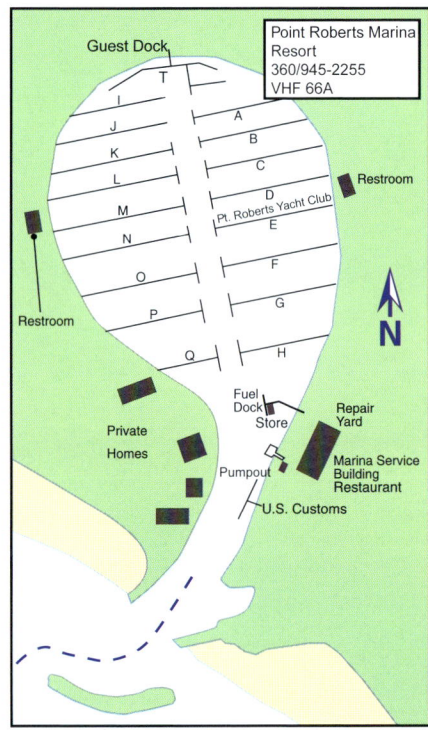

U.S. Customs Clearance Dock at Point Roberts; marina office and restaurant in the background.

Point Roberts Marina

See Area Map Page 175 - Maps Not for Navigation

NORTH PUGET SOUND

Point Roberts has a nearby park and excellent beaches to stroll.

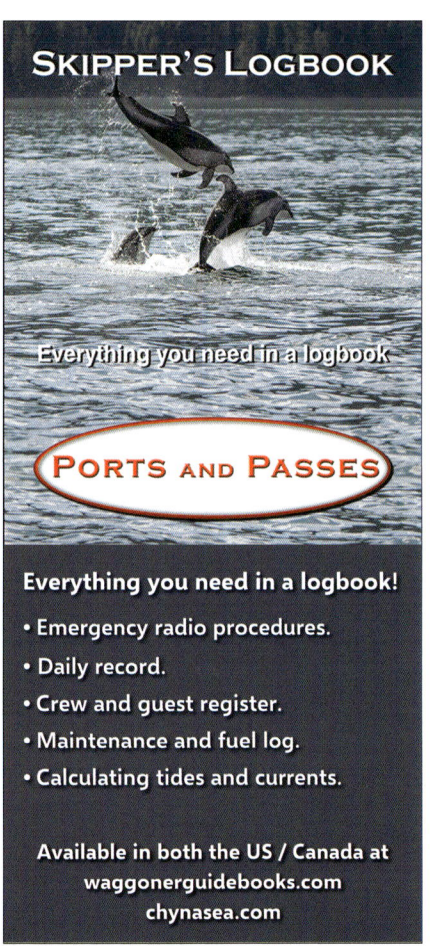

SKIPPER'S LOGBOOK

Everything you need in a logbook

PORTS AND PASSES

Everything you need in a logbook!
- Emergency radio procedures.
- Daily record.
- Crew and guest register.
- Maintenance and fuel log.
- Calculating tides and currents.

Available in both the US / Canada at
waggonerguidebooks.com
chynasea.com

NAUTICAL SLANG - COMMON EXPRESSIONS

Did you know that many common expressions spoken today came from seafaring terms and practices? Here are a few frequently heard phrases and their older nautical meanings:

"Cut and Run" – was the practice of securing sails of a square-rigged ship with old, disposable rope so it could be cut free for a quick departure. Boaters today most often think the phrase refers to cutting the anchor line for a quick escape.

"Devil to Pay" – refers to caulking the longest seam of the hull known as the "devil, with pay or pitch. This was one of the most difficult and unpleasant jobs aboard the ship, requiring squatting in the bilge(s) for many hours. Landlubbers of the day thought the phrase referred to Satan and created a moral interpretation.

"Dressing Down" – today this phrase refers to a reprimand for an officer or sailor. In earlier times, thin or worn sails were treated with oil and wax, which was called dressing down.

"Hard-up" – when the ships wheel was turned hard over to one side, the wheel could seize-up. With no way to relieve the seizing, the sailor was said to be hard-up or met with misfortune.

"Junk" – we use this word today for things that have no personal value. In seafaring days, junk referred to old rope not able to take a load. The rope was usually cut into pieces to make mops and mats.

"Overhaul" – was the need to send crew aloft to haul ropes/lines over the sails, called overhauling, to prevent the sails from being chaffed.

"Scuttlebutt" – was a water barrel with a hole cut into it so sailors could scoop out drinking water. The ship's gossip was often shared around the scuttlebutt.

"A Square Meal" – in seafaring days, the crew enjoyed a warm meal served on square wooden platters when the seas were calm. Today, the phrase refers to a meal that includes foods from all of the food groups.

"Taken Aback" – when the wind is on the wrong side of the sails and forces the ship astern, the ship is said to be taken aback, perhaps due to an inattentive helmsman.

"Tide Over" – in the absence of wind, a sailing ship would float with the tide until the wind returned, called a tide over. Today the phrase refers to a small supply used until one's main supply arrives.

"Under the Weather" – during seafaring days, this meant keeping watch on the windward or weather side of the bow. Sailors assigned to this station often became soaked with sea water and fell ill.

2023 WAGGONER CRUISING GUIDE

Strait of Juan De Fuca

STRAIT OF JUAN DE FUCA
Sequim Bay • Port Angeles • Neah Bay
Clallam Bay • Dungeness Spit

Scan the Latest
Juan de Fuca
Information

tinyurl.com/WG22xCh05

Race Rocks Lighthouse

The Strait of Juan de Fuca is about 100 miles long and 12 miles wide. Depending on the weather, it can be flat calm or extremely rough. The typical summertime pattern calls for calm mornings with a westerly sea breeze rising by mid-day, increasing to 30 knots or more late in the afternoon. If this sea breeze opposes an outflowing ebb current, the seas will be unusually high, steep, and close together. Often, however, the "typical" weather pattern does not prevail, and the wind blows around the clock. Or, it can be calm, even on a warm summer afternoon. Weather reports must be monitored. If wind is present or predicted, we stay off the strait.

CROSSING THE STRAIT OF JUAN DE FUCA

The Strait of Juan de Fuca has a well-earned reputation for being rough at times. It's true that a boat crossing the strait can take a beating that its crew will not want to repeat, but often the crossing can be almost flat. If conditions truly are foul, alternate routes exist. The secret to an easy crossing lies in picking your times and not being foolhardy. Routes suggested below are approximate and for reference only. They assume good conditions and the absence of current. Since current is always present, appropriate course adjustments will be needed.

Summer weather pattern. During the high summer cruising season, the "typical" weather pattern calls for near-calm conditions in the early morning when the air over the entire region is cool. As the summer sun heats the land, air over the land rises and colder ocean air funnels down the Strait of Juan de Fuca to replace the rising land air. This is called a sea breeze, and it usually develops in the late morning or early afternoon. By late afternoon the sea breeze can be quite strong, creating short, high seas, especially on an ebb. After sundown, as air in the interior cools, the sea breeze dies away.

Given this pattern, early morning crossings are preferred. Carefully monitor the official weather reports and forecast. If the morning report says the wind already is blowing 15 to 20 knots, and more wind is expected, don't cross. Wait until the wind subsides or take an alternate route.

Fog can develop unexpectedly. Sometimes it is only a thin mist, other times it can be pea-soup thick. Normally when the wind moves in, the fog blows out.

LOCAL KNOWLEDGE

DANGEROUS TIDE RIPS. Ebbing tidal currents can set up dangerous tide-rips at Point Wilson, and at the south end of Rosario Strait, at Cattle Pass, and off Discovery Island. Do not underestimate the viciousness of these tide-rips. Whenever possible, plan your passage to transit these danger spots near the turn of the tide or on a flood.

Point Wilson Tide-Rip. One of the more frustrating pieces of water we face in the Northwest is the infamous Point Wilson tide-rip just off Port Townsend. The rip usually (but not always) forms on an ebb tide, and may or may not be accompanied by westerly wind. The patch of rough water can extend for several miles north and west of Point Wilson. Usually, the rip doesn't form until well into an ebb cycle, so timing your arrival to coincide with slack water is best.

If, however, your timing is off, you can pick one of two routes around it.

The first is to hug the Point Wilson shore as closely as you dare, keeping close to shore until you pass McCurdy Point.

The other route is to stay close to the Whidbey Island shore (avoiding the shoal water off Partridge Point and stay east of Partridge Bank) until past Smith Island before turning toward your destination.

Point Wilson to San Juan Channel. The most direct route from Point Wilson to Friday Harbor is via San Juan Channel. A direct course between the two intersects Smith Island. Shoals, covered with dense kelp, extend westward from Smith Island for nearly 2 miles. Partridge Bank, between Point Wilson and Smith Island, should be avoided. Heavy kelp is an obstacle, and if the wind is up, seas are worse in the shallow water over the bank.

At Point Wilson you'll set a course of approximately 301° magnetic until you're abeam the Smith Island light, where you'll turn to a course of 330° magnetic to fetch Cattle Pass. (From Cattle Pass to Point Wilson reverse the process: run 150° magnetic until the Smith Island light bears abeam to port, then turn to 121° magnetic to fetch Point Wilson.)

When using this route, it's best to time your arrival at Cattle Pass for shortly after the current turns to flood. The current can run hard through Cattle Pass, so it's best not to fight it. Use the San Juan Channel current predictions.

If you do it right, you'll carry the last of a dying ebb out Admiralty Inlet, past Point Wilson, and well across the strait.

Just before reaching Cattle Pass, the current will turn to flood, flushing you nicely through the pass and into San Juan Channel. Since you can have 2 to 4 knots of current in Admiralty Inlet, and a couple knots of current in the strait, riding the ebb can save considerable time, even in a fast boat. The less time you're exposed, the less time you have to meet trouble.

To Rosario Strait or Deception Pass. From the mouth of Admiralty Inlet, plot a course that leaves Point Partridge bell buoy off Whidbey Island to starboard. If you're bound for Rosario Strait, stay out of the traffic lanes as much as possible. As noted above, the mouth of Rosario Strait can be filled with dangerous tide-rips on an ebb tide. Be prepared to favor the eastern shore.

To Haro Strait (Roche Harbor). Leaving Point Wilson, run a course of approximately 301° magnetic until the Smith Island light is abeam to starboard. Then turn to approximately 305° magnetic to run toward

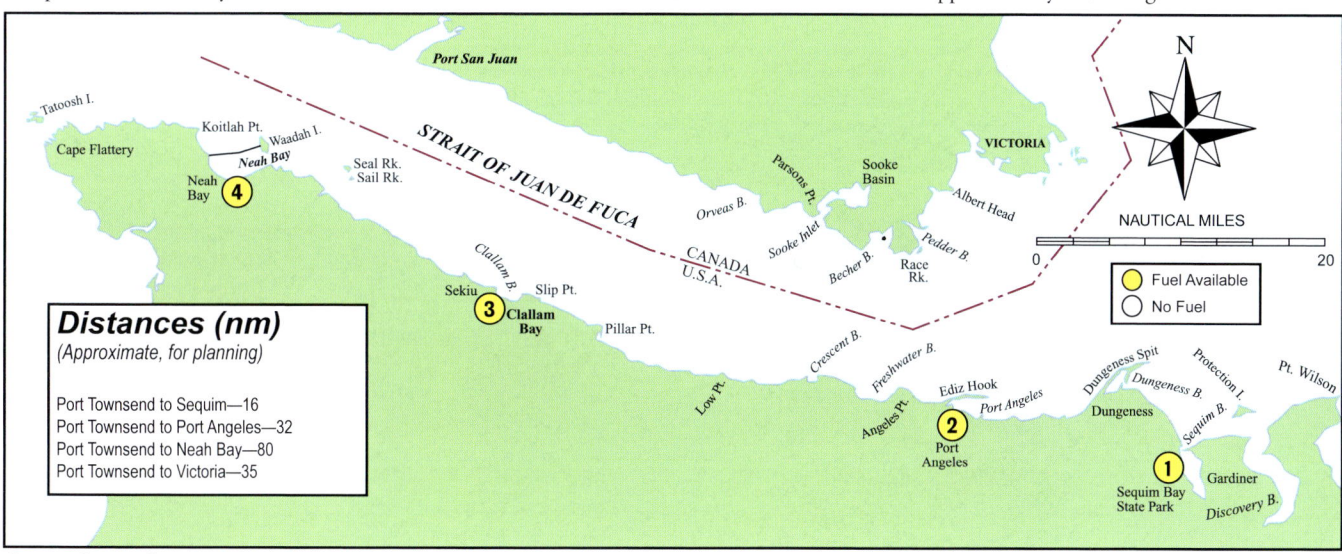

Distances (nm)
(Approximate, for planning)

Port Townsend to Sequim—16
Port Townsend to Port Angeles—32
Port Townsend to Neah Bay—80
Port Townsend to Victoria—35

Strait of Juan de Fuca

STRAIT OF JUAN DE FUCA

STRAIT OF JUAN DE FUCA GO-NOGO CHECKLIST

Tides & Currents - See Ports & Passes; Canadian Tides & Current Tables Vol. 5
- ☐ Phase of the moon – Spring or Neap Tide
- ☐ Flood or Ebb - Ebbing tidal currents can set up dangerous tide-rips at: Point Wilson, Cattle Pass, and South end of Rosario Strait

Weather System Predictions – via Internet or satellite
- ☐ Check NOAA Ocean Prediction Center forecasts for any approaching significant weather systems
- ☐ Check Windy.com, Predictwind.com, SiriusXM Marine, or Sailflow.com
- ☐ See Environment Canada and NWS NOAA forecasts for the Synopsis for East Entrance Juan de Fuca Strait, and Haro Strait

Weather & Seas Forecasts – via Internet, phone, or VHF
- ☐ See NWS NOAA Zone Area Forecasts for East Entrance Strait of Juan de Fuca, Northern Inland Waters Including San Juan Islands, and Admiralty Inlet; note wind speed and direction, wave height and interval, and trends
- ☐ See Environment Canada Forecast for Juan de Fuca Strait – East Entrance; Check for warnings, note wind speed, direction and trends

Observations & Present Conditions – via Internet, phone, or VHF
- ☐ Check Buoy Report for New Dungeness (46088); note wind and sea conditions
- ☐ Check Lighthouse and Station Observation Reports from Smith Island, Race Rocks, Port Townsend, Trial Island, and Entrance Island; note wind and sea conditions

Go-NoGo Decision
- √ Check wind direction in relation to direction of travel.
- √ Are you prepared to clear U.S. or Canada Customs?
- √ Is there a wind against wave or current situation?
- √ Are the more protected, but longer, alternate routes a better option?

Fail-Safe Contingency Plans
- √ Duck-in locations along the route: Dungeness Spit, and Oak Bay on Vancouver Is.

See the *Marine Weather* section in the Compendium chapter for telephone numbers, website addresses, VHF channels, and buoy numbers.

Lime Kiln Point on the west side of San Juan Island. Once near Lime Kiln Point, follow the San Juan Island shoreline north.

If you're returning south from Roche Harbor, follow the San Juan Island coastline until you're a little south of Lime Kiln Point, then turn to approximately 125° magnetic until the Smith Island light is abeam to port. At Smith Island turn to 121° magnetic to fetch Point Wilson.

Both the flood and ebb currents run strongly along the west side of San Juan Island. Even in a fast boat it is best to make this passage with favorable current. The Canadian Hydrographic Service book, *Current Atlas: Juan de Fuca Strait to Georgia Strait* illustrates these current flows in convincing diagram form. *Waggoner Tables*, published annually, provide the time schedule for the Current Atlas.

To Victoria. From Point Wilson, a course of approximately 275° magnetic takes you 30 miles to Victoria. Returning from Victoria, a course of about 095° magnetic should raise Point Wilson in time to make late-run corrections for the effects of current. In slow boats, the trip between Victoria and Point Wilson usually can be made on a single favorable tide. In all boats, utilizing favorable current can save significant time.

Even the best plan can go awry. While over the years we have made many easy crossings of the strait (only a few have been "memorable"), it's important to understand that conditions can change with little warning. When you're several miles offshore and the wind decides to kick up, you can't pull over until things improve.

The Strait of Juan de Fuca is not to be feared, but it should be respected. Be sure your boat is seaworthy, well-equipped, and in excellent condition. Carry plenty of fuel. Check the typically easterly flowing offshore weather systems. Let the weather and tide and current tables set your plans. Don't be afraid to wait, but be confident enough to seize opportunities as they arise.

Discovery Bay. Discovery Bay is west of Point Wilson. It is somewhat protected from the Strait of Juan de Fuca by Protection Island, a wildlife refuge. Discovery Bay is open and unobstructed, surrounded by forest and farm lands, with a few waterfront communities. The bay is seldom used by pleasure craft as an overnight anchorage. Gardiner, halfway down the bay, has a launch ramp. The WorldMark Club dock, along the west shore near Port Discovery, is available for timeshare members only. A small private community marina is located on the east shore at Cape George.

LOCAL KNOWLEDGE

SHOAL AREA: Sequim Bay has a large shoal in the middle of the entry channel with passage around the eastern and western sides. The marked channel, Red, Right, Returning to Sequim Bay, leads around the western side of the shoal area.

Sequim Bay. Sequim Bay is a large, beautiful bay with a State park, marina, and anchoring opportunities. The bay is protected by Travis Spit, which extends from the eastern shore. To enter, steer for the middle of this spit, then turn sharply west and run parallel to the spit before turning to the south at the tip of the spit. Current can run strongly in the channel during tidal exchange. The marked channel leads to the west of a shoal area just south of Travis Spit; favor the shore side of the channel when passing green channel markers 5 and 7.

Anchoring is possible in most of Sequim Bay with varying depths; one of the preferred is in a bight just south of John Wayne Marina on the west shore in 30 to 50 feet; Field Correspondents Sandy and Will Dupleich report good holding and protection from boat wakes and winds blowing in from the Strait of Juan de Fuca. Sequim Bay State Park is about 1.5 miles south of the John Wayne Marina entrance, on the west shore, with mooring buoys for boats 45 feet and under.

Actor John Wayne, who often visited Sequim Bay aboard his yacht Wild Goose, donated 22 waterfront acres to the Port of Port Angeles on condition that the Port build a marina on the site.

One of the first-come guest moorage docks at John Wayne Marina in Sequim Bay

① **John Wayne Marina.** 2577 W. Sequim Bay Road, Sequim, WA 98382; (360) 417-3440; (no VHF); rona@portofpa.com; www.portofpa.com. Open all year. Gasoline and diesel at the fuel dock. Guest moorage in approximately 22 side-tie spaces on two floats, and assigned slips as available; call the office to check on space availability. The office is closed between noon and 1:00 p.m. Services include 30 & 50 amp power, water, clean restrooms and showers; free Wi-Fi, laundry, pumpout, portapotty dump, and launch ramps.

The Dockside Grill restaurant is ashore and is reported to be excellent. Picnic area and beach access are nearby. Check-in at the first float inside the breakwater. John Wayne Marina is operated by the Port of Port Angeles. For those desiring onshore accommodations, the John Wayne Waterfront Resort (360-681-3853) has cabins and camp sites a short walk away.

① **Sequim Bay Marine State Park**. (360) 683-4235; Sequim Bay Marine State Park occupies 92 acres along the western shore of Sequim Bay. Open all year, day use and overnight mooring and camping; 6 mooring buoys (for boats 45 feet and under). Launch ramp with seasonal staging float. The dock with mooring float was closed due to unsafe conditions in 2021. Plans are to replace the dock, possibly in a new location in deeper water.

Facilities include restrooms, showers, portapotty dump, picnic sites, campsites, kitchen shelters, and launch ramp. Self-register and pay nightly mooring buoy fee on shore.

The Olympic Discovery Trail passes through the park and is accessible for walking or bicycling; see the Olympic Discovery Trail sidebar for more information.

John Wayne Marina

OLYMPIC DISCOVERY TRAIL

The Olympic Discovery Trail is a 130 mile long pathway for walking and bicycling that runs from Port Townsend to the town of LaPush on the Pacific Ocean. Segments of the impressive trail are accessible to boaters from the Sequim Bay area and Port Angeles area. To access the trail from John Wayne Marina, walk or bicycle ¾ mile along steep Whitefeather Way to the Johnson Creek Railroad Trestle Bridge, which has been converted for trail use. At Sequim Bay State Park (which has mooring buoys), the Olympic Discovery Trail passes through the park where you can walk or bicycle in either direction along the dedicated pathway. The trail passes in front of Port Angeles Boat Haven and at the City Pier boater facilities in Port Angeles. Bicycle rentals are available in Port Angeles.

The impressive Olympic Discovery Trail includes five original railroad trestles, the McPhee Tunnel near Lake Crescent, several river crossings, beautiful forests, and ocean views. The 780-foot trestle over the Dungeness River connects to a rare wooden truss bridge. For more information about the trail, visit the website at olympicdiscoverytrail.org.

[Leonard & Lorena Landon]

Dungeness Spit. Beautiful Dungeness Spit, 5.5 miles long, is the world's longest natural sand spit and is within the Dungeness National Wildlife Refuge. Hike the 10.2 mile long round-trip trail that takes you between the recreation area and the lighthouse at the end of the spit.

The spit provides protection from westerly weather, and convenient anchoring depths along its inner edge before an attached cross-spit forces the channel south. Shallow draft boats can continue into the inner harbor, where there is a launch ramp and protected anchorage. Dungeness Spit is open to hikers but has no public facilities. Dogs are not allowed ashore.

Contact the Wildlife Refuge Office (360) 457-8451 before going ashore. Land dinghies and kayaks in the designated area south of the Lighthouse between the yellow markers.

② **Port Angeles.** Port Angeles is a substantial small city on a bay protected by Ediz Hook. The Port Angeles City Pier, with visitor moorage, is near the south end of the business district. Guest moorage with full services is available at the breakwater-protected Port of Port Angeles Boat Haven marina at the southwest corner of the bay and City Pier.

Port Angeles is a U.S. Customs port of entry. The *Coho* car and passenger ferry runs from Port Angeles to Victoria (www.cohoferry.com). It is possible to moor the boat in Port Angeles, take the *Coho* ferry as a walk-on passenger in the morning, tour Victoria, B.C. for the day, and return to Port Angeles in the late afternoon.

The outer end of Ediz Hook is a Coast Guard station. Just west of the Coast Guard station is the Port Angeles Pilot Station, where Puget Sound Pilot tenders shuttle pilots to ships bound to or from Puget Sound ports.

2023 Waggoner Cruising Guide

STRAIT OF JUAN DE FUCA

See Area Map Page 181 - Maps Not for Navigation

Convenient side-tie guest moorage at Port Angeles Boat Haven

Port Angeles City Pier is located in the heart of downtown near cafes, shops, and the Waterfront Park, with access to the Olympic Discovery Trail.

Port Angeles has a number of attractions. The walkable town has many shops and restaurants to explore. The Feiro Marine Life Center, on the city pier, focuses on the marine life in the Strait of Juan de Fuca. Open daily, 10:00 a.m. to 5:00 p.m. in summers and 12:00 p.m. to 5:00 p.m. in winters. In late June, free summer concerts begin on the pier, Wednesdays 6:00 p.m. to 8:00 p.m. The Juan de Fuca Festival with music, workshops and crafts is on Memorial Day weekend. For general tourist information see the North Olympic Peninsula Visitor & Convention Bureau website: www.olympicpeninsula.org. The Olympic Discovery Trail is accessible at both Port Angeles moorage locations.

Farmers Market: Saturdays year-round, from 10:00 a.m. to 2:00 p.m. at the corner of Front Street and Lincoln Street.

② **Port Angeles Boat Haven**. 832 Boat Haven Drive, Port Angeles, WA 98362; (360) 457-4505; pamarina@olypen.com; www.portofpa.com. Open all year, ethanol-free gasoline and diesel at the fuel dock, and high-volume fuel delivery for larger vessels. The marina has concrete docks, side-tie guest moorage, and a guest arrival float. Maximum boat length 164 feet. Services include 30, 50, and 100 amp power, restrooms, Wi-Fi, showers, waste oil disposal, pumpout. Security system with locking gates. Call ahead for after-hours arrival. Reservations are accepted. Excellent 2-lane launch ramp with ample room for tow vehicles and trailers.

Customs clearance is available from a dedicated phone on the water side of the harbor office, (360) 457-4311. Haulout on a 70-ton Travelift. Groceries and laundry are nearby.

② **Port Angeles City Pier**. Foot of North Lincoln St., Port Angeles, WA 98362; (360) 417-4550; www.cityofpa.us. Six floats, one of which is ADA accessible, are at Port Angeles City Pier. Guest overnight side-tie moorage available for boats up to 80 feet. No power, no water; first-come, first-served. A self-registration pay station is located near the docks. Maximum 10-day stay. The floats are conveniently located near shopping and near the Waterfront Trail.

Crescent Bay. Crescent Bay is a possible anchorage if conditions on the Strait of Juan de Fuca become untenable. A little protection can be found close to the western shore, but swells can still work into the bay and make for an uneasy stay. Past the east end of Crescent Bay is the Salt Creek Recreation Area. Field Correspondent Jim Norris reports this is a great spot for tide pool exploring, with a nice beach.

Pillar Point. Pillar Point has a fishing resort with launch ramp and float but is not available for transient moorage. In a westerly the area close to and east of the point is a notorious windless spot–a "hole" in sailboaters' language. A Waggoner reader wrote to tell us anchorage is good along the eastern shore.

CLALLAM BAY AND SEKIU

Clallam Bay. Clallam Bay, with Sekiu on its western shore, is somewhat protected from westerlies and has convenient anchoring depths along the shore. A serious reef, marked by a buoy at its outer end well offshore, extends from the eastern point. Leave the buoy to port when entering the bay. Three marinas offer guest moorage.

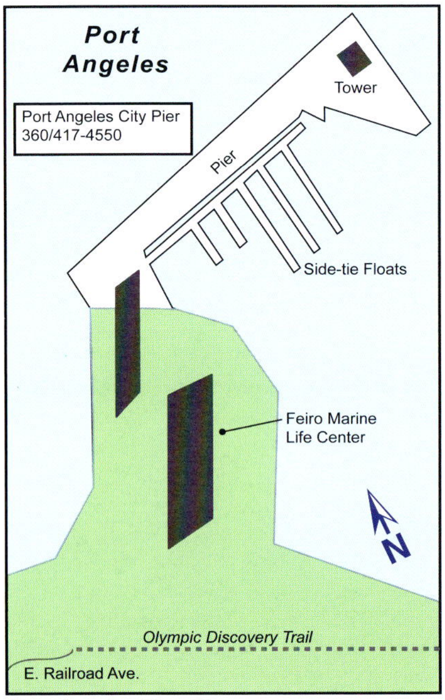

Port Angeles City Pier

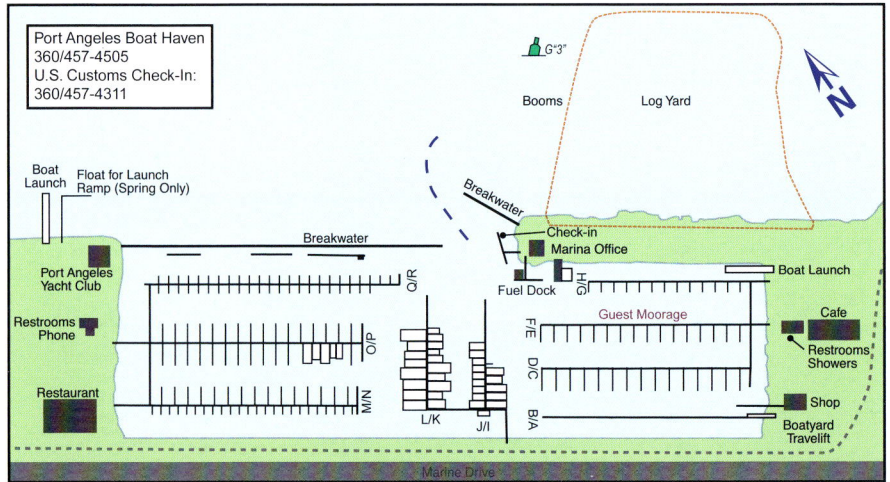

Port Angeles Boat Haven

www.WaggonerGuide.com

The Makah Museum collection houses 300-500 year old artifacts recovered from the Ozette Archeological Site.

③ **Van Riper's Resort.** P.O. Box 246, 280 Front Street, Sekiu, WA 98381; (360) 963-2334; www.vanripersresort.com. Open summers, closed winters. Guest moorage on five docks with 450 feet each. Facilities include restrooms, showers, free Wi-Fi, campground, concrete launch ramp. No power. Boat and motor rentals, charter service, ice, groceries, charts, and books. Nearby post office, restaurant and bar, and marine supplies.

③ **Mason's Olson Resort.** P.O. Box 216, 444 Front St., Sekiu, WA 98381; (360) 963-2311. www.olsons-resort.com. Open March through September. Gasoline and diesel at the fuel dock, shallow; check the tides. Side-tie guest moorage behind a breakwater; first-come, first-served; 35-foot maximum boat length. No power. Restrooms, showers, laundry; 4-lane concrete launch ramp; Wi-Fi near the office. Rustic cabins and camping available. Busy during salmon season. The Mason family owns and operates the resort.

③ **Curley's Resort.** P.O. Box 265, Sekiu, WA 98381; (360) 963-2281; (800) 542-9680; www.curleysresort.com. Open May through September, guest moorage while staying in one of the cabins. 750 feet of dock space, 30-foot maximum boat length. This is a private resort with moorage, motel rooms, and cabins for rent. Pets must remain on the boat.

NEAH BAY

The Makah Tribe town of Neah Bay is popular with sport fishermen, who trailer their boats in during the summer. It's also a good place to wait for a favorable weather window to round Cape Flattery and head down the Pacific Coast. Most boats bound to or from Barkley Sound, however, choose to stay along the Vancouver Island side of the Strait of Juan de Fuca. For cruising boats that do stop, moorage is at the Makah Marina docks, managed by Big Salmon Resort.

A long breakwater connects the mainland and Waadah Island, blocking ocean waves from getting in. Anchorage is good, sand bottom, throughout the bay. A second breakwater protects the Makah Marina. The Coast Guard station at the entrance to the bay serves the west end of the Strait of Juan de Fuca and the northern Pacific Ocean coast.

Neah Bay is not a U.S. Customs port of entry, although entrants with Nexus cards may be able to phone in for clearance. Those without Nexus must clear at a designated port of entry. Port Angeles is the nearest location.

The Makah Cultural & Research Center Museum features artifacts from the Ozette archaeological dig site. The museum is world-class—a must see. The Ozette dig unearthed a village site buried by a mudslide 500 years ago, before European contact. It is a time capsule of coastal Native life. The tools, clothing, furniture, weapons, and fishing implements are exquisitely preserved and displayed. Makah Days celebration is held in late August, all are welcome to attend.

Neah Bay's general store is well-stocked, except for spirits. Neah Bay is dry.

④ **Makah Marina**. P.O. Box 137, Neah Bay, WA 98357; (360) 645-3015; fuel sales, (360) 645-2749; www.makah.com/activities/marina; VHF 16 and 66. Open all year, guest moorage, 30 & 50 amp power, free Wi-Fi, potable water, restrooms, showers, laundry nearby, pumpout station, portapotty dump, 2-lane launch ramp with extended parking available for tow vehicles and trailers. Fuel dock with gas, diesel, and lubricants. Slips vary from 30-70 feet; side-tie for vessels up to 100 feet. Reservations are accepted April through mid-September. Shopping (on the rough and ready side) and lodging are nearby. The extraordinary Makah Museum (360) 645-2711 is within easy walking distance.

On shore, the administration building has restrooms and showers. Summertime moorage can be crowded with commercial boats and their gear.

④ **Big Salmon Resort.** P.O. Box 140, 1251 Bay View Ave., Neah Bay, WA 98357; (360) 645-2374; (866) 787-1900; www.bigsalmonresort.net. Open April 1 to September 15. Gas and diesel at fuel dock. Pumpout. Haulout to 30 tons and 2-lane concrete launch ramp with long-term parking. Guest moorage at Makah Marina. A small store carries tackle, some groceries, local charts. Motels are nearby.

If the fuel dock is closed for the season, fuel is available at the Makah Mini Mart's commercial dock just beyond the commercial fish offloading pier.

Stay Informed at WaggonerGuide.com/Updates

San Juan Islands

SAN JUAN ISLAND
Friday Harbor • Roche Harbor
Westcott Bay • Garrison Bay

LOPEZ ISLAND
Fisherman Bay • Spencer Spit • Watmough Bay

ORCAS ISLAND
Eastsound • Deer Harbor • Rosario Resort

Blakely Island • Sucia Island • Jones Island
Shaw Island • Stuart Island • James Island

Scan the Latest
San Juans
Information

tinyurl.com/WG22xCh06

Roche Harbor, San Juan Island

For many boaters, a cruise through the San Juan Islands begins with a passage out Guemes Channel from Anacortes.

The well-known **San Juan Islands** are the dream destination for thousands of boaters each year. The scenery is stunning, the fishing is good, the anchorages are plentiful, and the amenities—marine resorts, settlements, villages and towns—are many and varied. The islands contain large flocks of bald eagles. Sailing in the company of porpoises and whales is almost commonplace.

The San Juans have a feel about them that is different from most other coastal cruising areas. In the San Juans we don't just head down the coast to another bay, or out to a little clutch of islets for the night. Instead, we are cruising among the peaks of a majestic sunken mountain range, and each island peak is different from the others. We've truly left the bustle of civilization behind and found a corner of paradise.

The San Juans have so much to see and do that a first-time visitor can be overwhelmed. We have a short list of stops that we recommend. They are not the only places to experience, but nothing like them exists anywhere else. Our short list is as follows: Rosario Resort, Roche Harbor, English Camp (Garrison Bay), Stuart Island (Prevost Harbor and Reid Harbor), Sucia Island, Friday Harbor. You will make many other stops as well. But these six are highly recommended, especially for the first-time visitor, or when you have guests.

Rosario Resort is a mansion and estate built in the early 1900s by Robert Moran, a turn-of-the-20th-century pioneer ship builder. The facilities include a luxury resort hotel and marina. Roche Harbor is another century-old monument, this one built around limestone quarrying. It's now a deluxe resort and a not to be missed experience. English Camp is at Garrison Bay, a short distance from Roche Harbor. This is where the British garrison was stationed during the historic 1859–1872 Pig War. The blockhouse, formal gardens, and several buildings remain. They are now a National Historical Park, with an interpretive center. You can anchor in the bay and visit by dinghy.

Stuart Island is a gem. In both Prevost Harbor and Reid Harbor you can anchor, tie to a mooring buoy, or moor on the coveted, but space-limited, State Park docks. Whichever you do, you will be surrounded by beauty. A hike along a well-marked, up-and-down trail leads to the dirt road that runs out to Turn Point Lighthouse. Along the way are the Stuart Island one-room school, library, and museum.

Sucia Island, with its weather- and water-sculpted sandstone, its fossils and fascinating shoreline, is the definitive anchorage of the San Juans. The challenge will be choosing which of Sucia Island's five bays to stay in.

Friday Harbor is a lovely little town where you can browse the shops, or enjoy one of the many restaurants or pubs. Friday Harbor is the commercial hub of the San Juans, with more services than any other destination.

No, we've not mentioned the charming village of Eastsound on Orcas Island, or Lopez Village on Lopez Island, or the Shaw General Store at the Shaw Island ferry landing, or Spencer Spit, or a dozen other delightful places to see, although we certainly describe them in detail later in the chapter. This is the challenge with the San Juans. There are so many interesting choices.

Although summertime tourism is a major industry in the San Juan Islands, the settlements have retained a small village atmosphere. Minutes out of town, you will be on winding roads in pastoral farm country. Island people are easygoing and friendly, and many of them are highly accomplished. Movie stars and industrialist families have estates there. The late author Ernest Gann lived on San Juan Island. One famous author's book bio says simply that he lives on an island. What it doesn't say is that the island is in the San Juans. Warren Miller, producer of ski films, known and loved by snow skiers world wide, had a home in the San Juans; and television personality Oprah Winfrey had an estate on Orcas Island.

Drinking water is in short supply in the San Juan Islands. In almost every case you'll find no water for boat washing. Go to the San Juans with full water tanks, and conserve while you are there.

Personal Watercraft Restriction: Because some people were hot-dogging on their PWCs and harassing whales and other wildlife, San Juan County has banned PWC use in the San Juan Islands.

San Juan Islands National Wildlife Refuge: The San Juan Islands National Wildlife Refuge consists of 83 islands, islets, rocks and reefs. Boaters must remain 200 yards offshore from any refuge property.

San Juan Preservation Trust: This non-profit organization is instrumental in purchasing and receiving donated property in the San Juan Islands to protect and preserve land in its natural state for the benefit of wildlife, and for the enjoyment of all. Many of these properties are accessible by boat, with beach access, designated trails, and great views.

No Discharge Zone: All of the inside waters of Washington State from Puget Sound to the Canadian Border, including all of the waters of the San Juan Islands, are a No Discharge Zone (NDZ). It is illegal to discharge any (treated and untreated) black water sewage. Gray water from showers and sinks is not covered by this restriction.

Getting to the San Juan Islands. If you are approaching from the east, you'll enter the San Juans through one of four passes: Lopez Pass, Thatcher Pass, Peavine Pass, or Obstruction Pass.

At times the waters outside these passes can be turbulent, dangerously so, the result of tidal current and wind opposing each other. Make sure you have complete and accurate tide and current information. You can't go wrong with the official government publications, but our preferred tide book is Ports and Passes, available at marine supply stores or www.WaggonerGuide.com. Ports and Passes uses a tabular format, covering the area from Olympia to Southeast Alaska and is corrected for Daylight Saving Time.

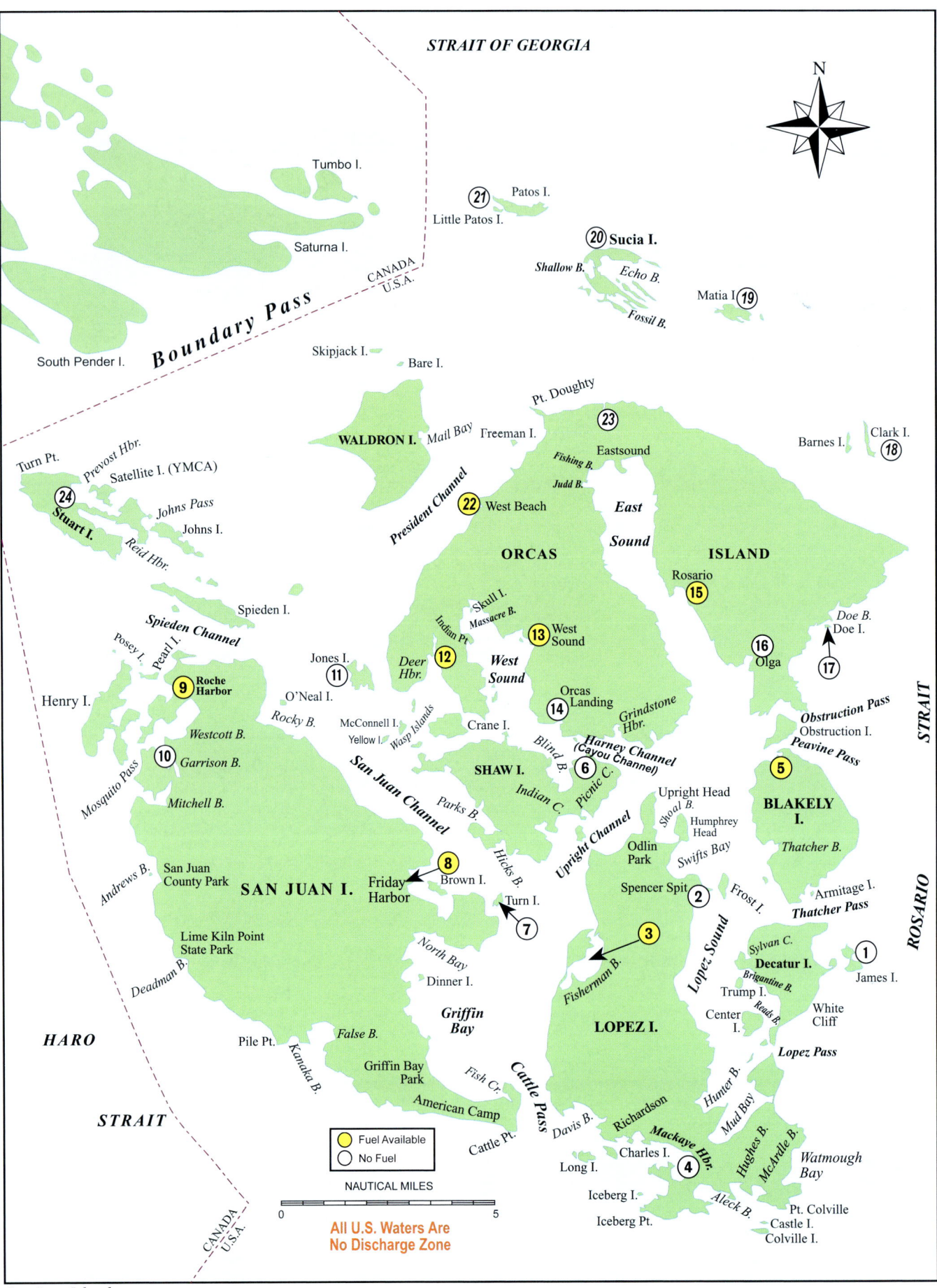

SAN JUAN ISLANDS

Reference Only – Not for Navigation

① **James Island Marine State Park**. (360) 376-2073; Open all year for day use, overnight mooring, and camping. James Island is a favorite spot, with trails to hike and wildlife to view. Visiting boats can use both sides of the 128-foot-long float located on the west side of the island. In the past, the float has been removed between October and March; the float is now available year-round. Beware that strong flood current can make docking challenging. Compost toilets located near the dock; no power or water. Strong currents and a rocky bottom make anchoring difficult in the west cove, use the float.

The east cove is exposed to wakes from passing traffic in Rosario Strait, but has 4 mooring buoys for boats 45 feet or less. Self-register and pay nightly mooring buoy fee on shore, or by phone as posted on the buoy. The park has a picnic shelter and 13 primitive campsites, nearby pit toilets. A Cascadia Marine Trail campsite is at Pocket Cove (high bank gravel beach). Excellent hiking, picnicking, scuba diving. Pack out all garbage. If at the dock, raccoons will go aboard unattended boats if food or garbage is left in the open. Best to stow food well and close the boat tight.

LOCAL KNOWLEDGE

TIDE-RIP: At the eastern entrance to Thatcher Pass, watch for tide-rips on ebbing current and southerly winds.

Thatcher Pass. Thatcher Pass runs between Blakely Island and Decatur Island, and is one of the main entrances into the San Juan Islands. Currents can run strongly. Washington State Ferries use Thatcher Pass, so keep a sharp lookout.

Decatur Island. Decatur Island is east of Lopez Island and south of Blakely Island. Decatur Island has three vacation communities and about 70 full-time residents. Reads Bay, Brigantine Bay, Sylvan Cove, and the unnamed bay between Decatur Head and Fauntleroy Point are anchoring locations around Decatur Island. All of the island's uplands, docks, and mooring buoys are private. Kimball Preserve on the southern tip of the island is the only publicly accessible area. The island's year-round and seasonal residents come and go by water taxi service or by private aircraft.

Sylvan Cove. Sylvan Cove, at the northwest corner of Decatur Island, has good holding bottom in convenient depths. The bay is truly beautiful, with New England-style buildings ashore. All the land is private, as are the mooring buoys, the dock, and float that serve homeowners on the island.

Brigantine Bay. The area between Trump Island and Decatur Island is pretty, and has anchorage in 24 to 42 feet. The dock and all the land ashore are private. Center Island has good anchorage which can be found by simply cruising around Center Island into Reads Bay until you find an area out of the prevailing wind.

Reads Bay. Reads Bay is located between Center Island and the south end of Decatur Island and includes the channel connecting to Lopez Pass. A charted cable area, shallow areas, and hazards awash make the north portion unsuitable for anchoring. The connecting channel is better for anchoring; watch for several charted shallow areas. Good holding on a mud bottom. Be prepared for water taxi and supply barge traffic transiting between Center and Decatur Islands, and Lopez Pass.

Kimball Preserve. South of Reads Bay is the Kimball Preserve area, made up of two small islands and the southern tip of Decatur Island. The southern tip of Decatur Island, the island to the southwest, and the isthmus connecting the two, are part of the San Juan Preservation Trust. The small rocky islet northwest of the isthmus is a Bureau of Land Management property, which joins the isthmus at low tide. The remains of a concrete structure are on the west side of the BLM island. The preserve is open all year, day use only, no facilities, no fires, no overnight camping, pack out all garbage. Anchor out. There is a dinghy or kayak beach landing area on the north shore of the isthmus. A half-mile trail along the south side of southern island continues across the isthmus and to the north end of the preserve property on Decatur Island. Excellent views in all directions can be found along the trail.

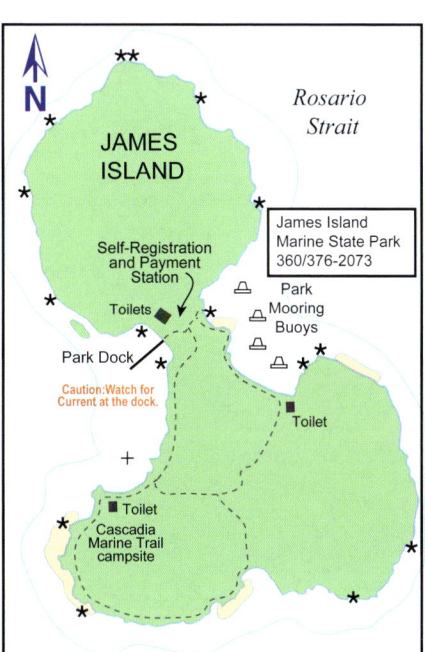

Eelgrass: located in some areas in less than 18 feet of water; anchor deeper to avoid.

Lopez Pass. Lopez Pass connects Rosario Strait to Lopez Sound. Currents can flow strongly through Lopez Pass with considerable turbulence; the area calls for careful navigation. Watch for traffic through the Pass as high-speed water taxis serving Decatur Island frequent the Pass.

Lopez Island. Lopez Island offers a variety of anchorages and moorages. On the northern end, sandy Spencer Spit is a favorite. Fisherman Bay, on the west side, has the village of Lopez, with marinas, a museum, a grocery store, and restaurants.

The southern end of Lopez Island is indented by several bays, and guarded by rocks and reefs. The geography is rugged and windblown, the result of the prevailing westerly winds from the Strait of Juan de Fuca. It's an interesting shore to explore when the wind is down.

Lopez Sound. Lopez Sound is the large body of water between Decatur Island and Lopez Island. This broad area has easy anchoring depths with few hazards. A selection of anchoring locations in Lopez Sound affords wind protection from a variety of directions. Among them are Hunter Bay and Mud Bay. Although Lopez Sound is surrounded by private homes and docks, it's very picturesque

Watch for current running perpendicular to the dock at James Island State Park.

James Island Marine State Park

SAN JUAN ISLANDS

See Area Map Page 188 - Maps Not for Navigation

Spencer Spit Marine State Park has buoys on the north and south sides of the spit.

and feels special. A variety of scenery captures the mind's eye, everything from wind swept slopes and rocky beaches, to tree-covered hillsides and open pastures. Crabbing and clamming are popular local past-times.

Mud Bay. South end of Lopez Sound. This large bay has ample room for anchoring with good holding in 12 - 14 feet over a mud bottom. Watch your depths, charted shallow areas in the bay. Good protection except in strong northeast and southeast winds. Buoys in the bay are private. Tiny Mud Bay County Park (360) 378-8420, located along the southeast side of the bay, is open all year for daytime use. No shore side signage at the park. The park beach is a popular departure point for kayakers. Clamming on the mud flats is reported to be good; crabbing good at times.

Eelgrass: located in areas near shore in less than 10 feet of water; anchor deeper to avoid.

Hunter Bay. Southwest corner of Lopez Sound. Hunter Bay is a good place to anchor, consistent depths of 15 feet over a mud bottom. The bay is surrounded by forest and protected from all but northeast winds. Located on the southeast side of the bay, just south of Crab Island, is a public launch ramp and public pier with a 45-foot float for day use, no overnight moorage. Crabbing is said to be good at times.

Eelgrass: is located in depths up to 24 feet, in four areas within about 500 feet of shore, 1) in the 3 1/2 to 4 3/4 fathom area on the southeast shore, 2) along the southwest shore, 3) in the west cove, and 4) along the northwest shore. Anchor away from shore to avoid eelgrass.

② **Spencer Spit Marine State Park.** 521 A. Bakerview Road, Lopez Island, WA 98261; (360) 468-2251; www.parks.wa.gov. On the northeastern shore of Lopez Island. Open all year, day use and overnight mooring and camping. The park has 6 mooring buoys on the north side and 2 mooring buoys on the south side of the spit; self-register and pay nightly mooring buoy fee on shore, or by phone as posted on the buoy. The buoys, for boats 45 feet and under, typically fill up quickly during the summer, but anchoring is good. Restrooms are located upland, no showers. Restrooms are closed from the end of October to March. Water is available at the bottom of the trail to the uplands.

Spencer Spit is a popular park. A saltwater lagoon, fed from the north side, is in the middle of the spit. If you are on the north side, you must walk around the tip of the spit and back down the south side to get to the upland areas of the park. The park has standard and primitive campsites. To reserve a campsite call (888) 226-7688. Rabbits abound, and interpretive signs aid exploration. Spencer Spit is a Cascadia Marine Trail campsite. Although the pass between Spencer Spit and Frost Island is narrow, it is deep and safe.

Swifts Bay. Swifts Bay, behind Flower Island and Leo Reef, is shallow, but a usable anchorage in settled weather. Anchor on a sand bottom in 10 to 20 feet.

Shoal Bay. Shoal Bay indents the northern tip of Lopez Island between Humphrey Head and Upright Head offering good, fairly protected anchorage. We think the best spot is behind the breakwater and off the private marina along the east shore. Numerous crab pot floats must be avoided in picking an anchorage.

Odlin San Juan Co. Park. (360) 378-8420; parks@sanjuanco.com. sanjuanco.com/495/Lopez-Island. West side of Lopez Island. Located between Flat Point and Upright Head. Open all year. Good bottom for anchoring, but exposed to northwest winds. Approximately five mooring buoys are available, a nightly use fee is payable at the park office, located up the road past the baseball field. Small float for boats 30 feet and under with a 2-hour limit, or take your small craft ashore. Campsites, restrooms, beach area and sea wall, baseball diamond, picnic sites, cooking shelter, fire pits. Boat ramp and trailer parking. Watch for current that runs strong through the bay, especially on a flood tide.

Upright Channel Park. A 20-acre San Juan County park with about 600 feet of sandy beach. Northwest side of Lopez Island 1/4 mile east of Flat Point. Day use only.

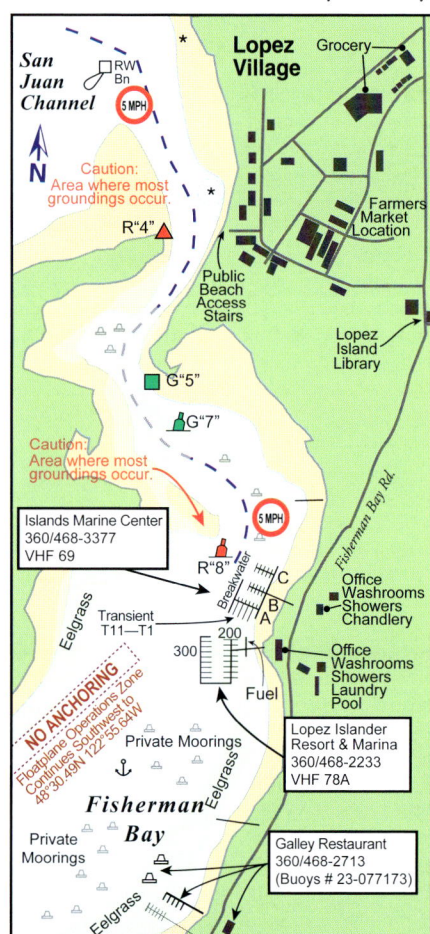

Spencer Spit State Park

Fisherman Bay, Lopez Island

See Area Map Page 188 - Maps Not for Navigation

SAN JUAN ISLANDS

Restrooms, 4 picnic sites. Private homes and beaches are to the west, please respect private property.

LOCAL KNOWLEDGE

SHOAL ENTRY: The entrance to Fisherman Bay should not be attempted by deep draft boats at less than half tide.

FLOATPLANE OPERATIONS ZONE: Remain clear of the floatplane operations zone on the northwest side of Fisherman Bay.

③ **Fisherman Bay.** Fisherman Bay extends southward about 1.5 miles into the western shore of Lopez Island. The entrance is winding and shallow, with a 5 mph speed limit; the entry day beacon, however, incorrectly states 10 mph. About 200 yards off the entrance, a non-lateral sector light marks the center of the entrance channel; you can pass on either side, but stay close to remain in the deepest water. Caution: watch for the charted rock awash approaching red Daybeacon 4. Leave this beacon to starboard, then follow the well-marked channel into the bay. Cutting any of the corners risks grounding.

The northernmost marina in Fisherman Bay is Islands Marine Center. The docks next door belong to the Lopez Islander Resort.

When entering or departing, resist the urge to cut inside any navigation marks. Departing, it's tempting to cut inside red nun Buoy 8, and there you are, aground. Remember: Red, Right, Returning, also means Red, *Left, Departing.*

Anchorage in Fisherman Bay is shallow, with a mud bottom. No anchoring in the designated 3,000 by 150 foot floatplane operations zone along the northwest side of the bay, from 48°30.78N 122°55.10W on the northeast end to 48°30.49N 122°55.64W on the southwest end.

Lopez Village is a little less than a mile away; the shoulder along the road was recently widened. You'll find excellent dining, well-stocked grocery stores, galleries, all the usual services, and the famous Holly B's Bakery. Another local favorite is Vita's Wildly Delicious, offering excellent deli foods and world-class wines. On your walk into the village, don't miss the lovely restored mansion that houses the library.

The Lopez Historical Museum in town is open noon to 4:00 p.m., Wednesday to Sunday, May through September, with exhibits inside and on the field outside. A farmers market takes up an entire field at the village, 10:00 a.m. to 2:00 p.m. on Saturdays, May through September.

Keep one hand free to wave to passing vehicles as you walk or cycle the roads. It's the custom on Lopez Island. Everybody waves.

A community funded fireworks display over Fisherman Bay is held on the 4th of July. Festivities include a barbeque and a country-themed parade.

Pumpout Service: The Port of Lopez' mobile pumpout service boat, named Blackwater, operates in and around Fisherman Bay; service began in August 2022; contact the vessel on VHF Ch 78 or call (360) 504-7982.

③ **Islands Marine Center.** 2793 Fisherman Bay Rd., Lopez, WA 98261; (360) 468-3377; imc@rockisland.com; www.islandsmarinecenter.com. Monitors VHF 69. Open all year, Monday through Saturday. Guest moorage along 1000 feet of dock space, 30 amp power, Wi-Fi, ATM, restrooms, showers, garbage, recycling, pumpout. Call or inquire online.

This is a well-run, full-service marina, with haulout to 25 tons, launch ramp, repairs, fishing supplies, and a fully stocked chandlery. One view guest room available for overnight lodging. Good depth at all docks.

Provisioning is fun at Lopez Village.

ISLANDS MARINE CENTER
YOUR HOME PORT IN THE SAN JUANS

IMC — ISLANDS MARINE CENTER, INC.

100 Slip Modern Marina with Water, ATM Power, Ice, Pumpout, High Speed Internet

Marine Parts • Napa Auto Supply

Fishing Tackle & Bait

Fully Stocked Chandlery

Pursuit, Ocean Sport & Alweld

Volvo, Mercruiser, Yamaha

Full Sales & Service

Factory Trained Service Department

Haulouts to 25 Tons

Restaurants & Shopping Nearby

P.O. Box 88 ❖ Fisherman Bay ❖ Lopez Island, WA 98261
Phone (360)468-3377 ❖ Fax (360)468-2283 ❖ VHF 69
E-mail imc@rockisland.com ❖ www.islandsmarinecenter.com
Call or Radio for Reservations

SAN JUAN ISLANDS

See Area Map Page 188 - Maps Not for Navigation

Islander Lopez Resort on Fisherman Bay has guest moorage, fuel, swimming pool, and much more.

③ **Lopez Islander Resort & Marina.** P.O. Box 459, 2864 Fisherman Bay Rd., Lopez, WA 98261; (360) 468-2233; (800) 736-3434; desk@lopezfun.com; www.lopezfun.com. Monitors VHF 78A. Open all year, gasoline & diesel at the fuel dock. Guest moorage in 64 slips plus 600-foot dock. Reservations recommended on busy weekends, call to reserve a slip. Services include 30 & 50 amp power, restrooms and showers, laundry, swimming pool (heated June through September), year-round Jacuzzi, free Wi-Fi in the lodge. Nearby bicycle and kayak rentals.

The resort has a good restaurant with an outdoor deck and sports lounge, a workout facility, a spa, massage, camping, and water-view lodging by reservation. Live music in the Tiki Bar most weekends June through September. The docks are solid, and the management is attentive. Shuttle service available for a fee.

Galley Restaurant. 3365 Fisherman Bay Rd., Lopez, WA 98261; (360) 468-2713; About one-half mile south of the Lopez Islander, the Galley has two mooring buoys for restaurant patrons marked with the restaurant name; tie-up dinghies at the restaurant's dock; northeast corner near the ramp. At press time the restaurant was still under renovation and closed to the public. Construction and permitting is ongoing, and the restaurant is not expected to be open for 2023.

④ **Mackaye Harbor.** Mackaye Harbor and Barlow Bay at the south end of Lopez Island are a good overnight anchorage for boats planning an early morning crossing of the Strait of Juan de Fuca. Swells from a westerly wind can make their way into the harbor.

A county dock/boat launch is located at the northeast end of Mackaye Harbor. The Southend General Store & Restaurant (360) 468-2315 is located a half mile away. The restaurant is open for lunch and dinner, call ahead for hours. The well-stocked grocery includes a collection of local foods, art and jewelry. Docks and mooring buoys in Barlow Bay are private. Dinghy or kayak ashore at Mackaye Harbor.

Dangerous Wreck: A sunken boat is on the east side of the entry to Barlow Bay, approximately at the 2 fathoms, 5 feet sounding. The wreck is visible at low tide. Mackaye Harbor is the site of a fish boat marina, and during the summer months a large fish boat fleet can be found in the harbor.

Eelgrass: located in some areas in less than 12 feet of water; anchor deeper to avoid.

Iceberg Island. An undeveloped state park in Outer Harbor. Open all year, day use only. Anchor out. No facilities, no fires, no overnight camping. Pack out all garbage. Do not disturb wildlife or alter the surroundings.

Aleck Bay. Aleck Bay is big and easy to get into. Beaches are private. Anchor close to the head of the bay in 30 to 36 feet. Open to easterlies. Strong westerlies can make their way into the bay due to the low terrain.

Hughes Bay. Hughes Bay is well protected from winds except southerlies. High surrounding terrain provides protection from the northeast and northwest. A few homes along the shore with private mooring buoys. No public buoys. Good anchoring depths ranging in the teens to 30 feet.

McArdle Bay. McArdle Bay provides good anchorage in 20 to 30 feet, but is completely exposed to southerly winds coming off the Strait of Juan de Fuca. Beautiful homes are on the hills above the bay, with lovely beaches below. No private or public buoys in the bay. Just outside, the chart shows a rock in the passage between Blind Island and Lopez Island. The rock is actually a reef.

Castle Island. Castle Island is part of the San Juan Islands National Wildlife Refuge. Boats must stay 200 yards from shore to protect wildlife; no shore access.

Watmough Bay. A beautiful high sheer rock wall is on the north side of Watmough Bay. The chart shows the bottom as rocky, but we have found excellent holding in blue mud in 12 to 18 feet about halfway in. Three San Juan County public mooring buoys are for boats 45 feet and under. No charge, limit 72-hour stay. The bay is sheltered from southerly and westerly winds, but we've

Lopez Islander Resort
On Scenic & Protected Fisherman Bay

Excellent Guest Moorage
Island Restaurant & Lounge
Pool, Jacuzzi & Boater's Showers

- Weekly live music
- Gas, diesel, power & water
- Adjacent pumpout facilities
- Laundry facilities
- On island golf
- Bicycle & Kayak rentals
- Workout facilities
- Village grocery & liquor store
- Water view hotel lodging

Lopez Islander Resort
Ch. 78A
(360) 468-2233
www.LopezFun.com

found waves work their way into the bay from freighters transiting Rosario Strait. Correspondent, Deane Hislop, warns that if current in the bay is holding the boat in a north/south direction, a wake will be on the beam.

A pretty trail leads back through the woods from the head of the bay. A second, steep trail leads to the top of Chadwick Hill from the northwest side of the beach. The head of the bay and the trails are part of a San Juan County Land Bank preserve, made possible by donations from private citizens and Bureau of Land Management.

Eelgrass: located in northeast entrance areas of the bay with 12 to 44 feet of water; anchor shallower or deeper to avoid.

LOCAL KNOWLEDGE

TIDE-RIP: Nasty tide-rips can form off the eastern entrance to Peavine and Obstruction Passes when the wind is blowing from the south and the tide is ebbing.

Obstruction Pass and Peavine Pass. Obstruction Pass runs between Obstruction Island and Orcas Island. Peavine Pass runs between Obstruction Island and Blakely Island. Both passes connect the inner San Juan Islands to Rosario Strait. Currents run to 6.5 knots, and can make these passes challenging. Peavine Pass is preferred, but be alert for occasional ferry traffic. The ferries usually use Thatcher Pass. Peavine Pass is their storm route, although sometimes it is used in fair weather as well.

Stop at Blakely Island Marina's short-stay fuel dock and visit the store for freshly-made donuts.

Blakely Island. Blakely Island is east of Lopez Island and Shaw Island. Both Blakely Island and tiny Armitage Island off the southeast corner of Blakely Island are privately owned, with no shore access. Anchorage is possible in Thatcher Bay, and, with care, behind Armitage Island. The Blakely Island Store & Marina, at the north end of Blakely Island, has guest moorage. Blakely Island is private, including the roads. Please confine your stays to the marina property.

⑤ **Blakely Island Store & Marina.** #1 Marina Dr., Blakely Island, WA 98222; (360) 375-6121; info@blakelyislandmarina.com; www.blakelyislandgeneralstore.com; Monitors VHF 66A. Moorage in 9 guest slips and in permanent slips as available; slips can accommodate boats to 70 feet; phone or make reservations online. Off-season guest moorage available; use the payment station located by the store. Fuel dock has gasoline and diesel, with a kiosk for self-serve credit card purchases from 6 a.m. to 8 p.m. during the summer months; no water. Moorage facilities include excellent concrete docks, 30 amp power, Wi-Fi, water, restrooms, showers, laundry and covered picnic area.

The store is open Labor Day weekend through September. The store cafe serves lunch daily during the summer months. Fresh donuts, made on site, are available in the morning. Beer on tap and wine by the glass. They also carry a good selection of books and some gift items.

The channel leading to the boat basin is shallow, (5 feet of depth on zero tide) and may restrict deep draft vessels at the bottom of a very low tide. Other than those conditions, you should have plenty of water. If in doubt, call the marina office for guidance.

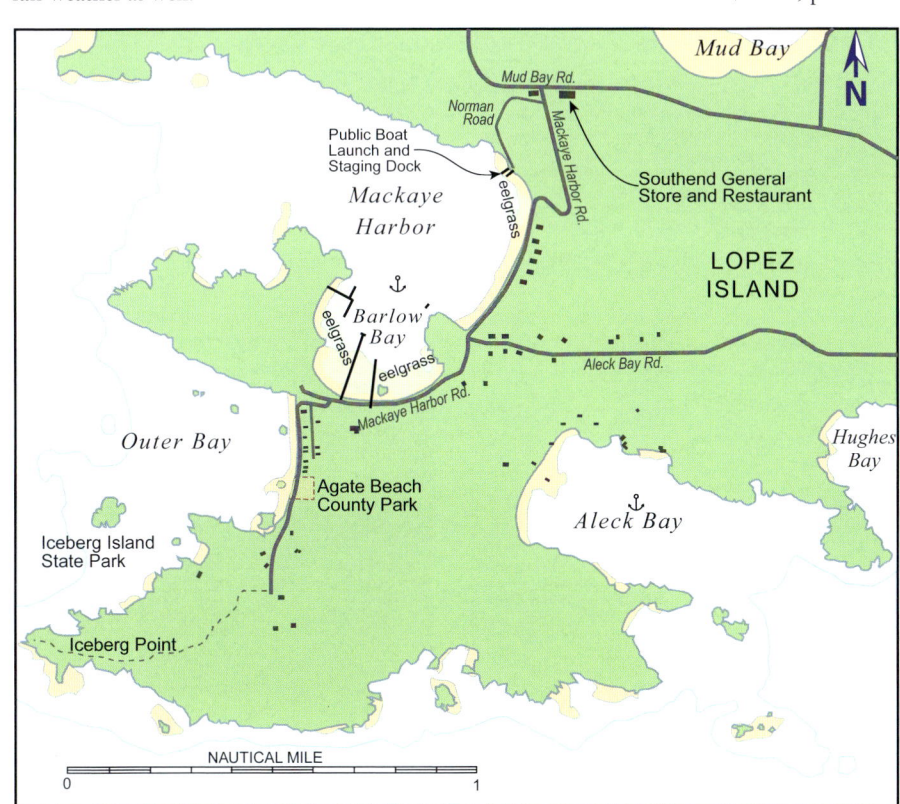

Mackaye Harbor, Outer Bay, Iceberg Point, and Aleck Bay

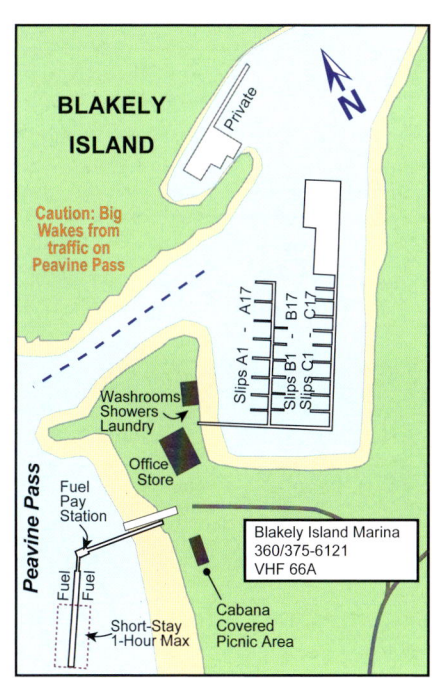

Blakely Island Marina

SAN JUAN ISLANDS

Shaw Island. The marina is adjacent to the Shaw Island ferry terminal. Resident boats occupy most of the dock space. Maximum length for short term guest moorage is 25 feet, call ahead at the Shaw General Store. It's better to anchor in Blind Bay and take the dinghy over. Tie up in a place that doesn't block a permanent boat. Wakes make their way into the moorage, either from the ferries or from boat traffic in the channel. Consider this when tying up to the dock.

Safety Note: Do not under any circumstances run the dinghy under the bow of a ferry tied up at the landing.

LOCAL KNOWLEDGE

Dangerous Rocks: Charted rocks obstruct the waters west of Blind Island. While it's possible to get through safely, our advice is do not pass west of Blind Island.

Blind Bay. Blind Bay, on the north side of Shaw Island, has good anchorage throughout the center portion. A few private mooring buoys are located in the southeast area of the bay. All of the Shaw Island uplands are private property; there is no access to the uplands or the road that circles the bay. Blind Island is a marine state park.

A privately maintained white daymark, located east of Blind Island, marks a rock that lies between Blind Island and the Shaw Island shore. Enter Blind Bay midway between that mark and Blind Island. The water shoals abruptly as you enter, but there's no danger unless you are too close to the island. Several rocks are just under the surface on the west side of Blind Island. Transit should not be attempted on the west side without local knowledge, there are rocks and reefs on the Shaw Island side. Crabbing can be good throughout the bay.

Blind Island Marine State Park. Blind Island is a minimally developed state park and Cascadia Marine Trail campsite, with 4 mooring buoys on its south side for boats 45 feet and under. Self-register and pay nightly mooring buoy fee on shore at Blind Island, or by phone as posted on the buoy. Toilets are on the island. Pack out all garbage.

⑥ **Shaw General Store.** P.O. Box 455, Shaw Island, WA 98286; (360) 468-2288; www.shawgeneralstore.com. Open year-round. Very limited short-term day-use guest moorage, maximum 25 feet, call ahead. Pumpout at the end of the main dock. Restrooms are adjacent to the ferry dock. Groceries, beer and wine, ice, gift items, local organic produce, and bins with bulk foods. The back area of the store is a coffee shop, which in earlier times, served as the island's post office. The Shaw General Store business, begun in 1898, is one of the oldest businesses in the San Juan Islands.

You'll enjoy anchoring in Blind Bay and taking the dinghy over to meet Steve and Terri Mason, who have run the store for many years; their daughter now operates the business. The store building was constructed in 1924. It's as charming as can be, with its straight-grain original wood floors, old shelving and displays, and posters and signs from days gone by. The store is a local hangout for Shaw Island residents.

Parks Bay. An excellent anchorage in a southern blow; Parks Bay is a fine anchorage, but you can't go ashore. Except for three privately-owned parcels at the north end and a single parcel at the south end, the land surrounding Parks Bay is owned by the University of Washington as a biological preserve, and is off limits to visitors. Stub pilings are at the closed end, but there is plenty of anchoring room, mud bottom, throughout the bay. Parks Bay Island, at the mouth of the bay, is no longer a state park. Unpredictable cell coverage.

Hicks Bay. Hicks Bay has good anchorage, although it is exposed to southerlies. When entering, take care to avoid a reef extending from the southern shore.

Indian Cove. Indian Cove, a popular anchorage area has a big open feeling. Exposed to the south but well protected to the north. Watch for drying rocks between Canoe Island and Shaw Island, and a shoal 200 yards west of the southern point of Canoe Island. The Shaw Island County Park, with launch ramp, has an excellent beach. Anchor in 15 to 40 feet with good holding.

Eelgrass: located in some areas in less than 24 feet of water; anchor deeper to avoid.

The County Park provides access to **Graham Preserve** and Reef Net Point County Park. Graham Preserve is a 99-acre San Juan Preservation Trust property with 1.2 miles of forested trails. The trailhead begins across the road from the entrance to Shaw Island County Park. After a short distance, the trail branches with a trail to the north leading to the Shaw Community Center, and a trail to

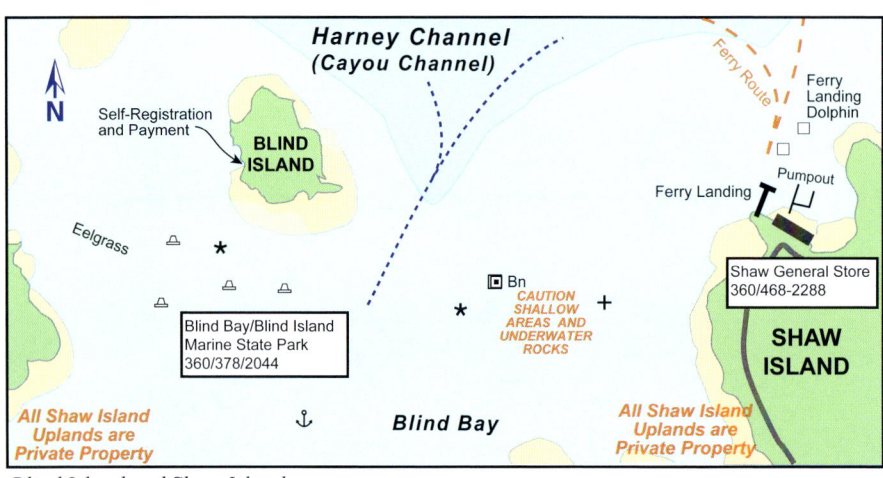

Blind Island and Shaw Island

Shaw General Store next to the Shaw Island ferry

Griffin Bay beaches provide access to American Camp trails.

American Camp trails lead to Cattle Point Lighthouse.

the south leading to a trailhead opposite the entrance to Reef Net Point County Park.

The half mile loop trail at Reef Net Point Park takes you along the shore of Reef Net Bay and past the remains of an historic log cabin. From Reef Net Point County Park, walk about 1/3 mile to the east on Squaw Bay Road to return to Shaw Island County Park.

Picnic Cove. Pretty little Picnic Cove is east of Indian Cove. All of Picnic Cove is in a larger charted cable crossing area and is not suitable for anchoring. Using a mid-channel entrance is best to avoid reefs on each side of the cove.

SAN JUAN ISLAND

San Juan Island is the second largest of the San Juan Islands, and has the largest population. Friday Harbor, the only incorporated town, is the seat of county government.

Cattle Pass. Cattle Pass is the local name for the narrow channel between the south end of San Juan Island and Lopez Island. It is the only southern entrance to the San Juan Islands, and connects with San Juan Channel. Whale Rocks lie just south of Cattle Pass. It's easy to get close to them if you're not careful. When we enter Cattle Pass from the south, we try to favor gong Buoy 3, marking Salmon Bank, to port, and make a course for the middle of the entrance. This avoids Whale Rocks.

After we clear Cattle Pass northbound, we've felt a definite tendency to favor the Lopez Island shore. Maybe it's just us. In any case, this course leads dangerously close to *Shark Reef*, about one-half mile north of Cattle Pass. We recommend sagging west a little toward Griffin Bay until past Shark Reef.

Tidal currents can run strongly through Cattle Pass, and the waters can be turbulent with rips and eddies. Watch out for a big ebb current flowing out of San Juan Channel against a fresh westerly wind in the Strait of Juan de Fuca. We've seen this ebb current as much as a mile outside Cattle Pass. Against a fresh westerly it will create high, steep seas, the kind you definitely want to avoid. Current predictions are shown under San Juan Channel in the tide & current books. In Cattle Pass, it's possible to run behind Goose Island and avoid foul current, but local knowledge is called for.

Fish Creek. Fish Creek is a tiny indentation near the southern tip of San Juan Island, lined with the docks and mooring buoys of the homes along its shores. Fish Creek has no public facilities, and swinging room is very restricted between the homeowners' floats.

American Camp. The 1,223 acre American Camp National Park occupies most of the southern tip of San Juan Island. Along the northeast shore of American Camp, just west of Fish Creek, are several beaches. A mud bottom shelf, 1 to 3 fathoms in depth, extends for nearly a mile along the shore, but is mostly covered in eelgrass. Protected from all except north through easterly winds, the anchorage is quiet and private. Watch for charted North Pacific Rock and a rocky shoal about 1/4 mile northwest.

When the U.S. border was in dispute with Great Britain (Canada), the two nations agreed to a peaceful joint occupation of San Juan Island until the boundary dispute could be resolved. In 1859, Capt. George E. Pickett (of American Civil War fame) landed on the southern end of the Island to establish American Camp. Pickett directed that clapboard buildings be shipped over from Fort Bellingham, including a hospital building, barracks, officers' quarters, and a laundress building. Conical tents shipped from Fort Steilacoom supplemented the buildings. Later, Colonel Henry Robert ordered the Corps of Engineers to start work on earthen fortifications on the ridgetop east of the camp. The American military presence on San Juan Island lasted for 14 years in less than comfortable conditions, while living conditions at English Camp on the north end of the Island were luxurious by comparison.

All that remains of American Camp today is the officers' quarters and the house-working quarters of the laundress. The beautiful grounds, with stunning views, are open to the public year-round at no charge. The American Camp Visitor Center is open Memorial Day to Labor Day.

Griffin Bay. You can anchor in several places in Griffin Bay. A stretch of beach inshore from Halftide Rocks is Griffin Bay Park, a public campground. American Camp, maintained by the U.S. Park Service as an historical monument to the 1859-72 Pig War, is a short walk from the campground. The Pig War resulted in setting the boundary between the U.S. and Canada in Haro Strait, keeping the San Juan Islands in the U.S.

Griffin Bay Park. North of American Camp at 48°28.566' N/123°00.603'W. Open all year. Pit toilets, rustic campsites, and a picnic area. Two inland campsites for boaters arriving by human- or wind-powered watercraft. Watch for shallow water and pilings. DNR property with 325 feet of beach front.

Griffin Bay, American Camp

SAN JUAN ISLANDS

See Area Map Page 188 - Maps Not for Navigation

Watch for current in the channel south of Turn Island and Turn Rock. Turn Island State Park lies just north of Turn Rock.

North Bay on the east side of San Juan Island has room for many boats, and the broad gravel beach at Jackson Park provides shore access.

North Bay Anchorage. North Bay at the northern end of Griffin Bay, offers anchorage for many boats, with protection from northerly and westerly winds. Good anchorage on a mud bottom in 20 to 30 feet of water, located off the beach northeast of Little Island. The anchorage is exposed to southerlies and easterlies. The long beautiful driftwood beach, northeast of Little Island, is Jackson Beach Park. A free public boat launch is located on the lagoon side of the beach. This anchorage offers aviation enthusiasts the opportunity to watch airplanes land and depart from Friday Harbor Airport.

⑦ **Turn Island State Park.** (360) 376-2073; In San Juan Channel, at the southeast entrance to Friday Harbor. Turn Island is open all year for day use and overnight mooring. Boat access only; *land only on the west or southwest beach.* Pets are not permitted on shore. Toilet and campsites. No fires. Pack out all garbage. Hiking, fishing, crabbing.

Turn Island is a beautiful park, completely wooded, with many trails. It's a popular stop for kayaks and beachable boats. Along the south side of the island the trees (madrona, cedar, hemlock, cypress) are bent and twisted, with much evidence of blowdown. The wind must howl though here in the winter.

Three mooring buoys, for boats 45 feet and under, normally available along the west side at the mouth of the pass, separating Turn Island from San Juan Island. Shoals quickly south of the southern most buoy. Currents can be quite strong in this pass, but these buoys are located safely out of the current. If you anchor to seaward of them, you will be in the current. We recommend the buoys. Self-register and pay nightly mooring buoy fee on shore, or by phone as posted on the buoy.

Correspondents James and Jennifer Hamilton have anchored off the southwest tip of Turn Island in about 10 feet of depth at zero tide. Although the current ran noticeably, the anchor held perfectly. Other boats, anchored farther out and closer to the eastern mouth of the pass, appeared to have less current.

Turn Island is part of the San Juan Islands National Wildlife Refuge. Do not disturb animals in their natural habitat.

WHALE WISE - WASHINGTON STATE

Southern Resident Orca Whales.

Washington State has enacted regulations governing whale watching and required safe distances from Southern Resident Orcas in Washington waters. These regulations apply to all vessels:

- It is illegal for vessels to get within 300 yards of a Southern Resident Orca.
- It is illegal for vessels to be within 400 yards of the path (behind and in front) of a Southern Resident Orca.
- There is a 7-knot speed limit within one-half nautical mile distance from a Southern Resident Orca.
- If a Southern Resident Orca comes within 300 yards of a vessel, the operator is required to disengage engine transmission(s) until the whale is a safe distance away.

Protecting Southern Resident Orcas is a high priority in Washington State. The physical and social differences between Southern Resident Orcas and Transient Orcas may be hard for most recreational boaters to identify, so practically speaking, it is best to stay well clear of all Orcas.

Marine Mammals & All Whales

A variety of whale species frequent Washington waters; and while these relatively new Washington State laws apply to Southern Resident Orcas, existing Federal and State regulations apply to other marine mammals in Washington waters. Give dolphins, porpoises, sea lions, seals, and other marine mammals the space they need. Coming too close can cause them stress and to abandon their young.

- Stay 100 yards from non-killer whales, dolphins, porpoises, and other marine mammals, and 200 yards if they are resting or with young.
- Turn off echo / depth sounders (voluntary) when not in use.
- Vessels are asked to avoid the Voluntary No-Go Zone on the West Side of San Juan Island, which extends ¼-mile offshore from Mitchell Bay to Cattle Point, and a ½-mile offshore at Lime Kiln Lighthouse.

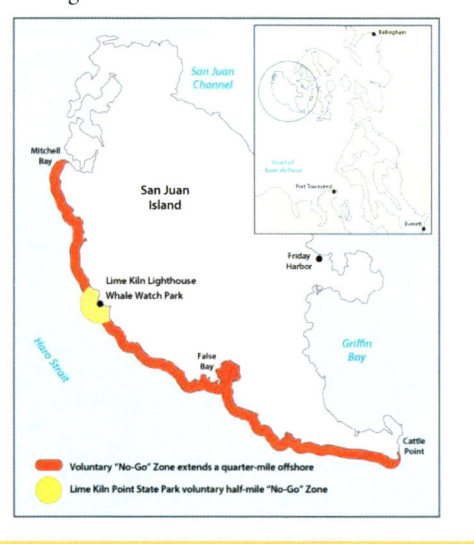

Friday Harbor is very popular with boaters and tourists.

Port of Friday Harbor has room for many guest boats with full amenities.

⑧ **Friday Harbor.** www.fridayharbor.org. Friday Harbor is the government and commercial center of the San Juan Islands. It is a U.S. Customs port of entry, and the terminal for ferries from Anacortes that also serve Sidney, B.C. The town swells with tourists during the summer months and has many boutiques, shops, galleries, restaurants and pubs to serve them. King's Market, a well stocked grocery store, is on the main street (Spring Street) two blocks up from the waterfront. Kings will drive you back to the marina with a sizable purchase.

Puget Sound Express (360-385-5288) has daily passenger only ferry service between Port Townsend and Friday Harbor; the boat, *Glacier Spirit,* operates early May to late September. Kenmore Air flies in from Lake Union and Boeing Field in Seattle, with a shuttle to Sea-Tac Airport. Friday Harbor Seaplanes flies in from their location on south Lake Washington in Renton. Check their websites for seasonal schedules.

Moor at the Port of Friday Harbor marina or anchor out. Anchorage is good in the cove north of the marina and to the west of Brown (Friday) Island. Do not anchor in the cable-pipeline area between San Juan Island and Brown Island. Our friend John Mifflin cautions that the water close to Brown Island contains several sunken wrecks, "requiring diver assistance when raising anchor."

Enter Friday Harbor around either end of Brown Island. An unlighted daybeacon marks the end of a drying reef off the southwest corner of Brown Island. Brown Island is privately owned, and has its own dock and floats.

Take care to avoid interfering with the ferries and the large number of floatplanes taking off and landing in the harbor. The fuel dock is located between the Port marina and the ferry dock. The floats just south of the ferry dock are owned by the condominium apartments ashore. Jensen's Marina, in the southeast end of the harbor, can handle repairs. Jensen's is owned by the Port of Friday Harbor and managed by Marine Services Group; 35-ton Travelift. No transient moorage. The Port marina office can provide a list of repair people. Kings Marine carries marine supplies, fishing gear and apparel.

Bus Transportation: San Juan Transit, next to the ferry landing, has scheduled service and tours all around San Juan Island; www.sanjuantransit.com; (360) 378-8887.

Taxi: Classic Cab, (360) 378-7519; Bob's Taxi, (360) 378-6777; Friday Harbor Taxi, (360) 298-4434; Rhodes Trips Taxi & Tours, (360) 298-6975; San Juan Taxi, (360) 378-8294.

Mopeds: Susie's Mopeds (800) 532-0087 (cars, mopeds, ScootCoupes).

Bicycles: Meat Machine Cycles (360) 370-5673.

Trolley: Friday Harbor Jolly Trolley Transportation (360) 298-8873. Offers guided rides to island attractions with hop on/hop off all-day passes.

Summer Concerts: Live music Saturdays at 2:00 p.m., July and August in the small park next to the marina.

Farmers Market: San Juan Farmers Market, Saturdays 10:00 a.m. to 1:00 p.m. mid-April through mid-October in the Brickhouse Plaza, 150 Nichols St., about 5 minutes from the marina.

THINGS TO DO

- **The Whale Museum**. In Friday Harbor. Learn about orca whales that frequent the San Juan Islands.
- **Lime Kiln Point** State Park. Watch for whales that often cruise by this park.
- **Tastings**. San Juan Vineyards has a tasting room near Friday Harbor. San Juan Island

Best Selection of Fishing Tackle & Marine Supplies in the San Juans!

Marinco Shorepower
Jabsco, Shurflo & Rule Pumps
Mustang, Onyx & NRS PFD's
SMI Crab & Shrimp Pots
NRS & Sealline Kayak Accessories
NOAA, CHS, & Maptech Charts
Nikon, Leupold & Orion Binoculars
GCI, MSR, Thermorest Camping Gear
Fishing Licenses & Discover Passes
Grocery, Deli, Wine & Spirits
Free Dock Delivery

Friday Harbor, San Juan Island, WA

KINGS MARINE
360-378-4593
110 Spring Street
1 block from Ferry above King's Market

NRS • NIKON • MSR • GCI • KERSHAW

Friday Harbor has a wide variety of excellent restaurants, pubs, and cafes.

Friday Harbor's Memorial Park marks the center of the downtown waterfront.

Distillery, with a variety of apple-based spirits, has a tasting room within walking distance of Roche Harbor.

- **San Juan Islands Sculpture Park.** More than 100 superb sculptures in iron, bronze, stone and wood displayed in a 20-acre park near Roche Harbor.
- **Pelindaba Lavender Farms.** Walk through fields of purple lavender and shop for all things lavender.
- **Saturday Farmers Market.** Fresh vegetables, flowers, plants, honey and more at the Brickworks in Friday Harbor.
- **English Camp.** See the gardens, hike the trails, learn the history in Garrison Bay.
- **American Camp.** Located on the southern tip of San Juan Island, American soldiers lived here during the joint U.S./British occupation of the island in the mid-1800s.
- **Roche Harbor Mausoleum.** Walk to this beautiful setting steeped in mythology.
- **Krystal Acres Alpaca Farm.** See alpacas and learn what they can be used for.
- **Susie's Mopeds.** Rent mopeds or electric bicycles. Office in Friday Harbor 360-378-5244.
- **The "Retirement of the Colors"** ceremony at Roche Harbor at sunset is unforgettable.
- **Friday Harbor Seafood.** Fresh shrimp, oysters, crab, or fish for sale on the main dock.
- **Shuttle Bus Tour.** Regular schedule in the summer. Ride the San Juan Transit bus (360) 378-8887, getting on and off at locations such as the Lavender Farm, Lime Kiln Point, and English Camp. Narrated bus tours available.

⑧ **Port of Friday Harbor.** P.O. Box 889, 204 Front Street, Friday Harbor, WA 98250; (360) 378-2688; tamih@portfridayharbor.org; www.portfridayharbor.org. Monitors VHF 66A. Certified Clean Marina. Open all year, gasoline and diesel at the fuel dock. Side-tie guest moorage along 1500 feet of dock, plus moorage on the guest dock and in unoccupied slips. Call or go online to make reservations. Reservations are accepted May 15 through September 15. Only 30% of the guest moorage space is available for reservations; 70% is first-come, first-served. If reservations are full, space may be available on the day you arrive.

The slips handle boats up to 60 feet. Longer boats (to 200 feet) side-tie along the breakwaters (see marina diagram). Breakwater

Photo by Matt Pranger

Stay, play and enjoy the whole day. Gather with friends so the fun never ends...

Where Friday Begins

PORT OF FRIDAY HARBOR

360-378-2688 * VHF 66A
www.portfridayharbor.org

This is the place for delicious ice cream in Friday Harbor.

Discover more cafes and shops along the back streets of Friday Harbor.

A has no power or water. Marina services include 120-volt 30 & 50 amp power, 240-volt 50 amp power, and three 240-volt 100 amp power. Guest docks G and H have been upgraded, including ELCI-protected shore power pedestals. On the south end of G dock, along walkway D, is a summer guest check-in station. A dinghy dock is located next to the main pier for boaters anchored out.

Free excellent Wi-Fi. Restrooms and showers. New restrooms are planned for the future to include individual rooms, with toilet, sink, and shower operated by debit or credit card. Excellent laundry open daily; tokens available in the office and laundry room.

A garbage compactor and recycling bins located behind the main office building. Key required for used oil drop. The Pumpty Dumpty pumpout service is available seasonally to come to your boat for a small charge, or you can use the self-serve pumpout carts. A stationary pumpout is located on a float between C and M docks. A large seasonal "Eco Barge" in which to empty vessel waste tanks is available on the outer "Breakwater A" for public use. When full, it is towed to the main pumpout station and then towed back into position on the breakwater. At low tides, deep draft vessels should not venture shoreward of the pumpout.

An ADA-compliant ramp connects the wharf above with the floats and slips below. A floating restroom is on the long float leading to guest moorage, dock G. A covered activity barge is available for groups or rendezvous. Ten or more vessels earn a group moorage discount, not applicable during the peak season months of July and August. Individual boats staying four nights get a fifth night free from September 15 to June 15. Check the Port's website for seasonal specials and events.

If you do not have reservations, call on VHF 66A for a moorage assignment, but wait until you are within sight of the marina before calling. It's recommended to call on VHF rather than by cell phone for quicker service. The office also appreciates a radio call when you vacate the slip. A dinghy float and day moorage are available. Nearby haulout and repairs.

This is one of the busiest marinas in the Northwest, and the pressure on staff and facilities is enormous. To their credit, they maintain the docks, showers and restrooms quite well.

Customs: U.S. Customs clearance is on Breakwater B. Tie up in the designated customs area and check in at the direct-phone kiosk on the dock. During the summer months the kiosk may be manned by a CBP agent. Occasionally customs officials will have you walk to the U.S. Customs office. The office has moved to the corner of Spring Street and First Street, about 3 blocks from the marina.

⑧ **Port of Friday Harbor Fuel Pier.** 10 Front Street, Port of Friday Harbor, Friday Harbor, WA 98250; (360) 378-3114; www.portfridayharbor.org. Between the Port of Friday Harbor marina and the ferry dock. Open 7 days a week, all year. Ethanol-free gasoline, diesel, oil, lubricants, propane, and ice.

Rocky Bay. Rocky Bay, close inshore from O'Neal Island, is a good anchorage and fairly well protected. Take care to avoid a drying shoal and a covered rock.

Lonesome Cove Resort. (360) 378-4477; located along the north shore of San Juan Island on Spieden Channel. Guest moorage for those staying in one of the on-shore accommodations. Five adorable cabins, Boat House, and Eagles Nest apartment; beautiful grounds and lovely views of Spieden Channel and Spieden Island. Maximum boat length 28 feet.

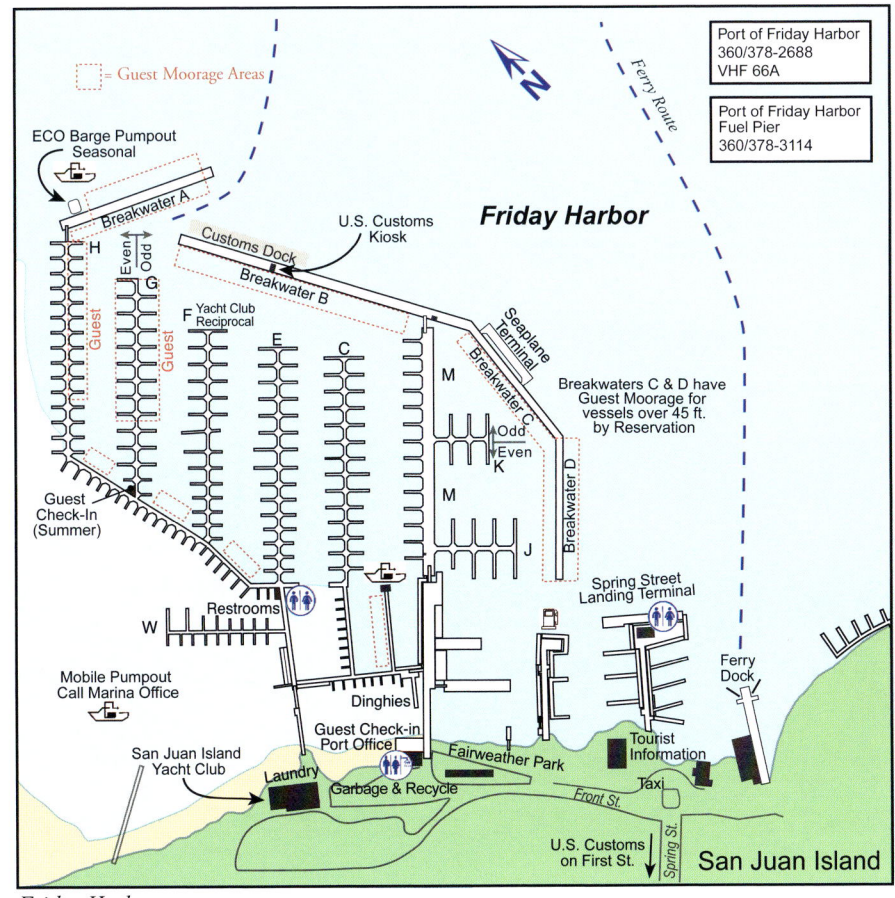

Friday Harbor

SAN JUAN ISLANDS

See Area Map Page 188 - Maps Not for Navigation

You will find nice moorage and plenty of anchoring space at Roche Harbor.

Open Bay beach is part of Henry Island Preserve.

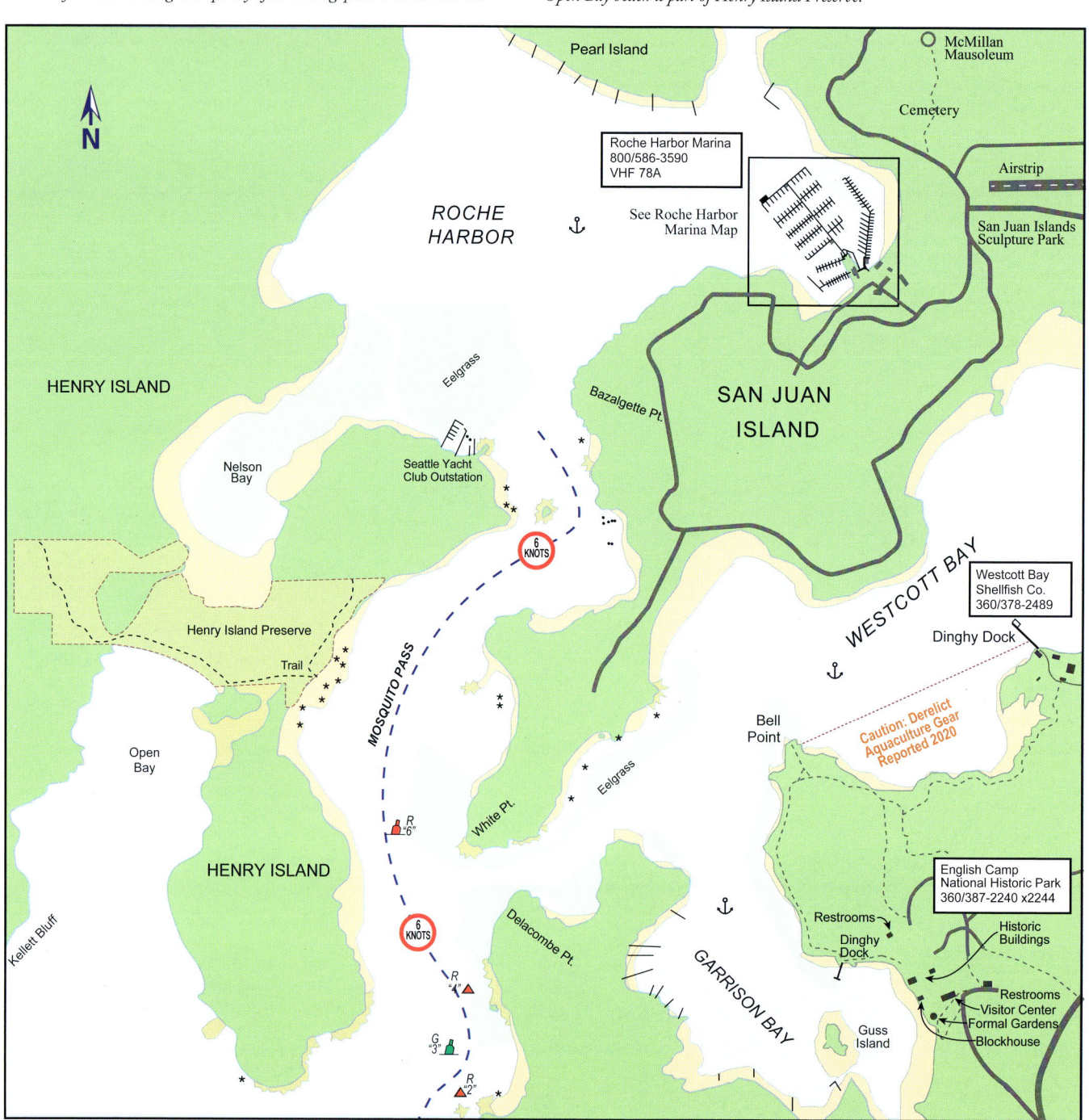

Roche Harbor, Westcott Bay, Garrison Bay, & Mosquito Pass

⑨ **Roche Harbor.** Roche Harbor, (pronounced Rohsh Harbor) on the northwest corner of San Juan Island, is popular, attractive, and has a number of interesting anchorages and moorages. From the north (Spieden Channel), enter Roche Harbor on the west side of Pearl Island. The passage east of Pearl Island is shallow, and is in line with dangerous rocks outside. From the south (Haro Strait), entry is through Mosquito Pass.

Roche Harbor is one of the busiest U.S. Customs ports of entry in the country for recreational boats. During the prime summer season, the floating customs office and the harbormaster's office are located on G-dock. The customs landing area on G-dock is noted with signs on the pilings. Moor between the signs only when clearing customs. On busy days, boats tend to create an informal line on the water, waiting for room on the customs dock. Be patient. It can be a challenge to maintain a place in line among boats at anchor, especially when a good breeze kicks up. Note that the seaplane dock is near the customs dock, and arriving seaplanes will need to cut through the line of boats.

One summer we watched as one of the area's large wooden sailing schooners pulled up to the dock to clear customs. The space was much too small to lie alongside. The captain commanded her crew of high school students to drop the anchor at the right time, as she turned stern-to the dock.

FLAG ETIQUETTE

The National Flag. Vessels should fly the National Flag in which they are registered. As a general rule, the ship's National Flag should be 1 inch for each foot of the vessel's overall length; be sure this flag is not too small in proportion to your vessel. The National Flag is properly flown from a staff pole at the stern of a power boat, and from the leech of the most aftersail of a sailboat. The Flag should be flown from 0800 to sunset, and at half-staff on Memorial Day until 12:00.

Courtesy Flag. As a courtesy, vessels should fly the National Flag of a foreign nation when cruising in their waters. Proper placement is on the mast of a power boat, or on the end of the starboard spreader for sailboats. For sailboats with more than one mast, the Courtesy Flag is flown from the starboard spreader of the forward mast. A power vessel without a mast, may fly the Courtesy Flag from the bow in lieu of a burgee; or preferably, on the starboard antenna strong enough to support it. For sizing purposes, use one-half inch for each foot of the vessel's overall length. The Courtesy Flag is raised after clearing customs.

Burgee. A burgee is a small flag with a symbol indicating membership in a yacht club or boat club. The burgee is flown from the bow on power boats and usually at the end of the lowest starboard spreader on sailboats. Only one burgee should be flown at a time, indicating the group or activity in which you are participating. Burgees can be sized to one-half inch for each foot of the vessel's overall length.

Quarantine Flag. A yellow flag signals that a vessel has not yet cleared customs and is awaiting inspection. Boaters should fly the yellow Quarantine Flag from the mast just prior to reaching a customs dock or assigned slip, and then remove the flag after clearing customs.

ROCHE HARBOR
MARINE SERVICES
PHILBROOK'S USA

- Marine Outboards
- Gas & Diesel Engines, Outdrives
- Electrical, Marine Heating Systems
- Watermakers, Marine Head Systems
- Yacht Care & Watch Programs
- Electronics
- Haul Out & Boat Storage
- Marine Parts Chandlery

360-378-6510
info@rocheharbormarine.com
www.rocheharbormarine.com

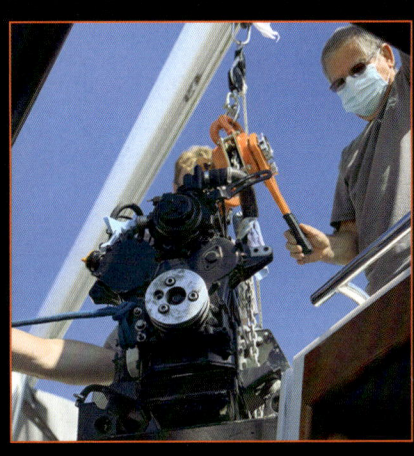

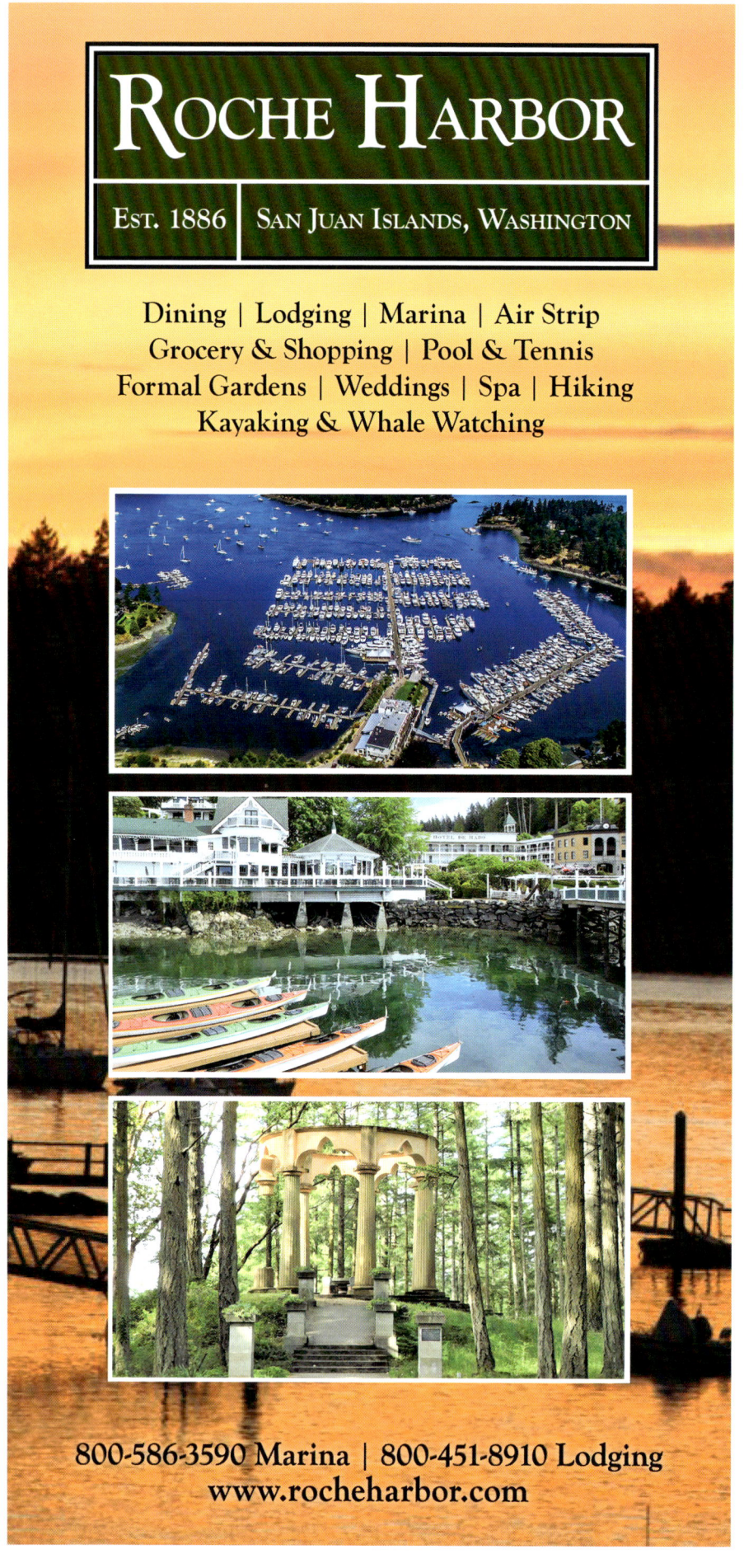

ROCHE HARBOR

Est. 1886 | San Juan Islands, Washington

Dining | Lodging | Marina | Air Strip
Grocery & Shopping | Pool & Tennis
Formal Gardens | Weddings | Spa | Hiking
Kayaking & Whale Watching

800-586-3590 Marina | 800-451-8910 Lodging
www.rocheharbor.com

With an audience watching, she backed down and tied off, stern-to. She placed a 133-foot vessel into less than 20 feet of dock space, impressive.

Note: During fall, winter, and spring, the customs and harbor offices are floated inshore to the main float, just west of the fuel dock. Approach as though you are going to the fuel dock. The customs dock is to starboard, marked with signs, just below the ramp. Once tied to the dock, all crew must stay on the boat until cleared. The U.S. Customs agents are particular about procedures here.

Many boats anchor in Roche Harbor, but we've heard of anchors dragging in strong winds. Check your set and use ample scope. Anchorage is also possible in Open Bay on Henry Island, although it is exposed to southerly winds.

Bus Transportation: San Juan Transit has scheduled service to Friday Harbor and all around San Juan Island. The pick-up area is on the road across from the Roche Harbor Market. Call (360) 378-8887; www.sanjuantransit.com.

Dogs: A very nice dog park is located at the top of the hill across the road from the village of homes and south of the sculpture park.

LOCAL KNOWLEDGE

ROCKS: The east entrance to Roche Harbor on the east side of Pearl Island is shallow with boat-eating rocks lurking below water 100 to 200 feet off the northeast corner of Pearl Island. Use caution when entering through the east entrance and remain mid-channel.

⑨ **Roche Harbor Marina**. P.O. Box 4001, Roche Harbor, WA 98250; (800) 586-3590; (360) 378-2155; marina@rocheharbor.com; www.rocheharbor.com. Monitors VHF 78A. Open all year, up to 250 guest slips, including moorage for boats to 150 feet. Make reservations online via Dockwa. The marina may have slips available on a first-come, first-serve basis depending on the time of year. Last-minute holiday moorage may mean Med-tying, stern-to on the cross docks. The dock crew provides plenty of help.

Ethanol-free gasoline and diesel at the fuel dock, open 9:00 a.m. to 6:00 p.m. Services include 30, 50, and some 100 amp power (ELCI-protected power on some docks), restrooms, showers, laundry, portapotty dump, propane, and free Wi-Fi (best reception is in the hotel lobby). Pumpout is at the north end of the fuel dock, or call for the "Phecal Freak," for a courtesy pumpout at your slip. Their motto: "We take crap from anyone." Tips are appreciated. The sister ship PT106 has been added to the fleet for pumpout service.

The moorage fee includes water, power, pumpout, trash disposal, and use of the pool and resort facilities. Excellent management.

SAN JUAN ISLANDS

When we visited at the end of a busy day at the end of summer, we found all the facilities, including the showers, to be clean and in good condition.

This is one of the most popular spots in the islands, and in our opinion is a must-see destination. The historic Hotel de Haro, the heated swimming pool, formal gardens, tennis courts, Afterglow Spa, well-stocked grocery store, gift shops, and excellent restaurant and lounge are something apart from the usual tourist fare. An informal café also is available. Try the Roche Harbor donuts at the café, made fresh each morning.

Be sure to take a walk up to the Afterglow Vista Mausoleum. You've never seen anything like it. Another good walk is up the small mountain behind the resort, past the limestone quarries, to a lookout. The trail is easy and well-maintained, and the view is excellent. The entire loop took us approximately a half-hour. If we had stopped to smell the flowers it would have taken an hour. The hotel lobby has complimentary walking tour maps. You can also purchase a pamphlet detailing the remarkable history of Roche Harbor. See the guest registry on display, and the pictures on the wall showing the history of Roche Harbor.

The San Juan Islands Sculpture Park is on the edge of the Roche Harbor property, across the road from the airstrip. The park is a display of outdoor sculpture—approximately 100 pieces —set in a large grassy field and along several trails through the woods. This description completely understates how impressive the display is. We spent an hour in the park and should have spent three more hours. It's magnificent.

Development of home sites on the hillside up from the hotel has been completed. Great effort was made to design the new construction in keeping with the classic century-old style of the existing buildings. Many of the units are available for overnight or longer stays. Contact Roche Harbor Lodging at www.rocheharbor.com. The Afterglow Spa offers massage and other treatments for the crew. Advance reservations recommended.

Located just under a mile west of the Resort at 12 Anderson Lane, is San Juan Distillery (360-472-1532). Open for tastings on Saturdays from 1:00 p.m. to 4:00 p.m. Their specialties include gins, liqueurs, flavored brandies and small batch ciders.

A lovely bell concert rings out from the church at 9:00 a.m., noon, and late afternoon. At sundown each evening during the summer season the marina conducts a formal retirement of the colors. The Roche Harbor flag is lowered, followed by the British flag to "God Save the King," and the Canadian flag to "O Canada." Then the cannon fires—BOOM!—and the U.S. flag is lowered to "Taps."

Dinghy Docks: Dinghy docks are at the bottom of the ramp to the main wharf, or to port just past the fuel dock.

Bus transportation: San Juan Transit has scheduled service all around San Juan Island, with regular stops at Roche Harbor. Guests can take the shuttle from the ferry landing in Friday Harbor to Roche Harbor; www.sanjuantransit.com; (360) 378-8887.

Mopeds: Susie's Mopeds is near the airstrip; www.susiesmopeds.com; (360) 378-6262.

Posey Island Marine State Park. www.parks.wa.gov. North of Roche Harbor. The less than 1 acre island is available for day-use. Anchor out and row ashore, or explore by dinghy or kayak from Roche Harbor. The two campsites are part of the Cascadia Marine Trail. Camping reservations are required for both campsites, which are for the exclusive use of boaters arriving by human- or wind-powered watercraft. One composting toilet, no other facilities. Water surrounding the island is shallow. Great sunset views on the west side.

Mosquito Pass. Mosquito Pass connects Roche Harbor to Haro Strait, and provides access to Westcott Bay and Garrison Bay. The flood current sets north in Mosquito Pass and the ebb sets south, out of Roche Harbor. Currents can be strong at times. The channel is narrow but well-marked. A 7 MPH speed limit is enforced in Mosquito Pass.

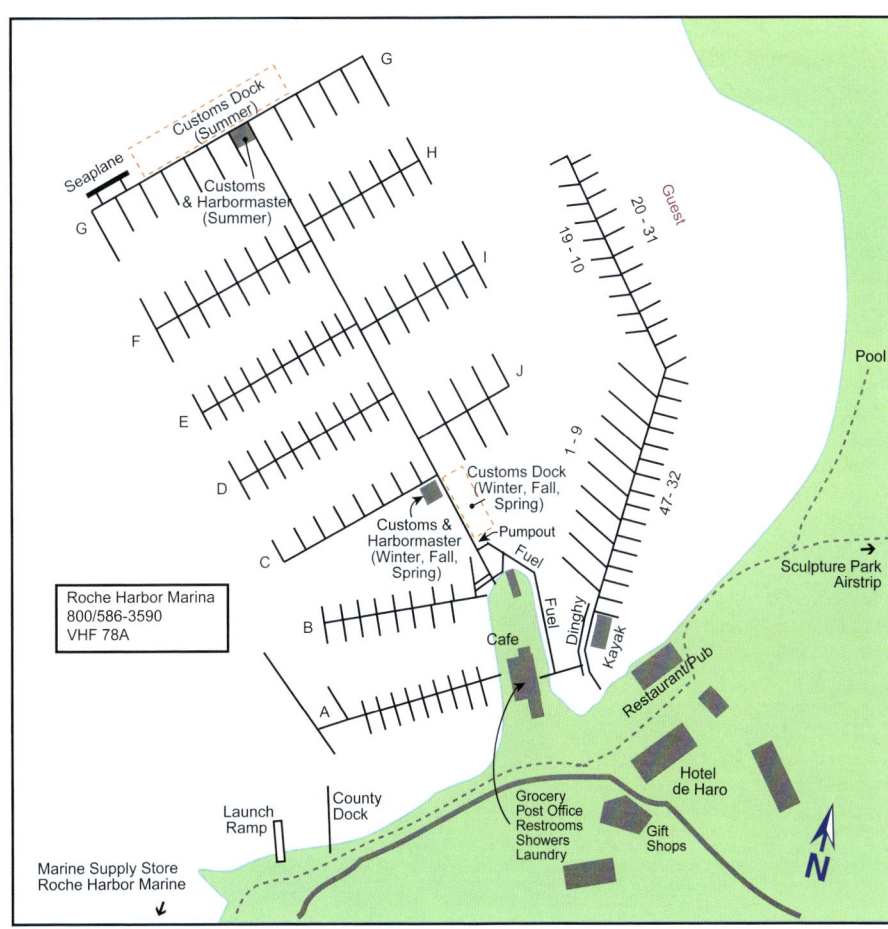

Roche Harbor Resort offers many amenities and attractions, spend at least 2 or 3 days to enjoy it all.

Roche Harbor Marina

SAN JUAN ISLANDS

See Area Map Page 188 - Maps Not for Navigation

Enjoy a meal or snack at Westcott Bay Shellfish Co.; use their dinghy dock or hike the trail from English Camp.

Westcott Bay. Westcott Bay is a large bay with good anchorage for many boats. Depths are consistently shallow throughout but adequate. Westcott is a quiet, scenic anchorage alternative to the often crowded Garrison Bay. Nearby English Camp National Historic Park, Westcott Bay Shellfish Co. (open to the public for sales), and Roche Harbor are all a dinghy ride away. Hiking trails connect English Camp Park with Westcott Bay Shellfish Co. The public beach near Bell Point reportedly has excellent clamming. Crabbing in the bay good at times.

LOCAL KNOWLEDGE

ANCHORING HAZARD: At minus tides, a field of abandoned oyster farm buoys and gear from a previous oyster farm in Westcott Bay appear in the area south of a line between Bell Point and the Westcott Bay Shellfish pier.

Westcott Bay Shellfish Co. (360-378-2489). Located on the southeast shore of Westcott Bay, open six days a week (closed on Tuesdays) during the summer months from 11:00 a.m. to 5:00 p.m., Memorial Day weekend through Labor Day; open Saturdays during the off season. Reservations are recommended during the peak season. Retail shellfish sales. As time permits, staff will show you how to shuck your oysters. Local bakery bread, cheeses, and charcuterie are available for purchase from their deli to enjoy with your hand-shucked shellfish along with beer, wine, sodas or water. Picnic tables overlooking the bay complete this unique experience. Anchor in the bay; boaters are welcome to tie dinghies (bow-tie only) to the Shellfish Company's working docks to go ashore and make purchases. Barbequed oysters are available on select days. During the 1970's, Westcott Bay oysters were known in oyster bars around the world. This family-run aquaculture farm continues the legacy of providing quality oysters as well as clams and mussels.

⑩ **Garrison Bay.** Garrison Bay, the site of English Camp, is a popular and excellent anchorage, with room for many boats.

⑩ **English Camp National Historical Park.** P.O. Box 429, 4668 Cattle Point Road, Friday Harbor, WA 98250; (360) 387-2240 ext. 2244; www.nps.gov. The grounds are open year-round until dusk. The Visitor Center, located in the old barracks, is open seasonally from 9:00 a.m. to 5:00 p.m. Anchor in the bay and dinghy to the park dock. British troops were garrisoned here during the 1859-72 Pig War, and the U.S. Park Service has restored the buildings and grounds as a historic site. You can tour the grounds, some of the buildings, and the cemetery, where several people from that era are buried. Rangers are on duty to provide information, and a film tells the history. It's a good stop for families with children. Restrooms, no other facilities. A steep trail leads to the top of 650-foot-high Young Hill, for marvelous views.

Mitchell Bay. A shoal extends from the south shore almost to the middle of the entry. A rock is at the outer end of the shoal. Leave this rock to starboard when entering. Large scale Chart 18433 shows the entrance clearly.

Snug Harbor Resort. 1997 Mitchell Bay Road, Friday Harbor, WA 98250; (360) 378-4762; sneakaway@snugresort.com; www.snugresort.com. Monitors VHF 66A. Snug Harbor is open all year. Moorage is for those staying in the resort's accommodations. No pets. Maximum boat length 60 feet. Depth at zero tide is 9 feet. Services include 30 amp power, Wi-Fi, restrooms, showers, garbage drop, recycling, barbecues, fire pits. Reservations recommended. The on-site convenience store has ice and limited groceries, gifts, propane, fishing and boating supplies. Mitchell Bay Coffee has free Wi-Fi, espresso, fresh pastries, waffles and soup. Canoes and kayaks available for guest use free of charge. Beautiful cabin accommodations.

Eelgrass: located in areas in 2 to 26 feet of water; anchor shallower or deeper to avoid.

Lime Kiln Point. Lime Kiln Point is a favorite place to watch for orcas, called "killer whales," that often cruise within a few yards of shore. Anchorage offshore from this park would be very difficult and is not recommended. A small interpretive center with information about orca whales is in the park. Best visited by taking the San Juan Transit shuttle bus from Roche Harbor or Friday Harbor.

San Juan County Park. 4289 West Side Road N., Friday Harbor, WA 98250; (360) 378-2992; www.sanjuanco.com. Open all year. Facilities include launch ramp and restrooms. No power, no showers. A popular park for kayak campers who can pull up on the beach.

Henry Island. A Seattle Yacht Club outstation (no reciprocals) is in Nelson Bay. Nelson Bay is shallow, so use your depth sounder and tide table before anchoring.

Henry Island Preserve. The Henry Island isthmus and some of the surrounding forest is part of the San Juan Preservation Trust. The isthmus forms the crossbar of the "H" connecting Little Henry Island and Big Henry Island. Public access to a one-mile hiking trail is available by dinghy and kayak on the beach at **Open Bay** and the beach along Mosquito Pass (see *Roche Harbor, Westcott Bay, Garrison Bay, & Mosquito Pass* map in this chapter). For more information go to sjpt.org. All property outside of the Preserve is private.

Unnamed Island #40. On the southwest side of San Juan Island, approximately 1 mile northwest of Pile Point. Open all year, day use only, no facilities. Anchor out at this undeveloped DNR (Dept. of Natural Resources) property. No fires or overnight camping. Pack out all garbage. Do not disturb wildlife or alter the surroundings.

Unnamed Island #38. On the southwest side of San Juan Island, near the center of Kanaka Bay. Open all year, day use only, no facilities. Anchor out at this undeveloped DNR property. No fires or overnight camping. Pack out garbage. Do not disturb wildlife or alter the surroundings.

LOCAL KNOWLEDGE

DANGEROUS REEFS: TowBoatUS reports the Wasp Islands are the number-one area for groundings in the San Juan Islands.

Wasp Islands. The Wasp Islands on the east side of San Juan Channel are a rock and reef-strewn area requiring careful navigation.

Yellow Island, a wildlife preserve, can be accessed by dinghy or kayak; land on the southeast beach below Dodd Cabin.

Jones Island Marine State Park is a wonderful family destination with beaches, hiking, camping, and wildlife.

The underwater hazards are charted but not all of them are marked, and the unwary can come to grief. Wasp Passage, however, is free of hazards, and the skipper who stays in the channel will have no problems.

All the major Wasp Islands are privately owned except Yellow Island, which is owned by The Nature Conservancy.

Yellow Island. (206) 343-4344; (206) 971-4337 Caretaker www.washingtonnature.org/yellowisland. Open 10:00 a.m. to 4:00 p.m. daily. Land dinghies on the southeast beach, below the wooden Dodd cabin. No landing permitted on the north side due to the sensitive ecosystem and wildlife. The east spit is closed in July and August for seal pupping when posted. No restroom facilities. No pets or food ashore. Temporary anchorage in the area between Yellow Island and McConnell Island; the bottom is rocky with a thin layer of gravel and sand. Visitors are to remain on the trail at all times. Interpretive signs were recently added for the self-guided tour. Groups of 6 or more need permission to land, contact the caretaker.

Eleven acre Yellow Island is owned by The Nature Conservancy and administered as a wildlife preserve. The Dodd cabin was built by Lew and Elizabeth Dodd between 1945 and 1947 with logs floated over from their Orcas Island property and windows from their chicken coop. Other materials consisted of scavenged driftwood from Yellow Island and pieces from decommissioned boats. The cabin remains virtually unchanged, and now serves as the caretaker's house for the island.

Northwest McConnell Rock. Northwest of McConnell Island. Part of the San Juan Islands National Wildlife Refuge. Boats must stay 200 yards from shore; no shore access.

⑪ **Jones Island Marine State Park.** (360) 376-2073; Open all year, day use and overnight mooring and camping. The cove at the north end of Jones Island is a good anchorage that is exposed to northerlies. Boats anchoring near the beach run sternties ashore, leaving swinging room for boats anchored in the middle. Currents can swirl through the bay, so leave ample room when you anchor.

Four mooring buoys, for boats 45 feet and under, are in the north bay. A seasonal 160-foot-long mooring float connects to a wharf that leads to shore. A portion of the float is reserved for dinghies and the Park Ranger's boat. The float is removed between October and March. Self-register and pay mooring buoy fee at the head of the dock. Composting toilet facilities are ashore. A well provides drinking water, but may run dry in late summer. Use the water sparingly.

Three mooring buoys are in the small bay on the south side of the island. Self-register and pay mooring buoy fee on shore, or by phone as posted on the buoy. No dock for shore access, kayak or dinghy ashore. In the middle of this bay, watch for a rock that lies awash at zero tide. The rock is shown on the charts, but the symbol is easy to overlook.

A lovely beach is on the east side of Jones Island.

Choose your anchorage based on which side of the island provides the best protection from the wind. We've had a pleasant night in the south anchorage when the wind was blowing from the north, while cruisers anchored in the north bay reported a difficult night.

The south bay is a Cascadia Marine Trail site, with 24 campsites and several camp shelters; toilet facilities at the campsite. Look for the fruit trees of a long-ago orchard, deer often go there. South bay is a popular kayak destination, with excellent views.

This is a wonderful park, popular for families with children. An easy trail connects the north and south moorages, with a 1.2-mile south loop trail branching off through forest and along rock headlands over the water. If you look carefully along this trail, you'll see low patches of prickly pear cactus growing along the way. At the north moorage especially, you probably will meet tame deer. If you dine at a picnic table they may try to join you. During the summer, mooring buoys and float space can be hard to get.

Caution: Raccoons will go aboard unattended boats at the dock if food is left in the open. Stow food away, and close the boat tightly. Raccoons are smart and can get into just about anything.

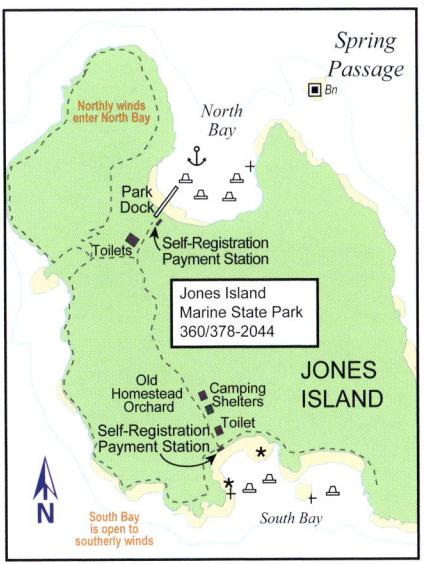

Jones Island Marine State Park

SAN JUAN ISLANDS

Orcas Island. Orcas Island is the largest island in the San Juans, deeply indented by Deer Harbor, West Sound and East Sound. Various locations around the island offer services ranging from floatplane flights, to groceries, to luxurious spa experiences, to boat repairs. The island hosts several festivals and has a seasonal Saturday farmers market in Eastsound. See www.orcasislandchamber.com/orcas-island-events for more information.

Getting Around: Car rental delivery service is available through "Orcas Island Shuttle" (360-376-RIDE), offering a variety of interesting vehicles. We spotted a 2-seater Miata with the company logo; cars can be delivered anywhere on the Island. For taxi service, call (360) 376-TAXI. San Juan Transit has shuttle bus service around the island on Fridays, Saturdays, and Sundays.

⑫ **Deer Harbor.** Deer Harbor is a quiet, protected bay on the west end of Orcas Island that is home to two marinas. Deer Harbor Marina is the first marina entering the bay from the south with guest moorage space, guest services, and outstations for several yacht clubs. At the north end of the bay is Cayou Quay Marina with permanent moorage only and no transient services. The entire bay north of Fawn Island has good anchorage. A charted Cable Area surrounds Fawn Island and extends westward to the shore of Orcas Island. Correspondent Roger Kutz reports an uncharted derelict vessel submerged in 45 feet of water at 48°37.136' N /123°00.401'W in Deer Harbor; anchors have been caught on this submerged vessel.

⑫ **Deer Harbor Marina.** P.O. Box 344, 5164 Deer Harbor Road, Deer Harbor, WA 98243; (360) 376-3037; mbroman@deerharbormarina.com; www.deerharbormarina.com. Monitors VHF 78A. Certified Clean Marina. Open all year, reservations accepted online through Dockwa during the summer months. Off season nightly moorage is first-come, first-served. Hail by radio for a slip assignment. Facilities include ethanol-free gasoline and diesel at the fuel dock. Guest moorage for vessels up to 120 feet; 30 & some 50 amp power, water, free Wi-Fi, with fast internet at all slips. Restrooms and showers, pumpout, laundry, and floating dock with BBQ for parties and rendezvous. Air service by Kenmore Air.

The docks are excellent, and the restrooms and showers are clean and spacious. A small store on the wharf offers groceries, beer, wine, espresso, Lopez Island Ice Cream cones, and has an ATM. A small cafe in the store offers breakfast items, grilled lunch items, and snacks during store hours. A gift shop on the dock has books and beach toys, open morning hours, during July and August. Kayaks for rent from an operator on site; guided kayak tours available. Whale watching, boat charters, and fishing charters available. Car rentals to explore the island are available through Orcas Island Rental Car (360-376-7433). We have driven to Turtleback Mountain for a hike, with an impressive view of the area.

A beautiful sand beach next to the wharf will entertain the little ones. At the north end of the beach is a small, lovely park. Both are within steps of Deer Harbor Marina and the adjacent accommodations. Marina guests have access to the resort's swimming pool. Matthew's Smokehouse (360-376-1040) at Deer Harbor Inn, a ten-minute walk north, serves BBQ dinners. A gravel pathway runs parallel with the country road most of the way to the Inn; it's a pleasant half-mile hike. The entire area has an easy and relaxed "vacation" feeling. The Island Pie, located across from the marina, has indoor and outdoor dining on the deck, offering great pizza, beer, cider and wine. Try the seasonal squash pizza, topped with feta cheese and drizzled over with a balsamic reduction; it's delicious.

Cell Phones: Cell phone service is spotty at the marina. A free courtesy phone is available in the laundry room.

A swimming pool, dining options, and beach toys for kids make Deer Harbor Marina a fun place.

LOCAL KNOWLEDGE

SPEED LIMIT: A 7-MPH zone marked by white cylindrical buoys extends from just west of Pole Pass eastward to Bell Island.

Pole Pass. Boats transiting between Harney Channel (Cayou Channel) and Deer Harbor usually go through Pole Pass, a narrow notch separating Crane Island from Orcas Island. Rocks obstruct the edges and approaches, and currents can run swiftly

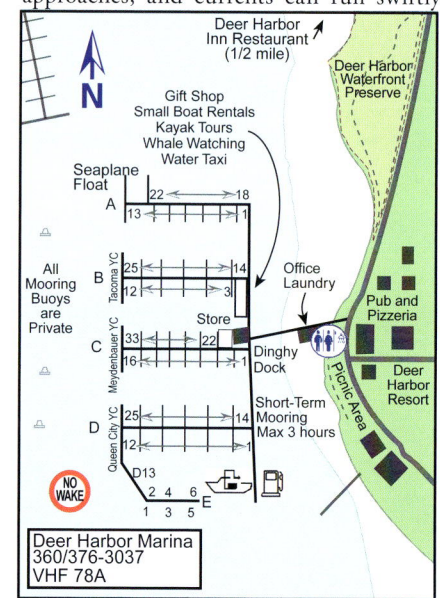

Deer Harbor Marina

Deer Harbor Marina

Whether you're here for a vacation or are looking for permanent moorage in a Pacific Northwest paradise, Deer Harbor Marina should be a key waypoint on your journey. Come enjoy the beauty of Deer Harbor throughout the season.

- Winter Rates at $9.00 per foot
- Fast internet at all slips
- Slips to 50'
- Guest side ties up to 110'
- 30 amp power/limited 50 amp
- New pool, showers & laundry
- Fuel dock (gas & diesel)
- Deli, groceries, beer, wine, ice cream, coffee, prep food, DVD rentals & ATM
- Whale watching, kayaks, bike & boat rentals, tours and charters
- Fresh water
- Pump-out
- Nearby restaurants
- Apparel, gifts, books, maps & charts

Deer Harbor Marina
Orcas Island, WA
Lat 48° 37' 135" • Lon 123° 00' 166"
CONTACT: 360.376.3037 • VHF 78A
EMAIL: mbroman@deerharbormarina.com
ONLINE: www.DeerHarborMarina.com

through the pass. A mid-channel course is safe. For most skippers, good sense dictates slow speeds. "No Wake" buoys are located along the Pass. Sometimes the sheriff is there, ticketing speeders.

⑬ **West Sound.** West Sound is the middle inlet of Orcas Island, where the Wareham family's West Sound Marina offers limited overnight moorage and complete service facilities. Next to the marina is the Orcas Island Yacht Club, with reciprocal moorage for visiting members. A day-use-only public dock is west of the Orcas Island Yacht Club dock.

Owners of the Kingfish Inn, Raymond and Holly Southern, continue the tradition of welcoming locals and visitors to the charming Inn overlooking West Sound. Located upland from the public dock in West Sound, the Inn offers four attractive suites with waterfront views and restaurant service open to the public, featuring local sourced ingredients. The Kingfish Restaurant is open Wednesday through Saturday; call (360) 376-4440 for reservations.

Good anchorage is available at the head of the bay (stay well clear of Harbor Rock, marked by a daybeacon). Anchorage is also good off the village of West Sound, and behind Double Island.

⑬ **West Sound Marina.** P.O. Box 119, 525 Deer Harbor Road, Orcas Island, WA 98280; (360) 376-2314; info@westsoundmarina.com;

Guest moorage, a chandlery, and repairs are available at West Sound Marina.

westsoundmarina.com. Monitors VHF 16, switch to 09. Open all year, except closed Sundays in the winter. Facilities include ethanol-free gasoline and diesel at the fuel dock, propane, 400 feet of guest moorage; call ahead same day for moorage. 30 amp power, restrooms, shower, pumpout. Recycling and used oil drop. Haulout to 30 tons with full service and repairs, including an enclosed area for major work. The chandlery has most boating supplies. When approaching, stay well off Picnic Island. A rock ledge extends into West Sound from the island. Once at the marina, stay close to the docks. The water shoals toward Picnic Island.

Victim Island. West side of West Sound. Open all year, day use only, no facilities. Anchor out at this undeveloped BLM property. No fires or overnight camping. Pack out all garbage. Do not disturb wildlife or alter the surroundings.

Massacre Bay. Located at the northwest end of West Sound, Massacre Bay has a number of possible anchoring locations in depths ranging from 40 to 60 feet. This is a large, wide bay open to southerly and southeasterly winds. Visiting Skull Island in Massacre Bay by dinghy or kayak is a favorite activity. Massacre Bay takes its name from the Haida raid on the Lummi in 1858. Cell coverage is limited or not available in areas of the bay.

Skull Island. North end of Massacre Bay. Open all year, day use only, no facilities. Anchor out at this undeveloped BLM property. No fires or overnight camping. Pack out all garbage. Do not disturb wildlife or alter the surroundings.

TURTLEBACK MOUNTAIN PRESERVE

Turtleback Mountain Preserve is a San Juan County Land Bank property. The 1,578-acre property offers over 8 miles of hiking trails and scenic vistas. There are two trailhead access points with parking, one at the North Trail off of Crow Valley Road, and the other at the South Trail off of Deer Harbor Road. Boaters can use the shuttle van at Deer Harbor Marina to access the trails at Turtleback Mountain. Trails at the South Trailhead are for pedestrians only; the North Trailhead allows horses and mountain bikes on a rotation basis – bikes on even calendar days and horses on odd calendar days. Trails vary from forested pathways and open meadows, to moderately steep outcroppings and ridges. No garbage disposal or water available; pack it in, pack it out.

The 8-mile trail network spans the "turtle's back," connecting the preserve's north and south trailheads. An additional 1-mile trail leads to the "turtle's head," with jaw-dropping views. Thanks to a partnership between the San Juan County Land Bank and the San Juan Preservation Trust, the piece between Turtlehead and Turtleback was connected, now referred to as "Turtleneck." Through the efforts of the San Juan County Land Bank, the San Juan Preservation Trust, the Trust for Public Land, and more than 1,500 private donors, Turtleback Mountain Preserve was established in 2007.

As with all Preserve properties, hikers are asked to stay on the trails to protect plant and wildlife species. Habitats include rare Garry oak woodlands, grasslands, and scattered wetlands.

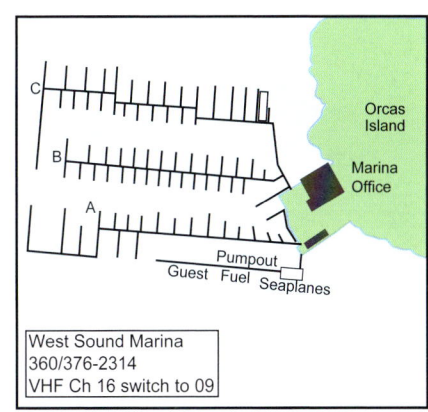

West Sound Marina

SAN JUAN ISLANDS

See Area Map Page 188 - Maps Not for Navigation

It's just a short walk to the village of Eastsound from the County Dock.

Brown Bear Baking in Eastsound has artisan breads and tempting pastries.

⑭ **Orcas Landing Public Dock.** (360) 370-0500 San Juan County Public Works. Orcas Landing has a public float next to the ferry dock for day use; no overnight stays. Be well-fendered and securely tied to the dock at Orcas Landing. Passing boat and ferry traffic in Harney Channel (Cayou Channel) throw a lot of wake towards the dock. The grocery store at the head of the ferry landing dock is well stocked and has a good selection of wine and cheese, sandwiches to-go, and baked goods. Don't miss the cider garden just up the hill at the Cider Works shop.

Grindstone Harbor. Grindstone Harbor is a small, shallow anchorage, with two major rocks in its entrance. One of these rocks became famous a number of years ago when the Washington State ferry *Elwha* ran aground on it while doing a bit of unauthorized sightseeing. Favor the east shore all the way in. Private mooring buoys take up much of the inner part of the bay, but there's room to anchor if you need to.

Guthrie Bay. Guthrie Bay indents Orcas Island between Grindstone Harbor and East Sound. It's a pleasant little spot with private mooring buoys around the perimeter and homes on the hillsides. Anchor in 24 to 42 feet.

East Sound. East Sound, the largest of Orcas Island's indentations, extends about 6 miles north from Foster Point. The shores on both sides are steep, and offer few anchorage possibilities. Rosario Resort is on the east side, a short distance north of the village of Olga. The only marina facility with guest moorage is Rosario Resort. The village of Eastsound is at the head, with several anchoring options. Fresh winds sometimes blow in East Sound, while outside the air is calm. Anchorage can be found at the head of the Sound in Fishing Bay, Judd Bay, and Ship Bay. A county public dock provides dinghy access to the village.

Eastsound. The village of Eastsound, at the head of East Sound, is the largest settlement on Orcas Island. Eastsound is a delightful village with a genuine San Juan Islands' character. In town are two well-stocked grocery stores, a hardware store, pharmacy, bakery, bookstores, gift shops, a selection of good restaurants, and an excellent museum. The welcoming and friendly village has everything within easy walking distance. Access to town is via the Eastsound County day-use dock. Be sure to visit the Farmers Market at the Village Green held on Saturdays from May through September.

Eastsound County Dock. A county dock located less than 1/4 mile south of the village of Eastsound on the western shore of Madrona Point in Fishing Bay, has a 40-foot day-use only float suitable for dinghies and small boats. The float is available April through October for stays up to 4-hours.

LOCAL KNOWLEDGE

EASTSOUND ANCHORING: A sign on the Eastsound dock announces that the bottom inshore, from a line between the dock and the small islet off the town, is sensitive eelgrass habitat. Boaters are asked to anchor seaward of that line.

Fishing Bay & Judd Bay. West of Eastsound village and at the head of East Sound are Fishing Bay and adjacent, Judd Bay. Anchorage can be found in Fishing Bay and the outer portion of Judd Bay in 20 to 45 feet of water over a mud bottom. Judd Bay has excellent holding over a sticky mud bottom in 40 feet of water. The bays are protected from all but southeasterly winds. The anchorage is semi-private with a few cabins and homes along the shore. A restored stone lime kiln from the late 1800's can be seen at the head of Judd Bay in the Judd Cove Preserve. The beach area is not accessible and watercraft landings are not allowed. Please view from the water. Private lands occupy the remainder of inner Judd Bay.

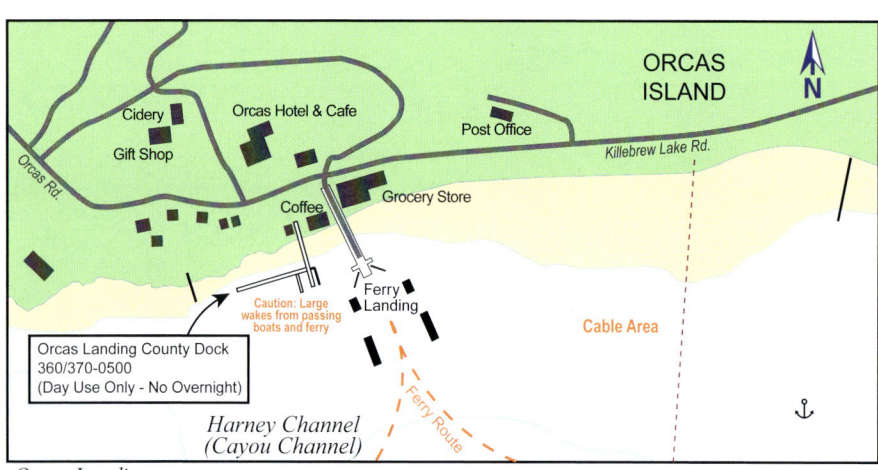

Orcas Landing

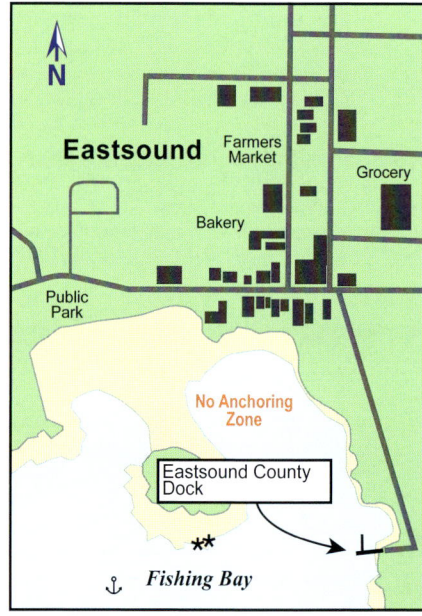

Eastsound

208   www.WaggonerGuide.com

See Area Map Page 188 - Maps Not for Navigation   SAN JUAN ISLANDS

Historic Moran Mansion is the anchor point at Rosario Resort & Spa, offering services and amenities for people of all ages.

⑮ **Rosario Resort & Spa.** 1400 Rosario Rd., Eastsound, WA 98245; (360) 376-2222; (800) 562-8820; harbormaster@rosarioresort.com; www.rosarioresort.com. Monitors VHF 78A. Open all year. Moorage for approximately 50 boats. 30 & 50 amp ELCI-protected power and 8 mooring buoys.

Buoys are for boats 50 feet and under, first-come, first-served. Boats on buoys pay a buoy fee and boats anchored out pay a landing fee for use of the marina amenities. Day use up to 2 hours is free on a space available basis, at the discretion of the Harbormaster, while dining and shopping at the resort. There's room to anchor, though the sound is exposed to southerlies.

Slip reservations are available online; note that boats 30 feet and under, and boats over 60 feet, not bookable online; call to make arrangements. Reservations strongly recommended during the peak season. A 200-foot breakwater dock accommodates larger vessels up to 180 feet. The outer end of the breakwater is for seaplanes only.

Moorage includes power, water, restrooms and showers. A pumpout cart is located on the dock. Excellent Wi-Fi. Fuel dock on site and garbage drop with recycling. Diesel and ethanol-free unleaded gasoline at the fuel dock (fuel dock by appointment October through April).

The resort offers a seasonal café, dining in the Mansion, a convenience store, and swimming pools. The Cascade Bay Grill and Store at the head of the dock is open from Memorial Day through mid-September and has snacks, sodas, beer and wine, gift items, and limited groceries. The Grill serves burgers, fish & chips, and casual fare, inside or out. Live entertainment scheduled periodically, check their website. Seaplane service to Seattle via Kenmore Air and NW Seaplanes.

The outdoor swimming pool, nearest the docks, welcomes families as does the spa-pool inside the resort's Mansion; the Mansion's outdoor pool below the hotel is for adults only.

For those wanting to explore Eastsound or the island, car rental delivery service is available through "Orcas Island Rental Car" (360-376-RIDE). "San Juan Transit" runs to Eastsound, Deer Harbor, Rosario and other locations on Orcas Island in the summer months on Fridays, Saturdays, and Sundays.

The centerpiece of the resort is the magnificent Moran Mansion, listed on the National Register of Historic Places. The mansion houses a restaurant, lounge and spa. Holiday buffets are an excellent way to spend your time while cruising the shoulder seasons. The mansion itself is a fascinating museum (open 8:00 a.m. to 9:00 p.m. daily), a chronicle of Robert Moran's history as a shipbuilder, the mayor of Seattle, then as the builder of Rosario. Christopher Peacock, longtime resident artist and musician and now resort manager, presents a slide presentation on the history of the resort, with musical accompaniment performed on the giant room-sized Wurlitzer pipe organ. The concert begins at 4:00 p.m. Tuesdays to Saturdays mid-June through mid-September, and Saturdays only through the winter. It's wonderful. Don't miss it. Moran State Park is about a 30-minute walk.

Figurehead: The beautiful figurehead above the marina is a replica from the wreck of the *America*, a wooden clipper ship converted to barge use. The ship went aground near False Bay on San Juan Island in 1914 while under tow from Seattle to Vancouver. During periods of small tides and slack water, the wreck's bones are still a dive site at False Bay (from *Northwest Dive News*).

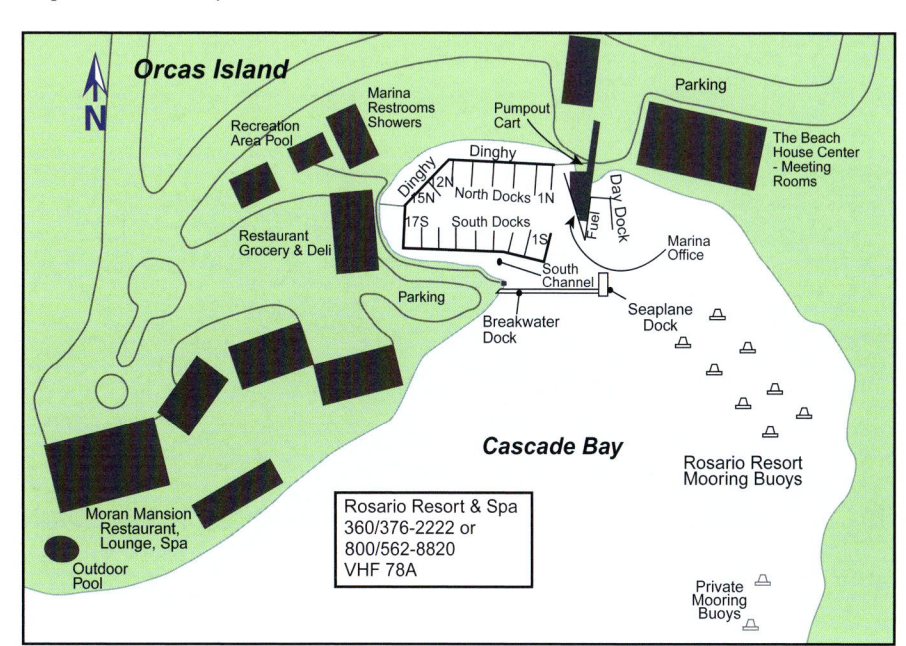

Rosario Resort

SAN JUAN ISLANDS

See Area Map Page 188 - Maps Not for Navigation

The public dock and pier at the charming village of Olga on Orcas Island

A country store and cafe await guests at Doe Bay Resort.

⑯ **Olga.** Olga, a tiny pastoral village, is near the entrance to East Sound, on the east shore. Olga has a dock and 105-foot-long mooring float, but no power, restrooms, or showers. The float is removed in winter. A box for overnight moorage payment is at the bottom of the ramp. Three-day overnight limit. Day-use stay up to two hours. Limited anchorage offshore exposed to southeasterly winds. Numerous private mooring buoys and charted cable area limit the possible anchoring opportunities.

A sign above the dock lists local stores and locations. Up the road you will find the Artworks co-operative, the James Hardman Gallery, and the Catkin Café housed in the reconstructed barreling plant building.

Twin Rocks. West of Olga. Open all year, day use only, no facilities. Anchor out at this undeveloped state park property. No fires or overnight camping. Pack out all garbage. Do not disturb wildlife or alter the surroundings.

Lieber Haven Resort. P.O. Box 127, Olga, WA 98279; (360) 376-2472; www.lieberhavenresort.com. In the middle of Obstruction Pass on the north shore. Owner Capt. Dave has built boats for 67 years and is a delight. He enjoys sharing stories and making people feel at home. Overnight moorage on the resort docks for cottage guests only; water and 30 amp power. Two rental cottages along a nice sandy, light gravel shoreline; kayak rentals. Store carries antiques and some marine supplies.

Obstruction Pass State Park. www.parks.wa.gov. Southeast tip of Orcas Island. Open all year, moorage at 3 buoys for boats 45 feet and under. Self-register and pay moorage buoy fee on shore, or by phone as posted on the buoy. Toilets, no power or showers. Good anchoring on a gravel bottom. Campsites with fireplaces, picnic tables, hiking trails.

⑰ **Doe Island Marine State Park.** (360) 376-2073; On the southeast side of Orcas Island. Normally open all year with five camping sites. This is a beautiful tiny island with a rocky shoreline dotted with tidepools. A trail leads around the island, through dense forest and lush undergrowth. Compost toilet; no power, no water or showers. Pack out all garbage. Adjacent buoys are privately owned. A 32-foot float was installed in 2019 at Doe Island. Moorage rates are payable 1:00 p.m. to 8:00 a.m.; use the self-registration payment station located upland. Currents run strongly between Doe Island and Orcas Island.

⑰ **Doe Bay Resort and Retreat.** 107 Doe Bay Road, Olga, WA 98279; (360) 376-2291; office@doebay.com; www.doebay.com. Doe Bay is an interesting off-the-beaten-path destination, with 2 guest buoys (call for reservations) and anchorage space for 3 to 6 boats. Dinghy ashore to the rocky beach to visit the general store and café. The creekside tubs and cedar sauna are available for a fee. Anchored guests can make reservations for the cafe.

The café has an intriguing menu and is open for breakfast, lunch and dinner, with indoor and outdoor seating. The general store has convenience groceries and items from local artisans. The resort has cabins, geodesic domes, yurts, a beautifully crafted treehouse, and campsites for rent. The waterfront Boat House, with hotel-style accommodations, opened in late-summer 2019. Doe Bay Fest, a popular music festival, is held in early August.

Stay Informed at WaggonerGuide/Updates.com

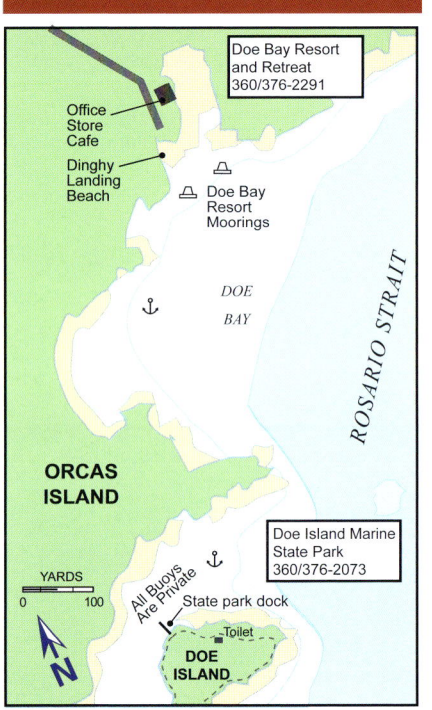

Doe Bay Resort has two mooring buoys for guest use.

Doe Bay

⑱ Barnes and Clark Islands. These two beautiful islands lie parallel to each other in Rosario Strait, between Orcas Island and Lummi Island. Barnes Island is privately owned, but Clark Island is a state park, with mooring buoys installed during the summer. Camping and picnicking sites are ashore, and trails meander along the island.

⑱ Clark Island Marine State Park. (360) 376-2073; Open all year, day use and overnight mooring and camping. Clark Island is exposed to Rosario Strait and the Strait of Georgia, and is best in settled weather. Mooring buoys are deployed between Clark Island and Barnes Island, and in the bay on the east side. The park has 9 mooring buoys for vessels 45 feet and under: 6 on the east side and 3 on the west side. Self-register and pay mooring buoy fee on shore, or by phone as posted on the buoy. Toilets, picnic sites, fire rings, and primitive campsites. No power, no water. Pack out all garbage.

Note: A nasty rock is in the entrance to the bay. Best to enter the bay from the northeast.

Visitor Report: Correspondents Bruce and Margaret Evertz spent a night on a buoy on the east side of Clark Island and ". . .woke up three times in the middle of the night hanging onto the mattress as we rolled in the wake of something big. Next time we'll try one of the buoys on the west side."

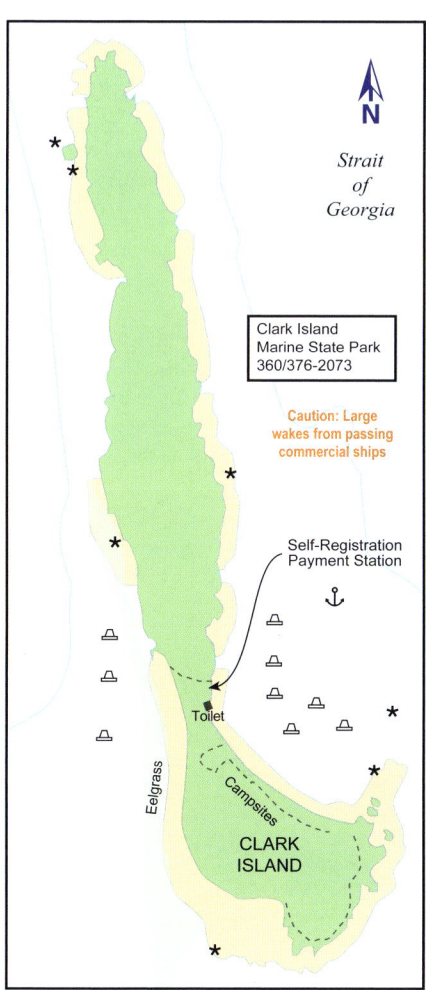

Though small, Matia Island has a cove for anchoring, two mooring buoys, and a dock.

⑲ Matia Island Marine State Park. (360) 376-2073; Open all year, day use and overnight mooring. Matia Island is part of the San Juan Islands National Wildlife Refuge. All access is restricted except the loop trail and the designated 5-acre moorage and picnicking area at Rolfe Cove. The rest of the island is off-limits to protect wildlife. Pets are not allowed on shore.

The favored Matia Island anchorage is in **Rolfe Cove**, which opens from the west. Strong currents can run through Rolfe Cove and the bottom is rocky. Be sure the anchor is well set and swinging room is adequate. Facilities include a 64-foot-long moorage float, 2 buoys (limit 45 feet), 6 campsites, toilet. Signage at the head of the dock states a limit of 4 boats on the dock. No power, water or showers. The mooring float in past years was removed in winter. The float, which was installed in 2019, is available year-round. Self-register and pay mooring fee at the head of the dock, or by phone as posted.

Those confident in their anchoring ability might try the little 1-boat notch between Rolfe Cove and Eagle Point, although you can't go inland from there. A stern-anchor will be required to keep the boat positioned. High cliffs surround this cove. It's very secluded and serene.

Anchorage is good in the bay indenting the southeast corner of the island. The remains of an old homestead are located at the head of that bay.

There is some disagreement about the pronunciation of Matia. Bruce Calhoun's book, *Cruising the San Juan Islands*, says it's pronounced "Mah-TEE-ah." We've been told, however, that a number of genuine old hands have always pronounced it "Mah-CIA," as in "inertia" or "militia." However the name is pronounced, Matia Island is a popular destination, beautiful and interesting.

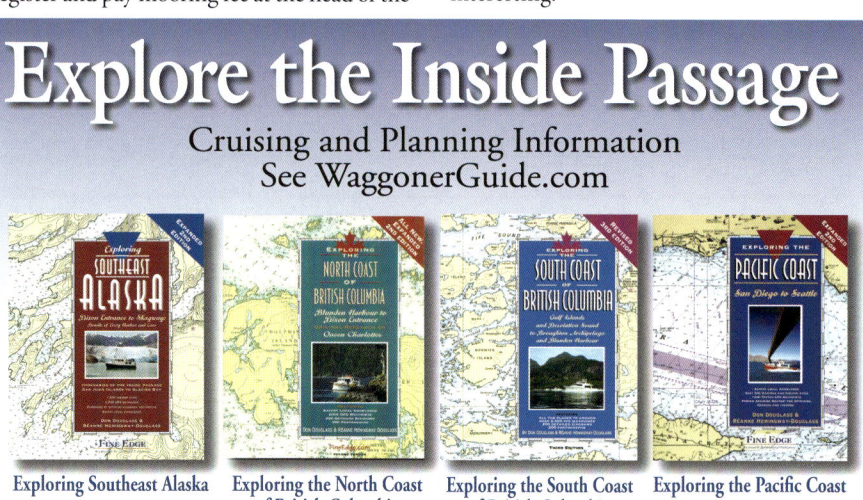

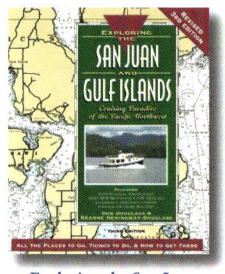

Clark Island Marine State Park

Explore the Inside Passage
Cruising and Planning Information
See WaggonerGuide.com

Exploring Southeast Alaska

Exploring the North Coast of British Columbia

Exploring the South Coast of British Columbia

Exploring the Pacific Coast

Exploring the San Juan and Gulf Islands

Fine Edge
Nautical & Recreational Publishing

The complete Exploring series by Don Douglass and Reanne Hemingway-Douglass is available at your local nautical bookstore, and WaggonerGuide.com or at 360-299-8500. In Canada available through Chynasea at 250-594-1184 and portsandpasses.com. Also on Amazon.

Exploring Vancouver Island's West Coast

2023 WAGGONER CRUISING GUIDE

SAN JUAN ISLANDS

See Area Map Page 188 - Maps Not for Navigation

Limestone outcropping at Shallow Bay

Fossil Bay has two Marine Park docks, a field of mooring buoys, onshore campsites, and restrooms.

㉑ Sucia Island Marine State Park. Open all year, day use and overnight mooring and camping. For information call (360) 376-2073; for campsite reservations call toll-free (888) 226-7688. Facilities include dock space, linear tie mooring systems, numerous mooring buoys, and toilets. Water, but no power, no showers. Potable water is not available Oct. 1 through early April. This probably is the most heavily used marine park in the system. As many as 500 boats can visit on one weekend in the high summer season.

Like Matia and Patos Islands, Sucia Island is made of sandstone carved by water and wind into dramatic shapes. Many fossils can be found in Sucia Island's sandstone. It is illegal to disturb or remove fossils.

The park has 55 primitive campsites and 2 group campsites, which can be reserved. Camping is permitted in designated areas only. A day use/picnic area, with picnic shelters, is on the neck of land separating Echo Bay and Shallow Bay, and can be reserved. The park has several miles of hiking trails and service roads. Fresh water is available at Fossil Bay and near Shallow Bay April through September. The most developed facilities are at Fossil Bay.

Sucia Island has several fingers that separate small bays. Facilities are as follows: Fox Cove: 4 mooring buoys; Fossil Bay: 2 docks, 13 mooring buoys; Snoring Bay: 2 mooring buoys; Echo Bay: 14 mooring buoys, 2 linear moorings; Ewing Cove: 4 mooring buoys; Shallow Bay: 8 mooring buoys. All mooring buoys are limited to boats 45 feet or less. Rafting allowed at the docks based on the size of boats. All docks and moorings are Washington State Parks facilities, self-register and pay a fee at the designated on-shore stations, or by phone as posted on the buoy. The mooring buoy count can change based on winter weather and repairs.

Shallow Bay. Shallow Bay is an excellent, popular anchorage. Lots of room except on minus tides. Mooring buoys take most of the obvious good spots, so if they are taken you'll be looking at the south side of Shallow Bay. Check the tides before anchoring, and be sure you'll have enough water under the keel at low tide. Easy entry as long as you pass between the two buoys marking the entrance. The best place to beach the dinghy is on the narrow neck of land separating Shallow Bay from Echo Bay. Sunsets in Shallow Bay are beautiful.

LOCAL KNOWLEDGE

DANGEROUS REEFS: A reef extends westward from Little Sucia Island nearly to the shoal water near West Bank. Sucia Island is surrounded by hazards. We strongly recommend zooming in on large scale charts.

Sucia, Patos, and Matia Islands

212   www.WaggonerGuide.com

Secluded Ewing Cove on the northeast area of Sucia Island Marine Park has mooring buoys that can be exposed to strong southeast weather.

Fox Cove. Enter Fox Cove from either side. Waters off the southern entry can be turbulent. At the west entry foul ground extends west farther than you expect. Tie to mooring buoys or anchor behind Little Sucia Island. A pretty spot with sandstone cliffs.

Fossil Bay. Fossil Bay is easy to enter, nicely protected and beautiful. Anchor out, tie to one of the mooring buoys, or moor at the docks. In winter one of the docks is moved to a more protected area of the park.

At the head of the outermost dock a plaque commemorates the yacht clubs that were members of the Interclub Boating Association of Washington, when Interclub worked to collect funds from ordinary citizens, then bought the island and gave it to the state as a state park. One of the points of land overlooking Fossil Bay is named for Ev Henry, the first president of Interclub, who conceived the idea and carried out the project.

Depths in Fossil Bay at zero tide are 6 feet at the outer end of the innermost dock, and they shoal rapidly toward the head of the bay. The park ranger told us depths are only 5 feet at zero tide near the outer dock. Be careful on low tides. Be aware of the reef that extends southeast from Ev Henry Point. A substantial day use shelter, excellent for group functions, has been built at the head of the dock. Call (360) 376-2073 for reservations.

Snoring Bay. Snoring Bay is easy to enter and has 2 mooring buoys. A good spot. As we understand the story, a park ranger was caught sleeping on duty in this bay, hence the name.

Echo Bay. Echo Bay is the largest of Sucia's bays. Although it is the most exposed, it is the most popular. Mooring buoys line the western shore, and 2 linear mooring systems are just outside the buoys. Picnic facilities are on the narrow neck of land separating Echo Bay from Shallow Bay.

The fine gravel beach at the head of Echo Bay is fairly steep, making dinghy landing much more convenient. We were able to step ashore without getting our feet wet.

The two long islands in Echo Bay (North Finger and South Finger Island) are privately owned. The south half of Justice Island (the small island off South Finger Island) is park-owned but closed to the public as a nature preserve.

Caution: A reader reported that he grounded his Cal 39 sailboat, which draws 6 feet 8 inches, on an uncharted rock in

Sucia Island Marine State Park

Limestone caves along Shallow Bay

SAN JUAN ISLANDS

See Area Map Page 188 - Maps Not for Navigation

Echo Bay at Sucia Island Marine Park has mooring buoys, two linear moorings, and anchoring space for many boats; shore access is by beach landing.

Echo Bay. The grounding occurred in the area marked 1 fathom, 5 feet extending from the small islet northwest of South Finger Islet, as shown on large scale Chart 18431. He sounded the area carefully after the grounding, and found the depths to be somewhat less than charted. The keel of his boat confirmed the soundings. On low tides especially, give the tip of this islet a good offing.

Despite occasional stories of anchor dragging in Echo Bay, we have found the bottom to be heavy, sticky clay, with excellent holding.

No-anchor Zone: A no-anchor zone is marked by buoys near the head of Echo Bay. They want to protect eelgrass from boat anchors and dragging chain rode. Mooring buoys in the bay use eco-friendly anchors that do not disturb eelgrass.

Ewing Cove. In our opinion, cozy little Ewing Cove, tucked in behind Ewing Island on the north side of Echo Bay, is the most charming of Sucia Island's bays. The cove has 4 mooring buoys and a lovely beach at the western end. We have reports of a rock in Ewing Cove's southern entrance, from Echo Bay. The rock is east of a white can that marks a fish haven. We're told the rock is black and hard to see, and feeds on propellers at low tide. Be extra cautious. Reader Bruce Farwell sent lat/lon coordinates of 48°45.794'N/122°52.924'W. We've found the narrow pass at the northwest end of Ewing Cove to be deep and easily run as long as you pay attention. Danger Reef lies just outside.

㉑ **Patos Island Marine State Park.** (360) 376-2073; Open all year, day use and overnight mooring and camping. Facilities normally include 2 mooring buoys (limit 45 feet) in Active Cove; one buoy was reported to be submerged in 2019. Current can run strong, making mooring to a park buoy, or anchoring, difficult. Toilets and primitive campsites. Self-register and pay mooring buoy fee on shore, or by phone as posted on the buoy. The remains of the dock that served the lighthouse on Alden Point are still there, but barely recognizable. A one-mile trail leads from the beach at the head of Active Cove to the lighthouse. Pack out all garbage. The island is a breeding area for birds.

㉑ **Active Cove.** The only possible Patos Island anchorage is in Active Cove, on the west tip of the island. The cove, with its sculpted sandstone walls, is one of the most scenic spots in the San Juans. Considerable current activity is outside the entrances.

Shallow Bay is a popular Sucia destination on the west side of the island.

Gravel beach landing area along the north shore of Shallow Bay

www.WaggonerGuide.com

West Beach Resort, on the west side of Orcas Island, offers seasonal transient moorage and seasonal buoys for guests.

Inside the cove the currents are reduced, but it's tight. Use the mooring buoys when possible. In 2019, correspondents, Brent and Peggy Ann Bierbaum, reported that the buoy nearest shore was under water and in need of replacement. If the mooring buoys are taken, anchoring gets interesting. A stern-tie to shore probably will be called for.

Freeman Island. On President Channel. Open all year, day use only, no facilities. Anchor out at this undeveloped state park property. No fires or overnight camping. Pack out all garbage.

㉒ **West Beach Resort.** 190 Waterfront Way, Eastsound, WA 98245; (360) 376-2240; (877) 937-8224; vacation@westbeachresort.com; www.westbeachresort.com. The resort is open all year, ethanol-free premium gasoline at the fuel dock (no fuel service in winter). 11 mooring buoys in the summer, and 4 buoys available in the winter. Docks and mooring buoys have Wi-Fi. Cabin and RV guests have priority on moorage and mooring buoys. Call or book online. Restrooms, showers, nightly beach bonfires, kids' activities, kayak and SUP rentals, epic sunsets. The pumpout station is free and accommodates boats up to 60 feet. Floats in deeper water accommodate larger boats. Larger powerboats and keel sailboats tie to mooring buoys. All of the docks, except the gas dock, are removed from mid-September to late May. Room for approximately four boats to moor at the fuel dock during the off season. The store has a little bit of everything, including groceries, ice, beer, wine, espresso, ice cream, and fresh-baked pizzas, hot dogs, and cinnamon rolls.

West Beach is a popular fishing resort with cabins, tent cabins, RV sites and camping. Private launch ramp (free for guests, a fee is charged for non-guests) and parking.

Point Doughty. A remote campsite on the Cascadia Marine Trail, with vault toilets, picnic tables, and a fire pit ring. A steep set of wooden stairs leads from the small rocky beach to the uplands. The beach is accessible by kayak or dinghy. Anchor in 40-50 feet on the south side of the point, best suited for northerly winds or in settled weather. Nearby YMCA Camp Orkila uses the site for environmental education. The adjacent 57-acre forested Natural Preserve, home to Bald eagles, is off-limits for hiking. Seals often haul out on the rocky shoreline.

㉓ **Brandt's Landing.** 340 Brandt-Landing Rd, Eastsound, WA 98245; (360) 376-4477; sjharbormaster@gmail.com; brandtslandingmarina.net. Located on the north end of Orcas Island a mile north of the village of Eastsound, the marina's floats are in a long narrow canal entered between North Beach and Terrill Beach. Open all year, with limited guest moorage available for overnight and hourly stays for vessels up to 50 feet. Off-season hours are 10:00 a.m. to 2:00 p.m.; contact the marina for moorage. Reservations accepted. Guest moorage slips are located at the far south end of the channel. Water, 30 amp power, and garbage drop. Enter on mid to high tide level; entry channel at the break water is some of the shallowest area.

Smuggler's Villa Resort. P.O. Box 79, Eastsound, WA 98245; (360) 376-2297; smuggler@rockisland.com; www.smuggler.com. No transient moorage. Smuggler's Village has condos for rent, a swimming pool and hot tubs. Reservations required. Good base for trailer boaters who can rent a condo for overnights and explore the northern San Juans during the day.

Waldron Island. In settled weather, anchorage is good in Cowlitz Bay and North Bay. Mail Bay, on the east shore, is rocky but usable. The mail boat from Bellingham used to arrive here, leaving the mail in a barrel hung over the water. In the 1890's, a stone quary opened at Point Disney, named after a sailmaker, Solomon Disney.

Cowlitz Bay. Cowlitz Bay has one of the loveliest sand beaches in the San Juan's. Three-quarters of a mile of shoreline and tidelands are part of the San Juan Preservation Trust and open to the public. The preserve begins about a half-mile west of the Waldron Island County Dock and continues to the low-bank and upland clearing areas, where you will find remnants of fallen cabins and fencing that once stood along the beach.

In 2019, no upland trails were found. The remainder of Waldron Island is private with no public facilities.

Departing Brandt's Landing on the north end of Orcas Island, with Sucia Island in the distance.

SAN JUAN ISLANDS

㉔ **Stuart Island Marine State Park. (360) 378-2044.** The center portion of Stuart Island, including Reid Harbor and Prevost Harbor, is a state park with campsites, potable water, and clean, spacious composting toilets. A trail and dirt road from Reid Harbor and Prevost Harbor lead out to the automated Turn Point lighthouse. The distance is about 3 miles, each way. It's an excellent walk, although the trail to the road goes over a mountain and will have you puffing. The view down into Reid Harbor is excellent.

Please respect private property and homes on the island. You can stop by the school house (1 room, K-8), the library and museum, which in our opinion are on the must-see list. The school house is modern, but the library and museum buildings go back to earlier days. The museum is filled with information about island life, which despite being close to big cities, is pretty primitive. There is no public electric power, for example. Every resident is responsible for his or her own electricity, and a few choose to do without. Ditto water and telephone, although cell phones have filled that void. Handmade postcards are for sale in the library on the honor system.

One island family, Ezra and Loie Benson and their children, have created a small business called Boundary Pass Traders. They operate the Treasure Chest, near the schoolhouse, and a second Treasure Chest along the road at Prevost Harbor. T-shirts and coloring books, with local scenes, are for sale. Strictly the honor system. Select the items you like and mail a check for your purchases, or you can pay online.

Prevost Harbor. Open all year, day use and overnight mooring and camping. Facilities include 256 feet of dock space, approximately 7 mooring buoys (limit 45 feet), a linear mooring system, 18 primitive campsites, toilets. Self-register and pay dock moorage, mooring buoy, and linear mooring fee at the head of the state park dock, or by phone as posted. The favored entrance to Prevost Harbor is around the west end of Satellite Island. A county dock on the northwest end of Prevost Harbor, suitable for dinghies, shortens the walk to the Island school and Turn Point lighthouse. No overnight stays at the county dock.

Caution: Two reefs in the Prevost Harbor entrance cover at high tide. One is off the Stuart Island shore and dries at 6 feet. The other is off Satellite Island and dries at 4 feet. The reefs are clearly charted, but when they cover, the route to the dock looks to be wide open. If you're entering at higher tide when the reefs are covered, don't wrap tightly to port around the tip of Satellite Island. That's where one of the reefs is lying in wait. Proceed a short distance straight into the harbor (but not too far; that's where the other reef is located), then turn to port.

Anchoring is good throughout Prevost Harbor; the west end is open to northerly wind and swell from passing ships.

Explore the shoreline of the harbor by kayak or dinghy. A grass airstrip is at the east end of the harbor, beyond the docks and houses. Rock formations and beaches are fascinating. Crabbing is reported to be good.

The passage to the east of Satellite Island is foul. It has been reported that, with care, these waters are passable at half tide or better, or by shallow draft boats; use caution. Shoreside State Park facilities are shared with Reid Harbor, on the narrow but steep neck of land that separates them.

Satellite Island East Cove. "The little cove on the eastern shore of Satellite Island has good holding in mud in about 40 feet. Wonderful view across Boundary Pass. Inside, Prevost Harbor was packed with boats; we were alone." [Hamilton]

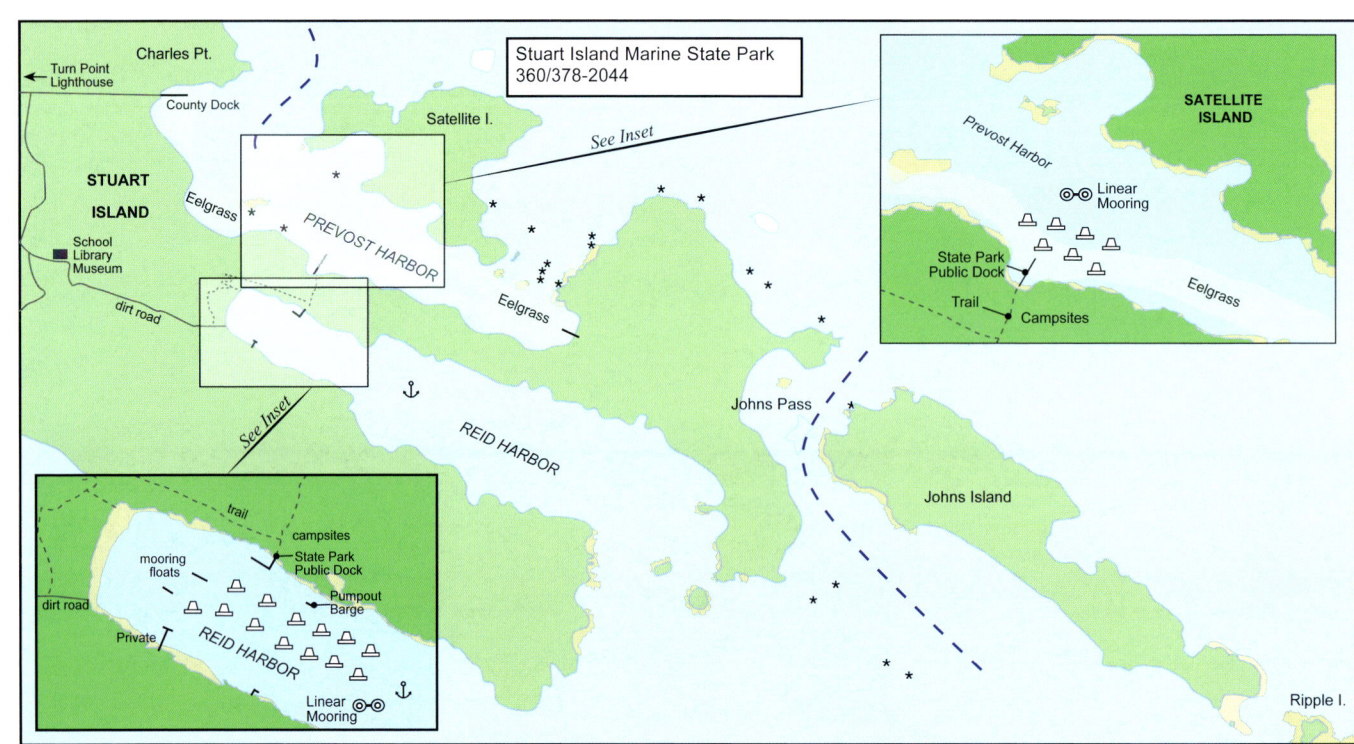

Hike the beautiful country roads on Stuart Island to get to the Turn Point Lighthouse

Stuart Island Marine State Park

Turn Point Lighthouse on Stuart Island

Gossip Island. "Reid Harbor had too many boats for our taste. Preferring a view anyway, we dropped anchor just outside, in the cove formed by Gossip Island and the unnamed island immediately northwest of Gossip Island. It was very private, with two white sand beaches nearby. Good holding ground for the anchor. Southerly swells rocked us a couple times. We had an excellent view through the islets to the Olympic Mountains, and of large ship traffic away off in Haro Strait." [Hamilton]

Johns Pass. Johns Pass separates Stuart Island and Johns Island, and is used regularly. At the south end of the pass foul ground, marked by kelp, extends about half of a mile southeast from Stuart Island. Boats heading southeast through Johns Pass should head for Gull Reef, then turn when well clear of the kelp. Anchorage is possible in Johns Pass and along the south side of Johns Island.

Reid Harbor. Open all year, day use and overnight mooring and camping. The entrance is straightforward. A 96-foot mooring dock is on the north shore, with a total of 192 feet of side-tie moorage. 13 mooring buoys (for boats 45 feet and under) dot the bay, and mooring floats (not connected to land) and a linear mooring system are within easy dinghy distance of the landing dock. Self-register and pay mooring fees at the head of the dock, or by phone as posted. Toilets, pumpout (manually operated pump), and portapotty dump are located on a float along the north shore. Reid Harbor is long and narrow, and protected by high hills. The bottom is excellent for anchoring, and the harbor holds a great number of boats. It's a popular destination. The setting is beautiful. Shoreside facilities are shared with Prevost Harbor, on the narrow but steep neck of land separating them. The county dirt road leading to the Turn Point Lighthouse, with its museum (and the school house, museum and library along the way), begins at the head of Reid Harbor. No dock at the head of the bay, but if tides are favorable you can beach your dinghy there without carrying it back through the mud.

Waggoner eNews
Boating, Maintenance Tips & Destinations
www.waggonerguide.com

SAN JUAN PRESERVATION TRUST LANDS

Did you know that the San Juan Preservation Trust protects and preserves 300 properties on 20 different islands in the San Juan's? These properties offer miles of trails and shoreline, with public access. Many of these sites are accessed only by dinghy or kayak, where you will find trailheads with Preservation Trust signage. Some areas, like Vendovi Island, offer a day-use dock.

The Mission of the Preservation Trust is to purchase and conserve unique properties with natural beauty that are vital to the ecosystem and/or has significant historic and scenic value. Caring for these lands connects people to nature and provides the same opportunity for future generations. Visitors are asked to stay on designated trails to protect flowers, plants, and animal habitat.

The San Juan Preservation Trust is a 501(C)(3) charitable organization. Funds come from contributions provided by individuals, families, and private foundations that support research, maintenance, and purchases of island property. Making a contribution entitles you to membership, which includes "The Island Dispatch," a quarterly print newsletter, along with e-newsletters, and priority when registering for events and outings.

Vendovi Island is a favorite among boaters, but other locations are often overlooked because these island access points are not widely known to the boating public.

Kimball Preserve is one of those hidden gems with spectacular views from the ridge trail along the southern tip of Decatur Island. The unnamed Island along with the southern tip of Decatur Island and the isthmus that connects the two are part of the San Juan Preservation Trust. Boaters can anchor in the channel between Kimball Preserve and Center Island and take the dinghy to the northern shore of the isthmus. A "no-trespassing" sign painted on a rock is left over from an earlier time and no longer applies. A trail leads up the hillside with fabulous ocean views. Decatur property north of Kimball Preserve is private. The rocky islet between the unnamed island and Decatur Island in the Preserve is an undeveloped Bureau of Land Management property.

A portion of Henry Island near Roche Harbor is another special place to visit. Henry Island Preserve is made up of the isthmus forming the crossbar of the "H" on Henry Island along with some of the surrounding forest. Public access to a one-mile trail is available by dinghy on the beach at Open Bay or at the beach along Mosquito Pass east of the isthmus, depending on weather conditions. The beach along the isthmus of Open Bay is spectacular and is part of the Trust property. The cabin along the beach is private; the grave marker is in memory of Henry W. Perkins (1835-1887). A trail along the Mosquito Pass side of the isthmus heads northward through the forest. Other property on Henry Island is private.

To learn more about the San Juan Preservation Trust, or to make a donation, or to view the map of Trust Properties that you can visit, go to www.sjpt.org. *[Lorena Landon]*

Gulf Islands

GULF ISLANDS
Victoria • Sidney • Butchart Gardens • Chemainus
Wallace Island • Pirates Cove • Nanaimo

SALTSPRING ISLAND
Ganges • Vesuvius • Fulford Harbour

NORTH & SOUTH PENDER ISLAND
Bedwell Harbour • Port Browning • Otter Bay

GALIANO ISLAND
Sturdies Bay • Montague Harbour

Scan the Latest
Gulf Islands
Information

tinyurl.com/WG22xCh07

*Princess Cove,
Wallace Island*

GULF ISLANDS

Gulf Islands are comprised of eight or ten large islands and many smaller ones. For convenience, the Gulf Islands section of this book includes the southern tip and the east side of Vancouver Island as far up-island as Nanaimo. We divide this area into Northern and Southern sections with Active Pass and Houstoun Passage, the boundary between the two. The largest of the Gulf Islands is Saltspring Island (also written as Salt Spring Island), seventy square miles in area, and many smaller islands and islets. This is prime cruising territory with marine parks, anchorages, distinctive small towns and thriving cities. The first settlers arrived during the Fraser River gold rush and over the years the Islands' sunny climate and isolated proximity to civilization attracted many venturesome individuals including pioneers, artists, millionaires and refugees.

Geologically, the Gulf Islands are made of sandstone that has been folded and uplifted until it sticks out of the sea. Like the San Juan Islands, the Gulf Islands are in the lee of mountains. They receive much summertime sun and little summertime rainfall. Water can be in short supply and boat washing is often not allowed, at least in the islands themselves.

The Gulf Islands are blessed with dozens of anchorages, from one-boat notches to open bays that hold many boats. Marine parks provide anchorage, mooring and docking possibilities, with facilities ashore. Private marinas run the spectrum from rustic to deluxe, many with excellent dining on-site or nearby.

The largest town in the Gulf Islands proper is Ganges on Saltspring Island. If your definition of the islands expands (as ours does) to include southern and eastern Vancouver Island, then Victoria, Sidney, Ladysmith and Nanaimo are larger than Ganges. The best provisioning stops are Victoria, Sidney, Ganges, Ladysmith, Chemainus, and Nanaimo. Fuel is available throughout the islands.

Navigation is straightforward, but pay attention. It's easy to get confused, and the waters are dotted with rocks and reefs. Know where you are at all times. Canadian Hydrographic Services electronic chart packs RM-PAC02 Vancouver Island East and V-PAC-A Vancouver Island East include BSB-raster and ENC-vector charts respectively for the Gulf Islands.

The waters of the Gulf Islands are often busy with a mixture of recreational vessels, commercial tour boats, inter-island ferries, and large ferries transiting between the mainland and the Gulf Islands. Sidney and Nanaimo are the major terminals for fast moving ferries between Vancouver and Vancouver Island.

Customs – Entering Canada. Vessels entering Canada are required to clear Canadian Customs at their first stop in Canada. Most boats will clear customs at Bedwell Harbour on South Pender Island, Victoria (includes Victoria Inner Harbour, Oak Bay and Cadboro Bay), Sidney, or Nanaimo. Bedwell Harbour is just 4 miles north of Stuart Island in the San Juan Islands, but its station is open only from May 1 through September 30. See the *U.S. and Canadian Customs Information* in the Compendium chapter for a more detailed explanation on the process of clearing Canadian Customs.

Gulf Islands National Park Reserve. The Gulf Islands National Park Reserve came into being in 2004. Many former provincial parks, and most of the uninhabited islands and islets south of Active Pass, were transferred to the new national park, plus a number of other properties that were purchased. Land continues to be purchased and added to the Reserve. Park lands have green and white location signs, or small yellow boundary signs bearing the stylized beaver symbol of Parks Canada. Dogs must be on leash. Camping is in designated areas only. Nominal usage fees are charged, often collected through honor boxes on shore. For more information see www.pc.gc.ca/gulf; gulf.islands@pc.gc.ca; (250) 654-4000; (866) 944-1744. For emergencies or to report problems on park lands, call toll-free (877) 852-3100.

Gulf Islands

Historic 1860 Fisgard Lighthouse at the entrance to Esquimalt Harbour

2023 Waggoner Cruising Guide

GULF ISLANDS

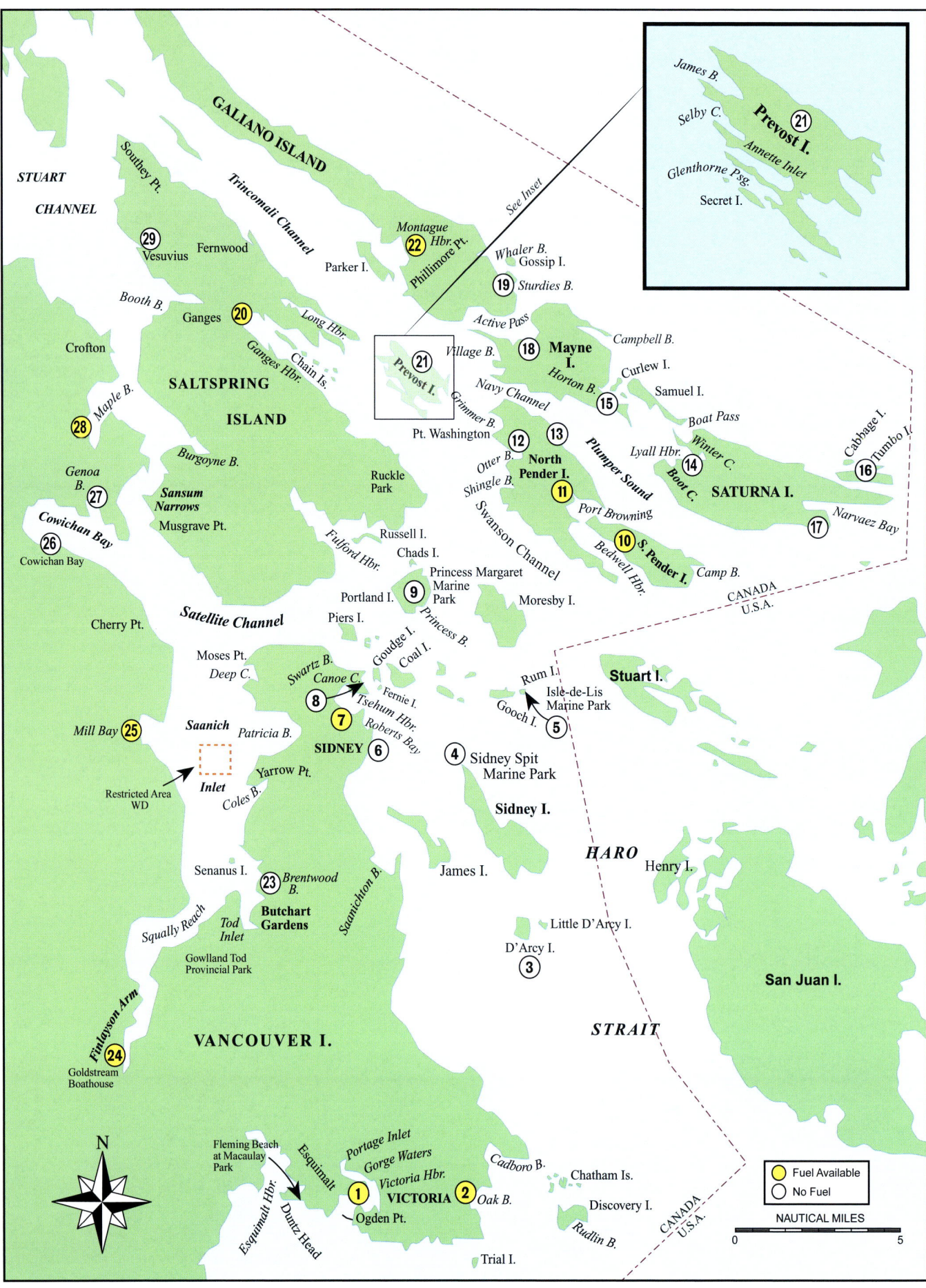

Reference Only – Not for Navigation

Southern Gulf Islands

VICTORIA AREA

Esquimalt Harbour. Esquimalt Harbour is a wonderful but often overlooked anchorage, with excellent holding in thick mud southeast of Cole Island, with room to swing. Protection is reasonable, even with big winds blowing in the Strait of Juan de Fuca. With this bottom you're not going anywhere, anyway, but you might be rocking and rolling at times due to swell or wind waves.

The Canadian Navy guards the entrance with a high speed inflatable and may advise you to keep 100 meters away from their ships and property. Anchor north of a line between the south end of Richards Island and the north end of Smart Island. Rafting is not allowed; and according to Sailing Directions, two anchors are required.

The British Navy once used Cole Island for munitions storage. The large brick buildings from the late 1800s on the island are still intact and make interesting exploration. Cole Island is a National Historic Site where visitors are welcome. A dinghy dock is located on the southwest side of Cole Island and boardwalk pathways connect all the buildings. For a map of the buildings on the island, go to www.coleisland.ca.

Security Zone: All vessels entering or departing Esquimalt Harbour are requested to contact QHM Operations on VHF channel 10 or by telephone (250) 363-2160. Give your vessel name, make, and direction of travel at Fisgard Lighthouse and Duntze Head. Fisgard Lighthouse was the first lighthouse on Canada's west coast (1860) and is still in operation.

You can anchor the dinghy off the beach at the lighthouse to tour Fisgard Light and the historic Fort Rodd Hill military site. Payment to enter the grounds should be made at the entrance gate to Fort Rodd Hill located above the lighthouse. The grounds are open from June through October. Gun emplacements, magazines, defensive walls and military houses from the late 1800's can be seen at Fort Rodd Hill; Fisgard Lighthouse contains archival photos and historical information about the lighthouse.

Fleming Beach at Macaulay Park. West of Victoria Harbour, in Esquimalt. Open all year. Facilities include launch ramp (fee charged) and washrooms. This is a charming little cove, protected by a rock breakwater, overlooked by most boating people. It is the home of Esquimalt Anglers' Association, a private sportfishing and fish enhancement group. The boarding floats at the launch ramp have room for temporary moorage while shopping nearby, or you can anchor out. Walkways and picnic areas have been built. Fleming Beach is adjacent to old coastal gun emplacements, which make for good exploring.

① **Victoria.** Victoria is the provincial capital of British Columbia, and the largest city on Vancouver Island. Vancouver Island is served by ferries from Port Angeles, WA to Victoria; from Tsawwassen to Sidney and Victoria through Swartz Bay; and from Vancouver (Horseshoe Bay) to Nanaimo. The fast-running Victoria Clipper passenger ferry connects Victoria and Seattle. Scheduled floatplanes also connect with Vancouver and Seattle, and other destinations.

Victoria is beautiful. The Empress Hotel, for which the word "majestic" could have been created, dominates the Inner Harbour. The Empress is flanked on the south by the B.C. provincial parliament buildings, themselves the embodiment of dignity, thoughtful deliberation, and orderly progress—the buildings, that is. Between the Empress and the parliament buildings stands the Royal British Columbia Museum, a must-see, especially for families. A giant ice-age mammoth dominates the entry, and the rest of the museum delights with a re-creation of Capt. Vancouver's ship, a Victorian town exhibit, a west coast seashore, a First Nations Big House and much, much more. Highly recommended.

The Maritime Museum of British Columbia (250) 385-4222 is located downtown in Nootka Court at 634 Humboldt Street, across from the Empress Hotel. This excellent museum is open 10:00 a.m. to 4:00 p.m. Tuesday through Saturday.

The Visitor Information Centre is on top of the causeway at the head of the Inner Harbour, across from the Empress Hotel. It's easy to find. The entire Victoria Inner Harbour is covered by Wi-Fi.

Inside Ogden Point, marinas and public wharves begin with Fisherman's Wharf and progress inward to the well-marked customs dock at Raymur Point. East of the customs dock is the Coast Victoria Harbourside Hotel & Marina. Next, in James Bay, comes the Causeway Marina, in front of the Empress Hotel. These docks are popular and fill first. Northward from the Causeway Marina comes Ship Point Marina. Continuing north are the Wharf Street Floats, and Johnson Street Marina. On the north shore of the Middle Harbour is the Victoria International Marina. With the exception of Harbourside Hotel & Marina and Victoria International Marina, all moorage facilities are managed by the Greater Victoria Harbour Authority. Details regarding these facilities are described below.

West Bay is home to three marinas, Westbay Marine Village, Sailors Cove, and Hidden Harbour, with permanent moorage and float homes. Two marinas in the Upper Harbour, Victoria Marina and Canoe Brewpub Marina & Restaurant, are permanent moorage only. The very substantial Point Hope Maritime Shipyard is located on the west side of Upper Harbour. **Johnson Street Bridge** separates Inner Harbour from the Upper Harbour, contact the bridge attendant on VHF 12.

For an interesting side trip, take the dinghy north under the Johnson Street Bridge, through Upper Harbour, Selkirk Water, and Gorge Waters to Portage Inlet. You'll travel through the industrial part of the city, then through park and residential areas. It's about a 3-mile trip; currents are a factor if you intend to row.

Harbor Master/Harbor Patrol: Contact Harbour Master/Patrol on VHF 18A or (250) 363-3578 office or (250) 380-8177 for 24-hour emergencies.

Customs: The customs dock is located at Raymur Point, just east of Fisherman's Wharf in front of the Harbourside Hotel & Marina. When arriving, check in using the dedicated phone at the customs dock.

Greater Victoria Harbour Authority: (GVHA) owns and operates several marine facilities, 3 of which have guest moorage: Causeway Marina, Ship Point Marina (large vessels), and Wharf Street Floats. Laundry, showers, and washrooms for all three guest facilities are located on the Broughton Street Pier–look for the gray building with a red roof. The Harbour Authority has a "meet and greet" program for visiting boats. When you enter the Inner Harbour, call on VHF 66A and they will direct you to available guest moorage.

Reservations: The Coast Victoria Harbourside Hotel & Marina, adjacent to the Fisherman's Wharf, accepts reservations. The Greater Victoria Harbour Authority accepts reservations and are recommended for larger vessels (60 feet and over), on special holidays, and during peak season months. Visit GVHA's website, gvha.ca, for more information about making reservations.

This is your view of the Empress Hotel from moorage at the Causeway Marina. Don't miss afternoon tea at the Empress.

GULF ISLANDS

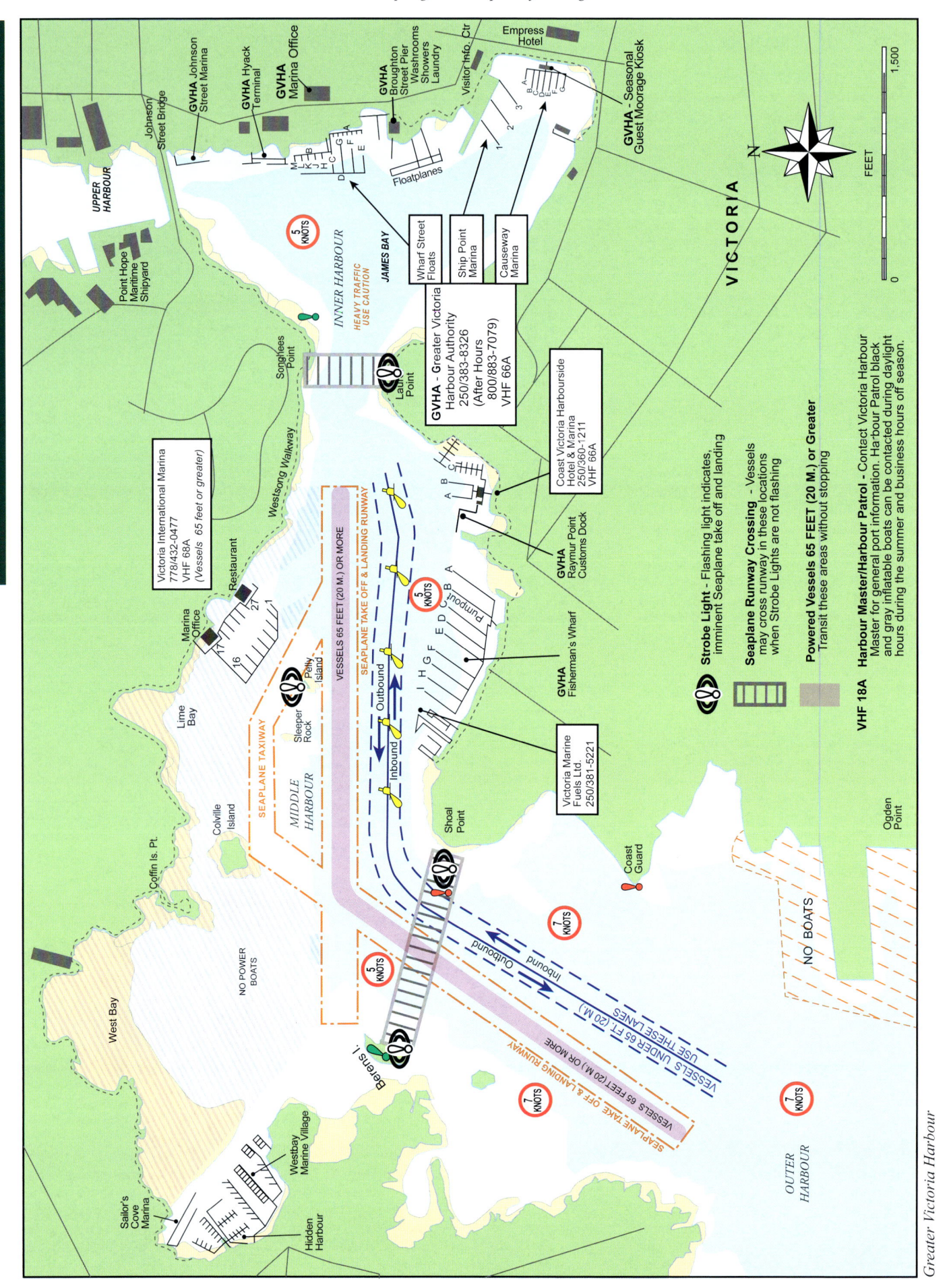

See Area Map Page 220 - Maps Not for Navigation

Greater Victoria Harbour

Symphony Splash: On the first weekend in August enjoy symphony music from a barge in the Inner Harbour, punctuated with cannons and fireworks. Over 40,000 people line the Inner Harbour for the evening event.

No Discharge Zone. Discharging raw sewage is prohibited in Victoria Harbour, defined as beginning at the Ogden Point breakwater. This applies to "black water" only. "Gray water," such as from dishwashing or showers, is okay (if biodegradable).

Pumpout: A for fee pumpout station is located on B-dock of Fisherman's Wharf. Tokens to operate the pump are available at Victoria Marine Fuels and the Harbour Authority seasonal kiosk at the Causeway Marina.

Taxi: Bluebird Cab (250) 382-2222; Victoria Cab (250) 383-7111; and Yellow Cab (250) 381-2222.

LOCAL KNOWLEDGE

Victoria Mandatory Traffic Lanes: All vessels 20 meters/65 feet LOA and less must enter and depart Victoria's Inner Harbour between Shoal Point and Laurel Point along the south shore, as shown in the accompanying harbor map. Inbound vessels favor the docks; outbound vessels a little farther out. The traffic lanes are marked by buoys (keep the buoys to port when entering and exiting). The more open water in the middle of the harbor is used by the large number of floatplanes that land and take off constantly. Because of the volume of boat and floatplane traffic, no sailing is allowed inside the breakwater. Sailboats under power must have sails lowered.

① **Greater Victoria Harbour Authority - GVHA.** 100-1019 Wharf Street, Victoria, BC V8W 2Y9; (250) 383-8326; (800) 883-7079 after hours; gvha@gvha.ca; www.gvha.ca. Monitors VHF 66A. The Greater Victoria Harbour Authority owns, manages, and operates a number of recreational and commercial marine facilities throughout Victoria Harbour. Three of the popular GVHA guest moorage marinas in the Inner Harbour include Causeway Marina, Ship Point Marina, and Wharf Street Floats.

GVHA's most popular guest location is the Causeway Marina located in front of the Empress Hotel. Ship Point Marina is adjacent to Causeway Marina with amenities for larger boats. Moorage rates at all three of GVHA's guest marinas are the same and can be viewed at gvha.ca. Washroom, shower, and laundry facilities for all of GVHA's guest facilities are located at Broughton Street Pier. GVHA's main office is located on the ground floor of an office building on Wharf Street, just above Wharf Street Floats. Seasonal guest registration kiosks are located at the bottom of ramp at Causeway Marina and Wharf Street.

GVHA commercial and permanent moorage facilities include **Johnson Street Marina** and **Hyack Terminal** in the Inner Harbour; **Fisherman's Wharf** and **Raymur Point Customs Dock** in the Middle Harbour; and the Cruise Ship Terminal and deep water facilities at Ogden Point. Fisherman's Wharf is reserved primarily for commercial and monthly moorage, no transient space. Johnson Street Marina is for monthly moorage only, primarily used by fish boats and commercial vessels. Hyack Terminal provides floatplane services, permanent moorage, and facilities for marine adventure tour operators.

GVHA accepts reservations online for guest moorage facilities and is the preferred method due to volume. Reservations are a must on special holidays and during the peak season. Visit GVHA's website, gvha.ca, or call them for more information about making reservations.

Broughton Street Pier - GVHA. Showers, washrooms, and laundry facilities for GVHA moorage guests are located at this location. Garbage and recycle drop are also located here. No moorage at the Broughton Street Pier. Water taxis and tour boats arrive and depart from this facility.

Causeway Marina – GVHA. Open all year with 2000+ feet of side-tie dock space for vessels up to 60 feet. 30 amp power, potable water, free Wi-Fi, garbage and recycling drop. Limited guest moorage space October 1 through May 15. Docks are gated all hours through the year. The check-in kiosk, located beside the ramp to shore, is open June 15 through September 15. These are the picturesque and popular docks directly in front of the Empress Hotel. Downtown Victoria beckons with fabulous restaurants, shopping, hotels, museums, and sightseeing. Public washrooms (no showers) are located under the Visitors Centre building. Private, clean Harbour Authority operated showers, laundry, and washrooms are at the Broughton Street Pier.

Ship Point Marina - GVHA. Open all year for larger vessels 60 feet to 280 feet; side-tie moorage. Docks are gated all-hours. Reservations highly recommended. Potable water, 30, 50, 100 amp single phase/208 & 3-phase/480 power. Free Wi-Fi, garbage and recycling drop. Public washrooms (no showers) are located under the Visitors Centre building. Private and clean Harbour Authority-operated showers, laundry and washrooms are at the Broughton Street Pier.

Wharf Street Floats – GVHA. Open all year for vessels to 375 feet, more than 1000 feet of side-tie visitor dock space. Limited guest moorage October 1 to the end of May. Potable water, 30, 50 & 100 amp power (single phase/208), garbage, free Wi-Fi. Power availability varies depending on location. Conveniently located downtown, just not quite as picturesque as the Causeway Floats in front of the Empress Hotel.

① **Victoria Marine Fuels Ltd.** (250) 381-5221; www.marinefuels.com. Fuel dock with gasoline and diesel, located at Erie Street Fisherman's Wharf at 1 Dallas Rd. Open all year, but with shorter winter hours, closed Christmas Day and New Year's Day. Store stocks snacks, food items, charts. This is the only fuel dock in the Inner Harbour.

① **Coast Victoria Harbourside Hotel & Marina.** 146 Kingston Street, Victoria, V8V 1V4; (250) 360-1211; coastvictoria@coasthotels.com; www.coasthotels.com. Guest moorage May through September, limited availability October through April; 30 & 50 amp power, potable water on the docks, washrooms and showers. Pumpout available for overnight guests. Marina guests have full access to the dining room and lounge, indoor/outdoor pool, Jacuzzi, sauna, and fitness facilities. Reservations accepted. Within walking distance of downtown.

① **Victoria International Marina.** 1 Cooperage Place, Victoria, BC V9A 7J9; (778) 432-0477; info@vimarina.ca; www.vimarina.ca. Monitors VHF 68A. On the north shore of Victoria Harbour, northeast of Pelly Island, two symmetrical one-story buildings sit on either side of this 28-slip marina designed to accommodate boats 65 to 175 feet in length. Six slips are leased for 40 years; seven slips are available for one-year renewable leases; seven slips for monthly leases with a 3-month minimum stay; and seven slips are reserved for guest moorage.

This is a world-class marina with first-class marina services, a crew lounge, and event space. The marina is designed and built with luxury yachts in mind. Due to Victoria Harbour traffic restrictions imposed by Transport Canada, this marina is for yachts 65 feet and over; smaller boats by special permit only. The trendy Boom & Batten Restaurant and Cafe (250-940-5850) is located next to the marina. The beautiful Westsong/Songhees Walkway meanders along the shore offering outstanding views. Three water-taxi landings are located along the Walkway with departures to Victoria's downtown waterfront.

THINGS TO DO

• **Royal British Columbia Museum.** (250) 356-7226. An excellent museum covering the human and natural history of British Columbia is just above James Bay in Victoria. Renovations may be underway and displays limited over the next several years.
• **B.C. Maritime Museum.** (250) 385-4222. Displays on B.C. maritime history and various rotating exhibits.
• **Afternoon Tea at the Empress Hotel.** (250) 384-8111. A special treat, high tea offers pastries and piano music in an elegant setting.
• **Afternoon Tea at Butchart Gardens.** (250) 652-4422; a public bus runs daily to

GULF ISLANDS

the gardens from Causeway Marina.
- **BC Parliament Building**. (250) 953-2033 visitor info. Take a guided tour of this government building; construction began in 1893; Neo-baroque Renaissance style.
- **Craigdarroch Castle**. (250) 592-5323. Tour the historic mansion at 1050 Joan Crescent, built by coal baron Robert Dunsmuir.
- **Victoria Chinatown**. Visit the oldest Chinatown in Canada and the second largest in North America; enjoy cafes and shops on Fisgard Street and Fan Tan Alley.
- **Victoria Bug Zoo**. (250) 384-2847. Visit the most amazing, rare, and unique collection of bugs from around the world; 631 Courtney Street.
- **Thunderbird Park**. (250) 356-7226. Visit the monuments and exhibits of the First Nation People, a reflection of the culture of the region. Buildings include St. Anne's Schoolhouse and the Mungo Martin House. Located next to the Royal BC Museum.
- **Emily Carr House**. (250) 383-5843. Learn about the renowned Canadian artist and writer Emily Carr, while visiting her childhood home at 207 Government Street.
- **Victoria Inner Harbour**. Watch street musicians, mimes, and artists. The waterfront comes alive in the summer.

② **Oak Bay.** Oak Bay is on the east side of the south tip of Vancouver Island, west of the Chatham Islands. The channels between the various rocks and reefs are well marked. This is the route taken by many tugs with tows, and commercial fish boats of all sizes. The Oak Bay Marina and a separate small repair yard are located behind the breakwater. Willows Beach, 0.7 miles north of Oak Bay Marina, has a charted restricted, no boating area.

② **Oak Bay Marina**. 1327 Beach Drive, Victoria, BC V8S 2N4; (250) 598-3369; (800) 663-7090 ext. 247; obm@obmg.com; www.oakbaymarina.com. VHF 66A. Open all year with gasoline and diesel. Customs clearance telephone at the fuel dock. Spectacular views of Mt. Baker. Guest moorage for boats to 70 feet; 15 & 30 amp power, washrooms, showers, laundry, Wi-Fi. Call ahead for availability or reserve through SwiftHarbour.com booking service.

The marina has excellent docks and a good licensed waterfront restaurant. Outdoor seating on the deck overlooking the marina. A coffee house for quick casual dining, and a gift shop with local products and sundry items. A small chandlery carries essential boating supplies. Repairs are at the Gartside Marine boatyard in a neighboring building, no haulout. The Oak Bay Beach Hotel is nearby for elegant dining. Complete shopping at quaint Oak Bay Village a short distance away. Regular bus service to downtown Victoria. Kayak tours and bike rentals available. Part of the Oak Bay Marine Group.

See Area Map Page 220 - Maps Not for Navigation

Temporary anchorage and access to the island can be found on the east side of D'Arcy Island Gulf Islands Park.

Discovery Island Marine Park. Open all year. An undeveloped park suitable for beachable boats only. The island was once the home of Capt. E.G. Beaumont, who donated the land as a park. The northern part of Discovery Island, adjacent Chatham Island, and some of the smaller islands nearby are Indian Reserve lands: no landing.

Chatham Islands. A favorite destination of kayakers and other small boaters, the Chain Islets and Chatham Islands lie 2 miles east of Oak Harbor and 0.5 mile north of Discovery Island. Due to the many rocks and reefs surrounding Chain Islets, Chatham Islands, and Discovery Island, the area is best explored by small boat. Chatham Islands and the north half of Discovery Island are Indian Reserves, respect these reserves and do not go ashore. The southern part of Discovery Island is a Marine Park with shore access.

In settled weather, small craft can find temporary anchorage in Puget Cove on Chatham Islands or in 5 to 6 meters of water in Alpha Islet Cove between Griffin Island and Discovery Island.

Cadboro Bay. Cadboro Bay is entirely residential except for the Royal Victoria Yacht Club, which has a breakwater-protected marina on the western shore. Moorage at Royal Victoria Yacht Club is for members of reciprocal clubs only. Customs clearance is available.

Anchorage in Cadboro Bay is excellent, mud and sand bottom. A 100-foot long concrete replica of Cadborosaurus, the elusive sea monster of Cadboro Bay, is prominent in the playground above the broad sandy beach at Cadboro-Gyro Park.

③ **D'Arcy Island (Gulf Islands National Park Reserve).** Open all year. This is an undeveloped island with no facilities other than some primitive campsites and a toilet. Dogs must be on leash. The island is surrounded by intimidating rocks, reefs, and shoals. Even if you study the chart carefully, kelp-covered rocks will pop up and surprise you. Approach with great caution. As far as we are concerned, there are no "good" anchorages at D'Arcy Island, only acceptable spots in the right weather. The cove on the east side of the island has depths of 10 to 25 feet with fair holding and some protection from west and northwest winds. The single Parks staff mooring buoy is in this cove. This cove is closest to the island's campsites and pit toilets. If conditions allow, the cove on the west side of the island, south of the light, will work. Two coves on the northwest end look okay, but we didn't put the anchor down to confirm.

D'Arcy Island was B.C.'s first leper colony; from 1891 until 1925 it housed Chinese lepers. The colony was closed in 1925 and the island reverted to provincial jurisdiction. Ruins from the colony located just south of the west side light remain. A rustic shore side trail runs from the east cove campsites around the south end of the island to the west side light. A well-marked trail cuts across the island from just south of the campsites to the colony ruins. Plans for the island as a federal penitentiary were never realized. D'Arcy Island remained undeveloped, and was established as a marine park in 1961. *A Measure of Value*, by Chris Yorath, provides a good history of D'Arcy Island. To the east, Little D'Arcy Island is private property.

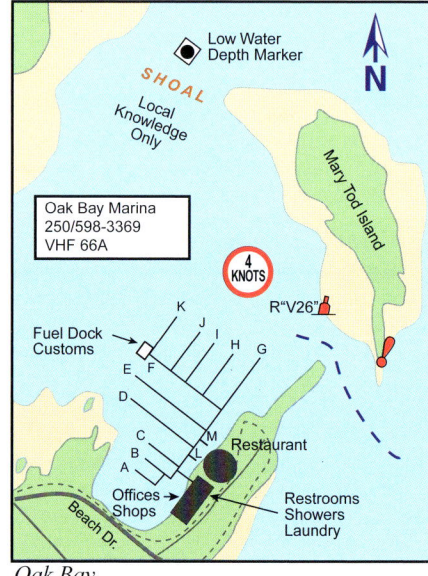

Oak Bay

224   www.WaggonerGuide.com

See Area Map Page 220 - Maps Not for Navigation

GULF ISLANDS

Enjoy an afternoon lunch on the sun-filled deck overlooking Oak Bay Marina.

Sculptures found along Sidney's promenade

④ **Sidney Spit (Gulf Islands National Park Reserve).** The park, open all summer, occupies about one-third of Sidney Island, and all of the mile-long Sidney Spit with its white sand and shell beach extending northwest from the island. The island is closed to visitors from November through February to facilitate traditional hunting by First Nations to control the fallow deer population. Anchor or tie to one of 12 mooring buoys, or moor on the seasonal dock. Anchoring depths are shallow and the area has considerable eel grass. Self-registration and payment box located at the dock. Buoys are limited to vessels of 50 feet or less in winds up to 30 knots; 40 feet for winds up to 37 knots; no mooring in large waves. In the summers, a passenger ferry runs between Sidney Spit dock and Sidney Beacon Ave dock.

Picnic and camping areas are ashore. Dogs must be on leash. An easily walked 2-km loop trail winds around the park through a dense forest of cedar, hemlock, fir, big-leaf maple and vine maple. A herd of fallow deer is reported to be on the island. A large saltwater lagoon is habitat for many animal and plant species and is off limits; markers show its borders. The remains of a brick-making factory are near the lagoon, where a beach is covered with broken red bricks.

⑤ **Isle-de-Lis at Rum Island (Gulf Islands National Park Reserve).** Open all year, anchoring only, campsites and a pit toilet. This is a small, undeveloped, and very pretty park with a walking trail and beaches. Dogs must be on leash. Rum Island is located at the east end of Gooch Island (private), where Prevost Passage meets Haro Strait. Anchorage is on either side of the gravel spit connecting Rum Island and Gooch Island. The northern anchorage is preferred. Rum Island is said to have come by its name honestly during Prohibition. In 1995 the warship HMCS *Mackenzie* was sunk in approximately 100 feet just north of Gooch Island to create an artificial reef for divers. It is marked with 2 cautionary/information buoys.

Saanichton Bay. Just off Cordova Channel between James Island and the east shore of Saanich Peninsula is Saanichton Bay. This large bay is open to the north but protected from south and west winds. Good anchoring in 15 to 30 feet with room to swing. Along the shore to the southeast is Cordova Spit Park with nice sand and gravel beaches. Along the western shore of the bay at Turgoose Point is the James Island public wharf with a small float. Most boat traffic transits Sidney Channel farther to the east so there is minimal boat wake. A large barge is normally moored in the bay but is not a factor for anchoring.

Roberts Bay. Good anchorage, centrally located about a mile from both Sidney and Tsehum Harbour. Anchor in the center of the bay where the large shallow bay gives separation from the homes lining the shore. Good holding on a flat mud bottom, but exposed to north and northeast winds. Large wakes from boats entering and exiting Tsehum Harbour occasionally find their way into the anchorage but the bay becomes settled in the evening.

THINGS TO DO

- **Shaw Centre for the Salish Sea.** Learn more about the ecosystem of the B.C. coastal waters.
- **Waterfront Lochside Regional Trail.** Rent bikes on this flat and easy-to-ride trail from Victoria to Sidney.
- **Sidney Street Market.** Thursday evenings on Beacon Ave; June to August, purchase food, produce, and art.
- **British Columbia Aviation Museum.** 1910 Norseman Rd, see early aircraft, warbirds, and modern aircraft.
- **Visit Gardens at Butchart Gardens.** (250) 652-4422; Public transportation runs from Sidney to Butchart Gardens. Tour the gardens during the day, have lunch, and enjoy Afternoon Tea in the original home of Butchart. Stay for the weekend to take in the special seasonal events.

⑥ **Sidney.** For boats crossing from Roche Harbor or the northern San Juan Islands, Sidney is a natural first stop to clear customs, stroll around, and restock with fresh produce, meat, spirits, and more. Downtown Sidney and nearby Tsehum Harbour have much to attract boaters, including excellent bakeries just up Beacon Avenue (Sidney's main street). The town also has art galleries, interesting shops, liquor stores, several bookstores, several museums, and three supermarkets. Summer concerts are held on the lawn at the base of Beacon Street. A paved walkway stretches 2.5 km along the Sidney waterfront between Port Sidney Marina and south beyond the Washington State Ferries terminal. It is part of the 29 km multi-use Lochside Regional Trail stretching from Swartz Bay to Victoria.

The Sidney Historical Museum occupies the lower floor of the old Post Office Building, at the corner of 4th and Beacon. The museum has an excellent exhibit of early history in Sidney, admission by donation. Highly recommended, especially for families. Located at the nearby Sidney airport is the BC Aviation Museum, a short cab ride away.

The Shaw Centre for the Salish Sea in the Sidney Pier building has outstanding exhibits of marine life from local waters.

For an entirely different feeling from downtown Sidney, try Tsehum Harbour, a short distance north of downtown. The pace in Tsehum Harbour is much slower, and many of the moored boats are funkier. This is where the fishing fleet moors, and where the boat yards are. Van Isle Marina is the major marina.

Something about Tsehum Harbour attracts good restaurants, too. Tsehum Harbour's only disadvantage is the long walk to major shopping. Regular bus service runs into Sidney, or you could take a taxi or rent a car. Thrifty Foods charges $5 per order for delivery.

Market: The Sidney Street Market takes over the lower part of Beacon Avenue Thursday evenings May through September, 5:30 p.m. to 8:30 p.m.

Customs: Sidney is the western terminus of the Washington State Ferries that run from Anacortes and Friday Harbor, and is a

GULF ISLANDS

See Area Map Page 220 - Maps Not for Navigation

Canada Customs port of entry. Customs can be cleared by telephone at Port Sidney Marina, Van Isle Marina or Canoe Cove Marina.

Wi-Fi: Shaw Go WiFi is available throughout the town of Sidney. You can select "Shaw Guest," create an account, and sign in at participating locations in town.

⑥ **Port Sidney Marina**. 9835 Seaport Place, P.O. Box 2338, Sidney, BC V8L 4X3; (250) 655-3711; admin@portsidney.com; www.portsidney.com. Monitors VHF 66A. Open all year. Facilities include 30, 50 & 100 amp power, water, excellent washrooms, showers, laundry, Shaw Go WiFi on the docks and free Wi-Fi in the comfortable marina lounge; a password is provided for marina guests. This is a popular marina, modern and well-maintained, adjacent to downtown Sidney. Reservations recommended. A for-fee pumpout, located between D and E docks, accommodates boats up to 40 feet. Mobile pumpout is available for larger vessels. Bikes (ebikes) available to rent. The marina is part of the Mill Bay Marine Group, with several marinas throughout B.C.

Call on VHF 66A low power before entering and exiting the breakwater. When approaching from the north, pass between the two buoys just outside the breakwater entrance. The easternmost of these buoys marks a reef. Do not try to enter between the north end of the breakwater and shore. If you are directed to the shore side of the long, main pier, do not stray outside the marked channel. The bottom has been dredged alongside the shoreside dock, but shoal water lies just a few feet inshore.

Customs: The customs check-in dock is on the end of G dock. Customs can be cleared by using the direct-line telephone on the dock. During summer months customs officers may be stationed there for inspections after calling in. Space at the dock is limited to one or two boats and once inside the breakwater maneuvering room is limited. The marina office has a video camera pointed at the dock and they can advise over the VHF if boats are waiting to clear customs.

Taxi: Sidney Taxi (250) 656-6666 and Yellow Cab (250) 656-1111.

⑥ **Sidney Beacon Ave. Public Wharf.** Sidney Beacon Avenue Public Wharf is used only for the summertime ferry to Sidney Spit Marine Park and does not have public dock space. A snack bar, café and a fresh fish market are at the end of the pier.

⑦ **Tsehum Harbour.** Tsehum Harbour (Tsehum is pronounced "See-um"), a shallow but navigable inlet about 1.5 miles north of downtown Sidney, contains a number of public, private, and yacht club moorages as well as chandleries. Enter favoring the Armstrong Point (south) side to avoid a marked rock.

This is the working waterfront of Sidney, with several excellent boatyards. Van Isle Marina, the first marina on the south side, has a customs check-in telephone, fuel, and guest moorage. Westport Marina has guest moorage, and many services including haulout and free showers. Other moorages in Tsehum Harbour are North Saanich Marina,

Enjoy a stroll along Sidney's waterfront promenade.

You will find friends frozen in time along the promenade

Capitol City and Sidney North Saanich yacht clubs, and private marinas. The main fuel dock is in Van Isle Marina. Fuel is also available at North Saanich Marina.

Speed limit: A speed limit of 4 knots is in force in Tsehum Harbour. Watch your speed and wake.

Repairs: Haulout and complete repairs are available.

LOCAL KNOWLEDGE

ROCKS: Stay close to the end of the dock when rounding the west end of the fuel and customs dock at Van Isle Marina. A substantial drying rock lies a short distance off, and each year a few boats manage to find it. The rock is marked by a beacon, but the rock extends toward the dock from the beacon.

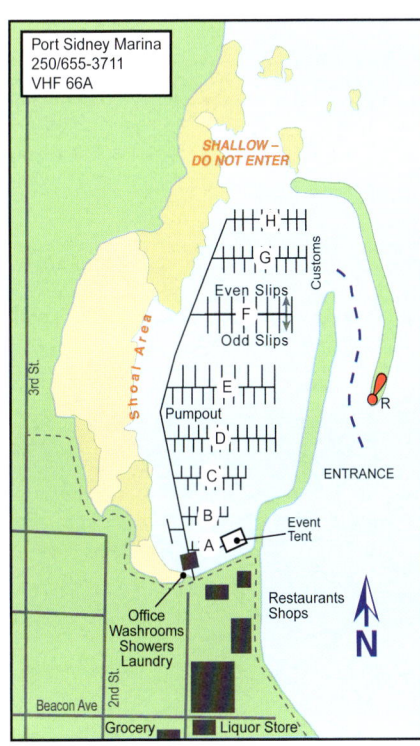

Port Sidney Marina

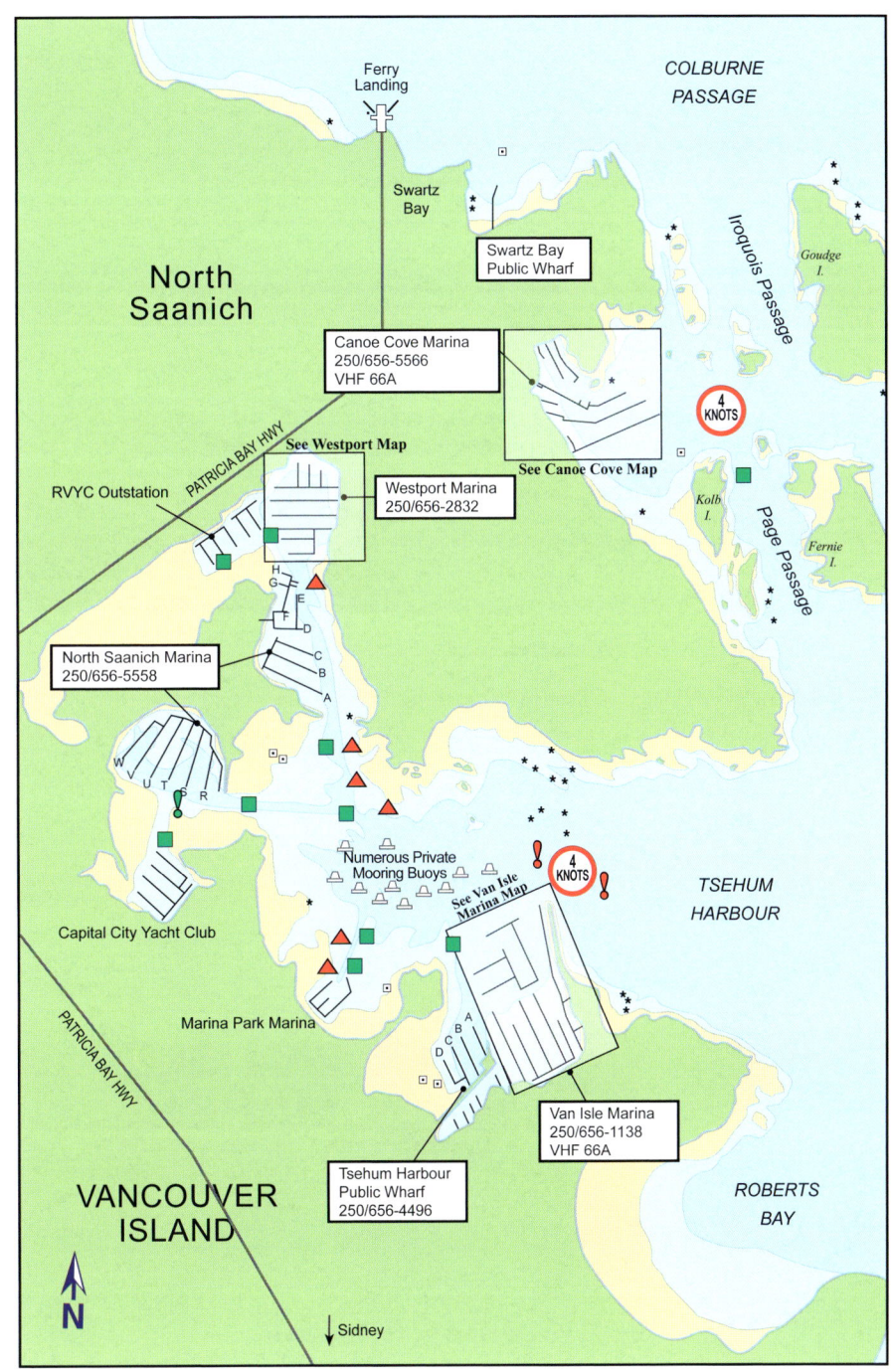

Tsehum Harbour

2023 Waggoner Cruising Guide

227

GULF ISLANDS

See Area Map Page 220 - Maps Not for Navigation

⑦ **Van Isle Marina.** 2320 Harbour Road, Sidney, V8L 2P6; (250) 656-1138; info@vanislemarina.com; www.vanislemarina.com. Monitors VHF 66A. Open all year, daily. Gasoline and diesel at fuel dock, customs clearance with dedicated phones in the small shed at the end of the fuel dock, free Wi-Fi, 15, 30, 50 & 100 amp power, excellent washrooms, showers and laundry. Self-serve dog wash on site. Pumpout and launch ramp. A business center with computer connections, copy machine, fax machine, and conference room is available for marina guests. Complimentary bicycle rentals and taxi vouchers to nearby locations. Groceries can be delivered to the marina by Thrifty Foods.

A side-tie dock, 451 feet long and 15 feet wide, runs parallel to the breakwater on the east side of the marina. It is set up for yachts up to 200' and more, with 100 amp power, telephone, cable, and internet connections. Large boat or small, it's best to call ahead for guest moorage availability.

Van Isle is a large and busy marina, about a mile from downtown. Full repair services, haulout to 45 tons, and dry storage are available. The Thrifty Foods in Sidney will deliver groceries to the marina. The Sea Glass Waterfront Grill is at the head of the dock, call (778) 351-3663 for reservations. The famous Latch Country Inn is a short walk away. The marina offers bicycles at no charge to ride into Sidney or on the popular Lochside Trail, nearby.

Since 1955 Van Isle Marina has been owned and managed by three generations of the Dickinson family. The family's long-term commitment to doing things right is evident. The staff is excellent, and the facilities are top-notch.

⑦ **Tsehum Harbour Public Wharf.** (250) 655-4496. Open all year, 1043 feet of dock space, 20 & 30 amp power, washrooms, shower, Wi-Fi available at the office. This is a commercial fish boat harbor that accepts very limited guest moorage. Customs clearance location.

⑦ **Westport Marina.** 2075 Tryon Road, Sidney, BC V8L 3X9; (250) 656-2832; westport@thunderbirdmarine.com; www.westportmarine.ca. Open all year. 15, 20, 30 & 50 amp power, washrooms, free showers, Wi-Fi. Guest moorage in unoccupied slips, call ahead for availability. Haulout to 55 tons. Well stocked chandlery, charts, limited groceries.

⑦ **North Saanich Marina.** 1949 Marina Way, North Saanich, BC V8L 6B3; (250) 656-5558; nsm@obmg.com; www.northsaanichmarina.com. VHF 66A.

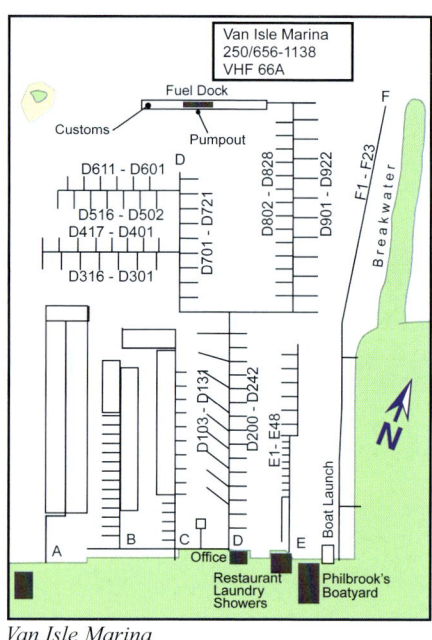

Excellence & Value in every Marina Experience.

CANADA CUSTOMS & FUEL DOCK

- 500 berths for annual, monthly or nightly moorage
- Service for boats 20' to 200'
- Fuel dock & marine store
- Canada Customs Port of Entry
- Haul outs & full repair facilities
- Yacht Park - 90 spaces for dry land storage and maintenance
- 15/30/50/100 amp shore power
- Casual Dining at Sea Glass Grill
- Business centre
- Laundry, showers & washrooms
- **NEW** Dog wash station
- Yacht brokerage & sales
- Free WiFi
- **NEW** Gas fire table & patio

Situated in beautiful Tsehum Harbour by Sidney, British Columbia, Van Isle Marina is just 5 minutes from ferries, Victoria International Airport and shopping.

VAN ISLE MARINA
family owned & operated since 1955

Tsehum Harbour, Sidney, BC | 250 656 1138 | info@vanislemarina.com

vanislemarina.com

Van Isle Marina

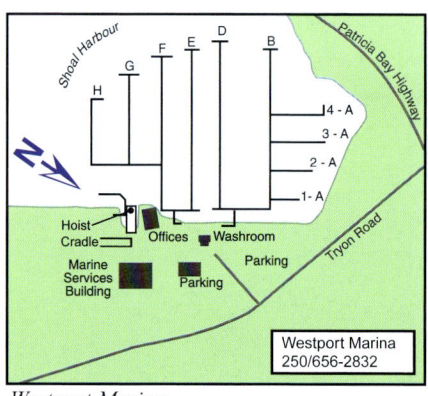

Westport Marina

228   www.WaggonerGuide.com

See Area Map Page 220 - Maps Not for Navigation

GULF ISLANDS

Open all year. Gasoline and diesel at the fuel dock; Wi-Fi. Washrooms at the main office. Permanent and guest moorage usually available for vessels to 70 feet; 15, 30 & 50 amp power.

Recent dock refurbishments, and a large dog walking area are among the marina's improvements. It's a short taxi ride to the nearby town of Sidney. Their store carries sundries, fishing tackle, boat cleaning supplies, and ice. Call ahead for moorage availability. Home of the Sidney North Saanich Yacht Club, with reciprocal moorage. The marina is part of the Oak Bay Marine Group, a company that owns several marinas on Vancouver Island.

⑧ **Canoe Bay.** Canoe Bay, commonly called Canoe Cove, is tucked in behind a group of islands, only some of which have navigable passages between them. The clearest passage is **John Passage**, along the west side of Coal Island. From John Passage turn west into **Iroquois Passage**, and follow Iroquois Passage between Fernie Island and Goudge Island into Canoe Bay.

Page Passage should be run only with local knowledge or close study of large-scale Chart 3479. Tidal currents can run strongly, especially on spring tides.

⑧ **Canoe Cove Marina & Boatyard.** 2300 Canoe Cove Road, North Saanich, BC V8L 3X9; (250) 656-5566; (250) 656-5515; www.canoecovemarina.com. Monitors VHF 66A. Open all year; 30 & 50 amp power, washrooms, showers, laundry, free Wi-Fi. This is a 450-berth marina with permanent and visitor moorage in unoccupied slips as assigned. Best to call ahead.

Navigate carefully on approach. A number of islands and rocks surround the entrance to Canoe Cove. They are well marked on the charts and easily avoided as long as you pay attention.

Porto Osteria Bakery & Cafe is in the center of the marina, and the excellent Stonehouse Restaurant is nearby. A short trail leads to the Swartz Bay ferry terminal for arriving or departing guests from Tsawwassen, on the B.C. mainland. A harbor taxi shuttle connects the marina with Sidney. Pacifica Paddle Sports (250) 665-7411 at Canoe Cove offers kayak, canoe, and paddleboard rentals along with lessons and tours.

Canoe Cove's major thrust is its environmentally friendly full repair facility, with an 83-ton Travelift, and extensive work areas. Chandleries are nearby. The staff and management are friendly and competent. Together with Vector Marine, Blackline

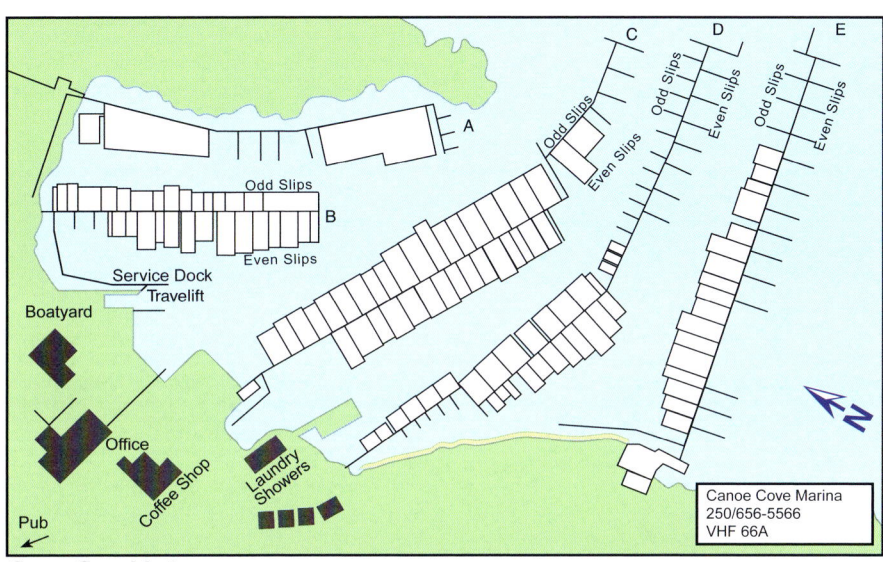

Canoe Cove Marina

Delta MARINE SERVICE
www.delta-marine.com

2075 Tryon Rd Sidney BC Canada
V8L 3X9 At Westport Marina
In Tsehum Harbour

- Retrofits
- Electrical
- Commissioning
- Mechanical Service
- Fiberglass & Gelcoat
- Welding & Fabrication
- Haul Outs
- Cabinetry
- Interior Design
- Vinyl Wrapping
- Custody & Provisioning
- Painting
- Detailing
- Varnishing
- Brightwork
- Customer Support 24/7/365

+1 250 656 2639
tracy@delta-marine.com

2023 Waggoner Cruising Guide   229

GULF ISLANDS

See Area Map Page 220 - Maps Not for Navigation

Marine, Raven Marine, Sea Power Marine Centre, Jespersen Boat Builders, Reyse Marine, and Lightship Marine Mobile, they can do anything. Be sure to visit the second-hand marine store, Tradewinds Boaters Exchange (778-351-0011) located past the boatyard at the marina.

Customs: 24-hour customs; call marina for directions to the customs dock.

Swartz Bay Public Wharf. Open all year, adjacent to the ferry terminal, with 85 feet of dock space. No facilities. Watch for heavy ferry traffic near Swartz Bay.

Piers Island Public Wharf. Open all year with 200 feet of dock space, no facilities.

⑨ **Portland Island (Gulf Islands National Park Reserve).** Formerly Princess Margaret Provincial Marine Park. Open all year, picnic and campsites, toilets, no other facilities. Dogs must be on leash and cleaned up after. In honor of her last visit to Victoria, Portland Island was donated to Her Royal Highness Princess Margaret, who later deeded the island to British Columbia. The park is now part of the Gulf Islands National Park Reserve.

Portland Island is wooded and hilly. Hiking trails follow the coastline. Easy-walking service roads and trails crisscross the center of the island. It would be easy to spend an entire day exploring. Reader Tyson Nevil says the coastline trail is easier to follow when walking in a counter-clockwise direction.

Anchor in Royal Cove (behind Chads Island) on the north side of the island, or in Princess Bay, behind Tortoise Island on the south side. The Royal Cove anchorage is exposed to the wakes of passing BC ferries, and Princess Bay also receives wakes. At Royal Cove you can have a quiet night if you can get well inside. Three red marked stern-tie rings are along the northeast shore in Royal Cove.

There's room for a couple of boats behind Brackman Island, off the southwest corner of Portland Island. Watch your depths at low tide. Brackman Island is a protected wildlife and bird sanctuary. No access is allowed above the high tide line and no pets are allowed.

Princess Bay is roomier and far more popular, but somewhat exposed to southerly winds. In summer it's usually fine. With its shallow depths, not much anchor rode need be paid out, and the boats squeeze in pretty tightly. Watch your depths as you approach the head of Princess Bay. The bottom shoals rapidly, farther from shore than you might expect. Dinghy docks in Royal Cove and Princess Bay provide shore access.

The host float in Princess Bay is staffed by yacht club volunteers during the summer. They answer questions and give out information.

The *G.B. Church*, a sunken freighter off the southwest shore of the island, is an artificial reef for divers. The freighter lies in 100 feet and is marked with bow and stern buoys.

PLUMPER SOUND AREA

Bedwell Harbour. Bedwell Harbour is home to Poets Cove, a luxury marina resort. North of the resort, anchorage is good (except in a southeasterly) off Beaumont Marine Park. Anchorage is also good in Peter Cove, on the west side of the harbour.

Anchorage is possible off Medicine Beach on the northwest side of Bedwell Harbour. A Nature Preserve is located next to the beach, and a short loop-trail on the bluff afords nice views. About 500 yards up the road from the beach is the adorable Slow Coast Coffee shop and Penderosa Pizza, along with a convenience store.

Customs clearance: The Canada Border Services Agency (Canada Customs) dock is adjacent to Poets Cove Marina and well marked. The customs dock was expanded in 2019 with ample side-tie moorage around a U-shape. The far end of the U is the seaplane dock. Open from May 1 to September 30. Except when landing your vessel, only the skipper can leave the boat until customs is cleared. The procedure is for the captain to go up the ramp to the direct-line telephones along the wall of the customs office. Have all of the vessel's paperwork and crew's passport information ready. Call in for clearance. In most cases the agent on the telephone will give you a clearance number, but you may be asked to standby for agents to inspect your vessel. Canpass or Nexus permits only from October 1 through April 30. See the *U.S. and Canadian Customs Information* section in the Compendium chapter for more information on clearing Canadian Customs.

Peter Cove. Peter Cove is at the southern tip of North Pender Island. It is a well protected little anchorage, but permanently moored boats make anchoring a bit tight. A significant reef guards the mouth of the cove. Enter and depart north of the reef.

⑩ **Poets Cove Marina.** 9801 Spalding Road, RR #3, South Pender Island, BC V0N 2M3; (250) 629-2100; (250) 629-2111 marina; marina@poetscove.com; www.poetscove.com. Monitors VHF 66A. Open all year, gasoline, diesel, and ice at the fuel dock. Guest moorage to 100 feet in 95 slips and side-tie; 30 amp power. Reservations recommended. If slips are filled, the "breakwater float" is available at a reduced rate. This float was not available in 2022; call the marina to check on the current status. Liquor store, cafe, pub with dining, heated pool, hot tub, spa, Eucalyptus Steam Cave, fitness center, and free Wi-Fi. Day passes for the pool are available for guests who anchor out. Coin-operated laundry machines are located adjacent to the pool.

The casual Moorings Cafe is located in the building adjacent to the pool and serves sandwiches, espresso, and baked goods. The cafe also sells liquor and convenience items. Syrens Bistro and Lounge, open April

GULF ISLANDS NO-GO ZONES

The Canadian government has enacted measures to protect Southern Resident Killer Whales (SRKW) in BC waters that include: minimum approach distance, no-go sanctuary zones, reduced speed, voluntary echo/depth sounder use limits, and fishing restrictions.

- **No-Go Zones (Red areas on the map) -** Two (2) Interim Sanctuary Zones have been established where general vessel traffic is prohibited from June 1 – November 30. Vessel traffic is not allowed off the southwest shore of North Pender Island and off the southeast end of Saturna Island. Check your charts, both areas are charted.

- **Restricted Fishing (Yellow areas on the map) -** recreational and commercial salmon fishing may be restricted from May until November - check the current regulations.

2022 Gulf Islands management measures

See Area Map Page 220 - Maps Not for Navigation   GULF ISLANDS

Beaumont Marine Park in Bedwell Harbour has mooring buoys, beaches, and hiking trails.

through October, serves lunch and dinner noon to 9:00 p.m. and has seating indoors or out on the patio. Aurora, a fine dining venue, serves breakfast and dinner, open seasonally.

Poets Cove has plenty of activities. Rent a bike, SUP, or kayak and explore the island; play a round of golf, or try the disc golf course.

Beaumont Marine Park (Gulf Islands National Park Reserve). In Bedwell Harbour, west side of South Pender Island, in Bedwell Harbour. Open all year. Facilities include 15 mooring buoys. Pay buoy fees at the honor box above the staircase at the beach, northwest of the buoys, no charge before 3:00 p.m. Mooring buoys accommodate boats up to 50 feet, or 40 feet depending upon wind conditions. Signage for size limits is posted on the buoys. Toilets, no showers or fresh water. Walk-in campsites, picnicking, excellent walking and hiking trails. Hike to the top of Mount Norman, elevation 800 feet, for a memorable view. Dogs must be on leash.

Enter from Swanson Channel from the south, or from Plumper Sound and Port Browning through Pender Canal (27-foot clearance).

Pender Canal. Pender Canal is a man-made dogleg channel between North Pender Island and South Pender Island, connecting Bedwell Harbour and Port Browning. The canal is crossed by a bridge with 27 feet of vertical clearance. Pender Canal is narrow, shallow, and often has a swift current running through it. Because of its dogleg shape, vessels approaching from opposite directions cannot see each other until they are in the narrowest section.

Before entering, broadcast your intentions on VHF 16, **LOW POWER**: *Securite, Securite, this is the 34-foot motor vessel Happy Days, northbound from Pender Canal, Bedwell Harbour to Port Browning. Any concerned traffic please advise, channel one-six.*

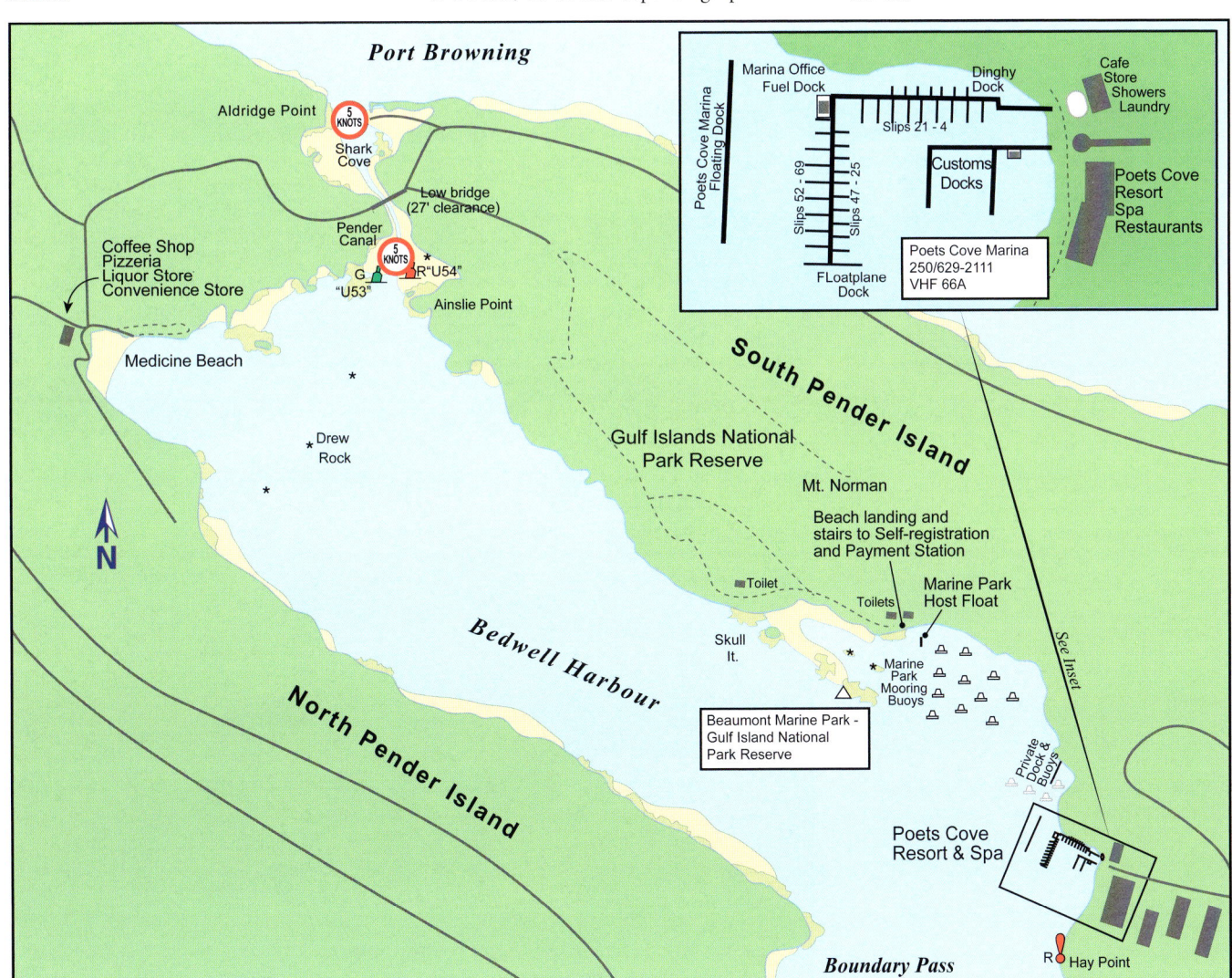

Bedwell Harbour

2023 Waggoner Cruising Guide   231

GULF ISLANDS

See Area Map Page 220 - Maps Not for Navigation

Port Browning Marina is a fun place with good pub food, a swimming pool, and friendly people.

"CAR STOPS" ON THE PENDER ISLANDS

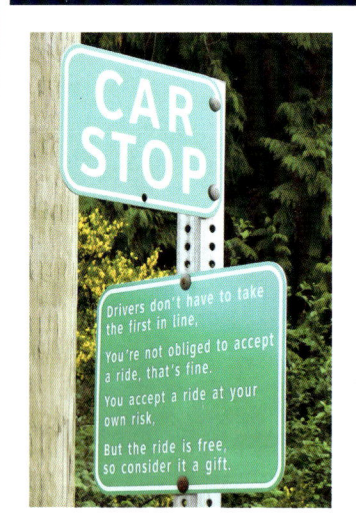

One day when walking back to Port Browning Marina with grocery bags in-hand, we paused at a bench near the entrance to Driftwood Centre; people in cars coming by kept stopping to ask if we wanted a ride. We soon realized we were standing next to a sign that read "Car Stop" with a cute poem that explained everything.

These "car stops" are found all over North and South Pender Islands, where willing locals stop to offer those on foot a ride. You don't have to accept the ride of course; but according to the poem, locals consider it a gift. For boaters, these "car stops" open up new possibilities to explore the islands. You can pick up an Island map at most Pender marinas; the green dots on the map show where all the "car stops" are located.

[Lorena Landon]

⑪ **Port Browning.** Port Browning has a resort (Port Browning Marina) with moorage and other facilities. Anchorage is good throughout the harbor. The Driftwood Centre shopping area is about a half-mile walk from the marina. The Center has a well-stocked Tru-Value Foods, a clothing shop, gift shop, book store, bakery, cafe, and liquor store. Tru-Value Foods will give you a ride back to the marina with purchases of $25 or more. The gas station at the Center carries marine supplies. Dog owners will love the outdoor complimentary dog wash facility at Driftwood Center.

The Nosy Point B&B, a grand old Victorian home, is just up the road from the marina. The Sea Star Vineyards Winery (250-629-6960) is 1.4 miles (2.25 km) northeast of Port Browning Marina. Check the website at seastarvineyards.ca or call for wine tasting hours and sales. The Twin Island Cider Co. is along the way, at the corner of Razor Point Rd. and Lupin Road; check hours for tastings at twinislandcider.com.

⑪ **Port Browning Marina.** P.O. Box 126, North Pender Island, BC V0N 2M0; (250) 629-3493; contact@portbrowning.ca; www.portbrowning.ca. Monitors VHF 66A. Canpass/Nexus-only reporting station. Open all year, 3000 feet of guest moorage; 30 & 50 amp power. The main dock and piers have recently been replaced. Water is not available at the docks.

A 300-foot wave-attenuator was added at the entrance to the marina, immediately west of red buoy U52, which marks shoaling and rocks; favor the wave-attenuator side of the channel when entering the marina.

Free Wi-Fi, ATM, excellent washrooms, laundry, and launch ramp. Seasonal swimming pool; beer & wine sales. Kayak and SUP rentals through Pender Island Kayak Adventures (250-629-6939). Safari-style glamping tents were added in July 2021. Electric bikes available to rent.

Port Browning Marina offers two dining venues: the licensed family Port Browning Pub (open daily, year-round), with large picture windows facing the bay; and the Bridgemans Bistro, with a separate entrance in the back of the building. Restaurant service is offered at Bridgemans on the weekends during the summer months, offering breakfast. The Bridgemans venue can be booked for special events and rendezvous for up to 100 people. Port Browning Marina is part of the Mill Bay Marine Group of properties.

Browning Harbour Public Wharf. Open all year, 89 feet of dock space, no facilities. Commercial fish boats have priority.

Shingle Bay (Gulf Islands National Park Reserve). This is a recent addition to the Gulf Islands National Park Reserve. Open all year, picnic tables, campsites, composting toilets. Dogs must be on leash and cleaned up after. See the remnants of the Shingle Bay fish reduction plant that operated intermittently between 1927 and 1959. It served as an important part of the local economy, employing 15 to 20 men at a time, mainly Pender Island residents.

Because the bay shoals rapidly, you must anchor well out, in line with the old reduction plant. Favor the north side, as a reef extends on the south. Anchorage is exposed to the southwest. The community park at the head of the bay is a welcome place to walk dogs, picnic, and access the island. A jungle gym is popular with children.

Port Browning

See Area Map Page 220 - Maps Not for Navigation

GULF ISLANDS

LOCAL KNOWLEDGE

GREEN BUOY AT OTTER BAY: A green spar buoy is off the corner of the marina docks. Red, Right, Returning means you leave this buoy to port as you enter. Do not pass between the buoy and the dock. A rock 2 feet below the surface at zero tide lurks between the buoy and the dock

⑫ **Otter Bay Marina.** 2311 McKinnon Rd., North Pender Island, BC V0N 2M1; (250) 629-3579; info@otterbay-marina.ca; www.otterbay-marina.ca. Monitors VHF 66A. Online reservations highly recommended during the peak season. Open May 15 to September 30. Four mooring buoys located in the bay south of the marina are used for guest moorage (summers only), contact the marina for reservations; buoys are numbered 1 through 4. Washrooms, showers, laundry; 15 & 30 amp power, 50 amp power on "A" dock. Garbage and recycling for overnight guests. Launch ramp on site. Two heated pools, fire tables, guest BBQs, and Wi-Fi included with moorage. Kayak and SUP rentals available.

This popular marina is on the west side of North Pender Island facing Swanson Channel; look for the tall flagpoles on the observation deck just past the ferry landing. The marina grounds are lovely and have a resort feel.

The upper family pool and lower adult pool are open mid-May through September 30.

The main building houses a great cafe with local baked goods, amazing coffee, and light fare for breakfast and lunch. There's also a gift shop featuring local artisan goods and branded apparel, along with convenience grocery items.

Many semi-private seating areas are located along the walkways among the colorful flower beds in the park-like grounds. An enclosed activity center, with a stone fireplace, is a nice

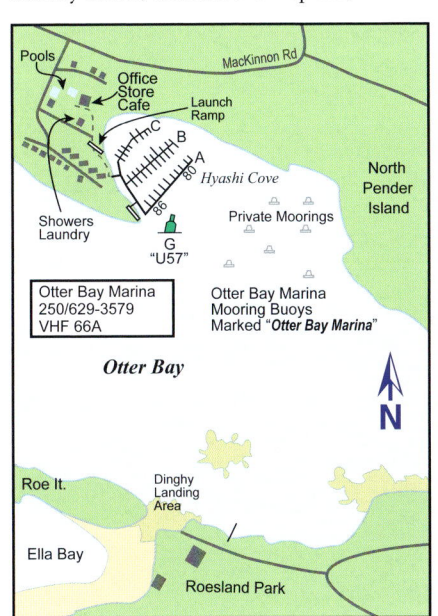

Otter Bay is one of the most relaxing marinas, with an inviting ambience.

venue for group events and rendezvous. For a short excursion, take the dinghy across the bay to Roe Islet/Roesland National Park, a lovely spot to stretch the legs. The 9-hole Pender Island Golf Course is about a 15-minute walk from the marina. Tee times are recommended but not required. The marina provides a golf course shuttle service.

Roesland/Roe Lake (Gulf Islands National Park Reserve). Located on North Pender Island, deep in Otter Bay. Correspondent Deane Hislop reports: "We set the anchor, good holding, and took the dinghy to the park's dinghy dock. We discovered a former 1908 farmhouse that now serves as the Pender Island Museum, offering a glimpse into the island's past. This is also the location of Parks Canada's field office. We took the short walk to the end of Roe Islet to take in an amazing view of Swanson Channel, Saltspring Island, and Vancouver Island. Then it was back along the islet and up Shingle Bay road to the Roe Lake trail head and through the forest to beautiful Roe Lake, making for a full day of hiking and exploring."

Port Washington Public Wharf. On North Pender Island. Open all year, 147 feet of dock space on two floats; no power or water. The northwest float is for transient boats; rafting permitted. The portion marked in yellow is a 15-minute load/unload area; eastern float is for local assigned moorage. Floats are subject to boat wakes from Swanson Channel. No facilities ashore. Watch for a rock off the southeast dock. The western most float is designated for aircraft.

Otter Bay Marina

OTTER BAY
MARINA
PENDER ISLAND, BC

Otter Bay Marina is located 5 miles from the US border on the west side of North Pender Island, just east of the Ferry Terminal in the heart of the Gulf Islands.

Our crew here at OBM is dedicated to providing you with excellent service

- 2 Heated Swimming Pools
- Boat & Kayak Launch
- 15, 30 & 50 Amp Power
- Wifi on the docks
- Potable Water (when available)
- Lawn Games
- Fire Pit area
- Store with Groceries, Books & Gifts
- Cafè including Baked Goods & Specialty Coffees
- Good selection of Local Beer, Wine and Ciders
- Event Spaces with covered areas and BBQ's
- Strong Cell Phone Signal
- Excellent Showers & Laundry Facility
- Dog Friendly Facility
- Nearby 9 Hole Golf Course–Shuttle Service

www.otterbay-marina.ca • (250) 629-3579 or VHF 66A • info@otterbay-marina.ca

2023 Waggoner Cruising Guide

⑬ **Hope Bay Public Wharf.** (250) 813-3321 Wharfinger. East side of North Pender Island, facing Navy Channel. Open all year, 150 feet of dock space, and two day-use mooring buoys marked "Hope Bay Store." Transient moorage is limited to approximately 45 feet located on the outside, southeast end of the dock; other spaces are permanent moorage only. No power, no water. Public restrooms are available in the building on the pier during business hours. If the dock is full (it often is), tie to a mooring buoy or anchor in 30 to 35 feet with good holding over a mud bottom, and dinghy in. Wakes from passing ferries make rafting undesirable, and depths on the inside of the dock are shallow at low tide. Peter, at the upland Goldsmith & Clock shop, is the wharfinger.

This historic landing has attractive buildings on the pier which house a number of small businesses, including the Pender Chocolates shop, the Pender Island Veterinary Clinic, The Hub cafe serving Mediterranean foods, Dockside Realty, and a gift shop in the conservancy office.

Breezy Bay Vineyards. (Formerly the Saturna Winery.) The owner of the vineyard property on Saturna Island put the property on the market in 2019; the property sold in 2020. The property is no longer open to the public. Anchorage is possible in the bay in settled weather.

Irish Bay. Irish Bay, on the west side of Samuel Island, is a good anchorage with scenic rock walls, but the island is privately owned. If you venture above the foreshore, the caretaker will shoo you off.

Winter Cove. A Gulf Islands National Park Reserve. Winter Cove, between Samuel Island and Saturna Island, has an attractive park on the Saturna Island side, and shallow anchorage. We think the best anchorages are behind Winter Point, north of the cable line, or just off the National Park Reserve lands. The charts show shallow water in the middle of the cove, but you can patrol around—carefully—with the depth sounder and find anchoring sites away from the preferred spots. The mooring buoys in the southwest corner of the cove are private. A public dinghy dock is on the eastern shore. It has been reported that a sunken boat lies in the middle of Winter Cove.

Minx Reef partially blocks the Plumper Sound approach to Winter Cove. Entering, we have found the best way to avoid the reef is to point the bow at the northern shore of Irish Bay, and run well past Winter Point before turning south into the cove.

The annual Canada Day (July 1) Saturna Island Lamb Barbecue at Winter Cove is a big event. The cove is packed with boats; islanders shuttle visitors ashore and back. For more information go to www.saturnalambbarbeque.com.

The annual Saturna Lions Club Dog & Dogs Show is in early September. Prizes for best dog and owner look-alike, best puppy, best tail-wagger, and more. Bribes encouraged. You don't need to be a member to attend. Register your dog in the morning before the event, held in Hunter Field at Winter Cove Park; it's an on-leash event. For more information and dates see www.saturnalionsclub.net.

Boat Pass. Boat Pass connects Winter Cove with the Strait of Georgia. Currents in Boat Pass can run to 7 knots past several nasty rocks and reefs. Take this pass only at or near high water slack, preferably after seeing it at low water so you know where the rocks are.

⑭ **Lyall Harbour.** www.saturnatourism.com Lyall Harbour, on Saturna Island, is a large, well protected anchorage, with a ferry landing and store near the entrance. Nearby **Boot Cove** is a beautiful spot with anchorage in 12 to 18 feet, but it is crowded with resident boats on mooring buoys, and can be subject to williwaws blowing over a low swale on Saturna Island.

Lyall Harbour is off the beaten path for the Gulf Islands. It is quiet and gradually being discovered. Your choice, anchor in the bay or tie at the dock. Nothing fancy. This is not Ganges. The Lighthouse Pub, located upland, has very good food with fish and chips being their signature item, though some say their lamb burger is to die for. Lamb carries a special reverence on Saturna Island. Dine inside or out on the deck. The beer is cold and the drink menu is imaginative and available by the drink or by the pitcher. You get the idea. The people are very nice. They say hello. They like your business. The Pub is family friendly.

You can rent bicycles at Saturna Cycle (250-857-4102) upland from the wharf. For an interesting island ride, visit the Saturna General Store & Freight (250-539-2936), a 2.5 km ride. An Outdoor Market is open seasonally on Saturdays in the store parking lot from 10:00 a.m. to 1:00 p.m. Two "glamping tents" are available for rent, which overlook the harbour in a beautiful treed setting. Check in at the Saturna Cycle shop.

⑭ **Lyall Harbour Public Wharf.** (250) 537-7293 wharfinger. Next to the ferry dock. Open all year, 200 feet of dock space. No power, no water. Showers and restrooms are located at the campground ¼ mile up the road from the wharf. Gasoline and diesel are available at the head of the wharf, and can be taken in 15-gallon jerry cans to the dock. Pay for fuel at the Saturna Cycle shop, just above the dock. Moorage is collected at the honor box at the top of the dock. Note, there are day rates and overnight rates.

Floatplanes arrive three times per day from the Vancouver airport for your guests.

Georgeson Passage. Georgeson Passage, between Mayne Island and Samuel Island, is short and pretty. Currents, based on Active Pass, are about half as strong as those in Active Pass, both flooding and ebbing. Still, they run vigorously. See the Georgeson Passage secondary station under Active Pass in the Tide & Current Tables Vol. 5, and Ports and Passes. If entering from the Strait of Georgia through the narrow pass between Campbell Point and Georgeson Island, be aware that a drying reef extends from Campbell Point into the pass. Favor the Georgeson Island side. Watch for rapids.

⑮ **Horton Bay.** The public wharf on the southeast end of Mayne Island is a Canpass/Nexus-only customs reporting station, and has room for a dozen 30-foot boats, plus rafting. Entering the area between Mayne and Samuel Islands requires some care but is completely navigable.

There is good anchorage in Lyall Harbour and limited guest moorage at the public dock.

A reef extends from Curlew Island into Robson Passage. The bay is filled with crab pots and private mooring buoys in the best part of the bay. We have received reports of current running through the bay.

⑯ **Reef Harbour (Gulf Islands National Park Reserve).** Reef Harbour, along with nearby Cabbage Island and Tumbo Island constitute a marine park. The park is open all year, 10 mooring buoys, pit toilets, no water, no showers. Dogs must be on leash. Caution, some buoys are close together, watch swinging space. No rafting on the buoys. Maximum vessel size: 50 ft for winds 30 knots or less; and 40 ft for winds of 37 knots or less. This is a pretty anchorage between Cabbage Island and Tumbo Island, out on the edge of the Strait of Georgia. Caution for rocks and reefs on the approaches. From west northwest, approach between two long reefs. Approaching from south, cross the reef on the Tumbo Channel side, between two patches of kelp, a short distance from the north tip of Tumbo Island. This should show 30 feet under the keel all the way across. Field Correspondent Jim Norris noted a gentle swell in the anchorage in settled weather but notes that it might be a lumpy anchorage in northwest winds at high tide when the protective reefs around Cabbage Island are submerged.

Cabbage Island has picnic sites, campsites, and a wonderful sandy beach. Crabbing is reportedly good. Cabbage Island is interesting to explore. It isn't very big, so you can walk around the entire island in a reasonable time. Though tiny, the island is hardly dull. The beaches are different on every side, ranging from white sand, to sandstone reefs, to an aggregate of small rocks embedded in sandstone, to fine gravel. Inland, you'll find forests of Arbutus (madrona), Garry oak and western red cedar.

Cabbage Island has nice sandy beaches and easy trails; anchorage is open to the north.

Tumbo Island, privately owned until recently, is now part of the Gulf Islands National Park Reserve. Trails lead through the island where you will find remnants of the island's commercial past in the forests and fields. Coal mining was attempted in the early 1900s, but the shafts flooded and the effort was abandoned. In the 1920s and 1930s foxes were raised on the island. The original fox farm homestead, on the flatter northeast end of the island, can still be seen. Field Correspondent Jim Norris reports good access to the trailhead just opposite mooring buoys 3 and 4, where you will find an information kiosk, map, and a rope to help climb up the smooth rock face. The landowner who sold Tumbo Island to the reserve has a life tenancy for the house and a small area surrounding the house located on the northeast end of the island. If someone is in residence there, please respect their privacy.

⑰ **Narvaez Bay (Gulf Islands National Park Reserve).** Picnic tables and toilet, camping in 7 sites, ideal for kayakers. Dogs must be on leash. Beautiful Narvaez Bay indents the rock cliffs on the south shore of Saturna Island, and is open to southeasterly winds and the wakes of passing ship traffic in Boundary Pass. Parts of the bay's shoreline were added to the Gulf Islands National Park Reserve, including the small peninsula parallel to the western shore, a short distance in.

You can anchor in the little bight behind this peninsula and have shelter from wind and waves, although a reader wrote that in a northerly, they experienced williwaw winds of 20+ knots from the head of the bay. The wind in the Strait of Georgia was only 12 knots. The holding ground is not very good. It appears to be loose mud, the kind that washes off easily. It felt like a thin layer on top of rock—fine for a picnic in settled weather, but chancy for overnight.

The neck of land separating the peninsula from the rest of Saturna Island holds the ruins of an ambitious homestead. We didn't find any buildings, although fruit trees and the remnants of fences are there. A dirt service road runs the length of the peninsula and leads up the hill to a main Saturna Island road.

ACTIVE PASS AREA

Active Pass. Active Pass separates Mayne Island and Galiano Island, and has long been one of the most popular fishing areas in the Gulf Islands. It also is the route taken by commercial traffic, including BC Ferries that run between Tsawwassen and Swartz Bay. Currents in Active Pass run to 7 knots on a spring tide. They flood eastward toward the Strait of Georgia. See the Tide and Current Tables Vol. 5, or Ports and Passes. Unless your boat is quite fast, slack water passage is recommended. If you are in the current, you can minimize turbulence by favoring Miners Bay.

Dinner Bay. Dinner Bay, between Crane Point and Dinner Point, looks to be a good anchorage, but is exposed to ferry wakes and northwest winds.

Village Bay. Village Bay is wide and deep, with convenient anchoring depths near the head. The bay is open to northwest winds and waves, but well protected from everything else. Village Bay has a ferry terminal.

⑱ **Miners Bay.** Capital Regional District (250) 539-3092 or (604) 765-3069; Neil Jensen is the wharfinger. The public wharf is located on the south side of Active Pass, and is subject to swirling tidal currents and wakes from passing ferries. A float is on each side of the wharf, best suited for smaller boats. Convenient anchoring depths are close to shore—most of the bay is quite deep.

A bakery, inn, pub, and two grocery stores are up the hill from the wharf. A small museum on Fernhill Road covers the history of this area with indoor and outdoor exhibits. Across from the museum, on Saturday mornings, from 10:00 a.m. - 1:00 p.m., the Mayne Island Farmers Market, has local produce, handicrafts, baked goods, and art work. Beginning in the 1800s, this was a popular stop for miners on their way to the gold mines. The Springwater Lodge (250-

Miners Bay Public Wharf

GULF ISLANDS

See Area Map Page 220 - Maps Not for Navigation

The public dock at Fulford is managed by the Harbour Authority of Salt Spring Island.

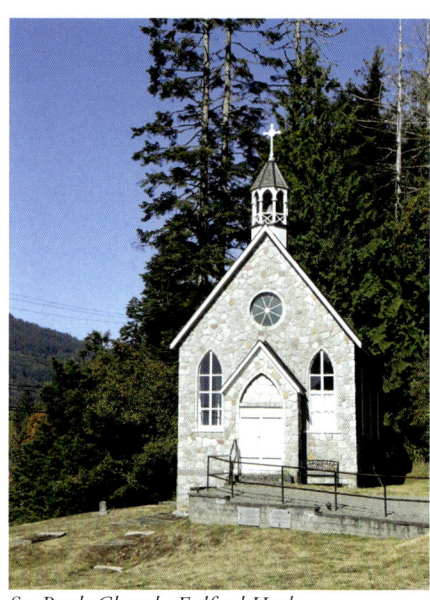

St. Pauls Church, Fulford Harbour

539-5521), built in 1892, overlooks the bay. It remains the oldest continuously operated hotel in British Columbia and offers outdoor patio dining; no indoor dining.

Customs: Miners Bay wharf is a Canpass/Nexus-only customs reporting station.

⑱ **Active Pass Auto & Marine.** (250) 539-5411. Open all year. Propane, tackle, bait, ice, snacks, ice cream, and some marine supplies. Located at the service station 200 yards from the dock.

⑲ **Sturdies Bay.** Sturdies Bay, on Galiano Island toward the eastern end of Active Pass, is a landing for ferries coming to and from Tsawwassen and continuing on to the other Gulf Islands. A public float is alongside the ferry dock. The community of Sturdies Bay, just up the road, has a grocery store and shops. Galiano Oceanfront Inn & Spa is south of the ferry landing with its own dock.

Sturdies Bay is a convenient stop to exchange crew arriving from or departing to the mainland on the BC Ferries. They can disembark the ferry, walk across to the provincial dock, and board the boat.

⑲ **Galiano Oceanfront Inn & Spa.** 134 Madrona Drive, Galiano Island, BC V0N 1P0; (250) 539-3388; info@galianoinn.com; www.galianoinn.com. Located in Sturdies Bay, north of the ferry landing. Open all year but dock in place May to October only, call for exact dates. Wi-Fi, but no power or water on the dock. The dock is subject to wakes from passing ferries in Active Pass. Set fenders accordingly. Reasonable dock rates; free if using the spa, restaurant, or inn.

This is a high-quality inn and spa, with casual fine dining, natural spa, and gardens. Pizza from a wood-fired oven is served for lunch and early dinner from a pizza terrace overlooking the bay (seasonal). Village shops are a block away with more choices for dining, shopping and liquor store. Smart cars are available for rental (inquire in advance).

If you're in Montague Harbour and want to dine at Atrevida Restaurant at the Inn, or have spa treatments, call for pick-up and reservations, (250) 539-3388.

The Kunamokst Mural from the 2010 Olympic games is displayed in the lobby of the Inn. The mural is made from individual tiles, each independently illustrated by a different artist. Collectively they form an image of an orca whale and calf. It's quite striking.

Whaler Bay. Whaler Bay is on the east side of Galiano Island, just north of Active Pass. It is full of rocks and shoal water. Enter carefully through a rock-strewn passage from the south, or through a more open passage around the north end of Gossip Island. Whaler Bay has a public wharf. Good protection is near the wharf, but there's very little swinging room.

Whaler Bay Public Wharf. (250) 539-2264. Open all year, 350 feet of dock space, no facilities. Commercial fish boats have priority.

MAYNE ISLAND, CAMPBELL BAY TO HORTON BAY

Campbell Bay. Campbell Bay, on the northeast side of Mayne Island, is entered between Edith Point and Campbell Point. It is open to southeasterly winds, but has anchoring depths near the head, mud bottom.

Bennett Bay (Gulf Islands National Park Reserve). Bennett Bay, south of Campbell Point, has good anchorage but is exposed to southeast winds. Curlew Island and Samuel Island are privately owned.

Note: Campbell Point, a portion of the waters of Bennett Bay, Georgeson Island, and the Belle Chain Islets including Anniversary Island, are part of Gulf Islands National Park Reserve. To protect sensitive ecosystems, access to Georgeson Island and the islets is prohibited.

SALTSPRING ISLAND, FULFORD HARBOUR TO LONG HARBOUR

Russell Island (Gulf Islands National Park Reserve). Russell Island is just outside Fulford Harbour. Anchor on the northwest side of the island, fair to poor holding, with views of mountains above Fulford Harbour. A trail leads through open meadows and a forest of Douglas fir, Arbutus (madrona) and Garry oak. The original house dates back more than a century. Readerboards explain the history. The island casts a spell upon all those who visit.

Fulford Harbour. Fulford Harbour is wide and open. A public dock for locals only is located on the north side of the ferry terminal. On the south side of the ferry terminal is a public float with transient moorage that is exposed to wind and ferry wash. No services at the float. The charming village of Fulford has a restaurant, a good grocery store at the Salt Spring Mercantile, and an assortment of art galleries and stores specializing in crafts and country clothing. Everything feels very "island."

By all means take a 15-minute walk down the road to St. Paul's Catholic church (called the Stone Church), built in 1880. The graveyard, with island history chiseled into its headstones, is adjacent. On one visit we found the church's door unlocked, and stepped inside. It was lovely. "This is where God lives," we thought.

Bus Transportation: Regular bus service on Saltspring Island connects Fulford Village, Ganges, Long Harbour, Vesuvius and Fernwood. For a schedule, call (250) 537-6758, or see the BC Transit website for Saltspring Island.

Fulford Outer Harbour - Harbour Authority of Salt Spring Island. (250) 537-5711 Open all year. www.saltspringharbours.com A public wharf and float is located

You'll find things nautical in the Gulf Islands.

Several small shops await your visit to Hope Bay Wharf on Plumper Sound.

immediately south of the BC Ferries terminal, managed by the Harbour Authority of Salt Spring Island.

The 54-foot public float provides moorage on both sides. Yellow painted rail is load unload only. Overnight moorage permitted. No water, no power. Payment envelopes, moorage rates, and a self-pay box are located on the wharf. Locals tend to use this float primarily for loading and unloading purposes.

Fulford Inner Harbour - Harbour Authority of Salt Spring Island. Located just north of the BC Ferries terminal is a public dock filled with local boats; no space for transient boats.

Isabella Island (Gulf Islands National Park Reserve). A smallish anchorage is available behind Isabella Island, a short distance west of the mouth of Fulford Harbour. Although exposed to the west, it's a cozy little spot for one or two boats. Anchor in 24 feet.

Ruckle Park. Beaver Point on Saltspring Island. Open all year, day use and overnight camping. No mooring facilities, exposed anchorage on each side of Ruckle Point. Probably the best of these anchorages is in the first cove south of Ruckle Point. Swinging room is limited, and the cove is exposed to ferry wakes and southeast winds. The anchorage is pretty and in settled weather could be a good day stop. This is an extensive park, with miles of shoreline and rocky headlands. Walk-in campsites. Great views.

Ganges & Salt Spring Island – Foodie Heaven!

Salt Spring Island has been a foodie heaven since the late 1800s. Back then, fresh produce grown on the island was delivered to Hope Bay, where it was loaded on the ferry and shuttled to Vancouver. Today, Salt Spring Island is home to brewers and vintners, farmers, cheesemakers, artisan bakers, and restauranteurs. If you love delicious food, Salt Spring Island is a fantastic destination.

FARMERS MARKET

Ganges hosts the best farmers market in the Gulf Islands. On Saturdays from April-October, the "Market in the Park" at Centennial Park is open for business. More than 100 vendors sell their wares, ranging from fresh produce to seafood to pastries and crafts. Everything is made locally.

The market is a great place for provisioning. We've found fresh seafood, unusual mushrooms, heirloom tomatoes, ripe melons, berries, a variety of sprouts, and more. Always a favorite, visit Brigitte's French Patisserie, with superb desserts. Fair warning, it's best to go early since many items sell out by closing time.

WINE AND BEER

Salt Spring has two wineries: Garry Oaks Estate Winery, and Salt Spring Vineyards. Each has a tasting room. Both Garry Oaks and Salt Spring Vineyards require car transportation. Each winery hosts a variety of tasting events throughout the summer, some including food pairings or live music. Check their websites for a schedule of events.

The Sip and Savour Festival in September celebrates Salt Spring Island's food and wine. If beer is your preference, stop by one of B.C.'s smallest breweries, Salt Spring Brewing Co., outside of Ganges. You can enjoy beer on tap, or pick up a bottle or growler. The beer is organic and made with locally grown ingredients— even the hops are from Salt Spring Island.

STILL HUNGRY?

If you're willing to travel beyond walking distance from Ganges, another world opens up. Salt Spring Auto Rentals (250 537-3122) located at Salt Spring Marina, provides maps highlighting more than 40 destinations on Salt Spring Island. Many of these places are artisan food businesses, ranging from cheese makers to beekeepers. One of our favorites is Salt Spring Island Cheese Company near Fulford Harbour. A tour includes petting the goats and sampling some of their 20+ cheeses in a tasting room overlooking the production facility.

[Mark Bunzel]

GULF ISLANDS

LOCAL KNOWLEDGE

DANGEROUS ROCKS & REEFS: Enter Ganges Harbour (5-knot speed limit), leaving all the Chain Islands to starboard; *do NOT* cut through any of the islands. No shortcuts. There are rocks and reefs throughout. The entry channel itself can be a 'minefield' with crab pot floats, many in dark colors; considerable boat traffic, and a charted, busy floatplane operations area.

There are two similarly named dangers in Ganges Harbour. *Money Maker Reef* is northwest of Third Sister Island near the entrance to the Harbour; *Money Makers Rock* is 2 miles to the northwest and is now covered by the south end of Salt Spring Marina's breakwater.

The dangerous shallow area, between Salt Spring and Ganges marinas, is a shallow area with at least one pinnacle rock off of Ganges Marina C-dock, known locally as Zachary Rock. Some charts may have this rock incorrectly named Money Makers Rock. The exact location and water depth of Zachary Rock and the surrounding shallow area remain uncertain. Use extreme caution when approaching Ganges Marina's north docks and Salt Spring Marina. The water depth at zero tide could be as shallow as 4 feet 3 inches.

㉠ **Ganges.** Ganges, at the head of Ganges Harbour, is a favorite destination. This bustling seaside village has marinas, good anchorage, shops, banks with ATM's, galleries, restaurants, and two large supermarkets with marina delivery. There is a dedicated centrally located dinghy dock. Thrifty Foods is the closest to the marinas. Above the store, entered from the street side, is "The Local," a liquor store associated with Thrifty Foods that also delivers to the marinas. Country Grocer (Liquor Agency in the store), at 374 Lower Ganges Road, has a "boaters van" (250-538-2398) with pick-up, drop-off services at any Ganges marina daily, from 10:00 a.m. to 6:00 p.m. Mouat's, a huge old hardware and household goods general store with a separate gift shop and apparel section, is a long-standing favorite. They also have fishing and marine supplies.

The sprawling Salt Spring Island Saturday Market, also called the Farmers Market, is held in Centennial Park at Grace Point on Saturdays 9:00 a.m. to 4:00 p.m., April through October. A Tuesday farmers market, no crafts, is held in the same location, 2:00 p.m. to 6:00 p.m. from June to the end of October. Although boats and tourists are important to summer trade, Ganges is not just a summer resort village. It's a bustling center of year-round local commerce.

Boats can anchor out in the bay. All buoys in the harbour are private. Moorage is available at Salt Spring Marina, Ganges Marina, or the town's Kanaka Wharf. Larger vessels might side-tie along the 240-foot-long floating breakwater that extends into the bay from the Coast Guard dock. A floatplane float, pumpout station, and some power and water are on the breakwater. Because of the breakwater's high freeboard, it is best suited to larger boats. If the wind blows (especially a southeasterly), expect some movement.

The Saltspring Island Sailing Club's docks, to port as you approach Grace Point, have some space for reciprocal clubs. It's about a 1-mile walk to town. The Centennial Wharf public dock behind Grace Islet is permanent moorage only with some guest "hot berths" available if you call the Harbour Authority office. Off Mouat's store, the Kanaka Wharf is within close proximity to shopping; Kanaka dock moorage frequently opens up during the day as boats come and go.

More than 40 artists' studios are in Ganges and scattered around Saltspring Island. In addition to painters and sculptors, they include artisan cheese makers, bakers, wineries, distilleries, and now a microbrewery. Rental cars and vans are available at Salt Spring Marina. A local map identifies stops and hours.

Artspring: Locally supported arts and theater, an easy walk from the village. See www.artspring.ca.

Bird Sanctuary: While you can anchor a short distance south of the Sailing Club's docks, Walter Bay and the spit that creates it are a sanctuary for black oystercatchers. Please leave the sanctuary area alone.

Swimming Pool: The Rainbow Road Indoor Public Pool is an easy walk away. Call (250) 537-1402 for hours.

Bus Transportation: Regular bus service on Saltspring Island connects Fulford Harbour, Ganges, Long Harbour, Vesuvius and Fernwood. For a schedule, call (250) 538-4282.

Shuttle: A free shuttle goes to Upper Ganges Shopping Center with a well-stocked grocery, drug store, and liquor store; call (250) 538-2398.

Taxi: Silver Shadow Taxi (250) 537-3030

Car Rental: Salt Spring Car Rentals (250) 537-3122

THINGS TO DO

- **Studio Tour.** Map available at the Visitor Centre. Rent a car, van, or moped at the Salt Spring Marina and visit some of the 40 artist studios. Most are open every weekend.
- **Salt Spring Island Cheese Company.** See the many steps needed to make artisan

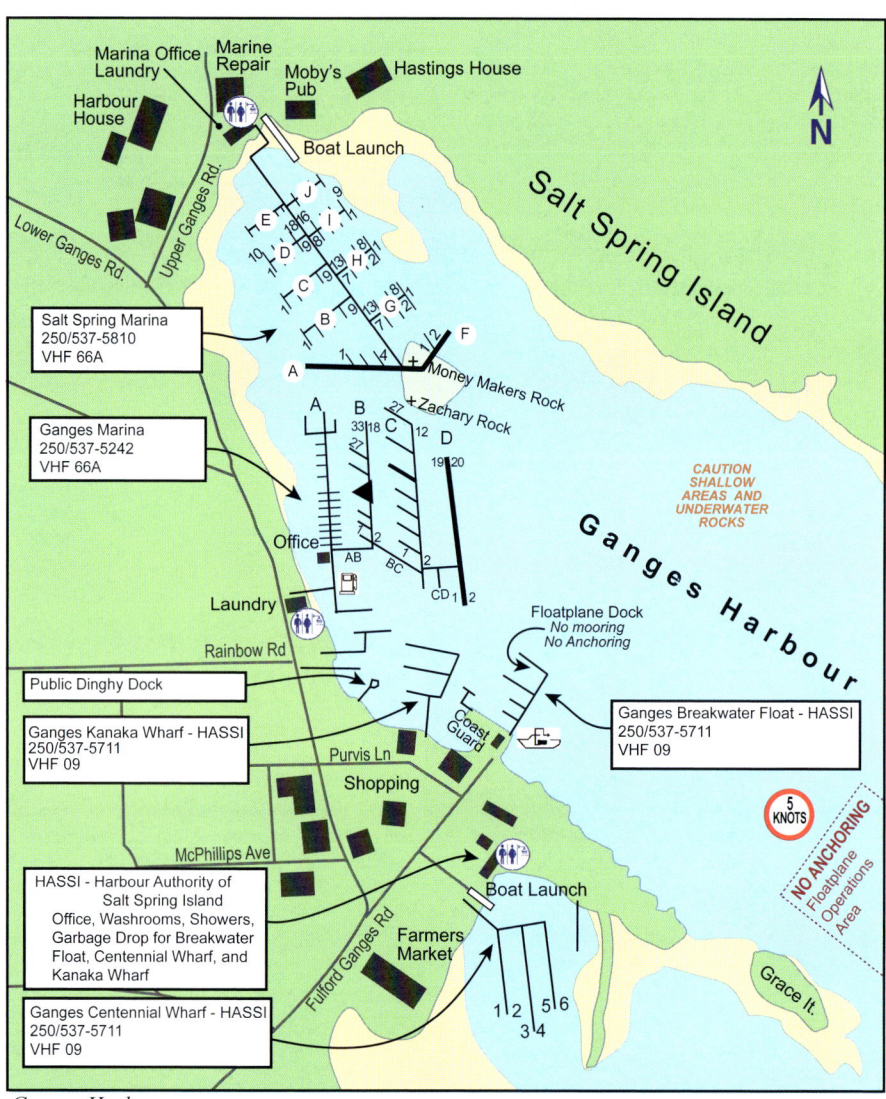

Ganges Harbour

Rotary Park is a starting point to explore and discover Ganges.   *Follow the boardwalk pathway to shops and eateries.*

cheese. Then taste 20 different cheeses.
- **Wine Tasting.** Wineries are on Saltspring Island and they regularly have tastings. Wine and farm tours available at TourSaltSpring.com.
- **Salt Spring Island Saturday Market.** The largest farmers market in the islands.
- **Hastings House.** Reserve for an elegant dinner or a bistro lunch. Walk the grounds of this manor style resort.
- **Barb's Buns.** Delicious coffee and fresh baked goods. Bring some back to the boat. Their breakfasts and lunches are also very good.
- **Embe Bakery.** A "old style" full service bakery serving up freshly baked breads, pastries, dessert pies, and meat pies.
- **Salt Spring Wild Cider House.** (250) 931-5554. Restaurant and tasting room, with many varieties of cider from locally sourced apples and pears.
- **Tree House Cafe.** Popular eclectic hangout with tree in center, features international eats and live music.

⑳ **HASSI - Harbour Authority of Salt Spring Island.** 127 Fulford Ganges Road, Salt Spring Island, BC V8K 2T9; (250) 537-5711. Monitors VHF 09. www.saltspringharbours.com.

The Harbour Authority of Salt Spring Island manages eight marina facilities on Salt Spring Island: Ganges Centennial Wharf; Ganges Breakwater Float (which also includes the Wharfhead where the Coast Guard building is located); Ganges Kanaka Wharf; Vesuvius Bay; Fulford Inner Harbour; Fulford Outer Harbour; Burgoyne Bay; and Musgrave Landing. The Harbour Authority office and wharfinger are located at Ganges Centennial Wharf. Proof of liability insurance coverage of 2 million required.

⑳ **Ganges Centennial Wharf - HASSI.** (250) 537-5711. Monitors VHF 09. www.saltspringharbours.com. This is the Grace Point facility. Mostly commercial and permanent moorage, but sometimes guest space is available, call the Harbour Authority Office.

⑳ **Ganges Breakwater Float - HASSI.** (250) 537-5711. Monitors VHF 09. www.saltspringharbours.com. This is the dock below the Coast Guard station. Moorage on the outside of the long floating breakwater or in several slips on the inside. Be sure to avoid the marked seaplane and Coast Guard areas. Limited 30 amp power and water. Pumpout at the dock. Washroom, shower and garbage drop at the Harbour Authority office at Centennial Wharf. Two hours free moorage before 4:00 p.m.

Wharfingers collect moorage daily, or pay in the drop box at the head of the docks or at the Harbour Authority office.

⑳ **Ganges Kanaka Wharf - HASSI.** (250) 537-5711. Monitors VHF 09. www.saltspringharbours.com. These docks are immediately north of the floating breakwater, with 1400 feet of visitor moorage, water, 30 amp power. Good free Wi-Fi on the docks or from nearby cafés. Three-day maximum stay from May 15 to September 15. Washroom, shower and garbage drop, with recycling, located at the Harbour Authority office at Centennial Wharf, about a block away. Free moorage for 2 hours. Boats come and go all day and moorage opens up after crews complete their shopping. The white bull rail area is not available for overnight moorage on specific days; check the posted signage.

Wharfingers collect check or cash for moorage daily, or pay in the drop box at the head of the docks, or at the Harbour Authority office.

LOCAL KNOWLEDGE

EXPLORING ISLANDS: Explore Third Sister Island by dinghy to see the midden shell beach and creative driftwood outhouse.

⑳ **Ganges Marina.** 161 Lower Ganges Road, Salt Spring Island, BC V8K 2L6; (250) 537-5242; gangesmarina@gmail.com; www.gangesmarina.com. Monitors VHF 66A. Moorage for vessels up to 120 feet. Open all year, premium gasoline, diesel, and limited lubricants at fuel dock; ample guest moorage. Reservations required, call or make reservations online. Pet owners required to provide a deposit. Docks were rebuilt in 2021, along with new ramps; new fuel pumps installed; and new machines placed in the refurbished laundry. Facilities include 30 & 50 amp power, washrooms, showers, laundry, free Wi-Fi, garbage drop. Proof of liability insurance coverage is required. Groceries, restaurants, propane, and other services nearby.

A floating breakwater, 500 feet long and 24 feet wide, can handle vessels to 400 feet.

⑳ **Salt Spring Marina.** 124 Upper Ganges Rd., Salt Spring Island, BC V8K 2S2; (250) 537- 5810; (800) 334-6629; info@saltspringmarina.com; www.saltspringmarina.com. Monitors VHF 66A. Reservations required; available online through Swift Harbour. Docks were replaced and expanded in 2020. The floats have guest moorage for a variety of boat sizes in a configuration that includes a floating breakwater covering Money Makers Rock. Electrical service is ELCI-protected, one of the first in BC. 30 & 50 amp power, washrooms, showers, laundry, and free Wi-Fi. Water, ice, recycling, garbage drop, mobile pump-out station, and concrete launch ramp. Marina security gate. No long term parking. At certain times of the year, when in short supply, water use at the docks may be restricted to certain hours.

Adjacent Moby's Pub (take-out & off-sales) has a terrific menu, music and dancing. Moby's has both indoor and outdoor dining. Check their website. Harbours End has full-service repairs with haulout to 40 feet (250-537-4202). Car, van, scooter, and bicycle rentals (250-537-3122).

Long Harbour. Long Harbour lies parallel to Ganges Harbour, but is much narrower. The BC ferry from Tsawwassen lands there. Good anchorage is beyond the ferry dock, taking care not to anchor over a charted cable crossing. Royal Vancouver Yacht Club has an outstation in Long Harbour.

PREVOST ISLAND

㉑ **Prevost Island.** Prevost Island is a favorite of many. Annette Inlet and Glenthorne Passage, on the northwest end, are particularly attractive. The bays indenting from the southeast also look inviting, but with a southeaster always possible and with ferry traffic flying by in Swanson Channel, they might get a little lumpy.

Acland Islands. The passage between the Acland Islands and Prevost Island is a pleasant anchorage, with dramatic sheer rock walls on the Prevost Island side. Anchor in 25 to 35 feet with enough room to swing, or stern-tie to Acland Island.

Glenthorne Passage. Glenthorne Passage is the westernmost of the northern bays on Prevost Island. Well protected anchorage in 15 to 30 feet, good holding. Even though cabins line Secret Island, the surroundings are agreeable and the anchorage is popular. In summer months the sun sets in the narrow passage between Glenthorne Point and Secret Island.

Annette Inlet. Annette Inlet is a little wider than Glenthorne Passage, with few houses and a good sandy beach at the head. As you approach, note the charted rock that dries at 0.9 meter, off the mouth of the inlet. A rock at the point is marked by a small, private beacon. Approach from the Glenthorne Passage side and wrap around the point, leaving the beacon to starboard. The head of the bay shoals to drying flats. Anchor in 8 feet (zero tide) anywhere, gray mud bottom. Southeast winds can blow across the low swale separating Annette Inlet from Ellen Bay on the other side of Prevost Island, but there isn't enough fetch to build waves.

Selby Cove & James Bay. A house and dock are on the right side as you enter Selby Cove. Anchor in 18 feet and be sure of your set. We found poor holding in one spot. James Bay is the most northeast bay, open to northwesterlies. It is a little deep for anchoring until close to the head. The lands surrounding James Bay and a portion of the north shore of Selby Cove are part of Gulf Islands National Park Reserve, as are the lands surrounding Richardson Bay and the Portlock Point light station at the southeast corner of Prevost Island. Ferries do not serve Prevost Island, thus it is less populated than the larger islands.

MONTAGUE HARBOUR

㉒ **Montague Harbour.** Montague Harbour is a popular stopping spot in the central Gulf Islands. It is well protected and has an outstanding marine park. Depending on wind direction, you can find good anchorages around the bay.

Entry is unobstructed, either from the southeast, past Phillimore Point, or from the northwest, between Parker Island and Gray Peninsula.

Montague Harbour will hold a huge number of boats. We have anchored there during high season surrounded by more than 100 boats, yet no one was crowded. Anchor in about 40 feet over a mud bottom. The marina has a fuel dock, store, gift shop, scooter and kayak rentals, and restaurant. For-fee Wi-Fi is available throughout the harbor; cell phone reception is poor.

No Discharge Zone, Gray Water okay.

Customs: Montague Harbour is a Canpass/Nexus-only call-in customs clearance location.

Dining: A range of dining choices are available. Everybody enjoys the Hummingbird Inn Pub. A visit to Hummingbird Pub begins with a memorable ride on the Hummingbird Pub bus. Catch the bus on the road above the marina, about 300 yards to the right of the intersection. The bus also stops at the front gate of the marine park. Check the Hummingbird Pub website or signs at the marina and park entrance for the scheduled times for bus pick-up. The Hummingbird Pub serves food and is family friendly. The entertaining bus ride is worth the trip.

The Pilgrimme Restaurant (250-539-5392) operates in the former location of the French restaurant La Berengerie. It gets great reviews from visiting boaters. Call for reservations, or go to pilgrimme.ca. Walking distance from Montague Harbour Marina.

Located inland, at 743 Georgeson Bay Rd., is the impressive Woodstone Manor and Restaurant (250-539-2849), open for lunch and dinner Thursday-Sunday. The Michelin Star chef prepares outstanding European cuisine. The hotel will pick up dinner guests from Montague Harbour.

LOCAL KNOWLEDGE

SHOAL: A shoal extends southeast from the tip of Gray Peninsula into Montague Harbour. We've seen a boat thoroughly grounded on that shoal, awaiting a rising tide. Continue well into the harbor before turning east to anchor or pick up a mooring.

㉒ **Montague Harbour Marine Park.** Montague Harbour Marine Park, at the north end of Montague Harbour, is beautiful, exceptionally well-maintained and very popular. The park is open all year. It has excellent white sand beaches on the south side and astonishing rock beaches on the north and west sides. If you walk along the beach on the north side, opposite the head of the lagoon, you'll find a midden beach with numerous shells. There's no hint of the midden on the trail above, but it's obvious from the beach. A tiny, secluded beach is on Gray Peninsula, facing Parker Island. The park has walk-in campsites, a picnic area and toilets. A dock with a 300-foot-long float is for dinghies and

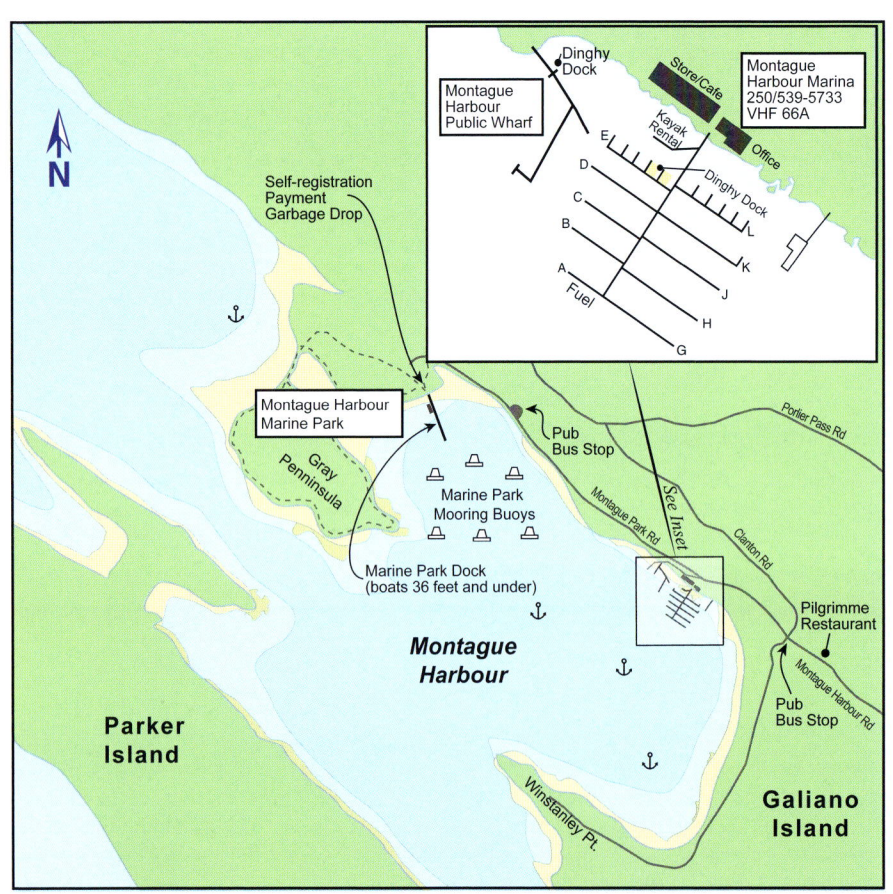

Montague Harbour

Pilgrimme Restaurant is near Montague Marina.

Montague Marina has moorage, fuel, store, and a restaurant.

boats up to 11 meters (36 feet). Designated dinghy area is on the shore end of the float. There are approximately 39 mooring buoys off the dock. No boat size limitation is marked on the buoys but as a practical matter, be careful not to endanger other boats or damage buoy equipment. An honor box for paying moorage is at the top of the stairs. The Park Ranger will also accept VISA and MasterCard and will visit your boat in late afternoon/early evening to collect your payment. The park has anchorage for many boats on both sides of Gray Peninsula depending on wind direction. Garbage disposal for a fee is available, located up the stairs from the dock.

㉒ **Montague Harbour Marina.** 3451 Montague Rd, Galiano Island, BC V0N 1P0; (250) 539-5733; montagueharbourmarina@gmail.com; www.montagueharbour.com. Monitors VHF 66A. Open May 1 to September 30. Guest side-tie moorage, 15 & 30 amp power, no water at the docks, free Wi-Fi, and washrooms. Reservations strongly recommended during the high season. Garbage and recycle drop for overnight moorage guests. Dog friendly. Licensed restaurant, with daily specials. Groceries, marine supplies, and gift shop. Diesel and ethanol-free gasoline at the fuel dock. Fuel is available during the off-season on Saturdays from 10:00 a.m. to 2:00 p.m. or by arrangement. Moped, kayak, and boat rentals (250) 889-4764.

The store carries an expanded variety of goods, including smoked fish, meats, and local produce, fishing tackle, a good selection of books, souvenirs, and hand-dipped ice cream cones. Cappuccino bar service available. The licensed Crane & Robin is open for lunch and dinner. Check their happy hour specials. Dinghy dock available for any boaters on anchor or mooring buoys who want to enjoy the marina's shopping and dining. Check in at the office, located across from the store, if you plan to leave the property. Limited Wi-Fi for anchored boats is available for a fee.

㉒ **Montague Harbour Public Wharf.** Open all year, 160 feet of dock space, no facilities. 2-hour complimentary tie-up for dinghies and boats. Fee for additional stays, pay at self-registration payment box at head of the ramp. Video monitoring and the wharfinger enforce the 2-hour free limit. Surveillance ensures that everyone has an opportunity to use the dock. Wharfinger always greets you with a smile.

Walker Hook. Walker Hook, on the west side of Trincomali Channel, has a beautiful beach on its eastern shore, where it connects with Saltspring Island. Anchor in 24 feet. An approach between Atkins Reef and Saltspring Island takes the worry out of identifying just where the various rocks are.

Fernwood Public Wharf. This Capital Regional District managed dock is located on the Trincomali Channel side of Saltspring Island 1.6 nm north of Walker Hook, opposite Victoria Shoal, and about 1 nm south of Wallace Island. Open all year, 44 feet of dock space, maximum stay 24 hours, no facilities. The float is at the end of a long pier and is exposed to Trincomali Channel and possible rough conditions.

Two eateries are located just 50 meters from the head of the wharf: Fernwood Café (250) 931-2233, open year-round (hours vary off season); and Twig & Buoy (250) 931-8944 also open year-round. You will find excellent food at both venues, offering lunch, dinner, and breakfast menu items; including pizzas to go. For those anchored at Wallace Island, consider ordering a pizza for pickup via dinghy.

MONTAGUE HARBOUR MARINA
LAT. 48°53'N LONG. 123°24'W

MARINA & FUEL DOCK
Transient Moorage— May to September
30/15amp Power, Wifi & Garbage with Moorage
Fuel Dock with Gasoline and Diesel
RESERVATIONS HIGHLY RECOMMENDED

GENERAL STORE & MARKET
Coffee Shop, Ice Cream, Produce, Meat, Seafood
Fishing Gear, Bait, Ice, Books, Clothing & Gifts

GALIANO ISLAND, BC   FIVE DINING OPTIONS

250.539.5733
INFO@MONTAGUEHARBOUR.COM

VHF 66A
MONTAGUEHARBOUR.COM

GULF ISLANDS

See Area Map Page 220 - Maps Not for Navigation

SAANICH INLET

Saanich Inlet extends south into Vancouver Island for about 12 miles. The northern part of the inlet is fairly civilized, especially along the Saanich Peninsula shore to Brentwood Bay, where Butchart Gardens is located. For a beautiful and often-overlooked trip, continue south through Squally Reach and Finlayson Arm. Boat traffic usually is minimal.

Holding Tank Pumpout Service: J.R. Pump Out, a mobile pumpout boat, serves the Brentwood Bay/Butchart Gardens area of Saanich Inlet. Because of a sill at the mouth of the inlet, Saanich Inlet does not exchange its water well and is growing increasingly lifeless along the bottom. Saanich Inlet is not a good place to pump overboard. J.R. Pump Out at (844) 507-3451 or VHF 88 (seasonally). During the summer season the pumpout boat goes out every evening. In winter, every two weeks.

Restricted Area: In Saanich Inlet, Area Whiskey Delta (WD) is restricted when the government is conducting certain operations. Before entering, listen to the continuous marine broadcast or call the Coast Guard on VHF 83 to ensure the area is not restricted before entering.

Deep Cove. When entering Deep Cove, stay clear of Wain Rock, which lies 0.2 mile off Moses Point. The remains of a public wharf are in the south part of the cove. Deep Cove Marina is adjacent to this pier and is for permanent moorage, yacht charters and sales. No guest moorage.

The Chalet restaurant is located along the north shore in Deep Cove; boaters can anchor in front of The Chalet restaurant and land the dinghy on their private beach to enjoy lunch or dinner at the restaurant. Call ahead for reservations (250) 656-3541, open Wednesday-Sunday. This is a unique venue overlooking Deep Cove and Saanich Inlet. The home was built as a teahouse for the B.C. Electric Rail Line in 1913 and has been a restaurant ever since. After coming ashore, leave your boots behind and slip on your nice shoes; this is a fine dining venue with prices to match. Remains of several pilings in front of The Chalet help locate the restaurant; see www.deepcovechalet.com for more details.

Patricia Bay. Patricia Bay, locally called Pat Bay, is open, but all the facilities are reserved for the Canadian Government's Institute of Ocean Sciences. It is here that the Canadian Hydrographic Service develops and maintains charts and related publications for western Canada and the Arctic.

Coles Bay. Coles Bay is east of Yarrow Point. It is good for temporary anchorage but open to southerly winds. If approaching from the north, the Canadian Small Craft Guide recommends that you give Dyer Rocks, off Yarrow Point, a 0.5-mile berth to avoid shoals extending south from the rocks.

LOCAL KNOWLEDGE

DANGEROUS ROCKS: A reef, marked by red nun Buoy U22, is a short distance off the Brentwood Bay ferry dock. Approach Brentwood Bay Resort & Marina from the north, leaving buoy U22 to starboard. Dangerous rocks lie on the other side of the buoy, and west and south of the resort's docks. Locals report that these rocks are hit frequently.

㉓ **Brentwood Bay.** Butchart Gardens is one of the main attractions around Brentwood and is well worth a visit. Another popular attraction is the Victoria Butterfly Gardens (877) 722-0272 located about two miles from Brentwood Bay.

The village near the highway has some shopping. Moorage is at Brentwood Bay Resort & Marina and limited moorage at Portside Marina and Angler's Anchorage Marina.

The Mill Bay ferry departs a short distance south of Sluggett Point. The Seahorses Cafe, with a dinghy dock, is north of the ferry dock. Nearby Blue's Bayou Café to the south has Cajun/Creole style food. Open for lunch and dinner, reservations recommended (250) 544-1194. The Brentwood Bay Public Dock, next to the Cafe, is suitable for dinghies and small watercraft.

Pumpout: Pumpout is available by reservation throughout Brentwood Bay for free (donations appreciated) through J. R. Pumpout, (844) 507-3451 or VHF 88. This program is funded by Butchart Gardens.

㉓ **Portside Marina.** 789 Saunders Ln., Brentwood Bay, BC V8M 1C5; (250) 652-2211; portsidemarina@shaw.ca; portsidemarina.net. Open all year with limited guest moorage for boats up to 50 feet, reservations accepted. 30 amp power, water, washrooms, showers, and laundry. The marina is located in Brentwood Bay north of the BC Ferries terminal and next to the Seahorses Café. A small marine ways and boatyard that specializes in wooden boat building and repair is adjacent to the marina. Pacifica Paddle Sports (250-665-7411) is located at the marina and has rental kayaks, canoes, and SUPs.

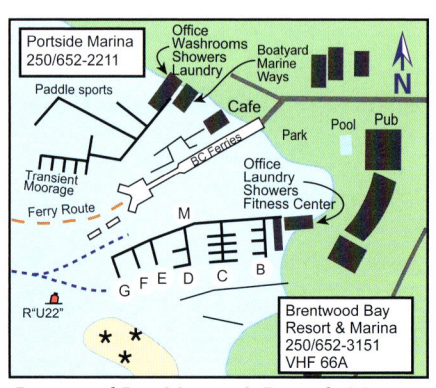

Brentwood Bay Marina & Portside Marina

㉓ **Brentwood Bay Resort & Marina.** 849 Verdier Ave., Brentwood Bay, BC V8W 1C5; (250) 652-3151; (888) 544-2079; marina@brentwoodbayresort.com; www.brentwoodbayresort.com/marina/. Monitors VHF 66A. The reservation-only marina has 22 slips of guest moorage and side-tie moorage for vessels to 125 feet, 15, 30 & 50 amp power, water, washrooms, laundry, garbage, recycling, showers, adult pool with drinks and pub food service, sushi and sake, cold beer & wine off-sales in the pub, free Wi-Fi. Live music and beer samplers on Sundays.

This is a highly rated resort and spa, with excellent views of Saanich Inlet, beautiful landscaping. A shuttle boat runs to Butchart Gardens for a fee (make reservations at the marina office), or it's a short dinghy ride away. Kayak and SUP rentals and eco-adventure tours available.

㉓ **Anglers Anchorage Marina.** 905 Grilse Ln, Brentwood Bay, BC V8M 1B5; (250) 652-3531; info@anglersanchoragemarina.com; www.anglersanchoragemarina.com. Some guest moorage available in slips to 50 feet; side tie up to 160-foot vessels. 15, 30, & 50 amp power; washrooms, showers, laundry, garbage drop, pumpout. Wi-Fi signal strongest near the office. Reservations recommended, call or see

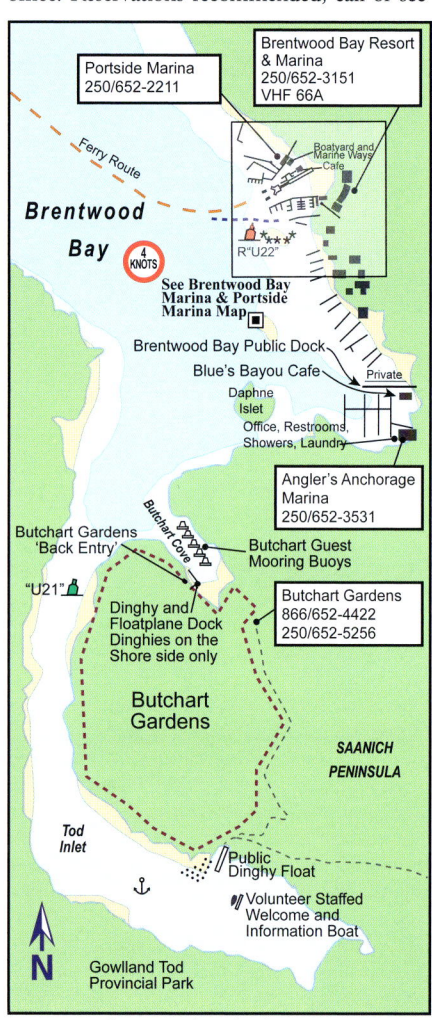

Brentwood Bay and Tod Inlet

The Gardens at Butchart are easily accessed by boat; special events are hosted on the grounds.

their website. The popular Blue's Bayou Cafe is located next door; call (250) 544-1194 for cafe reservations.

㉓ **Butchart Gardens**. 800 Benvenuto Avenue, Brentwood Bay, BC V8M 1J8; (250) 652-5256; (866) 652-4422; www.butchartgardens.com. Locally named **Butchart Cove** just outside the mouth of Tod Inlet is the back door to the celebrated and astonishing Butchart Gardens. The Gardens are a must-see attraction. They are lighted at night, creating an entirely different effect from the day. On Saturday evenings during the summer a fireworks display is held on a large field in the gardens, all done at ground level accompanied by music. Fireworks were suspended in 2022, check their website for the current status and other events.

Concerts are held throughout the summer at Butchart Gardens. Afternoon Tea, held in the former Butchart home, is a delight and includes a selection of teas and petit fours. A little known secret is — The Dining Room restaurant will prepare special picnic baskets to enjoy on the grounds during the summers — see their website for the menu.

The Gardens' dinghy dock is in tiny Butchart Cove with 4 free mooring buoys for boats 40 feet and under (a fifth mooring ball for vessels 18 feet and under) that are first-come, first-served, maximum 24 hour stay. Eyes for stern-ties are set into the rock wall. Most visitors put the anchor down in adjacent Tod Inlet and go by dinghy to the dinghy dock. Dinghy dock is closed from December 1 to January 6.

Tod Inlet. Tod Inlet reaches back behind Butchart Gardens into Gowlland Tod Provincial Park, and has ample anchoring room. Anchor in water deeper than 20 feet to protect eelgrass. Green can Buoy U21 marks a rock. Leave the buoy to port when entering. The inlet is narrow when seen from Brentwood Bay, but opens somewhat after a bend. In the narrow sections you should plan to run a stern-tie to shore. Boats in the more open sections around the bend often can swing without a stern-tie. On Saturday nights the inlet is crowded with boats that come to see the fireworks display at the Gardens.

The dinghy dock on the southeastern shore of the inlet is provided by the Marine Conservation Society and BC Parks, look for the green Marine Ecology float building. A trail to the south leads to the main entrance of Butchart Gardens, about a 10 minute walk. Stay left at the 'Y' in the trail. It's also a short dinghy ride to Butchart Cove where you can tie to the shore side of the dinghy dock and pay admission to the gardens at the backdoor entrance. The dinghy dock in Tod Inlet serves as an access point for the Gowlland Tod Provincial Park with hiking trails connecting through the Gowlland Range. During the summer months, volunteers set up a float in Tod Inlet to provide information and answer questions. The float is staffed by members of the Capital City Yacht Club on behalf of BC Parks.

No Discharge Zone, Gray water okay.

Finlayson Arm. Goldstream Boathouse is located at the head of Finlayson Arm, at the edge of drying flats off the mouth of the Goldstream River. The shoal water seems to be extending farther north, so come in close to the docks. If the approach is made from mid-channel, an unsuspecting skipper could run aground. Unique homes dot the hillsides and shoreline along Finlayson Arm. Look for the cute 'crooked little house' on a small point just before the power lines on the western shore at 48°31.14'N/123°32.5'W.

㉔ **Goldstream Boathouse.** 3540 Trans-Canada Hwy, Victoria, BC V9B 6H6; (250) 478-4407; www.goldstreamboathousemarina.com. Open all year, gasoline and diesel at fuel dock. Minimal guest moorage available, but even during the summer season they usually have room, call ahead. Complete repair facility and haulout by trailer up to 50 feet, small convenience store, 2-lane concrete launch ramp, 15, 30 & 50 amp power, washrooms, no showers. The store was refurbished in 2019.

㉕ **Mill Bay.** Mill Bay is a good anchorage. The west shore provides a lee from the usual summer west or northwest winds. The bay is, however, open to southeast winds. Just north of the Mill Bay Marina is a spar buoy zone marking a no-anchoring area. A charted pipeline extends from the northwest corner of the bay.

㉕ **Mill Bay Marina.** 740 Handy Road, Mill Bay, BC V0R 2P1; (250) 743-4303; contact@millbaymarina.ca; www.millbaymarina.ca. Monitors VHF 66A. 700 feet of guest moorage to accommodate boats to 300 feet; 30 & 50 amp power, water, gasoline, diesel, pumpout, laundry, showers, free Wi-Fi. Reservations recommended in season, available online. Wide roomy slips and side-tie moorage on concrete docks. State-of-the-art marina with great views of Mt. Baker and friendly service.

Picnic tables and propane barbeques for guest use are on the docks. The Bridgemans Bistro restaurant, open for lunch and dinner, and brunch on weekends, is a hit. Soft drinks, ice cream. Live music on Sundays. Blue Dog Kayaking (250) 710-7693, located at Mill Bay Marina, offers kayak and SUP rentals, instruction, and expeditions.

The Mill Bay Shopping Centre is a short walk up the hill. The Center has a supermarket, drug store, liquor store, the Bru-Gos Coffee Shop, a hardware store, bank and a women's wear shop called Wear It's At, with lots of boat themed clothing. The gas station has propane refills. A pizza shop and Visitor Centre are also located there.

A public launch ramp is on the north side of the marina. Spar buoys north of the marina and boat launch, located in front of the Brentwood College School (a college prep boarding school), mark a no-anchoring area. The no-anchoring area protects an ocean loop geo-exchange system used for heating and cooling the school's buildings.

㉕ **Mill Bay Community Wharf.** Open all year, 50 feet of dock space, no facilities. Three hour maximum stay, no overnight moorage.

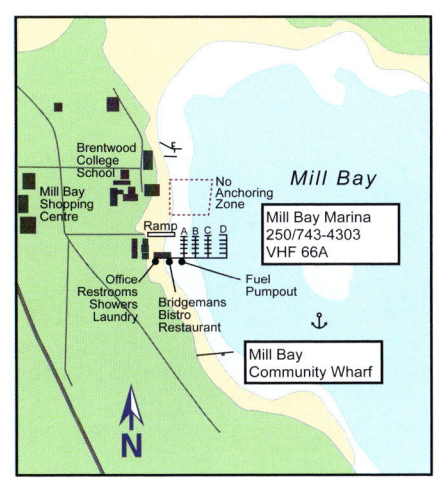

Mill Bay

Cowichan Bay Fishermen's Wharf

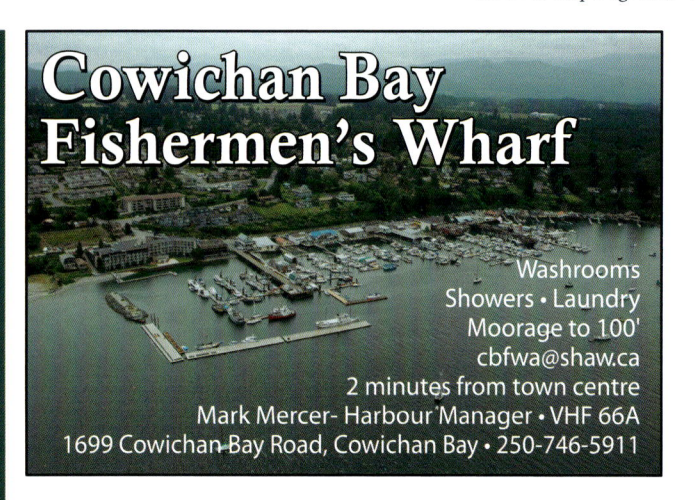

Washrooms
Showers • Laundry
Moorage to 100'
cbfwa@shaw.ca
2 minutes from town centre
Mark Mercer- Harbour Manager • VHF 66A
1699 Cowichan Bay Road, Cowichan Bay • 250-746-5911

True Grain bakery is definitely worth a visit in Cowichan.

㉖ **Cowichan Bay.** www.cowichanbay.com. The waterfront village of Cowichan Bay is located near the southwest corner of Cowichan Bay. Docks at Fishermen's Wharf are behind a floating breakwater. The floating breakwater dock is not connected to land. A dinghy is needed for shore access. Two privately owned marinas are west of the public wharf and offer limited guest moorage. Hecate Park, at the other end of town, has a launch ramp and ample trailer storage.

In settled weather anchorage is possible but not advised. We are told crabbing and prawning are good. The annual Cowichan Bay Regatta is held the first weekend in August, a popular event drawing many participants. The village is full of life. It has numerous shops and businesses, including liquor stores and good restaurants, not one of them part of a major chain. Interesting little shops are tucked away everywhere. The True Grain Bakery is a favorite. Udder Guys Ice Cream has some of the best ice cream on the coast. The Cowichan Bay Maritime Centre, built on a wharf extending from shore, has many interesting displays. Classic Marine Store (250-746-1093) is a well-stocked marine chandlery with marine parts, supplies, gifts, and fishing gear. Don't miss the Classic Café located in the store, offering delectable bites.

A grass tennis court, just like Wimbledon, is 3 miles west of town at 2290 Cowichan Bay Rd (250) 746-7282. Non-members can book a court online at info@lawntennis.ca during the season (May-Sept. 15); open daily. For winery and distillery tours of the area, see CheersCowichan.com (250) 710-7391.

㉖ **Cowichan Bay Fishermen's Wharf Association.** P.O. Box 52, Cowichan Bay, BC V0R 1N0; (250) 746-5911; cbfwa@shaw.ca. Monitors VHF 66A. First-come, first-served. Open all year, 900 feet of dock space for vessels to 100 feet, 30 amp power, free Wi-Fi, clean washrooms, laundry, showers, free pumpout, garbage and recycling drop, waste oil disposal. Short-term shopping stops are encouraged until 2:00 p.m.; check-in at the harbor office.

㉖ **Oceanfront Suites at Cowichan Bay.** 1681 Cowichan Bay Rd., Cowichan Bay, BC V0R 1N0; (250) 715-1000; info@oceanfrontcowichanbay.com; www.oceanfrontcowichanbay.com. Full service resort hotel. Moorage at the dock for hotel guests; no hourly stays. Dock suitable for shallow draft boats only. No power on the docks. The Oceanview restaurant overlooking the bay is open seasonally. Located immediately south of the Fishermen's Wharf dock. Watch your depths on very low tides.

㉖ **Pier 65 (Dungeness Marina).** 1759 Cowichan Bay Rd., Box 51, Cowichan Bay, BC V0R 1N0; (250) 748-6789. Office hours vary. 80-foot transient moorage dock, maximum boat length 70 feet; 30 amp power in one box with 4 receptacles; water at the dock. Call ahead for available space; reservations accepted. New showers as of 2022.

㉖ **Bluenose Marina.** 1765 Cowichan Bay Rd., P.O. Box 40, Cowichan Bay, BC V0R 1N0; (250) 748-2222; info@thebluenosemarina.com; www.thebluenosemarina.com. Open all year. Docks were upgraded in 2022. Guest moorage available on a 100 foot dock, reservations accepted. 30 & 50 amp power; washrooms, showers, laundry. Nearby launch ramp, public playground, and kayak shop. The Vine restaurant and Udder Guys Ice Cream shop are nearby.

㉗ **Genoa Bay.** Genoa Bay indents the north shore of Cowichan Bay. Anchorage can be found off the marina docks. The Genoa Bay Marina has guest moorage.

㉗ **Genoa Bay Marina.** 5000 Genoa Bay Rd., Duncan, BC V9L 5Y8; (250) 746-7621; (800) 572-6481; info@genoabaymarina.com; www.genoabaymarina.com. Monitors VHF 66A mid-May through end of October. Open all year, guest moorage along 1200 feet of dock space by reservation. C Dock has been widened, allowing more space for social gatherings. Excellent washrooms, showers and laundry; 15, 30 & 50 amp power. Potable water on the docks is locally

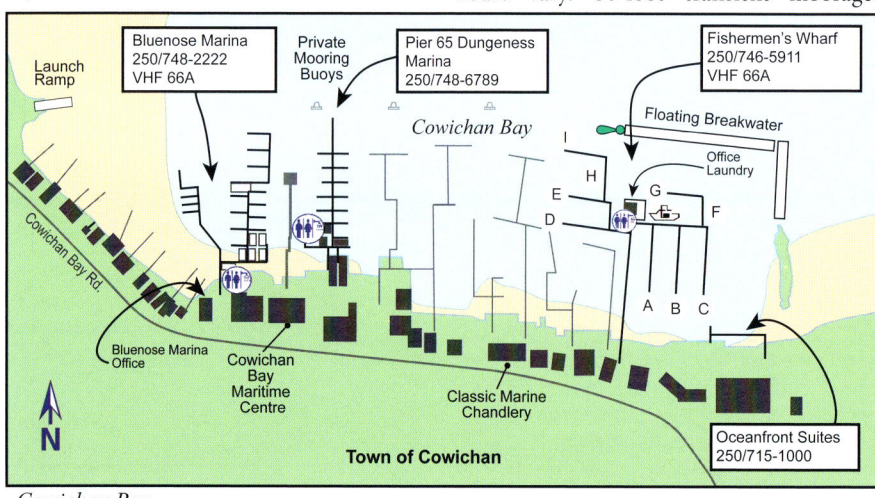

Cowichan Bay

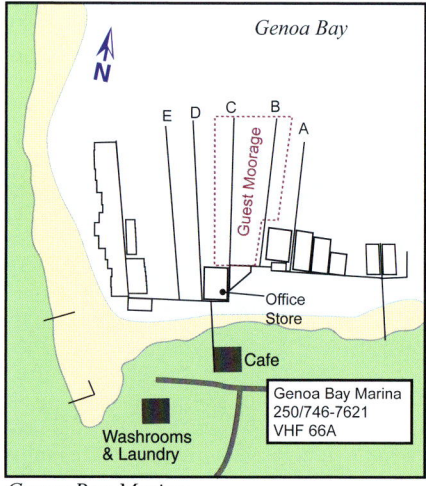

Genoa Bay Marina

See Area Map Page 220 - Maps Not for Navigation   GULF ISLANDS

Genoa Bay Marina side-tie guest moorage

Genoa Bay is a quiet, protected marina and anchoring destination with a great cafe.

produced; quantity of use may be limited. Launch ramp, covered picnic shelter, Wi-Fi.

This is a popular summer stop. The Genoa Bay Gallery has lovely paintings, prints, and sculptures. The "breakfast cabana" on the dock offers coffee, fresh baked goods, and other breakfast items most mornings, from the third weekend in June through Labor Day. Their blueberry waffles are a favorite. The unusually good marina store carries convenience items, souvenirs, books, and snacks. Good crabbing in the bay. Ask at the office about the nearby "Mad Dog" trail that takes you to the top of Tzouhalem Mountain. Bicycle rentals available at the marina.

The upland Genoa Bay Cafe is often busy, reservations recommended. The menu offers unique local cuisine with prices to match.

Musgrave Landing - Harbour Authority of Salt Spring Island. (250) 537-5711 saltspringharbours.com/musgrave-landing/. Musgrave Landing is on the southwest corner of Salt Spring Island, at the mouth of Sansum Narrows. It is managed by the Harbour Authority of Salt Spring Island. Musgrave Landing is a popular stopover, although it has only a small public float for visitor moorage, no facilities, and very restricted anchorage nearby. Upland you'll find good hiking along miles of logging roads. On a pleasant roadside walk we picked a bouquet of thistle, foxglove, dandelion, fern, salal, nicotiana and pearly everlasting for the galley table. A housing development, with private dock, is on Musgrave Point.

SANSUM NARROWS TO DUCK BAY

Sansum Narrows. Sansum Narrows connects Satellite Channel to the south with Stuart Channel to the north, and leads between high hills on Saltspring Island and Vancouver Island. The wind funnels down the axis of the narrows, turning at the bends. It also funnels down the valleys leading to the channel, so wind directions can be erratic. Currents seldom exceed 3 knots; usually they are less.

Speed Limit: 7 knots in the narrowest parts of the fairway.

Burgoyne Bay - Harbour Authority of Salt Spring Island. saltspringharbours.com/burgoyne-bay/; Burgoyne Bay has ample anchorage in 18 to 30 feet at its inner end, but is subject to williwaws that blow across a low swale on Saltspring Island. Most of the bay is too deep for convenient anchoring. A 65-foot public float for visitor moorage is at the head of the bay, next to the anchorage, no facilities. One side of the float is available for guest moorage stays up to 48 hours. The other side is reserved for local use.

㉘ **Maple Bay.** Maple Bay is a major pleasure boat center, with public moorages and all necessary facilities and services. Birds Eye Cove, off the southwest corner of Maple Bay, is home to the Maple Bay Yacht Club, with reciprocal moorage, and the Maple Bay Marina and Birds Eye Cove Marina. Anchoring is good in Birds Eye Cove, but avoid anchoring on the east side of the cove, opposite the marina docks. Markers designate

DISCOVER THE HAND OF MAN AT MAPLE BAY

An extensive private collection of world culture is tucked just above the small community of Maple Bay. This exceptional museum recently opened for public viewing. Boaters can easily visit the museum by mooring their boat at Maple Bay Marina and go by dinghy to nearby Maple Bay Public Wharf. A steep but short quarter-mile hike up the road from the municipal wharf brings you to the Hand of Man Museum.

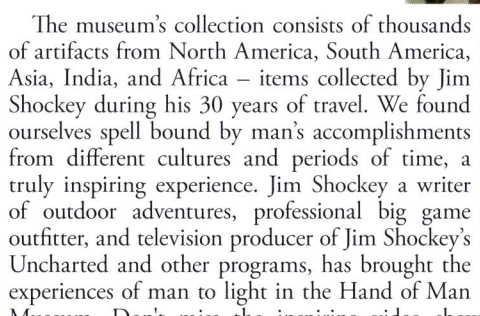

The museum's collection consists of thousands of artifacts from North America, South America, Asia, India, and Africa – items collected by Jim Shockey during his 30 years of travel. We found ourselves spell bound by man's accomplishments from different cultures and periods of time, a truly inspiring experience. Jim Shockey a writer of outdoor adventures, professional big game outfitter, and television producer of Jim Shockey's Uncharted and other programs, has brought the experiences of man to light in the Hand of Man Museum. Don't miss the inspiring video shown in the African room. Jim's hunting and traveling adventures have spanned six continents and 50 countries. Through his adventures, he became an avid collector of Tribal Art and Tribal Artifacts from around the world.

The Hand of Man Museum (888-826-1011) is open daily, located at 6759 Considine Avenue and serves as a witness to the traditions and historic tools used by man to harvest and gather over the centuries. Upon arrival at the wharf, walk across the road where you will find a trail cut through the blackberry bushes, this will put you onto Maple Bay Road; continue up the hill and turn right onto Considine Avenue and walk one more block; it's worth the hike!

[Lorena Landon]

2023 Waggoner Cruising Guide

GULF ISLANDS

See Area Map Page 220 - Maps Not for Navigation

Birds Eye Cove with Maple Bay Marina; the no anchoring zone is in the middle

The Lion Rampant Pub in Maple Bay and its guest dock for patrons

the no anchoring navigation channel.

Birds Eye Cove Farm, located a half-mile south of Maple Bay, is a favorite local attraction. The Farm raises beef, pork and chickens as well as providing farm-fresh eggs. Visitors can purchase eggs, meat pies and meat dishes from the "Gypsy Wagon" open daily from 10:00 a.m. to dusk. A self-payment box is inside the wagon. Food items are created on their spit grill and wood-fired oven. It's a treat to see the 300 acres of beautiful rolling fields. Social events are held in the large hand-cut timber frame barn and there are two timber frame cabins to rent. For more information go to www.birdseyecovefarm.com or call (250) 748-6379.

One of the best farmer's markets on Vancouver Island is held in downtown Duncan on Saturdays at the Market Square, look for the Clock Tower. The market is open year-round, spring/summer hours 9:00 a.m. to 2:00 p.m. Taxi service is available through Duncan Taxi (250) 746-4444.

㉘ **Maple Bay Marina.**
6145 Genoa Bay Rd., Duncan, BC V9L 5T7; (250) 746-8482; (866) 746-8482; info@maplebaymarina.com; www.maplebaymarina.com. Monitors VHF 66A. Open all year, phone for reservations;

Birds Eye Cove and Maple Bay Marina

check in at the store for moorage payment. Slip assignment is made when calling on VHF 66A upon approach. Gasoline, diesel, lubricants, propane and pumpout service at the fuel dock; open daily from 8:00 a.m. to 7:00 p.m. in the summers; hours vary in the shoulder season. High-flow fuel pumps available. 15 & 30 amp power, some 50 amp; garbage, washrooms, showers, laundry, water, waste oil disposal, and free Wi-Fi for guests.

A lovely picnic shelter provides space for yacht club group functions. Mariners Market & Espresso Bar has coffee, convenience groceries, and local crafts. The chandlery has a few marine supplies. It has been reported that docks at Maple Bay are deteriorating and showing their age, as are the washrooms and laundry facilities. Finger floats on G & H docks were improved in 2022. Plans are in the works to make further improvements.

A 50-ton Travelift provides haulout for boat repairs at the adjacent Valet Yacht Services (250) 252-3232; quality@valetyachtservices.ca.

The Shipyard Restaurant & Pub has good food, with daily specials and live music on Friday evenings. The pub offers off-sale beer and wine.

Hiking trail maps are available in the office for Mount Tzouhalem. Harbour Air has scheduled floatplane service to Vancouver Harbour and Vancouver Airport.

㉘ **Birds Eye Cove Marina.** 6271 Genoa Bay Rd., Duncan, BC V9L 5Y8; (250) 746-5686; office@birdseyemarina.com. The marina was sold in November 2019; permanent moorage only, no transient moorage or fuel service.

㉘ **Maple Bay Public Wharf.** Connie Crocker Wharfinger, (250) 715-8186. Open all year for day-use and overnight; first-come, first-served. Located in Maple Bay, not in Birds Eye Cove, which extends from the south side of Maple Bay. Moorage along 300 feet of dock space; no power. Self-registration and payment box at the head of the ramp. A nice beach is nearby. An underwater park is about 200 feet off the end of the dock. The wharf is operated by the North Cowichan Municipality. The Lion Rampant Pub (250-746-5422), with a 50-foot guest dock for patrons, is nearby.

Don't miss visiting the Hand of Man Museum (888) 826-1011 located at 6759 Considine Ave, Maple Bay; it's a steep but short quarter-mile hike up the road from the public wharf. The museum is outstanding, home to thousands of artifacts from all over the world collected by Jim Shockey during his 30 years of travel as a guide and writer.

Crofton Public Wharf. Open all year, 1000 feet of dock space, 20 & 30 amp power, washrooms, showers, laundry, garbage drop. Breakwater protected. The docks are usually full with local boats, rafting permitted. Crofton is the pulp and paper mill town on the west side of Stuart Channel. The public dock is next to the terminal for the ferry to Vesuvius on Saltspring Island. Walking distance to all services including groceries, restaurants, fishing supplies and licenses. Playground two blocks away. Nearby outdoor swimming pool, tennis courts, hiking trails.

㉙ **Vesuvius.** Located on the northwest side of Saltspring Island, the village of Vesuvius is the terminus for the ferry to Crofton on Vancouver Island. Vesuvius has a public wharf, coffee shop with tasty lunch items, and the popular Seaside Restaurant all within easy walking distance. Vesuvius Bay has anchorage that is open to the northwest with limited protection to the south and southeast. The bay is regularly rocked with wakes from the arriving ferry. More protected anchorage can be found nearby in Duck Bay.

㉙ **Vesuvius - Harbour Authority of Salt Spring Island.** (250) 537-5711 saltspringharbours.com/vesuvius-bay. The public wharf at Vesuvius, located behind the ferry landing, has side-tie visitor moorage on a 40 foot float; no power, no water. Self-registration, moorage rates and payment box are located at the wharfhead; first 2 hours stay at no charge 8:00 a.m. to 4:00 p.m. This is a popular well-used location.

Duck Bay. Just north of Vesuvius Bay, Duck Bay has good anchorage with steep, wooded cliffs rising on its east side. The bay is well-protected, except from northwest winds. A number of private docks, mooring buoys and homes surround the bay.

NORTHERN GULF ISLANDS

Stuart Channel. Stuart Channel runs from Sansum Narrows to Dodd Narrows. It is bordered on the west side by Vancouver Island, and on the east side by Saltspring, Penelakut (Kuper), Thetis and De Courcy Islands. Stuart Channel tends to be littered with drift because of extensive log towing to Crofton, Chemainus and Ladysmith. Keep a sharp watch ahead.

㉚ **Chemainus.** Chemainus is on the Vancouver Island side of Stuart Channel. It has a good public wharf, floats, and mooring buoys. Chemainus Bay, south of the Municipal Dock, is filled with commercial log boom operations and commercial maritime activities. The bay is not suitable for anchoring.

Chemainus is filled with boutiques, galleries, antique shops, and interesting-looking restaurants. More than 30 of the town's buildings have large, well-done murals, most of them depicting Chemainus' distant past as a Native seasonal campground and its more recent history as a mining, logging, and mill town. In recent years, the mural project has focused on celebrating Canadian artist Emily Carr's work. Chemainus is Canada's largest permanent outdoor art gallery.

Chemainus has grown so popular that a large parking area has been built for tour buses, and in they roll, filled with visitors from around the world. Don't miss Waterfront Park and the Chemainus Museum. Horse-drawn tours are available. Two 49th Parallel grocery stores are located on Oak Street. The original historic general store is immediately above the municipal dock, and the newer fully-stocked store is about half a mile up the road at 3055 Oak Street; call (250) 246-3551 for dock-side deliveries, a fee is charged. Also on Oak Street is the Chemainus Bakery with a good selection of fresh baked goods.

A ferry crosses between Chemainus and Thetis Island, about a 10-minute walk from either Thetis Island Marina or Telegraph Harbour Marina. This is a good way to visit Chemainus. If you take in an evening show in Chemainus, be sure you can get to the ferry before the last departure. Chemainus Water Taxi is another option (250) 246-7866 or (250) 246-9559.

Live Theater: The Chemainus Theatre, with a Playbill Dining Room, hosts live matinee and evening performances year-round (closed Mondays). Highly recommended. Call for tickets in advance: (250) 246-9820 or (800) 565-7738.

㉚ **Chemainus Municipal Wharf.** P.O. Box 193, Chemainus, BC V0R 1K0; (250) 715-8186; (250) 246-4655; harmen.chemainus.munimarina@gmail.com. Monitors VHF 66A. Day and overnight moorage; 30 & 50 amp power, water, washrooms, showers, garbage drop for overnight guests, pumpout and Wi-Fi. Make moorage reservations directly with the marina by phone or email; they have no relationship with third-party

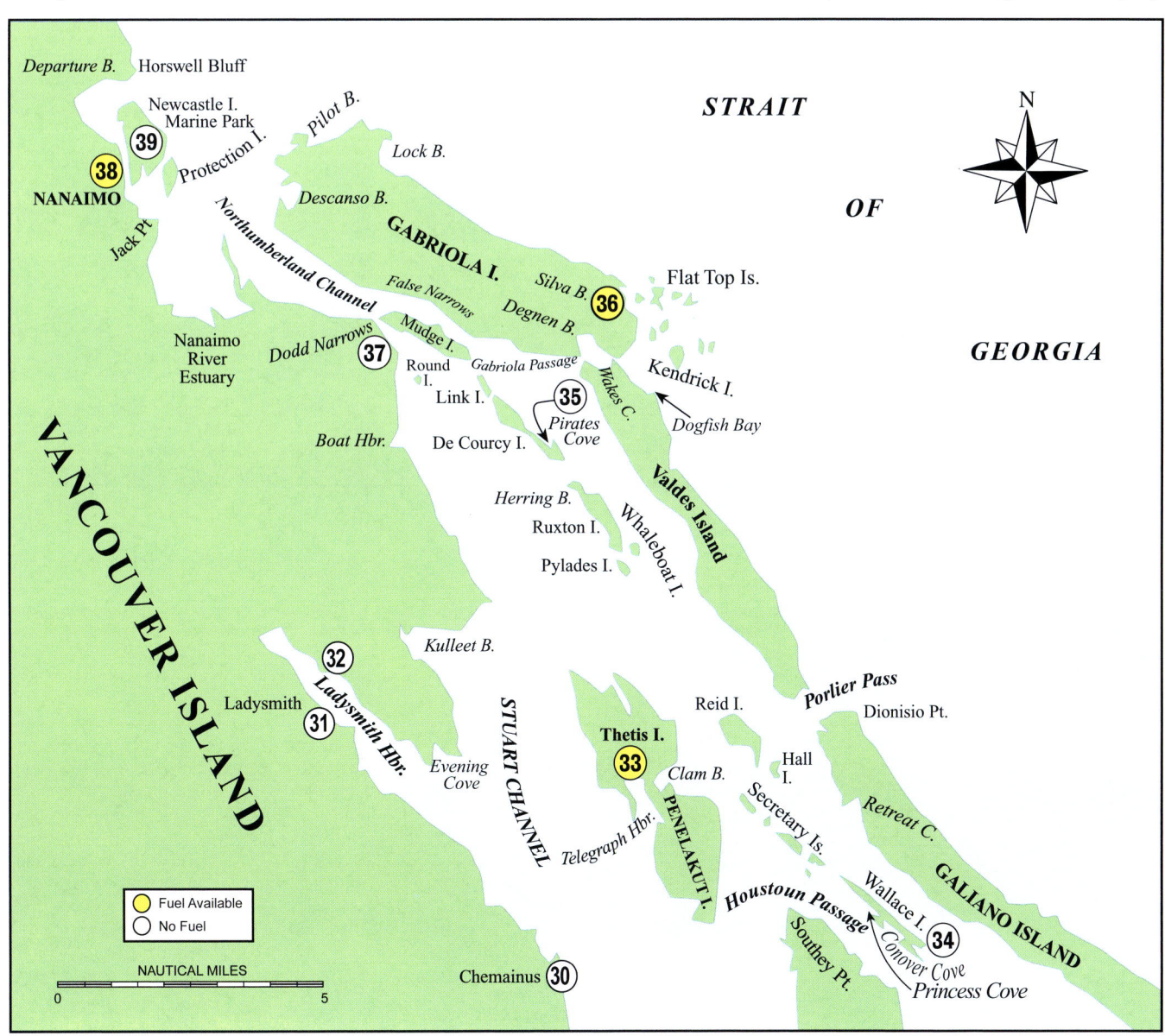

Northern Gulf Islands

GULF ISLANDS

See Area Map Page 247 - Maps Not for Navigation

The small town of Chemainus has a surprisingly good selection of eateries and activities.

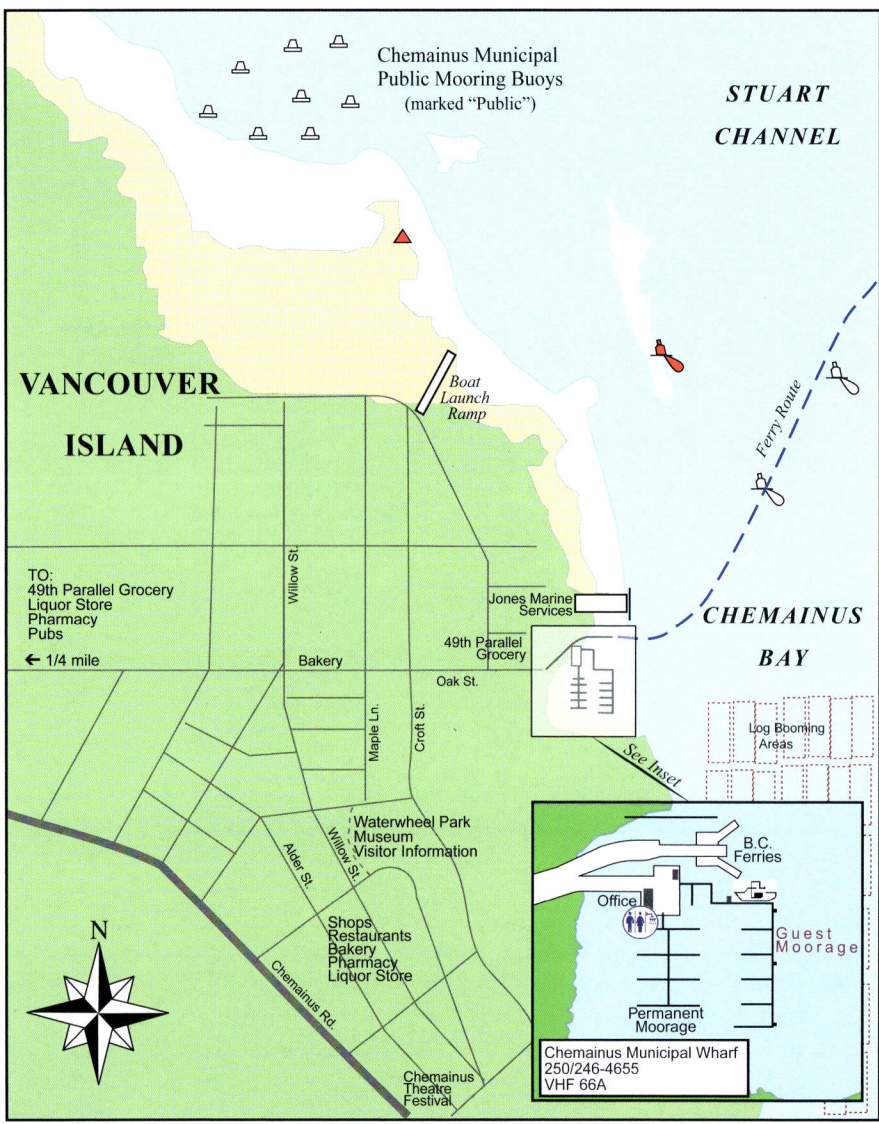

Chemainus

booking services. A nice laundromat is 1½ blocks away at 9870 Cross Street. This marina, with slips and side-tie, is next to the ferry terminal. Reservations recommended. Every two hours from morning to night, the ferry arrives and rolls things around a little. It's not bad, but first-time visitors should be aware of the wake.

Visitor boats will tie along 175 feet on the outside of the main dock or moor in slips on the inside of the main dock. Because Chemainus is a popular day stop, landing fees have been instituted—$6 under 40 feet; $12 over 40 feet. They found that the docks were full during the day then empty at night, and they need moorage income to maintain the facility.

Mooring Buoys: Eight mooring buoys are available off the park at the entrance to the bay. One boat per buoy, 45-foot maximum length. Cost is $12 per night if you pay at the Chemainus Municipal Dock office; $20 if they have to come out to collect. Private mooring buoys are also in the bay; look for the buoys labeled 'public.'

Jones Marine Services Ltd. Box 29, Chemainus, BC V0R 1K0; (250) 246-1100. Fuel service for commercial vessels only.

Evening Cove. Evening Cove, at the mouth of Ladysmith Harbour, is a possible anchorage. Correspondent Bruce Evertz reports: "We found good protection from northwest winds, but did have a few wakes from passing boats. There are several houses around the bay so it's not a good spot to take Fido ashore."

㉛ **Ladysmith Harbour.** Ladysmith is on Vancouver Island, approximately 6 miles north of Chemainus. Ladysmith is an active sawmill town. Logs are stored on the north side of the harbor and in front of the mill on the south side.

Ladysmith itself is about one-half mile from Ladysmith Community Marina and Fisherman's Wharf, up the hill and across the highway. Before reaching the highway, the big blue building you see once served as a railroad equipment repair facility. The tracks are still there.

The main street of Ladysmith looks as if time passed it by. Movie scenes have been filmed here. A large and friendly 49th Parallel Grocery is several blocks west from the main downtown area, and will deliver to the docks. A private liquor store is next door to the grocery.

The Old Town Bakery at 510 First Avenue (main street through town) is "to die for," with the widest variety of fresh-baked cinnamon buns we've ever seen. We had an excellent and reasonably priced deli lunch there, too. Buoma Meats, at 412 First Avenue, is an old-fashioned butcher shop, all weights in pounds and ounces. The Beantime Cafe serves fresh roasted coffee. A broad selection of restaurants are in town. Several restaurants will deliver to the marinas.

Ladysmith Community Marina, run by the Ladysmith Maritime Society, behind Slag Point on the south side of the harbor, is the first major set of docks. Ladysmith Fisherman's Wharf is adjacent, followed by Ladysmith Marina farther into the harbor. Raven Point Marina, on the north shore, sometimes has transient moorage available. Ladysmith Yacht Club, located at Ladysmith Marina has reciprocal moorage. Near the mouth of Ladysmith Harbour, the long float in Sibell Bay on the north side of the Dunsmuir Islands is a Seattle Yacht Club outstation, member boats only; no reciprocal moorage.

Good anchoring is in Sibell Bay, at the head of Ladysmith Harbour, and in the small bay between north Dunsmuir Island and Bute Island. Sibell Bay is a bit more exposed then the other two possible anchorages. There is ample swinging room with good holding at the head of Ladysmith Harbour. The bay between North Dunsmuir Island and Bute Island is well protected with room for a few boats. A community dock on the west side of Bute Island has a 40-foot concrete float, which provides access to a loop trail on the island. Maximum 3-hour stay on the dock, no charge.

Sealegs Kayaking Adventures (250-245-4096), located upland from Ladysmith Community Marina, offers equipment sales, tours, and lessons. Concerts are held in the park at Transfer Beach.

Note: Visitors will find that many of the shops in Ladysmith are closed Saturday through Monday, so plan accordingly.

Repairs: Ladysmith Marine Services (250-714-6206) offers marine repairs and haulout to 40 feet.

No-Discharge Zone. Gray water okay.

㉛ **Ladysmith Fisherman's Wharf.** P.O. Box 130, Ladysmith, BC V9G 1A1; (250) 245-7511 or (250) 618-4720 after hours; office hours 10:00 a.m. to 1:00 p.m. Monday through Saturday. lfwa@telus.net; www.ladysmithfishermanswharf.com. Open all year, 1200 feet of dock space, 30 amp power, garbage drop, washrooms, showers, laundry services, waste oil disposal, trailer parking. Marine repairs, tidal grid and launch ramp. Limited transient moorage. Commercial fish boats have priority during the winter months. Stairs lead up the hill toward the town of Ladysmith, about one-half mile away.

㉛ **Ladysmith Marina.** 901 Gladden Rd., Ladysmith, BC V9G 1K4; (250) 245-4521; ladysmithmarina@obmg.com; www.ladysmithmarina.com. Monitors VHF 66A. Open all year, washrooms, showers, and a public laundry. 30 & 50 amp power. Picnic area. This marina has permanent moorage, but guest moorage is often available in unoccupied slips, call ahead for availability; reservations accepted. Dock A on the east side of the marina is occupied by the Ladysmith Yacht Club, with reciprocal moorage. The marina is part of Oak Bay Marine Group, a company that owns several marinas. Future plans include a boardwalk and new office buildings upland.

The picture says it all - a trip to the Ladysmith Bakery is well worth the hike up the hill.

Ladysmith Harbour

GULF ISLANDS

See Area Map Page 247 - Maps Not for Navigation

Ladysmith Community Marina is a very welcoming destination with side tie guest moorage.

Check the cafe hours at the Marina

㉛ **Ladysmith Community Marina.** P.O. Box 1030, Ladysmith, BC V9G 1A7; (250) 245-1146; info@lmsmarina.ca; www.lmsmarina.ca. Monitors VHF 66A. Call or make reservations online. Open all year, 950 feet of guest moorage with 30 amp power, water, cube ice and block ice. Purchase tokens at the office to operate the pumpout. Free Wi-Fi. Garbage and recycling (donations are appreciated).

The impressive Ladysmith Maritime Society Welcome Centre, on a float at the docks, has a fireside lounge, washrooms, showers, laundry, and the seasonal Oyster Bay Cafe, which is open daily from mid-May to Labour Day. Adjacent to the Oyster Bay Cafe is the Sea Life Centre with interpretive displays and an underwater portal to view the marine life. The cross dock by the Welcome Centre is for dinghies 10 feet and under.

These are the first set of docks on the southwest side as you enter Ladysmith Harbour. The docks are very good and the historical displays, including restored museum boats and equipment, are fascinating. The Harbour Heritage Centre, an art gallery, and the Ladysmith Maritime Society with a naval display, are up the hill in the large blue building. The town of Ladysmith is a short walk farther up the hill.

The community is justifiably proud of this facility and its large meeting spaces. A large covered 40 X 20 foot picnic area with tables and grills, located on the docks, can accommodate up to 100 people. At the end of the day it is not unusual for a group to gather round, some grilling their dinners and some visiting others. Dine on the Dock programs are often held on Fridays during the summers and frequently sell out. Music and food on the Dock events are held in July and August. Their BBQ's and Open Mic Nights are popular.

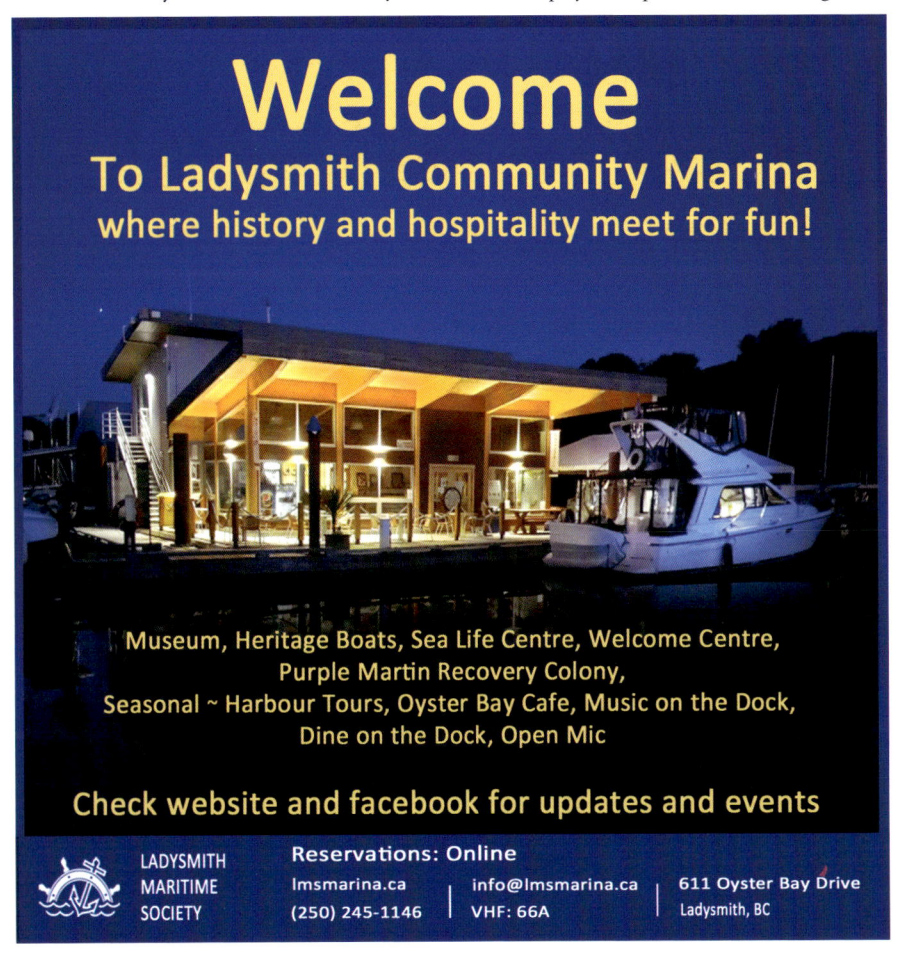

Welcome
To Ladysmith Community Marina
where history and hospitality meet for fun!

Museum, Heritage Boats, Sea Life Centre, Welcome Centre, Purple Martin Recovery Colony,
Seasonal ~ Harbour Tours, Oyster Bay Cafe, Music on the Dock, Dine on the Dock, Open Mic

Check website and facebook for updates and events

LADYSMITH MARITIME SOCIETY

Reservations: Online
lmsmarina.ca
(250) 245-1146
info@lmsmarina.ca
VHF: 66A
611 Oyster Bay Drive
Ladysmith, BC

NO DISCHARGE ZONES B.C. WATERS

BRITISH COLUMBIA - discharge of black water is not allowed in the following areas. Approved holding tanks are required in these areas. Macerator treatment systems, even if approved, do not qualify. Unless otherwise noted, Gray water is not included in the regulations.

– Pirates Cove (no gray)
– Prideaux Haven
– Roscoe Bay
– Smuggler Cove
– Squirrel Cove
– Tod Inlet
– Victoria Harbour
– Carrington Bay
– Cortes Bay
– Gorge Harbour
– Ladysmith Harbour
– Mansons Landing
– Montague Harbour
– Pilot Bay
– Burrard Inlet/False Creek

Main street Ladysmith has a wide selection of shops and eateries.

One of several dining options in Ladysmith.

Check the website for more information. The Ladysmith Community Marina is run by the Ladysmith Maritime Society and is a true community marina, with over 250 volunteers. As guests, we could feel their enthusiasm.

㉜ **Raven Point Marina.** 4760 Brenton-Page Rd., Ladysmith, BC V9G 1L7; (250) 245-2312; (877) 860-6866; www.ravenpoint.ca. Monitors VHF 66A. Open all year. Permanent moorage to 66 feet, with limited guest moorage in slips, and side tie as available; 30 amp power, water, free Wi-Fi, garbage drop, and recycling. Laundry and showers. Reservations recommended. The dinghy dock is next to the ramp at the head of G dock. Previously known as Page Point Marina, this site was refurbished in 2021, including the Inn and restaurant. Raven Point Marina offers stunning views and personable service.

Tent Island. Tent Island is off the south tip of Penelakut Island (formerly Kuper Island), at the junction of Houstoun Passage and Stuart Channel. The small bay on the west side of Tent Island is a popular anchorage in settled weather.

Find Your Dream Itinerary
with *Waggoner* as your Guide

The 2023 Waggoner Guide includes cruising itineraries for the boater's dream vacation trip to many of the best places throughout Puget Sound, San Juan Islands, Gulf Islands, Desolation Sound, and Southeast Alaska.

Itineraries include helpful information for navigating the waters to each destination along with ideas and suggestions for things to do when you get there.

WAGGONER

WaggonerGuide.com • 360.299.8500 • Anacortes

GULF ISLANDS

See Area Map Page 247 - Maps Not for Navigation

Watch for floatplane and boat traffic in Telegraph Harbour.

View of Telegraph Harbour from outdoor seating at Thetis Island Resort

Preedy Harbour. Preedy Harbour indents the southwest corner of Thetis Island, due west of Telegraph Harbour. The ferry from Chemainus calls there. From the south, enter between Hudson Island and three long, thin reefs, marked with red (starboard hand) lights and day beacons. From Stuart Channel enter between Hudson Island and Dayman Island. Reefs, marked by green buoys on the Dayman Island side and a light on the Hudson Island side, extend from both these islands. Because the Hudson Island light is positioned upland from the toe of its reef, favor the Dayman Island buoys.

Entry from the north is clear as long as you stay mid-channel. For all three entries, check the chart carefully so you know where the reefs are, and how to avoid them.

A day-use-only community dock is in the northeast corner of Preedy Harbour, near the ferry landing. Anchorage is good in this area, keeping in mind the ferry comings and goings.

㉝ **Telegraph Harbour.** Telegraph Harbour is one of the Gulf Islands' most popular stops. It is located across Stuart Channel from Chemainus, between Thetis Island and Penelakut Island (formerly Kuper Island). Two marinas are in Telegraph Harbour: Thetis Island Resort and Telegraph Harbour Marina. Both marinas are walking distance to an inter-island ferry to Chemainus. While you're at Telegraph Harbour, you may enjoy walking the roads of Thetis Island. You'll find a number of interesting stops, including the Howling Farm Market.

Note the shoal areas on the east side of the channel across from the Thetis Island Resort. Depths are shallower than charted.

Penelakut Island (formerly Kuper Island) is an Indian Reserve.

Howling Wolf Farm Float. (250) 246-2650 Located at the north end of Telegraph Harbour (corner of Marine Dr, and Pilkey Point Road). The Howling Wolf Farm has a dinghy float for those wanting to access the farm's stand to purchase pies, baked goods, jams, and produce. The float is usable at mid- to high-tides and goes dry at low tides. The farm stand is open daily from 9:00 a.m. to 6:00 p.m., early April through October. A Farmers Market is held at the farm stand location on Saturdays from 10:00 a.m. to 2:00 p.m., June through early September. Visitors will find local crafts and foods from 19 participating vendors.

LOCAL KNOWLEDGE

ENTRANCE CHANNEL: On very low tides hug the breakwater outside the Thetis Island Resort's fuel dock as you enter Telegraph Harbour. The channel has about 9 feet of depth at zero tide. Don't cut the corner, give Penelakut Island side a good offing.

㉝ **Thetis Island Resort.** 46 Harbour Rd., Thetis Island, BC; (250) 246-3464; marina@thetisisland.com; www.thetisisland.com or check facebook. Monitors VHF 66A. To port, this is the first marina as you enter Telegraph Harbour. Open all year, gasoline and diesel at the fuel dock, propane on shore, over 3000 feet of side-tie dock space, 15 & 30 amp power and some 50 amp. Washrooms, showers, and laundry. Wi-Fi on the docks; get the password at the restaurant or the fuel dock. A cell phone booster covers the restaurant and deck areas. No water at the docks. Docks are reported to be showing their age and in need of repair or replacement.

Music is held at the restaurant on most weekends during July and August. The marina has a liquor store, convenience groceries, snacks, ice, and post office. It's a 10- to 15-minute walk to the BC Ferries to Chemainus.

The fully-licensed restaurant has inside and outside dining. The restaurant has good food and an excellent selection of beers, porters, stouts, and single-malt scotches.

The Resort has its own water desalination system, no water at the docks however. A covered picnic and barbecue area with seating is available for groups.

㉝ **Telegraph Harbour Marina.** Box 7-10, Thetis Island, BC V0R 2Y0; (250) 246-9511; (800) 246-6011; sunny@telegraphharbour.com; www.telegraphharbour.com. Monitors VHF 66A. This is the marina at the back of the bay. Although close to drying flats, the docks have at least 6 to 8 feet on all tides. Open 7 days a week, mid-June through mid-September, and weekends only from Easter through mid-June. In winter no facilities are available except moorage and electricity. Moorage along 3000 feet of dock; 15 & 30 amp power, washrooms, showers, laundry, Wi-Fi, garbage drop, recycling, limited water.

The store carries convenience groceries including a variety of specialty meats, deli items to go, and fresh-baked pies. The marina has pre-ordered homemade pizzas and fresh baguettes. Books and other items

Telegraph Harbour

See Area Map Page 247 - Maps Not for Navigation

GULF ISLANDS

North Cove on Thetis Island has anchorage for a number of boats; two street ends for shore access.

for sale. Everyone loves the old fashioned soda fountain, where you can still get guilt-filled hard ice cream and milk shakes.

The marina is clean and well-maintained. Staff helps arriving boats land. They have a playground for kids, a dog run, a large covered area for group functions, and a picnic area with tables and barbecues. It's a 10 to 15 minute walk to the BC Ferries to Chemainus.

Rendezvous: Many rendezvous are held here in spring or early fall, best to call ahead for reservations on weekends and during the peak season. A few rendezvous fill the marina, but most do not. Moorage space is usually available.

The Cut. The Cut is a straight drying pass connecting Telegraph Harbour with Clam Bay. Red, Right, Returning assumes you are returning from Clam Bay. The Cut is suitable only for dinghies, kayaks, and shallow draft boats at high tide. Signs at each end purport to show the depth, but they read approximately 3 feet too deep. We took the dinghy through at the bottom of a 4.3-foot tide, sounding the shallow spots with a leadline. Although the two signs said 6 feet of water was in the channel, we found only 2 to 2.5 feet in the shallow spots near the Telegraph Harbour entrance and at a couple of narrow places on the Clam Bay side. Locals are often seen along The Cut collecting clams.

North Cove. North Cove indents the north end of Thetis Island and is a good anchorage, although it is open to northwesterly winds. A substantial rock breakwater protects a private float and boathouse at Fraser Point, the entrance to North Cove. Camp docks are in the southwest corner of the cove. Anchor in 24 to 36 feet (zero tide) along the south shore. High tide covers fingers of rock that extend from the south shore, but the rock reappears when the tide drops. Don't get too close. Stay clear of the rocks in the middle of the entry. The charts show them as ++, for dangerous rocks 6 feet or less beneath the surface.

Cufra Inlet. Cufra Inlet, about a mile long, extends into Thetis Island from the southeast corner of North Cove. Most of the inlet dries, but is good for dinghy exploring at higher water.

Clam Bay. Clam Bay is a large, relatively open bay with good anchoring in convenient depths. Reader Jerry Williams, who lived there, says his favorite spot is the little bight on the north shore, between Leech Island and Thetis Island. The mouth of the Clam Bay is partly blocked by Centre Reef. Rocket Shoal is in the middle of the bay. Lacking familiarity, the safest entry is south of Centre Reef, between Buoy U42 and Penelakut Spit, which extends from Penelakut Island. Check the charts. Clam Bay is at one end of The Cut, the drying channel that separates Thetis Island from Penelakut Island.

Welcome to Thetis Island Resort
Marina • Restaurant

Restaurant with Family Dining
Dining on the Deck • Covered BBQ and Picnic Area
Rental Suites Overlooking the Harbour
Convenience Store • Liquor Store
Showers & Laundry Facilities
Free Dinghy Tie-Up
Free Wi-Fi

We welcome rendezvous groups.

250.246.1443 • VHF 66A
N48 65.6, W123 40.1
www.thetisisland.com • thetisislandresorts@gmail.com

2023 Waggoner Cruising Guide

GULF ISLANDS   See Area Map Page 247 - Maps Not for Navigation

Stern-ties are the rule at popular Pirates Cove Marine Park.

Read the Local Knowledge regarding the process for safely entering Pirates Cove.

Southey Bay. At the north tip of Saltspring Island, tucked in beside Southey Point, is a little notch that Tom Kincaid used as an anchorage in past years. An increasing number of private mooring buoys have restricted swinging room, but it's still a possible anchorage.

Secretary Islands. The Secretary Islands have several nice little anchorages, with the emphasis on *little*. One of the easiest is in the notch on the Trincomali Channel side between the two Secretary Islands.

Mowgli Island. Mowgli Island, off the northwest tip of the Secretary Islands, has good anchorage in a cozy bay between it and the first Secretary island. Swinging room is limited. We suggest a stern-tie across the gravel beach to driftwood ashore. The island is surrounded by reefs. They are easily seen at low tide, but be cautious at high tide.

㉞ **Wallace Island Marine Park.** www.env.gov.bc.ca/bcparks/explore/parkpgs/wallace/ Open all year. Wallace Island, a marine park purchased with the help of the local boating community, is a low and beautiful tree-covered island in Trincomali Channel. Enter from Houstoun Passage. You'll find sheltered anchorage and a dock at Conover Cove, anchorage for many boats in locally-named Princess Cove, and room for a couple of boats just inside Panther Point. The park has toilets, campsites and picnic areas, and trails crisscrossing the entire island. It's a fine place to walk through the forest and stretch the legs. Raccoons roam the area—especially at night, lock up all food items aboard and pack out refuse. Old cabins set in an orchard near Conover Cove are locked shut, awaiting funds for restoration. One cabin is festooned with carved name boards from visiting yachts. Please respect the two private properties on the island.

㉞ **Conover Cove.** A reef directly offshore from the entrance to Conover Cove on Wallace Island can be avoided by going around either end. Especially from the southeast, give the reef ample room. When you leave, remember the reef is there. We are told that each year boats depart at high tide and drive up on the rocks. A dock for boats 36 feet and under provides access to the island, a nominal fee is charged. An honor-system pay-box is located at the head of the ramp. Conover Cove is fairly shoal at the dock and shoals even more toward both ends of the bay. You can anchor and stern-tie to pins, with chain, set in the rocks on shore. Be sure to check your depths. The entrance to Conover Cove is shallow at low tide.

㉞ **Princess Cove.** Princess Cove is just northwest of Conover Cove, and has room for quite a few boats to anchor. 18 long chains, with large links for stern lines, are attached to existing pins set in the rock along the shoreline. If anchoring in the cove, set the anchor carefully in 18 to 24 feet (deeper toward the mouth of the cove), and maintain an anchor watch if the wind comes up. A dinghy dock is on the west side of the cove for convenient access to hiking.

㉞ **Panther Point.** Panther Point is the southeast tip of Wallace Island. There's room for one or perhaps two boats in 30 to 36 feet just inside the mouth of the cove. If you anchor any farther inside, a rock on the north side will restrict your swing. The anchorage is exposed to southeast winds but protected from other winds.

Retreat Cove. Retreat Cove, a small notch protected by off-lying Retreat Island, indents Galiano Island across Trincomali Channel from the south tip of Wallace Island. The approach around the north side of Retreat Island is shallow and foul with rocks and reefs. Enter only from the south. The head of Retreat Cove shelves sharply. Anchor in 18 to 24 feet, but plan your swing to avoid the shelf. An 80-foot-long public dock, no facilities, is on the southern shore of the cove. Local boats take much of the space on the dock.

North Galiano. North Galiano is on the west side of Galiano Island. It lies to the northeast of Hall Island and has anchorage and a small public dock, no facilities.

Dionisio Point Park. Open all year, day use and overnight camping, toilets, no power, no showers. Anchor only. The park overlooks Porlier Pass. It has sandy beaches, rocky headlands and forested uplands. Anchorage is open to Strait of Georgia swell and northerly winds.

Porlier Pass. Porlier Pass separates Galiano Island and Valdes Island. Several times a year, currents on large tides reach 9 knots. Current predictions are shown in the Tide and Current Tables Vol. 5, and Ports and Passes. The current floods north into the Strait of Georgia, and ebbs south into the Gulf Islands. The best time to transit is at slack water. A study of the chart shows it is safest to transit Porlier Pass on the south sides of Black Rock and Virago Rock, staying toward the Galiano Island side of the pass.

From the Strait of Georgia, begin your approach near Lighted Bell Buoy U41. South of the buoy, pick up the range on Race Point and Virago Point. Follow that range into Porlier Pass to clear the rocks extending from the northeast tip of Galiano Island. Once clear of the rocks, you can turn to follow a mid-channel course between Virago Rock and Galiano Island.

Lighthouse Bay. Located at the entrance to Porlier Pass, Lighthouse Bay provides anchorage that is protected from most winds. Porlier Pass current can be running fast while waters are calm in Lighthouse Bay. Anchor south of the charted cable crossing. Ruins of cannery buildings are on the west shore, and the remains of a light keeper house, wharf, and shed are on the east shore.

De Courcy Group. The De Courcy Group has several interesting small anchorages. **Whaleboat Island,** just off the southeast shore of Ruxton Island, is a relatively

Explore ashore at Pirates Cove Marine Park; check out the treasure chest.

Pirates Cove Marine Park is a popular location; take care entering, and prepare to stern tie.

undeveloped provincial park. The preferred anchorage is south of the island, taking care to avoid a drying rock. The north end of **Ruxton Island** has **Herring Bay**, one of the more attractive small anchorages in the northern Gulf Islands, and frequently used when the anchorage at **Pirates Cove** on De Courcy Island is full (which it often is in the summer). Herring Bay has a white sand beach to enjoy. The De Courcy Group is named after Michael de Courcy, captain of the H.M.S. Pylades, who charted these waters from 1859 to 1861.

Whaleboat Island Marine Park. Just south of Ruxton Island. No facilities. Whaleboat Island is undeveloped, but provides an extremely limited alternate anchorage to Pirates Cove Marine Park. The preferred anchorage is south of the island, taking care to avoid a drying rock.

Pylades Island. Reader Jerry Williams, who grew up on Pylades Island, tells us the little hole just north of the dot islet off the northeast corner of Pylades Island is "magical." Most of the land is private, please do not take dogs ashore. A drying shoal is between Pylades Island and the dot islet, so approach from the north. In Whaleboat Passage, between Pylades Island and Ruxton Island, note the drying rock off Pylades Island. Jerry Williams reports that the rock is farther from shore than one might think and recommends favoring the Ruxton Island side.

Herring Bay. Herring Bay indents the northwest end of Ruxton Island, off Ruxton Passage. The bay is bordered by weather-carved sandstone walls and has a beautiful sand beach on the southeast side. Good anchoring in 24 feet, much to explore.

A charted rock ledge that dries at 1 foot is in the west entrance to Herring Bay at 49°05.08'N/123°43.01'W. We use the north entrance exclusively.

㉟ **Pirates Cove Marine Park.** Pirates Cove is open all year, campsites, pit toilets, hand pump water (boil before use) on the south beach, no other facilities. It's a lovely little harbor, protected from seas but not all winds, with room for many boats (on a short scope). 24 stern-tie chains are set into the sandstone cliffs that encircle the bay; the boat's stern-tie line is run through a large link in the chain. Do not use trees for stern tie. Two dinghy docks are for shore access, one on the northeast and the other on the southwest side of the cove. Dinghies may go ashore at the south end beach. The small marina on the right as you enter is private.

Most of the land is a marvelous provincial park. The cove is surrounded by a forest of Douglas fir, Garry oak and Arbutus (madrona). Well-maintained trails lead through the forest and along the rock shoreline with its sculpted sandstone formations and tide pools. Be sure to stay on designated trails to avoid brushing against poison oak, a rash-causing plant species protected by the Provincial Marine Park. Pirates Cove has only a fair holding bottom of sticky mud. If the wind comes up during the night, you can expect a fire drill as boats drag anchor. It's best to stern-tie. When departure time arrives, be prepared to spend extra time cleaning the anchor as it comes aboard.

No Discharge Zone, No Gray Water Discharge.

LOCAL KNOWLEDGE

DANGEROUS REEFS: The entrance to Pirates Cove is guarded by a reef that extends parallel to the shoreline to a point a little beyond a concrete beacon. When entering, you must leave this beacon to port. A range, consisting of a white-painted arrow on the ground and a white × on a tree above, shows where to make your approach. Align the × on the tree above the arrow on the ground and proceed slowly until just past the concrete beacon to port. Turn sharply to port and leave the red Spar Buoy U38 to starboard. The entry is shallow. At lower tides deep-draft boats should be especially cautious.

On Ruxton Passage, the little notch at the south end of De Courcy Island is also part of the park, and you can anchor there. The beach is good for dinghy or kayak landing, and campsites are ashore. Additional anchorage is available at Whaleboat Island Marine Park, nearby. Another "Pirates Cove overflow" notch is just north of Pirates Cove off Link Island.

Boat Harbour Marina. 2275 Kendall Road, Nanaimo, BC V9X 1W8; (250) 802-9963; marina.boatharbour@gmail.com; www.boatharbourmarina.ca; Joe, the wharfinger, is a delight. Located across Stuart Channel from De Courcy Island. Open June-September, 9:00 a.m. to 5:00 p.m. Long-term moorage with transient space; max boat size is 100 feet; minimum charge of 32 feet for all transient vessels. Two-day minimum stay. 30 & 50 amp power, water, garbage drop, Wi-Fi. Restrooms and showers. Call or book reservations online 48 hours in advance. Four mooring buoys also available by reservation. Floatplane service available through Vancouver via Pacific Coastal Airlines.

Boat Harbour Marina has substantial concrete floats and quality metal ramps and pilings. The marina offers customized tours for groups of 8 or more. You can opt for hikes through the private upland trails, with a picnic at the lake, or you might choose cooking classes, catered parties or pig roasts. A pig and beef roast event is held on July 1, Canada Day. A gazebo is available for group gatherings.

The anchorage area in Boat Harbour is within a private 'water lot' and is a no discharge zone. Anchorage allowed only with a permit by calling or texting (250) 802-9963 for application. The no-anchoring zone is marked with a line of spar buoys and posted signage. All of **Kenary Cove** dries on low tide.

The small community of Cedar on Yellow Point is two and a half miles (4 km) from Boat Harbour Marina. The popular English-style pub, Crow & Gate (250-722-3731), is located on Yellow Point Road. A Farmer's Market is held on Sundays at the Woodbank School.

Garbriola Passage has light traffic; check tides and currents before heading to Silva Bay.

GABRIOLA PASSAGE TO NANAIMO

Gabriola Passage. Gabriola Passage (Gabriola is pronounced "GAY-briola") is the northernmost entrance to the Gulf Islands from the Strait of Georgia. From Bowen Island on the east side of the strait, it is 14 miles to Gabriola Passage, the shortest crossing between the lower mainland and the islands.

Tidal currents on spring tides can run to 8 knots in Gabriola Passage, both flood and ebb. Typical maximum currents are around 4 knots. Transiting is best at slack. The current sets east on the flood and west on the ebb. Times of slack and maximum currents are given in the Tide & Current Tables, Vol. 5 and Ports and Passes.

Degnen Bay. Degnen Bay, on Gabriola Passage at the south end of Gabriola Island, is a good anchorage but very crowded with boats on moorings. Entering Degnen Bay, favor the east side, close to Josef Point, to avoid rocks in the middle. A petroglyph of a killer whale is on a slab of rock near the head of the bay. Correspondents John and Lorraine Littlewood report additional petroglyphs on the United Church grounds. A public dock provides access to Gabriola Island. All other docks are private.

Degnen Bay Public Wharf. Has 190 feet of dock space, which is usually filled with local boats. Power and garbage drop, but no other facilities.

Wakes Cove. Wakes Cove, on Gabriola Passage at the north end of Valdes Island, has a beautiful provincial marine park occupying almost the entire north end of Valdes Island. The park has trails and historical interpretation information. It is served by a small dock, approximately 40 feet, for RCMP and BC Parks personnel. The park is accessible by dinghy and kayak. Anchorage is a little iffy.

Dogfish Bay. Kendrick Island, on the northeast side of Valdes Island, creates a narrow and shallow bay known locally as Dogfish Bay. Dogfish Bay is well protected and the holding ground is good. West Vancouver Yacht Club has an outstation on Kendrick Island, members only, no reciprocal moorage. The yacht club's dock and their field of private mooring buoys occupy some of the bay's anchoring area, but there is still room for a few boats to anchor.

Drumbeg Provincial Park. South end of Gabriola Island, overlooking Gabriola Passage. Open all year, day use only. Toilets, no other facilities. Has shelving sandstone rocks and a small sandy beach.

Flat Top Islands. The Flat Top Islands are appropriately named, and from the north or east they're a little hard to tell apart. If approaching from the Strait of Georgia, pass north of Thrasher Rock Light. The light marks the northern end of Gabriola Reefs. All the Flat Top Islands are privately owned.

LOCAL KNOWLEDGE

DANGEROUS ROCK: When entering Silva Bay between Vance Island and Tugboat Island, leave the beacon marking Shipyard Rock to port. Do not turn at once for the Silva Bay floats or other facilities. Shipyard Rock is larger than it appears on the charts. Continue instead until about halfway to Law Point before making your turn. Give the rock plenty of room.

㉟ **Silva Bay.** Silva Bay is a popular destination in the Flat Top Islands area, well protected, with good holding bottom. From the north, enter through Commodore Passage between Gaviola Island and Vance Island; from the south enter through Commodore Passage between Acorn Island and Tugboat Island. From Commodore Passage, enter Silva Bay between Tugboat Island and Vance Island, leaving Shipyard Rock to port; notorious Shipyard Rock lies along the south side of this passage. Entering Silva Bay from the south through Sear Island Passage between Gabriola Island and Sear Island is possible only on mid- and high-water tides.

Check the community bus schedule for pick up at Page's Inn for a visit to the Island's village core. Nester's Food Market (250-247-8755) will deliver groceries to marinas at no charge. Paula Maddison, a resident of the island, offers cheese making classes, call (250) 247-9635 to inquire.

Anchoring: Anchoring is tight. Much of the bay is filled with private mooring buoys and is charted as a no anchoring zone. A designated floatplane departure and landing area is located along the front of the docks, where anchoring is not allowed.

㊱ **Silva Bay Resort & Marina.** 3383 South Road, Gabriola Island, BC V0R 1X7; (250) 247 8662 ext. 8; info@silvabay.com; www.silvabay.com. Monitors VHF 66A. Open all year with guest moorage, 30, 50, & 100 amp power, water on the fuel dock, garbage drop; washrooms are located in a trailer upland. Reservations recommended. Diesel and mid-grade gasoline at the fuel dock. A marine carpentry shop is located upland in the blue colored buildings above the marina. Daily floatplane flights to Vancouver.

The Silva Bay Bar & Grill was destroyed by fire in October 2017. Dan Chen and family, owners of the marina property, have started redevelopment of the uplands. Clearing and fencing for construction was completed

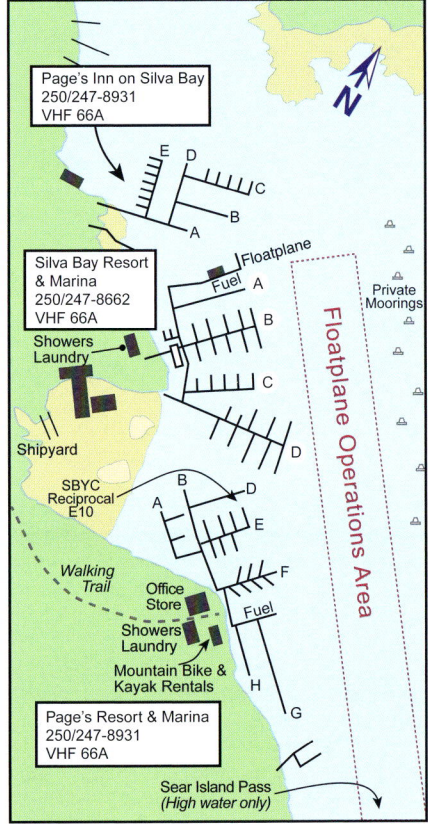

Silva Bay

GULF ISLANDS

in 2022. Plans include a new restaurant, a rebuild of the general store, and an elegant 16-room hotel. Green spaces and patios will overlook the stunning views. Completion is expected by summer of 2024.

㊱ **Page's Resort & Marina.** 3350 Coast Road, Gabriola Island, BC V0R 1X7; (250) 247-8931; info@pagesresort.com; www.pagesresortgroup.com. Monitors VHF 66A. Open all year. Visitor moorage accommodates vessels to 40 feet; two slips accommodate vessels up to 60 feet; one slip can accommodate a 75-foot vessel. Reservations accepted online. Mid-grade marine gasoline and diesel at the fuel dock. 15 & 30 amp power, washrooms, showers, laundry, garbage, recycling, bicycle and kayak rentals, ice, free Wi-Fi.

Cottages and tent sites for rent. Campers and RV guests share the one shower facility per gender with boaters. The grounds are well maintained and include a picnic area. Cab service and a community shuttle bus service can take you to Gabriola Island's shopping center, or you can rent bicycles at Page's. Page's has kayak and SUP rentals too.

For those interested in books, Page's carries a range of titles, especially books about local subjects by local authors. The office/store carries essential groceries, sundry items, bait, and cruising guides. The store's freezer is stocked with ready-made dinners that can be prepared back at the boat or on the barbeque. Selection of liquors, wine, and craft beers and ciders. Food includes items from Woodfire

Scenic Silva Bay has guest moorage at two marinas, or plan to anchor out.

Restaurant; deli sausage rolls and bacon; and coffee from a micro roaster on Gabriola Island. The Woodfired pizzas are designed to stay crisp when warmed up in the microwave. Other delights include artisan cheese making classes on site. Local resident Paula Maddison teaches classes in cheese making. Craft cider tasting is also available on the island; see gabbiescider.com.

㊱ **Page's Inn on Silva Bay.** 3415 South Rd., Gabriola Island, BC V0R 1X7, (250) 247-9351; info@silvabayinn.ca; www.pagesresortgroup.com. This lovely Inn, formerly the Boatel, is owned by Page's Resort & Marina. Meeting space is available on the top floor. Located west of Page's Marina, the docks at Page's Inn offer transient moorage for boaters staying ashore in one of the suites. The onsite food truck, Fire Truck Grill, features grilled meats and seafood. A farmers' market selling produce, food, and Gabriolan art is held on the grounds on Sundays during the summers.

SILVA BAY • GABRIOLA ISLAND • BC

PAGE'S RESORT AND MARINA
SINCE 1943

Experience Island Life and Discover New Passions at Our Full-Service Resort & Marina

- Silva Bay Sunday Market
- Live Music
- West Coast Eats
- Food Trucks
- Kayak Rentals
- Fuel Dock

- Local Artwork & Handicrafts
- Beers, Wine & Spirits
- Seaside Cottages & Suites
- Picnic Grounds
- Leisure Packages
- Groceries

PAGESRESORTGROUP.COM • VHF 66A • 250-247-8931

2023 Waggoner Cruising Guide

GULF ISLANDS

See Area Map Page 247 - Maps Not for Navigation

Busy Dodd Narrows deserves careful timing and transit.

False Narrows. False Narrows is east of Dodd Narrows, and is an alternate connection between the Gulf Islands and Northumberland Channel. If you choose to make this passage, you will be traveling between reefs in a shallow channel that is best used at half tide or better. Local knowledge says if you strictly follow the two ranges shown on the chart you'll be okay. Go slowly to keep your wake down. Maximum currents in False Narrows are about half of those in Dodd Narrows. Watch for thick kelp beds.

㊲ **Dodd Narrows.** Currents in Dodd Narrows run to 9 knots as water swirls through the narrow deep passage between cliffs. The narrows are best taken at slack water. For the hour or so before the predicted turn, boats collect at each end waiting for the right time. These boats include commercial craft, even tugboats with log tows or large barges, so the period around slack water can get pretty interesting. Generally, the boats on the upstream side go first, catching the last of the dying fair current. When they are through, boats on the other end go through, picking up the beginnings of the new (for them) fair current. It all works well as long as no one gets impatient. Vessels will be transiting in both directions during and around slack periods.

Check for traffic by viewing AIS targets on both sides of the narrows and listen on VHF 16 for Securité calls from traffic that might pose a safety concern for other vessels. Tugboats with log tows and large commercial vessels will typically announce their intentions on VHF 16. In recent years, VHF 16 has been flooded with Securité calls from boats that may not need to announce themselves, so if your boat does not pose a safety concern for others, there is no need to make a Securité call. If you do make a call, be sure to use 1-watt low power. Don't be in a hurry, and don't try to pass a slower boat. Dodd Narrows is short. Travel single-file and leave room between your boat and the boat ahead and share the channel with opposing direction traffic.

LOCAL KNOWLEDGE

STAND-ON GIVE-WAY: In passages with current, the vessel traveling with the current (in the same direction as the current) is the stand-on vessel; and the vessel traveling against the current is the give-way vessel.

Northumberland Channel. Northumberland Channel is the passage from the Gulf Islands to Nanaimo. It begins at False Narrows and runs northwest between Gabriola Island and Vancouver Island. Northumberland Channel exits in the Gulf of Georgia, or, at Jack Point, makes the turn to Nanaimo. Because of considerable log boom towing in the area, watch for floating debris. If you are not yet ready for civilization, you might lay over at Pilot Bay, on the north end of Gabriola Island.

Pilot Bay. Pilot Bay is on the north end of Gabriola Island. It's a good anchorage in a southeasterly, but is open to northwesterlies.

No discharge zone, gray water okay.

Gabriola Sands Park. North end of Gabriola Island. Open all year, day use only. Toilets, but no other facilities. This park fronts on Taylor Bay and Pilot Bay. It has a sandy swimming area and a playfield. Good for kids.

Sandwell Park. Northeast side of Gabriola Island. Open all year, day use only, toilets but no other facilities. This is a small seafront park with a sandy beach and forested uplands.

㊳ **Nanaimo.** As you pass Jack Point the city of Nanaimo opens up. Head for the prominent high rise condominium building, easily seen from Jack Point. The harbor is wide and sheltered from the Strait of Georgia by Protection Island and Newcastle Island.

The Nanaimo Port Authority public marina with guest moorage at Inner Basin and W.E. Mills Landing, is at the south end of the business district near Nanaimo's famous Bastion (blockhouse), with access to downtown Nanaimo. The Bastion was built in 1853 by the Hudson's Bay Company, and is Nanaimo's oldest man-made landmark still standing. A Thrifty Foods supermarket, London Drug, ATM, B.C. liquor store, Starbucks and several fast-food and sandwich shops are in the Port Place shopping mall near the Port Authority marina. The Nanaimo Museum is in the Conference Centre, one block from the public marina.

Additional moorages are in Newcastle Island Passage, the channel leading behind Newcastle Island to Departure Bay. The Nanaimo Yacht Club has reciprocal guest moorage. Waterfront Suites & Marina has guest moorage and Stones Marina occasionally has room for transient boaters. Newcastle Island Marine Park has a dock with moorage (no power or water) and mooring buoys.

Repair and haul-out facilities capable of handling any needed job are located along Newcastle Island Passage, known locally as Newcastle Channel.

Nanaimo is a natural point of departure for boats headed across the Strait of Georgia or north to Campbell River or Desolation Sound and beyond. It is the second largest city (behind Victoria) on Vancouver Island. Shops of all kinds line the narrow, winding streets of old town Nanaimo. We've prowled through several impressive bookstores—new and used—in downtown.

Nanaimo offers excellent dining, from

False Narrows can be an alternate to Dodd Narrows, but follow the range marked channels and check the tide and current predictions, as it is shallow.

casual to elegant. Several restaurants are on the water in the marina. A winding promenade takes walkers along the waterfront for 4 km (2.5 miles), from the marina to the B.C. Ferry Terminal in Departure Bay. Theaters and tennis courts are nearby.

An 1853 cannon, intended in its day to protect the Bastion but used instead to welcome ships into the harbour, is fired at noon each day at the Bastion beginning in May. It's a ceremony complete with a piper in full regalia and a booming explosion with a cloud of white smoke. Beginning in June the Brigadoon Dance Academy's highland dancers perform from 11:15 a.m. to 11:45 a.m. Get there early and bring your camera.

Nanaimo is home to the Annual 'World Championship Bathtub Race' held during the third weekend in July. The event is preceded by a parade of bathtub race participants, games, food, and concerts. See www.bathtubbing.com.

Floatplane Activity: Beware of floatplane arrivals and departures when motoring in the charted air operation area. A flashing white light, located on the Eco Barge pumpout dock, indicates air operation.

Customs: Canada Customs is marked at the end of E dock on the north side, just behind the fuel dock area.

Chandlery: Harbour Chandler, south of the boat basin, is an excellent chandlery. At the north end is Stones Boatyard Marine Store.

Markets: Just north of the Bastion, a farmers market, often with entertainment, is open 9:00 a.m. to 2:00 p.m. on Saturdays, May to mid-September.

Taxi: AC Taxi, (250) 753-1231

LOCAL KNOWLEDGE

SATELLITE REEF: Buoy *PS* is west of Satellite Reef. When entering from Northumberland Channel, stay west of Buoy *PS* when continuing north. Satellite Reef dries at zero tide and should be considered hazardous at all times.

THINGS TO DO

- **Nanaimo Bastion.** Located above the marina, the Bastion is the oldest standing building in Nanaimo. You can explore it, or watch the cannon ceremony at noon.
- **Newcastle Island (Saysutshun).** Hike to the sandstone quarry or rent a kayak, SUP, or bike. A foot ferry provides regular access to Newcastle Island from the Nanaimo waterfront or take your dinghy. A children's playground was recently added. Walking tours and a traditional tribal salmon bake are available on the island by reservation. Beautiful campsites are also available by reservation; water and restrooms at the park. See www.newcastleisland.ca for reservations information
- **Nanaimo Museum.** Just up from the marina at 100 Museum Way. Learn the history of Nanaimo from its First Nations roots to the discovery of coal in the area.
- **Petroglyph Provincial Park.** A taxi ride from the docks. See carvings of animals and sea creatures immortalized in the sandstone hundreds and thousands of years ago.
- **Dinghy Dock Pub.** On Protection Island. Take your dinghy or the ferry ($9). Great sun deck, good food, and of course cold beer.
- **Walk or bike** the multi-use Harbourfront Walkway trail along the downtown waterfront, and on north along the Newcastle Channel.

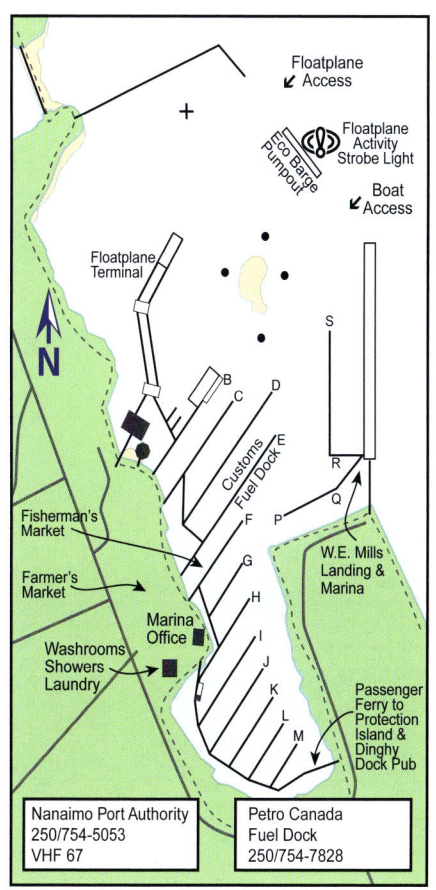

Nanaimo Harbour & Newcastle Island Passage

Nanaimo Port Authority

2023 Waggoner Cruising Guide

GULF ISLANDS

See Area Map Page 247 - Maps Not for Navigation

Nanaimo's 4 kilometer long Waterfront Promenade takes hikers to Departure Bay.

③⑧ **Nanaimo Port Authority.** 100 Port Drive, P.O. Box 131, Nanaimo, -BC V9R 5K4; (250) 755-1216; (250) 754-5053; marina@npa.ca; www.npa.ca. During July and August call (250) 755-1216. Monitors VHF 67 (not 66A). Open year-round. Three hours of moorage for a nominal fee, call on VHF 67 for slip assignment. Fewer spaces have been reserved for guest moorage than in the past. Reservations recommended. Reservations must be made 48 hours in advance. Rafting is permitted along side commercial fish boats only. Dock assistants are available during the summer months to help you tie up. Numerous commercial fish boats are in the basin during the winter months, but pleasure craft moorage is available. Water at selected docks in the winter. Customs clearance available at the customs dock, just behind the fuel dock.

A floating breakwater dock is in the center of the harbour entrance, and the Eco Barge pumpout and portapotty dump is tied to the shore side of this dock. No charge for the Eco Barge. Arriving and departing vessels must pass south of the floating breakwater dock. The northern entrance is reserved for aircraft.

The Port Authority harbour is actually two marina facilities: **Inner Boat Basin** and **W.E. Mills Landing & Marina** (formerly and locally known as Cameron Island Marina). We have used both and are happy either place. All of the Nanaimo commercial district is within a five-minute walk.

Seasonally, fresh fish is sometimes sold at the Nanaimo Fisherman's Market dock at the entrance to the Inner Boat Basin. Fish & chips and Mexican food are available at seasonal floating cafes on the docks.

Dinghy Dock. There is no designated dinghy dock, if arriving by dinghy, call the marina office on VHF 67 for tie-up instructions.

No Discharge Zone, Gray water okay.

③⑧ **Inner Boat Basin** is mostly permanent moorage with some guest space. Facilities include extensive dock space, 20 & 30 amp power on all floats, some 50 & 100 amp power, water, free Wi-Fi, waste oil disposal, and pumpout. Washrooms, showers with heated tile floors, and laundry are next to the wharfinger office.

③⑧ **W.E. Mills Landing & Marina.** Larger vessels and ships will tie on the outside of the breakwater pier, smaller boats on the inside. Facilities include 20, 30, & 50 amp power and water. Free Wi-Fi. Washrooms, showers, and laundry are located in the Inner Boat Basin near the marina office, a short dinghy ride but a long walk. Wakes from boats headed for the fuel dock or the Inner Boat Basin rock boats at W.E. Mills Landing & Marina. The docks have a security gate that is open 7:00 a.m. to 11:00 p.m. Between 11:00 p.m. and 7:00 a.m., you'll have to use the combination supplied by the dock help or call security to let you in. Watch the current when landing at W.E. Mills Landing & Marina. Usually there's no problem, but be aware.

③⑧ **Petro-Canada Coastal Mountain Fuels.** 10 Wharf St., Nanaimo, BC V9R IP2; (250) 754-7828. Open all year, gasoline and diesel at the fuel dock. Lubricants, accessories, ice, snacks. At the end of "E" dock, open daily from 7:30 a.m. to 5:00 p.m.

③⑧ **Waterfront Suites & Marina.** 1000 Stewart Ave., Nanaimo, BC V9S 4C9; (250) 753-7111; moorage@waterfrontnanaimo.com; www.waterfrontnanaimo.com. Open all year, moorage to 100 feet, 30 & 50 amp power, washrooms, showers, laundry, Wi-Fi available in the hotel lobby, 24-hour service and security. Reservations encouraged. The docks are modular and staff can configure a dock for odd sized boats. Often has space for transient boats when the other marinas are full.

③⑧ **Stones Marina.** 1690 Stewart Ave., Nanaimo BC V9S 4E1; Marina (250) 753- 4232; email@stonesmarina.com; www.stonesmarina.com. Open all year, 30 & 50 amp power, washrooms, showers, laundry, cable & internet. Limited transient overnight moorage by reservation only. The marina office is located in the white building up the driveway and along the main road. The marina complex has a pub and restaurant, liquor store, marine supplies store, boatyard, yacht charters, and day-use guest moorage dock. The 140 foot float in front of the pub restaurant has side-tie space for vessels visiting the Stones Marina complex. **Stones Boatyard & Marine Store** www.nanaimoboatyard.ca (250-716-

Nanaimo's fuel float is at the center of Inner Boat Basin and W.E. Mills Landing is in the distance.

Upland from the docks at Nanaimo you will find shops, restaurants, and a seasonal market along the promenade.

Below the Nanaimo marina office, you will find the popular Penny's Palapa floating restaurant.

9065) are located in the Stones Marina complex. The do-it-yourself or yacht services boatyard with 83-ton Travelift is available for scheduled and emergency repairs. Stones Boatyard & Marine Store is under separate ownership.

Caution: Waters are shallow around the day-use guest dock and Travelift; check your depth.

㊳ **Departure Bay Gas N Go.** 1840 Stewart Ave., Nanaimo, BC V9F 4E6; (250) 591-0810. Open all year. Fuel dock with gas and diesel at north end of Newcastle Channel. Small store carries snacks, tackle, some lubricants.

㊴ **Newcastle Island (Saysutshun) Marine Park.** www.env.gov.bc.ca/bcparks/explore/parkpgs/newcastle/ Open all year, moorage with 1500 feet of dock space, excellent washrooms and showers. No power, no water. Anchoring is prohibited in Mark Bay; 43 mooring balls are available for vessels 40 feet and under (some are limited to 30 feet). A nightly mooring fee is paid onshore at the head of the dock. Extensive anchorage is still available just beyond Mark Bay and the docks. Several small bays, beaches, and playing fields. Many hiking trails. Walk-in campsites and picnic areas. Seasonal kayak, canoe, SUP and bicycle rentals. A passenger ferry connects the island with Nanaimo.

The 1931 pavilion houses a dance floor, snack bar, visitor center, and excellent interpretive displays on the natural and human history of the area.

This is an extraordinary park. The pulpstone quarry astonishes. The bays and beaches intrigue. Before European settlement, Newcastle Island was a summer campsite for First Nations people. Since European settlement, it has supported a shipyard and been mined for coal. In the early 1870s it was quarried for sandstone that built the San Francisco Mint. Between 1923 and 1932 its sandstone was quarried for pulpstones, giant cylinders that ground wood into pulp for making paper. Before WWII, Japanese fishermen ran herring salteries here. Through it all, Newcastle Island has been a popular holiday spot.

You might see rare albino raccoons, and dozens of bunny rabbits. If moored at the dock, raccoons will try to board vessels searching for food. Secure your boat well, and don't leave any food or garbage out. Arrive early enough to get literature from the visitor center. Try to spend the night. The lights of Nanaimo are beautiful. The Dinghy Dock pub is a short dinghy ride away.

Stay Informed at WaggonerGuide.com/Updates

Newcastle Island has miles of excellent walking trails.

Pulp stones from the sandstone quarry on Newcastle Island

Strait of Georgia

EAST VANCOUVER ISLAND
Schooner Cove • French Creek • Comox

HORNBY ISLAND
Tribune Bay • Ford Cove

LASQUETI ISLAND
Jedediah Island • False Bay • Squitty Bay

TEXADA ISLAND
Sturt Bay • Anderson Bay

Scan the Latest
Strait of Georgia
Information

tinyurl.com/WG22xCh08

Nanoose Harbour Entrance

STRAIT OF GEORGIA

Strait of Georgia. The Strait of Georgia is not to be trifled with. It's a big body of water, 110 miles long and 15 to 20 miles wide. Pleasure craft cross the strait all the time, but locals know better than to go out when the wind is blowing. They are especially careful when wind blows against strong currents.

When conditions are right, the strait need not be intimidating. The "typical" summertime fair weather wind pattern calls for calm mornings followed by a rising northwesterly sea breeze by early afternoon. By mid-afternoon the sea breeze can be 20 to 25 knots. In the evening the wind dies down. We have crossed early in the morning and in the evening and had no problems.

Frequently though, the typical pattern doesn't hold. If a weak frontal system passes over the area, the higher pressure behind the front will produce northwesterlies of 20 to 25 knots, sometimes reaching gale force. These winds can blow around the clock for three days or even longer, effectively closing the strait to small craft.

Summer afternoon southwesterly winds known as Qualicums can blow across the strait between Qualicum Beach and False Bay at the northern tip of Lasqueti Island. Qualicum winds resulting from the passage of a cold front can reach 40 knots but are short-lived.

When wind opposes current in Sabine Channel, between Lasqueti Island and Texada Island, 8-foot seas can result. Malaspina Strait can be rough, especially when wind is against current. Currents from Howe Sound and Burrard Inlet meet off Point Atkinson, and create rough seas. Wind makes them worse.

Check for winds on the Strait of Georgia.

When the wind is up it produces a difficult 4- to 5-foot chop—sometimes higher—in the middle of the strait away from land influences. These aren't long, lazy ocean swells. Strait of Georgia seas are steep and close together. In southeasterly winds, the largest seas are found near Chrome Island and Cape Mudge, both locations with significant fetch. When the wind blows from the northwest, the largest waves are found in Sabine Channel and near Sand Heads. A well-handled boat might run with these seas, but taken on the bow or beam they are no fun at all.

Sometimes, the afternoon winds never materialize and the strait can be crossed all day. It's best to avoid being forced into crossing at a specific time or on a specific day. Wait for calm conditions and know that they don't always appear in the morning and evening. When the conditions are right, go. Be cautious yet decisive.

Even in calm conditions, you may find tide-rips off many of the points and wherever passes or channels join the strait. When the current flows out of a pass or inlet into the strait, confused seas result. Add wind, and big confusion results. While the ebb current flows from inlets into the strait, note that the flood current flows out of the Gulf Islands into the strait. At the eastern mouths of Active Pass, Porlier Pass, and Gabriola Pass, look for rough seas on the flood, especially when the wind is blowing.

Weather patterns do exist and the bad spots are known. The skipper who monitors the VHF continuous marine broadcast will gather a sense of what is happening, where it is happening, and why it is happening. Go and no-go decisions get easier.

Here are a few tips for a safe and comfortable crossing, or cruise on the Strait of Georgia:

- **Buoy Reports** - Monitor the buoy reports for Halibut Bank (Buoy 46146, off Gibsons) and Sentry Shoal (Buoy 46131, between Comox and Campbell River and below Mitlenatch Island). These reports provide frequent updates on sea state and wind conditions. They can be found online on Environment Canada's website, on the continuous marine broadcast, or by calling Dial-A-Buoy at (888) 701-8992 or (301) 713-9620.

- **Lightstation Reports** - Monitor lightstation reports. Lightstations are at Chrome Island, Merry Island and Entrance Island. The lightkeepers provide information on visibility, wind speed and direction, and sea state, updated every three hours and broadcast on the VHF WX channels. Or call on VHF 82.

CROSSING STRAIT OF GEORGIA GO-NOGO CHECKLIST

Tides & Currents - See Ports & Passes; Canadian Tides & Current Tables Vol. 5
- ☐ Time your crossing to be near mid-Strait at slack
- ☐ Flood or ebb; avoid wind against current conditions
- ☐ Ebbing currents flow out of inlets into the Strait, except in Gulf Islands
- ☐ Flooding currents from both north and south directions meet at Mitlenach Island

Weather System Predictions – via Internet or satellite
- ☐ Check NOAA Ocean Prediction Center forecasts for any approaching significant weather systems
- ☐ Check Windy.com, Predictwind.com, SiriusXM Marine, or Sailflow.com
- ☐ See Environment Canada forecast for the Synopsis report for Strait of Georgia North of Nanaimo and Strait of Georgia South of Nanaimo

Weather & Seas Forecasts – via Internet, phone, or VHF
- ☐ See Environment Canada Forecasts for Strait of Georgia North of Nanaimo and South of Nanaimo; check for warnings and note forecast wind speed and direction

Observations & Present Conditions – via Internet, phone, or VHF
- ☐ Check Buoy Reports for Halibut Bank (46146) and Sentry Shoal (46131); note wind speed and direction
- ☐ Check Lighthouse and Station Reports from Chrome Island, Merry Island, and Entrance Island; note wind speed and direction
- ☐ Check the status of Restricted Area Whisky Golf north of Nanaimo

Go-NoGo Decision
- √ Check wind and wave direction in relation to direction of travel. Straight line crossing is the shortest distance, but may not be the most comfortable.
- √ Will the typical summer weather pattern with afternoon winds affect conditions?
- √ Is Restricted Area Whisky Golf active?

Fail-Safe Contingency Plans
- √ Duck-in locations along the route: lees may lie off Texada Island and Lasqueti Island

See the *Marine Weather* section in the Compendium chapter for telephone numbers, website addresses, VHF channels, and buoy numbers.

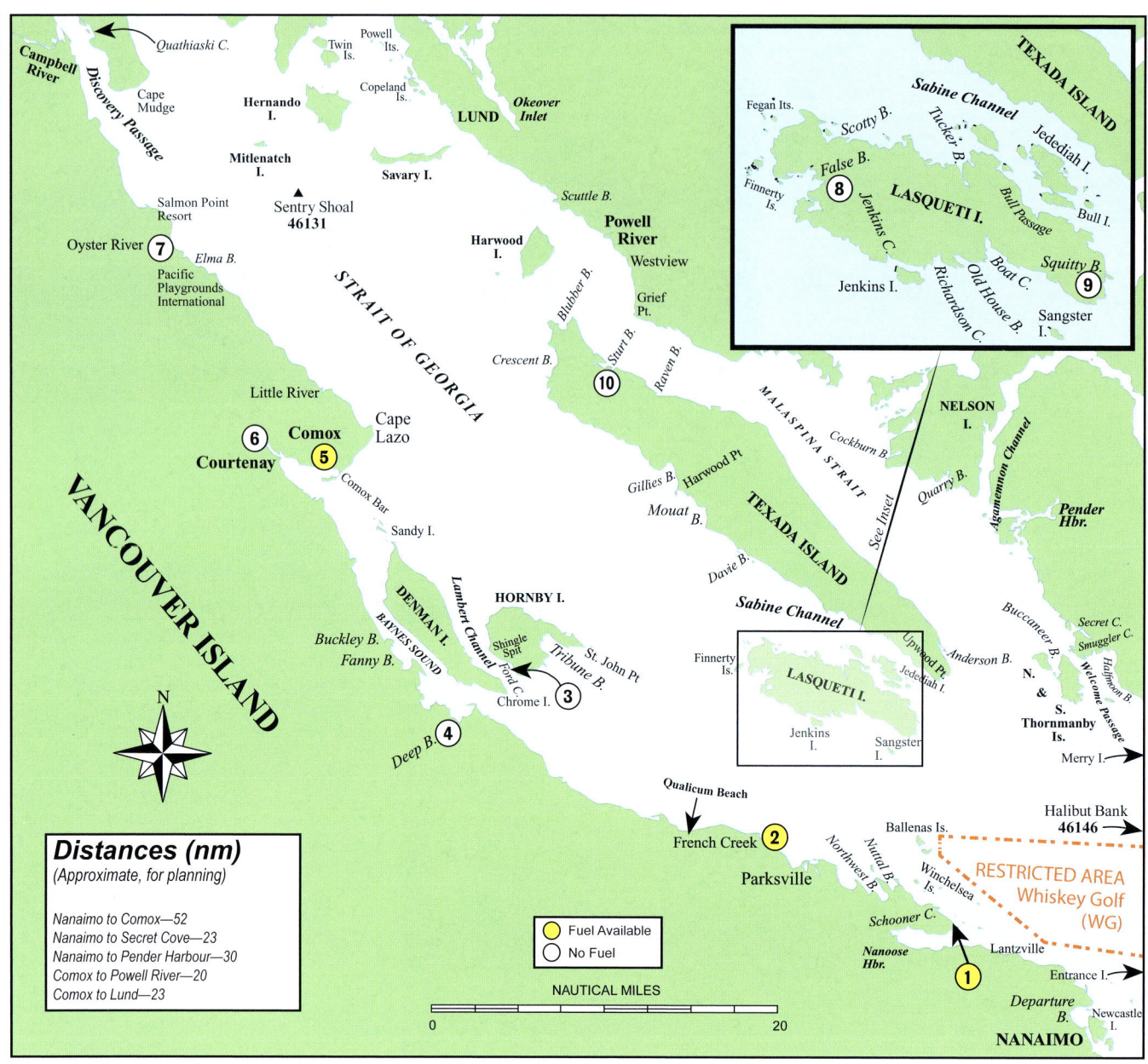

STRAIT OF GEORGIA

Reference Only – Not for Navigation

- **Qualicum Beach** - The area between Qualicum Beach and Lasqueti Island can be subject to southwesterly winds coming through the Alberni "notch" in the Vancouver Island mountains. Check Chrome Island for local southwesterly winds. Old salts also recommend checking winds at Cape Beale, on the west coast of Vancouver Island. If a strong southwesterly wind is blowing there, often it will flow right over Vancouver Island through the Alberni "notch," affecting the waters off Qualicum Beach.

- **Lees** - Take advantage of lees along the way. For example, you may choose to go up one side or the other of 27-mile Texada Island to stay in the lee of a southwesterly or northeasterly wind. Always be prepared to turn around and go back if things do not look right.

Whiskey Golf. Boats headed north from Nanaimo often must navigate through or around the restricted area "WG" (Whiskey Golf) when it is "live." Whiskey Golf is a deepwater range jointly operated by the Canadian and U.S. Navies, and is used to test torpedoes and various ships' systems. Buoys and moorings may be laid anywhere within WG. Use extreme caution when transiting. The area consists of a network of underwater sensing devices joined by cables to a control site on Winchelsea Island. Torpedoes are fired from range vessels or aircraft along a predetermined course, and are tracked from the Winchelsea control center. No explosives are used; however, a hazard exists due to the possibility of the torpedo homing on vessels. After the run, the torpedoes are recovered either by helicopter or range vessels. Unauthorized craft are not permitted in the area while the range is in operation.

Typically, the range is active Mondays through Fridays, sometimes Saturdays, 7:00 a.m. to 5:30 p.m. For information on range area status, contact Winchelsea Control on VHF channel 10 or 16; or listen on VHF Weather 1 or 3. For next day planned range activity and status, call (250) 468-5080. The Coast Guard (VHF channel 83A) also knows if the range is active. If unsure, contact Winchelsea Control by phone or VHF, or the Canadian Coast Guard.

The Whiskey Golf restricted area is on the direct course across the Strait of Georgia from Nanaimo to Secret Cove, Smugglers Cove, Pender Harbour, and other destinations along the Sunshine Coast. We once saw an oblivious skipper cross right through the active range. Winchelsea Control made multiple calls to the offending vessel with no response. A patrol helicopter quickly flew over, hovered just in front of the offending vessel, and redirected it to safe water. Such encounters are best avoided.

See Area Map Page 264 - Maps Not for Navigation

STRAIT OF GEORGIA

Fairwinds Marina with guest moorage, fuel, a cafe, and nearby golf and hiking, off Strait of Georgia

The Canadian Navy established a safe transit route along the edges of the restricted area when the range is in use. After clearing Nanaimo Harbour or Departure Bay (being careful to avoid Hudson Rocks and Five Finger Island), head directly for the Winchelsea Islands. Pass east of Winchelsea Islands within 1000 yards. Turn to pass east of the Ballenas Islands within 1000 yards. Once well past the Ballenas Islands, steer a course for your destination on the mainland side of the strait, or northwest along the Vancouver Island side.

Nanoose Harbour. All of the waters and foreshore of Nanoose Harbour west of Wallis Pt. are a military Controlled Access Zone administered by the Department of National Defence. The harbour is open to the public within the limitations of the Controlled Access Zone regulations. All vessels entering the harbour are required to register their arrival, intended duration of stay, and departure from the harbor by contacting the Queen's Harbour Master at (250) 213-3325 or (250) 363-7584. Contact Winchelsea Island Control when south of Maude Island on VHF 10 or 16 before entering the harbour. Pleasure craft anchoring is only permitted south of a line west of Datum Rock and in the vicinity of Fleet Point. The docks and mooring buoys along the north shore are for Royal Canadian Navy and U.S. Navy vessels engaged in activity on the Winchelsea (Whiskey Golf) torpedo range and pleasure craft mooring and access is prohibited.

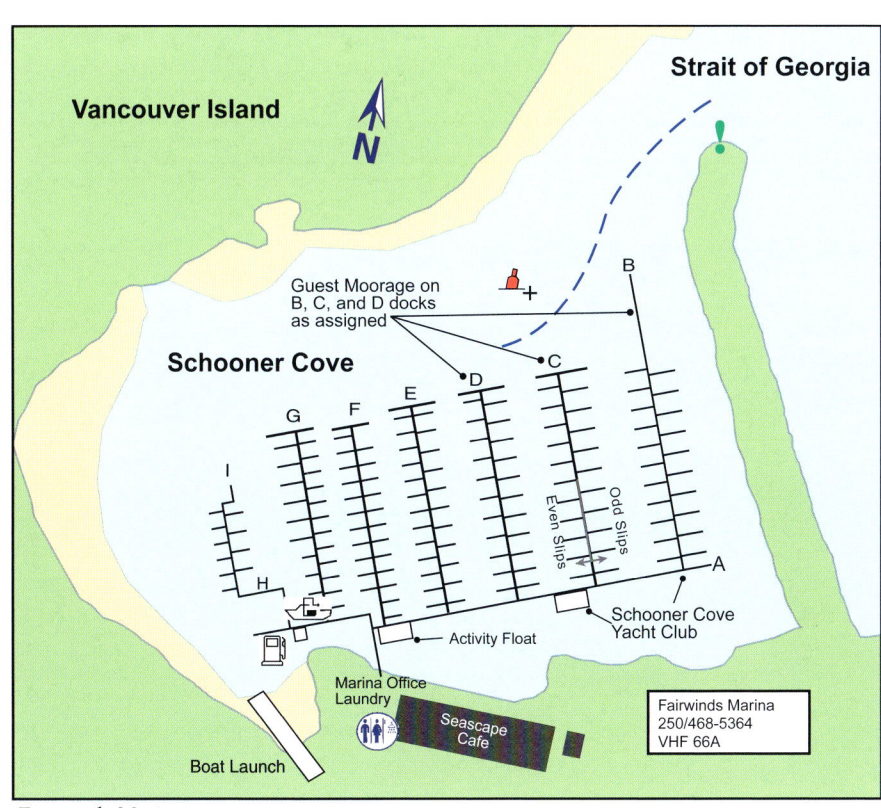

Schooner Cove. Schooner Cove is north of Nanoose Harbour. The cove is well-protected with a breakwater on the northwest entrance. The Fairwinds Marina fills most of the cove.

① **Fairwinds Marina.** 33521 Dolphin Dr., Nanoose Bay, BC V9P 9J7; (250) 468-5364; marina@fairwinds.ca; www.fairwinds.ca. Monitors VHF 66A. Fairwinds Marina, located at Schooner Cove, is open all year with gasoline and diesel at the fuel dock; pumpout and boat launch on site. Guest moorage for vessels up to 100 feet, 15, 30 & 50 amp power. Washrooms, showers, and laundry are complimentary with moorage. Reservations are a must. Proof of liability insurance coverage of 2 million is required. Bicycles, including eBikes, are available for rent. A series of hiking/biking trails are nearby; ask the marina for a map.

A major renovation of the large upland building was completed in September of 2020. The marina office, restrooms, showers, and laundry are located on the first floor. The expansive Seascape Cafe, along with a bar and coffee shop are located upstairs, offering beautiful views overlooking the marina and beyond.

Easily accessed off of Ballenas Channel and Strait of Georgia, the marina has picturesque views of the Strait of Georgia and Coast Mountains. Watch for a rock marked by a red buoy just inside the breakwater. Keep the buoy well to starboard when entering. The outstanding Fairwinds Golf club is nearby, call for the courtesy shuttle.

Schooner Reef. Schooner Reef is a short distance northward off the mouth of Schooner Cove and has caught a number of boats unaware. The light marking the reef is on the southernmost of its rocks. More rocks lie up-island from the light.

Nuttal Bay. Nuttal Bay is protected from southeasterly winds but exposed to northwesterlies. To enter Nuttal Bay, leave Dorcas Rock Buoy *P27* to port. Do not pass between Dorcas Rock Buoy *P27* and the land south of it. Buoy *P27* lies a good deal farther out than one might expect. If you are traveling up- or down-island, locate that buoy and pass to seaward of it.

Northwest Bay. Northwest Bay is home to a private moorage only marina with no services for transient boaters, and an active log dump and booming operation. The bay is protected from southerly winds but open to the north and northwesterly winds and seas. Suitable anchorage depths can be found at the head of the bay and in a bight along the west shore.

Mistaken Island. Privately owned and posted with "No Trespassing" signs.

Parksville. Parksville has a nice beach, but shoal water extends out some distance. No facilities are available for boaters.

Fairwinds Marina

STRAIT OF GEORGIA

② **French Creek Harbour Authority.** 1055 Lee Rd., Parksville, BC V9P 2E1; (250) 248-5051; hafc@frenchcreekharbour.ca. Monitors VHF 66A. Open all year with gasoline & diesel. Commercial vessels have priority for moorage, but room may be available for pleasure craft. No reservations; rafting is required. Washrooms and shower (with deposit), 20 & 30 amp power. A key from the office is required for waste oil and garbage disposal. Office hours are 8:00 a.m. to 5:30 p.m. Restaurant, pub, marine supplies, nearby launch ramp and haulout. A fish market in the large white processing building sells fresh seafood. Groceries are at the mall, a 15-minute walk away.

French Creek is the only breakwater-protected harbor in the 25-mile stretch between Northwest Bay and Deep Bay. The breakwater has recently been extended. French Creek is the western terminus of the passenger ferry to Lasqueti Island.

Hornby Island. Hornby Island has anchorages in Tribune Bay, Ford Cove, and south of Shingle Spit (where a small ferry runs to Denman Island). Tribune Bay and Shingle Spit are exposed to southeast winds.

A seasonal dock for dinghies and shallow draft water craft is located next to the ferry terminal. The dock is for guests dining at the Thatch Pub and Restaurant located above the dock. The fully licensed Pub and Restaurant has live entertainment, (250) 335-0136; thatchpub.com.

The annual Hornby Festival, held in early August, is a well-organized event drawing professional, award-winning musicians, song writers, and artists from around the country and across the border; see hornbyfestival.com.

Tribune Bay. Tribune Bay is a wonderful place to visit and justifiably popular. Anchor offshore in 20 to 45 feet; eelgrass reported to be in 18 feet or less. Dinghy to a splendid sand beach and enjoy Tribune Bay Provincial Park. Take the 3-mile hike to Helliwell Provincial Park on St. John Point.

Locals call their community Ford's Cove, charts refer to the harbour as Ford Cove.

Caution: Tribune Bay has excellent protection from northwesterlies, but in a southeasterly the bay can get very rough.

Note: Dogs are not allowed on the beach at Tribune Bay.

③ **Ford Cove.** Located on Hornby Island, Ford Cove is a delightful community with ample guest moorage. A green spar buoy marks the southern end of Maude Reef. You'll see a rock breakwater and a floating breakwater. To enter, leave the rock breakwater to starboard. No fresh water on the dock. Good anchorage on rocky bottom.

A well-stocked grocery (250) 335-2169 is upland from the docks and sells fresh take-out pizza year-round. A seasonal fish & chips restaurant is located above the store. The store and eatery along with cottages, campsites, and RV parking make up the small resort called Ford's Cove Marina & Store.

There are numerous trails in the area. A well-traveled 1.5 mile trail leads northwest along the shore to Shingle Spit and the popular Thatch Pub.

③ **Ford Cove Harbour Authority.** 10800A Central Rd., Ford Cove, Hornby Island, BC V0R 1Z0; (250) 335-0003; VHF 66A; fordcoveharbour@gmail.com; www.fordcoveharbour.com. Open all year, guest moorage in unoccupied slips as assigned and side-tie along the inside floating breakwater. 20 & 30 amp power, toilets, garbage drop, no water, no showers. No power on the breakwater. Reservations accepted online for slips via credit card payment. Moorage on the breakwater is first-come, first-served; no rafting on the breakwater. A loading dock is located near the ramp. Kayak and boat rentals.

Baynes Sound. Chart 3527 shows navigation aids not shown on Chart 3513. These aids are buoys marking extensive shoals off Gartley Point, Union Point, Denman Point and Base Flat (Buckley Bay); 2 buoys near Repulse Point; and 2 buoys

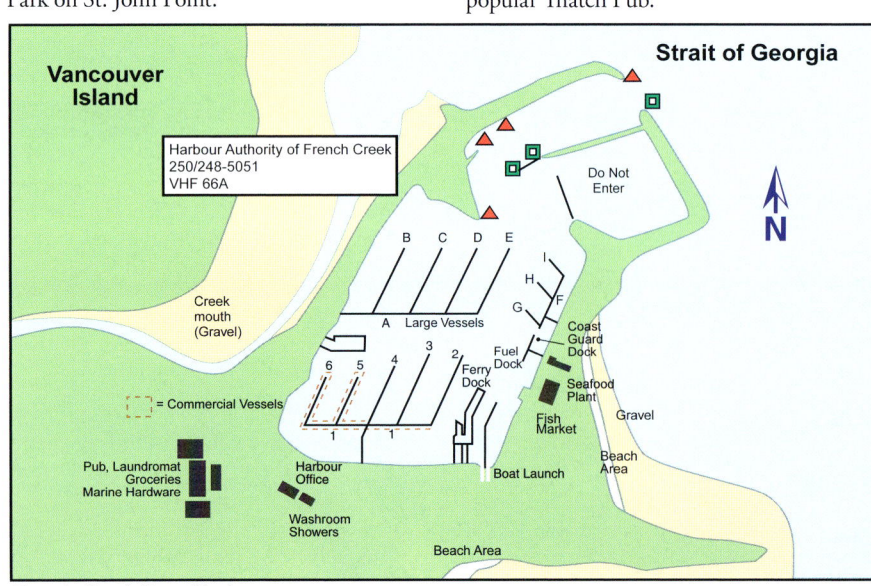

French Creek Boat Harbour

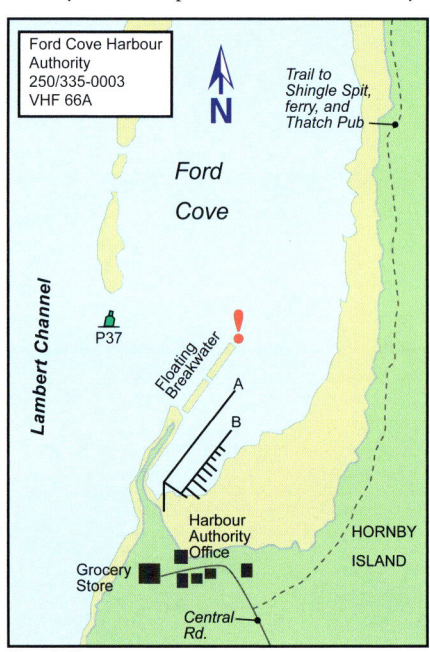

Ford Cove

STRAIT OF GEORGIA

marking the shoal off Mapleguard Point. Baynes Sound, a 12-mile-long refuge, is protected from the Strait of Georgia by Denman Island. A ferry to Denman Island crosses from Buckley Bay. Comox is at the north end of Baynes Sound and Deep Bay is at the south end. The northern entry to Baynes Sound is across the Comox Bar, marked by buoys and a lighted range on the Vancouver Island shore. The southern entry is past Chrome Island.

LOCAL KNOWLEDGE

NAVIGATION NOTE: A considerable shoal extends into the mouth of Baynes Sound outside Deep Bay. The shoal, and shoaling along the shoreline of Denman Island, opposite, are marked by buoys shown on Chart 3527, but not on Chart 3513.

④ **Deep Bay.** Anchorage is good in Deep Bay, though in deeper water than most boaters like. Derelict boats, which occupied a portion of the best space, have recently been removed. The Ship & Shore Cafe, which once sold convenience supplies, is now a full restaurant under new ownership.

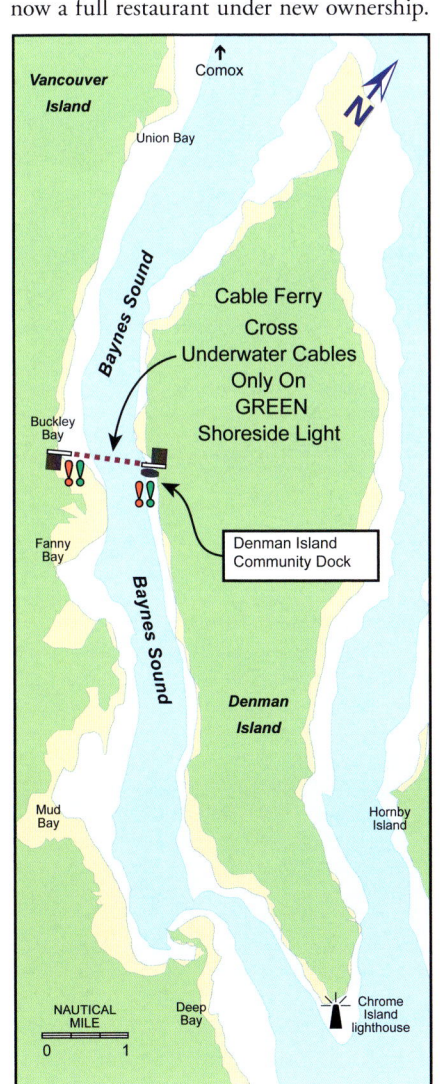

Denman Island

Denman Island Community Dock just south of the ferry dock has guest moorage and buoys.

The restaurant is located near the head of the public wharf. Washroom and laundry facilities nearby.

④ **Deep Bay Harbour Authority.** 164 Burne Rd., Bowser, BC V0R 1G0; (250) 757-9331; deepbay-mgr@shawcable.com; www.dbha.ca. The government wharf and floats are open all year with moorage along 1130 feet of dock. Garbage drop, 20 & 30 amp power, free Wi-Fi, free pumpout, waste oil disposal, tidal grid, and guest dock. Washrooms and showers. The pumpout is located at the loading zone on the main pier. Space is very limited and rafting is required, call ahead to see what is available.

Fanny Bay. Fanny Bay is primarily a camping area, with a small public float.

Denman Island. Denman Village is a one-third mile walk up a steep hill. The Denman General Store with groceries, a post office, and liquor store is in Denman Village. A small museum, community center, bistro, and a craft shop are also in the Village.

The north end of Denman Island stretches out into a long spit, dotted with small islands and rocks. One of these islands, Sandy Island, is a provincial park. Off the south end of Denman Island is Chrome Island lighthouse, a dramatic landmark.

LOCAL KNOWLEDGE

CABLE FERRY: The *Baynes Sound Connector* cable ferry runs between Buckley Bay and Denman Island. Red and green lights are at each terminal. When the green lights are illuminated, vessels may cross the ferry lane. When red lights are illuminated, the ferry is in transit and vessels may not cross the ferry lane.

Denman Island Community Dock. www.denmanisland.com. A public dock and 60-foot float are alongside the landing for the cable ferry that runs to Buckley Bay on Vancouver Island. Six hours of moorage is free, 5-day maximum stay. No power or water.

Moorage not permitted in yellow painted areas. 5 mooring buoys available; rafting not permitted at the dock or on the buoys. Self-registration and payment box at the top of the ramp.

Boaters need to check the red/green light at each of the Denman-Buckley cable ferry terminals before crossing the ferry route in Baynes Sound.

The Denman-Buckley ferry runs on three underwater cables across Baynes Sound.

2023 WAGGONER CRUISING GUIDE 267

STRAIT OF GEORGIA

See Area Map Page 264 - Maps Not for Navigation

Trails, beaches, and proximity to Comox make Sandy Island Marine Park a popular destination.

Warm sand on bare feet always feels great.

Sandy Island Marine Provincial Park (Ja'ji7em and Kw'ulh). This park includes the Seal Islets, and is accessible only by boat. Anchor in Henry Bay, south of Longbeak Point. Anchorage is steep-to, anchor in 70-80 feet with excellent holding on a mud bottom. Picnic areas, swimming, fishing, hiking trails, and wilderness campsites. Sandy Island is a popular overnight stop for kayakers. The one mooring buoy in front of Sandy Island is for use by the park host. At low tide it is possible to walk along the sandy spit all the way to its end, halfway to Comox.

LOCAL KNOWLEDGE

NAVIGATION TIP: If you follow the buoyed channel over the Comox Bar in a fresh southeasterly you will have 4- to 5-foot seas on your beam. In these conditions it's better to ignore buoys P54 and P52 and instead work your way south until you can turn to fetch the inner Buoy P50 while running with the seas. The chart indicates ample depths. Large scale Chart 3527 shows Buoy P50, but small scale Chart 3513 does not.

Comox Bar. The Comox Bar nearly joins Denman Island and Cape Lazo, with a shallow channel (least depth 15 feet) across the bar. A lighted range—white, with red vertical stripes—is on the Vancouver Island shore. The range's lights are visible in cloudy weather and at night, but in sunlight they are hard to see. Lighted red Bell Buoy P54 marks the Strait of Georgia end of this channel. Red Buoys P52 and P50 show the course across the bar.

⑤ **Comox.** Comox is a busy little city, population 13,600, with breakwater-protected marina docks. HMCS Quadra, a Canada Sea Cadet camp, is on Goose Spit, across the bay from Comox. The Comox Valley is a popular retirement area and more recently has attracted young families and new businesses.

From Baynes Sound the entrance to Comox is well marked, but be careful of drying flats off Gartley Point and in the inner half of the bay. The breakwater in front of the town will be clearly visible. As the harbor map shows, the breakwater shelters three facilities: the Comox Harbour Authority, Comox Valley Marina; and the Comox Municipal Marina with a Gas N Go fuel dock. A launch ramp and two tidal grids are behind the breakwater. The Harbour Authority public docks, where pleasure craft are welcomed, is around the east end of the breakwater.

Showers and laundry are in the Harbour Authority's building at the head of its docks. A beautiful pavilion with meeting space overlooks the Comox Harbour and serves as a nice venue for club rendezvous. A Splash Park located behind the pavilion is a hit with the kids. Seasonal food trucks are located near the pavilion.

Comox has good shopping and a number of restaurants within walking distance of the marina. The downtown area includes a supermarket and chandlery. Don't miss the gelato shop near the supermarket. Regular bus service runs from the Comox Mall to the town of Courtenay with more shops, restaurants and a museum. You can also go by dinghy up the river to Courtenay. See the Courtenay section for more information.

Marine services at Comox include Desolation Sound Yacht Charters (250) 339-7222 offering cleaning, maintenance, hull inspection, and bright work (after-hours calls accepted); Comox Marine & Woodworking (250) 941-6699 with marine supplies, electrical, and a broad range of marine components; Wills Marine Supply (250) 941-7373 offering electrical, mechanical, diving and repair services.

When you're in Comox, take the short walk to the Filberg Heritage Lodge & Park. It's a 9-acre estate built in the 1930s by logging baron R. J. Filberg, furnished and maintained in its original splendor. The heavy wood construction, fabulous gardens, and interesting outbuildings (root cellar, chicken coop, dairy barn, potting shed, and so forth) are must-see attractions. Weddings and art shows are held there. The seasonal Summer

Comox Marine & Woodworking
Free delivery to Comox Harbour
- Complete victron packages
- Electrical components, solar panels
- Marine chandlery and online store
- Electric outboard motors and batteries
- Composting toilets

Authorized distributor for **victron energy** and **torqeedo** Electric Outboard Motors

Shop comoxmarine.ca
Shop at comoxmarine.ca sales@comoxmarine.ca 250-941-6699
1766 Ryan Rd East, Comox, BC

Comox Valley Harbour

Comox Valley Marina 250/339-2930
Gas N Go 250/339-4664 VHF 66A
Comox Municipal Marina 250/339-3141
Comox Valley Harbour Authority 250/339-6041 VHF 66A

www.WaggonerGuide.com

Comox Park at the harbour has a Splash Park

Comox harbour has fuel, and three marinas with guest moorage; it is a popular destination.

Kitchen, located on the grounds, is open Thursday through Sunday; call (250) 339-2750 or email summerkitchen@filberg.com for hours and seating reservations.

Floatplanes: A floatplane landing and takeoff zone is southwest of the marina breakwaters, with regularly scheduled flights. It does not affect anchoring behind Goose Spit or the approach to the marinas.

Festival: The Filberg Festival, an arts, crafts, food, and entertainment celebration, draws 20,000 to 25,000 visitors each year. It's held at Filberg Park, east of the public floats in Comox Harbour. Dates coincide with Comox Nautical Days and B.C. Day long weekend in early August. The park will be closed the week prior to the festival and the week following. Special events also can result in closures. Call first to confirm they are open (250) 941-0727. www.filbergfestival.com.

⑤ **Comox Valley Marina.** 1805 Beaufort, Box 20019, Comox, BC V9M 1R9; (250) 339-2930; manager@comoxvalleymarina.com; www.comoxvalleymarina.com. Side-tie moorage at a guest dock and in unoccupied slips. Water, 15, 30 & 50 amp power, shower, washroom, free Wi-Fi, 24-hour access to laundry, garbage, and nearby floatplane service. The amenities building and marina office are on the float at the base of the ramp. For after hours guest moorage, contact Comox Valley Harbour Authority.

⑤ **Gas N Go Marine Ltd.** 11 Port Augusta St., Comox, BC V9M 7Z8; (250) 339-4664; (888) 575-4664; gasngomarine@gmail.com; www.gasngomarine.com. Monitors VHF 66A. Open all year. Fuel dock with gasoline & diesel.

⑤ **Comox Municipal Marina.** 1809 Beaufort Ave., Comox, BC V9M 1R9; (250) 339-3141, Jess Whetter, wharfinger. Permanent moorage, with some transient moorage as available when a permanent tenant is away; 15 & 30 amp power, washrooms, Wi-Fi. Call ahead for availability.

⑤ **Comox Valley Harbour Authority.** 121 Port Augusta St., Comox, BC V9M 3N8; (250) 339-6041; info@comoxharbour.com; www.comoxharbour.com. Monitors VHF 66A. Located at east end of the Comox breakwater. Guest moorage available on 2100 feet of docks, 20, 30 & 50 amp power. Holding tank pumpout, garbage drop, cardboard recycling, waste oil disposal, free Wi-Fi (get the password at the office). Clean washrooms, showers, laundry, and an air-conditioned lounge with a bucket of biscuits for visiting boat dogs.

Note: Fold-up wagon carts are available at the marina for picking up groceries; ask at the front desk (please do not take grocery store carts to the marina; use the marina's fold-up carts).

This is a working waterfront facility, only two blocks from downtown Comox. In the summer, harbor staff move the fishing boats to one float and set aside the other docks for overnight pleasure craft. Fresh seafood may be available "off the boat," usually in the evening. The Harbour Authority staff works hard to make visiting pleasure boaters feel welcome and comfortable.

⑤ **Comox Harbour.** Anchorage can be found in Comox Harbour; with northerly winds, anchor south of the marina breakwater, taking care to avoid channel entrances on either end of the breakwater; in southerly winds, the favored anchorage is tucked into the cove north of Goose Spit; there are a number of boats on permanent moorings in this area. Mud bottom. The harbour is not as well protected as charts might suggest and can get uncomfortable in southerly winds.

⑥ **Courtenay.** For an adventurous outing, ask at the Harbour Authority office for local knowledge regarding taking the dinghy 3.3 nautical miles up the Courtenay River to the town of Courtenay. A drying river channel, marked by ranges, leads through the delta to the river mouth. The mouth is blocked by a weir that dries at 7 feet; without the weir the slough would empty completely at low tide.

A small private marina is on the left (southwest shore) just after passing the weir. Next is an opening bridge with a vertical clearance of 6.9 feet. Just before you reach the fixed Lewis Bridge, Courtenay Slough leads off to the right. Inside, an extensive Comox Valley Harbour Authority float parallels the shore, and a city float is at the head.

Enter the slough at high tide only. The slough's Harbour Authority dock is gated and locked. Harbour Authority registered guests may pick up a re-entry key at the Harbour Authority office in Comox. The weathered remains of a restaurant and small craft floats are just beyond the entrance to the slough. Excellent shopping and several restaurants are within easy walking distance. If the tides aren't cooperating, you can take the bus (250-339-5453) or taxi (250-339-7955) into Courtenay.

Museum: We highly recommend a visit to the Courtenay & District Museum (250-334-0686), a 4-block walk from the slough. There, hung from the ceiling, is the 40-foot-long skeletal reconstruction of an 80-million-year-old elasmosaur, excavated from the banks of the nearby Puntledge River. This is the most dramatic exhibit in an outstanding paleontological display. Other things to see are dinosaur footprints, an extinct marine reptile that resembles a 15-foot-long alligator, and an ancient fish they call a "sabre-toothed salmon." The museum is impressive; families with inquisitive children will be rewarded. There's much more than we can cover here. The museum is in the old brick post office building at 4th St. and Cliffe Avenue.

DESOLATION SOUND
YACHT CHARTERS, SERVICES & MARINE SUPPLY

- Bareboat Charters
- Power & Sail Training
- Yacht Management
- Marine Supply Store
- Certified Marine Mechanical
- Scheduled Maintenance

250-339-7222
desolationsoundyachtcharters.com

250-941-0396
marinesupply@dsyc.ca

LOCATED AT THE COMOX VALLEY MARINA

Stern tie pins are found around Deep Bay at Jedediah Island.

Cape Lazo. Cape Lazo is marked by a high cliff. *Be sure to stay to seaward of Buoys PJ and PB.* The buoys are well offshore, but shoals studded with boulders reach almost all the way out to them. Somewhere just north of Cape Lazo is the point at which the tidal currents change direction and begin flooding south from the north end of Vancouver Island, rather than north from Victoria.

Little River. Little River, 3 miles up-island from Cape Lazo, is the western terminus for the ferry to Westview/Powell River. Marginal moorage for a few small craft can be found behind the ferry dock.

Oyster River. A channel, dredged annually and marked by pilings, leads to the protected Pacific Playgrounds Marina next to the mouth of the Oyster River.

⑦ **Pacific Playgrounds Resort & Marina.** (250) 337-5600; info@PacificPlaygrounds.com; www.PacificPlaygrounds.com; open year-round, secure marina with transient and permanent moorage up to 40 feet, a few 46-foot spaces; 15 amp power, water at the docks, restrooms, showers; reservations accepted. Call ahead to make sure space is available, they are often fully booked. Payment made at the upland office open 9:00 a.m.-8:00 p.m. summer months. Payment can also be made at the dockside "fishing shack" summer hours 6:00 a.m.-8:00 p.m.; hours vary off-season. Located 16 miles south of Campbell River (49° 52' N / 125° 7' W), Pacific Playgrounds is accessed through a channel alongside, and south of Oyster River. This is a challenging entrance, check the tide tables; marina personnel advise that a minimum tide of 7 feet is needed for a boat with a 4.5 foot draft; the depth is shallowest at the outermost channel marker; access is not advised during high winds and swells Oyster River Plaza is a short walk from the marina, with shops, cafes, a supermarket, and other services. A beautiful trail from the marina leads to a one-lane timber truss bridge over Oyster River.

⑦ **Salmon Point Resort.** (250) 923-6605; sales@salmonpoint.com; www.salmonpoint.com. Gas, propane, launch ramp, store, laundry, pool, jacuzzi and kids' activity areas. Located 15 miles south of Campbell River on the western shore of Discovery Passage, this marina, built behind a riprap breakwater, has room for powerboats up to 32 feet. The entrance is very shallow and dries at low tide. "Stay-aboards" (overnighting on boat) not permitted. The resort is an RV park primarily serving recreational fishermen, with 1 to 2 bedroom cottages, rental RVs, and a licensed restaurant and pub on site.

LASQUETI ISLAND

Lasqueti Island is often overlooked by pleasure craft as they hurry across the strait between Nanaimo and the Sunshine Coast, or run along the Vancouver Island shore between Nanaimo and Campbell River. The island has a number of good anchorages. A convenience store is at the village of False Bay, located upland from the ferry landing on the left. The shores of Lasqueti Island are indented by a number of bays that invite anchorage. Along the south shore are Boat Cove, Old House Bay, Richardson Cove and Jenkins Cove, all of which are somewhat open to southerlies, but offer good protection from northerlies or in settled weather. This part of the Lasqueti shoreline is rugged and beautiful. Squitty Bay is at the southeast end of Lasqueti Island—tiny, but with a public float. Several little doghouses for anchoring can be found in Bull Passage. Little Bull Passage, between Jedediah Island and Bull Island, has a number of good anchorages in both ends, and is passable for most boats. Other anchorages are Boho Bay, Tucker Bay and Scottie Bay. Spring Bay is only partially protected from the north by a group of small islands offshore.

⑧ **False Bay.** False Bay is the primary settlement on Lasqueti Island with a public float offering limited dock space and a floatplane tie-up. A passenger-only ferry runs between False Bay and French Creek on Vancouver Island. Island residents transport not only themselves by ferry but also bring a large quantity of supplies, everything from food and clothing to appliances. It's quite a scene when the ferry arrives at False Bay. An open-air market is held at the arts center, a quarter mile up the road from the ferry landing, from mid-June to September.

Buoys adjacent to the ferry landing are private and fill most of the anchoring area near the public float. The preferred anchorage is the north shore of the bay, an easy dinghy ride to the public float. On warm summer afternoons strong winds, called Qualicums, can blow through False Bay; waves break at the dock, making tie-up difficult. If you must tie in these conditions, make sure you have robust dock lines and fenders. Kevin Monahan, a long-time resident of Lasqueti Island, reports that southwest gale force winds at Cape Beale often serve as a presage of Qualicum winds arriving at False Bay.

⑨ **Squitty Bay.** Squitty Bay is a tiny, narrow and shallow notch at the southeast corner of Lasqueti Island. It would be harrowing to enter Squitty Bay in a roaring southeasterly, but at other times entry should be easy. Rocks border the north side of the entrance; favor the south side. The unnamed point on the south side of Squitty Bay is an ecological reserve, noted for prickly pear cacti and Rocky Mountain juniper. The public dock, 150 feet long, may be largely occupied by local boats. Rafting is permitted. Ashore, the trees in this

The public dock at False Bay on Lasqueti Island is a hub of activity when the foot-ferry arrives.

area are bent and broken, obviously by strong winds. Tall trees are rare. A walk along the road is fascinating.

Bull Passage. Bull Passage and the islands that lie off the south end of Jedediah Island are rugged and scenic.

Little Bull Passage. Between high rock cliffs, Little Bull Passage is narrow and beautiful. Watch for the charted rock on the Jedediah Island side. It hides at high tide. Our notes say, "The east end of Little Bull Passage is absolutely fabulous. So much variety and strength in the rock walls and islands. Worth a side trip just to see the sights."

Jedediah Island. Jedediah Island is a marine park. Although good anchorages are scarce and tight, Jedediah Island is increasingly popular. One of the best anchorages is in the little notch, called Deep Bay, opposite the south end of Paul Island, where chains have been installed around this small bay to facilitate stern-ties. It is impractical that all these stern-ties could be used at the same time in this tiny, v-shaped bay, except for the smallest of boats. The large number of stern-ties are provided to allow different options for boaters. Long Bay just south of Deep Bay is usable, too. Long Bay goes dry a short distance inside the mouth. Codfish Bay on the southeast side of Jedediah Island has room for two or three boats to stern-tie. If nothing looks good at Jedediah Island itself, Boho Bay at Lasqueti Island, about 1 mile away, is an alternative.

One interesting spot is the narrow and protected steep-sided notch at the southeast end of Jedediah Island. Although its sheer walls might discourage much on-shore exploration, it is possible to scramble from the head of the notch up the bluffs on the north side. You will be rewarded not only with access to the rest of the island but also an excellent view toward Texada Island. [*Hamilton*]

For easy access to the island, take the dinghy ashore at Deep Bay and hike the short, well-marked trail across the island. A map of the island is posted at the head of the trail from both Deep Bay and Long Bay. A trail also leads from Codfish Bay. A visit to the old homestead on the east side of Jedediah Island is an exciting adventure and should not be missed. The homestead is frozen in time and left undisturbed. Please respect the property and leave things as found for others to enjoy.

The island was owned by several families over the years. The Foote Family first purchased the island in 1890. Alan and Mary Palmer, the last owners, didn't want this island paradise to be developed so sold Jedediah Island to the Provincial Government in 1994 to be used as a Marine Park. A plaque on the island commemorates their generous forethought. You can learn more about the history of Jedediah Island in the book - *Jedediah Days, One Woman's Island Paradise*, by Mary Palmer.

TEXADA ISLAND

Texada (pronounced "Tex-AY-da") Island has three main anchorages: Anderson Bay on Malaspina Strait at the south end; Blubber Bay at the northern tip; and Sturt Bay, a couple miles south along the Malaspina Strait (eastern) side. Although it has a ferry landing and public float, **Blubber Bay** is dominated by an enormous quarry and is not inviting, but anchorage is possible if needed. Texada Island has a long history of mining including iron, copper, silver and gold. In more recent years, Texada has been a continuous source of high quality limestone.

The Texada Blues & Roots Festival is held in late July at Gillies Bay Ball Park. Also held at Gillies Bay is the popular Sandcastle Weekend, the first weekend in August.

Anderson Bay. Anderson Bay is at the south end of Texada Island on Malaspina Strait. It is a beautiful spot, lined with sheer rock walls. Anchor in 24 feet near the head.

The safest approach is from the southeast. In our opinion, the pass between Texada Island and the unnamed 20-meter island is not as open as the charts suggest. We explored this pass at the bottom of a 1.6-foot low tide and found rock shelves extending from the Texada Island side well into the pass. Be especially careful of the reef that extends from the southwest point of Texada Island. The reef dries at low tide, but at higher stages of tide it could be a nasty surprise.

⑩ **Sturt Bay.** Locally called Marble Bay, on Malaspina Strait near the north end of Texada Island; it has the best anchorage and moorage on Texada Island. Anchorage is in the bay, but beware of forest and mining equipment said to be lying on the bottom.

The full service grocery store has liquor, good meats and produce. A farmers market is held Sundays at Gillies Bay Ballpark. The Texada Island Museum, housed in a wing of the local school at 2003 Waterman Ave., covers the history of Texada mining and quarrying; open Wednesdays from 10:00 a.m. to noon.

Caution: Sturt Bay is a welcome haven if a northwesterly is kicking up Malaspina Strait, but not suitable in a fresh southeasterly. Blubber Bay provides better anchorage in a southeasterly.

Texada Boat Club. (604) 414-5897, or (604) 223-1122; texadaboatingclub.ca; VHF 66A. Located in the SE corner of Sturt Bay, behind a breakwater, the Texada Boat Club has floats for members and visitors. The first three floats (docks 1, 2, 3) as you enter the bay are marked for members only; the last float (dock 4) is marked for visitors and has first-come first-serve side-tie space on both sides. Water, 15-amp power, and garbage drop for a per bag fee. Self-register and make payment (cash only) at the harbormasters office, lower level of the first house on the left about 130 yards/meters up the road. Bob Timms is the harbormaster.

Van Anda (Vananda). A 50-foot public dock is located in Van Anda Cove. Guest moorage at the dock can be lumpy in northwesterlies. Nearby Sturt Bay is preferred.

Harwood Point Regional Park. Gillies Bay, Texada Island. Anchor out only and dinghy in to a 40-acre park. Grass fields, picnic tables, campsites, pit toilets.

Texada Boat Club in Sturt Bay on Texada Island has guest moorage for visiting boats.

Vancouver B.C. & Sunshine Coast

WHITE ROCK TO VANCOUVER
Boundary Bay • Fraser River • Steveston

VANCOUVER AND HOWE SOUND
False Creek • Vancouver Harbour • Indian Arm
Horseshoe Bay • Gibsons

GOWER POINT TO SECHELT INLET
Buccaneer Bay • Smuggler Cove • Secret Cove
Pender Harbour • Egmont • Sechelt Rapids • Sechelt

JERVIS INLET
Blind Bay • Ballet Bay • Hotham Sound • Jervis Inlet
Princess Louisa Inlet

MALASPINA STRAIT TO SARAH POINT
Grief Point • Westview • Lund • Copeland Islands

Scan the Latest Vancouver & Sunshine Coast Information

tinyurl.com/WG22xCh09

Pender Harbour

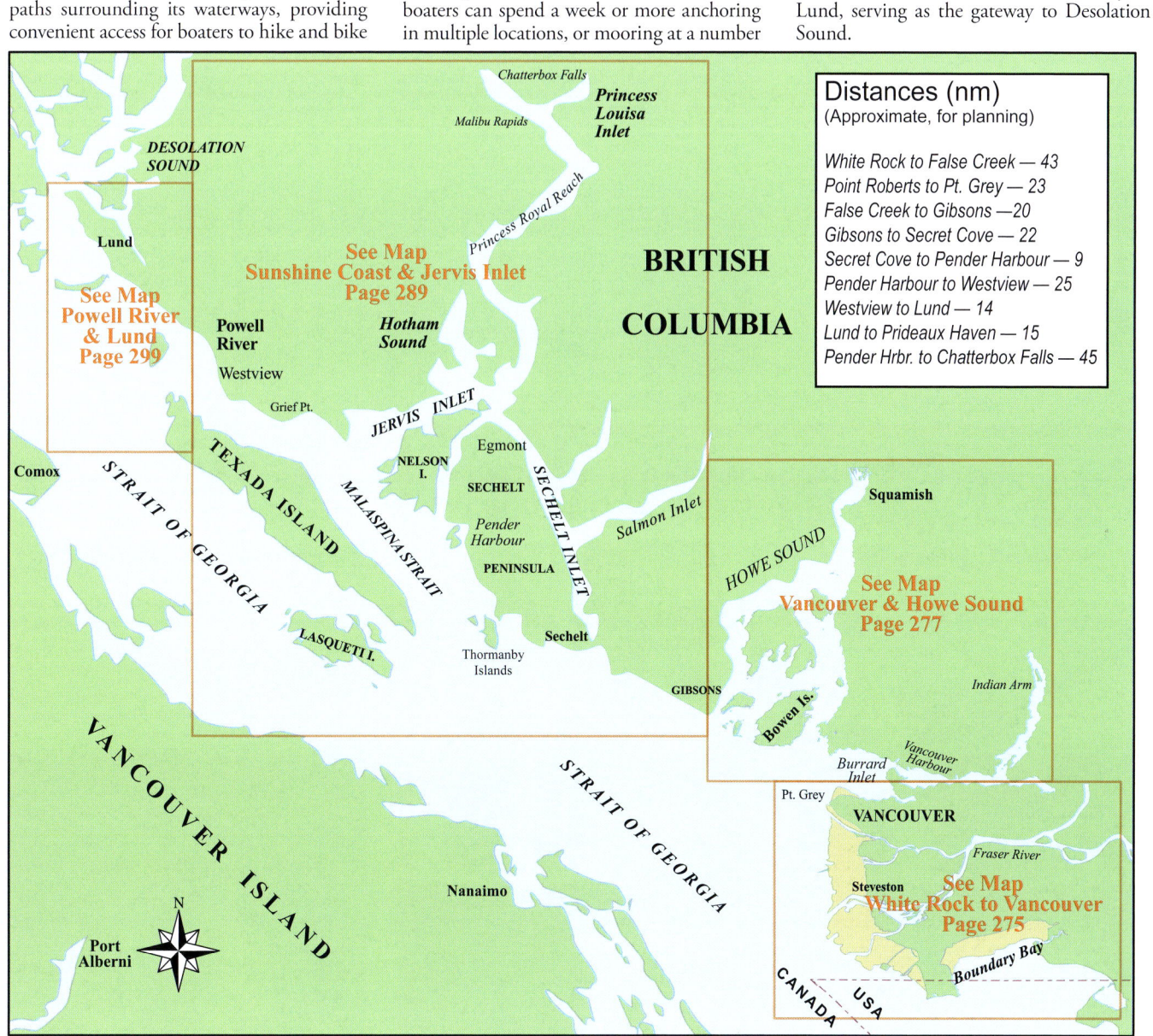

VANCOUVER B.C. & SUNSHINE COAST

The journey from Boundary Bay on the U.S./Canadian border northward to the city of Vancouver and along the Sunshine Coast to Lund is an extensive cruising area that offers a wide variety of destinations.

The border town of White Rock B.C., on the east side of Boundary Bay, is lined with cafes and shops along a sandy beach, accessed by a public pier. Heading north, the Fraser River offers charming fishing villages along its banks like Steveston located inside the river delta, and New Westminster farther up the river. River current and river sediment extending off shore bring new challenges and experiences for the boater.

Most pleasure craft choose to go north through the Gulf Islands, then pick a good weather window to cross the Strait of Georgia to the City of Vancouver or Howe Sound. The shortest distance across the Strait from Gabriola Pass to Howe Sound is 14 miles. Listen for the weather report for the Halibut Bank buoy. The metropolitan city of Vancouver has beautiful parks and bike paths surrounding its waterways, providing convenient access for boaters to hike and bike throughout the city. Restaurants, museums, and shops abound and are accessible from all marinas. A short distance away is Indian Arm, with charming bedroom communities. Cruise a short distance north from Vancouver into Howe Sound, and boaters find themselves in a different world, with stunning scenery and far fewer boats. Bowen Island and the charming community of Gibsons at the mouth of Howe Sound are favorite stops.

Continuing north along the Sunshine Coast, Pender Harbour, is a delight with its many coves, nooks, and crannies, where boaters can spend a week or more anchoring in multiple locations, or mooring at a number of different government and private resorts.

Princess Louisa Inlet is one of the most sought-after destinations, with its granite-face cliffs and stunning Chatterbox Falls. The park dock and mooring buoys provide convenient overnight stays. The community of Egmont, on Sechelt Peninsula, serves as a good jumping off point.

Next stop, Powell River is a good refueling and reprovisioning stop. The town has a marine supply store, a lovely beach, and some great restaurants. At the north end of the Sunshine Coast is the small community of Lund, serving as the gateway to Desolation Sound.

A waterfront pedestrian and separate bike path fronts Coal Harbour and takes you all the way to Stanley Park.

Distances (nm)
(Approximate, for planning)

White Rock to False Creek — 43
Point Roberts to Pt. Grey — 23
False Creek to Gibsons — 20
Gibsons to Secret Cove — 22
Secret Cove to Pender Harbour — 9
Pender Harbour to Westview — 25
Westview to Lund — 14
Lund to Prideaux Haven — 15
Pender Hrbr. to Chatterbox Falls — 45

Vancouver B.C. & Sunshine Coast

Boundary Bay. The U.S./Canada border runs through Boundary Bay. Crescent Beach is located to the northeast up the Nicomekl River. Point Roberts, Washington, is to the southwest. White Rock and the Semiahmoo First Nation's reserve are on the southeast shore. The southeastern section of Boundary Bay, straddling the U.S./Canada border is known as Semiahmoo Bay. The northern tip of Boundary Bay is known as Mud Bay.

① **White Rock.** White Rock, in Canada, is almost due north of Blaine, in Boundary Bay. A long pier, with floats at the outer end, crosses tide flats. The waterfront village has interesting restaurants, shops, and galleries.

① **City of White Rock Pier.** (604) 626-5330. White Rock is a Canada Customs port of entry; call (888) 226-7277. The south side of the eastern float has about 50 feet of space reserved for transient moorage, 2 hours maximum stay, no power or water. Repairs were made to the pier in 2019.

② **Crescent Beach.** North of White Rock, the Nicomekl River empties into Boundary Bay, creating a channel that leads to the village of Crescent Beach and the Crescent Beach Marina. The channel is marked by port and starboard daymarks. The marina is located just beyond the Burlington Northern Railway swing bridge that crosses the river to Blackie Spit. Depending on tide, bridge clearance ranges from 9 to 20 feet. The bridge is manned 7 days a week, from 6:30 a.m. until 10:30 p.m., and will open to 3 horn blasts. Hail the bridge on VHF 66A or call (604) 538-3233.

② **Crescent Beach Marina Ltd.** 12555 Crescent Road, Surrey, BC V4A 2V4; (604) 538-9666; info@crescentbeachmarina.com; www.crescentbeachmarina.com. Monitors 66A. Open all year, hours vary in the off-season. Gasoline & diesel at the fuel dock. Guest moorage for boats to 50 feet; call first. Haulout on hydraulic trailers to 30 tons, 15, 20 & 30 amp power, washrooms, ice, repairs, chandlery, launch ramp, showers, laundry, pumpout, dry storage. Used oil drop.

Canoe Passage. Canoe Passage is the southernmost mouth of the Fraser River. The seaward entrance is marked by a government buoy, but private dolphins mark its winding path through Roberts Bank. Although mainly used by commercial boats with local knowledge, Canoe Passage can be used by small craft, especially at half tide or better on a rising tide. The swing bridge connecting Westham Island with the mainland is manned 24 hours a day, and opens to 3 whistle blasts. Contact the bridge tender on VHF 74 or by telephone at (604) 946-2121. Locals who use the passage re-mark the channel yearly, after major runoff has moved the sand bars.

South Arm Fraser River. Sand Heads marks the mouth of the South Arm (also called the **Main Arm**) of the Fraser River. The South Arm is the Fraser's major entry, and is protected on its north side by the Steveston Jetty. Currents in the Fraser River can run to 5 knots, depending on the volume of water in the river, which in turn depends on rain and snow melt upstream. Large flood tides will at times slow or reverse the current.

Caution: An on-shore wind meeting an ebb current, combined with heavy outflow from the river, will create dangerously steep and high seas in the river mouth. Friends who keep their boats on the river tell of their entire boat being airborne in these conditions.

The lower part of the Fraser River is delta country, low and flat. The marshlands are havens for wildlife, and you'll see many eagles. The river itself contains much drift. The river is used heavily by fish boats, tugs towing barges or log booms, Coast Guard boats, work boats of all description, and freighters. Water-oriented industrial companies are located along the shores.

Relatively few cruising boats go up the Fraser River, in part because the entire coast between Point Grey and Point Roberts is uninteresting to view, and hostile in any kind of wind. Most of the marinas on the Fraser River, with the exception of Steveston, exist primarily for permanent moorage tenants, with few facilities for visitors.

③ **Steveston.** The first stop on the Fraser River is Steveston, a long, slender harbor on the north side of Cannery Channel, protected by a sand island (Steveston Island). Although Steveston is primarily a fishing town with moorage and other services for commercial fishermen, it has become a lively tourist destination as well. Transient moorage is available at the Steveston Wharf and at Imperial Landing located a third of a mile east of the wharf. Steveston has a fuel dock. Antique shops, bookstores, plenty of dining and all the other facilities of a small city are ashore. The streets of Steveston are quaint; the local movie industry sometimes films scenes there. Steveston has much to offer above and beyond its attractive shops and cafes. The excellent Gulf of Georgia Cannery Museum on the west end of the Public Wharf is a must see, as is the Britannia Shipyards National Historic Site on the east end of the village, reached by a beautiful promenade along the shoreline. Hikers and bicyclists make use of the extensive trail system that leads to the North Arm of the Fraser River and to the City of Richmond. For a short hike, walk the trail west of town to Garry Point Park with beach access and great views over the South Arm and the Gulf Islands.

③ **Steveston Harbour Authority Wharf.** 12740 Trites Rd., Richmond, BC V7E 3R8; (604) 272-5539; www.stevestonharbour.com. Open all year, 30 amp power, water, washrooms, and showers. No Wi-Fi. Side-tie transient moorage is available by reservation only on the east side of the unlabeled float, east of the fish sales float (the eastern most

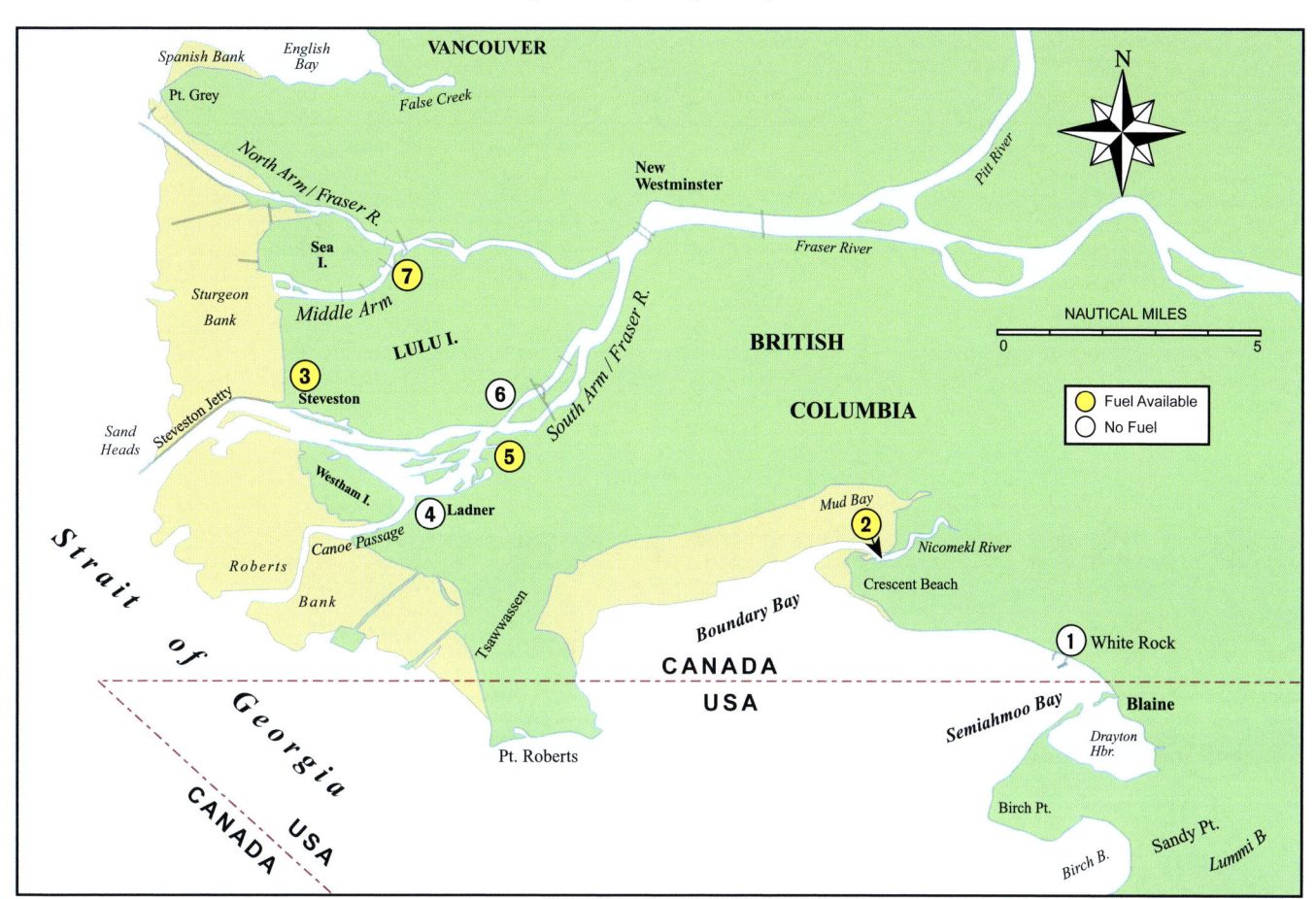

White Rock to Vancouver

Wharf float.) All transient guests must register and make payment by phone; the Harbour Authority office is located more than a mile away, at their Paramount Basin site. A key to the showers is provided upon request. Showers and public washrooms are located next to the Gulf of Georgia Cannery Museum. Hourly stays for dining or shopping are permitted on the west side of the 3rd Ave. Pier at no charge; no overnight; call the office before tying up.

③ **Steveston Chevron.** (604) 277-4712. Fuel dock with ethanol-free gasoline, diesel, washrooms. Limited marine supplies, lubricants, snacks.

③ **City of Richmond Imperial Landing.** Located a third of a mile east of the Steveston Harbour Authority docks; parksprograms@richmond.ca; www.richmond.ca/parks. A Richmond City Parks Department facility (604) 244-1208. Transient side-tie moorage on this substantial 600-foot concrete dock, first-come, first-served; 30 amp power, no water, no washrooms, or showers. First three hours are free. Rates for stays over three hours are posted at the automated pay-station at the head of the ramp. Maximum stay is three consecutive days. This dock offers a more secluded moorage option when visiting the community of Steveston. Charted depths are deeper off the west end of this dock than around the Steveston Harbour docks.

Caution: Hazardous submerged piles are reported near the inside (shore side) of the east half of the dock.

④ **Ladner.** Ladner is a pretty town. Leave the main branch of the Fraser River and take Sea Reach to Ladner Harbour, fronted by float homes. Moorage for fish boats is on the port side, and pleasure craft are welcome when the fleet is out. Strongly favor the south shore as you enter Ladner Harbour, skirting the docks of marinas and businesses located along River Road. A drying mud bank, studded with deadheads, extends a considerable distance from the north side of the harbor.

④ **Ladner Yacht Club.** (604) 946-4056; www.ladneryachtclub.ca. Reciprocal boats only if space is available. Water, restrooms, 30 amp power, secured marina.

Deas Slough. A little farther up the river from Ladner, Deas Slough is home to Captain's Cove, located behind Deas Island. A low bridge blocks passage any farther up Deas Slough, except for small boats with no masts.

⑤ **Captain's Cove Marina.** 6100 Ferry Rd., Ladner, BC V4K 3M9; (604) 946-1244; info@captainscovemarina.ca; www.captainscovemarina.ca. Permanent moorage only. Haulout to 60 tons, and a do-it-yourself yard for repairs.

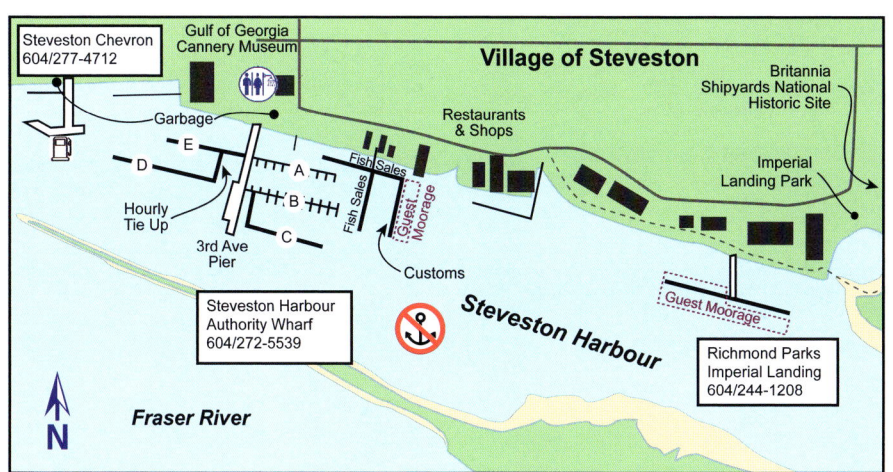

⑥ **Shelter Island Marina Inc.** 6911 Graybar Rd., Richmond, BC V6W 1H3; (604) 270-6272; infodesk@shelterislandmarina.com; www.shelterislandmarina.com. Open all year, some guest moorage, call ahead. Washrooms, showers, laundry, water, 15, 30, & 50 amp power, several Travelifts for boats up to 220 tons, chandlery with hardware section in the marina office and a full-service chandlery across the parking lot. Restaurant and pub with free Wi-Fi, beer and wine store, and a full liquor store two blocks away.

Shelter Island Marina is behind Don Island at the south entrance to Annacis Channel. It is a busy facility with a number of boat repair companies.

New Westminster. New Westminster is located at the confluence of the North and South Arms of the Fraser River, and is heavily industrialized along the waterfront.

Tom Kincaid has run the river past New Westminster to the Pitt River, where he spent the night at the Pitt Meadows Marina. A few friends have continued to the Harrison River, running up the Harrison River to Harrison Lake and Harrison Hot Springs. All recommend having a fast boat and a knowledgeable pilot aboard before attempting to run either of these rivers. The Fraser River beyond Richmond is poorly marked, and sand bars are constantly changing. The river is navigable as far as Hope during high water stages, but mariners should rely on local knowledge before attempting this run.

North Arm Fraser River. The North Arm of the Fraser River is lined with boatbuilding and repair yards and other businesses that serve the marine community. A jetty runs through Sturgeon Bank along the south side of the North Arm, parallel to the Point Grey shoreline. A dredged basin, known locally as "Coward's Cove" or the "Chicken Hole," is on the north side of the channel, just before the North Arm enters the Strait of Georgia. The basin gives good protection to skippers while they assess conditions out on the strait.

⑦ **Richmond Chevron.** 7891 Grauer Rd., Richmond, BC V7B 1N4; (604) 278-2181. Beneath Arthur Laing Bridge. Open all year, gasoline, diesel, lubricants and waste oil disposal.

Middle Arm Fraser River. The Middle Arm of the Fraser River runs along the south side of Sea Island, which is almost entirely taken up by Vancouver International Airport. The west entrance is blocked by Sturgeon Bank with no marked channels. We have seen a small, fast cruiser enter the Middle Arm, but the tide was high and perhaps the skipper had local knowledge (or maybe was just lucky). Prudence dictates entry from the North Arm only. The Delta River Inn Marina and Vancouver Marina are on the Middle Arm near a low swing bridge connecting the city of Richmond with the airport.

⑦ **Pier 73 Marina & Yacht Club.** 3500 Cessna Drive, Richmond, BC V7B 1C7; (604) 970-4882; info@pier73marina.com; pier73marina.com. Located 8 miles up the North Arm of the Fraser River in Moray Channel at the Pacific Gateway Hotel Vancouver Airport. Open all year, limited guest moorage, call ahead. This fully refurbished marina has slips from 30 to 80 feet, 30 & 50 amp power, water.

⑦ **Vancouver Marina.** #200-8211 River Road, Richmond, BC V6X 1X8; (604) 278-9787; (604) 278-3300 fuel dock; mooring@vancouvermarina.com; www.vancouvermarina.com. Monitors VHF 66A. Open all year, request for moorage available online. Gasoline & diesel at the fuel dock, 15, 20 & 30 amp power, garbage, pumpout, recycling and waste oil disposal, washrooms, no showers. They carry marine supplies, snacks, bait, and ice. 24-hour security. Located in the heart of Richmond on the Middle Arm of the Fraser River. The adjacent Galleon Marine has outboard services and parts.

⑦ **Skyline Marina.** 8031 River Road, Richmond, BC V6X 1X8; (604) 273-3977; www.skylinemarina.ca. Open all year, no transient moorage. The marina has a boatyard and 30 ton Travelift.

THE NEW-OLD MARTIN MARINE

Largest Supply of Marine Hardware on the North Shore. Free Parking.

Interlux

1176 Welch Street, North Vancouver, BC V7P 1B2
Phone: 604-985-0911 • Toll Free: 1-866-985-0911 • info@martinmarine.ca

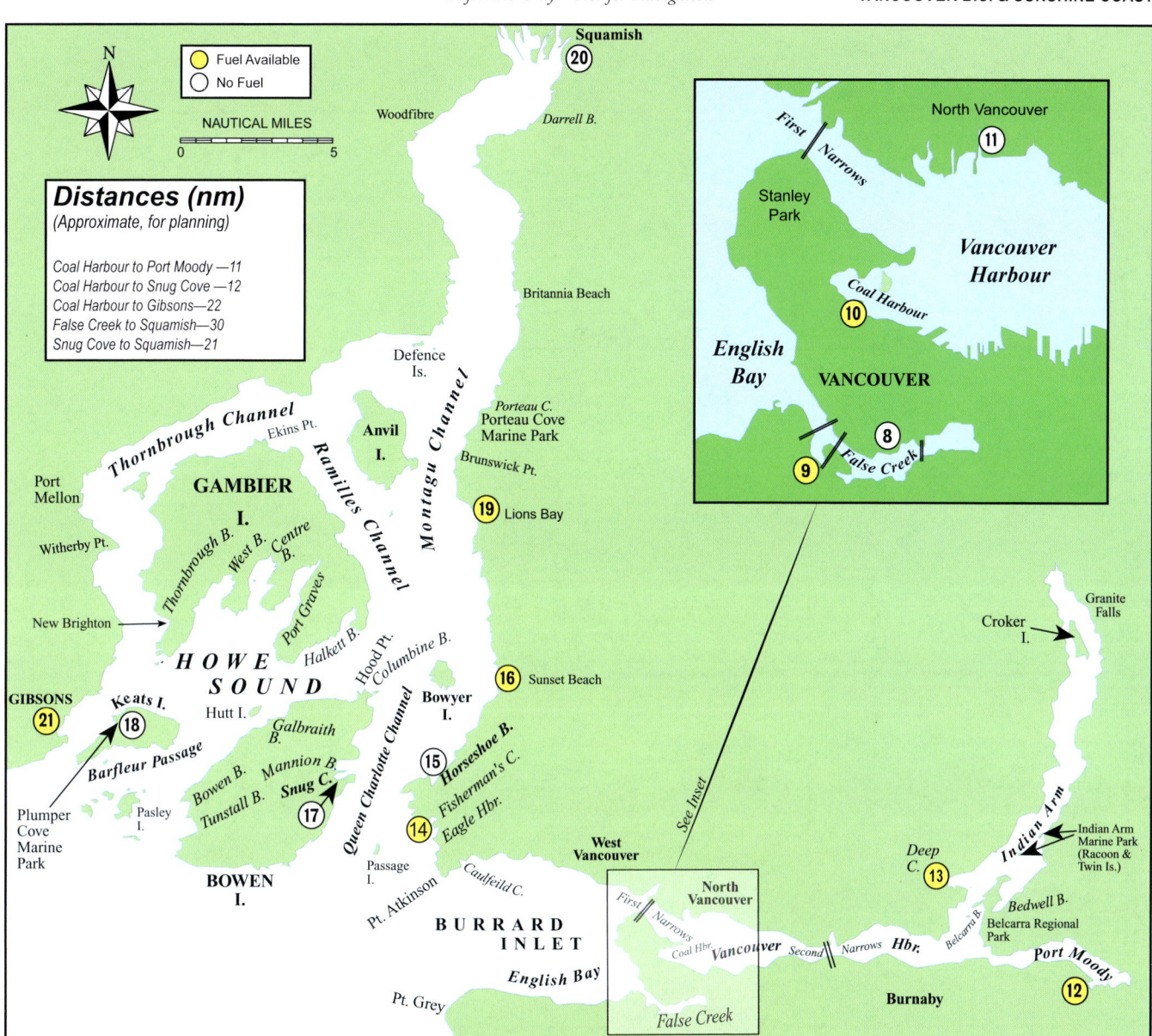

Vancouver and Howe Sound

⑦ **Milltown Marina.** 9191 Bently Street, Vancouver, BC V6P 0B9; (604) 697-9191; admin@milltownmarina.com; www.milltownmarina.ca. Office open Tuesday through Saturday. Permanent and transient moorage for vessels up to 80 feet, 30 & 50 amp power, water, restrooms, showers, garbage, and recycle drop. Propane refills. This is one of Vancouver's newest marinas located on the Fraser River near the Vancouver International Airport.

A restaurant is located upland. Milltown Marine Services (604-264-8020) is next door near the marina.

VANCOUVER

Vancouver is the largest city in British Columbia, and the major deepwater port on the west coast of Canada, handling cargo from across Canada and around the world. The city is clean, safe, and thoroughly cosmopolitan. Its architecture is exciting. Vancouver's parks, museums, hotels, and dining are wonderful.

If you are approaching Vancouver from the south, you could go up the North Arm of the Fraser River to a number of marinas in the Richmond area, and take a bus into the city. If you are approaching from the north, you could tie up at Horseshoe Bay on the north shore of West Vancouver, or at Snug Cove on the south side of Bowen Island. A private foot ferry runs between Snug Cove and Granville Island during the summer months; contact Bowen Island Land & Sea Taxi at (604) 484-8497. Or take the BC Ferries from Snug Cove to Horseshoe Bay, then board a bus for the trip into Vancouver—or as far south as White Rock if that's where you wanted to go. The Vancouver transit system is excellent and affordable.

For moorage in Vancouver proper, choose either the Vancouver Harbour area or the False Creek area. Each has advantages, and each is good. Once you're settled, Vancouver's bus and light rail system allows you to get around the entire area with minimum delay. A Costco store is located near the northeast end of False Creek at 605 Expo Blvd. (604) 622-5050.

Anchoring restriction: A permit, at no cost, is required for all vessels anchoring in False Creek (see False Creek area description for details).

Taxi: Black Top & Checker (604) 731-1111; Vancouver Taxi (604) 871-1111; and Yellow Cab (604) 681-1111.

Point Grey. Point Grey marks the southern entrance to Burrard Inlet. When approaching from the south, cutting too close to Point Grey risks grounding on Spanish Bank. Leave the buoys to starboard when entering.

Spanish Bank. Spanish Bank is an extensive drying bank off the north shore of Point Grey. The outer edge of the bank is marked with buoys. Royal Vancouver Yacht Club has its main clubhouse and sailboat moorage about 3 miles from Point Grey along the south shore of English Bay. A launch ramp is close to the former Kitsilano Coast Guard station near the entrance to False Creek.

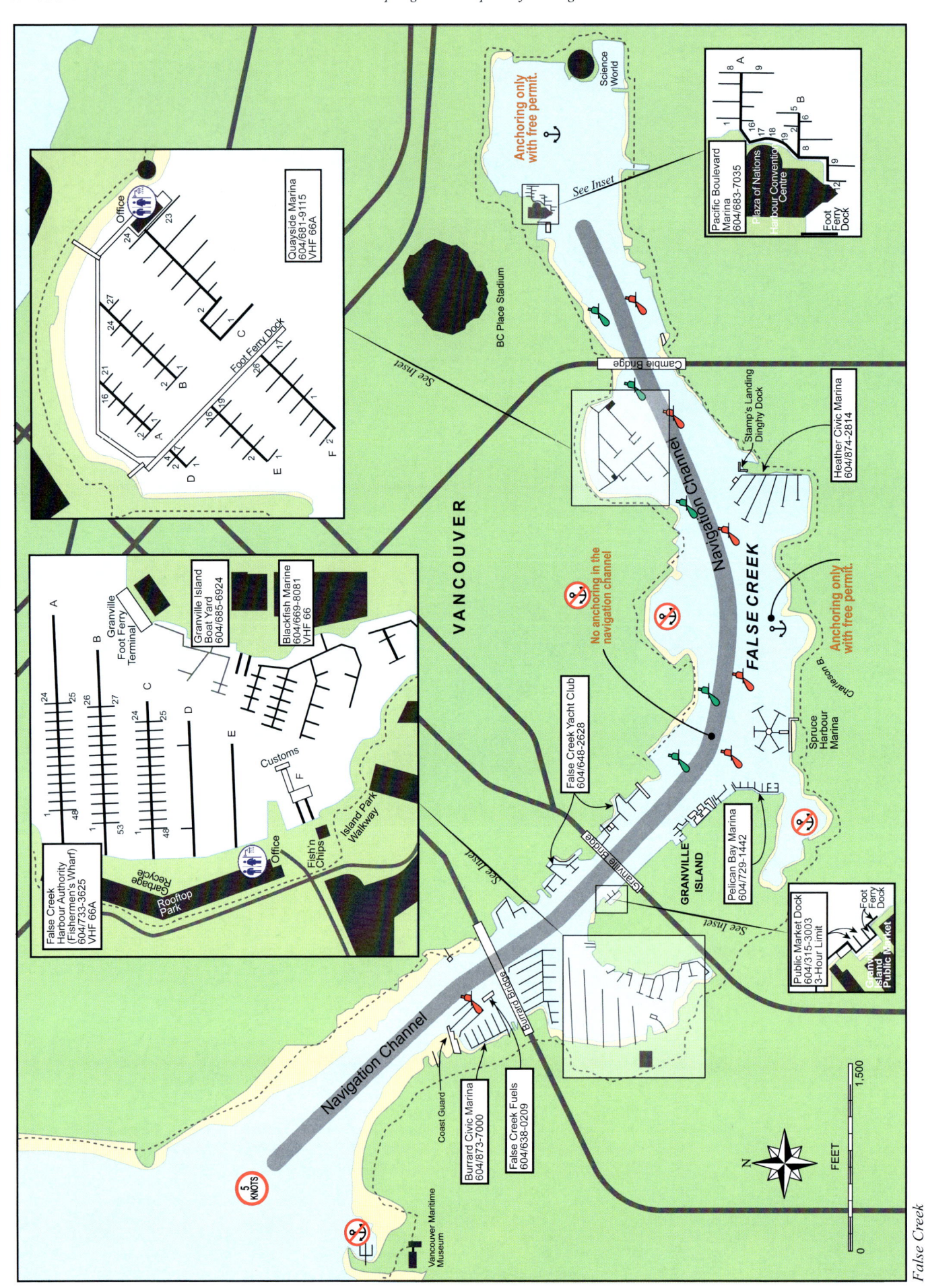

VANCOUVER B.C. & SUNSHINE COAST   See Area Map Page 277 - Maps Not for Navigation

False Creek

Quayside Marina
604/681-9115
VHF 66A

Pacific Boulevard Marina
604/683-7035

False Creek Harbour Authority (Fishermen's Wharf)
604/733-3625
VHF 66A

Granville Island Boat Yard
604/685-6924

Blackfish Marine
604/669-8081
VHF 66

False Creek Yacht Club
604/648-2628

Heather Civic Marina
604/874-2814

Pelican Bay Marina
604/729-1442

Spruce Harbour Marina

Public Market Dock
604/315-3003
3-Hour Limit

Burrard Civic Marina
604/873-7000

False Creek Fuels
604/638-0209

278
www.WaggonerGuide.com

FALSE CREEK

False Creek is an ideal centrally located bay with a number of marina moorage options, well-protected anchorage and a full service boatyard with Travelift. A well-monitored anchoring permit system helps to keep anchoring space available and prevents permanent anchorage abuses. Anchoring permits (free) are required for day anchoring longer than 8 hours and overnight anchoring. Permits can be picked up at Heather Civic Marina or online at http://vancouver.ca/streets-transportation/anchoring.aspx. The permit is valid for 14 days April-September and for 21 days October-March. Boats without permits are subject to ticketing and fines up to $500.

False Creek Yacht Club, on the north shore of False Creek, usually has guest slips available. Quayside Marina, also on the north shore, has excellent facilities with guest slip and side-tie moorage. Foot ferries stop at Quayside. On the south shore, the Fishermen's Wharf marina, managed by the False Creek Harbour Authority, has transient moorage and good facilities. It is a short walk from the marina to the Granville Island Market, shops, and restaurants. False Creek is covered by Wi-Fi.

Blackfish Marine, on the west side of Granville Island near the Granville Market, sometimes has moorage available in unoccupied slips, reservations required. To reach these docks, turn south just before the Tap & Barrel Bridges Restaurant when you enter False Creek and work your way towards their docks. On the east side of Granville Island the Pelican Bay Marina, next to the Granville Island Hotel, has some guest moorage.

Granville Island is an active and vibrant place, full of people. You'll find an excellent food market (similar in many ways to Seattle's Pike Place Market, except bigger and better), with many restaurants, galleries, shops, and a variety of marine supplies, both on the island and a short walk away. Docks face the waterway and are posted for a 3-hour maximum stay; register with security at (604) 315-3003.

Two harbor foot ferry franchises serve False Creek, it's a great way to tour the harbour. These foot ferries do not stop to pick up passengers from boats anchored in the bay.

Fuel: Fuel is available at the False Creek Fuels.

Pumpouts: Pumpouts are located at Burrard Bridge Civic Marina, False Creek Harbour Authority Fishermen's Wharf, False Creek Yacht Club, Heather Civic Marina (under the large "Monk's" sign), and Quayside Marina.

The City of Vancouver and the Vancouver Park Board started a free mobile pumpout service pilot project, which has been ongoing to provide service during the summer months. To schedule the service, contact False Creek Mobile Pumpout Skookum Yacht Services at (778) 683-7867; pumpout@skookumyachtservices.com.

No Discharge Zone. Gray Water Okay.

A pedestrian promenade encircles False Creek with unsurpassed views.

Vancouver Maritime Museum. 1905 Ogden Avenue in Vanier Park, Vancouver, BC V6J 1A3; (604) 257-8300; www.vancouvermaritimemuseum.com. Vancouver Maritime Museum is on the south shore of English Bay at the entrance to False Creek.

The museum's docks are for display boats only. The vessel St. Roch, which explored the Northwest Passage, is on display in its own building. The False Creek Ferry stops at the museum docks.

⑧ **False Creek Yacht Club**. 1661 Granville St., Vancouver, BC V6Z 1N3; (604) 648-2628 dockmaster; (604) 682-3292 administration & event scheduling; www.fcyc.com; welcome@fcyc.com. Washrooms, showers, laundry, pumpout, free Wi-Fi, 30 amp power, and lounge. Open all year on the north side of False Creek, directly under the Granville Street Bridge. Reciprocal and public guest moorage in unoccupied slips as assigned. Limited moorage for boats over 50 feet. Call the dockmaster for reservations. The yacht club, once active as the Vancouver Boating Welcome Centre, is still pleased to share their local knowledge with boaters. A passenger foot ferry runs regularly to Granville Island.

⑧ **Quayside Marina**. 1088 Marinaside Crescent, Vancouver, BC V6Z 3C4; (604) 681-9115; qsmarina@ranchogroup.com; www.ranchovan.com/marina. Monitors VHF 66A. Open all year for vessels to 120 feet, 30, 50 & 100 amp power, water on the docks, washrooms, showers, laundry, pumpout, garbage and recycling, ice, security. Wheelchair accessible. Online Reservations are available on their website. Slip sales and long-term lease information also found on their website.

The Quayside (pronounced "Keyside") Marina is on the north shore of False Creek, in the middle of Vancouver's cosmopolitan Yaletown district. Most of the slips are for permanent moorage, but guest moorage is available on a 500-foot-long float extending from shore, or in vacant slips. Colorful Aquabus foot ferry boats come and go from their spot near the head of that float as do the small passenger False Creek Ferries. Moorage reservations are essential during high season and requested year-round. Although it's a bit of a walk from the guest dock to the office, check in promptly after you arrive. For provisioning, visit the Urban Fare Market, a block away, at 1688 Salt Street. Costco, located at 605 Expo Blvd., is a short walk or taxi ride away.

⑧ **Pacific Boulevard Marina**. Box 26, 750 Pacific Blvd., Vancouver, BC V6B 5E7; (604) 683-7035; info@pacblvdmarina.com; www.pacblvdmarina.com. Permanent moorage marina with transient space when available for vessels up to 40 feet; 30 & 50 amp power, water, security gates. Located at the northeast end of False Creek. Reservations requested no more than one week in advance. Transient space is most likely available during March and April. Sea-Doo and pontoon boat rentals.

⑨ **Burrard Civic Marina**. 1655 Whyte Ave., Vancouver, BC V6J 1A9; (604) 733-5833 (604) 505-5833 harbourmaster cell; burrard.marina@vancouver.ca. The first marina in False Creek, with over 420 berths. Open 7 days a week all year. Operated by the City of Vancouver. Permanent moorage with some space for transient boats in vacant slips to 36 feet (occasionally up to 45 feet). Call for availability. Water, 15 amp power, washrooms, showers, pumpout, waste oil disposal, security gate with key-card, free Wi-Fi. The marina is convenient to the Vancouver Maritime Museum, walking and bike paths, and the False Creek foot ferries.

⑨ **False Creek Fuels**. 1655 Whyte Avenue, Vancouver, BC V6J 4N1; (604) 638-0209; fillup@falsecreekfuels.com; www.falsecreekfuels.com. Monitors 66A. Just west of the Burrard Street Bridge, the fuel float carries gas, diesel, oil, lubricants. Open 7 days a week. Waste oil and fuel disposal. Accommodates vessels to 165 feet. The store has drinks, snacks, ice cream, sandwiches (seasonal), and a coffee bar. It also has ice, bait, tackle and marine supplies.

⑨ **False Creek Harbour Authority Fishermen's Wharf**. Fishermen's Wharf. 1505 W. 1st Ave., Vancouver, BC V6J 1E8; (604) 733-3625; info@falsecreek.com; www.falsecreek.com. Monitors VHF 66A. Open

VANCOUVER B.C. & SUNSHINE COAST

See Area Map Page 277 - Maps Not for Navigation

False Creek is alive with pleasure craft, paddle craft, fish boats, and aqua bus ferries.

Burrard Marina and Fishermen's Wharf in False Creek

24 hours a day year-round. Located on the south shore of False Creek, west of Granville Island. Contact the Harbour Authority office for docking instructions prior to arrival. 20 & 30 amp power on all docks; 50 & 100 amp power on some. Contact the Harbour office for access to locked power connection boxes. Water, washrooms, showers, laundry, ice, pumpout, recycling, waste oil disposal, free Wi-Fi, and 24-hour security. Ramps between shore and the floats are wide, long and compliant with Canadian Disability Policy Alliance.

A fish sales dock is just east of the Harbour Authority office, where you may purchase fresh seafood directly from fish boats as scheduled. The upland Go Fish Seafood Shack's fish & chips are not to be missed, take-out or enjoy at the outdoor bar and picnic tables. Expect long lines around noon time.

A rooftop park with fountain and tables is above the Harbour Authority offices and Lockers. The Vancouver Maritime Museum in Vanier Park is a short walk away. The popular Shakespeare Festival, under the tents in Vanier Park, is held early June through mid-September. Granville Island, with its excellent market, shops, cafes and theaters is within easy walking distance from Fishermen's Wharf.

Customs Clearance. A courtesy customs clearance area is located in the yellow painted bull-rail area on the 'T' end of F-dock. There is no dedicated phone, you will need to use your cell phone.

⑨ **Blackfish Marine.** 1815 Maritime Mews; Vancouver, BC V6H 3W7; (604) 669-8081; info@blackfishmarine.com; www.blackfishmarine.com. Open all year, moorage in unoccupied slips as available, 30 & 50 amp power. Located on the west side of Granville Island.

⑨ **Granville Island Boat Yard.** (604) 685-6924; www.granvilleislandboatyard.com. A full service boatyard with 55 ton Travelift is located on the west side of Granville Island. The boatyard has repair service trades people available and welcomes do-it-yourself.

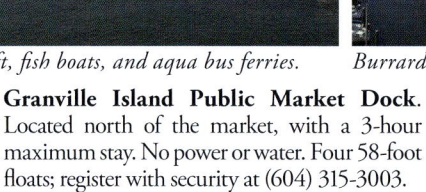

Granville Island Public Market Dock. Located north of the market, with a 3-hour maximum stay. No power or water. Four 58-foot floats; register with security at (604) 315-3003.

⑨ **Pelican Bay Marina.** 1708 W. 6th Ave., Vancouver, BC V6J 5E8; (604) 729-1442; pelicanbaymarina@gmail.com. Open all year, adjacent to the Granville Island Hotel on the east end of Granville Island. Moorage in unoccupied slips when available, call ahead. Water, 15, 30 & 50 amp power, washroom, ice.

⑨ **Heather Civic Marina.** 600 Stamps Landing, Vancouver, BC V5Z 3Z1; (604) 874-2814; heather.marina@vancouver.ca; www.vancouver.ca/streets-transportation/heather-civic-marina.aspx. Permanent moorage only marina, with restaurants and pub nearby.

A passenger foot ferry runs to both sides of False Creek. The Heather Civic Marina office issues anchoring permits for False Creek.

LOCAL KNOWLEDGE

STRONG CURRENTS: Currents run strongly in both First and Second Narrows. Use caution, especially because of the heavy traffic that frequents the area.

⑩ **Vancouver Harbour (South).** Vancouver Harbour is entered under the Lions Gate Bridge through First Narrows, in the northeast corner of Burrard Inlet. Because of heavy commercial traffic, strong currents and narrow channels, sailing craft must be under power from westward of First Narrows until eastward of Second Narrows. Fishing, water sports, rowing, and anchoring in the area is also prohibited; 15 knot speed limit in the waters around First Narrows. In First Narrows, a strong ebb current meeting a fresh onshore breeze can create high, steep seas. Current predictions are shown in the Tide and Current Tables Vol. 5, and Ports and Passes. Monitor VHF 12 for Vessel Traffic Services (VTS) information. Stay off to the side and clear of commercial traffic.

Watch for drifting logs and floatplane traffic. Approaching Coal Harbour, leave Burnaby Shoal and the Chevron fuel barge to starboard. Observe a 5-knot speed limit in Coal Harbour.

Once into Vancouver Harbour, your best bet for moorage is along the southern shoreline in the Coal Harbour area. Vancouver Rowing Club, located adjacent to Stanley Park, has moorage for members of reciprocal yacht clubs. Stanley Park is nearby.

Bayshore West Marina, next to the Harbour Ferries docks, offers some guest moorage.

Coal Harbour Marina, just east of the Bayshore Hotel, makes a visit to Vancouver a real pleasure. It is first class in every way, and is an excellent base for a few days in town.

These marinas are close to downtown Vancouver, a pleasant walk or short cab ride away. Wright Mariner Supply, occupying a floating structure in the Coal Harbour Marina, sells a complete range of marine supplies, clothing, charts, and books.

Robson Street's shops, galleries and wide range of restaurants are just a few blocks away.

Anchoring restriction: Pleasure craft may not anchor in Vancouver Harbour between First Narrows and Second Narrows.

⑩ **Harbour Green.** A Vancouver City Parks Board dock, located east of Coal Harbour Marina. The dock at this site was closed in 2022 for renovation. Construction began in the fall of 2021, with an anticipated completion date of summer 2022; however, in August of 2022, the dock was still closed. Guests will have easy access to Harbour Green Park, the promenade, and area shops and cafes once the dock is completed.

⑩ **Coal Harbour Chevron.** (604) 681-7725. Fuel barge in Coal Harbour open 7 days a week 7:00 a.m. to 11:00 p.m., gasoline & diesel; washrooms for customers.

⑩ **Coal Harbour Marina.** 1525 Coal Harbour Quay, Vancouver, BC V6G 3E7; (604) 681-2628; guestservices@coalharbourmarina.com; www.coalharbourmarina.com. Monitors VHF 66A. Open all year, guest moorage for

A spectacular promenade leads from Canada Place to Coal Harbour.

Coal Harbour Marina guest moorage puts you in the middle of Vancouver.

boats to 330 feet; reservations in season highly recommended. Facilities include 30, 50 & 100 amp single/3-phase power, Wi-Fi, pumpout, washrooms, showers, laundry. This is a first-class marina with wide concrete docks, 24-hour staff, security gates, a restaurant, marine supply store, and easy access to downtown Vancouver.

⑩ **Bayshore West Marina.** 450 Denman St., Vancouver, BC V6G 3J1; (604) 689-5331; info@bayshorewestmarina.com; www.bayshorewestmarina.com. Open all year, mostly permanent moorage with limited guest moorage to 80 feet; 30, & 50 amp power, garbage, recycling, Wi-Fi, washrooms, and pumpout. Reservations available online. Located in Coal Harbour between Stanley Park and the Westin Bayshore Resort. Restaurants and shopping within easy walking distance. The slips and fairways are wide for easy maneuvering.

⑪ **Vancouver Harbour (North).** With the exception of the redeveloped Lonsdale area, the north shore of Vancouver Harbour is mostly heavy commercial. Transient moorage is available at The Creek Marina and at the City of North Vancouver's St. Roch dock. Both are near the Lonsdale area which has a selection of restaurants and pubs, grocery, and shopping. SeaBus foot ferry service at Lonsdale Quay in North Vancouver runs to downtown Vancouver. The crossing takes 12 minutes and connects with other transportation options in downtown Vancouver. More info at: Vancouver transit planning at www.translink.ca.

A number of good marine repair shops are in The Creek Marina and at Lynnwood Marina, just west of Second Narrows.

Saturday Summer Concerts: July through August at Shipbuilders' Square at the foot of Lonsdale. Shipyards Night Market: May through September from 5 to 10 p.m. on Fridays. Live music, fresh food and locally made products.

Caution: The SeaBus north terminus is just west of Lonsdale Quay with frequent arrivals and departures of two foot-passenger catamaran SeaBus ferries.

⑪ **St. Roch Dock.** (604) 982-3910; www.cnv.org/piers. 80 feet of floating dock for short-term and overnight moorage. Located east of Lonsdale Quay with its "Q" on top of the tower, just below the historic yellow crane and next to the re-developed 700x50 feet Burrard Dry Dock. This pleasure craft float is conveniently located but exposed to Vancouver Harbour on the south. No charge for the first 3 hours of stay. Thereafter, call the City of North Vancouver (604) 982-3910 to make payment.

The City of North Vancouver has two other docks nearby. The Goldsworthy Pier float has 36 feet of day-use only space with stays limited to 3 hours at no charge. The Burrard Dry Dock is for large vessels and requires prior arrangement scheduling and a signed agreement.

⑪ **The Creek Marina.** (Formerly Mosquito Creek Marina) 415 West Esplanade, North Vancouver, BC V7M 1A6; (604) 987-4113; mcmb_dockmaster@squamish.net; www.mosquitocreekmarina.com. Limited guest moorage in unoccupied slips during the summer. Reservations required via their online request form. 15, 30 & 50 amp power (100 amp on Dock A), washrooms and laundry, Wi-Fi, 50-ton Travelift, water, pumpout by reservation, marine repairs, security gates, 24-hour security. On-site cafe located in a double-wide trailer near the office.

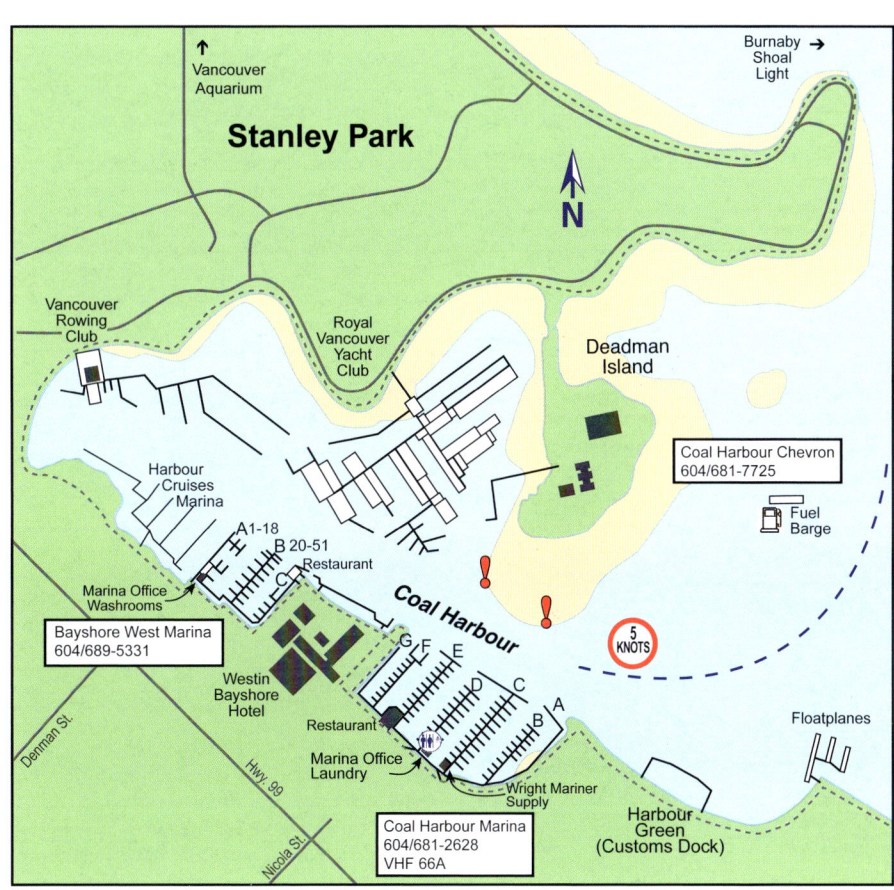

Coal Harbour

The marina is operated by the Squamish Nation. A mixture of open moorage and covered moorage with a variety of slip sizes. Know your assigned slip and study the marina dock diagram before entering the marina as dock and slip signage is lacking.

A foot path connects the marina with Lonsdale Quay shopping, with restaurants and a farmers market. Several boat repair companies with complete services are on-site. It's a 10-minute walk to the SeaBus foot ferries to downtown Vancouver.

⑪ **Lynnwood Marina.** 1681 Columbia St., North Vancouver, BC V7J 1A5; (604) 985-1533; info@lynnwoodmarina.com; www.lynnwoodmarina.com. Moorage for repair customers only. The marina has 15 & 30 amp power, complete repairs, and haulout to 60 tons.

THINGS TO DO

- **Granville Market.** On Granville Island, a delight to the senses with flowers, spices, teas, fruit and other food markets, restaurants and crafts.
- **Foot Ferries.** Crisscross the water from False Creek. Travel to different attractions or stay aboard to tour the entire harbor area. Some ferries allow bicycles.
- **Vancouver Maritime Museum.** Learn more about B.C. maritime history from Vancouver to the Arctic. See tugboats, fireboats and even pirates. Easily reached by foot ferry.
- **Stanley Park.** Several bike rental shops are on Denman Street, near Coal Harbour. Rent a bike and ride the trail along the seawall. Or, take a walk around the park. While in Stanley Park, learn more about B.C.'s First Nations people in Klahowya Village and ride the Spirit Catcher Miniature Train.
- **Vancouver Aquarium.** Located in Stanley Park. Excellent. Don't miss the cute sea otters.
- **Science World.** The distinctive domed glass building on False Creek with imaginative exhibits and hands-on experiments for young and old.
- **Bloedel Floral Conservatory.** In Queen Elizabeth Park. Tropical plants; colorful birds flying about; 4600 Cambie Street.
- **Fly Over Canada.** Sit in flight-motion seats before a spherical screen and fly over Canada; open daily from 10:00 a.m. to 9:00 p.m. at Canada Place; tickets available at flyovercanada.com.
- **Museum of Anthropology.** On the University of British Columbia campus. Study of First Nations people and other B.C. cultures.
- **Deeley Motorcycle Exhibition.** Over 250 motorcycles on exhibit, spanning 115 years and 59 different manufacturers; 1875 Boundary Road.
- **Yaletown or Gastown.** Key shopping areas with many shops and boutiques.

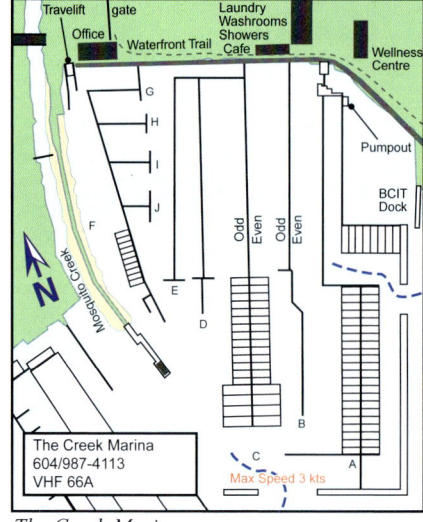

The Creek Marina

BURNABY, PORT MOODY, INDIAN ARM

Second Narrows. To proceed eastward from Vancouver Harbour to Burnaby and Port Moody, you first must go through Second Narrows. On spring tides, flood currents can reach 6.5 knots and ebb currents 5.5 knots. The narrows are not to be treated lightly. Wind and current opposing each other can create standing waves and difficult seas. The best advice is to go through near times of slack, although on small tides the current should present few problems for boats with adequate power. Current predictions are shown as a secondary station in the Tide and Current Tables Vol. 5, and Ports and Passes.

Due to extensive heavy displacement commercial traffic, monitor Vessel Traffic Service on VHF channel 12. Sailing is not permitted in Second Narrows; pleasure craft are to stay to the side of the channel. Listen for a "Clear Narrows" securite' call by Vessel Traffic Service. When issued, all vessels are to remain clear and not interfere with the passage of a large-draft vessel transiting Second Narrows.

Cates Park. Cates Park is at Roche Point, near the entrance to Indian Arm. The park has a paved launch ramp, beach, trails, playground, changing room, and picnic shelter. Temporary anchorage only.

Barnet Marine Park. The park at the east end of Burrard Inlet is the site of an old sawmill. The park has no public float, but anchorage is good just east of the fishing pier. Enjoy the sandy beach, or stretch your legs on "Drummond's Walk."

Port Moody. Port Moody ends in drying flats, but a dredged channel on the south shore leads through the flats to Rocky Point Park. The park has a launch ramp, swimming pool and picnic areas, and is the location of the Port Moody Museum. A large designated anchorage area (permit required) is located at

Power house on upper Indian Arm

the head of the bay with protection from all except northwesterly winds. There is a 10 knot speed limit in Port Moody east of a line drawn north of the Pacific Coast Terminals, and a 5 knot limit within 300 meters of Rocky Point boat launch.

Port Moody DAA Anchorage. Port Moody DAA (604) 469-4552. A designated anchorage area in Port Moody has space for approximately 20 boats. Boats in this designated anchorage area must have $2 million liability insurance and register online at portmoody.ca/en/recreation-parks-and-environment/anchoring.aspx to reserve space. Anchor within the designated area marked by four buoys upon receipt of email permit confirmation. A nominal fee is charged for each day, with a maximum stay of 21 nights in a 40-day period. Checkout time is noon.

⑫ **Reed Point Marina.** 850 Barnet Highway, Bldg. #1, Port Moody, BC V6H 1V6; (604) 937-1600; office@reedpoint.com; www.reedpoint.com. Open all year, mid-grade gasoline and diesel. Washrooms, showers, pumpout, haulout to 55 tons, chandlery, sundries, restaurant, marine supplies and service. Permanent moorage only.

INDIAN ARM

Indian Arm extends 11 miles into the Coast Range mountains, which soar to 5000 feet. The classy town of Deep Cove is tucked inside the cove that has the same name located in Indian Arm. Waterfront homes extend along the western shore of Indian Arm, accessed by a road that runs half way up Indian Arm to Best Point. From Best Point northward, the uplands are part of Indian Arm Marine Park, covering both sides of the forested mountain terrain. The waters in Indian Arm generally are calm, but can be ruffled by local downdraft winds off the mountains. Indian Arm is a little secret that Vancouver boaters cherish. It feels remote, yet it is close to the city.

There are two 5-knot speed limit zones in Indian Arm. The first zone is Indian Arm South, beginning at Boulder Island extending

Deep Cove Yacht Club docks are just north of the public dock.

The quaint small town of Deep Cove is enjoyable and fun to explore.

north to Jug Island. The second zone, Indian Arm North, begins at Croker Island and extends to the north end of Indian Arm.

Indian Arm Marine Park (Say Nuth Khaw Yum). In 1996 the Indian Arm Marine Park was expanded from the Twin Islands and Racoon Island to include most of the fjord. Croker Island and Granite Falls are part of the park.

Belcarra. Belcarra Regional Park is located northwest of Port Moody on the east shore of Indian Arm. This beautiful park is popular for hiking, swimming, and picnicking, with Sasamat Lake at the center of the park. Approximately 16 miles of hiking trails and nearly 6 miles of cycling trails. Anchorage is good in Belcarra Bay with nice depths on a flat bottom. The public float is for loading and unloading only.

Strathcona. The small Strathcona municipal float is at the mouth of Indian Arm across from Belcarra, behind White Rock and the Grey Rocks Islands. The float dries at low tide.

⑬ **Deep Cove.** Deep Cove is a city of about 5,000 people. The public float provides access to shopping in the town of Deep Cove for vessels up to 36 feet, no overnight moorage. The commercial village, adjacent to the public float, is upscale. Deep Cove is the location of the Deep Cove Yacht Club. Deep Cove Northshore Marina has moorage, fuel, and other amenities. Speed limit in Deep Cove is 5 knots.

⑬ **Deep Cove Public Wharf.** The dock is 145 feet long, and is within walking distance of grocery stores, restaurants, live theater, and other facilities. Day use moorage for boats up to 36 feet, purchase hourly moorage tickets from the ticket machine at the wharf; no overnight moorage.

Deep Cove DAA Anchorage. A designated anchorage area (DAA) with 4 mooring buoys is located in Deep Cove to limit the amount of time boats can remain in Deep Cove. Anchoring on the hook in Deep Cove is not permitted. Boaters need to register and pay a mooring fee to moor on a buoy; maximum stay is 72 hours. Buoys are limited to boats 40 feet or less. Apply for a permit at least one week prior to your arrival; go online at nvrc.ca/node/212504 to submit a request. Proof of $2 million liability insurance is required. Permits are processed during business hours 8:00 a.m. to 4:30 p.m., Monday-Friday. For questions, contact the Park Ranger at (604) 671-7960.

⑬ **Deep Cove North Shore Marina.** 2890 Panorama Drive, North Vancouver, BC V7G 1V6; (604) 929-1251; info@deepcovemarina.com; www.deepcovemarina.com. Open all year, gasoline and diesel at the fuel dock, limited guest moorage in unoccupied slips and side-tie. Call ahead. Facilities include washrooms, showers and laundry. Deep Cove Village with restaurants and shopping is located a mile to the west.

Bedwell Bay. Bedwell Bay has the best anchorage in Indian Arm. The bay is sheltered from southerly winds. The anchorage can be crowded during peak season. Speed limit 5 knots.

Twin Islands and Racoon Island. The larger of the Twin Islands has a dinghy float on its east side, and picnic and sanitary facilities ashore. Anchorage offshore is quite deep (between 80 and 150 feet). Twin Islands and Racoon Island are used by kayakers and canoeists who pull their craft ashore.

Granite Falls. Granite Falls, the largest of the falls entering Indian Arm, tumbles off a cliff along the east bank. A small day dock makes access easy and serves campsites ashore. Anchorage is fair just offshore. The climb up the cliff is good exercise for cramped muscles. Because of the questionable anchoring bottom, overnight anchoring is not recommended if outflow winds are expected.

Wigwam Inn. The Wigwam Inn, at the head of Indian Arm, was a luxury resort whose rich history goes back to 1906. Today it is a Royal Vancouver Yacht Club outstation. RVYC members only. Burrard Yacht Club and Deep Cove Yacht Club have outstations nearby—members only, no reciprocals.

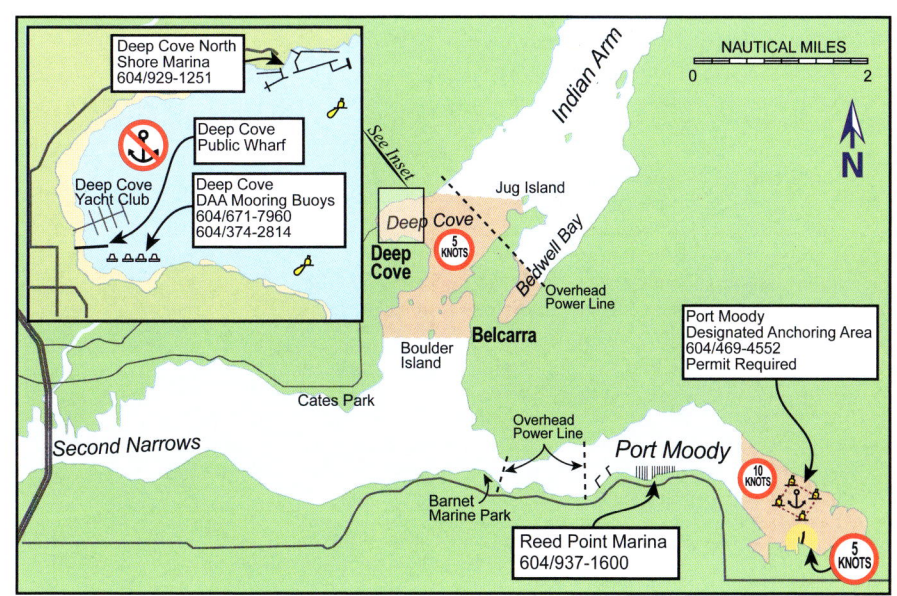

Indian Arm & Port Moody

VANCOUVER B.C. & SUNSHINE COAST

POINT ATKINSON TO HORSESHOE BAY

Caulfeild Cove. Caulfeild Cove is a tiny bight, protected from nearly all winds and seas, tucked into the shoreline just east of Point Atkinson. A 52-foot public float lies along the east side of the cove with 6 feet of depth alongside.

LOCAL KNOWLEDGE

TIDE-RIPS: The waters just off Point Atkinson can be very rough, especially on a large ebb flowing against a fresh onshore wind. Often, a course well to seaward is called for, and even that can be heavy going. Point Atkinson is well known to Vancouver boaters, who give this area great respect.

Point Atkinson. Point Atkinson is the north entrance to Burrard Inlet.

Eagle Harbour. Eagle Harbour is the home of the Eagle Harbour Yacht Club. No guest moorage.

Fishermans Cove. Fishermans Cove, the home of West Vancouver Yacht Club, is filled with Thunderbird Marina. West Vancouver Yacht Club has some guest moorage for members of reciprocal clubs.

Important: Enter on the northwest side of the 39-meter island and Eagle Island, leaving the flashing red light to starboard. A "false entrance" between the 39-meter island and Eagle Island could put you in real trouble.

The passage from Eagle Harbour east of Eagle Island is shown clearly on ENC chart CA570009 but not on smaller scale ENC chart CA470072.

The daymark in the northern mouth of the passage east of Eagle Island should be left to starboard by craft approaching from the north side of Eagle Island. Vessels northbound from Eagle Harbour should leave the daymark to port.

⑭ **Thunderbird Marina.** 5776 Marine Drive, West Vancouver, BC V7W 2S2; (604) 921-7434; thunderbird@thunderbirdmarine.com; www.thunderbirdmarine.com. Permanent moorage only. Haulout to 25 tons for boats to 50 feet. Do-it-yourself or use trades people boatyard. Thunderbird Marine Supplies carries marine supplies and hardware, open Tuesday through Sunday. Marine electrical, electronics, and other marine services onsite.

⑭ **Fishermans Cove Marine Fuels.** 5908 Marine Drive, West Vancouver, BC V7W 2S2; (604) 921-7333; Gas and diesel. Convenience store with supplies, snacks, and ice cream.

HOWE SOUND

Howe Sound is a 23-mile long, deep-water inlet off the Strait of Georgia, with Squamish at its head. About 12 miles from Vancouver, Howe Sound is the "backyard" for Vancouver area boaters. Stunning Coast Range mountains surround Howe Sound.

Most boaters visit the communities and anchorages in the southern portion of Howe Sound. The town of Gibsons, on the west shore, is served by ferry from Horseshoe Bay, and offers two marinas and a fuel dock. Good restaurants, fun gift shops, a grocery and farmers market are available in Gibsons.

The village of Snug Cove on Bowen Island is another delightful destination with boutiques, pubs and cafes, two grocery stores and hiking opportunities. Bowen Island is served by ferry at Snug Cove. Smaller marinas dot the eastern shore of Howe Sound, frequented by runabouts and sport fish boats.

The south end of Gambier Island has several anchorages, including Port Graves, with room for a large number of boats. Two yacht club outstations are on the north side of Gambier Island. Keats Island, near Gibsons, offers anchorage and moorage at Plumper Cove Marine Park, with upland park areas. On the eastern shore of Howe Sound, Porteau Cove has a lovely beach and detached 60-foot Park float and one mooring buoy.

Continuing north, the population becomes sparse in a wilderness setting with few anchorages. The water turns emerald green north of Anvil Island with stunning views of the Coast Range mountains. Glimpse views of the Sea-to-Sky highway, carved into the granite outcroppings, give testament to this wilderness environment. "**Mariners Rest**," an islet off Mariners Rest Point, is a Provincially designated burial site for ashes at sea, look for the silver cross and anchor on the islet. Ashes are not buried on the islet, but rather at sea nearby, going ashore is not permitted.

In the distant northwest shore of Howe Sound are several large pulp and paper operations. Log booming areas fill the waters in front of these operations. Watch for considerable drift that may be present in Howe Sound.

The town of Squamish is at the head of Howe Sound. Squamish is a vibrant town that has attracted young families, and brings in tourists seeking hiking opportunities and special attractions like the Sea to Sky Gondola near town, and Whistler Blackcomb, a world-class ski resort, located farther north. Moorage is available at the Squamish Port Authority docks and at the adjacent Squamish Yacht Club docks, where guests are welcome from just about any yacht club. Squamish has excellent pubs and cafes, groceries, hardware and other necessities.

⑮ **Horseshoe Bay.** Horseshoe Bay is the eastern terminus of ferries serving the Gulf Islands, Sunshine Coast, and Vancouver Island. Sewell's Marina, a breakwater-protected public marina, is located to the west of the ferry docks. Horseshoe Bay is very active with BC Ferries traffic and with small fish boats coming and going. There is limited transient moorage and no anchoring. Boaters transiting this area are urged to use caution because of the steady procession of large ferry boats.

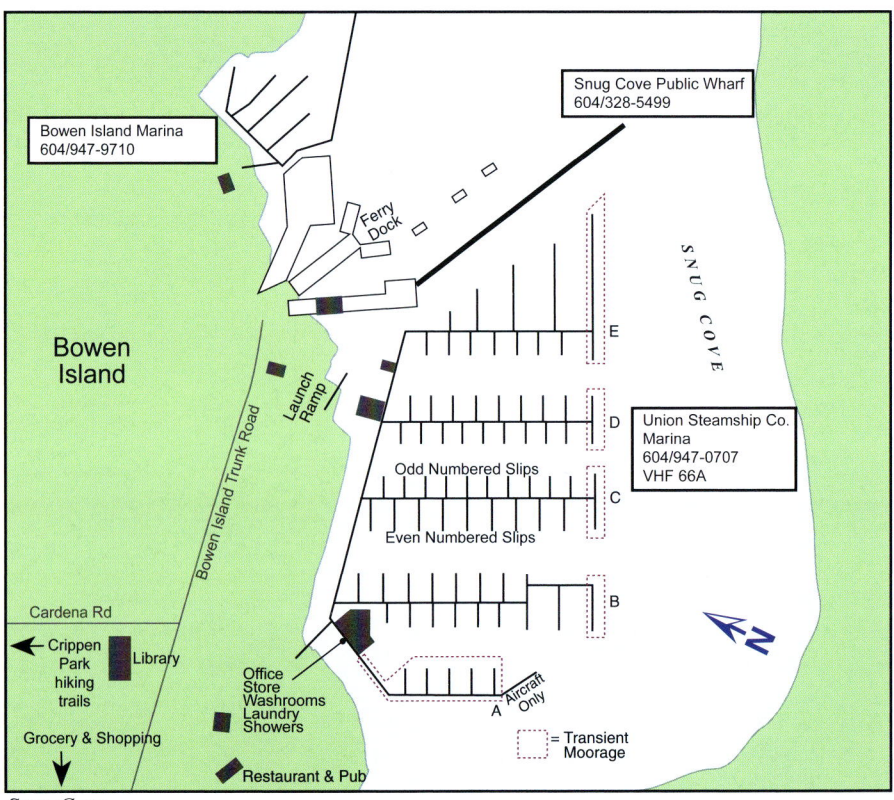

Snug Cove

⑮ **Sewell's Marina Ltd.** 6409 Bay St., West Vancouver, BC V7W 3H5; (604) 921-3474; info@sewellsmarina.com; www.sewellsmarina.com. Open all year, gasoline and diesel fuel, ice, limited 15 & 30 amp power, concrete launch ramp, frozen bait. Limited guest moorage, mostly for boats 45 feet and under, call ahead. Fishing charters. Restaurants, groceries, and a post office nearby.

⑮ **Horseshoe Bay Public Wharf**. (604) 925-7129. Guest float, approximately 100 feet, on the south side of the wharf for short-term tie-up, maximum 4 hour stay. A float on the east end of the wharf is a 10-minute pick-up, drop-off area.

⑯ **Sunset Marina Ltd.** 34 Sunset Beach, West Vancouver, BC V7W 2T7; (604) 921-7476; sunsetmarina@shawlink.ca; www.sunsetmarinaltd.com. Open from March 1 to October 15. Gasoline, guest moorage to 24 feet, haulouts to 25 feet (power boats only), repairs, launch ramp with long term parking, washrooms. They carry marine supplies, tackle, and bait.

Bowen Island. Bowen Island is served by ferry from Horseshoe Bay. Snug Cove has a public wharf and two marinas. It's a wonderful destination with shops, a number of good restaurants, and a 600-acre park. A co-op store up the hill from the harbor has provisions. On the northeast corner of Bowen Island, Columbine Bay and Smugglers Cove offer good anchorage. Galbraith Bay has a public float. Anchorage in Bowen Bay and Tunstall Bay.

⑰ **Snug Cove**. Snug Cove on Bowen Island is a favorite stop. It has a public dock and two marinas, and is served by ferry from Horseshoe Bay. From there you can take a bus to downtown Vancouver. Or take the seasonal foot ferry that runs directly to Granville Island.

The commercial village at Bowen Island has several boutiques, restaurants, grocery store, bakery/coffee house, pharmacy, wine store and liquor agency, and a couple of pubs. Bowen Island residents are artistic, interesting, and eclectic, and the local shopping reflects the character of the population.

Pubs: Visit Bowen Island Pub located in an impressive building up the hill, and don't miss the Copper Spirit Distillery with a selection of locally crafted vodka, gin and whisky.

Dock Dance: The annual Dock Dance, a benefit dance for the local volunteer firefighters, is held in early August. Participants take over the dock at Snug Cove for a party that literally rocks the dock with music and dancing.

Golf: The 9-hole par 35 Bowen Island Golf Club is challenging and beautiful, with greens that are devilishly hard to read. Call (604) 947-4653. Union Steamship Co. provides transportation for its guests.

Ferry Noise: Ferry propellers make underwater noise that can sometimes be heard throughout Snug Cove. If you hear what you think is an onboard pump cycling ON whenever a ferry is at the dock, realize that it may actually be noise transmitted from the ferry's props to your hull.

⑰ **Bowen Island Marina.** 375 Cardena Dr., RR 1 A-1, Bowen Island, BC V0N 1G0; (604) 947-9710; www.bowen-island.com. Moorage for boats on an annual basis. No overnight transient moorage. Located on the starboard side when entering Snug Cove. Shops with ice cream, pies, pastries, tacos, gifts and kayak rentals.

⑰ **Snug Cove Public Wharf.** (604) 328-5499. This wide concrete dock, with 350 feet of space, is next to the ferry landing in Snug Cove and exposed to ferry wash. No water or electricity. First-come, first-served in areas that are not reserved for load/unload and water taxis. Some areas are reserved for monthly moorage from mid-September to mid-June. Self-registration and payment at the top of the ramp on the pier. Day use and overnight stays.

⑰ **Union Steamship Co. Marina**. P.O. Box 250, Bowen Island, BC V0N 1G0; (604) 947-0707; marina@ussc.ca; www.unionsteamshipmarina.com. Monitors VHF 66A. Open all year, ample guest moorage; call for reservations. Pumpout, 30 & 50 amp power, a boaters' lounge with washrooms and showers, laundry, free Wi-Fi. The washroom and shower building, one of the finest on the coast, also includes a comfortable lounge with big screen TV and a computer station, all near the showers and laundry.

This is an excellent place to stop. Rondy Dike, an architect by training, and his wife Dorothy have restored the Union Steamship Co. landing into a wonderful destination resort. Their daughter, Oydis Dike Nickle, now manages the resort and marina. The staff is attentive and standing by to help. A lovely boardwalk leads from the marina, connecting several shops, cafes, and Doc Morgan's Pub & Restaurant. Easy walking trails are found through the adjacent 600-acre park. It seems that everyone who stays at Union Steamship has a good report. Reservations recommended.

The marina has 8 cottages available on the hillside.

Mannion Bay. Located north of Snug Cove, with anchorage in the northwest and southwest areas of this large bay. There are a number of private buoys in the northern part of the bay. The southern part is shallow. Most of the shoreline is a voluntary no-anchor zone to protect eelgrass. The zone is marked by 8 cylindrical buoys. Boaters are encouraged to anchor outside the marked eelgrass area. There is reasonable protection from southeast winds in the southwest portion of the bay; however, anchorage in Mannion Bay is rolly from ferry traffic and when the inflow or outflow winds are strong in the channel. Anchorage is limited to 48 hours.

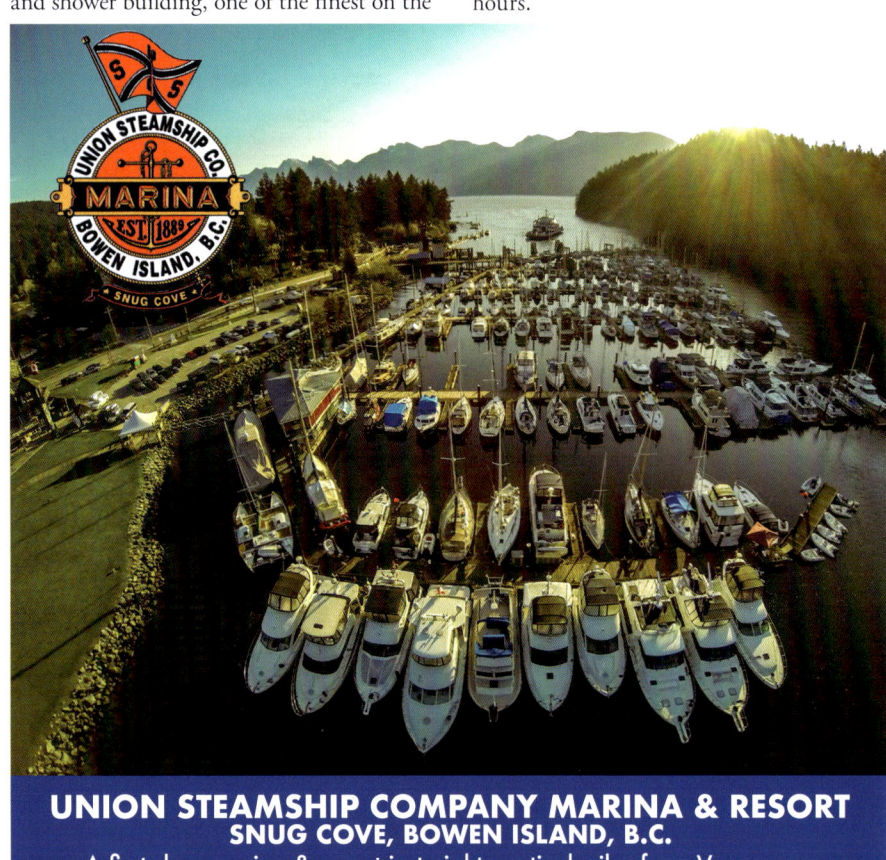

UNION STEAMSHIP COMPANY MARINA & RESORT
SNUG COVE, BOWEN ISLAND, B.C.
A first-class marina & resort just eight nautical miles from Vancouver.
Guest moorage to 210', Doc Morgan's Restaurant, Chandlery & Gift Shop.
www.ussc.ca 604.947.0707 VHF 66A marina@ussc.ca

VANCOUVER B.C. & SUNSHINE COAST

See Area Map Page 277 - Maps Not for Navigation

Plumber Cove with its Marine Park dock and mooring buoys is a great place to stay.

Mount Gardner Park Public Dock. A Bowen Island municipal dock; (604) 947-4255. Galbraith Bay, northwest side of Bowen Island. Has 110 feet of space for loading and unloading, max 15 minutes.

Gambier Island. Gambier Island has three significant inlets, all opening from the south: West Bay, Centre Bay, and Port Graves. A smaller inlet, Halkett Bay, is at the southeast corner of the island. Thornbrough Bay, on the west side of the island, has a public dock. We are told that boats often tie to log booms on the western (Port Mellon) side of the island. In the summertime the water around Gambier Island warms to swimming temperatures. We know, we tried it.

Gambier Harbour Public Wharf has 100 feet of dock space.

Burrard Yacht Club and Thunderbird Yacht Club have outstations at Eakins Point at the north end of Gambier Island. Members only, no reciprocals.

West Bay. Favor the west shore when entering West Bay to avoid the reef extending from the eastern shore. West Bay once was a major log booming site and the bottom is apt to be foul with old cable and equipment.

Anchorage in West Bay is in at least two places. The first is on the north side of the reef, close to the reef. The second is in the bight at the northeast corner of the bay. Easy anchoring depths are close to shore in this bight, but because of real estate development, you probably shouldn't run a stern-tie to shore.

Centre Bay. Most of Centre Bay is deep, but the little bight on the west side, just inside the entrance, has 18- to 24-foot anchoring depths, and is delightful. Royal Vancouver and West Vancouver yacht clubs have outstations in Centre Bay. The docks belonging to the Centre Bay Yacht Station are at the head of the bay.

Port Graves. Port Graves is definitely the most scenic of Gambier Island's inlets and has good anchoring depths at the head. Because of real estate development in West Bay and Centre Bay, Port Graves is the best anchoring spot on the island. A small float at the public wharf, located at the head of the bay, is used for dinghy tie-up. The marked yellow side-tie is reserved for a water taxi. The adjacent floats belong to a Christian camp and are private. The wharf is under the auspices of the Sunshine Coast Regional District (604) 885-6802. A 2.5-mile trail near the head of the wharf leads to Lost Lake.

Halkett Bay. Halkett Bay at the southeast corner of Gambier Island has one mooring buoy, labeled B.C., Parks, and has room for 4 to 5 boats to anchor; beware that chop can be somewhat active in southerly winds. In 2018, 5 stern-tie pins, with chain, were installed along the western shoreline within the park boundary by BC Parks and the BC Marine Parks Forever Society. Approach along the east shoreline as rocks lie on the west side of the bay. A dinghy dock provides access to Halkett Bay Marine Park with pit toilets, primitive campsites, and trails.

Halkett Bay Fircom Dock. A Sunshine Coast Regional District dock (604) 885-6800. Fircom dock is located on the southeast side of Gambier Island, along the west shore south of Halkett Bay. The 52-foot float is available on a first-come, first-serve basis for 24 hours at no charge. No water, no power. The Fircom Market, located upland, sells fresh produce on Friday evenings and Saturday mornings, seasonally.

Brigade Bay. Brigade Bay is on the eastern shore of Gambier Island. Anne Vipond, reporting in Pacific Yachting, suggests that because of deep water fairly close to shore, a stern anchor be set toward the beach and the main anchor set offshore.

Thornbrough Bay. The New Brighton Public Wharf in Thornbrough Bay has 390 feet of dock space.

⑱ **Plumper Cove Marine Park.** The Park is in a cove formed by Keats Island and two small nearby islands. The park has 400 feet of dock space and approximately 7 mooring buoys for boats 13 meters or less. No rafting. Park mooring buoys are large yellow cylinder shaped; other moorings are private. Field Correspondent Jim Norris reports wave action at the dock from passing boats and BC Ferries. The bay has anchorage for several boats. A rock, marked by a yellow buoy, lies a dozen yards off the dock.

Porteau Cove. Porteau Cove is on the east shore of Howe Sound in Montagu Channel at latitude 49°33'N. The park is open all year; toilets, launch ramp, walk-in campsites, hiking trails and a picnic area. Tiny Porteau Cove itself has a 60-foot mooring float, not connected to land, and 1 mooring buoy. Two shallow-water buoys near the float mark shallow areas and are not mooring buoys. Sunken ships and man-made reefs provide excellent scuba diving. White caution buoys mark the yellow-buoyed diving area. Watch your depths; some of the cove dries at low tide. Anchoring within the park is prohibited.

⑲ **Lions Bay Marine Ltd.** 60 Lions Bay Ave., P.O. Box 262, Lions Bay, BC V0N 2E0; (604) 921-7510; www.lionsbaymarina.com. Open all year, except closed December 15 to January 15. In winter, closed on Tuesday and Wednesday. Gasoline, diesel and propane available. In summer they have transient moorage for boats up to 32 feet on 400 feet of dock space. Haulout to 30 feet (powerboats only) with repairs on site. Groceries and a post office are nearby.

⑳ **Squamish.** www.squamish.ca. The town of Squamish, pop. 20,000, is nestled against the Coast Range mountains at the north end of Howe Sound, between Vancouver and Whistler. Since the 2010 Winter Olympics at nearby Whistler, Squamish has become a vibrant town with young families and outdoor enthusiasts. A bus transit service (604-892-3567) runs to Whistler and the Sea to Sky Gondola, or you can rent a car. The Sea to Sky Gondola is about 2.5 miles from the docks and the views from the top are outstanding. At the top, a suspension bridge leads over a canyon to a trail with scenic overviews. There are many hiking and rock climbing opportunities near and around the gondola base station. The Squamish shopping district is about one-quarter mile from the docks where you will

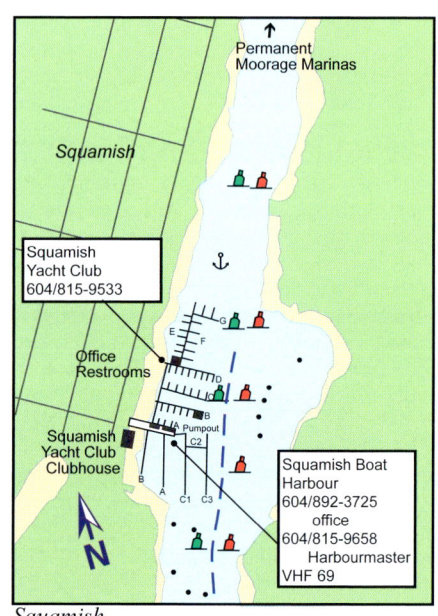

Squamish

find excellent pubs and restaurants. There are two grocery stores within a half-mile walk of the docks. A Saturday Market is held in a parking lot at the north end of Junction Park, April through October.

Summertime inflow winds usually begin between 11:00 a.m. and noon. By 2:00 p.m., the wind can make landing tricky. Best to go to Squamish in the early morning. The Harbour Authority docks are your best bet for moorage or the adjacent yacht club for reciprocal moorage from any yacht club. The Blue Heron Marina (604-898-3733) and Sea To Sky Marina (604-892-9282) are private permanent moorage marinas located farther up the channel beyond the Harbour Authority and yacht club. On a recent visit, we saw a sailboat anchored in the channel just north of the yacht club docks.

Transit Mamquam Blind Channel between the head of Howe Sound and the Squamish marinas with caution, preferably on a mid or high tide. The channel has a lighted range. On entry, follow the range, favoring the starboard side until abeam Stawamus River, then favor the port (west) side of the channel through the charted quarter mile shallow area. Stay close to the piling painted green/white/green at the charted shallowest area. The channel in front of the public dock and yacht club is marked with private red and green spar buoys

⑳ **Harbour Authority of Squamish Boat Harbour.** P.O. Box 97, Squamish, BC V8B 0A1; (604) 892-3725 or (604) 815-9658 Harbourmaster. VHF 69. Open all year. Located near downtown Squamish next to the Squamish Yacht Club. 80 feet of side-tie summer guest, transient moorage; maximum boat length 55 feet. Pumpout, 15 and 30 amp power, washrooms, showers, garbage, and boat launch. First-come, first-served; call ahead to check availability. Expect a relaxed, informal experience. They don't get many visitor boats.

⑳ **Squamish Yacht Club.** 37778 Logger's Lane, P.O. Box 1681, Squamish, BC V8B 0B2; (604) 815-9533, yacht club port captain; reciprocals are available for just about any yacht club, must display yacht club burgee. Guest moorage on docks D17-19 (the yellow zone) on a first-come, first-serve basis; call ahead to check available space. Maximum boat length 45 feet. 15, 20 and 30 amp power, water, restrooms, showers and garbage. Guest key assigned. Docks are within walking distance to downtown.

Shoal Channel (The Gap). The Gap is a sandy shoal with a least depth of approximately 5 feet at zero tide, between Keats Island and Steep Bluff, at the mouth of Howe Sound. Although waves off the Strait of Georgia tend to break on this shoal, if you know your draft and the state of the tide you can approach Gibsons from the strait via The Gap and have no problems—unless it's rough, and then you should go around Keats Island. Stay mid-channel. Boulders line the edges of the passage. The distance to Thrasher Rock, outside Gabriola Pass in the Gulf Islands, is approximately 16 miles. Use Chart 3463 for the crossing, changing to Chart 3526 as you approach Popham Island. This approach, with Howe Sound islands backed up by the Coast Range mountains, is magnificent.

Correspondent Pat Shera says you can cross Shoal Channel at anything but low tides using a natural range. Keep the FlG (flashing green) light located east of the Gibsons Harbour entrance just barely visible in line with the base of Steep Bluff in the foreground. This transit takes you across the shoals with a minimum depth of 7 feet at zero tide. Travel along the 20- to 30-foot depth contour from either side until this natural range lines up, then stay on the range until you reach 20- to 30-foot depths on the other side. Not recommended when a strong southerly is blowing.

㉑ **Gibsons.** Gibsons is a charming seaside village, a good place to take the day off and stretch your legs. The lower Gibsons downtown area is filled with shops, restaurants, and pubs ranging from elegant to funky. The Sunshine Coast Museum & Archives is excellent. Hours are 10:30 a.m. to 4:30 p.m., Tuesday through Saturday.

The nearest supermarket is SuperValu in upper Gibsons. You'll need a ride. Be sure to see Fong's Market & Gifts in lower Gibsons, one of the more unexpected places on the coast. They have many of the essential grocery items, a good selection of Asian foods and a broad array of bowls, tea pots and other imported items. Stop by Sandy's Bake Shoppe for pies, bread, pastries and pasties. Mike's Artisan Gelato is another favorite in town, one of the best gelato selections outside of Vancouver. The Gibsons Market is just up from Gibsons Marina and sells local produce, meats, and cheese; an aquarium is located upstairs in this two-story building.

As you enter the marina complex at Gibsons, you will see The Gibsons Landing Harbour Authority public dock to the north. Gibsons Marina and Fuel Dock are ahead and to the south. There are several private docks and a private marina behind the breakwater at Gibsons. A shoal extends from the shore between the public dock and the fuel dock. Approach each moorage directly from seaward.

Some boats anchor outside the breakwater and to the east of the pier, in front of the townsite. This is unprotected and suitable only in settled weather.

Sea Cavalcade: The Sea Cavalcade festival, featuring food, dancing, fireworks, and other events, is held each July. See www.seacavalcade.ca. For information about other events and activities, call the Gibsons Visitor Centre at (604) 886-2374.

㉑ **Gibsons Landing Harbour Authority.** P.O. Box 527, Gibsons, BC V0N 1V0; (604) 886-8017; glha@telus.net; www.gibsonsha.org. Monitors VHF 66A. Open all year, guest moorage, 15, 30, 50 and 100 amp power but mostly 15 amp with 30 amp receptacles on most docks. Three-ton crane, washrooms and showers, laundry, pumpout, garbage

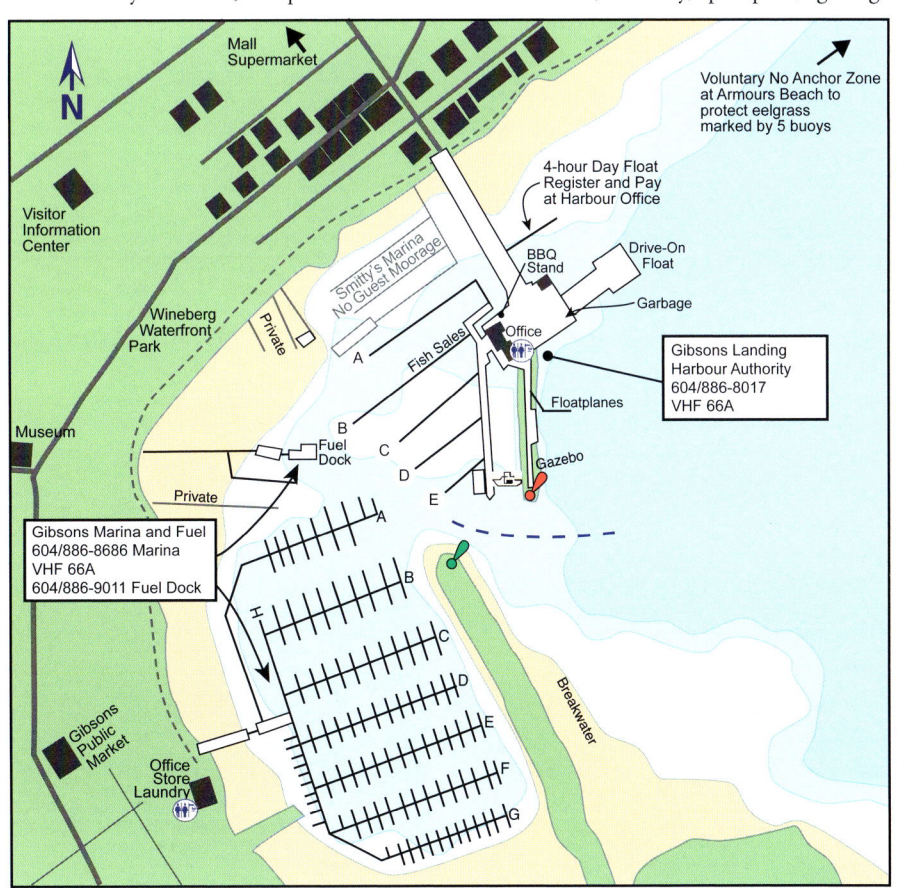

Gibsons

VANCOUVER B.C. & SUNSHINE COAST

Gibsons harbour has fuel and guest moorage in two marinas, all within walking distance of town.

dumpster. Docks inside the breakwater are first-come, first-served; call ahead to check on available space. Fairways are narrow, fender both sides of your vessel.

The public wharf has been upgraded with beautiful offices, improved shoreside amenities, and surveillance television security. Much of the moorage space is taken by permanent tenants, but they work to fit visitors in. Reservations accepted for vessels over 50 feet, which are assigned to the concrete float outside the harbour breakwater, located on the northeast side of the pier. Water on the float. A year-round 80-foot long float for short-term stays up to 4 hours is on the shore side of the wharf outside the breakwater protected harbour, adjacent to the large vessel reserved moorage. Register and pay at the Harbour Authority Office.

㉑ **Gibsons Marina and Fuel Dock**. P.O. Box 1520, Gibsons, BC V0N 1V0; (604) 886-8686 (marina), (604) 886-9011 (fuel dock). Monitors VHF 66A. Moorage primarily for 26- to 40-foot vessels; maximum vessel 80 feet. Anchoring is possible north of the harbour, but boat wakes may keep you rocking. Open all year except Christmas Day. Reservations accepted. 15 and some 30 amp power, free Wi-Fi, washrooms, showers, laundry, and a chandlery. Pumpout, recycling, and concrete launch ramp. The fuel dock has gasoline and diesel. The store on the fuel dock has lubricants, snacks, and ice cream.

GOWER POINT TO SECHELT INLET

From Howe Sound to Pender Harbour the coast is largely a barren run. The exceptions are Buccaneer Bay, Secret Cove, Smuggler Cove, and to a lesser extent, Halfmoon Bay. When the weather gets up, the going can be wet and slow; but with a weather eye, the passages can be easy.

Trail Bay. A rock breakwater protects a small moorage at **Selma Park** on the south shore of Trail Bay. We once waited out a nasty southeasterly, riding on the hook in this hideout.

Welcome Passage. Welcome Passage separates South Thormanby Island from Sechelt Peninsula and is used by boats of all types bound up or down the Sunshine Coast. The passage west of Merry Island is deep and easily navigated.

LOCAL KNOWLEDGE

STRONG CURRENTS: Currents run to 3 knots at the north end of Welcome Passage and 2 knots off Merry Island at the south end. When wind and current oppose each other, the waters can be rough and uncomfortable. Watch for drift.

Halfmoon Bay. Sunshine Coast Regional District facility (604) 885-2261. A public pier, with a 75-foot float, is at the head of Halfmoon Bay. It is very shallow on the land end of the mooring float. Side-tie available on the outside of the float. Onshore, you can walk about a half block through a residential neighborhood to an area with a store (a longtime landmark) and a cafe with fresh bakery goods. Henry Hightower, a resident of Halfmoon Bay, provided us with the following insider's view of the facilities and anchorage possibilities. He writes:

"The store at the Halfmoon Bay government wharf is well stocked, and has the best bacon and free-range eggs, as well as fresh and packaged meat, fruit, vegetables and staples, fishing gear, beer, wine and liquor, convenience store stuff, and a gift shop." After visiting, we agree.

If a strong wind is blowing or forecast, there will almost certainly be at least one tug with a log boom waiting for favorable weather, positioned across the open south side of Priestland Cove between the shore and the charted rocks. There is quite a bit of room to anchor behind its shelter.

Priestland Cove is southeast of the government dock.

㉒ **Smuggler Cove.** Smuggler Cove has a narrow entrance through the rocks, but opens to a beautiful anchorage that is protected from most weather. We have received reports that the cove is not protected from northwesterlies. First-timers should study the charts carefully before entering the cove to avoid rocky shoals extending from the south shore. Inside is Smuggler Cove Marine Park, which has no facilities for boaters or campers, but does have trails through the park's 457 acres of woodlands. A favorite activity is paddling a kayak or dinghy among the little islets and coves. Reduce swinging room by taking one of many stern-ties (38), with lengths of chain, set in the rock ashore. Additional stern-ties were added in 2018 and old-stern-tie installations upgraded by BC Parks and the BC Marine Parks Forever Society.

Story has it that Larry Kelly, "King of the Smugglers," hid unemployed Chinese workers in the late 1800's and transported them into the U.S. for a fee. Official entry was forbidden at that time. During Prohibition (1920-1933) the cove was used by rum runners.

No Discharge Zone. Gray water okay.

Buccaneer Bay. Buccaneer Bay is between North Thormanby and South Thormanby Islands, and has a beautiful white sand beach at the south end and west side.

Be careful to enter Buccaneer Bay by leaving the Tattenham Ledge Light Buoy Q51 to port. The buoy is well north of South Thormanby Island, but it marks the end of Tattenham Ledge and should be respected.

Once in Buccaneer Bay, anchor in 30 to

Gibsons offers a nice selection of interesting cafes, a bakery, and yogurt shop.

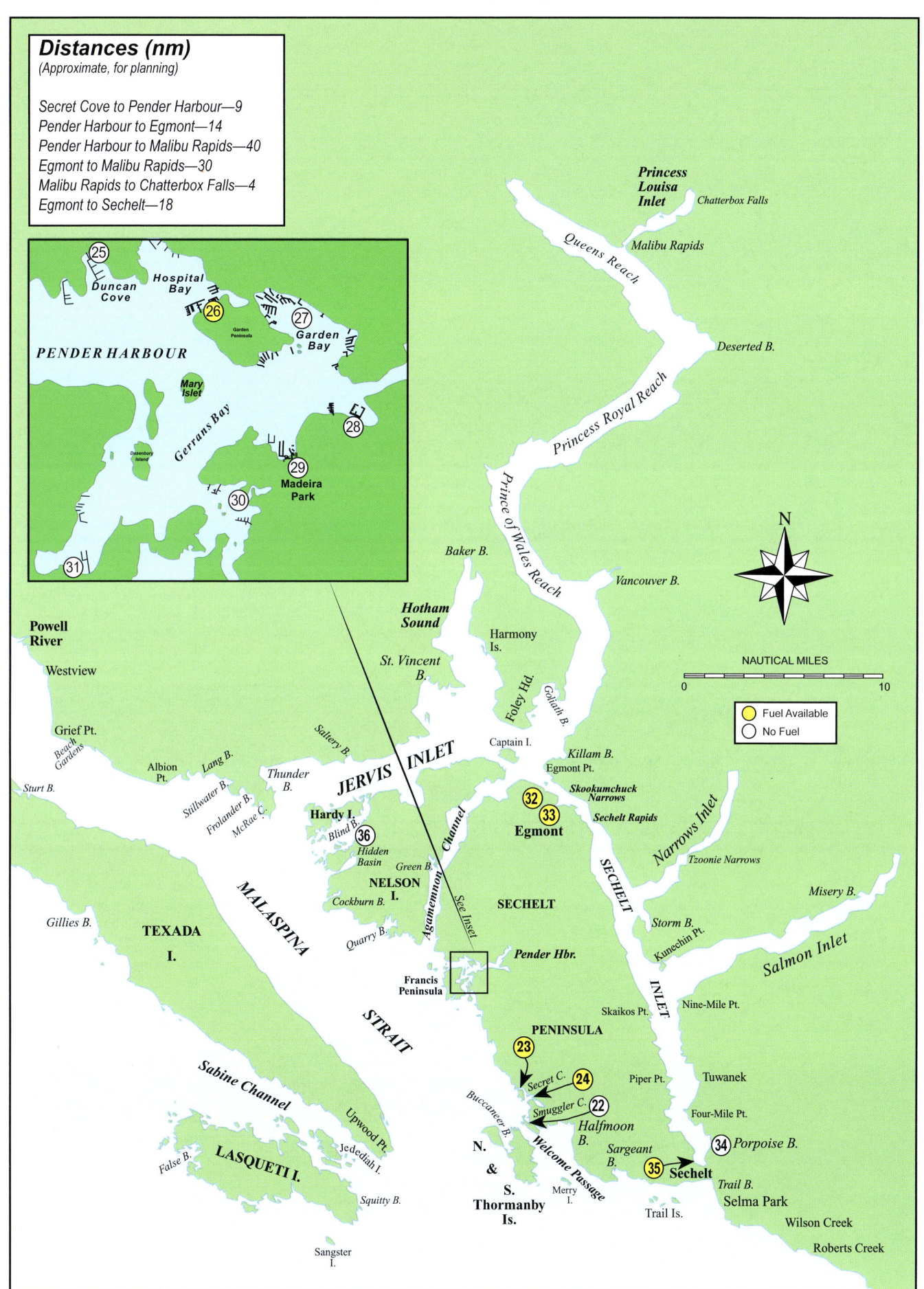

Reference Only – Not for Navigation   VANCOUVER B.C. & SUNSHINE COAST

Distances (nm)
(Approximate, for planning)

Secret Cove to Pender Harbour—9
Pender Harbour to Egmont—14
Pender Harbour to Malibu Rapids—40
Egmont to Malibu Rapids—30
Malibu Rapids to Chatterbox Falls—4
Egmont to Sechelt—18

Sunshine Coast and Jervis Inlet

40 feet behind the Surrey Islands or in 20 to 30 feet in Water Bay. The Surrey Islands anchorage is particularly cozy and attractive.

A private moorage is in Water Bay. During the day small boat traffic to and from the dock will rock you some, but it dies down at night. The dock is posted for loading/unloading.

Watching your depths, you can also snug up to the shoaling waters off Gill Beach at the south end of the bay. In a southeasterly, you'll get some wind but no seas. There's no protection from a northwesterly, however. One year, we anchored in calm conditions only to have a northwesterly come in around midnight and ruin our night's sleep. It was pretty bouncy.

Secret Cove. Secret Cove has three branches, each with excellent weather protection and easy anchoring depths. Unfortunately, the Secret Cove bottom is notorious for anchor dragging in strong winds, so be sure you are well set if you do anchor.

Enter Secret Cove north of a light on a small rock in the middle of the entrance. Inside are the three arms. The southern arm has a very narrow entrance but adequate depths inside. This arm is lined with private docks that restrict swinging room in the middle. You can find room to anchor, however, off the Royal Vancouver Yacht Club outstation docks about halfway in. The center arm has Buccaneer Marina. The north arm is occupied almost entirely by Secret Cove Marina, but there is still plenty of room for anchoring, using stern-ties to shore if needed; a few chains and ropes are found along the west shore. A public float is adjacent to Secret Cove Marina.

㉓ **Secret Cove Public Wharf.** Managed by the Harbour Authority of Pender Harbour (604) 883-2234. Dock has 144 feet of moorage with 20 amp power and water. Plans are in the works to upgrade power for 2023. Self-registration, payment box located on the wharf. Primarily used by local commercial fish boats and the Thormanby water taxi.

㉓ **Secret Cove Marina.** 5411 Secret Cove Road, Halfmoon Bay, BC V7Z 1B7; (604) 885-3533; info@secretcovemarina.com; www.secretcovemarina.com. Monitors VHF 66A. Request reservations online. Open Victoria Day weekend through Canadian Thanksgiving. This is a full service marina in the north arm of Secret Cove, with gasoline and diesel fuel, guest moorage, 15, 30, & 50 amp power, washrooms, clean showers, liquor agency, restaurant, store with groceries and nice selection of beverages, gift items, branded clothing, block and cube ice, boating and fishing supplies, Wi-Fi. Kayak and paddleboard rentals. This marina resort is well managed and continues to receive excellent reviews. Kendra and Andreas Tize purchased the marina in 2021.

The La Bettolina restaurant is delightful, offering farm to table dining, open Thursday through Monday; call (778) 888-4702 for reservations.

㉔ **Buccaneer Marina & Resort Ltd.** 5535 Sans Souci Rd., Halfmoon Bay, BC V0N 1Y2; (604) 885-7888; buccaneermarina@telus.net; www.buccaneermarina.com. Open all year, gasoline and diesel fuel, limited guest moorage with 15 amp power, chandlery, engine and outboard repairs (weekdays), haulout to 40 feet, paved launch ramp with long term parking. Fishing tackle and one of the few places with live herring bait. Water taxi to Thormanby Islands. Located in the center arm of Secret Cove. Owned and operated by the Mercer family since 1968. Jerry Mercer passed away in 2022, he will be missed.

Bargain Bay. Although its entry is actually off the Strait of Georgia, Bargain Bay is properly a part of the complex of bays that make up Pender Harbour. Enter between Edgecomb Island to the east and Francis Peninsula to the west. The entry is easy and open until you are part way inside, where a drying reef and an underwater rock extend from the west shore to the middle of the channel. Another underwater rock lies off the east shore. Pass between the two rocks and proceed into the bay.

Bargain Narrows, called Canoe Pass, is a drying channel spanned by a bridge with 4 meters (13.12 feet) vertical clearance. The pass runs between Bargain Bay and Gerrans Bay inside Pender Harbour.

---

secretcove MARINA

The Sunshine Coast's best kept secret for moorage, fuel, dining & supplies . . .

Marina
visitor moorage up to 150', with water, power

Fuel Dock

Services
showers, recycling
Gigabit Wifi

Store
B.C. liquor agency
groceries, meats & produce
marine supplies
hardware & tackle,
baked goods, organic coffee
books & magazines
charts, clothing
giftware

Close to Smugglers Cove & the beaches of Thormanby Island

monitoring VHF channel **66A** @secretcovemarina
www.secretcovemarina.com • info@secretcovemarina.com
1-866-885-3533
5411 Secret Cove Road, Halfmoon Bay, BC
reservations recommended in summer months

The Upper Deck Restaurant
Upscale Italian dining by Chefs Adam Pegg and Anthony Santi

Pender Harbour has anchorage and many marinas with guest moorage.

Hospital Bay Public Wharf in Pender Harbour has transient moorage.

PENDER HARBOUR

Pender Harbour is a natural stopover for boats heading north or south in the Strait of Georgia. For northbound boats, it's just the right distance for a day's run from Nanaimo, Silva Bay, or Howe Sound. For boats southbound from Desolation Sound, it's a good place to prepare for the long, exposed legs across the Strait of Georgia or down the Sunshine Coast. Boats bound to or from Princess Louisa Inlet often use Pender Harbour both going and coming.

Pender Harbour has good marinas, good anchorages, good eating, and good shopping. It has fuel and a haulout and repair facility. Diving services available through Wet Dock Divers (604-740-5969). The harbor is nestled against steep mountains; the scenery is beautiful. It's a good place for walking and hiking. If you carry trail bikes, the Madeira Park Public Wharf has a map of the nearby Suncoaster Trail, built and maintained by volunteers.

Pender Harbour is not a single large bay. It is a complex of coves, each with its own personality. Duncan Cove has a marina resort along the north shore. Gerrans Bay has marinas and anchorage. Hospital Bay and Garden Bay have marinas, fuel, shopping and dining. The best anchorages are in Garden Bay and Gerrans Bay, and in the bay between Garden Peninsula and Madeira Park. John Henry's Resort & Marina is the only place for fuel in Pender Harbour. Madeira Park, in the southeast corner of Pender Harbour, has moorage, haulout and repairs. A shopping center is a short walk from the Madeira Park dock.

Pender Harbour has several drying and underwater rocks throughout, but most of them are marked. With Chart 3535 (or good electronic charts) and a little care, you should have no problems.

Pender Harbour Music Festivals: The Pender Harbour Music Society sponsors a concert series throughout most of the year; check their website for dates and tickets at www.penderharbourmusic.ca or call (604) 989-3995.

Transportation: There's no bus or taxi service. Use your dinghy, or try the **SloCat Harbour Ferry**, based in Madeira Park, (604-741-3796) or VHF 66A, for excursions or shopping trips.

㉕ **Pender Harbour Resort and Marina.** 4686 Sinclair Bay Road, Garden Bay, BC V0N 1S1; (877) 883-2424; (604) 551-2742 (phone or text); info@phrm.ca; www.phrm.ca. Open all year with moorage to 50 feet. New docks, with a new configuration, were installed in 2018. Transient moorage is in unoccupied slips. Reservations accepted through "Swift Harbour" online booking. No VHF monitoring; boaters will receive a text message for slip assignment. Water, 15 & 30 amp power, Wi-Fi, showers, laundry, launch ramp, garbage and recycling drop. Marina guests have access to all resort amenities, including heated seasonal swimming pool, fire pit, gazebo, and sports field. Cottages, motel rooms, yurts, campsite, small boats, stand-up paddleboards, and kayaks are available to rent. There is a small store in the office with snacks, essentials, bait and gifts.

Hospital Bay. Hospital Bay is on the west side of Garden Peninsula, facing the mouth of Pender Harbour. The harbor is home to the former Fisherman's Resort and Marina (now part of John Henry's), John Henry's store and fuel dock. Hospital Bay Public Wharf is next door. Hospital Bay is also the site of the St. Mary's Columbia Coast Mission Hospital building, built in 1929.

A narrow isthmus divides Hospital Bay from Garden Bay with a walkway between the two. Dan's Grill, an old-fashioned diner (previously LaVerne's) is located here. Dan's, which opened in July 2018, carries on the tradition of tasty burgers, milkshakes, fish n' chips, and offers breakfast all day.

㉖ **John Henry's Resort & Marina.** P.O. Box 68, Garden Bay, BC V0N 1S0; (604) 883-2336 ext. 1; info@johnhenrys.ca; www.johnhenrys.ca. Monitors VHF 66A summers only. Reservations available online or call ahead. Open all year with 2300 feet of moorage; water, 20, 30 & 50 amp power, washrooms, showers, laundry, Wi-Fi, garbage, recycling, ice, launch ramp. Gasoline, diesel, and propane at the fuel dock. Moorage guests receive a fuel discount. Oceanfront cottage rentals available. Kenmore Air provides floatplane service from Seattle.

This is a quiet, well-cared-for marina and resort with a lovely lawn. The store above the fuel dock has convenience groceries, sandwiches, charts, books, a liquor agency, post office, and ATM. The store also carries tackle, bait, and ice. The store at the fuel dock carries snack items, fishing tackle, and boat supplies.

The cafe has indoor and outdoor seating for take-out food orders.

Hospital Bay Public Wharf. P.O. Box 118, Madeira Park, BC V0N 2H0; Harbour Authority of Pender Harbour; (604) 883-2234; penderauthority@telus.net. Across from the fuel dock in Hospital Bay, 200 feet of first-come, first-served side-tie transient moorage both sides of the southern-most float. Mostly 20 amp power, with one 30 amp receptacle; power upgrades planned for 2023. Water on the docks. Portapotties are in the pocket park 200 feet up the road.

㉗ **Garden Bay.** Garden Bay is at the northeast corner of Pender Harbour. The Garden Bay Hotel hasn't been a hotel for a long time, so don't look for rooms to rent.

Seattle Yacht Club, Burrard Yacht Club and Royal Vancouver Yacht Club have outstations in Garden Bay—members only,

Secret Cove

no reciprocals. Many boats anchor out in Garden Bay and dinghy either to the marinas, John Henry's, or to Madeira Park. The Garden Bay holding ground is good and protection is excellent in most weather.

Garden Bay Provincial Park Marina has about 50 feet of frontage on the north shore. The park has a dinghy dock, toilets, and a network of excellent walking trails, but no other facilities for boaters. Garden Bay Lake, a popular swimming destination, is within walking distance of the Provincial Park.

Garden Bay Marina. P.O. Box 90, Garden Bay, BC V0N 1S0. Upland facilities burned down in November of 2020. The docks are closed; no public moorage.

Gunboat Bay. Gunboat Bay, surrounded by high, steep mountains, is entered through a narrow channel with a least depth of 4 feet. An underwater rock lies just to the north of the centerline of the entry channel. Currents in the entry channel are quite strong except at slack water. Although the bay is open and good for anchorage before it peters out into drying flats, few boats anchor there because Garden Bay is so much easier.

㉘ **Sunshine Coast Resort & Marina.** P.O. Box 213, Madeira Park, BC V0N 2H0; (604) 883-9177; (888) 883-9177; vacation@sunshinecoast-resort.com; www.sunshinecoast-resort.com. Open all year with moorage for boats to 100 feet, call for reservations, 15 & 30 amp power, water, washrooms, showers, free Wi-Fi, hot tub on the deck, laundry, bait, small boat and kayak rentals, and a hillside lodge with 16 truly outstanding rooms.

The entire property is tidy and well-maintained. Ralph Linnmann is the manager.

A steep mountainside rises above the docks. The laundry, showers, and road to town are a considerable climb up the hill, although the office and additional showers are in the lodge about halfway up. The marina is in the small bay to the right as you approach Gunboat Bay, about a half-mile north of Madeira Park shopping. You can walk to Madeira Park down the hill (and back up to return) or take the dinghy (we'd take the dinghy). Transportation to the challenging Pender Harbour Golf Club.

㉙ **Madeira Park.** If you want to provision, Madeira Park is where you'll do it. The Harbour Authority Public Wharf is close to two grocery stores (the well-stocked IGA, and the Oak Tree Market with excellent meats and cheeses). The IGA is open 7 days a week 8:30 a.m. to 7:00 p.m., and 8:30 a.m. to 8:00 p.m. in July and August; delivery to the wharf by request. Garbage disposal is available for a fee per bag. A

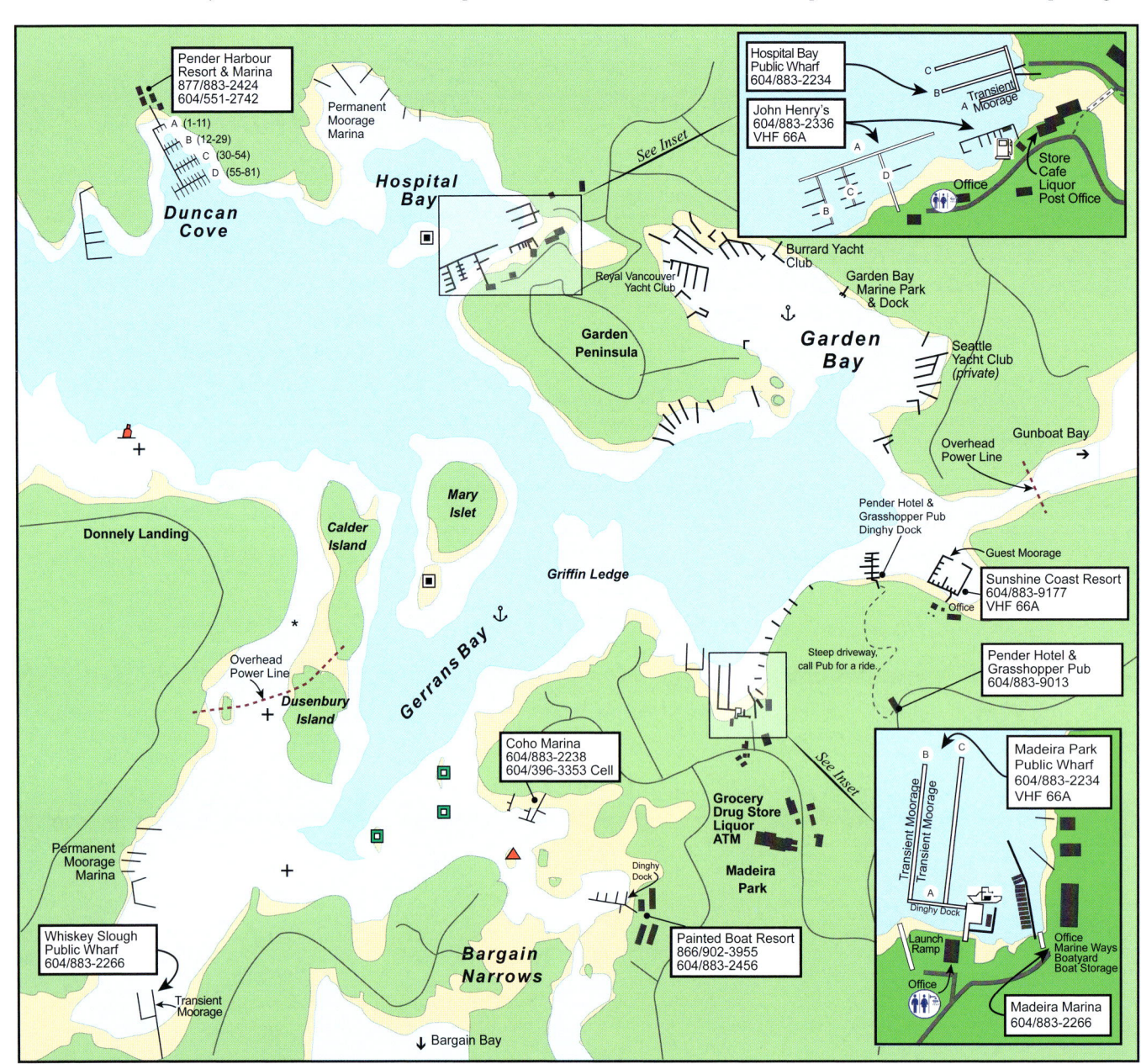

Pender Harbour

It's a short pleasant walk to shopping from Madiera Park Public Wharf.

Dinghy dock at Madiera Park Public Wharf, with access to shops and grocery stores

drugstore, liquor store, bank with ATM, book store, and veterinarian are close by. No laundromat. Madeira Park has a full-service medical clinic. The Grasshopper Pub has been rebuilt and has temporary moorage at their dock while dining or shopping at their liquor store.

㉙ **Madeira Park Public Wharf.** P.O. Box 118, Madeira Park, BC V0N 2H0; (604) 883-2234; Harbour Authority of Pender Harbour; penderauthority@telus.net. Monitors VHF 66A. Open all year, 600 feet of first-come, first-served transient moorage space located on both sides of B-dock. 20, 30 and 50 amp power; plans are in the works to upgrade power for 2023. Water, washrooms, showers, free Wif-Fi, garbage drop for fee, recycling at no charge. Pumpout with reservation. Floatplane dock available for moorage between 4:00 p.m. and 9:00 a.m. (be prepared to be out by 9:00 a.m.). The dinghy dock (south side of A-dock) faces the shore, adjacent to the launch ramp. No dinghy check-in is needed and no charge for daytime dinghy tie-up for the first hour. Marine repair, chandlery, and mechanics nearby.

Madeira Park Public Wharf is a destination in its own right. A small park with a gazebo and benches overlooking the marina is ideal for relaxation or a picnic. Two well-stocked grocery stores and a liquor store within walking distance make this a great place to provision. Stores allow customers to use their shopping carts to haul items to the Wharf, where the carts may be left. This well-managed facility is a popular destination.

㉙ **Madeira Marina.** P.O. Box 189, Madeira Park, BC V0N 2H0; (604) 883-2266; madeiramarine@telus.net. Open all year. Marine railway with haulout to 40 tons, complete marine repairs, parts, indoor painting facility for boats up to 30 feet, and chandlery. Prompt, competent repair service.

Pender Harbour Hotel & Grasshopper Pub. 12671 Sunshine Coast Hwy, Madeira Park, BC V0N 2H0; (604) 883-9013; penderharbourhotel.com. Located in Madeira Park high above Welbourn Cove. The Hotel's private dock has space for temporary moorage while visiting the Grasshopper Pub or shopping at their liquor store. Call for moorage and courtesy pickup at the dock; it's a short but steep walk up the driveway to the Hotel and Pub. Good food and drink with outstanding views.

Gerrans Bay. Gerrans Bay is one of the larger bays in Pender Harbour with suitable anchoring depths. It is quieter and less traveled than other areas of Pender Harbour. The bay is dotted with rocks that are charted and or marked. It is mostly residential, with some of the homes obviously in the commercial fishing business. Two marinas, Coho Marina and Painted Boat Resort & Marina, and the Whisky Slough Public Wharf, have moorage for transient boaters. A private marina with no transient moorage is located on the west shore near the southwest head of the bay. Anchoring can be found in the southwest head of the bay or in the northeastern half of the bay over a mud bottom with good holding.

㉚ **Coho Marina and RV Resort.** 12907 Shark Lane, Madeira Park, BC V0N 2H0; (604) 883-2248; (604) 396-3353 cell; info@cohomarina.com; www.cohomarina.com. Open all year with guest moorage for boats to 40 feet in unoccupied slips, reservations accepted. Located on the east side of Gerrans Bay, the marina approach is through marked and charted rocks and reefs. 15 & 30 amp power, water, restrooms, showers, and laundry; 5-minute walk to Madeira Park shopping center, with grocery stores and liquor.

㉚ **Painted Boat Resort Spa & Marina.** P.O. Box 153, 12849 Lagoon Rd., Madeira Park, BC V0N 2H0; (604) 883-2456; (866) 902- 3955; reservations@paintedboat.com; www.paintedboat.com. Open all year with limited guest moorage for those staying in resort accommodations, ask about moorage space when making room reservations. The approach from east Gerrans Bay winds through rocks and reefs. We suggest entering carefully with a bow watch. The docks have 15, 30 & 50 amp power and water, no washrooms, no showers. This is a first-class resort. The upscale Lagoon Restaurant is open seasonally for dinner, with dinghy tie-up space near shore for restaurant patrons. The full-service spa is available to those who have made an appointment. The swimming pool is for lodge guests only.

㉛ **Whiskey Slough Public Wharf.** P.O. Box 118, Madeira Park, BC V0N 2H0; (604) 883-2234; penderauthority@telus.net. Limited first-come, first-served side-tie transient moorage, with the best chance to find open space on the eastern most float towards shore. 20 & 30 amp power; plans are in the works to upgrade power for 2023. Limited access to potable water, no facilities or services upland. Mostly commercial fish boats here.

Agamemnon Channel. Agamemnon Channel runs northeast between Nelson Island and the mainland, and is the shortest route for those heading for Princess Louisa Inlet, Egmont, or Sechelt Inlet. The only reasonable anchorage is at Green Bay. A private marina is in Agamemnon Bay.

Green Bay. Green Bay is a well-protected small bay on the northwest side of Agamemnon Channel. Prime anchorage is at 30 feet in the cove on the west side of Green Bay in front of the lake shown on the chart. A stream with a waterfall runs from the lake to the cove. A drying reef nearly closes the pass to the back cove to the north of the prime anchoring area. Holding is fair on a hard mud bottom. Use caution approaching and within Green Bay as it is not well charted. Sailing Directions warns of rocks on the east side of the entry to Green Bay which are not shown on the chart. A large uncharted rock/pinnacle with 6 feet of water at zero tide is located mid-channel off a cabin with a small float, on the northeast side of Green Bay, east of the prime anchoring area. We entered favoring the west side of Green Bay. Several cabins, some with private docks, cling to the shore. The gentle sound of the waterfall makes for a restful anchorage.

VANCOUVER B.C. & SUNSHINE COAST

See Area Map Page 289 - Maps Not for Navigation

Backeddy Resort & Marina on Sechelt Inlet is your last stop on the way to Princess Louisa Inlet.

SECHELT INLET

Egmont. Egmont, on the Sechelt Peninsula, is near the entrance to Skookumchuck Narrows and Sechelt Rapids. Sechelt Inlet lies beyond the rapids. Backeddy Resort & Marina and Bathgate General Store & Marina both have fuel. Backeddy Resort & Marina fronts on Skookumchuck Narrows; Bathgate is closer to the rapids, behind a well-marked reef in Secret Bay. The public dock is adjacent. Beautiful West Coast Wilderness Lodge, with fine dining, is immediately south and up the hill from Backeddy Resort & Marina. It's an easy walk between the two, and the view from the dining room and deck at West Coast Wilderness Lodge is a knockout. One of our correspondents reports that their dinner was as good as the view—world class, they said. We agree.

The Egmont Heritage Centre is a short walk up the main road from the marinas.

LOCAL KNOWLEDGE

STRONG CURRENTS: Strong currents can whip through Backeddy Marina. Use caution when docking. Sechelt Rapids currents in the Tide and Current guides will give you an idea of the current direction and force.

DANGEROUS ROCKS: The red triangle day beacon off Backeddy Marina's south docks means Red, Right, Returning for the channel outside. Approaching the docks, leave the beacon to port or you will run up on a rock shelf that extends from shore.

㉜ **Backeddy Resort & Marina.** 16660 Backeddy Rd., Egmont, BC V0N 1N0; (604) 883-2298; (800) 626-0599; info@backeddy.ca; www.backeddy.ca. Monitors VHF 66A. Open all year with guest moorage and services, reservations recommended. Gasoline and diesel fuel, 400 feet of moorage for vessels up to 120 feet. 15 & 30 amp power, washrooms, showers, laundry, garbage drop with fee, Wi-Fi, water at the fuel dock. 8 geodesic domes for luxury camping, oceanfront cabins, and a concrete launch ramp. Floatplane access for Kenmore Air and West Coast Air. Small convenience store on site with ice. Backeddy Pub open for lunch and dinner, hours vary between October and April, call ahead.

The marina is opposite the Sutton Islets. This is a well-run marina, its rustic exterior hides the well-appointed pub and accommodations. Kayak and bicycle rentals available at the marina. Tours for Princess Louisa Inlet leave from the Backeddy dock. Water taxi service available. The Backeddy fuel dock is the first and last on the way to and from Princess Louisa Inlet.

㉜ **West Coast Wilderness Lodge.** 6649 Maple Road, Egmont, BC V0N 1N0; (778) 280-8610; lodge@wcwl.com; www.wcwl.com. This beautiful luxury lodge is located within easy walking distance from Backeddy Marina and offers a fine dining venue for boaters and lodge guests. Open for breakfast and dinner during the shoulder seasons; breakfast, lunch, and dinner during the summer. Reservations highly recommended during peak season, July and August. The float below the lodge is for seaplanes; however, dinghies may tie-up while dining at the lodge, contact on VHF 68A. A steep trail leads from the dock to the lodge. Adventure tours can be booked through the Egmont Adventure Centre located below the Lodge (778-280-8619). Moorage can be found near the Lodge at Backeddy Marina or at Egmont Public Wharf.

㉝ **Bathgate General Store, Resort & Marina.** 6781 Bathgate Rd., Egmont, BC V0N 1N0; (604) 883-2222; info@bathgate.com; www.bathgate.com. Contact on VHF 16. Open all year, gasoline and diesel at the fuel dock, limited guest moorage, 15, 20 & 30 amp power, showers, washrooms, laundry. Reservations recommended. Shallow depths at the fuel dock restrict access. The store has fresh produce and a good selection of groceries, propane, marine supplies, liquor agency, bait and tackle, block and cube ice. It's the only well-stocked store for miles. Deluxe wheelchair-accessible waterfront motel unit available. Short and long term parking.

The reef in Secret Bay can confuse a first-time visitor, especially one who isn't that familiar with navigation aids. Remember: Red, Right, Returning. When entering, leave the red daymark well to starboard and you'll have no problems. If you still aren't sure, just remember to go around the ends, not between the two beacons.

㉝ **Egmont Public Wharf.** Managed by the Egmont Harbour Authority, 604-883-9652 or 604-883-9463, two public floats and one

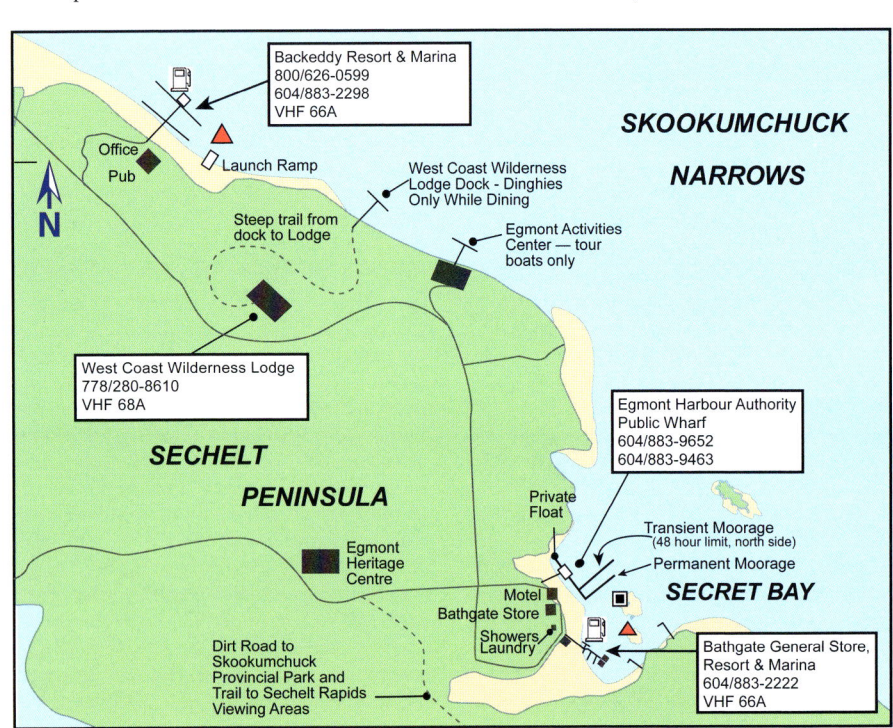

Egmont (Backeddy, Bathgate, Egmont Marinas & Wilderness Lodge)

See Area Map Page 289 - Maps Not for Navigation   VANCOUVER B.C. & SUNSHINE COAST

Enjoy a picnic lunch with great views at Backeddy Resort.

Sechelt Rapids running at a 12 knot flood, less than full boil at almost 16 knots

private float are accessed from the public wharf. The small float northwest of the wharf is private with no public access. The two large floats south of the wharf are public with permanent moorage on the southerly of these two floats and 150 feet of transient moorage for up to 48 hours on the northerly side of the north float. Self-registration and payment is at the head of the ramp. Water; 20 & 30 amp shore power. Rafting encouraged, two boat deep limit.

Sechelt Inlet. Beautiful Sechelt Inlet, with few anchorages and limited facilities for pleasure craft, is often passed by—especially with Princess Louisa Inlet at the end of nearby Jervis Inlet. Sechelt Rapids also serve as a gate to keep out all but the determined.

To explore Sechelt Inlet and its arms, use Chart 3512 (1:80:000) or Chartbook 3312. The inlet is shown at 1:40,000 in Chartbook 3312. Sechelt Inlet extends about 15 miles south of Sechelt Rapids. It ends at Porpoise Bay, the back door to the village of Sechelt, where there is a public float and easy anchorage. Two arms, Salmon Inlet and Narrows Inlet, run from the eastern side of Sechelt Inlet into the heart of the Earle Mountain Range. A number of provincial park sites are in Sechelt Inlet, most of them best suited to small boats that can be pulled up on the beach.

Inflow winds can blow from south to north in Sechelt Inlet and up Salmon Inlet and Narrows Inlet. Even when the northern part of Sechelt Inlet is near calm, the southern part can be increasingly windy. In Salmon Inlet and Narrows Inlet, the inflow winds will grow stronger as the inlets deepen and narrow. Outflow winds can develop at night, but in the summer they often don't unless a strong southeasterly is blowing out on the strait.

The tidal range does not exceed 10 feet in Sechelt Inlet, and the times of high and low tide are 2 to 3 hours after Point Atkinson. Two secondary ports, Porpoise Bay and Storm Bay, are shown in Tide & Current Tables, Vol. 5. Current predictions for Tzoonie Narrows, in Narrows Inlet, are shown under Secondary Stations in Tide & Current Tables, Vol. 5 and Ports and Passes. Depths at the head of the Inlet are shallow enough for easy anchoring over a mud bottom. Usually there are other boats at anchor and a number of private buoys, but it's a large area with ample space.

For a complete description of Sechelt Inlet cruising, including excellent hiking trails, see our sister publication, *Cruising the Secret Coast,* by Jennifer and James Hamilton.

LOCAL KNOWLEDGE

DANGEROUS CURRENTS AND INCORRECT TIDE DATA: We've had reports that some current tables contained in electronic navigation programs don't agree with the printed tables for Sechelt Rapids. Use the Canadian Hydrographic Service or Ports and Passes tables.

Sechelt Rapids. On large tidal exchanges, Sechelt Rapids can run 16.5 knots, the world record holder. Sechelt Rapids, also known as the Skookumchuck Rapids (Sechelt is pronounced "SEE-shelt"; skookum means "big" or "strong," and chuck means "body of water"), provide the only water access to Sechelt Inlet.

Times of turn and maximum current are shown in the Tide and Current Tables, Vol. 5 and in Ports and Passes. Sechelt Rapids can be extremely dangerous except at or near slack water. At full flow the rapids are boiling cauldrons with 8-foot overfalls and 12- to 16-knot currents. Even an hour before slack, when many other rapids may have calmed down, the Sechelt Rapids can be menacing. Traverse the rapids only at slack water. Be aware of where you are time-wise in the lunar cycle. When close to, or on a full moon or new moon, the period of slack water is short. When the rapids are running at full strength this area is deadly.

Lacking prior experience, do not go through without accurate charts for Sechelt Rapids and Secret Bay. Sailing Directions says the best route through the rapids is west of Boom Islet (choked with kelp, but safe) and west of the Sechelt Islets light.

We, however, have run a dogleg course without discomfort through the middle of the channel, between the Sechelt Islets and the unnamed islet directly north of the Sechelt Islets. This area is where dangerous whirlpools can develop on ebbs, so be careful. Give Roland Point a wide berth, especially on a flood.

Either direction, Sechelt Rapids are just fine at slack, and if you time it well (easily done) you'll slide through with no problems at all. But when the rapids are running, their roar can be heard for miles. Lives have been lost there.

Before making your own entrance it can be instructive to walk to the rapids from the public dock in Egmont to watch the channel in full boil.

Sechelt Rapids Viewing. On flood current watch standing waves and kayakers surfing the waves from Roland Point Viewing Area; on ebb current watch whirlpools from the North Viewing Area. Viewing times are 30 minutes of max current. The 4 km long trail is an easy walk from Bathgate, with minimal elevation gain; walking time is about 1 hour each way.

㉞ **Poise Cove Marina**. 5991 Sechelt Inlet Rd., Sechelt, BC V0N 3A3; (604) 885-2895. Open all year with limited guest moorage for boats to 25 feet, limited 15 amp power, concrete launch ramp for boats 25 feet or less. No long term parking. Located on the east side of Sechelt Inlet near Porpoise Bay Marine Park.

㉞ **Choquer & Sons Ltd.** 5977 Sechelt Inlet Rd., Sechelt, BC V0N 3A0; (604) 885-9244; choquerandsons@telus.net. Good docks with guest moorage for boats to 75 feet, deep enough for sailboats, 15 & 30 amp power, bathroom, showers. Launch ramp and trailer lift. Full marine repair. Their primary business is a machine and metal fabrication shop upland.

㉟ **Lighthouse Pub & Marina**. 5764 Wharf Rd., Sechelt, BC V0N 3A0; (604) 885-9494; info@lighthousepub.ca; www.lighthousepub.ca. Located at the south end of Sechelt Inlet with easy access to Sechelt village. Docks with slips from 16 to 40 feet plus side-tie moorage, 30 amp power, showers, laundry, washrooms. Call ahead for moorage, make payment at the pub. The long and often empty dock extending from the pub is reserved for Harbour Air floatplanes. The dock to the east, marked 'Day Use' is used for transient side-tie. Dinghies may tie-up on the fuel dock, near shore, when dining at the pub or visiting in town. For taxi service call (604-885-3666). Gasoline and diesel at the fuel dock. Lighthouse Marine Store (778-458-3625) carries marine hardware, charts, fishing supplies, snacks, ice. Look for the lighthouse on top of the pub. We've heard the food at the pub is excellent. Three 2-bedroom "Bed & Boat" cottages are available for rent, reservations at bedandboatcottages.com.

㉟ **Royal Reach Marina & Hotel.** 5758 Wharf Rd., Sechelt, BC V0N 3A0; (604) 885-7844. Open all year, moorage to 30 feet is for hotel guests only, limited 15 amp power, must call ahead. Located at the head of Sechelt Inlet. Watch your depths at low water.

㉟ **Porpoise Bay Government Wharf.** 5770 Wharf Street, Sechelt, BC V0N 3A0; (604) 740-7528 Wharfinger, or (604) 885-1986 City. Next to the Lighthouse Pub & Marina. This dock usually is completely taken by local boats, but space does become available from time to time; call ahead regarding available space. Docks accommodate boats up to 30 feet; 20 & 30 amp power, water, pumpout, and grid. Self-registration and payment box at the head of A-dock. Dinghies may tie-up if space allows.

Narrows Inlet. Narrows Inlet is mostly 150 to 180 feet deep except at the head, where the Tzoonie River makes a delta. Tzoonie Narrows, about a third of the way along, is a spectacular cleft in the high mountains that surround the inlet. Tidal currents run to a maximum of 4 knots through Tzoonie Narrows, but the passage is free of hazards. All but the slowest or lowest-powered boats could run them at any time. Arguably the best anchorage in this area is in Storm Bay at the mouth of Narrows Inlet. Storm Bay is very pretty with a dramatic rock wall on its eastern shore. Anchor behind the little islets at the entrance or near the head of the bay.

Tzoonie Narrows Park. This park takes in both sides of the narrows and is good for swimming, fishing, diving, and picnicking. Walk-in campsites. The 1-meter islet shown on the chart is a long, narrow reef with large extensions under the surface. You can anchor inside the reef, or in the deep bight on the other side of Narrows Inlet.

Salmon Inlet. Salmon Inlet is very deep, although anchorage is good in Misery Bay, where the water is warm enough for swimming. A drying shoal almost blocks the passage across the inlet at Sechelt Creek. The shoal can be passed safely by staying close to the north shore.

Ballet Bay on Nelson Island is a popular anchoring spot on the Sunshine Coast.

MALASPINA STRAIT TO JERVIS INLET

Quarry Bay. Quarry Bay faces the Strait of Georgia and is too deep and exposed to be a destination of first choice. If you must anchor there, you could work your way in among the rocks in the southeast corner of the bay. It would be a good idea to run a stern-tie to keep from swinging onto a rock. At the north end of Quarry Bay a little cove, surrounded by homes, is well protected and has good anchoring depths. It would be a good hideout. Chart 3512 shows a stream connecting this cove with Quarry Lake. Three rocks in this cove are shown in Chartbook 3312.

Cape Cockburn. An unmarked drying rock is a short distance off Cape Cockburn. Give the cape a good offing.

Cockburn Bay. Cockburn Bay is completely plugged by drying rocks and is accessible only by small craft at or near high water.

Hidden Basin. Hidden Basin is blocked by drying shoals and rocks, and currents run strongly through the restricted entrance. Chartbook 3312 (1:40,000) shows Hidden Basin better than Chart 3512 (1:80,000). Entrance to Hidden Basin should be made—carefully—at high water slack. Secure anchorage is available once inside.

㊱ **Blind Bay.** Blind Bay once had a number of good anchorages, especially along the Hardy Island side. Most of them now are taken with private homes and their docks, so the choices are fewer. One good spot on the south side is popular Ballet Bay. On the north side, Hardy Island Marine Park (formerly Musket Island Marine Park) has anchoring. Nearly all anchorages require a stern-tie. Use your chart and depth sounder, watch for rocks, and go slowly.

㊱ **Ballet Bay.** Ballet Bay, on Nelson Island, is a popular, well-protected anchorage in Blind Bay.

Ballet Bay can be entered from the north, but many rocks obstruct the path and close attention is called for. The easier entry is from the west, between Nelson Island and Clio Island. If you do enter from the west, the rock shown at the point before you turn into Ballet Bay truly is there, and farther offshore than you might expect. Give it a wide berth. Some of the many rocks around Ballet Bay are marked with sticks or cairns, but don't count on all of the rocks being marked. Not all the rocks are charted. Go slowly and pay attention.

The center of Ballet Bay is good-holding mud, but the bottom grows rockier toward shore. It has been reported that cables and debris lie on the bottom. Note the charted cable crossing areas.

Hardy Island Marine Park. Formerly Musket Island Marine Park. Located behind Fox Island, near the western entrance to Blind Bay. The upland area of the park is on Hardy Island. A beautiful spot.

Anchor behind the tiny islet, or in the bay that opens up to the north of the islet. In most cases you'll stern-tie to shore. The bottom can be rocky, so be sure you have a satisfactory set. You also can anchor in the narrow, vertically sided, almost landlocked cove indenting Hardy Island immediately northwest of the park itself.

Rock has been quarried on the peninsula high above the cove. It's quite dramatic. The area is poorly charted and some of the depths are deeper than charts show.

Telescope Passage. Telescope Passage connects Blind Bay with Jervis Inlet, but is partly blocked by underwater rocks that extend from the 70-meter island at the north entrance. Strongly favor the Nelson Island side until past the 70-meter island. Then, trend toward the middle of the passage to avoid charted and uncharted rocks along the Nelson Island side. When approaching Telescope Passage from Jervis Inlet, you might be confused (we were) by the presence of a tiny islet almost 100 feet high just outside the entrance. Check the chart closely; the islet is shown as the smallest oval imaginable with (26), for 26 meters high, directly beside it.

JERVIS INLET

Jervis Inlet extends 46 miles into Coast Range mountains and is the route to fabled Princess Louisa Inlet. Jervis Inlet is 1 to 1.5 miles wide and often more than 600 feet deep. Steep-to shores, with mountains rising directly above, make for few good anchorages. Currents in Jervis Inlet are light, and are often affected by winds. Watch for drift. Heading up-inlet, Backeddy Resort & Marina and Bathgate Marina in Egmont are the last fuel stops.

Once beyond Foley Head and Egmont Point, you'll find only indifferent anchorages at Vancouver Bay, Deserted Bay, and Killam Bay. The 30 miles of Princess Royal Reach, Prince of Wales Reach, and Queen's Reach do not have usable anchorages. Unlike the other deep fjords that penetrate from the sea, however, Jervis Inlet has a spectacular prize at the end: Princess Louisa Inlet.

Pictograph: Correspondent Pat Shera reports a good pictograph of what appear to be a group of salmon and other figures on the north side of Princess Royal Reach, midway between Osgood Creek and Patrick Point.

McRae Cove. Indenting the south end of the peninsula to the east of McRae Islet where Jervis Inlet joins Malaspina Strait, this small cove can be a day or overnight stop. The bay has consistent depths that are shallow for deep draft vessels. Watch for charted rocks at the entry and drying area at the head of the cove. The cove is scenic with windows to Malaspina Strait. A couple of homes occupy the north shore. This is a well-protected cove that is larger than it appears on the charts and has room for two or three boats.

Thunder Bay. Thunder Bay, immediately inside the north entrance to Jervis Inlet, has anchorage in the protected cove on the south shore, and in the open cove at the northwest corner. Correspondent Capt. Fred Triggs reports that in the southern cove, the rock drying at 2.1 meters appears to be farther offshore than charted. The cove looks a little small on the chart, but Capt. Triggs says it has room for several boats and good holding. The shores are lined with vacation cabins. Mooring floats restrict anchoring room. Rocks extend from the point as you approach. Give the point a good offing. At low tide the charted rock looks like a small haystack. If you stay off the west shore you'll be fine.

Saltery Bay. Saltery Bay has a public float, picnic sites and a seasonal take-out eatery. It is the ferry landing for road travel along the Sunshine Coast. The Saltery Bay Provincial Park, with beach access, is about half a mile to the west. A log booming operation, with signs warning boaters of cables, fills most of the possible anchoring area in the bay, and what remains has several private mooring buoys. An underwater cable area is to the west of the ferry landing.

Harmony Islands Marine Park with stern tie pins along the island on the lower left.

Saltery Bay Harbour. (604) 487-0196. Public floats are located adjacent and east of the ferry landing. Visitor moorage is available along 650 feet of space on three floats on a first-come, first-serve basis. The western most float is 240 feet long with stays limited to 48 hours on the outer western portion of the float. No power, no water. Most of the space is taken by local boats. Space for smaller boats can usually be found. Commercial vessels have priority.

Saltery Bay Provincial Park. Open all year, anchor only or moor at the public dock, a 1-km walk from the park entrance. Picnic facilities and a dive rinse station are located above the small sandy beach. Most of the shoreline is rock, however, and very impressive. In Mermaid Cove, scuba divers can look for the underwater statue of the mermaid. The dive reef is marked by white buoys. A launch ramp is a short distance west of Mermaid Cove.

St. Vincent Bay. Much oyster culture activity. Sykes Island and Junction Island may have anchorage.

Hotham Sound. Hotham Sound is a beautiful 6-mile-long body of water surrounded by high, rugged mountains that rivals Princess Louisa Inlet for beauty, but with far fewer boaters. Friel Lake Falls tumbles 1,400 feet down a sheer mountainside near Harmony Islands. The Sound is generally sheltered from most strong winds; however, williwaws can blow down from the mountains.

Good anchorages in Hotham Sound are few. Suitable anchorage is found in Harmony Islands Marine Park, Baker Bay, and at the head of Hotham Sound.

Harmony Islands Marine Park. The Harmony Islands in Hotham Sound are lovely. Four islands comprise the Harmony Islands Group. Three of the islands, the southern-most and the two northern-most, are part of the Marine Park. The middle island is private property and is not part of the park. The northwestern-most island was acquired by BC Parks (with substantial help from BC Marine Parks Forever Society) in 2018.

The middle island is privately owned with a house and private dock that is posted with "Private" signs. Please respect the private property and do not access or land on the middle island (including stern-ties).

Anchorage is possible in the south half of the channel east of the islands, where you can find depths of 40 to 60 feet to drop the anchor and then stern-tie to one of the 6 pins imbedded at the high-tide line of the rocky east shore of the south island, see map. Don't tie on the privately owned middle island. If you are setup for deeper anchoring, it is possible to anchor in the northern part of the channel and stern-tie. Anchorage for smaller vessels may be found in locally-named Kipling Cove, a nook surrounded by the two northern islands and the middle island. The bottom is rocky and a private dock occupies the south portion of the cove. Stern-tie to

Harmony Islands Marine Park

shore on either of the northern islands, which are owned by BC Parks.

In settled weather it is possible to anchor in the rocky and exposed nook on the west side of the islands – watch for reefs and rocks. We have been told that williwaws can make anchoring interesting.

Dark Cove. Dark Cove is a little notch between Foley Head and Goliath Bay, and was recommended to us by an experienced sailboater we met at Princess Louisa Inlet. We motored through Dark Cove the next day but didn't stop. At 90 feet deep, Dark Cove isn't ideal for anchoring, although protection behind Sydney Island is excellent.

Malibu Rapids. Malibu Rapids mark the entrance to Princess Louisa Inlet. The rapids are narrow and dogleg-shaped, and boats at one end cannot see boats at the other end. It is courteous—and wise—to warn other vessels via VHF Channel 16 that you are about to enter the rapids, and the direction you are traveling. First, be sure to set your VHF radio to LOW POWER. The transmission can be brief: *"Securité, Securité. This is the 34-foot motor vessel Happy Days, inbound to Princess Louisa Inlet. Any concerned traffic please respond on channel one-six."*

A VHF securite call is a notice of safety to boaters. When making a securite call at Malibu Rapids, it is for safety reasons and not for any right-of-way statement. Rules of the road for vessels operating in current flow are determined by current flow direction. Vessels traveling with the current are the 'stand-on' and vessels traveling against the current flow are the 'give-way.' The path through Malibu Rapids is 'S' shaped. While it might be tempting to 'cross over' the opposing traffic path to get a look at the rapids, this may create a conflict with boats coming in the opposite direction.

Currents in Malibu Rapids run to 9 knots and create large overfalls. Run this passage at slack water. High water slack occurs about 25 minutes after high water at Point Atkinson, and low water slack about 35 minutes after low water at Point Atkinson. High water slack is preferred because it widens the available channel somewhat. High slack or low, before entering or leaving Malibu Rapids, local knowledge says to wait until the surf created by the overfall subsides entirely.

Important: Use the Volume 5 Canadian Hydrographic Service or Ports and Passes tide tables for Point Atkinson tides.

Princess Louisa Inlet. Princess Louisa Inlet, 4 miles long, is the "holy grail" for cruising people from all over the world. Entered through Malibu Rapids, the inlet is surrounded by 3000-foot-high mountains that plunge almost vertically into 600-foot depths below. Entering Princess Louisa Inlet is like entering a great cathedral. The author Earle Stanley Gardner wrote that no one could see Princess Louisa Inlet and remain an atheist. It is one of the most awesome destinations on the coast. What words can describe this place? All the superlatives have been used up on lesser subjects.

Please observe a no-wake speed limit. Larger wakes bounce off the sides of the inlet.

Malibu Club, a Young Life Christian summer camp for teenagers, is at the entrance to the inlet, just inside Malibu Rapids. The kids and staff are welcoming and polite. Tours are possible. It's probably best to visit by dinghy after your boat is settled at Macdonald Island or the park dock at Chatterbox Falls.

As you clear Malibu Rapids and motor up Princess Louisa Inlet, you will be treated to waterfalls streaming down the mountainsides. About halfway along, 4 mooring buoys are behind Macdonald Island.

Princess Louisa Park is at the head of the inlet, surrounded by a bowl of high sheer cliffs that astonish even repeat visitors. The 650-foot-long park dock will hold a large number of boats. The dock is available at no charge; maximum boat length is 55 feet and stays are limited to 72 hours. Snug up close to the boat in front to leave room for others. The float at the end of dock is for floatplanes. Five mooring buoys were recently installed just south of the dock along the eastern shore.

If the dock is full, you will need to make use of one of these five buoys, or one of the four mooring buoys at Macdonald Island. Buoys can accommodate boats up to 70 feet; buoys are marked. Anchorage is possible at Macdonald Island but may not be practical due to depths and lack of swinging space. A dinghy dock is provided on the mainland shore opposite Macdonald Island for visitors to access a 1 km loop trail. Trail map at the Kiosk.

Since most people don't stay longer than a day or two, there's good turnover. A boat at anchor or on a mooring buoy need only wait for the twice-daily departure of boats from the dock running for slack at Malibu Rapids. Space then can be found before the next fleet arrives from the rapids. Water (not potable) is available all the way out the dock (May 1 - Oct 30) but no power. Up-inlet thermal winds can develop on warm afternoons. Be aware if you're out in the dinghy.

The park is beautifully developed and maintained. Use the shoreside toilets. Limit generator use to 9:00 a.m. to 11:00 a.m. in the morning and 6:00 p.m. to 8:00 p.m. in

Princess Louisa Marine Park

A trail leads from the head of the dock to Chatterbox Falls at Princess Louisa Marine Park.

the evening. Quiet hours are 11:00 p.m. to 7:00 a.m. The water is warm enough for swimming, even by adults who usually don't go in anymore. Field Correspondents Dan and Karin Leach report that a "Do Not Swim During Lion Mane Jellyfish Season" sign is posted at the dock,

No discharge zone. Gray water okay.

There's a covered fire pit for group get-togethers. For those who wish, a short walk to the pools near the base of Chatterbox Falls will yield a bracing bath/shower followed by a power rinse.

A delightful waterfall-fed pool is hidden in the forest on the north side of the inlet. From the dock you can see a large boulder that marks the spot. Land the dinghy on the small beach just beyond the boulder and walk a few steps to the pool. A bather we met yelped when he jumped in, but a moment later said the water was fine.

No hook-and-line fishing. Princess Louisa Inlet is a rockfish conservation area.

Trapper's Cabin is about a 2-hour very demanding hike from the dock area. The cabin is now completely collapsed. The trail is steep, and often muddy and slippery. We're not kidding about the hike being demanding, serious injuries have occurred.

With a fast boat, Princess Louisa Inlet could be seen in one day. Zoom up for the morning slack at Malibu Rapids, see the sights for a few hours, and zoom out on the afternoon slack. That, however, would be seeing Princess Louisa Inlet but not experiencing it. Something good happens to people when they're at Princess Louisa Inlet. We suggest at least three days for the trip: one day up 46-mile-long Jervis Inlet; the next day at the park; and the third day back down Jervis Inlet on the morning slack.

Princess Louisa Society. The Princess Louisa Society was formed to buy and preserve the area around Chatterbox Falls for perpetuity. The Society gave the property to B.C. Parks, but maintains an active role in the care of the facilities. Fundraising continues to maintain and develop the facilities at docks and in the area. Annual memberships are $40 U.S. or Cdn.; life memberships are $200 U.S. or Cdn. The Society website is www.princesslouisa.bc.ca.

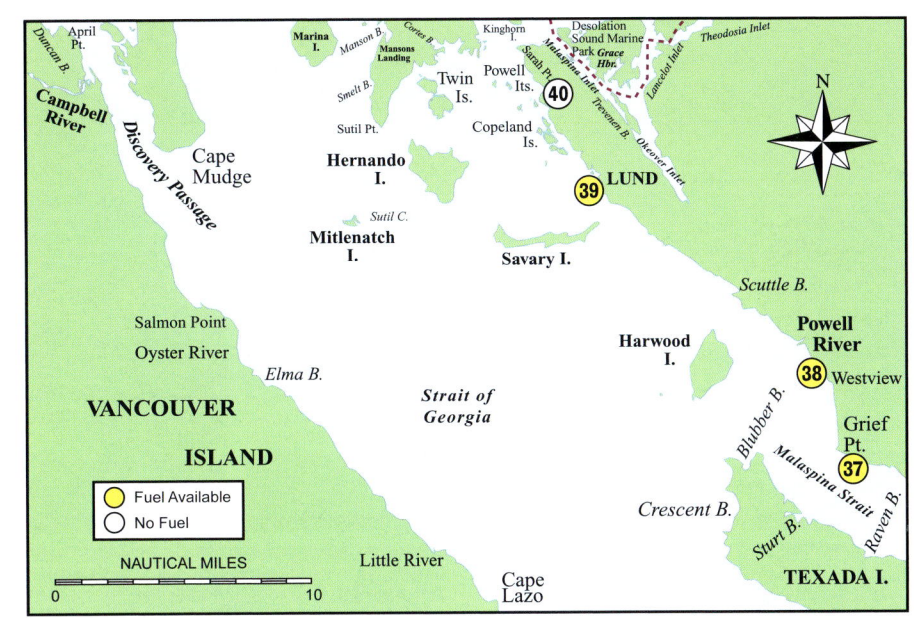

Powell River & Lund

MALASPINA STRAIT TO SARAH POINT

Malaspina Strait, 36 miles long, separates Texada Island from the mainland. Although the strait looks protected from the open water of the Strait of Georgia, storms can create high seas. Especially on an ebb tide, confused seas often build up off the mouth of Jervis Inlet and extend almost to Texada Island. Grief Point, at the north end of Malaspina Strait, is another bad spot in a southeasterly. Other than the mouth of Jervis Inlet, however, Malaspina Strait poses no threat in settled weather.

McRae Cove faces Malaspina Strait, just west of Scotch Fir Point at the mouth of Jervis Inlet. The cove is well protected but shallow. The charts show a straightforward entry between the 27- and 29-meter islands, then along a 36-meter island. Anchoring is in the vicinity of the 36-meter island in 6 feet at zero tide. Don't go much farther in—the bottom shoals quickly.

㊲ **Beach Gardens Resort & Marina.** 7074 Westminster St., Powell River, BC V8A 1C5; (604) 485-6267; (800) 663-7070; beachgardens@shaw.ca; www.beachgardens.com. Monitors VHF 66A July & August. Reservations accepted. Open all year, moorage, 15 & 30 amp power, water, free Wi-Fi, washrooms, showers, coin laundry, fitness center, indoor pool, ice, well-stocked beer and wine sales store. Gasoline, diesel and lube oil at the fuel dock, seasonal only. This is a breakwater-protected marina with good docks, just south of Grief Point. Deluxe waterfront rooms are available. Kayak and paddle board rentals available.

Beach Gardens Resort features a new building overlooking the marina and fronting the older buildings of the resort. The laundry, beer and wine store, and the excellent Seasider Bistro, (604) 485-0996, are on the bottom level with beautiful views of Malaspina Strait. Check www.theseasider.ca for hours of operation. A market with a coffee bar is within walking distance of the marina. Free shuttle service from the marina to Powell River Town Centre Mall is available in July and August. The city bus stop is a short walk away.

BEACH GARDENS
RESORT & MARINA
POWELL RIVER, BC

DELUXE OCEANFRONT ACCOMMODATION

- 55 Berth Marina - Permanent + Transient Moorage
- Cold Beer & Wine Store
- Showers, Ice + Coin Laundry
- Better Bodies Fitness Centre
- Free Marina Guest WiFi
- Seasonal Fuel Dock + Shuttle
- On-site Distillery, Salish Sea Spirits (SalishSeaSpirits.ca)

Steps from **THE SEASIDER** bistro • wine bar • patio

7074 Westminster St. Powell River, BC

1.800.663.7070 beachgardens.com

Beach Gardens Resort & Marina

2023 Waggoner Cruising Guide   299

VANCOUVER B.C. & SUNSHINE COAST

See Area Map Page 299 - Maps Not for Navigation

Westview Harbour docks are sheltered by a substantial rock breakwater.

The BC Ferries terminal is adjacent to Westview Harbour docks.

Grief Point. Grief Point marks the northern end of Malaspina Strait on the mainland side. The seas around Grief Point get particularly rough when the wind blows.

㊳ **Westview/Powell River.** The guest moorage facility at Westview Harbour consists of two basins referred to as Westview and South Harbour; these two basins are accessed through the shared south entrance and the floats are used by working vessels and transient pleasure craft. Fuel, water and power are available at the Westview and South Harbour basins. A harbour basin north of the ferry landing is for permanent moorage only and has a separate entrance. Restaurants and marine supplies are nearby in the Westview community. Grocery stores and a major shopping center are a taxi ride away, or use the free shuttle from the marina. The BC Ferries landing is mid-way between the north and south basins.

The section adjacent to the ferry loading area between the two main moorage areas, north and south, has been redeveloped and now houses the harbor office, new washrooms, showers, and laundry. Access to excellent restaurants, the Willingdon Beach Trail, and the historic "Townsite" district makes Powell River a destination worth visiting.

An excellent stock of marine and fishing supplies is available at nearby Marine Traders chandlery. Shops and a range of restaurants are on the main commercial streets, a short walk away. The Chopping Block, an old-fashioned butcher shop, is at the north end of Marine Avenue. Their meats, seafood, homemade smoked sausage, and cheese are delicious. The Town Centre Mall, with Save-On Foods, Safeway, Shoppers Drug Mart, Walmart, liquor store and other shops, is located some distance away, up a steep hill on Courtenay Street (they call it Cardiac Hill). It's a hike. Another shopping center has a QF grocery store that will deliver to the marina. Save on Foods also makes deliveries.

The original Powell River townsite is a couple of miles up the road from Westview. Visitors can walk or bicycle along the shoreline through a beautiful forested trail starting at Willingdon Beach on the north end of downtown Powell River. Numerous pieces of historic logging equipment are on display along the Willingdon Beach Trail, serving as a fascinating outdoor museum complete with interpretive signage. For energetic hikers, you can access the old "Townsite" district above the Mill off the end of the trail. Take a taxi for the return trip to Powell River. "Townsite" is the original settlement of Powell River and is a designated National Historic District. Four hundred of the original buildings from the early 1900s remain. Many have been refurbished and are still in use. A row of large oak trees and grand homes from the era stand proudly overlooking the mill and Malaspina Strait. Several cafes are found in "Townsite" and a brewery offering craft beer samplers.

In Powell River, history buffs may want to visit the small history museum adjacent to Willingdon Beach. The Blackberry Festival is in early August. Check the town's website (www.discoverpowellriver.com) for a schedule of activities.

㊳ **Westview Harbour.** 6790 Wharf Street, Powell River, BC V8A 1T9; (604) 485-5244; jkinahan@powellriver.ca. Monitors VHF 66A. Open all year, potable water, 30 & 50 amp power, washrooms, large showers, laundry. Waste oil disposal, recycling, and garbage drop for moorage guests. Free Wi-Fi and pumpout. Leave the daymark inside the harbor entry to port when entering. Guest moorage is available at both Westview Harbour and South Harbour basins, which share the same south entrance. Westview Fuels is the demarcation between the two moorage areas. First-come, first-served; call ahead for available space.

Rafting may be required or stern-tie to the main dock. South Harbour (floats 7-11) can accommodate vessels up to 150 feet (20-foot draft at zero tide). A short trail connects the South Harbour basin and the Westview Harbour basin.

Washrooms, showers, and garbage drop are available at both Westview and South Harbour; the newest facilities are located at Westview with the older more basic facilities at South Harbour basin.

Two-hour complimentary moorage, call ahead. Free scheduled shuttle to the mall picks up outside the harbor office four times per day during the ten-week season. Schedule is posted at the marina office.

㊳ **Sunshine Coast Fuels Ltd.** (formerly Westview Fuels). P.O. Box 171, Powell River, BC V8A 4Z6; (604) 485-2867 or 4188. Monitors VHF 66A. Gasoline, diesel, lubricants, washrooms, and ice. Located between Westview Harbour and South Harbour. Locally owned and operated fuel supplier.

Westview Harbour

Boardwalk Restaurant offers great views overlooking the docks at Lund.

The pathway along Lund's waterfront is full of surprises.

Dinner Rock. Dinner Rock, exposed at all tides, is approximately 0.2 mile off the mainland shore, slightly southeast of Savary Island. In 1998 a 1000-lb. cross was erected on the rock. It is a memorial to the five people who died there in October 1947, when the vessel *Gulf Stream*, proceeding in darkness with rain falling, struck the rock and sank.

Savary Island. Savary Island is a 4-mile-long sandy island that lies approximately east and west, and is served by water taxi from Lund. The island is a favorite destination for Vancouverites. The small public dock on the north shore is for loading and unloading only. Anchorage is good, sand bottom, within easy dinghy distance of shore. Savary Island has no real protected harbor, but the beaches are some of the best in B.C.

In summer months Riggers, a licensed pub-style restaurant, and a small general store are open. From the public dock turn right and follow the road for about one-half mile. Bicycles can be rented nearby. A number of years ago Bob Hale anchored off the north shore for the night and "got away with it."

By contrast, Tom Kincaid once anchored overnight in the same area, but by morning the wind had come in from the north and he was on a lee shore.

We visited Savary Island recently and anchored in 50-70 feet just off the dock and mooring field. We took the dinghy to shore and explored the island. The gently sloping beach makes landing and mooring the dinghy a challenge. Visiting by water taxi from Lund might be a better idea if you plan to spend the day there.

Nearby **Hernando Island** is surrounded by rocky shallows, and is seldom visited by cruising boats. Renowned authors Lin and Larry Pardey, however, report excellent anchorage with protection from southeast winds in **Stag Bay**, northwest of the pier. Anchor in 18 to 24 feet on a firm sand bottom.

Mitlenatch Island. Roughly west of Hernando Island, Mitlenatch Island appears to be an uninviting rock out in the middle of the Strait of Georgia. It is in fact a thriving and ruggedly beautiful wildlife refuge, with a small, protected anchorage on its east side. Park volunteers spend a week in turn each year on the island doing trail maintenance and guiding tours. Visitors are asked to stay on the trails to avoid disturbing birds. Pets are not permitted on the island. Those who visit will be rewarded, as this note from Correspondents John and Lorraine Littlewood suggests:

"If you can get there on a calm clear day in September, you'll see an incredible variety of wildlife, from Goshawks to huge sea lions. An additional benefit is water so clear that we could actually watch our Bruce anchor deploy. It hit the bottom in about 20 feet, flipped over, bit, and buried itself. This was on only 2:1 scope, although we later paid out to our normal 3:1."

We thank reader Sharl Heller for increasing our awareness of Mitlenatch Island.

㊴ **Lund.** Lund is the north end of the Pacific Coastal Highway, the road that leads all the way to the tip of South America. Lund is a busy place in the summer, a jumping-off point for Desolation Sound with fuel, provisions, and pumpout. The historic Lund Resort, with restaurant and pub, is at the head of the fuel

Mitlenatch Island is a wildlife refuge with an observation blind and trails. Best visited in settled weather. Small boats can anchor in the cove.

VANCOUVER B.C. & SUNSHINE COAST

Lund is a popular stop going to, or coming from Desolation Sound.

No anchoring in Finn Cove near Lund.

dock. A convenience store is located behind the hotel.

Lund is the mainland's closest launch site to Desolation Sound. Long-term auto, trailer and tow vehicle parking available. Lund Auto & Outboard is a few blocks away at the top of the hill. Nancy's Bakery is in the modern, larger building overlooking the public docks. Nancy's pastries, pizzas, and other specialties are a favorite. Nancy's also has good Wi-Fi. Upstairs from Nancy's is Pollen Sweaters, specializing in locally made sweaters, and Terracentric Adventures, a kayak tour operator. With commercial fishing in decline, the docks and shoreside facilities were upgraded to make them more inviting to visiting pleasure craft. Rafting may be required.

Fuel: The busy Lund Resort fuel dock has gasoline and diesel.

Garbage: The A&J's garbage shack, with a garbage bin, accepts garbage for a fee charged by weight.

㊴ **Lund Small Craft Harbour.** P.O. Box 78, Lund, BC V0N 2G0; (604) 483-4711 or (604) 414-0474; lundharbour-wharfinger@ twincomm.ca; www.lundharbourbc.wordpress.com. Monitors VHF 73. Open all year, first-come, first-served; call when outside the breakwater for slip assignment. 1500 to 1700 feet of breakwater-protected dock space, 20, 30 & some 50 amp power. Water at the docks for overnight guests. The harbor has one of the only pumpout stations in the area. Garbage drop, with a fee per bag, is above the fuel dock. No oil disposal. Excellent washrooms and showers. Wide concrete launch ramp with 4 lanes, good for most launchings down to about 5 feet above zero tide, some say 3 feet.

Enter north of the floating breakwaters. The northern dock located inside the breakwater is reserved for pleasure craft. Rafting is the rule, fender both sides to be prepared. Don't give up if the docks appear full. Office hours are 8:00 a.m. to 11:00 a.m. and 3:00 p.m. to 5:00 p.m. October to May, 8:00 a.m. to 5:00 p.m. June and September, 8:00 a.m. to 8:00 p.m. July 1 to Labour Day. Moorage is free for the first hour, 1 to 3 hours are charged at the half-day rate. Radio ahead for a slip assignment when near the entrance, even for short stays.

The floating concrete breakwater (no power or water) protects the inner docks. You can side-tie to the breakwater floats on the inside, and dinghy to the marked dinghy dock area below the ramp. Overnight moorage is charged on the breakwater.

Local knowledge says to be aware of a shallow spot, 4 feet at zero tide, near the launch ramps.

㊴ **Lund Resort.** 1436 Highway 101, Lund, BC V0N 2G0; info@lundhotel.com; www.lundresort.com. Permanent moorage only on their private, gated dock; guest moorage is no longer offered. For inquiries, call (604) 483-7777. The fuel dock (604-414-0471) has gasoline, diesel, and lubricants. Water for a fee.

The historic hotel, which dates back to 1905, has been restored and remodeled with a pub and separate dining area. The hotel has 31 rooms, ranging from budget-sensitive to four boutique oceanfront rooms overlooking the water. Rooms were not available in 2022 due to staffing and covid concerns. Check with the resort for availability.

The hotel, pub, general store, and fuel dock are under the ownership and management of the Tla'amin Nation. A new building was recently constructed behind the hotel to house the store, which carries convenience groceries, gifts, and a wide selection of wine, beer, and liquor. Public laundry facilities and showers are located in the store building. Tug Guhm Gallery & Studio, well known for lifelike seal heads carved from a single block of stone, is in the lower part of the hotel.

Finn Cove. Just northwest from the village of Lund, tucked between Sevilla Island and the mainland, is Finn Cove. There is a public float on the northwest side of the cove detached from land with no access to shore. Jack's Boatyard, with haulout and storage, is located on the east shore of the cove. Finn Bay Road leads from Lund to Finn Cove.

Finn Cove is a No Anchor Zone. Likewise, the harbour at Lund and the waters extending seaward well beyond the breakwaters is a No Anchor Zone.

㊴ **Lund Water Taxi.** (604) 483-9749. Scheduled service to Savary Island. Inquire about charter service to other locations.

㊴ **End Of The Road Parking.** P.O. Box 94, 1440 Lund Rd., Lund BC V0N 2G0; (604) 483-3667. Daily and long-term vehicle and trailer parking in secure lots off-site.

㊴ **Lund Automotive & Outboard Ltd.** 1520 Lund Hwy, Lund, BC V0N 2G0; (604) 483-4612. Long-term tow vehicle and trailer parking in secure lots. Call ahead for reservations. Mechanics are on staff for mechanical and electrical repairs and they are an authorized service facility for several engine brands. Haulout to 30 feet.

㊴ **Jack's Boatyard (Finn Cove).** 9907 Finn Bay Road, P.O. Box 198, Lund, BC V0N 2G0; (604) 483-3566; info@jacksboatyard.

Lund Harbour

ca; www.jacksboatyard.ca. Located 1/3 of a mile northwest of Lund in Finn Cove, owner Jack Elsworth created this do-it-yourself boatyard. The yard is equipped with a 50-ton Travelift and a custom-made 30-ton lift. The large upland boatyard and storage area is accessed by the 30-ton lift, while the 50-ton lift services the lower and smaller yard area with limited space for larger boats. The larger upland boatyard has plenty of room that allows you to work at your own pace. The boatyard has a list of local marine specialists.

You can stay on your boat while working on it; water, power, washrooms, showers, laundry, garbage and recycling drop are available. Wi-Fi is available in the upland boatyard.

Jack's haulout lifts and those in Campbell River are the only haulout lifts until Sointula's marine ways near Port McNeill, and Shearwater's Travelift some 200 miles north.

Copeland Islands Marine Park is a great place to explore by kayak.

Copeland Islands. The Copeland Islands (locally known as the Ragged Islands) are a provincial park. Anchorage is possible in several nooks and coves among the islands, although some of the coves are exposed to wakes from boats transiting Thulin Passage. Because of remnants of booming cable on the bottom, a buoyed trip line to the anchor crown is a good idea. Check your swing when you anchor. 19 stern-tie pins, with chains, were installed by BC Parks and the BC Marine Parks Forever Society in 2018, making it easier for boaters to visit the Copeland Islands. Please watch your wake in Thulin Passage. There are environmentally sensitive areas in the Copeland Islands.

Sharpe's Landing. A private marina with no facilities for transient boaters is in a small bay on the north end and east side of Thulin Passage. Please watch your wake as you go by.

㊵ **Bliss Landing Estates.** (604) 414-9417; (604) 483-8098; bliss@twincomm.ca. Located in Turner Bay, north of Lund. Open May through October. First-come, first-served guest moorage for boats under 60 feet. The site is a former cannery town, which is now a private community with seasonal guest moorage. The docks belong to the development. Transient moorage is in unoccupied slips or side-tie at the south side of the southerly docks. Washrooms, showers, laundry, 30 & 50 amp power, water, free Wi-Fi. Docks are exposed to westerly winds; moor bow-out. It's about a 15-minute dinghy ride to Lund.

Copeland Islands Stern-tie Anchor Pins

The private community docks at peaceful Bliss Landing Estates has limited guest moorage.

2023 Waggoner Cruising Guide

Desolation Sound & Discovery Passage

DESOLATION SOUND
Prideaux Haven • Homfray Lodge • Toba Inlet
Pendrell Sound • Refuge Cove • Teakerne Arm

CORTES ISLAND
Squirrel Cove • Cortes Bay • Von Donop Inlet
Gorge Harbour

QUADRA ISLAND
Rebecca Spit • Heriot Bay • Octopus Islands
Okisollo Channel

DISCOVERY PASSAGE
Campbell River • April Point • Brown Bay
Gowlland Harbour • Small Inlet

Scan the Latest
Desolation Sound &
Discovery Passage
Information

tinyurl.com/WG22xCh10

Desolation Sound, Homfray Channel

DESOLATION SOUND & DISCOVERY PASSAGE

Desolation Sound - Captain George Vancouver had it all wrong when he explored and wrote about this area during his cruise in 1792. He named it Desolation Sound, saying, "there was not a single prospect that was pleasing to the eye." Granted, his crew did have a challenging time with weather, fleas, and even shellfish poisoning. In reality, Desolation Sound, located today literally just beyond the end of the road, is a place of extraordinary beauty. It's one of the Northwest's most dreamed-about and sought-after cruising destinations.

Officially, Desolation Sound is the body of water north of Sarah Point and Mary Point, and south of West Redonda Island. When most people think of cruising these waters they consider Desolation Sound to include the entire area north of Cape Mudge and Sarah Point, and south of Yuculta Rapids and Chatham Point, including Discovery Passage (Campbell River).

For those departing from the Seattle or Vancouver areas, the trip to or from Desolation Sound might take as long as a week, depending on boat speed, weather, and stops along the way.

Desolation Sound is not a huge area. Even slow boats can go from one end to another in a day. But Desolation Sound offers a wilderness setting, generally easy waters, many bays and coves to explore and anchor in, and marinas where fuel and supplies are available. On the west side of these cruising grounds, Campbell River on Vancouver Island is a vibrant small city. Campbell River has complete supplies and even a boatyard for haulout and repairs. Lund, on the B.C. mainland, is at the eastern entry to Desolation Sound. Lund is a quaint, small village that has several services vacationing boaters are apt to need, including a nearby boatyard and lift. Lund also is the northern terminus of Highway 99, a road that extends to Tierra del Fuego on the tip of South America. Small marinas scattered throughout Desolation Sound offer fuel, water, and limited supplies.

Since it is close to the point where the tidal currents meet on the inside of Vancouver Island, the water in Desolation Sound is not regularly exchanged with cold ocean water. During the summer, water temperatures of 70° to 80°F are not unusual in some of the bays, making for comfortable swimming.

Navigation is straightforward, with few hazards in the major channels. Closer to shore it's a different story, but the rocks and reefs are charted.

The most popular time to cruise Desolation Sound is from mid-July through the end of August, when the prospects for sunny, warm weather are best. It's also when the anchorages and facilities are most crowded. June weather can be cool and rainy, but crowds are not a problem. It's then that the waterfalls are most awesome and the resorts and businesses, while open and stocked, are the least harried.

If your calendar permits, the very best time to cruise Desolation Sound might be early- to mid-September. By then the high-season crowds have departed, yet summer usually hangs on for a last and glorious finale. Stock in the stores may be thin and the young summertime help has headed back to school, but the low slanting sunlight paints the hills and mountains with new drama, and the first colors of autumn make each day a fresh experience. Watch the weather closely. Leave before the fall storm pattern begins, although usually that's not before October.

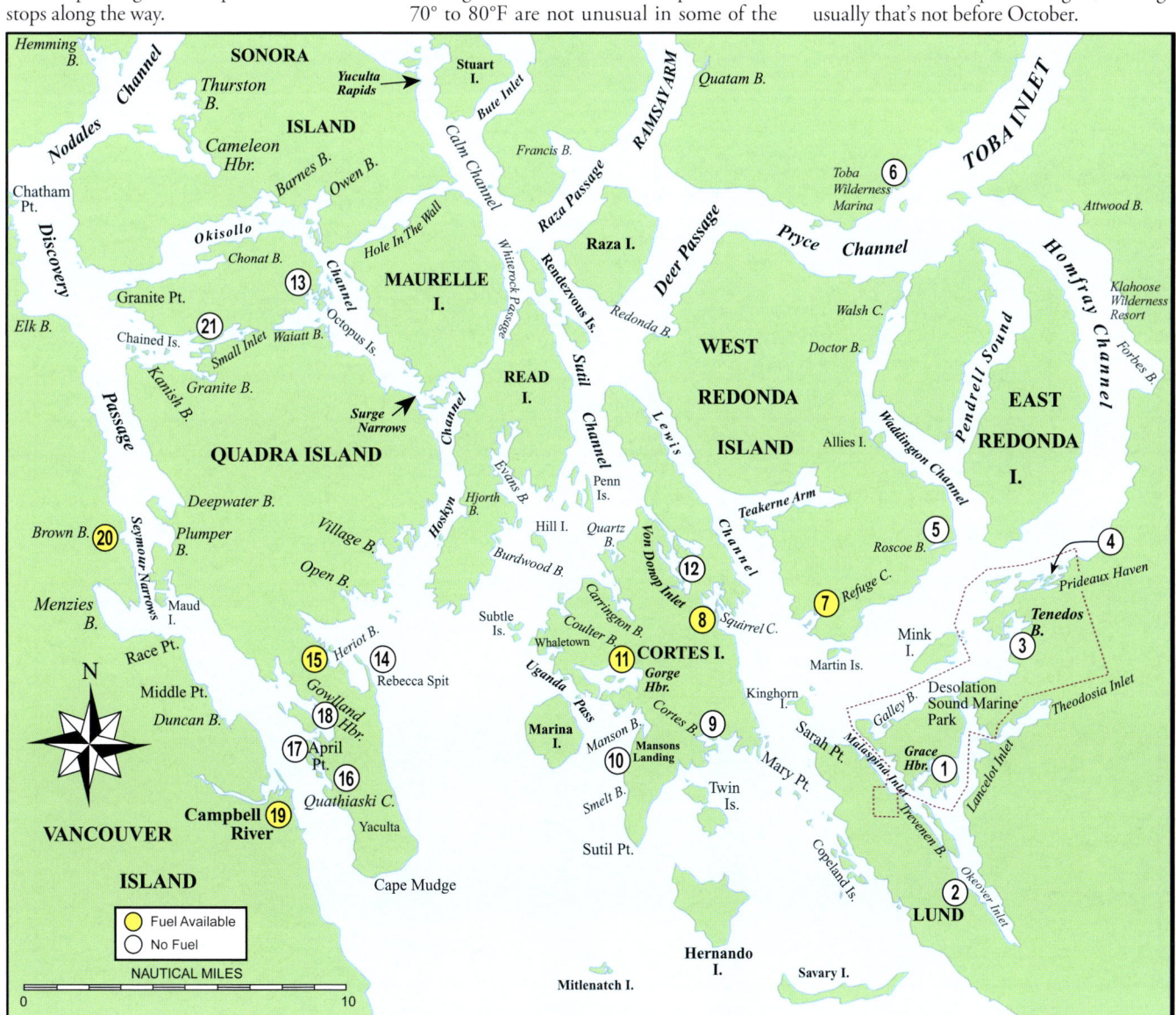

Desolation Sound and Discovery Passage

DESOLATION SOUND & DISCOVERY PASSAGE See Area Map Page 305 - Maps Not for Navigation

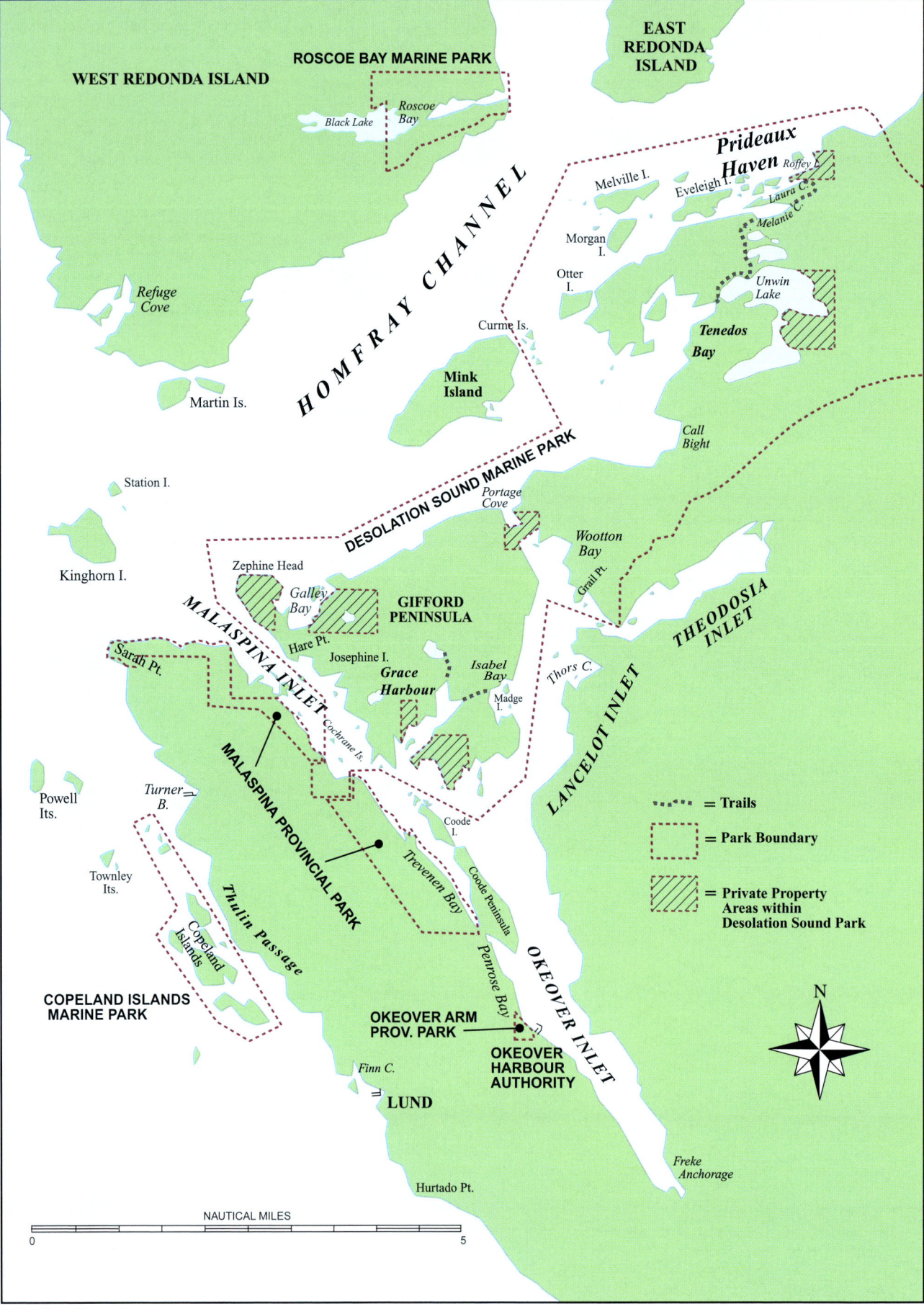

Homfray Channel

DESOLATION SOUND & DISCOVERY PASSAGE

The view of Okeover Harbour Authority docks from the Laughing Oyster Restaurant.

Navigation Note: Tide information for locations in Desolation Sound is shown in Ports and Passes and Canadian Tide and Current Tables, Vol. 5 (shown as secondary ports based on Point Atkinson Tides). Currents for Beazley Passage, Hole in the Wall, and Discovery Passage are shown in Vol. 6 and Ports and Passes as are corrections for Upper Rapids and Lower Rapids in Okisollo Channel, along with Owen Bay tides and Okisollo Channel secondary port tide corrections.

Sarah Point. For boats running north through Thulin Passage, Sarah Point, at the tip of the Malaspina Peninsula, is the dramatic entrance to Desolation Sound. The high hills of the Malaspina Peninsula hide the Coast Range mountains. But on a clear day, once Sarah Point is cleared, the mountains come into magnificent view.

MALASPINA INLET

Malaspina Inlet, Okeover Inlet, Lancelot Inlet and Theodosia Inlet all are entered between Zephine Head and Myrmidon Point. On a spring flood tide you will most likely find current at the mouth of Malaspina Inlet, all the way to Grace Harbour. Much of Gifford Peninsula, to the east of Malaspina Inlet, is Desolation Sound Marine Park. Several good anchorages are in this area. You'll also find rocks and reefs, most of them covered in kelp in summer and easily identified. They'll keep you alert, though.

Aquaculture occupies several otherwise inviting anchorages, but there are still plenty of choices in this area. Malaspina Inlet is popular with kayakers. Be mindful of your wake.

① **Grace Harbour.** Grace Harbour is a popular anchorage. The inner bay is surrounded by forest and almost completely landlocked, with anchorage for quite a few boats. Many of the anchorages are along the shore, so be prepared to run a stern-tie. In 2018 BC Parks and the BC Marine Parks Forever Society added 10 stern-tie pins, with chains, for a total of 16 stern-ties in the harbour. A fire pit is in a little park-like area at the north end. A rock, shown on the charts, is in the middle of this innermost bay. The anchor just skids across the rock before finding holding ground on the other side. On a crowded summer weekend, the empty spot in the middle is there for a reason.

Cochrane Bay. Located on the west side of Malaspina Inlet, Cochrane Bay along with the two small islands in front of the bay, are within the Desolation Sound Marine Park. The only safe entrance into the bay is from the south. Correspondent Deane Hislop reports that there appears to be an entrance on the north side, but it's not safe due to uncharted rocks that lie below the surface. Set the hook in 35 feet of water over a sand and gravel bottom. A short trail on the western shore of the bay leads to the Sunshine Coast Trail system.

Trevenen Bay. The head of Trevenen Bay looks like a good anchorage on the chart, but the bay is largely taken by aquaculture.

Penrose Bay. Anchorage at the head of the bay. The Okeover Harbour Authority docks are on the west shore to the south.

② **Okeover Harbour Authority.** okeoverharbour@gmail.com; Okeover Inlet borders the Desolation Sound Marine Park area. The Okeover Harbour Authority docks are located on the western shore of Okeover Inlet a short distance south of Penrose Bay with road access to Lund. Oysters and other seafoods are grown in several places along beautiful Okeover Inlet.

The docks at Okeover are managed by the Okeover Harbour Authority (604) 483-3258, contact via VHF 66A. Docks located behind the L-shaped breakwater are for local working boats. The large outer breakwater (440 feet each side) provides plenty of space for transient moorage, no power, no water; the seaward side of the breakwater is exposed to northerly winds. Moorage is on a first-come, first-serve basis; payment made to wharfinger or fill out the self-registration envelope and deposit at the office door-drop. Office located on the wharf is open 12:30 p.m.-6:30 p.m. daily during the summer months, hours vary during the off-season. Launch ramp on-site.

The Laughing Oyster Restaurant (604) 483-9775 is located above the docks. It is an excellent restaurant with outstanding cuisine, lovely surroundings and a stunning view. Reservations recommended. It's one of those gems not to be missed.

Lancelot Inlet. Isabel Bay in Lancelot Inlet is popular. The best anchorage is behind Madge Islands, with a beautiful view and room for one or two boats among the large rock formations. Good anchorage is also in Thors Cove. The bay is deep, except in nooks or close to shore.

Correspondent Pat Shera, from Victoria, wrote to tell us that in Isabel Bay he fouled his anchor on a section of bulldozer track at the head of the anchorage, just west of the north tip of Madge Island. If you have Chartbook 3312, it's where the 4.2-meter sounding is shown. He says another section of track was high and dry on a nearby rock.

Theodosia Inlet. Theodosia Inlet has a narrow, shallow, and kelp-choked entrance, but is navigable by most boats at all stages of the tide. Once inside, the bay opens up. Logging activity takes away from the remote feeling of the bay. Boomed logs can occupy much of the shoreline. Anchorage is in a number of gunkholes along the shoreline.

Wootton Bay. At the head of Lancelot Inlet is Wootton Bay. Good anchorage is located in the cove at the north end of Wootton Bay near the neck of land separating Wootton Bay from Portage Bay. The anchoring cove has swing room for 2 to 3 boats in 40 to 55 feet of water with good holding. The neck of land to Portage Bay, along with land about ¼

DESOLATION SOUND
YACHT CHARTERS, SERVICES & MARINE SUPPLY

- Bareboat Charters
- Power & Sail Training
- Yacht Management
- Marine Supply Store
- Certified Marine Mechanical
- Scheduled Maintenance

250-339-7222
desolationsoundyachtcharters.com

250-941-0396
marinesupply@dsyc.ca

LOCATED AT THE COMOX VALLEY MARINA

DESOLATION SOUND & DISCOVERY PASSAGE

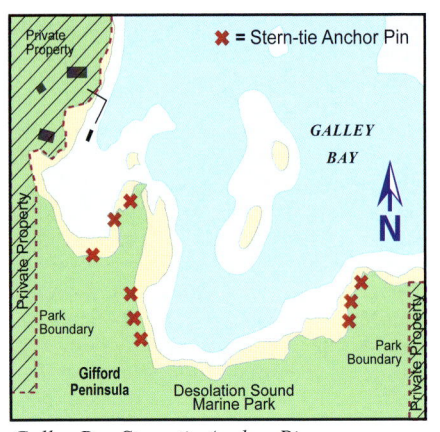

See Area Map Page 305 - Maps Not for Navigation

Galley Bay Stern-tie Anchor Pins

Prideaux Haven is a popular destination in Desolation Sound and stern-tie is the rule.

mile to either side is private property and is not part of the park. Stern tie is not possible in the anchoring cove, because the shore and uplands to the north are private. The shore to the east is part of the Desolation Sound Marine Park. However, drying shoals prevent stern ties. Water temperatures in Wootton Bay on Memorial weekend can be in the high sixties.

MINK ISLAND AREA

Galley Bay. Galley Bay is just east of Zephine Head. It is a good anchorage, particularly in the eastern end. In 2018, 9 stern-tie pins, with chain, were installed in the area by BC Parks and the BC Marine Parks Forever Society.

Mink Island. Mink Island is private property, but you'll find excellent anchorage in the bay that indents the southeast shore, particularly if you work in behind the little island in the center of the bay. You'll probably run a stern-tie to shore.

Curme Islands. Wolferstan describes navigation in the Curme Islands, east of Mink Island, as "challenging." The Curme Islands are extremely tight with shallow waterways, but with anchoring possibilities if the boat uses 4-way ties to hold position. For most people, dinghies and kayaks are probably the way to go.

③ Tenedos Bay. Tenedos Bay (also called Deep Bay) is a favorite, for a couple of reasons. First, it's a good, protected anchorage, with a landlocked basin behind Bold Head. Second, it's just a short dinghy ride to a 1/4 mile trail that leads to Unwin Lake, a popular freshwater swimming hole. The trail continues beyond Unwin Lake to two smaller lakes and all the way to Melanie Cove and Prideaux Haven, a 1 to 2 hour journey.

In addition to the landlocked basin noted above, you'll find anchorages in coves along the shore of Tenedos Bay. 14 stern-tie pins, with chain, are located around the bay; installed by BC Parks and the BC Marine Parks Forever Society. The center of Tenedos Bay is too deep (300 to 600 feet) for anchoring.

Caution: As you enter Tenedos Bay, a nasty rock lies submerged off the south side of Bold Head. Especially if you are headed to or from Refuge Cove, Mink Island, or around Bold Head to Prideaux Haven, this rock is right on your probable course. The rock lies farther offshore than you might expect. Give it an extra wide berth, just to be sure. A number of rocks are charted. All are easy to avoid if you are aware of them.

Otter Island. A very narrow but navigable channel runs between Otter Island and the mainland. Ample space for a few boats to anchor on the north side, using stern-ties to shore.

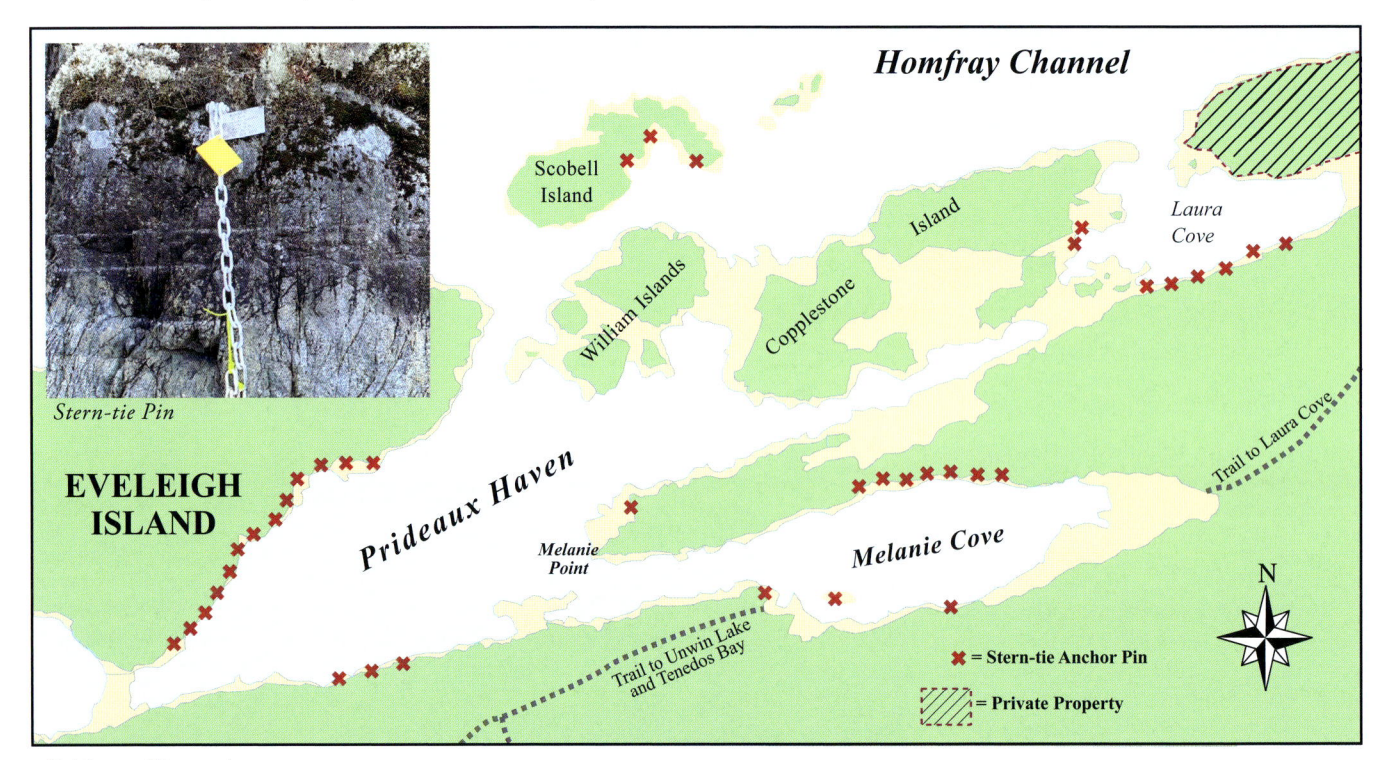

Stern-tie Pin

Prideaux Haven Area

PRIDEAUX HAVEN AREA

The coves that make up the area generally known as Prideaux Haven are the most popular spots in Desolation Sound, with several requiring stern-ties to increase the number of boats accommodated. The area is described in great detail by M. Wylie Blanchet in her classic book, *The Curve of Time*.

At the head of Melanie Cove you can find the remains of Mike's place, and in Laura Cove traces of old Phil Lavine's cabin site are visible (both from *The Curve of Time*). The evidence, however, is getting pretty faint.

The entire clutch of islands and shallow waterways invites exploration by dinghy or kayak. The narrow pass between Scobell Island and the William Islands, for instance, is beautiful. During high season, the only thing missing is solitude. You'll have lots of company. There is some cell phone reception in the area, including Prideaux Haven.

No Discharge Zone. Gray water okay.

Eveleigh Island. Anchorage is in Eveleigh Anchorage, the western cove behind Eveleigh Island. A drying reef connects Eveleigh Island with the mainland. Entry to the other Prideaux Haven anchorages is around the east end of Eveleigh Island. A reef almost, but not quite, closes this entrance. Use Chart 3555 (recommended) or Chartbook 3312. Smaller scale Chart 3538 (1:40,000) shows the entry but with too little detail to inspire confidence. After rounding Lucy Point, strongly favor the Eveleigh Island side of the passage to clear the reef.

④ Prideaux Haven. Boaters will find numerous stern-tie installations throughout the Prideaux Haven area including: along the southeast shore of Eveleigh Island; along the southeast shore of Scobell Island; on the north and south shores of Melanie Cove; and on the south and west shores of Laura Cove.

No Discharge Zone. Gray water okay.

④ Melanie Cove. Melanie Cove is perfectly protected, with ample room along both shores for boats to anchor and stern-tie. There are approximately 7 stern-ties along the north shore and 3 stern-ties along the south shore; installed by BC Parks with the help and support of BC Marine Parks Forever Society stern-tie project. A few boats can anchor in the middle without a stern-tie.

Mike's cabin once stood at the head of the cove as described in *The Curve of Time* by M. Blanchet. A half-mile trail, starting on the north side at the head of Melanie Cove, leads to Laura Cove. The trail is well-worn, but a number of trees have fallen across the trail requiring some scrambling.

Another trail from Melanie Cove leads to Unwin Lake at Tenedos Bay. The trailhead begins on the south shore of Melanie Cove, look for the small wooden trail sign on the point near the cove entrance. The trail is steep in places and takes 1-2 hours to reach Tenedos Bay. For a shorter hike, take the left fork in the trail to a small lake overlook, a trail sign points the way.

④ Laura Cove. Laura Cove has a fairly narrow entrance, with a least depth of approximately 10 feet at zero tide. Rocks extend from both sides. Enter cautiously. Once you're inside, the bay is beautiful. A few cherry trees and English Ivy mark Old Phil, the Frenchman's cabin site mentioned in *The Curve of Time*, at the head of this bay. Anchorage is to the east of Copplestone Point. The west end of the cove is a maze of rocks and reefs. In 2018, 6 stern-tie pins were installed along the south shore and 2 stern-tie pins on the northwest end of the cove by BC Parks and the BC Marine Parks Forever Society.

Roffey Island. If you can't find a place at Prideaux Haven, Melanie Cove, or Laura Cove, try the little bay behind Roffey Island. Room for one or more boats away from the crowd.

Homfray Channel. Homfray Channel curves from the south end of West Redonda Island and around East Redonda Island, until it merges with Toba Inlet. The only bays of consequence are Forbes Bay and Atwood Bay. The center of Atwood Bay is too deep

---

DESOLATION SOUND MARINE PARK TRAILS

Melanie Cove to Laura Cove – 0.6 miles each way with an elevation gain of 287 feet. Approximate travel time of 45 minutes one way to Laura Cove. Two cairns on a large flat rock near the head of Melanie Cove indicate where you can tie-off the dinghy and access the trailhead. The trail is easy to follow with red surveyor's tape at a few spots along the way. The hike is moderate to difficult, with a number of fallen trees across the trail that require climbing over or under. The hike takes you past an established second growth forest with carpets of moss.

Melanie Cove to Lake Overlook – a half-mile trail leads from Melanie Cove up 360 feet to an overlook at one of two small lakes north of Unwin Lake. Melanie Cove Trailhead is at 50°08.44N 124°40.67W and is marked with a small rustic wooden "Trail" sign. A stern-tie installation is along the south shore of Melanie Cove near the trail sign where you can tie-off the dinghy. The trail is moderately difficult with some downed trees and limbs across the trail. About .4 miles from Melanie Cove, the trail branches with signs that mark the way to "Lake Overlook" and mark the way to "Unwin Lake."

Melanie Cove to Tenedos Bay via Unwin Lake – a two-mile trail goes between Melanie Cove and Tenedos Bay and passes along the northwest shore of Unwin Lake. This trail joins the Melanie Cove to Lake Overlook trail as described above, along with the Tenedos Bay to Unwin Lake trail described below. The trail passes two small lakes just north of Unwin Lake.

Tenedos Bay to Unwin Lake – an easy, less than a quarter-mile trail begins at the northeast corner of Tenedos Bay at 50°07.42N 124°41.38W with an elevation gain of 130 feet. There is a pit toilet at the trailhead and a rustic campsite. The trail is moderate with an easy section from Tenedos Bay to a bridge at Unwin Lake. After the bridge, the trail north along Unwin Lake shore is moderate. There are several spots to access the Lake for a warm-water swim. The main trail from Tenedos to the bridge is short enough and wide enough to portage a light weight kayak or canoe to explore large Unwin Lake.

Grace Harbour to Isabel Bay – a one-half mile trail is reported to lead from the east cove in Grace Harbour to Isabel Bay.

Grace Harbour to a small lake – a one-third mile trail is reported to lead from the north cove in Grace Harbour to a small lake northward.

DESOLATION SOUND & DISCOVERY PASSAGE

See Area Map Page 305 - Maps Not for Navigation

for convenient anchoring, though we've successfully anchored in the nook indenting the north shore. Bob Stephenson, the former owner of Desolation Sound Yacht Charters, says Forbes Bay can be good for anchoring.

In Bill Wolferstan's book, *Desolation Sound and the Discovery Islands*, he tells of two Native pictographs on the west shore of Homfray Channel—one of a single fish, the other unidentified. Actually, there are several pictographs located about 10 feet above the high water line located across the channel from Lloyd Point.

Klahoose Wilderness Resort. (250) 935-8539; VHF 66A. Office hours 9:00 a.m. to 5:00 p.m. Monday-Friday. Located just north of Forbes Bay. Beautiful and remote location with 250 feet of moorage and two mooring buoys. Moorage is for guests who have booked overnight stays at the lodge or in one of the cabins. Potable water, showers; Wi-Fi at the lodge. No power at the dock. Guests can sit on the covered porch and enjoy a beautiful view up the channel. All inclusive accommodation packages with Wildlife Cultural Tours or Grizzly Bear Viewing Tours. Reservations recommended during the high season.

WADDINGTON CHANNEL

⑤ **Roscoe Bay/Roscoe Bay Marine Park**. Roscoe Bay, on West Redonda Island where Waddington Channel meets Homfray Channel, is an excellent, protected, and popular anchorage. The bay is divided into an inner cove and an outer cove, separated by a drying shoal easily crossed by shallow draft boats at half tide or better. If in doubt, go in on a rising tide. At high tide most sailboats can get in. 12 stern-tie pins, with chains, were added in 2018 by BC Parks and the BC Marine Parks Forever Society for a total of 22 stern-ties in Roscoe Bay.

The inner cove is pretty, and except for the other boats enjoying the bay with you, it's a good example of what cruising in these waters is all about. Dinghy ashore and take the short hike up to the knob dividing the two bays.

At the head of the inner cove, an old logging road with a short stream beside it connects with Black Lake. During summer months, the water in Black Lake is warm and excellent for swimming or bathing. Trout fishing is reportedly good. If you carry your dinghy up the road, you can launch it along the lake's shoreline.

On the north shore of Roscoe Bay is the beginning of a challenging trail to the top of 2165-foot high Llanover Mountain. The trailhead is near a rock face where a stream empties into the bay at approximately 50°09.65N 124°46.22W. According to alltrails.com, there is a sign at the start of the trail. The trail is not always well-maintained. Trees may be down and there are muddy areas. Views from the summit are outstanding. A round trip takes several hours.

No Discharge Zone. Gray water okay.

Walsh Cove Marine Park has anchoring space for a number of boats, but have your stern-tie set up ready.

Pendrell Sound. With summer water temperatures dependably in excess of 68°F, Pendrell Sound has been called the "warmest saltwater north of Mexico." Major oyster culture operations are in the sound, providing seed oysters to growers all along the coast.

Strings of cultch material (often empty oyster shells) are suspended from floats in the bay until the oyster spat adheres to them, at which point they are shipped.

The favored anchorage is at the head of Pendrell Sound, probably stern-tied to trees ashore. Wear good shoes and sturdy gloves when you're clambering around on the rocks.

Another anchorage is on the western shore, about three-quarters of the way up the sound, tucked in behind a small islet at the outfall from a saltwater lagoon.

Speed Limit Zone: A 4-knot speed limit is in effect throughout the north half of Pendrell Sound to protect seed oyster growing operations

Elworthy Island. A delightful cozy anchorage lies behind Elworthy Island, a mile north of Church Point, roughly across Waddington Channel from the entrance to Pendrell Sound. The aquaculture noted on charts no longer is present. The island is called Alfred Island by Wolferstan, but in 1992 it was renamed Elworthy Island for seaman Richard Elworthy, who died serving freedom in 1942. A handsome plaque is set into rock on the northeast corner of the island. Enter the anchorage from either end, but watch for a drying rock near the north entrance. The south entrance shallows to about 12 feet. The island's shoreline is covered with oysters.

Allies Island. Allies Island is connected to West Redonda Island by a drying reef. The north cove is pretty well choked with aquaculture; anchorage is possible in the south cove. The south cove offers a secluded anchorage for 1 to 3 boats and is exposed to the southeast. The rocks around the cove are full of oysters.

Doctor Bay. Doctor Bay is mostly filled with aquaculture. Correspondent Fred Triggs reports good anchorage in 35-40 feet north of the aquaculture operation. We've also heard reports that the aquaculture operation allows pleasure boats to tie up to some floats; check with an employee for instructions.

Walsh Cove Marine Park. Walsh Cove Marine Park is a beautiful little spot with room for several boats to stern-tie along the rocky shore. 15 stern-tie pins, with chain, were installed in 2018 by BC Parks and the BC Marine Parks Forever Society. See Walsh Cove reference map for locations. Enter Walsh Cove from the south. At the north end of the cove, a rock-strewn reef connects Gorges Island to West Redonda Island. The middle of the cove is deep. The cove is well protected from down-channel winds but open to up-channel winds from the south. Two sets of Native pictographs are at Butler Point.

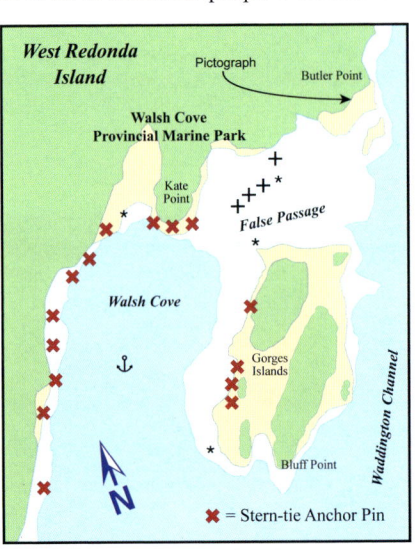

Walsh Cove Stern-tie Anchor Pins

Toba Wilderness Marina

See Area Map Page 305 - Maps Not for Navigation   **DESOLATION SOUND & DISCOVERY PASSAGE**

You won't find any towns in Toba Inlet. What you will find are outstanding views and wilderness.

⑥ **Toba Wilderness Marina.** (250) 830-2269; inquiries@tobawilderness.com; www.tobawilderness.com. Contact VHF 66A ahead of time for tie-up instructions upon approach. Marina moorage is seasonal and runs from June through September. Reservations highly recommended during July and August, with a minimum 2-day advance notice.

This is a quiet marina, located behind Double Island at the mouth of Toba Inlet. The views up Toba Inlet are breathtaking. The marina has 1400 feet of moorage, on concrete floats, for vessels up to 200 feet. No requirement for rafting. Enjoy the attractive Welcome House located upland for afternoon and evening get-togethers. 5 km of hiking trails, Wi-Fi, free ice, washroom, showers, and garbage drop-off (1 bag only per day with overnight moorage). Abundant clean clear water is available on the dock, with 30 and 50 amp power.

Scheduled floatplane service available through NW Seaplanes and Corilair. Secure long-term moorage and boat watch available. Please do not go into the water while hiking to the base of the falls, as this is the source of the marina's drinking water.

This marina is not setup for day visits or tours. Overnight guests only please. Anchoring in the bay adjacent to the dock is not recommended. Field Correspondent Dale Blackburn recommends that rendezvous groups spread out the arrival times of participating boats so that marina host Kyle can direct vessels to assigned spaces.

Toba Inlet. Toba Inlet extends 20 miles into the 8,000-foot-high Coast Range mountains until it ends in drying flats at the mouth of the Toba River. The water is very deep right up to the rock wall shores. Look for two Native pictographs in Toba Inlet: one along the west shore 1 mile south of Brem Bay and another on the north shore 3.6 miles east of Brem Bay. Magnificent waterfalls crash into the sea, especially early in the season when the snowpack is rapidly melting. Toba Inlet reminds us of the inlets north of Cape Caution. Limited anchorage is possible at the head of the inlet, and in Brem Bay off the mouth of the Brem River. We observed a boat stern-tied in a small bight off the north shore near a river inlet at approximately 50°26'N/124°32'W.

Correspondent Gil Flanagan reported that he has anchored, stern-tied, on the northeast side of Brem Bay, at the mouth of a cove created by a rock breakwater not shown on the chart. The views were beautiful.

Toba Inlet's most dramatic waterfalls are on the south side of the inlet, about 3 miles past Snout Point, which is located opposite Brem Bay.

LEWIS CHANNEL

Lewis Channel runs between West Redonda Island and Cortes Island and is where you will find some of the more popular stops on the Desolation Sound area: Refuge Cove, Squirrel Cove, and Teakerne Arm.

Toba Wilderness Marina

A relaxing environment with well maintained hiking trails and waterfalls just a few miles from beautiful Desolation Sound and the lovely warm waters of Pendrell Sound. After the sunset places its glow on the surrounding mountains, spend the evening under the Welcome House with new friends. Quiet and beautiful.

- New concrete floats • Wi-Fi • 30 & 50 amp power
- Dockside moorage for vessels up to 200'
- Plentiful clean, clear water
- Scheduled float plane stop for Kenmore Air
- Stop for Northwest Seaplanes, Corilair
- Boat Watch available (secure personalized service)

By Reservation – Minimum two days in advance
inquiries@tobawilderness.com
250-830-2269 • Please call VHF 66A on approach.

2023 WAGGONER CRUISING GUIDE

DESOLATION SOUND & DISCOVERY PASSAGE

See Area Map Page 305 - Maps Not for Navigation

Guest side-tie moorage, fuel, a well-stocked store, and liquor store are all within easy reach at Refuge Cove.

⑦ **Refuge Cove**. Refuge Cove, with a public marina, fuel dock, shops and well-stocked store, is a good resupply stop in the heart of Desolation Sound. The prime season starts June 1st. The busiest times during July and August are between 11:00 a.m. and 3:00 p.m. For easiest moorage and fuel dock use, early morning and late afternoon are recommended. Several homes, joined by boardwalks, surround the cove. Ample moorage is available. A floating dock, just off the fuel dock, is for overflow moorage, with no power or water. Dogs should be on a leash. A pet path is beside the used-book stand. Anchorage is possible toward the head of the bay.

Traffic can be heavy during high season. Approach slowly, and wait your turn for dock space or fuel. Turnover is rapid; you shouldn't have to wait long. Refuge Cove is a scheduled stop for floatplane service.

Garbage Barge: Around mid-June, an enterprising chap named Dave Cartwright moors a barge near the mouth of Refuge Cove. He accepts bagged garbage at $2 per pound and responsibly takes it away. If you have accumulated garbage from several days in Desolation Sound, this is one of the few places to dispose of it. Tips appreciated.

⑦ **Refuge Cove General Store.** General Delivery, Refuge Cove, BC V0P 1P0; (250) 935-6659; refcov@twincomm.ca; www.refugecove.com. Guest moorage along 2000 feet of side-tie dock space. No reservations; first-come, first-served. Refuge Cove does not monitor VHF radio. Open June-Sept. 15. Purified water, 15 amp power available 24 hours, July and August; 9 am to 5 pm in the shoulder season; no power or water in the winter. Fee-based Wi-Fi. Washrooms, showers, and laundry are up by the store. The fuel dock has gasoline, diesel, and propane.

The store carries groceries, fresh produce, deli items, including cheeses and meats, hand-dipped ice cream, a complete liquor agency with interesting wine selections, some marine supplies and fishing gear, charts, cube and block ice, a selection of books and magazines. It is also a post office. The store has limited operating hours in the fall.

Most businesses, including the art gallery and gift shop, are open June through August. The cafe has fresh bakery items; open for breakfast, lunch and dinner. Licensed for wine and beer with Happy Hour specials.

Teakerne Arm. Teakerne Arm is a deep inlet extending from Lewis Channel into West Redonda Island. Anchorage is just inside the entrance in Talbot Cove, or in front of the waterfall from Cassel Lake at the head of the north arm, or in the south arm. Both arms are deep, except very close to shore.

The area near the waterfall is a provincial park, with a dinghy float connected to shore by an aluminum ramp. Anchorage is in 90 to 150 feet. A cable in fair but serviceable condition hangs down the rock wall west of the waterfall for stern-ties. Several rings are set in the rock just above the high tide line and on either side of the dinghy dock. The waterfall is stunning, about 2½ stories high. Taking the short, vigorous hike from the dinghy float to Cassel Lake for a swim is a popular pastime. The water warms in the summer.

Talbot Cove. Talbot Cove is near the entrance to Teakerne Arm, on the south shore. The cove is marked with large yellow propane floats for a commercial operation. Anchor with a stern-tie in the southeast corner.

CORTES ISLAND

Cortes Island, with approximately 1,000 permanent residents, is part of the Discovery Islands archipelago, lying roughly halfway between Powell River and Campbell River. Desolation Sound lies to the east of Cortes Island. The island is only 15 miles long and 8 miles wide, with three small communities: Whaletown, located northwest of Gorge Harbour; Mansons Landing to the south; and Squirrel Cove on the east side of the island. Although accessible via BC Ferries, Cortes Island has a remote, quiet character. When not arriving by private boat, one must take a ferry to Vancouver Island, then a ferry from Campbell River to Quadra Island, drive across Quadra, to then take another ferry to Cortes Island. June Cameron describes the early days on Cortes Island in her book, *Destination Cortez Island*, a recommended read. Published in Canada by Heritage House and in the U.S. by Fine Edge Publishing.

Public docks can be found at Whaletown, Mansons Landing, and Squirrel Cove; the marina resort in Gorge Harbour is a popular destination and fills in the peak season. Von Donop Inlet and the surrounding area makes

Replenish
Refuel
Refresh
in the Heart of Desolation Sound

Refuge Cove

- Complete Groceries including Fresh Produce, Meats, Dairy Products, Deli
- Gas, Diesel, Oil, Propane
- Large Liquor & Wine Selection
- Block & Party Ice
- Showers, Laundry, Post Office
- Gifts, Books & Charts
- Fishing Tackle & Bait
- Wireless Internet
- Float Plane Service
- Year-round Overnight Moorage
  – no reservations necessary
  – 4hr courtesy stopover

Seasonal Hours
June: 9am-5pm
July & Aug: 9am-6pm
Sept. 1-15: 9am-5pm

Winter Hours
Sept. 16 - May 31
1pm - 3pm M,W,F

Famous Friendly Service

250-935-6659
refcov@twincomm.ca

up the Ha'Thayim Marine Park, with protected anchorage areas, hiking opportunities, and coves to explore by dinghy or kayak. Other harbours and coves around the island provide protected anchorages as well.

The island was named in 1792 during the expedition of Galiano and Valdes, after Hernan Cortes, the Spanish conqueror of Mexico. Sutil Channel, to the west, was also named by Galiano and Valdes for the Nahua woman who was the interpreter, adviser, and mistress of Hernando Cortes during his conquest of Mexico.

⑧ **Squirrel Cove**. Squirrel Cove is made up of an outer bay and an inner bay. The outer bay provides access to the public wharf and the Squirrel Cove Trading Co. general store dock. The inner bay, consisting of two anchorage areas, has better protection and during the summer is often full of anchored boats. A saltwater lagoon is at the head of the inner bay. A connecting rapids runs into the lagoon at high tide and out of the lagoon at low tide. Be sure to plan an exit strategy if you enter the lagoon by dinghy.

The Cove Restaurant, with a take-out menu, is located upland; open daily beginning the second weekend in June. Seating is available in the licensed restaurant, or sit out on the deck and enjoy the lovely view.

A farmers market is held Sundays from 11:00 a.m. to 3:00 p.m.

At one time the inner bay was used for log booming. The late June Cameron wrote an article in Pacific Yachting telling of a tangle of sunken logs on the bottom. Our side-scan sounder showed the bay filled with logs scattered like matchsticks.

In 2019, a Waggoner reader reported fouling their anchor in fish-farm debris at position 50°8.0467'N/124°55.5680'W, about where Chart 3554 shows a fish-farm.

A trail leads from the northwest corner of Squirrel Cove to Von Donop Inlet.

The large building on the west shore is a Native Cultural Centre and offices.

No Discharge Zone. Gray water okay.

⑧ **Squirrel Cove Public Dock.** Harbour Authority of Cortes Island, Box 329, Manson's Landing, B.C., V0P 1K0; (250) 293-0007 or (250) 935-0263; www.cortesharbours.ca; hacimgr@gmail.com. Open all year with 200 feet of floating dock that is often filled with local boats. First-come, first-served; commercial vessels have priority. There's always room for the dinghy. Rafting is encouraged. 15, 20, & 30 amp power. Self-registration and payment at the honor box located at the head of the ramp or pay with credit card, or Paypal at the Harbour Authority website. Garbage drop for a fee (cash).

The dock is close to the Squirrel Cove Trading Co. store. A full-time diver is nearby for maintenance and recovery, phone number posted at the dock.

At very low tides the ramps from the wharf to the floats are quite steep. Local boats often take much of the dock space, although by being patient we've found room. A public mooring ball is available in front of the store.

⑧ **Squirrel Cove Trading Co. Ltd.** P.O. Box 1, Squirrel Cove, BC V0P 1T0; (250) 935-6327; squirrelcovetrading@yahoo.ca; www.squirrelcove.com. Open all year. Washrooms, showers and laundry are in a separate building

The public dock at Squirrel Cove has limited space for overnight and short stays to visit the store.

How Fresh Tomatoes Get To Refuge Cove

Have you ever thought about how a remote marina like Refuge Cove can have such a well-stocked store with fresh produce? Boaters who come to cruise the Desolation Sound region know that the store at Refuge Cove will be ready for them, stocked with all the basics and even fresh produce. But how is it done? We discovered how on a recent visit to this cove of refuge, tucked along the western shore of West Redonda Island.

We stopped at the store in late May, hoping to resupply our galley with tomatoes and other fresh fruit. The storekeeper informed us that a shipment would be arriving that afternoon. Loading boxes of canned goods, along with breads and fresh produce can be a day-long task, especially with the added logistics of transporting supplies to an island. This realization prompted our questions – "Where do the supplies come from and how do you get them here?"

We got the full story that went something like this — We must first motor our barge across Lewis Channel to the public wharf at Squirrel Cove on Cortes Island, where a truck with a load of fresh supplies will be ready to meet us. The truck, of course, had to take the ferry from Campbell River on Vancouver Island to Quathiaski Cove on Quadra Island, then drive across Quadra Island to Heriot Bay to get on another ferry to Whaletown on Cortes Island, and then drive across Cortes Island to Squirrel Cove. Once we arrive at the public wharf at Squirrel Cove, we unload the truck and start stacking a makeshift sled with a yoke and rope that is used to carefully lower the sled, as it slides down the ramp to the dock below. We then start loading the barge, carefully stacking the boxes onto pallets for weight and balance. The process is repeated over and over again until all the boxes and produce have been unloaded from the truck. Then we are off once again, motoring across Lewis Channel in the hopes that the weather will hold for a safe crossing. Back at Refuge Cove, we pull the barge alongside the dock underneath a hoist, where the pallets of supplies are lifted up to the storefront. But we're not done yet, everything must be stacked neatly on the store shelves and arranged in baskets for that added customer appeal.

After hearing their story, we came to more fully appreciate the effort it takes to keep a remote island store stocked with goods throughout the busy cruising season. So next time you bite into that perfectly ripe tomato at Refuge Cove, think about how far that tomato traveled to get there – then slice, dice and enjoy.

[Lorena Landon]

DESOLATION SOUND & DISCOVERY PASSAGE

See Area Map Page 305 - Maps Not for Navigation

Busy Mansons Landing public dock has space for visits by dinghy.

just west of the store. Potable water at the dock. Gasoline, diesel, propane and kerosene available upland. Gas and diesel available at the dock via hoses from the upland pumps. The dock is 6 feet below the local tide chart and only accessible at high tides by small craft, plan accordingly.

Liquor, ice and an assortment of groceries; limited selection of fresh items. Picnic tables available. Books, marine hardware, post office, pay phone, Wi-Fi, ATM. The expanded hardware section downstairs has just about anything a person might need. Amazon packages can be delivered to the store address in c/o your name.

A crafts shop and gallery is next to the store, stocked with island-made (or designed) goods and clothing. Artists take turns staffing the shop. A Sunday market, with crafts, local produce, baked goods and musicians, runs from 11:00 a.m. to 3:00 p.m., summers only.

⑨ **Cortes Bay.** Cortes Bay is well protected, but in some places the soft mud bottom doesn't hold well. Use Chart 3538 when approaching. Several charted rocks and reefs near the entrance have claimed the inattentive. These include Central Rock, north of Twin Islands, several rocks around Three Islets, and a rock off the headland midway between Mary Point and the entrance to Cortes Bay. To be safe, we always pass south of Three Islets.

Pay close attention to the beacon in the middle of the narrow entry to Cortes Bay. This beacon, with its red triangle dayboard, marks the south end of a nasty reef. Leave the beacon to starboard (Red, Right, Returning) as you enter. If you doubt the existence of this reef, one look at low tide will convince you. A small public wharf is at the head of Cortes Bay. It is usually full during the summer. Rafting is required.

Seattle Yacht Club has an outstation on the south shore of Cortes Bay, at the location of a former marina. Royal Vancouver Yacht Club has an outstation on the north shore. No reciprocals at either outstation.

Local knowledge says good holding ground is east of the Royal Van outstation, off the mouth of a small drying cove. During a 30- to 40-knot southeasterly blow, we saw several boats anchored successfully off the SYC outstation as well.

No Discharge Zone. Gray water okay.

Twin Islands. Twin Islands, located off the southeast side of Cortes Island, are really a single island divided by a drying spit. Anchorage is possible close to the drying spit on either side.

Sutil Point. Sutil Point is the south end of Cortes Island. A long, drying spit dotted with boulders extends south from the point, almost to buoy *Q20*. Give this buoy plenty of sea room.

A fresh southeast wind, especially if it is blowing against an ebb current (see Point Atkinson tides), will set up high steep seas south of Sutil Point and east past Mitlenatch Island. Sutil Point can be dangerous in a southeasterly.

Smelt Bay Provincial Park. One mile north of Sutil Point on the west side of the peninsula. Good temporary anchorage is close to shore. The park has 23 campsites, picnic tables, and a white sand beach.

⑩ **Mansons Landing.** Mansons Landing on Manson Bay, located on the south side of Cortes Island has good anchorage, a public dock, a marine park, a lagoon, and a community village one mile from the public dock. The east shore of Manson Bay, the uplands and the lagoon to the east, are all part of the Mansons Landing Marine Park. The public dock also on the east shore provides access to the park and the road to the village. Anchorage is good north of the public dock. The entire area is exposed to the south.

The one mile walk to the village is uphill on a very lightly traveled road. The village has a well stocked co-op grocery store with a wide selection of organic foods and a café with Wi-Fi. The post office, community center, and take-out restaurant with outdoor seating, and a small store are across from the co-op. A small museum and visitor information center, housed in the historic Mansons Landing store building, are beyond the community center on the road to the west. A farmers market is held Fridays from 12:00 p.m. to 3:00 p.m at Mansons Hall Community Center (250-935-0015). Don't miss the homemade pies and root beer floats at the community center cafe.

No Discharge Zone. Gray water okay.

⑩ **Mansons Landing Marine Park.** Open all year, 117 acres. The park has no dock of its own, but can be reached from the Mansons Landing public dock, or you can anchor out. Hague Lake, with warm water and swimming beaches safe for small children, is a 10-minute walk from the public dock. The lagoon reportedly has clams and oysters.

⑩ **Mansons Landing Public Dock.** (Harbour Authority of Cortes Island), Box 329, Manson's Landing, B.C., V0P 1K0; (250) 293-0007; www.cortesharbours.ca; hacimgr@gmail.com. Open all year with a 240 foot float that is often filled with local boats. First-come, first-served; commercial vessels have priority. 20 & 30 amp power. First hour is free; up to 4 hours are at half-rate; thereafter, full-rate; rates apply to dinghies. Self-registration and payment in the honor box at the head of the ramp, or pay by credit card on their website. Garbage drop for a fee (cash). North end of the float is reserved for floatplane and load/unload.

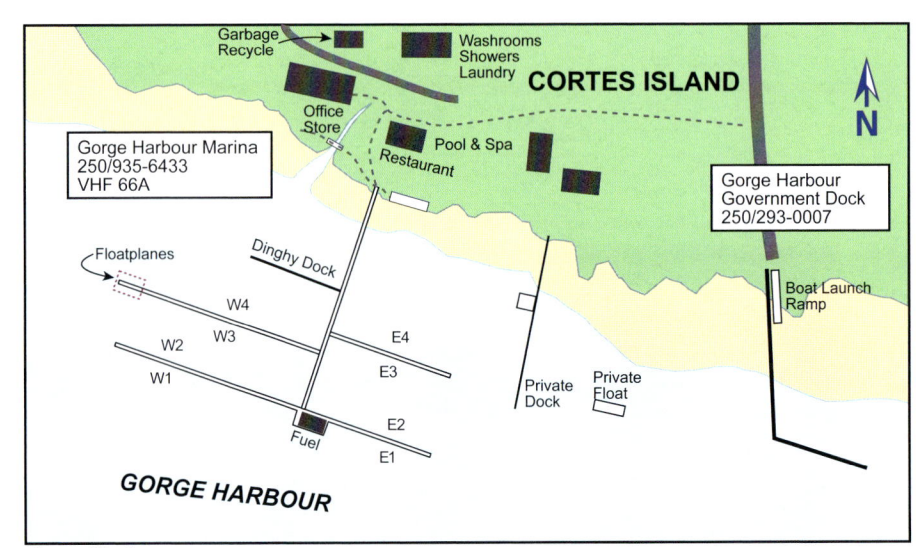

Gorge Harbour

See Area Map Page 305 - Maps Not for Navigation   **DESOLATION SOUND & DISCOVERY PASSAGE**

Gorge Harbour has several areas with good anchoring, all are scenic and protected.

⑪ **Gorge Harbour** is a large bay with many good spots to put the hook down. The entry is through a narrow cleft in the rock cliff. Orange-colored Native pictographs, including a stick figure man, a man on what appears to be a turtle or fish, and several vertical lines, are on the rock wall to port as you enter. You have to look closely to identify them. Current runs through the entrance, but boats go through at any time. Inside you'll find good, protected anchorage. Several aquaculture operations are in the harbour. A field of private buoys is to port. The Gorge Harbour Marina Resort, on the northwest shore, has many amenities, including a restaurant. If the marina is full, anchor in the protected bay in 55 to 60 feet.

No Discharge Zone. Gray water okay.

⑪ **Gorge Harbour Marina Resort.** P.O. Box 89, Whaletown, BC V0P 1Z0; (250) 935-6433 ext. 4; moorage@gorgeharbour.com; www.gorgeharbour.com. Monitors VHF 66A. Open all year, gasoline and diesel at the fuel dock, guest moorage along 1800 feet of dock. Reservations are recommended May 15 to September 15; held-back moorage space is released daily at 3:30 p.m., first-come, first-served. Facilities include 30 & 50 amp power, water, swimming pool, hot tub, barbecue areas, washrooms, showers, laundry, and Wi-Fi.

The marina resort was purchased by the Klahoose Tribe in August of 2021; they plan to expand the fuel dock and moorage facilities in the future. A well-stocked convenience store has canned goods, meats, dairy products, ice, and propane. The store has a large selection of wine and liquor and is reported to have the best produce on the island, organic and vegan items available. A dinghy dock is available for boats anchored out to access the store.

Four lodge rooms and a poolside cottage for rent. Garbage disposal is available for marina guests for a fee, no charge for recycling. Complete recycling instructions available. The resort has an RV park, 2 trailer rentals, and campground. Floatplane service to the marina. Kayaks and stand-up paddleboards for rent.

The resort features a pool and hot tub surrounded by attractive landscaping. A patio with a fireplace and barbecue area are available for guest use. Both overlook the harbor. Live music is often performed in the evening on the patio, as well as weekly movie nights for families. There is a nice children's play area. Many boaters consider Gorge Harbour Marina & Resort to be on the list of special destinations. The Gorge Harbour Marina farmer's market is open from 10 a.m. to 1:00 p.m. on Saturdays during summer.

The Floathouse Restaurant always gets excellent reviews. The atmosphere is cozy and conducive to multi-table conversations. Open from May through September, with reduced hours in winter. During peak season the restaurant offers breakfast, lunch, appies (3:00 p.m. to 5:00 p.m.), dinner and a Sunday brunch. The restaurant has a covered bar and cocktail area; an open section has seating overlooking the harbour. Restaurant reservations recommended in the high season.

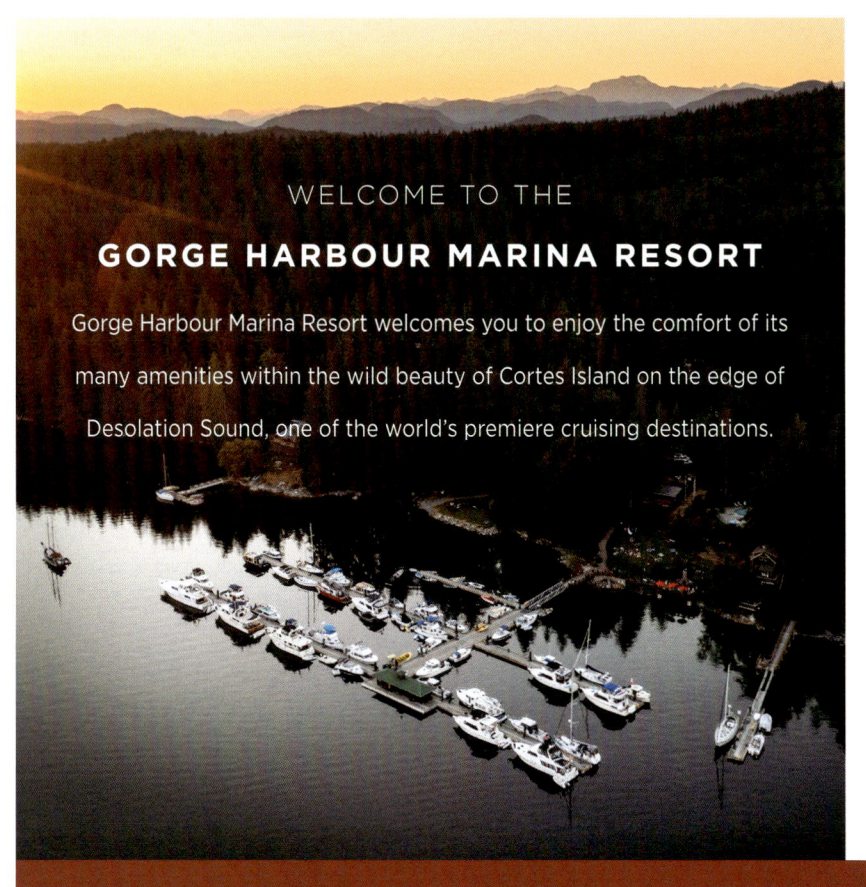

WELCOME TO THE
GORGE HARBOUR MARINA RESORT

Gorge Harbour Marina Resort welcomes you to enjoy the comfort of its many amenities within the wild beauty of Cortes Island on the edge of Desolation Sound, one of the world's premiere cruising destinations.

GORGE HARBOUR

Moorage · Accommodations

RV & Camping · Kayak & Paddle Board

Rentals · Marine Gas & Diesel

Car Gas · Propane

Grocery & Liquor Store

Restaurant · Pool & Hot Tub

Showers · Laundry · Internet

Phone: 250-935-6433 | reserve@gorgeharbour.com | www.gorgeharbour.com

DESOLATION SOUND & DISCOVERY PASSAGE

See Area Map Page 305 - Maps Not for Navigation

⑪ **Gorge Harbour Public Dock.** (Harbour Authority of Cortes Island), Box 329, Manson's Landing, B.C., V0P 1K0; (250) 293-0007; www.corteshabours.ca; hacimgr@gmail.com. Located a short distance east of the Gorge Harbour Marina. Open all year with a 100 foot float that is often filled with local boats. First-come, first-served; commercial vessels have priority. Self-registration and payment honor box at the head of the ramp. Garbage drop for a fee (cash) as scheduled via truck pick up; see posted schedule upland. Boat launch ramp located adjacent to the dock.

Uganda Passage. Uganda Passage separates Cortes Island from Marina Island. The pass is narrow and winding, but well marked and easy to navigate as long as you pay attention. Red, Right, Returning assumes you are returning from the south. See the Uganda Passage map showing the route through the passage. Shark Spit is long and low, with a superb sand beach. Swimming is good. Anchorage is south of the pass, on either the Cortes Island side or the Marina Island side.

Whaletown. Whaletown is the terminus of the ferry between Cortes Island and Quadra Island. The ferry dock is on the north side of the bay, and a 200-foot public float is on the south side. Watch for several marked and unmarked rocks, normally covered by kelp. The public float is mostly taken up by local boats. First hour free; stays up to 4 hours at half rate; stays over 4 hours at full day rate. Self-registration and payment box located on the wharf at the head of the ramp.

Subtle Islands. The two Subtle Islands are separated by a drying shoal. Good anchorage is off this shoal on the east side, particularly in settled weather. The little bay on the north side is very deep except at the head. It has a lovely (and exposed) view to the north. The islands are privately owned and marked with "stay off" and "keep away" signs.

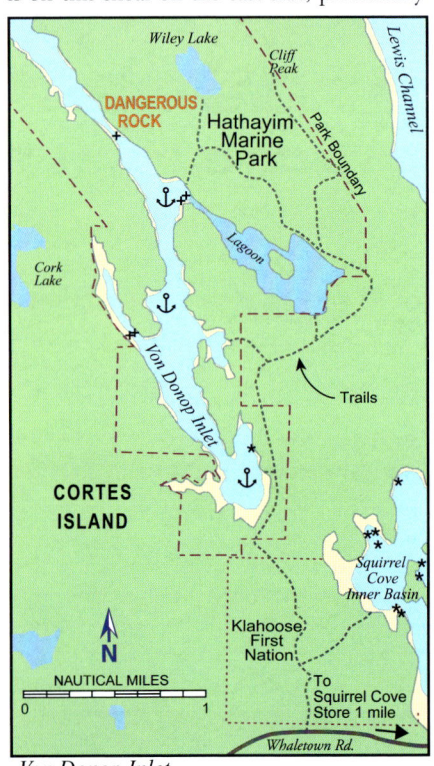

Coulter Bay. Coulter Bay is pretty, but as the chart indicates, much of the bay is too shallow for anchoring. Most of the good spots are taken by local boats. You could anchor in the tiny nook behind Coulter Island, beside a little unnamed islet to the west. Some cabins are nearby, but they are screened from view.

Carrington Bay. Carrington Bay is pretty, and well protected except from the north. The bottom is rocky so be sure your anchor is properly set before turning in for the night. Carrington Lagoon, at the head of the bay, is interesting to explore. You can portage a kayak across the logs that choke the entrance to the lagoon. The late June Cameron, in *Destination Cortez*, says the lagoon entrance was blasted out of rock. A foot-bridge now crosses the entrance.

A good anchorage is to the right, near the entrance to the lagoon, with a stern-tie ashore. We've seen other boats anchored in the little bight a short distance to the left of the lagoon entrance and behind the tiny island just off the eastern shore of the bay. The best anchorage is in the lee of Jane Islet or in the lee of the 58-meter islet.

No Discharge Zone. Gray water okay.

Quartz Bay. Quartz Bay is unusually pretty, with good holding bottom. The eastern cove of the bay has several homes and a few private docks along the shoreline. You can anchor with swinging room in 30 to 42 feet near the head, but you're in their front yards. The western cove has some aquaculture, one cabin on the shore, and anchoring depths near the south and west shores. You may have to run a stern-tie to shore. It is exposed to north winds, but it's a nice spot.

⑫ **Von Donop Inlet.** Von Donop Inlet, on the northwest tip of Cortes Island, is a 3 mile long landlocked inlet entirely within the Háthayim Provincial Marine Park. The inlet is entered through a 2-mile long channel with a narrow neck mid-way along the channel. Caution at the neck for rocks in the middle of the channel; hug the south side of the channel. Best entry and exit is at high-water slack. Once inside, several coves provide protected anchorage. The largest of these coves takes up the entire head of the inlet and has room for many boats. The bottom in this area is sticky mud. It is ideal for holding, but requires extra cleaning time when departing. The lagoon at the northeast end of the inlet can be explored by dinghy at high-water slack. The outlet of this lagoon has reversing tidal overfalls. All of the uplands are park lands. Several maintained trails lead from the head of the Inlet to the lagoon, lakes, Squirrel Cove, and a longer trail leads to the road to Squirrel Cove Store and Gorge Harbour. The trailhead is on the southeast shore at the head of the inlet.

LOCAL KNOWLEDGE

DANGEROUS ROCK: About halfway into Von Donop Inlet, a rock lies in the narrowest part of the channel. Look for two prominent rock outcroppings covered with lichen, moss and grass on the left side of the channel. The rock is opposite the second, or inner, of these outcroppings. Hug the right side and keep that rock to port, even if tree branches try to brush the starboard side of the boat or rigging.

⑫ **Háthayim Provincial Marine Park** (Von Donop). This 3155-acre park includes Von Donop Inlet, Robertson Lake and Wiley Lake.

Read Island. The east side of Read Island is indented from the south by **Evans Bay**, where several little notches are worth exploring as anchorages. Most have drying flats at their heads. A small public float is near the entrance to Evans Bay and is usually filled with local boats. No amenities upland. **Bird Cove** is one of the best protected anchorages. Bird Cove has a wilderness feel despite a couple of homes along the shore. .

The north end of Evans Bay splits into two coves. The westerly cove is too deep for anchoring. The easterly cove is well protected with good anchoring depths; a fishing lodge and cabin are ashore.

Hill Island. Hill Island is privately owned. According to Sailing Directions, a private lodge with a floating breakwater is in Totem Bay. The island is not open to the public.

Burdwood Bay. Burdwood Bay has several possible anchorages, particularly on the lee side of the little islands that extend from the south side of the bay, and in a notch in the north end. Burdwood Bay is not particularly pretty, but could be a hideout in a storm.

Hoskyn Channel. Hoskyn Channel runs between Read Island and Quadra Island and connects at the north with Whiterock Passage and Surge Narrows.

Von Donop Inlet

Uganda Passage

Middle entrance to Waiatt Bay in Octopus Islands Marine Park

Good anchorage is at the head of the bay in Von Donop Inlet.

Bold Island Anchorage. Bold Island is just north of Village Bay on the west side of Hoskyn Channel. Enter through Crescent Channel. Anchorage is in the basin at the northwest corner of Bold Island, approximately between the two drying reefs. Two oyster farms are in the area with one along the northwest shore of Bold Island. The bay opens to the south with views across Read Island. The anchorage might be exposed to southerlies.

Hjorth Bay. Hjorth Bay, on Hoskyn Channel along the west side of Read Island, is a good anchorage except in a strong southerly. Anchor in 50 to 60 feet, probably with a stern-tie to shore. A small cabin is on shore behind the island.

Surge Narrows Settlement. A public wharf and floats located about three-quarters of a mile northeast of Surge Point serves the residents of Read Island. The floats have about 180 feet of side-tie space; the outermost end is reserved for floatplanes. A buoy marking a drying rock is northwest of the floats. The general store and its adjacent dock closed many years ago.

Whiterock Passage. Whiterock Passage is narrow, and the dredged channel is bounded on both sides by drying shoals studded with angry boulders. Least depth at zero tide is 5 feet. Maximum currents are 2 knots. Running Whiterock Passage at half tide is a good idea—it exposes the shoals on both sides but provides a little extra depth. The uninitiated tend to avoid Whiterock Passage, but it's easy to run if you pay attention and know how. Here's how:

Carefully study Chart 3537 with its detail of Whiterock Passage at a scale of 1:10,000. As the charts show, two ranges are on the Read Island side of the passage. Going either direction, one will be a leading range as you enter, and the other a back range as you depart. Approaching, find the leading range and stay exactly on it. Proceed slowly and watch astern as the back range comes into view. When the back range lines up, turn the appropriate direction and let the back range keep you on course as you complete your transit.

Remember that the course lines on the charts are true, not magnetic. You must subtract the magnetic variation from the true heading to get the magnetic course. Before entering, make sure you have a clear view astern from the helm to view the back range markers.

Rendezvous Islands. The Rendezvous Islands have a number of homes along their shores. Anchorage may be possible in a bight between the southern and middle islands, but a private float and dolphins restrict the room available.

CALM CHANNEL

Calm Channel connects Lewis Channel and Sutil Channel to the south, and with Bute Inlet and the Yuculta Rapids to the north. It is appropriately named, often being wind-free when areas nearby are breezy.

Frances Bay. A logging road and logging dump area are located on the westerly side at the head of the bay, indicating past logging operations. Logging operations have not been seen here in recent years. Boats have anchored at the head of the bay in the eastern portion. It has been reported that the bottom is rocky throughout the rest of the bay and an anchor fouling cable is near the log dump.

Church House. Church House is an abandoned Indian Reserve opposite the entrance to Hole in the Wall on Calm Channel, and near the mouth of Bute Inlet. The white-painted church, an often-photographed landmark, has collapsed in a heap.

Redonda Bay. Redonda Bay has the ruins of an old wharf left over from logging days, but otherwise is not a good anchorage. The wharf is no longer usable and the ramp leading from the float to the wharf is gone. Several rocks in the bay are charted.

Bute Inlet. Bute Inlet, approximately 35 miles long, is very deep. Except in small areas near the mouths of rivers and at the head of the inlet, it is not good for anchorage. Usually, the bottom drops away steeply, making a stern-tie to shore necessary. Anchorages should be chosen with an eye to strong inflow winds during the afternoon, followed by calm, then by icy outflow winds in the morning. Correspondents Gil and Karen Flanagan explain:

"The glaciers around Bute Inlet were melting and there are a lot of them. The water was milky by Stuart Island, and got darker and darker the farther up we went, turning from light green to gray to brownish. We saw considerable drift, including complete trees with roots sticking 8 feet or so into the air. At times we had to slow to idle, shift to neutral and coast through bands of drift. Jack Mold, the caretaker at Southgate Camp, said what we experienced was normal. Waddington Harbour, at the head of Bute Inlet, has a lot of good anchoring spots in 10 to 50 foot depths. We anchored as close to the northeast shore as we could get, and still were at least 100 yards from the beach (don't bother trying to stern-tie). There is no protection from wind, but we had no wind. We didn't see much driftwood on the beach, either. We doubt if inflow winds blow hard or long, probably because even on hot days the massive ice fields in the mountains above preclude high land temperatures.

Because of the ice fields, we had an overnight low in the upper 40s on September 1. It was 10 to 20 degrees lower than temperatures we had been experiencing in Desolation Sound. The morning air was cold enough that we needed heavy coats, even in the sun. Mountains 6,000 to 7,000 feet high rise directly from the head of the inlet. They have snowfields, and are spectacular. The milky water, drifting logs, huge harbor and high mountains create an environment that felt wild and different from anywhere we have been on the coast. We spent only 19 hours in Waddington Harbour, which wasn't long enough to take the dinghy up either river. We did see a grizzly bear on the beach near our anchorage. We definitely will go back." [*Flanagan*]

Reader Richard McBride sent a note about a tiny anchorage he calls "The Nook," just outside Orford Bay:

"It is a small crack in the mountain wall about 100 feet wide at the opening and about 150 feet deep, with a little waterfall at the head. This is a terrific spot for a couple of small boats to tuck in. Lat/lon 50°34.368'N/124°52.439'W."

DESOLATION SOUND & DISCOVERY PASSAGE

See Area Map Page 305 - Maps Not for Navigation

OKISOLLO CHANNEL/ SURGE NARROWS

Owen Bay tides and Okisollo Channel Secondary Port tide corrections are contained in Canadian Tide and Current Tables Vol. 6, and Ports and Passes. Okisollo Channel runs along the east and north sides of Quadra Island, from Surge Narrows to Discovery Passage.

Surge Narrows & Beazley Passage. Surge Narrows and Beazley Passage should be run at or near slack water. Spring floods set eastward to 12 knots and ebbs set westward to 10 knots. Current predictions are shown under Beazley Passage in the Canadian Tide and Current Tables Vol. 6, and Ports and Passes.

Although Beazley Passage, between Peck Island and Sturt Island, has the strongest currents in the Surge Narrows area, it is the preferred route between Hoskyn Channel and Okisollo Channel. Especially on an ebb current in Beazley Passage, watch for Tusko Rock, which dries at 5 feet, on the east side of the pass at the north end. Stay well clear of Tusko Rock.

Sailing Directions says the duration of slack at Surge Narrows varies between 5 and 11 minutes.

The passage north of the Settler's Group is usable following the deeper channel, avoiding the charted rocks and shoals.

Cozy anchorages with stern tie in protected coves at Octopus Islands Marine Park

⑬ **Octopus Islands Marine Park.** This is a beautiful, popular anchorage and exploration area, wonderfully protected. The park includes all of Waiatt Bay, the uplands south of Waiatt Bay, and all but the two large islands in the Octopus Islands group. The two islands charted on Chart 3539 as 50 meter and 71 meter islands are private and not part of the park. Octopus Islands Marine Park was expanded and Chart 3539 shows its present boundaries. Much of the upland areas to the north of Waiatt Bay are not part of the park and are private property.

You can enter Waiatt Bay from Okisollo Channel with care for the rocks, but the usual entry is by a narrow channel from the north. Anchor in Waiatt Bay or any of several coves in the Octopus Islands group and run a stern-tie to shore. At the end of the narrow channel as you enter from the north, a rock, clearly shown on Plans Chart 3537, obstructs part of the entry to the first cove on the right. This rock is easily seen as a white smear under the water.

Waiatt Bay. Waiatt Bay is broad and protected, with convenient anchoring depths throughout. The entire bay is part of the Octopus Islands Marine Park. The bay's entrance is choked with islets and rocks, and Sailing Directions (written for large vessels) warns against entering. With the aid of large scale Plans Chart 3537, however, a small boat can pick its way in along the south shore, or

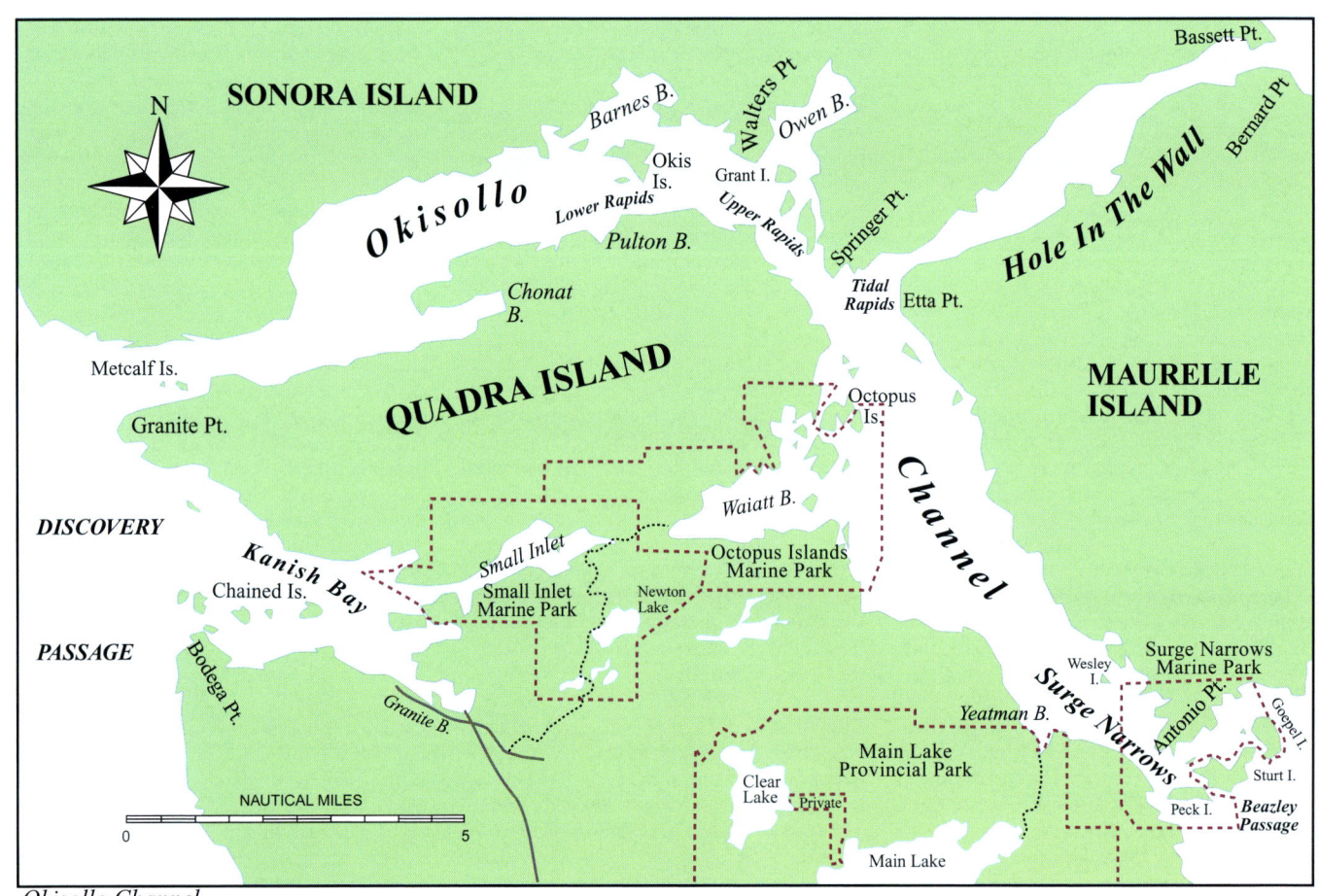

Okisollo Channel

in the middle of the islets, or along the north shore. The chart shows the possibilities. You might anchor in a notch along the shore, or at the head of the bay.

A half-mile easy trail connects the head of Waiatt Bay with Small Inlet. About half way between Waiatt Bay and Small Inlet, a sign points the way to Newton Lake with a less traveled trail branching to the northwest. Follow the Newton Lake sign direction, which also takes you to Small Inlet. A trail sign at the head of the cove in Small Inlet marks the end of the trail between Waiatt Bay and Small Inlet. From here, the trail to Newton Lake follows the south shore of Small Inlet cove before becoming difficult and steep. It is one mile from the trail head at Small Inlet cove to Newton Lake. Don't confuse a small pond, a short distance before Newton Lake, for the real thing. The crystal clear waters of Newton Lake invite a fresh water swim. From Newton Lake a two-mile trail continues to Granite Bay Road and Granite Bay.

Hole in the Wall. Hole in the Wall connects Okisollo Channel with Calm Channel to the east. Boats accumulate on each side of the rapids at the western entrance to Hole in the Wall, waiting for slack water. In general, boats on the upstream side will catch the last of the fair current when the rapids calm down, leaving room for the boats on the other side to pick up the new fair current in the opposite direction. Slacks occur 50 to 55 minutes before Seymour Narrows, and last about 4 minutes (Seymour Narrows currents are shown in Canadian Tide and Current Tables Vol. 6, and Ports and Passes). The flood current sets northeast. Maximum currents run to 12 knots on the flood and 10 knots on the ebb.

LOCAL KNOWLEDGE

DANGEROUS CURRENTS: Upper Rapids and Lower Rapids in Okisollo Channel can be dangerous and should be run at or near slack. Slacks occur 50 to 55 minutes before slack at Seymour Narrows.

Upper Rapids. These are the first rapids in Okisollo Channel north of Hole in the Wall, and they are dangerous unless run at or near slack water. Slack occurs 55 minutes before Seymour Narrows (Seymour Narrows currents are shown in Canadian Tide and Current Tables Vol. 6, and Ports and Passes). At full rush on a spring tide, the rapids running at 9 knots are frightening to watch. A wall of white water stretches nearly across the channel almost until slack. When it's time to go through, steer a little east of mid-channel to avoid Bentley Rock. Chart 3537 makes the course clear.

Barnes Bay and several small indents in this part of Okisollo Channel could be good anchorages, except for the large amount of log booming and aquaculture. Owen Bay is the preferred anchorage.

Drew Harbour has good anchoring for many boats; Rebecca Spit Park has excellent beaches.

LOCAL KNOWLEDGE

STRONG CURRENTS: Currents run strong through the islands that separate Owen Bay from Upper Rapids. If you explore these islands, exercise caution to avoid getting sucked into the rapids.

Owen Bay. Owen Bay is large and pretty. Our recommended anchorage is in the second little notch on the west side of the bay. This notch is quite protected, and has room for about 5 boats if the spots are well chosen and stern-ties are used. Enter Owen Bay through a narrow channel between Walters Point and Grant Island. A reef, marked by kelp, extends from Walters Point nearly halfway across this channel. It will inspire you to hug the Grant Island side. Correspondent Pat Shera adds that there is good holding and shelter near the small public float on the east side of the bay. Shera also says that the northeastern head of Owen Bay has "acres of good holding on a flat bottom." That area, however, is subject to being hit by strong (and cold) outflow winds from Bute Inlet. He was "kissed by the Bute" one sleepless night and knows what he's talking about.

Lower Rapids. Lower Rapids turns at virtually the same time as Upper Rapids—55 minutes before Seymour Narrows (Seymour Narrows currents are shown in Canadian Tide and Current Tables Vol. 6, and Ports and Passes). Currents run to 9 knots on spring tides, and you must steer a course to avoid Gypsy Shoal, which lies nearly in the middle. Transit at slack water only.

We recommend avoiding Lower Rapids altogether by going through Barnes Bay, north of the Okis Islands. At times other than slack you will still see considerable current, but you will avoid the hazards of Lower Rapids.

Barnes Bay. Barnes Bay and several small indents in this part of Okisollo Channel could be good anchorages, except for the fair amount of aquaculture. Anchorage may be possible to the west in **Chonat Bay** and in the notch behind **Metcalf Island.**

QUADRA ISLAND, SOUTH

⑭ **Drew Harbour/Rebecca Spit Marine Park.** Drew Harbour is large, and in the right winds the open harbor can be lumpy. The preferred anchorage is in the bight immediately inside the north tip of Rebecca Spit. A drying shoal defines the south side of this bight. The shoal extends a considerable distance from shore, and it could fool you at high tide. If the preferred bight is full, anchor south of the drying shoal in 24 to 36 feet, although it isn't as protected. Nearly all of Drew Harbour has good anchoring. The south half has a flat bottom and is more protected in southerly winds. There is plenty of room for many boats, with ample swinging room.

Rebecca Spit Marine Park is popular. The Drew Harbour side of the spit has a lovely sand beach. Trails with picnic tables run the length of the spit. The exposed Sutil Channel side has a beach of remarkable small round boulders.

The silvered tree snags on the spit are the result of subsidence during a 1946 earthquake. It is believed that the mounded fortifications were defenses built 200 to 400 years ago by the local Salish tribe against attacks from the Native Kwakiutl.

LOCAL KNOWLEDGE

AQUACULTURE BUOYS: A field of about 6 white aquaculture buoys are along the southeast shore of Quadra Island just south of Rebecca Spit. The buoys are about 0.75 nm off shore.

Stay informed at WaggonerGuide.com/Updates

DESOLATION SOUND & DISCOVERY PASSAGE

See Area Map Page 305 - Maps Not for Navigation

Heriot Bay Inn & Marina has fuel and a delightful pub.

Taku Resort & Marina has views of Drew Harbour and Rebecca Spit.

⑮ **Heriot Bay.** Heriot Bay has a public wharf, a supermarket, the Heriot Bay Inn & Marina, and the Taku Resort. During the summer high season the public dock usually is full with boats rafted several deep. Anchorage area north of the public wharf is filled with private mooring balls. Transient anchorage is found further east in 50 to 60 feet of water. The Heriot Bay Inn & Marina is between the ferry dock and the public dock. Just south of Heriot Bay, in Drew Harbour proper, Taku Resort has excellent docks and facilities. Heriot Bay Tru-Value Foods, a short walk from the Heriot Bay or Taku resorts, is the best-stocked grocery store in Desolation Sound, with complete groceries, including fresh vegetables and meats, a post office, gift shop, and liquor store; Java Bay Cafe is located in the same building. Free grocery delivery to the docks from Tru-Value Grocery (250) 285-2436. Bicycles can be rented from a shop on the road above Taku Resort. The Quadra Island Golf Course is a short ride away.

⑮ **Heriot Bay Public Wharf.** (250) 285-3622; www.qiha.ca. Monitors VHF 68A. Open all year; power, water, portable toilets, Wi-Fi, garbage drop, launch ramp. The floats are often filled with local boats; occasional guest moorage in slips as assigned and available; call ahead to inquire. Watch for ferry wash on the outer face. Heriot Bay Inn and shopping nearby. The dock is managed by the Quadra Island Harbour Authority.

⑮ **Heriot Bay Inn & Marina**. P.O. Box 100, Heriot Bay, BC V0P 1H0; (250) 285-3322; (888) 605-4545; info@heriotbayinn.com; www.heriotbayinn.com. Monitors VHF 66A. Open all year, gasoline, diesel, propane, ice and fishing tackle. Guest moorage available on 1800 feet of side-tie dock, mostly 15 amp power with some 30 amp, washrooms, showers, laundry, limited Wi-Fi. Reservations recommended June through September. Fairways between the finger floats are narrow, larger vessels should 'starboard-tie' on the outside of Float 1. The outer docks and fuel dock are subject to wakes from passing ferries.

The hotel is delightful. This 1913 historic hotel has ten rooms, three cabins, and a suite. The restaurant has outdoor seating overlooking the bay, and the pub has live music on many nights. The gift store off the lobby has local guidebooks, local artisan jewelry, crafts, and souvenirs. The office can provide contact information for local tours and fishing guides. Heriot Bay Tru-Value Foods is a short walk up the hill. Bicycle and kayak rentals nearby.

In 2008 a group of 20 Quadra Island residents ("old hippies," one of them said) bought the property and set about making improvements. Among them they had all the needed skills: carpentry, electrical, painting, administrative, whatever else was required. In recent years the Heriot Bay Inn's public areas have been upgraded with lovely flower beds and walkways. The goal of this working community is to maintain the property with the spirit of welcoming the traveling public.

⑮ **Taku Resort & Marina.** P.O. Box 1, Heriot Bay, BC V0P 1H0; (877) 285-8258; info@takuresort.com; www.takuresort.com. Monitors VHF 66A. Open all year. Approximately 600 feet of guest moorage, reservations accepted. Docks were renovated in 2022. Potable water, 30 amp power, and Wi-Fi. Wi-Fi may be spotty. Garbage drop for overnight moorage guests. Washrooms, coin showers, laundry and a 14-room resort are ashore, as are RV sites, tennis, volleyball, badminton and horseshoes. The docks are exposed to southeast winds across the bay, but the inside moorage is protected. The views and proximity to Rebecca Spit Marine Park make this a popular marina. A shopping center and Tru-Value Foods grocery store is a short walk away. A kayak tour operator is on site and a bicycle rental store is just up the road. The resort offers kayak and paddleboard rentals. The facilities and service are high quality. Lynden McMartin is the manager.

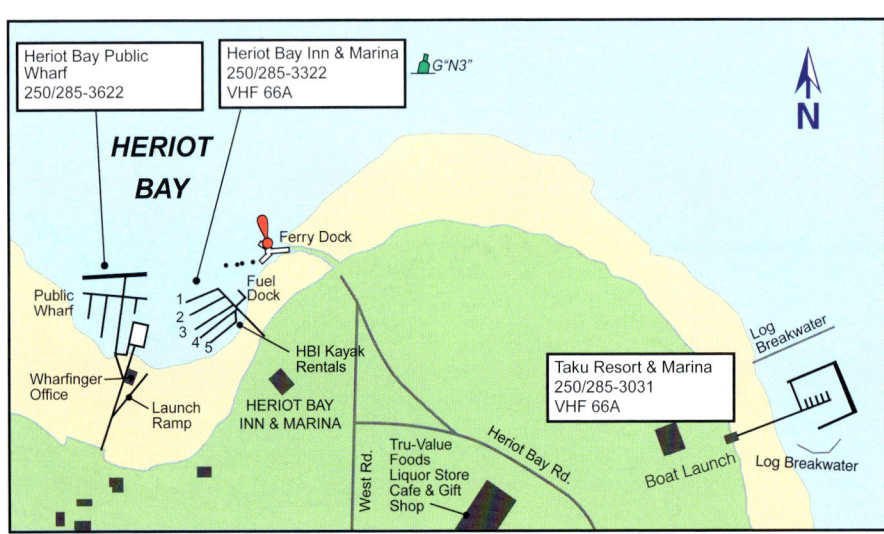

Heriot Bay

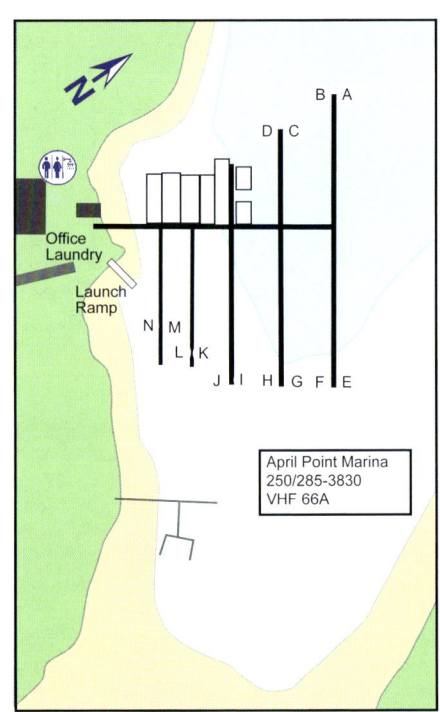

April Point Marina

DISCOVERY PASSAGE

Discovery Passage is approximately 20 miles long, and separates Quadra Island and Sonora Island from Vancouver Island. It is the main route for commercial traffic north and south along the east side of Vancouver Island. Cape Mudge is the south entrance to Discovery Passage. At the north end, Discovery Passage connects with Johnstone Strait at Chatham Point. An enormous amount of water flows through Discovery Passage, flooding south and ebbing north. Tide-rips are frequent.

Cape Mudge. The area around Cape Mudge and Wilby Shoals is a famous hot spot for salmon fishing and often full of small fishing craft during the summer months. Several resorts in the area cater to sport fishermen. Guides are available for hire in Campbell River.

On a flood tide, a backeddy often sets up at Cape Mudge running north along the western edge of Wilby Shoals all the way to the Cape Mudge Lighthouse.

LOCAL KNOWLEDGE

CAPE MUDGE TIDE-RIPS: A strong southeasterly wind against a large, south-flowing flood tide can set up high and dangerous seas. Lives have been lost off Cape Mudge in such conditions. Cape Mudge has been a graveyard for vessels of all sizes, particularly in the winter months. If a southeaster is blowing, Sailing Directions recommends entering at or after high water slack.

Yaculta. The First Nations settlement of Yaculta, located on Quadra Island, is the site of the Nuyumbalees Cultural Centre (250-914-8762), with regalia and historical artifacts and photos. Open Thursday-Sunday, June 15 through September 15. The Centre is a 3-block walk south from the public dock. We urge a visit.

Yaculta Public Dock. Located at 50°01.4'N on the east side of Discovery Passage. Public dock with 220 feet of float; 30 amp power and water. No charge. Not recommended for overnight stays, exposed to winds and boat wakes, use at your own risk. Near the Yaculta village and the Nuyumbalees Cultural Centre. Moorage space on the more protected inside of the floats is normally occupied by local boats.

⑯ **Quathiaski Cove.** Quathiaski Cove (known locally as Q-Cove) is the Quadra Island landing for the ferry to Campbell River. A public dock is next to the ferry landing and may be rolly from ferry wakes and passing vessels. A seasonal snack stand is in the ferry parking lot; a pub and restaurant are a short walk away. A shopping center with a good grocery store, a tasty informal café, pizza restaurant, bank with an ATM, and a variety of stores to peruse are a few blocks up the hill from the ferry landing. The grocery store will deliver to the dock. The Visitor Centre is next to the bank. A farmers market adjacent to the Visitor Centre is open Saturday mornings during the summer months.

Because of ferry traffic, the best anchorage is farther north in the cove behind Grouse Island. Fingers of current from Discovery Passage work into Quathiaski Cove at some stages of the tide, so be sure the anchor is well set.

⑯ **Quathiaski Cove Public Wharf.** (250) 285-3622; www.qiha.ca. Adjacent to the ferry landing. The dock has 20, 30 & 50 amp power, water, Wi-Fi, pay telephone, and launch ramp. Above the dock are washrooms and shower facilities, with a number to call for the keycode after hours. The dock has considerable mooring space, but we often find it crowded with local and commercial fish boats. Commercial fish boats have priority. South side of the south float is for seine fishing vessels. Managed by the Quadra Island Harbour Authority.

⑰ **April Point Marina.** 866 April Point Rd. Quathiaski Cove, BC V0P 1N0; (250) 285-3830; info@aprilpointmarina.com; Monitors VHF 66A. Moorage open year round. The marina is located in the cove a half mile southeast of April Point. The marina has moorage for vessels up to 200 feet; 30, 50, & 100 amp power. Call for reservations. Water at the docks, and garbage for marina guests. Laundry; restrooms and showers. Floatplane service by Kenmore Air.

Approaching, you will see a red spar buoy at the entrance to the cove. The buoy marks a shoal, keep the buoy to starboard as you enter (Red, Right, Returning). The proper channel will appear narrow, especially at low tide. You will be strongly tempted to leave the buoy to port, which might put you aground.

Limited anchorage can be found in the cove near the marina. A rock-strewn passage, suitable for kayaks and dinghies only, leads between the cove and adjacent Gowlland Harbour.

April Point Resort is a 10-minute walk from the marina, or an easy commute by dinghy. The docks in front of the Resort lodge are for dinghies and tour boats only.

April Point Resort & Spa (250-285-2222) is under separate ownership from the marina. Located on April Point, the resort is a vacation destination from an earlier time, which is now showing its age. Notable stars from previous generations, like Bob Hope and John Wayne, vacationed here. Guests will find accommodations and seasonal dining. The spa may be open depending on staffing. The resort is owned by North Coast Hotel Resort Ltd, which operates a number of high-quality resorts. Painter's Lodge, north of Campbell River on the west side of Discovery Passage, is a North Coast Hotel resort, with dining, a swimming pool, hot tub, and tennis courts.

Steep Island Lodge. P.O. Box 699, Campbell River, BC V9W 6J3; (250) 830-8179; info@steepisland.com; www.steepisland.com. Open May 15 to September 30. Guest moorage for those staying in lodge accommodations. Water at the dock, no power. This is a beautiful resort with private cabins. It is on the east side of Steep Island, off the northwest corner of Gowlland Island. Fishing and kayak charters available. Floatplane service. Jacuzzi. Dinner is all-inclusive and by reservation only.

⑱ **Gowlland Harbour.** Gowlland Harbour is a large, protected bay behind Gowlland Island. Before entering, study the chart so you can avoid Entrance Rock north of Gowlland Island.

You'll find good anchoring depths at the north end of the bay, but it's much prettier at the south end. Good protection can be found behind Stag Island, although homes and docks are along the shoreline. Good anchoring is also behind Wren Islet, Crow Islet, and the Mouse Islets, all of them a little northwest of Stag Island. These islets, which are protected as provincial park preserves, make good picnic spots. Deeper water anchoring with more swing room and fewer homes along the shore can be found at the southeast end of the harbour.

April Point Marina has quiet moorage in the snug cove.

DESOLATION SOUND & DISCOVERY PASSAGE

⑲ **Seascape Waterfront Resort**. Due to storm damage, this facility closed to the public in 2022. Floats are partially sunk and unsafe. Upland facilities, including cabins are also closed. It is unlikely that this facility will open to the public in the future.

CAMPBELL RIVER

Campbell River calls itself the "Salmon Capital of the World," and is working to become an important tourist destination. While dozens of guideboats take sportfishermen to prime fishing areas in Discovery Passage and off Cape Mudge, lunker-size salmon are still caught from marina breakwaters and the public fishing pier.

Campbell River has complete shopping, dining, and marine facilities, all close to the waterfront. Fisherman's Wharf and the Coast Marina are close to Tyee Plaza with drugstore, liquor store, excellent laundromat, and more. Discovery Harbour Marina is part of the extensive Discovery Harbour Centre with grocery and big-box general merchandise stores, liquor store, fast food, restaurants, and pubs. Buses leave hourly from a shelter at the mall, providing a convenient way to visit other areas of town.

An attractive promenade runs the length of the shoreline from Fisherman's Wharf to Discovery Harbour Marina. The recently extended promenade now connects the two shopping areas.

As you approach Campbell River from the south you will find four marinas, with transient moorage, each protected by a breakwater. The southernmost marina is Fisherman's Wharf (formerly the Government Dock, now Campbell River Harbour Authority).

Coast Marina is the second breakwater protected marina, offering guest moorage as you progress northward. The BC ferry runs between Quathiaski Cove on Quadra Island and Campbell River lands adjacent to Coast Marina. Coast Marina is closest to downtown Campbell River.

The third marina is Discovery Harbour Marina with considerable moorage, including slips and side-tie. The 52-acre Discovery Harbour Centre adjoins the marina for convenient shopping, including Ocean Pacific Marine Supply, a well-stocked chandlery. Adjacent to the shopping center is a repair yard with 110-ton Travelift haulout.

The fourth marina (north side of Discovery Harbour) named Discovery Harbour Authority Small Craft Harbours is located behind the same breakwater that protects Discovery Harbour Marina. This fourth marina is located on the north side of Discovery Harbour Fuels sales dock and provides transient moorage and a boat ramp. All four marinas monitor VHF 66A.

Located one half-mile up the Campbell River is Freshwater Marina and Boatyard, offering permanent moorage, repair services and a 50 ton Travelift.

Marine Parts & Supplies: Well-stocked Ocean Pacific (250-286-1011) has overnight delivery from major suppliers in Vancouver for just about anything.

Museums: The Campbell River Museum & Archives, at 470 Island Hwy, is in the "don't

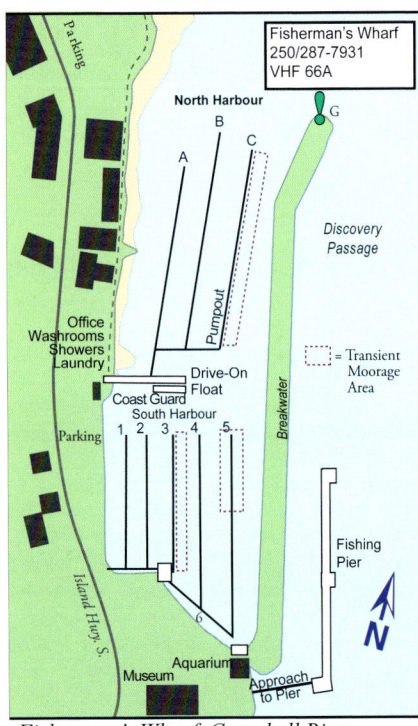

Campbell River

Fisherman's Wharf, Campbell River

See Area Map Page 305 - Maps Not for Navigation   **DESOLATION SOUND & DISCOVERY PASSAGE**

miss" category. The care and imagination of the exhibits remind us of the Royal British Columbia Museum in Victoria, only smaller, and without the giant ice age mammoth.

The Maritime Heritage Centre, a short walk south from Fisherman's Wharf, features a number of fishing and maritime exhibits.

The Discovery Passage Aquarium is just above the docks at Fisherman's Wharf. It is small, but the exhibits are well done. Younger crew will enjoy it.

Farmers market: Sundays, May through September, 10:00 a.m. to 2:30 p.m. in the fishing pier parking lot at the Fisherman's Wharf docks. Fresh farm produce, baked goods, fresh fish, all the things you'd expect.

⑲ **Fisherman's Wharf (Campbell River Harbour Authority).** 705 Island Highway, Campbell River, BC V9W 2C2; (250) 287-7931; fishermans@telus.net; www.fishermanswharfcampbellriver.com. Monitors VHF 66A. Open all year, water on docks, 20, 30, limited 50 & one 100 amp power, pumpout, ample dock space, washrooms, showers, tidal grids, Wi-Fi, garbage, recycling. Reservations accepted; proof of liability insurance required. All docks are side-tie and rafting is the rule throughout the harbour, be prepared. Docks A, B, and C are in the North Basin and docks 1-6 are in the South Basin. Docks A,B,1,2 and the west side of 3 are reserved. Transient space is located on dock 5, the east side of 3, and the east side of C. The pumpout is on dock C in the north basin in the area marked "Loading Zone."

This was almost entirely a commercial fish boat moorage basin until the harbor authority took over operation. Several improvements have been made to attract pleasure craft. The building above the drive-on float houses the harbour office, washrooms and showers. Crabby Bob's seafood cafe, on finger 6 on the south wharf, also sells fresh and frozen seafood. Other boats sell fish on the floats between fingers 2 & 3. Call the office for a heads-up on what's available. Office hours are 8:00 a.m. to 5:00 p.m., 7 days a week. If the office is closed, take an empty space in one of the designated transient moorage areas and register in the morning. Take a stroll along the fishing pier, stop at the take-out food window, and enjoy the views.

⑲ **Coast Marina.** 1003 Island Highway, Campbell River, BC V9W 2C4; (250) 287-7455, or (250) 204-3900; coastmarina@gmail.com; www.coastmarina.ca. Monitors VHF 66A. The Coast Marina is located behind the middle of Campbell River's three breakwaters, and has facilities for boats to 180 feet in length. Open all year, guest moorage, 30, 50 & 100 amp power, washrooms, showers, excellent laundry across the street in the plaza, garbage, recycling, water, and free Wi-Fi. Owner and manager, Derik Pallan, is a delight and always makes you feel right at home. Moorage requests available online through Swift Harbour booking services, or inquire by phone.

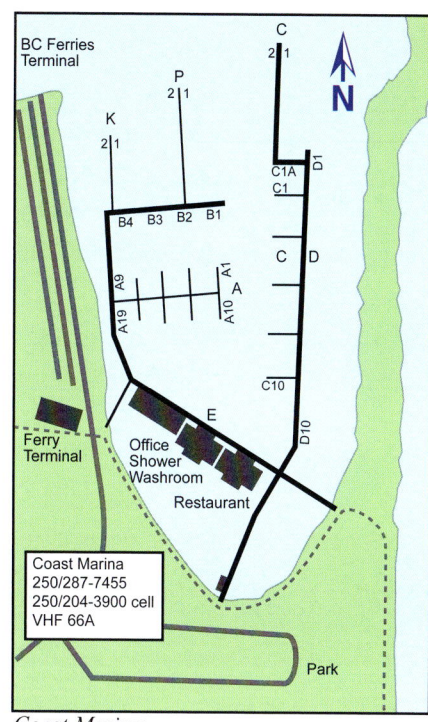

Coast Marina

The marina has wide concrete gated docks with power and water to each slip. The marina is just steps away from Foreshore Park and downtown Tyee Plaza shopping. Dockside Fish & Chips is a fully licensed restaurant with indoor and outdoor seating right on the docks. CR Whale & Bear Excursions office on site, available for bookings.

OCEAN PACIFIC
MARINE STORE & BOATYARD

The North Island's Largest Marine Supply Store & Boatyard

LOCATED IN DISCOVERY HARBOUR MARINA, CAMPBELL RIVER

www.oceanpacificmarine.com

ABYC CERTIFIED TECHNICIAN

Our Full-Service Boatyard Offers:
- 110 Ton Travelift
- ABYC Certified Marine Technicians & Electricians
- CWB Certified Welders
- Certified Diesel Mechanics
- Fibreglassers, Painting and Detailing
- Shipwrights & Fine Wood Workers
- Emergency Services Available

Toll-Free: **800-663-2294**
Local Phone: 250-286-1011
102-1370 Island Highway
Campbell River, B.C. V9W 8C9

2023 WAGGONER CRUISING GUIDE   323

"Everything a boater needs is here."

- 24 Hr Video Surveillance
- On-site Security
- Washrooms & Showers
- Power & Water
- Modern Guest Docks
- Fish Cleaning Facilities
- Fishing Guide Services
- Internet Available
- Laundry Facilities
- Block & Cubed Ice
- Garbage Disposal

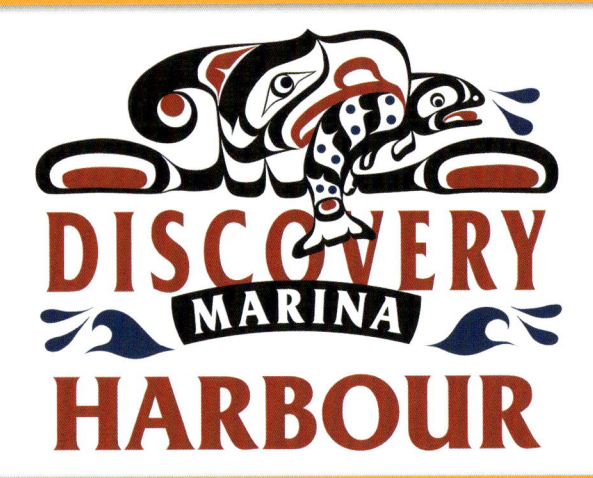

DISCOVERY HARBOUR MARINA

DISCOVERY HARBOUR FUELS

- Guaranteed Fuel Supply
- Ethanol Free Gasoline
- Competitive Pricing
- Friendly Knowledgeable Staff
- 14 Fuel Filling Pump Dispensers
- Full Line of Oil & Filters
- Ice & Convenience Store Items
- Propane Bottle Exchange
- Fishing Gear

Discovery Harbour Marina: phone 250.287.2614 ~ fax 250.287.8939
www.discoveryharbourmarina.com ~ email info@discoveryharbourmarina.com

Discovery Harbour Fuels: phone 250.287.3456 ~ fax 250.287.3442
www.discoveryharbourfuel.com ~ email info@discoveryharbourfuel.com

See Area Map Page 305 - Maps Not for Navigation   **DESOLATION SOUND & DISCOVERY PASSAGE**

Discovery Harbour north basin with Discovery Harbour Fuels and Small Craft Harbours

Discovery Harbour south basin with permanent and guest moorage at Discovery Harbour Marina

⑲ **Discovery Harbour Marina.** Suite 392-1434 Ironwood St., Campbell River, BC V9W 5T5; (250) 287-2614; info@discoveryharbourmarina.com; www.discoveryharbourmarina.com. Monitors VHF 66A. Open all year, with a mixture of slips and side-tie. Washrooms, showers, and laundry accessed with a key fob. For-fee Wi-Fi, garbage drop, ample guest moorage, with 20, 30, 50 & 100 amp single/3-phase power. In-slip pumpout service. The G, H, I and J floats have side-tie moorage that can handle mega-yachts, additional side-tie on docks C and D. Finger piers have recently been added to docks A and C with 30, 40, and 50-foot slips. All docks have security gates.

This is the largest of Campbell River's four breakwater-protected marinas. The marina has excellent docks, landing assistance and friendly people.

The marina office, with showers, washrooms, and laundry, is in a two-story floating facility at the foot of the north ramp on K dock; the facilities are accessed with a key fob. Floating washrooms are also near E dock to save the long walk to the main washrooms. The docks can be busy with whale and bear tour operators. Water taxi located on the main dock.

The extensive Discovery Harbour Centre shopping plaza is adjacent to the marina, with everything you would expect to find in a major center, including the Superstore Grocery; a loonie is needed to unlock a grocery cart. When the cart is deposited back in place, the loonie is returned. A selection of restaurants, pubs, and hair salons are nearby.

⑲ **Discovery Harbour Fuels.** Box 512, Campbell River, BC V9W 5C1; (250) 287-3456; info@discoveryharbourfuel.com; www.discoveryharbourfuel.com. Monitors VHF 66A. Located straight ahead as you enter the Discovery Harbour breakwater. Open year round. Ethanol-free gasoline, diesel, and propane-exchange. Fresh water fill. Canadian Hydrographic Services nautical charts and tide and current tables. Fishing gear, marine parts, ice, kerosene, and convenience supplies. This is a popular stop with ample space at the fuel dock.

⑲ **Discovery Harbour Authority Small Craft Harbours.** (250) 287-7091. Monitors VHF 66A. This marina was formerly for commercial boats only but is now open to recreational vessels; the marina is managed by the Discovery Harbour Authority. Open all year with 4000 feet of dock space located north of the fuel sales just inside the Discovery Harbour breakwater. Transient moorage with mandatory rafting; permanent slips for commercial vessels; launch ramp on site. 30 & 50 amp power and two 100-amp stations; no reservations, may call ahead for availability. Washrooms, showers, laundry, garbage drop with recycling and waste oil disposal; no Wi-Fi. Payment made at wharfinger office on site open 8 a.m.-4 p.m. daily; after hours use envelope payment drop at office door. Marina has a night watchman and camera surveillance.

Freshwater Marina and Boatyard. 2705 N Island Hwy, Campbell River, BC V9W 2H4; (250) 286-0701 admin@freshwatergroup.ca Marina; (250) 203-2635 travellift2018@gmail.com Boatyard; www.freshwatermarina.ca. Open all year Monday – Friday. Freshwater Marina is located about half a mile up the Campbell River from Discovery Passage; the Marina and Boatyard are accessible on a 6 foot tide or better for small craft and higher tides for larger vessels. River pilots are available, contact Freshwater Marina. Permanent moorage is available for vessels up to 65 feet, dryland storage for smaller craft. Tide dependent launch ramp. No transient moorage. Freshwater Boatyard has a 50 ton Travelift and do-it-yourself boatyard that also welcomes trades contractors.

Seymour Narrows. Currents in Seymour Narrows run to 16 knots on the flood and 14 knots on the ebb, flooding south and ebbing north.

Northbound, you can wait for slack either in Menzies Bay on the Vancouver Island side, or in the good-size unnamed bay behind Maud Island on the Quadra Island side. South of Maud Island the flood forms a backeddy along Quadra Island, easily sweeping northbound boats toward Maud Island. Southbound, Plumper Bay is a good waiting spot on the east side, as is Brown Bay on the west side. Brown Bay has a floating

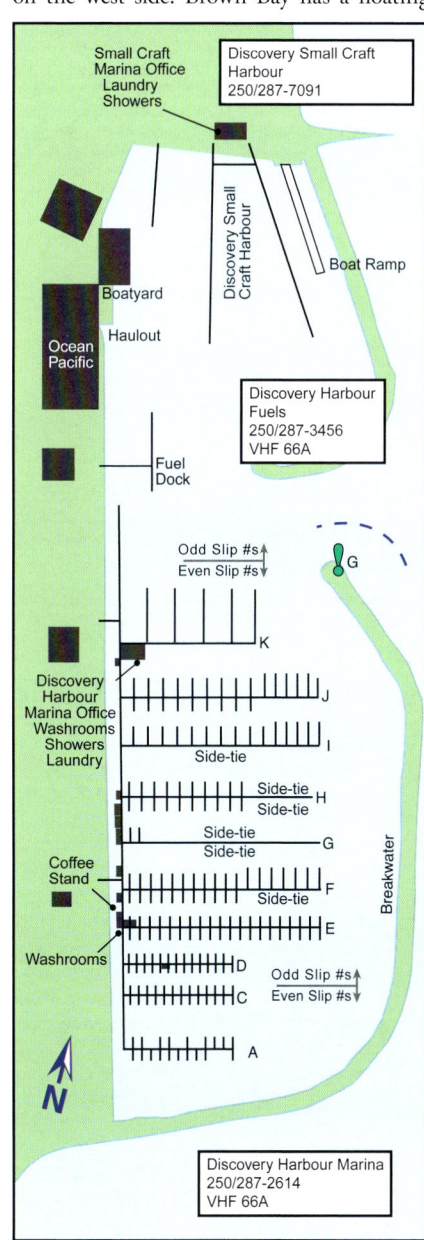

Discovery Harbour

325 DESOLATION SOUND & DISCOVERY PASSAGE

2023 waggoner CRUISING GUIDE   325

breakwater, and a marina with a fuel dock and restaurant.

Both **Deepwater Bay** and **Plumper Bay** are too exposed and deep to be attractive as anchorages. **Menzies Bay** may have good anchorage, being careful to go around either end of a drying shoal which almost blocks the entrance. This area is used as a booming ground for the pulp mill in Campbell River.

Seymour Narrows is the principal route for northbound and southbound commercial traffic, including cruise ships. Give large vessels ample room to maneuver. Before going through, we urge you to read the Sailing Directions section on Seymour Narrows. Especially on a flood, Sailing Directions counsels against the west side because of rough water. Monitor the passage times of commercial traffic on VHF 71, the area Vessel Traffic Services (VTS) frequency.

The warship HMCS *Columbia* was sunk off Maud Island to create an artificial reef.

⓴ **Brown's Bay Marina & RV Park.** 15021 Brown's Bay Road, Campbell River, BC V9H 1N9; (250) 286-3135; marina@brownsbayresort.com; www.brownsbayresort.com. Monitors VHF 12 & 66A. Open all year, gasoline and diesel, side-tie moorage to 100 feet along 2000 feet of dock, 50 slips for boats to 24 feet, 15, 30 & 50 amp power, free Wi-Fi, washrooms, showers, laundry, ice, cable television, phone, garbage drop, marine & RV store, boat launch. Several rental cabins available.

This marina is on Vancouver Island, at the north end of Seymour Narrows. Enter around the north end of the breakwater. Strong currents can sweep through the marina; be sure to take the current into account when maneuvering, and tie your boat to the dock securely. Concrete breakwater sections were added in 2022.

The store has a variety of snack items, clothing, and fishing gear. The seasonal floating restaurant offers all-you-can-eat crab on Thursdays and Fridays, when available, along with their annual Luau. For other scheduled events like the Log Carving Exposition and the Annual Pig Roast, call or check their website.

Kanish Bay. Kanish Bay has several good anchorages. You could sneak behind the **Chained Islands**, and with some thought and planning find a number of delightful spots, especially in settled weather. A charted large aquaculture, or at least the buoyed anchor points for same, lies mid-channel between 61-meter island and the entrance to Granite Bay. The small bay between Granite Bay and Small Inlet offers protection from westerlies. An aquaculture operation is in the mouth of this bay.

Correspondents James & Jennifer Hamilton anchored in the cove behind Bodega Point, just south of the 2-meter rock. "Really beautiful. Birds calling. Good holding in sticky mud.

Granite Bay. Granite Bay is well protected from all except strong northwest winds. Good bottom and room for several boats to anchor. The shore to the north is part of Small Inlet Marine Park, and the shore on the south has a few houses.

SEYMOUR NARROWS

Seymour Narrows is a wide pass, clear of hazards, and offers a direct route north past the important provisioning town of Campbell River. It is the easiest connection from the Strait of Georgia to Johnstone Strait or Cordero Channel.

Most commercial vessels stay clear of Seymour Narrows except at slack. A ship or barge-towing tug cannot afford to go sideways for even a few seconds. Small fishboats and recreational vessels, however, often transit Seymour Narrows within an hour of the turn, especially if going with the current. We always take Seymour Narrows going with the current and we've rarely had an anxious moment.

Smaller tides, where maximum current is predicted at six knots or less, can be taken at any time for most boats (again, going with the current). Larger tides should be taken within a half-hour of the turn. If it's a strong current cycle, in the 14- to 16-knot range, arrive at the pass within 15 minutes of slack water and the current will be manageable. The strongest current doesn't extend very far in either direction, so the transit past whirlpools lasts only a few minutes.

Hydrographers say the strongest currents at the Narrows are in the vicinity of Ripple Rock (slightly west of mid-channel, directly beneath the hydro lines strung between Vancouver Island and Maud Island). On a flood, the strongest turbulence will be along the west wall and in the area south of Ripple Rock. On an ebb, the turbulence and the set starts between Maud Island and Ripple Rock. The ebb current sets northwest to the west wall.

Northbound vessels: On small tides, northbound vessels should arrive off the Maud Island light an hour before the end of the ebb, or an hour prior to high water slack, before the ebb begins. Once into the narrows, steer toward the tongue of the current stream (east of mid-channel) to avoid the whirlpools and eddies north of Maud Island up to North Bluff. On big tides, low-powered vessels will find it prudent to be at the Maud Island light at high water slack, or just a few minutes into the north flowing ebb.

If the slack is at low water, arrive at the pass before the end of the ebb. Slack on large tides is not very long, five to ten minutes at most. You'll want to be past Brown Bay before the southflowing flood gets underway. It can be brutal in a slow-moving boat. You may find a back eddy along the eastern shore. On a large flood, Seymour Narrows can reach 16 knots, no place to be in any kind of boat.

Southbound vessels: Southbound boats should be opposite Brown Bay within an hour of the beginning or end of a neap (small) flood. On a large spring flood, it would be wise to be opposite Brown Bay within a half-hour of its end or beginning. Keep well off the sheer rock wall on the west shore of the narrows. Current turbulence can set a vessel onto that wall. The worst turbulence is usually south of Ripple Rock, especially if wind is against current. Stay on your side of the channel (i.e. to starboard) to be clear of any tugs or large ships headed the other way. The good news about Seymour Narrows is that there are no obstructions and just one strong, main stream.

Note how the current is pushing the barge to one side in Seymour Narrows.

Granite Bay Park Dock. The Strathcona Regional District (250-830-6700) public dock has a 230 foot float with side-tie space that is mostly occupied by local boats. Self-registration and payment box at the head of the dock. Two 15 amp shore power receptacles located at the base of the ramp offer power during limited hours. No other services at the dock. A launch ramp (limited to boats 20 feet or less) and trailer parking are located at the park. Granite Bay and the dock are open to strong northwesterlies.

㉒**Small Inlet.** A narrow but easily-run channel with a least depth of 8 feet leads from the northeast corner of Kanish Bay to Small Inlet. This inlet, surrounded by steep, wooded mountains, is beautiful, although we can confirm that a strong westerly from Johnstone Strait can get in and test your anchoring. Once through the kelp-filled entrance channel, a number of good anchorages can be found along the north shore. A couple of boats can fit behind a little knob of land near the southeast corner. The chart shows 3 rocks in this anchorage—actually, it's a reef with 3 high points. You also can anchor in the cove at the head of Small Inlet, behind two small islands.

A half-mile easy trail connects the cove at the head of Small Inlet with Waiatt Bay. The trail head is at the head of the cove in Small Inlet with a trail sign pointing east to Waiatt Bay. To the west, a trail to Newton Lake follows the south shore of Small Inlet cove with two dinghy landing sites, one at the rock outcropping across from the two islands forming the cove, and the other at a rocky shore midway between the previous rock outcropping and the head of the cove. The trail to Newton Lake is a one-mile steep and sometimes difficult forest trail. Don't confuse a small pond, a short distance before Newton Lake, for the real thing. The crystal clear waters of Newton Lake invite a fresh water swim. From Newton Lake a two-mile trail continues to Granite Bay Road and Granite Bay.

㉑ **Small Inlet Marine Park.** Located on the west side of Quadra Island bordering Octopus Islands Marine Park on the east, Small Inlet Marine Park has good anchoring opportunities in Small Inlet itself and in nearby Granite Bay and Kanish Bay. The marine park includes upland areas and trails. See *Okisollo Channel* map in this chapter.

Granite Point. If you are traveling between Discovery Passage and Okisollo Channel, you can safely steer inside Min Rock, north of Granite Point, and run close to Granite Point itself. You will be treated to the sight of some extraordinary rock formations on Granite Point.

Rock Bay Marine Park (Otter Cove). Otter Cove is just inside Chatham Point. It's a useful little anchorage, with convenient depths and protection from seas rolling down Johnstone Strait. If you need a place to hide until the wind or seas subside, it's a good spot.

LET'S TALK TRASH

Boaters seem to be anxious about trash, getting it off their boat that is – we don't seem to mind paying $7 per pound for wine, $2 per pound for toilet paper, and we are ready to pay $1 per pound for gas. So why do we sometimes feel hesitant when asked to pay by the pound to get rid of our garbage? We pay for garbage service at home, so why resist paying for the same service at small, remote communities that we visit?

Getting rid of trash in remote locations can't be cheap. Garbage collection services at marinas and communities like Lund, Refuge Cove, and Gorge Harbour must pay someone to collect mounds of garbage, transport that garbage by truck, and then load it on a ship to be taken elsewhere, it's an expensive proposition that returns little to no profit for their service. Trash is collected not only for island residents, but for those of us who come to enjoy the beautiful beaches, trails, anchorages, and marinas of Desolation Sound. It's no wonder that someone waiting around for our stinky garbage gets a little testy when customers fail to be less than appreciative of their services.

No, we don't want to carry trash around on our boat for weeks, so supporting garbage services when we find them is vitally important. Here are a few services at some key locations in Desolation Sound:

Lund – Boaters can dispose of their trash and recycle for a fee at A & J's Garbage Shack garbage bin (604-414-6097) near the new grocery store at Lund, located behind the Lund Hotel. Cost is $1 per pound for recycling and $2 per pound for garbage. Summer Hours are 9 am to 3:30 pm daily. If the attendant is not present, use the scales located in front of the shack for weighing your trash and deposit the fee in the self-payment box. The service is monitored by cameras, with signage that says "smile for the many cameras that watch over Lund." Garbage at A & J's is collected and driven 35 miles to the Powell River Transfer Station. A & J's costs for transporting and disposing of trash is a service, not a profitable business.

Refuge Cove – Boaters will find a Garbage Barge anchored at the mouth of Refuge Cove near Centre Island providing garbage collection service beginning each season around mid-June. Enterprising Dave Cartwright will accept your bagged garbage for $1 per pound (cash only); pull up by dinghy and he will weigh your bags. Plastic recyclables accepted. He appreciates friendly conversation and your thoughtful tips; after all, he is sitting there among mountains of bags all day to accept your unwanted trash. Check out his website at davesgarbage.wordpress.com.

Gorge Harbour – Boaters and island residents can take their garbage and recycle to the head of the Government Public Dock (look for the red railed pier in Gorge Harbour located east of Gorge Harbour Marina), where Reusary will be waiting with her truck on Mondays from 10 am to Noon and on Fridays from 2 pm to 4pm to collect your garbage – the fee is $1 per pound for garbage and .50 per pound for recycle. She transfers the garbage to the appropriate dump site and processing station.

Yes, talking trash is an important aspect of boating and a necessary service among other services for which we are happy to make payment; we want these services to be there in the future.

Boaters should keep in mind that small communities simply do not have municipal garbage collection and transfer station facilities. Starting at Pender Harbour going northward, you will be paying to get rid of your garbage with the exception of major towns like Campbell River, Powell River, Port McNeill, and Port Hardy. Boaters staying at one of the three government docks in Pender Harbour can take their trash to the Office in Maderia Park for a disposal fee of $2 per small bag and $5 for a large bag. Some marinas in Pender Harbour include garbage disposal in their moorage fees.

Johnstone Strait

JOHNSTONE STRAIT
Yuculta Rapids • Stuart Island • Dent Rapids
Nodales Channel • Shoal Bay • Blind Channel
Sidney Bay • Greene Point Rapids
Whirlpool Rapids • Sunderland Channel
Forward Harbour • Port Neville

Scan the Latest Johnstone Strait Information

tinyurl.com/WG22xCh11

JOHNSTONE STRAIT

Reference Only – Not for Navigation

The southern tip of Stuart Island marks the northern boundary of Desolation Sound. North of Desolation Sound, you'll find colder water, harsher weather, fewer services, and a greater number of rocks, reefs and tidal rapids. You should have good ground tackle and know how to use it.

Fewer boats venture north of Desolation Sound. Many stay out for four to eight weeks or more. Most boats are coastal cruisers or long-range, blue-water capable. The farther north you go, the more remote conditions become, all the way to Alaska.

It is possible to do a quick two- to three-week trip from Seattle to this area, although it might require long days on the water to get there. The reward is experiencing beautiful cruising grounds few others will see.

Garbage Drops. While occasionally you will find a lack of garbage drops in Desolation Sound and south, garbage becomes a much greater problem farther north. Garbage must be hauled from marinas and settlements to authorized dumps, usually on Vancouver Island. Since marinas must pay for hauling and disposal, most charge a fee for garbage, if they accept it at all. Those that do will sometimes take recyclables at no charge. Use as little glass as possible, wash and flatten cans, and pack paper out.

Fresh Water. Fresh water can be a problem even in Desolation Sound, and northward the supplies are fewer. Many marinas prohibit boat washing. Some marinas limit the amount of water for filling tanks. Check with marina staff before washing the boat or filling the tanks.

Some stops, such as Lagoon Cove or Blind Channel, have sweet spring water from deep wells. In some places, the potable water has a brown cast from cedar bark tannin. We don't know of anybody who has had a bad experience from it. As an added protection, water can be filtered with a 3-stage filter system available at most marine supply stores and online.

Prices. The season is short and the costs are high. Everything must be brought in by water taxi, barge, or air. Don't be upset when prices are higher than at home. Remember, too, that during the season the marina personnel's workday starts early and ends late, and calls for a smile at all times.

Provisions. Going north there are major shopping centers and large grocery stores in Campbell River, Port McNeill, and Port Hardy. There are small stores with many items and the essentials in Telegraph Harbour, Echo Bay, Sullivan Bay, Sointula, and Alert Bay. You will not starve, though you may not always find those special ingredients for a unique recipe, like Old Bay for a prawn boil.

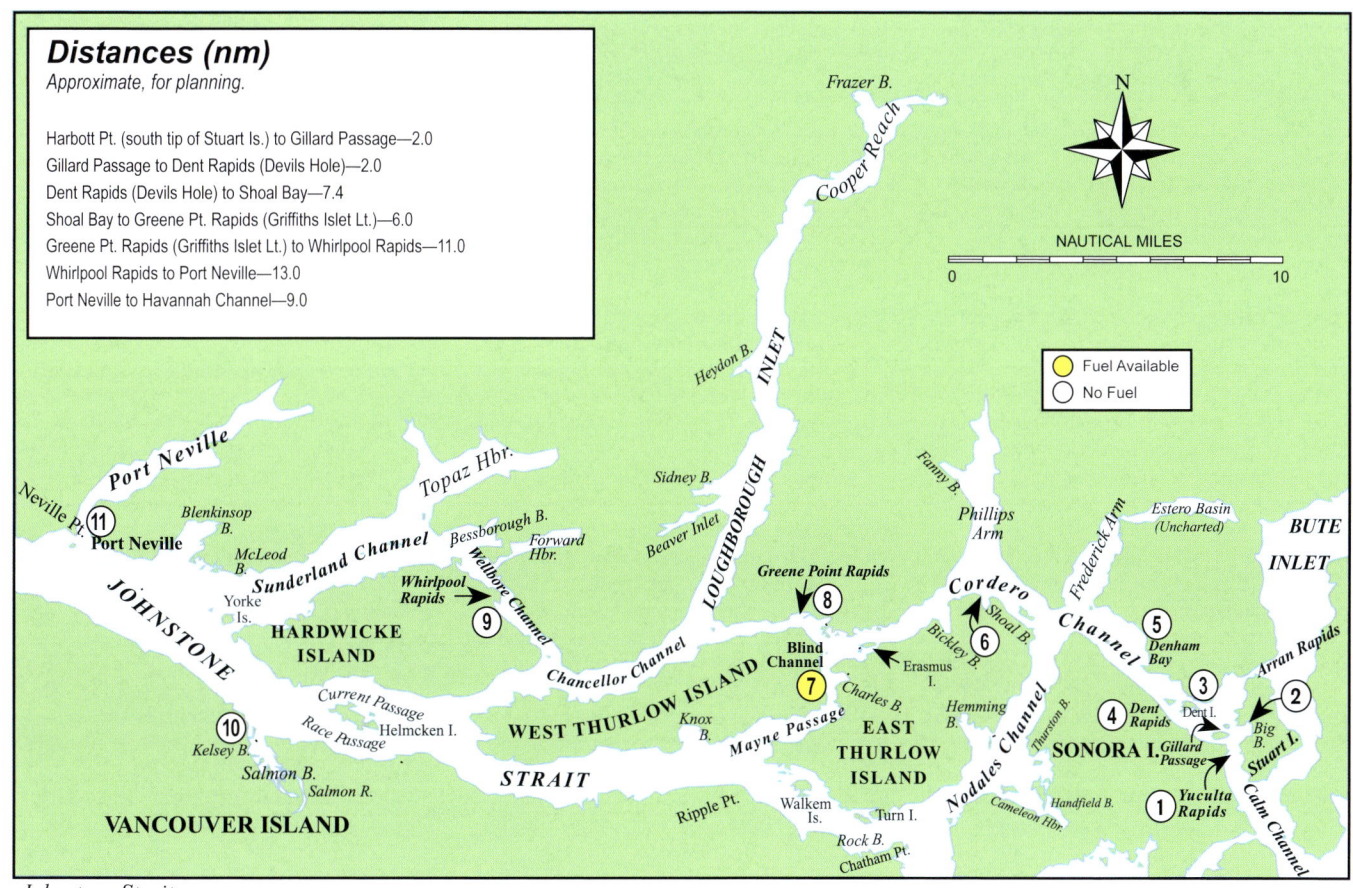

Chatham Point marks the Southern end of Johnstone Strait.

Distances (nm)
Approximate, for planning.

- Harbott Pt. (south tip of Stuart Is.) to Gillard Passage—2.0
- Gillard Passage to Dent Rapids (Devils Hole)—2.0
- Dent Rapids (Devils Hole) to Shoal Bay—7.4
- Shoal Bay to Greene Pt. Rapids (Griffiths Islet Lt.)—6.0
- Greene Pt. Rapids (Griffiths Islet Lt.) to Whirlpool Rapids—11.0
- Whirlpool Rapids to Port Neville—13.0
- Port Neville to Havannah Channel—9.0

Johnstone Strait

Recommended books. Peter Vassilopoulos' cruising guide, *Broughton Islands Cruising Guide,* is excellent. The book covers the waters from Yuculta Rapids to Port Hardy, and is packed with maps, history, and hundreds of aerial color photos.

Exploring the South Coast of British Columbia, by Don Douglass and Réanne Hemingway-Douglass, is another excellent book covering this area.

Local Knowledge: The Skipper's Reference, Tacoma to Ketchikan by Kevin Monahan, is a compilation of useful navigation and trip-planning information, including mileage and conversion tables. It has a comprehensive section on tidal rapids, recommended strategies, and how to calculate timing for transit. We use the mileage charts regularly. Monahan's excellent Johnstone Strait diagrams are included in this section.

THE INSIDE ROUTE TO THE BROUGHTONS

Most cruisers heading north choose the sheltered inside route through Cordero Channel, Chancellor Channel, Wellbore Channel and Sunderland Channel rather than face a long, possibly rough passage in Johnstone Strait against the prevailing northwest winds. Often the Johnstone Strait route is taken on the way home with the winds from astern and ideally on a flood tide. The inside route runs from the north end of Calm Channel (the south tip of Stuart Island), through five sets of rapids: Yuculta Rapids, Gillard Passage, Dent Rapids, Greene Point Rapids, and Whirlpool Rapids. The route includes an open stretch of approximately 13 miles in Johnstone Strait (which cannot be avoided) between Sunderland Channel and Havannah Channel, after which the currents of Chatham Channel must be negotiated. Careful planning is paramount. You need to know the times of slack water at each rapids, and you need to know how long it will take to get to each rapids.

Up-to-date charts and a copy of the Canadian Tide and Current Tables Vol. 6 or Ports and Passes are critical for safe navigation. Using the corrections shown in the Reference and Secondary Current Stations in the front part of the Tide and Current Tables (back of Ports and Passes), you must be comfortable calculating the times of slack water at the various rapids. For anchoring or transiting shallow channels, use the corrections in the Reference and Secondary Ports pages to calculate times and heights of tides.

The calculations can be daunting at first, but an evening spent reading the excellent instructions will clear matters considerably. For clarifications, don't be shy about asking a few old salts on the docks. They (we) love to help.

Since the waters north of Desolation Sound flood southward from the top of Vancouver Island and ebb northward, the northbound boat (if it wishes to clear a number of rapids in one run) has a timing problem. Assuming a start with Yuculta Rapids, all the rapids to the north will already have turned before slack water occurs at Yuculta. It is best to approach Yuculta Rapids before the southbound flood turns to the northbound ebb, and utilize two backeddies (described below) to help your way against the flood for the two or so miles to Gillard Passage and Dent Rapids. Done correctly, you'll go through Dent Rapids against the last of the flood current, and let the new ebb current flush you out Cordero Channel.

The ebb will already have been running 13 miles away at Greene Point Rapids, which turned earlier. Depending on your boat's speed, the ebb could be at full force when you arrive. Rather than go through in these conditions, many choose to overnight at Blind Channel Resort. Shoal Bay and the Cordero Islands are other good places to wait for Greene Point Rapids to turn to slack.

The next day you can depart before high water slack and push through Greene Point Rapids in the dying flood current. Then you'll hurry to Wellbore Channel, to take Whirlpool Rapids early in the favorable ebb current. If this is done early in the morning, it is possible the wind will not have started building for the stretch in Johnstone Strait. With luck it can be a pleasant run down Sunderland Channel and into Johnstone Strait for the 13-mile run to Havannah Channel. How well this works depends on the speed of your boat, the time of day, the conditions, and the flexibility of your schedule.

Southbound the options are greater. Take your first rapids against the last of the dying ebb, and let the new flood current flush you south. Each rapids in succession turns at a later time. Given the right conditions even a slow boat can take all the rapids on one tide, with only a few hours' wait if the boat arrives at any given rapids when they are running too hard to risk transit.

Note: Canadian Tide and Current Tables *do not adjust* for Daylight Saving Time. Ports and Passes tide and current times are adjusted for Daylight Saving Time.

Caution: A tight schedule is not justification for taking a chance with bad conditions. The dangers are real.

Guest side-tie moorage at Stuart Island Community Dock; Store with view deck upland

① **Yuculta Rapids.** The Yuculta (pronounced "YEW-cla-ta") Rapids separate Stuart Island and Sonora Island. Taken at slack they are benign, but at full force on a spring tide, especially against an opposing wind, they can be extremely dangerous. Northbound, Sailing Directions recommends that slow and low-powered boats arrive at the rapids an hour before high water slack, and use a backeddy along the Stuart Island shore until off Kellsey Point. Then cross to the Sonora Island shore to use a prevailing northerly current. This should position the boat to go through Gillard Passage and Dent Rapids satisfactorily. If you are late and unsure about transiting Dent Rapids, wait in Big Bay for the next slack.

② **Big Bay (Stuart Island).** For decades, Big Bay on Stuart Island has been a major fishing resort center. The public floats are behind a plank and piling breakwater at the head of Big Bay. The former Big Bay Marina is now a private fishing resort with no services for cruising boats. The Stuart Island Community dock has moorage and a store. Big Bay has seen an increase in development of exclusive, high-end fishing resorts and lodges over the past few years. Many boats criss-cross the bay during the summer and peak fishing seasons.

② **Stuart Island Community Dock.** P.O. Box 5-6, Stuart Island, BC V0P 1V0; (250) 202-3625; postmaster@stuartisland.info; www.stuartislandca.info. Monitors VHF 66A. Moorage, water, liquor, laundry, post office, store, ice, fishing guides, good cell phone coverage, free Wi-Fi. No power, no fuel. Staff is on call 24 hours a day in season.

The docks were rebuilt and expanded to accommodate boats to 100+ feet. Be aware of flood current swirling around the docks when arriving and departing. The store carries convenience items, liquor, and sundries. Store hours are 9:00 a.m. to 6:00 p.m. seven days a week in season. A large deck with a covered picnic area connects to the store.

A well-marked road and trail lead to Eagle Lake. The trail continues past the Lake to Bassett Cove on the other side of the island. It's a good walk, through beautiful forest.

See Area Map Page 329 - Maps Not for Navigation

JOHNSTONE STRAIT

LOCAL KNOWLEDGE

SHALLOW AREA: Note that there is a charted shallow area a fair distance off Stuart Island Community docks. Approach from the southwest. Charts indicate that the shallows are marked by kelp. If there is any kelp, it is not noticeable. The deep water end of Float B is reserved for floatplanes. Watch for floatplanes landing and departing in the waters just off the Community Dock.

Fisherman's Landing, a popular stop for mega yachts and recreational boats of all sizes

Gillard Passage. Currents run to 13 knots on the flood and 10 knots on the ebb. Transit near slack water. Times of slack are shown in Canadian Tide and Current Tables Vol. 6 and Ports and Passes. Pass south of Jimmy Judd Island. Big Bay is a good place to wait if the current is too strong.

If you're lucky, you might find the trees on and near Jimmy Judd Island filled with eagles that swoop down to the swirling waters to feed on hake, whose air bladders have brought them to the surface. It's a real sight.

③ **Fisherman's Landing & Lodge.** P.O. Box 5-3, Stuart Island, BC V0P 1V0; (250) 202-0187; www.thefishermanslandingandlodge.com; fishermanslandingandlodge@hotmail.com. Monitors VHF 66A (previously known as Morgans Landing). Additional concrete docks were installed in 2020 for a total of more than 1,600 feet of side-tie guest moorage. 30, 50, 100, and 200 amp power. Wi-Fi, water, washrooms, showers, laundry, and ice. Reservations recommended. The 50-foot float on the west end is for floatplanes. Happy Hours are held on weekends. The dining room is being renovated and will not be open in 2023. Meals will be by reservation. Facilities include accommodations, eco tours, and guided fishing charters. This is an upscale fishing lodge located at the mouth of the little bay that separates Dent Island from the mainland. Floatplane and water taxi service available. Plans are in the works to add a fuel dock.

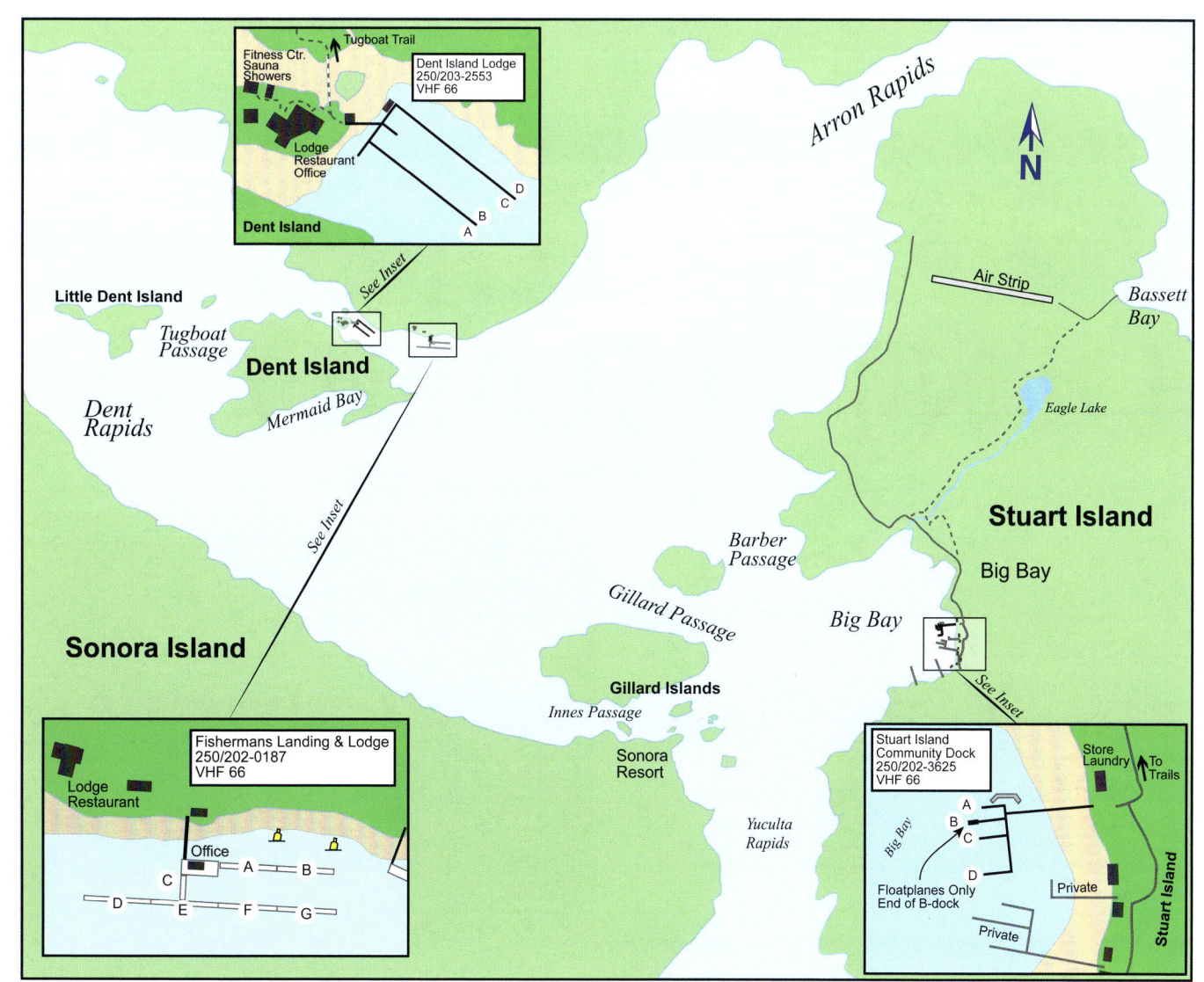

Discovery Passage Rapids Area

2023 WAGGONER CRUISING GUIDE

JOHNSTONE STRAIT

See Area Map Page 329 Maps Not for Navigation

③ **Dent Island Lodge.** P.O. Box 8, Stuart Island, BC V0P 1V0; (250) 203-2553; info@dentisland.com; www.dentisland.com. Monitors VHF 66A. Open late June to mid-September, guest moorage for boats to 200 feet on wide, stable concrete docks, 30 & 50 amp power at every dock pedestal, plus single-phase 100 amp power upon request. Reservations required. Potable water on the docks, Wi-Fi, good cell phone service, fishing guides, restaurants, gift shop, sauna, showers, exercise room, hot tub.

The service at Dent Island Lodge is first class, with moorage and dinner prices to match. The main lodge was recently removed and completely rebuilt for a bigger and better lodge that opened in late June of 2018. The new lodge takes advantage of the gorgeous views. The enlarged dining room and other spaces flow out to the rapids of Canoe Passage.

The professional staff treats you like a special guest in a small, quiet, private retreat. At the end of the day after the guide boats have returned from fishing, an elegant appetizer table is set out. The dinner menu in the main dining room offers a wide menu selection. The less formal Rapids Outdoor Grill is a small-plate-style dining area with a view of Canoe Pass rapids. Tables surround the kitchen and the chef personally prepares each dish directly in front of you. Both dining options are popular; reservations highly recommended.

A hiking trail, rough in places, is a good place to work off some of the calories.

The lodge is at the back of a little bay separating Dent Island from the mainland, next to Canoe Pass rapids, where 10- to 12-knot whitewater tidal currents churn. A spacious deck overlooks the pass. Another deck, screened by forest, holds a hot tub.

The lodge has a fast jet boat for eco-explorations and thrilling rides in the rapids. They offer tours to the head of Bute Inlet, including runs up the rivers in the inlet. Resort manager Justin Farr is an experienced fishing guide in these waters, and he knows every swirl, overfall and calm spot. The boat turns in its own length and dances through rough waters. The tour will make you respect the waters around Dent and Arran Rapids. Salmon charters can be arranged by the resort.

Schedule arrivals and departures to coincide with slack water in Gillard Passage, and approach from the southeast. Watch for a shoal area 0.9 meter deep at zero tide on the east side of the entry. Stay mid-channel.

Dent Island Lodge is a special place for special occasions, or just enjoy a relaxing vacation.

DENT ISLAND

The boater's destination of choice!
- protected moorage
- power & water
- wireless internet
- fine dining
- hot tub, sauna & gym
- seaplane & water taxi service
- reservations required

ph: 250-203-2553   Radio Ch 66A   info@dentisland.com

Denham Bay is a charming, cozy resort with guest moorage and hiking trails..

Boat name signs at Mermaid Bay

Mermaid Bay. This small bay located on the southwest side of Dent Island is best know for its collection of boat name signs tacked to trees on the north side of the bay. Some of the signs are surprisingly high up in the trees, a few are draped along the rocky shore, but all are big and well-made. The bay is well-positioned for temporary anchorage while waiting for timing of Dent Rapids to the north, or Gillard and Yuculta Rapids to the south. Good anchorage can be found in 5 to 9 fathoms. In 2022 a collection of docks were stored at the head of the bay. Cell service throughout the rapids area is good.

④ **Dent Rapids**. Currents run to 9 knots on floods and 8 knots on ebbs. Time corrections are shown under Reference and Secondary Current Stations in Tide and Current Tables Vol. 6 and Ports and Passes. Per Sailing Directions, "In Devils Hole, violent eddies and whirlpools form between 2 hours after turn to flood and 1 hour before turn to ebb." People who have looked into Devils Hole vow never to run that risk again. Favor the Sonora Island shore of Dent Rapids.

Tugboat Passage, between Dent Island and Little Dent Island, avoids the potential problems of Devils Hole, and the current is less. Use the large-scale inset on Chart 3543, and favor the Little Dent Island side.

Arran Rapids. Arran Rapids separate the north side of Stuart Island and the mainland, and connect Bute Inlet with Cordero Channel. Current predictions for Arran Rapids are shown in Canadian Tide and Current Tables Vol. 6, and Ports and Passes. Arran Rapids are unobstructed, but tidal streams run to 13+ knots. These rapids have a long history of killing the unknowing or foolhardy. Run Arran Rapids at slack water only, if at all. We have hiked from Big Bay to Arran Rapids and watched the water during a spring tide. The enormous upwellings, whirlpools, and overfalls were frightening.

⑤ **Denham Bay.** (250) 883-7480 or (250) 883-9415; denhambay@gmail.com; www.denhambay.com. Monitors VHF 66A. Dehnam Bay is located in a lovely setting with park-like grounds offering several well-appointed vacation cabins. Be sure to stay clear of Secord Rock located approximately 400 yards offshore lying northwest of Horn Point; there is currently no buoy marking this rock. Open May 15 to October 15, water, Wi-Fi, no power.

Approximately 500 feet of moorage space; call ahead for assistance with line handling. Moorage reservations accepted, or call ahead for space. Managers Claudia and Joe Hancock provide a warm welcome. The docks can accommodate boats up to 95 feet as space allows. New owners, Ryan and Monica Peterson, plan to extend the dock for additional guest moorage for 2023. A beautiful outdoor kitchen area with granite countertops is available for cabin guests, and boaters moored at the marina can make use of a separate shore-side kitchen area. A smoker is on site for guests to use by contacting the managers. Happy Hour held on Fridays. Ice, ice cream, and gifts available in the shop. The grounds are a delight, with lovely walkways and a shore-side boardwalk, pet friendly. Hiking trails are in the area, one of which leads to a couple of waterfalls.

Frederick Arm. Frederick Arm is deep, with almost no good places to anchor. You can anchor in several nooks along the eastern shoreline, or near the head, where the bottom shoals rapidly.

Estero Basin. If the crowds are getting to you, uncharted Estero Basin, at the head of Frederick Arm, is where you can avoid them. The narrow passage into the basin, called "The Gut," is passable only at high water slack (very high water slack, we now are told), and slack doesn't last long. A dinghy with outboard motor is a good way to go, and you may have to drag it part of the way. We have not been in Estero Basin, but Wolferstan has. He writes convincingly about the strong currents in The Gut and the eerie stillness of the 5-mile-long basin with its uncharted rocks. Friends tell us that Estero Basin is absolutely beautiful, usually deserted, with small islands, sheer cliffs, and water that grows fresher the farther you go. "Bring your lunch and shampoo," we're advised.

Waggoner reader Patrick Freeny reported that he had just enough water for his inflatable dinghy on a 13-foot tide. On a 10-foot tide the dinghy had to be dragged in. Dinghies or skiffs only, no larger boats.

NODALES CHANNEL

Thurston Bay Marine Park. Thurston Bay Marine Park is large enough to hold many boats without feeling too crowded. We've had good overnight anchorages in Handfield Bay, and in 36 feet behind Block Island.

The landlocked inlet behind Wilson Point, on the south side of Thurston Bay, is best entered at half tide or higher. Wolferstan calls this inlet Anchorage Lagoon. At the entrance, least depth at zero tide is 2 feet or less. We tiptoed in near the bottom of a 2.9-foot low tide with the depth sounder showing 6 feet (our boat drew 3 feet). Inside we found four boats at anchor in a pretty setting, with 9 to 10 feet of depth. This is a good place to know your vessel's draft and the tidal range during your stay. Be bear aware when ashore.

LOCAL KNOWLEDGE

DANGEROUS ROCKS: Note that in the entrance to Cameleon Harbour, Douglas Rock, which dries at 1.5 meters, is detached from Bruce Point. Give Bruce Point ample room.

JOHNSTONE STRAIT

Handfield Bay. Enter via Young or Burgess Passages, located to port as you enter Cameleon Harbour. Chart 3543 (1:40,000) makes it clear that you should enter Handfield Bay leaving Tully Island to port. Once inside you'll find excellent protection, good anchoring depths, and shore access. The rock north of Tully Island is usually easy to spot at half tide. Handfield Bay is a favorite stop for many cruisers.

Cameleon Harbour. Cameleon Harbour is a big, open bay with ample protected anchorage, depending on where you need the shelter.

Hemming Bay. Enter leaving the Lee Islands well to starboard to avoid Menace Rock in the middle of the bay. Most of Hemming Bay is deep, but you can find anchoring depths near the head. Correspondent Deane Hislop reports a large booming operation on the north shore with signage warning of cables across the bottom; anchorage is possible at the southwest side of the bay, but the beauty of the bay is spoiled by the logging operation.

⑥ **Shoal Bay.** Shoal Bay has a public float with good anchorage off the outboard end. The water shallows dramatically at the head of the bay. Shoal Bay is protected from most winds blowing down Cordero Channel, but is open to wakes from passing boats. It has a beautiful view up Phillips Arm. Rafting is mandatory, unless otherwise posted; set out fenders on both sides. The docks fill quickly during the summer, so arrive early or be prepared to anchor out. No power or water at the docks. Mark MacDonald is the wharfinger.

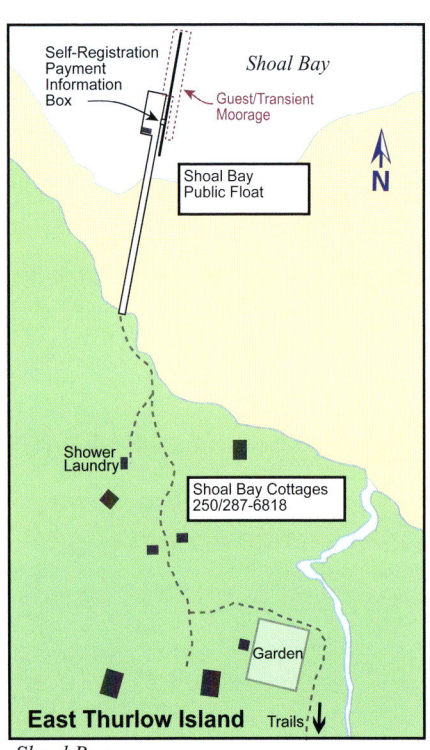

Shoal Bay

⑥ **Shoal Bay Cottages.** General Delivery, Blind Channel, BC V0P 1B0; (250) 287-6818; shoalbay@mac.com; www.shoalbay.ca. Open May 1 to October 1; self-registration payment box on the dock; cash or check. Free limited Wi-Fi near the cottages. Showers and laundry available to boaters. Guest cabins through Shoal Bay's website and Airbnb. A covered deck with breathtaking views up Phillips Arm is a great place to meet and greet.

A large vegetable patch, adorned with sculptures, is available for garden-deprived cruisers who like to get their hands dirty. All tools are provided. Pay by donation for what you pick. Mark's wife Cynthia is a talented potter, and her locally thrown and fired pottery is available for sale. Her work adorns the property.

For exercise, take the challenging hike up the mountain to the abandoned gold mine. Ask Mark for directions. Be bear aware.

Phillips Arm. Phillips Arm is deep, with little protection along the shores. Fanny Bay looks good on the chart, but has log booming activity. A northwest wind can blow through a saddle in the mountains at the head of **Fanny Bay**. On an earlier visit we found a stiff breeze in the bay; in Phillips Arm the air was calm. Large logging operations are located near the head of the inlet. A friend, much experienced, tells us not to anchor in the area of Dyer Point. The bottom there is foul with a tangle of sunken logs. *[Hale]*

Bickley Bay. Bickley Bay on Cordero Channel has anchoring depths toward the head of the bay. Favor the east shore to avoid a shoal area. Friends who have cruised in the area extensively warn of poor holding ground and won't go in anymore. Phil Richter at Blind Channel Resort also warns of poor holding. Caution advised.

Cordero Lodge. The Lodge and restaurant closed in 2017. Current owners of the property do not have plans at this time to rebuild the facility. Some of the floats have been removed and the remaining buildings have started to collapse.

Crawford Anchorage. Crawford Anchorage, between Erasmus Island and East Thurlow Island, is chancy at best, with a rocky and poor holding bottom. Friends report they have anchored in Crawford Anchorage successfully, using a Bruce anchor and a stern-tie to Erasmus Island. We tried anchoring with indifferent results. Enter Crawford Anchorage from the west—rocks lie in the eastern entrance. Rocks also lie southeast of Mink Island.

Mayne Passage (Blind Channel). Mayne Passage connects Cordero Channel with Johnstone Strait. From Johnstone Strait, the entrance can be hard to spot, hence the local name "Blind Channel." The current in Mayne Passage reaches 5 knots at springs, flooding north and ebbing south. Chart 3543 (1:40,000) shows rips in the northern part of Mayne Passage, and Sailing Directions warns of whirlpools and overfalls. Passages near slack are recommended. Blind Channel Resort, on the west shore of Mayne Passage, is popular. On the east side of Mayne Passage, Charles Bay is a good anchorage.

Charles Bay. On the east side of Mayne Passage, Charles Bay has convenient anchoring depths around Eclipse Islet in the center of the bay. Just east of Eclipse Islet, however, the bay shoals to drying flats.

LOCAL KNOWLEDGE

STRONG CURRENTS: Current runs across the face of the floats at Blind Channel Resort and landing can be a little tricky. At the fingers themselves, the current runs from north to south about 90 percent of the time, regardless of the current in the middle of the channel. A short distance off the fingers, however, the current usually runs from south to north. You can verify the current direction at the docks by observing which way the fingers press against the pilings at the outer ends. Call on the VHF for docking instructions. One of the staff always comes down to help with landings. They know what to do.

Mark, Shoal Bay Cottages owner, manages the Shoal Bay Public Wharf, with guest moorage.

See Area Map Page 329 - Maps Not for Navigation   JOHNSTONE STRAIT

Family owned and operated Blind Channel Resort is a welcome stop.   *Blind Channel Resort has fuel, a restaurant, store, and hiking trails*

⑦ **Blind Channel Resort.** Blind Channel, BC V0P 1B0; (888) 329-0475; info@blindchannel.com; www.blindchannel.com. Monitors VHF 66A. Open all year, gasoline, diesel, propane. Ample moorage on 2000 feet of dock, 15, 30 & some 50 amp power, washrooms, showers, laundry, UV-treated spring water; fiberoptic Wi-Fi installed late 2022. Garbage drop for a fee, no charge for glass and cans. Floatplanes stop here. This is a complete, well-run, and popular marina and resort, with water taxi, adventure tours, accommodations, well-stocked store, fresh-baked goods during the high season, post office, liquor agency, gift items. The nice gazebo overlooking the marina is a welcome addition in rainy weather. Several events are held throughout the summer months, check their website for the season's schedule.

The resort is surrounded by hiking trails, developed and maintained by Interfor. One trail leads to an 900-year-old cedar, 16 feet in diameter. It's a good hike and a splendid old tree. Recommended.

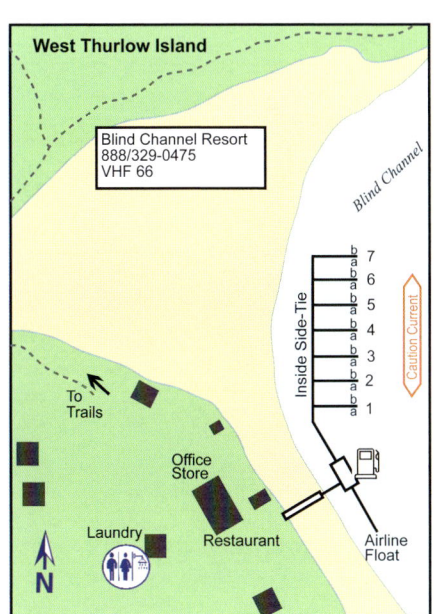

The fully-licensed Cedar Post Restaurant (open mid-May through Labor Day) is excellent. Breakfast, lunch, and dinner are offered daily during the peak season. The Grill Shack on the seaside patio is open for lunch and for happy hour starting at 5:00 p.m. in July and August. Don't miss the home-made baked goods available in the store.

This is a real family enterprise, now spanning four generations. Edgar and the late Annemarie Richter bought Blind Channel in the early 1970s. Edgar designed and built all the buildings, and Annemarie's distinctive and lovely artwork decorates the restaurant; photographs and verses adorn the docks.

What they built, with long hours and hard labor, is a long way from what they bought over 40 years ago.

Their son Phil Richter is general manager. Phil and Jennifer's sons Eliot and William grew up working on the docks and in the dining room. Eliot is now a partner in the business and lives on-site. You will most likely see Eliot's children running around the property helping and having fun.

The tidal current-turbine generator that was installed in Mayne Passage near the resort, for a research project, has since been removed. This previous in-water generator may still appear on some nautical charts.

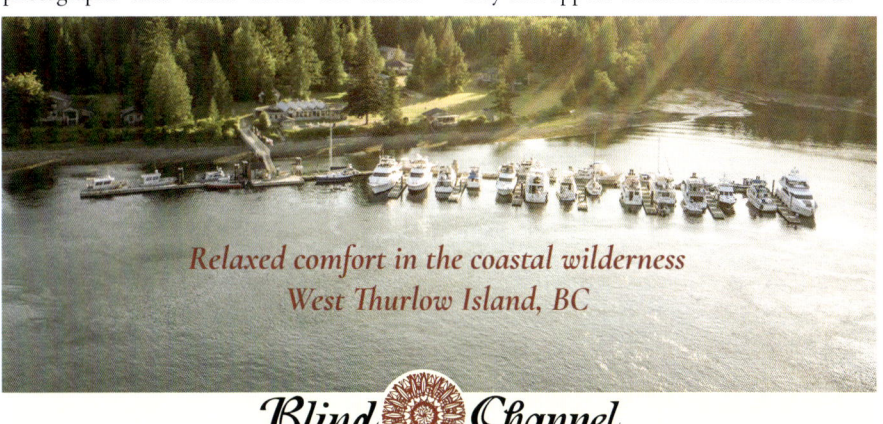

Relaxed comfort in the coastal wilderness
West Thurlow Island, BC

Blind Channel
RESORT

Full Service Marina & Fuel Dock with power, potable water, gas, diesel & propane.

Dine at the Cedar Post Inn: Grilled lunch, happy hour & dinner.

Well stocked store: groceries, liquor, ice & fresh baked goods.

Amenities: WIFI, showers, laundromat, tours, water taxi & post office.

Accommodations

Enjoy the ambiance.
Hiking Trails • Tours • Water Taxi

info@blindchannel.com | 1-888-329-0475 | www.blindchannel.com

Blind Channel Resort

2023 WAGGONER CRUISING GUIDE   335

JOHNSTONE STRAIT

See Area Map Page 329 Maps Not for Navigation

Sidney Bay off Loughborough Inlet

Expect to find other boats and ships on Johnstone Strait.

Cordero Islands Anchorage. Field Correspondent Dale Blackburn reports that this is a good anchorage for overnight, or to wait for favorable conditions in nearby rapids. Enter from the south between the two smaller islands that form the southern boundary of the anchorage, being careful to clear the charted rock to starboard. Anchor in 30-40 feet in the east or northwest coves with good holding in sand and mud and for the best protection from winds and current.

⑧ **Greene Point Rapids.** Currents in Greene Point Rapids can run to 7 knots on spring tides. On small tides, currents are much less. Sailing Directions warns of "considerable overfalls, whirlpools and eddies," and recommends transiting near slack. Current predictions are in Tide and Current Tables Vol. 6, and in Ports and Passes. When eastbound on flood tides, low-powered boats, and boats with tows, are cautioned against being set against Erasmus Island. When transiting northwest bound and waiting for slack water, anchorage can be found in Cordero Islands Anchorage, described above.

Loughborough Inlet. Loughborough (pronounced "Loch-brough") Inlet, off Chancellor Channel, is deep, with steep-to sides and few good anchorages. Protected anchorage can be found in **Beaver Inlet**, a short distance from the mouth on the western shore, but there may be log booming activity with significant commercial activity, making this inlet less than scenic. Edith Cove in Beaver Inlet is occupied by a float home and log raft. If you don't mind anchoring in 75 to 100 feet, the middle of the bay appears to have a soft bottom and is more scenic than the head.

Sidney Bay. Sidney Bay indents the western shore of Loughborough Inlet, where resident homesteaders Dane Campbell and Helen Piddington operate a rustic 200-foot float for visiting boats, located on the south side of the bay 50°30.88'N/125°36.06'W. Payment can be made at the float shed, or across the bay at their home on the north shore. A picnic table and book exchange are in the float shed. Dane most likely will be ready to receive your painter line and provide good conversation. Correspondent Deane Hislop writes, "It's well protected from the wind and a beautiful location. We've stayed many times." Dane is a soft spoken commercial fisherman that we have found quite interesting to talk to.

In 1975 he and his wife moved to Sidney Bay, where they raised their two children. Helen's book, *The Inlet*, describes life and their experiences in Loughborough Inlet." Her other book, *The Rumble Seat*, describes growing up in the 1930's near Victoria BC. The Landons report that Helen's health is failing; boaters may wish to visit this pioneer out-station, one of the last remaining from a bygone era, before it too passes with time. Field Correspondent Jim Norris visited in 2022 and reported that Dane is still welcoming boaters.

WELLBORE CHANNEL

⑨ **Whirlpool Rapids.** Whirlpool Rapids on **Wellbore Channel** has currents to 7 knots. The time of turn is based on Seymour Narrows, and corrections are shown under Secondary Current Stations in the Tide and Current Tables Vol. 6, and Ports and Passes. The flood sets southeast and the ebb sets northwest. When the current is running, expect strong whirlpools, upwellings and back eddies on the downstream side. The turbulence occurs south of Carterer Point on the flood, and north of Carterer Point on the ebb. It is best to transit within a half-hour of slack, although on small tides boats seem to go through anytime.

At low tide you might see bears on the beach near the south entrance to Wellbore Channel.

Forward Harbour. The entrance to Forward Harbour is narrow but unobstructed. Most of the harbor is 60 to 90 feet deep. Douglas Bay is a pretty anchorage, sheltered from Johnstone Strait westerlies that turn and blow through Sunderland Channel.

The bottom of Douglas Bay drops off quickly, and you may find yourself anchored in 60 feet of water instead of 30 feet—a good reason to carry at least 300 feet of anchor rode. We've had a report that a southeast wind can make for a rough time for boats anchored along the northern shore. Field Correspondent Jim Norris reports cell reception outside and east of Douglas Bay, along the north shore.

A trail leads from Douglas Bay to a white sand beach at Bessborough Bay. The trail is reportedly well-marked and easy to walk with blue rope marking the trailhead at each end.

If Forward Harbour is too full, good anchorage can be found in the little bay on Hardwicke Island, directly across from the mouth of Forward Harbour.

Bessborough Bay. Although you can find anchoring depths in the southeast corner, the entire bay is open to strong westerlies blowing up Sunderland Channel.

Topaze Harbour. Big and pretty enough, but little shelter for small boats.

Sunderland Channel. Sunderland Channel connects Wellbore Channel with Johnstone Strait. If the westerly is blowing and whitecaps are in Sunderland Channel, it will likely be worse in Johnstone Strait. Many boats wait out these conditions in Forward Harbour.

All of the channels northwest of Yuculta Rapids—Nodales Channel, Mayne Passage, Chancellor Channel, and Sunderland Channel—lead to Johnstone Strait. Each provides some protection and a chance to observe conditions on Johnstone Strait before venturing out. A strong westerly wind opposed by an ebb current can make Johnstone Strait difficult.

Harbour Authority docks at Kelsey Bay have limited transient moorage.

WWII era ruins on Yorke Island afford great views of Johnstone Strait.

JOHNSTONE STRAIT

Johnstone Strait is a seductive and difficult body of water. The strait begins at Chatham Point in the east, and stretches 54 miles along the northeast side of Vancouver Island to Blinkhorn Peninsula. It is the shortest route up- or down-island. Especially on the Vancouver Island side, Johnstone Strait is bounded by steep, high and beautiful mountains. On a clear day the scenery is awesome.

That is the seductive part. The difficult part is what the wind and current in Johnstone Strait do to each other. The flood current flows eastward, down-island, toward Discovery Passage and Campbell River. The ebb current flows westward, up-island, toward Queen Charlotte Strait and the North Pacific Ocean. A residual ebb surface current exists in Johnstone Strait, increasing the west-flowing ebb current's strength and duration. In the summer, the prevailing wind in Johnstone Strait is a westerly, often a gale-force westerly, funneled by the mountains. The result is a classic wind-against-current heaping up of the seas.

Conditions are worst where the meeting of currents creates tide-rips, even in calm conditions. This stretch begins at Ripple Shoal, east of Kelsey Bay. It extends westward past Kelsey Bay, through Race Passage and Current Passage, and across the mouth of Sunderland Channel. Especially on an ebb, when the westerly is blowing you don't want to be there—period. Leave the heroics to others. Johnstone Strait can take all the pleasure out of a pleasure boat. Monahan's Local Knowledge diagrams, later in this chapter, illustrate Johnstone Strait's trouble spots.

Despite the potential problems, we have run the length of Johnstone Strait, both directions, many times, and often had an excellent ride. But we listened to the weather and went when conditions were calm or near-calm. If the wind had come up, we were prepared to run for cover in a bay or seek out a friendly point to hide behind until conditions improved. We always keep a bail-out point in mind. Conditions can change quickly.

Watch for drift in Johnstone Strait. There's considerable current activity, and many shear lines where scrap wood, tree limbs, logs, and even entire floating trees accumulate.

Turn Island. Turn Island is off the southern tip of East Thurlow Island, at the intersection of Johnstone Strait and Discovery Passage. Anchor behind Turn Island, about where the 5.8-meter sounding is shown on the chart across from Turn Bay, with good holding and room to swing. The anchorage has nice views to Johnstone Strait and the mountains on Vancouver Island. *[Hamilton]* Charts show a log dump north of this anchorage. Reader Kelly Calvert reports snagging a logging cable when they anchored in small Turn Bay behind Turn Island.

Knox Bay. Knox Bay is located on the north side of Johnstone Strait, near the mouth of Mayne Passage. Knox Bay would be a poor choice for an anchorage, but a good hideout to escape a strong westerly in the strait. The northwest corner of the bay is best protected. Unfortunately, it is deep and occasionally has log booming.

Fanny Island. When the Environment Canada weather station was moved from Helmcken Island to Fanny Island a few years ago, Johnstone Strait weather reports improved dramatically (Helmcken Island could report 8 knots of wind when it was blowing 30). We're told, however, that while Fanny Island reports of northwest winds are fairly accurate, south and east winds can be reported less than what's actually going on.

Helmcken Island. Helmcken Island has protected anchorage on its north side in Billygoat Bay. Currents in this part of the strait run at 5 knots. When opposed by wind from the opposite direction large, dangerous seas can build rapidly. Billygoat Bay is a good place to hide out. Anchor in approximately 30 feet, although Correspondents James and Jennifer Hamilton found only poor holding over rock. Instead, they recommend the cove northwest of Billygoat Bay. They go up to the head of the cove, where they have found calm water, with an "awesome" view eastward. The cove is unnamed in Sailing Directions or on the chart. The Hamiltons call it Helmcken Cove.

⑩ **Kelsey Bay.** (250) 282-0178. Sayward Harbour Authority. Kelsey Bay, on the north side of Vancouver Island, has a breakwater southeast of the harbor, made of old ship hulks—the Union Steamship *Cardena* and three WWII frigates: *HMCS Runnymede, HMCS Lasalle,* and *HMCS Longueil.* Enter leaving the light green breakwater to starboard and the old ships to port. Watch for current entering the breakwater. Transient moorage is on A, B, and C docks, maximum length 60 feet. Water, 20 and 30 amp power, garbage drop, recycling, oil disposal. Restrooms and showers. Most of the moorage is occupied by commercial fish boats. Rafting may be required. Moorage is paid at the honor box at the top of the ramp, an attendant is on site during the summer months. We found the docks to be clean and well maintained.

A small gift shop on the pier at the neighboring Futures Society facility doubles as a tourist office, (250) 282-0018. Smaller boats can tie up at the 200-foot dock located behind the pier; water depths range from 8-15 feet. The small village of Sayward is approximately one mile south, with some services, including a coop grocery and a store at Sayward Valley Resort.

Yorke Island. Located in the middle of Johnstone Strait, west of Hardwicke Island, Yorke Island is the site of several gun emplacements which were installed in 1937. These ruins from WWII were originally intended to block enemy backdoor approach to the Strait of Georgia and the cities of Vancouver and Victoria. Well maintained trails by BC Parks lead from the south cove

JOHNSTONE STRAIT

See Area Map Page 329   Maps Not for Navigation

The house on Milly Island at the entrance to Port Neville looks like a lighthouse.

Port Neville pier and floats are public but uplands are private property.

on the island to various gun and battery sites. The main gun emplacement is at the highest point on the island with great views of the Strait and is visible from passing boats. Yorke Island is a haunting place to visit and worth the stop in the right conditions. Maps of the island and more historical information can be found at www.wikipedia.org/wiki/Yorke_Island_(Canada). Temporary anchorage can be found in 30 to 45 feet of water, east of the unnamed cove on the south side of the island. The cove is often covered with kelp and the bottom is rocky with poor holding. Wind and current are a consideration. Leaving the boat unattended is not recommended. Charted rocks lie south of the cove.

Blenkinsop Bay. Blenkinsop Bay has reasonably protected anchorage along the north shore of Johnstone Strait, but swells from westerly winds work into the bay. The chart shows tide-rips off Blenkinsop Bay. The chart isn't kidding. McLeod Bay and an unnamed bay inside Tuna Point are possible temporary anchorages.

⑪ **Port Neville.** Strathcona Regional District. Port Neville is an excellent spot to duck into if the weather in Johnstone Strait deteriorates. It is an 8-mile-long inlet with three distinct areas of interest to recreational boaters: first is the 2-mile entrance channel with a government dock and anchorage; second is the 3-mile long main bay with anchorage throughout; and third is the 2-mile long inner bay with large drying flats. There are no public facilities or services in the area.

Entrance Channel: Current runs strong throughout (3 knots per Sailing Directions) in the entrance channel. A government dock and float are a short distance inside the entry channel, along the eastern shore. Check for current before approaching the dock, it can make for a challenging landing. No power or water at the dock and no charge for overnight stays.

At the head of the dock is a readerboard with the history of the area. All of the uplands are private property, posted with no trespassing signs.

Anchoring is possible and popular in the channel across from the government dock. Farther up the channel is a shallow and rocky area. A few homes and a private dock are on the west shore opposite the government dock.

Main Bay: The huge main bay three miles long and over half a mile wide has room for a fleet of boats to anchor. Pick your spot just about anywhere; see the anchoring comments section at the end of this write up. Northwest winds do come into the bay over and around the mountains to the northwest. There has been logging activity on the hillsides and booming is possible but does not interfere with anchoring choices. On the west side of Robbers Nob, near the tip, several petroglyphs can be seen below the high tide line. The property above the high tide line is private.

Inner Bay: Beyond Hanatsa Point near Baresides Bay is a shallow channel leading to the Inner Bay which is seldom visited. A logging camp with booming may be active at the head of the inner Bay.

History: For years Olaf "Oly" Hansen, at the government dock post office, could be reached by radio for a report on conditions on Johnstone Strait. Oly died in January, 1997 at age 87, another legend gone from the coast. Oly's widow Lilly lived on in the family house for a few years, but finally had to move down-island. In 2003, shortly after her 90th birthday, she too left us. Their daughter Lorna (Hansen) Chesluk raised her daughter Erica in the house at the head of the wharf. Lorna was the postmaster, and she happily looked out on the strait and gave a report if you called on the radio.

The post office was closed in 2010, and Lorna moved to Campbell River to be closer to family. The Hansen family had lived at Port Neville since 1891. Until it closed, the Port Neville post office was the longest continuously-operating post office in the province. Yet another page of coastal history is turned. The wonderful old store building at the head of the wharf is now private property.

Anchoring Comments: Correspondents Elsie and Steve Hulsizer report after trying several anchoring locations in Port Neville, their preferred spot is in the entrance channel across from the public dock where the water is protected from northwest winds by hills. Correspondents James and Jennifer Hamilton recommend anchoring in Baresides Bay, directly south of the MSh symbol on Charts 3545 and 3564 where you will be in 15 feet of water at zero tide, about 200 feet from shore. Excellent holding. Not the most protected but out of the worst of westerly winds.

Forward Bay. What appears to be a small anchoring spot on Johnstone Strait between Bush Islets and West Cracroft Island reportedly has no holding due to a sandy bottom and eelgrass. It is open to easterly winds, and westerly winds reportedly wrap around West Cracroft Island and into the spot. Sides shallow quickly.

Boat Bay. With room for several boats, Boat Bay has good anchoring in about 30 feet of water. Located on the south shore of West Cracroft Island toward the west end of the island and opposite Robson Bight, Boat Bay is a good spot for an overnight stay or to escape strong westerlies; open to easterlies. A private glamping operation with tent pads is on shore.

LOCAL KNOWLEDGE

RESTRICTED AREA: Robson Bight, on the Vancouver Island side near the north end of Johnstone Strait, is an Ecological Reserve, a gathering place for Orcas. Unauthorized vessels (meaning yours and ours) are not allowed. Stay outside of the Reserve's boundary lines noted on the charts.

Robson Bight. The Robson Bight Ecological Reserve is a restricted area that runs 0.5 mile offshore and for 5 miles off Robson Bight. It is part of a reserve for Orca whales. The Reserve is not centered on the Bight and extends more to the east. The Reserve is shown on most charts but may be hard to see. If you stray into the restricted area, wardens will intercept your boat and instruct you to leave immediately.

JOHNSTONE STRAIT

See Area Map Page 329 - Maps Not for Navigation

MONAHAN'S LOCAL KNOWLEDGE

West of Port Neville, the ebb begins along the mainland shore and takes almost two hours to completely cover the strait from one side to the other.

Turn to flood occurs in Sunderland Channel 1h 40m before Johnstone Strait Central and 1h 20m before Camp Point.

Current Passage turns to ebb 50m after Johnstone Strait Central, but 1h 15m before Camp Point.

To avoid heavy weather in Johnstone Strait (especially when wind opposes currents) Sunderland, Wellbore and Cordero Channels offer calmer conditions.

Turn to ebb at Vansittart Point occurs up to 30m before Current Passage, almost two hours before Camp Point.

Freshet conditions in mainland rivers may encourage a premature turn to ebb in the vicinity of Mayne Passage.

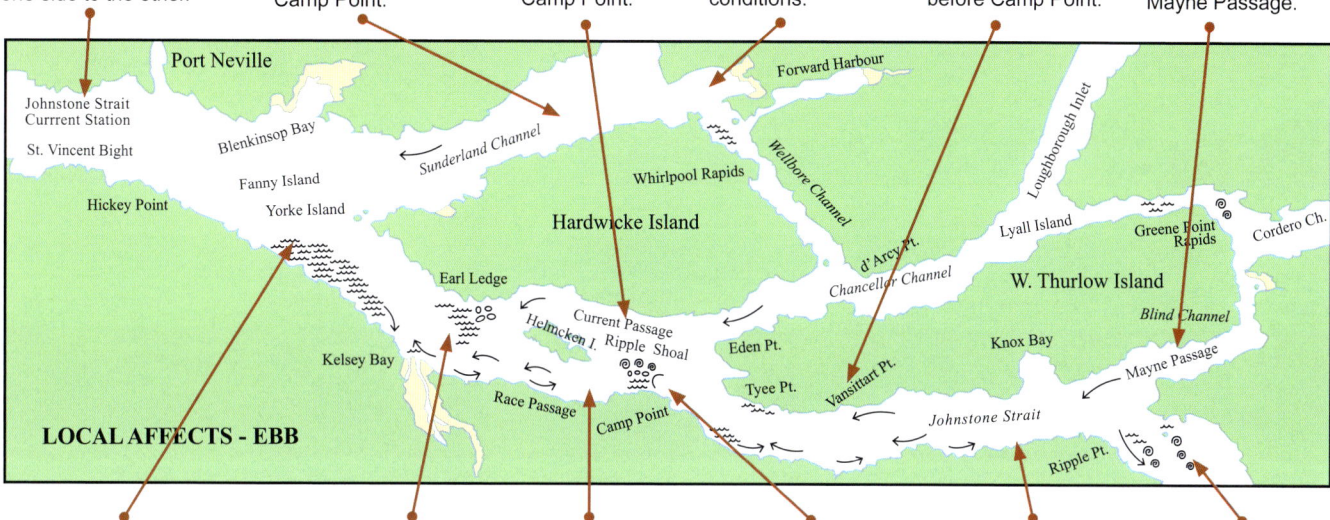

LOCAL AFFECTS - EBB

When waves from gale force westerlies oppose a strong ebb current, large seas propagating southward are generated in this area. In this case, smaller boats should seek shelter at Port Neville or enter the harbour at Kelsey Bay and wait for the contrary current to moderate.

A steep underwater ridge extends southward from Earl Ledge across the channel to the Vancouver Island shore. Deep tidal currents meet this steep topography and are deflected to the surface, causing extreme turbulence west of Helmcken Island during large tides.

Tide rips and conditions dangerous to small craft are generated in this area during large tides, especially when strong westerlies oppose the ebb current.

Stay clear of Ripple Shoal. Dangerous whirlpools form to the west of the shoal during the ebb.

Immediately adjacent to the shore, back eddies may run in the opposite direction to the main flow. However, at headlands between back eddies, the ebb current is strong right up to the shore.

Tide rips and turbulent conditions are generated in this area during large tides, especially when strong westerly winds oppose the ebb current.

Near Port Neville, the mainland and Vancouver Island shores turn to flood up to one hour before the center of the channel.

In Current Passage, turbulence is weaker near the north shore.

To avoid heavy weather in Johnstone Strait (especially when wind opposes currents) Sunderland, Wellbore and Cordero Channels offer calmer conditions.

Stay clear of Ripple Shoal. Dangerous whirlpools form to the east of the shoal during the flood.

First ebb current in eastern Johnstone Strait begins between Mayne Passage and Vansittart Point, up to two hours before turn to ebb at Camp Point.

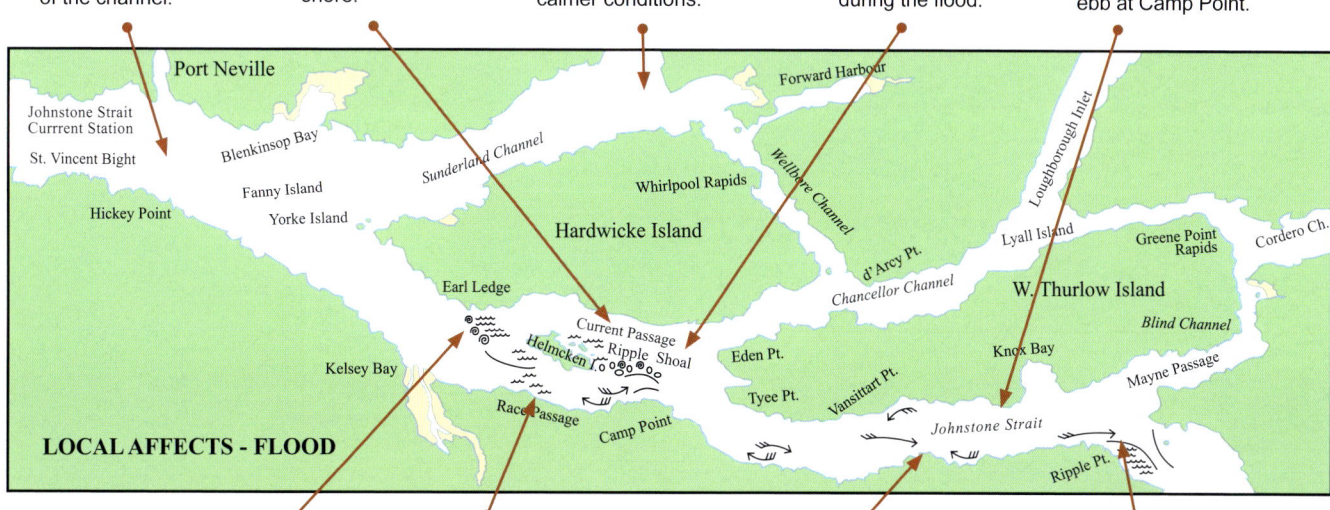

LOCAL AFFECTS - FLOOD

Tide rips and conditions dangerous to small craft are generated in this area during large tides, especially when strong southeasterlies oppose the flood current.

The ebb current in Current and Race Passages persists approximately 1h 20m longer than in Sunderland Channel.

Immediately adjacent to the shore, back eddies may run in the opposite direction to the main flow. However, at headlands between back eddies, the flood current is strong right up to the shore.

Tide rips and turbulent conditions are generated in this area during large tides, especially when strong southeasterlies oppose the flood current.

Legend: Boils (upwelling), Whirlpool, Turbulence (Tide Rip), Direction of ebb current, Direction of flood current

Copyright © Kevin Monahan, *Local Knowledge: A Skipper's Reference, Tacoma to Ketchikan*

2023 WAGGONER CRUISING GUIDE

The Broughton Region

THE BROUGHTON ISLANDS
Echo Bay • Lagoon Cove
Glendale Cove • Sullivan Bay
Jennis Bay • New Vancouver

WEYNTON PASSAGE
Bauza Cove • Telegraph Cove
Beaver Cove • Pearse Islands

BROUGHTON STRAIT
Port McNeill • Alert Bay • Sointula

QUEEN CHARLOTTE STRAIT
Beaver Harbour • Port Hardy • Bear Cove

Scan the Latest Broughtons Information

tinyurl.com/WG22xCh12

*Echo Bay
Cramer Pass*

THE BROUGHTON REGION

"The Broughtons" is an all-encompassing term for the inlets, islands and waterways on the mainland side of Queen Charlotte Strait, north of Johnstone Strait. This area includes the islands adjoining Blackfish Sound and Fife Sound. It also includes Knight Inlet, Kingcome Inlet, Tribune Channel, Drury Inlet, and Mackenzie Sound. For convenience we include Havannah Channel and Chatham Channel. Locals call this area the Mainland, to distinguish it from the Vancouver Island side from Sayward (Kelsey Bay) to the top of Vancouver Island, which they call North Island.

Most boaters include the towns of North Island among their stops when visiting the Broughtons, transiting across Queen Charlotte Strait for fuel and supplies. We have included North Vancouver Island in this Broughton Region chapter. The northeastern tip of Vancouver Island is served by Highway 19. Port Hardy is the northern most community on Vancouver Island and is the end of the road, marked by a statue of a carrot with a chunk bitten out. The carrot is a symbol of government road building promises, dangled in front of North Island since 1897. The road was not completed until 1979. The towns of Port McNeill, Alert Bay, Sointula, and Port Hardy on North island serve as major re-supply stops, including groceries, fuel, water, and repairs. Kelsey Bay and Robson Bight to the southeast are covered in the Johnstone Strait chapter.

Hospitals: Port McNeill and Port Hardy have fully-staffed hospitals. A Community Health Centre is located in Alert Bay on Cormorant Island.

The Broughtons, or the Mainland, is one large, complex cruising ground. It offers anchorages from raw and wind-swept Fife Sound and Blackfish Sound, to the gentler waters of Simoom Sound, Greenway Sound and Drury Inlet. A few small resorts—no two of them alike—are found throughout the Broughtons. Most cruisers anchor out some of the time and enjoy the social side of marina life the rest of the time. During the course of a cruising holiday, most cruisers either stop at or overnight at all the marinas: Lagoon Cove, Echo Bay, Sullivan Bay, and New Vancouver, along with docks at Jennis Bay, Health Bay, and Minstrel Island.

Lacy Falls in Tribune Channel near Watson Cove and Kwatsi Bay

The rich history of the Broughtons begins with Native habitation dating back thousands of years. On Mound Island, 14 depressions in the earth are evidence of Native Bighouses and Longhouses, each of which held extended families. We're told that trading beads, the colorful glass beads exchanged for valuable pelts by early traders, can sometimes be found on beaches throughout the Broughtons. The ruins of two uninhabited native village sites in the Broughtons can be visited, one at Karlukwees on Turnour Island and Mimkwamlis on Village Island. Pictographs can be found in several locations in the Broughtons and their locations are noted in this chapter. The village of New Vancouver on the north tip of Harbledown Island is home to native peoples with settlements along Knight Inlet. At New Vancouver you will find a dock with guest moorage; ask about a tour of the bighouse.

The Broughtons were homesteaded in the late 1800s and early 1900s. Families were raised on rude farms. The men rowed across Queen Charlotte Strait to Alert Bay, or rowed—*rowed*—200 miles south to Vancouver or Victoria to conduct business and bring back supplies.

In most cases, the forest has erased all traces of the homesteaders' now-abandoned efforts. One notable exception is remarkable "Monks' Wall," at the north end of Beware Passage. There, hidden in the trees, are the remains of rock walls from William and Mary Anne Galley's wilderness trading post that was active from the late 1800s until after the First World War.

The Broughtons are a destination. Take your time and don't hurry through. See Billy Proctor's museum in Proctor Bay. Marvel at Lacy Falls on Tribune Channel. Anchor out in the coves and lagoons. Visit the marinas and meet the locals who run them.

Ask questions, read the history, and take time to explore. If you spend your entire cruise in the Broughtons, you might just scratch the surface.

Marinas: Marinas in the Broughtons are different from marinas elsewhere on the coast. They're small and sometimes family run; each marina has its own character and charm. Some cruisers develop friendships with the owners,

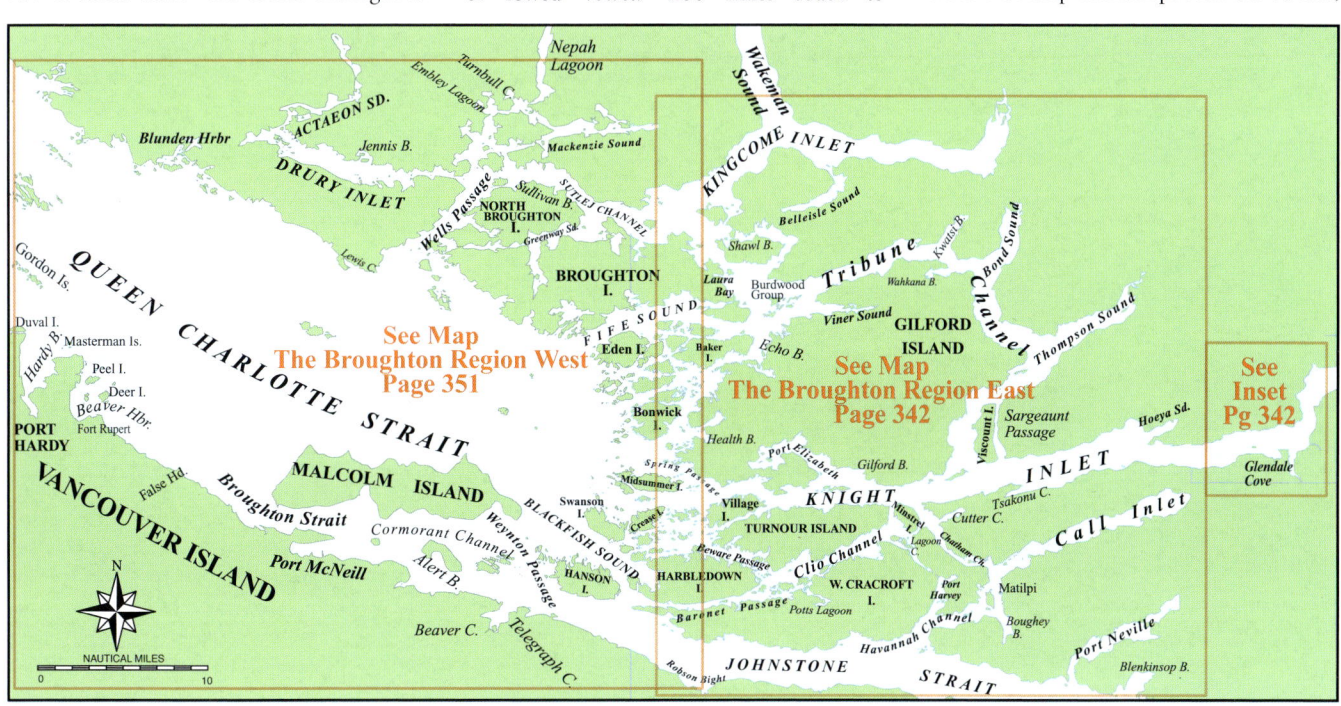

The Broughton Region

2023 waggoner CRUISING GUIDE 341

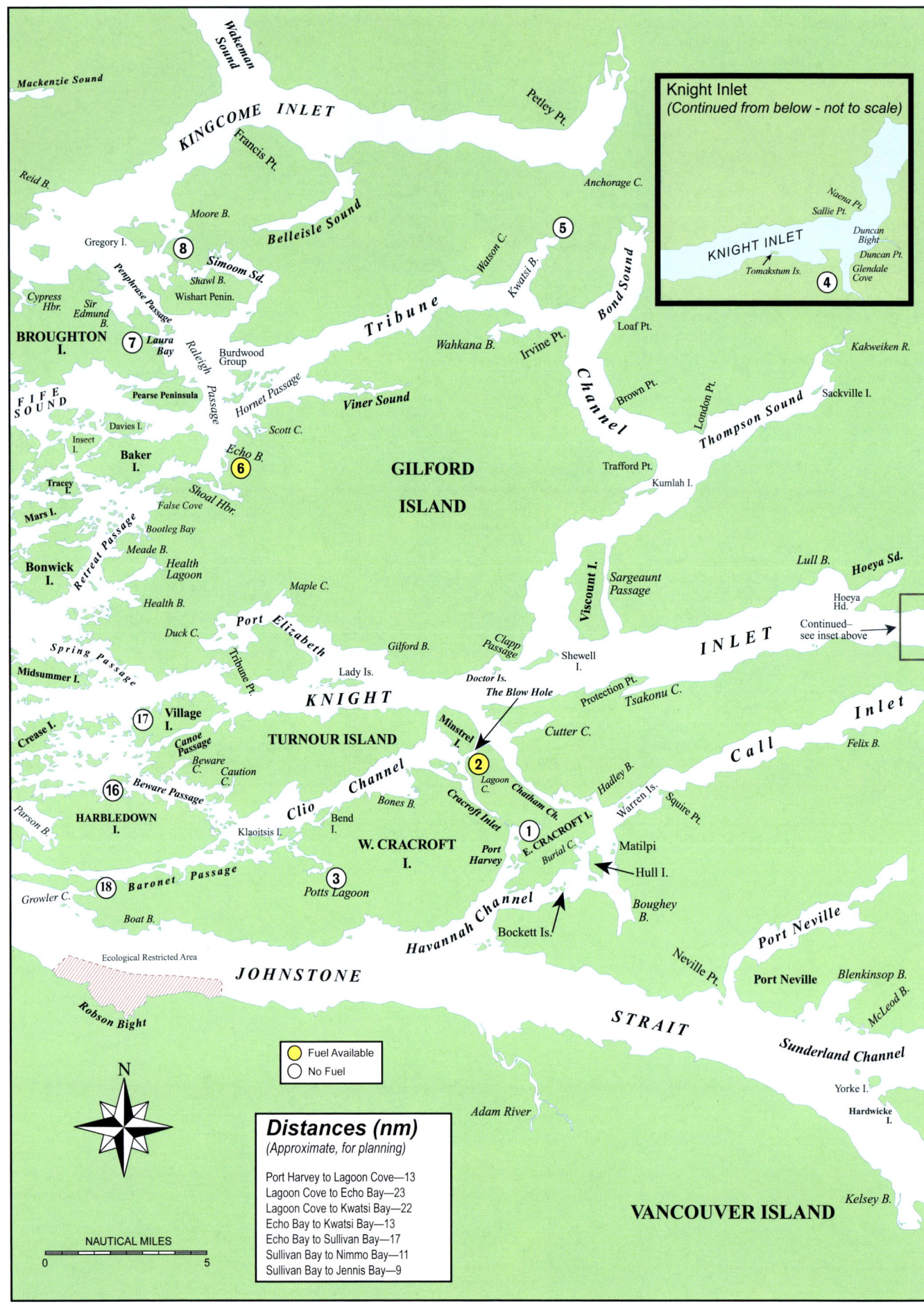

THE BROUGHTON REGION

Reference Only – Not for Navigation

Knight Inlet
(Continued from below - not to scale)

- Naena Pt.
- Sallie Pt.
- Duncan Bight
- KNIGHT INLET
- Tomakstum Is.
- Duncan Bight
- Glendale Cove ④

Map Labels

- Mackenzie Sound
- Wakeman Sound
- KINGCOME INLET
- Petley Pt.
- Reid B.
- Francis Pt.
- Moore B.
- Belleisle Sound
- Anchorage C.
- Gregory I.
- ⑧ Simoom Sd.
- Shawl B.
- Watson C.
- ⑤
- Cypress Hbr.
- Sir Edmund B.
- Penphrase Passage
- Wishart Penin.
- Kwatsi B.
- Bond Sound
- Loaf Pt.
- Kakweiken R.
- BROUGHTON I.
- ⑦ Laura Bay
- Raleigh Passage
- Burdwood Group
- Tribune Channel
- Wahkana B.
- Irvine Pt.
- Brown Pt.
- London Pt.
- Thompson Sound
- Sackville I.
- FIFE SOUND
- Pearse Peninsula
- Hornet Passage
- Viner Sound
- Trafford Pt.
- Davies I.
- Scott C.
- Kumlah I.
- Insect I.
- Baker I.
- Echo B. ⑥
- GILFORD ISLAND
- Lull B.
- Hoeya Sd.
- Tracey I.
- Shoal Hbr.
- False Cove
- Mars I.
- Bootleg Bay
- Viscount I.
- Sargeaunt Passage
- Hoeya Hd.
- Continued– see inset above
- Bonwick I.
- Retreat Passage
- Meade B.
- Health Lagoon
- Maple C.
- Health B.
- Duck C.
- Port Elizabeth
- Gilford B.
- Clapp Passage
- Shewell I.
- INLET
- Spring Passage
- Tribune Pt.
- Lady Is.
- Doctor Is.
- The Blow Hole
- Protection Pt.
- Tsakonu C.
- Midsummer I.
- KNIGHT
- Minstrel I.
- Cutter C.
- Call Inlet
- Crease I.
- ⑰ Village I.
- TURNOUR ISLAND
- ② Lagoon C.
- Chatham Ch.
- Hadley B.
- Felix B.
- Canoe Passage
- Beware C.
- Caution C.
- Clio Channel
- Cracroft Inlet
- ① E. CRACROFT I.
- Warren Is.
- Squire Pt.
- ⑯ Beware Passage
- Bones B.
- Bend I.
- Matilpi
- Parson B.
- HARBLEDOWN I.
- Klaoitsis I.
- W. CRACROFT I.
- Port Harvey
- Burial C.
- Hull I.
- Boughey B.
- Growler C.
- ⑱ Baronet Passage
- Potts Lagoon ③
- Bockett Is.
- Port Neville
- Boat B.
- Havannah Channel
- Neville Pt.
- Port Neville
- Blenkinsop B.
- Ecological Restricted Area
- McLeod B.
- JOHNSTONE
- Robson Bight
- STRAIT
- Sunderland Channel
- Adam River
- Yorke I.
- Hardwicke I.
- Kelsey B.
- VANCOUVER ISLAND

Legend

- 🟡 Fuel Available
- ⚪ No Fuel

Distances (nm)
(Approximate, for planning)

- Port Harvey to Lagoon Cove—13
- Lagoon Cove to Echo Bay—23
- Lagoon Cove to Kwatsi Bay—22
- Echo Bay to Kwatsi Bay—13
- Echo Bay to Sullivan Bay—17
- Sullivan Bay to Nimmo Bay—11
- Sullivan Bay to Jennis Bay—9

NAUTICAL MILES 0 — 5

The Broughton Region - East

Public dock at the entrance to Blow Hole on Minstrel Island

Range markers in Chatham Channel guide you safely through.

and come back year after year to catch up. Owners of these wilderness marinas make do with what they have in regards to power and water. Power is normally an additional charge and can be more expensive than elsewhere. Most of the power is generated on site using expensive fuel powered generators managed by the marina.

Wi-Fi: Internet in the Broughtons is provided by satellite, and bandwidth is often limited. Marina owners request that visitors refrain from downloading videos, sending large email attachments, using Zoom, or engaging in other high bandwidth activities.

Potluck Happy Hour: Two of the marinas in the Broughtons have a potluck hors d'oeuvre— or even a potluck dinner—gathering around 5:00 p.m. Bring your own beverages, leaded or unleaded and your own plate with utensils. It's an ideal time to meet other boaters and exchange information. You'll want to carry a stock of suitable fixings for your hors d'oeuvre or potluck contribution. The fixings don't have to be fancy. If you're down to Doritos and salsa, they'll be hoovered into mouths in short order. If you enjoy preparing something special, this is a good time to show your stuff.

Good Books: Tide Rips and Back Eddies; and Full Moon, Flood Tide. Both by Bill Proctor, edited and illustrated by Yvonne Maximchuk. Published by Harbour Publishing. These books are highly recommended reading before or during a cruise to the Broughtons. If you are hungry for a little more, consider Yvonne's book, *Drawn to Sea,* for more insights on life and the people of this area.

HAVANNAH CHANNEL

Havannah Channel leads northward to Call Inlet, Chatham Channel and Knight Inlet.

① **Port Harvey.** Port Harvey offers ample anchorage, serving as a good stop for a northbound run up Johnstone Strait, or a starting point for an early morning southbound passage. Protected from all but the strongest winds, it has convenient anchoring depths with good holding at the head of the bay, with room for a number of boats. The small notches and coves in the outer part of the bay are susceptible to strong winds and waves from Johnstone Strait. Strong winds can blow through Cracroft Inlet.

A large-marine ways used to launch barges constructed on site, along with other marine industrial operations, occupy the western shoreline. These industrial operations make the bay less than scenic, but Port Harvey provides needed shelter when the weather in Johnstone Strait kicks-up. All of the docks and moorings are private. The previous Port Harvey Marine Resort is private property no longer open to the public.

Port Harvey Marine Resort. The Port Harvey marina property was sold in March of 2020 and is no longer operating as a public marina open to boaters.

Bockett Islets. Tom Kincaid has anchored for a few hours among the Bockett Islets awaiting favorable current in Chatham Channel.

Boughey Bay. Anchorage is toward the south end of Boughey (pronounced "boogie") Bay. John Chappell (*Cruising Beyond Desolation Sound*) says easterly winds can spring up suddenly in the bay.

Matilpi. Matilpi (pronounced MAT-il-pi) is a former Indian village site. It is beautiful, with a white shell beach backed by dense forest. Anchor behind the northern of the two islands, or between the islands. Protection is excellent.

Burial Cove. Burial Cove is pretty, though open to most winds. It is well-protected from seas and has good holding in 25 feet. A few houses are on shore. We've anchored there twice. A large set of private docks are along the northeast shore.

Call Inlet. Call Inlet is approximately 10 miles long, and runs through beautiful, steep-sided mountains. You can find anchoring depths in the **Warren Islands**, near the mouth of the inlet. Anchorages are open to views up Call Inlet; and open to westerly and easterly winds. Holding is fair; preferred locations are on the east and west ends of the island chain away from upland buildings and a work barge with heavy equipment. The Islands are a pretty stop, where you can wait for the current to change in Chatham Channel, or for an overnight stay in settled weather. Correspondent Deane Hislop reports "two wonderful nights anchored in a depth of 35 feet; views of the islands and Call Inlet are outstanding."

Chatham Channel. Chatham Channel is easier to run than it appears from the chart. The southern section is the narrowest, with the least room in the channel, and requires the greatest attention. The current floods east and ebbs west. Near slack water is the most pleasant time to transit this southern section.

Slacks are based on Seymour Narrows predictions. Correction factors for the times of slack water are found under Secondary Stations in the Tide and Current Tables, Vol. 6, and Ports and Passes. Chart 3545 (1:40,000) shows the area. Chart 3564 (1:20,000), with its 1:10,000 inset of the southern section, shows the two range locations.

We have found that in some lighting conditions, or if the trees are not trimmed, the ranges are hard to locate from the far ends of the lower channel. Going either direction, a sharp-eyed crew should sight astern at the back range until it grows difficult to see. By then the leading range should be visible. Maximum currents in the southern section run to 5 knots on a spring tide, with no significant swirls or overfalls. In our experience, the current usually is much less than shown (but not always; twice, we have found considerable current). Chatham Channel can be taken at times other than slack water, but you should know what you are doing, and in the southern section *keep your boat lined up on the range.* Keep your eyes open. We encountered a bear swimming across Chatham Channel one morning.

Cutter Cove. Cutter Cove, located across from Minstrel Island Resort (now closed) at the north end of Chatham Channel, is very pretty and a good anchorage. A fresh west or northwest wind can enter the cove. No swells, but aggressive little whitecaps. The bottom looks flat, as if it's pure mud. "At least one noisy old rock is down there, though, because the anchor chain dragged across it all night long." *[Hale]* Anchor in 24 feet (zero tide).

Minstrel Island Harbour. Minstrel Island Harbour is well protected from all winds and offers anchorage for a number of boats. A 160-foot dock, along with a re-purposed 90-foot dock, are available year round for guest moorage at no charge; both docks are detached from land. No power, no water, and no garbage drop. There are no upland services. Boaters may go ashore by dinghy or kayak to the public uplands; other surrounding property is private.

THE BROUGHTON REGION   See Area Map Page 342 - Maps Not for Navigation

This site has a long and varied history. Its name comes from the late 19th century when a survey ship visited the area with a minstrel troupe onboard, who provided musical entertainment. During the early 1900's, Minstrel Island had a hotel, dance hall, store, and school along with a machine shop and boat repair services. An old pier was once the center for freight deliveries, including mail for residents of The Broughtons. In later years, the docks served as a popular destination for motor yachts and floatplanes.

The pier, floats, and upland buildings deteriorated for over a decade. In 2019 the pier and old docks were removed by Small Craft Harbours, part of the Fisheries & Oceans Department, which maintains the facility primarily as a refuge for commercial vessels; recreational vessels are welcome to stay at the floats.

Popular Happy Hour at Lagoon Cove is held at the historic workshop.

LOCAL KNOWLEDGE

CAUTION: Entering Lagoon Cove from Blow Hole, give the Islet and shoal across the channel from Perley Island a wide berth as the shoal extends farther west than charts indicate. Look for a private orange and/or green round plastic float which should pass to your port side entering Lagoon Cove.

The Blow Hole. The Blow Hole is a short, shallow, easily-navigated channel between Minstrel Island and East Cracroft Island. The channel gets its name from strong westerly winds that sometimes blow through. Near the west end a reef, shown clearly on Chart 3564, extends from East Cracroft Island on the south side of the channel. Brave the kelp and favor the north side of the channel and you'll have no problems.

② **Lagoon Cove.** Lagoon Cove has good anchorage along the shorelines, although the middle of the bay is a little deep for most boats. Lagoon Cove Marina is on the east side of the bay. Locals recommend against anchoring on the west side of the bay, which they say is foul with logging cable. We got a note from a reader who said at least one cable can be found on the east side as well.

② **Lagoon Cove Marina.** c/o Minstrel Island P.O., Minstrel Island, BC V0P 1L0; (778) 819-6962; info@lagooncovemarina.com; www.lagooncovemarina.com. Monitors VHF 66A. Open all year. Reservations accepted; a portion of the docks are held open for drop-ins. Two additional dock sections were added in 2022. Lagoon Cove has gasoline, diesel; 15, 30, & 2×30 amp power, water, washrooms and showers; gift shop. A Starlink dish provides fast internet connections. Kenmore Air, Corilair, and NW Seaplanes service to Seattle.

A do-it-yourself burn barrel is available for burnable garbage (no fair just dropping a bag of garbage in, for someone else to deal with). The fuel dock office carries fishing tackle, prawn and crab traps, ice, and ice cream. Complimentary coffee service is available on the dock each morning. A separate store with the name "Edgewater Emporium" carries Lagoon Cove branded clothing.

The entire property has a whimsical quality about it. The workshop is a "historic" workshop full of old tools. A totem pole is made from pieces of outboard motors and all sorts of other junk. Two "exercise stations," one of them a wood pile where you can lift weights, the other an old-fashioned lawnmower, invite the eager. Several hiking trails are maintained. A pet path is available for the four-legged crew. Be bear aware.

Lagoon Cove Marina is one of the most popular stops on the coast and fills during the summer months. Happy hour appetizer

Lagoon Cove Marina
Easy to find, hard to leave

www.lagooncovemarina.com
778-819-6962 (text or call)
info@lagooncovemarina.com

Moorage for boats large & small • Daily potluck happy hour
Wi-Fi on the docks • 24 hour 15, 30, & 2x30 power
Clear spring water • Diesel & gas • Hiking trails
Morning Coffee • Washrooms & showers • Book exchange
Clothing & gift shop • Friendly, relaxed atmosphere

See Area Map Page 342 - Maps Not for Navigation   THE BROUGHTON REGION

Side-tie floats at popular Lagoon Cove; anchorage can be had in south of the marina.

The office and fuel dock at Lagoon Cove

potlucks for marina guests are held almost every day in the "historic" workshop. Guests bring treats from their boats. Happy hour often morphs into a casual potluck dinner. Ping-Pong under the fruit trees is also a popular pastime.

Owners, Jim and Lou Ryan, of Lagoon Cove, along with their daughter Kelley and son-in-law Dan, are committed to "enhancing but not changing" this popular destination, as evidenced by ongoing improvements.

CLIO CHANNEL

Cracroft Inlet. Cracroft Inlet is on the south side of Dorman and Farquharson Islands. While we have not anchored there, it is reportedly well protected, with good holding bottom on either side of the large charted rock. Lagoon Cove, on the other side of Farquharson Island, can be reached by taking the dinghy around the east end of the island. The passage is shallow, so check the tide.

Bones Bay. The entire bay is fairly open, although you may find temporary anchorage behind the islets along the south shore. Watch for rocks around the islets. A floating fishing lodge is moored behind these islets.

Bend Island. Bend Island is connected to West Cracroft Island by a drying ledge, but good anchorage is in either end. Friends have anchored in the tiny nook just east of Bend Island, with a stern-tie to shore.

③ **Potts Lagoon.** The outer bay behind Klaoitsis Island and the 119-meter headland is open for anchorage; the previous log booming operation has been removed, only the landing site remains. A small float at the landing site serves as a good dinghy dock to access the logging roads for hiking. Two inner bays provide good protection from all winds. The inner bay to the southeast of the 41-meter island is the more popular and spacious with anchoring depths of 18 to 24 feet. Ruins from an old pier along with a few float homes add to the character of this hidden scenic anchorage. A smaller but more private cove is found to the northeast of the outer cove.

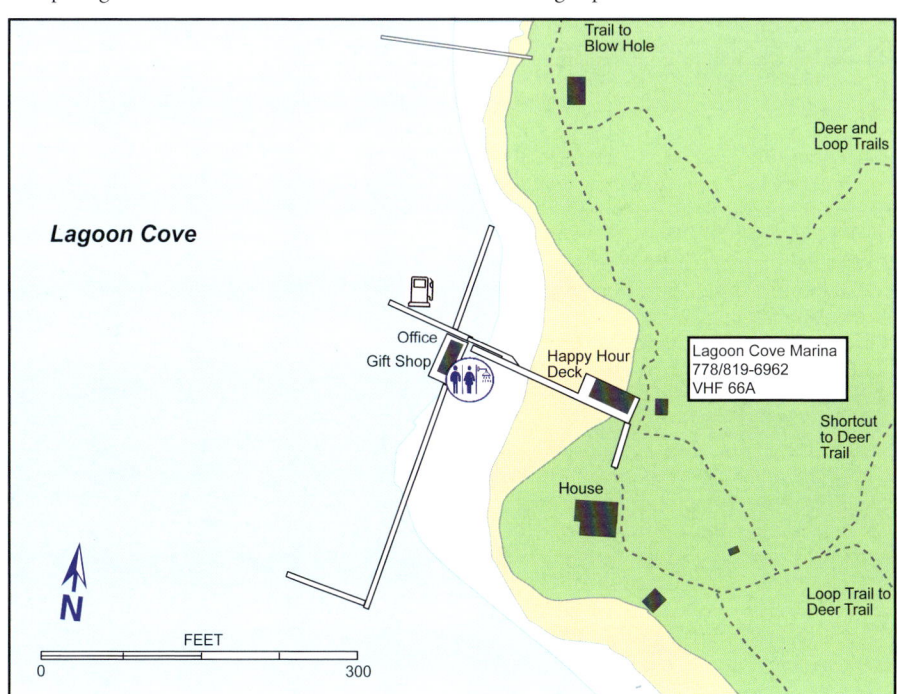

Klaoitsis Island. Anchorage might be found in the bay northwest of Klaoitsis Island, and in a notch on the south shore of Jamieson Island. Currents can run through these anchorages. For most boats, Potts Lagoon is a better choice.

Knight Inlet. Knight Inlet (locally called Knight's Inlet) extends from its mouth at Midsummer Island to its head, at the mouth of the Klinaklini River. The inlet is about 70 miles long and 2 miles wide, the longest of the fjords indenting the B.C. coast. Along most of its length, the shores rise steeply to 6,000-foot-high mountains. Anchorage is iffy at best, so for many, the inlet's upper reaches are explored mainly by fast boats able to make the round trip in a single day. Boats with limited fuel capacity should top off at Lagoon Cove before making the trip. Extensive logging activity has put considerable debris in the water. Watch carefully.

The section above Glendale Cove is reported to be more dramatic than Jervis or Bute inlets. Reader John Tyler reports, "Even with the distances involved, it's well worth the time to cruise up there."

Tsakonu Cove is a pretty anchorage with open views to the west and up Knight Inlet. It is protected from westerly inflow, but exposed to the east. It can be blowing summertime inflow outside the cove while much calmer inside. Anchor near the head of the cove in 50 to 70 feet with good holding. Driftwood logs on the shore suggest that outflow winds in Knight Inlet probably roar into Tsakonu Cove, accompanied by substantial seas. In 2019, the log dump on the south shore was not active. "Late one August afternoon we were pushing against 20 to 30 knot westerly winds on Knight Inlet when we pulled in to Tsakonu Cove for the night and found 5 to 8 knot winds inside the cove." *[Landons].*

Lagoon Cove

Lagoon Cove Marina
778/819-6962
VHF 66A

2023 WAGGONER CRUISING GUIDE   345

Knight Inlet on the way to Glendale Cove

Hoeya Sound. Hoeya Sound is pretty, but deep and completely exposed to the westerly winds that are prevalent in the summer.

④ **Glendale Cove.** Glendale Cove on Knight Inlet is a popular destination for recreational boaters and commercial tour operators. It has one of the highest concentrations of Grizzly Bears, also referred to as Brown Bears, on the west coast of British Columbia. Bears feed on tidal area sedge in the spring; and by mid-August, feed on salmon.

In May of 2017, the DAFN Glendale Cove Water-Based Grizzly Bear Viewing Management Plan was put into effect to create a sanctuary for bears by strictly managing the number of people accessing the bear viewing areas, and to limit boat traffic in Glendale Cove. Too many boats can easily crowd and displace the bear population. The Da'naxda'xw/Awaetlatla First Nations Band (DAFN) serve as Guardians and closely monitor all activities in the Cove, their traditional native territory. All of Glendale Cove waters and uplands are included in the managed area. The DAFN Keogh Indian Reserve (I.R.) #2 area is in the southeast corner of the Glendale Cove and is a Do Not Enter Zone.

When entering Glendale Cove, boaters should contact the "Glendale Cove Guardians" on VHF 68 to receive a copy of the Bear Viewing Guidelines brochure and map. All bear viewing is done from your vessel, kayak, or dinghy. No shore access at any time; dogs should not be taken on shore in Glendale Cove. The nearest beach access is at Duncan Bight to the northeast and Siwash Bay to the west.

There is a 5-knot speed limit throughout the cove (including dinghies). Boaters should be respectful of boat speed, noise, distance, and viewing time. Viewing is limited to 6 small craft at a time, maintaining a distance of 50 meters (164 feet) from shore. Commercial tour operators have prescribed time slots for viewing. Recreational boaters should contact "Glendale Cove Guardians" prior to viewing bears. Being good stewards and respectful boaters is important for the future preservation of Grizzly Bears.

Knight Inlet Lodge, located on the east side of Glendale Cove, is a private resort providing Grizzly Bear tours for their guests, seventy percent of whom visit from Europe and twenty percent come from Australia. Reservations are booked well in advance for this distinctive lodge. The Lodge does not provide transient moorage and does not offer any services for boaters visiting the area. A couple of small tour operations also operate in the area. Tour operators and private boaters alike all abide by the same bear-viewing regulations.

Anchorage is available in two small bights along the western shore of Glendale Cove. Anchor at least 200 meters (656 feet) from the waterline so as not to disturb bears that come to feed along the shore. Anchorages are protected from inflow westerly winds but are exposed to northeast outflow wind. Holding is good. About 4 nautical miles west of Glendale Cove is a small bay with possible anchoring behind Tomakstum Island on the south shore of Knight Inlet.

Wahshihlas Bay. Located at the mouth of the Sim River, Wahshihlas Bay is a possible anchorage. Although we've never tried it, Correspondents Bruce and Margaret Evertz have. "It was settled weather and we anchored in the northwest corner, just off the shoal. There were some snags to avoid. If we expected any winds we could have moved away from the shoal a little and anchored with a stern tie to shore or to some old pilings. The bay is far from 'bomb proof,' but we felt secure with the weather we had." [Evertz]

Port Elizabeth. Port Elizabeth is a great big bay bounded on the west by low hills that let westerlies in. A substantial log booming operation is in the cove in the northwest corner. You can find good anchorage near the booming site and along the western shore, west of the largest of the three islands. The two smaller islands are joined on the west by drying flats.

Correspondents John and Lorraine Littlewood provided us with the following extra information:

"The unexpected difficulty with the anchorage in Duck Cove at the west end of Port Elizabeth is that in any winds from 0 to 180 degrees you will feel the full force. We were getting gusts to 30 knots in a southeaster, supposedly sheltered. The only real shelter is in the extreme southeastern end of Port Elizabeth, except in a northwest blow." [Littlewood]

Sargeaunt Passage. Sargeaunt Passage connects Knight Inlet and Tribune Channel. The passage runs between steep-sided mountains with a shallow narrow neck near the middle. Some current is noticeable at the narrows. The shoal at the narrows extends from the east shore across much of the passage. Favor the west shore. The shallowest point is at the south end of the narrows with a minimum depth of approximately 9 feet at zero tide; much less than charts indicate. Anchorage is possible at either end of the narrows, although one cruiser warned of logging cables fouling their anchor and a deadhead marked with a red float was sighted on the southeast side.

Tribune Channel. Tribune Channel borders the east and north sides of Gilford Island. Several anchoring locations can be found along Tribune Channel but most are deep or best in settled weather. The only marina on Tribune Channel is at Kwatsi Bay. Lacy Falls on the north shore of Tribune Channel can be stunning. Two small native pictographs are clearly seen on a rock face about 20 to 30 feet above the high waterline on the east side of Miller Point.

Glendale Cove

Bear viewing from your boat is good at Glendale Cove and well-managed by DAFN First Nation.

Kumlah Island Anchorage. Kumlah Island is in Tribune Channel, roughly across from the mouth of Thompson Sound. Waggoner reader Joel Erickson found suitable anchorage in 16 to 24 feet behind Kumlah Island, between it and Gilford Island. We haven't spent the night, but would consider anchoring there in settled weather. The view is beautiful.

Thompson Sound. Thompson Sound is surrounded by forested mountains so steep that the hillsides are scarred by many landslides. Earlier editions of the Waggoner said Thompson Sound has no good anchorages, but Correspondents John and Lorraine Littlewood set us straight with this email: "There is excellent anchorage at the head of Thompson Sound, on the shelf between the mudflats at the mouth of the Kakweiken River. You can explore the river for a couple miles at high tide; there is lots of bear sign, and we don't mean black bears, either!"

A reader reported that when they tried to anchor, they found the shelf dotted with crab trap buoys, leaving no room. They anchored briefly in the lee of Sackville Island, with a stern-tie to shore.

Bond Sound. In the past, we reported that Bond Sound had no good anchorages. But inspired by Bill Proctor's wonderful book, *Full Moon, Flood Tide*, readers Jim and Marsha Peters anchored their Grand Banks 42 *Dev's Courage* at the head of the sound in settled weather and took the dinghy some distance up the Ahta River. They said it was beautiful. Correspondents Steve and Elsie Hulsizer say to go up about two hours before high water. Another reader, Bill Cooke, told us that cutthroat trout fishing is good at the head of the sound. Correspondents John and Lorraine Littlewood add this note from an early September cruise:

"Bill Proctor's book, *Full Moon, Flood Tide,* led us to the Ahta River at the head of Bond Sound, an absolutely pristine salmon spawning river teeming with every sort of wildlife, from very large, dead salmon that have just completed their life cycle, to much larger hairy brown mammals that feed on them (and just about anything else they want to). The place is like something from a fairy tale. It is not all that easy to find and explore, but very much worth it. Anchorage is tricky just off the drying bar at the mouth of the rivers (there are two: Ahta Creek on the left as you face the estuary and the Ahta River on the right). The Ahta River, with a smaller opening, is deep, fast and clear. Don't tell a soul."

Note: Strong winds can funnel through Bond Sound, making it mostly unsuitable for overnight anchorage. A substantial building in Bond Sound is home to an Indigenous cultural camp for youth.

⑤ **Kwatsi Bay.** The inner cove of Tribune Channel's Kwatsi Bay is a stunning anchorage. This serene cove is surrounded by a high bowl of granite rock faces, waterfalls, and forested steps, one of the most impressive in the Broughtons. Sunrises and sunsets are magnificent. Rain will bring a number of waterfalls to life and will turn the waters darker with tannin. The bay is deep, over 100 feet in much of the inner cove. The favorite area for anchoring is in the northeast corner of the cove in 50 to 80 feet of water.

Kwatsi Bay Floats. Kwatsi Bay Floats were closed for the 2021 and 2022 boating seasons while the new owners considered plans for construction. To-date, plans do not include guest moorage for the general boating public. Rumor has it that future plans include accommodations and eco tours.

Max Knierim and wife Anka Fraser carved out a place to live in beautiful Kwatsi Bay, where they raised their daughter Marieke and son Russell. After 24 years of welcoming boaters at the marina docks, the decision was made to retire. The Kwatsi Bay Marina property was subsequently sold in 2021. Sadly, Max passed away that same year, a devastating blow to the family. While Max and Anka will be missed at Kwatsi, countless memories endure.

Watson Cove. Watch for a charted rock in the entrance, and favor the north shore when entering. A 30 to 40 foot shallow shelf is just outside the entrance. Watson Cove is surrounded by shear rock walls, dense forest, and beautiful waterfalls on the north side. Although open to westerly winds and reportedly foul with logging debris, the cove is accessible for anchoring in 50 to 60 feet.

Land your dinghy at the rock slab about 200 feet before the head of the cove on the south shore, where you will find a large rusty anchor pin set into the rocky shoreline. Immediately above this landing, you will find a very rustic trail (bring boots) leading to the 1000-year-old cedar tree mentioned in Billy Proctor's *Full Moon, Flood Tide*. The tree is a memorable sight.

Lacy Falls. Just west of Watson Cove, Lacy Falls washes down an expanse of smooth black rock and tumbles into the sea. The boat can be brought up close, but not too close. The bottom at the base of the falls is rocky. Note: During dry periods, water does not fan across the rocks.

Wahkana Bay. The inner cove of Wahkana Bay is attractive, but 120 feet deep except near shore. The south shore has spots where you can anchor in 48 to 72 feet with swinging room, however. Parts of the east shore are reported

Watson Cove one of the few anchorages on Tribune Channel

THE BROUGHTON REGION

See Area Map Page 342 - Maps Not for Navigation

Viner Sound has several mooring buoys at the head of the inlet.

to be foul with logging debris and old pilings beneath the surface. The head of the inner cove shoals rapidly so watch out. Wind can blow through the saddle that reaches to Viner Sound.

Viner Sound. Three-mile long Viner Sound is a fjord-like inlet. The entrance is wide and deep and the head of the inlet is a ¾ mile long drying area. The middle ¾ mile section is narrow and shallow with a few anchoring options and two sets of mooring buoys.

The indent on the north side, a short distance down the narrow channel, will hold one boat near the opening. Just inside that indent the water shoals immediately. Further up the narrow channel, two public mooring buoys are in the little cove on the north side and two older mooring buoys are in the indent immediately to the south of the cove. One of the two older buoys is half submerged.

The long shoaling area shown on the chart at the head of Viner Sound is real. Watch your depths as you explore. A trail reportedly goes from the north cove to a lake.

Scott Cove. Scott Cove once was a busy logging camp, but the camp is now closed. This was the location of Pierre's Bay Marina, which moved to Echo Bay in 2008. We're told a surprising number of people still show up every summer mistakenly looking for Pierre's Bay Marina in Scott Cove.

LOCAL KNOWLEDGE

POWELL ROCK WARNING: A nasty drying rock lies off Powell Point, the southwest corner of Scott Cove. A boat running between Tribune Channel and Echo Bay or Cramer Passage could easily run up on this rock. Give Powell Point, and the rock, a big, wide offing.

⑥ **Echo Bay.** Echo Bay has been a gathering place for thousands of years; and for more than 100 years, it has been a center for loggers, fishermen, and now summertime boaters. More recently, Pierre and Tove Landry bought the Echo Bay Resort; and over the course of several decades, improved and upgraded the facilities, creating one of the premier destinations in the Broughtons, complete with a fuel dock, store, and event hall. In June of 2020, Pierre's Echo Bay Marina was sold to KHFN First Nation, who now operate the marina. The Haliwud Water Taxi (250-974-8062) is available for local transport. Sea Wolf Adventures offers Indigenous and Wildlife Tours.

Echo Bay has much to offer. Visit Billy Proctor's museum of local artifacts. A short trail leads from Echo Bay Marina

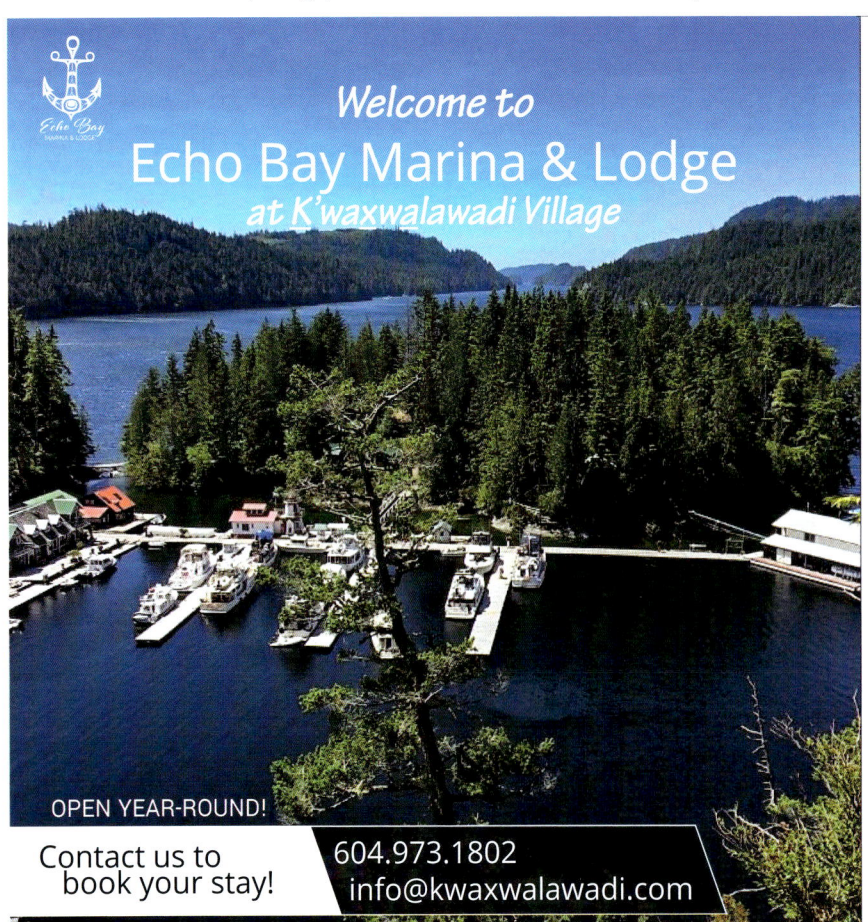

Welcome to Echo Bay Marina & Lodge at K'waxwalawadi Village

OPEN YEAR-ROUND!

Contact us to book your stay!
604.973.1802
info@kwaxwalawadi.com

Welcome to K'waxwalawadi, Echo Bay Lodge & Marina

The Kwikwasut'inuxw Haxwa'mis First Nation purchased Pierre's at Echo Bay in 2020! New owners, same great destination with all the amenities in place to welcome our guests:

- Fuel
- Moorage
- Grocery Store
- Post Office
- Walking Trails
- Rental Suites
- Laundromat & Showers
- 15, 30 & 50 Amp Power
- Family & Pet Friendly
- All Size Yachts Welcome

We're located in the heart of Kwikwasut'inuxw Haxwa'mis territory in the Broughton Archipelago
50°45.115'N/126°29.730'W
VHF Channel 66A "Echo Bay Marina"

kwaxwalawadi.com

See Area Map Page 342 - Maps Not for Navigation

THE BROUGHTON REGION

Echo Bay with the marina floats on the right and Cliffside floats and floating homes to the left.

to the museum. The trail has recently been re-routed and improved for a lovely walk through the forest. Or you can take the dinghy to Shoal Harbour to visit the museum and see local author and artist Yvonne Maximchuk's SeaRose Studio, www.yvonnemaximchuk.com.

A deep midden at Echo Bay Marine Park, at the head of the bay, shows evidence of an ancient First Nation's village. The village was occupied for thousands of years and was still inhabited during the Hudson's Bay Company era. In later years, a schoolhouse stood on shore, but the school-age population of the area fell below the threshold needed to keep the school open. The school closed in 2008, and was removed in the fall of 2014.

The dock at the head of Echo Bay Marine Park has been condemned and is now closed. The holding bottom can be poor; anchor with care. The beach is often used as a landing for dinghies and kayaks.

Slow down: The wakes from passing vessels and the following wake from approaching vessels can get inside the bay and set things a-rocking. Please slow down well outside the marina when approaching.

⑥ **Echo Bay Marina & Lodge.** c/o General Delivery, Simoom Sound PO, BC V0P 1S0; (604) 973-1802; info@kwaxwalawadi.com; kwaxwalawadi.com. Monitors VHF 66A. Cell phone coverage is spotty in the area. Marina moorage, lodging, and fuel open year-round. Power on the docks available early July to mid-September. Gasoline, diesel, and propane at the fuel dock. 15, 30 & 50 amp power; rental cabins, store, ice, water, washrooms, showers, and laundry. Please check in at the store before using the shower or laundry to pay the nominal fee. The store carries basic grocery items and gifts. Limited Wi-Fi and cell phone coverage. Ample guest moorage; reservations recommended during the busy summer months; make reservations online. Floatplane service by Kenmore Air and NW Seaplanes.

This is a busy destination in the Broughtons, with wide, sturdy docks. The protected bay, with dramatic sheer rock faces, is beautiful.

Echo Bay is a social place. Happy Hour gatherings are common, and guests are encouraged to use the dining hall for impromptu happy hours and movie nights. Bring your favorite movie to show. Visitors enjoy sitting around a cozy fire pit located on shore above the docks and on the colorful Adirondack Chairs at the bottom of the ramp.

The Kwikwasut'inuxw Haxwa'mis First Nation (KHFN) purchased Pierre's Echo Bay Lodge & Marina in June of 2020. Echo Bay on Gilford Island in the beautiful Broughton Archipelago is the heart of the KHRN's traditional territory. The marina is within a short boat ride from KHFN's main village of Gwa'yasdams. The KHFN has plans to integrate their culture into their eco-tours and other services at Echo Bay. Owners of Echo Bay can put boaters in touch with local First Nation Grizzly Bear tour operators. Tours are by boat with occasional hikes along river inlets.

Caution: beware of current that can run swiftly around the floats.

⑥ **The Cliffside at Echo Bay.** Pierre and Tove Landry own The Cliffside property and rent out cabins at The Cliffside for long-term stays. The KHFN, owners of Echo Bay Lodge & Marina, have permission to use the floats at The Cliffside for overflow moorage from Echo Bay. No power or water at the floats. A ramp to shore leads to a trail through the woods to Billy Proctor's Museum. Use the dinghy to cross over to the KHFN docks to visit the store, pay moorage, and attend activities.

Shoal Harbour. Shoal Harbour has good, protected anchorage, mud bottom. We would anchor just to the right, inside the entrance. Study the charts and use caution when transiting the narrow entrance. Watch the depths; the main head and northern arm shoal quickly.

Billy Proctor's Museum. Open 9:00 a.m. to 5:00 p.m. A trail, rough in places, leads from Echo Bay. An easier trail begins at The Cliffside. By boat, if you leave Echo Bay and turn left toward Shoal Harbour, you can follow the shoreline around the peninsula and into a cozy bay with a home, small dock and marine railway haulout. This is where

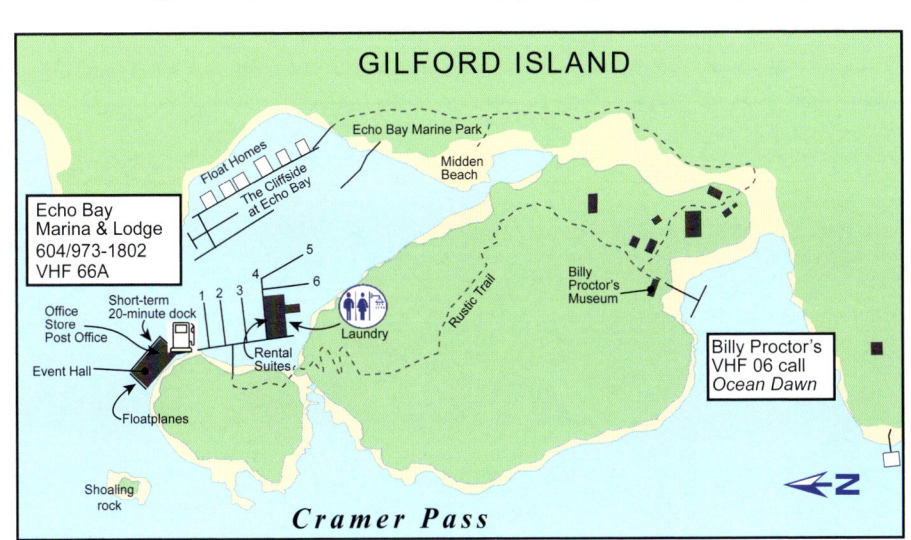

Echo Bay

Hike the short trail to visit Billy Proctor's museum.

2023 WAGGONER CRUISING GUIDE

THE BROUGHTON REGION   See Area Map Page 342 - Maps Not for Navigation

legendary Billy Proctor, who has logged, trapped and fished on the coast all of his many years, lives and has his museum.

Over a lifetime, Billy Proctor has collected a treasure of Chinese opium bottles, Chinese and Japanese beer bottles, engine plates, tools, arrowheads, bone fish hooks, a 1910 mimeograph machine from Minstrel Island, a crank telephone, a scale from the old Simoom Sound post office, and thousands of other artifacts of the coast's past. In a structure he built from lumber he milled himself, the remarkable collection is displayed. Out the front door is another building he put up himself, housing a small book and gift shop, and more treasures. Everything has a story, even the windows and doors.

Billy built a replica of a hand logger's cabin, circa 1900. All the wood came from a single cedar log he found floating. Recently, he built a small schoolhouse and filled it with items from the old Echo Bay schoolhouse. Visitors can write on the old blackboards and look through old pictures. The kids love it.

No admission charge for the museum or schoolhouse, but a box marked "donations," which go to salmon enhancement, is next to the door. Billy also has an excellent selection of books on the area, including his own.

If you want to call ahead, try *Ocean Dawn* on VHF 16 or 06. Hike the occasionally challenging trail from Echo Bay. Meet Billy and go have a look. We think you'll be glad you did.

LOCAL KNOWLEDGE

PYM ROCKS WARNING: When crossing from the vicinity of Echo Bay bound for Fife Sound and destinations to the northwest, Pym Rocks, off the northwest tip of Baker Island, lie very close to your probable course. Give Horsford Point, Ragged Island, and Pym Rocks wide offing.

Burdwood Group. The Burdwood Group is a beautiful little clutch of islands, a gunkholer's dream. The group is dotted with rocks and reefs, and Chart 3515 (1:80,000) doesn't show a lot of detail. With a sharp lookout, however, small boats can slowly maneuver among the islands. Anchorages are scarce, deep and rocky, and recommended in settled weather only. Given the opportunity, the cruising boat should at least patrol through these islands.

Pictographs on Kingcome Inlet

Simoom Sound. Simoom Sound is a dogleg inlet, very scenic, but most of it is too deep for anchoring. The best anchorages are in **O'Brien Bay** at the head of Simoom Sound, and in **McIntosh Bay** and the bays adjacent, along the north shore. You'll be in 48 to 60+ feet in O'Brien Bay, and 18 to 36 feet in the McIntosh Bay area. We spent a quiet night in McIntosh Bay behind the small island. The views took our breath away. In an emergency you could find anchorage off the northeast corner of Louisa Islet, and near the mouth of a creek on the Wishart Peninsula side.

⑦ **Laura Bay.** Laura Bay is a pretty anchorage. Anchorage is in two areas: one with a challenging entry is in the long neck that extends westward behind the outer bay; the other is in the cove north of the small islet between Trivett Island and Broughton Island.

Laura Bay is charted as the long neck westward from the outer bay and has anchorage for only one or two boats. A drying reef extends from the south shore a short distance inside the entry to the neck of the bay and extends somewhat past the middle of the channel. The reef extends farther into the channel than the charts indicate. Approaching the reef, favor the north side at dead slow with an alert bow watch.

Laura Cove is our name given to the cove between Trivett Island and Broughton Island. The cove is lovely with room for several boats; a stern tie may be needed. Entering the cove, leave the island to starboard. Charts incorrectly indicate good water on both sides of the islet.

Correspondent Deane Hislop reports that Laura Bay and Laura Cove are favorite locations for commercial crabbers. Recreational boaters have been known to snag pot lines that stretch under water over a hundred feet.

Sir Edmund Bay. Sir Edmund Bay should be entered east of Nicholls Island to avoid a rock west of the island. This rock is farther offshore than you might expect. Fish farms take up considerable space, but anchorage is possible in a cove at the northwest corner of the bay, and in another cove at the south corner.

The northwest cove is 48 to 60 feet deep until well in. Then it shoals to 30 feet before the shelf is reached. An all-chain anchor rode would yield a small enough swinging circle; boats with combination chain and rope may need to stern-tie to a tree. The cove is not very pretty and wouldn't be our first choice.

The southern cove has anchorage behind a charted drying rock. Some years ago, we visited near the bottom of a 7-foot low tide and failed to locate the rock. Others who have anchored there say the cove is a good spot, however. Until we know more we neither recommend nor discourage anchoring.

Laura Cove is the favored anchorage in Laura Bay

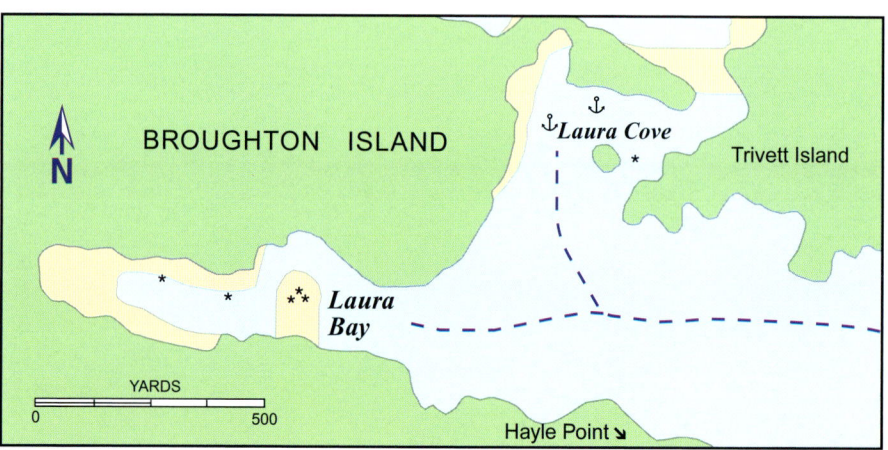

Laura Bay

⑧ **Shawl Bay & Moore Bay.** Shawl Bay and Moore Bay are a short distance inside the entrance to Kingcome Inlet on the east side. The bays are connected by a narrow channel that reportedly is navigable at half tide or better. Moore Bay has no marinas. Anchorage is behind Thief Island in the south part of Moore Bay, or in 36 feet close behind the 55-meter island near the north shore. Two other nooks along the east shore might also be workable anchorages, depending on the weather. Along the north shore, near where a stream from Mt. Plumridge enters the bay, the Ministry of Forests installed a dinghy dock and four campsites with picnic tables and an outhouse.

Shawl Bay Marina. c/o General Delivery, Simoom Sound, BC V0P 1S0; Frank at (778) 363-3481; shawlbaymarina@gmail.com. Shawl Bay Marina was closed in 2016 for renovations, which began in 2017. Construction continued through 2021 and 2022. Guest moorage is planned to be open in 2023, with approximately 175 feet of dock space for about four boats in a U-shaped configuration, with an outside tie on the northeast end. Non-potable water on the docks, no power. Limited Wi-Fi. Call ahead for moorage space. Open to self-contained boats, no shower or restroom facilities.

Reid Bay. Reid Bay, on the western shore just inside the entrance to Kingcome Inlet, is open, deep, and uninteresting. It is no place to anchor. Just south of Reid Bay, however, an unnamed cove has possibilities. It is rather pretty and has good protection from westerlies. The chart indicates depths of approximately 6 fathoms throughout the bay, but our depth sounder showed 60 to 80 feet, except about 36 feet close to the head. If you go into this cove, give a wide berth to the point at the south entrance. We saw one uncharted rock just off the point; Chappell's guidebook says there are two.

KINGCOME INLET

Kingcome Inlet extends 17 miles inland between high and beautiful mountains, terminating at the delta of the Kingcome River. The water is milky from glacier runoff and the surface band of water can be surprisingly fresh. Just beyond Petley Point at the head of the inlet, a magnificent new pictograph, a real work of art, is painted high on a rock cliff on the north shore. It is the work of Native artist Marianne Nicolson. The pictograph is brilliant red in color, and measures 28 feet wide and 38 feet high. A half mile south of the new pictograph, there is a much older Native pictograph. The book, *Two Wolves at the Dawn of Time*, by Judith Williams, describes the project. The book's prose is a bit rich, but the story is interesting.

Kingcome Inlet's great depths and sheer rock walls allow virtually no suitable anchorages in the upper portions, except in settled weather.

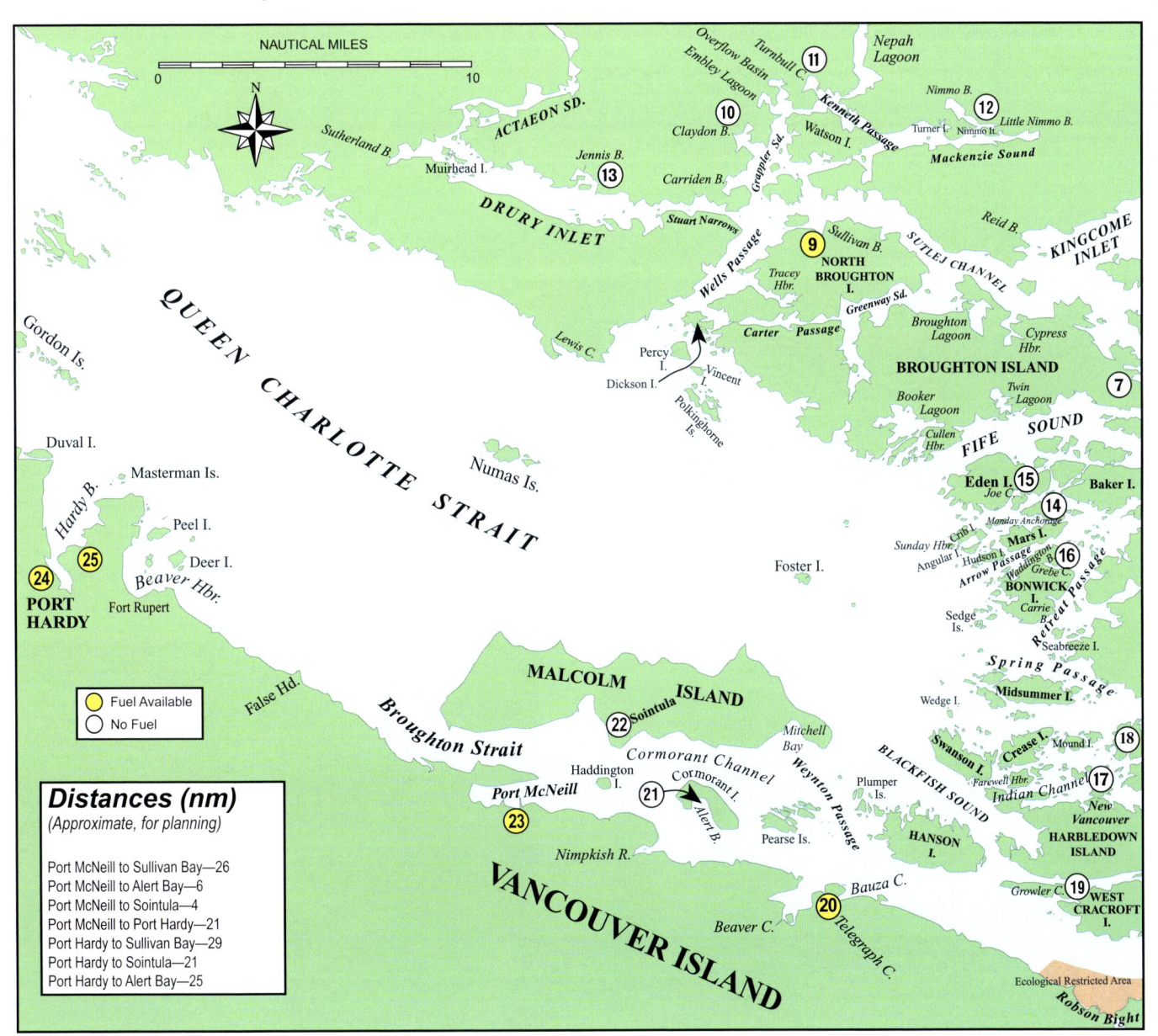

The Broughton Region - West

THE BROUGHTON REGION   See Area Map Page 351 - Maps Not for Navigation

Wakeman Sound. Wakeman Sound branches off Kingcome Inlet and extends about 7 miles north into the mountains. Although it has no good anchorages, on a clear day the scenery is beautiful. Wakeman Sound is a center for logging activity. Watch for drift in the water.

Belleisle Sound. Belleisle Sound branches off Kingcome Inlet to the south. Entry is between two high green mountains—the kind that make you feel small. Belleisle Sound is beautiful and remote-feeling, but generally too deep for easy anchoring. Only a small area just inside the entrance is usable. Chappell and Sailing Directions warn that strong westerlies can blow through. On the day of our visit the surface was mirror-calm. The water was warm and people on another boat took a swim, right out in the middle. We spent the night in Belleisle Sound without difficulty, anchored and stern-tied to the little islet across from the entrance. [Hale]

SUTLEJ CHANNEL

Cypress Harbour. Cypress Harbour is a pretty spot, but a large fish farm occupies part of Miller Bay, and two log booms are present in Berry Cove farther in. Good anchorage, removed from the fish farm and log boom, is in lovely Stopford Bay in the southeast corner of Cypress Harbour. Be sure to avoid the charted rock. We've had a report of a stretch of logging cable lying on the bottom a short distance before the rock is reached. Watch the depths in Stopford Bay; the bottom grows increasingly shoaled until it becomes drying flats. Recommended if you want a quiet, tucked-away anchorage.

Correspondent Deane Hislop reports that the Forest Service Recreation site on Clawston Point offers 5 camp sites with picnic tables, fire pits, and a pit toilet.

Broughton Lagoon. "The entrance to Broughton Lagoon is a reversing tidal rapids. At Alert Bay high slack, water pours in through the narrow passage, trying to fill the lagoon. At Alert Bay low slack, water pours out at a ferocious rate. The calmest time to enter Broughton Lagoon is about 1 hour 15 minutes after Alert Bay high slack. For about 30 minutes around that time the rapids are at their least flow. Use the north entry channel only. The other channel often dries. This is a beautiful lagoon. It has plenty of width and depth for powerful dinghies. Not recommended for larger craft without local knowledge." *[Tom Taylor]*

Greenway Sound. Greenway Sound has several good anchorages. The bay behind Broughton Point, at the east end of Carter Passage, is nice.

Depending on conditions, anchorage is in a number of little nooks on both sides of Greenway Sound and behind Simpson Island, near the head of the sound. Leave Simpson Island to starboard when approaching the head of Greenway Sound. For exercise, Broughton Lakes Park, with access from a dinghy dock on the west shore of the bay due east of Greenway Point, received much work in recent years and has excellent hiking. The bay itself is a little deep for anchoring, so anchor elsewhere and take the dinghy over. Good trout fishing at the lakes (fresh water license required), beautiful views.

Cartwright Bay. This bay is open to the wakes from passing traffic in Sutlej Channel, but offers easy anchorage at its inner end.

⑨ **Sullivan Bay Marina Resort.** Box 6000, Port McNeill, BC V0N 2R0; (604) 484-9193; sullivanbaymarina@gmail.com; www.sullivanbay.com. Monitors VHF 66A. Seasonal moorage and store; fuel open year-round with gasoline, diesel and propane. No garbage drop. Beer cans, pop cans, wine bottles and water bottles are accepted for recycling. Amenities include 15, 30 & 50 amp power, water, washroom, showers, laundry, exercise room, and Starlink internet for a fee. Guests often gather around "Sullivan Square" at 5:00 p.m. for drinks and appies.

All of the marina buildings are on floats and date from the mid-20th century. Golfers can try to make a hole in one at the 1-hole golf course. Depending on tide and wind, the floating target is 100 to 140 yards out.

Sullivan Bay is legendary among cruising boaters. It has ample moorage (3000 feet), a

---

SULLIVAN BAY · MARINA RESORT
WELCOME TO OUR UNIQUE FLOATING VILLAGE!

Sullivan Bay, a part of the magical Broughton Archipelago. With the beauty of nature at every turn, visitors are bound to see whales, dolphins, eagles, and many more wonders.

The Marina Offers:
- Gasoline, Diesel, Propane
- Showers & Laundry
- 15, 30 and 50 Amp Power
- Starlink Internet $10 per boat
- Fishing Tackle
- Boat Babysitting Our Specialty
- Exercise Room

- Liquor Agency
- Well-stocked Store with Fresh Baked Goods Daily
- Regular International & Local Float Plane Service
- Restaurant
- Stay 2 Nights and Get the 3rd Night's Moorage Free

Cruise on over and enjoy the marina and hospitality.

SullivanBayMarina@gmail.com
WWW.SULLIVANBAY.COM
604.484.9193
VHF CH. 66A

SULLIVAN BAY MARINA
BOX 6000
PORT MCNEILL, B.C. V0N 2R0

The small community at Sullivan Bay is entirely on floats.

Walk all the floats at Sullivan Bay for a morning jaunt.

well-stocked grocery store with liquor agency, bait and tackle; open 9:00 a.m. to 5:00 p.m. and on demand 7:00 p.m. to 8:00 p.m. They also offer fresh-baked pastries and cinnamon buns.

The Town Hall Restaurant is open Monday, Wednesday, and Friday with a fixed price, buffet-style dinner; we have received rave reviews, especially over the prime rib dinner, call for reservations. Limited menu lunch service is available Tuesdays, Thursdays, and Saturdays. "Wing Nights" are held on Saturday evenings.

This is a popular turnaround point for Broughtons cruisers. Daily floatplane service to Seattle and elsewhere. Boat sitting available.

The annual July 4th celebration and parade on the docks is hugely popular. Reservations recommended.

A community of handsome vacation float homes occupies a portion of the Sullivan Bay moorage. Bill & Laura Swanson are the managers, along with their young son, Gabe, assistant manager in training.

Atkinson Island. Find anchorage in either end of the passage south of Atkinson Island.

GRAPPLER SOUND

Grappler Sound, north of Sutlej Channel and Wells Passage, has several good anchorages.

Kinnaird Island. The bay in the northeast corner of the island is reported to be good in settled weather.

Hoy Bay. Some anchorage is possible in Hoy Bay, behind Hopetown Point, west of Hopetown Passage.

LOCAL KNOWLEDGE

HOPETOWN PASSAGE CURRENTS: One of two passages to Mackenzie Sound is Hopetown Passage with dangerous currents. If Hopetown Passage is attempted at all, it should be done cautiously, at high water slack in a shallow draft boat. Kenneth Passage is less challenging and the preferred channel for entering Mackenzie Sound and Nimmo Bay.

Hopetown Passage. The eastern entrance to Hopetown Passage is blocked by a drying reef. Strong currents, tidal overfalls and shallow depths make this a challenge. Explore by dinghy first.

Carriden Bay. Carriden Bay is located just inside Pandora Head, at the entrance to Grappler Sound. The holding is reportedly good, if a little deep when away from the shoreline. One reader calls Carriden Bay "a special spot." As you look in, the spectacular knob of Pandora Head rises on the left, and when you're in, you see a beautiful vista of mountains out the mouth of the bay. This vista makes Carriden Bay exposed to east winds, however. It could be an uncomfortable anchorage in such winds.

⑩ **Claydon Bay.** This is a popular anchorage. Entering or leaving, favor the Morton Point side. Foul ground, shown on the chart, extends from the opposite side of the entry. In Claydon Bay you can pick the north arm or south arm, depending on which way the wind is blowing. An islet is in the entry to the north arm. Leave this islet to starboard when entering. Note also that the drying reef surrounding the islet extends a considerable distance southeast of the islet. The northern arm has room for about a dozen boats; holding is good with a thick mud bottom. Crabbing is reportedly good.

Woods Bay. Woods Bay is deep until close to shore, and exposed to westerly winds. This bay has been reported to be a good spot in settled weather, but we think other anchorages in the area are more appealing.

Embley Lagoon. The lagoon is too shallow for anything but dinghies, but an interesting exploration.

Get all the latest cruising updates at:
WaggonerGuide.com/Updates

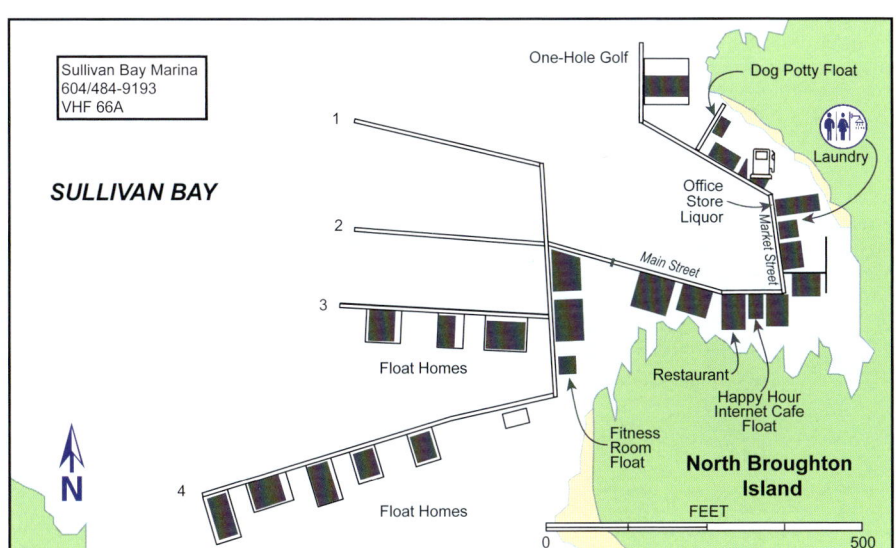

Sullivan Bay Marina Resort

THE BROUGHTON REGION

⑪ **Turnbull Cove.** Turnbull Cove is a large, popular, and beautiful bay, with lots of room and good anchoring in 30 to 50 feet. Avoid the areas in front of recent slides. The bottom there probably is foul with debris. Chappell warns that an easterly gale can turn the entire bay into a lee shore, so be aware if such winds are forecast.

The Ministry of Forests built a trail from Turnbull Cove over the mountain to Huaskin Lake. Correspondents Brett and Sue Oemichen report that an old steam donkey, somewhat hidden by trees, is to the right of the dinghy landing near the trailhead to the lake. A large float for swimming, a picnic table, a tent platform, and a fire pit are at the lake. It's really nice. The trail goes straight up and straight back down, and it's muddy in places. Steps and even a handrail are on the lake side. They make a big difference. The lake is scenic and looks as if it goes forever.

Approach: Currents of 2+ knots flow through the channel leading to the entry. Currents are not hazardous, but they can come as a surprise. The west side of the entry is charted as clear, but lots of kelp is growing there. A mid-channel course is recommended.

Nepah Lagoon. The adventuresome might want to try Roaringhole Rapids into Nepah Lagoon. Transit, by dinghy with an outboard motor, should be attempted only at high water slack, which lasts 5 minutes and occurs 2 hours after the corresponding high water at Alert Bay. The channel is only 3 feet deep at low water. Nepah Lagoon doesn't appear to have any usable anchorages, except possibly a little notch about a mile from the rapids.

MACKENZIE SOUND

Kenneth Passage. Kenneth Passage has sufficient depths at all stages of tide, however be careful of a covered rock off Jessie Point. Currents can be quite strong and whirlpools sometimes appear. Slack water entry is advised, especially on spring tides. The best advice is to take a look and decide if conditions suit you and your boat.

Steamboat Bay. Steamboat Bay is a good anchorage, with room for a few boats. The bay shoals to drying flats all around. Watch for the drying rocks along the east shore at the entrance.

Burly Bay. Burly Bay is a good anchorage, mud bottom, but the muddy shoreline makes going ashore difficult. The little notch just to the west of Blair Islet is better. Blair Islet has ample room for two boats to swing at anchor in 20-30 feet, mud bottom. At low tide, a drying, rocky bar separates Blair Islet from Burly Bay. At high tide, you can take the dinghy across the rapids just around the corner to explore the east end of Hopetown Passage. From the open water on the north side, the views of Mt. Stephens are stunning.

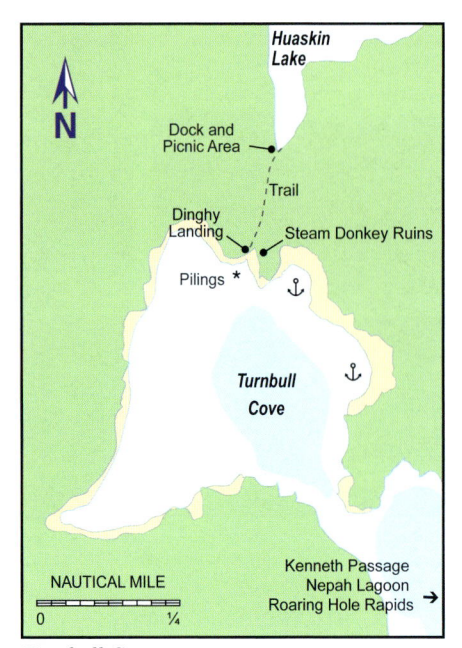

Turnbull Cove

Little Nimmo Bay and Nimmo Bay. Little Nimmo Bay is a pretty anchorage, and the rock-strewn entrance is not as difficult as it appears on the chart—except on a low tide. The Nimmo Bay Wilderness Resort is located there. Anchor in 24 feet, mud bottom. Several small waterfalls tumble through the forest. With care it is possible to go through to Nimmo Bay, which has roomy anchorage offering 15-40 foot depths, with a sticky, mud bottom. At low tide, an extensive, drying flat forms from the head of the bay. In late summer, the bear watching here is excellent with numerous bears roaming the beaches at low tide.

⑫ **Nimmo Bay Wilderness Resort.** Box 696, Port McNeill, BC V0N 2R0; (800) 837-4354; connect@nimmobay.com; www.nimmobay.com. VHF 10. Nimmo Bay Wilderness Resort is a luxury destination resort.

Resort services are available by advance reservation from May through August with reservations accepted beginning April 15th. Visiting boaters with advance reservations may enjoy a gourmet dining experience and spa treatments at the lodge. Moorage is only for guests with reservations for resort services and adventure tours. Anchoring out is also an option in Nimmo Bay or Mackenzie Sound. Floatplane service available from Kenmore Air and NW Seaplanes.

DRURY INLET

Drury Inlet is much less visited than other waters in the area. The entrance, off Wells Passage, is clearly marked on the charts, as is Stuart Narrows, 1.5 miles inside the entrance. Good anchorage is in two arms of Richmond Bay (choose the one that protects from the prevailing wind); near Stuart Narrows; in Jennis Bay; and in Sutherland Bay, at the head of Drury Inlet. Approach Sutherland Bay around the north side of the Muirhead Islands, after which the bay is open and protected.

Our sister publication, *Cruising the Secret Coast*, available at WaggonerGuide.com, by Jennifer and James Hamilton, devotes an entire chapter to exploring Drury Inlet and Actaeon Sound, with details about interesting hikes.

Helen Bay. Helen Bay is just east of Stuart Narrows. It is reportedly a good anchorage. Halibut are said to be caught in the area.

Stuart Narrows. Currents in Stuart Narrows run to a maximum of 7 knots, although on small tides they are much less. Times of slack are listed under Alert Bay, Secondary Current Stations, in the Tide & Current Tables Vol. 6, and Ports and Passes. The skipper of a tug towing a log boom through Stuart Narrows advised us that he times slack for 10 minutes after both high and low tides at Alert Bay, which is in line with the tide and current tables information. The only hazard is Welde Rock. You will most likely see the kelp. Get way over to the south side of the channel. The current flows faster south of Welde rock, although passage can be made north of the rock as well. Leche Islet should be passed to the north. A study of the chart shows a rock patch to the south.

Note that Stuart Narrows is well inside the mouth of Drury Inlet.

Nimmo Bay Wilderness Resort, a luxury destination resort.

See Area Map Page 351 - Maps Not for Navigation   THE BROUGHTON REGION

A view of Jennis Bay, the Jennis Bay Floats, and Drury Inlet in the background.   *Jennis Bay Floats on the left and float homes on the right*

Richmond Bay. Located just south of the west entrance to Stuart Narrows, Richmond Bay contains three coves. The southwest inner cove is filled with a float house and a large work float. The best anchorage is in 50 feet just off the work float.

⑬ **Jennis Bay.** Jennis Bay is the site of a logging camp and booming ground, with good anchorage in the cove northwest of the Jennis Bay floats.

⑬ **Jennis Bay Floats.** P.O. Box 456, Port McNeill, BC V0N 2R0; (778) 762-3037, jennismarina@gmail.com; www.jennisbay.com. Limited monitoring of VHF 66A; "preference is to just come on in." Jennis Bay is a historic logging camp with a quaint, rustic feel. Logging is still active in the area. Moorage available year-round, 300 feet of transient moorage space for up to 11 boats depending upon size and rafting options. No power at the docks. One hose tap for spring water, and one hose tap for cedar water for boat washing. Burn barrel for trash. Kayaking and miles of logging roads for exploring. Happy Hour potlucks are ad-hoc, organized by visiting pleasure boaters at the covered gathering area.

From Drury Inlet, enter Jennis Bay around either end of Hooper Island. If entering during limited visibility, the west end may be safest. Keep to a mid-channel course to avoid rocks along the shores. Leave the floating log breakwater and yellow buoys to starboard entering the marina.

Caution: Obstructions in the water lie about 500 feet southeast of the marina's log boom breakwater, consisting of a float plus a separate standing boom, neither of which are lit.

Davis Bay. Davis Bay looks inviting on the chart, but is not very pretty and is open to westerlies. Enter on the south side of Davis Islet, strongly favoring the Davis Islet shore. Anchoring depths of 24-30 feet.

Muirhead Islands. The Muirhead Islands, near the head of Drury Inlet, are rock-strewn but beautiful. They invite exploring in a small boat or kayak. The cove on the northeast side, behind the dot island, is a suitable anchorage, as is the cove on the south side, immediately west of the 59-meter island.

Actress Passage and Actaeon Sound. Actress Passage, connecting Drury Inlet with Actaeon Sound, is rock- and reef-strewn, narrow and twisting. Careful navigation is required. There are two theories: some feel high water slack is best to have more water; others feel low water slack is best to allow a better chance of seeing the rocks and hazards in the water. One approach is to enter Actress Passage between Dove Island and the mainland to the north, avoiding the charted rock. Tugs and tows and other commercial traffic, however, use the shorter channel east of Dove Island, splitting rocks marked with sticks at the entrance to Drury Inlet.

Once into Actress Passage, the overriding navigation problem is the area between Skeene Point and Bond Peninsula, where a careful S-shaped course around the rocks is required, hence the local name Snake Passage. Another choice is to follow Chappell's suggestion of crossing from Skene Point to Bond Peninsula, and working past the charted hazards around the corner.

In our sister publication, *Cruising the Secret Coast*, the Hamiltons have extensively explored this area and present specific directions for this passage and the area.

WELLS PASSAGE

Tracey Harbour. Tracey Harbour indents North Broughton Island from Wells Passage. It is pretty and protected. No anchorage is viable, however, until near the head of the bay. There, you can find anchorage on mud bottom in Napier Bay, or on rocky bottom in the bay behind Carter Point. You're apt to find log booms in Napier Bay, and leftover buildings from an old logging operation. Anchor near the head of the cove behind Carter Point. The cove is beautiful and cozy-feeling, but the bottom feels like a thin layer of mud on top of rock and it wouldn't take much to drag the anchor.

Carter Passage. Since Carter Passage is blocked in the middle by a boulder-strewn drying shoal, it is actually two harbors, one off Wells Passage and one off Greenway Sound, with good anchorages in each end. The west entrance has tidal currents to 7 knots, and should be taken at or near high water slack. A reef extends

Morris Islet at the east entrance to Stuart Narrows has a direction and distance sign to Jennis Bay.

2023 WAGGONER CRUISING GUIDE   355

THE BROUGHTON REGION

See Area Map Page 351 - Maps Not for Navigation

Wells Passage connects western Broughtons with Queen Charlotte Strait.

from the south shore, so keep north of mid-channel. Two pleasant anchorages are in this west end.

The east entrance, off Greenway Sound, is somewhat easier, in terms of both tidal currents and obstructions.

Dickson Island. Dickson Island is near the mouth of Wells Passage. The small anchorage on the east end of the island provides good protection from seas, but the low land allows westerly winds to blow across the bay. Two other bays along the west side of Broughton Island are too exposed to westerly weather to be good anchorages.

Polkinghorne Islands. The Polkinghorne Islands are outside the mouth of Wells Passage. A channel among the islands is fun, particularly on the nice day. The anchoring bottom we've found is not too secure, so an overnight stay is not recommended. [Kincaid]

FIFE SOUND

Cullen Harbour. Cullen Harbour is on the south side of Broughton Island, at the entrance to Booker Lagoon. It is an excellent anchorage, with plenty of room for everyone. You might rock a little if the wind is blowing from northwest. The bottom is mud, and depths range from 24 to 50 feet. Cell service.

LOCAL KNOWLEDGE

BOOKER LAGOON: Booker Passage, the entrance to Booker Lagoon, has strong current with turbulent waters. The narrow channel should be transited at or near short slack water periods. Best to survey the passage by dinghy while the mothership awaits in Cullen Harbour.

There are reports of rocks and reefs in the western-most cove in Booker Lagoon. Charts for the area show one rock awash, reef areas, and a foul area near the center at the entrance to the west cove arm. Proceed cautiously with a bow watch.

Booker Passage. This narrow channel is the main passage to Booker Lagoon, it is bounded by reefs on both sides. Currents run strong at 7 knots or more on big tides. Considerable turbulence and eddies form on both ebb and flood current. Transit only at or near slack water which can be as short as 10 minutes. Use the Sunday Harbour secondary station and add about one hour for tide level; see Canadian Tide and Current Tables Vol. 6, or Ports and Passes. The channel is about 50 feet wide and depths are as charted.

The narrower and shallower channel on the northwest side of Long Island has equally strong current, turbulence and eddies. Favor the southeast side of the channel to avoid heavy kelp at the narrowest section.

Booker Lagoon. The entrance to Booker Lagoon is from Cullen Harbour through Booker Passage. The lagoon is quite large and deep in the middle. All four arms have good anchoring opportunities with convenient depths over sticky mud bottom. Pick the one with the best protection for anticipated weather. Surrounding hillsides have patches of second growth timber interspersed with native forests. The aquaculture pens that once occupied the four arms have been removed. Booker Lagoon is a secluded coastal paradise. Watch for a couple of partially submerged buoys off the south shore of the entrance to the west arm, they are likely remains from one of the aquaculture pens and difficult to see. Explore around, then anchor in one of the arms, perhaps away from other anchored boats; it's that kind of place.

Deep Harbour. In the past the inner part of Deep Harbour was blocked by boomed logs and the center of the bay taken over by aquaculture pens. It is now clear and there are little nooks around the edges with room for one boat.

BROUGHTON ARCHIPELAGO

Much of the Broughton Archipelago is now a marine park. Some of the islands are private, however, so use discretion when going ashore.

Our journal, written while at anchor after a day of exploring, reads, "A marvelous group of islands and passages, but few good anchorages. We navigated around Insect Island and through Indian Passage. Very pretty—many white shell beaches. Rocks marked by kelp. A different appearance from Kingcome Inlet or Simoom Sound. The trees are shorter and more windblown. The west wind is noticeably colder than farther east. Fog lay at the mouth of Fife Sound; a few wisps blew up toward us. Great kayaking, gunkholing country." [*Hale*]

This large group of islands west of Gilford Island does have anchorages, including Sunday Harbour, Monday Anchorage, and Joe Cove. The area is dotted with rocks, reefs, and little islands, which in total provide good protection, but also call for careful navigation.

M. Wylie Blanchet (*The Curve of Time*) was blown out of Sunday Harbour, and we've heard mixed reports about Monday Anchorage. Chappell wasn't impressed with

Booker Passage leads to Booker Lagoon with several good anchorage bays and coves.

either one. Joe Cove is considered to be a good anchorage. Large scale charts should be studied carefully before going into these waters. Currents run strongly at times through the various passages.

Sunday Harbour. Sunday Harbour is formed by Crib Island and Angular Island, north of the mouth of Arrow Passage. The bay is very pretty, although exposed to westerly winds. We would anchor in the middle for a relaxing lunch on a quiet day. The little cove in the northeast corner looks attractive but is full of rocks.

⑭ **Monday Anchorage.** Monday is a large and fairly open anchorage between Tracey Island and Mars Island. There are a number of bays, bights and coves with varying depths. Correspondent Deane Hislop set the hook between the most eastern islet and Tracey Island in 30 feet of water and spent time exploring tide pools and a large midden on Tracey Island. When entering the anchorage from the south, beware of the foul ground shown on the chart, extending from Tracey Island to starboard.

⑮ **Joe Cove.** Joe Cove, perfectly protected and private feeling, indents the south side of Eden Island. The best anchorage is near the head. A little thumb of water extends southeast near the head of the cove, but access is partially blocked by several rocks. It is possible, however, to feel your way in by hugging the shore to starboard as you enter. The passage is narrow but clear. The float in the cove has deteriorated to the point where it is no longer safe to use; a sign warning not to use the float has been posted.

East of Eden (Lady Boot Cove). Lady Boot Cove is what Don and Reanne Douglass call this nice little anchorage in *Exploring the South Coast of British Columbia*. Locals

Current runs strong through Booker Passage

Joe Cove has protected anchorage; the deteriorated float is no longer usable.

tell us the correct name is East of Eden. The cove indents the northeast corner of Eden Island, with Fly Island directly off the mouth. As the chart shows, the southern indent is shoaled and foul with a drying reef. The northern indent is beautifully protected with room for 3-4 boats; room to swing is limited so a stern-tie is best.

RETREAT PASSAGE

Seabreeze Cove. This otherwise unnamed lovely little anchorage in Gilford Island was suggested by Correspondents James and Jennifer Hamilton. It lies behind the 70-meter island due east of Seabreeze Island, at the western entrance to Retreat Passage. Their report: "We anchored in 18 feet south of the 70-meter island and held very well in sticky mud. Some southwest winds did blow through, but nothing major. The water was barely rippled. Caught three big Dungeness crabs overnight."

Be aware that the bottom shoals rapidly once past the 70-meter island.

Bootleg Bay. South of False Cove, a thumb-like island protrudes northwest from Gilford Island. The cove south of that island has about 30 feet at the entrance, shoaling gently toward the head. No name appears on the charts. According to Chappell it is known locally as Bootleg Bay. A wrecked fish boat has been reported at the head of the bay. Anchoring depths 20-40 feet.

⑯ **Waddington Bay.** Waddington Bay indents the northeast corner of Bonwick Island. The bay is popular, with room for several boats. It has good holding in 18 to 30 feet. The approach is off the little pass that connects Retreat Passage and Arrow Passage. Turn to leave the 46-meter island to starboard, and go on in. Be sure you have the right island; they all look

PLANNING HAPPY HOUR

Happy Hour is the primary social gathering when cruising the Broughtons. This fun tradition typically begins around 5:00 p.m. at family-run marinas like Lagoon Cove and Sullivan Bay. If a Happy Hour is not scheduled it often happens spontaneously at places like Echo Bay, when a group visiting on the dock start bringing out hors d'oeuvres to share. All of a sudden someone gasps, "Hey, we ought to have a Happy Hour!" The drinks start flowing and more food emerges.

I always make sure we have plenty of items for whipping up a jaw-droppingly impressive Happy Hour hors d'oeuvre, preferably something that will stack or mound to 8-12 inches high or more What is my secret? A good supply of cream cheese and crackers! At the beginning of the season I make a special trip to my local warehouse store for bricks of cream cheese. I also buy a variety of crackers, boxes of them. I stock onion soup mix, different spice combinations, canned smoked salmon, canned crab, and even canned shrimp. Dried cherries, cran-raisins, dried apricots, and a few syrups help add color and flavor.

Some captains and crew bring a dip with fresh caught crab, or they show up with a bowl of fresh prawns caught that morning. A variety of recipes show up too, the pea salad like my mother used to make, or the spicy coleslaw served in an antique bowl. Our best galley advice for cruising in the Broughtons? Be ready and go bold for Happy Hour. Mix it up, mound it high, and watch it fly. Fellow cruisers will love the end result!

THE BROUGHTON REGION   See Area Map Page 351 - Maps Not for Navigation

Health Bay village has a longhouse and a small community dock.

alike. The approach is wide enough, but rocks are all around and careful piloting is called for. Know your position at all times. Waddington Bay shoals at the head. The wind direction and your depth sounder will tell you where to put the hook down. Wind will get in when the westerly is blowing, but there's no fetch for seas to build. This is a tranquil anchorage—a good place to hide out for a few days.

Grebe Cove. Grebe Cove indents the east side of Bonwick Island off Retreat Passage. The cove shallows to 40 to 50 feet about 200 yards from the head, and 30 to 40 feet near the head, mud bottom, with good depths side to side. A saddle in the hills at the head might let westerlies in, but the seas would have no fetch. On one visit, a couple in a 20-foot pocket cruiser called out, "Great anchorage! The otters will entertain you!" A collection of work boats, fish boats, and small ships are permanently moored along the south shore.

Carrie Bay. Carrie Bay indents Bonwick Island across Retreat Passage from Health Bay. The head of the bay is pretty and protected from westerly winds. The bottom shoals rapidly from 40 to 50 feet in much of the bay to around 20 feet at the head. Good holding in sand and shell bottom.

Health Bay. (250) 949-6012. The Health Bay Indian Reserve, with a small dock offering overnight moorage with power, fronts on Retreat Passage, ask for Charlie. Health Bay itself is strewn with rocks.

Anchorage is best fairly close to the head of the bay, short of the first of the rocks. Reliable cell signal is available in Retreat Passage in front of the Health Bay community.

BLACKFISH ARCHIPELAGO

The name Blackfish Archipelago does not appear on the charts or in Sailing Directions, but generally refers to the myriad islands and their waterways adjacent to Blackfish Sound.

Goat Island Anchorage. You'll find a good anchorage in the cove that lies off the southeast corner of Crease Island.

Enter Goat Island Anchorage between Crease Island and Goat Island, leaving Goat Island to port and Crease Island to starboard. The chart makes the preferred entry clear. Caution for the charted shoals northeast of Goat Island as you approach the preferred entrance. Chart 3546 in raster mode appears to mislabel a smaller island to the south of Goat Island, along Village Channel, as Goat Island. Vector mode charts correctly show Goat Island as the small island immediately southeast of a short peninsula on Crease Island.

INDIAN RESERVE (IR) LANDS

When navigating the BC Coast, boaters often see "IR" or the words "Indian Reserve" on charts. Many wonder what this designation means, as there may, or may not be, evidence of habitation.

Indian Reserve (IR) are tracts of land set aside under the Indian Act and treaty agreements for the exclusive use of an Indian band. Reserves are governed by one or more band Chiefs and Councils. A single band may control one or several reserves, while some reserves are shared between multiple bands. Band members possess the right to live on reserve lands, and band administrative and political structures are frequently located there. Reserve lands are not strictly "owned" by bands but are held in trust for bands by the Crown.

Of the 638,000 First Nations people who reported being Registered Indians, nearly half live on one of the 3,100 Indian Reserves in Canada. Many reserves, especially on BC waters, are small, remote, non-contiguous pieces of land that may or may not have year-round resident population. Some are used only seasonally by the band. In the Broughtons, Health Bay (Gilford Island) and New Vancouver (Harbledown Island) are examples of communities with small populations of band residents. In fact, both of these communities have docks that welcome visiting boaters. Others, such as Mamaliliculla (Village Island) and Karlukwees (Turnour Island) are settlements that are not currently inhabited but have historic buildings and structures from previous habitation. See separate entries in the Waggoner Guide for more information on these sites. Many others have no local names, buildings or other signs of habitation except, perhaps, a centuries-old midden. They may only be marked by signs indicating the named band territory.

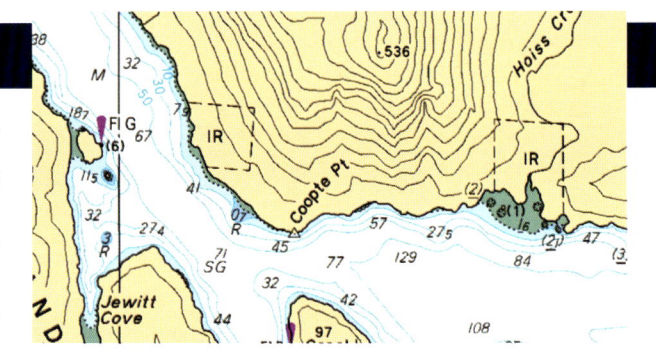

Regardless of whether First Nations people are present, all of these lands should be treated as private land and respected by visitors. Some Reserves, such as Mamaliliculla on Village island, require formal permission to visit and charge a fee to see the village. All of these reserve lands are protected by British Columbia's Heritage Conservation Act (http://www.bclaws.ca/civix/document/id/complete/statreg/96187_01), which prohibits damage to the sites or removal of material that constitutes part of the site. For personal safety and out of respect for First Nations property, visitors should not enter abandoned buildings.

Indian Reserves recognize and respect the 10,000-year inhabitation of the BC Coast by First Nations people. Each site is unique and some offer escorted tours. Check the Waggoner Guide for information about contacting Band offices for permission to visit. If you visit, please respect these places that are sacred to the people to whom they are entrusted. Take only photos and leave only footprints.

Use of the Mimkwamlis private dock and access to the uplands at Village Island is by permission only.

The native village ruins at Village Island are accessible with prior permission; a donation to the Native Band is requested.

Anchor in 12 to 18 feet on a sometimes rocky bottom, wherever it looks good. The cove is excellent for crabbing. Weed on the bottom might foul some anchors. A reader reported that their anchor found a large diameter line on the bottom, probably left over from earlier logging. Where there's one cable there might be more. It would be a good idea to rig a trip line to the crown of the anchor. The view to the southeast is very pretty.

Leone Island. A bay lies between Leone Island and Madrona Island. Tom Kincaid has anchored there and recommends it. "'Friends, with extensive experience, also recommend it. We, however, tried to set our anchor four times over a 2-day period, and failed each time. Twice the anchor did not penetrate large, leafy kelp. Once it refused to set in thin sand and reedy weed. On the last try the anchor seemed to set, but it dragged with only moderate power in reverse." [*Hale*]

Mound Island. The cove behind Mound Island is a good anchorage, paying mind to the rocks (shown on the chart) that line the shores. Tom Sewid at Village Island told us that 14 depressions in the earth were once the sites of big houses. Correspondent Pat Shera reports that the depressions are obvious, just inland from the beach at the western end of the island.

⑰ **New Vancouver. (Tsatsisnukwomi)** (250) 974-2703. VHF 78. Moorage, with 30 amp power (15 amp breakers). Cash only payment. Washrooms, showers and laundry are located in a building upland from the pier. Three rooms for overnight accommodations are located in the same building. Visitations to New Vancouver were not permitted in 2021 and 2022 due to Covid considerations. Boaters should check with the Band Office for the current status regarding visitations and guest moorage.

New Vancouver, traditionally known as Tsatsisnukwomi Village, is on the north side of Harbledown Island, a short distance west of Dead Point, the entrance to Beware Passage. The location is marked IR on the chart, for Indian Reserve. It is the ancestral home of the Da'naxda'xw Native Band, who moved from Knight Inlet in the 1960s. Efforts are underway to protect eelgrass in the area, anchor in deeper water. The band is welcoming and offers cultural tours of the village and Bighouse for a fee; the tour is very interesting and inspiring.

Farewell Harbour. You'll find good anchorage in Farewell Harbour close to the Berry Island side. The Farewell Harbour Marine Resort, shown on the chart, is actually a luxury fishing resort and doesn't cater to visiting yachties.

Da'naxda'xw Tribal Band members lead guided tours of their Bighouse at New Vancouver.

Chiefs Bathtub. The Chiefs Bathtub is located on Village Channel on the north side of Berry Island, at approximately 50°36.45'N /126°39.56'W (NAD 83). It's a sculpted-out depression in a rock cliff, a little below the high water line. According to Tom Sewid, up-and-coming chiefs had to sit in this bathtub four times a day for four days as the cold waters of the tide washed in. If you take the dinghy to see the tub more closely, don't touch the pictographs on the rock. Skin oils deteriorate the paint.

⑱ **Village Island.** Mamalilikulla First Nation, 1441B 16th Ave Campbell River, BC V9W 2E4; (250) 287-2955; viband@mamalilikulla.ca; Mamalilikulla.ca.

A site on the western shore of Village Island is often known incorrectly as Mamalilaculla. It is the uninhabited village of Mimkwamlis and the ancestral home of the Mamalilikulla First Nation. Uplands are protected Indian Reserve property and access is by permission of the Mamalilikulla First Nation Band office. The Band requests a fee of $20 per person to tour the village site, with its empty school building, collapsing houses, fallen totem poles and Bighouse remains. Tours typically available May-September. If you see the watchman boat at the dock, you may go ashore to request permission and make payment. All fees go to clean up of the village site and support the Band's guardian watchmen program. Self-guided tours are allowed when a watchman is not on duty as long as you make payment and have prior permission from the Band office.

Anchor in the bay north of the village site; be sure of your set. A 160-foot private dock is located in the bay north of the village to provide improved access for band members, and visitors with permission to go ashore. Tie-up is allowed only by permission from the Mamalilikulla First Nation. The moorage fee of $1 per foot is payable at the dropbox located upland from the ramp; short-term stays, no overnight moorage.

Mimkwamlis is protected under the Heritage Conservation Act; respect the village property; leave all artifacts and remains as they lie; and do not enter any of the buildings. No camping or fires ashore; leave only footprints.

THE BROUGHTON REGION

See Area Map Page 351 - Maps Not for Navigation

The Broughtons Archipelago has many opportunities for anchoring.

Native Anchorage. Native Anchorage is located at the southwest corner of Village Island. It's no place to be in a southerly storm, but in all other winds it's a fine anchorage. Put the hook down in 18 to 24 feet. Excellent mud bottom.

Canoe Passage. Canoe Passage runs east-west between Turnour Island and Village Island. The waterway dries at low tide, but can be transited at higher tides, depending on a vessel's draft.

Beware Passage. Place names from Chart 3545 for Beware Passage might scare you away; Beware Passage, Caution Rock, Caution Cove, Beware Rock, Beware Cove, and Dead Point. Beware Passage is aptly named, but you can get through safely. Sailing Directions recommends transiting at low water when rocks are visible.

There are two routes through Beware Passage; Care Island route and Harbledown Island route. Both routes are shown on our Beware Passage map. Locals suggest using either route at low water slack, when rocks can be seen and current isn't making course changes difficult. We recommend proceeding dead slow with a careful watch on depth sounder and a bow watch. Assuming a passage from east to west, both routes start by entering just off Nicholas Point on Turnour (pronounced "Turner") Island.

There are several pictographs on a rock face 300 yards west of Nicholas Point. North of the pictographs is a midden beach, which is the site of the early native village of Karlukwees. Boaters can anchor off the beach and come ashore by dinghy or kayak to visit the site; please respect the land and leave things as found. Watchmen are present on occasion. Around 1850, the Tlawitsis Band moved here from Klaoitsis Island located just south of Beware Passage. The Tlawitsis lived here until the 1960's and were active in the fishing industry.

After Nicholas Point and the pictographs, both routes follow mid-channel between Kamano Island and the unnamed islet north of Kamano Island. At the west end of Kamano Island, the two routes separate.

For Harbledown Island route, turn to heading 275º magnetic when the west end of Kamano Island is abeam your port side. Proceed to the Harbledown Island side of Beware Passage and a narrow channel between Harbledown Island and a pair of small islands that lie just offshore from Harbledown Island. This narrow channel has kelp, and a charted shoal on the Harbledown Island side. Exit this narrow channel on a heading of 305º magnetic. Turn to port and continue northwest on Beware Passage when Dead Point is on a course of 273º magnetic.

For Care Island route, when the west end of Kamano Island is abeam your port side, turn to a heading of approximately 346º magnetic. Turn to a heading of approximately 266º magnetic when you see a forested rock outcropping on Turnour Island shore to your starboard. Check your GPS chartplotter to confirm this critical turn to the west making sure you avoid the rock awash to port and the charted rock that dries at 1.2 meters. Proceed, favoring the Care Island side until past Care Island. Then turn to heading 271º magnetic. For both routes, pass between Beware Rock and the charted rock that dries at 0.9 meters and proceed to Dead Point.

Caution Cove. Caution Cove is open to prevailing winds, but the bottom is good. Caution Rock, drying at 4 feet, is in the center of the entrance. The rock is clearly shown on Chart 3545, as are the rocks just off the drying flats at the head of the cove. A logging operation may be operating in the cove.

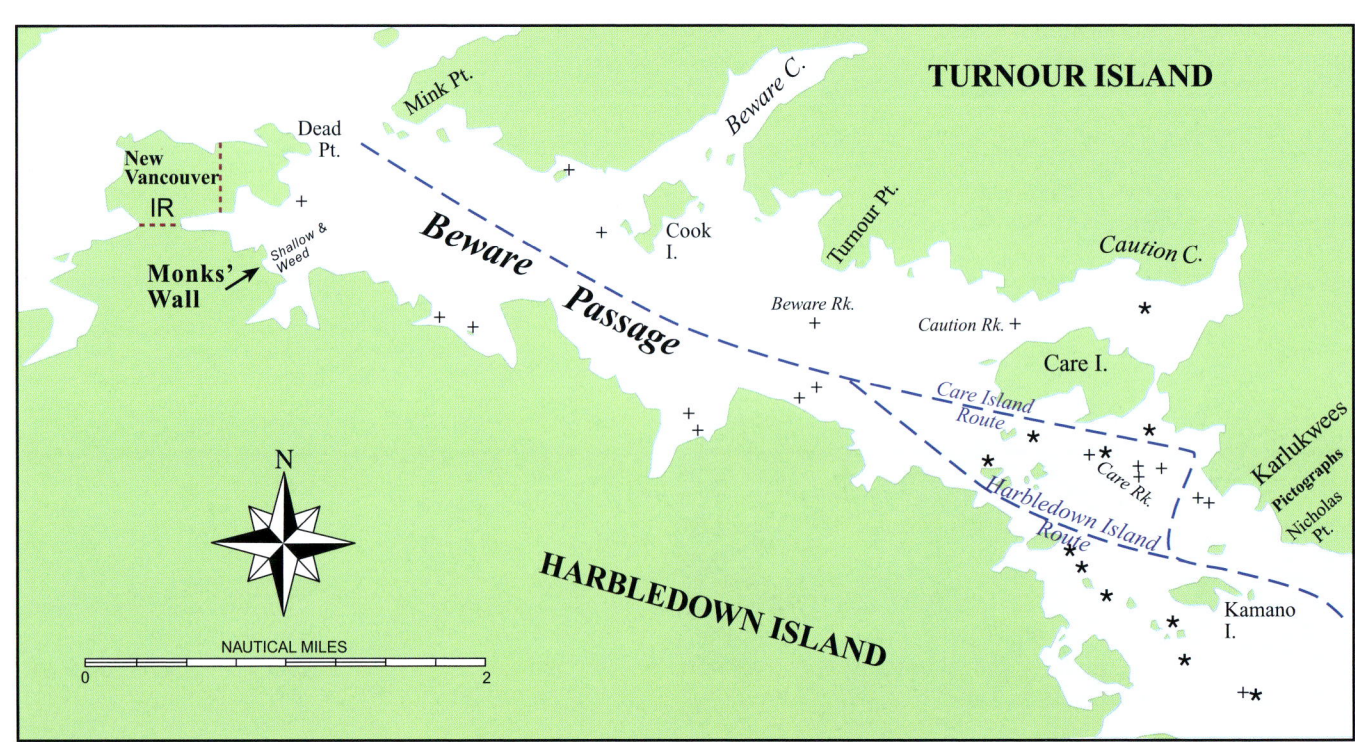

Beware Passage

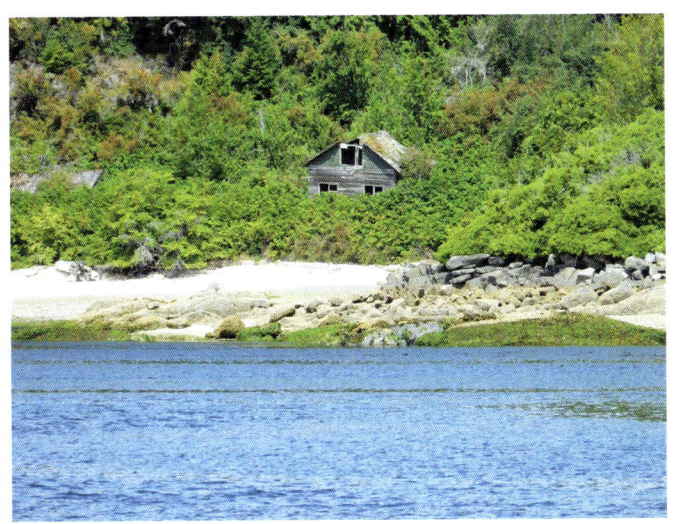

The village of Karlukwees, located along Beware Passage, is the traditional territory of the Tlowitsis First Nation.

Nature is slowly reclaiming the once massive but still intriguing Monks' Wall.

Beware Cove. Beware Cove is a good anchorage, very pretty, with protection from westerlies but not southeasterlies. Easiest entry is to the west of Cook Island, leaving Cook Island to starboard.

Monks' Wall. The ruins of a once massive and mysterious rock wall lies hidden just inside the treeline on Harbledown Island, at the north end of Beware Passage.

The wall was built by white settlers, William Herbert Galley and his wife Mary Anne Galley. In the late 1800s, Galley acquired 160 acres on Harbledown Island and built a trading post there. According to Galley's great-granddaughter, great-grandfather Galley married Mary Anne Wharton in 1889. Together they cleared the land, planted 125 fruit trees, and kept cows, pigs, chickens, ducks and sheep. The homestead was defined by carefully-built rock walls, straight and solid. An archway marked the entrance to the trading post. It is said that Mary Anne Galley carried rocks in her apron. Those rocks are big. Some apron. Some great-grandmother.

Monks' Wall is located on the west side of Beware Passage, a short distance south of Dead Point. It is on the point of land separating two large, shallow bays, at lat. 50°35.40'N and lon. 126° 35.12'W. Anchor in the bay north of that point of land and row the dinghy in. The bottom shoals when approaching the cove, and is dense with weeds that could foul a propeller. Working from north to south, identify the third little nook on the point of land. It's a definite indent. The ruins of the magnificent walls are just inside.

If you hike through the woods around the area you'll find more walls; taken together they're impressive. All built by hand. Straight and true. Enveloped now by the relentless forest. The archway has since collapsed.

Although Monks' Wall is a misnomer, it looks like the name will stick. Our thanks to Galley great-granddaughter Kathy Young for her historical background, and to Billy Proctor for his quickly-drawn map that showed us where to find the site.

Request: The wall and the lesser walls in the surrounding forest are a treasure. Please, no souvenirs, no destruction, no litter.

Dead Point. The unnamed cove just inside Dead Point offers protection from westerlies.

LOCAL KNOWLEDGE

CURRENT DIRECTIONS: Current in Baronet Passage floods west and ebbs east, the opposite of the flows in Johnstone Strait a mile south, and in Knight Inlet 4 miles north.

Baronet Passage. Baronet Passage is very pretty. It's partially obstructed by Walden Island, with the preferred passage in the deeper channel to the north of Walden Island. This is a well-used passage for boats heading to and from Blackfish Sound.

⑲ **Growler Cove.** Growler Cove, on the west end of West Cracroft Island, is an excellent anchorage, with ample room and good protection from westerlies and easterlies. It is popular with commercial fishermen who work Johnstone Strait and Queen Charlotte Strait. During prime commercial fishing months of July and August, Growler Cove is apt to be full of commercial boats, with little room for pleasure craft.

If you're approaching from the east, enter along West Cracroft Island, favoring the island as you work your way in. We saw an extensive kelp bed, not shown on the chart, off the point that leads to the entrance. We would keep clear of that kelp. If you're approaching from the west, enter between Sophia Islands and Baron Reef, both shown on the chart. Inside, keep a mid-channel course, favoring the north side to avoid a charted rock about halfway in. Good anchoring near the head in 18 to 24 feet.

Hanson Island. The rugged and beautiful north shore of Hanson Island is indented by a number of bays and coves that are a gunkholer's paradise. The most popular anchorage is in Double Bay. Enter only along the west side of the bay. The bay behind Spout Islet, to the east of Double Bay, is also a good anchorage. Correspondent Deane Hislop writes: "We spent a night in the beautiful bay to the east of Spout Islet. The holding was good and provided protection from the summer afternoon westerlies. The view of the whales in Blackfish Sound, the Miriam Range, and 1238-meter Mt. Mathison were spectacular.

Growler Cove is a well-protected anchorage on the west end of West Cracroft Island.

THE BROUGHTON REGION

Queen Charlotte Strait. Queen Charlotte Strait is about 15 miles wide. The prevailing winds are from the northwest in the summer and the southeast in the winter. In the summer, winds are often lighter in the morning.

Typically, by late morning or early afternoon a sea breeze will begin, and by mid-afternoon it can increase to 30 knots with very rough seas. The sea breeze usually quiets at sundown.

Tom Taylor, owner of the now-closed Greenway Sound Marina Resort, has crossed the strait between Wells Passage and Port McNeill hundreds of times, and tells us that in good weather he could go (in a fast boat) as late as 2:00 p.m. Any given day can go against the norm, however. Skippers should treat Queen Charlotte Strait with great respect.

Weather information: The wind report from Herbert Island, in the Buckle Group, can be a good reference for approaching northwesterly winds. If it's not blowing at Herbert Island, there's a good chance Queen Charlotte Strait will be okay. If Herbert Island is windy, however, Queen Charlotte Strait probably will be next.

Bauza Cove. Bauza Cove is an attractive but deep bay with good protection from westerly swells. It is open to the wakes of passing traffic in Johnstone Strait.

㉐ **Telegraph Cove.** Telegraph Cove is postcard picturesque. The boardwalk is lined with old, brightly painted buildings on pilings, including a good restaurant and pub. The old homes are now cottages for resort guests. The place is the embodiment of the word "charming." A whale museum is located at the end of the docks and a whale watch excursion boat leaves several times each day. Tide Rip Grizzly Tours takes groups up Knight Inlet by fast boat to see grizzly bears. Charter fishing boats head out to fish for salmon, and a kayak operator takes groups out to the islands and Johnstone Strait.

The Telegraph Cove Resort moorage is to starboard as you enter. Moorage is primarily for small boats, but some room is available for larger boats at the dock near the entrance. To port as you enter, Telegraph Cove Marina has some side-tie guest moorage for larger boats,

This historic building at the entrance to Telegraph Cove houses the Whale Interpretive Centre.

and a considerable number of guest slips for boats to 30 feet.

Be advised, though, that Telegraph Cove isn't very big. There's room to maneuver, but "spacious" is not the word that comes to mind, especially when the wind picks up.

㉐ **Telegraph Cove Marina.** 1642B Telegraph Cove Rd., Telegraph Cove, BC V0N 3J0; (250) 928-3163; (877) 835-2683; reservations@ telegraphcove.ca; www.telegraphcove.ca. Monitors VHF 66A. Open all year, 70 slips to 30 feet. Mostly permanent moorage with some guest moorage. End-ties possible for boats 50 foot plus. Several slips have 15, 30 & 50 amp power; seasonal potable water. Concrete launch ramp. Showers, laundry, and washrooms. Garbage with recycling, Wi-Fi available for a fee. Reservations required, call or see moorage request form online. Generators may not be run in the marina. It's an easy walk around the cove to amenities and tour operators, such as whale watching, grizzly bear viewing, and kayak tours.

㉐ **Telegraph Cove Resort.** Box 1, Telegraph Cove, BC V0N 3J0; (250) 928-3131; (800) 200-4665; info@TelegraphCoveResort.com; www.telegraphcoveresort.com. Open seasonally with gasoline (no diesel), launch ramp, restaurant, pub, two coffee shops, general store with gifts and fishing tackle. Slips for boats to 25 feet. Larger boats may be able to overnight on the fuel dock, check with management. Moorage request form online. No power or water. Cabins and campsites available for rent. The resort maintains the historic boardwalk, with cottages and buildings from when this was a telegraph station during the early 1900s. Attractions include fishing charters, whale and bear watching tours, and the Whale Interpretive Centre. The restaurant and pub are good.

Beaver Cove. Fairly deep anchorage can be found along the shores of Beaver Cove, the site of an old sawmill. Logs may be boomed in the bay, and the bottom is almost certainly foul with sunken logs and debris.

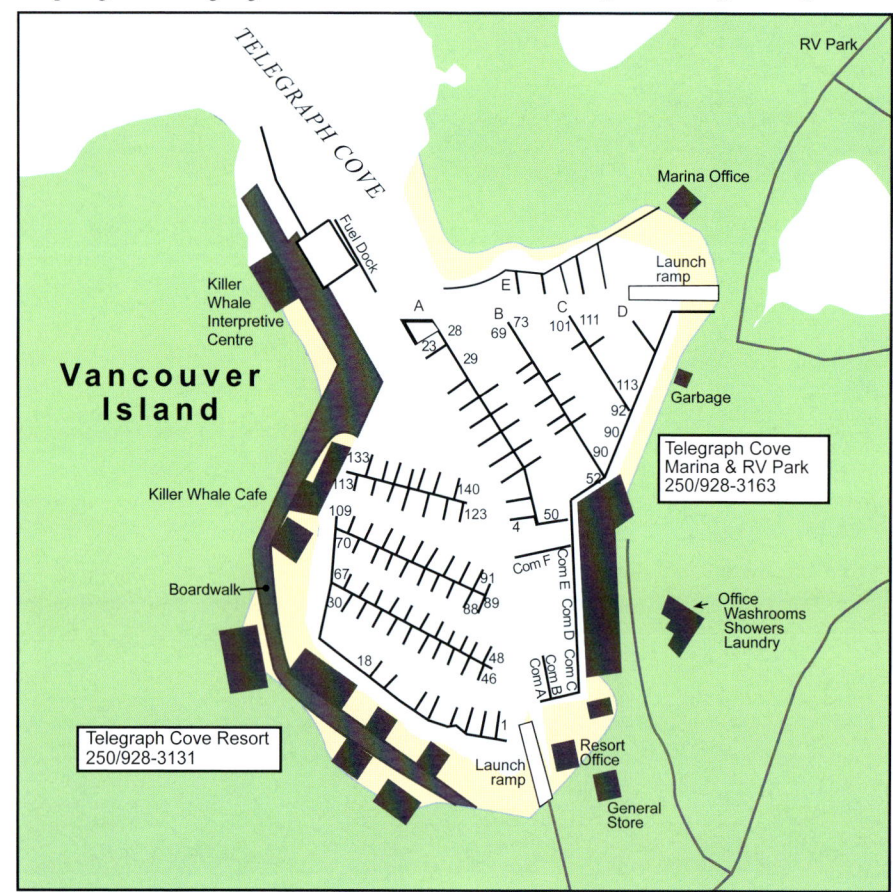

Telegraph Cove

See Area Map Page 351 - Maps Not for Navigation

THE BROUGHTON REGION

Pearse Islands (Cormorant Channel Marine Park). Careful piloting is called for when exploring this area because of rocks, reefs, and strong currents in the narrow channels between the islands. Correspondents James and Jennifer Hamilton report:

"We anchored in 30 feet (zero tide) just north of the 72-meter islet, about where the 9.8-meter sounding is on Chart 3546. A little wind blew through from the northwest, but we saw very little boat traffic. It was a lovely spot with an excellent view down Broughton Strait. Good holding—the anchor set instantly with 150 feet of rode out. It looks like excellent dinghy-exploring country, but it had been a long day and we didn't have the strength.

The next morning the current was really whipping through the passage, but we held just fine. When we left, we found the current very strong off the tip of the 88-meter island, with whirlpools and upwellings." [Hamilton]

Correspondent Pat Shera reports that when the current is flooding east in Broughton Strait, a strong westward countercurrent is present when approaching the Pearse Islands from the south.

㉑ **Alert Bay.** One can learn more about native culture here, in less time, than anywhere on this part of the coast.

Chart 3546 shows Alert Bay in good detail and shows where current runs up to 4 knots. Protected moorage is available in the Boat Harbour basin at the head of the bay.

A small public float is in front of the main part of town. The float is exposed to all winds, and currents can run swiftly, but it is convenient when provisioning at the nearby grocery. Deeper in the bay, the breakwater-protected Boat Harbour basin, northwest of the ferry landing, has moorage. Anchorage is

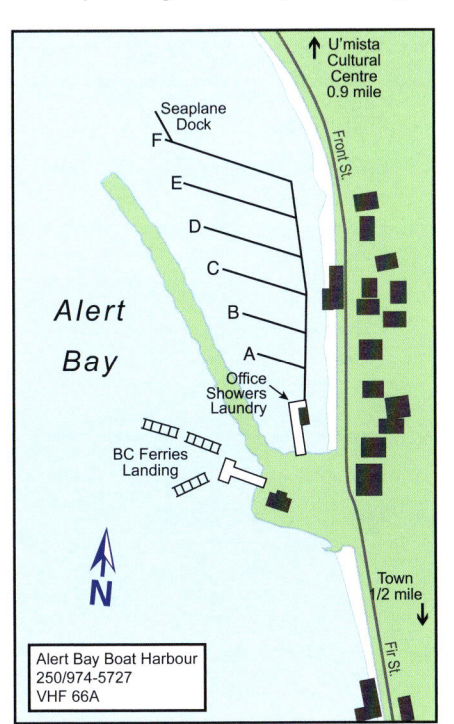

Alert Bay Boat Harbour

Alert Bay Boat Harbour
250/974-5727
VHF 66A

THE SPIRIT OF U'MISTA

The heritage of the Inside Passage is a rich tapestry of man's life on the land and his utilization of its waters for both transportation and sustenance. Today we enjoy the beauty of the islands and animals, the fjords and waterfalls. And, occasionally, nature's bounty, hauled to the surface in a crab pot or caught on the end of a fishing line. But for thousands of years, since long before Europeans arrived, the area was carefully occupied by First Nations people.

The First Nations people depended on the environment around them in ways often lost in modern life. Their beliefs and customs are inextricably linked to the Inside Passage. A glimpse into their culture reveals a belief in family and clan and an interest in preserving life and land. They believe in sustaining their people by maintaining nature's balance.

They are also a giving people, always ready to share. Perhaps there is no better example of their culture of sharing than their potlatch ceremonies.

Potlatches bring together neighboring families and nearby tribes. Cultural traditions, like songs and dances, are performed and ceremonial regalia, like coppers, masks and robes, are shown off. Feasts are prepared. Gifts, ranging from blankets to berries, are given. Successful potlatches can be reminisced about for years. Potlatches may celebrate marriage, birth, death or other rites of passage. Regardless of the reason for celebration, potlatches are a vehicle for giving. The more a family shares, the better the event is remembered.

In 1885, the government of Canada banned potlatches. Unwilling to give up centuries old traditions, the celebrations secretly continued. But in the early 1920s, a new Director of Indian Affairs gave orders to enforce the potlatch laws. First Nations members were arrested and some were jailed for up to two months. Regalia was confiscated, packed and shipped to Ottawa for storage. Some masks were kept for the personal collection of the Superintendent General of Indian Affairs.

Beginning in the 1960s, the Canadian government slowly repatriated the items they had taken. They reached an agreement where the regalia would be returned and placed on display in two museums, the Nuyumbalees Cultural Centre near Cape Mudge, and the U'mista Cultural Centre in Alert Bay. When a person returns from a restricted life, they are said to have "u'mista," and the same can be said for the potlatch regalia that has now been returned to the First Nations people.

Today, the spirit of u'mista is alive in the coppers, robes and masks on display in the U'mista Cultural Centre.

2023 Waggoner Cruising Guide

Alert Bay
Discover our World

Arts | Culture | Heritage

U'mista Cultural Centre
Alert Bay Visitor Centre
and Art Gallery
Alert Bay Museum
Big House & World's
Tallest Totem Pole
'Namgis Burial Ground with
stand of totems
Traditional dance performances
in Big House

Activities

Whale watching
Fishing
Nature Trails
Traditional Canoes
Skate Park
Cultural Playground

Health

Hospital and Health Centre
Personal Care Services

Business

Full service Marina
Accommodations -
Hotels, B&B's Cabins
Campground
Grocery Store | Pharmacy
Restaurants | Pubs
Liquor Store | Post Office
Churches | Banking | Hair Salon

For general inquiries and cultural planning:

Alert Bay Visitor Centre

Phone: (250) 974-5024
Fax: (250) 974-5026
E-mail: info@alertbay.ca
www.alertbay.ca

U'mista Cultural Centre
For events and cultural activities check here
www.facebook.com/Umista.Cultural.Society
(250) 974-5403 or 1-800-690-8222 | www.umista.ca

available in the bay; be sure to anchor clear of the ferry dock and its approach.

The Alert Bay village is about a half-mile walk from the Boat Harbour. At the top of the dock, take a right and walk along the waterfront. The village has a grocery store, pharmacy, pub, liquor store, restaurants, salon and spa, ATM, post office, and walk-in emergency clinic. An excellent Visitor Centre is on the water side of the road, about midway into the commercial area. It's open 7 days a week during the season. You will get good information about the attractions in Alert Bay: the world's tallest totem pole (whose top blew off in a 2007 winter storm); the U'mista Cultural Centre and gift shop; the Ecological Park, where you can see culturally modified cedar trees (trees partly stripped of bark to make baskets, regalia, and clothing); the burial grounds; and the Anglican church that dates back to 1879. Brochures give information and map routes for self-guided tours. Interpretive displays have been installed. U'mista Cultural Centre is about a one-mile walk to the left from the Boat Harbour docks. Five awakwas (places to meet) along the way represent the five clans of the 'Namgis First Nation.

Cruisers moored at Port McNeill can walk-on the BC ferry to Alert Bay. Catch the morning ferry from Port McNeill and return on afternoon or evening ferry from Alert Bay. Bring your camera. The entire town of Alert Bay is walkable and photogenic.

Hiking trails: Cormorant Island has an extensive system of predator-free hiking trails. Ask for a map in the Visitor Centre or harbor office.

Seafest: Fourth weekend in July along the boardwalk. Table vendors, music, fun contests, and Artfest.

Alert Bay 360: B.C. Day is the first Monday of August. Observe or take part in the paddling race around Cormorant Island.

㉑ **Alert Bay Boat Harbour.** 20 Fir Street, Bag 2800, Alert Bay, BC V0N 1A0; (250) 974-5727; boatharbour@alertbay.ca; www.alertbay.ca. Monitors VHF 66A. Excellent docks, 30 amp power, water, pumpout. This is the breakwater-protected public wharf and floats in Alert Bay, located next to the ferry landing. The harbor manager's office features showers and flat-rate laundry with nice machines.

㉑ **U'mista Cultural Centre.** P.O. Box 253, Alert Bay, BC V0N 1A0; (250) 974-5403; (800) 690-8222; info@umista.ca; www.umista.ca; www.facebook.com/umista.cultural.society. We doubt that anyone could see this collection of historical coppers, masks and other ceremonial regalia without being affected. Open daily 9:00 a.m. to 5:00 p.m. from Canada Day to Labor Day, and Tuesday through Saturday, 9:00 a.m. to 5:00 p.m. in winter.

The displays portray the history of the area and the significance of the potlatch. In 1885 the government attempted to outlaw potlatch ceremonies, but the law was generally ignored and unenforced. In 1921, however, 45 people in the village were charged with violating a revised version of the law. Twenty-two people received suspended sentences, in an agreement where potlatch paraphernalia and ceremonial regalia, including masks and coppers, were turned over to the Indian Agent at Alert Bay. The items were sent to museums; some ended up in the personal collection of a government official. The people of Alert Bay successfully negotiated the return of their property in the 1960s, with the stipulation that museums be constructed for their display in Alert Bay and in Yaculta, near Cape Mudge. The result in Alert Bay is the U'mista Cultural Centre.

If you can, schedule your visit to see the T'sasala Cultural Group (250-974-8097) dance performances held in July and August at the 'Namgis Bighouse: admission charges for adults and children 4-12; no charge for children under 4. They explain and perform traditional dances, complete with regalia and masks. The audience joins in a dance at the end. Afterward, a visit to the U'mista Cultural Centre takes on greater importance. The artifacts on display are extraordinary. You can participate in a variety of free drop-in programs such as cedar bark weaving, traditional medicine, and story telling, to name a few. Check their Facebook page for free events and classes during the summer. The children's play area is a natural playground of trees and rocks that kids can climb.

Malcom Island Lions Harbour in the foreground and the village of Sointula to the upper right

㉒ **Sointula.** Sointula is a pleasant stop with amenities including an Info Centre, Co-op grocery store and bakeries. The Malcolm Island Lions Harbour Authority Small Craft Harbour has space in the summer for visiting boats in both the north and south sections. The Sointula Co-op, across the road from the south docks, carries charts and a good selection of marine hardware. A Co-op grocery store in the village, closed on Sundays and Mondays, has a small liquor agency. The Co-op does not use plastic bags. Bring your own bags for purchases. A farmer's stand, actually a box on the side of the Info Centre, carries local items including eggs and breads and uses an honor box for payment. The hotel in town has an ATM and restaurant. Coho Joe's is a popular cafe and coffee shop in the village.

Sointula means "place of harmony" in Finnish, and was settled by Finnish immigrants as a utopian cooperative shortly after the turn of the 20th century. Utopia didn't last, but the Co-op store is a reminder of earlier days. There's no doubting the Finnish influence as you walk around—the town is clean, well-maintained and orderly. You'll find well-tended lawns and gardens, with unique wood fencing.

Schedule time to see the museum. It's nicely done, and volunteers on duty love to share the town's history.

Sointula is a place where drivers wave as they go by, and are apt to stop and ask if you'd like a ride. It's a place where people put down what

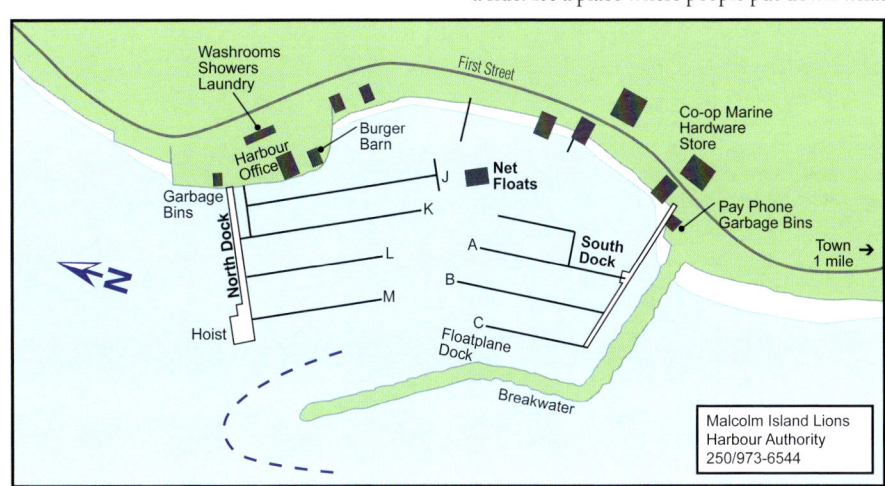

Malcolm Island (Sointula)

THE BROUGHTON REGION

See Area Map Page 351 - Maps Not for Navigation

they are doing to chat briefly and exchange a small joke or two.

You can also visit Sointula by walking on the BC ferries from Port McNeill.

Note: the concrete float that used to be next to the BC Ferries dock in front of the town center has been removed.

㉒ **Malcolm Island Lions Harbour Authority**. P.O. Box 202, Sointula, BC V0N 3E0; (250) 973-6544; milha@cablerocket.com; www.sointulaharbour.com. Monitors VHF 66A. Excellent docks with 20 & 30 amp power, some 50 amp; water, laundry, showers, garbage drop, Wi-Fi. Office hours are 8:30 a.m. to 2:30 p.m. in summer, 8:30 a.m. to 12:30 p.m. in winter. Downtown Sointula is an easy bike ride away, loaner bicycles are available at the Harbour Office.

Sointula's extensive public docks are behind a rock breakwater at the head of Rough Bay, 1 mile north of the ferry landing. The docks are divided into north and south sections. Both sections are available to visiting boats and it's an easy walk on the road between the two. Each set of docks has a garbage drop. The north docks also have washrooms, showers, and laundry, built and maintained by the Malcolm Island Lions Club. Solar panels on the roof provide the hot water. Both sections have potable water on the docks. All moorage is first-come, first-served, side-tie only, no reservations, rafting allowed. Moor where it makes sense. Pay at the office in the north section. Lorraine Williams is the manager. The office staff is happy to provide you with more information on the town.

The Burger Barn, a local favorite, with good hamburgers, wraps, and fish & chips, is in the bright red building in the parking lot.

Tarkanen Marine Ways (250) 973-6710, capable of major and emergency work, is located near the boat basin. Tarkanen has three marine ways with varying size cradles that can accommodate vessels up to 60 feet. With the closing of the Quarterdeck Boatyard in Port Hardy, this is the only marine ways between Campbell River or Lund and Shearwater. It is often busy serving commercial fishing boats. Tarkanen Marine Ways was completely rebuilt after a fire, and subsequently re-opened for business.

Mitchell Bay. Mitchell Bay, near the east end of Malcolm Island, is a good summertime anchorage, protected from easterlies and northwest winds. Not suitable in south or southwest winds. A public dock managed by the Malcolm Island Lions Harbour Authority is located on the east side of the bay; first-come, first-served. The L-shaped public dock has approximately 150 feet of moorage on the outside. Inside portion of the docks are usually occupied by smaller, local boats. Self-registration and payment box located at the head of the ramp. Don't miss visiting the bright 'Red Net Shed' at the head of the pier, where you can purchase antiques and other collectibles. A log boom area is north of the public dock.

㉓ **Port McNeill.** Port McNeill is a modern small city on Highway 19, which runs the length of Vancouver Island. It has banks, stores, hotels, restaurants, marine supplies, marine repairs services, and transportation to the rest of Vancouver Island. With most services located within easy walking distance of the boat harbor, Port McNeill is an excellent resupply point for boats headed north, south, or into the Broughton Islands. A Saturday Market is held from 9:00 a.m. to 1:00 p.m. on the lawn in front of the Port Authority and Visitor Center building.

Port McNeill has three marinas: the North Island Marina, Federal Docks, and the Town of Port McNeill Harbour Municipal floats. All are protected by an extensive breakwater. The Port Harbour docks are the first, to port as you round the end of the breakwater. North Island Marina and fuel dock is to starboard. Federal Marina is tucked between the Port Municipal floats and the breakwater, and managed by the Port McNeill Municipal office. All three facilities are close to shopping, restaurants and a modern laundromat with free Wi-Fi. The well-stocked IGA is in a shopping center a few blocks from the docks. The IGA has a van and will make deliveries or you can wheel grocery carts to the marinas. Fishing tackle, post office, large liquor stores, drug store and more are within a few minutes' walk. An auto parts store is just beyond the head of the North Island Marina docks and carries marine parts, batteries and lubricants. A short distance from the harbor is Progressive Diesel with factory trained service representatives and access to parts for several major brand marine engines. Parts that are not available locally can be ordered and often flown in the next day. While there is no boat yard in Port McNeill, there are a number of resources for marine services and repairs. Both marina offices can provide a list of boat service providers. The Shop-Rite marine and logging store handles outboard repairs.

Regular floatplane service connects down island. Kenmore Air and NW Seaplanes fly to Seattle from North Island Marina. The Port Hardy International Airport, with air service north and south, is a 30-minute taxi ride from Port McNeill. Taxi service available through Wavin' Flags Taxi (250-230-7655). During prime season, moorage can be tight, anchorage is possible across the bay from the marinas with good holding in thick, sticky mud. Be sure to see the Port McNeill & District Museum, which showcases the history of logging in the area. It is a short walk from the docks. Nearby, the world's largest burl is on display. BC Ferries operates a ferry from Port McNeill with service to Sointula and Alert Bay. Many visitors moor their boat in Port McNeill and walk-on the ferry to Sointula and Alert Bay.

㉓ **North Island Marina.** 1488 Beach Dr., Port McNeill, BC V0N 2R0; (250) 956-4044; (855) 767-8622 Reservations; www.northislandmarina.com. Monitors VHF 66A. Winter contact phone is (250) 956-3336. Open all year with 2100 feet of guest moorage for vessels to 280 feet. 30, 50 (120/208 volt) and 100 amp (single and three phase) power, water, Wi-Fi. Garbage, and recycling at the head of the dock. The main dock has a security gate; get the passcode from the marina office.

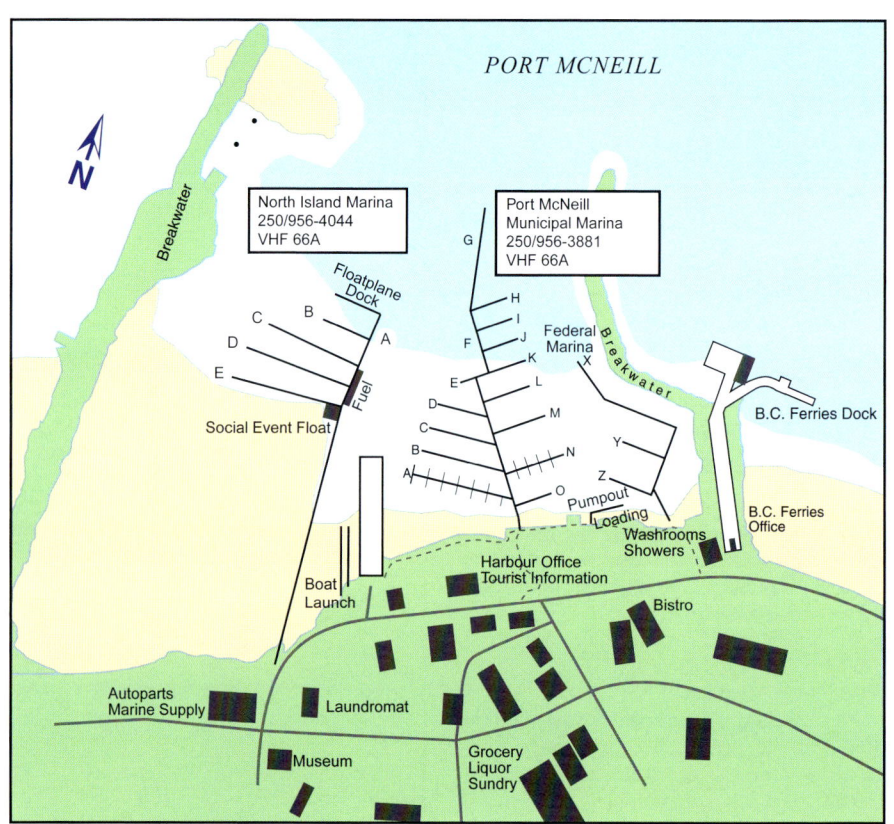

Port NcNeill

NORTH ISLAND MARINA
PORT McNEILL
BRITISH COLUMBIA

Gateway to the Broughtons and Northern BC

Friendly Service

- Transient and Guest Moorage for yachts up to 285'
- In berth fueling for Marine Diesel, Marine Gas, Avgas and Jet Fuel
- Propane
- Laundromat, Chandlery and Parts Store
- BBQ and Patio Area
- Free WiFi

Marina: 250-956-4044 • Winter: 250-956-3336 • VHF 66a

For reservations visit www.NorthIslandMarina.com

THE BROUGHTON REGION   See Area Map Page 351 - Maps Not for Navigation

Port McNeill harbour marinas and town with full-services in the background. The BC Ferries terminal has service to Alert Bay and Sointula.

Reservations highly recommended. The fuel dock has gasoline, diesel, 100 LL and Jet A aviation fuel, propane. A long fuel hose and reel allows for in-berth fueling.

The dock store has ice, lubricants and some marine parts. This is a well-staffed marina located adjacent to the municipal marina. You can't miss the large "Happy Hour" float with wind-break and awning cover, which has become the gathering place for special events. The 10-foot long custom made charcoal grill is started each evening during the summer season for your steak, burgers, or just-caught salmon. The custom-made tables have built-in stainless tubs for ice to keep beverages chilled.

North Island Marina offers many services, including a courtesy car, and pick-up and drop-off at the Port Hardy airport, about 24 miles away.

The marina staff can arrange for other services, including boat watch. For those who need to return home, North Island Marina is a good spot to leave your boat. Kenmore Air and Northwest Seaplanes leave directly from the North Island Marina floatplane dock with flights to Seattle. Bruce and Nancy Jackman have owned and operated the marina for many years. Their son Allan and other family members continue to be involved with the management and care of the marina.

PORT MCNEILL
Gateway to The Broughtons

HARBOUR OFFICE & INFORMATION CENTRE
Call on 66A for a slip assignment
Pumpout - Showers

PORT McNEILL BRITISH COLUMBIA

Phone: 250-956-3881 • Fax: 250-956-2897 • info@portmcneillharbour.ca • www.portmcneill.ca

㉓ **Port McNeill Harbour.** 1594 Beach Drive, P.O. Box 1389, Port McNeill, BC V0N 2R0; (250) 956-3881; info@portmcneillharbour.ca; town.portmcneill.bc.ca/harbour. Monitors VHF 66A. When approaching, call on the VHF for a slip assignment. Open all year, guest moorage, 20, 30, 50 & 100 amp power, water, washrooms, showers, pumpout, waste oil disposal, garbage drop. This is a well-managed, friendly, and inviting marina with guest moorage room for all sizes of boats. No reservations; first-come, first-served. The marina office works to get everyone in when calling upon arrival.

The marina office is in the Visitor Centre building, above the marina. The BC Ferries landing, with service to Alert Bay and Sointula, is east of the marina. The Harbour showers are located above the BC Ferries landing and are $5 per day, payable at the Harbour Office. The port expects to complete new shower facilities by spring 2023. A passcode for the combination lock to the showers is provided with payment. Carts are available at the head of the dock for the short trip to the nearby grocery and liquor store.

A 108-foot loading dock is available for short-term stays of up to 1-hour. Contact the Harbour Office on VHF 66A for permission to use the dock. Water is available at this dock along with a for-fee pumpout. Vessel captains must remain with the boat while on this dock.

㉓ **Port McNeill Federal Docks.** (250) 956-3881; info@portmcneillharbour.ca; town.portmcneill.bc.ca/harbour. Located behind the breakwater within Port McNeill Harbour. These are working docks, mostly taken by government and commercial vessels. Managed by Port McNeill Harbour Office with guest moorage first-come, first-served, subject to rafting.

www.WaggonerGuide.com

Beaver Harbour is the ancestral home of the Kwakiutl First Nations people and the location of historic Hudson's Bay Company at Fort Rupert.

Storey's Beach in Fort Rupert

Beaver Harbour. The islands in Beaver Harbour are picturesque. The west side of the Cattle Islands is protected; anchor on a mud bottom in 30 to 45 feet. Patrician Cove has been recommended to us. Several white shell midden beaches are located throughout the islands. Reader Jack Tallman reports fresh northwesterly winds get in and can make for a "troublesome night."

Our sister publication, *Cruising the Secret Coast* by Jennifer and James Hamilton, devotes a chapter to Beaver Harbour and the Native village of Fort Rupert.

Fort Rupert. Located in Beaver Harbour past Thomas Point. Exposed to north and east winds, but with several areas that serve well for day anchorage or overnight in settled weather. The town of Fort Rupert consists of two distinct areas, the newer town on the southwest shore of Beaver Harbour and the Native Reserve on the southernmost shore. Both areas are accessible by dinghy or kayak. Storey's Beach Park on the southwest offers a sandy beach and picnic tables. The south shore is the site of the Kwakiutl Band Longhouse and cemetery with exceptional carvings and paintings by Calvin Hunt, a well-known Master Carver and local resident. Visitors are welcome at the community carving shed located near the Longhouse and at Calvin Hunt's art gallery located on Copper Way.

Anchor off the south beach in 16 to 30 feet of water and dinghy to shore, look for the public gazebo for a landing spot. Position the dinghy appropriately for the charted extensive drying beach. A short trail leads to the cemetery and Longhouse; the small Fort Rupert General Store is nearby.

This area was once the site of a Hudson's Bay Company fort, built in 1849, first commanded by William Henry McNeill. The fort burned down in 1889. One of the remaining eight-pound cannons is displayed in front of the Longhouse.

㉔ **Port Hardy.** Port Hardy is the northernmost community on Vancouver Island. Moorage is at the seasonal Seagate T-Floats, formerly called the City Dock (summer only), Quarterdeck Marina, and Port Hardy Harbour Authority.

The seasonal Seagate T-Floats are adjacent to the Coast Guard wharf, and have the closest access to town and shopping. If the floats are full, you can anchor out and take the dinghy in.

The Quarterdeck Marina and the Harbour Authority floats are a mile or so farther into Hardy Bay, past a narrow entry channel. It's a one-mile walk from this inner bay to downtown. Stryker Electronics Ltd. (250) 949-8022, with marine electronics, repairs and a chandlery is across the street.

A large Save-on Foods supermarket (250-949-6455) is at Thunderbird Mall. For items with "Regular price/Member price" shelf tags, we found that non-members can get the Member price by asking the checker for a tourist card. The store will deliver large orders to the Seagate Summer Floats, Harbour Authority floats, and Quarterdeck Marina, with a delivery charge of about $12 for three boxes.

Port Hardy is clean and friendly. A park is along the shore with a seaside promenade past tidy waterfront homes. The Visitor Centre is next to the park. Be sure to read the sign commemorating completion of the Carrot Highway. A nearby library houses a small but excellent museum. Taxi transportation is available in the area; Town Taxi (250) 949-7877; Waivin Flags Taxi (250) 230-7655.

Port Hardy has city amenities, including a hospital and airport with scheduled flights to and from Vancouver. Nearby Bear Cove is the terminus for the BC Ferry that runs to Prince Rupert during the summer. Coastal Mountain Fuels is in Bear Cove. There is a recreational boat marina in Bear Cove with portapotties and two lane boat ramp.

Historic canon from Hudsons Bay Company days at Fort Rupert

THE BROUGHTON REGION

See Area Map Page 351 - Maps Not for Navigation

Caution for shallow and shoaling areas entering Port Hardy's inner harbour.

Dining: Port Hardy has several restaurants. We've had a good lunch and dinner at the Quarterdeck Pub at the Quarterdeck Marina. Cafe Guido has excellent coffee, sandwiches and baked goods. The Book Nook, the West Coast Community Craft Shop and The Drift are co-located with Cafe Guido. A local favorite, The Sporty Bar & Grille is down the street. A recent addition to Port Hardy is the beautiful Kwa'LiLas Hotel, formerly the Port Hardy Inn. Three Native tribes; Nakwaxda'xw People, Gwa'sala People, and Kwakiutle People came together to completely rebuild the structure, making extensive use of local cedar as an expression of native culture. The Kwa'LiLas Hotel houses the fine dining Ha'me' Restaurant with an excellent menu. Ha'me' is open for lunch and dinner; (250) 949-8884 for reservations.

Museum: The museum on the main street in town is small but superb. It also houses the finest collection of local history and local interest books we've seen. We recommend it.

Fuel: Fuel is available on the east side of Hardy Bay at Coastal Mountain Fuels in Bear Cove, and at Quarterdeck Marina farther in the bay.

Walkway & Nature Trail: A walking trail with picnic tables and viewpoints starts near the Quarterdeck Marina, leads past the Glen Lyon Inn, and continues along the edge of Hardy Bay. At the head, you can turn north and walk to the Quatse River estuary, or take the Quatse River loop through the woods to the Quatse River Salmon Hatchery (www.quatsehatchery.ca or call (250) 949-9022 to arrange a tour). The trail is very easy, and much of it is wheelchair-accessible. It's a great side-trip that offers a different perspective of Port Hardy. [*Hamilton*]

LOCAL KNOWLEDGE

FLOATPLANE OPERATIONS FLASHING LIGHTS: Two floatplane pilot-activated white flashing lights in Port Hardy's inner harbour, when flashing, indicate floatplane aircraft take-off and landing activity. Both lights are charted, one is located on the east shore 300 yards south of red and green inner harbour entrance markers, and the other is located on the tip of the south shore breakwater.

DANGEROUS REEF: South of the Port Hardy Seagate T-Floats in the outer bay, yellow buoys mark a large drying reef. If proceeding to the inner bay, pass well east of the reef.

㉔ **Fisherman's Wharf** - Port Hardy Harbour Authority. 6600 Hardy Bay Rd., Port Hardy, BC V0N 2P0; (250) 949-6332; (250) 949-0336 cell; porthardyharbour@gmail.com; www.porthardy.ca. Monitors VHF 66A. The finger floats have mostly 20 amp power, some 30 amp. The main float has increased the number of 30 and 50 amp outlets. Although this basin is primarily for commercial fishing vessels, there is limited room for pleasure craft in the summer when the fleet is out. The facility has washrooms, pumpout, and launch ramp; no showers or laundry.

㉔ **Quarterdeck Inn & Marina Resort.** 6555 Hardy Bay Rd., P.O. Box 910, Port Hardy, BC V0N 2P0; (250) 949-6551; (250) 902-0455; marina@quarterdeckresort.net; www.quarterdeckresort.net. Monitors VHF 66A. Open all year, gasoline, diesel, propane, guest moorage, 15, 30 & 50 amp power, washrooms, showers, laundry, Wi-Fi access, liquor store. During winter the fuel dock and marina office are closed on Sundays. The Quarterdeck Pub & Restaurant is on the same property.

Quarterdeck's 40-room hotel is attractive and well-appointed. It has full wheelchair access, ocean views, and a covered walkway to the pub, with a nice area for families.

The boatyard and Travelift are no longer operating.

㉔ **Seagate T-Floats** -Port Hardy Harbour Authority. (250) 949-6332; (250) 949-0336 cell; porthardyharbour@gmail.com; www.porthardy.ca. Monitors 66A. Seasonal floats with 30 amp power, water, and garbage drop. Close to town and shopping. Side-tie for boats up to 60 feet. Docks are best used in settled weather as the area is exposed to the north. New anchors and chain for the floats were installed in 2020. Docks are managed by Port Hardy Harbour Authority; moorage payment can be made with credit card by telephone or to Harbour Authority staff who come to the floats twice daily. This is a convenient place to stop and fill water tanks before heading around Cape Caution or into the Broughtons.

㉕ **Coastal Mountain Fuels** (Bear Cove). 6720 Bear Cove, Port Hardy, BC V0N 2P0; (250) 949-9988. Monitors VHF 16. Open all year, gasoline, diesel, kerosene, propane. Despite commercial appearance, they welcome pleasure boats. Washrooms, bait, ice, waste oil pump and disposal. Located near the BC Ferries terminal. Launch ramp and convenience store.

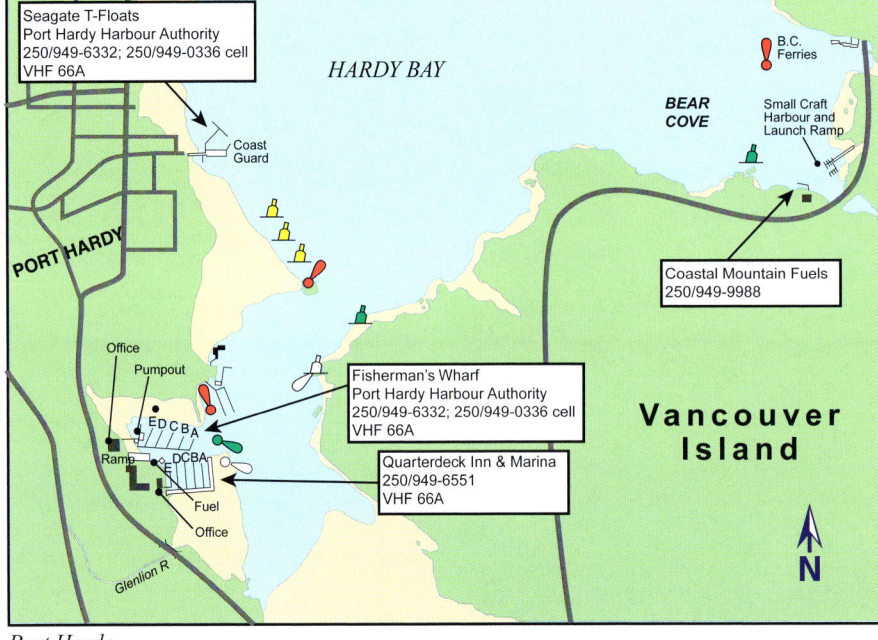

Port Hardy

West Coast of Vancouver Island

HARDY BAY TO QUATSINO SOUND
God's Pocket • Goletas Channel • Nahwitti Bar
Cape Scott • Sea Otter Cove

QUATSINO SOUND TO KYOQUOT
Winter Harbour • Quatsino Narrows • Coal Harbour
Brooks Peninsula • Bunsby Islands

KYUQUOT SOUND TO ESPERANZA INLET
Clear Passage • Zeballos • Esperanza • Tahsis Narrows

NOOTKA SOUND TO HOT SPRINGS COVE
Tahsis • Critter Cove • Friendly Cove • Estevan Point

CLAYOQUOT SOUND
Bacchante Bay • Ahousat
Lemmens Inlet • Tofino

BARKLEY SOUND
Ucluelet • Broken Group
Port Alberni • Bamfield

Scan the Latest
West Coast
Vancouver Island
Information

tinyurl.com/WG22xCh14

Brady's Beach, Barkley Sound

WEST COAST OF VANCOUVER ISLAND

Reference Only – Not for Navigation

Cruising West Coast Vancouver Island. For many, the area from Port Hardy, at the top of the east coast of Vancouver Island, down the west coast of Vancouver Island to the mouth of the Strait of Juan de Fuca, is the finest cruising ground in the Northwest—except, perhaps, Alaska. Little can compare with the variety, beauty, ruggedness, remoteness, and sheer satisfaction of this voyage. Please allow enough time when you make the trip. Plan for three weeks, two weeks at a minimum. This is a large cruising area to cover and you may have to allow for being weathered in.

The West Coast is broken into five inlets and sounds that snake their way into the heart of Vancouver Island. Mountains rise all around. Rocks lurk in the waters. Fish and wildlife abound. Only the hardy (and occasionally the foolhardy) are out there with you. This is Northwest cruising writ large.

Except for the rounding of Cape Scott and the long run down the Strait of Juan de Fuca, the distance between inlets and sounds is in the 20 to 30 mile range. Wait for good weather and dash around. Once inside, let the wind outside blow. You're safe.

Clockwise or counter-clockwise? Most boats travel the west coast of Vancouver Island traveling counter-clockwise. For sailboats, the prevailing summertime westerly winds combine with the westerly swells of the Pacific Ocean, and create some splendid downwind offshore sailing. Most powerboats have an easier time running with the seas than into them, so they prefer the prevailing conditions. "Prevailing," though, does not mean guaranteed, and the wind can blow from the south.

The difficulty with a counter-clockwise trip is the time it takes. To go down-island on the outside, you first must go up-island on the inside, and the weeks go by. Those who do not have the luxury of time to circumnavigate Vancouver Island can cruise the West Coast by running out the Strait of Juan de Fuca to Barkley Sound. They begin their explorations from Barkley Sound, traveling clockwise up the coast, perhaps only as far as Nootka Sound and then back down the coast. They must pick their weather for outside passages up-island into the prevailing swells, but that can be done. And if weather delays a passage for a day or even a few days, at least the time is spent on the West Coast, not in traveling up the Inside Passage.

Strait of Juan de Fuca. For boats coming from Puget Sound or Vancouver/Victoria, the Strait of Juan de Fuca can be a difficult body of water. The typical summer weather pattern calls for calm conditions in the early morning, with a sea breeze building by afternoon, often to 30+ knots. When wind and tidal current oppose, large, steep seas result.

On the American side, boats can leave Port Townsend at first light and get to Sequim Bay, Port Angeles, Pillar Point or even Neah Bay before the wind builds. From there they can cross to the Canadian side for the run to Ucluelet Customs the next day. Weather permitting, a fast boat can make it in one day.

On the Canadian side, boats can depart Victoria or Sooke at first light, and reach Port San Juan or even Barkley Sound, conditions and boat speed permitting. The distance from Victoria to Bamfield is approximately 92 nautical miles.

These thoughts are for typical conditions.

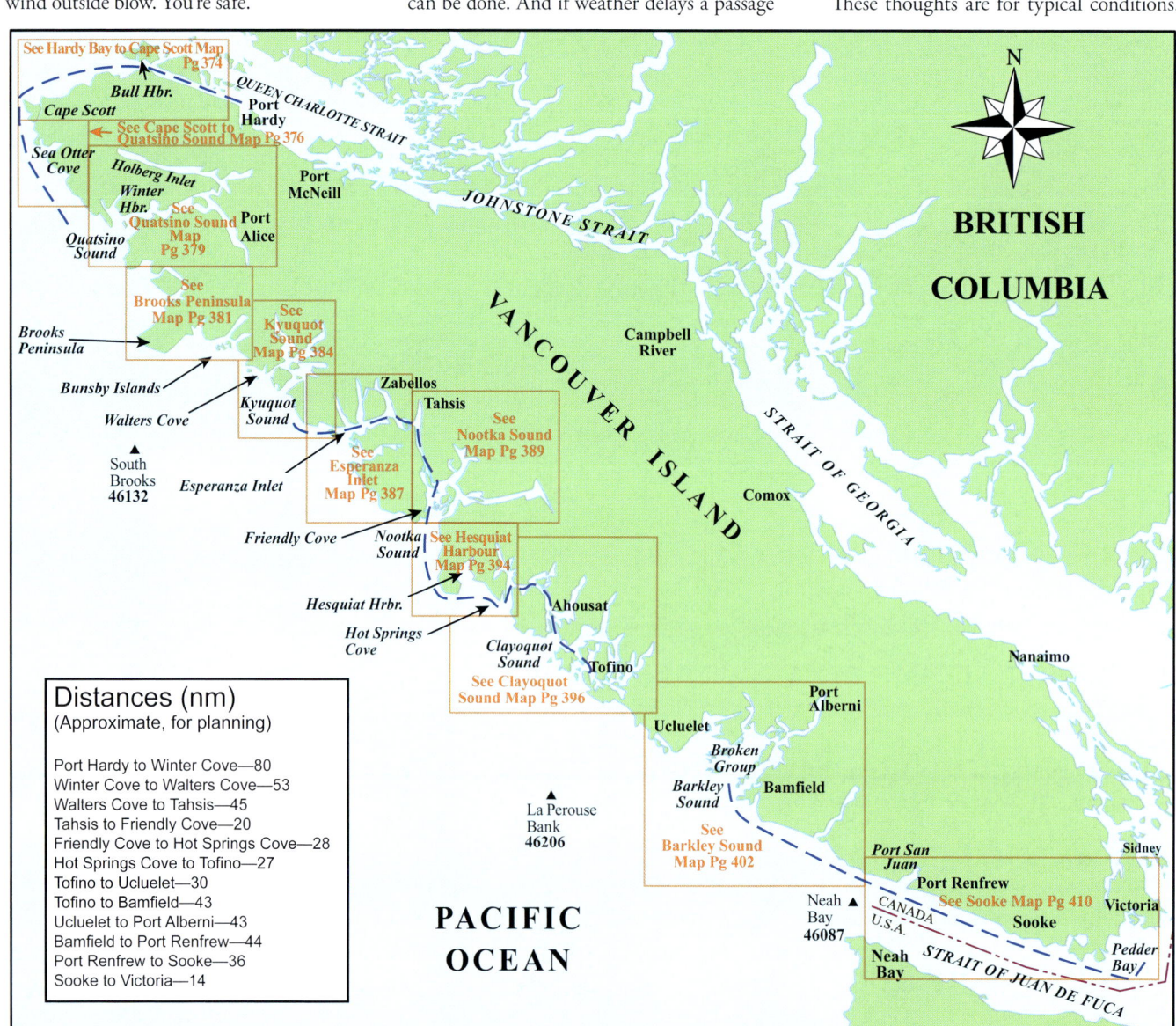

Distances (nm)
(Approximate, for planning)

- Port Hardy to Winter Cove—80
- Winter Cove to Walters Cove—53
- Walters Cove to Tahsis—45
- Tahsis to Friendly Cove—20
- Friendly Cove to Hot Springs Cove—28
- Hot Springs Cove to Tofino—27
- Tofino to Ucluelet—30
- Tofino to Bamfield—43
- Ucluelet to Port Alberni—43
- Bamfield to Port Renfrew—44
- Port Renfrew to Sooke—36
- Sooke to Victoria—14

West Coast Vancouver Island

Variations often change typical conditions. We have seen the strait windy all day and calm all day. Listen to the weather broadcasts, watch the barometer and sky, and be cautious.

The boat. Large or small, a boat for the West Coast should be seaworthy, strong, and well-equipped. The seas encountered on the offshore passages will be a test, especially at Cape Scott, Brooks Peninsula, Tatchu Point, Estevan Point, the entrance to Ucluelet, Cape Beale, and in the Strait of Juan de Fuca.

The wind accelerates as it is diverted at the capes and points, and the ocean's currents grow confused. Between wind and current, the seas grow noticeably higher and steeper. Even on moderate days, a boat can suddenly be surrounded by whitecaps. At Cape Scott and off Brooks Peninsula, pyramid-shaped waves can appear, break (or crumble into foam), and sweep past.

These 'rogue' waves can come from directions different from the prevailing seas. Assuming a summertime westerly wind and a course in following seas, they can grab the broad sterns of many powerboats and make broaching a hazard. A double-ender, especially a double-ended sailboat with a large rudder, will not be affected as much. In fact, sailing in these seas with a 25-knot breeze from astern could be high points of the trip. But a planing-hull powerboat skipper will pay close attention to the waves and their effect.

It is at times such as these that the skipper and crew know they are in serious water, and that their boat and equipment must be dependable. It is no place for old rigging, uncertain engines, sticky steering, intermittent electrical power, broken antennas, small anchors, unswung compasses, or clogged pumps. For a lifelong city-dweller, the West Coast is a wild coast with open seas and rocks a mile offshore. It pays to be prepared.

There are essentially no repair services between Port McNeill/Port Hardy and Ucluelet. Where service is available, it is oriented towards sport fishing vessels, with limited capabilities and parts to service inboard engines, onboard auxiliary systems and electronics. Even if you have the parts, the shop will very likely not have the time to help you since their bread and butter is the sport and commercial fishery.

You, the owner and operator of the boat, must decide which systems are critical to continuing the voyage and carry your own spares and learn how to install them. Parts not common to sport fishing vessels may be available from Campbell River, the nearest large town with an industrial base. Make sure that you have the maintenance and parts books available and the tools needed. With the right parts and tools, another cruiser may be able to help.

Most consider radar all but essential. The local boats, even the little ones, have radar. A GPS chartplotter will add to your navigational peace of mind. Even on clear days in mild conditions, GPS can identify turning points and confirm visual navigation. A chartplotter can take the anxiety out of navigating among ugly black rocks. In thick weather or fog, radar and electronic navigation will raise the comfort level aboard dramatically.

Weather. Winter on the West Coast is stormy, and not a place for pleasure craft. In early spring, conditions begin to improve, and by June or July the pattern of calm early mornings followed by rising westerly winds establishes itself. In the evening, the winds subside. That said, even in summer, serious storms can hit the West Coast.

Northwest winds coming down the coast tend to turn inland at the entrances to sounds and inlets. Sailors making a downwind run along the coast will often be able to carry that wind into the sounds, ending their day with a glorious sail on smooth water.

Fog can be a problem, particularly in August and September. We've heard the month of August referred to as "Foggust." The typical fog forms in early morning and burns off in late morning or early afternoon—just as the westerly fills in. If an outside passage is planned but the morning is blanketed in fog, the skipper will appreciate having radar and a chartplotter. It is also important to have your day's route layed out and saved on your chartplotter, complete with waypoints.

Plan for rain and cool temperatures as well as sunshine during a visit of two to four weeks or more.

The Coast Guard broadcasts continuous weather information from several locations along the way. The reports are limited in scope to weather that affects the West Coast, and include wind and sea state reports from lighthouses and weather-monitoring stations. In surprisingly short time, a visitor who's paying attention learns how to interpret the weather broadcasts and decide whether the time is right for an outside passage.

Lighthouse weather reports are particularly valuable. These reports include visibility, wind speed and direction, human-observed sea state, and swell height and direction. Reports are issued every three hours, but light keepers can often be reached on VHF 82 for up-to-the-minute weather information.

Fuel. Although the West Coast is a wilderness, it is a wilderness with fuel. Gasoline and diesel are available all along the way, within workable ranges for virtually any boat capable of safely being out there. The fuel stations exist to serve the fishing fleet and the pockets of permanent residents, especially Native communities. Fuel can be found at Winter Harbour, Coal Harbour, Fair Harbour, Zeballos, Esperanza, Tahsis, Critter Cove (gasoline only), Moutcha Bay, Ahousat, Tofino (gasoline and biodiesel), Ucluelet, Bamfield, Poett Nook (gasoline only), Port Alberni, Port San Juan, Sooke, and Victoria.

Ice. Although finding block ice can be a challenge, it is available at select locations on the west coast. Where commercial fishing is allowed, the fish processing plants may have flaked ice for the fish boats, which take it on by the ton. A polite inquiry usually will yield enough ice for the icebox or cooler—sometimes for a charge, often not. Fish ice is "salt ice," and not recommended for the cocktail hour.

Water. Water can be found at most communities. Ask locals before filling the tank.

Fresh vegetables. Uneven quality. Best to plan ahead and stock accordingly. Port Alice, Port Alberni, Tofino and Ucluelet are the only towns with real supermarkets.

Public docks. Every community has a public dock with moorage fees collected by a local resident. At some of the docks the local resident isn't around, or doesn't bother to come collecting. Accept the no-charge tie-ups where you find them, pay gladly where the charge is collected.

Reference books and guidebooks. The Canadian Tide and Current Tables, Vol. 6 gives tides and currents south to Port San Juan. Vol. 5 covers the Strait of Juan de Fuca and inland waters of Strait of Georgia and Puget Sound. Ports and Passes covers the entire west coast and Strait of Juan de Fuca. Sailing Directions, volume PAC 202 includes West Coast Vancouver Island and PAC 201 includes Strait of Juan de Fuca. They are the official government publication and should be considered essential. Note that Sailing Directions is intended for large vessels. A cove listed as good for anchoring may be too deep or exposed for small craft, but a passage listed as tortuous may be easily run by small craft.

For guidebooks, we recommend carrying the most current edition of the *Waggoner Cruising Guide* for updated information on facilities (only the Waggoner is updated each year). Three other good guidebooks exist, and all three are carried in the Waggoner Store. The three are very different. Look for the one that most matches your cruising style.

The first is Don and Reanne Douglass' *Exploring Vancouver Island's West Coast*. The book is clear, easy to understand, and describes a large percentage of bays and coves along the West Coast. Not every bay described is a desirable anchorage, but the Douglasses tell the reader what to expect if forced to enter.

The second is Anne and Laurence Yeadon-Jones' *Dreamspeaker Cruising Guide, Vol. 6: The West Coast of Vancouver Island*, 2nd edition published in 2017 by Fine Edge in the U.S. and Harbour Publishing in Canada. They favor stern-tieing and tight anchorages which some boaters may not care for, particularly since stern-tieing is rarely necessary on the west coast.

Supplemental Reading: *Voyages to Windward* by Elsie Hulsizer, paperback edition, 2015. Well-told stories of West Coast adventures packed with information about the coast's history, people, and natural history. Excellent photos. Provides a good sense of

WEST COAST OF VANCOUVER ISLAND

Reference Only – Not for Navigation

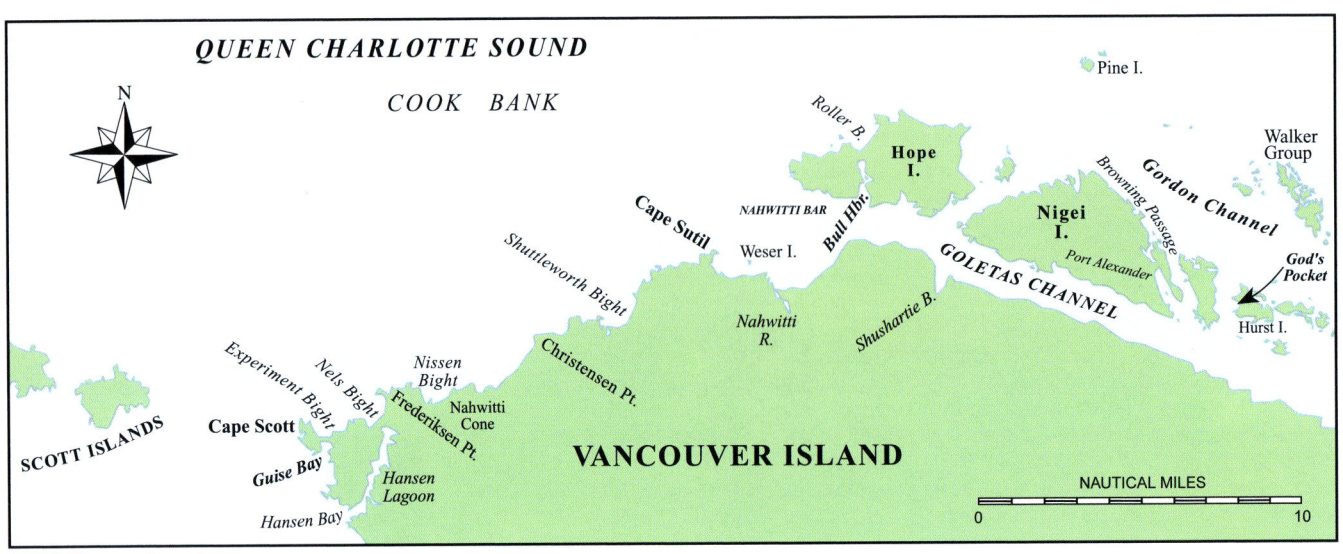

Hardy Bay to Cape Scott

what it's like to cruise this challenging and interesting coast.

Charts. The Canadian Hydrographic Service electronic raster charts are available for all of West Coast Vancouver Island and Haida Gwaii as a package, PAC-01 and vector charts package, V-PAC-B. Canadian Hydrographic Service has more than 30 charts that cover the coast between Port Hardy and Trial Island. Buy them all. Let the few that you don't use be insurance that you will have the chart you need, regardless of where you are. The charts are of excellent quality and easy to read. The West Coast is no place for approximate navigation.

Coast Guard. The Canadian Coast Guard stationed along the West Coast is simply incredible. They watch like mother hens over the fleets of fish boats, pleasure boats and work boats, ready to deploy helicopters and rescue craft instantly. They know what the weather is doing and where the traffic is. They know where to find help. A call to the Coast Guard brings action.

Local communities can often respond even faster than the Coast Guard. In the area off Kyuquot Sound, for example, we were told that a call to Walters Cove on VHF 06 or 14 would bring help a-running. Be sure to call the Coast Guard on channel 16, too.

Insurance. Insurance policies for most inshore boats do not cover the west coast of Vancouver Island. Read your policy and check with your agent about extending the coverage for the period of your trip.

Customs Clearance. In the past, Canada Customs and Border Services has been available in Ucluelet from June 1st to September 30 at the 52 Steps dock. However, the service was not available in 2020, 2021, and 2022. The other nearest CBSA port of entry is in Victoria. There are no other Canada Customs and Border Services on West Coast Vancouver Island. The nearest U.S. Customs and Border Protection port of entry is at Port Angeles, there is no U.S. Customs services at Neah Bay.

Communications. Cell phone service is found in Ucluelet, Bamfield, Tofino, Hot Springs Cove, many locations in Clayoquot Sound, most locations in Barkley Sound and in many locations in Quatsino Sound. Wi-Fi services that might be found at marinas, coffee shops, and restaurants are usually satellite based, which is slower than you may be used to.

Oregon's Secret. Many of the boats cruising the West Coast come from Oregon. For years it's been their playground, their little secret. The reason is obvious. After the trip along the Washington coast, their first stop is the west coast of Vancouver Island. In good weather it's a long but easy run. Boats from the population centers of Puget Sound or Vancouver/Victoria usually find it easier to enjoy cruising in the protected waters inside Vancouver Island.

Trailer Boats. Launch ramps are available on each of Vancouver Island's sounds and inlets. Many kayakers choose whatever part of the West Coast they wish without making a summer of it. The West Coast truly is kayak country, with kayak delivery services from small speedboats with kayak racks, to the coastal freighters *Frances Barkley* and *Uchuck III*.

HARDY BAY TO CAPE SCOTT

We will start from the north as though leaving from Port McNeill or Port Hardy, both excellent ports with provisioning and other services. Most importantly, you can watch the internet for the right weather window. Many cruisers like to watch for a 1-3 day settled weather window for the trip leg from the top of Vancouver Island south past Brooks Peninsula.

Goletas Channel stretches west-northwest 23 miles between Duval Point (entrance to Hardy Bay) and the western tip of Hope Island. At the west entrance of Goletas Channel the notorious Nahwitti Bar blocks westerly swells from entering. Goletas Channel's shorelines are steep-to. Winds can funnel between them and grow stronger, but in usual summer conditions the channel, while it can get pretty

God's Pocket Resort has space for a few boats and is a good jumping-off point when rounding Cape Scott.

www.WaggonerGuide.com

Sunset at Nahwitti Bar

choppy, is not known for dangerous seas. Be alert, however, for turbulence and debris in the water where Christie Passage, Browning Passage and Bate Passage join Goletas Channel. The mouth of Hardy Bay can be slow going as you pick your way through drift. Bull Harbour indents Hope Island at the west entrance to Goletas Channel. It is the usual waiting point for slack water on Nahwitti Bar.

God's Pocket is a favorite layover in Christie Passage on the west side of Hurst Island, just off Goletas Channel. Boats bound around Vancouver Island probably will not see God's Pocket unless to escape a chop in Goletas Channel. But boats planning a direct crossing of Queen Charlotte Sound to Haida Gwaii (Queen Charlotte Islands), or boats bound past Cape Caution, find God's Pocket to be a good departure spot. God's Pocket is a local name, not shown on the chart.

God's Pocket Resort. P.O. Box 130, Port Hardy, BC V0N 2P0; (250) 949-1755; info@godspocket.com; www.godspocket.com. Monitors channel 16 & 10. This is primarily a diving resort with friendly people. Room for three to four boats at the dock, or anchor out. No power or water on the docks. No washrooms and no showers. Breakfast, lunch and dinner are available for the resort's diving guests; others can be accommodated on an as-available basis, call ahead.

Port Alexander. Port Alexander, indenting Nigei Island west of Browning Passage, is a good anchorage for boats bound for Cape Scott or around Cape Caution. Anchor near the head in 50 to 60 feet. The beach is good for dog walking. Northwesterly and westerly winds blow in across the island, but has no fetch for seas to build. The west side of the bay seems more protected than the east. The accumulation of large logs on the beach indicates that this is no place to be in a southerly storm. Marginal cell service.

Clam Cove. Clam Cove is a local name, not shown on the chart, for an anchorage on the Gordon Channel side of Nigei Island, where Browning Passage meets Gordon Channel. The entrance is approximately 0.7 miles southeast of Hougestal Point. The entrance is guarded by rocks; kelp marks the shallow spots. The basin has room for several boats, with protection from all winds. Readers Kim and Bill Halley report that two derelict boats are on the southeast side of the cove; watch for lines strung across the cove in front of these boats.

An easily-walked trail leads from the south end of Clam Cove to Port Alexander. A cluster of float homes is located at the north end of the inner-most part of the cove.

Shushartie Bay. "We stopped for breakfast in Shushartie Bay after rounding the top end of Vancouver Island (clockwise circumnavigation). A 30-knot southeasterly wind was blowing against a strong flood current, making Goletas Channel very rough. We went deep into the bay and dropped the hook in 50 feet just inside the 30-meter line, west of some dolphins marked 'Dns' on the chart. Holding was good in thick mud. This is no Prideaux Haven, but considering the conditions outside, the swell that came in wasn't too bad. The Douglasses description of Shushartie Bay is fairly negative, and we don't know how it would be in a westerly. But it worked for us that day." [*Hamilton*]

Bull Harbour. Bull Harbour is a lovely bay almost landlocked in Hope Island. It is the place to wait for weather and for slack water on Nahwitti Bar.

Enter Bull Harbour around the east side of Norman Island, which blocks the southern entrance. A light marks the entrance. 3-knot speed limit inside the harbour. Parts of Bull Harbour grow quite shoal on a low tide. Check the depths and tide tables before anchoring for the night. The bottom is mud and holding is excellent. Sailing Directions says the southern portion of the harbor is reported to be foul with old chain and cable. During the fishing season, commercial fish boats often crowd the harbor. The entrance should be kept clear for floatplane landings and departures. The Coast Guard station, once active here, has been decommissioned.

All of Hope Island, including Bull Harbour, at the west end of Goletas Channel, is the property of the Tlatlasikwala Native Band. Boaters may tie-up at the Band's dock in mid-harbour but may not go ashore on Hope Island, all of which is private Indian Reserve land. Moorage is first-come, first-served. The northern most section of the dock is reserved for floatplanes. A detached float just past Norman Island near the harbour entrance is also available for moorage. Payment for moorage can be mailed to the Band at Tlatlasikwala First Nation (250) 902-0815, PO Box 339, Port Hardy, BC V0N 2P0. See their website at www.tlatlasikwala.com.

Westerly winds can enter Bull Harbour, as can southeast gales. If you are anchored, be sure the anchor is well set with adequate scope.

Nahwitti Bar. Nahwitti Bar should be attempted only at or near slack. Slack water and current predictions are shown in Tide and Current Tables, Vol. 6. Maximum tidal currents over the bar reach 5.5 knots. From seaward, the bar shoals gradually to a least depth of approximately 35 feet. When ocean swells from deep water hit the bar, friction from the shallowing bottom slows the water there, while the top of the swell continues its pace. As a result the waves grow high and steep. If a strong ebb current opposes westerly winds, dangerous and heavy breaking seas will develop.

It is often said that the ideal time to cross Nahwitti bar is at high slack water, when the typical westerly wind blows with the flood current. This tends to keep seas down and permits crossing a few minutes before the slack. The subsequent ebb current flows to 3 knots along the coast all the way to Cape Scott.

A crossing at high slack is not without its disadvantages, though. First, the ebb that follows will oppose the prevailing westerly wind, and could build a steep chop along the run to Cape Scott. Second, if you cross Nahwitti Bar at slack, you are almost guaranteed to arrive at Cape Scott around mid-tide, when currents there could be kicking up the seas. One alternative is to take the inner route around Nahwitti Bar prior to high or low slack at the bar, timing your arrival at Cape Scott for high or low water.

Thus the wise skipper considers all factors before crossing Nahwitti Bar: current direction and speed, weather, time of day, and vessel speed. At least 30 minutes should be allowed to get through the swells on the bar. Even fast boats usually must proceed slowly. At slack water in windless conditions, we found impressive swells extending 2.5 miles out to Whistle Buoy *MA* before they died down.

Nahwitti Bar Inner Route. A September 1992 *Pacific Yachting* article by June Cameron describes a quieter inner route that avoids Nahwitti Bar altogether. While in Bull Harbour, an old and grizzled commercial

WEST COAST OF VANCOUVER ISLAND

fisherman told us he hadn't gone across the bar in years, and we were nuts if we didn't take the inner route. Cross to the bay on the south shore of Goletas Channel and work in behind Tatnall Reefs. Follow the Vancouver Island shoreline around the bay, passing on either side of Weser Island. If the westerly is blowing, you can hide in the little nook behind Cape Sutil. We did it and it works. We don't plan to cross Nahwitti Bar again. [*Hale*]

Cape Sutil to Cape Scott. Sailing Directions says the distance from Cape Sutil to Cape Scott is 15 miles, but this understates the actual running distance after crossing Nahwitti Bar. A more realistic distance would be measured from Whistle Buoy *MA*, and would be approximately 16.5 miles. Although the run across the bottom of Queen Charlotte Sound is exposed to westerlies, except for the relentless Pacific swell the early morning conditions are often quiet. Rocks extend as much as a mile offshore all along the way. Stay well off.

According to Sailing Directions, temporary anchorage can be found in Shuttleworth Bight, Nissen Bight, Fisherman Bay (southwest corner of Nissen Bight), Nels Bight, and Experiment Bight. Study the chart before entering, and watch the weather.

Cape Scott is the westernmost point of Vancouver Island. Dangerous rocks extend 0.5 mile offshore, northward and westward. The cape itself is a low piece of land connected by a narrow neck with the main body of Vancouver Island. The Cape Scott Light, on a square tower 13 feet high, is on higher ground about a quarter-mile inland from Cape Scott.

Currents flowing on both sides of the cape meet at Cape Scott. Especially when opposed by wind, the currents can produce heavy seas and overfalls, dangerous to small craft. Even in calm conditions, seas can emerge seemingly from nowhere, the result of colliding currents. With its seas, rocks, and shortage of convenient hidey-holes, Cape Scott is not a place to treat lightly. A vessel in trouble at Cape Scott could be in serious distress, and quickly.

It is with good reason that guidebooks (including this one) and magazine articles emphasize the dangers and cautions at Cape Scott. The waters can be treacherous. Yet in settled summer conditions, a well-managed seaworthy vessel, with a good weather eye, can make a safe and satisfying rounding. The standard advice is to round Cape Scott at slack. Other factors may persuade a skipper to round at times other than slack. Each situation, each boat, is different. What worked yesterday may not work today. A careful skipper, fully aware that safety of the vessel and crew truly are at risk at Cape Scott, must judge conditions and make the right choices.

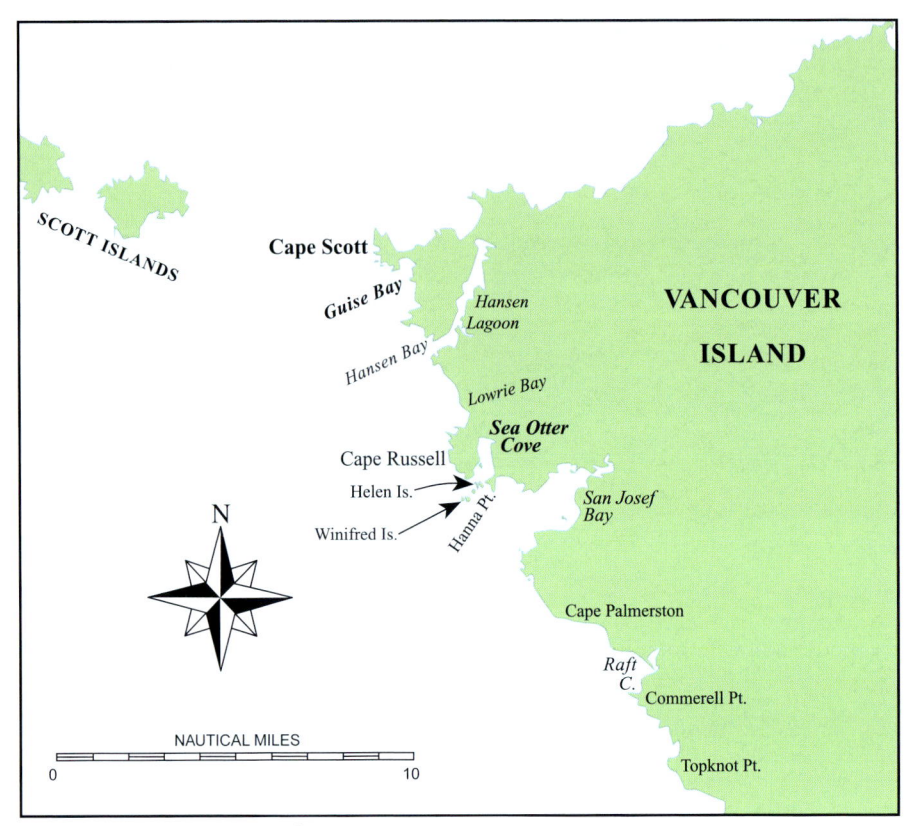

Weather information: The Cape Scott lighthouse weather report is regularly updated with wind speed and direction, sea conditions, and visibility information. The automated weather station on Sartine Island provides wind speed and direction. Listen to the continuous marine broadcast for the latest weather information.

Cape Scott to Quatsino Sound

CAPE SCOTT TO QUATSINO SOUND

Depending on the courses chosen, the run from Cape Scott to the entrance of Quatsino Sound is approximately 28.5 miles. To stay clear of off-lying rocks and reefs, the general advice is to follow the 20-fathom curve all the way down the coast. Douglass says he prefers the 30-fathom curve for an extra margin of safety. We are inclined toward Douglass' 30-fathom standard. In moderate conditions with excellent visibility, we felt comfortable in 25 to 30 fathoms. Had conditions worsened, we would have moved out.

With the summer westerly in place, the run between Cape Scott and Quatsino Sound is a downhill sleigh ride. Powerboaters, especially those with planing hulls, will have to saw away at the helm and play with the throttle to stay in harmony with the relentless procession of rollers. They will arrive tired. The sailboaters will have all the fun, especially if the boat and crew can handle a spinnaker. They too will arrive tired, but exhilarated.

Given the conditions, many boats make a direct passage between Cape Scott and Quatsino Sound, and leave the bays between for another day. Sailboats, after a long passage at 6 knots, will be apt to put into one of those bays, particularly Sea Otter Cove. Boats heading clockwise, toward Cape Scott, might also be more apt to investigate the shoreline, choosing to spend the night in Sea Otter Cove. They could make an early departure the next morning and round Cape Scott before the westerly fills in.

Weather information: At the north end, the

Rounding remote Cape Scott is a part of the West Coast Vancouver Island experience.

See Area Map Page 379 - Maps Not for Navigation

WEST COAST OF VANCOUVER ISLAND

Cape Scott lighthouse weather report informs mariners of wind and sea conditions. At the south end, the Quatsino lighthouse report does the same. Listen to the continuous marine broadcast for the latest weather information.

Guise Bay. Guise Bay is just south of Cape Scott. Sailing Directions says the entrance to Guise Bay is encumbered with rocks, and local knowledge is called for. The chart suggests that entrance is possible, but Douglass says that the rocks are often covered with foam and a strong heart is needed. Correspondents Gil and Karen Flanagan, however, put in to Guise Bay, and here is their report:

"Guise Bay is a great anchorage. The shore is so interesting we would consider overnighting there. The walk to the lighthouse is well used, and pretty easy. The anchorage area is about 600 yards long by 600 yards wide. The swell that day was only a few inches. Behind the island, the main south entrance channel is 1000 feet wide and 42 feet deep. If it is a reasonably nice day, don't pass it by." [Flanagan]

Hansen Bay. Hansen Bay was the location of a Danish settlement around 1900. Supply vessels could anchor in good weather only. The settlement failed. Sailing Directions says Hansen Bay "affords no shelter," although commercial fish boats do hole up there.

Sea Otter Cove. Sea Otter Cove, south of Cape Scott, is described in Sailing Directions as "indifferent shelter." Nevertheless, Sea Otter Cove is a favorite of fish boats, and well-known to yachtsmen. The rocks and islets outside the entrance are awesome in their ruggedness. Inside, you feel safe but surrounded by hostile ground. Sea Otter Cove is an exciting place to be. We recommend it.

Enter from the south, between Hanna Point and the Helen Islands. Watch for swells breaking near and almost across the entrance, but careful attention to the chart will bring you through. The channel is narrow, and grows shallower as you go in. Deep draft vessels should be careful if they anchor there due to the shallow depths. Four storm mooring buoys are in place; least depth is about 8 feet at zero tide.

Tiny community of Winter Harbour.

San Josef Bay. San Josef Bay is protected from northerly winds, but open to westerly and southerly winds. Anchor in settled weather.

QUATSINO SOUND

Quatsino Sound is the northernmost of the five sounds that indent the west coast of Vancouver Island. Despite fish farms and logging operations, Quatsino Sound still provides scenic coves and interesting anchorages. With the exception of North Harbour and Winter Harbour on the north side near the entrance, Quatsino Sound is probably the sound least explored by cruising yachts.

Quatsino Sound is the first quiet anchorage after the 50-mile run from Bull Harbour, and a welcome sight it is after anxiety at Cape Scott and hours of rolling seas. The entrance is straightforward. Using large-scale Chart 3686, identify South Danger Rock and Robson Rock (both of them well away from land), stay close to Kains Island, and proceed into Forward Inlet. North Harbour and Browning Inlet are good anchorages, or you can continue to Winter Harbour.

For those coming from Haida Gwaii or the Central Coast, Quatsino Sound offers the opportunity to do major provisioning, either at Port Alice or by taking a bus to Port Hardy from Coal Harbour.

VHF: We are told the fishermen work on channels 73, 84, and 86.

Cell phones: There is cellular service throughout most of Quatsino Sound except Forward Inlet north of Montgomery Point.

① **Winter Harbour.** Winter Harbour once was a commercial fishing outpost, and B.C. Packers owned the first major set of docks as you enter, including the fuel dock. With the closing of fishing, their docks and fuel facility have been taken over by the company that owns and runs the Outpost store. Today Winter Harbour has 12 full time residents and about 70 summer residents.

Beyond the Outpost and its facilities is the campground of the Winter Harbour Lodge, followed by the Qualicum Rivers Fishing Resort (the large white building), and finally, the Winter Harbour Authority public dock.

The library, located above the public dock, has irregular hours. Pay phones are on the far side of this building. A post office and book exchange is located in a small building to the right of the public wharf. For-fee Wi-Fi is available in Winter Harbour.

Van Isle 360: The Van Isle 360 sailboat race, held in odd-numbered years, visits Winter Harbour. They fill the docks when they arrive.

① **Outpost at Winter Harbour, Grant Sales Ltd.** 108 Winter Harbour Rd., Winter Harbour, BC V0N 3L0; (250) 969-4333; winterharbour@telus.net; www.winterharbour.ca. Monitors VHF 19. Open all year, moorage for boats to 75 feet, gasoline, diesel, oil, laundry, washrooms & showers, general store, water at fuel dock, campsites. The showers are in a small building on a dock near the Outpost. The general store has frozen foods including some frozen meat, canned goods, packaged foods and ice. Produce is limited. Grocery availability may depend on delivery schedules. The Outpost also carries liquor, clothing, charts, fishing equipment, and miscellaneous tools. The liquor agency has a decent wine selection. Wi-Fi can be purchased and used at an attractive patio area overlooking the harbor. Greg Vance is the owner. Two-bedroom units available for shoreside accommodations.

A community boardwalk skirts the shoreline at Winter Harbour.

2023 Waggoner Cruising Guide

WEST COAST OF VANCOUVER ISLAND

① **Winter Harbour Authority.** (800) 960-2646 Harbormaster; Monitors VHF 69. Moorage on 450 feet of dock, water, waste oil disposal, garbage drop, recycling, 15, 20, & 30 amp power. Power is run to the dock by extension cord; quality varies. Moorage is first-come, first-served; make payment at the adjacent fishing lodge, where you will find the harbourmaster. Cruisers may need to go to the Outpost to use the for-fee Wi-Fi. A tidal grid is available. Qualicum Rivers Resort (800-960-2646), the fishing lodge next door, operates June through September and sells flaked ice to cruisers.

A sign on the dock asks shallow draft boats to allow deeper draft boats priority on the outer side. Larger boats also anchor to the north of the public dock and at the head of Winter Harbour.

North Harbour. North Harbour, north of Matthews Island in Forward Inlet, is an excellent anchorage, popular with boats planning a morning departure from Quatsino Sound. A small float house is moored close to shore and does not significantly interfere with anchorage. North Harbour is sheltered and quiet, yet close to the mouth of Quatsino Sound.

Browning Inlet. Browning Inlet is narrow and sheltered from seas and swells, with good holding in 18 to 30 feet. Crabbing is reportedly good. In strong northwesterlies, winds blow from the valley to the north. In those conditions North Harbour or Winter Harbour are preferable.

Koskimo Bay. Koskimo Bay has a couple of anchorages, one behind Mabbott Island and one at Mahatta Creek. The Koskimo Islands are at the east end of Koskimo Bay.

Mabbott Island. The little area behind Mabbott Island would be a cozy spot to drop the hook if the large fish farm and float house didn't take much of the anchorage.

Mahatta Creek. In Koskimo Bay. Work your way east of the mouth of the creek, anchor in 30 to 45 feet. At high tide you can explore the creek. Waves can build across the sound in strong northwesterlies. On those days it's best to move north to East Cove.

Koskimo Islands. Explore by dinghy. The narrow passage between the largest of the islands and Vancouver Island can be run (carefully), but with safe water just outside the islands we see no need to.

Koprino Harbour. Most of Koprino Harbour is too deep for pleasure craft to anchor, but the area of East Cove, near the northeast corner of Koprino Harbour, is excellent.

East Cove. East Cove is tranquil, snug and tree-lined, with good dinghy access to shore—cruising as it should be. If East Cove were in Desolation Sound instead of Koprino Harbour, it would be filled with 25 boats every night, all stern-tied to shore. But because East Cove is on the west coast of Vancouver Island, you will probably be the only boat at anchor and won't need a stern-tie. Another cove, almost as delightful, is just to the north, behind a group of little islets. The largest of these islets is identified on the chart as Linthlop Islet.

Pamphlet Cove. Pamphlet Cove, part of a provincial recreation reserve, is located on the north side of Drake Island, about 3.5 miles west of Quatsino Narrows. Pamphlet Cove is scenic and protected, an ideal anchorage. You can go ashore and enjoy the reserve. At high tide several small lagoons make for good exploring by dinghy or kayak.

Julian Cove. Southeast of Drake Island and east of Kultus Cove. Protection is excellent and holding is good. Probably the most pristine cove in Quatsino Sound, Julian Cove has room for four or five boats. Beautiful forested hills surround it without a clearcut in sight. At the head of the bay a stream crosses a marsh and salmonberries grow along the shore. Watch for bears. Entry is direct and easy.

Smith Cove. It's been reported that a large float and separate float house, with cables running to shore, occupies much of Smith Cove. Nearby Julian Cove is a better choice.

Atkins Cove. Atkins Cove is well protected except south. Good holding over a mud bottom.

"Early Bird Cove," Douglass' name for the almost-landlocked cove accessed through the narrows on the north side of Atkins Cove, is also a good anchorage. We went through the narrow, shallow entrance strongly favoring the west shore. On an 8.5-foot high tide we saw depths of 6.5 feet.

Neroutsos Inlet. "The wind blows hard every afternoon in Neroutsos Inlet," one knowledgeable local told us. Neroutsos Inlet is long and straight-sided, with little diversion along the way. A former pulp mill is at Port Alice near the south end.

② **Port Alice.** Port Alice, properly Rumble Beach, but locally called Port Alice, is a friendly, former cellulose-mill town struggling to adjust to the recent sale and subsequent closure of the mill. Amenities include a liquor store, and a grocery market that almost qualifies as a supermarket (and the best grocery shopping between Port Hardy and Tofino). Restaurants are scarce. Fuel is available from a service station near the public dock at the north end of town for a $20 fee. A tricky 9-hole golf course is located at the site of the former mill, the real Port Alice, about a mile south of the town. Showers and laundry are available at the campground half a mile south of the yacht club and Rumble Beach Marina.

Visitors are warmly welcomed in Port Alice. It is a delightful stop and a good alternative to a bus ride into Port Hardy from Coal Harbour for provisioning.

② **Rumble Beach Marina.** (250) 209-2665; (250) 284-3391. Open all year with moorage to 100 feet. This marina, just south of the Port Alice Yacht Club, is the best moorage prospect in Port Alice. Potable water, garbage drop, laundry, and showers. No power. Fuel can be delivered to the dock April-September by prior arrangement with Port Alice Petroleum, call (250) 284-3530.

The marina is operated by the city and is within walking distance of all Port Alice amenities.

② **Port Alice Yacht Club.** You must belong to a yacht club with reciprocal privileges to tie up here. A log breakwater protects the yacht club and the public dock/launch

Harbour Authority float at Winter Harbour

Julian Cove is an outstanding anchorage.

378   www.WaggonerGuide.com

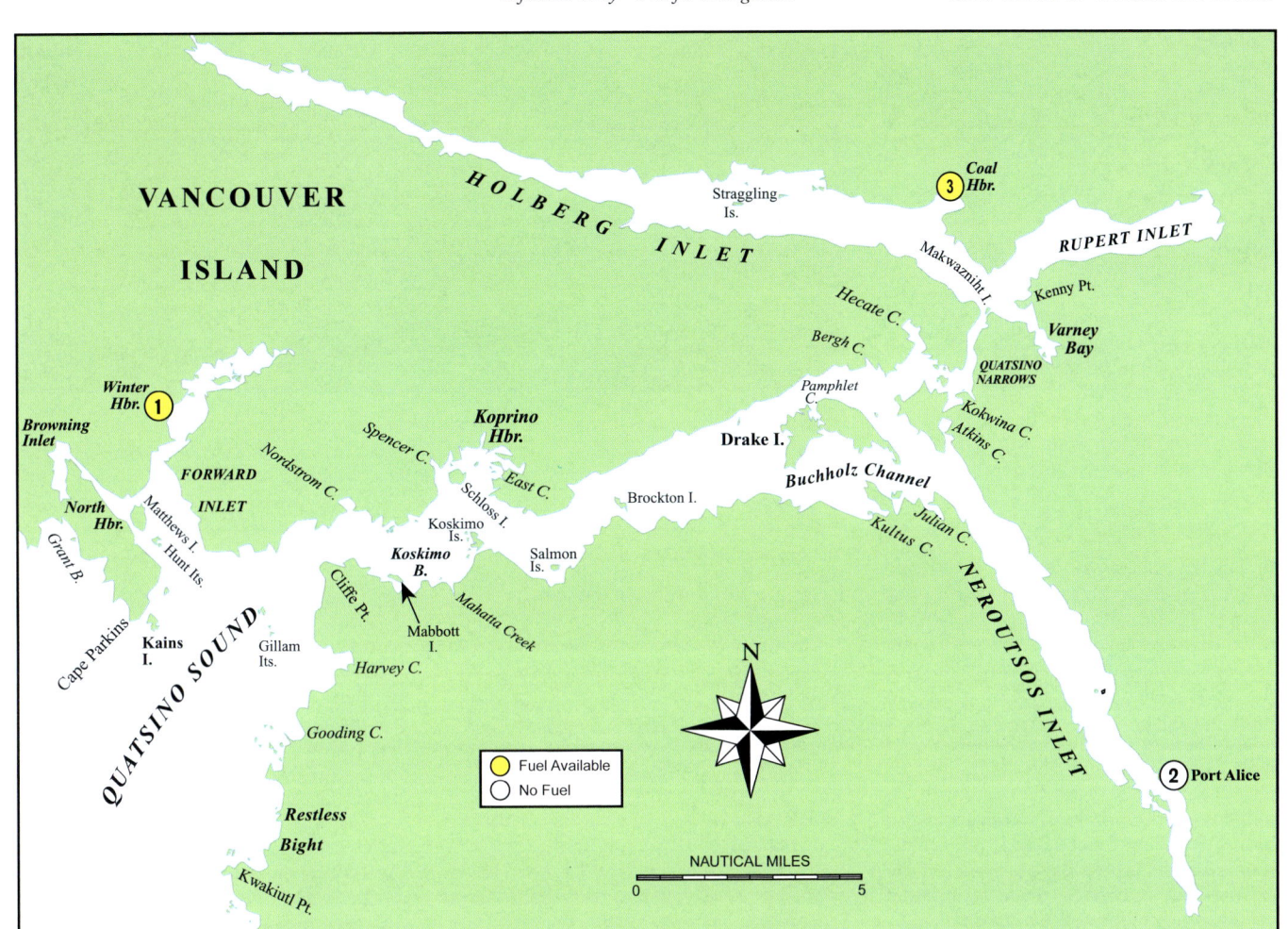

Quatsino Sound

ramp to the south. Moorage is available in members' vacant slips. Slips are generally not available in July and August. Boats that have been trailered to Port Alice cannot stay at the yacht club.

Although the yacht club is designed primarily for smaller boats, it may have room for larger boats if two adjacent moorage spaces are open. A volunteer worker may point you to your slip, help you tie up, then show you around town. Good water and 20 amp power on the docks. If you come in after hours, the gate is locked but the phone numbers of volunteers are posted. A public park with picnic tables and playground equipment is immediately to the north. We were told that boats can anchor south of the Frigon Islets.

Quatsino Narrows. Quatsino Narrows connects with Rupert Inlet and Holberg Inlet, and the village of Coal Harbour. With tidal streams near Makwazniht Island running to 9 knots on the flood and 8 knots on the ebb, it is best to take the narrows near slack. Predictions for Quatsino Narrows are shown as a secondary station based on Tofino in Canadian Tide & Current Tables Vol. 6, and Ports and Passes. You'll find considerable turbulence near Makwazniht Island. The range on the eastern shore of the narrows is for large ships with 30-foot drafts; small boats need not stay on the range. Turbulence, though less than that found near Makwazniht Island, is present near the south entrance to Quatsino Narrows. At slack water, watch for tugs with log boom tows.

Varney Bay. Varney Bay, at the mouth of the Marble River and east of the north entrance to Quatsino Narrows, is scenic, tranquil and protected. A dinghy ride up the Marble River is worth a trip through Quatsino Narrows. Anchor inside Kenny Point behind the 3-meter island, and watch for rocks and deadheads as you enter. Varney Bay is a fish preserve. No fishing. Correspondents Gil and Karen Flanagan add this report: "After you cross the rather large delta, the Marble River flows through a canyon. The river has undercut some of the canyon walls, forming fantastic caverns. We went up the river about 2.7 miles to a rapids, where we found a huge cavern, measuring at least 30 feet by 30 feet. A must-see." To ensure enough water to safely cross the delta and reach the cavern, plan to be at the rapids as close to high tide as possible.

Rupert Inlet. Rupert Inlet is the site of the giant Utah Mines open pit copper mine, now closed and flooded.

③ **Coal Harbour**. Coal Harbour has a small village with launch ramp, marina, and museum. It is 8 miles by road from Port Hardy.

Thrice-daily bus service to Port Hardy, with connections to Port McNeill, leaves from the village.

During World War II, Coal Harbour was a Royal Canadian Air Force seaplane base. The large building on the waterfront was the hangar. The Coal Harbour Whaling Station, the last whale-processing site on the West Coast, later operated out of these same facilities. Whaling operations ceased in 1967. The hangar and adjacent land now serve as seaplane storage, launching facilities, and water taxi service.

Three rooms in the hangar make up a museum, with artifacts, newspaper clippings and photographs from Coal Harbour's years as an RCAF base and a whaling station. Ask at the desk to see it. If you're lucky you'll get a guided tour. No charge. The large whale jawbone shown in photos of Coal Harbour has been repaired and is on display in the hanger. Recommended.

③ **Quatsino First Nations Dock**. 322 Quattishe Road, Coal Harbour, BC V0N 1K0; (250) 949-6870; Moorage, gas, diesel, water, some 20 amp power. Showers and laundry facilities available beyond the wharfinger office. The floats can be busy with commercial boats. Floats can accommodate vessels up to 60 feet.

2023 Waggoner Cruising Guide 379

WEST COAST OF VANCOUVER ISLAND

See Area Map Page 381 - Maps Not for Navigation

Holberg Inlet is 18 miles long, narrow and deep, a classic fjord. It has few places to anchor, and not much for the cruising yachtsman. With its 36-mile round trip and no facilities or attractions, it is seldom traveled by cruising yachts.

Quatsino Village. The public dock at Quatsino Village is mostly for smaller boats and loading/unloading. We tucked into the only larger space available only to be shouted at by a taxi boat operator who appeared to have plenty of space to maneuver. We walked into the village and to the 1898 Anglican church, open for visitors. A small museum and snack shop are open one hour per day, several days a week. Chart 3681 shows the details for entry. Room to anchor off the dock if necessary.

BROOKS BAY

Brooks Bay is between Quatsino Sound and Brooks Peninsula. It's about 19 miles from a departure point south of Kains Island (at the entrance to Quatsino Sound) to a point about 2 miles west of Solander Island. Depending on the course chosen, it's another 22 to 25 miles from Solander Island to Walters Cove—a total of at least 40 miles in the open sea. If wind and seas are favorable, those heading south will want to seize the opportunity to round Brooks Peninsula. They can be excused for not exploring Brooks Bay. If the weather is unfavorable, Brooks Bay is a good place to explore while waiting for a weather window. If you have the time, it is recommended.

Two inlets, Klaskino Inlet and Klaskish Inlet, are beautiful and have good anchorage, although portions of Klaskino Inlet have been logged. Brooks Bay is dotted with unmarked (but charted) rocks and reefs that make navigation exciting. Plot courses carefully.

④ **Klaskino Inlet.** Assuming an approach from the north, leave Lawn Point approximately 2 miles to port. (Lawn Point's grassy-looking slopes are in fact covered with low bushes). Continue, leaving Scarf Reef to port. Then turn to leave Rugged Islets to starboard. Turn to pass midway between Buoys *M17* and *M18*, then turn to enter Klaskino Inlet.

For a quick anchorage, skirt around Anchorage Island into Klaskino Anchorage or into the small bight north of Klaskino Anchorage.

If you'd like to explore further, go through Scouler Pass. Use the more open northern channel, leaving Buoy *M23* to port. The kelp will be close enough to hold your attention. Anchor in the bight between the 67- and 53-meter islands, in the area shown as 7 meters at zero tide. The drying flats of the river mouth come up sharply. Be sure you don't swing onto them.

Correspondent Gil Flanagan went all the way to the head of Klaskino Inlet (about 4 miles from Scouler Pass), and recommends the anchorage behind the little island near the head. He says shore access is excellent, with logging roads for walking. Make noise; bears frequent the woods.

Leaving Klaskino Inlet, the safest route is back between Buoys *M17* and *M18*. Although it's possible to take a route westward through Steele Reefs, it is not the safest and can be unnerving with surf crashing over the rocks.

⑤ **Klaskish Inlet.** If you run from Quatsino Sound directly to Klaskish Inlet, your probable course will take you very near to Hughes Rock, which dries 5 feet. Hughes Rock is clearly shown on the chart. Don't run over it.

Consider anchoring in magnificent Klaskish Basin, reached through a knockout, must-see narrow gorge with vertical rock sides overhung with dense forest. Once through, you are separated from the rest of the world. All the mooring buoys shown on the chart have been removed.

Brooks Peninsula. Brooks Peninsula and the waters off Cape Cook are, together with Cape Scott, the most hostile on the west coast of Vancouver Island. Like rounding Cape Scott, rounding the Brooks is a milestone in a circumnavigation. The peninsula itself is a mountainous, rectangular promontory that extends 6 miles out from Vancouver Island, like a growth on the side of an otherwise handsome face. Rocks and reefs guard much of the shoreline. Tangles of driftwood make beaches impassable. Cliffs rise from the beaches. At the tops of the cliffs, wilderness. Much of the peninsula is a provincial park, preserved for its wildness. Twenty thousand years ago, when glaciers covered most of Vancouver Island, the Brooks Peninsula remained ice-free. Plant species wiped out in glaciated areas are still found here.

Cap on the Cape: When a cloud forms on top of Brooks Peninsula over Cape Cook, it often means that strong northwesterly winds will follow.

Cape Cook & Solander Island. Cape Cook is the northwestern tip of Brooks Peninsula.

The entrance to Klaskish Basin is narrow.

Docks at Rumble Beach Marina are within walking distance to Port Alice.

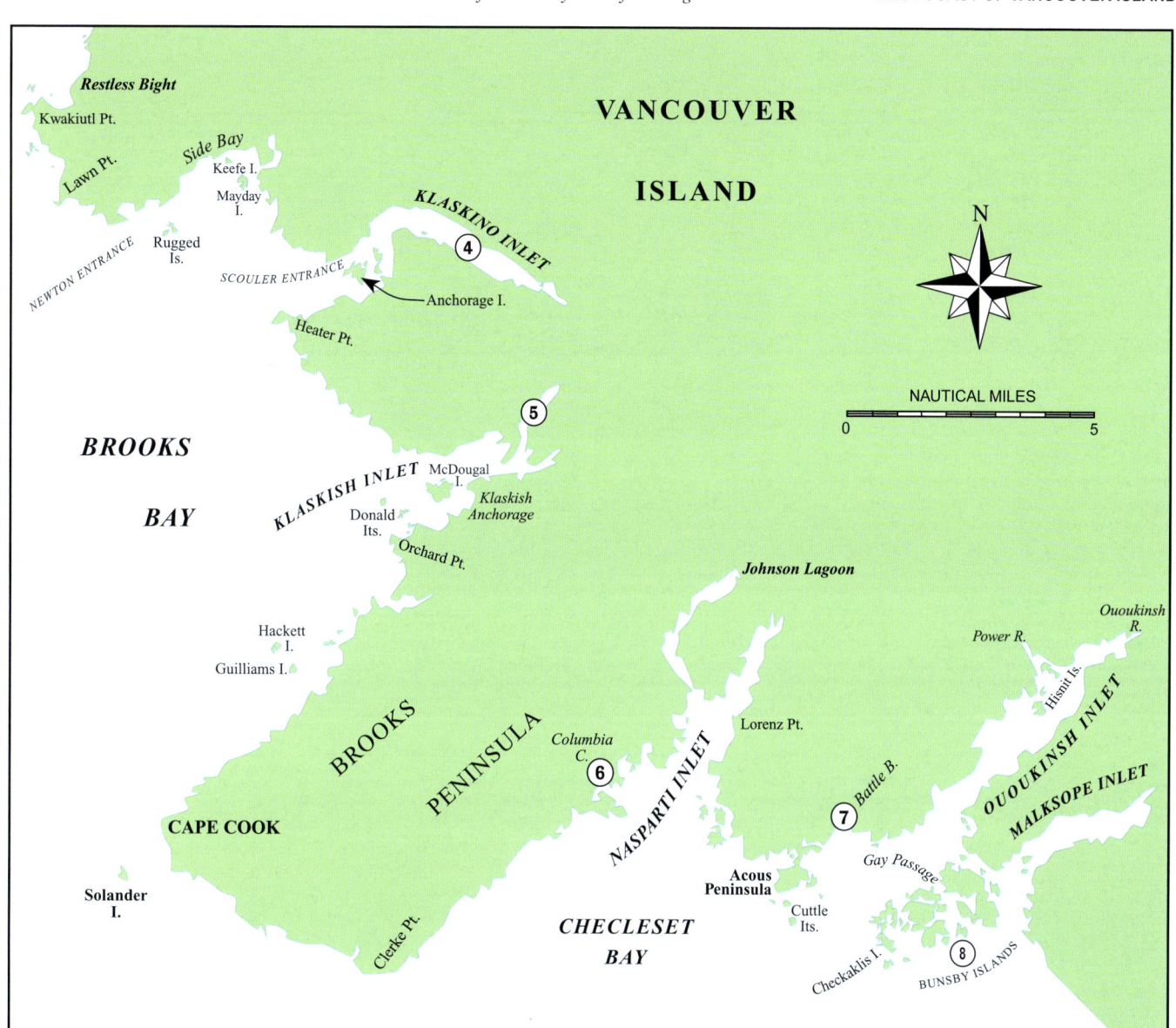

Brooks Peninsula

Rocks and shoals extend offshore from Cape Cook nearly to Solander Island.

The Cape Cook/Solander Island area can be a dangerous patch of water. When conflicting currents meet accelerating winds, conditions can sink a boat. Cape Cook has driven back large ships. The marine weather broadcasts often talk of "local winds off the headlands." The headland they have in mind is Cape Cook. While no headland on the West Coast should be taken lightly, Cape Cook (and Cape Scott) should be given the greatest respect. If conditions sound questionable, wait. When your opportunity comes, seize it.

On all but the quietest days, the safe route past Cape Cook is well offshore from Solander Island. If you are one of the rare lucky ones to round the Brooks on a quiet day and can approach Solander Island more closely, you'll see Steller sea lions hauled out on the base of the island and puffins swimming near your boat.

Weather information: An automated weather station on Solander Island provides wind speed and direction, updated hourly. Listen to the continuous marine broadcast for the latest weather information.

Clerke Point. Clerke Point marks the southeast corner of Brooks Peninsula. Shoals extend at least 0.5 mile offshore. Following the 20-fathom curve will leave ample room for safety. The pyramid-shaped seas we had battled at Solander Island disappeared completely by Clerke Point.

Once past Brooks Peninsula, the winds slacken, the weather warms and conditions improve.

CHECLESET BAY

Checleset Bay has a number of anchorages, including the Shelter Sheds, Columbia Cove, and the Bunsby Islands. If you have just rounded Brooks Peninsula, Shelter Sheds or Columbia Cove are good stops. Columbia Cove is exceptional.

Shelter Sheds. The Shelter Sheds are lines of reef extending from Brooks Peninsula into Checleset Bay. Fishermen have found shelter in their lee, hence the name. Correspondent Gil Flanagan reports that Shed 4 has by far the finest beach his family has found—better even than West Beach at Hakai. The water was near 70° F. A trail leads to Columbia Cove, but Correspondents Steve and Elsie Hulsizer report that windfall has made the trail difficult, especially the first 200 yards.

⑥ **Columbia Cove.** Beautiful Columbia Cove is known locally as Peddlers Cove. Neither name is on the chart. The cove is immediately north of Jackobson Point, snugged up against the base of Brooks Peninsula. Depths in Columbia Cove are shallower than charted.

Be sure to enter between Jackobson Point and the 215-foot island. Columbia Cove has experienced some silting over the years and anchoring room has become limited. The mouth of the cove, between Jackobson Point and the 215-foot island, is safe in a northwesterly. In southerlies, winds and waves

WEST COAST OF VANCOUVER ISLAND

make this area uncomfortable, leaving room for only about three boats in the cove itself. Columbia Cove is a voluntary no-discharge zone. Please volunteer.

The name Columbia Cove comes from Captain Robert Gray's ship Columbia, which overnighted here twice. If you think Columbia Cove is crowded with three boats, now imagine it with the Columbia, the schooner Adventure, and the ship Margaret, of Boston, all at the same time. A sometimes muddy trail across the small peninsula formed by Jackobson Point leads to a beautiful sandy ocean beach. Great beachcombing. Take the dinghy up the stream to the trailhead, but watch the tide. You can be stranded, with a long walk across tideflats dragging your dinghy or kayak.

Weather Note: When strong winds from the northwest are forecast south of Brooks Peninsula, the Brooks provides a lee for Columbia Cove and adjacent waters. Winds may be strong but seas will be quiet. It's a good place to wait out a northwest gale. It's not a good place to wait out a southeast gale.

⑦ **Battle Bay.** Battle Bay, north of the Bunsby Islands, has acceptable anchorages roughly off the Indian reserve, and in the nook that makes up the northeast shore. Approach the Longback Islands before making your turn into Battle Bay. One interesting anchorage is immediately west of Battle Bay, against the east shore of Acous Peninsula. To reach that anchorage, leave the Skirmish Islands to starboard as you approach. From there you'll look across a sea of islands and rocks to the Bunsbys.

The Indian Reserve on the Acous Peninsula is the former home of the Checleset Band, now located in Walters Cove. You can find fallen totem poles serving as nurse logs, and the depressions of old Longhouses.

⑧ **Bunsby Islands.** "Did you get to the Bunsbys?" That's what people ask when they learn you've been down the west coast of Vancouver Island. Don't disappoint them by saying no. The Bunsby Islands are rocky, rugged, and beautiful. They were named

Brooks Peninsula is famous for high winds and rough water. It demands respect.

for a character in the Charles Dickens novel *Dombey and Son.* A number of other features in the area also carry names from that novel.

Study the chart and know your location at all times. Enter the Bunsby Islands only through Gay Passage. Two anchorages are off this passage: either the cove in the southern island or the slightly larger bay in the northern island. Enter the northern island's bay favoring the north shore to avoid a shoal extending from the south side. In this larger bay, note the rock directly beneath the 6-fathom sounding. The lagoon adjacent to this bay may be fine for an adventuresome trailerable boat.

The cove on the west side of Gay Passage is guarded by two rocks that dry 4 feet. The rocks are easy to identify and avoid if you're paying attention. The cove has room for several boats.

Checleset Bay has a large population of sea otters, the successful result of a 1969 effort to re-establish these delightful creatures. From the Bunsbys, where they were first re-introduced, the sea otters have spread up and down the coast, as far south as Barkley Sound and as far north as the Cape Caution area on the mainland. You'll sometimes see them in "rafts," groups of otters hanging together, in kelp beds.

If weather allows, take the dinghy or kayak around the islands. The rugged, windswept rocks and islets are too stunning to try to describe. It's easy to get disoriented. Carry a chart, compass, handheld GPS and handheld VHF radio.

KYUQUOT SOUND

With the exception of the outer islands and Rugged Point, Kyuquot (pronounced "Ki-YU-kit") Sound is protected and pretty, surrounded by high mountains, with easy waters. On the inside, Dixie Cove and Don Douglass' "Petroglyph Cove" (known locally as Blue Lips Cove) are excellent anchorages, and several others are attractive. The settlement of Walters Cove is a favorite.

From the south, enter Kyuquot Sound past Whistle Buoy *M38.* Leave the buoy to starboard, and proceed through Kyuquot Channel. Most visiting pleasure craft, however, will approach from the north and stop at Walters Cove before entering Kyuquot Sound proper.

⑨ **Walters Cove.** For communication, call on VHF channels 06 or 14. The little settlement of Walters Cove has almost everything you might need after a week or two of working your way along the coast: outpost hospital, ice, charts, a small general store, pay phone, a restaurant and coffee shop, relaxed and friendly people, happy kids and lazy dogs. The store at the public dock, on the south side, is open Monday, Wednesday and Friday; and the store above the dock, on the Kyuquot side, is open evenings only. The Kyuquot Inn Restaurant, also known as Java The Hutt, is open daily with free Wi-Fi for customers; cash only.

One thing Walters Cove does not have is liquor. Walters Cove is dry, by vote of the Kyuquot Native community, and there's not a drop to be bought. Nor is liquor in evidence, even on the dock.

Another thing you won't find is fuel. Be sure you have enough fuel in your tanks. The nearest fuel is in Fair Harbour.

From seaward, the safest approach to

Solander Island off Cape Cook, the Cape of Storms, on a rare calm summer afternoon.

The Bunsby Islands are not to be missed. The rugged scenery and sandy beaches are a highlight of the west coast of Vancouver Island.

Walters Cove in all weather is to enter via Brown Channel. Go through Brown Channel and turn on a course to leave Ahmacinnit Island to starboard (caution for charted rocks and reefs). Work your way past the east side of Walters Island and into Walters Cove.

Boats coming south from the Bunsby Islands probably will follow a route along the Vancouver Island shoreline, leaving McLean Island to port and the rock just east of McLean Island to starboard. Turn to port to pass Chief Rock Buoy *M29* to port (caution for charted rocks and reefs). Enter Walters Cove after passing the east side of Walters Island.

Take note of the charted rock awash at 10 ft (50°03'06"N/ 127°27'07"W). This rock is along your probable shoreline passage course. At a depth of 10 feet at zero tide the rock is not a concern for most boats, but you should know it's there.

Entry to Walters Cove can be a tricky matter. Although it is marked by buoys and a daybeacon, the channel past the east side of Walters Island is easy to misread, and the unwary skipper could be on a rock. When following the rule of Red, Right, Returning, entry is safe. The one daybeacon along the way marks the narrow passage that leads directly into Walters Cove. Don't cut it close. Remember that beacons are attached to the earth; rock extends well into the passage from the beacon. Use a mid-channel course favoring the north side between the beacon and the 51-meter island opposite. The chart makes the route clear.

Several locals insist, "Don't anchor in Walters Cove!" The bottom, they say, is foul with debris. Furthermore, the floor of the bay is crisscrossed by high voltage submarine electrical cables, a Telus phone line, and the water lines serving the community.

Instead of anchoring, tie up at the Walters Cove Public Wharf to port as you enter. Long mooring floats are on each side of the public wharf. The general store and post office is at the head of the wharf. Open Monday, Wednesday, and Friday 1:00 p.m. to 5:00 p.m. Stock arrives once per week.

Java the Hutt Coffee Shop, which began its life as a "boat-through" rather than "drive-through" coffee shop on the Kyuquot Inn dock, is now located in the renovated school house at the inn with an expanded menu. They serve coffee, pastries and a variety of burgers and salads. Free Wi-Fi is provided. Showers are available at the inn. Owner Eric Gorbman is among one of the friendliest people on the coast.

The best time to arrive at Walters Cove is Thursday afternoon. The *Uchuck III* arrives that day, sometime around 5:00 p.m., depending on the other stops they have scheduled. Walters Cove becomes a bustle of activity when the ship lands, with skiffs arriving from all over the cove and outlying areas.

Watching the *Uchuck III* unload its cargo is a slice of West Coast life you won't want to miss. Everyone pitches in. Fuel barrels, boxes, even washers and dryers are loaded off the boat's starboard side into waiting skiffs. Pallets of groceries are loaded off the port side onto carts on the dock.

Because the ship overnights at Walters Cove, passengers spend the night at lodges and B&Bs. For dinner, passengers eat at the Java The Hutt Coffee Shop. When there is space, the Java The Hutt also feeds boaters, guests at the lodges, and anyone else who asks by mid-afternoon. Dinner is delicious. Guests eat family-style at a long table.

For medical matters, contact the VIHA (Vancouver Island Health Authority) outpost hospital at Walters Cove, (250) 332-5289.

Good water is available at the store for a small fee.

The Kyuquot Band Native community of approximately 200 is across the bay, served by its own public dock. We met a resident of the Native community who told us that she operates a small store near the head of the dock selling snacks, soft drinks, some groceries and native crafts.

All transport is by boat in Walters Cove, and from an early age the Kyuquot children (and Native children all along the coast) are accomplished boat handlers. Their outboard-powered craft seem to have but two directions: forward and reverse; and two throttle settings: full-power and off.

Walters Cove has been a popular gathering place for decades. Years ago it was home to five fish camps in the summer. When people were stuck in port waiting for the weather to break, the talk flowed. Long ago Walters Cove got its local name of Bull---t Bay, BS Bay in polite company. A cafe in Walters Cove was called the BS Cafe.

⑨ **Walters Cove Resort.** (250) 332-5274; (250) 287-2223; gofishing@walterscoveresort.com; www.walterscoveresort.com. Monitors VHF 78A. Open in summer with moorage for those staying at the lodge; water, ice, Wi-Fi. No power. Reservations required. This is a first class fishing lodge. Fishing charters and fish packing available.

Barter Cove. Barter Cove, in the Mission Group islands outside Walters Cove, is open, unprotected and not as interesting as anchorages inside Kyuquot Sound. Leave Ahmacinnit Island and the tiny islet east of Ahmacinnit Island to starboard, and feel your way in.

Kamils Anchorage. Kamils Anchorage in the Mission Group islands is more exposed than Barter Cove. Enter, very carefully, through Favourite Entrance.

Amos Island. From Walters Cove, the easiest entrance to Kyuquot Sound is around the east

The public wharf at Walters Cove. The building at the head of the wharf is a post office and well-stocked store.

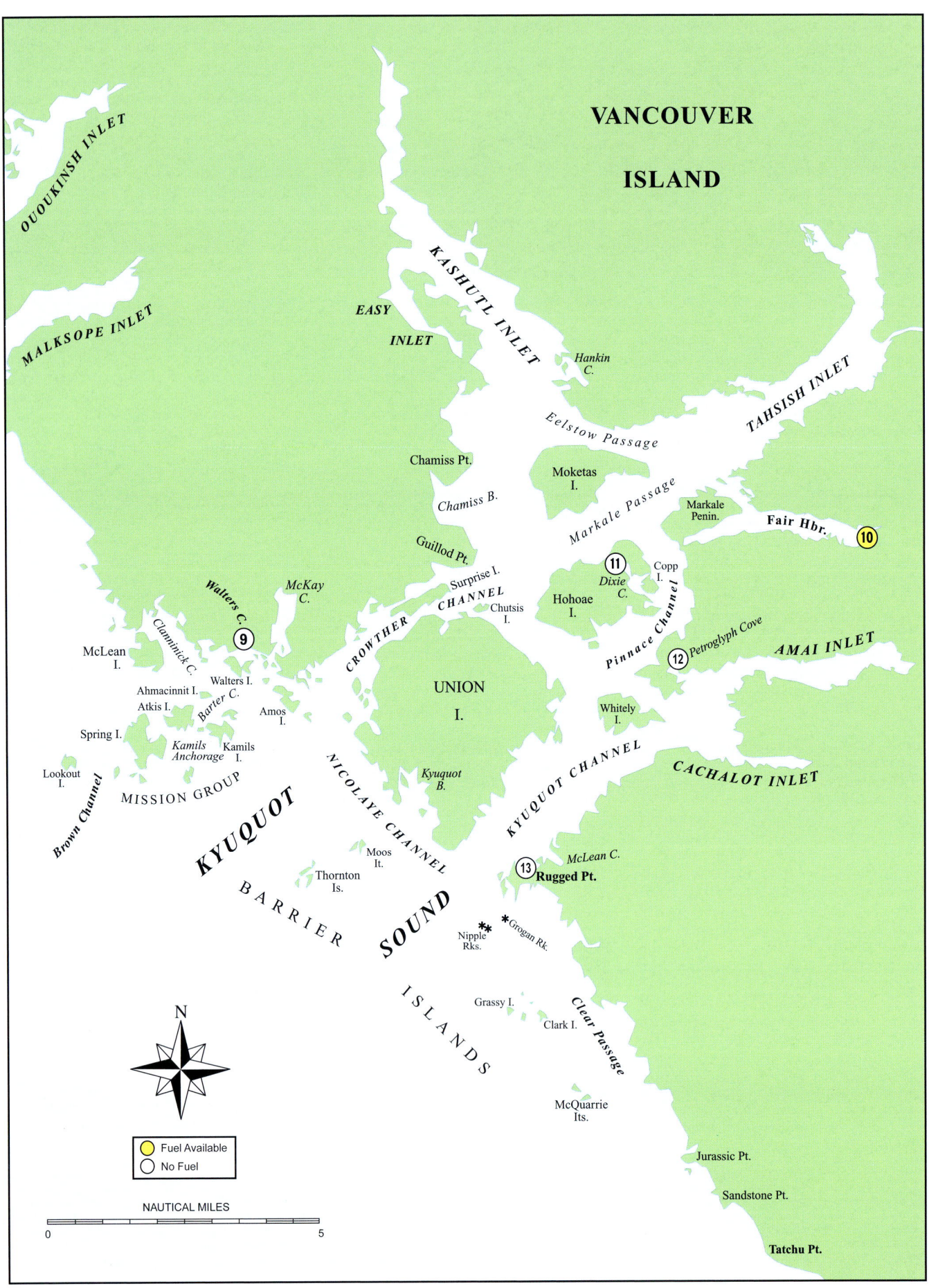

Kyuquot Sound

side of Amos Island into Crowther Channel. Use Chart 3651 to identify the channel between Walters Cove and Nicolaye Channel, then Chart 3682 to find the route past Amos Island. The passage east of Amos Island is deep but narrow, and bounded by rocks. The first time through can be unsettling, but after you've done it once, it's easy.

Surprise Island. Surprise Island, steep, round, and logged off to stumps, is located in Crowther Channel. On the south side of Surprise Island, Crowther Channel is deep and open, but on the north side a narrow passage is interesting. At zero tide least depths in this passage are approximately 18 feet. A ledge of rock, shown on the chart, extends from the north shore. Favor the Surprise Island side all the way through.

Hankin Cove. Hankin Cove is located near the mouth of Kashutl Inlet, on the east side. It is a beautiful little cove with good holding and completely protected. Stands of small trees covering the hillsides show evidence of past logging. Correspondents Gil and Karen Flanagan anchored in the southeast cove, and add, "Chart 3682 is way off on the shoal in this cove. The shoal extends only halfway across from the east shore. Depths are 12 to 18 feet along the west shore, almost to the south end of the cove."

⑩ **Fair Harbour.** Enter Fair Harbour south of Karouk Island, leaving the two lighted beacons to port. The passage north of the island has two reported rocks, not shown on the chart.

Fair Harbour has a wide launch ramp at the head, with a small campground and ample parking. A dirt road leads from Zeballos to Fair Harbour, the only road access to Kyuquot Sound. This is a popular trailer boat launch point. A good-sized public wharf, with a long float, is at the head. If the float is full, anchor in approximately 60 feet.

⑩ **Fair Harbour Marina & Campground.** (250) 483-3382; fairharbourmarina@gmail.com; www.gatewaytokyuquot.com. Open all year. Limited moorage, gas, diesel, propane, water, garbage drop, boat launch. No power on the docks. This is the only fuel in Kyuquot Sound. A small store carries fishing tackle, ice, convenience food. For-fee Wi-Fi; complimentary for paying customers.

⑪ **Dixie Cove.** Dixie Cove indents the east side of Hohoae Island, and is a wonderful anchorage. Enter south of Copp Island, through a narrow but deep passage to the first of two anchorages. The outer anchorage is approximately 30 feet deep, with good holding. Another narrow passage leads to the inner cove, completely secluded, with rock cliffs on one side. Depths here are approximately 18 feet, mud bottom with excellent holding. Landing on shore is a problem, so you're restricted to the boat. As a place to put the hook down, though, Dixie Cove is highly recommended.

⑫ **Petroglyph Cove** (Blue Lips Cove). In his excellent book, *Exploring Vancouver Island's West Coast*, Don Douglass describes this previously-unnamed anchorage and calls it "Petroglyph Cove." In the second edition of his book, Douglass acknowledged that others had not been able to find the petroglyphs. Hulsizer reported finding what looked like a faded pictograph (red ochre painting) and noted that the local name for the cove is Blue Lips Cove—because when residents went swimming the water was so cold their lips turned blue. Petroglyph, Pictograph or Blue Lips, the cove is located near the mouth of Amai Inlet, roughly due west of Amai Point. The narrow entry is hidden until you're right on it. The channel shallows to a least depth of 12 to 18 feet, but has no hazards. Once inside you are protected. While in our opinion Petroglyph Cove is not as pretty as Dixie Cove, it is an excellent spot.

Volcanic Cove. Exposed to the north, small, no room to swing. Temporary only for small boats, in our view.

⑬ **Rugged Point Marine Park.** Rugged Point marks the southern entrance to Kyuquot Sound. Our notes read, "Wow!" The beaches on the ocean side are spectacular, and deserve a visit. Anchor along the inside beaches in 18 feet on a kelp-covered hard sand bottom, and dinghy ashore. The Pacific swell, though diminished, can get into the anchorage. The anchorage is protected from southeasterlies and westerlies but is subject to occasional nighttime outflow winds. Be sure you anchor far enough offshore to avoid swinging onto shallows if outflow winds develop.

A trail, now upgraded with a boardwalk, leads through the park to the ocean beaches. Bear and cougar prints have been sighted, so be noisy. Once on the ocean beach, you will find a series of paths leading around headlands all the way to the Kapoose Creek. Some of the paths are steep and involve climbing ladders or using ropes for assistance.

Cachalot. Cachalot, the site of a former industrial whaling center, makes an interesting lunch stop or afternoon exploration. Locate it by finding the abandoned pilings between Cachalot Inlet to the east and Cachalot Creek to the west. Although pronounced locally as "catch a lot," the name means sperm whale in French (and in French would be pronounced "caa-shaa-low"). The whaling center operated between 1907 and 1926, then served as a pilchard reduction plant until the 1940s.

Anchor off the old pilings in 30 to 60 feet of water and take the dinghy ashore. You'll find old whale bones, crockery, and miscellaneous hardware on the beach, and rusty equipment in the forest. Next to the creek, a ferrocement statue of a sperm whale serves as a memorial to the whales that were processed at this site. The statue was placed there by Vancouver Island artist Wayne Adams in the 1970s. Hulsizer gives the history of the site in her book *Voyages to Windward*.

When anchoring, avoid the drying shoal on the north end of the site near the river and be sure to anchor in at least 30 feet of water to avoid your anchor being entangled in kelp.

Kyuquot Sound to Esperanza Inlet. Depending on the course chosen, it is approximately 13.5 miles between Rugged Point and the entrance to Gillam Channel, which leads into Esperanza Inlet. In good visibility the route through Clear Passage is smooth and interesting. In poor visibility, we would head seaward from Rugged Point to entrance Buoy *M38*, then turn southeastward toward Gillam Channel.

Clear Passage to Tatchu Point. Clear Passage takes you about 4 miles along the coast in waters protected by the Barrier Islands, past a steady display of rugged rocks and rock islets. The channel is free of hazards. To enter Clear Passage, leave Grogan Rock to starboard, watching carefully for the rock to port, marked by kelp, that dries at 4 feet. Heading down-island, we got a little close to Grogan Rock, and the depths came up sharply. We moved off to port and they went back down. You will have no trouble identifying Grogan Rock. It is an awful 23-foot-high black pinnacle and it commands attention. Lay a course to take you north of McQuarrie Islets, and exit Clear Passage leaving McQuarrie

Fair Harbour, home to Fair Harbour Marina with the only fuel in Kyuquot Sound.

WEST COAST OF VANCOUVER ISLAND

See Area Map Page 387 - Maps Not for Navigation

At anchor in lovely Hankin Cove

Islets to starboard. The rocks and islets along Clear Passage all look alike. It helps to plot a waypoint at the spot where you intend to turn to exit past McQuarrie Islets. Clear Passage is also a good route when heading north. Leave McQuarrie Islets and Grogan Rock to port.

The island just south of Grassy Isle is a good place to hunt fossils. "We anchored south of Clark Island and took the dinghy ashore to a shell beach on the southeast corner of the island. The fossils were just lying on the beach. We recommend doing this on a calm day only. With a more detailed metric chart, it might be possible to find anchorage between Grassy Isle and Clark." [*Hulsizer*]

Local fishermen say the waters from Jurassic Point past Tatchu Point can be an "ugly patch of water." Use caution and careful judgment.

⑭ **Rolling Roadstead** (Catala Island Provincial Park). Rolling Roadstead offers acceptable anchorage in fair weather. From the west the approach can be tricky. Douglass describes the approach in his book. Careful navigation is called for, including the finding and identifying of the various rocks and reefs in the entrance. The hazards are easily identified, either by the breaking surf or kelp growing in the shallows. With the hazards accounted for, the entry is reported to be safe. All agree that it should be run in fair weather only, with good visibility.

If you're coming down from Tatchu Point, especially in a fresh westerly, it's easier to enter via Gillam Channel, leaving Black Rock and Entrance Reef to port and approach Rolling Roadstead from the southwest. Anchor in the lee of the point of land that juts abruptly from Catala Island.

Catala Island, which protects Rolling Roadstead, is a provincial marine park. The beach on Catala Island is beautiful. Several sea caves are accessible.

Gillam Channel. Gillam Channel, more than one-half mile wide and well-buoyed, is the safe entrance to Esperanza Inlet. Approaching, leave the entrance buoy *M40* and buoy *M42*, which marks the west end of Blind Reef, to starboard. Leave buoy *M41* to port, and continue into Esperanza Inlet.

ESPERANZA INLET

Esperanza Inlet is on the west side of Nootka Island, and ultimately connects with Nootka Sound. The inlet is part of the "inside route" through this portion of the coast. This route is served by three communities—Zeballos, Tahsis, and Gold River—and by the Esperanza Mission, with its fuel dock and excellent water. The waterways are beautiful, and contain several good stopping places. Tahsis Narrows connects Esperanza Inlet with Tahsis Inlet on the Nootka Sound side, and is not difficult to run.

Nuchatlitz Inlet. Reader Don Thain reports that Mary Basin is a delightful and protected anchorage with good holding in mud. A pretty waterfall on Laurie Creek is reachable by dinghy on a 7-foot tide. The inner basin is a tidal lagoon.

⑮ **Nuchatlitz Provincial Park.** Nuchatlitz Provincial Park is a beautiful and interesting stop with a well-protected anchorage. It's a favorite among kayakers and campers. The area contains a number of archeological treasures, including burial canoes on land and burial caves on the outer islands.

The entry to Nuchatlitz is very complex with numerous rocks and reefs; a careful study of the charts is warranted. Inside, a large bay has a uniform bottom with approximately 30- to 40-foot anchoring depths. In good weather, if you choose an anchoring spot where you can see over the islands towards the northwest, you may be rewarded with a magnificent sunset. The anchorage can be absolutely calm when the wind dies in the evening, but you can hear the surf breaking on the outer islands.

The abandoned Indian village of Nuchatlitz is on the shore of a 44-meter island marked Indian Reserve, above a marvelous beach. At low tide you can walk the drying sand bar from the reserve island to a second 44-meter island to the west. Although the village was moved from this site to Espinosa in the 1980s, the site is still visited by the band. Local kayak tours use it as a landing site.

A number of private homes dot the shores of a privately-owned unmarked island on the south side of the anchorage. Private buoys mark the route past submerged rocks to homes on the island's back side and to a shallow lagoon. Use Chart 3676, which reflects hydrographic survey work performed between 1992 and 1996 at the cost of many survey launch propellers.

The easy but long entry to Nuchatlitz is from the northeast, passing east of Rosa Island. From there the chart makes the course clear: Follow the winding channel east of the 37-meter and 34-meter islands, and east of the two red spar buoys *M46* and *M48* (Red, Right, Returning). At Buoy *M48* the bay opens up. Both Douglass and Yeadon-Jones describe a second, more direct entrance, leaving the light on the 37-meter island (known locally as Entrance Island) to starboard as you enter.

⑯ **Queen Cove.** Queen Cove is a short distance inside the entrance to Port Eliza, the first inlet to port as you enter Esperanza Inlet. It is a safe and satisfying spot to put the hook down and go exploring, although not as beautiful as Nuchatlitz on the east side of Gillam Channel. Queen Cove is a popular anchorage among island circumnavigators. Anchor here and you'll soon have company. The cove is well protected, and has excellent holding in 20 to 40 feet. It is large enough for several boats to swing. We have received reports that the Queen Cove Band collects a fee for anchorage. A cabin with a dock is at the north end of Queen Cove. The Park River enters at the north end, and makes for good dinghy exploration.

The most protected anchorage is the nook at the south end of Queen Cove, between the little island and the rock that dries at 3.4 meters (11 feet). Swinging room is a little restricted, but the anchorage is workable. We overnighted in Queen Cove, anchored in the wider and much more exposed northern area. At 5:00 p.m. the wind came in, and built to about 25 knots before dying at sundown. We sailed back and forth on our anchor, but we didn't budge. [*Hale*].

Espinosa Inlet. Espinosa Inlet is deep and high-walled. No place to anchor. The Native village of Ocluje is located at its head.

Newton Cove Resort. (877) 337-5464; info@nootkamarineadventures.com; www.nootkamarineadventures.com. Monitors VHF 06. Call for advance reservations. Newton Cove Resort near the mouth of Espinosa Inlet is a fishing resort with services and facilities for resort guests only.

⑰ **Zeballos.** www.zeballos.com. Zeballos (pronounced "Ze-BAH-los") is the most unexpected town on the west coast of Vancouver Island. While other settlements range from fishing camp (Winter Harbour) to bustling town (Tofino), Zeballos stands alone.

The trip up Zeballos Inlet is an especially scenic one, with bulbous-topped odd-shaped

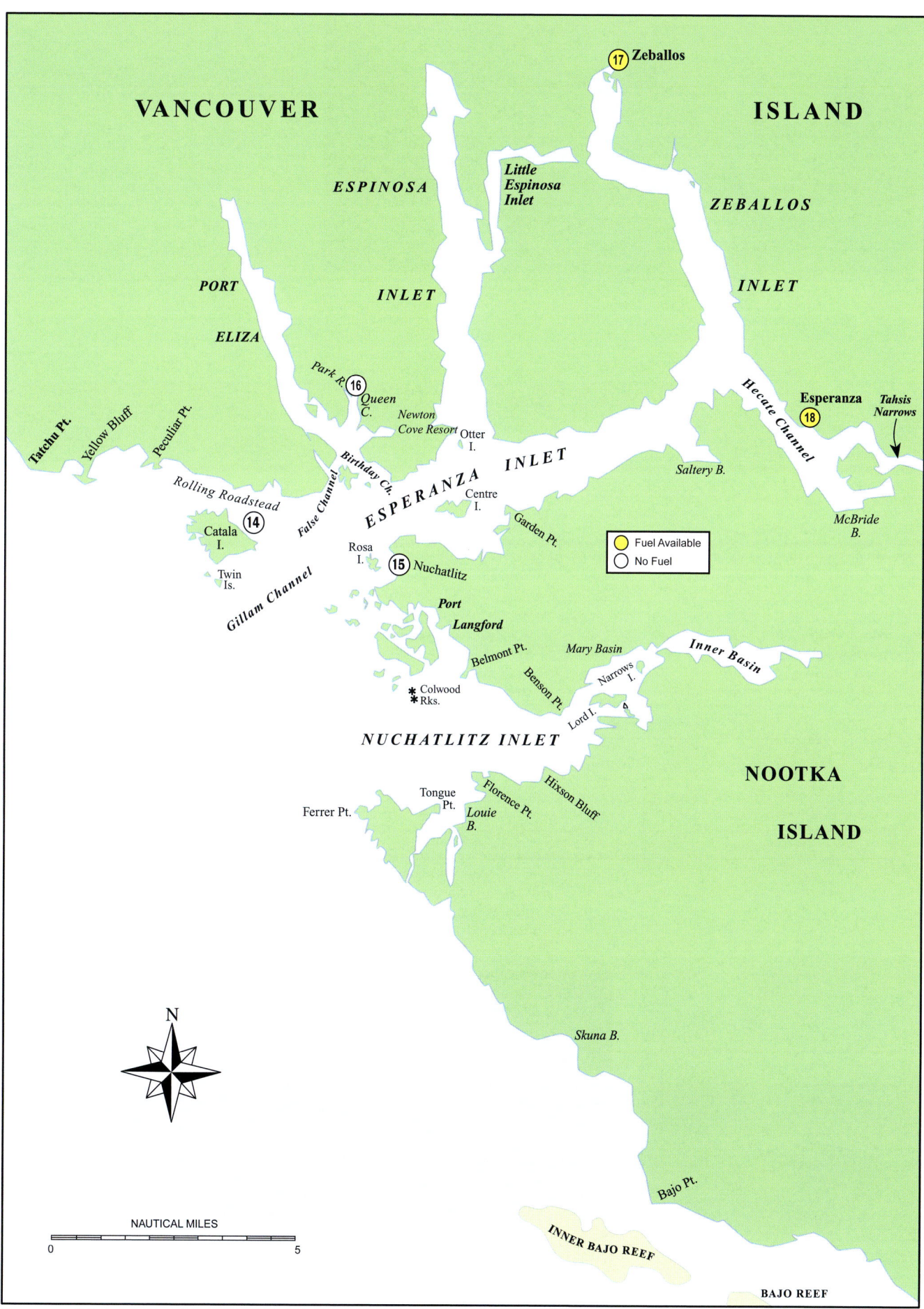

Esperanza Inlet

WEST COAST OF VANCOUVER ISLAND

See Area Map Page 387 - Maps Not for Navigation

Zeballos is bounded by impressive mountains.

mountains, and sheer rock faces rising above the shores. Zeballos is a mining town that looks like Cicily, Alaska, the fictional town made famous by the television show *Northern Exposure*, with wandering streets, false-fronted buildings, and a museum. The town is built at the mouth of the Zeballos River, next to mountains that go *straight up*.

The museum, located on the main road heading out of town, is one of the town's main attractions. It's small but fascinating, with mining paraphernalia, photographs, and a full-scale model of a mine entrance. In past years the museum was staffed by a full-time curator, but in recent years it has not always been open regularly. If you arrive at the museum during the workweek and no one is there, inquire at the municipal hall and someone will give you a tour.

The town constructed a boardwalk trail through the Zeballos River estuary. It's a beautiful walk along the river.

Much gold has been taken out of the highly mineralized mountains around Zeballos. Over dinner at the hotel on our first visit, we talked with a wildcat prospector whose eyes burned bright as he told of pockets of gold still waiting to be taken. He insisted that he didn't have gold fever, *but he knew where the gold was*. [Hale]

Tie up at the public dock, to the right of the fuel dock as you approach. Pay telephones are at the head of the dock and on the seaplane dock. The village has a wharf to the left of the fuel dock, but it is for large vessels, loading and unloading only. The small float next to the wharf is for short-term (a few hours) tie-up. A bird-viewing platform overlooks the estuary.

A fish-processing plant is shoreward of the fuel dock and is one of the town's economic mainstays. It's a good place to purchase chipped ice.

Provisioning: Cruising boaters often ask whether they should stop at Zeballos or Tahsis for provisioning. The answer is you may need to stop at both for everything you need. At present, no good store exists in Zeballos. The store near the fuel dock carries ice cream and convenience foods, as well as frozen meat and bread, and liquor. The Rosa Island General Store also offers limited items including staples, snacks, and cigarettes. Fruits and vegetables may be in short supply at both stores. Zeballos is a good place to spend the night. The inlet leading to the town is long and beautiful. There's no point going both ways in one day.

⑰ **Zeballos Fuel Dock Inc.** P.O. Box 100, Zeballos, BC V0P 2A0; (250) 761-4201. Open all year. Gasoline, diesel, propane, kerosene, petroleum products, some marine supplies. Candace Saulkner is the owner.

⑰ **Village of Zeballos Municipal Wharf.** (250) 761-4229. Open all year. For large vessels, loading and unloading only. The small float next to the wharf is for short-term (a few hours) tie-up. Some overnight moorage with permission. Access to power and water if absolutely necessary.

⑰ **Zeballos Small Craft Harbour.** P.O. Box 99, Zeballos, BC V0P 2A0; (250) 761-4333. Monitors VHF 06. Open all year with 400 feet of moorage, 30 amp power, year-round washrooms & showers, water, waste oil collection, all tide launch ramp, long term parking (launch ramp is run by the village). A sign on the east side of the easternmost dock warns of shallow water, but the Hulsizers report finding 2.7 meters when sounding the depth with a lead line at low tide.

⑱ **Esperanza (Nootka Mission).** P.O. Box 368, Tahsis, BC V0P 1X0; (250) 483-4162; www.esperanza.ca. info@esperanza.ca Monitors VHF 06. Fuel dock open all year from 7:00 a.m. to 9:00 p.m. with gasoline, diesel, lube oil. Excellent water, phone service and free Wi-Fi for one hour for customers. A small store, with fishing gear and limited groceries, is on the fuel dock; no alcohol or tobacco. Moorage is available at the dock for boats up to 120 feet in front of the old boathouse, except during the month of July; call ahead. The mission runs camps for local children. When a camp is in session, facilities may not be available.

Esperanza is the home of the Nootka Mission. Its story goes back to 1937, when the Shantyman Mission began a hospital at Esperanza. This was in the tradition of the Mission, founded in northern Ontario in 1907 to serve shanty dwellers in outlying areas. The Esperanza hospital no longer operates and the property is now owned by the Esperanza Ministries Association, serving people of the west coast of Vancouver Island.

Zeballos

The floats at Zeballos are well maintained, with power and water.

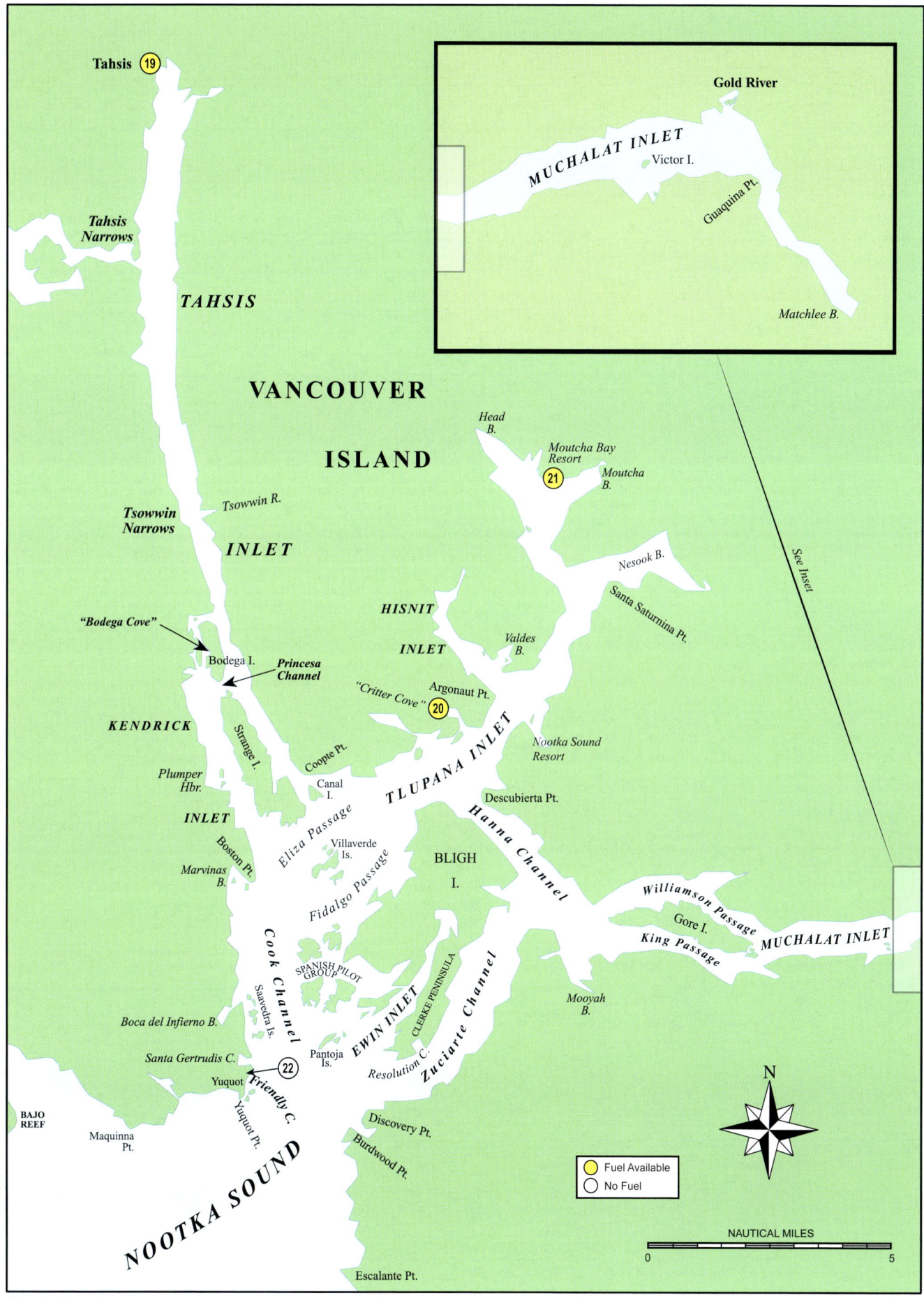

Reference Only – Not for Navigation **WEST COAST OF VANCOUVER ISLAND**

Nootka Sound

WEST COAST OF VANCOUVER ISLAND

The property is immaculately kept. The fuel dock is an important source of revenue.

Inquire about availability for visiting boaters. Showers, washrooms, some 15 amp power, water, ice, and laundry are available. Sometimes, fresh Esperanza-grown produce and canned cheesecake are available for purchase.

Tahsis Narrows. Tahsis Narrows connects the Esperanza Inlet side of Nootka Island with the Nootka Sound side. From the chart, one would think reversing tidal currents rage through the narrows four times a day, but they do not. The narrows are deep and free of hazards, with little tidal current activity. Passage can be made at any time.

TAHSIS INLET

Tahsis Inlet (Tahsis is pronounced with a short-a, as in cat) is long and narrow, and bounded by mountains. The wind funnels and blows up-inlet or down, depending on conditions. The normal situation in prevailing westerly winds is for light or outflow winds in the morning and strong inflow winds in the afternoon, building stronger as you approach the town. But during extended periods of warm weather, strong outflow winds can also develop, especially at night and early morning. Gale-force easterlies rarely reach upper Tahsis Inlet, making it a good place to wait out a storm.

⑲ **Tahsis.** At the head of the inlet the sawmill town of Tahsis once had full facilities, but the mills closed and have been dismantled. The loss of the mills just about killed the town. Now, Tahsis is struggling but surviving. Outsiders bought the houses at bargain prices, which, at least initially, gave the economy a small boost. Through it all, the Westview Marina has remained an outstanding operation.

In town, the Tahsis Supermarket has consolidated many of the operations previously run by others. The Supermarket sells groceries, liquor and fuel. It also has a small cafe. This is a small town, and grocery selection is limited. Tahsis Building Centre, a hardware store, is just north of the Supermarket. A post office is located at the other end of town, near the seaplane dock.

The Tahsis library, in the municipal building, has free Wi-Fi and an excellent view. It's a wonderful place to while away a stormy afternoon.

⑲ **Westview Marina & Lodge.** P.O. Box 248, Tahsis, BC V0P 1X0; (250) 934-7672; (800) 992-3252; info@westviewmarina.com; www.westviewmarina.com. Monitors VHF 06. The fuel dock has gasoline, diesel, lubricants, and marine parts. Mechanic available 24/7. Washrooms, showers, laundry, free Wi-Fi, small store with ice and good gift selection, licensed restaurant with patio, and the Island Attitude Coffee Café. The Café is seasonal and opens Mother's Day weekend. Moorage with 15, 30 & 50 amp power and potable water. Kayak rentals and eco tours. Courtesy car available. Email your provisioning list a week ahead and they'll have it ready for you.

This marina, at the head of Tahsis Inlet, is set up to serve the summer flotilla of small sportfishing boats. Cruisers are welcome, too, and the marina has just about anything a cruising boater might need. Reservations recommended May to September, but the marina will always try to fit you in. The restaurant has live music and steak dinners on Friday nights, June through September. Each year, we hear good things from readers, praising the facilities and the treatment they receive. The marina is neat and attractive, the people helpful, and the fuel dock easy to approach.

Tsowwin Narrows. The major navigation danger in Tahsis Inlet is Tsowwin Narrows, created by the outfall from the Tsowwin River. A beacon marks the edge of the shoal. Pass between that beacon and another beacon on the west shore of the inlet. Remember that beacons are attached to the earth, and shoal water can extend into a channel from a beacon. Give each beacon a good offing. While we did not see much debris, Tahsis Inlet is reported to have considerable drift and deadheads, depending on logging activity. Keep a close watch on the water ahead.

Princesa Channel. Princesa Channel runs between Bodega Island and Strange Island, and connects Tahsis and Kendrick inlets. A route through Princesa Channel gets a boat out of the Tahsis Inlet chop and cuts some distance off a passage for southbound boats heading to Friendly Cove, but the Tahsis Inlet entrance to Princesa Channel is narrow and partly guarded by underwater rocks.

From Tahsis Inlet to Kendrick Inlet (east to west) the problem is the flood tide. The flood current flows northward into Tahsis Inlet, and a boat entering Princesa Channel will find a definite northward set to its course. This northward set will tend to put the boat onto a submerged rock charted about 200 feet north of the Princesa Channel light, at the east entrance to Princesa Channel. Don and Reanne Douglass, in their book *Exploring Vancouver Island's West Coast*, believe the rock is closer to 100 feet from the light. Whether 100 feet or 200 feet, the rock is not far away. The goal is to wrap around the Princesa Channel light but avoid yet another charted rock south of the light, while not being set onto the rock 100 to 200 feet north of the light. Chart 3675 shows the rocks clearly. Study the chart and you will understand not only the challenge but the decisions required to meet the challenge.

We ran Princesa Channel in a stout flood current and had no problems. In our case, we ran south in Tahsis Inlet until the Princesa Channel light bore 235° magnetic, then turned toward the light. We kept the light on our nose (we had to crab to make good our course) until the light was close aboard, then laid off to starboard to give the light 50 feet of clearance, and entered the channel. The key was to be aware of the rock 100 to 200 feet north of the light and keep our course south of that rock. Once past the light we held a mid-channel course and waltzed on through. [*Hale*]

Bodega Cove. Douglass calls this previously unnamed anchorage "Bodega Cove" and we see no reason to argue. Bodega Cove lies at the head of Kendrick Inlet, between Nootka Island and Bodega Island. The area has been logged, so the scenery is not that of primeval forest. Protection is excellent, however, and the shores are accessible. A reef extends from the Nootka Island side of the entrance. Favor the eastern, Bodega Island, side.

The recommended approach is to divide the entry channel in half, then split the eastern, Bodega Island, portion in half again (in other words, three-quarters of the way toward the eastern shore), and run down that line.

A large log dump and booming ground is on Nootka Island near the head of Kendrick Inlet. When it's in operation, you can watch huge machines dumping piles of logs into the water.

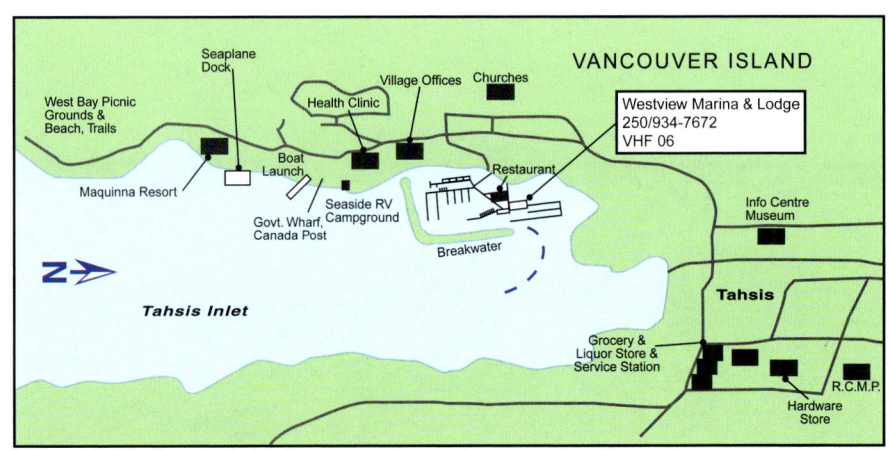

Tahsis Inlet

NOOTKA SOUND

Nootka Sound is where European influence in the Northwest began. Although Captain Cook first landed at Resolution Cove in 1778, it was at Friendly Cove that Captain Meares built the *Northwest America*, 48 feet on deck, the first ship ever built on the west coast, and launched it in 1788.

The long arms (Muchalat Inlet and Tlupana Inlet) that reach out from Nootka Sound have few anchorages, and they tend to be deep. The Port of Gold River is at the head of Muchalat Inlet. The town of Gold River is 9 miles from the dock. Trailerable boats, most of them here for salmon fishing in Nootka Sound, are launched at Gold River.

㉑ **Critter Cove.** Critter Cove is the name given by Cameron Forbes to this previously unnamed spot about 1 mile south of Argonaut Point on Tlupana Inlet. Cameron has established a sportfishing resort in the cove and named it after his nickname of "Critter," when he played hockey. The inner cove is no longer suitable for anchoring.

㉑ **Critter Cove Marina.** P.O. Box 1118, Gold River, BC V0P 1G0; (250) 412-6029; info@crittercove.com; www.crittercove.com. Fuel dock carries mid-grade gasoline, oil, ice, bait, coffee, convenience food, fishing tackle, and ocean-themed pottery. Fuel dock hours are 10:00 a.m. to 6:00 p.m. in June, and 8:00 a.m. to 9:00 p.m. in July and August. Moorage, cabins, lodge rooms, suites, restaurant, showers, washrooms. No power or water on the docks. Showers are for overnight guests only.

Cameron Forbes, one of the nicest guys you'll meet, has quite a sportfishing camp here. Most of Critter Cove is on floats, including the licensed restaurant and some of the accommodations. The Critter Cove Cafe is open for breakfast, lunch and dinner. Boaters who are not overnight guests are welcome at the cafe. There are also self-contained beach cottages on the land adjacent to and behind the floating portion of the resort. Most of the boats at Critter Cove are trailered into Gold River, where they are launched. They do have room for a few visiting cruisers.

Nootka Sound Resort. (877) 337-5464; VHF 06 info@nootkamarineadventures.com; www.nootkamarineadventures.com. Nootka Sound Resort is fishing resort; facilities and services are for resort guests only.

Hisnit Inlet. Hisnit Inlet extends north from Tlupana Inlet. Hisnit is one of the few anchorages in Nootka Sound that is well-protected, shallow enough for convenient anchoring, and large enough for a number of boats. Two submerged rocks lie almost mid-channel a short distance into Hisnit Inlet. Do not be deceived by the open and safe appearance of the inlet as you arrive or depart. Favor the south shore.

The view of mountains up the stream at the head of the inlet is stunning. A marble quarry once operated on the east shore. Piles of white marble are visible on the beach and in the nearby forest. The quarry itself is buried under fallen trees and is difficult (and dangerous) to locate. Near the head of the inlet on the same east shore is a large rock shaped like a human head.

Anchorage at the head of the inlet is in 40 to 60 feet. It is open but protected. The shoreline is accessible.

㉑ **Moutcha Bay Resort.** (877) 337-5464; info@nootkamarineadventures.com; www.moutchabay.com. Moutcha Bay Resort is a full service marina, with moorage to 150 feet available to those staying in Moutcha accommodations. Fuel dock with gasoline, diesel and propane, water, 15 & 30 amp power, pumpout, Wi-Fi, and a concrete launch ramp. Washrooms and showers are at the top of the docks. The docks are beautifully built, wide and stable. A small store carries limited groceries, gift items, and ice.

The restaurant is good and features local seafood, meat, and produce. Fishing charters, guided and unguided, are available on a fleet of rental boats. Fish processing and packing is offered. Yurts, chalets, and campsites can be rented. The staff is helpful and courteous. This is a luxury resort with facilities to match.

Ewin Inlet. Ewin Inlet indents the south side of Bligh Island some 3 miles, with no anchorages until the head is reached. The cove to the west at the head of the inlet is quite protected and has depths of 30 to 40 feet. "We rounded the little islet in the cove at low tide, about 100 feet off, and the depth sounder abruptly but briefly showed a depth of 15 feet. We suspect it found an uncharted rock." [*Hale*]

The Island Attitude Coffee Café at Westview Marina.

It is a short walk from Friendly Cove to this beautiful beach looking west towards the ocean.

WEST COAST OF VANCOUVER ISLAND

Resolution Cove. Historic Resolution Cove is on Bligh Island, near the south end of Clerke Peninsula. In March, 1778, Captain Cook anchored his two ships there and found and fitted a new foremast for the *Resolution*. A flagpole and plaques commemorating Cook's visit have been placed on a knoll above the cove. Anchor in 40 to 50 feet, either with a stern-tie to shore or enough room to swing. You'll probably make your visit a short one. Swells from the ocean wrap around the Clerke Peninsula into the cove.

Santa Gertrudis Cove. The western cove in Santa Gertrudis Cove is an excellent anchorage: cozy, good holding, protected. As you enter you will see an island in the northern cove. A submerged rock extends from that island a considerable distance toward the south shore, farther than we expected. Be sure to identify this rock and give it room as you favor the south shore. There is sufficient room to pass between this rock and the drying rock shown off the south shore on the chart. The north cove of Santa Gertrudis Cove, around the island, is foul and tight.

㉑ **Friendly Cove.** Friendly Cove is where Captains Vancouver and Quadra met in 1792 and attempted to negotiate the final details of the Nootka Convention of 1790, in which Spain relinquished to England all its claims to Northwest lands. Hulsizer, in her book *Voyages to Windward*, gives an interesting and succinct explanation of the complicated events in Friendly Cove that brought Spain and Great Britain to the brink of war before they worked out their differences in the Nootka Convention.

Friendly Cove is shallow and fairly protected from typical summertime winds, with good anchoring for four or five boats on a sand bottom. Outflow winds can make Friendly Cove bumpy. Nearly all the land ashore belongs to the Mowachaht Band, and a fee (cash only) must be paid for landing. The band has summertime staff on hand who monitor VHF 66A and collect the fee. The landing fee is the same, whether you dinghy in from an anchored boat or tie up at the wharf and floats on the west side of the bay.

When you anchor, be aware that the *Uchuck III* delivers tourists and freight to the dock regularly. To watch the *Uchuck III* wind its way through anchored boats is awe-inspiring—and terrifying if you're on one of the boats.

A trail runs through campgrounds and above the ocean beach. It passes the Native graveyard and leads to a lake that's good for swimming. Six rental cabins, small and rustic, are just beyond the lake. The spired Catholic church is filled with Native carvings, and has two marvelous stained glass windows. They depict the transfer of authority over the area from Spain to England in 1792, and were a gift from the government of Spain. A carved welcome figure stands on the far shore of the cove, facing the open sea.

㉒ **Nootka Light Station.** You can walk from the Friendly Cove beach to the Nootka Light Station on San Rafael Island. A well-maintained series of stairs leads up from the beach to the light station. Once at the station, be sure to sign the guest book.

Nootka is a repeater station for Prince Rupert Coast Guard radio, and has considerable radio equipment. Every three hours from early morning until nightfall, the Nootka station reports weather conditions for the marine weather broadcast, including estimated wind strength and sea conditions offshore.

Thanks to the miracle of the Fresnel lens, the light uses only a 35-watt LED bulb to cast a beam that can be seen for 15 miles.

The Nootka Light Station and its light keepers are powerful arguments for retaining manned light stations along the coast. They are invaluable for timely and accurate weather information, and for communication in areas that may not have good cell phone coverage. The lightkeepers monitor VHF channel 82. We are told that many of the lightkeepers maintain an open Wi-Fi signal for visiting boaters.

Estevan Point. Estevan Point is the southwest corner of Hesquiat Peninsula, another of the headlands where winds and seas build and become confused. Estevan Point can be ugly in a storm, but in more settled conditions does not present the challenge found at Cape Cook or Cape Scott. In fog, the problem with Estevan Point is its low, flat terrain, which makes its shoreline a poor target for radar. The rocks more than a mile offshore make Estevan Point unforgiving for the navigator who is off-course.

From Nootka Sound, a rounding of Estevan Point first must clear Escalante Rocks and Perez Rocks, both of them on the west side of Hesquiat Peninsula. Unfortunately for the navigator, no single chart shows all of Estevan Point from Nootka Sound to Hesquiat Bay in large scale. You will be forced to plot your course on small scale Chart 3603, which doesn't give much close-in detail. Once at Estevan Point, you can use Chart 3674 to continue to Hot Springs Cove.

Especially with the lack of a single good large scale chart for the west side of Hesquiat Peninsula, the general advice is to give Estevan Point "lots of room." Give Escalante Rocks and Perez Rocks lots of room, too. This applies when heading north as well.

Weather Information: The Estevan Point lighthouse provides updated wind, sea, and atmospheric conditions every three hours. Listen to the continuous marine broadcast for the latest weather information.

Hesquiat Harbour. Hesquiat Harbour is protected from westerly winds, and Hesquiat Bar (24 feet deep) knocks down the Pacific swell. Crossing the bar may be unsafe in a southeasterly; storm seas can break over it. Anchorage depths can be found in **Boat Basin** located at the northeast end of Hesquiat Harbour; but Rae Basin provides better protection since Boat Basin is open to the south. Most of the upland areas around Hesquiat Harbour and Boat Basin are included within the Hesquiat Peninsula Provincial Park. **Rae Basin** is a well-protected anchorage in the northeast corner of Boat Basin and offers bear viewing opportunities at low tide. Rae Basin consists of an outer basin anchorage and an inner basin anchorage. Most boats will prefer anchoring in the outer area of Rae Basin. Anchorage is possible for shallow draft vessels in Rae Basin's inner area. At a tide of 11 feet or higher, you can dinghy into Hesquiat Lake from Rae Basin.

From Boat Basin or Rae Basin, you can take the dinghy to **Cougar Annie's Garden** for an interesting educational tour. Pioneers Ada

Climb the stairs to the Nootka Light Station for a view of Friendly Cove.

COUGAR ANNIE'S GARDEN IN HESQUIAT HARBOUR

Cougar Annie
In 1915, the wily pioneer Cougar Annie set foot on the beach at Boat Basin in Hesquiat Harbour with her husband and three children. For seventy years, while bearing 8 more children and outliving three more husbands, she cleared and cultivated land, trapped small animals, and defended her turf and family from cougar and bear. Ada Anne (Cougar Annie) was successful in creating a mail-order garden nursery in addition to her other endeavors. As she grew old, her extensive gardens became overgrown until visionary Peter Buckland established the Boat Basin Foundation, which provided needed funding to restore the expansive gardens. His creativity has infused over 33,000 hours of labor to build more than a mile (2,100 meters) of cedar boardwalk and over 20 structures, built entirely from cedar windfall on the property.

Touring The Gardens
A tour of the property will take the better part of an afternoon or morning, winding past magnificent 500- to 1,000- year old cedars, Cougar Annie's gradually fading home, and Peter's structural sculptures. This is a real highlight of West Coast Vancouver Island. To arrange a visit, contact boatbasinfoundation@gmail.com with an estimate of your arrival dates. You can confirm or adjust your arrival date with Peter by email, using cell service with data via a nearby cell tower in Hot Springs Cove.

Tour Guide
You will find Peter's house at the head of Hesquiat Harbour in Boat Basin. Peter will welcome you ashore and accompany you to Cougar Annie's Garden and the Boat Basin Foundation, which provides education in temperate rainforest ecology. The tour fee is $30 per person with a $120 minimum, payable only by credit card, or you may be able to make payment by engaging in 2-hours of volunteer work on the property.

Where To Anchor
Anchorage can be taken in Boat Basin, or you can duck into the front portion of Rae Basin. At higher tides, it is even possible to enter the furthest reach of Rae Basin, but this maneuver is only for skippers who are confident of their ability to navigate by depth sounder. Bear wander the shores at low tide; and at a tide greater than 11 feet, you can dinghy up the creek to Hesquiat Lake.

Entering Hesquiat Harbour
Boaters should use caution when entering Hesquiat Harbour, seas can break over the 24-foot deep Hesquiat Bar; check weather and consult charts before heading to this very special place. Cougar Annie's Garden is a short distance northwest of popular Hot Springs Cove at Maquinna Marine Provincial Park.

- Mary Campbell, Correspondent

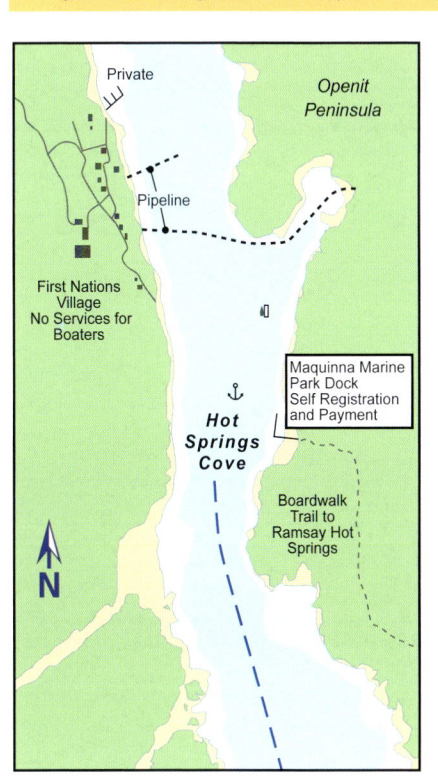

Hot Springs Cove

Anne (Cougar Annie), and husband William Rae-Arthur, cleared land for a homestead in 1915 at Boat Basin where they raised their three children and established a large garden. Today, the garden is maintained as a heritage site with research studies in temperate rainforest ecology. Tours are arranged through the Boat Basin Foundation (www.boatbasin.org); email boatbasinfoundation@gmail.com or call (250) 726-5096 a couple of days before your arrival. Admission is charged to help pay for the restoration and ongoing research there; credit card payment preferred. Correspondent Mary Campbell reports that the visit is well worth the $30 donation fee. Land or anchor your dinghy off the beach in front of Peter's house and cabin located along the north shore of Boat Basin. Peter, who acts as guide, will accompany you along the trail to Cougar Annie's Garden.

Hot Springs Cove Area. Hot Springs Cove is adjacent to Sydney Inlet, the northern entrance to Clayoquot Sound. Depending on the points of departure and arrival and the exact course chosen, the distance from Nootka Sound around Estevan Point, past Hesquiat Peninsula, and east to Hot Springs Cove, is approximately 30 to 31 miles. When traveling south, once you are past Chief Matlahaw Point, you can duck into the lee of Hesquiat Peninsula to avoid the worst of the ocean swells.

㉓ **Hot Springs Cove.** www.env.gov.bc.ca/bcparks/. Hot Springs Cove is home to **Maquinna Marine Provincial Park** and Protected Area, and **Ramsay Hot Springs**. The park and hot springs are reasons why cruising boats do the West Coast. The challenge of getting to Hot Springs Cove is sufficient to make the reward—a soothing bath in comforting water (no soap, please)—worth the entire trip. In earlier times, most visitors came the hard way, up from Barkley Sound or down from Cape Scott. Now tour boats, floatplanes, and even helicopters carrying visitors who have arrived without effort at Tofino, visit Hot Springs Cove many times a day. An hour by high-speed boat, and they are there.

The cove is easy to enter. Chart 3674 shows that the mouth is open and the channel free of dangers. The marine park public dock is approximately 1.7 miles farther into the cove from the hot springs themselves. You can anchor in 24 feet, or boats less than 12

Hesquiat Harbour

meters (40 feet) can tie to the Park dock; self-registration and fee payment box on shore at the Park Information Shelter. Hot Springs Cove is within the Ahousat First Nation territory; the Ahousaht Stewardship Program may collect donation fees for anchorage, look for the yellow *Ahous Hakoon* vessel; they can answer questions and will provide you with a receipt.

A 1.2-mile walk along a well-maintained boardwalk leads to the hot springs. A $3 per person park fee is payable at a drop box near the head of the dock. In the past, visiting craft had a tradition of bringing a plank to add to the boardwalk. On the plank would be carved the name of the boat and the year of the visit. Many of the planks showed remarkable artistic talent.

Construction began in 2020 to replace and widen the boardwalk from the dock to the hot springs and was completed in late 2021. Approximately 50 of the previously carved boards with boat names, considered historic, were kept to be used in a special feature at the park yet to be determined.

The hike through the rainforest to the hot springs is easy and beautiful. Toilets are available at the end. A changing room in which clothes may be doffed and a bathing suit put on is above the hot springs. The place is popular.

Although a constant stream of bathers hike the trail and soak in the springs during the day, savvy boaters staying the night know that if they come before 9:00 a.m. or after 6:00 p.m., they will share the springs only with other boaters.

Note: pets not permitted beyond the start of the boardwalk; alcoholic beverages not permitted within the park.

The hot springs were closed during 2021 and 2022 due to Covid concerns; at press time it was not known if the springs would be open for the 2023 season, check BC Parks website at bcparks.ca/parks/maquinna-marine/. Hot Springs has campsites, often used by kayakers. A cell phone tower in the Native village across from the Park now provides four to five bars of cell phone service (Bell).

The B&B vessel, the *InnChanter*, which is open for meals on a space available basis, plans to be in Hot Springs Cove for 2023; check their website at innchanter.com.

CLAYOQUOT SOUND

Clayoquot Sound is a series of inlets and passages with entrances at both its north and south ends. By traveling inside Clayoquot Sound you can explore many coves and anchorages, and avoid 20 miles of ocean swells. Tofino is the only major town, although fuel and some groceries are available at Ahousat. There is cell coverage around Tofino and Hot Springs Cove, but coverage is spotty in outlying areas and inlets.

Much of Clayoquot Sound is within the traditional territory of the Ahousaht First Nation, who have established a Stewardship Guardian Program. First Nation representatives of the **Ahousaht Stewardship Program** collect donation fees at various anchorages within the Clayoquot Sound in support of their programs which include care for beaches and trails, search and rescue support, management and cultural interpretation for visitor access, and training in first aid. Receipts for payment are provided via a representative aboard the *Ahous Hakoon* vessel. Guardians monitor VHF channel 65A and may be contacted if you are in need of support. For more information call Ahousaht Stewardship Operations at (250) 731-6957.

Sydney Inlet. Sydney Inlet is the northern entrance to Clayoquot Sound. It is adjacent to Hot Springs Cove and leads approximately 11 miles into the mountains of Vancouver Island, with several good anchorages. Rounding Sharp Point after leaving Hot Springs Cove, be aware of two charted but unmarked off-lying rocks. The first is fairly close to Sharp Point and easy to avoid. The second is about 0.2 mile off. Most boats will choose to pass between the two rocks. Be sure you know where you are. Once in Sydney Inlet, the fairway is open and unencumbered. Reader Don Thain reports that sea otters are now well established in Sydney Inlet and that crabbing is poorer where the sea otters have colonized.

Sydney Inlet Unnamed Cove. This is the cove that lies behind the 65-meter island about 0.5 mile south of Hootla-Kootla Bay, at latitude 49°21.85'N on the east shore of Sydney Inlet. (Douglass, in both editions of *Exploring Vancouver Island's West Coast*, mistakenly calls this cove Hootla-Kootla, but the chart leaves it unnamed and calls the next cove to the north Hootla-Kootla.) Enter from the south. You'll see a beautiful white beach. Although the water is a little shallow near the beach, it's the prettiest spot in the cove. You could also anchor at the north end of the cove, behind the 65-meter-high island. Do not attempt to enter the cove at the north end. It is foul.

Young Bay. Young Bay, on the east side of Sydney Inlet, is a lovely place to anchor, although a little deep until you get close to shore. The middle is 50 to 60 feet deep, but along the shore it's easy to find 35- to 40-foot depths. On the south shore a stream connects with Cecilia Lake, one-half mile away. A rough trail leads up the stream to the lake. Trout fishing at the lake is reported to be good. A copper mine and a pilchard reduction plant both operated here in the past. Only a few concrete platforms and pieces of machinery remain.

Enter Young Bay right down the middle, to avoid shoals that extend from either side. Once inside you will see a small islet with trees on it. Pass to the south of that islet.

Bottleneck Bay (Coyote Cove). This is an otherwise unnamed bay that cruising guide author Don Watmough fell in love with. Bottleneck Bay is located just north of Young Bay, east of Adventure Point. The entrance is narrow but deep. Inside, the high, treed hills make the feeling of seclusion complete. Easy anchoring in 30 feet.

Holmes Inlet Nook. An intimate back cove in Holmes Inlet, with room for 2 to 3 boats over a mud bottom; anchoring depths of 20 feet. Swinging room is tight so you may want to stern-tie.

Hootla-Kootla Bay. Hootla-Kootla Bay is located about 0.25 mile north of the 65-meter-high island on the east shore of Sydney Inlet, approximately 1.6 miles from the mouth of the inlet. This cove is known locally as Baseball Bay, but the chart shows it as Hootla-Kootla Bay. The entrance is shallow, and is partly blocked by a charted rock just south of mid-channel. Divide the channel north of the rock in half, and enter the northern half "mid-channel." "Least depth on the depth sounder was 12.5 feet near the bottom of a 3.6-foot low tide at Tofino. Anchorage is good once inside." [*Hale*]

Riley Cove. Riley Cove is just east of Starling Point, on the northwest tip of Flores Island. It may not be the best choice for an anchorage. The cove is open and uninteresting, and a little deep for anchoring until close to the head. At the head, Riley Cove is divided into two smaller coves; the cove to the west has a sandy beach. A rock, not shown on the chart, is just off the point that separates the two coves. A shoal extends from the east shore near the entrance of Riley Cove. Favor the west shore.

Steamer Cove. Steamer Cove is on the north side of Flores Island, behind George Island. The small cove at the southwest corner of Steamer Cove is well protected and has easy anchoring depths.

㉔ **Bacchante Bay.** Bacchante Bay, at the east end of Shelter Inlet, is a dramatic anchorage, with steep cliffs on both sides, an inviting grassy meadow at the head and a snow-capped mountain beyond. The narrow, shallow entrance is hidden until you are close. Bacchante Bay is part of Strathcona Provincial Park. Minimum depth at entry is 18 feet; a shallowing bar, just outside the entrance, has a minimum depth of 16 feet.

Bacchante Bay has ample room to anchor in 40 to 50 feet. Holding is excellent. If you run to the head of the bay, watch for abrupt shoaling off the meadow. At high tide explore Watta Creek by dinghy.

Readers Mike and Sandy Cecka report fouling their anchor in Bacchante Bay. They anchored on the west side of the bay, below steep cliffs. We've had no problem anchoring in the middle of the bay.

Hayden Passage. Hayden Passage is on the west side of Obstruction Island, and connects Shelter Inlet with Millar Channel. Tidal current predictions are shown with Hayden Passage as a secondary station based on Tofino in the Tide and Current Tables, Vol. 6 and Ports and Passes. The flood sets southeast; the ebb, northwest. Be sure to pass west of the red daymarker beacons (Red, Right, Returning).

Because the flood currents meet at Hayden Passage, you may find that the currents don't behave as predicted. The cautious passage would be at slack water. If transiting sometime other than slack water, maintain a constant watch for current set, and crab as needed to stay in the channel.

Sulphur Passage. Sulphur Passage connects Shelter Inlet and Millar Channel on the east side of Obstruction Island and is far more tortuous than Hayden Passage. The northern portion of Sulphur Passage is the tricky part. There, the channels twist and turn and are bounded by

---

Covid Considerations

At Press Time, closures remain in the Clayoquot Sound area:

Lone Cone Trail and campground/hostel is closed until 2024.

Hesquiat Peninsula Provincial Park remains closed.

Maquinna Marine Park Hot Springs remains closed.

See **WaggonerGuide.com/Updates** for the latest on marinas and destinations.

Lennard Island Lighthouse near Tofino

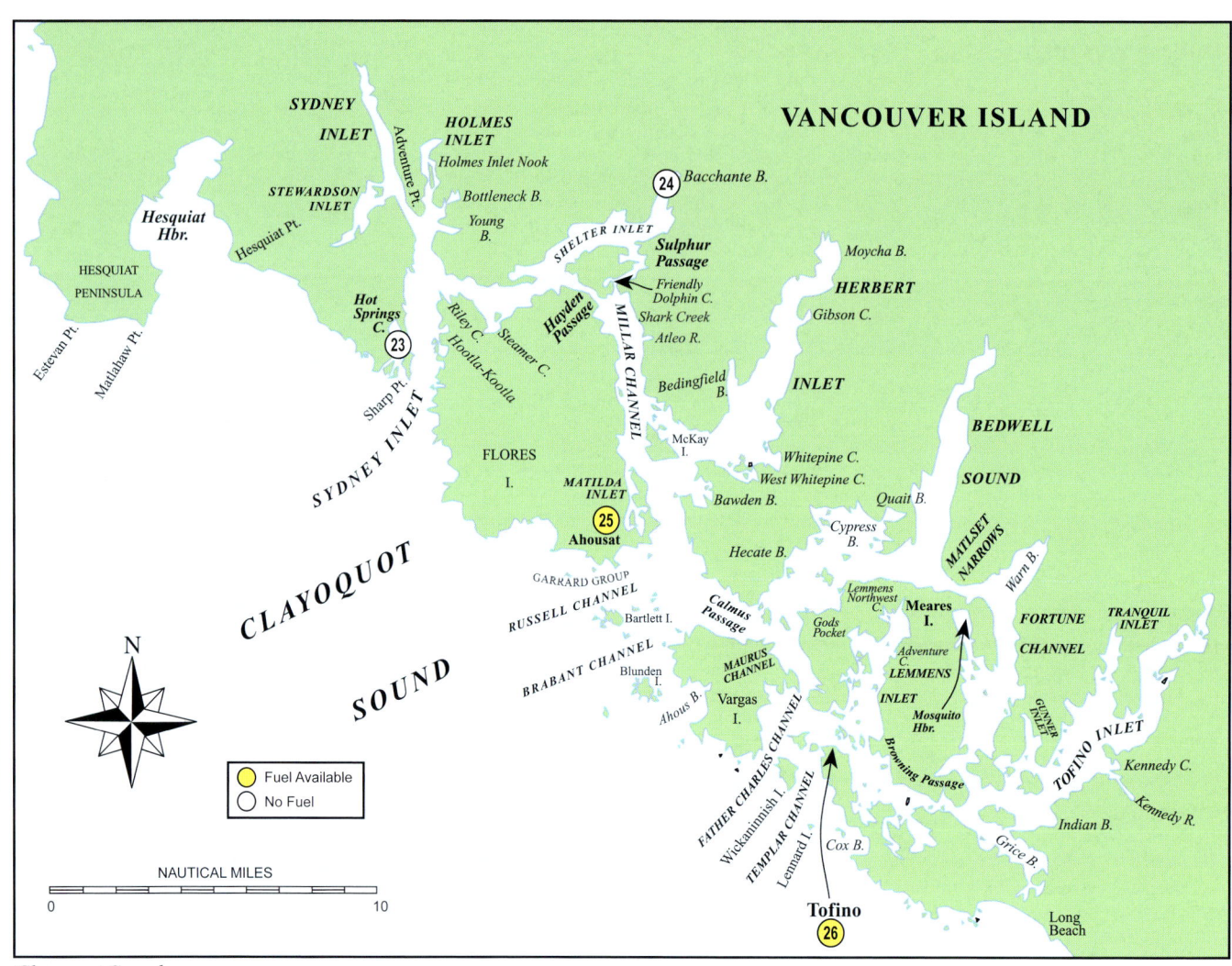

WEST COAST OF VANCOUVER ISLAND Reference Only – Not for Navigation

Clayoquot Sound

submerged rocks. Don Douglass ran Sulphur Passage along the east side of the 38-meter island in the northern portion, and reported it to be a period of "high anxiety." Locals favor passing on the west side of 38-meter island, where the Landons found a minimum depth of 35 feet on the south end of the narrow channel, between 38-meter island and Obstruction Island. Tidal current predictions are in Tides & Currents Vol 6 and Ports & Passes as a secondary station based upon Tofino.

Friendly Dolphin Cove. Friendly Dolphin is Douglass' name for the cove that indents Obstruction Island, just inside the south entrance to Sulphur Passage. The cove is pretty, private and appealing. Well protected from wind and current. Anchor near the head in 40 to 50 feet, probably with a stern-tie ashore to control swinging, or in 50 to 60 feet with room to swing. Space for 3 or 4 boats. The Landons reported a pleasant stay early in the season.

Shark Creek Falls. 49°22.95'N/126°04.00'W. "This is a kayakers' secret: a beautiful 70-foot-high waterfall in a chimney, accessible at high tide by dinghy only. It is located in Millar Channel, just north of Atleo River. Anchor north of the small island and dinghy in. Best in late afternoon when sunlight makes a rainbow on the rocks behind the falls." [*Hulsizer*]

Matilda Inlet indents the southeast corner of Flores Island and is bordered on the east by McNeil Peninsula. Anchorage is possible near the head of Matilda Inlet. From the anchorage, a warm springs in Gibson Marine Park can be visited (best at high tide; at low tide it's a muddy hike) or a trek made to the beach. Don Watmough describes the area in fond detail. The Native community of Marktosis is on McNeil Peninsula. Across the inlet and a short distance north are the store and fuel dock of Ahousat.

㉕ **Ahousat.** General Delivery, Ahousat, BC V0R 1A0; (250) 670-9575. Ahousat, with its general store, fuel dock and marine ways, is on the west shore of Matilda Inlet, at the southeast corner of Flores Island. Ample moorage for transient boaters; high dock with metal facia, may need to adjust fenders. Gasoline and diesel at the fuel dock, washrooms, 15 amp power, showers and laundry, haulout to 30 feet. Potable water, pay phone, post office, and motel rooms are available. The store is a rough-and-ready place, with a cougar head on the wall, but with luck, it may have what you need: groceries, miscellaneous hardware and marine supplies. No charts or liquor.

Marktosis (Maaqtusiis). Marktosis is the Native village across Matilda Inlet from Ahousat. Carved Native canoes can be seen on the beach and at the shed by the Government Wharf. Docks at the wharf are filled with commercial fish boats and sport fish boats; transient moorage is limited. Permits for the Wild Side Trail can be purchased at the fuel dock; the trail is mostly boardwalk to White Sand Cove (www.wildsidetrail.com). You can anchor south of Ahousat in the bay near the "slightly warm" springs, and take the dinghy back to the village. Leave the dinghy at the Government Wharf and touch base with the band office before exploring further. The Ahous Fuel Bar (250-670-6803) has gas and diesel; rocks make the approach hazardous; larger boats should enter only at high tide.

Gibson Marine Park. Gibson Marine Park is at the head of Matilda Inlet, past Ahousat. At one time, Hugh Clarke, at the Ahousat General Store, hacked out a trail from the head of the inlet to the hot springs. Boots are necessary on the trail, which transits some boggy areas. Clarke recommends going in at

Well-protected Quait Bay, just inside this narrow entrance, has anchorage for many boats.

half tide on a rising tide, to avoid tramping across the mud flats. Correspondent Gil Flanagan tells us that you can hike for many miles on the ocean beach to the west. The only problem, Flanagan says, are bands of gravel that make barefoot walking uncomfortable. He adds that the beach is popular with kayakers and tourists from Tofino. The park requests that dogs are kept out of the park as there have been incidents of wolves killing the dogs.

Herbert Inlet. The run up Herbert Inlet is even more spectacular than many other inlets along the coast. High mountains and rock walls line the shores. Deep alpine river valleys lead away into the mountains. Snowcapped peaks can be seen in the distance.

West Whitepine Cove. Although unnamed, both Watmough and Douglass call this delightful anchorage West Whitepine Cove, and we shall do the same. West Whitepine Cove lies to the west of Whitepine Cove, near the mouth of Herbert Inlet. Entry to the inner bay is along the south side of the 67-meter island. We entered slowly, strongly favoring this island. Rocks were visible underwater and easily skirted. Once inside, the cove is lovely and protected. Bears are reported to frequent the south shore.

A charted rock is in the cove, off the tip of the little peninsula that extends southeast from the 94-meter island. When anchoring, stay away from it.

Gibson Cove. Gibson Cove indents the west side of Herbert Inlet, about 5 miles north of Whitepine Cove. Since Gibson Cove is not on the way to anyplace else, we suspect it sees few visitors. Those who do visit are in for a treat. Gibson Cove is beautiful, but a little deep for anchoring. Although it appears protected, strong afternoon westerlies can bring wind and waves.

Quait Bay. The entrance to nearly landlocked Quait Bay is located on the northeast side of Cypress Bay. Watch for the numerous crab pot buoys in Cypress Bay. From Cypress Bay, enter Quait Bay passing 45-meter island off your starboard side, favoring the port-side of the channel. The chart makes the course clear. A large floating lodge, with no services for boaters, is just inside the entrance on the left. Quait Bay has room for many boats. Anchor nearly anywhere in 20-40 feet of water. Southwesterly winds do find their way into the bay.

The most popular spot is in the little cove in the east corner in about 10 feet. A submerged concrete structure (49° 16.603N 125° 50.843W) lies in the mouth of the two nooks at the back of this cove. The structure dries at 2 feet. A private 40-foot float is located on the north shore.

For a peek at what life is like for Clayoquot Sound's year-round floating home residents, take your dinghy out the entrance of Quait Bay, enter the unnamed cove south of Quait Bay (49° 15.86N 125° 51.57W) and continue all the way to the head of the cove to visit Wayne Adams and Catherine King in their floating garden on their magenta and turquoise floating home. Wayne and Catherine must hold the record for interviews and feature articles about Clayoquot Sound residents.

Matlset Narrows. Matlset Narrows runs to a maximum of 4 knots on spring tides. The flood sets east. Sailing Directions warns of strong tide-rips in the vicinity of the Maltby Islets at the east end of the narrows. We ran the narrows against a west-flowing ebb. We saw definite current activity, but had no problem. We suspect any tide-rips would be on a flood.

Calmus Passage to Heynen Channel. The route from Millar Channel to Heynen Channel via Calmus Passage and Maurus Channel is the beginning of shallower water. The channels are well marked by buoys and beacons but the navigator must stay alert, keep an eye on the depth sounder, and know the vessel's position at all times. Large-scale Chart 3685 is extremely helpful.

Lemmens Inlet. Lemmens Inlet indents Meares Island, just a few miles from the town of Tofino. Be sure to use large scale Chart 3685 while navigating around Tofino and into Lemmens Inlet. The entry channel to the inlet is amply deep, but bordered by drying flats. Once inside, you have your choice of three possible anchorages—although float homes now are moored in all of Lemmens Inlet's coves, so anchoring may be a challenge. Watch for numerous crab pot buoys throughout the Inlet.

Adventure Cove. Adventure Cove, where Capt. Robert Gray built the small schooner *Adventure* in 1792, is filled with history. The beach is easy to land on. While walking in the woods we could almost feel the presence of Gray's Fort Defiance and the shipbuilding activity. Though the area is now overgrown with large trees, some say you can feel as though *something went on here*. Don and Reanne Douglass describe the history well. Hulsizer discusses it more thoroughly in *Voyages to Windward*. Unfortunately, floathouses take up most of the cove, leaving little room for anchoring. Discarded fish farming equipment on the beach makes beach access challenging. A reader tells us an uncharted rock lies SSW of the island in the mouth of Adventure Cove.

Lemmens Northwest Cove. Lemmens Northwest Cove is Douglass' name for this anchorage in the northwest corner of Lemmens Inlet. It is identified on the chart by the 39-meter island. Two charted drying rocks east of 39-meter island and a large oyster farm obstruct entrance to the cove. Rows of oyster aquaculture farming fill the area on both sides of these two drying rocks to the shoreline to the northwest. Enter the cove with 39-meter island on your port side and the oyster farm very close on your starboard side. Caution for the charted shoals on the northeast side and north tip of 39-meter island. Bow watch is recommended. Once inside, you'll find good anchoring depths and adequate protection; caution for the charted shallow spot. Several float homes are tucked into various areas of the cove.

Gods Pocket. Gods Pocket is the cove northwest of Lagoon Island, on the west side of Lemmens Inlet. Protection is good, with anchorage in 25 to 30 feet. Aquaculture is in the cove with buoys set in half of Gods Pocket. Three or four float homes are tucked into bights along the northern shore.

Fortune Channel. Fortune Channel connects Tofino Channel with Matlset Narrows, which in turn connects with the waters of upper and western Clayoquot Sound. In Fortune Channel you can choose from three good anchorages: Windy Bay, Heelboom Bay and Mosquito Harbour. Chances are, you won't see much boat traffic in this area.

WEST COAST OF VANCOUVER ISLAND

Mosquito Harbour. Although not as scenic and cozy as Heelboom Bay, Mosquito Harbour is big and open and easily entered. Anchor in 20 feet behind the Blackberry Islets. Approach on either side of the Wood Islets, but from Fortune Channel you'll probably approach by way of Plover Point or Dark Island. Kelp marks the rocks off the north end of Dark Island. Note the location of Hankin Rock. We would trend toward Plover Point before turning to enter Mosquito Harbour.

Heelboom Bay. Heelboom Bay, located near the south end of Fortune Channel, is a good anchorage, surrounded by lush evergreen forests. Room for 3-4 boats. We found outstanding holding in 35 feet. This Bay was the site of a major protest against logging in Clayoquot Sound and is considered almost sacred by some residents. Approaching, favor the east shore and stay well clear of rocks off the western shore. One of these rocks is considerably detached from the shoreline. Chart 3685 helps understanding.

Windy Bay. Windy Bay is beautiful. The south shore is heavily forested, and the north shore is sheer rock wall. Westerly winds accelerate over the saddle at the head of the bay, but they have no fetch to build up seas. With 15 knots of wind outside Windy Bay, we had gusts to 30 knots inside. Anchor in 30 to 35 feet with excellent holding.

Browning Passage and Tsapee Narrows. Rocks abound and shoals threaten. The larger scale Chart 3685 will show you the way. If you are coming from Heynen Channel or Lemmens Inlet, the course will be clear: Pass west of Morpheus Island and east of Buoy Y35, and continue down Browning Passage and through Tsapee Narrows. Note that currents on springs can run to 5 knots near Morpheus Island and 4 knots at the narrows. Go slowly. Look ahead and identify all buoys, islands and visible rocks well in advance. Keep a close reference between your charts and your navigation electronics. Done this way, the passage should not be difficult.

If you are departing Tofino, leave Buoy Y29, opposite the 4th Street dock, to starboard, and run toward Arnet Island until you can safely turn to run south, along the west side of Riley Island. Favor Riley Island to pass clear of the rocks shown on the chart. Once south of Riley Island you are in Browning Passage.

TOFINO INLET

Island Cove. Island Cove is easy to enter around either side of Ocayu Island. Study the chart to avoid the rocks that lie off the southwest shore of the approach. Unfortunately, the hillsides surrounding Island Cove have been logged down to the water's edge and the cove isn't very pretty. Anchor in 40 to 50 feet, close to the west shore.

Gunner Inlet. It's tricky to get into the inlet and not very scenic when you make it. Approach favoring the east shore and use a small low islet with a distinctive white top as your leading mark. Make an S-turn around the islet and follow the chart in. Anchoring depths vary, 20-60 feet.

Tranquilito Cove. Tranquilito Cove is the name Douglass gave this unnamed cove on the east side of Tranquil Inlet, near the head. This cove is secluded and beautiful. The rock wall on the north side has been strikingly sculpted by glaciers. Favor the northern side of the entry to avoid a shoal that extends from the point of land on the south side. Anchor in 20 feet.

Cannery Bay. Cannery Bay, at the mouth of the Kennedy River, provides good protection and is easy to get in. Despite its flat terrain, it's rather pretty. Consider the nook just to port as you enter. Anchor in 15 to 20 feet over mixed mud and sand with excellent holding.

Kennedy Cove. Kennedy Cove is easy to enter by favoring the 68-meter island. Anchor wherever you like in 15 to 30 feet. It's a pretty spot. A private dock and water slide is on the north shore, labeled "ruin" on some charts. Farther in the bay is a private gazebo overlooking the cove from IR Land.

㉖ **Tofino.** If you come from up-island, Tofino will be your first major town since Port McNeill or Port Hardy, and it's more vibrant than either of them. During the summer season, Tofino's bustle and busyness may surprise you. After growing accustomed to the slower life up-island, Tofino, with its commerce, tourists, fast traffic and loud engines, can cause culture shock. Welcome to the city.

As long as you're in the city you might as well spend some money. You can choose from several good restaurants, the kind that serve meals without french fries. Gift shops and galleries—at last!—are available for mementos and presents. The Co-op store, close to the waterfront, is a complete supermarket and will deliver if asked. The Co-op also carries clothes. Showers are available at the 4th Street Dock and at the laundromat at 4th & Campbell. Set expectations for the laundromat by first checking the online customer reviews. Common Loaf is all-organic and features a local favorite: peasant bread. SoBo, open for lunch and dinner, uses locally grown ingredients in their dishes; reservations recommended (250) 725-2341. The "1909 Restaurant" at Tofino Resort & Marina is also excellent. For a guided food tour, contact Tofino Food Tours at (800) 656-0713.

Be sure to allow enough time to see all the sights that Tofino has to offer. The Tofino Botanical Gardens (250) 725-1220 located 1.5 miles out of town, is worth a visit and is open daily. A network of paths and boardwalks are contained within the 12 acres of gardens, forest, and shoreline. Tofino is known for its beautiful beaches and has several surf shops in town. You often see surfboards strapped to bicycles, as surfers make their way to the beaches. Surf reports are given for North & South Chesterman Beach and Cox Beach. Other beaches include Mackenzie, Middle, and Tonquin Beaches, with Tonquin being the closest to Tofino.

The Tofino Transit Shuttle (250-725-2871) on Campbell Street can take you out to the beaches, or call the Tofino Water Taxi (250-725-8844). Bike rentals are available next to the Tofino Bus station. A dedicated bike path follows the highway south of town; the planned extended bike path to Ucluelet was completed in 2022. Bus service runs between Tofino and Ucluelet.

The Big Tree Trail on nearby Mears Island is another worthwhile excursion. A dinghy dock on the west side of the island is available while hiking the 3 km loop trail, which takes about 2 hours. A small fee to hike the trail is collected by a guard on duty, or you can use the on-site payment box. Some of the largest trees in B.C. are found here, ranging in age from 1,000 years to 1,500 years old. The largest tree is known as "the hanging garden."

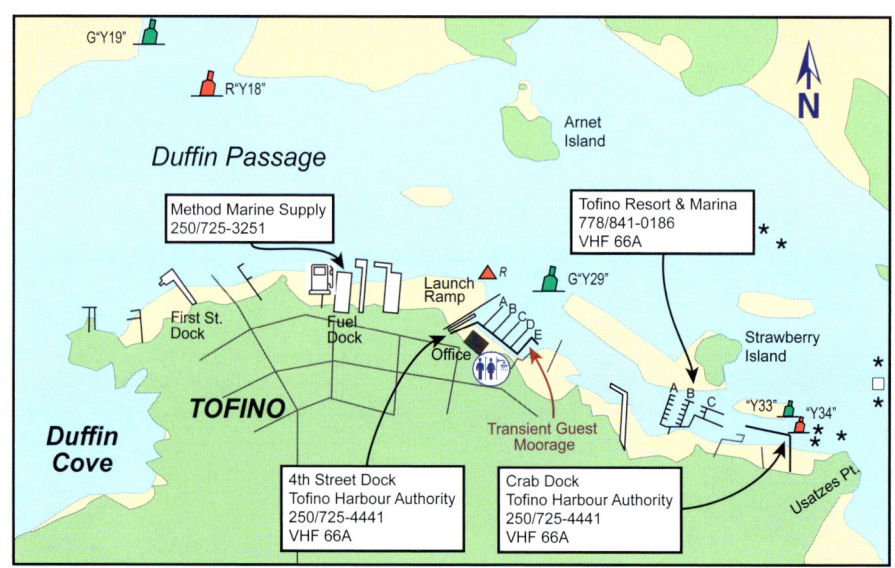

Tofino

Tofino's waterfront as you enter Duffin Passage; fuel is at the docks on the far left of this picture.

The Tofino Water Taxi makes stops at the Big Tree Trail.

Opitsaht First Nations Village, located on the southwest end of Mears Island, is the oldest, continuously run Native settlement. A campground/hostel above the beach is a starting point for the popular Lone Cone Trail to the summit of Lone Mountain, contact (250) 725-2169 or go to www.LoneConeTrail.ca for more information. The Water Taxi from Tofino can take you to the Opitsaht Dock.

Hot Springs Cove, located 28 nautical miles northwest of Tofino, is a popular destination. The high-speed Tofino Water Taxi makes runs to Hot Springs Cove and is a nice option for visitors arriving in Tofino by private boat or by car.

From seaward, enter Tofino via Templar Channel. While Chart 3673 gives a good overall view for the close navigation needed, we strongly recommend large scale Chart 3685. Note how the buoyed fairway twists and turns to avoid shallows. Identify each buoy as you proceed, and leave the buoys off the proper hand.

From the north, enter Tofino via Deadman Pass, narrow and bordered on both sides by drying flats. Be sure to use large scale Chart 3685. Note that while you may be returning to Tofino, the buoyage system in Deadman Pass is not. As you head south in Deadman Pass you will leave the red buoys to port.

The approach to Tofino, whether through Templar Channel or Deadman Pass, is one of the few places on this coast where you need to carefully watch the currents. Time your arrival for slack water to avoid the strong currents that swirl around the docks.

Stay close to the docks once at Tofino. A serious drying reef lies a short distance off.

Anchoring can be a challenge because of strong currents that sweep through the harbor. Although Tofino has several public docks, moorage for visiting boats is limited. The District of Tofino Dock (called the Whiskey Dock) near Grice Point is closest to the Co-op and the liquor store, but is busy day and night with water taxis and locals. Moorage may be available at the Method Marine Supply fuel dock. It tends to be full during the busy season, but you can check.

The most popular moorage is the Tofino Harbour Authority 4th Street Public Dock. Farther east, the Tofino Resort & Marina may have space, but without advance reservations the docks often are taken by their sport fishing guests. The easternmost public dock is called the Crab Dock. The Crab Dock is a longer walk from the commercial district, however. Currents can make landing on a flood tide tricky. Do not proceed eastward past the Crab Dock. A major rock blocks the channel.

㉖ **Tofino Harbour Authority 4th Street Public Dock**. P.O. Box 826, Tofino, BC V0R 2Z0; (250) 725-4441; info@tofinoharbour.ca; www.tofinoharbour.ca; Monitors VHF 66A. Open all year, 20 & 30 amp power, water, for fee pumpout, washrooms, showers, laundry, for fee Wi-Fi. This is the closest moorage to Tofino, convenient to the commercial district. Watch the current. Office open daily 11:00 a.m. to 1:00 p.m. in summers; open Tuesday, Wednesday and Thursday during the off season.

A shoal extends into the channel from a piling east of the easternmost dock, and leads across the ends of B, C and D docks. Dredging was completed in 2017. Minimum depth is 8 feet at 0 tide.

This is a commercial fishing harbour with some recreational and transient moorage. The "L" end of E-dock is designated for transient vessels. The remainder of E-dock is for recreational boats over 25 feet and includes both transient and long-term moorage. The shore side of the main spine float connecting all the labeled floats is for recreational vessels less than 25 feet. Approximately 50 feet of transient moorage is located on the east side of the deep-water end of A-dock. Sixty feet of active loading/unloading space is located on the west side of the shore-end of A-dock, just below the ramp. All transient moorage is first-come, first-served. Rafting encouraged up to two deep. Permanent spaces used for guest moorage as assigned by the harbourmaster. The Harbour Authority tries to fit everyone in.

The dock water system operates by a 'loonie' timer, similar to pay showers. Make sure all the other faucets are closed, then feed a loonie into the timer, which pressurizes the dock system for about 15 minutes. Water pressure is good and one dollar should get you about 100 U.S. gallons of water. Be all set up before you start the system. Car day parking available for purchase.

WHALE WISE - JUAN DE FUCA

Southern Resident Killer Whales

The Canadian government has enacted measures to protect Southern Resident Killer Whales in Critical Habitat areas of BC waters. Critical Habitat BC waters include the Strait of Georgia, the southeast portion of the Gulf Islands, Boundary Pass, Haro Strait, Strait of Juan de Fuca, and offshore from West Coast Vancouver Island up to Tofino.

- Three (3) Interim Sanctuary Zones have been established where general vessel traffic is prohibited from June 1 – November 30. Two are in the Gulf Islands and the third is Swiftsure Bank at the east entrance to Strait of Juan de Fuca.
- Vessels must remain at least 400 meters from all killer whales when in Southern Resident Killer Whale Critical Habitat areas (orange area on map above).
- Three "Enhanced Management Areas" have been established (Strait of Juan de Fuca, Fraser River mouth, southern Gulf Islands) where all vessels are asked to reduce their speed to less than 7 knots when within 1 km of killer whales.
- When safe to do so, vessel operators are asked to turn off echo sounders and turn engines to neutral idle if a whale is within 400 meters.

Marine Mammals & All Whales

Existing Canada regulations protect all marine mammals in BC waters. Give dolphins, porpoises, sea lions, seals, and other marine mammals the space they need. Coming too close can cause them stress and to abandon their young.

- Stay 100 yards from non-killer whales, dolphins, porpoises, and other marine mammals, and 200 yards if they are resting or with young.

WEST COAST OF VANCOUVER ISLAND

See Area Map Page 396 - Maps Not for Navigation

㉖ **Method Marine Supply.** Box 219, 380 Main Street, Tofino, BC V0R 2Z0; (250) 725-3251; sbernard@methodmarine.ca; www.methodmarine.ca. Open all year. Gasoline, bio-diesel, lube oils, propane, water, ice, divers' air, vacuum waste oil disposal. Moorage has electrical hookup, but moorage often is fully reserved in the busy season. This is a modern, well-run facility, with a good chandlery that carries a wide range of equipment and supplies, including sport fishing gear, fishing licenses, bait, snacks, foul weather wear, and charts. Storm Light Outfitters, a well-stocked outdoor gear store, is right behind, up on the street.

㉖ **Tofino Resort & Marina.** 634 Campbell St, Tofino, BC V0R 2Z0; (844) 680-4184; (778) 841-0186; marina@tofinoresortandmarina.com; www.tofinoresortandmarina.com. Monitors VHF 66A. This is a high-end resort with secure gated docks, open all year. 15 & 30 amp power, water, showers, laundry, Wi-Fi and fitness room. Most of the slips and side-tie are for smaller boats with limited side-tie moorage for medium sized boats on the 'T' ends of several docks. There is a side-tie area for yachts up to 130 feet with 100 amp power. Reservations requested. The fuel dock has marine gasoline, no diesel. Harbour Air Service available from the dock. The upland '1909 Restaurant' offers fine dining, with casual eats available at the adjacent 'Hatch Pub'. Adventure tours to Hot Springs Cove, hiking excursions through National Parks, and whale/bear watching are offered through the upland resort/marina office. The resort is co-owned by former Canucks player Willie Mitchell.

㉖ **Tofino Harbour Authority Crab Dock.** P.O. Box 826, Tofino, BC V0R 2Z0; (250) 725-4441; info@tofinoharbour.ca; www.tofinoharbour.ca; Monitors VHF 66A. Julie is the harbormaster. This is the easternmost dock on the Tofino waterfront. Some transient recreational moorage for vessels up to 40 feet, 20 & 30 amp power, water, Wi-Fi. First-come, first-served. Use caution upon approach as there are rocks off the northeast end of the docks and a shoal located just north of the dock; check your charts.

CLAYOQUOT SOUND TO UCLUELET

It is approximately 19 miles from Lennard Island, at the southern entrance to Clayoquot Sound, to Whistle Buoy *Y42* offshore from Ucluelet Inlet. These 19 miles cross the ocean face of the Pacific Rim National Park; but since you'll probably be about 3 miles out, you won't see much of the park. Sailing Directions says to stay 2 miles off the coast; Watmough likes 3 miles. So do we. Plot a waypoint for Whistle Buoy *Y42*, go 3 miles offshore from Lennard Island, turn left, and make for the buoy. In fog, radar is a big help in avoiding the many fish boats that work these waters. Sport fishing boats that travel full speed even in thick fog are especially worrisome. Absent a GPS and radar, in fog we would go out to at least 30 fathoms deep and follow the 30 to 40 fathom curve to Buoy *Y42*.

Weather Information: The Lennard Island lighthouse, just outside of Clayoquot Sound, and the Amphitrite Point lighthouse, just outside of Barkley Sound, provide a picture of outside weather conditions. Listen to the continuous marine broadcast for the latest weather information or you can attempt to call the lighthouse keepers on VHF 82.

Amphitrite Point. Amphitrite Point, at the end of the Ucluth Peninsula, can present a challenge. The essential navigation problem is to get around Amphitrite Point while staying well clear of Jenny Reef, shown on the chart, yet staying off the Amphitrite Point shoreline. The problem is made more difficult in fog, when the radar may lose Buoy *Y43* against the shoreline.

Carolina Channel is the entry suggested by Sailing Directions, except in thick weather, when Carolina Channel can be too rough for safe navigation. The outer entrance to Carolina Channel is marked by Whistle Buoy *Y42*, about 0.5 mile offshore. The channel leads past Bell Buoy *Y43*, which lies but 300 meters off the rocky shore. In reduced visibility, life can get interesting when you're trying to raise Buoy *Y43*. If you have trouble seeing the buoy against the rocky shoreline, the light structure on the east side of Francis Island could serve as a leading mark.

Find Your Dream Itinerary
with *Waggoner* as your *Guide*

The 2023 Waggoner Guide includes cruising itineraries for the boater's dream vacation trip to many of the best places throughout Puget Sound, San Juan Islands, Gulf Islands, Desolation Sound, and Southeast Alaska.

Itineraries include helpful information for navigating the waters to each destination along with ideas and suggestions for things to do when you get there.

WAGGONER

WaggonerGuide.com • 360.299.8500 • Anacortes

www.WaggonerGuide.com

As you approach Carolina Channel, leave Whistle Buoy *Y42* close to starboard, and turn to a course of 037° magnetic to raise Buoy *Y43*. After passing close south of Buoy *Y43*, Sailing Directions suggests using the summit of South Beg Island as a leading mark. It should bear approximately 075° magnetic. Run approximately 0.2 mile until the eastern extremity of Francis Island is abeam, then round Francis Island and enter Ucluelet Inlet.

BARKLEY SOUND

Depending on your direction, Barkley Sound is the first sound on the way north or the last sound on the way south. Barkley Sound is named after English Capt. Charles William Barkley, who in 1787 sailed into the sound on his ship *Loudoun*, which he had illegally renamed *Imperial Eagle* (Austrian registry) to avoid paying a license fee to the East India Company. With Capt. Barkley was his 17-year-old bride, Frances Trevor Barkley. Capt. Barkley came to trade with the Indians for furs. You'll find reminders of the Barkleys in many names around Barkley Sound, including Imperial Eagle, Loudon and Trevor Channels.

Barkley Sound is roughly square in shape, measuring 15 miles across its mouth and approximately 12 miles deep, not counting the 20-mile-long canal to Port Alberni. The sound is dotted with rocks and islands, and the waters are famous for their excellent fishing. A cruising boat could spend weeks in Barkley Sound, fishing, exploring, and moving from one nook to another. In fact, many boats do just that, coming directly from Puget Sound, Oregon, or the Strait of Georgia region.

During the summer months, fog often forms just offshore. In minutes, it can sweep in, even with no wind. It is essential, therefore, that the navigator know the vessel's position at all times. GPS and electronic navigation will prove useful in foggy conditions. Radar is a big help. Most boats cruising Barkley Sound, large and small, have radar. Even with electronic help, the navigator must remain alert and aware.

If approaching from up-island, you will probably enter Barkley Sound from Ucluelet. Note that a course across Sargison Bank from Ucluelet to the Broken Group takes you very close to a rock that lies approximately 0.7 miles east of Chrow Island. The rock is shown on the chart not with a rock symbol, but by a depth of 0.5 meters. It is easy to overlook while scanning the chart for hazards.

If approaching from the Strait of Juan de Fuca or Oregon, leave Cape Beale at least one-half mile to starboard, which will leave the offshore rocks a safe distance off. The Canadian Customs dock may or may not be available, check the CBSA website. Due to the uncertain availability of Canadian Customs, we recommend clearing customs in Victoria. A good option is to enter Imperial Eagle Channel, leave Effingham Island to port, and proceed west between Clarke and Benson Islands to Loudoun Channel and Ucluelet.

In Barkley Sound you will find superb exploring everywhere: Pipestem Inlet, the Pinkerton Islands, Julia Passage, the Chain Group, the Deer Group and the famous Broken Group. Settled summer weather makes it possible to anchor in any of hundreds of coves or nooks and explore by dinghy.

We do not cover all the areas mentioned above, an unfortunate consequence of limited exploration time. Other references—especially Douglass' *Exploring Vancouver Island's West Coast* are excellent resources. In the end, your own inquisitiveness and derring-do will determine the range of your exploring.

Ucluelet. Ucluelet is pronounced "You-CLOO-let." With moorage, fuel, provisions, repairs and good dining, the village of Ucluelet (pop. approx. 1800) is the commercial center of Barkley Sound. The channel leading into Ucluelet is well buoyed. Following the rule of Red, Right, Returning, you will have no problems. Spring Cove, to port a short distance inside the channel, is where fish boats used to discharge their catches. The plant deep in the cove is closed and the docks are posted with No Trespassing signs. Spring Cove is a good anchorage.

Ucluelet has one fuel dock, located on the town side. Several fish processing plants and public docks used by large commercial boats are also on the town side of the inlet. Small public docks used by the Ucluelet Native Band are on the east side of the inlet, across from town.

West of the north tip of Lyche Island, the Ucluelet Small Craft Harbour is the principal marina, and the one we recommend. Another marina to consider is Island West Resort, on the west side of the inlet just before the turn to the small craft harbor. The docks are built almost entirely for trailerable boats. They have no designated guest dock, so call ahead by phone.

In town, halfway up Ucluelet Inlet, Pioneer Boat Works (250-726-4382) has a marine railway for haulout and repairs. Their chandlery, next to the ways, has a good stock of marine supplies, commercial and sportfishing tackle, and charts. Cruisers will find what they need there.

Around the winding streets of Ucluelet you will find gift shops, art galleries, including an excellent Native Gallery, and the Ucluelet Aquarium. The Co-op Grocery is up the hill. Restaurants include casual to fine dining. Don't miss the excellent bakery and the Ucluelet Brewery. Visit the kayak museum inside the old Wreckage building, called "Manke at The Wreckage," located at 1754 Peninsula Rd. above the Ucluelet Small Craft Harbour.

It's a pleasant bike ride out the road to the Coast Guard Station at Amphitrite Point Lighthouse. The 2.6 km Lighthouse Loop Trail is especially nice, with scenic view points that begin beyond He-Tin-Kis Park, near the Coast Guard Station. The 5 km Big Beach Trail overlooks the ocean and rocky shore. The 1 km Ancient Cedars Trail is north.

Ucluelet Harbour

WEST COAST OF VANCOUVER ISLAND   *Reference Only – Not for Navigation*

Barkley Sound

The 52 Steps dock at Ucluelet has side-tie guest moorage on both sides of the float.

In Ucluelet Inlet, Lyche Island can be passed on either side. If passing on the west side (the town side), check Chart 3646 and leave the buoys and beacons off the proper hands.

Customs: CLOSED IN 2020, 2021, AND 2022. In the past, the 52 Steps Dock in Ucluelet was the only customs reporting station on the west coast of Vancouver Island. Customs reporting at this location was seasonal, open June 1 to September 30 and has not been operational since the 2019 season. Check with Canada Border Service Agency at www.cbsa-asfc.gc.ca

㉗ **Eagle Marine, Ltd./Columbia Fuels**. 1231 Eber Road, Ucluelet, BC V0R 3A0; (250) 726-4262; www.columbiafuels.com. Open 7 days a week all year, summer 7:30 a.m. to 6:00 p.m., winter 8:00 a.m. to 5:00 p.m. Gasoline, diesel, lubricants, water, ice, bait, tackle, convenience items, garbage drop.

Whiskey Landing. 1645 Cedar Rd, Ucluelet, BC V0R 3A0, Canada; (250) 726-2270; www.whiskeylanding.com; info@whiskeylanding.com. Guest moorage for hotel guests.

㉘ **Ucluelet Small Craft Harbour.** 200 Hemlock St., Ucluelet, BC V0R 3A0; (250) 726-4241; (250) 725-8190; kcortes@ucluelet.ca. The marina has 30 amp and some 50 amp power, water, washrooms, tidy showers and laundry, pumpout, garbage drop, recycle, waste oil disposal, and for-fee Wi-Fi. The outside basin, before entering the large main basin, has three floats that are usually for commercial boats, with a pumpout at the bottom of the ramp. Docks B & C in the main basin are marked for commercial boats only; docks D, E & F are for recreational and commercial boats. The facility is completely protected, well maintained, and quiet. It's where most cruising boats tie up. The staff is attentive and helpful. Kevin Cortes is the wharfinger.

㉘ **Island West Resort.** Box 879, 1990 Bay St., Ucluelet, BC V0R 3A0; (250) 726-7515; fish@islandwestresort.com; www.islandwestresort.com. Open all year, reservations accepted. Limited moorage for larger boats up to 40 feet, call ahead. A busy sportfishing resort, often fully reserved a year ahead for July and August. Limited 15 amp power, washrooms, seasonal showers and laundry, free Wi-Fi, portapotty dump, launch ramp, marine supplies, ice, convenience groceries, excellent pub. Fishing charters.

㉙ **52 Steps Dock.** (250) 726-4241; (250) 725-8190; kcortes@ucluelet.ca. Located on the west side, north of the fuel dock and south of town, open all year with moorage on both sides of a 450 foot float. Water, no power, no restrooms or showers. This facility is managed by the Small Craft Harbour wharfinger. Pay by phone or when the wharfinger makes his rounds at the dock, twice daily.

WESTERN BARKLEY SOUND

The western part of Barkley Sound, from Ucluelet to Pipestem Inlet and over to the Pinkerton Islands, is relatively open and easily run. As long as you stay in the middle, Newcombe Channel and Macoah Passage present no problems. They lead to the Stopper Islands and, beyond them, to Pipestem Inlet. Pipestem Inlet is where the magical falls at Lucky Creek await.

Stopper Islands. The Stopper Islands are quite pretty and beg exploration by dinghy or kayak. Anchor between Larkins Island and the large island.

Toquaht Bay Marina. www.secretbeachcampground.com. On the west side of Toquaht Bay behind a breakwater constructed of orange railroad tankers. Boat launch and moorage for trailerable boats.

Pipestem Inlet. Pipestem Inlet is long, beautiful and bordered by high mountains. Most of the inlet is too deep for anchoring, but there are several good anchorages near the mouth and at the head of the inlet. Anchorages near the mouth are behind **Bazett Island** in the southwest cove and southeast cove. The southwest cove has a fish farm work float and a number of large yellow buoys. The southeast cove is in the little thumb-shaped inlet; an adjacent shore provides stern-tie opportunities. A third anchorage option at the mouth of the inlet is on the north side of **Refuge Island**, a bit east of the 16-meter island. These anchorages are within easy dinghy commute to Lucky Creek. At the head of the inlet, you can tuck behind 32-meter island, or continue to the very end to anchor in a basin formed by a shoaling area.

㉚ **Lucky Creek.** The late John Schlagel, fearless longtime explorer, did not suggest that we see Lucky Creek, he instructed us to see Lucky Creek, and he was right. This is a window-of-opportunity trip and the window corresponds with high tide.

We suggest taking the outboard-powered dinghy up to the falls an hour before high water and coming out an hour after. Correspondents Steve and Toni Jefferies report that a minimum plus 7-foot tide is needed to navigate the entry bar and creek to the falls. There are many shoals along the creek.

The entrance is directly across Pipestem Inlet from Bazett Island. After crossing the shallow entry (bordered by meadow grass and wildflowers), the channel winds through marvelous mature forest, with overhanging cedars. The deeper part of the channel tends to follow the outside of the bends, river-style.

"When you arrive, tie the dinghy off to the side and climb up to a series of pools. Be careful, the rocks can be slippery. And remember, you can't tarry too long, the falling tide will close you in.

You probably won't be alone at Lucky Creek. The lodges and resorts in the area are fully familiar with Lucky Creek and the boat drivers know the channel well. We got to Lucky Creek a half-hour after high tide, and the guests were all leaving—at top speed in the narrow waterway that was unfamiliar to us. They came right at us and swooped past, all smiles and happiness as we splashed through their wakes. No matter, the trip was worth it." [*Hale*]

Entrance Inlet. Entrance Inlet indents Vancouver Island at the northeast corner of Mayne Bay. Anchor in the outer basin in 40 feet. During the day you will have boat traffic from the fishing resort in Cigarette Cove.

Cigarette Cove. You can anchor in Cigarette Cove, but the resort takes up much of the space. The entry is narrow and bounded by rocks. If you pay attention, you will have no problems.

Southeast Cove. This cove is open to the west, but is good in settled weather. Anchor in 35 to 40 feet.

Pinkerton Islands. Far from the wildness of the outer islands, the Pinkerton Islands are north of the Broken Group, next to Vancouver Island. The Pinkertons are small and protected, with narrow channels, and are ideal for gunkholing. Watch for rocks. The easiest anchorage is in the cove northwest of Williams Island. Unless several boats want to share the cove, no stern-tie is required. A study of the chart will suggest a number of other possibilities, most of which will require a stern-tie to shore.

WEST COAST OF VANCOUVER ISLAND   *See Area Map Page 402 - Maps Not for Navigation*

Take the train to visit Historic McLean Mill, a working steam-powered mill.

UPPER BARKLEY SOUND

Effingham Inlet. Sailing Directions says Effingham Inlet is high, steep and deep, with few if any anchoring possibilities. Correspondents Bruce and Margaret Evertz explored Effingham Inlet and here is their report:

"We found anchorage in the bay on the west side of Effingham Inlet about one-quarter of the way in. The center of the bay is fairly flat and approximately 75 feet deep. Our anchor set well at 49°00.959'N/125°10.659'W. Another secure spot would be at the south corner of the bay in 30 to 40 feet with a stern-tie. We were told that boats often anchor on the north side of the small peninsula near John Islet, at the entrance."

"While several oyster farms are in the lower part of Effingham Inlet, we saw few signs of man farther in. It isn't Princess Louisa, but like Pipestem Inlet it's still pretty. The sides are high, steep and forested, with many interesting cliffs. We saw only two waterfalls. We didn't see many anchoring opportunities unless you want to stern-tie, and there were many small bights for that. We were told that afternoons can be windy, but the trees grow right to the high water line so we don't think the winds amount to much." [*Evertz*]

㉛ **Jane Bay/Franks Bay.** This bay, known locally both as Jane Bay and Franks Bay, is not named on the chart. It is located at the back of Barkley Sound, connected by a narrow but safe passage with Vernon Bay at 48°59.80'N/125°08.80'W. Anchor, carefully, near the head before the flats shoal too much. A water line is clearly marked with yellow buoys. Or tie up at Eagle Nook Lodge.

㉛ **Eagle Nook Resort (Vernon Bay).** P.O. Box 289, Ucluelet, BC V0R 3A0; (604) 357-3361; samantha@eaglenook.com, www.eaglenook.com. Monitors VHF 73. Marina is immediately to starboard as you enter the bay. Moorage to 100 feet, 30 & 50 amp power, water, Wi-Fi, washrooms and showers. Reservations recommended, especially for larger boats. Open June to mid-September. An elite high-end restaurant. Guided fishing and kayak tours are available to visiting boaters. Moorage is for those staying in the resort's accommodations; minimum 3-night stay. Well-maintained walking trails lead through the forest. Corporate retreat packages.

Useless Inlet. Useless Inlet contains a number of aquaculture leases and recreational float homes. Entry to the inlet is made interesting by a series of large rocks that are covered except at lower stages of the tide. The rocks were covered when we were there and the wind rippled the water, making them hard to see. The obvious safe entry is along the north shore, to avoid the rocks in the middle. We attempted that route twice but didn't feel comfortable. We did see several trailerable sport fishing boats roar in and out of Useless Inlet, running between the rocks in the middle. They knew where the channel was; we didn't.

Correspondents Bruce and Margaret Evertz went into Useless Inlet. They report that "Useless Nook," described in the Douglass book, has an oyster farm in it, and a sign on shore that says, "No anchorage or trespassing in bay—oyster farm."

Rainy Bay Cove. Located on the north side of Junction Passage on Seddall Island. Tucked behind the smaller Boyson Islands, a narrow passage leads into Rainy Bay Cove, home to a quiet community of float cabins along the western shore. Good anchorage at the north end of the cove to the west of the shoaling nook; anchoring depths of 30 feet over a mud bottom.

ALBERNI INLET

Alberni Inlet begins between Chup Point and Mutine Point, where it meets with Trevor Channel and Junction Passage. The inlet continues some 21 miles into the heart of Vancouver Island to the town of Port Alberni. Alberni Inlet is narrow and high-sided. A well-protected detached public float is in San Mateo Bay, near the mouth of the inlet, and in Hook Bay about half way up the inlet. China Creek Marina, about 6 miles down-inlet from Port Alberni, has limited guest moorage for larger vessels. Tidal current flows are less than 1 knot both directions, but the surface current can flow as fast as 3 knots when wind and current direction are the same.

In the summer, an up-inlet thermal wind develops at 1:00 p.m. ("You can set your clock by it," says a friend in Port Alberni), and will increase to 25 to 30 knots by mid-afternoon. The wind produces a short, uncomfortable chop. We would run Alberni Inlet in the morning.

Port Alberni. In our opinion, the McLean Mill National Historic Site, accessed via a 1954 diesel locomotive train, is the highlight and reason to visit Port Alberni. Port Alberni offers several moorage options for pleasure boaters. Port Alberni is also very popular as a saltwater trailer boat destination, giving trailer boaters safe and easy access to Barkley Sound, one of the most diverse and interesting cruising grounds in the Northwest. It's a 21-mile run down the Alberni Inlet to Barkley Sound.

To get to Port Alberni from the mainland, trailer the boat to the BC Ferries terminal at Tsawwassen, near the U.S. border, or to the Horseshoe Bay terminal, north of Vancouver. Large, comfortable ferries will take you to Nanaimo's Duke Point or Departure Bay terminals. (Or, if you are coming from the south, take the private ferry Coho from Port Angeles, Wash. to Victoria.) Our trailer boat friends tell us the fares for trailered boats are not inexpensive, so be prepared. From the Duke Point ferry terminal at Nanaimo, an easy and often beautiful 1½- to 2-hour drive on

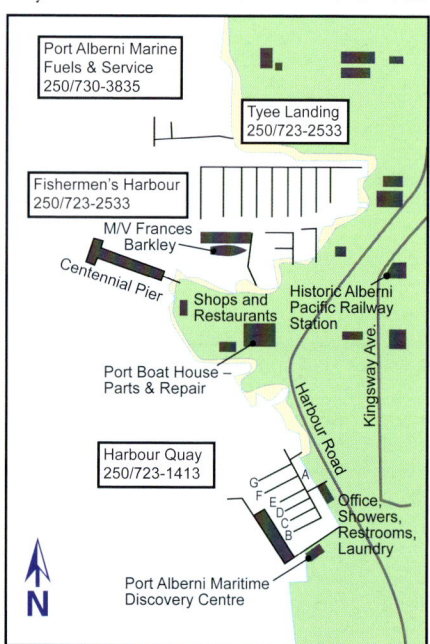

Port Alberni

paved highway will take you to Port Alberni.

Along the way, be sure to stop at Cathedral Grove for a walk through a towering forest of 1000-year-old cedar, hemlock and Douglas fir. The trail is easy and well-maintained. If you hurry along, you can walk it in 20 minutes. If you linger to absorb more of the majesty, it could take about an hour. Interpretive signs explain everything.

To reach Port Alberni you do have to go over a 1230-foot-high mountain pass, with an 8 percent grade on the east side and a 6 percent grade on the west. Be sure your rig has enough power and brakes.

Once at Port Alberni, you'll find good launch ramps at Clutesi Haven Marina at the mouth of the Somass River, and at China Creek, located 6 miles down the Alberni Inlet. Long-term parking is available at both locations. All the marinas are operated by the Port Alberni Port Authority; www.portalberniportauthority.ca.

In Port Alberni you'll find complete services including hospital, shopping, marine supplies and a boatyard. The "Port Boat House" (250-724-5754) provides service for trailerable boats.

In years past, a 1954 diesel locomotive and train cars ran from downtown Port Alberni to the McLean Mill National Historic Site, the only working steam-operated sawmill in Canada. The train is no longer operational, but visitors can arrive by taxi, call United Cab at (250) 723-2121. The McLean Mill is a fascinating tour, with interpretive signs to explain what you are looking at. The cookhouse, blacksmith shop, workers' housing and other buildings have been restored. Mill demonstrations and a guided theatrical experience are offered as scheduled. Logs are in the mill pond. A trip to the McLean Mill is a step back in time. The entire family will enjoy it. Call (250) 723-1376. Better yet, for latest information and schedules see www.alberniheritage.com.

For information on other attractions and events, contact the Alberni Valley Chamber of Commerce, (250) 724-6535.

Salmon Festival: Port Alberni's Salmon Festival & Derby (www.salmonfestival.ca) is held Labour Day weekend each year at Clutesi Haven Marina. We are told that the Somass River is the third largest salmon stream in B.C. Only the Fraser River and the Skeena River have larger returns.

Haulout: Alberni Engineering and Shipyard has haulout and complete repairs for boats to 100 feet. Call (250) 723-0111.

Fuel: Marine gasoline and diesel are available at Tyee Landing in Port Alberni and in China Creek.

San Mateo Bay. Located at the junction of Trevor Passage and Junction Passage on the east side. A 70-foot public float, managed by Port of Alberni Port Authority, offers overnight side-tie moorage at no charge. Moorage available on both sides of the float, which is detached from shore. The float, tucked behind Bernard Point, provides shelter from most winds. Depths in the bay are too deep for anchoring.

Uchucklesit Inlet. A branch near the entrance of Port Alberni Inlet, Uchucklesit leads northwest to Snug Basin. The east shore of this deep inlet is lined with float homes, summer cabins and year-round residences; watch your speed and wake. The variety of homes makes for an interesting cruise. About half way up the inlet on the east shore near Cass Creek is the small community post office on floats; this is also the landing for the *M/V Barkley Sound* passenger vessel. No services for pleasure boaters. Anchorage can be found in **Snug Basin**, with good protection in depths of 50-60 feet over a flat mud bottom.

Green Cove. Located east of Cheeyah Island at the entrance to Uchucklesit Inlet, Green Cove offers protected anchorage from all except northwesterly winds which have fetch. Anchorage depths are as charted, with a flat mud and sand bottom. Upland homes and cabins dot the shoreline, some with fanciful names. In 2018 the Landons noted a non-operational fuel dock just inside the cove entrance on the north shore of Strawberry Point peninsula. No log booms were observed in the cove.

Limestone Bay. Located on the west side of Alberni Inlet, just north of the entrance to Uchucklesit Inlet. Use only the southwest entrance into the bay. The small bay has space for one or two boats to anchor at the northwest head of the bay. Two float cabins, both with log breakwaters, are not a factor for anchoring. Anchoring depths of 12 feet over mixed mud and sand, protection from northerlies but open to south westerlies.

㉜ **China Creek Marina & Campground.** (250) 723-9812; www.campchinacreek.com; chinacreek@alberniport.ca. Open April through September, 88 slips and 2300 feet of side-tie moorage, 4-lane launch ramp. Proof of $2 million liability insurance required. Gasoline, diesel, propane, 15, 20 & 30 amp power, washrooms, showers, laundry, ice, garbage drop, fish cleaning stations, playground. Campsites and RV sites are adjacent. Shallow depths with shifting sandbars make the marina entrance challenging. Moorage is for camping guests but does include camping on your boat.

Hook Bay. Located about half way up Port Alberni Inlet on the west shore, Hook Bay provides protection from up-inlet winds. Anchor in 30-40 feet over a flat bottom. A 50-foot public float, managed by the Port Alberni Port Authority, is available for overnight moorage at no charge; side-tie on both sides of the float, which is not connected to shore.

㉝ **Harbour Quay.** 2900 Harbour Rd., Port Alberni, BC V9Y 7X2; (250) 723-1413; www.portalberniportauthority.ca; harbourquay@alberniport.ca. Harbour Quay has 15 slips and 2000 lineal feet of side-tie moorage. Proof of $2 million liability insurance required. 20 & 30 amp power, washrooms, showers, laundry, potable water on the floats, garbage drop and secured gate access. This is a breakwater-protected marina close to downtown. The docks have been reconfigured to create more side-tie moorage, making it attractive for larger boats. Check ahead for availability. Adjacent to the Maritime Heritage Discovery Centre, located in a genuine west coast lighthouse.

㉝ **Fishermen's Harbour.** 3140 Harbour Rd., Port Alberni, BC V9Y 7X2; (250) 723-2533; www.portalberniportauthority.ca; fishermensharbour@alberniport.ca. Open all year, 7600 feet of moorage. Proof of $2 million liability insurance required. 20, 30 and some 50 amp power, water, washrooms & showers, garbage drop and pumpout. Shipyard, marine ways and a two-ton electric winch on site. Fishermen's Harbour is adjacent to downtown Port Alberni, with all the services of downtown close by. They never turn anyone away, but be prepared to raft. June is the busiest month.

㉝ **Tyee Landing.** 3140 Harbour Rd., Port Alberni, BC V9Y 7X2; (250) 723-2533; www.portalberniportauthority.ca; fishermensharbour@ alberniport.ca. 160 feet of side-tie moorage is located north of Fishermen's Harbour and to the shore side of the fuel dock. Contact the Port Authority for availability. Proof of $2 million liability insurance required.

Harbour Quay provides moorage for pleasure boaters visiting Port Alberni.

WEST COAST OF VANCOUVER ISLAND

See Area Map Page 402 - Maps Not for Navigation

㉝ Port Alberni Marine Fuels & Services. 990-3300 Harbour Rd., Port Alberni, BC V9Y 7X2; (250) 730- 3835; At the end of the Tyee Landing dock, located just north of Fishermen's Harbour, this fuel facility is a recent addition. Marine gasoline and diesel including high-speed diesel. Convenience store. Open Monday through Friday 9:00 a.m. to 5:00 p.m.; Saturday, Sunday, and holidays 9:00 a.m. to 3:00 p.m.

㉞ Clutesi Haven. (250) 724-6837; www.portalberniportauthority.ca; clutesihaven@alberniport.ca. Open all year. Moorage sometimes available, call ahead. Proof of $2 million liability insurance reequired. Water, 15, 20 & 30 amp power, washrooms, garbage drop, 4-lane launch ramp. Clutesi Haven is located behind a breakwater near the mouth of the Somass River. Best suited to boats 40 feet or less. This is a popular launching spot for trailerable boats. Hotels, pubs, and liquor store are nearby. Groceries are 5 blocks away.

BROKEN GROUP

The Broken Group extends from the wind-and-wave-lashed outer islands to peaceful islands deep inside Barkley Sound. The Broken Group is part of the Pacific Rim National Park, to be preserved in its natural state in perpetuity. For many Northwest boaters, a holiday spent in the Broken Group is the fulfillment of a lifelong dream.

Boats visiting the Broken Group will find dozens of little nooks and bights to put the hook down, depending on weather and the mood on board. Reanne & Don Douglass, and the Yeadon-Jones all describe a number of them in their guides. The major anchorages are Effingham Bay, Turtle Bay and Nettle Island.

Pets: The Broken Group is part of Pacific Rim National Park. In order to protect native flora and fauna, pets are not permitted on shore anywhere in the Broken Group.

Effingham Bay. Effingham Bay is large, pretty, and protected. On the nights of our visits we have shared the bay with 10 to 20 other boats, yet everyone had room to swing and we didn't feel crowded. The chart shows the entrance. Anchor in 30 to 50 feet, good holding. Sunsets, seen out the mouth of the bay, can be dramatic. Because Effingham Bay is open to the west, westerly winds can make the anchorage a bit bumpy.

Take the time to dinghy ashore and hike to the east side of Effingham Island, where you will find a lovely sand beach. The trail begins at the end of the little thumb of water at the head of Effingham Bay, marked by some posts decorated with crab pot floats. The trail is narrow and requires some clambering over tree roots. Watch for plastic markers hanging from branches that show the way to go. Be wolf and bear aware. Make noise as you walk. When in a group, act in unison to send a clear message to the wolves that they are not welcome.

A variety of float homes and vacation homes line the north shore in Uchucklesit Inlet.

Back away slowly, do not turn your back on a wolf.

The trail across the island takes about 15 minutes. A sea cave is located in the area, but is inaccessible at high tide. Late in the day the view eastward from the beach—the sea, with the mountains of Vancouver Island painted in low reddish light—is inspiring.

Benson Island. In settled weather you can take anchorage off the east shore of Benson Island, in the cove opposite the water faucet icon on the chart. A trail leads across the island to a scenic rocky beach with a blowhole that sounds just like a whale blowing.

Clarke Island. Temporary or settled weather anchorage can be found on the east side of Clarke Island.

Turret Island. The cove formed by the 36-meter island on the southwest side of Turret Island is okay for anchoring, though the bottom is thick with kelp. The surrounding area has interesting rock formations and is good for exploring by dinghy or kayak.

㉟ Turtle Bay. Turtle Bay is a local name for the bay formed by Turtle Island, Willis Island, and Dodd Island, offering room for many boats to anchor. Joes Bay, an appendage of Turtle Bay, indents Turtle Island. It is the little nook where Salal Joe, the Hermit of Barkley Sound, made his home.

Entrance to Turtle Bay can be taken from the north, off Peacock Channel, between Dodd Island and Chalk Island. A study of the chart shows the entrance channel bounded by rocks and drying rock outcroppings along the way.

Some boaters prefer the less narrow entrance between Chalk Island and Turtle Island and then between Walsh Island and Turtle Island.

For either route, a careful entry, proceeding slowly and identifying the hazards, will bring you in safely. Anchor in 25 to 30 feet on a mud bottom, good holding.

Nettle Island. Nettle Island has three good anchorages—one in the large bay that indents the southern shore, and the other two in the channel between Nettle Island and Reeks Island to the east. In Nettle Island's large bay we prefer the eastern portion, off the park ranger's float cabin. The center of the bay is a little deep (50 to 60 feet, depending on state of tide), but you can find depths of 20 to 30 feet near the shore north of the ranger's cabin. Reader Dick Drinkow reports that the park ranger warns that boats have grounded on the shelf, and recommends anchoring in the center of the bay.

There are two other anchorages along the east side of Nettle Island, opposite Reeks Island. Both of these nooks will hold a couple of boats each, and some say they are delightful. The charted rocks are easy to identify and avoid.

Outer Islands. The outer islands of the Broken Group are marked by twisted trees, the result of relentless onshore winds, especially in the winter. If your needs include the desire to navigate "at the edge," the outer islands can satisfy that need. Here, you'll have your opportunity to run in wind and fog, with the Pacific Ocean swells beating against the rocks. Navigate carefully. The low islands are easy to get mixed up. Rocks and reefs are charted, but they're everywhere. This is beautiful, raw country. The kayakers have it best. The favored anchorage is at Wouwer Island.

Wouwer Island. Wouwer Island is breathtaking, both in its scenery and gunkholing. At half tide or higher, most boats can make it through the slit between Batley Island and Wouwer Island. A bow watch will only scare you, though necessary.

We anchored temporarily in a nook south of two islets, west of the slit between Batley and Wouwer Islands. A trail leads across the island to a lovely beach with great beachcombing.

EASTERN BARKLEY SOUND

㊱ Poett Nook. Poett Nook is on the eastern shore, at lat 48°53'N. It doesn't look like a nook when you see it. It is a spacious, rather pretty bay, with good anchoring in 25 to 35 feet. The entry is narrow but deep. The Poett Nook Marina, a large sport fishing resort, is on the eastern side of the bay.

㊱ **Poett Nook Marina & Campground.** Mailing: P.O. Box 1083, Port Alberni, BC V9Y 7L9; (250) 758-4440; (250) 720-9572; poettnookmarina@gmail.com; www.poettnook.com. Gasoline at the fuel dock, washrooms, showers. No power, non-potable water. A small store carries convenience food, ice, and tackle. Fee-based garbage drop. This is a busy small-boat sportfishing resort, with 123 RV/camping sites and berths for 174 boats. Maximum length 36 feet. Most boats launch at Port Alberni or China Creek.

Robbers Passage. Robbers Passage leads between Fleming Island and Tzartus Island in the Deer Group, and is a likely route for boats bound between points near the head of Barkely Sound and Bamfield. A rock that dries 1 meter is in the western approach to Robbers Passage. Although the rock is clearly charted, people at the Port Alberni Yacht Club swear this is one rock that moves. Give the rock a wide berth. The S-shaped channel leading into Robbers Passage requires close attention, but with attention it is safe. A study of large-scale chart 3668 will make the route clear. Inside the passage, the Port Alberni Yacht Club has its floating clubhouse and docks. Several large buoys might be mistaken for mooring buoys. These buoys are not designed for mooring and have dragged when boats tied to them.

Port Alberni Yacht Club. Consider spending at least one night at the Port Alberni Yacht Club. The facility is clean and well-maintained, and the folks are friendly and helpful. They have a wealth of local knowledge to share. Be sure to walk the beautiful trails around the peninsula behind the yacht club. The moorage charge is modest and goes back into the facility. All are welcome; no yacht club membership needed. Washrooms, showers, and non-potable water available. Power available to yacht club members only. Note that upland trails and facilities are private property and are for yacht club members and paying overnight guests. If you anchor out, do not come ashore.

Fleming Island. The day was sunny with only a gentle breeze, so we left the boat at the yacht club and motored the dinghy around Fleming Island. The impossibly rugged shoreline is dotted with sea caves. We were told that some of the caves extend far into the rock. For thousands of years the First Nations people in Barkley Sound put some of their dead in bentwood boxes and hid them in sea caves. We were fascinated by the stories.

We did, however, ease the dinghy through a narrow cleft in the rock and up to the mouth of one cave. The opening loomed above us, and we could see the floor of small boulders rise and disappear in darkness. The rock walls of the cleft were covered with orange and purple sea stars. Other neon-hued sea life waved in the surge. The word impressed does not begin to describe the effect on us. [Hale]

Tzartus Cove. Tzartus Cove (our preferred anchorage on Tzartus Island) is the name Douglass gives to this excellent anchorage about 0.5 mile north of Marble Cove. Rocks extend from both shores, so go right down the middle when you enter. Anchor near the head in 25 to 30 feet. Sea caves are nearby. Reader Dick Drinkow reports that a bit of northwest swell can get into the cove and that kelp fouled their anchor.

Marble Cove. Marble Cove is on the west side of Tzartus Island, and often is mentioned as a good anchorage (we would choose instead the cove one-half mile north). A rock stack between two islands and reddish rocks on the shore add to the scenic nature of the cove. A float house is on the north side of Marble Cove. Anchor in 25 to 30 feet off the gravel beach on the island opposite the float house. This is a good place to explore tidepools at low tide.

Grappler Inlet. Grappler Inlet joins near the mouth of Bamfield Inlet and leads to Port Désiré, a protected anchorage with a launch ramp and a public dock. Although Grappler Inlet is beautiful, it is surrounded by homes.

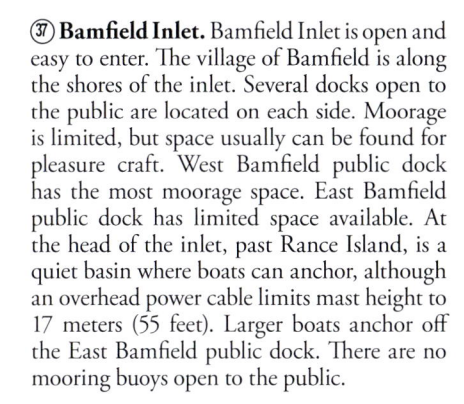

㊲ **Bamfield Inlet.** Bamfield Inlet is open and easy to enter. The village of Bamfield is along the shores of the inlet. Several docks open to the public are located on each side. Moorage is limited, but space usually can be found for pleasure craft. West Bamfield public dock has the most moorage space. East Bamfield public dock has limited space available. At the head of the inlet, past Rance Island, is a quiet basin where boats can anchor, although an overhead power cable limits mast height to 17 meters (55 feet). Larger boats anchor off the East Bamfield public dock. There are no mooring buoys open to the public.

㊲ **Bamfield.** They call the inlet "Main Street." The village of Bamfield covers both sides of the inlet, and the west side is not connected by road with the east side. You cross by dinghy or water taxi (250-728-1212). The Bamfield General Store, with liquor agency, is on the west side of the inlet. The Post Office is next to the store. A boardwalk runs along the homes and businesses on the west side, and folks get around by walking. The seasonal Boardwalk Bistro located near the West Bamfield public dock serves espresso drinks and delicious salmon burgers (open Thursday-Sunday).

The east side has roads that tie its businesses and homes together. They connect with the 60-mile-long dirt logging road that leads to Port Alberni. The east side has a hardware store and a marine store, motel with a pub, and a convenience grocery store with a cafe. The trail to Cape Beale begins on the east side of the inlet. Anchorage and a launch ramp are at nearby Port Désiré.

A small Outpost Hospital is located on the east side. It is set up to treat illness or injury, deliver babies, and dispense medication. The hospital is operated by registered nurses, and a visiting physician calls on a regular schedule. They work closely with the Coast Guard for emergency helicopter transport when needed. A fee schedule accommodates non-Canadians who need medical attention.

Fiber optic cables have been installed at Bamfield, and some docks and lodges may now offer Wi-Fi.

The large building on the east side of the inlet near the entrance houses the Bamfield Marine Research Science Centre. The Centre is owned by five universities in British Columbia and Alberta, and began operation in 1971. Visitors may walk the campus but office and research buildings are closed to the public. The Research Centre once served as the eastern terminus of the transpacific cable that connected North America with Australia. Its first message was sent on November 1, 1902; its last message was sent in 1959. See their website at www.bms.bc.ca.

Bamfield offers several events during the year, including the Music by the Sea Festival (250) 882-4527, with classical and jazz musicians from all over. See musicbythesea.ca for dates or call (250) 888-7772. The festival welcomes boaters. The first time you

The Port Alberni Yacht Club docks are in Robbers Passage.

WEST COAST OF VANCOUVER ISLAND

See Area Map Page 402 - Maps Not for Navigation

attend, they will award you a festival burgee to fly from your boat. Come a subsequent year, and they'll give you a second burgee with one star on it. Repeat as many times as you want and get as many burgees as your number of visits, each with more stars. The experience of sitting in the Marine Research Science Centre's Rix Auditorium and watching the sun set over Barkley Sound through floor to ceiling glass windows while listening to wonderful music is well worth repeating.

While in Bamfield, don't miss the Kiixin Tour (pronounced Keein). The Native village of Kiixin, located near Pachena Bay, is a National Historic Site with remains of a traditional First Nations village. Tours are provided by the Huu-ay-aht First Nation, open late-May to mid-September. A tour bus leaves from the East Bamfield Public Dock to the trail head. Hike through old-growth rain forest to a beautiful protected beach with tide pools. Evening tours include a gathering at the beach with a sharing of history, song and drumming. The trail is uneven and muddy in places. Book tours online at kiixin.ca/book-a-tour or call (250) 735-3432.

For an independent hiking adventure, visit Brady Beach, it's the locals' best kept secret. The beautiful sandy beach offers marvelous beach walks and sunset views. The beach is accessed via a gravel road behind West Bamfield Public Dock.

㉛ **East Bamfield Public Dock**. (250) 728-3231; hfnmarket@gmail.com hfndevelopmentlp.org; Located on the east side at the south end, 100 feet of guest moorage on the outside of the western-most float for vessels up to 15 meters (50 feet); water, for-fee garbage drop, 20 & 30 amp power at one stanchion located under the ramp. No washrooms. Dinghy landing space can usually be found. Preferred method to register and pay is at nearby upland "The Motel - Bamfield" (250-728-3231) or self-registration and pay with cash at the box located at the top of the ramp. Managed by the Huu-ay-aht Development Limited Partnership which also manages the nearby convenience store and "The Motel - Bamfield."

㉛ **Kingfisher Marina**. 211 Nuthatch Rd., Bamfield, BC V0R 1B0; (250) 728-3231; frontdesk@hunayaht.com. Located on the east side of the inlet opposite the "Y54" red spar buoy. Open all year, limited side-tie guest moorage behind the fuel dock. Gas and diesel at the fuel dock. Laundry service, Wi-Fi, and ice. No power, no water. Waterfront suites are available upland.

㉛ **West Bamfield Public Dock**. (250) 720-7548 wharfinger; bhadockmanager@gmail.com. Side-tie moorage on both sides of 500 feet of floats, 20 & 30 amp power, water. No washrooms, no garbage drop. Reservations recommended during July and August. Self-registration and payment box located at the head of the ramp. If the public docks are full, contact Bamfield Lodge (250-728-3419) located directly behind the public docks. **Bamfield Lodge** accepts overflow moorage at their dock as space allows.

㉛ **Harbourside Lodge**. (250) 728-3330; (604) 328-1656; requests@harboursidelodge.com; www.harboursidelodge.com. VHF 06 & 72. Open June to mid-September with guest moorage, 30 & 50 amp power, water, washroom, and showers. Gasoline and diesel. Located on the west side of the inlet, just past the public dock. Convenience store has ice, bait, tackle.

㉛ **McKay Bay Lodge**. (250) 728-3323; mckaybay@island.net; www.mckaybaylodge.com. Located on the west side of the inlet at the south end. Transient moorage as space available; lodging guests have priority; call ahead. They usually have space early and late in the season but are often full in July and August. Gasoline, limited quantity of diesel, tackle, ice. Reservations are taken for dinner at the lodge. Washroom, guest rooms.

Dodger Channel. A small basin on the south portion of the channel, just east of Haines Island off the southwest corner of Diana Island, provides anchorage in settled weather; anchorage is open to the northwest and southwest. A drying rock lies on the west side of the north entrance to Dodger Channel. The south entrance from Trevor Channel is shallow, with rocks on both sides. Correspondent Mary Campbell reports that the south basin anchorage serves well as an early morning departure point from Barkley Sound. "It's the perfect anchorage for a good night's sleep before the run down the Strait of Juan de Fuca and has shallow depths, good crabbing and good views of the open sea. Diana Island is reminiscent of beaches in the South Pacific."

BARKLEY SOUND TO BECHER BAY

The final leg of a counter-clockwise circumnavigation of Vancouver Island is from Barkley Sound into the Strait of Juan de Fuca. On the Canadian side, Port Renfrew is the only protection between Barkley Sound and Sooke.

The typical summer weather pattern calls for calm conditions in the early morning, with a westerly sea breeze building by afternoon, often to 30+ knots.

Currents in the Strait of Juan de Fuca can be strong. This can speed up the passage, especially for sailboats. Or, they can substantially slow the trip. When the wind blows against the current, steep, sometimes-dangerous seas result. Pay attention to the current when planning to transit the Strait of Juan de Fuca.

Several weather resources make the trip less nerve-racking. Lighthouses at Cape Beale, Pachena Point and Carmanah Point provide regular weather updates. Automated stations at Shearingham Point and Race Rocks report hourly wind speed and direction. The Neah Bay weather buoy (46087) provides regular wind speed updates, and the New Dungeness buoy (46088) provides wind speed, direction, and sea state. Put together, you can get a picture of conditions on the Strait before venturing out.

Cape Beale. Cape Beale, surrounded by off-lying rocks, marks the eastern entrance to Barkley Sound. Trevor Channel exits at Cape Beale, and is the safest entry to, or exit from, Barkley Sound in thick weather or poor visibility. Seas can be difficult off Cape Beale when an outflowing current from Barkley Sound meets the longshore current outside. The collision of currents, combined with wind and shallow depths around the cape, can make for heavy going.

The usual advice is to round Cape Beale in early morning, before the summertime westerly wind gets up.

The West Bamfield village store and their docks with the Coast Guard station in the background

408 www.WaggonerGuide.com

Pacific Gateway Marina, the only protected marina between Sooke and Bamfield

The local lightkeepers have provided this bit of local knowledge: A nasty reef is one-quarter of a mile in front of the lightstation. Beware of coming in close to take photos. Lightkeepers have had to summon the Bamfield Lifeboat crew a good many times to rescue overturned sports-fishing and pleasure craft occupants.

Nitinat Narrows. Nitinat Narrows connects Nitinat Lake with the Pacific Ocean. Nitinat is popular with kite sailors, campers, and hikers that access the West Coast Trail. Entrance to the narrows is obstructed by rocks and a shallow bar. An onshore wind can cause breaking seas. A crossing of this bar and negotiation of the narrows to Nitinat Lake is considered a supreme Northwest navigation challenge by a small number of adventurers. Each year a few boats do make it through. Boaters can contact Carl at Carl's Crab Shack, VHF Ch 68, for local advice on timing slack at Nitinat Narrows.

Many years ago Don Douglass took his 32 Nordic Tug across the bar, through the narrows, and into Nitinat Lake. His guidebook, *Exploring Vancouver Island's West Coast,* describes the experience, including the comment that his crew refused to ever try it again.

㊳ **Port San Juan.** For shelter off the Strait on the Canadian side consider Port San Juan, about halfway between Victoria and Barkley Sound. Port San Juan is a rectangular notch in Vancouver Island, with Port Renfrew on the eastern shore near the head of the bay. The breakwater protected marina at Port Renfrew offers year-round moorage and services. A public dock at Port Renfrew has limited moorage for smaller boats. The village and surrounding area has a grocery, pub, and several cafes.

The historic hotel and pub, at the head of the public dock, is a great place to relax over drinks. Port Renfrew is at the end of the road; hundreds of hikers, kayakers and sight-seers pour through town during the summer months.

Thrashers Cove. About one-third of a mile north of Quartertide Rocks, just off Hobbs Creek along the west shore of Port San Juan is a small bight with good anchoring depths and fair protection from northwesterly winds. Upland areas are part of the Pacific Rim National Park Reserve and the West Coast Trail. On shore you will see trail hikers camped for the night. A permit is required to visit the Park Reserve and hike the trail.

Woods Nose. Anchorage can be found close to shore behind Woods Nose on the south shore of Port San Juan. Woods Nose head breaks up the swell. Trees ashore block southerly winds, but the anchorage is open to northerly and westerly winds. In 2018, Landons reported that a private float and crab trap buoys occupied much of the desirable anchoring area.

㊳ **Port Renfrew Community Dock.** 17280 Parkinson Rd., Port Renfrew, BC V0S 1K0; (250) 647-5431. VHF 06 & 68 "Medd-O Base." Floats with room for 20 boats are installed from mid-May through mid-September. All are taken by charter boats. No electrical power; water is on the wharf but not on the floats. Best to call ahead for availability and reservations. Stan Medd is the harbormaster.

㊳ **Pacific Gateway Marina.** (250) 412-5509; contact@pacificgatewaymarina.ca; www.pacificgatewaymarina.ca. VHF 66A. Open year round. 60 slips designed for sport fishing boats and 200 feet of side-tie for larger vessels. Larger vessels should call ahead for availability. Reservations highly recommended. Water; 30 amp power available on A and B docks only. Washrooms with toilets; showers planned for the future. Ice and free Wi-Fi. Gasoline and diesel on the fuel dock. Launch ramp. This marina is owned and managed by the Mill Bay Marine Group. The marina has the only breakwater protected moorage in the area. Bridgemans West Coast Eatery is open year-round, overlooking the marina with views of Port San Juan. Bridgemans will cook your catch of the day for $15 per person; pre-book with the restaurant. SUP and sea kayak tours and rentals available nearby. A general store with groceries is within walking distance of the marina. The Botanical Beach Provincial Park is 3 km away. Ask about jeep rentals.

Renfrew Marina and RV Park. 7505 Gordon River Rd., Port Renfrew, BC V0S 1K0; (250) 483-1878; info@portrenfrewmarina.com; www.portrenfrewmarina.com. Open seasonally May through September. Monthly and daily moorage for small craft when available. First-come, first-served. Marine gasoline and launch ramp. Renfrew Marina is located at the head of Port San Juan, 1-mile up the Gordon River. River bar access is only navigable by shallow draft smaller vessels at mid to high tide (3 foot plus) with local knowledge; check tides.

SOOKE AND BECHER BAY

㊴ **Sooke Harbour.** Enter between Company Point and Parsons Point. The harbor is protected by Whiffen Spit, which nearly blocks the passage. Enter by keeping Whiffen Spit close to port. Two intersecting ranges mark the entrance channel. Follow the marked channel to town on the west bank. An area just inside Whiffen Spit, with charted depths of 7 meters (3 ¾ fathoms), has good anchorage, although wakes from passing boats make it rolly. Sooke Harbour Marina is the first set of docks. Just north of that is Jock's Docks, then Prestige Resort and a little farther up is Sooke Harbour Authority wharf with guest moorage. Sooke Harbour Marina and Jock's Docks have moorage for smaller vessels. Two day-use floats are located at the north end of the city boardwalk north of the of Harbour Authority city floats. Currents run quite strongly along the city waterfront, take care when landing.

Sooke Basin, the innermost harbor, is seldom visited by pleasure craft. The shallow channel follows the curve of the shoreline east of Middle Ground, between Eliza Point and Trollope Point. Notices to Mariners advises that entry to Sooke Basin be made after low water during daylight hours, when the drying banks are visible. Sooke is 15 miles closer to Barkley Sound than downtown Victoria, and often used as a departure point for boats heading up the west coast of Vancouver Island.

Sooke has a wide variety of services close to the Harbour Authority city floats, including a marine railway and machine shop, groceries, fuel, and restaurants. Just

WEST COAST OF VANCOUVER ISLAND

Reference Only – Not for Navigation

Sooke Harbour Authority floats are often full with local boats.

south of the Harbour Authority docks is the beautiful Prestige Oceanfront Resort, which houses the West Coast Grill. Shops, grocery, and restaurants are in town about half a mile north from the Harbour Authority docks. Follow the road the full half-mile distance or take the trail to the boardwalk for the last quarter-mile. The trail to the boardwalk starts in McGregor Park and follows the shoreline before climbing a hill into town.

No customs clearance is available in Sooke. The nearest Canadian Port of Entry is Victoria.

㊴ **Sooke Harbour Resort & Marina**. 6971 West Coast Road, Sooke, BC V9Z 0V1; (250) 642-3236; reservations@sookeharbourmarina.ca; www.sookeharbourmarina.ca. Open all year with side-tie guest moorage to 50 feet along outside breakwater. Inside docks are for boats up to 25 feet. First-come, first-served. Services include washrooms, showers, 30 & 50 amp power, Wi-Fi on shore, and 2-lane concrete launch ramp. This is the first marina as you come into the harbor.

㊴ **Jock's Dock**. 6947 West Coast Rd., Sooke, BC V9Z 0V1 (778) 425-2703. Open all year; 60 slips for small sport fishing boats and runabouts; occasional guest moorage when available; first-come, first-served, call ahead. Water at the docks; two launch ramps, fishing charters. The upland Crab Shack (250-642-4410), open May to October, sells smoked fish, prawns and live crab.

㊴ **Sooke Harbour Authority.** 1800 Maple, Sooke, BC V9Z 1H5; (250) 642-4431; (250) 893-6578 cell; sookeharbour@telus.net. Open all year, first-come, first-served guest moorage along both sides of 400 foot A-dock, 20 & 30 amp power, water, garbage drop, used oil disposal; no washrooms or showers. Rafting required. Gate-secured floats are well maintained. Watch for current when approaching the floats. Walking distance to town via the park boardwalk.

Sunny Shores Resort & Marina.
5621 Sooke Rd., RR 1, Sooke, BC V9Z 0C6; (250) 642-5731; www.sunnyshoresresort.com. Gasoline and diesel at fuel dock. Guest moorage for 6 to 10 smaller boats, call ahead for availability. Docks are in an advanced stage of deterioration. Washrooms, showers, laundry, 15 amp power, haulout. Motel accommodations and campground. Store carries ice, fishing tackle, limited groceries. Taxi to town 3 miles away.

Becher Bay. Becher Bay is a good alternative to Sooke for boaters wishing to avoid a difficult entry in fog. Although Becher Bay is farther east than Sooke, the time not spent winding your way past Whiffen Spit makes up for it. Campbell Cove on the west side of Becher Bay is a pleasant anchorage, but be careful of a drying rock near the south end. It's a good departure point for the run to Barkley Sound. Kelp is on the bottom; be sure of your set. Murder Bay, at the north end, is another recommended anchorage, also with kelp, though. Another pleasant anchorage lies to the east of Wolf Island. For a bit of gunkholing, enter between Wolf and Lamb Islands. Be sure to avoid the submerged power cable when anchoring.

㊵ **Becher Bay Marina & Campground**. 241 Becher Bay Rd., Sooke, BC V9Z 1B7; (250) 642-3816. Open May 1 to September 30. Limited guest moorage by reservation only, maximum boat length 30 feet. Services include washrooms, no showers, 2-lane concrete launch ramp, no power. Smokin' Tuna Cafe on site. RV parking.

Pedder Bay. Pedder Bay is a mile-long inlet, shallow and narrow, just south of William Head. No anchoring in bay due to submerged utility pipes. A launch ramp with floats is at the head.

㊶ **Pedder Bay Marina.** 925 Pedder Bay Drive, Victoria, BC V9C 4H1; (250) 478-1771; pbm@obmg.com; www.pedderbay.com. Monitors VHF 66A. Open all year, gasoline only at fuel dock. Permanent and visitor moorage available for vessels up to 35 feet, call ahead for larger boats. Washrooms, showers, laundry, 30 amp power, free Wi-Fi, 3-lane concrete launch ramp, year-round RV resort, camping, coffee shop, chandlery with bait, tackle, and ice. Careful when approaching, watch the wind. Located between Pearson College and Dept. of National Defence (don't stop there; it's a prison). The marina is part of Oak Bay Marina Group, a company that owns several marinas on Vancouver Island.

WaggonerGuide.com/Updates

Sooke

Pedder Bay Marina

Cape Caution

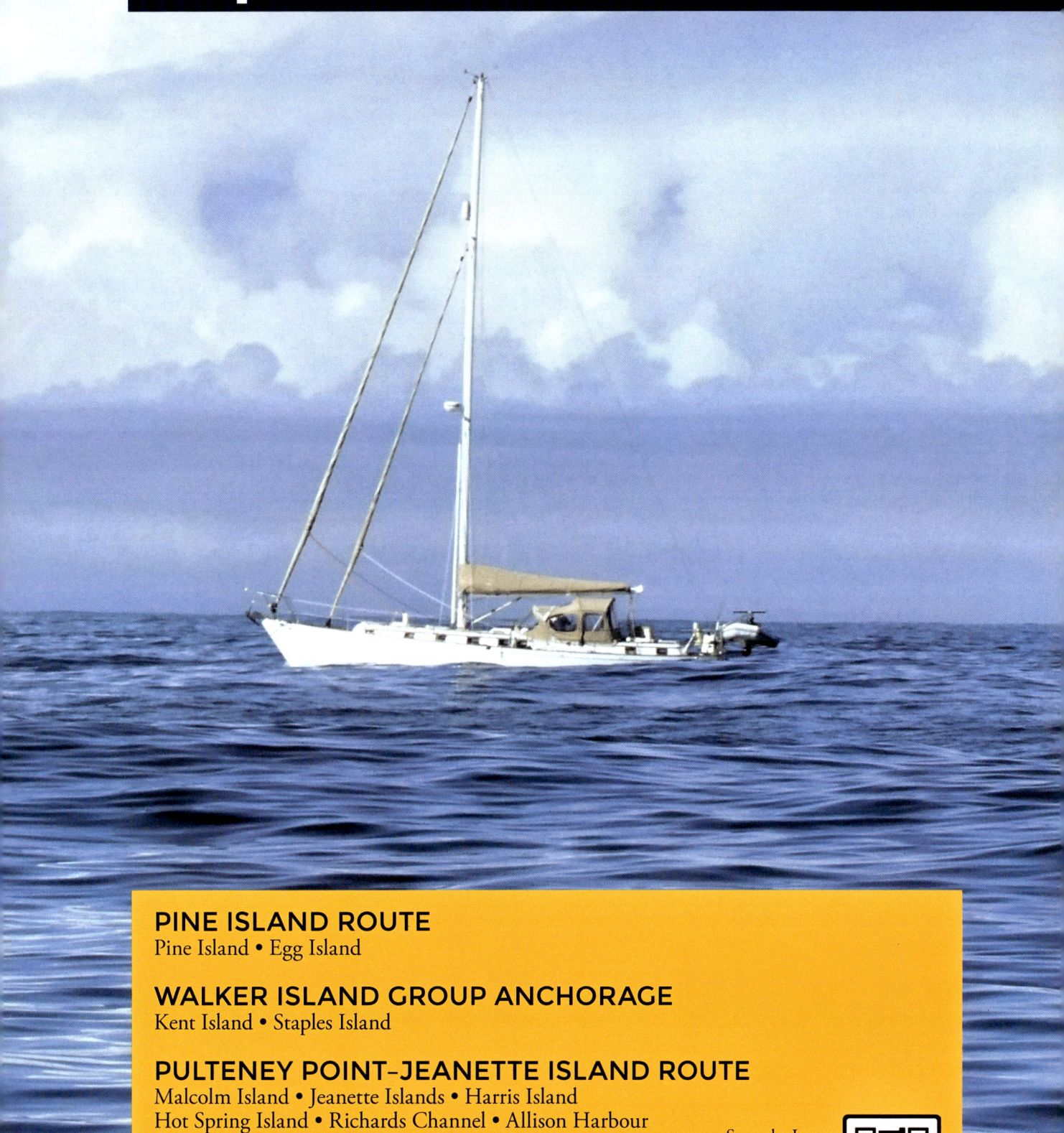

PINE ISLAND ROUTE
Pine Island • Egg Island

WALKER ISLAND GROUP ANCHORAGE
Kent Island • Staples Island

PULTENEY POINT–JEANETTE ISLAND ROUTE
Malcolm Island • Jeanette Islands • Harris Island
Hot Spring Island • Richards Channel • Allison Harbour

MAINLAND ROUTE
Blunden Harbour • Allison Harbour • Miles Inlet
Nakwakto Rapids • Southgate Group

Scan the Latest
Cape Caution
Information

tinyurl.com/WG22xCh15

CAPE CAUTION

See Area Map Page 413 - Maps Not for Navigation

Cape Caution, for some, is a fearsome barrier to exploring the remote and beautiful northern areas of British Columbia and on to Southeast Alaska. Like many of the challenging cruising areas of the Inside Passage, careful planning, attention to the weather reports, patience and time can lead to a smooth and uneventful crossing. We have met cruisers who may wait for days for the right settled conditions. Good weather for a crossing happens more often than you might think.

To get to the central and northern B.C. Coast you first must round Cape Caution. Although the distance in open water is only about 40 miles, the seas can be high and steep. The bottom shoals from 100+ fathoms off the continental shelf to 20-70 fathoms in Queen Charlotte Sound itself, causing seas to heap up. The problem is made worse when these seas are met by the outflowing ebb currents from Queen Charlotte Strait, Smith Sound, Rivers Inlet and Fitz Hugh Sound.

We've refined our "go, no-go" decisions to six factors: weather forecast; time of day; lighthouse wind and sea reports; flood or ebb tide; size of tidal exchange (spring tide or neap tide); and the automated combined wave (wave and swell) height reports from the West Sea Otter Buoy. We have learned that our tolerances are different for head seas versus following seas. Generally, we can tolerate higher wave conditions with following seas than head seas with waves over the bow.

Weather Forecast. Regardless of other factors, we want a favorable forecast or we're not going. Fog, while limiting visibility, often indicates little to no wind, favorable for a crossing if you are skilled at operating your radar. Radar is very helpful as it is not unusual to have opposing traffic in this area during periods of settled conditions.

Time Of Day. The typical summertime weather pattern calls for calm early mornings, followed in late morning or early afternoon by a rising westerly sea breeze, sometimes to gale force. "Typical," however, does not mean every day. We've seen windy mornings and flat-calm late afternoons.

Lighthouse Wind And Sea Reports. From south to north, lighthouses, and automated stations, at Scarlett Point, Herbert Island, Pine Island, Egg Island, and Addenbroke Island report conditions approximately every four hours, posted on the Continuous Marine Broadcast. Pine Island and Egg Island are the most relevant. Addenbroke Island, inside the mouth of Fitz Hugh Sound, often reports quiet conditions when Pine Island and Egg Island are much rougher. Scarlett Point, just off the north part of Vancouver Island, usually is quieter than Pine Island and Egg Island.

Flood Or Ebb Tide. Flood tide is preferred. On a flood, the incoming swells and prevailing westerly wind are aligned and the seas are flattened. The ebb is the reverse: outflowing ebb currents meet the westerly swells, making them higher and steeper. One year we made the mistake of crossing the mouth of Rivers Inlet in a mounting sea breeze that was blowing against a strong outflowing ebb, and we took a beating. We *will not* do that again.

Size Of Tidal Exchange. If possible, cross during a time of neap tides (half moon). If that can't be done, try to cross on a flood. If that can't be done, try to cross at the end of one tide, when currents are growing less, and the beginning of the next tide, while currents are still low. Avoid crossing the mouth of Rivers Inlet on an ebb.

West Sea Otter Buoy. When West Sea Otter Buoy reports seas 1.3 meters or less, with a dominant wave period greater than 8 seconds, crossing is likely to be pleasant. Combine this information with the weather forecast, lighthouse reports, and flood and ebb tides.

VTS Radio Note. South of Cape Caution, Victoria VTS, channel 71, controls large vessel traffic. North of Cape Caution, traffic is controlled by Prince Rupert VTS, channel 11. Especially in reduced visibility, one radio should be monitoring VHF 16 and a second radio should be scanning channels 11 and 71.

Cell Coverage. Cell service with data is available south of Cape Caution. North of Cape Caution there is no cell service until you get to Bella Bella/Shearwater.

Pine Island Route. This is the most popular route from Vancouver Island. It begins at Scarlett Point at the mouth of Christie Passage on Gordon Channel, and ends at Penrose Island Marine Park at the north end of Rivers Inlet. The distance is approximately 40 miles. Boats often provision and refuel in Port McNeill or Port Hardy, and move to a departure point near Christie Passage for a crossing the next morning. God's Pocket in Christie Passage, Port Alexander in Browning Passage, or Clam Cove in Gordon Channel just west of Browning Passage, are often used. Another good spot is the cove between Staples Island and Kent Island in the **Walker Island Group**.

The Pine Island route leads westward in Gordon Channel to Pine Island, then northward past the tip of the Storm Islands, past Egg Island, and on to Smith Sound, Rivers Inlet or Cape Calvert. This route will give Cape Caution an offing of 1.5 to 2.5 miles.

Gordon Channel is a principal passage for commercial vessels. In thick weather or fog, having radar, GPS and AIS is extremely helpful. Especially in low visibility or fog, most commercial traffic can be avoided by crossing Gordon Channel to the Redfern Island/Buckle Group side, and favoring that side to Pine Island.

Pulteney Point to Jeanette Islands Route. If Queen Charlotte Strait is behaving, this can be a good route from Port McNeill, on Vancouver Island, to the mainland side. From Pulteney Point at the west tip of Malcolm Island, turn to a course of 309° magnetic. This will leave the charted kelp patch to port. Twenty miles later you will arrive at the Jeanette Islands on the mainland side of Queen Charlotte Strait. Proceed through Richards Channel until Buoy *N31*

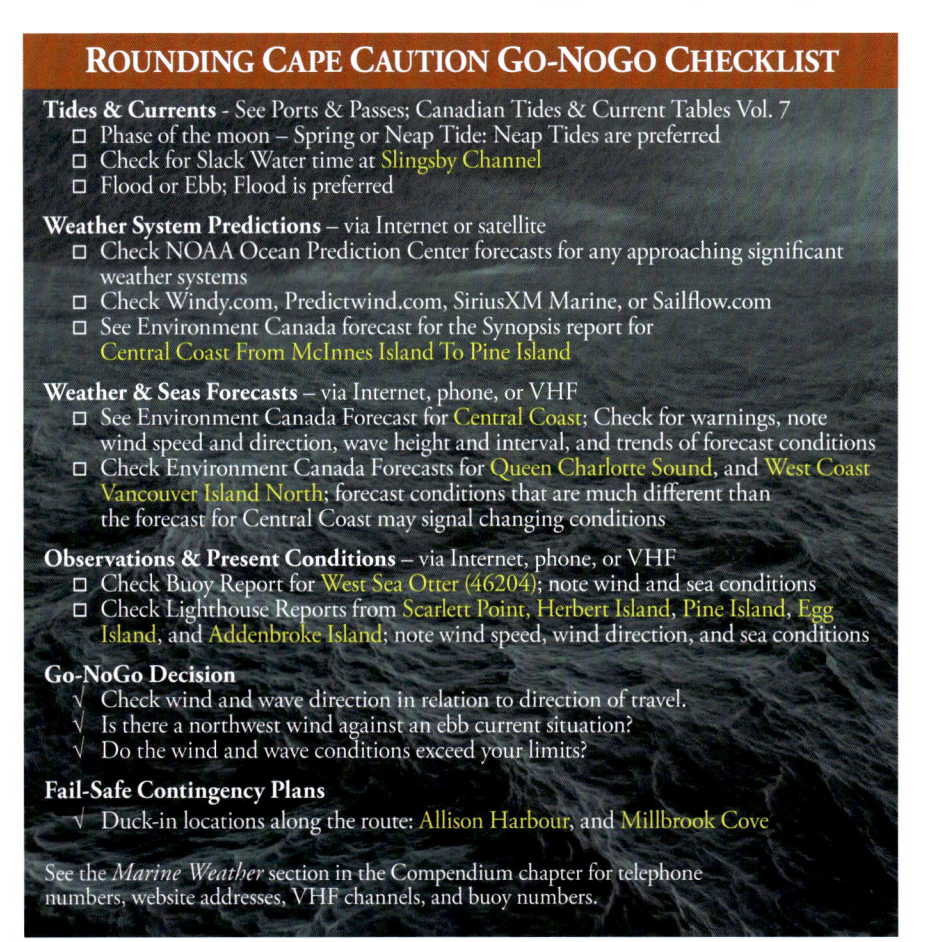

ROUNDING CAPE CAUTION GO-NOGO CHECKLIST

Tides & Currents - See Ports & Passes; Canadian Tides & Current Tables Vol. 7
- ☐ Phase of the moon – Spring or Neap Tide: Neap Tides are preferred
- ☐ Check for Slack Water time at Slingsby Channel
- ☐ Flood or Ebb; Flood is preferred

Weather System Predictions – via Internet or satellite
- ☐ Check NOAA Ocean Prediction Center forecasts for any approaching significant weather systems
- ☐ Check Windy.com, Predictwind.com, SiriusXM Marine, or Sailflow.com
- ☐ See Environment Canada forecast for the Synopsis report for Central Coast From McInnes Island To Pine Island

Weather & Seas Forecasts – via Internet, phone, or VHF
- ☐ See Environment Canada Forecast for Central Coast; Check for warnings, note wind speed and direction, wave height and interval, and trends of forecast conditions
- ☐ Check Environment Canada Forecasts for Queen Charlotte Sound, and West Coast Vancouver Island North; forecast conditions that are much different than the forecast for Central Coast may signal changing conditions

Observations & Present Conditions – via Internet, phone, or VHF
- ☐ Check Buoy Report for West Sea Otter (46204); note wind and sea conditions
- ☐ Check Lighthouse Reports from Scarlett Point, Herbert Island, Pine Island, Egg Island, and Addenbroke Island; note wind speed, wind direction, and sea conditions

Go-NoGo Decision
- √ Check wind and wave direction in relation to direction of travel.
- √ Is there a northwest wind against an ebb current situation?
- √ Do the wind and wave conditions exceed your limits?

Fail-Safe Contingency Plans
- √ Duck-in locations along the route: Allison Harbour, and Millbrook Cove

See the *Marine Weather* section in the Compendium chapter for telephone numbers, website addresses, VHF channels, and buoy numbers.

is abeam to port. Alter course slightly to leave Harris Island to starboard and Allen Rocks Lighted Whistle Buoy *N33* to port. A course of approximately 293° magnetic will take you to a common intersection point west of Cape Caution.

Caution in Richards Channel. On an ebb, especially a big ebb, Richards Channel can be difficult. One year, although the wind was calm, a big ebb set up a 2.5-knot outflowing current that opposed the incoming swells, creating larger and more threatening seas. We aborted our crossing and anchored instead in Allison Harbour.

Mainland Route. The mainland route offers more shelter in case of a blow and lets you visit Blunden Harbour, Allison Harbour, Miles Inlet, and Milbrook Cove in Smith Sound. You could even take a major side trip through famed Nakwakto Rapids (at slack) and spend time in Seymour Inlet and Belize Inlet. Many boats prefer the mainland route for its greater interest and possibility of shelter. The major cautions are Richards Channel on an ebb (above) and the waters off Slingsby Channel on an ebb.

Slingsby Channel Caution. Slingsby Channel is the primary drain for the hundreds of miles of inlets behind Nakwakto Rapids. What Slingsby Channel does to Queen Charlotte Strait on a big ebb can be terrifying. Outer Narrows at the mouth of Slingsby Channel runs to 9 knots on an ebb. The water fire-hoses into Queen Charlotte Strait, where it collides with the Pacific Ocean's incoming swells. If a westerly is blowing against this vast outpouring, conditions can be as bad as the worst at Cape Mudge.

Outer Narrows currents turn 10 minutes before Nakwakto Rapids, both flood and ebb. We departed our anchorage in Allison Harbour at 8:00 a.m., not realizing that two hours earlier the maximum ebb at Nakwakto Rapids was 11.4 knots. Shortly after 8:00 a.m. Slingsby Channel was still roaring. Although not a breath of wind was stirring, we found ourselves in large, steep seas that lifted the bow high, then crashed us down into the troughs. We pressed on, hoping not to meet a log in the bottom of a trough, and got through without injury or damage. The turbulence diminished but persisted all the way to Cape Caution, which we rounded at 10:10 a.m., a half-hour after the turn to flood in Slingsby Channel.

Summing up. Rounding Cape Caution is more than simply rounding the Cape itself. From the departure points to arriving in Fitz Hugh Sound, you will transit different areas with varying weather and sea conditions. The total experience involves planning for and choosing a route through the various sections. These sections include: staging and anchoring the night before; transiting of Queen Charlotte Strait; avoiding conditions off Slingsby Channel; rounding the Cape itself; and passing outside or inside Egg Island. You might include in your plan a stop in Smith Sound. You will need to choose the day's stopping point: Millbrook Cove, Penrose Island Marine Park (Fury Cove, Fry Pan, Big Fry Pan), Goose Bay, or go all the way to Pruth Bay. Patience and diligence in planning is the key. Start the planning process well ahead of time; start watching the forecast weather and the subsequent buoy and lighthouse observations a week ahead to familiarize yourself with conditions and place names.

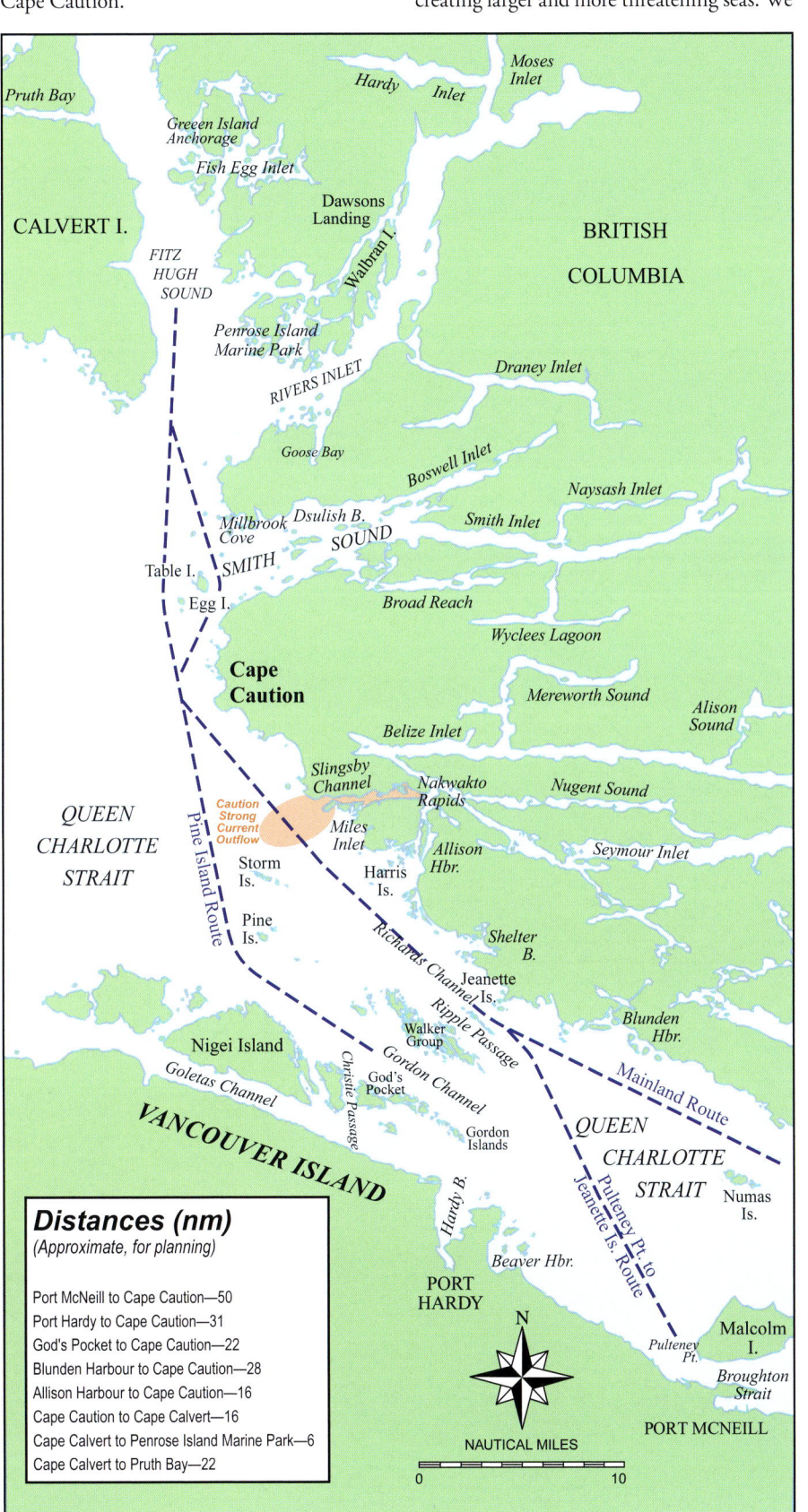

Distances (nm)
(Approximate, for planning)

- Port McNeill to Cape Caution—50
- Port Hardy to Cape Caution—31
- God's Pocket to Cape Caution—22
- Blunden Harbour to Cape Caution—28
- Allison Harbour to Cape Caution—16
- Cape Caution to Cape Calvert—16
- Cape Calvert to Penrose Island Marine Park—6
- Cape Calvert to Pruth Bay—22

Cape Caution

Northern B.C. Coast

BLUNDEN HARBOUR TO SLINGSBY CHANNEL
Allison Harbour • Miles Inlet • Nakwakto Rapids

SMITH SOUND
Table Island • Millbrook Cove
Ahclakerho Channel

Scan the Latest Northern B.C. Coast Information

tinyurl.com/WG22xCh16

RIVERS INLET & FISH EGG INLET
Dawsons Landing • Penrose Island Marine Park

FITZ HUGH SOUND & FISHER CHANNEL
Pruth Bay • Ocean Falls • Shearwater

BURKE & DEAN CHANNELS, BELLA COOLA
Eucott Hot Springs • Elcho Harbour

SEAFORTH CHANNEL & MILBANKE SOUND
Roscoe Inlet • Reid & Jackson Passages • Fiordland

FINLAYSON CHANNEL TO PRINCE RUPERT
Klemtu • Butedale • Bishop Bay • Hartley Bay

*Fiordland
Mathieson Channel*

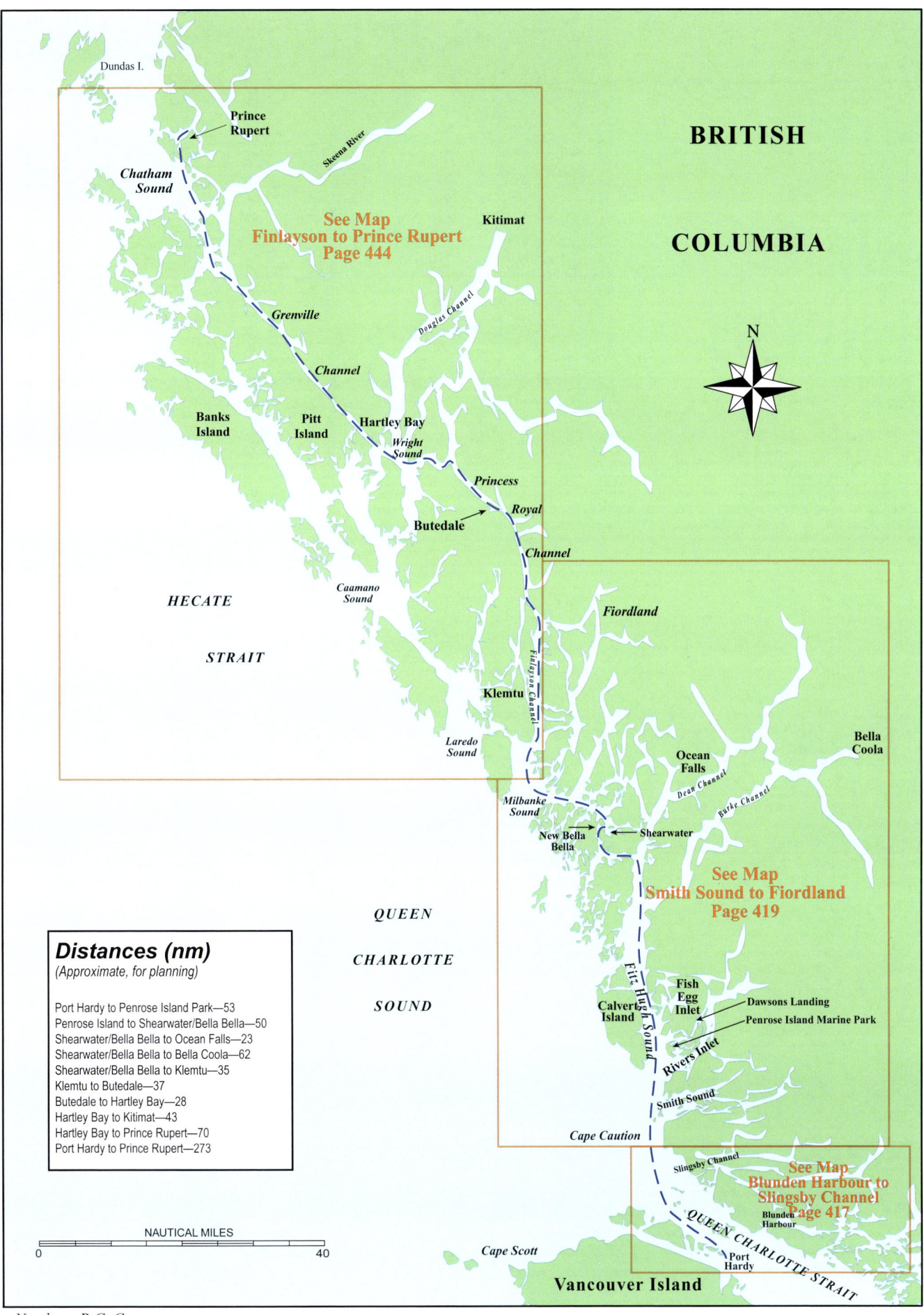

Reference Only – Not for Navigation NORTHERN B.C. COAST

NORTHERN B.C. COAST

BRITISH COLUMBIA

Dundas I.
Prince Rupert
Skeena River
Chatham Sound
Kitimat

See Map Finlayson to Prince Rupert Page 444

Grenville Channel
Douglas Channel
Banks Island
Pitt Island
Hartley Bay
Wright Sound
Princess Royal Channel
Butedale
Caamano Sound

HECATE STRAIT

Fiordland
Klemtu
Finlayson Channel
Laredo Sound
Ocean Falls
Dean Channel
Bella Coola
Burke Channel
Milbanke Sound
New Bella Bella — Shearwater

See Map Smith Sound to Fiordland Page 419

QUEEN CHARLOTTE SOUND

Fitz Hugh Sound
Calvert Island
Fish Egg Inlet
Dawsons Landing
Penrose Island Marine Park
Rivers Inlet
Smith Sound
Cape Caution

Slingsby Channel
See Map Blunden Harbour to Slingsby Channel Page 417
Blunden Harbour
Cape Scott
Port Hardy

QUEEN CHARLOTTE STRAIT

Vancouver Island

Distances (nm)
(Approximate, for planning)

Port Hardy to Penrose Island Park—53
Penrose Island to Shearwater/Bella Bella—50
Shearwater/Bella Bella to Ocean Falls—23
Shearwater/Bella Bella to Bella Coola—62
Shearwater/Bella Bella to Klemtu—35
Klemtu to Butedale—37
Butedale to Hartley Bay—28
Hartley Bay to Kitimat—43
Hartley Bay to Prince Rupert—70
Port Hardy to Prince Rupert—273

NAUTICAL MILES 0 — 40

Northern B.C. Coast

2023 Waggoner Cruising Guide 415

NORTHERN B.C. COAST

Planning a Trip to the Northern B.C. Coast. Most cruisers limit their voyages to the waters south of a line that runs between Wells Passage on the mainland to Port Hardy on Vancouver Island. North of this line the northern part of Queen Charlotte Strait is a natural barrier. It takes time, a strong boat, and good navigation skills to proceed farther up the coast. To be fair, a lifetime of cruising could be spent south of that line with complete satisfaction.

But—to those with the time and inclination—the coast north of Wells Passage is a special experience. The scenery is magnificent, the population is small and self-sufficient, the fishing can be exceptional and you can even take a warm soak at one of several hot springs. You can anchor in bays with no other boats and take in the scenery all by yourself.

This is the part of the coast where you'll find the famous names: Nakwakto Rapids, Rivers Inlet, Fish Egg Inlet, Hakai, Bella Bella, Ocean Falls, Ivory Island, Fiordland, Butedale, Grenville Channel, Prince Rupert. It's a coast filled with history and possibilities. If it's wilderness you seek, you can find it here.

Be self-reliant. Between Port Hardy and Prince Rupert, there are few marinas with services for pleasure boats. Be glad the facilities are there, and don't complain if they're a little rough and maybe a bit more expensive. Don't expect marina help to come down to take your lines as you land.

Most facilities and businesses are set up to take credit cards. ATMs are limited except for a machine at Shearwater and sometimes in Klemtu, and you have full banking in Prince Rupert. Cell phone coverage is in and near populated communities only. To determine whether you have cell phone coverage or roaming in this area, check with your provider. There are several areas with cell phone coverage between Port Hardy and Prince Rupert. Generally speaking you will find coverage at Shearwater/New Bella Bella, Klemtu, Hartley Bay, Kitimat, and Bella Coola. Some boats rent or purchase satellite phones when cruising this area. Satellite based messaging devices, such as the Garmin InReach system, with weather forecast delivery options, are useful in isolated areas with no VHF radio reception. Land line pay phones are in Bella Coola, Shearwater, New Bella Bella, Ocean Falls, and Klemtu.

Insurance. Some vessel insurance policies don't cover these waters without a special rider. Check with your marine insurance broker before you leave.

The boat. Not many small boats cruise the northern coast. You'll sometimes see jerry cans filled with extra fuel or water lashed to the rails or in the cockpits. Radar and GPS should be considered standard equipment. This is remote country. The boat should be in top mechanical condition. Complete spares should be carried.

Many anchorages along this coast are 60 to 90 feet deep, with shallower water too close to shore to swing in comfort. You'll need ample anchor rode—300 feet should be considered the minimum.

Bottoms often are rocky. Because of its resistance to bending and its ability to set and hold in nearly any bottom, including rock, Bruce is a popular anchor. Manson Supreme, Rocna, CQR, Ultra and Delta anchors also are popular. You don't see as many Danforth style anchors. Danforth style anchors are good in sand and mud, but they have trouble setting in rock, and once wedged they are easily bent.

Be sure to carry at least two anchors. Whatever the style of anchors chosen, they should be big, strong, and ready to deploy.

Fuel and water. Fuel is plentiful, both gasoline and diesel, all the way up the coast. Rivers Inlet has gasoline and diesel at Dawsons Landing. You can get gasoline and diesel at Bella Coola, Shearwater, New Bella Bella, Klemtu, Kitimat, Hartley Bay, and Prince Rupert. The longest distance between fuel stops is roughly 70 miles.

Water is available all along the way. Some of it may be tinged brown from cedar bark tannin, but people have been drinking cedar water for decades with no ill effects. The dock at Ocean Falls has sparkling clear, purified water. New Bella Bella, Klemtu and Hartley Bay have multi-million-dollar water treatment plants that deliver clear, pure water.

Weather. Bring clothes for all conditions, from cold and rainy to hot and sunny. Expect wet weather at least part of the time. The residents of Ocean Falls call themselves "The Rainpeople" for good reason. Some years have been so wet that a few boats quit their cruise.

Plan for clouds down on the deck, for fog, for rain (both vertical and horizontal), and for storms. Leave enough flexibility in the schedule to anchor through serious foul weather. Be sure the boat is well-provisioned and equipped with generator or battery power to spend several days at anchor in one location.

Plan on sunshine, too, maybe a lot of sunshine. It can get *hot*. Bring bug spray, and equip the boat with screens on doors, hatches, opening ports, and windows.

You should have a heat source while underway and a heat source to be used at anchor. A hydronic system, with heat exchanger and furnace, can be used for both. There are various combinations of different heaters that can provide warmth.

Sailboaters will want some sort of cockpit protection, from a companionway dodger to full cockpit enclosure. Keep the cabin warm and dry, or you'll be miserable.

Marinas. There aren't many marinas on this coast. In Rivers Inlet, Dawsons Landing has moorage, fuel and supplies. The Native band stores at New Bella Bella and Klemtu have a good grocery selection. Shearwater, near New Bella Bella, has moorage, a restaurant and pub, groceries, chandlery, fuel, water, haulout and repairs. Ocean Falls has moorage, power, water, Wi-Fi and a pub in nearby Martin Valley. Farther north, Hartley Bay has fuel, water, and limited moorage. Prince Rupert has just about everything.

If you're in a jam, you could seek help at one of the sportfishing lodges along the coast, but remember that their business is serving their fly-in fishing guests, not recreational boats.

Dogs and hiking. Shorelines often are steep and rocky along this part of the coast, with few good places to walk the dog or take a walk yourself. Although we have seen many pets on board, we've met a number of cruisers who feel it's just too difficult to get a dog ashore. People who enjoy regular walks and hikes will find their options limited. All agree that the coast is beautiful, but some would welcome more opportunity for exercise.

Repairs. While it's best to carry complete spares and know how to fix whatever goes wrong, nobody can be ready for everything. Parts and mechanics can be flown in anyplace along the coast between Port Hardy and

Northern B.C. Coast has everything from sandy beaches and rocky shores, to tall mountains and fiords.

Reference Only – Not for Navigation

NORTHERN B.C. COAST

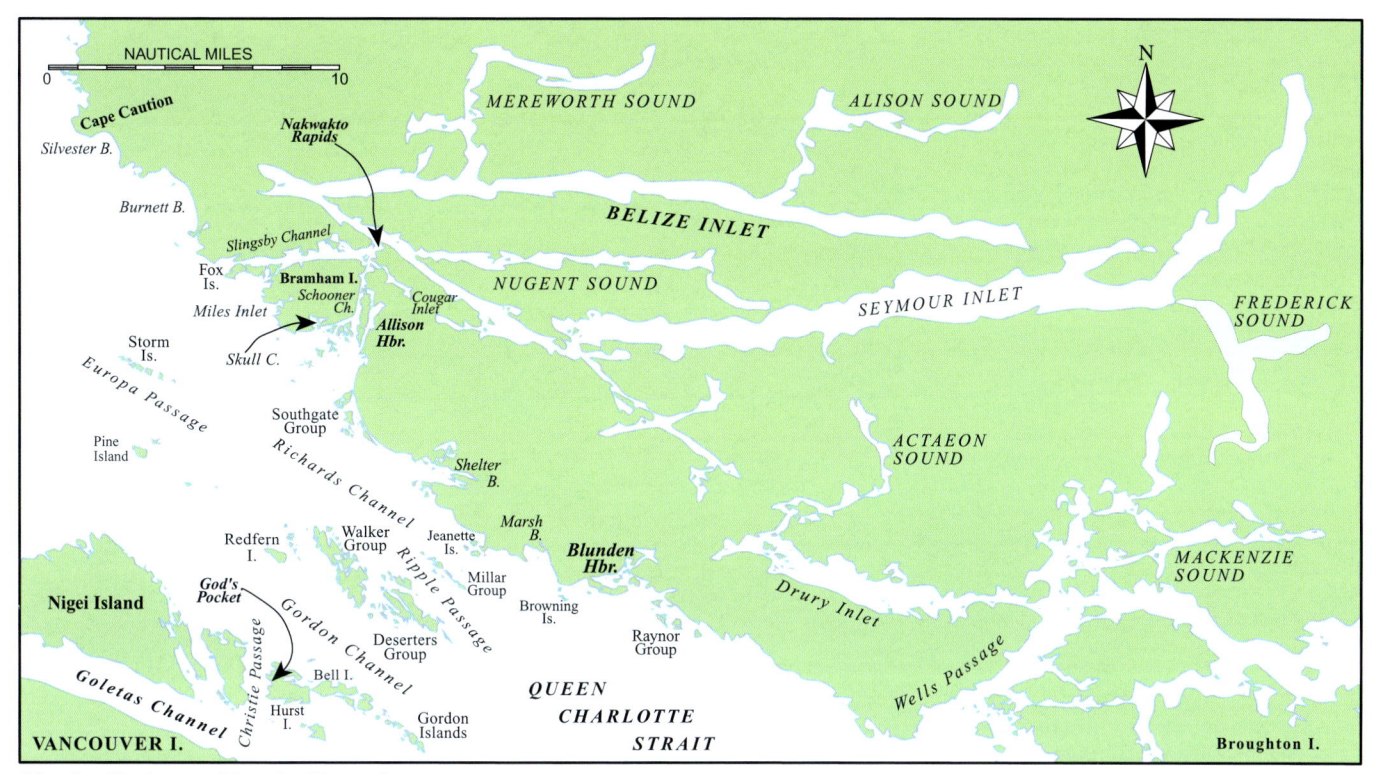

Blunden Harbour to Slingsby Channel

Prince Rupert. The only full-service shipyard is at Shearwater. Parts can be easily flown in to New Bella Bella. Kitimat has facilities and a yard for repairs. Prince Rupert has full services, though they primarily serve the fishing fleet.

Charts and reference books. Canadian Hydrographic Service (CHS) has more than 65 charts that cover the coast from Wells Passage to Prince Rupert. Vector (ENC) digital charts for Northern BC Coast are available from CHS individually or in chart pack PAC-B. This chart pack includes the west side of Vancouver Island, Northern BC Coast, and Haida Gwaii. Raster (BSB) digital charts for Northern BC Coast are available from CHS individually or in chart pack PAC03, which includes Queen Charlotte Sound, Hecate Strait to Portland Canal. Navionics includes Northern BC vector charts with their Canada coverage. Coastal Explorer users may purchase the CHS west coast vector and raster chart packs from Coastal Explorer.

Tides and currents are shown in Ports and Passes and Canadian Tide and Current Tables, Vol. 7. North of Cape Caution you may want to consider getting the 3-volume set of Sailing Directions for the North Coast, PAC 200, 205, and 206.

An in-depth guidebook is *Exploring the North Coast of British Columbia, 3rd Ed.*, by Don Douglass and Réanne Hemingway-Douglass. *Cruising the Secret Coast*, by Jennifer and James Hamilton includes anchorages in some of the most scenic, out-of-the-way locations for this area.

Blunden Harbour is a beautiful anchorage, with room for many boats. It's a good starting point for an early morning rounding of Cape Caution.

BLUNDEN HARBOUR TO SLINGSBY CHANNEL

The entrance to Blunden Harbour is approximately 11 miles northwest from the mouth of Wells Passage.

Blunden Harbour. Blunden Harbour is a lovely, well-protected bay, with excellent holding ground. As you approach the entrance it is important to identify Siwiti Rock and leave it to starboard. Study the 1:15,000 Blunden Harbour inset on Chart 3548 or your chartplotter. Note the several rocks along both sides of the passage into Blunden Harbour. These rocks make a somewhat serpentine route necessary as you go in.

Anchor anywhere in the large basin, or between Moore Rock and Byrnes Island. We feel that Moore Rock is closer to Byrnes Island than the chart suggests. All of the north shore uplands is part of the Pahas First Nations Band; no trespassing on shore. Byrnes Island is a First Nations burial ground, trespassing is prohibited. A large "no trespassing" sign warns against exploring the uplands.

You can explore Bradley Lagoon in the northeast corner of Blunden Harbour. Those who have say it's interesting. Take the dinghy through the rapids at high water slack. Cell service with data is available in the harbour.

Southgate Group. The Southgate Group is a cluster of islands at the corner of the route between Blunden Harbour and Allison Harbour. A passage between Southgate Island and Knight Island makes for a scenic, sheltered shortcut. Basins on either

2023 Waggoner Cruising Guide   417

side of the narrows appear just right for anchoring. Chart 3921 shows the passage in large detail.

Allison Harbour. Allison Harbour is large, long and nicely protected, with room for many boats. Log booms may be tied to shore. Crabbing is said to be good. The best holding ground is toward the head, in 20 to 25 feet. *Favor the western shore as you enter and leave, to avoid a rock that lies almost mid-channel, about halfway in.*

Murray Labyrinth. This one is for the brave, who will be rewarded. *Exploring the North Coast of British Columbia* has a good description of Murray Labyrinth, and *Best Anchorages of the Inside Passage,* authors Kelly and Vipond describe Murray Labyrinth in glowing terms. Waggoner Correspondents Lorraine and John Littlewood report:

"The inner cove is a special place to us and nearly a perfect anchorage. It's guarded by what looks to be an impossibly tortuous, kelp-choked entrance, so most boats pass on by (in 10 years, we've not seen another boat there). It's not that hard, though, and the reward is that extreme rarity on the coast: a landlocked, completely protected anchorage with access at any tide and endless exploration potential by kayak or dinghy.

We took our 43-foot Ocean Alexander in twice, and other boats before. It was a piece of cake each time—just keep a bow watch and go dead slow, in and out of gear as necessary to give yourself plenty of time to react. All obstacles are plainly visible or charted. Use the south entry only. Do not attempt to enter or leave through the northern passage in anything other than a kayak or dinghy. It's foul, and what appear to be two rocks are really one rock with the middle part awash at low tide." [*Littlewood*]

Skull Cove. Skull Cove is on Bramham Island, roughly opposite Murray Labyrinth. It is one of the prettier anchorages you will find. If approaching from the south, we would pass behind Southgate Island and follow the eastern mainland shore almost to City Point. Then we would turn northwest, leaving Town Rock to port, and go through the passage between the Deloraine Islands and Murray Labyrinth, thus avoiding all the rocks and reefs that lie offshore. If approaching from the north, follow the Bramham Island shore.

Enter Skull Cove on the east side of the unnamed island and take anchorage in the cove immediately to port, in 20 to 25 feet. The view on the west side of the island is superb.

Miles Inlet. Miles Inlet indents the west shore of Bramham Island and is beautiful. The narrow passage is lined with silver snags. The trees are not tall, suggesting wind from winter storms blows strongly in the inlet. The entrance is narrow, but using McEwan Rock as a reference, the entrance is easy to locate. Off-lying rocks are on each

Boat name signs attached to trees on Turret Rock in Nakwakto Rapids

side of the entrance. Go directly down the middle. Once inside, anchor in a little nook on the north side of the entrance channel or at the T intersection. The two arms of the T shoal rapidly, but the north arm has more room.

Schooner Channel. Schooner Channel, along the east side of Bramham Island, is narrow and requires constant attention to avoid rocks and reefs. With attention, however, the channel is not difficult to run. Watch tidal currents closely. The flood runs to 5 knots and the ebb to 6 knots. Schooner Channel currents are shown in Ports and Passes and Canadian Tide and Current Tables, Vol. 6, as a secondary station based on Nakwakto Rapids.

An unnamed bay opposite Goose Point at the north end of Schooner Channel is mentioned in Sailing Directions as a good anchorage for small craft.

LOCAL KNOWLEDGE

Tide-Rip: Mike Guns, a commercial fisherman with much experience in these waters, reports that when an ebb current opposes a westerly wind, the entrance to Outer Narrows and Slingsby Channel is on par with the worst conditions that Nahwitti Bar or Cape Mudge can produce. He has seen "noticeable turbulence" as long as 3 hours after maximum ebb at Nakwakto Rapids. Take this patch of water seriously.

Slingsby Channel. Slingsby Channel runs between the mainland and the north side of Bramham Island. Currents in Outer Narrows, between the Fox Islands and Vigilance Point, run to 7 knots on the flood and 9 knots on the ebb. Outer Narrows is shown as a secondary station based on Nakwakto Rapids in Canadian Tide and Current Tables, Vol. 6 or Ports and Passes.

Enter Slingsby Channel via a narrow, scenic channel that runs between Fox Islands and Bramham Island, thus avoiding Outer Narrows entirely. The channel is easy to run, and deeper than the chart shows.

Treadwell Bay. Treadwell Bay is a good, protected anchorage at the east end of Slingsby Channel. It is often used by boats awaiting slack water at Nakwakto Rapids. Favor the east shore as you enter to avoid rocks off the Anchor Islands. The rocks are shown clearly on the charts. Inside, beware of rocks shown on the chart off the south shore of the bay.

Nakwakto Rapids. Nakwakto Rapids is among the world's fastest. Especially on spring tides, they must be transited at slack water only. At neap tides the window of safety opens a little wider. We have been told that high water slack is much preferred over low water slack. On big tides in particular, take this advice very, very seriously.

During the full rush of a maximum tidal current, the sound and action of the rushing water give the impression that Turret Rock actually trembles. Brave mariners have nailed boards with their boat names to trees on Turret Rock. Favored passage is on the west side.

Behind Nakwakto Rapids lie the extensive waterways of Seymour Inlet, Belize Inlet, Nugent Sound, and Alison Sound.

Note: Our sister publication *Cruising the Secret Coast*, by Jennifer and James Hamilton, devotes three chapters to the approaches to Nakwakto Rapids and the extensive waters of Seymour Inlet and Belize Inlet.

NORTHERN B.C. COAST

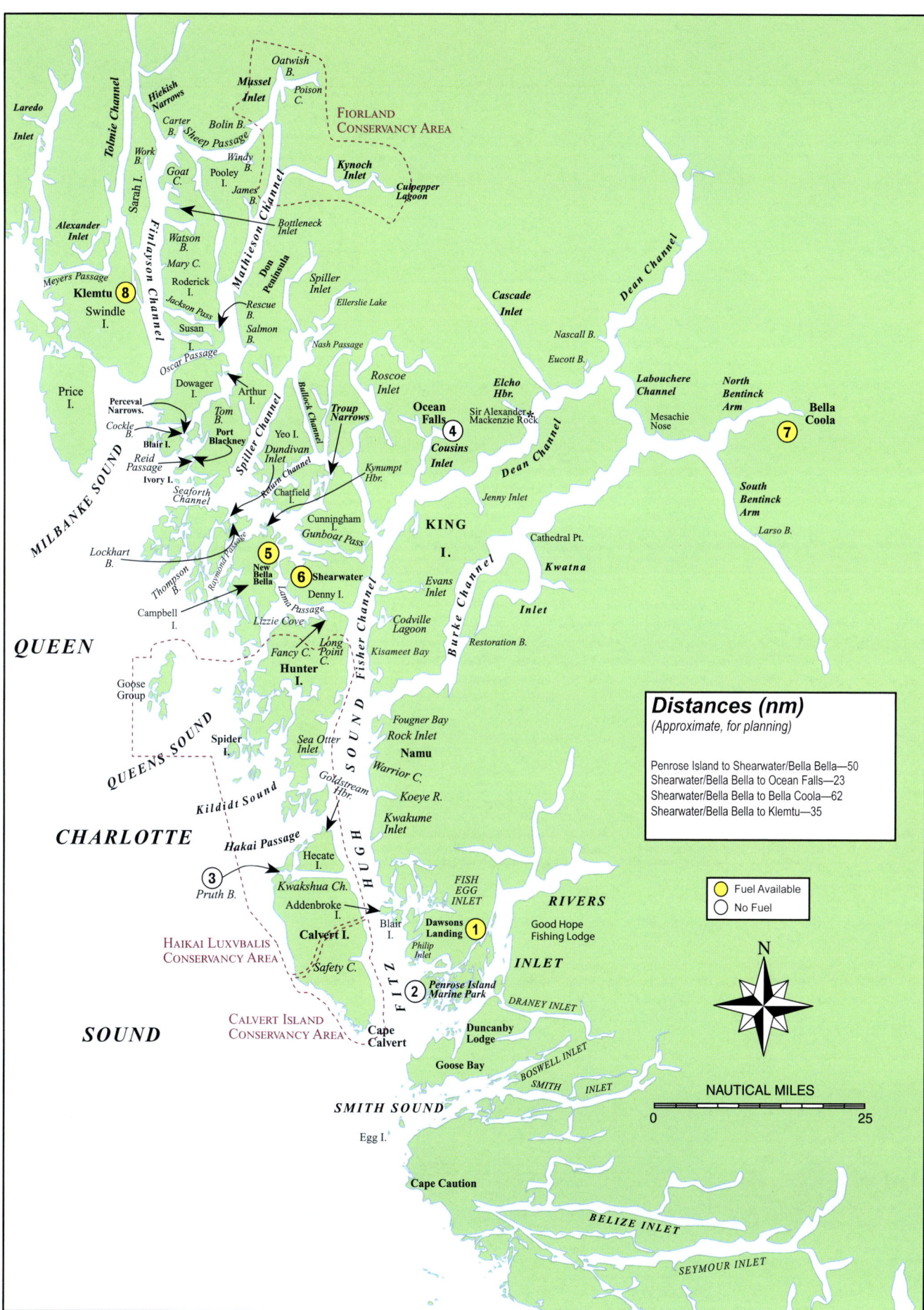

Reference Only – Not for Navigation

Distances (nm)
(Approximate, for planning)

Penrose Island to Shearwater/Bella Bella—50
Shearwater/Bella Bella to Ocean Falls—23
Shearwater/Bella Bella to Bella Coola—62
Shearwater/Bella Bella to Klemtu—35

○ Fuel Available
○ No Fuel

Smith Sound to Fiordland

2023 Waggoner Cruising Guide 419

NORTHERN B.C. COAST

See Area Map Page 419 - Maps Not for Navigation

Smith Sound

SMITH SOUND

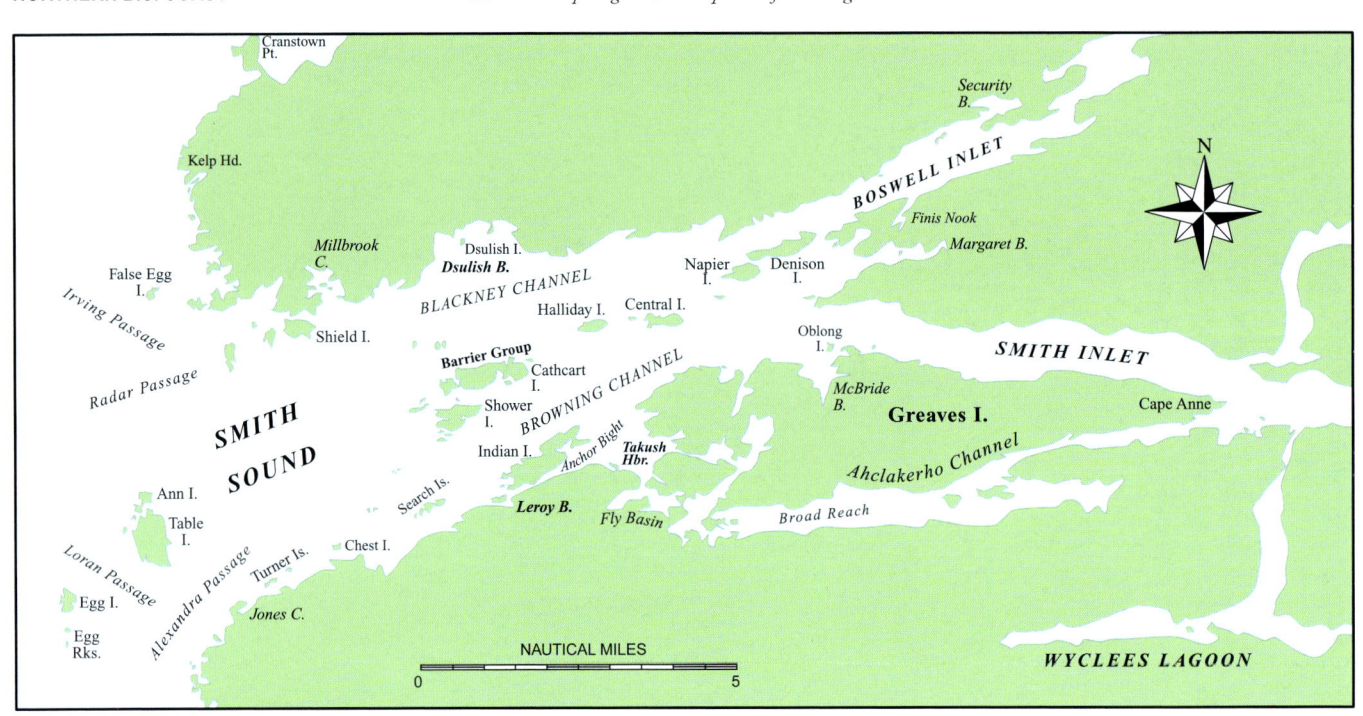

Smith Sound doesn't see many pleasure boats, but it's reputed to be full of fish. We visited during an opening for gillnet commercial salmon fishing, and the boats turned out in force. Picking our way among the nets required close attention, but all went well.

You're on your own in Smith Sound itself. There are no resorts or settlements. Several bays are good for anchoring, although only one, Millbrook Cove, really appeals to us.

From the south, enter Smith Sound through Alexandra Passage, between North Iron Rock and Egg Rocks. From the west, enter through Radar Passage. From the north, enter through Irving Passage. We suggest that you plot waypoints to keep clear of rocks. This is especially true in reduced visibility.

Table Island. Table Island is in the mouth of Smith Sound, and the casual visitor would not think of it as an anchorage. But fish boats anchor there and have no problems. A boat waiting to make a southerly dash around Cape Caution could find this anchorage useful, as could a boat seeking shelter from a westerly in Queen Charlotte Sound. The Hulsizers report spending a rolly night at this anchorage.

Jones Cove. Jones Cove is on the south shore of Smith Sound, near the mouth. The cove is cozy and well protected and often used by commercial fish boats. Anchor in 20 feet with limited swinging room. Depending on the rise and fall of the tide and the presence of other boats, you may choose to run a stern-tie to shore.

Fly Basin. Fly Basin is on the south side of Smith Sound at 51°16.35'N/127°36.20'W. "It is very private and protected, but entry requires care. Study of the chart will show that you should favor the western shore until opposite the point of land extending from the eastern shore. Then swing to the east side of the channel. The charted rocks can be difficult to see except at low water. Once in, anchor in 15 to 25 feet (zero tide) in the eastern section of the bay, excellent holding in mud." [*Hamilton*]

Correspondents John and Lorraine Littlewood report the western basin is also good. Work your way in past the rocks, and anchor in pristine surroundings on a good mud bottom. They begged us to not tell a soul about this anchorage, but since we are friends we feel safe letting you in on it.

McBride Bay. This bay is on the north side of Greaves Island, at the east end of Browning Channel. It is deep until near the head, which has 30 to 40 foot anchoring depths. Protection is excellent, but swinging room is a little limited.

Ahclakerho Channel. Ahclakerho Channel leads along the south side of Greaves Island. The current runs hard in the channel. Transit at slack water, especially on big tides. Slack appears to be around the time of high and low water at Bella Bella. Correspondent Gil Flanagan reports: "This is an overlooked gem. The narrow part of the channel is probably 200 feet wide. The anchorage on the east side of the 78-meter east Ahclakerho Island gives good protection from west winds in Smith Sound. We stern-tied among numerous rocks and small islands. It was beautiful."

Crossing Smith Sound at Blackney Channel to anchor in Millbrook Cove.

Millbrook Cove is a quiet, protected anchorage.

Goose Bay Cannery built in 1926, now a private fishing lodge

Margaret Bay. Margaret Bay is at the head of Smith Sound, on the point of land that separates Boswell Inlet and Smith Inlet. Chambers Island, rather small, is in the middle of the bay, about halfway in. West of Chambers Island depths are too great for anchoring. East of the island they shallow to 50 to 55 feet. The head shoals sharply, and old pilings take up much of the room at the head. Protection is excellent.

Ethel Cove. Ethel Cove is just outside the mouth of Margaret Bay. It looks right out to sea, however, and we found a very low surge coming in. Get close to shore or anchor in 50 to 60 feet farther out.

Finis Nook. Finis Nook is located near the mouth of Boswell Inlet, on the south shore, sort of "around the corner" from Margaret Bay. It is nearly landlocked and completely protected; it seems a perfect anchorage. A log boom blocks the back bay, however, and a float house is on the east side, with the wreck of a fish boat. Anchoring depths in the area not already taken are approximately 35 feet. We were disappointed, and went back to Millbrook Cove to overnight. (In *Cruising the Secret Coast*, the Hamiltons like Finis Nook).

Dsulish Bay. Dsulish Bay, with beautiful white sand beaches, is on the north shore of Smith Sound. A trail reportedly leads to Goose Bay to the north. The best anchorage is behind the 46-meter island, deep inside the bay. It is a little open but workable. We have seen fish boats anchored along the west side of Dsulish Bay. In the right conditions it would be a good lunch stop, though we're not so sure about overnight.

Millbrook Cove. This is the outermost anchorage on the north side of Smith Sound. To us it is the favored anchorage. The cove is completely landlocked, with 25 to 35 foot depths, good holding ground, and ample room.

Getting in will hold your attention, at least the first time. Find the red spar buoy *E6* marking Millbrook Rocks. The buoy has a small radar reflector on top. Leave this buoy to starboard (Red, Right, Returning), and aim the boat toward the 30-meter island. Keep a sharp lookout for rocks on both sides, especially the west side, as shown on the chart. The 30-meter island can be passed on either side, although the east side is a little deeper.

Once in, watch for a drying rock a short distance off the northeast corner of the 30-meter island. Minding your depths, anchor anywhere.

RIVERS INLET

Note: Cruising the Secret Coast, by Jennifer and James Hamilton, contains an entire chapter devoted to cruising the parts of Rivers Inlet not covered here, with a little overlap.

Rivers Inlet is a famed salmon fishing area and, at one time, had 18 salmon canneries. All the canneries are closed now and most are sinking into ruin. Absent its commerce of former years, Rivers Inlet is prime cruising ground. The scenery is beautiful and the anchorages excellent. The area is served by Dawsons Landing and private fishing lodges.

Open Bight. Open Bight, well named, is just inside Cranstown Point at the entrance to Rivers Inlet. Anchorage, with protection from westerlies but not easterlies or northerlies, is along the south and west shores. The west shore is preferred. We would put the hook down outside the kelp line in 25 to 30 feet, within view of a stunning white shell midden beach. Gentle swells will rock the boat.

Home Bay. Home Bay, on the south shore a short distance inside the mouth of Rivers Inlet. A sunken ship and rusty equipment is reported to be on the shore. Readers Kim and Bill Halley report that debris lies on the sea bottom, with the opportunity to foul an anchor.

Just west of Home Bay is another nook, which Douglass calls West Home Bay in *Exploring the North Coast of British Columbia*. The bay has anchorage behind the first of two islets inside. Contrary to Douglass' illustration, however, low tide reveals rocks that foul the western side of that first islet. We would pass the islet only to the east.

Cow Island Group. Anchoring possibilities lie in the unnamed group of islands just west of Cow Island. Larger boats will find good anchoring in deep water in the unnamed cove marked with 29-meter and 35-meter soundings. The large island with the 105-meter hill is at the north end of this cove. Smaller boats can creep into the unnamed cove east of the deep water cove. This cove is marked with a 9-meter sounding in the mouth and a 16-meter sounding inside. The Black Gold Fishing Resort is moored on the eastern shore. The little nook at the northeast end of the cove offers quiet anchorage in 60 to 120 feet, but be careful when you enter this nook. A reef extends northward nearly halfway across the entrance, much farther than the chart suggests. Favor the north side.

LOCAL KNOWLEDGE

GOOSE BAY NO WAKE: Slow down and reduce wake when passing the Black Gold floating Fishing Resort on the west side of Goose Bay, near 53-meter and 54-meter islands across the bay from Duncanby Lodge.

Duncanby Lodge. (604) 628-9822; (877) 846-6548; www.duncanby.com. Duncanby is an all-inclusive fishing resort. The restaurant and docks are no longer open to the general boating public. No fuel service.

Goose Bay. Anchorage is good in 20 to 50 feet on a sticky bottom across the bay from the cannery buildings. Crabbing is reported to be good.

Goose Bay Cannery. This is a private facility; moorage at the dock is for members only, with posted no trespassing signs. The historic cannery in Goose Bay, built in 1926, processed and canned salmon from 1927-1957; 350 people once worked and lived at the cannery. The cannery now serves as a private fishing lodge.

Hemasila Inlet. "Entry to the inner basin looks impossible on the chart, but isn't. The charted rock is central in a 200-foot-wide channel and is visible except at very high tides. Favor the east side—it has slightly more room and the shore is steep. We anchored in 35 feet just north of the 9.1-meter sounding with plenty of room to swing. Holding was excellent in thick mud. It was sheltered and pretty, with a small creek at one side and a small waterfall at the other side. Watch for a rock 2.5 meters deep at zero tide in the mouth of the inlet where the R symbol and 24 meter sounding are located." [*Hamilton*]

Taylor Bay. Taylor Bay indents the east shore of Walbran Island and has tranquil, lovely anchorage in 35 to 50 feet, although swinging room is limited. Anchor all the way in or try the nook behind the north end of the inner island, between the inner island and Walbran Island. Protected from most winds except east and southeast.

NORTHERN B.C. COAST

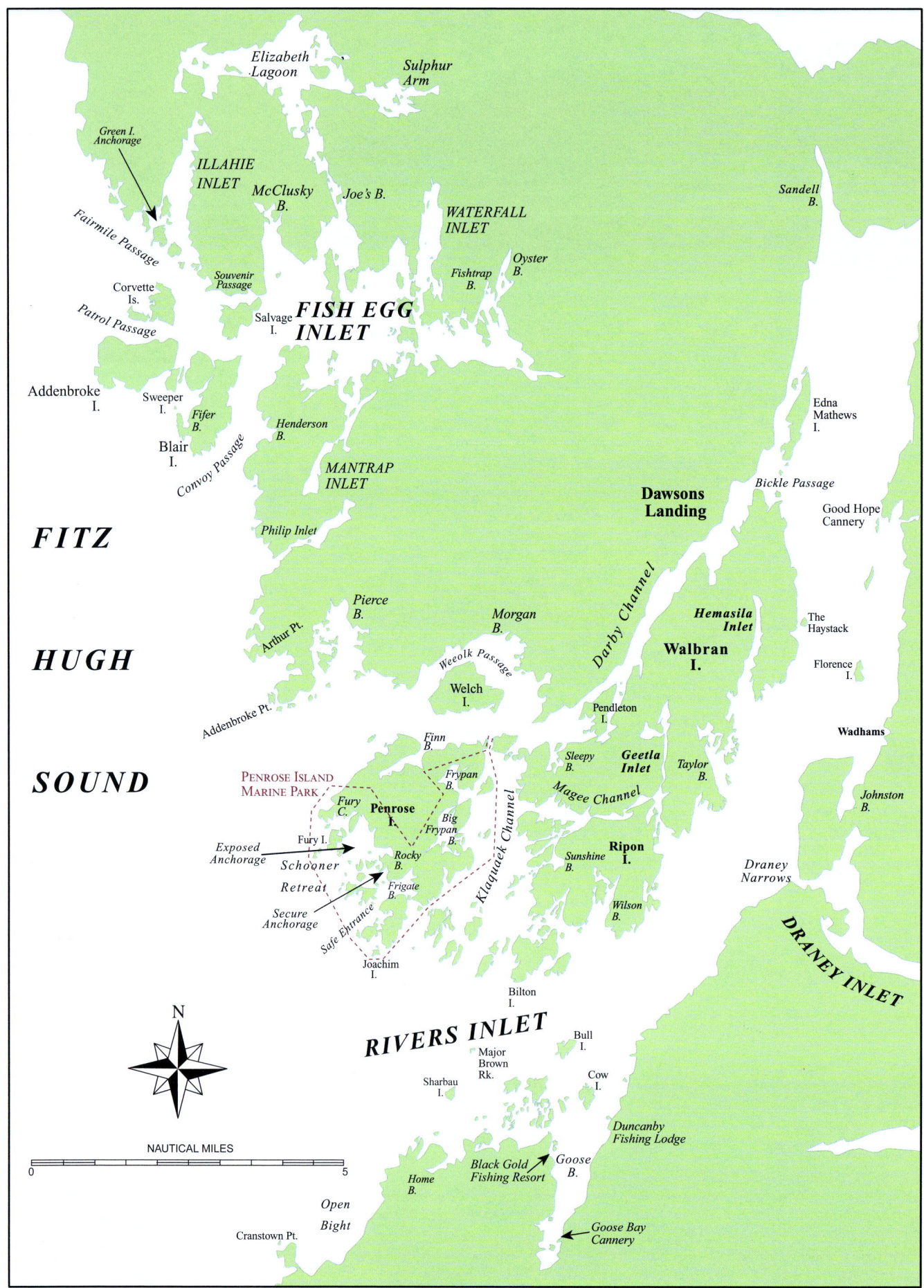

See Area Map Page 419 - Maps Not for Navigation

Rivers Inlet & Fish Egg Inlet

Draney Narrows & Draney Inlet. The current runs hard in Draney Narrows. We looked in 1½ hours before the predicted turn and decided against it. Fifteen minutes before the turn the narrows were flat. Predictions are shown in Canadian Tide & Current Tables, Vol. 7 and Ports and Passes as a secondary station based on Prince Rupert Tides.

Draney Inlet, approximately 24 miles long, is surrounded by high, steep mountains. It's beautiful. Because it is not on the way to anyplace else, it sees little pleasure craft traffic. Good anchorage in 30 to 35 feet is available in Fish Hook Bay, a short distance inside the narrows. When we visited, a float home with two floating outbuildings was on the south shore of Fish Hook Bay, near the entrance. A large sign read, "Warning, Private Property, No Trespassing." A convincing watchdog greeted our boat with don't-mess-with-me barks and growls. We didn't argue.

Note: Our sister publication, *Cruising the Secret Coast*, by Jennifer and James Hamilton, devotes a chapter to Draney Inlet, with much information about anchorages and what to see.

Johnston Bay. Johnston Bay, on the east shore of Rivers Inlet just south of Wadhams, is a former cannery site. The bay is quiet and beautiful, but deep until very near the head. As the chart shows, a reef lies in the center of the outer part of Johnston Bay, and a rock is close to the eastern shore at the entrance. Favor the western shore all the way in and you'll have ample depths of 30-50 feet.

Sandell Bay. "North shore of Rivers Inlet, where the inlet takes that east bend. Anchor well into the bay in 25 feet, zero tide. Excellent holding in mud/sand/rock/shell. Kind of like a cement mix, and held like it, too. Sandell Bay looks exposed on the chart, but is actually protected. It was blowing 30 knots in Rivers Inlet when we came in, and from the anchorage we could see a line of whitecaps out there. But hardly any wind or fetch reached us." [Hamilton]

Good Hope Cannery. Good Hope Cannery is the large, white building visible when cruising past Draney Inlet. The facility is a high-end fly-in sport fishing resort. No services for cruising boats.

① **Dawsons Landing** (Dawsons Landing General Store). (604) 629-9897; dawsonslanding@hotmail.com; dawsonslanding@gmail.com www.dawsonslanding.ca. Monitors VHF 06. Located at the north end of Darby Channel in Rivers Inlet. Phone service is spotty; it's often best to communicate by email. Open all year; gasoline and diesel fuel. Guest moorage, hardware, groceries, liquor, charts, ice, fishing licenses, and gear. The store has limited hours of operation. Washroom, showers, laundry, and post office. Two rental cabins with kitchenettes. Satellite based Wi-Fi available for a fee, pay at the general store. Locally produced water available on the dock. A helipad takes up part of the south end dock. They have scheduled air service from Wilderness Seaplanes and NW Seaplanes.

Dawsons Landing is owned by Rob and Nola Bachen, and has been in the family since 1954. This is a real general store, with an excellent stock of standard grocery items and an astonishing accumulation of tools and hardware. One year, for example, we needed an in-line fuse holder to replace a spare we had used. Dawsons had it.

The floating village of Dawsons Landing with guest moorage, store, cabins, and fuel.

Note that instead of cleats, you'll tie to loops of rope set into the planks. Absent bull rails, it's easier and safer to clear the docks of snow in the winter. The one dock with bull rails is used by floatplanes and the Grumman Goose.

Smoked salmon: It's almost worth a trip to Dawsons Landing simply to stock up on the Bella Coola Valley Seafoods smoked wild Pacific salmon that Nola carries in the store. Several smoke flavors to choose from; time of year varies depending on the commercial fishing season.

Supplying Rivers Inlet for Over 65 Years

DAWSONS LANDING
GENERAL STORE LTD.

A GENUINE OLD-TIME GENERAL STORE

Fuel • Complete Grocery
Well-Stocked Liquor Agency
Block & Cube Ice
Bottled Water • Water on Dock
Internet Hookup
Bait • Souvenirs
Moorage • Post Office
Showers & Laundry
Rental Cabins
Scheduled Air Service

We Freeze Fish

IN THE MIDDLE *of the* **WORLD-FAMOUS RIVERS INLET FISHING GROUNDS**

WWW.DAWSONSLANDING.CA
dawsonslanding@gmail.com • Phone 604/629-9897
Proprietors Rob & Nola Bachen • Dawsons Landing, BC V0N 1M0 • VHF 06

NORTHERN B.C. COAST

See Area Map Page 419 - Maps Not for Navigation

Impromptu gathering on the docks at Dawsons Landing.

Darby Channel (Schooner Pass). Darby Channel, locally called Schooner Pass, borders the west side of Walbran Island, and is easily run. Southbound boats should favor the west shore of the channel to avoid being lured into foul ground behind Pendleton Island. The rock off the southwest corner of Pendleton Island is clearly marked by a beacon and easily avoided.

②**Penrose Island Marine Park.** This Provincial park consists of narrow channels and well protected coves on Penrose Island - Fury Cove, Frypan Bay, and Big Frypan Bay - conducive for exploration by dinghy or kayak.

No Discharge Zone: The discharge of blackwater (sewage) is prohibited within the park.

② **Fury Cove.** The cove behind Fury Island is a beautiful and a popular anchorage, with a perfect white shell beach. Fury Cove, as it is commonly called, is entered by leaving Cleve Island to port, then turning to port towards the narrow entrance.

Fury Cove is a good place to spend the night before a southbound rounding of Cape Caution, or when headed north after crossing Cape Caution. It is popular and occasionally fills up; consider Big Frypan Bay as an alternative. While at anchor, you can look across the beach and see the conditions on Fitz Hugh Sound. Inside, avoid the charted rock that dries at 10 feet close to Fury Island. Consider taking the dinghy to shore to explore the beach and tide pools. A cabin used by kayakers is nestled in the woods on the north shore of Fury Island.

Cleve Island is mentioned in Sailing Directions, but shown on the chart only as a 61-meter island—no name. **Breaker Pass** separates Fury Island from Cleve Island. We have run through the pass in calm weather, but we could tell it wouldn't take much of a southwesterly for Breaker Pass to live up to its name.

No Discharge Zone: No black water overboard discharge.

②**Frypan Bay.** Frypan Bay, spacious, scenic and well protected, is at the northeast corner of Penrose Island. Anchoring depths, along the south shore, are 25 to 40 feet and, in the middle, 50 to 85 feet with good holding. This anchorage is a favorite of many cruisers. The narrow entrance has an uncharted shoal on the port side shore as you enter.

②**Big Frypan Bay.** Located on the east side of Penrose Island, this large bay has ample room for numerous boats; anchoring depths of 68 feet on a sand-mud bottom. Shallower depths can be found in a couple of coves within the bay. The short, narrow entrance to Big Frypan is straight-forward and easy to transit.

Finn Bay. Finn Bay, on the north side of Penrose Island, is well protected. An abandoned sport fishing camp is in the bay. Anchoring depths of 36-66 feet can be found in the bay.

Sunshine Bay. Tucked in the middle of Ripon Island, the bay is entered through a narrow channel off of Klaquaek Channel. The charted shoal on the south shore at the neck of the entrance is not as extensive as depicted on the charts. Anchoring depths are 25 to 30 feet over a flat mud bottom. This intriguing bay is home to a hidden community of float-homes. During the off-season, this bay is the parking location for several fishing lodge buildings.

Pierce Bay. Exercise caution, because Pierce Bay contains dangerous rocks not necessarily shown on the chart. One of the rocks is east of the south tip of the largest island, at 51°31.665'N/127°45.667'W. This rock is in relatively open water, and could surprise a person. Another is off the northwest point of the large island, where the anchorage opens up.

Philip Inlet. Philip Inlet indents the mainland side of Fitz Hugh Sound approximately 3 miles south of Addenbroke Island. The entrance can be hard to identify. Use caution when entering: ledges of rock extend from each side

Supplies, mail, and guests arrive at Dawsons Landing on historic Grumman Goose

Front-row seat at Dawsons Landing to all sorts of activity.

www.WaggonerGuide.com

Green Island Anchorage has room for several boats in a well protected bay with a view of Fitz Hugh Sound - not the entrance.

Fury Cove is well protected with sandy beaches and windows to Fitz Hugh Sound.

of the inlet near the mouth. About halfway in, a small island creates a rock-strewn, tight and tricky narrows. A bow watch is recommended. Field Correspondents Jim Norris and Anita Fraser report: "We came here to hide from an approaching southeast gale. We entered midway on the flood and found the entrance narrow in one spot, but well charted on Chart 3934. Least depth was 18 feet at half tide with very slight current. We anchored in 55 feet in the middle of the bay with good holding. The next morning Addenbrook Island lighthouse reported southeast 15 knot winds; we had northwest 3 knots."

Fifer Bay. Fifer Bay indents the western side of Blair Island, with lovely 6- to 12-foot anchorage for small craft at the head of the southernmost cove. There's room for one boat if it swings, more if all stern-tie to shore. When entering, favor Sweeper Island to avoid the rocks lying off the southern side of the entrance. When clear of the rocks, turn south and work your way into the anchorage.

FISH EGG INLET

Fish Egg Inlet indents the east side of Fitz Hugh Sound, behind Addenbroke Island. This is beautiful cruising country, and is becoming one of the popular spots on the coast. Those who say you'll be all alone are wrong. The gunkholing possibilities are many.

Mantrap Inlet. Once you're inside, Mantrap Inlet offers good anchorage. The entrance, however, is narrow, made narrower by an uncharted ledge of rock that extends from the west shore. Consider going through at half tide or higher, dead slow, with a lookout.

Oyster Bay. Oyster Bay, next to Fish Trap Bay at the head of Fish Egg Inlet, is a nice anchorage with a remote feel to it. We had a late and relaxed lunch there, anchored in 20 feet near the head of the bay. Recommended. [*Hale*]

Fish Trap Bay. Awfully tight, but room for one boat, stern-tied. At lower water levels the Native fish trap is clearly visible.

Waterfall Inlet. Pretty spot, but we couldn't find any comfortable anchorages. We felt that the west entry, leaving the 99-meter island to starboard, was safest. Go slowly and watch for rock ledges that extend from each side of the narrow pass.

Joe's Bay. Joe's Bay has become quite popular. When we visited in early July one year, five other boats were already anchored. Joe's Bay is worth the crowds, though. It's tranquil, tree-lined and snug. Anchoring is straightforward in the southern basin; rocks and reefs make the northern portion somewhat trickier. A stern-tie to shore might be called for to keep the boat from swinging onto a rock. Once anchored, the tidal rapids leading to Elizabeth Lagoon and Sulphur Arm are worth exploring with the dinghy.

Souvenir Passage. Sailing Directions says that Souvenir Passage is very narrow at its eastern end and the chart shows a rock on the north shore. We have found good water all the way by favoring the south side of the passage.

Illahie Inlet. The head of Illahie Inlet would be a delightful anchorage in 30 to 40 feet, mud bottom, with good protection. Favor one shore or the other as you enter Illahie Inlet. Rocks lie in the middle of the channel, partway in.

Green Island Anchorage. With room for several boats, this well protected anchorage off Fitz Hugh Sound has several nooks and view corridors to provide a more open feel from this cozy anchorage. While there is no cell reception, conditions on Fitz Hugh Sound can be seen from the anchorage. Anchor in 25 to 40 feet of water over a soft mud bottom. Look for the weathered handmade Green Island sign as you investigate the network of channels. It's a great place to explore by kayak or dinghy.

The short, narrow entrance to Big Frypan Bay is easy to transit.

Entrance to the very well-protected Sunshine Bay on Ripon Island

FITZ HUGH SOUND

Fitz Hugh Sound begins at Cape Calvert and continues north to Fisher Channel. Boats crossing Queen Charlotte Sound from the south will find the ocean swells quickly vanish once Cape Calvert is behind them. A southwesterly can still make things nasty, especially in a south flowing ebb current. Even in settled conditions, expect to find rougher water where Hakai Passage joins Fitz Hugh Sound.

Northbound boats that don't stop at Rivers Inlet probably will stop in Fifer Bay, Safety Cove, or Pruth Bay. Green Island Anchorage is another good choice for passing traffic.

Safety Cove. Safety Cove is a steep-walled, uninteresting bay that indents Calvert Island approximately 7 miles north of Cape Calvert. The bottom shoals sharply a fair distance from the head of the bay. Sailing Directions recommends anchoring immediately when the depth reaches 100 feet. If you press in to find shallower water, watch your swing or you could find yourself aground on the shelf at low tide. Despite its name and regular use, Safety Cove is not our first choice of anchorages in the area.

③ **Pruth Bay.** Pruth Bay is at the head of **Kwakshua Channel,** some 7 miles north of Safety Cove. Pruth Bay has long been a favorite stopover point. It offers ample room, 40- to 50-foot anchoring depths, and a flat bottom with good holding. Storms coming off the ocean can make the bay quite windy.

This entire area is part of the **Hakai Luxvbalis Conservancy Area**, a huge provincial park that includes the northern half of Calvert Island, the southern two-thirds of Hunter Island, and Goose Island.

Correspondents James and Jennifer Hamilton have anchored in about 50 feet with good holding in the unnamed cove west of Keith Anchorage, on the south shore of Kwakshua Channel, a short distance east of Pruth Bay. Anchor in this cove or one of the others that indent that shore, in Pruth Bay itself, or in the bay north of the thumb of land marked by Whittaker Point.

Southbound, we often overnight at Pruth Bay before rounding Cape Caution. Hakai Beach Institute provides free Wi-Fi in the bay, handy for downloading weather information.

Note: Our sister publication, *Cruising the Secret Coast*, by Jennifer and James Hamilton, devotes a chapter to this area. It describes anchorages not included in the *Waggoner*, and includes coverage of anchorages at the mouth of Hakai Passage.

The beaches near Pruth Bay are arguably the best beaches anywhere on the west coast.

③ **Hakai Beach Institute.** In 2010 the luxury fly-in fishing resort at the head of Pruth Bay was purchased by the Tula Foundation and became the Hakai Beach Institute. The facility is now used for research and as a conference center. Visitors are welcome to moor their dinghies and use the marked walk-way and trail to the Pacific side of the Institute's grounds.

No fuel or commercial services are available at Hakai Beach Institute. When arriving by dinghy, moor only at the clearly marked "dinghy dock" section of the float. The Institute requests that visitors sign the guest log at the Welcome Centre, at the head of the dock. A public washroom is adjacent.

The grounds are immaculate. Follow the signs for the trail to West Beach, one of the finest beaches on the coast. The trail is substantially covered with a boardwalk, but unfinished and muddy in some places. Carry

Easy trail from Pruth Bay brings you to West Beach.

HAKAI BEACH INSTITUTE – PRUTH BAY

Pruth Bay has always been a good overnight stop along the Inside Passage. The bay, at the head of Kwakshua Channel, is well protected and scenic. But the real attractions are West Beach and North Beach, two of the most beautiful sand beaches in the Northwest.

The uplands at Pruth Bay are home to the Hakai Institute ecological labs and observatory under the umbrella of the Tula Foundation. The Institute conducts long-term scientific research, working in conjunction with Canadian and U.S. universities and government agencies. The dock at Pruth Bay accommodates the Institute's fleet of boats to transport personnel and equipment. The Institute's outstanding work and well-organized collaboration have been recognized by the United Nations, which designated the Tula Foundation as the Northeast Pacific Regional Collaborative Center" of Ocean Science, covering the Pacific Coast from Baja California to the Aleutian Islands.

Due to its location, the Hakai Beach Institute is totally off the grid. Electricity is generated by a 50 kw solar farm feeding into a nearly 10,000 amp hour battery bank. Water is collected on site. Sewage is heavily treated before being released. And perhaps most welcome for visiting boaters, internet is piped in through nine satellite links and distributed wirelessly throughout the property and anchorage (please, no streaming video or other bandwidth intensive tasks).

We are fortunate to have people like Eric and Christina, principals of the Tula Foundation, focused on understanding our environment and sharing the beauty of this area with visiting boaters. Boaters may tie up their dinghy behind the main docks, sign in at the upland kiosk, and hike the well-maintained boardwalk and gravel pathway to beautiful West Beach.

You can learn more about the Hakai Beach Institute and the work of the Tula Foundation on their website at hakai.org

bug spray. After a pleasant and flat hike of almost a half-mile, you hear the ocean and break out of the forest to a beautiful beach, with white sand extending in both directions. On a sunny day it seems almost tropical. On an overcast day, with crashing waves, it carries the beauty and furor of the wild Pacific Ocean. A less-developed trail leads north to North Beach, a sandy beach facing Hakai Pass; and a longer more challenging trail leads south to nine scenic west facing beaches.

Visiting boats are welcome to anchor in Pruth Bay, as long as they stay 100 meters from the dock so seaplanes have room to maneuver. Free Wi-Fi covers some of the bay. Wi-Fi internet use is limited to 300 MB of data per device per day. The best reception is close to the head of the bay.

Meay Inlet. Meay Inlet leads north from Kwakshua Channel to Hakai Pass. Immediately after the turn past Whittaker Point is a small scenic cove with room for 4 or 5 boats. The Hamiltons, in *Cruising the Secret Coast*, named this cove Whitaker Point Cove and report anchorage in 40 to 60 feet, with good holding in mud mixed with shell.

The Hakai Lodge (hakai-lodge.com) fly-in fishing resort, owned by the principals of NW Seaplanes, is in a nearby cove from late June until September. The resort has almost daily floatplane service to the Renton/Seattle area, making this a good place to drop off or pick up crew or parts. The lodge serves meals to visiting boaters, reservations required 24-hours in advance for breakfast, lunch, and dinner. Reservations also accepted for guided fishing tours. Email ccarlson@hakailodge.com or hail on VHF 16 for meal reservations. This is a seasonal resort, floats are removed in the off-season.

Hakai Passage. Hakai Passage is one of the great fishing spots, yielding 50- to 60-pound salmon and large bottom fish. Since Hakai Passage opens to the Pacific Ocean, it can get rough. Treat it with respect. On an otherwise pleasant afternoon we overheard two well-managed boats discussing on the radio whether the swells they were facing in Hakai Passage began in Japan or just Hawaii.

Goldstream Harbour. Goldstream Harbour is a lovely little anchorage at the north end of Hecate Island. Enter from the east favoring Hat Island, which extends from the south shore about 0.2 mile inside. Don't favor Hat Island too closely, though; rocks extend out from it. Hat Island is not named on the chart, but its height (39 meters) is shown. Once past Hat Island, pass Evening Rock, which dries at 1.2 meters, leaving it to starboard. Evening Rock lies about 300 feet off the northwest corner of Hat Island (it helps to refer to the chart as you read these instructions). Inside, the middle of Goldstream Harbour is about 30 feet deep. Rocks extend out from the shore, so pick your anchoring spot carefully to swing safely. This is a nice protected spot with an opening in rocks to look out at the conditions in Hakai Pass.

Ward Channel. Ward Channel connects Hakai Passage with Nalau Passage. Running it is straightforward as long as you follow the chart to keep track of the rocks.

Edward Channel. Edward Channel, west of Ward Channel, also connects Hakai Passage with Nalau Passage, but the southern entry is much tighter than Ward Channel. Pass between the 27-meter and 31-meter islets, staying well clear of the detached rock that dries at 1.6 meters off the south tip of the 27-meter islet. Don't try the south entry with larger scale charts. It doesn't show enough detail where you need it. The primary reason to be in Edward Channel is the lovely anchorage of Lewall Inlet.

NORTHERN B.C. COAST

See Area Map Page 419 - Maps Not for Navigation

Lewall Inlet. Lewall Inlet indents the east shore of Stirling Island and is a delightful anchorage. Run all the way to the bend and anchor in 10 to 20 feet, north of the north shore of the entry channel. Stay well off the little treed islet near the south shore. A ledge of drying rock reaches out from that islet.

Uncharted rock: An uncharted rock lies mid-channel just north of the anchorage bend at approximately 51°46.150'N/128°06.266'W. The rock dries on a +2 foot tide. Use extreme caution if going north of the bend at the anchorage.

Nalau Passage. Nalau Passage, scenic and open, separates Hunter Island and Stirling Island, and connects Fitz Hugh Sound with Kildidt Sound. A conservative, mid-channel course has no hazards. The western entrance, however, is made interesting by drying rocks offshore from the north side of the passage. Eastbound boats crossing Kildidt Sound may have anxious moments finding the exact entrance. We used the following waypoint for the western entrance successfully: 51°47.10'N/128°07.20'W.

SPIDER ISLAND AREA

Cruising the Secret Coast, by Jennifer and James Hamilton, contains extensive coverage of these cruising grounds, including Kildidt Sound, Kildidt Inlet, the Goose Group, the McNaughton Group, and other wild areas between Hakai Passage and Seaforth Channel.

Kildidt Sound. Kildidt Sound is remote and beautiful with many anchorage possibilities. Consult *Cruising the Secret Coast* for more information on the numerous islets and anchorages in this area.

Serpent Group. Correspondents James and Jennifer Hamilton have anchored successfully in the cove on the easternmost side of the 57-meter island, southwest of the 31-meter island. Their anchorage was tranquil, but when they dinghied ashore and climbed to the seaward side they found windblown trees barely holding to the shore.

Kildidt Narrows. Kildidt Narrows is the reversing tidal rapids at the entrance to Kildidt Inlet. Waggoner correspondents and Canadian Hydrographic Service, indicate that the Sailing Directions times are incorrect. High water slack occurs approximately 1.5 hours after high water at *Bella Bella*. The time difference for low water slack varies with the height of the tide. For a low water of 0.4 meter, slack occurs approximately 2 hours after low water at *Bella Bella*; for a low water of 2.5 meters, slack occurs approximately 1 hour after low water at *Bella Bella*.

For complete coverage of Kildidt Narrows and Kildidt Inlet, see *Cruising the Secret Coast*.

Wind swept and rocky, Edna Island in the Breadner Group is scenic and off the beaten path.

Brydon Channel. Brydon Channel connects Kildidt Sound and Spider Anchorage. Westbound across Kildidt Sound, lay a course well south of Lancaster Reef, then turn north toward the Brydon Channel entrance. When studying the chart, you will see the easternmost dogleg in Brydon Channel is foul with rocks. Mike Guns, a commercial fisherman with much experience in these waters, told us the safe route through is to hug the northwest end of the 72-meter island at the eastern end of the channel. This keeps you clear of the rocks farther out. See the reference map.

Brydon Anchorage. Brydon Anchorage extends northward into Hurricane Island at the west end of Brydon Channel at 51°50.25'N/128°12.25'W (NAD 83). Correspondents James and Jennifer Hamilton anchored in 30 feet near the very head. They

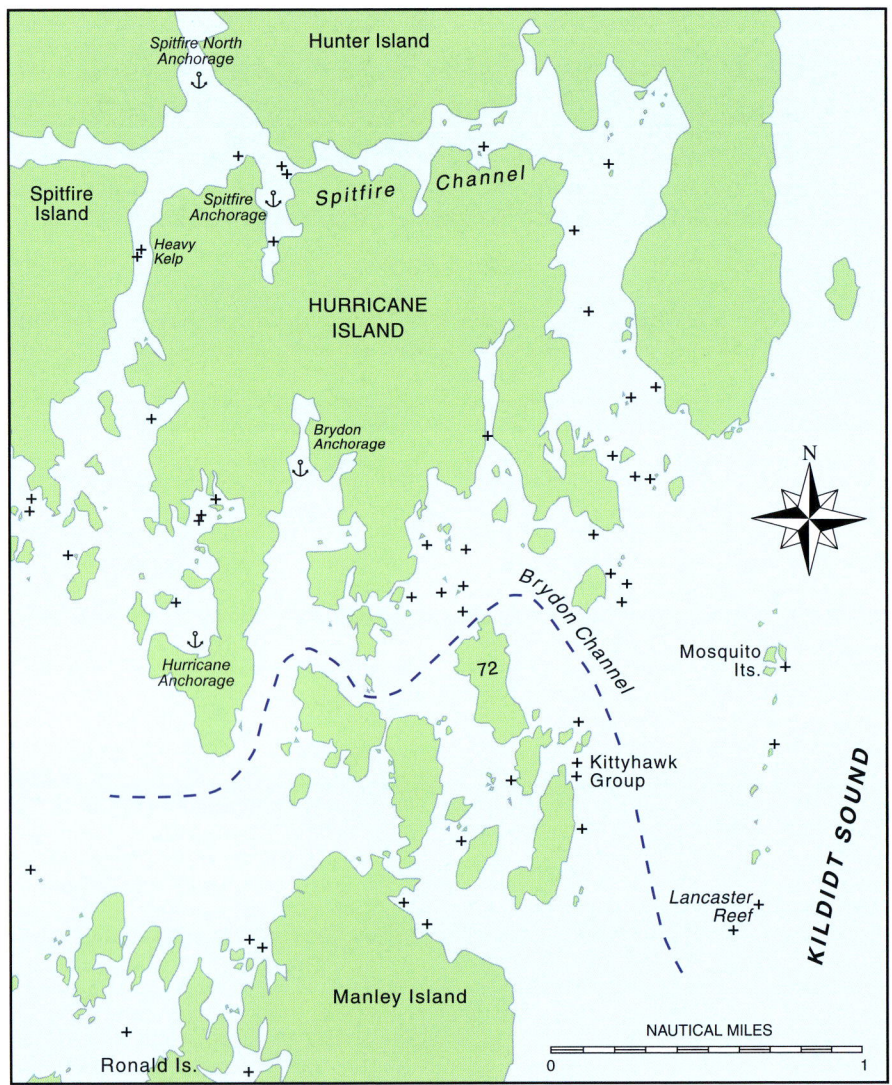

Brydon Channel

report, "An amazing view to the south, not a soul around. It was an astonishingly quiet and beautiful anchorage—like no other. Most places remind us of somewhere else. This one stands alone." [*Hamilton*]

Spider Island area. This area is beautiful, raw, remote feeling, and little visited. The waters are also full of rocks. This is perfect gunkholing country, a paradise for kayakers.

You have a choice of two ways to get there, outside or inside. The outside route goes out the mouth of Hakai Passage into Queens Sound, then bends northwest toward the west side of Spider Island. Breadner Point, on the west side of Spider Island, is a famous hot spot for spring salmon. South of Spider Island, enter through Fulton Passage, or north of Spider Island through Spider Channel.

The inside route goes through Nalau Passage, across Kildidt Sound, and through rock-choked Brydon Channel into Spider Anchorage. An alternate to the Brydon Channel portion is Spitfire Channel, along the north side of Hurricane Island. Spitfire Channel has one spot so tight, however, we recommend you explore by dinghy before committing the mother ship. Near high tide, and with a lookout on the bow, we squeezed through in a 52-foot Grand Banks.

The following information is an overview of the main places. It would take several days to poke around all the delights of this area.

Passage between Spider Anchorage and Spitfire Channel. This passage separates Spitfire Island and Hurricane Island. The passage is clear until the north end, where rocks extend from Spitfire Island. This area is fairly well covered with bull kelp floating on the surface and thick leaf kelp below. We went in near the top of a high tide without difficulty. Next morning we departed 1½ hours after a 3.3-foot low tide and gathered a heavy glop of leaf kelp on our props and rudders. A low-powered fin keel sailboat could have been stopped dead. This passage is best run near high water.

Hurricane Anchorage. "Hurricane Anchorage" is Douglass' name for the otherwise unnamed cove in the hook formed by the south end of Hurricane Island. As shown on the reference map, enter north of the group of islets that make up the hook. Well protected and scenic.

Spitfire West Anchorage. This is Douglass' name for the otherwise unnamed cove that indents Hurricane Island, immediately west of the Spitfire Channel narrows. Several people have recommended it to us. Douglass says the bottom offers only fair to poor holding, however.

Spitfire North Anchorage. This is our name for the otherwise unnamed cove that indents Hunter Island, west of the Spitfire Channel narrows. Mike Guns recommended it to us. We would anchor in the outer part only. At low water the mouth leading to the inner lagoon appeared to be impassable or nearly so. The east side of the outer cove had a bottom that felt like a thin layer of mud on top of rock, and we dragged easily. The west side of the cove yielded good holding in 50 to 55 feet.

Spitfire Channel. Spitfire Channel separates Hurricane Island and Hunter Island, and except for the narrows at the west end, is easily run. The narrows are another matter. A medium-size cruiser can go through these narrows without difficulty, but with great caution and a sharp lookout. Underwater rocks extend into the channel, especially from the north side. Plan your transit at high water slack—high water, to get the greatest width possible; slack because we wouldn't want current pushing us where we didn't want to go. Least depth is 1.9 meters (approximately 6 feet) at zero tide.

Southbound in Spider Channel, approaching the Stopper Group islands on the way to Spider Anchorage

Bonsai tree on wind-swept island near Spider Anchorage and Spitfire Channel

FITZ HUGH SOUND, CONTINUED

Kwakume Inlet. Kwakume Inlet is a beautiful and roomy anchorage, but study your chart closely before entering. A rock awash at zero tide is shown outside the entrance, and you'll want to steer a course to avoid it. Mike Guns, a commercial fisherman with 35 years' experience in these waters, says the preferred approach is from the north. He recommends favoring the mainland shore, to pass between the rock and the shore.

Once past the rock, pass between the larger islet in the entrance and the little dot islet south of the larger islet. Inside, two rocks are shown a short distance along the north shore, one of them dries at 1.5 meters. Near the head of the main basin and south of its islet, another rock is shown, this one dries at 1.8 meters.

The south cove immediately inside the entrance has been recommended as an anchorage, or anchor in 25 to 30 feet (zero tide) at the head of the inlet, between the shore and a rock shown as drying at 1.8 meters.

If you can get into it, the inner basin is unusually secluded and snug feeling. Be aware, however, that the short fairway leading to the inner basin is narrow, and that a substantial drying rock lies in the middle, with more rocks on each side. *High water only, this little pass, dead slow bell, with alert lookouts.* We favored the north side.

Having a high tide when we arrived in early evening, we felt our way into the inner basin for the night. We were treated to glass-smooth water and the most plaintive loon's call we've ever heard. As we slipped out at high water early the next morning we were stopped cold by a wolf's cry—a long lonesome troubled howl, repeated just once. [*Hale*]

Koeye River. A charted rock lies north of Koeye Point. Enter north of that rock and wrap around into the cove behind the point. A lodge is near the point. A float is anchored near the middle of the cove.

A few years ago we talked with the lodge caretaker, who told us that an onshore wind blowing out of Hakai Passage creates large seas that roll into the bay. He also said this is grizzly bear country. Later, we talked with a boat that experienced the seas mentioned above. The skipper said the seas were awful. They had come back from the mine and had much trouble getting from the dinghy to the boat. Stay away in a westerly.

Although in our opinion Koeye (pronounced "Kway") River is not a good spot for overnight anchoring, several people have told us a dinghy trip up the river to the mine ruins is beautiful. At the mine you'll find two open pits connected by a tunnel. The remains of a shop are there, and a huge old 1-cylinder steam engine. The buildings on the point at the mouth of the river are a Bella Bella Native band summer camp and there is a Longhouse within the bay along the shore. [*Hale*]

Sea Otter Inlet & Crab Cove. Sea Otter Inlet, on Hunter Island, has two arms that form a "T" at the entrance. Crab Cove, the northern arm, was recommended by a park ranger at Pruth Bay. Anchor near the head in 30 to 35 feet. The south arm is prettier than Crab Cove and more private feeling. Anchor near the head of the south cove in 35 to 40 feet.

Kiltik Cove. Mouth of cove at 51°53.80'N /128°00.05'W. Kiltik Cove indents the east side of Hunter Island, approximately across from Namu. It is extremely well protected. The bottom shoals abruptly just past the tiny rock islet on the east shore of the arm. We would anchor in 35 to 40 feet a short distance north of that rock.

Warrior Cove. Warrior Cove is on the mainland (east) side of Fitz Hugh Sound, approximately 1.5 miles south of Namu. With a typical westerly wind, a following sea will chase you into the cove, but the seas subside when you pass the 82-meter island (in a southeast gale a lump may get in). The inner cove is pretty and protected. Scout around for just the right spot, and put the hook down in 20 to 25 feet, good holding.

Namu. The falling-down cannery at Namu went through a transition. For many years caretakers Pete and Rene (pronounced "Reenie") Darwin, and Rene's longtime friend Theresa, managed the facility. They created a unique destination on a collection of floats, complete with a covered common area, gift store, workshop, greenhouse, and docks. They transformed the uplands of the old cannery with art and creative landscaping. Pete and Rene have moved on, physically moving their floats to Lizzie Cove on Lama Passage. See Lizzie Cove entry for more information.

Anchorage is still available at Namu or in nearby Rock Inlet.

Navigation note: The beacon is gone from Loo Rock, between the Namu floats and the entrance to Rock Inlet, but Loo Rock still exists. Watch for other possible obstacles in the area.

Rock Inlet. Rock Inlet extends northeast from Whirlwind Bay (Namu), and it's a good, protected spot. Entering or departing, be sure to identify Verdant Island, near the mouth, and pass east of it. Keep a mid-channel course and watch for rocks. The chart shows the way. Inside, anchor in 25 to 40 feet. The bottom is rocky in some areas.

FISHER CHANNEL

The north end of Fitz Hugh Sound divides into Burke Channel and Fisher Channel. Burke Channel leads eastward to Bella Coola, which is connected by road to Williams Lake and the highways inland. Bella Coola has facilities and is mentioned often by the few residents on this part of the coast, but is little visited by pleasure craft.

Fisher Channel is a continuation of the Inside Passage route, although the Inside Passage soon leads west and north, via Lama Passage or Gunboat Passage, to Bella Bella and Shearwater. If you remain in Fisher Channel you will reach Cousins Inlet. Ocean Falls, at the head of Cousins Inlet, is the most complete and interesting ghost town on the coast.

Humchitt Island. Humchitt Island is immediately off the south tip of King Island, at the intersection of Fitz Hugh Sound, Burke Channel and Fisher Channel. "With 15-knot southeasterlies blowing up Fitz Hugh Sound, we overnighted in the cove on the northeast shore of Humchitt Island. The seas were 2 to 3 feet outside, but our anchorage was tranquil and calm, with an amazing view up Fisher Channel. Anchor in 10 to 20 feet, moderate to good holding over rock, with a 150-foot swing radius." [*Hamilton*]

Kisameet Bay. Kisameet Bay is on King Island, about 3.5 miles north of the mouth of Burke Channel, roughly east of Fog Rocks. The northernmost part of the bay, behind the island, is the preferred location. It's quiet and fully protected from wind and sea, with a 'window' out into Fisher Channel to observe conditions. This is a very pleasant place to hide out. Anchor in 30 to 40 feet. We overnighted in this anchorage before heading south to cross Cape Caution.

Nature is working to reclaim the once active Namu Cannery site off Fitz Hugh Sound.

This sandy beach at Sagar Lake is reached by trail from Codville Lagoon.

Codville Lagoon. Codville Lagoon is a provincial park on the east side of Fisher Channel. It is a popular anchorage, protected and pretty. Strong winds can work their way to the back cove. The narrow entrance is hard to locate, but Codville Hill, its moonscape of three peaks and barren rock slopes, is a good landmark. Favor the south side of the entrance to avoid a rock off the north shore. Anchoring depths of 40 to 50 feet at the eastern head of the inlet. A 1.2 km boardwalk trail with muddy sections runs from the northeastern shore of the anchorage to sandy beaches at beautiful Sugar Lake. Field Correspondent Jim Norris warns of vicious sand fleas. This is bear country. Make noise as you walk.

The Trap. The Trap is located behind Clayton Island on the west side of Fisher Channel, about 2 miles south of Lama Passage. North entrance at 52°02.35'N/127°56.80'W. South entrance at 52°01.05'N/127°56.80'W. We read about this spot in Iain Lawrence's *Far Away Places* (now out of print). Southbound on a windy, rainy afternoon we decided to tuck in for a look. The passage behind Clayton Island is as Lawrence describes it: deeper than charted, but protected from westerly winds. Lawrence says the bottom is rocky and requires a stern-tie to shore to prevent swinging. The Trap itself is the bay at the very south end of the passage. Lawrence says this bay empties at low tide, revealing a labyrinth of ancient fish traps.

Long Point Cove. Long Point Cove is located on the west side of Fisher Channel, approximately 1 mile south of Lama Passage. Although Sailing Directions mentions Long Point Cove as a good anchorage for small craft, it isn't as scenic or interesting as other anchorages in the area. On entering, favor the west shore to avoid a rock that dries some 250 to 300 yards north of Long Point. The rock is shown on the chart.

④ **Ocean Falls (Cousins Inlet).** Ocean Falls is a favorite destination. Although a ghost town, Ocean Falls is a busy ghost town. The winter population of 25 swells to 100 in the summer, but services are limited. Two bed and board inns offer services to their guests.

A right turn at the top of the ramp from the Small Craft Harbour leads to Ocean Falls proper. The small gift store in the corner of the marine ways building and the Old Bank Inn are the only operating businesses in Ocean Falls.

The dam dominates the head of the inlet and supplies electrical power for Ocean Falls, Shearwater, and New Bella Bella. The dam also provides water and power for the town's multi-million dollar hatchery and rearing pen facility for Atlantic salmon smolt for fish farms. Some 30 large green fiberglass rearing pens have been installed beside the former Crown Zellerbach mill site. Mixing ponds, where freshwater and saltwater are blended in exact proportions for the developing smolt, have been blasted out of the rocky mountainside leading to the dam. High tech has arrived in Ocean Falls. In early 2018, a computer-based cryptocurrency "mining" entity leased a building with a computer processing facility, which requires large amounts of electrical power.

A trip to Ocean Falls is not complete without a hike to the dam with vistas of Link Lake and views of the once busy mill town below. A walk through this "ghost town" can't help but stir the imagination. Make noise—you might meet a bear. Trout fishing in Link Lake is said to be excellent.

A left turn at the top of the dock leads visitors on a 1.5-mile road to Martin Valley. It's an easy, scenic stroll. The first house you come to is Saggo's Saloon, which changed ownership in 2022; renovations are planned for the pub, anticipated to be completed sometime in 2023.

The houses in Martin Valley were taken over by the province when Ocean Falls was abandoned. They have since been sold to people who enjoy the beauty and solitude of the area. Visitors as well as locals arrive at Ocean Falls by ferry service from Bella Bella, Shearwater, and Bella Coola (check BC Ferries for the scheduled service). A water taxi based in Ocean Falls takes passengers to various destinations on the central coast, call Ken and Shelly (250) 289-3396.

Crabbing is excellent off the old mill site. Halibut and salmon can be caught in Cousins Inlet. Consider dropping a prawn trap in Wallace Bay on your way up the inlet. We think Ocean Falls is a "don't miss" stop for its unique charm and beauty. Air service to and from Ocean Falls is available through Wilderness Seaplanes.

④ **Ocean Falls Small Craft Harbour.** General Delivery, Ocean Falls, BC V0T 1P0; (250) 289-3374, wharfinger Eva Prine. Open all year, public dock with ice, potable water,

Ocean Falls and Small Craft Harbour

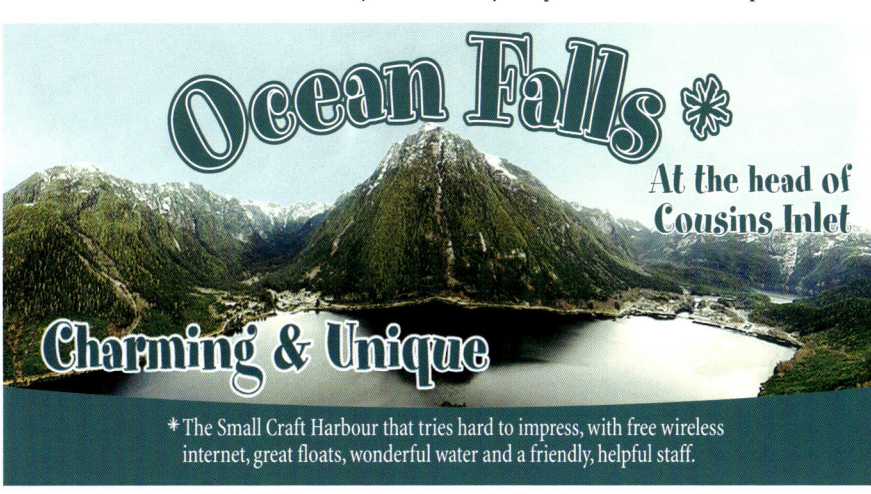

Ocean Falls ✺
At the head of Cousins Inlet
Charming & Unique

✺ The Small Craft Harbour that tries hard to impress, with free wireless internet, great floats, wonderful water and a friendly, helpful staff.

2023 Waggoner Cruising Guide

NORTHERN B.C. COAST

See Area Map Page 419 - Maps Not for Navigation

The Small Craft Harbour at Ocean Falls is in the lower left; remnants of the town are in the center; the dam and Link Lake are in the distance.

free Wi-Fi, 20 & 30 amp power, no fuel. The Harbour Manager is John Bole (250) 289-3315, who oversees maintenance. Recent upgrades include new decking and electrical stanchions.

Ample dock space with reasonable rates and all the Link Lake water you need. The water is sweet and pure and has gone through a further purification process.

"The Shack," a yellow float house next to the ramp, is where boaters register and pay for moorage. Long-term plans for this government small craft harbour include replacing the aging "shack" and float with a kiosk for moorage payments.

Located in the downstairs corner of the marine ways building is a little gift shop owned by Les & Toni LeMarston, who also own the marine ways. Upstairs is the late "Nearly Normal" Norman's collection of items left behind by former residents of Ocean Falls. If the door is not open, ask around, a local will open up for visitors. Children love visiting the "Fairy Rock" located a short 3/4 mile distance from the docks on the road to Martin.

Children take great delight in finding the tiny fairies and coins hidden in the Rock. Be sure to let the wharfinger know if you plan to visit Fairy Rock so the fairies can be alerted; you can contribute coins at The Shack in support of this long-standing tradition at Ocean Falls. Another fun tradition is the Annual Salmon Derby Barbecue weekend held in late August, a popular event drawing participants from other nearby communities. Tickets for the barbeque can be purchased at The Shack.

No garbage drop: Recycling bins for plastic, glass, tin, aluminum and burnables are located at The Shack. Take everything else with you.

Weather radio channel WX 1: The signal is spotty. If necessary, walk along the dock with a handheld VHF until you find reception.

④ **Old Bank Inn**. (250) 289-9624; info@lemarston.com. Les and Toni LeMarston purchased the former fishing lodge near the historic Ocean Falls Hotel and converted the lodge into a cozy bed and board guesthouse offering six comfortable rooms with breakfast, lunch and dinner included in the daily rate. You guessed it, the building was originally the bank in Ocean Falls. Toni sells delicious homemade bread and cinnamon buns, or stop by to purchase ice cream cones.

Lama Passage. Lama Passage leads westward and northward from Fisher Channel to New Bella Bella and Shearwater. Cruise ships and BC Ferries use this passage regularly. Keep a sharp lookout ahead and astern.

Fancy Cove. Fancy Cove is on the south shore of Lama Passage and is a delightful little anchorage. Don and Reanne Douglass write about the cove in their book *Exploring the North Coast of British Columbia*. This nearly landlocked cove is well protected. Anchor in 10 to 25 feet.

Fannie Cove. Fannie Cove is in Cooper Inlet on the south shore of Lama Passage. It's a beautiful little spot, with an obvious anchoring nook on its eastern shore just inside the entrance. Unfortunately, the holding ground is only fair. We tried twice to get a good set in the little nook and once farther out, but each time we dragged without much effort. We would overnight in settled weather only. Study the chart before entering. Leave Gus Island and the little dot islet west of Gus Island to port as you approach.

Lizzie Cove. Lizzie Cove is a well protected anchorage with an entrance that is not well charted and with rocks that are difficult to locate. The cove has room for a number of boats sheltered from nearly all winds.

Two routes, Hogan Rock Route and Gus Island Route bring you into Lizzie Cove from Lama Passage. Bow watch is required.

Hogan Rock Route - leave Hogan Rock and the awash rock northwest of Hogan Rock to port; proceed south-southwest passing the reef that dries at 3-meters to port; then turn west-to pass 41-meter island to port; and wrap around the 41-meter island. Give the northwest end of 41-meter island shoal a wide berth.

The falls at Ocean Falls

See Area Map Page 419 - Maps Not for Navigation   NORTHERN B.C. COAST

Fuel Dock at Bella Bella

Grocery Store in Bella Bella complete with bakery and meat department.

Gus Island Route – leave Gus Island to port; proceed south-southwest; then turn northwest, passing 41-meter island to port and the reef that dries at 2.1-meters to starboard; and wrap around the 41-meter island. Give the northwest end of 41-meter island shoal a wide berth.

Lizzie Cove is home to Pete and Rene Darwin who welcomed visiting boaters at their floats in years past. Their floats are now closed to the public. Pete and Rene Darwin moved their floats, BBQ shelter, and gift shop from Namu to Lizzie Cove a number of years ago. Their self-sufficient gardens are impressive and include a hothouse with fruit trees.

Jane Cove. Jane Cove, on the south shore of Lama Passage in Cooper Inlet, offers shelter but lacks scenic quality. Study the chart carefully before entering to avoid shoals and rocks. Fannie Cove, despite its marginal holding, or Fancy Cove, which is spectacular by comparison, are preferred.

⑤ **Bella Bella.** New Bella Bella (Waglisla) is a major Native village, with fuel, potable water, garbage drop, and a grocery store and nice cafe; cell phone service is good. The village has a hospital. The closest laundromat is at Shearwater. The BC Ferries terminal is located south of town.

The main pier and floats are busy with water taxis and local boat traffic. Moorage is filled with commercial and local boats; there is no transient moorage but always room for a dinghy. The fuel dock (250-957-2440) has gas and diesel, call ahead for service. The attendants are courteous, but religious about closing during their lunch hour. You may have to be patient. New Bella Bella's water treatment plant provides a steady stream of clear, potable water at the fuel dock.

A new, large grocery store opened in 2018 and includes a bakery and meat department. This is a fun place to shop for gifts and food items to re-stock your galley. The supply barge arrives weekly on Sundays. Just north of this store is the Waglisla Senior Centre, with native artwork. The locals are friendly and eager to share their stories. Visitors are also welcome to tour the K-12 Bella Bella Community School.

Guests at Shearwater can take the water taxi to New Bella Bella to shop at the band store or to drop off or pick up passengers or parts from the airport. Scheduled airline service runs throughout the day.

The New Bella Bella airport is about 2 miles from the village. You can walk along the road or take a taxi. The taxi is often standing by before or after a flight or call (250) 957-2582 or on VHF channel 14. They know the schedules. Wilderness Seaplanes serves New Bella Bella with multiple flights per day.

Old Bella Bella. Old Bella Bella is on Denny Island on the northeastern shore of Lama Passage. The excellent docks and lovely buildings ("Whistler North") house the Coast Guard Search and Rescue vessel *Cape Farewell*, its crew and support staff, and Fisheries and Oceans personnel. No transient moorage.

Lizzie Cove offers protected anchorage but with a challenging entry.

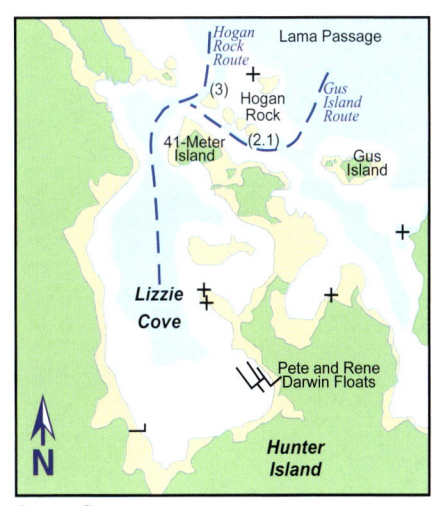

Lizzie Cove

2023 Waggoner Cruising Guide

Kliktsoatli Harbour. Shearwater Resort & Marina is located in Kliktsoatli Harbour, 2 miles east of New Bella Bella on the north side of Denny Island. Good anchorage can be found on the eastern shore.

⑥ **Shearwater Resort & Marina.** (250) 957-2666; moorage@shearwater.ca; hotel@shearwater.ca; www.shearwater.ca. Monitors VHF 66A, the fuel dock monitors VHF 08. Open all year, 1700 feet of guest moorage (200 feet added in 2019), 15, 30 & 50 amp power on the main spine float and on part of the T-ends. Free Wi-Fi. Potable water is available on the guest dock. Seasonally, there are two waterlines for different uses; one carries potable water, and the other is for washdown. In 2022, the hoses had laminated labels. Please be sparing and sharing with the potable water. During prime season, register and pay for moorage at the dockside harbourmaster's office, or at the hotel during shoulder season. Moorage reservations are highly recommended during the busy summer months. Cellular service is good.

The fuel dock has diesel, gasoline, lubricants, propane, Avgas and Jet A. Please reduce your wake around the fuel dock and moorage docks. On shore you'll find an ATM, washrooms, showers, laundry, ice, restaurant, pub, haulout, launch ramp, facilities for waste oil dump, garbage drop and recycling center. Garbage drop is for registered moorage guests only. A well-stocked grocery store, liquor store, and marine supply store are on site along with a post office, coffee pastry bar, and gift shop. The showers and laundry room, in the building across from the store, are excellent.

The popular pub, with live entertainment, has a nice deck for outdoor dining. It's a great place to meet other boaters and locals, who often share a table.

In 2021, the Heiltsuk Nation purchased the resort assets, including the marina, accommodations, fuel dock, restaurant, and store, with plans to add ecotours. They are doing an excellent job maintaining the facility and grounds.

Shearwater is the most complete marine facility between Campbell River and Prince Rupert. The shipyard can haul boats to 70 tons and handle almost anything, from toilet repairs to electronics to repowers. They can order parts for you and coordinate their arrival by air if needed. Shearwater has its own 3,000-foot airstrip for private aircraft. Scheduled airline service to Port Hardy and Vancouver is available at New Bella Bella. Shearwater is also a stop for the BC Ferries system. Hunter Helicopter Tours (778-899-0513 or 604-533-9733) can provide airport transfers and sightseeing excursions. The Sea-Bus water taxi connects Shearwater and New Bella Bella (Waglisla) with a 10-minute, 2.5-mile ride. In calm weather you can scoot over in a dinghy. Shearwater is the crossroads of the northern coast and gets a full range of visitors.

The marina was the site of a WWII Royal Canadian Air Force seaplane base. The large historic hangar now serves as the shop. In 2013, Craig Widsten, the former principal owner of the resort, created two special tributes to the heritage of Shearwater and the surrounding area. When a wall of the shop needed replacement, Craig had it rebuilt and commissioned muralist Paul Gartua to paint the images of seventeen people who had an impact on the growth and development of Shearwater. They include tribal leaders, medical professionals, the original manager of the Hudson's Bay Co. outpost, and even

Enjoy lunch at Shearwater Marina pub.

Craig's father, Andrew, the founder of Shearwater. Measuring 120 feet wide and 22 feet tall, the mural is quite striking.

Craig also installed a cenotaph to commemorate Shearwater and New Bella Bella residents' war service. He commissioned the casting of a 17-foot scale replica of the Stranraer flying boat that was based at Bella Bella during WWII. Nearby, a carved Eagle pole commemorates First Nations veterans, and an obelisk commemorates other veterans from the area.

Kakushdish Harbour. Kakushdish Harbour, long and narrow, extends into Denny Island immediately east of Kliktsoatli Harbour (Shearwater). An overhead power cable with 23 meters (75 feet) vertical clearance crosses the entrance. "We favored the north shore through the entrance bar and saw a minimum depth of 11 feet, zero tide. Anchor in 20 to 25 feet, good holding in mud. The anchorage was surprisingly deserted and tranquil." [*Hamilton*]

LOCAL KNOWLEDGE

NAVIGATION NOTES: The trickiest spot in Gunboat Passage is the narrow fairway between Denny Point and Maria Island. Use caution to navigate away from the rocks. A second tricky spot is the reef that extends from the southern shore toward Dingle Island. Watch the currents in this area. A red nun buoy marks the outer end of this reef. Red, Right, Returning assumes you are returning eastbound, from the sea. The third tricky spot is the range at the west end of Gunboat Passage. Entering or departing, stay on the range.

Gunboat Passage. Gunboat Passage connects Seaforth Channel with Fisher Channel and is a scenic route between Ocean Falls and New Bella Bella/Shearwater. The passage is littered with reefs and rocks, but all marked with new, upgraded aids to navigation installed by the Canadian Coast Guard in 2019.

Beales Bay. The entrance looks tricky on the chart, but if you leave the small islet to port as you enter, you'll have good water.

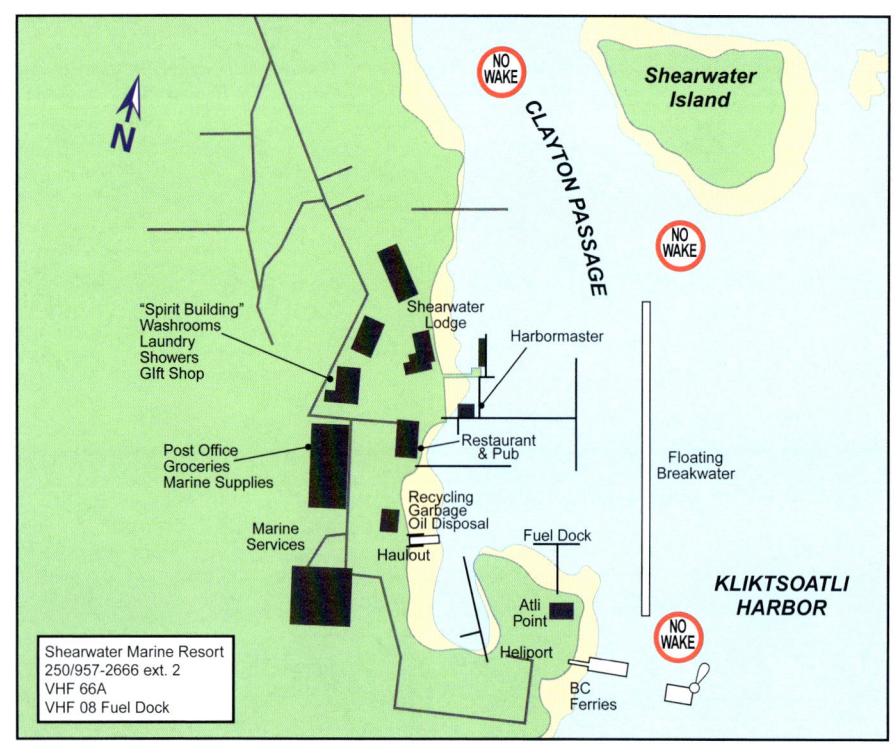

Shearwater Marine Resort

Anchor inside in 30 to 40 feet. Stay well clear of the mouth of Beales Lagoon. At least two detached drying rocks lie in the cove off the lagoon's mouth. Excellent protection.

Gosse Bay. Gosse Bay is west of Maria Island, a good anchorage on the west side of the westernmost cove.

Forit Bay. Forit Bay, on the eastern approach to Gunboat Passage, is an excellent, protected anchorage in 15 to 25 feet. The entrance, however, is encumbered by a large rock between Flirt Island and the point of land that marks the inner part of the bay. The rock is not visible at high tide, but is visible through the water at a little less than half tide.

Enter Forit Bay by wrapping around the north tip of Flirt Island, leaving the island to port.

BURKE CHANNEL, DEAN CHANNEL, BELLA COOLA

Burke Channel and Dean Channel border the south and north sides of King Island and plunge deep into the Coast Range mountains. This is some of the most beautiful and awe-inspiring country imaginable, but after seeing so much beautiful country all along the B.C. coast, we expected it to be just more of the same. We were wrong. A circumnavigation of King Island will astonish you. Gone is the raw coast with its low, wave-pounded islands. A short distance up either channel puts you inland, bounded on each side by high mountains. If you're going to spend some time on this coast, see these waters.

LOCAL KNOWLEDGE

EBB CURRENT: On warm summer days, heating of inland air produces an up-channel sea breeze in Burke Channel that can begin as early as 10:00 a.m. and blow strongly until sundown. Make your runs early and find shelter before the wind starts blowing.

TIDE-RIPS: The surface water in Burke Channel is often in an almost constant ebb, the result of fresh water flowing toward the sea. When this surface ebb meets a spring flood, tide-rips, whirlpools, and general confusion results.

Burke Channel. Burke Channel leads 38 miles inland, beginning at Edmund Point, just north of Namu. From Edmund Point to Restoration Bay, the lower reaches of Burke Channel are subject to strong tidal currents and heavy tide-rips, but in the upper reaches the tidal streams are weak.

The north end of Burke Channel divides into South Bentinck Arm and North Bentinck Arm (Bella Coola is at the head of North Bentinck Arm), and Labouchere Passage, which leads to Dean Channel. When the ebb current is flowing and the up-channel sea breeze is blowing, expect rough seas at the confluence of these channels. Early morning, before the B.C. interior heats up, is often the calmest time of day.

All these cautions make Burke Channel sound impenetrable, which isn't the case. The prudent skipper simply will avoid being out there in the wrong conditions.

The best anchorage along Burke Channel is at the head of Kwatna Inlet, with a second-best choice being the small cove just north of Cathedral Point.

Fougner Bay. Fougner Bay is near the mouth of Burke Channel on the south side, just east of Edmund Point. The outer part of the bay is somewhat protected, with anchorage in 40 to 60 feet. To us it feels uninviting. An inner cove, however, is a perfect spot.

Find the 4.1-meter sounding back in the bay. That's the cove. To get in, the chart shows good water by leaving the + symbol (indicating a dangerous underwater rock 2 meters or less at zero tide) to starboard. Once clear of the rock, loop into the back cove. Very cozy and protected. Study the chart carefully before entering Fougner Bay. The rocks off the entry are easy to avoid, but you want to know where they are and where you are.

Kwatna Inlet. Kwatna Inlet extends some 12 miles into the mainland and is too deep for anchoring until near the head. Watch carefully for the drying flats at the head. We are told by several people that it is an excellent place to put the hook down.

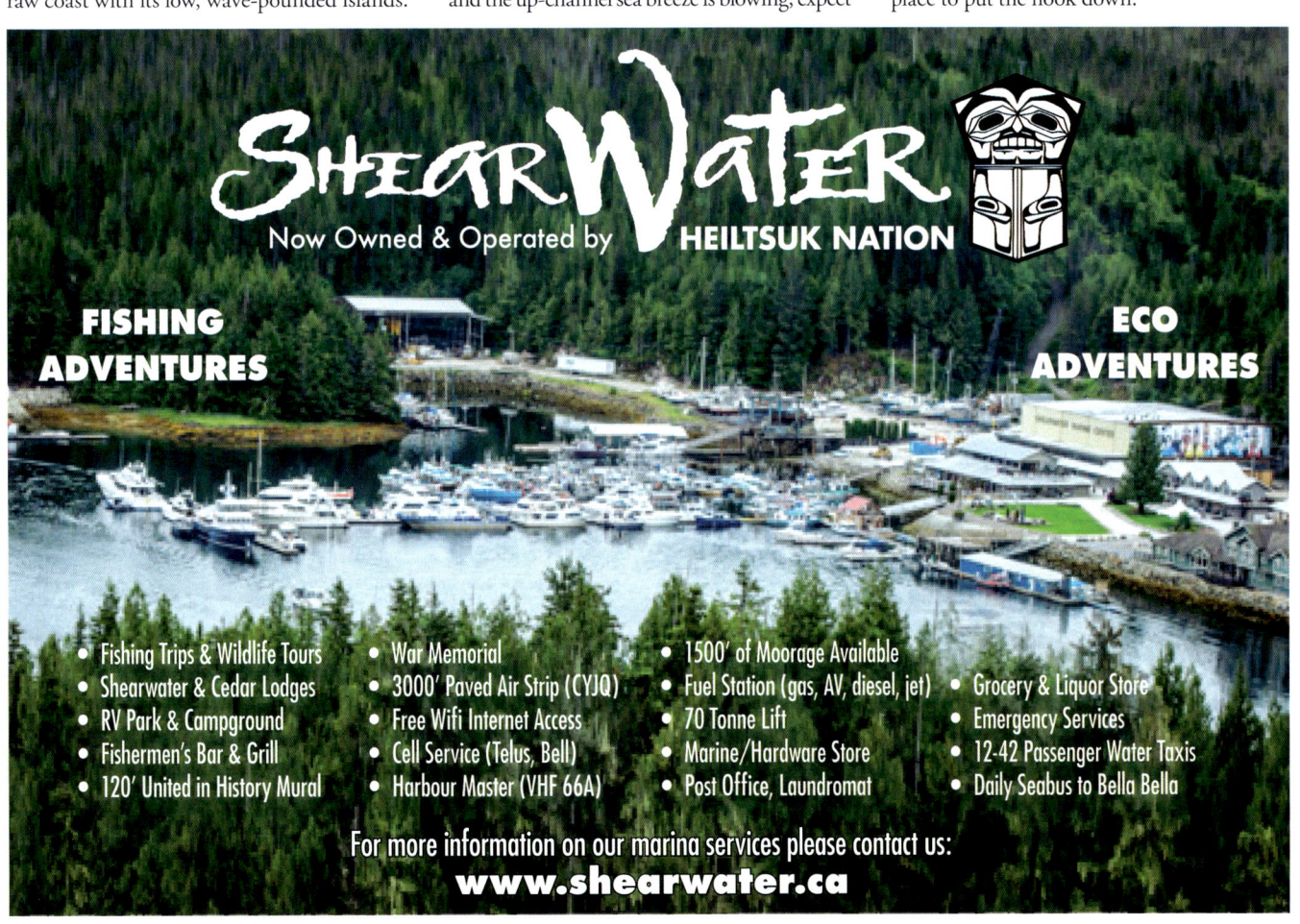

ShearWater

Now Owned & Operated by HEILTSUK NATION

FISHING ADVENTURES

ECO ADVENTURES

- Fishing Trips & Wildlife Tours
- Shearwater & Cedar Lodges
- RV Park & Campground
- Fishermen's Bar & Grill
- 120' United in History Mural
- War Memorial
- 3000' Paved Air Strip (CYJQ)
- Free Wifi Internet Access
- Cell Service (Telus, Bell)
- Harbour Master (VHF 66A)
- 1500' of Moorage Available
- Fuel Station (gas, AV, diesel, jet)
- 70 Tonne Lift
- Marine/Hardware Store
- Post Office, Laundromat
- Grocery & Liquor Store
- Emergency Services
- 12-42 Passenger Water Taxis
- Daily Seabus to Bella Bella

For more information on our marina services please contact us:
www.shearwater.ca

NORTHERN B.C. COAST

See Area Map Page 419 - Maps Not for Navigation

The Bella Coola docks look more spacious in this photo than when we were trying to raft off in 20-knot winds.

Cathedral Point. Cathedral Point, a weather reporting station, marks the north entrance to Kwatna Inlet, and is easily identified by its white building and tower.

Just north of the point, a tiny cove with dramatic granite walls makes a good anchorage in 25 feet. The cove has excellent protection from up-channel winds, but the mass of large logs on the south beach suggests that down-channel winds and seas blow right in. We patrolled the cove but did not stay. Early Correspondent Bill Hales, from Victoria, anchored for the night and reported a pleasant experience.

South Bentinck Arm. South Bentinck Arm, 25 miles long, lies between high mountains. The relatively few cruisers who have gone all the way up the arm say it is beautiful. We have gone as far as Larso Bay, which has good anchorage in 35 to 70 feet. The mountains across from Larso Bay are beautiful. Correspondent Gil Flanagan found one of the largest red cedars in B.C. by walking about 1 km up a logging road that begins in the north part of the bay. The tree is on the right side of the road, marked with a plaque.

Tallheo Hot Springs. Tallheo Hot Springs is about one-quarter mile north of the mouth of Hotsprings Creek on the west shore of South Bentinck Arm, a short distance south of Bensins Island. A concrete and rock pool is tucked into a little rocky grotto above the high-tide line; the waters are odorless. Anchorage is exposed.

North Bentinck Arm. The water in North Bentinck Arm is green and milky, the result of the Bella Coola River emptying into the head of the arm. We found no good anchorages, so you have to hope for room at the Bella Coola docks. Watch for drift. Windy Bay is on the south side of North Bentinck Arm, near the junction with Burke Channel. When we crossed the mouth of Windy Bay in early afternoon we learned how it got its name. Whew!

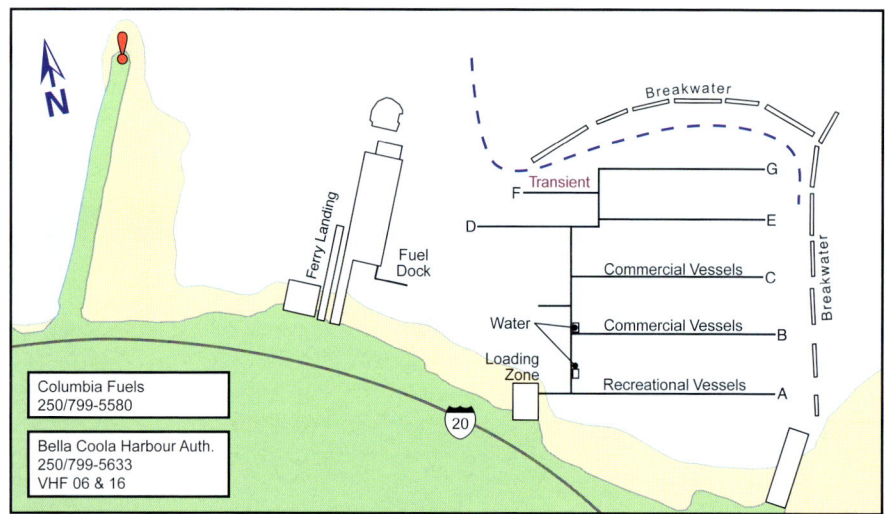

Bella Coola

LOCAL KNOWLEDGE

WEATHER TIP: The wind can blow almost constantly at Bella Coola, making for rough seas going in or out. There aren't many places to hide from the weather, either. Be aware of the tendency for strong inflow and outflow winds before deciding to go to Bella Coola.

⑦ **Bella Coola.** Bella Coola is seldom visited by yachts but interesting nonetheless. The government floats are run by the Bella Coola Harbour Authority, and they are making improvements. Water is available on the docks, shore power, washrooms, and showers are available as well.

The Columbia Fuels fuel dock is adjacent to the public floats.

Correspondent Gil Flanagan says the best way to visit is to overnight in Larso Bay in South Bentinck Arm or Eucott Bay on Dean Channel, and come over in the morning. A visitor at the Seattle Boat Show recommended anchoring in Bryneldsen Bay, near the north end of Labouchere Channel, and going to Bella Coola early the next morning. Bryneldsen Bay is behind the thumb of land that extends southeast, approximately 0.8 miles from Ram Bluff. The bay is not named on the charts but does show an anchor symbol.

The town of Bella Coola is 3 kilometers (about 2 miles) from the dock. Taxis may be available. The Bella Coola Estuary makes for a beautiful stroll. Stay on the water side of the road, since it's wider and safer for walking.

We urge you to see the Bella Coola Museum, housed in buildings dating from 1892 and 1898. It is on the edge of town along the road from the marina. Bella Coola is where, in 1793, Alexander Mackenzie touched saltwater on his transcontinental crossing of Canada. Much of the museum's display is about Mackenzie. We bought a booklet of Mackenzie's journal entries (including comment about the unrelenting wind) in the Bella Coola and Dean Channel area.

The town has provincial and federal government offices, a post office, hospital, motel, liquor store, laundromat, showers, and a well-stocked co-op grocery store and Moore's Organic Market. Take a tour of the area on the Bella Coola Valley Bus for $2.50; call (250) 799-0079 before 8:00 p.m. the day before you want to ride the bus.

Correspondents Bruce and Margaret Evertz add the following: "A worthwhile attraction in this area are the petroglyphs. The Native band wants them preserved, so they are not marked on any maps. Guides may be available. You can get information about them at the museum."

Correspondents Gil and Karen Flanagan report that rental cars are available (Bella Coola Vehicle Rentals 250-957-7072). "We put about 150 miles on a Dodge Caravan, all

www.WaggonerGuide.com

About 0.8 nm southwest of Hokonson Pt. on Dean Channel is a petroglyph - what message do the symbols convey?

This monument marks Sir Alexander Mackenzie Rock, where Mackenzie ended his overland westward explorations in 1793.

on good paved roads. The spectacular drive to Tweedsmuir Park inland is rated as one of the 10 most scenic drives in Canada."

Bella Coola is the B.C. Interior's window on the coast. Each year, a remarkable number of boats are trailered from the Interior to Bella Coola, where they stay the summer, either tied to the dock or on trailers.

⑦ **Bella Coola Harbour Authority.** P.O. Box 751, Bella Coola, BC V0T 1C0; (250) 799-5633; bellacoolaharbour@gmail.com. They try to monitor VHF channels 06 & 16. Open all year with guest moorage. Facilities include 30 amp power, water, washrooms, laundry and showers (showers closed November through March), Wi-Fi and tidal grid. Garbage drop for a fee. Launch ramp. Fuel dock adjacent. The harbor office is at the head of the pier. Office hours June through September 8:00 a.m. to 6:00 p.m. and off season Monday through Saturday 8:00 a.m. to 12:00 p.m.

Float "A" is dedicated for visiting pleasure craft 14 meters and longer. The float is exposed to westerly winds. Smaller boats can tie up there, but if a boat 14 meters or longer arrives, the smaller boats will have to move.

Bella Coola is a popular launch point for trailerable boats; boat launch floats make launching and retrieving easier.

The marina is tight and the wind can blow almost constantly. Rafting is required. If necessary, take temporary moorage at the loading zone. Put out lots of fenders, both sides. Of all the places we have landed, Bella Coola is one of the most challenging.

The floats are located south of a rock breakwater, behind a floating log breakwater. They are home port to a large number of commercial fish boats. All of A dock and the south side of B dock are reserved for pleasure craft. You may have to raft to a permanent boat. The channel on the land side of A dock is narrow, especially at low tide. Feel your way in and find a spot.

Now that the local Harbour Authority is running the facility, more interest is devoted to visiting boaters. Even so, Bella Coola is not a "resort marina." Self-reliance is the key.

Columbia Fuels Fuel Dock. (250) 799-5580. Open Monday through Friday 9:00 a.m. to 4:00 p.m. all year. Call (250) 305-8333 for off-hours service. Gasoline, diesel, lubricants. Dwayne Saugstad is the manager. Dwayne's great-great-grandfather led the original band of Norwegian settlers to Bella Coola. Dwayne's great-grandfather remained, as did Dwayne's grandfather, Dwayne's father, and now Dwayne and his two children. All have called or presently call Bella Coola their home. Six generations.

Labouchere Channel. Labouchere Channel connects the north end of Burke Channel with Dean Channel. **Mesachie Nose**, at the confluence of the two channels, is a magnificent glacier-smoothed rock prominence on the north shore. Tidal currents combined with winds and surface water runoff can create very difficult seas in this area. If the water is flat, see Mesachie Nose, up close.

The waters of Labouchere Channel itself are generally smooth and wind-free. The scenery, with waterfalls spilling from high mountains, is fabulous. Our notes say, "So many waterfalls!"

LOCAL KNOWLEDGE

WEATHER TIP: Strong up-channel sea breezes can develop when warm temperatures in the Interior heat the air and suck cold ocean air up the various inlets. This sea breeze can begin as early as 10:00 a.m. and last until sundown. Because summertime freshets often create a nearly permanent ebb surface current, an ugly chop can develop when the wind blows against the current.

Dean Channel. Dean Channel connects with Fisher Channel at the mouth of Cousins Inlet (Ocean Falls) and continues 53 miles northward. It is bordered on both sides by high mountains; Burke Channel offers some of the finest scenery along the coast. In Dean Channel we felt as if we were high up in the mountains on a huge lake, like we should be chewing gum to clear our ears. The concept of being at sea level in these surroundings was hard to grasp.

The principal points of interest on Dean Channel are Elcho Harbour, Sir Alexander Mackenzie Rock, and Eucott Bay and hot springs. Cascade Inlet is stunning, but not a good place to anchor.

Jenny Inlet. If Jenny Inlet were someplace else it might be interesting. But we found it ordinary, too deep for anchoring, with a logging camp near the head. Elcho Harbour, 8 miles farther up Dean Channel, or Cousins Inlet (Ocean Falls), 5 miles down-channel, are better choices.

Elcho Harbour. If you are looking for a scenic spot, Elcho Harbour qualifies. It's stunning. The inlet reaches a little more than 2 miles back between steep high mountains, and appears perfectly protected from all winds. Waterfalls plummet from the sides. A lovely bowl is at the head of the inlet, with the obligatory stream that creates an estuary and mudflat. Anchor in 90 to 110 feet off a delightful waterfall on the west side, about one-third of the way in. Or anchor at the head in 90 feet before it shelves up to mudflat. Take the dinghy back out to Sir Alexander Mackenzie Rock for a little history.

Sir Alexander Mackenzie Rock. Sir Alexander Mackenzie Rock is marked by a cairn at the mouth to Elcho Harbour. On 22 July 1793 Mackenzie completed his overland journey across North America to the Pacific Ocean, and marked his accomplishment with ochre paint on the rock. Later, the inscription was carved into the stone. You can bring the boat right up to the monument rock, watching for underwater rocks close to shore, and take your own picture of it. Or you can anchor out and dinghy ashore, leaving somebody aboard in case the wind kicks up.

Apparently, Mackenzie ended his westward trek here because the waters beyond were Bella Bella tribal country, and his Bella Coola Indian guides could not guarantee safety. A few miles west on the north side of Dean Channel, ochre pictographs on white cliffs are thought to be boundary markers. They are a short distance east of Frenchman Creek. We found the pictographs about 0.6 nautical miles south of the daymark near Hokonson Point.

NORTHERN B.C. COAST

See Area Map Page 419 - Maps Not for Navigation

Eucott Bay off of Dean Channel has room on a shallow bottom for a number of boats. Hot Springs are along the shore on the right side of this picture.

Eucott Bay. Eucott Bay is a gorgeous spot, about as pretty as any we have anchored in. The mountains along the eastern and northeastern sides remind us of Yosemite. Photographers, bring your camera—Half Dome in Eucott Bay is impressive. Grassy shores ring the entire bay and afford good opportunities to spot wildlife. The entire bay is shallow, watch your depth when picking your anchoring spot. Holding is good on a mud bottom,. Stay mid-channel at the entrance and watch for a deteriorating float mid-channel at the neck of the entrance.

Eucott Hot Springs is near the head of the bay, inshore of a line of pilings. A soaking basin formed by several large boulders, sealed with concrete, has room for 6 people to soak. Water at the hot springs can be too hot for soaking if the flow of hot water coming in from the pipe is not restricted. A stick jammed into the concrete end will help cool the pool. Take insect repellent and boots for the muddy shore at low tide.

Craig Widsten, former owner of Shearwater Marine Resort, told us that in 1948 his father and he journeyed to Eucott Bay to pack mud and hot spring water for sale to health and beauty fanatics in Europe. We're sure it was elegant—hot spring water and mud from the remote Canadian coast, to smooth away the wrinkles and cure what ails you.

Nascall Bay. Nascall Hot Springs is near the mouth of Nascall Bay. You'll recognize the buildings by their blue roofs. Previous owners had ambitious development plans, but they didn't work out. The facility is private with posted No Trespassing signs.

SEAFORTH CHANNEL, MILBANKE SOUND, FINLAYSON CHANNEL

LOCAL KNOWLEDGE

Navigation Note: Although Seaforth Channel is connected with the sea, west of Lama Passage the buoyage system defines "returning from the sea" as returning from south to north, not west to east. If you are outbound in Seaforth Channel, west of Lama Passage you will leave red aids to navigation (buoys, beacons, lights) to starboard (Red, Right, Returning from the south). If you are inbound in Seaforth Channel, west of Lama Passage, leave red aids-to-navigation to port.

"Returning from the sea" changes at Lama Passage. East of Lama Passage, inbound vessels will leave red buoys, beacons and lights to starboard.

Seaforth Channel. Seaforth Channel connects the New Bella Bella/Shearwater area with Milbanke Sound to the west and is part of the Inside Passage route. Ivory Island is at the western entrance.

Troup Passage. Troup Passage runs between Chatfield Island and Cunningham Island, and leads to Roscoe Inlet. Troup Narrows is at the northern end. Near the southern end of Troup Passage an unnamed bay sometimes called Discovery Cove is an excellent anchorage.

Discovery Cove. Discovery Cove at lat 52°13.50'N, unnamed on the charts, is the only major indent of Cunningham Island from Troup Passage. It was first recommended to us by John and Evonne MacPherson, who spent many summers cruising the coast in their perfectly-maintained 45-foot Grenfell, Malacandra. The chart shows rocks on the southwest shore of the entry, but if you go in along the northeast shore you'll have no problems. This is one of the most beautiful coves on the coast. It is surrounded by mountains and seemingly immune to any storm winds that might be about. Anchor in either of the two nooks along the north shore or the area to the east.

Hot Springs pool at Eucott Bay

Roscoe Inlet has some of the most awe-inspiring scenery on the coast.

Troup Narrows. Troup Narrows, with maximum tidal currents of only about 2 knots, is easily run. Assuming a passage from south to north, identify the reef that dries 15 feet near the south entrance to the narrows. Leave the reef to port, and slide west to the beautiful rock cliffs of Chatfield Island. Stay on the Chatfield Island side until the point of land on Cunningham Island is abeam, then trend east to the far shore of Cunningham Island to avoid the reef that extends from the 65-meter island. Study the chart to find the rocks you must avoid.

Roscoe Inlet. Roscoe Inlet is drop-dead beautiful. Beginning where Johnson Channel meets Return Channel, Roscoe Inlet winds some 21 miles back through high mountains that plunge straight down into the sea. Exquisite bowls and valleys lead into the mountains. Sheer cliffs tower overhead. In some places you can bring the boat alongside a vertical granite wall that rises to a mountain peak 3600 feet above and still have more than 450 feet of water below. Dramatic.

Good anchorages are scarce. For a day trip, we suggest motoring up in the morning, dropping the hook for lunch at the head of the inlet, and motoring back in the afternoon. You can overnight, of course.

Other than the head of the inlet, in our opinion **Boukind Bay** is the easiest anchorage along the way. A large, 25- to 30-foot-deep area allows plenty of room to swing. If an inflow wind is blowing, however, it might be a little bouncy. **Quartcha Bay** is a visually stunning anchorage, although deep until close to the sides or the mud flats at the head. Waterfalls tumble down the mountain sides. From near the head you can look back into two glacier-polished bowls of rock (called cirques) and extensive meadows. Correspondent Gil Flanagan reports that evidence of ancient fish traps can be found on the large tide flats. **Shack Bay** and **Ripley Bay** are exposed to inflow winds, and deep until very close to shore. We didn't like them. **Clatse Bay**, at the south end of Roscoe Inlet, is a good anchorage. Go all the way to the head and anchor in 40 to 50 feet.

Bugs: Several readers have warned about ravenous deer flies. Bring insect repellent.

Briggs Inlet. Briggs Inlet challenges Roscoe Inlet for beauty with high mountains and granite faces. Briggs Inlet is immediately west of Roscoe Inlet, reaching 11 miles north from Return Channel. Entering, the first two or three miles of the inlet are much the same as Return Channel with forested hillsides, some of which are filling in with second growth after past logging. After the first narrows higher mountains appear. Good anchorages can be found at Emily Bay and Briggs Lagoon.

First Narrows at 2.6 miles into the inlet, the current floods north and ebbs south. Current is laminar with a few smaller whirlpools. Keep slightly to the west side of the channel to avoid rocks on the point to the east. For more information on the First Narrows, see *Exploring the North Coast of British Columbia* by Don Douglass and Reanne Hemingway-Douglass.

Second Narrows separates the inlet from the lagoon. Second Narrows is very narrow with a charted rock along the north shore. Second Narrows leads to Briggs Lagoon with a number of anchorage opportunities. For more information about entering the Lagoon and anchoring options, see the *Exploring the North Coast of British Columbia* guidebook.

Emily Bay is located on Briggs Inlet between First and Second Narrows. It is the best and easiest anchorage with high mountains surrounding a large flat bottom bay. At the head of the bay, a stream from nearby Lake Emily flows into the bay. Check the charts when entering the bay for charted rocks on both sides of the deeper entry fairway. Except for the charted 1¼ fathom shallow area, protected anchorage can be found nearly anywhere in the bay in 7 to 10 fathoms with good holding.

Morehouse Bay. Morehouse Bay, indenting Chatfield Island off Return Channel, has a lovely one-boat anchorage (more, if all are stern-tied to shore) in a cove at the very back, or room for more boats in 60-foot depths outside the back cove. To enter the outer anchorage, leave the 53-meter island to port and the 44- and 59-meter islands to starboard. The more secluded back cove is in the south part of the bay, behind the 59-meter island. Leave a large rock, shown as a 1.2-meter depth, to starboard as you enter. The entry is easy—just be sure you know where that rock is. Anchor in 25 to 35 feet.

Wigham Cove. Wigham Cove, on the south shore of Yeo Island, is a popular anchorage and an excellent place to overnight before transiting Seaforth Channel. Favor the west shore as you enter, until abeam the islets in the middle of the bay. Then turn to pass north of the islets to the favored anchorage in the northeast nook of the cove, which has room for several boats. We have shared this anchorage with a 60-footer and a 43-footer with no crowding at all.

Dangerous rock: Be careful if you enter the southernmost nook of Wigham Cove. A dangerous underwater rock with a depth of 0.5 meters at zero tide is reported lying close to and just east of the northernmost of the three drying rocks that extend from the eastern shore of the entrance to Wigham Cove. When entering this nook, favor the islets to the east.

Spiller Channel. Spiller Channel and Bullock Channel run north from Seaforth Channel on either side of Yeo Island and lead to famed Ellerslie Lagoon, whose entrance rocks have bumped many a boat. Neither run is particularly scenic. Compared with other areas, the hillsides are low.

Neekas Cove, across the channel from the north tip of Yeo Island, is the only easy anchorage in the southern part of Spiller Channel. Yeo Cove, near the south entrance to Spiller Channel, has a rock-studded entry and only limited anchorage deep in the southeast corner. Tate Lagoon, which leads into Don Peninsula, has a treacherous entrance. This lagoon is shown as unnamed on the charts. Douglass describes both places.

The top of Spiller Channel is a little better. The hidden anchorage Douglass calls "Nash Narrows Cove" is lovely. Decent anchorage can be found in the bay immediately south of Ellerslie Lagoon.

McInnes Island Lighthouse on Milbanke Sound is a reference point for Environment Canada weather forecast areas.

Neekas Cove. Neekas Cove is opposite the north tip of Yeo Island in Spiller Channel. The cove is narrow and pretty, but deep until close to the head, where the bottom shelves rapidly. Anchor in 50 feet (zero tide) if cautious; 35 feet if braver; less, at your peril. Watch for bears on the shore here.

Nash Passage. Nash Passage (Douglass' name for this otherwise unnamed winding channel), separates Coldwell Peninsula from a good-sized unnamed island on the approach to Ellerslie Bay, just before Spiller Inlet. The chart shows rocks, but the ones to watch out for dry at 4.3 meters, so they should be visible much of the time.

Nash Narrows Cove (Douglass' name again), is the little cove at the turn of Nash Passage. It is beautiful, and would be a good spot to put the hook down.

A peninsula separates Ellerslie Lagoon from a substantial bay immediately to the south. Anchorage is in the inner bay, east of an islet in the middle of the fairway. Pass either side of the islet. Our preferred spot is in 60 feet (zero tide) on the south side, under a towering cliff. The north side of the bay might get down to 40-foot depths, but isn't as protected or cozy feeling.

Ellerslie Lagoon. Because of dangerous rocks, a spring tide high water entry is called for. Two sets of narrows lead in. Ellerslie Lake pours a lot of water into the lagoon; expect the outflowing current through the narrows to last longer than usual.

Spiller Inlet. Spiller Inlet extends northward from the top of Spiller Channel. The sides are steep and the water is deep until near the head, where the depths shoal rapidly to a shelf. Near the head of the inlet, the granite cliff on the east side has fractured and fallen away to create Weeping Woman, a Picasso-like natural sculpture on the mountainside. It's quite dramatic.

Bullock Channel. Bullock Channel is a straight run between Return Channel and the top of Yeo Island. Study the chart and favor the Coldwell Peninsula side of the channel. The shoal areas on the Yeo Island side have a tendency to be right where you think you should be going.

The only good Bullock Channel anchorages are on the Coldwell Peninsula side—one at the south end, the other at the north end (where we overnighted). We checked the purported anchorages on the Yeo Island side, but they weren't satisfactory. We found poor holding in the northernmost anchorage, and rock, rock, rock in the bight a little south of the north anchorage.

The water is warm near the top of both channels. In colder waters we like our cabin heat in the morning, but we had no need for it there. [Hale]

Bullock Channel North Cove. This is Douglass' name for the otherwise unnamed anchorage behind the 39-meter island at the north end of Bullock Channel, on the Coldwell Peninsula side. We found excellent overnight holding in 50 feet (zero tide) opposite the west opening to the cove. The chart shows a rock awash at zero tide in this west opening. Enter and depart this cove from the north.

Bullock Spit Cove. Again, Douglass' name for this unnamed anchorage located inside the 70-meter island on the Coldwell Peninsula side, near the south entrance to Bullock Channel. As the chart shows, you don't want to go very far in or you'll run aground. We found good holding in 35 feet just south of the tip of the island.

Kynumpt Harbour. Kynumpt Harbour indents the north tip of Campbell Island, east of Raymond Passage. Sailing Directions says the local name is Strom Bay. The entrance is open and easy, but study the chart carefully to identify and avoid rocks on the western and southern shores. The northernmost indent on the eastern shore is reported to be a good anchorage, as is Strom Cove, the arm that extends to the southeast. We poked around Strom Cove to find a good lunch stop, but saw mostly 55 to 75 feet on the sounder. At those depths, even a 3:1 scope would swing us too close to rocks near shore, so we anchored in the outer bay, 40 feet, west of Spratt Point.

Dundivan Inlet. Dundivan Inlet indents Dufferin Island west of Raymond Passage. It's a pretty spot with several islets to break up the scenery, but the water is deep except near hazards. Two arms make up Lockhart Bay, near the head. The western arm is the more attractive anchorage. For overnight we would run a stern-tie to a tree. The eastern arm is deep (60 feet) until very near the head and requires a stern-tie. Dundivan Inlet would not be our first choice unless weather was ugly and we were looking for a place to hole up.

Raymond Passage. Raymond Passage connects Seaforth Channel with Queens Sound and sees few pleasure craft. The passage is open, free of hazards, and connects with Codfish Passage at the south end. If you're looking for a raw and exposed wilderness experience and have the boat and navigation skills to manage it, Raymond Passage is a good choice.

Thompson Bay. Thompson Bay is on the west side of Potts Island. Examine the area on your chartplotter or study Chart 3938. This entire area is beautiful and seldom visited. At the northeast corner of Thompson Bay an excellent, protected cove indents Potts Island. Enter the cove from the north, at 52°09.75'N/128°20.75'W.

To get from Raymond Passage to Thompson Bay, run a course of approximately 239° magnetic from the southern tip of Alleyne Island to the 45-meter island, then turn to a course of approximately 292° magnetic to Agnew Islet. You will leave Seen Island approximately one-quarter mile to the south. Rocks will be all around you, but stay in the pass and you will have water.

St. John Harbour. Enter from the north, leaving red buoy *E46*, marking Rage Reefs, to starboard. Several floating fishing resorts are around Dyer Cove. We prefer the back cove; be sure to avoid the drying shoal. The shallowest point of the channel is at least 7 feet deep. Holding is good.

Milbanke Sound. Milbanke Sound is the shortest route north or south for boats trying to make time along the Inside Passage. In quiet conditions Milbanke Sound is easy. But if the wind is blowing the crossing can be brutal.

From Seaforth Channel to Finlayson Channel, leave Ivory Island to starboard and lay a course that passes north of Susan Rock and west of Vancouver Rock Buoy

E54. From there, lay a course to the mouth of Finlayson Channel. Our course took us fairly close to Jorkins Point and the east side of Swindle Island. Total distance was about 12 miles. We've seen boats pass east of Vancouver Rock and take Merilia Passage. This saves about a mile.

Tuno Creek Anchorage. At the south end of Reid Passage, Blair Inlet extends nearly 2 miles eastward into the Don Peninsula. Tuno Creek empties into the head of Blair Inlet. Anchor south of the creek in 25 to 30 feet, good holding over mud. Strong westerly winds will probably reach the anchorage, but wind protection is good from other directions.

Reid Passage & Port Blackney. If there's much wind at all, most pleasure craft headed north or south will avoid Milbanke Sound and use the Reid Passage route east of Ivory Island. Chart 3910 makes navigation straightforward. At the south end, be sure to identify all the rocks and islets, and Buoy E50. In the middle of Reid Passage, pass to the east of Carne Rock. Port Blackney, at the north end of Reid Passage, has two anchorages, Boat Inlet and Oliver Cove, that can be used before crossing to Perceval Narrows.

Boat Inlet. Boat Inlet, at the southwest corner of Port Blackney, has a delightful basin for anchorage, with an untouched feeling. The passage that leads to the basin is shallow, however, and rocks encumber the south shore and middle of the channel. Favor the north shore all the way in, with an alert lookout for underwater rocks. The little bay on the north shore at the east end of the passage is shallow and rocky. Stay out. Depending on your vessel's draft, wait for half tide or higher before running Boat Inlet.

Oliver Cove. Oliver Cove Marine Provincial Park, on the east side of Port Blackney, is a safe and pretty anchorage. Enter carefully, avoiding a charted rock in the middle of the fairway and another on the south side. Put the hook down in 35 feet. A few years ago we saw a bear and her cubs on the rocky shore.

Perceval Narrows. The Inside Passage route leads across Mathieson Channel between Port Blackney and Perceval Narrows. Tidal current predictions are found as a secondary station under Prince Rupert in Tide and Current Tables, Vol. 7 and Ports and Passes. From south to north, lay a course that gives Cod Reefs a good offing to port as you leave Port Blackney. Then turn to approximately 270° magnetic and cross Mathieson Channel toward Martha Island, leaving Lizzie Rocks to starboard. We found turbulence in Mathieson Channel off Lizzie Rocks on an ebb tide.

Cockle Bay/Lady Douglas Island. Cockle Bay, a short distance north of Perceval Narrows, has a beautiful beach and good protection from westerlies. You can find 30- to 35-foot depths along the south shore and 60 to 90 feet in the middle, as shown on the chart.

Ivory Island Lighthouse overlooks Milbanke Sound and Seaforth Channel.

Tom Bay. Tom Bay is on the east side of Mathieson Channel at lat 52°24.20'N. It's a good anchorage, though scarred by recent logging. As with most bays on this coast, Tom Bay shoals at the head. Anchor in 60 to 70 feet.

Dowager Island & Arthur Island. The coves north of Arthur Island, approximately 1.5 miles south of Oscar Passage on the west side of Mathieson Channel, are mentioned in Sailing Directions as a small boat anchorage. Neither cove is very scenic and driftwood clogs the eastern cove. We would choose Rescue Bay on Susan Island, Salmon Bay to the north, or Tom Bay to the south.

Salmon Bay. Salmon Bay is on the east side of Mathieson Channel, opposite the mouth of Oscar Passage. It is deep until the very head, where the bottom comes up to 50 to 60 feet. The bay is cozy and we heard a loon—always a soothing sound.

Oscar Passage. Oscar Passage is the wide-open Inside Passage route between Mathieson Channel and Finlayson Channel. On an ebb, however, the seas can heap up where Oscar Passage joins Finlayson Channel, the result of swells from Milbanke Sound meeting outflowing current. Larger vessels often use Oscar Passage rather than Jackson Passage.

Rescue Bay. Rescue Bay is the most popular anchorage in this area. It is well protected with good holding, and has room for many boats. Study the chart carefully before entering, and steer a determined mid-channel course between the two islands and their reefs that mark the entrance. Once inside Rescue Bay, scout around with the depth sounder and pick your spot carefully. We saw one boat on the western side find the bottom at low tide, after being too eager to get the anchor down.

Note the drying rock in the southeast corner of the bay. Note also the drying reef that extends from the east side of the bay, south of the round islet. The reef covers at high water, and we anchored a little close to it. After checking things out by dinghy and seeing how near the reef was, we re-anchored farther out. At low water the reef showed itself. We were glad we had moved.

Jackson Passage. Jackson Passage is the scenic route between Mathieson Channel and Finlayson Channel. The passage is easily navigated, except for a tight spot at Jackson Narrows at the eastern end, where the depth shows as low as 12 feet on the charts. The fairway through the eastern end of Jackson Narrows is quite narrow and shallow; kelp marks the rocks. Larger vessels may prefer Oscar Passage to the south. While neither the chart nor Sailing Directions shows the current directions, our observations from several transits indicate the flood current sets east and the ebb current sets west.

Jackson Narrows is blind. Before entering, either direction, it's a good idea to call ahead on VHF channel 16, low power, to announce your intentions *(Securité, securité, this is the 34-foot motor vessel* Happy Days, *about to enter Jackson Narrows westbound. Any eastbound traffic please advise, channel one-six)*. One year, to our astonishment, a boat approaching from the other end called back on channel 16. Since we were about to enter, the other boat waited until we got through. Strongly favor the south shore all the way through the narrows, and keep a sharp lookout. A transit near high water slack would be the least anxious, although we have gone through at low water slack with no difficulty.

James Bay. James Bay, on the west side of Mathieson Channel, is open to southerly winds, but gets you out of the chop in the channel. It is a pretty spot; an area on the south shore hillside has been logged, however, second growth is starting to fill in. The bottom shoals abruptly in the northwest corner. Anchor in 75 feet, where the little anchor symbol is on the chart.

FIORDLAND AND KHUTZE CONSERVANCY AREAS

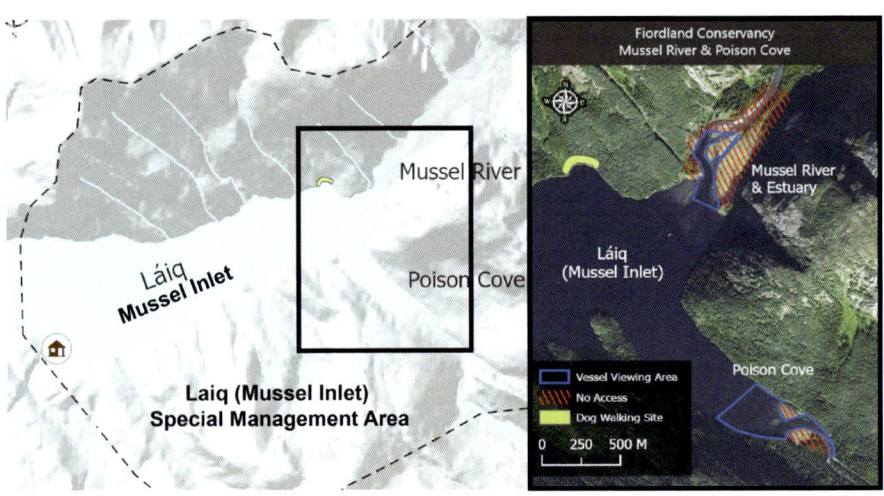

Fiordland Conservancy. British Columbia's impressive Fiordland encompasses Kynoch Inlet and Mussel Inlet along with their estuaries and the surrounding soaring peaks of the Coast Mountains. The Fiordland Conservancy is a massive scenic wilderness, covering nearly 200,000 acres of uplands and 18,752 acres of foreshore. Accessible by boat, mariners are privileged to view this incredible area, which is co-managed by BC Parks and the Kitasoo Xai'xais First Nation.

The Fiordland Conservancy, located at the northern reaches of Mathieson Channel, is home to wildlife including both grizzly and black bears. All estuary systems within the Fiordland Conservancy are sensitive, important ecosystems. Mussel Inlet and Poison Cove offer the most valuable habitat for bears.

Within the **Mussel Inlet** area, there are two designated water-based bear viewing sites that have been set aside with special provisions – the Mussel Estuary at the head of Mussel Inlet, and the **Poison Cove Estuary** at the head of Poison Cove. Anchoring and viewing bears outside these designated viewing areas is allowed all year.

From May 1 through August 14, pleasure boaters may enter the Mussel Estuary and Poison Cove Estuary for water-based wildlife viewing purposes, with a maximum of 16 people allowed at any one time. Pleasure boaters who wish to enter the Mussel Estuary or Poison Cove Estuary for water-based viewing during the peak season, August 15 through October 15, may do so only with a permitted guide (KX Guardians or BC Park Rangers). During peak season, boaters are to contact Kitasoo Xai'xais Guardians on VHF Ch 6 regarding their intentions before entering upper Mussel Inlet and Poison Cove. Radio contact is best achieved when entering the eastern arm of Mussel Inlet. Going ashore is not permitted at any time of year, except at the designated campsite and dog walking area which are outside the estuary bear viewing areas. The estuaries are closed to all bear and wildlife viewing October 16 through April 31. Pets are not permitted in the estuary viewing zones at any time.

The Kitasoo Xai'xais Guardian Program is intended to preserve this unique pristine area and help prevent bears from being displaced (a Watchmen Cabin is located about a half mile east of Barrie Point in Mussel Inlet along the south shore). While viewing bears, boats are to remain at least 50 meters or 160 feet away from the bears. Since the potential exists to negatively impact bears and wildlife, boaters are asked to limit their viewing time to 20 minutes. Approach and depart at slow boat speeds of 3 knots or less.

Similar to Mussel Inlet, **Kynoch Inlet** is a remote glacially carved fiord within the Fiordland Conservancy, featuring massive granite cliffs, fertile estuaries, and splendid waterfalls. Radio contact with Kitasoo Xai'xais Guardians is NOT required to enter Kynoch Inlet.

Because Fiordland Conservancy is an undeveloped wilderness area with no facilities, visitors should be totally self-sufficient and properly equipped. The village of Klemtu serves as a convenient staging area for trips into this very special wilderness. For more information, contact BC Parks area supervisor at 250-982-2701, or the Kitasoo Xai'xais Stewardship Authority in Klemtu at 250-839-1096.

Khutze Conservancy. Located north of the Fiordland Conservancy in Khutze Inlet off Graham Reach, Khutze Conservancy encompasses the Khutze River Watershed, old-growth forests, and scenic mountains of high value to grizzly bears and other wildlife, covering nearly 85,000 acres. The Khutze Conservancy is under the joint management of BC Parks and the Kitasoo Xai'xais Nation. Boaters are to contact the Kitasoo Xai'xais Guardians on VHF Ch 6 from July through October 15 before entering the Khutze water-based wildlife viewing area (a Watchmen Yurt is located on Green Spit). Anchoring and viewing bears outside the designated viewing area is allowed all year. Within the designated viewing area, a maximum of 16 people is allowed at any one time; public bear viewing is water based only. Public access to the Interpretive Site on land is allowed only with a permitted guide. Pets are not allowed in the viewing area. Dogs can go ashore on the north side of the inlet, approximately 1.5km northwest of the river mouth, across from Pardoe Point.

[Lorena Landon]

Kynoch Falls on Kynoch Inlet in Fiordland is a great photo opportunity with your boat.

FIORDLAND CONSERVANCY

The Fiordland Conservancy was established in 1987, and is some of the most striking country on the coast. The mountains are sheer and beautiful and the wildlife abundant, but anchorages are just about nonexistent. Fortunately, good anchorage can be found in Windy Bay, only a short distance away.

Fiordland begins just east of Bolin Bay at the north end of Sheep Passage, and includes Mussel Inlet and Kynoch Inlet. We include Bolin Bay in this section because it is so pretty, and Windy Bay because it is the best anchorage near Fiordland.

Windy Bay. Windy Bay is on the south shore of Sheep Passage, near the eastern end. The chart shows anchorage in the middle, but more protected anchorage is in 60 feet in what we call Cookie Cove, just east of the little island at the northeast corner of the bay. Excellent holding. Room for several boats in the bay.

Bolin Bay. Bolin Bay is set in a bowl of sheer rock mountains with a beautiful drying flat at the head. We didn't anchor, but we did find a few spots with depths of 35 to 60 feet near the head of the bay, which is steep to. With care you might get a safe amount of scope out and stay off the flats. The center of the bay is deep. Windy Bay is a better choice.

Mathieson Narrows. Mathieson Narrows connects Mathieson Channel to Sheep Passage and Mussel Inlet. The narrows is 275 yards wide and free of obstructions. With high mountains on either side, strong winds can funnel through the narrows.

Some turbulence can be present in the vicinity of Mathieson Narrows where the flood stream that flows north through Mathieson Channel and the flood that flows east through Sheep Passage meet.

Oatwish Bay. Oatwish Bay is at the north end of Mussel Inlet. Amazing Lizette Falls will have you reaching for the camera. The bay is too deep for anchoring. We enjoyed lunch there, drifting, engines off.

Poison Cove. At the northeast end of Mussel Inlet lies Poison Cove and Mussel Cove/Mussel River. This is a protected wildlife area for bears and mountain goats which is jointly monitored by BC Parks and the Kitasoo First Nation. When arriving at Mussel Inlet, boaters should contact Kitasoo Guardians on VHF Channel 06. Anchoring is permitted; going ashore is permitted only with a guide. There a two water-based bear viewing areas within Mussel Inlet, the Mussel River Estuary and the Poison Cove Estuary. A maximum of 16 people are allowed in these estuaries at one time. For more information go to www.env.gov.bc.ca/bcparks/explore/parkpgs/fiordland/ or call the Kitasoo Stewardship in Klemtu at (250) 839-1096. The run to the east of Mussel Inlet to Poison Cove left us awestruck.

Kynoch Inlet. Located off Mathieson Channel, Kynoch Inlet is a spectacular deep water fiord with unsurpassed beauty. Words such as amazing, awesome, incomparable and magnificent suggest but do not capture the grandeur of this inlet. Black rock mountains rise straight up and waterfalls spill down the mountain faces. The inlet is so narrow and the sides are so steep that our GPS lost its satellites. The only anchoring in the Inlet is in deeper water off the drying flats of Kainet Creek. Correspondents Elsie and Steve Hulsizer reported in 2018 that waters off Kainet Creek have silted, and they touched bottom with a 6 foot keel where the chart showed 10 meters. They also reported strong inflow afternoon winds blow up Kynoch Inlet; and suggested planning a visit to Culpepper Lagoon during neap tides to provide longer slack water intervals for entering and exiting.

Culpepper Lagoon. Enter or depart Culpepper Lagoon around high water slack. The late Captain Brian Pemberton, who has been in and out many times, reported that current in the entrance turns at high water for nearby secondary tide station Tom Bay. Correspondent Bill Hales reports a least depth of 10 to 15 feet at the entrance.

Scenic Bolin Bay isn't that well protected.

Lizette Falls and hanging Lizette Lake emptying into Oatswash Bay in Fiordland.

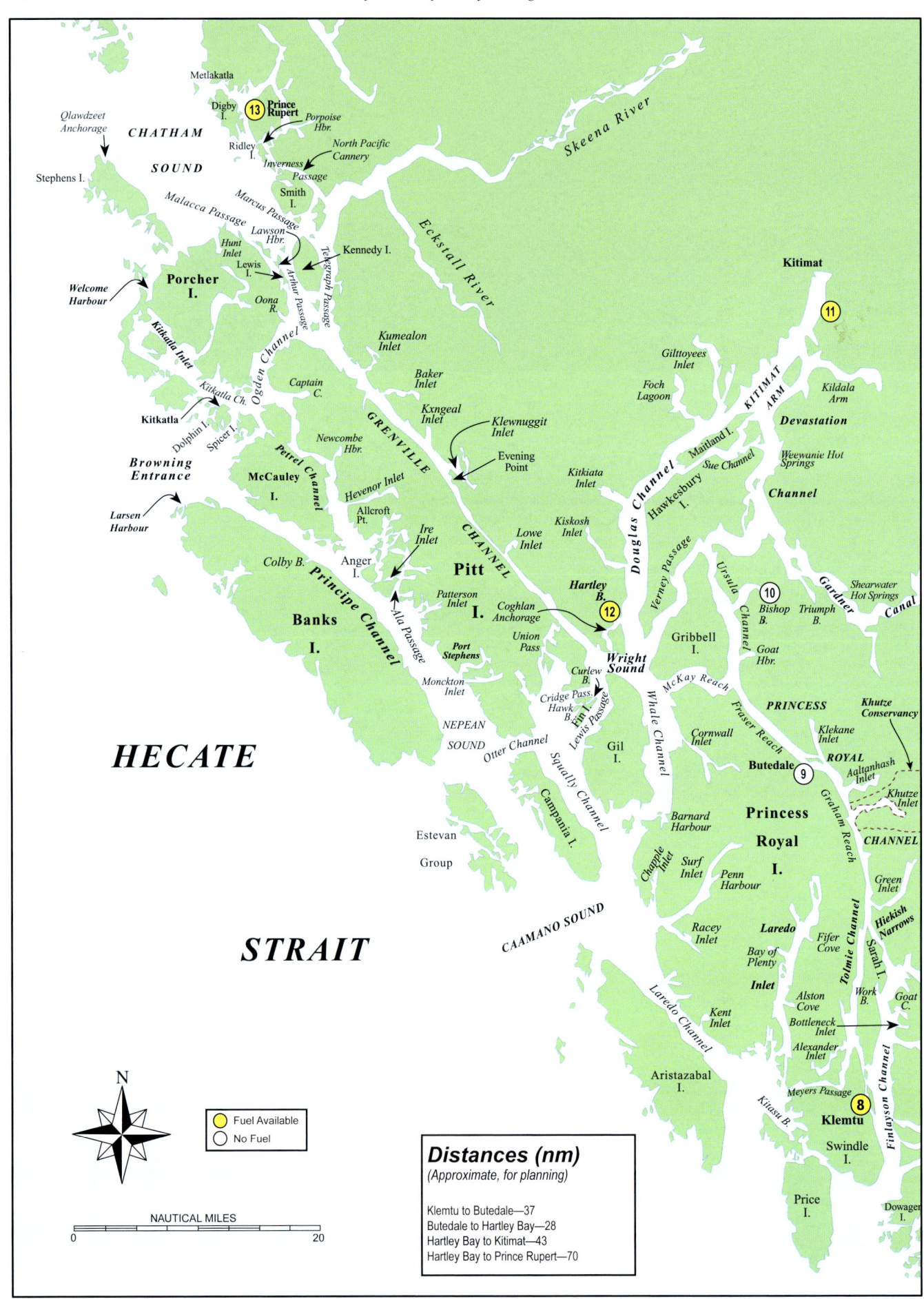

NORTHERN B.C. COAST   *Reference Only – Not for Navigation*

NORTHERN B.C. COAST

444

Distances (nm)
(Approximate, for planning)

Klemtu to Butedale—37
Butedale to Hartley Bay—28
Hartley Bay to Kitimat—43
Hartley Bay to Prince Rupert—70

Finlayson Channel to Prince Rupert

444   www.WaggonerGuide.com

The Native village of Klemtu has the Kitasoo Band Store with groceries and fuel.

Tours of Klemtu's Longhouse are available.

FINLAYSON CHANNEL TO PRINCE RUPERT

Nowish Cove. Nowish Cove is on the east side of Finlayson Channel, south of Jackson Passage, at the entrance to Nowish Inlet. Despite being shown as an anchorage, we weren't impressed. The bottom is 85 feet deep and currents from Nowish Narrows swirl through the bay. If protection is needed from a southerly storm, we would consider this cove. Otherwise, if we were looking for a place to hide and had the time, Bottleneck Inlet, 11 miles farther north, is a better choice.

⑧ **Klemtu.** (250) 839-1255 or 1096; kitasooband@gmail.com The fuel dock (250-839-1233) and the well-stocked Kitasoo band store are at the north end of town. The store is open Monday through Saturday, closed for lunch 12:00 p.m. to 1:00 p.m., limited hours Sundays. Boaters may tie-up at the fuel dock when shopping for groceries at the band store as space permits. The band store carries a good selection of groceries and other essentials (no liquor); the stock can thin a few days after scheduled ferry deliveries. The store receives supplies only once every two weeks. The band store has an ATM.

You'll find gasoline, diesel, propane, stove oil, and ample clear water from the village's water treatment system. The fuel dock faces the channel and wakes from passing boat traffic are apt to bounce you against the dock. Be sure you are well-tied and well-fendered. If the attendant is not in the office shack on the pier, try calling First Nations Fuel on VHF 06. Klemtu is the last fuel stop until Hartley Bay, approximately 65 miles north. In several recent instances, Hartley Bay has temporarily run out of fuel. Choose fuel stops accordingly.

An 11-foot-wide, 210-foot-long concrete dock is available in the bay near the village for first-come, first-served moorage without charge; no power or water at the docks. The docks may be filled with local fish boats and nets are often stacked on the floats. Be prepared to anchor, being mindful of large drying shoals on the south and west sides of the bay.

BC Ferries and Wilderness Seaplanes have scheduled service into Klemtu. The village has a K-12 school, good cell phone coverage, and a medical clinic.

If you'd like to see the extraordinary Bighouse overlooking the harbor, contact the Kitasoo Band Office at (250-839-1255) or George Robinson on VHF Ch 6. Tours are $10 per person. A pedestrian walkway runs around the harbor from the fuel dock to the Bighouse. For accommodations and wildlife eco tours, contact the Spirit Bear Lodge at (250) 339-5644.

Clothes Bay. Clothes Bay is south of Klemtu on the west side of the channel between Swindle Island and Cone Island. The bay is well protected except from southeasterly winds. We anchored for the night behind the north tip of Star Island at the mouth of the bay. At low tide, we discovered that the charted "something," extending from Base Point north of us, was a substantial drying reef. The bay has good holding but limited room for only a couple of boats. Being near Klemtu, there is cell phone service in the bay.

Alexander Inlet. Alexander Inlet extends 5 miles into Princess Royal Island, beginning where Meyers Passage and Tolmie Channel meet. If you're fed up with the throngs of boaters and crowded anchorages on this part of the coast (we're joking), here is where you can escape. The early sections of Alexander Inlet are bordered by steep mountains, and are beautiful. The head, however, is surrounded by low hills and is rather ordinary. But, being 5 miles off the beaten path, chances are you'll be the only boat.

The chart shows the inlet well. The only tricky part is near Bingham Narrows. After clearing the drying reef before you reach Bingham Narrows, sag to the west shore to avoid the drying rocks, marked by kelp, just before the narrows themselves.

The head of the inlet is wide open, with ample room to avoid the rock that dries at 2.4 meters lying off the west shore. Anchor in 30 to 35 feet with outstanding holding.

One of the hilltops looks like the profile of a woman lying on her side, and we called it Sleeping Woman. See if you agree. We saw a pair of birds that our field guide identified as red-throated loons, not seen as often as common loons. A lagoon pours into the very head of the inlet, making fluffs of white foam on the water's surface. We rowed over and took pictures, but didn't take the time to explore further. It's very pretty.

The next morning our final note, written after the previous day's notes called the head of Alexander Inlet rather ordinary, reads, "This is a neat spot." [Hale]

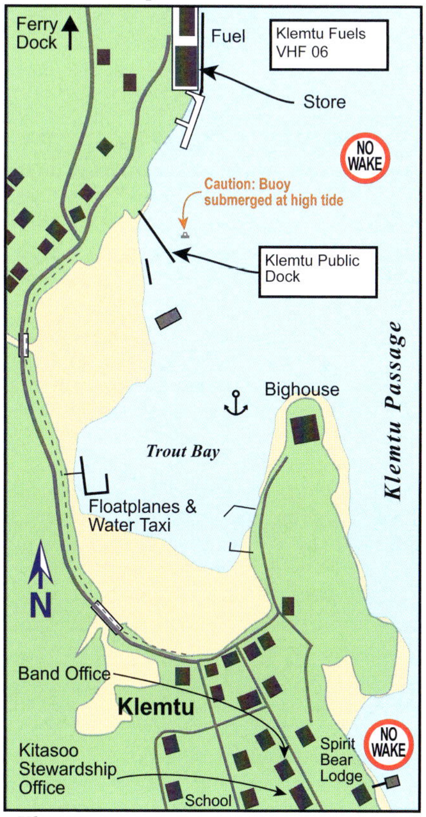

Klemtu

OUTSIDE ROUTE – PRINCESS ROYAL ISLAND & PITT ISLAND

At this point we step away from the main Inside Passage route to describe the routes west of Princess Royal and Pitt Islands. Those continuing through Finlayson or Tolmie Channels, past Butedale, and through Grenville Channel will find that information resuming on page 450.

Without question, the preferred Inside Passage route to Prince Rupert and beyond is through Finlayson or Tolmie Channels (past Klemtu), past Butedale, and up through Grenville Channel. The waters are protected, the scenery is outstanding, and there's enough boat traffic that if you have a problem, somebody will be along to help out.

An alternate route is on the outside of Princess Royal and Pitt Islands. This route is popular with sailors and adventuresome power boaters. It's as beautiful as the traditional route, but wilder and much less traveled, with more islands and anchorages but fewer waterfalls. Sailors will find more consistent and stronger winds due to the wider channels and lower hills. There's even room for tacking. Because of their remoteness, we recommend these passages for more experienced cruisers only.

From south to north, the outside route first leads up the west side of Princess Royal Island. It begins by running west through Meyers Passage (near Klemtu), then through Laredo Channel and Whale Channel, and rejoins the Inside Passage at Wright Sound. To cruise the outside of Pitt Island, the route runs west from Wright Sound (south end of Grenville Channel), and north through Principe Channel and Petrel Channel, then east through Ogden Channel to rejoin the Inside Passage.

On the outside of either island you could travel all day and only see one or two other pleasure boats, although you're sure to see a few fish boats, perhaps a tug and barge or even a cruise ship. You'll find good anchorages on the outside. In many cases you'll be the only boat.

Weather permitting, you could travel the traditional Inside Passage going one way and all or part of the outside route going the other. The inside and outside routes are roughly the same distance. However, if you take only part of the outside route, going back and forth between the inside and the outside, your total trip will be longer. If you are considering the outside route, carry Sailing Directions PAC 206, and *Exploring the North Coast of B.C.*, by Don Douglass and Réanne Hemmingway-Douglass. The *Waggoner Guide* describes only the most direct outside routes and focuses on good anchorages. The other books cover a wider area and describe places that require caution and may be more challenging than some skippers would like. If you have the desire for a coastal cruising challenge, with the boat and skills to meet that challenge, the west coast of Princess Royal Island and Pitt Island are excellent cruising areas.

If winds are favorable, sailboats (or slower powerboats) can cut almost a day off their time on the outside route with an open water passage that avoids Klemtu and Meyers Passage. Northbound exit Seaforth Channel, cross Milbanke Sound, and transit Catala Passage. Or, go around McInnes Island, then north up Laredo Sound to Laredo Inlet. This open water route has no stops until you reach Higgins Passage, so pick your weather window carefully. Pay careful attention to your navigation in Catala Passage. The islands and rocks are easily confused, especially in fog. Watch for cruise ships and freighters that occasionally use Laredo Sound.

WEST SIDE OF SWINDLE ISLAND

Higgins Passage. Higgins Passage connects the north end of Milbanke Sound to Laredo Sound, between Swindle and Price Islands. The middle section of the passage, however, has strong currents, many turns, and dries on a six foot tide. Anchorage can be found in the western end of Higgins Passage. From Laredo Sound, enter Higgins Passage south of Kipp Islet. **Grant Anchorage** is deep and not well protected from southeast winds. Proceed through the anchorage and anchor in 30 to 40 feet on the west side of **Lohbrunner Island.** This anchorage is well protected from all winds, mud bottom.

Kitasu Bay. Kitasu Bay is between Wilby Point and Meyers Passage. Several anchorages are available, ranging from good to excellent. The bay itself is exposed to northwesterly winds, which blow straight down Laredo Channel into **Parson's Anchorage**. In southeasterly or southwesterly weather, however, Parson's Anchorage provides good holding.

The **Marvin Islands** provide shelter from northwest winds. Anchor on the southeast side of the islands in about 50 feet. Several boats can anchor in this location and be protected from moderate winds. Gale force northwesterly winds can make this anchorage uncomfortable.

Jamieson Point Anchorage (also known as Coward's Cove) is just east of Jamieson Point and provides total protection from all winds. Stay mid-channel when entering to avoid a rock on the west side of the entrance. This rock is usually marked by kelp. Once inside, anchor in 30 to 40 feet over a sticky mud bottom.

The eastern basin of **Osment Inlet** provides good anchorage in most weather but the bottom is rocky and irregular.

WEST SIDE OF PRINCESS ROYAL ISLAND

Meyers Passage. Meyers Passage separates Swindle Island and Princess Royal Island and is the low-anxiety way to travel between Finlayson Channel and Laredo Sound. The only tricky spot is kelp-choked Meyers Narrows. Although the narrows are not difficult to run, kelp may be present. Current can run to 3 knots in the narrows.

We went through slowly, avoiding the kelp as best we could. When we got through we said, "Piece of cake."

Meyers Narrows Cove. Field Correspondents Jim Norris and Anita Fraser report that there's good anchorage in 45 feet in the unnamed cove on the south shore of the Narrows.

LOCAL KNOWLEDGE

NAVIGATION NOTE: Red spar Buoy E70 is in the middle of the tight spot in Meyers Passage. Pass north of the buoy, midway between the buoy and the north shore. Currents to 3 knots flood east and ebb west. Sailing Directions says least depth is encountered at Meyers Narrows. Kelp shows the places to avoid.

Meyers Passage Anchorage. On the south shore of Swindle Island, about ¼ mile west of the entrance to Meyers Narrows is an unnamed charted anchorage; anchor in 45 to 60 feet of water with good holding. Open to Meyers Passage to the north and west, with good views of the occasional boat traffic.

Corney Cove. This charted anchorage located on the north shore of Meyers Passage has room for one or two boats if stern-ties are used. Due to limited swing room, a single larger boat will need a stern-tie as well. Anchor in 50 to 65 feet of water over a thin loose mud bottom, with poor to fair holding. Upslope anchoring is favored in the deep-water center with stern-tie. You might even find the remnants of a previous stern-tie above the granite face on the right side as you enter the cove. A creek flows into the head of the cove near a charted rock awash. Well protected from wind and current, with a window onto Meyers Passage.

Laredo Channel. Laredo Channel separates Princess Royal Island and Aristazabal Island, and connects Laredo Sound at the south end with Caamaño Sound and Campania Sound at the north end. Aristazabal Island, on the west side of Laredo Channel, is incompletely charted and considered extremely challenging.

While several inlets lead off Laredo Channel into Princess Royal Island, Laredo Inlet at the south end and Surf Inlet at the north end are the major indents.

Laredo Inlet. Laredo Inlet is about 20 miles long, and is well protected from westerly storms. If you're approaching from the south, such as from Meyers Passage, the closest entry is through Thistle Passage. Rocks extend first from the east side of the narrows, then from the west side. They aren't shown well on the chart. We went through at the top of a 12.8-foot tide. We didn't see any sign of the rocks and they were not marked by kelp. Caution advised. The chart shows 4½ fathoms least depth at the north end of the narrows.

The eastern entrance to the narrows at Meyers Passage.

Palmer Anchorage. Fisherman Mike Guns suggests Palmer Anchorage at the south end of Thistle Passage as a good wait-and-see temporary anchorage in a northwest gale, but it's deep, and not what we'd select as the best overnight cruising anchorage.

While several overnight anchorages are available in Laredo Inlet, we think you'll be choosing between Quigly Creek Cove, Alston Cove, Bay of Plenty, and perhaps Fifer Cove. We spent the night in Alston Cove and explored Fifer Cove and Bay of Plenty.

Quigley Creek Cove. From the top of Thistle Passage, turn east just beyond the first small island, leaving the remaining islands to port, then follow the shore into a landlocked basin at the mouth of Quigley Creek. The basin has a depth of about 60 feet at zero tide. A beautiful spot, protected by surrounding islands from wind and waves. This is one of the few outer channel anchorages that you might share with another boat.

Alston Cove. Mouth 52°45.10'N/128°45.75'W. Lovely Alston Cove is easy to enter and is surrounded by mountain peaks. We put the hook down in sticky brown mud just onto the 6½-fathom area on the north side of the cove, near the flats.

When we departed the next morning we were glad to have the anchor washdown system. It took a long time to hose the chain and anchor clean.

Fifer Cove. Mouth 52°52.15'N/128°45.15'W. Fifer Cove is surrounded by mountain peaks and is very scenic, but most of the cove is too deep for easy anchoring.

To enter, wrap around Tuite Point, leaving it to starboard. We found 40- to 50-foot depths near the head of the cove, off the stream mouth. Correspondents James and Jennifer Hamilton report the creek shoals out much farther than the chart indicates or they expected, and holding was poor.

Kohl Island Anchorage. "Kohl Island is in Weld Cove, directly south of Bay of Plenty. The bight at the northwest tip of Kohl Island is a sheltered anchorage with mountain views. Approach between Kohl and Pocock Islands and turn west when clear of the rocks off the north tip of Kohl Island. The anchorage is at 52°49.00'N/128°46.09'W between two uncharted rocks. One rock rarely covers and the other is awash at 12 feet. We dropped the anchor between the rocks and pulled back 150 feet to stern-tie onto Kohl Island. Holding was good in 10 to 20 feet over mud and shell." [Hamilton]

Bay of Plenty. Bay of Plenty was recommended to us by Correspondents Mike Guns and Laurie and Anita Dowsett. On our chart, Guns drew the entrance channel south of the 120-foot island, and north of the little islet in the middle of the Bay. Anchor in 30 feet, short of the flats. Those flats, by the way, come out a long way. The bay is open to southwest storms.

Field Correspondent Jim Norris reports good anchorage, but his empty crab pot had him renaming this spot "Bay of Not so Much."

Buie Creek. The Hamiltons report that a spectacular two-level waterfall is a short distance up Buie Creek at the head of Laredo Inlet. To visit, anchor temporarily off the head of Laredo Inlet at 52°58.128'N/128°39.763'W in 90 feet with a 250-foot swing radius, moderate holding.

Kent Inlet. Kent Inlet is on the east side of Laredo Channel. Once inside, Kent Inlet is scenic and appears to be well protected. To get inside, however, you must go through Philip Narrows, which is guarded by rocks. Sailing Directions says currents through Philip Narrows run to 8 knots at spring tides, and recommends a transit at slack water only.

We arrived at Kent Inlet near high water slack, so we went in. Kelp marked the rocks at the entrance, off Laredo Channel, and they were not a problem. Kelp did *not* mark the rocks a short distance east of Loap Point. Rocks are out in the middle, exactly where you think you want to be. Stay south of those rocks. Give them room.

At slack water Philip Narrows was easy. Correspondents Laurie and Anita Dowsett recommended anchoring either near the west shore immediately inside Phllip Narrows, or in the back basin off the tidal waterfall. Favor the north shore to get to the back basin. Note the rocks on the south side when entering the back basin. The water in Kent Inlet was dark with rain runoff when we visited; we couldn't see more than a foot or two into it. We had good depths all around the point that defines the back basin. This anchorage is beautiful, marred only by many diseased trees.

LOCAL KNOWLEDGE

CHARTPLOTTER ERRORS: In Surf Inlet, one of our chartplotters placed our boat several hundred feet from where it actually was. Navigate cautiously in this area. Chart data in remote areas may be from very old surveys.

Whales are a welcome sight; keep your camera ready.

NORTHERN B.C. COAST

See Area Map Page 444 - Maps Not for Navigation

One of the many interesting bays in Weinberg Inlet on Campania Island.

Surf Inlet. Beautiful Surf Inlet stretches 13 miles into Princess Royal Island at the north end of Laredo Channel, ending at a stunning waterfall over a dam that separates Bear Lake from the inlet.

An abandoned concrete power house is on a point below the dam at the head of Surf Inlet. A road leads to a point below the falls. We've been told that if you can get a dinghy or kayak up to the dam (the road looks like the way to go), you can go up Bear Lake to an old mining camp that is surprisingly intact.

Chapple Inlet, at the mouth of Surf Inlet, has a few anchorage possibilities, but Surf Inlet itself has only one, Penn Harbour.

Penn Harbour. Penn Harbour is beautiful and spacious, with a straightforward entry and ample anchoring room in 40 to 50 feet near the head. A stream cascades into the east end and makes little white icebergs of foam on the surface—except that on the night of our visit the icebergs weren't white, they were tan. The water was brown and the anchor turned brown as it penetrated the surface. It disappeared altogether within a foot or two.

Chapple Inlet. Chapple Inlet leads north from the mouth of Surf Inlet, and has anchorage possibilities. These include a little nook on the west shore at Doig Anchorage, another nook behind Chettleburgh Point, and in Kiln Bay. Entry to Chapple Inlet is easy at Mallandaine Point. Follow a midchannel course along the east shore.

At **Doig Anchorage**, try the area just north of the point at 52°55.10'N/ 129°07.80'W. We didn't verify the depths, but we saw three rafted powerboats anchored and stern-tied to shore.

Behind **Chettleburgh Point**, we would anchor in 60 feet, with ample swinging room. This is where you will appreciate an all-chain anchor rode so you can swing in a smaller circle on shorter scope. If you move closer in for shallower water, you'll probably want to run a stern-tie to shore.

In **Kiln Bay**, anchor in 60 feet, north of the little island.

LOCAL KNOWLEDGE

CHARTPLOTTER ERRORS: In Emily Carr Inlet, one of our chartplotters placed our boat several hundred feet from where it actually was. Navigate cautiously in this area.

Emily Carr Inlet. Emily Carr Inlet is on the north side of Surf Inlet, right at the mouth. The inlet is beautiful, and the main body of the inlet is open. With close attention it should present no problems. A reef, however, extends from Webber Island nearly across Holgate Passage, making the entry from Chapple Inlet a little tricky.

We went through Emily Carr Inlet from north to south, then turned northeast to complete our circumnavigation of Princess Royal Island. Although the winds were light, we got into a nasty tide-rip off the 207-foot island south of Duckers Island and wet the boat down pretty thoroughly. It wasn't fun. We crowded over close to Duckers Island and found calmer water. [*Hale*]

Barnard Harbour. Mouth, west side of Borde Island, 53°04.90'N/129°07.75'W; east side of Borde Island, 53°05.20'N/129°06.65'W.

Barnard Harbour is big, open, and beautiful. It was a center for fly-in sport fishing lodges, but these lodges have since moved. Anchor in Cameron Cove along the west shore in 30 to 35 feet or in 40 to 60 feet off the mouth of Barnard Creek.

Campania Island. Campania Island, with its bald, knobby mountaintops, is recognizable from miles away. Several inlets on Campania Island's west shore provide sheltered anchorages, interesting views, and opportunities for exploration by kayaks and dinghies. All are well charted.

McMicking Inlet. McMicking Inlet, in Estevan Sound on the west side of Campania Island, is one of the few places in the outer channels where, at least in July and August, you might have competition for the best anchoring spots. The looming granite mass of Pender Mountain makes for a dramatic anchorage, and twisted cedars growing among the rocks add to the scenic character. Use Charts 3724 and 3912. Although the entrance to McMicking Inlet is open to the south, islets, rocks and reefs diminish any swells. Enter south and east of a chain of islets and drying reefs extending from the south end of Jewsbury Peninsula. Anchor north of the narrows.

Weinburg Inlet. Located off Estevan Sound on the west side of Campania Island. Weinberg Inlet is the delightful maze of islets and lagoons that include Anderson Passage and Dunn Passage, and unnamed bays, coves, and basins. Approximately 4 miles of passageways lead from Estevan Sound to the head of Weinberg Inlet.

At the head of **Anderson Passage** is a large basin where there is good anchorage with swinging room for several boats. This is the easiest way to enter Weinberg Inlet in limited visibility. Larger boats can anchor in the center of the basin in about 13 fathoms. Small boats can anchor in the more scenic and intimate southeast nook.

Dunn Passage leads to a series of bays and coves with anchoring depths from 30 to 90 feet. The head of Dunn Passage provides good anchorage among a labyrinth of rocks and islets. There is room for one or two boats, but swinging room is limited. Field Correspondent Jim Norris reports spending three nights anchored here waiting out a southeast gale, with good holding but limited swinging room on a 5 to 1 scope. The Landons anchored in the southeast set of basins with a selection of scenic locations with depths of 30 to 90 feet.

WEST SIDE OF PITT ISLAND

This route leads from the south end of Grenville Channel.

Otter Channel. Two possible anchorages appear to be available on the south tip of Pitt Island (the north side of Otter Channel). The first is Dillon Bay, where we saw a sailboat anchored. The second is Saycuritay Cove.

Saycuritay Cove. The small cove east of Fleishman Point on the southwest corner of Pitt Island. Approach from 53°12.67'N/129°33.54'W, heading north. Favor the Pitt Island shore beyond the islet at the entrance, and wrap around the north side of the first of the three small islets inside. Minimum depth on entry is 10 feet. Anchor in 25 feet with room to swing between the first and second of the three small islets. Holding is good over a soft bottom, with reasonable wind protection and views out between the islets. Good anchoring depths also are at the 6-fathom sounding on the chart. The ruins of an old settlement, now a kayaker camp, are on the east shore of the bight in the north side of the large islet that makes up the south shore of the cove." [*Hamilton*]

Watch for bears foraging along the shore.

Signs like this one at Newcombe Harbour mark several anchorages.

Monckton Inlet. Monckton Inlet indents Pitt Island at lat 53°18.65'N. The inlet is well protected, with three anchorage possibilities. The first is in 60 feet on the back side of Monckton Point, a short distance inside the inlet on the north side. If you can get in and out near high water, this would be a marvelous, snug anchorage. With propellers and rudders hanging down, however, low water access is scary.

The second anchorage is about three-quarters of the way into the inlet in the bay that extends north almost a mile behind Roy Island. Go up near the head, past the two rocks marked with a + on the chart. Anchor with lots of room in 40 to 50 feet, mud bottom. We tried to find the two rocks mentioned above, but didn't see them. They were not marked by kelp. Be aware.

The third anchorage is at the very head of Monckton Inlet in 50 to 60 feet, mud bottom. It's not very interesting.[*Hale*]

Kooryet Bay. Kooryet Bay, on Banks Island, roughly across Principe Channel from Monkton Inlet, can provide a convenient escape when fog sets in or winds kick up in Principe Channel. Inside the bay you'll have a good vantage point for watching changing conditions in the channel. In southerly winds, anchor in the south cove. In northerly winds, anchor off the creek bed or northwest of Kooryet Island.

Patterson Inlet/Princess Diana Cove. Patterson Inlet is narrow, beautiful, and appears well protected. The head of the inlet divides into a north arm and a south arm. The south arm is very pretty, with a stunning rock wall on the north side near the entry. The bottom is 90 feet deep, though, and a grown-over log booming ground is near the head. We see no need to anchor in the south arm.

The north arm is known as Princess Diana Cove. We overnighted there. It was a perfect anchorage, 25 to 30 feet deep, thick mud bottom. Anchor in the middle. Rocks and reefs sneak up along the shores.

Note: A reader tells us this bay was not good in a southeast gale.

Ire Inlet. Ire Inlet is entered from Ala Passage at latitude 53°30'N. The entry is narrow and quite dramatic, but the fairway is clear. The hillsides are covered with remarkable trees, tall and straight with very short limbs. They look like green pipe cleaners. The trees on top of the rock mountain on the north side of Ire Inlet are twisted and have few limbs. From our distance they looked like bonsai trees.

The little cove on the south shore has rocks as shown on Chart 3984 but not on 3741. Not a good spot. A much better anchorage is between the little islet and the head of the inlet in 20 to 25 feet. Pass north of the little islet. Rocks lie off the south side, and a large drying shoal extends from the south shore of the inlet.

If you visit Ire Inlet (recommended), study the chart carefully before entering Ala Passage. A number of islets and drying rocks must be identified and located. Know where you are at all times and check for fallen trees before entering.

Azimuth Island. Mike Guns put us onto this one. A small unnamed island lies southwest of Azimuth Island, and a convenient anchorage is behind that island at 53°31.45'N/129°59.50'W on the chart. Anchor in 60 to 65 feet. Be sure to enter this anchorage from the north. The southern entry is foul with rocks.

Tangent Island. Tangent Island lies in a cluster of islands located north of Anger Island, near the intersection of Petrel and Principe Channels. The cove on the east side of Tangent Island provides good protection, with a view to the mountains of Pitt Island to the east. Although the anchorage is 100 feet deep, it has good holding and is well protected. Tangent Island also provides an opportunity to refresh your geometry. Enter via Markle Passage, passing between Sine Point to the west, Tangent Point to the east and Logarithm Point to the south.

Colby Bay. Colby Bay is on Banks Island, the west side of Principe Channel, at latitude 53°32.10'N. Go down the middle and anchor in 30 feet where the bay opens up. You'll be surrounded by mountains and protected from northwest or southeast gale winds in Principe Channel. Mike Guns, who first recommended Colby Bay to us, called this spot "a joy."

Petrel Channel. Petrel Channel begins at the south tip of McCauley Island and winds along the west side of Pitt Island to Captain Cove. It has four anchorages, all on the Pitt Island side.

Allcroft Point. Just south of Allcroft Point, at lat 53°35.65'N, is an unnamed bay that gets you off Petrel Channel. Anchor in 75 to 90 feet when you get to the wide spot. The chart shows a rock awash at zero tide obstructing access to the back cove. You may prefer Hevenor Inlet.

Hevenor Inlet. Hevenor Inlet stretches 5 miles into Pitt Island's mountains and you have to go all the way to the head of the inlet for suitable anchorage. The hills on both sides have been clearcut, but already are green again. Anchor in 35 to 60 feet off the falls (you'll see them) or off the mouth of the lagoon.

Newcombe Harbour. Newcombe Harbour is a fine, well-protected anchorage. Motor straight in and anchor off the drying flats in 40 to 50 feet. We wouldn't bother with the little nook on the east shore, a short distance inside the entrance. It is rather tight and not that exciting. With such good, easy anchorage only a little farther in, it's not worth the effort. The log booms reported in the Douglass *Exploring the North Coast of British Columbia* were not there when we visited.

Captain Cove. Captain Cove is a cozy, protected anchorage at the northwest corner of Pitt Island, near the south entrance to Ogden Channel. Anchor in 60 to 80 feet in the large basin behind the 84-foot island, or in the 5-fathom basin along the south shore, behind the little dot islet. We have anchored twice in the 5-fathom basin and once behind the 84-foot island. If you don't mind 70 to 80 feet, the anchorage behind the island is excellent.

The public dock in Kitkatla. When maneuvering, stay close to the dock.

Well-protected Bottleneck Inlet is a popular stop going north or south.

Kitkatla. (250) 848-2214. Kitkatla is a Native village on the north end of Dolphin Island, west of Ogden Channel. The dock has 20 & 30 amp power but no other amenities. Most of the dock is taken by local boats. Fuel is available by jerry jug; pay in advance at the band office.

Kitkatla is a pleasant community. Ann's B&B has a nice display of small baskets and conical hats, which Ann wove in years past. Several small convenience stores operate out of homes.

Don't plan to stop at Kitkatla on weekends. Most of the village goes shopping in Prince Rupert.

We left Bully Island to port and went up Kitkatla Channel, leaving the Kitkatla Islands to starboard. Sailing Directions says a church spire is a significant Kitkatla landmark from the water, but new construction makes the spire less significant. Green Buoy *E95* marks the end of a rocky shoal when you get close to the moorage area, and a little island lies beyond. Leave Buoy *E95* to port and turn toward shore. Head for the large loading dock, leaving the little island to starboard. Go slowly. Kelp marks the shallow spots. Once past the island, run right along the public dock or as close as the rafted boats allow. Rocks lie along the island.

Deep draft boats beware: Depth alongside the dock is approximately 6.5 feet at zero tide.

Spicer Islands. Located off Beaver Passage, between Spicer Island and South Spicer Island. Follow the channel to the well-protected, roomy basin. Anchor in 25 feet, good holding. The Spicer Islands are used by many as an overnight jumping off point for crossing Hecate Strait for Haida Gwaii.

Larsen Harbour. Larsen Harbour, at the northwest corner of Banks Island, is a scenic anchorage. Low-lying rocks surround the anchorage and storm-battered trees line the shore. Field Correspondent Jim Norris reports that there is no significant kelp blocking the entrance and that the anchorage is well-protected from swells originating in Hecate Strait but not from northwest winds which can build steep waves at the entrance. Jim also reports that there are no buoys in the harbour, contrary to some other guidebooks.

Conditions on Hecate Strait are visible from within the anchorage, making it a good place to stage a trip across the strait to Haida Gwaai. Anchor in 15-25 feet, with fair holding on a rocky bottom with patchy kelp.

Welcome Harbour. Welcome Harbour is on the east side of Henry Island. A maze of rocks and islets guard the entrance; navigate carefully. The channel on the west side of Dancey Island leads to Secret Cove. Welcome Harbour is a favorite of many Prince Rupert boaters.

INSIDE PASSAGE ROUTE, CONTINUED

Mary Cove. Mary Cove is on the east side of Finlayson Channel across from Klemtu. It is a pleasant little cove, but it appears open to southwest winds. Anchor in 50 to 55 feet of water inside the cove. A salmon stream empties into Mary Cove.

Bottleneck Inlet. Bottleneck Inlet, at latitude 52°42.8'N on the east side of Finlayson Channel, is an outstanding anchorage. It is protected and beautiful, and large enough for a number of boats. The north side of the inlet has superb rock walls. The chart shows a least depth of just over a fathom in the narrow entry, and a rock shelf extends from the south shore at the narrow part. Favor the north shore. Deeper draft vessels should enter cautiously at low tide. The chart fails to show a 13-15 fathom hole a short distance inside the entry sill. The bottom then comes up to 25-30 feet.

Although we have anchored in Bottleneck Inlet several times now, one night in particular was memorable. That was the night a forewarned on-shore gale struck the coast. At 1:30 a.m. the winds hit. We could see clouds racing overhead and hear the wind roaring in the trees above us, but except for four tongues of strong wind that slammed into our boat between 1:30 a.m. and 4:00 a.m., the air around us was almost calm. [*Hale*]

Goat Cove. Goat Cove indents the eastern shore near the north end of Finlayson Channel. An inner basin is reached by running through a narrow neck. Inside, Sailing Directions says good anchorage can be had in 17 fathoms, which is pretty deep. Don Douglass likes this inner basin, too, and would anchor near the head in 36 feet. We don't like it at all. We went in during a gathering storm, and wind gusts found their way to us with nothing to stop them. The bottom shoaled too quickly for us to anchor in 36 feet and pay out scope to stand up to the wind. "Oversold!" we decided, and left. We must add that since then, we have met other cruisers who like Goat Cove, so perhaps it comes down to what the weather is doing. [*Hale*]

Work Bay. Work Bay is on the west side of Finlayson Channel near the north end. The bay appears open to southerly winds, but we anchored there in the southerly storm that chased us out of Goat Cove, and found no wind and only remnants of a few rollers from Finlayson Channel. In our opinion Work Bay has room for just one boat at anchor unless all boats stern-tie. The bay is 40 to 50 feet deep. With only a 3:1 scope (150 feet) of anchor rode out, you must be in the center or you will swing onto shore or onto the drying shelf at the head of the bay.

Lime Point Cove. Lime Point Cove, on Griffin Passage, is an indentation just south of the north end of Pooley Island. For years it has been passed by after the area above the cove was logged. New growth has filled in and once again it is a quiet, scenic anchorage, although exposed to southerlies passing up through Griffin Passage. Anchor in the shallow areas of the cove in 36 to 70 feet.

Carter Bay. Carter Bay is on the north side of Sheep Passage at the east entry to Hiekish Narrows. The bones of the steamship Ohio, which ran up on Ohio Rock in 1909, are there. Knowing he was sinking, the captain of the Ohio made it across the mouth of the narrows and into Carter Bay, where he grounded the ship. Of the 135 passengers and crew, only four were lost. Anchoring depths of 54 feet near the head of the bay. The anchorage is exposed to southwest winds.

Picturesque Khutze Inlet has anchorage at Green Spit. The uplands are part of the Khutze Conservancy with a Watchman Program.

Butedale, the former cannery site, is privately owned; permission is needed to use the dock.

Hiekish Narrows. Hiekish Narrows connects with Sheep Passage and Finlayson Channel at the south end, and Graham Reach, the continuation of the Inside Passage, at the north end. Current predictions are given under Hiekish Narrows in Ports and Passes and Canadian Tide and Current Tables, Vol. 7. Currents run to 4.5 knots on the flood, 4 knots on the ebb. The flood sets north. The water behind Hewitt Island appears to be a possible anchorage, but the current runs strongly through it.

Graham Reach & Fraser Reach. Graham Reach and Fraser Reach are wide, straight and deep, and lined with beautiful waterfalls. Cruise ships make this their highway. The principal stopping point for pleasure craft is Butedale.

Horsefly Cove. Horsefly Cove is a short distance inside the mouth of Green Inlet on the east side of Graham Reach. The cove is cozy and protected, but 80 to 90 feet deep. You may have to stern-tie to shore to restrict your swing.

Swanson Bay. Swanson Bay is on the east side of Graham Reach. This bay is exposed, but interesting. Ruins of an old sawmill and pulp mill are on the beach and back in the trees. A 3-story concrete building is just inside the treeline. Farther back, a tall red brick chimney is hidden in the trees. Although the chart shows the chimney as a landmark, summer foliage has almost obscured it from view.

We had trouble finding a comfortable place to anchor at Swanson Bay, settling finally for the shallower water off the creek mouth. Current from the creek kept the boat from swinging. Ashore are the ruins of what once was a formidable shipping center. We have seen a photo of a long wharf at Swanson Bay, with a large square-rigger tied alongside. The wharf is gone, and only a few pilings remain. Unfortunately, the dense forest inhibited our exploration on land.

Our notes show that Swanson Bay shipped its first load of pulp in 1909, and in the 1920s had a population of 500. Its last shipment was in 1934. The notes don't show the source of this information, so no guarantees.

A few years ago we saw a black-colored wolf on the south shore of Swanson Bay. It watched as our boat slowly approached. Then, with a dismissive air it ambled back into the forest. [*Hale*]

Khutze Inlet. Khutze Inlet stretches eastward from Graham Reach nearly 5 miles to a beautiful and rich river estuary at the head. Khutze Inlet, Khutze River estuary, and surrounding uplands are part of the K'ootz/Khutze Conservancy. The estuary is a prime habitat for wildlife including grizzly bears with bear viewing opportunities, especially during salmon spawning season. The Klemtu based Kitasoo/Xai'xais Nation are the stewards of the conservancy and estuary, and along with BC Parks, have developed guidelines for access to the estuary. The estuary includes waters, drying flats, and uplands along the Khutze River from the river mouth to 3 km upriver. Within the estuary, public bear viewing is water-based only; maximum of 16 people at one time; no paddleboards, jet-skis, or jet boats; no dogs ashore (dogs can go ashore on the north side of the inlet 1.5 km northwest of the river mouth); no drones; and no camping. From July through October 15, all visitors to the inlet and estuary are to check in with the Kitasoo Guardian on VHF Ch 6. A watchmen yurt is located on Green Spit. For additional information, contact Kitasoo Stewardship at (250) 839-1096.

There is a stunning anchorage at the head of the inlet at the mouth of the Khutze River with views across the drying river flats into a broad valley with mountains on both sides. Don't get too close to the flats. The water can be murky and the bottom comes up sharply. A long and beautiful waterfall tumbles down the mountain to the right. The outfall stream forms an alluvial fan off its mouth. The bottom of the alluvial fan shifts as the river outfall changes mud deposits and at least one boat has gone aground when it swung too close to shore. Check the bottom carefully and completely before setting the hook and check the tide predictions. The bottom is steep-to and anchoring can be in deep water.

You can also anchor behind Green Spit near the mouth of the inlet along the south shore, just west of a stream mouth. The chart shows the right spot.

⑨ **Butedale.** Inside Passage Marine Corporation; skennedyau@gmail.com. Located on Princess Royal Island, at the south end of Fraser Reach, Butedale is the site of an historic cannery. Only four original buildings from the former large cannery remain.

The Butedale property was purchased in 2013 and plans to re-develop the property have been ongoing. The uplands are a construction site and remain closed to visitors. We don't know what the future holds for this boater stop; additional investors are currently being sought to accelerate development.

Only visitors registered with the Inside Passage Marine Corporation may tie up at the private floats; tying up is at boater's own risk. To request permission to visit, email Shawn Kennedy at skennedyau@gmail.com or text him at (604) 649-1665.

New floats were installed in 2019 and 2020 with side-tie moorage space for 4 to 5 vessels. Site construction vessels have priority; guest moorage is available only by permission. Untreated lake water is available from a hose near the ramp. A caretaker may be onsite. At this time, there are no other facilities at Butedale.

Anchorage is possible, though the bottom near the dock may be foul with cable from earlier cannery operations. The nearby waterfall is lovely. Spirit Bears are sometimes seen in the area.

Klekane Hot Springs. Located about 5 miles northeast of Butedale at the north end of Klekane Inlet on the east side of an estuary at the head of the Klekane Inlet at 53°14.77'N/128°40.86'W. Hike in at high tide and be bear aware. Look for the cedar building with a green metal roof, which covers a concrete block pool.

In 2022, the pool was reportedly in poor condition, with cracks in the concrete block construction resulting in little water in the pool for soaking. The spring waters are odorless.

When Butedale was a cannery from 1919 into the 1960's, workers regularly came to soak in the pool. The springs are seldom visited today. Anchoring near the Hot Springs and accessing the site may be difficult.

The hot springs pool at Bishop Bay is covered with a shelter. A boardwalk path leads from the dock to the pool.

⑩ **Bishop Bay Hot Springs.** Bishop Bay Hot Springs is located at the head of Bishop Bay, on the east side of Ursula Channel. This is one of the don't-miss stops along the northern B.C. coast. Local residents have done an outstanding job building and maintaining the bathhouse and boardwalk. A voluntary use fee was put in place, along with an honor box upland on the way to the hot springs. At the bathhouse, the hot spring water is an agreeable temperature and odor-free. The boardwalk parallels the shoreline through fabulous, moss-covered and moss-hung forest.

The dock is small, maximum boat size is 30 feet; larger boats should anchor out. Fish boats sometimes raft-up at this dock. Anchoring is only fair to poor, because the bottom slopes quickly to deep water. A stern-tie would make anchoring more comfortable. A short distance south of the dock a shoal, not shown on the charts, extends into the bay from the shoreline. Be aware of that shoal and plan your swing to stay well off it. The mooring buoy which may be marked "Private" is actually for public use, use at your own risk. We have seen some boats drag on the mooring ball.

Shearwater Hot Springs. Located on the north side of Alan Reach in Gardner Canal within a small bay between Shearwater Point and Europa Point. These odorless springs are also known as **Europa Hot Springs**. Two rock mortar pools, one covered by a bathhouse and a smaller pool outside, are situated just above the high tide line. Anchorage and 2 mooring buoys in the bay.

Verney Passage. Verney Passage, along the west side of Gribbell Island, must be one of the more beautiful places on earth. It is lined, both sides, with raw, polished rock mountains, 3500 feet high. Great glacier-carved bowls, called cirques, are hollowed into the mountains. From the water you can see their forested floors and sheer rock walls. Especially on a sunny day, a visit to Bishop Bay Hot Springs should include a circumnavigation of Gribbell Island, to see Verney Passage.

Weewanie Hot Springs. Midway up Devastation Channel, Weewanie Hot Springs is in a beautiful bay north of Weewanie Creek, surrounded by sheer rock walls and forest. One mooring buoy reported to be in the bay.

The Kitimat Aquanauts Scuba Club built the rustic bathhouse and concrete soaking tub. Land a dinghy on the rocky beach and follow the trail past a campsite to the bathhouse. Or, land the dinghy on the rocks just below the bathhouse, tie to a log ashore, and climb up to the bathhouse. We've found Weewanie Hot Springs quiet and tranquil, less crowded than popular Bishop Bay.

Proper hot spring etiquette is to pull the plug on the lower tub, drain, then replug. The tub will fill again from the hose connected to the underground hot springs.

⑪ **Kitimat.** Kitimat, pop. 10,000, is a small city located at the head of Douglas Channel. While it has shopping for nearly everything one might need, the town itself is located about 5 miles from the nearest marina, MK Bay Marina. Taxi service (Coastal Taxis, 250-632-7250), if available, is about $25 each way. We suspect a person needing to get to town for shopping could find a ride.

Kitimat is a classic company town, built by Alcan in the 1950s to make aluminum. In the middle of the shopping area, the small Kitimat Museum and Archives has several exhibits that show how the town was built, including the massive tunnels and hydroelectric power dam for the smelting plant. The Alcan plant was one of the largest non-defense construction projects of the 1950s. Today, new owners continue updating and operating the plant.

Just a few miles west on Douglas Channel you can see the clearing and construction for a Liquid Natural Gas plant, which is nearing completion. When completed, this will be the terminus for an LNG pipeline beginning in the Interior north of Prince George. The gas will be processed, chilled into liquid form, and loaded on ships for distribution.

⑪ **MK Bay Marina.** 4935 Kitimat Village Rd, Kitimat, BC V8C 2G7; (250) 632-6401; contact@mkbay.ca; www.mkbaymarina.ca. Monitors VHF 68. Open all year, 420 feet of guest side-tie moorage on D-dock and occasional slip moorage. 20, 30 & 50 amp power, water, washrooms, showers, laundry, and free Wi-Fi. Call ahead to reserve space; guest moorage space can be tight during the peak season. The convenience store has deli items, fishing supplies, and ice. Pizza at the marina on Thursdays. Gas and diesel fuel, haulout to 20 tons, and launch ramp on site.

The marina is on the east side of Kitimat Arm. Boats on the seaward side of the dock should consider extra fenders. Inflow winds, common in the afternoon, produce significant chop. Walkways were recently upgraded and new washing machines installed. A full-service campground opened in August 2019, and the marina added approximately 100 new slips. An overnight guest house is available at the marina. The marina is co-owned by The Mill Bay Marine Group and Haisla Nation.

LOCAL KNOWLEDGE

WEATHER TIP: When crossing Wright Sound in an outflow wind in Douglas Channel, it is better to lay a course to Juan Point, at the north end of Gil Island. We tried this route in an outflow wind, and found it much smoother than our previous crossing, in which we tried a direct (and wet) route between Point Cumming and Cape Farewell.

Wright Sound. Wright Sound is at the junction of Grenville Channel, Douglas Channel, Verney Passage and McKay Reach. All these passages pour their currents into Wright Sound, where the waters collide and mix. Especially on an ebb, not much wind is needed to make conditions ugly.

Coghlan Anchorage. Coghlan Anchorage is behind Promise Island, and is connected by Stewart Narrows with Hartley Bay. The anchorage is open to the south, but still somewhat protected. Anchor in 35 to 40 feet just north of Brodie Point. The protection and holding ground is excellent, if not scenic. Anchorage is also possible on the shore opposite Brodie Point, off Otter Shoal.

⑫ **Hartley Bay.** Band Office, 320 Hayimiisaxaa Way, Hartley Bay, BC V0V 1A0; (250) 841-2500; fuel dock & marina (250) 841-2675; hbvc@gitgaat.ca. Open all year. Gasoline and diesel, pure water (from the water treatment plant) at the fuel dock, 30 amp power on the floats. Garbage drop, but only separated recycling accepted. Major credit cards accepted.

Hartley Bay, near the south end of Douglas Channel, is a friendly and modern-looking village that is home to the Gitga'at First Nations people; population 130. A no-charge government dock behind a rock breakwater has limited transient moorage. The Cultural Centre is upland near the fuel dock. No liquor. No pay phone, but cell phones work.

Fuel dock hours are Monday through Thursday 8:00 a.m. to 12:00 p.m., and 1:00 p.m. to 5:00 p.m.; Friday through Sunday on call, VHF 06, Hartley Bay Fuel. Hartley

Hartley Bay is a pleasant boardwalk community with a government dock behind the breakwater.

Bay has run out of fuel several times in recent years. Boats that must take on fuel at Hartley Bay should call ahead to ensure availability.

It is a pleasure to walk the Native village of Hartley Bay where homes and public buildings are all connected by a series of wide, substantial boardwalks. There are no roads in town except for the wide boardwalks used occasionally by ATV's and Smart Cars; residents generally get around by bicycle or on foot. For supplies and groceries locals must ride the foot ferry to Prince Rupert, an 80-mile journey one way. This interesting community has a small fishing fleet and a fish hatchery. A trail along Kukayu River leads to the fish hatchery, where visitors are welcome. Continuing farther along the trail we discovered the "local swimming hole" where you can hike down the stairs to enjoy a natural pool. Rumor has it that locals know where you might see a "Spirit Bear," stop by the Band Office for more information (250-841-2525).

Fin Island. Fin Island lies between Lewis Passage and Cridge Passage, immediately west of Gil Island. Fin Island is fairly low and not particularly interesting, but it has two workable anchorages, Curlew Bay and Hawk Bay. Hawk Bay is the better of the two.

Curlew Bay. Curlew Bay indents the northeast corner of Fin Island. It isn't a destination anchorage by any means, but it will do in settled weather or a southerly. The bay appears open to a northerly and to outflow winds from Douglas Channel. The chart shows shoaling a short distance west of the narrows. We anchored in 20 feet at the east end of the narrows. The anchor bumped twice on what felt like rock, then set solidly. [*Hale*]

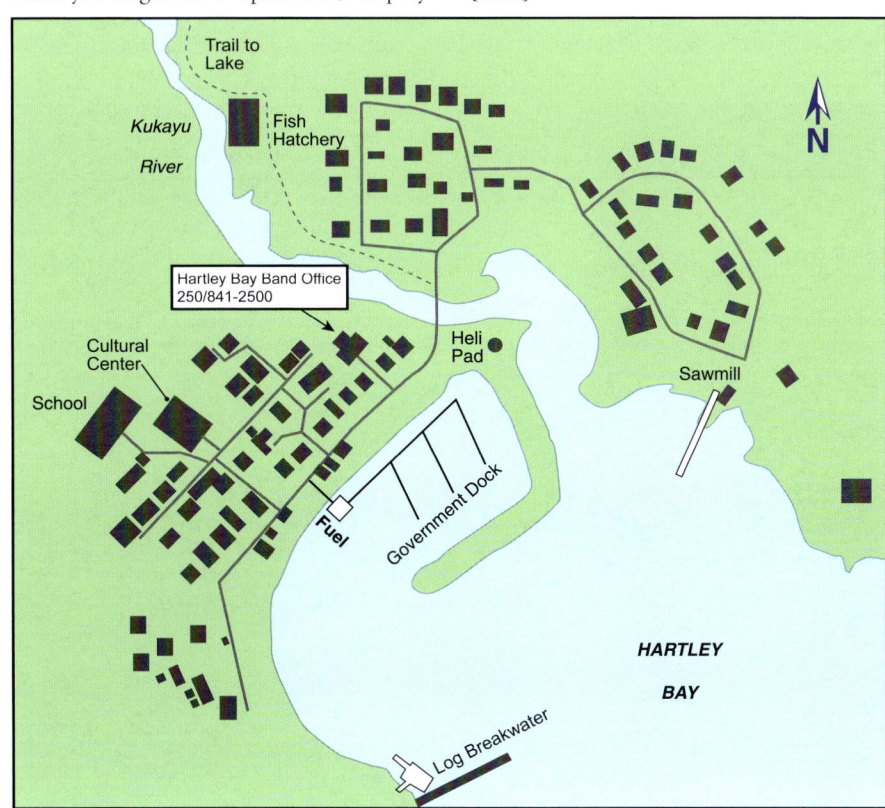

Hawk Bay. Hawk Bay, on the west side of Fin Island, is more scenic and has more room than Curlew Bay. The anchorage is somewhat open to westerly winds and you'll swing around if it's blowing. Anchor in the middle in 60 feet.

Grenville Channel. Grenville Channel is a straight and unobstructed 45-mile-long channel running between Wright Sound in the south and Arthur Passage in the north. The Sailing Directions indicate that currents in Grenville Channel reach a maximum of 2 knots, but between Lowe Inlet and Evening Point, in the narrowest portion of the channel, we've seen as much as 3 to 4 knots on the flood and up to 6 knots on the ebb, especially near Lowe Inlet. Canadian Hydrographic Service does not provide current predictions for Grenville Channel but does provide corrections for high and low water at Lowe Inlet, based on Bella Bella. These corrections can be found in Ports and Passes and the Canadian Tide and Current Tables, Vol. 7. NOAA provides secondary corrections for Grenville Channel, but they are based on Wrangell Narrows and are suspect. Virtually all software predictions for currents in Grenville Channel are based on the NOAA data, and are equally suspect.

Tidal currents flow in and out of each end of Grenville Channel. According to Sailing Directions, flood currents meet near Evening Point, about 25 miles from the south entrance, and ebb currents separate about one mile further to the northwest. This advice is misleading because it is true only in certain circumstances.

Height of the tide at each end of the channel is what drives the flood current to the central parts of the channel. The timing and strength of these currents would be reasonably predictable if that was all there was to it. But many other factors combine to make the currents in Grenville Channel very difficult to predict. High water occurs at different times and reaches different heights in Wright Sound and Chatham Sound. Depending on which end has the higher tide, the strength of the current, and even its direction, may change significantly.

The meeting and separating points of flood and ebb are also variable. The wind regime in Chatham Sound and Wright Sound may be considerably different and may have a strong influence on tidal heights. When onshore winds pile up water in Chatham Sound, Wright Sound may be under the influence of outflow winds from Douglas Channel, diminishing the height of the tide. This scenario forces the meeting point of the currents to the southeast.

When the Skeena River is in flood, vast amounts of fresh water are deposited into the northern end of Grenville Channel. This forces the meeting point of the currents far to the southeast, and when combined with certain wind conditions, pushes it nearly all the way to Wright Sound.

Finally, though Grenville Channel appears to be well protected, when strong currents in

Hartley Bay

the northern, more open part of Grenville Channel oppose strong winds from the NW or SE, a heavy chop develops, making travel very uncomfortable. At those times, conditions in the northern end of Grenville Channel may actually be worse than in the open waters of Chatham Sound.

Be sure to give Morning Reef, north of Evening Point, a wide berth.

Grenville Channel is a major waterway on the Inside Passage. You may see tugs with tows, all types of fish boats and large commercial vessels, the BC Ferries, and cruise ships. In limited visibility, radar is essential and AIS is helpful. We monitor Prince Rupert Vessel Traffic Service on VHF 71 when approaching Prince Rupert Harbour. Large vessels have Call-in Points shown on the charts. Their check-ins with VTS will help you develop a mental picture of the large vessels that may be a factor on your passage, especially those approaching from ahead or overtaking from astern.

Union Passage. Union Passage, on the west side of Grenville Channel, is served by Hawkins Narrows from Grenville Channel, and Peters Narrows from the south. It is one of those places people talk about but not many visit. The problem is the two sets of narrows. The chart shows 8-knot currents in Hawkins Narrows and 7-knot currents in Peters Narrows. Hawkins Narrows slack is shown as 5 minutes in duration. Neither the chart nor Sailing Directions say much about Peters Narrows. Once inside, the scenery is not remarkable.

The currents often are much less than shown, and the window of least current much wider than 5 minutes. We entered Union Passage through Hawkins Narrows at low water slack, poked around for a few minutes, then departed the way we came. The day was windy, rainy and cold. Our spirit was with the great explorers, but our resolve that day was weak. [Hale].

The entrance to Hawkins Narrows is at latitude 53°22'N. The channel is open until the inner end is approached. There, a rock awash at zero tide lies off the eastern shore. Favor the western shore to avoid it.

Lowe Inlet (Verney Falls). Lowe Inlet, a provincial park 14.5 miles from the southern entrance to Grenville Channel, is an excellent spot to overnight. You can anchor either in the outer basin or in Nettle Basin, the cozier inner cove. Walt Woodward, in his book *How to Cruise to Alaska Without Rocking the Boat Too Much*, recommends anchoring directly in front of Verney Falls where they pour into Nettle Basin. Current holds the boat in place, and you are treated to a wonderful view of the falls. Depending on the time of year, you may see bears fishing in the falls. Holding ground is only fair, so be sure the anchor is well set and you have ample scope for high tide. An alternative is to anchor far enough from the falls that the current, while still enough to hold the boat steady, is not very strong.

Douglass, in *Exploring the North Coast of British Columbia,* likes the Verney Falls anchorage, but also suggests an anchorage along the south shore of Nettle Basin, off the shelf formed by a creek that empties into that area. We tried to put the hook down in 60 feet off that shore, but found that we would swing too close to the shelf. After two tries in wind squalls and heavy rain showers, we moved out to the middle and anchored in 100 feet with 300 feet of rode out. Shortly after we were settled another boat came in, tried to anchor as we earlier tried, then moved out to the middle as we had. Our holding ground was excellent. We had trouble tripping the anchor the next morning. Lowe Inlet is beautiful. "If you're looking for a scenic spot, this is it." [Hale]

Klewnuggit Inlet. At approximately 120 feet, Klewnuggit Inlet is too deep for most boats to anchor. We talked with some folks, however, who found excellent crabbing near the head of the inlet.

East Inlet. East Inlet is adjacent to Klewnuggit Inlet. The inner cove of East Inlet is a superb anchorage, surrounded by high mountains and protected from seas. In a storm, however, winds might swirl through. Anchor near the head of the inner basin in 50 to 55 feet. You can also find anchorage in the little cove on the south shore, just inside the entrance to the inner basin.

We anchored at the head of East Inlet, a perfect night in a perfect place. Mountains reflected in the calm water. A small stream drained from a lake into the head of the inlet, and waterfalls poured down from the sides. We found an inukshuk, a small, stonehenge-like marker, next to the stream mouth. [Hale]

Kxngeal Inlet. Kxngeal Inlet, on the north side of Grenville Channel approximately 4 miles northwest of Klewnuggit Inlet, is a beautiful bowl in the mountains. Favor either shore as you enter to avoid a nasty rock that dries 16 feet in the entrance. The inlet is at least 130 feet deep until it shelves at the head, and when it shelves, it shelves right now. Trees are at the head of the inlet, with logged areas on each side. The shelf is on a line with the points where the trees begin. Anchor in 90 feet.

Watts Narrows. Watts Narrows is a short passage that connects Baker Inlet with Grenville Channel. A dogleg turn near the inner entrance makes the passage blind. Before entering, either direction, announce your intentions on VHF 16, low power. Sound the ship's horn as you approach the turn. The current runs swiftly through the narrows, but people tell us they have gone through in the presence of current without trouble. We have waited for slack water, which occurs about the times of high and low water at Prince Rupert. As the chart shows, the narrows are narrow, but they are deep. A mid-channel course will get you through safely.

Baker Inlet. Baker Inlet, entered through Watts Narrows, is wonderful. The best overnights are at the head of the inlet, 60 feet, good bottom, mountains all around. Remote and beautiful.

Kumealon Island/Kumealon Inlet. The little cove behind Kumealon Island is a good anchorage for a small number of boats. The much larger Kumealon Inlet, immediately south, also is good. Behind Kumealon Island, anchor in 15 to 25 feet north of the island, near the head.

Kumealon Inlet is well protected and has beautiful scenery. Anchor in the inner basin,

Small boats can anchor just beneath Verney Falls where the current prevents you from swinging into the rocks. If the salmon are running, the bear viewing is fantastic.

behind the little island. Find a good spot and put the hook down in 50 to 70 feet. A reader reported that two uncharted rocks lie close to shore near the southeast corner.

Oona River. The village of Oona River, a tiny Swedish fishing and boatbuilding community, indents Porcher Island at the east end of Ogden Channel. A public dock is behind a stone breakwater, and is served by a narrow channel through drying mudflats. From the white buoy, line up on the private range markers on the rock jetty and proceed along the markers set in the entrance. Use caution, but depths should be adequate for most pleasure vessels. Call "Oona River" on VHF channel 06 for additional information, though you may not always get an answer. Cell phones work near Oona River.

Arthur Passage to Chatham Sound. Assuming a northbound route, begin your run west of Watson Rock (west of Gibson Island) at the northern entrance to Grenville Channel. Continue north to a waypoint off the flashing light on the southwest shore of Kennedy Island. Then turn westward slightly to run past the southwest corner of Hanmer Island and leave Bell Buoy *D9*, marking Cecil Patch, to port. Continue to a waypoint in the passage west of Genn Island, then to a waypoint east of Holland Rock.

From Holland Rock, run to a waypoint west of Barrett Rock at the entrance to Prince Rupert Harbour. The entire area is well-buoyed, but it is easy to get the buoys confused.

LOCAL KNOWLEDGE

WEATHER TIP: Chatham Sound can be downright ugly when the wind blows. Especially on an ebb, when the onshore wind meets the combined ebb current and Skeena River runoff. Seas can get high, steep and close together. Listen to the hourly weather updates. If it's blowing at Holland Rock, conditions can be rough.

Lawson Harbour/Kelp Passage. Kelp Passage is on the west side of Lewis Island, across Arthur Passage from Kennedy Island.

Lawson Harbour indents the top of Lewis Island. Neither would be our first choice for scenery, but each serves as an anchorage if needed. A reef extends from the western shore inside Lawson Harbour. Anchor near the south end of the reef in 35 to 40 feet.

In Kelp Passage, anchor in the area marked 8.8 meters on Chart 3947, mud bottom. The small basin at the south end of Kelp Passage provides good protection in a northerly wind.

Qlawdzeet Anchorage. A large bay on the north end of Stephens Island, well protected from all but northerly winds. This anchorage is often used by fishing vessels and has plenty of room for a number of boats. Anchorage can be found in the main bay or tucked into small bights. Use Chart 3909.

Porpoise Harbour. (250) 628-9220; info@peharbour.ca. Located at Port Edward, Porpoise Harbour gives priority to long-term, year-round customers. Transient moorage available on a first-come, first-serve basis, best to call ahead, 15 & 30 amp power, water, garbage drop, washrooms, showers, laundry. Approach using the range south of Ridley Island marked with a buoy for Porpoise Channel.

The harbor is close to the North Pacific Cannery, a museum showing what cannery life was all about. Bus service to Prince Rupert is available. A large drying tidal area connects Porpoise Channel with Inverness Passage.

North Pacific Cannery. (250) 628-3538; www.northpacificcannery.ca info@northpacificcannery.ca. Hours: 10:00 a.m. to 5:00 p.m., May-September. The North Pacific Cannery Museum is located about 5 miles up Inverness Passage from Chatham Sound. The North Pacific Cannery is the oldest standing cannery on the West Coast and is a National Historic Site. The cannery operated from 1889 to 1968. Visitors can tour the cannery buildings including the processing plant; check in at the museum entrance. Guided tours are available three times daily, July through August; and Tuesday through Sunday during May, June, and September. Public transportation to Port Edward, site of the North Pacific Cannery, is available via the Prince Rupert transit city bus or via taxi service.

NORTH PACIFIC CANNERY
A CENTURY OF SALMON

Imagine a century ago, when hundreds of fishing boats would be out on the Skeena and Nass Rivers for 4-5 days per week, 24 hours per day during the salmon runs, in all kinds of weather and sea conditions. Tender boats would shuttle the salmon catch back to the docks of the North Pacific Cannery. Picture a dock with thousands of silvery salmon being cued up for processing. It was tough work done by specialists of different ethnic backgrounds. In the beginning the work was all manual, even the cans were made by hand. As time went on, new machines and processes improved the efficiency and ability to can more salmon.

The North Pacific Cannery was more than just a cannery. It was a small town, processing salmon for over 90 continuous years from 1889 to 1968, and remains the oldest standing cannery on the West Coast. A tour of the North Pacific Cannery is a glimpse back in time, where you get a sense of how these hardy people fished, processed the salmon, and lived in different housing areas onsite. As you tour the buildings and grounds, you can almost hear and feel what it must have been like.

The North Pacific Cannery museum captures what cannery life was like for the Japanese, Chinese, First Nations, and Europeans working in this plant. You can walk from building to building and see how a cannery worked, see the company store, office building, and rows of houses. You can tour the cannery on your own, or take one of the group tours to learn more about the canning process and the social aspects of life here.

The North Pacific Cannery is located 22 km south of Prince Rupert. You can rent a car in town or take the local bus which stops right in front of the cannery. Allow about 3 hours for a docent's tour of the facility. The Crew Kitchen, a small café at the cannery, sells baked goods and is open for lunch. Don't forget to stop by the gift shop.

NORTHERN B.C. COAST

LOCAL KNOWLEDGE

SPEED LIMIT: A 5-knot speed zone in Prince Rupert Harbour is enforced within 600 yards of the Prince Rupert shore. It is up to you to gauge the distance as there are no speed limit buoys.

⑬ **Prince Rupert.** As you approach Prince Rupert, it's a good idea to monitor Prince Rupert Traffic (VTS) on VHF 71 in case a large ship decides to depart while you're coming in. The fairway gets narrow in places. This is especially important in poor visibility.

As you approach, the large coal and grain loading areas are part of the Port of Prince Rupert's Ridley Terminals. From Barrett Rock at the entrance to Prince Rupert Harbour, it is another 5.5 miles of slow speed travel to town. Four marinas serve Prince Rupert: Fairview at the south end, the Cow Bay Marina in front of Atlin Terminal, Prince Rupert Rowing and Yacht Club in the middle, and Rushbrook at the north end. The Rushbrook Floats, Fairview Small Craft Docks, and Porpoise Harbour are all managed by the Port Edward Harbour Authority, (250) 628-9220.

Fairview is primarily a commercial boat moorage facility, although some pleasure boats do tie up there. It is fairly far from downtown. Rushbrook, at the north end, has better facilities for pleasure boats; but during the commercial fishing months, many fish boats occupy the slips. The walk from Rushbrooke to town is long but manageable. Most pleasure boats go directly to Cow Bay Marina and the Prince Rupert Rowing and Yacht Club, located at Cow Bay. Both these marinas quickly fill during the peak summer months. Reservations are recommended. Demand for moorage at Prince Rupert continues to be high. Plans are underway to open a new marina west of Cow Bay Marina in the near future. Good anchorage is in Pillsbury Cove, across the harbor. Northwest Fuels operates a large fuel dock in Cow Bay, just past the Prince Rupert Rowing & Yacht Club.

Prince Rupert ("Rainy Rupert"), population 12,500, offers just about anything you need for your boat. What isn't there can be flown in. Fuel and waste oil disposal are available at Northwest Fuels in Cow Bay.

Restaurants, a pub, and fish market are near the marinas. A shopping mall is a pleasant walk uptown, or you can take a cab. A Walmart is now located in the mall. A large Safeway is located between Cow Bay and the mall. The Save-On-Foods market, farther uptown, is another option for provisions, and they will deliver to the docks for a fee. The provincial liquor store is close to the Safeway parking lot. A smaller, private liquor store is at Cow Bay. Be sure to visit Rupert Meats, offering an excellent selection of house-made fresh and smoked meats and fish.

The Museum of Northern British Columbia is excellent, and sponsors a variety of informative day and evening programs during the summer. Highly recommended. Several restaurants are in town and in the Cow Bay area, some of them quite good. The Port Interpretive Centre, located on street level in Atlin Terminal, gives free tours about the past, present and future of the Port of Prince Rupert. Recommended.

Located above Cow Bay, Sea Sport Outboard Marine and Clothing has an excellent selection of clothing, fishing equipment, safety gear, and marine parts. They also have a machine shop on site.

The King Coin laundry in the center of town is self-serve laundromat, or use their drop-off/pickup service. Rupert Cleaners, located 1.5 blocks from Safeway, also has drop-off laundry service in addition to pickup and delivery service at your boat.

Just beyond the mall, at 617 2nd Ave. is Gary's Lock and Security Shop. Gary Weick, the longtime owner, collects things. His shop is a museum. In the window are wonderful toys from the 1930s and 40s, Canadian Pacific Railroad conductors' caps, old photos—and a stuffed and rare, mounted fur-bearing trout. It was caught in Lake Superior, from depths so great trout grow fur to keep warm. This trout's fur is white. Everything is explained on the sign next to the specimen. You have to see it.

For a glimpse back in time take the bus to Port Edward for a tour of the North Pacific Cannery on Inverness Passage, now a museum (250-628-3538). You'll see how the workers lived during the late 1800s and early 1900s.

For an exciting tour to the Khutzeymateen Grizzly Bear Sanctuary at the head of

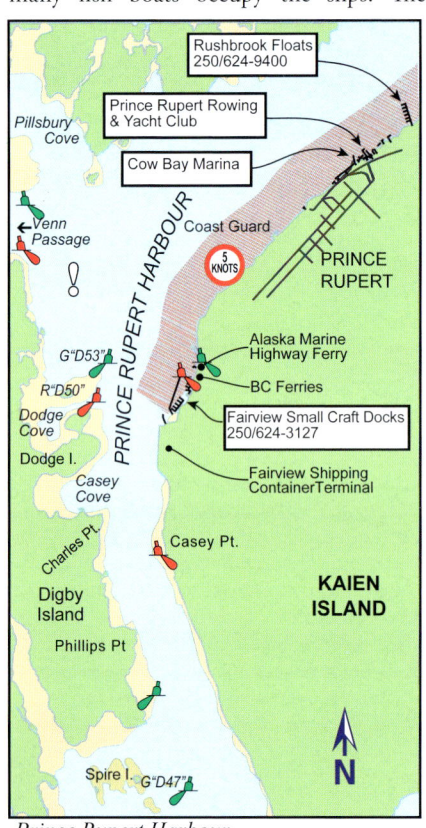

Prince Rupert Harbour

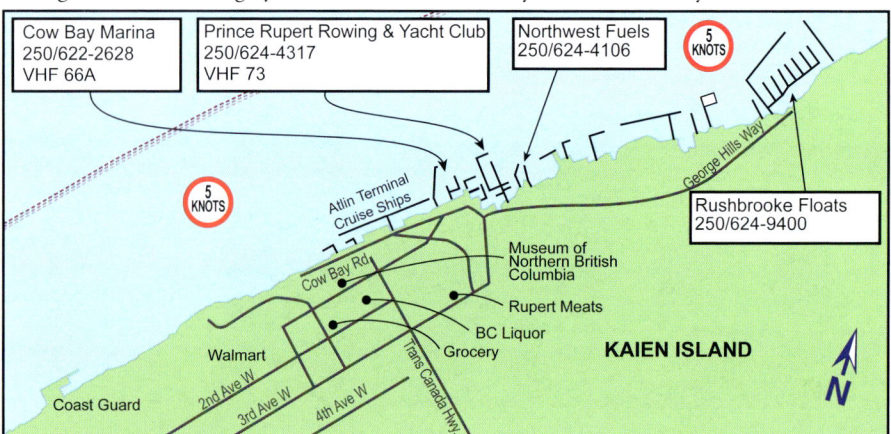

Prince Rupert Waterfront

456

Khutzeymateen Inlet, contact Prince Rupert Adventure Tours at (250) 627-9166.

Prince Rupert has become a major deepwater seaport, in heavy competition with Vancouver, Puget Sound, and California. Prince Rupert is closer to Asia than any other west coast port, and CN Rail owns tracks from Prince Rupert to Memphis, Tennessee. Transit time from Asia to the heartland of the U.S. is cut by at least two days. Prince Rupert can handle the largest container ships now afloat.

Prince Rupert is the last major city in British Columbia before transiting Dixon Entrance on the way to Ketchikan and Southeast Alaska. While there is good shopping and liquor stores in Prince Rupert, vessels bound for Alaska may want to wait to provision until Ketchikan to avoid customs issues with liquor, produce, and meat. On the way south from Alaska, Prince Rupert is the best place to stock up on produce, meat and liquor.

Customs Clearance: Lightering Dock previously served as a customs clearance phone location. The dock has been removed and the property purchased by the City of Prince Rupert, with plans to construct a marina to serve the public. Construction is on hold indefinitely due to lack of funding.

Most southbound boaters clear customs by calling from their slip at Rushbrooke, the Prince Rupert Rowing and Yacht Club, or Cow Bay Marina; call 888-226-7277. Customs agents have the option of calling out a local officer for an inspection.

Airport: The Prince Rupert airport is located on a separate island from the city and all passengers use an airport shuttle. The shuttle center is located downtown in the Prestige Hotel Building. There is only one shuttle trip for each flight. Shuttle service is included in the airline ticket fare. Shuttle schedule and more information can be found on the airport website www.ypr.ca.

Trailer and Vehicle Storage: For those trailering boats to Prince Rupert and looking for places to store their tow vehicle and boat trailer, contact: Coastal Propane (250) 624-5011; Bandstra Transport (250) 624-6826; Bridgeview Marine (250) 624-5809.

Car Rentals: National, (250) 624-5318. Located on the west end of town in the Highline Hotel.

Cruise Ships: A cruise ship will call once or twice a week during the summer. When a ship is in town, the streets and stores are apt to be crowded.

Fairview Small Craft Harbour. (250) 624-3127; info@peharbour.ca. Open 7 days a week 5:00 a.m. to 8:00 p.m. during the summer; 8:30 a.m. to 5:00 p.m. Monday through Friday the rest of the year. This is the first set of docks as you approach Prince Rupert. Commercial vessels primarily, but sometimes room for a few pleasure boats. Water, 15 & 30 amp power, garbage drop, and washrooms. First-come, first-served.

⑬ **Cow Bay Marina.** (250) 622-2628; www.cowbaymarina.ca. Monitors VHF 66A. Open all year with moorage for boats up to 80 feet and can accommodate larger yachts up to 140 feet on the breakwater docks; 30, 50 & 100 amp power, washrooms, showers, laundry, water, garbage drop, recycling, and free Wi-Fi. The showers and laundry facilities for marina guests are located in the white building at the bottom of the ramp near docks A and B. Reservations recommended, email or fill out the moorage request form online. This 51-slip marina is located in Cow Bay in front of the Atlin Terminal building. Be sure to fender well as wakes from passing boats find their way into the marina despite the posted "no wake" sign. The marina is close to the center of town.

⑬ **Prince Rupert Rowing and Yacht Club.** P.O. Box 981, 121 George Hills Way, Prince Rupert, BC V8J 1A3; (250) 624-4317; info@prryc.com. Monitors VHF 73. Open all year, call or email for reservations; 30 & 50 amp power, water; Wi-Fi, washroom and showers; garbage drop, with recycling. Fish-cleaning station. Waste oil dump at the Northwest Fuels facility next door.

This is more of a marina than a traditional yacht club. There is no reciprocal moorage. Although reservations are not accepted, visitors are encouraged to call at least 24 hours ahead to get on a wait list for moorage. Cell phones work for calling the Yacht Club from Hartley Bay and Oona River. As you approach, call on VHF 73. During the peak season, dock attendants help arriving guests with their lines and provide directions to slip assignments.

Most of the docks have recently been replaced, including the main spine dock, with new shore power upgrades and a private security gate access system. The dockside potable water system was included in the 2021 marina improvements. Be aware that you will be squeezed in more tightly than at most marinas. If the commercial salmon fishing fleet is in the midst of an opening, the boats will come and go all night, and moorage at the outermost docks can be pretty bouncy. Put out lots of fenders.

Look for the bright red roof. The yacht club is close to good dining in Cow Bay or

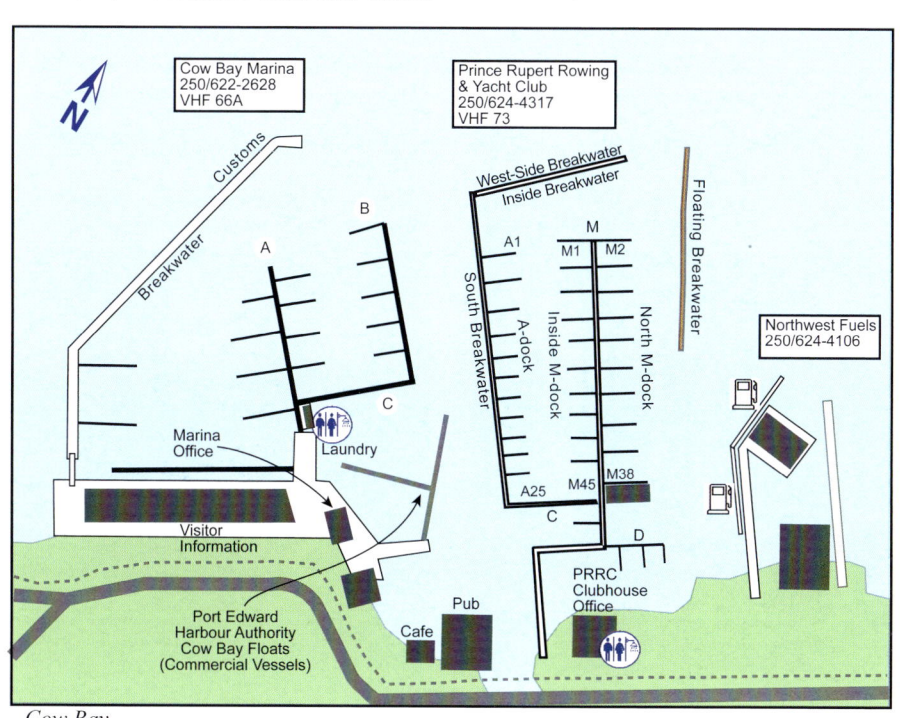

Cow Bay

NORTHERN B.C. COAST

Cow Bay Marina is just one block from shops and restaurants and three blocks from town.

you can walk or take a cab uptown for more restaurants and shopping.

⑬ **Northwest Fuels Ltd.** (250) 624-4106. Located in Cow Bay next to the Yacht Club. Open daily during the summer months; Monday through Friday in the off season. Petro Canada gasoline, diesel, lubricants, washrooms and showers. Block, cube and salt ice. Small convenience store on the pier with a surprising number of marine and fishing tackle items. Garbage drop, waste oil disposal. Propane is available a few blocks away. This fuel dock is often busy; be prepared to wait for a space to clear.

⑬ **Rushbrook Small Craft Harbour.** (250) 624-9400; info@peharbour.ca. Open all year, water, 15 amp power, washrooms, and single pay shower. Commercial vessels have priority in the summer, but there may be room for pleasure craft. Rafting required. Located about a mile north of town. Rushbrook has the only launch ramp in Prince Rupert. First-come, first-served. The office upland is open Monday through Friday, and open daily during the fishing season.

Pillsbury Cove. Pillsbury Cove, on the west side of Prince Rupert Harbour, is an excellent anchorage: level bottom, great holding, beaches and tide pools, and lots of crab. When the marinas in Prince Rupert are all full or you prefer anchoring, this is a good choice.

Prince Rupert is a 3-mile dinghy ride away. Field Correspondent Jim Norris notes that entering Pillsbury Cove can be intimidating due to the extensive aquaculture floats crowding the east side of the entrance channel; hug close to these floats on your starboard side as you enter.

Cow Bay shops and restaurants near Cow Bay Marina and Rowing Club

THINGS TO DO

• **Cow Bay.** Several good restaurants and shops. One casual favorite is Cowpuccino's for coffee, fresh baked goods and excellent Wi-Fi.

• **Khutzeymateen Sanctuary.** Also called "Valley of the Grizzly," this is the only park of its kind in Canada. It contains one of the largest populations of grizzly bears—about 50 —in British Columbia. Located 45 km NE of Prince Rupert.

• **North Pacific Cannery.** The oldest, most completely preserved cannery remaining of 200-or-so that once dotted B.C.'s northwest coast. A bus or car ride away from town.

• **Museum of Northern British Columbia.** An impressive collection about the northwest coast. A First Nations Longhouse describes the history of the people and area going back to the last ice age. It contains well-preserved, historical Tsimshian and other First Nations works of art, clothing, baskets and more. A short walk from the marinas.

• **Firehall Museum.** Focused on the history of the local fire department since 1908. A rebuilt red fire truck from 1925 sits in the middle of the museum.

• **Kwinitsa Railway Museum.** Authentic railway station with artifacts from the early 1900s, the heyday of the Grand Trunk Pacific Railway. On the waterfront.

• **Farmer's Market.** In town on Sunday afternoons during the summer season.

• **Earl Mah Aquatic Center.** A short walk from Cow Bay.

• **Seafest.** The town's biggest annual festival, held each June.

• **Port Interpretive Centre.** Hands-on activities let visitors explore the growth of Prince Rupert's commerce including, containers, coal and grain.

• **Rushbrook Trail.** Hike the 1.8 mile trail that follows the coastline along a former railway line. The trail starts at Cow Bay.

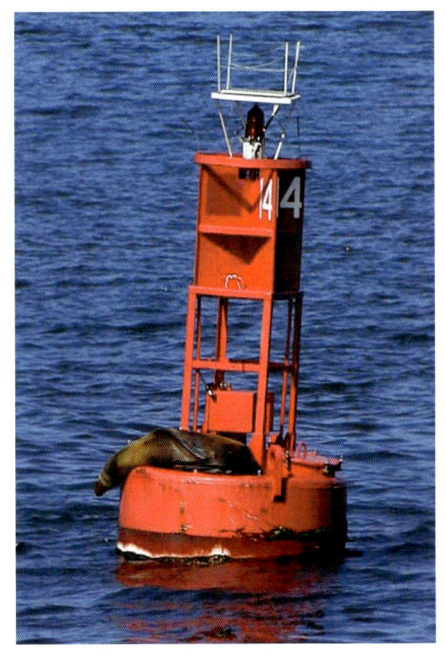

Haida Gwaii

*Windy Bay
Lyell Island*

GRAHAM ISLAND
Masset • Port Clemes
Skidegate • Daajing Giids (Queen Charlotte)

MORESBY ISLAND, HEADING SOUTH
Sandspit Harbour • Louise Narrows • Skedans Bay • Dana Passage • Hoya Bay

GWAII HAANAS NATIONAL PARK RESERVE
Tanu Island • Louise Narrows • Hotspring Island • Rose Inlet

ANTHONY ISLAND (SGANG GWAAY)
Nan Sdins • Grays Cove

Scan the Latest
Haida Gwaii
Information

tinyurl.com/WG22xCh17

HAIDA GWAII

See Area Map Page 461 - Maps Not for Navigation

Haida Gwaii. Located 130 miles north of Vancouver Island and 65 miles west of the B.C. coast's mainland islands, Haida Gwaii offers some of the Northwest's most spectacular cruising. Haida Gwaii is an archipelago of over 150 islands, best explored by boat. It is remote and pristine with a unique geological history. Glaciers once covered this area and receded 2,000 years before the rest of British Columbia, resulting in an ecosystem with some species of plants and animals not seen anywhere else. It has been referred to as the "Galapagos of the Northwest" with hundreds of species of birds, unique species of bears and many trees and plants growing in areas from the rain forests of the western coast to the dry forests on the eastern coast.

Haida Gwaii means "Islands of the People" in the language of the first people to settle here. The Haida were revered and respected along the coast as ambassadors and warriors, with a unique culture. The islands had a population of more than 10,000 until the 1800s when many succumbed to smallpox and other diseases from Europe. By 1900, only 350 remained. A visit to Haida Gwaii and the Gwaii Haanas National Park will take you to a place where you can see what remains of this once great culture. As you walk the trails through the rain forest and moss-covered rock canyons around the old villages you may even feel the presence of the people who inhabited this rugged and beautiful area.

Haida Gwaii experienced the impact of an imbalance caused by western man. In the 1800s sea otters were hunted almost to extinction. Their pelts were highly valued around the world and greed took over. In time the sea urchin population grew out of control without the sea otters to keep them in check. Later, the health of the kelp beds was affected by the overabundance of sea urchins. Nature's balance was thrown off. Today the symbol of Haida Gwaii is the sea otter and the sea urchin, a reminder to keep the ecosystem in balance.

Fishing and crabbing are allowed within the Gwaii Haanas Reserve except in designated closed areas, which are described at orientation. Appropriate fishing licenses required.

Permits. The Gwaii Haanas National Park Reserve, a Protected Area, was created in 1987 and encompasses the southern third of the Haida Gwaii archipelago. The Reserve is jointly managed by the Haida and the government of Canada. It is unique in Canada, covering both land and sea. A visit to Gwaii Haanas requires a permit for the time you will be in the Reserve. A fee per person, per day is payable when obtaining the permit. No charge for youth 17 years old and under. There is no limit on the number of days you may stay within the Reserve; however, after six days, it is more cost effective to purchase a Season Pass.

Only 100 visitors are permitted in Gwaii Haanas National Park Reserve at once. Advance reservations are recommended to ensure you'll get a permit. An orientation is required for all visitors, either in advance by DVD or at the **Haida Heritage Centre** (250-559-7885) in Skidegate. Telephone and video conference orientations were offered for reopening after Covid. The Haida Heritage Centre has a lovely gift shop. Orientation sessions are typically available from 9:00 a.m. until 4:30 p.m., Monday-Friday, and occasionally held on Saturdays. Orientation sessions can be scheduled by appointment when staff is available. It is recommended that you book your orientation time slot when you make your permit reservation. A permit tag is issued at the time of orientation and must be carried ashore within the Park Reserve. The excellent orientation covers the history of Gwaii Haanas as well as the procedures to visit the different sites within the park. All protected sites are managed by Haida Watchmen. They can be reached on VHF 06 prior to going ashore at each site. They manage the number of visitors on shore at a time. They also provide interpretive talks about the site and are very welcoming. Pets are not allowed on shore at the Watchmen sites.

A fee is not required between October 1st and April 30th, but visitors must register and attend an orientation session. Check the Parks Canada Gwaii Haanas website for more information. Call (877) 559-8818 (8:30 a.m. to 4:30 p.m. Monday through Friday after April 2nd) for more information or to arrange for a permit (www.pc.gc.ca/gwaiihaanas). As a convenience, orientation sessions are generally offered in early March in Vancouver BC, Victoria, or Sidney; check their website for the year's schedule. If planning to enter Gwaii Haanas from the south, it may be possible to get an orientation package by mail for a fee; contact the Haida Heritage Centre.

Getting to and from Haida Gwaii. Separated from mainland British Columbia by Hecate Strait; from Vancouver Island by Queen Charlotte Sound; and from Alaska by Dixon Entrance, getting to Haida Gwaii by boat requires crossing some of the Northwest's most feared bodies of water. Hecate Strait is notorious for rough water. With shallow depths in the northern portion, ranging from 50 to 115 feet, winds can quickly whip up big, uncomfortable seas. Tides move large volumes of water through Hecate Strait and Dixon Entrance. When wind blows against current, dangerous conditions can result. Particularly during spring tides, be mindful of possible wind-against-current situations. Nevertheless, we have had several smooth passages by timing the transit to the correct conditions and forecast.

There are basically three options for getting to and from Haida Gwaii; Crossing Hecate Strait from mainland BC Coast is the shortest open water route and the most common; Crossing Queen Charlotte Sound from Vancouver Island is the most direct but the longest open water route; Crossing Central Dixon Entrance to the north is only possible when departing Haida Gwaii as there are no Canada customs clearance locations in Haida Gwaii.

Crossing Hecate Strait. Shearwater, Bella Bella, and Klemtu in the south, and Prince Rupert in the north, are the popular starting points. There are a number of anchorages on the islands between Hecate Strait and BC mainland's Inside Passage. Routes from these anchorages offer the shortest open water crossings, ranging from 85 miles for southerly departure points and 65 miles from the northerly departure points. Many boats depart for Haida Gwaii from Prince Rupert. This route offers the shortest crossing (roughly 60 to 65 miles of open water), allowing boaters to minimize their exposure to potentially hazardous weather. Prince Rupert is a major city, and has anything a cruising boater might need before heading out to explore Haida Gwaii. With fuel, provisions, and internet access for weather information, Prince Rupert makes a logical starting point. After leaving Prince Rupert, several anchorages provide a place to spend the night and wait for better weather before crossing Hecate Strait. Larsen Harbour, anchorages in the Spicer Islands, and Welcome Harbour are good choices. In the past we have been warned of extreme kelp in Larsen Harbour. More recently we have been told that Larsen Harbour is easily navigable. It is the shortest point of crossing

Orientations for Gwaii Haanas National Park are held at the Haida Heritage Center in Skidegate.

Reference Only – Not for Navigation

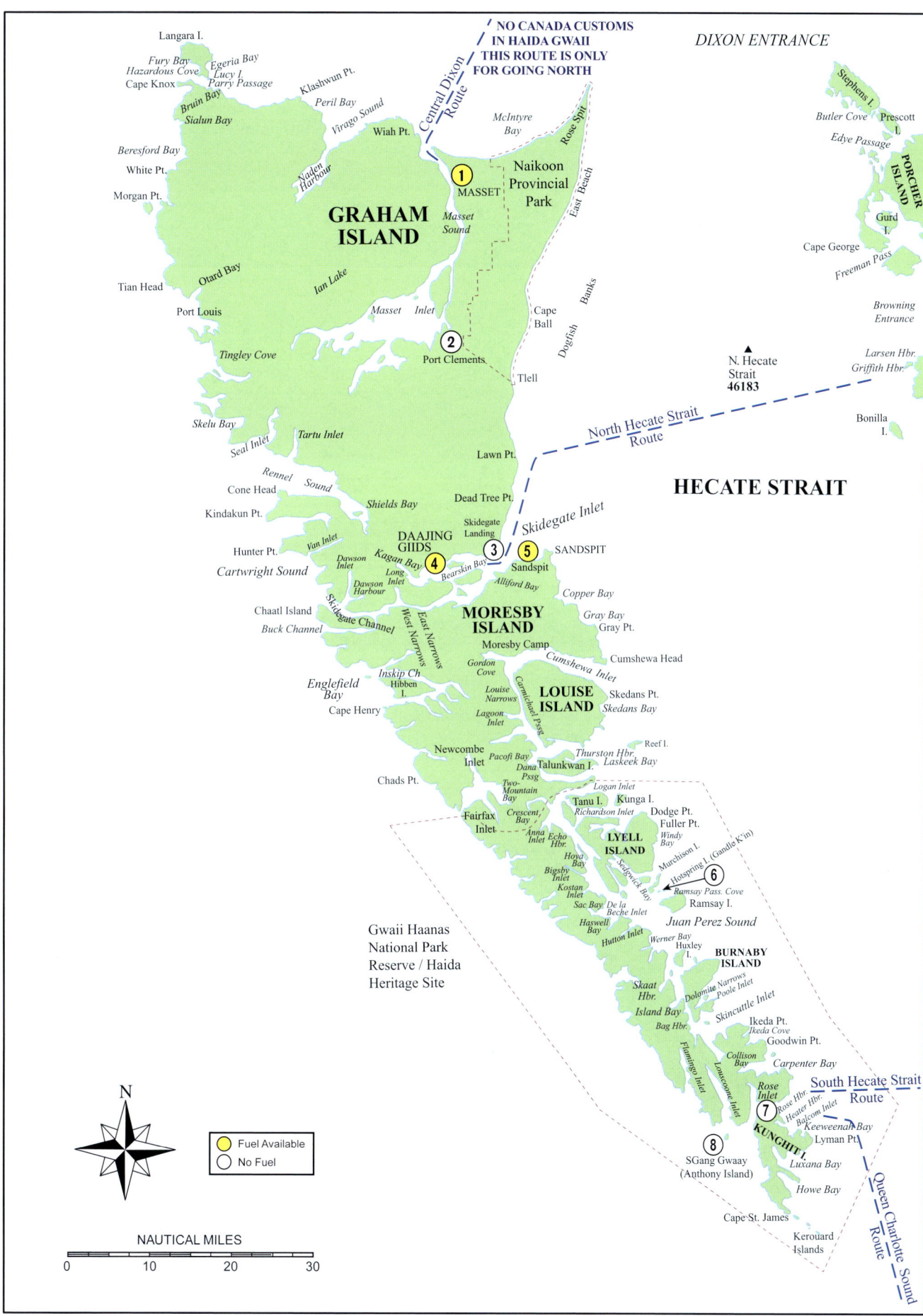

HAIDA GWAII

HAIDA GWAII

to Lawn Point on Graham Island. During one of our trips, we anchored in the Spicer Islands. For our early morning departure we listened for the wind and wave report from the North Hecate Strait weather buoy Station 46183 and navigated directly across Hecate Strait, passing the buoy on the way to Lawn Point. Note the shoal area leading north from the entrance to Skidegate Inlet. If headed to Sandspit Harbour or Daajing Giids, follow the deeper channel to Skidegate Inlet or Shingle Bay. In settled conditions and higher tides, we have crossed just north or south of Bar Rocks near the green can buoy.

Shearwater, Bella Bella, and Klemtu have provisions, fuel, water, and internet access and are good southern starting locations. Departing from Shearwater, Bella Bella, or Klemtu, boaters can take one of several routes from the Inside Passage to what Douglass terms the Outer Passage, where you will find several anchorages on Aristazabal Island before crossing Hecate Strait to Rose Harbour on Moresby Island. Because Rose Harbour is within the Gwaii Haanas National Park Reserve, you will be required to have a permit and have already completed the required Park orientation. This 85 mile crossing can be done in one long summer daylight day. This route crosses the southern area of Hecate Strait, which is not as shallow as the northern portion.

There are no services at Rose Harbour, so boaters landing in Rose Harbour need to have fuel, provisions, and water until arriving in Daajing Giids (Queen Charlotte) or Sandspit. Correspondent Mary Campbell has had four smooth crossings along this route. She suggests Borrowman Bay or Weeteeam Harbour for overnight anchorages. This route is also a good option when returning from Haida Gwaii after your stay in Gwaii Haanas Park.

Crossing Queen Charlotte Sound. Haida Gwaii can also be accessed from Vancouver Island to the south. The trip is long— about 160 nautical miles—and exposed to the full brunt of the open Pacific Ocean. Sailboats and slow powerboats will have to make an overnight passage. For faster boats in settled weather, the trip can be completed in a very long day. Keep in mind, however, that sea conditions may not be conducive to high-speed operation. Also remember that fuel is not available anywhere south of Sandspit. You will need a Gwaii Haanas National Park Reserve permit and have completed the required orientation. From the south, plot a route from the area north of Vancouver Island to Houston Stewart Channel and Rose Harbour. Use West Sea Otter weather buoy, Station 46204, and the South Hecate Strait weather buoy Station 46185 for wind and wave reports for the area. This might also be your return route when leaving Haida Gwaii for points south.

Crossing Central Dixon Entrance. Boats returning to British Columbia from Alaska may be tempted to cross Dixon Entrance to Masset instead of Prince Rupert. Unfortunately, there are no Canadian Government customs offices anywhere in Haida Gwaii. Boats southbound from Alaska must first clear customs in Prince Rupert. Boaters going north from Haida Gwaii and into Alaska may cross Dixon Entrance and proceed to Ketchikan for required U.S. Customs clearance. Keep in mind that you may not anchor or make landfall anywhere in U.S. waters before clearing customs in Ketchikan. From Masset to Ketchikan is approximately 85 miles, which can be done in one long day. Check weather, current, and conditions in Dixon Entrance carefully. Use Central Dixon Entrance weather buoy, Station 46145 for wind and wave reports.

Fuel. Fuel is available at Masset on the north end of Graham Island, at Sandspit, and in the village of Daajing Giids in Skidegate inlet. Cruising in Haida Gwaii is wilderness cruising with no major repair services or boatyards.

Water. Masset, Port Clements, Sandspit, and Daajing Giids have potable water. Parks Canada maintains fresh water hoses at Hoya Bay (near Shuttle Island) and at Louscoone Inlet; water at both locations is untreated.

Garbage Drops. In the remote and protected areas all trash must be carried out with you.

Insurance. Not all vessel insurance policies cover Haida Gwaii, check with your insurance agent to ensure that you have coverage for this area.

Provisioning. Groceries are available in Masset, Skidegate, Daajing Giids, and Sandspit. Deliveries are usually once a week. Selection may be limited.

Trailering. BC Ferries serve Masset, Skidegate, Sandspit, and Alliford Bay. Check www.bcferries.com for schedules and rates. Boat launches are located at Alliford Bay, Sandspit, Masset, and Copper Bay. Trailering small boats to Haida Gwaii may save time and money and can minimize weather delays.

Resources. Don and Reanne Douglass *Exploring the North Coast of British Columbia* is a helpful cruising guide for Haida Gwaii.

GRAHAM ISLAND

① **Masset.** During the summer months, Masset, the northernmost community on Haida Gwaii, is a hub of sport fishing operations. The local airport offers regular flights to Vancouver, and floatplanes run regularly from Prince Rupert. You'll find restaurants, a liquor store, three grocery stores, a hardware store, pubs, car rentals and an internet cafe.

Local businesses cater to tourists, with sightseeing trips and fishing charters. Hikes give boaters the opportunity to stretch their legs and see a different side of Haida Gwaii. The 9-hole Dixon Entrance Golf Club is 5 kilometers outside of town. The Dixon Entrance Maritime Museum showcases the maritime history of the area.

① **North Arm Transportation.** (250) 626-3328; nat@northarm.bc.ca; www.northarm.bc.ca. Open all year. Located at the government dock. Gas, diesel, and lubricants available.

① **Delkatla Slough Harbour Authority.** (250) 626-5487. Open all year, first-come, first-served, primarily a commercial boat facility. Power and water on the docks, garbage drop, tidal grid. Rafting required.

Refuge Cove. Known locally as 7-mile Cove, Refuge Cove provides good protection from weather and has 600 feet of dock space. This is a good place to wait out a storm, or to wait for favorable currents to enter Masset. Use caution entering Refuge Cove. The fairway is narrow, about 100 feet wide, with 6-foot depths at zero tide. In stormy conditions, swells can break across the entrance channel, making it impassable. Fishing outside Refuge Cove is reportedly excellent.

Langara Island. The northernmost island in the archipelago, is known for its exceptional salmon fishing. Sport fishing lodges on the island cater to fly-in guests. Several anchorages are available, although they are typically busy with sport fishing boats.

Marina at Masset on Graham Island

Waterfront pathway at Daajing Giids (Queen Charlotte) with views of Bearskin Bay.

Masset Sound. Masset Sound connects Masset to Port Clements and Masset Inlet. Currents run to 5.5 knots, although the Douglasses report little turbulence. Boats, particularly slow boats, should use caution when transiting the area. Vessels entering Masset Sound should do so on a flood, and exit on an ebb.

② **Port Clements.** Port Clements is a small town south of Masset. It has a grocery store, post office, health clinic, liquor store, restaurants, and a pub. A museum showcases the history of logging on Haida Gwaii. Local businesses offer sightseeing tours and fishing trips.

Several miles from town, a hiking trail leads to the Golden Spruce heritage site, where a sacred, golden-colored Sitka Spruce tree stood until a logger-turned-conservationist famously cut it down to protest logging. John Vaillant's book, *The Golden Spruce,* tells this story with a lot of interesting facts about Haida Gwaii.

② **Port Clements Small Craft Harbour.** P.O. Box 198, Port Clements, BC V0T 1R0; (250) 557-4295; www.portclements.ca. Open all year. Transient moorage, 20 & 30 amp power, garbage drop, unpaved boat launch. First-come, first-served, rafting required. Register at office three blocks away. Ice, a pay phone and groceries are available at the nearby Bayview Market.

SKIDEGATE, DAAJING GIIDS, AND SANDSPIT

③ **Skidegate.** Skidegate offers lodging, restaurants, groceries, and shops with local crafts. In fair weather boats can anchor offshore and dinghy in. Visiting cruisers may want to visit Skidegate by road from Daajing Giids.

④ **Daajing Giids (Queen Charlotte).** Queen Charlotte, on the south end of Graham Island, has many services and supplies. Groceries, restaurants, pubs, a liquor store, ATM, marine supplies, a hardware store, rental cars, lodging, a post office, and an internet café are available. Local outfitters offer guided tours which can be an option to see the protected areas.

A visitor center is just east of the Harbour Authority floats. The staff is friendly and can answer most questions about the area. Many summer events are hosted at a "square" just below the visitor center.

The grocery store is located approximately ½ mile west of the Harbour Authority. It is restocked each Monday. The post office, laundromat, and liquor store are in the same complex. A farmers market is held each Saturday near the community center and library.

Anchorage, in 20-35 feet, is good in Bearskin Bay, although it is open to wind and chop from the east.

④ **Queen Charlotte Harbour Authority.** P.O. Box 68, Daajing Giids, BC V0T 1S0; (250) 559-4650; harbour@qcislands.net. Open all year with moorage, 15 & 30 amp power, washrooms, showers, and garbage drop. A tidal grid is available for haulouts, and nearby there is a boat launch for trailerable boats. Water is available, but not on all docks. Improvements to the docks and washroom facilities were completed in 2022.

④ **Fast Fuel LP.** (250) 559-4611; sales@fastfuel.ca; www.fastfuel.ca. Located at the Inland Air pier. Open 8:00 a.m. - 5:00 p.m. mid-June to late August, open all year for call outs. Gas and diesel. Call ahead for lubricants.

Skidegate Channel. Skidegate Channel is the narrow, shallow, and winding channel between Graham and Moresby Islands, connecting Hecate Strait with the Pacific Ocean. East and West Narrows are particularly challenging, though daybeacons make transiting easier than in the past. Because of the difference in tidal swings on the Pacific and Hecate Strait sides of Haida Gwaii, tides and currents in Skidegate Channel are complex and

Queen Charlotte Harbour Authority floats, with Bearskin Bay anchorage in the background

HAIDA GWAII

See Area Map Page 461 - Maps Not for Navigation

difficult to predict. It's best to plan on arriving at McLellan Point roughly three hours after low water in Queen Charlotte (Daajing Giids).

Alliford Bay-Skidegate Ferry. Graham Island and Moresby Island are separated by Skidegate Inlet and Skidegate Channel. A small ferry runs daily from Alliford Bay near Sandspit on Moresby Island, to Skidegate Landing on Graham Island. Boaters visiting the two main islands by rental car should be aware of the last ferry sailing of the day. The last sailing from Moresby Island is normally 5:35 p.m., and the last sailing from Graham Island at Skidegate is normally 6:10 p.m. For the current ferry schedule, go to bcferries.com.

⑤ **Sandspit.** Sandspit, on the northeast end of Moresby Island, is a settlement with a launch ramp and well-protected marina, restaurants, pubs, liquor store, lodging, post office, and laundromat. The grocery store, about 4 km northeast from the marina, is restocked each Monday and Friday.

Sandspit has hiking and biking trails, the Willows Golf Course, (Haida Gwaii's only 18-hole golf course), and an airport with scheduled commercial service to Vancouver. Airport shuttle service and freight delivery is provided through Eagle Transit (250) 559-4461.

⑤ **Sandspit Harbour.** P.O. Box 477, Sandspit, BC V0T 1T0; (250) 637-5700; sandspitharbour2@outlook.com; www.sandspitharbour.com. Monitors VHF 06, 08, 09, 73. Open all year with guest moorage to 100 feet, 15, 30, 50 & 100 amp power, seasonal water, pumpout, pay phone, showers, washroom, garbage drop, launch ramp and free Wi-Fi. Marina office hours are the same as the Fuel Dock hours listed below. This is the most modern marina in Haida Gwaii. Reservations strongly recommended in the summer for vessels over 45 feet. Bridgeview Marine for repairs is located across the road.

⑤ **Sandspit Harbour Fuel Dock.** Operated by and located at Sandspit Harbour. Open June through August 7:00 a.m. to 9:00 a.m. and 6:00 p.m. to 9:00 p.m. and Sept. through May 9:00 a.m. to 12:00 p.m. Gas and diesel.

⑤ **Bridgeview Marine.** 537 Beach Road, Sandspit, BC V0T 1T0; (250) 637-5432; www.bridgeviewmarine.com. Open all year 8:00 a.m. to 5:00 p.m., Monday to Friday. Haulout to 36 feet. Marine supplies, mechanics with extensive outboard and stern drive experience, limited diesel and inboard experience.

Moresby Camp. Moresby Camp has road access to Sandspit, a public float, and a boat launch.

Gordon Cove. Gordon Cove, just south of Moresby Camp, is a an excellent anchorage. Good holding in 15-30 feet.

Louise Narrows. The small boat passage at Louise Narrows is scenic, shallow and narrow, only 30 feet across in some places. It is best to travel through the passage before high water and while the gravel banks are still visible. This way, you can see the channel, and if you inadvertently run aground, the rising tide will float you off.

When we transited we saw depths of less than five feet under the keel. It was

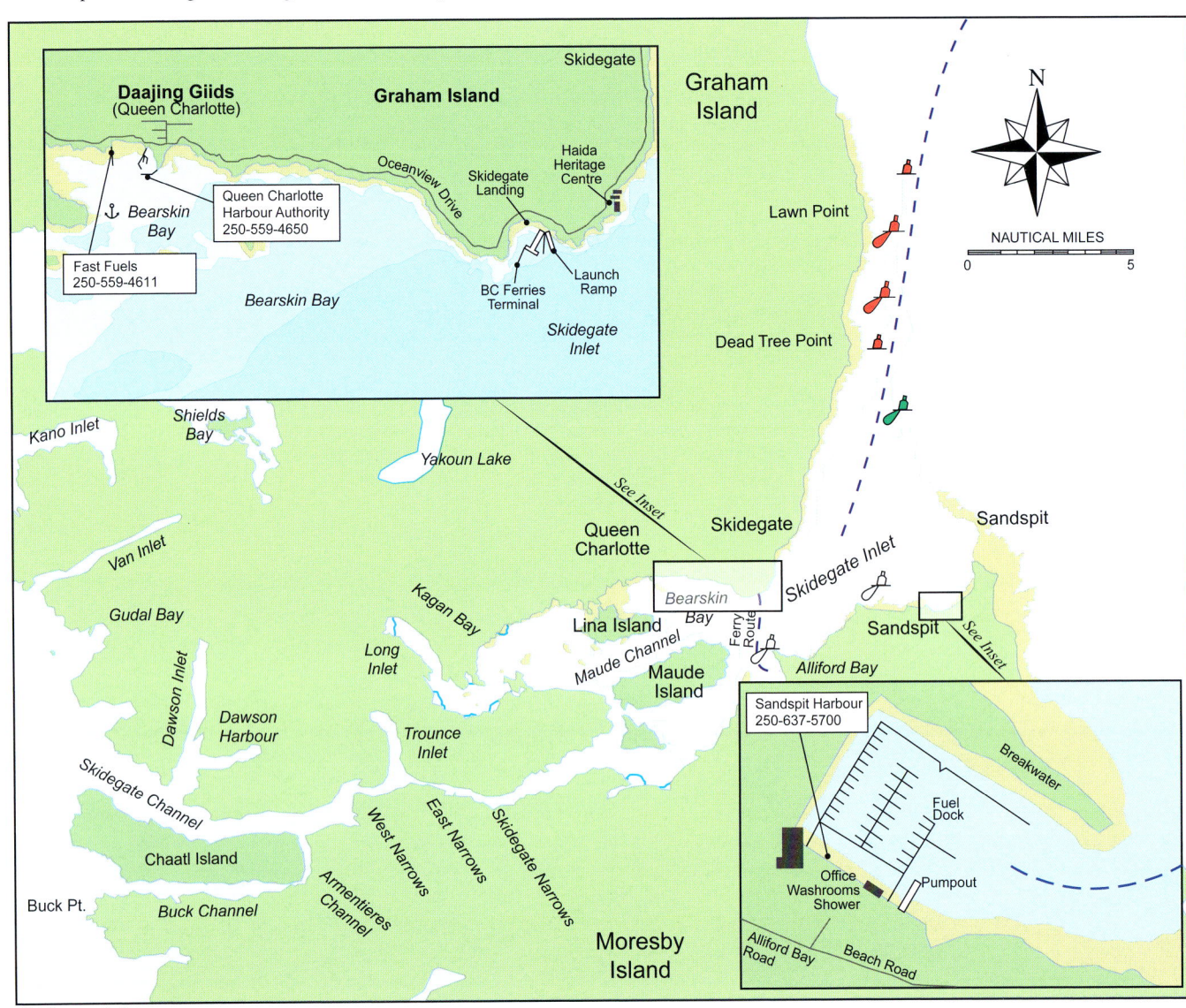

Skidegate Inlet

manageable, but added a bit of excitement. Given the limited space for maneuvering within the narrows, boats transiting Louise Narrows should make a sécurité call on VHF 16 low power before entering.

Skedans Bay. Skedans (or K'uuna Llnagaay) is situated on the eastern tip of Louise Island. It faces south onto Skedans Bay from a crescent beach that forms the neck of a small peninsula. As the furthest north of all the Watchmen sites, its relative accessibility makes it one of the most often visited. Skedans Bay is not within the protected area of the Gwaii Haanas National Park Reserve but visitors are still required to have had an orientation and to pay the day visit fee.

The procedure for visiting all Watchmen sites is to contact the Haida Watchmen on VHF 06 before coming ashore. If the site already has visitors, the Watchmen may ask you to stand by on board until the next group can come ashore.

K'uuna Llnagaay means Village at the Edge, but it was also known by the Haida as Grizzly-Bear-Town because of the large number of grizzly bear carvings found there. Visiting traders named it Skedans, a corruption of the name of its chief, Gida'nsta.

In the mid-1800s, almost 450 Haida lived here in about 26 Longhouses. Records show there were 56 monumental cedar sculptures, including frontal poles, single and double mortuary poles, memorial poles and mortuary figures.

K'uuna Llnagaay is one of the few remaining village sites with some standing poles and remnants of large Longhouses. Crests featured on the poles, such as rainbow, frog, eagle, beaver, and two-finned killer whale, signify which families lived there. A path winding through the old village allows you to appreciate the artistry of the poles, now in varying stages of decay, and provides a glimpse of what Haida life might have been like many years ago.

We anchored in 45 feet, about one mile southeast of the Watchmen site, and took the dinghy to shore. The anchorage immediately south of the Watchmen site was smaller and more exposed to northerly wind than we liked.

Mortuary Poles on SGang Gwaay (Anthony Island)

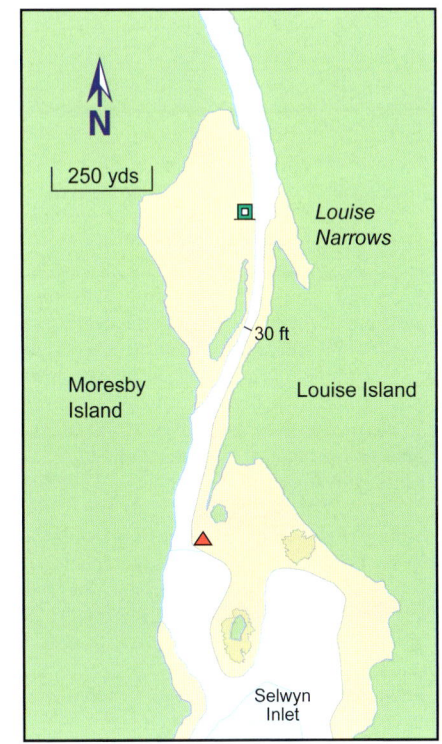

Thurston Harbour. Thurston Harbour on Talunkwan Island is a well-protected anchorage conveniently located between Skedans Watchmen site to the north and Tanu Watchmen site to the south. Anchor here following an afternoon visit to Skedans and get an early morning start to visit Tanu. There is plenty of room and good holding. While located near Gwaii Haanas Park, this anchorage is outside the park boundary and does not require a reservation or daily fee.

Dana Passage. Dana Passage is a narrow and scenic route between Talunkwan and Moresby Islands. At the narrowest section, the passage is only about 100 feet wide, but depths are at least 30 feet throughout.

GWAII HAANAS NATIONAL PARK RESERVE

Tanu Island. The beautiful and haunting village of T'aanuu Llnagaay is located on the east shore of Tanu Island, on Laskeek Bay. T'aanuu means eelgrass, which commonly grows in shallow water around the village. T'aanuu Llnagaay follows the shoreline of two beaches divided by a rocky shoal. In the mid-1800s, the village population was about 550, with 25 Longhouses, 31 mortuary columns, and 15 mortuary houses. Present-day visitors notice the many logs on the ground and may mistake them for windfalls; these, however, are the posts and beams of old Longhouses. The Longhouses faced the shoreline, and were dug into the ground for protection from the weather. Large, rectangular pits mark their locations. Though there are no standing poles here, on close inspection you can see ancient carvings made smooth by time and furred by moss. Walking amidst the ruins, surrounded by the protective rainforest, one gets a strong sense of the people who lived there. Contact the Haida Watchmen on VHF 06 for permission before coming ashore.

Fair weather anchorage can be found just off the landing beach, in 35-50 feet. Holding is marginal and currents run strongly. When the wind is blowing from the north, swells roll in from Hecate Strait.

Crescent Inlet. The head of secluded Crescent Inlet has sheltered anchorage with good holding. The inlet has beautiful views of mountains and old growth forest. Bears frequent the meadow at the head of the inlet. Moresby Explorers, a tour company, maintains a small floating lodge in Crescent Inlet. The inlet is outside the protected area, anchorage here does not require a reservation or payment.

Anna Inlet. Beautiful, knobby mountains surround Anna Inlet. The narrow entrance is difficult to see but easily navigated. Steering a mid-channel course, we never saw depths less than 35 feet at zero tide. Anchor in 50-60 feet at the head of the inlet.

Echo Harbour. Picturesque and well protected, Echo Harbour just off Darwin Sound offers good anchorage. Take your dinghy around the corner to the head of the cove where you will find a waterfall and wildlife viewing. Correspondent Mary Campbell reports seeing kingfishers standing watch over the stream outflow and bears roaming the beach looking for clams. Douglass reports finding evidence of an old homestead and apple trees on shore. Watch for bears.

Hoya Passage. Currents run to 2 knots, flooding north and ebbing south.

Hoya Bay. Hoya Bay, also known as Freshwater Cove, located off Hoya Passage, has a public float with untreated fresh water available. For overnight stays, anchor out or use one of the two public mooring buoys.

De la Beche Inlet. According to Douglass, De la Beche Inlet has two interesting

Louise Narrows

HAIDA GWAII

anchorages, De la Beche Cove and Sac Bay. De la Beche Cove is a small nook on the south shore of De la Beche Inlet, landlocked by an island. Douglass reports adequate holding at the head of the bay.

Sac Bay. Sac Bay juts out to the south from De la Beche Inlet, good holding and spectacular mountain scenery.

③ Windy Bay. Windy Bay, or Hlk'yah GaawGa, is a fair weather anchorage used to visit the historic fishing village called Hlk'yah Llnagaay (Falcon Town). Near here in 1985, the Haida blocked logging roads in their protest to put an end to logging on Lyell Island and protect the area that became Gwaii Haanas. The Longhouse is named "Looking Around and Blinking House" to honor this victory. An old growth forest contains trees over 1000 years old and more than 200 feet tall. A trail leads through huge Sitka spruce and western red cedar trees, draped with mosses and lichens. The Haida Watchmen can point out culturally modified trees where the bark was stripped for making baskets or hats. Some of these trees show where test holes were cut in them to check their suitability for making a canoe or carving a pole.

In August 2013, the Legacy Pole, the first new monumental pole in 130 years, was raised in Windy Bay. This pole was carved to celebrate the 20 years of co-management of the Reserve by the Haida Nation and the government of Canada. It is visible from the water.

We anchored just offshore from the Watchmen cabin, on the 3.7 meter sounding, in 20-30 feet, fair holding on a rocky bottom. Contact the Haida Watchmen on VHF 06 before coming ashore.

④ Hotspring Island. Hotspring Island is one of the most popular stops in Haida Gwaii. The hot springs, located on the south side of the island, were struck by a magnitude 7.7 earthquake that shook the area in October of 2012 and changed mother nature's plumbing. For several years, the flow of hot water ceased entirely. In 2015, pools of hot water appeared below the high tide line, and in 2016 some of the pools began filling again. By 2017, three pools were full, with the hottest one near the Watchmen dwelling, and the other two nearby pools linked by a new boardwalk. In addition to the attractive boardwalk, changing facilities and a bathhouse were added at the site. 2018 saw the return of more boaters to once again enjoy this fabulous destination.

Haida Watchmen are on site and require boaters to call on VHF channel 06 before coming ashore. The anchorage directly off the hot springs is exposed, with marginal holding on a rocky bottom. A better anchorage is between Hotspring and House islands.

Ramsay Passage Cove. Fairly well-protected alternative to Hotspring Island anchorages, but requires a 1.5-mile dinghy ride.

Dolomite Narrows. Dolomite Narrows is the narrow, shallow neck within Burnaby Strait and is poorly charted. One section dries completely on a 2-foot tide. Currents run to several knots. Small, privately maintained range markers show the route the locals take, but the markers are often missing or hard to locate.

The Narrows are famous for the fabulous assortment of tidal life to be seen. Bat stars in a rainbow of colors, blood stars, and other amazing creatures rarely seen in the Pacific Northwest carpet the shallows. Correspondent Mary Campbell suggests anchoring in Bag Harbour to the south, or pick up the buoy just north of the narrows, and transit the narrows at low tide in your dinghy or kayak. This allows you to see how you feel about bringing your big boat through at high water slack, depending on the condition of the range markers and the expected depths. Alternatively, you can take the longer, more exposed route around Burnaby Island rather than chance grounding.

Bag Harbour. Bag Harbour is a secure anchorage at the south end of Dolomite Narrows. It's a good place to wait for appropriate conditions for a northbound transit of Dolomite Narrows, or relax after a transit.

Ikeda Cove. Ikeda Cove is a lovely, protected anchorage with excellent holding. A grassy meadow is a haven for wildlife. We spotted deer, a bear and cub, and a pair of sandhill cranes. Remains of cabins, wharves and machinery can be found on shore.

Collison Bay. Good protection but some swell can find its way into the bay. Anchor behind the islet on your starboard when entering the inner part of the bay. Holding and anchoring depths are good. The Landons waited-out a strong southeasterly for two days and watched a spectacular whale show at the entrance to the inner bay.

Heater Harbour. Located on the east side of Kunghit Island, Heater Harbour offers reasonable protection in settled weather with plenty of swinging room. The north and northwest arms are kelp gardens and you may need to spend time de-kelping your anchor; holding is good. Correspondent Mary Campbell reports that on a kayak trip up the northwest arm she spotted sandhill cranes and black-tailed deer.

Rose Harbour. Once a bustling whaling station, Rose Harbour is now a small, quiet community and the only piece of privately owned land within Gwaii Haanas. Remnants of the old whale rendering facilities can still be seen on the shoreline. Local residents provide lodging and meals for commercial tour groups; the boating public can join the group for meals if space is available with advance notice. Contact "Rose Harbour Kitchen" on VHF Ch 6.

Rose Inlet. Open to the south, this large inlet with suitable anchoring depths is protected from most conditions except southerly weather. Correspondent Mary Campbell suggests good anchoring can be found at the head of the inlet or east of Denny Rocks; beachcombing and crabbing are good.

Louscoone Inlet. Louscoone Inlet at the south end of Moresby Island has several possible anchorages. Small Cove, east of Crooked Point, is reportedly rocky and filled with kelp. Etches Point Cove, between two unnamed islands northwest of Etches Point, is the best anchorage. The Douglasses report another small and unnamed cove with limited swinging room 1 mile northwest of Etches Point Cove and 0.4 mile north of Cadman Point.

Untreated fresh water is available from a hose on a buoy (52° 11.70N 131° 15.40W) shown on Chart 3857; boil before consuming.

⑤ Anthony Island. Anthony Island or SGang Gwaay, on the northwest side of Kunghit Island, is recognized worldwide as a historic UNESCO World Heritage Site. Nan Sdins (also known as Ninstints) is a former Haida village and the major attraction. Filled with the largest collection of original Haida heraldic and mortuary poles, Nan Sdins offers a remarkable look into the Haida culture. The poles at Nan Sdins have been reset upright for the last time. Going forward, when a pole naturally falls it will be left to decay, following the tradition of the memory fading for the chief or family depicted by the pole, and for whom it was created.

Anchorage is not permitted directly off the totem park. Instead, anchor in Grays Cove, or in the cove on the northwest corner of the island. Vessels with deeper draft will prefer anchoring in Grays Cove. If anchored in the northwest cove, look for the bright orange fishing floats on the beach. These floats mark the boardwalk trail through the woods to the Watchman cabin for check-in. Call the Haida Watchmen on VHF 06 for permission to come ashore.

SGang Gwaay and the Nan Sdins Village Site is one of the top 10 places to visit on the entire coast. You might feel the spirits of the Haida as you walk through the woods to Nan Sdins. You emerge from the wood into a grove of carved poles. From the beach you can see what it must have been like when the Haida pulled their long war canoes up in front of the village. Nan Sdins should not be missed.

Grays Cove. Grays Cove, on the eastern shore of SGang Gwaay, is about a quarter-mile south of Nan Sdins, with a good dinghy landing beach and trail to the site. While well-protected from west and northwest weather, it is open to the south and east. The bottom is rocky and notorious for poor holding. Set well and check your set; anchor watch is advised.

Reference Only – Not for Navigation

HAIDA GWAII

SGang Gwaay (Anthony Island) and the Nan Sdins Village is a UNESCO World Heritage Site; the beach is lined with old mortuary poles.

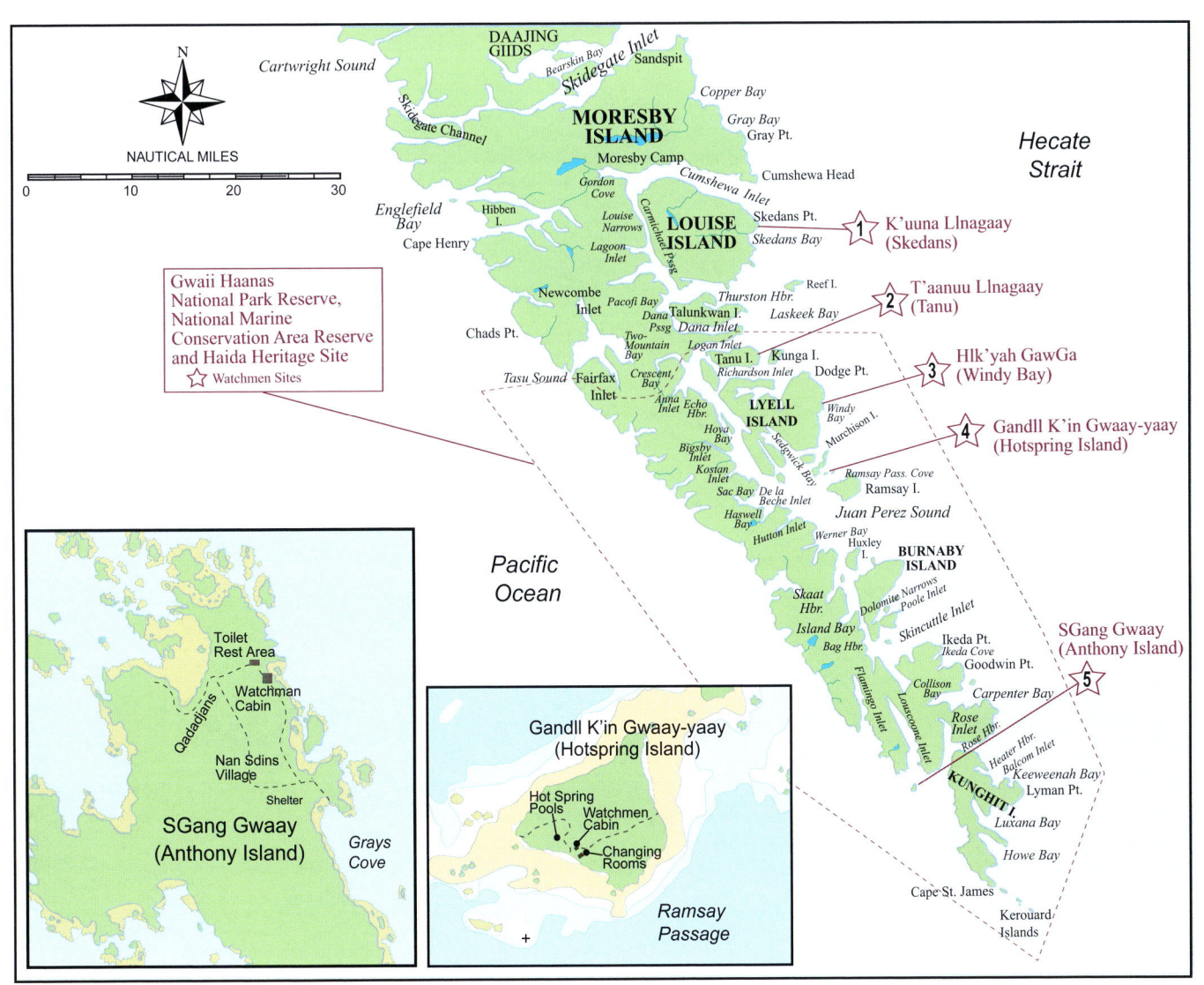

Gwaii Haanas

Dixon Entrance

VENN PASSAGE TO METLAKATLA BAY
Du Vernet Pt. • Metlakatla, BC

TONGASS PASSAGE ROUTE
Port Simpson • Tongass Passage
Lincoln Channel

NORTH DUNDAS ISLAND ROUTE
Green Island • Holliday Passage • Danger Passage

CROSSING DIXON ENTRANCE SOUTHBOUND
Clearing Canada Customs

Scan the Latest Dixon Entrance Information
tinyurl.com/WG22xCh18

Green Island Lighthouse Chatham Sound

On to Southeast Alaska! This chapter covers the departure routes from Prince Rupert and Chatham Sound, the options for the open water crossing of Dixon Entrance, and the approach to Ketchikan.

The distance from Prince Rupert to Ketchikan (via Venn Passage) is 82 nautical miles. Depending on the speed of your vessel, the weather and sea conditions, a stop in Prince Rupert before crossing Dixon Entrance might be required. Foggy Bay is 50 miles from Prince Rupert and could be an option for an overnight stop. It's a beautiful anchorage with good protection.

Vessels must report arrival into U.S. waters in Alaska to U.S. Customs and Border Protection (CBP) by one of three means: CBP ROAM/CBP One App; telephone call to CBP Small Boat Reporting Office if all aboard are enrolled in a Trusted Traveler Program such as Nexus, Global Entry, or I-68; or by reporting in-person to a CBP Officer in Ketchikan. U.S. cellular coverage is usually found near Cape Fox. Vessels that have reported arrival, completed clearance, and have a clearance number from CBP by phone or ROAM/One may proceed to their destination. Those that need to report in-person in Ketchikan and need more than one day to reach Ketchikan will need to contact CBP in Ketchikan (907-225-2254) in advance for permission to anchor one night in Foggy Bay. For more information about clearing customs see the *U.S. And Canadian Customs Information* section in the Compendium chapter and *Customs Clearance* topic in the Southeast Alaska chapter.

Before leaving British Columbia, however, consider some of the excellent cruising in Portland Inlet and Portland Canal, just north of Prince Rupert. Portland Canal is one of the longest fjords in North America and defines the border between the U.S. and Canada. It is beautiful and remote. Farther up the canal, the water becomes increasingly opaque, almost milky, the result of glacial run-off. The outpost of Stewart, B.C., with Bear Glacier just above town, has a public dock, a "yacht club," and other services. Stewart, B.C. is so remote that there is no VHF weather radio reception.

Hyder, Alaska is on the other side of the canal, less than a mile from Stewart. Hyder does not have a U.S. Customs office for clearance. Ketchikan is the closest CBP office. The typical strategy is to explore British Columbia on the way north, then go to Ketchikan for customs clearance. When headed home from Southeast Alaska, explore the areas south of Ketchikan, such as Misty Fjord or Hyder. Then go to Prince Rupert for customs clearance into Canada.

Both the United States and Canada require vessels to check in with customs authorities prior to anchoring, mooring, or going ashore.

In addition to Portland Canal, Observatory Inlet has a number of good anchorages. This area was the base camp for Captain George Vancouver when his expedition explored this area in 1793.

Cruising in Portland Canal is covered in detail by Don and Reanne Douglass in their cruising guide, *Exploring the North Coast of British Columbia,* published by FineEdge.com.

DIXON ENTRANCE GO-NOGO CHECKLIST

Tides & Currents - See Ports & Passes or Canadian Tides & Current Tables Vol. 7
- ☐ Phase of the moon – Spring or Neap Tide; Neap Tides preferred
- ☐ Check for slack water time at Kelp Island Passage, Duke Island and Port Simpson

Weather System Predictions – via Internet or satellite
- ☐ Check NOAA Ocean Prediction Center forecasts for any approaching significant weather systems
- ☐ Check Windy.com, Predictwind.com, SiriusXM Marine, or Sailflow.com
- ☐ See Environment Canada and NWS NOAA forecasts for the Synopsis for Dixon Entrance East

Weather & Seas Forecasts – via Internet, phone, or VHF
- ☐ See Environment Canada Forecast for Dixon Entrance East; Check for warnings, note wind speed and direction, wave height and interval, and trends
- ☐ See NOAA NWS Forecast for Clarence Strait; check for warnings; note wind speed, direction and sea conditions

Observations & Present Conditions – via Internet, phone, or VHF
- ☐ Check Buoy Reports for West Dixon Entrance (46205), and Central Dixon Entrance (46145); note wind speed and direction, wave height and interval, and sea conditions.
- ☐ Check Lighthouse and Station Reports for Rose Point, Triple Island, Green Point, and Dundas Island; note wind speed, direction, and sea condition

Go-NoGo Decision
- ✓ Check wind direction in relation to direction of travel.
- ✓ Do the wind and wave conditions exceed your limit?
- ✓ Is there a wind against wave or current situation?

Fail-Safe Contingency Plans
- ✓ Duck-in locations along the route: Moffett Islands, Port Simpson, Tongass Passage, Brundige Inlet, Dundas Island, Foggy Bay

See the *Marine Weather* section in the Compendium chapter for telephone numbers, website addresses, VHF channels, and buoy numbers.

Crossing Dixon Entrance: Heading North. Several options exist for transiting Chatham Sound and crossing the open water of Dixon Entrance.

A stop at Prince Rupert can be a welcome break after the long passage up Grenville Channel and through northern British Columbia. Prince Rupert is one of the last fuel stops in Canada, and some boats may need to take on fuel before proceeding the 82 miles to Ketchikan.

If conditions are favorable, some boats bypass Prince Rupert entirely. This saves several hours of transit time. Anchorages are available in the Moffatt Islands, Qlawdzeet Anchorage on Stephens Island, and Brundige Inlet on Dundas Island, or in Foggy Bay after crossing Dixon Entrance (with a call to U.S. Customs and Border Protection in Ketchikan, (907) 225-2254).

The first route option is the shortest but the most exposed. A second route is a variation on the first: Cross Chatham Sound on a northwest heading and pass through the Moffatt Islands. They're beautiful and protected, but require good situational awareness to navigate among the many small islands, islets, and rocks. Several anchorages are tucked among the islands, pleasant enough for an overnight at anchor. At Dundas Island cross to Cape Fox and follow the coastline to Foggy Bay to overnight. The next morning continue up Revillagigedo Channel to Ketchikan.

The third choice is a longer route. First travel along the east side of Chatham Sound, then cross Portland Inlet. Sometimes referred to as the "mainland route," it offers some protection, and minimizes the open water crossing by harbor hopping along the shoreline. Attention needs to be focused on the effect of outflow wind and current from Portland Inlet.

The longer routes offer more shelter and duck-in points. The best choice depends on weather and current conditions. It is critical to develop a good picture of the currents, wind speed and direction, and ocean swells from Environment Canada and NOAA weather forecasts, buoy reports, and lightstation reports. Monitoring these resources for several days prior to crossing Dixon Entrance can give a skipper a good understanding of what to expect during a crossing.

Weather planning. Planning a Dixon Entrance crossing starts with NOAA and Environment Canada forecasts. Use NOAA's "Dixon Entrance to Cape Decision" forecast and Environment Canada's "Dixon Entrance East" forecast.

Given a favorable forecast, several weather reporting stations are useful in determining if conditions are acceptable. The Central Dixon Entrance Buoy (Buoy 46145) provides regularly updated wind speed, direction and sea state information. This information can be accessed by listening to the continuous marine broadcast, using the Dial-a-Buoy service (888-701-8992), or (301) 713-9620, or

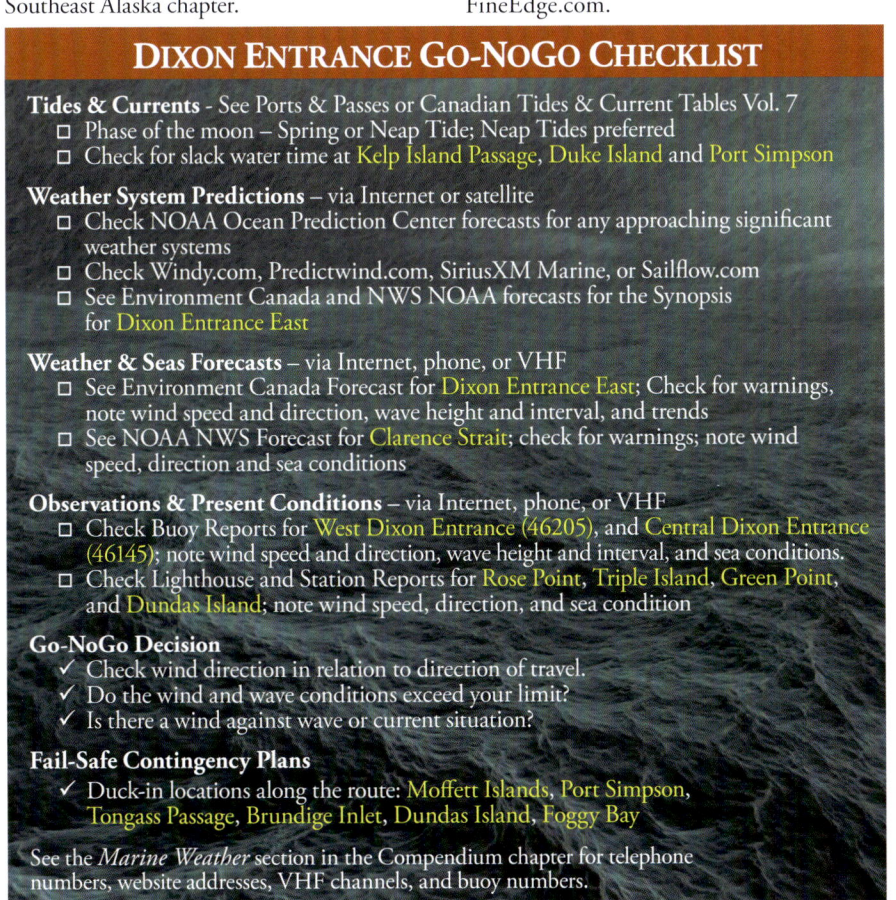

DIXON ENTRANCE   *Reference Only – Not for Navigation*

Distances (nm)
(Approximate, for planning)

Prince Rupert to Port Simpson - 26
Prince Rupert to Brundige Inlet - 32
Prince Rupert to Lincoln Channel - 33
Prince Rupert to Foggy Bay - 50
Prince Rupert to Ketchikan - 82

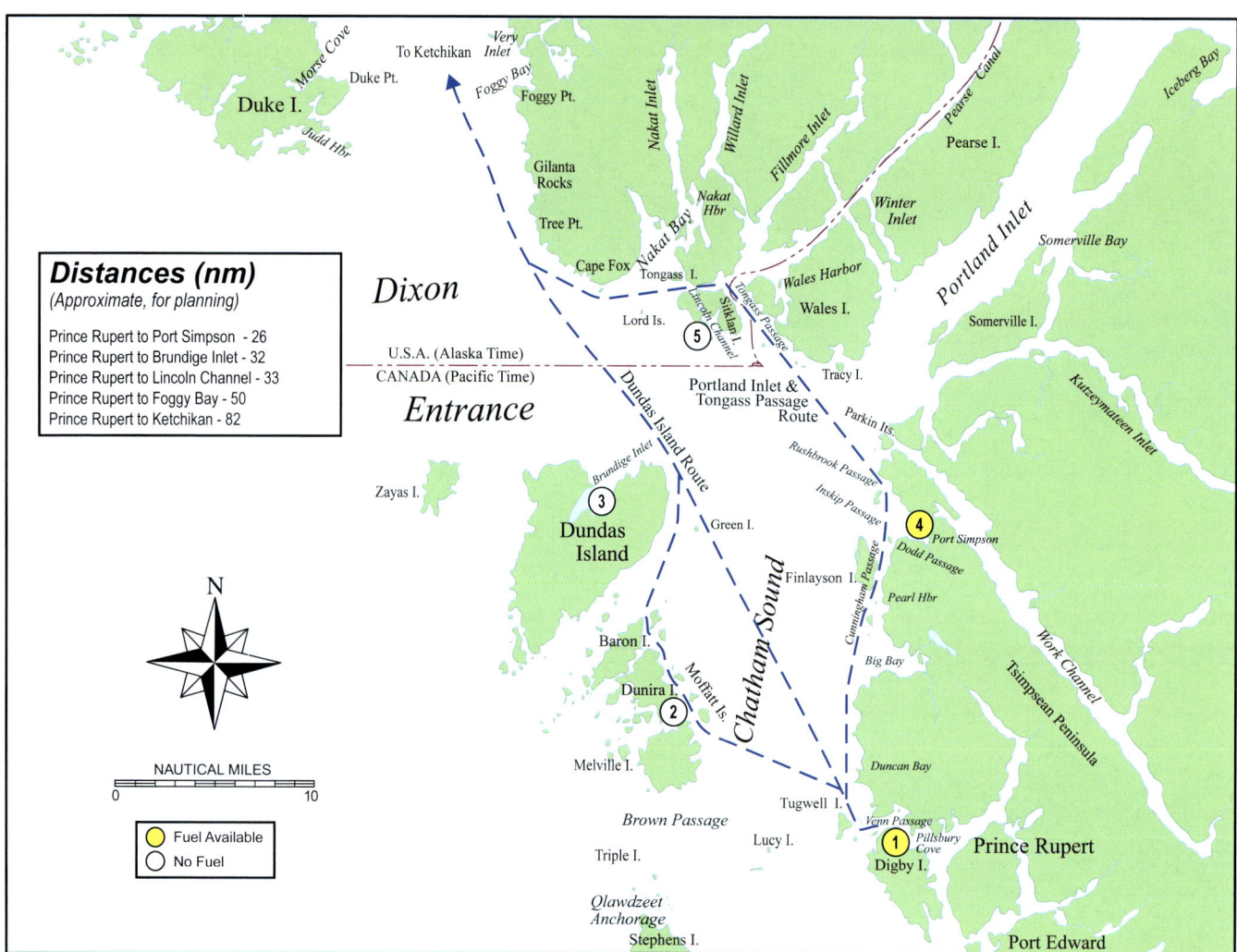

Dixon Entrance

checking online at www.ndbc.noaa.gov.

Automated, land-based weather stations at Lucy Island, Grey Islet, and Rose Spit provide wind speed and direction, updated hourly. The Green Island and Triple Island lightstations are staffed with lightkeepers year round. These lightkeepers provide updated weather observations every three hours, including wind and sea conditions. Listen for their reports on the continuous marine broadcast, or visit www.weather.gc.ca. You may also be able to call them directly on VHF 82.

Mariners are also using Apps like PredictWind.com, SailFlow.com, and Windy.com which give visual representations of forecast winds and sea conditions to judge the open ocean crossing. These Apps require a good internet connection.

Consider reading a weather book or taking a weather course to help understand and interpret weather data. Much data is available, even if the only source is the VHF continuous marine broadcast. The key is to understand the information as it streams by, and to use reports from multiple stations to paint a complete picture for the area you are interested in. An outflow wind from Portland Inlet blowing against a flood current, for example, will make for rough conditions as far away as Dundas Island. Even with the best preparations, conditions can change. Have a backup plan, such as using Brundige Inlet as a duck-in point before crossing. Be sure your vessel and crew are ready for changing weather conditions.

① **Venn Passage to Metlakatla Bay.** Venn Passage and the route through Metlakatla Bay is suitable for recreational boats of 75 feet or less. The route through Venn Passage is narrow and twisting, with shoals on each side. Buoys and range markers help navigation. Depths can be less than 10 feet, so some skippers time their passage for mid- or high-tide.

This route saves about 12 miles, compared with going south from Prince Rupert Harbour and rounding Digby Island. It's the channel favored by the fishing fleet, and it can be busy. The route requires careful situational awareness and attention to the depth sounder and chartplotter. Even the buoys are suspect. In the past some have been dragged hundreds of yards out of position by log tows. Use caution when passing the landing for the ferry to the airport at Du Vernay Point. It is a regularly enforced no-wake zone. A no-wake zone in front of the village of Metlakatla is also enforced. Spend time studying the charts to understand this route before attempting.

From Prince Rupert, head west to Grindstone Point and enter the channel. Follow the buoys and range markers. Note when heading west through Venn Passage, the range markers will be astern (back ranges). You will need either a clear view astern, or a stern watch with clear communication to the helm. At Tugwell Island, a turn to the north takes you into Chatham Sound toward Dundas Island, or along a route that follows the shoreline toward Port Simpson and Portland Inlet.

Dundas Island Route. The shortest route across Dixon Entrance is to depart Metlakatla Bay, take a direct course towards Green Island, then head up Holliday Passage. Round the top of Dundas Island and turn toward Mary Island. Proceed via Tongass Narrows to Ketchikan. If Dixon Entrance is too rough, you can anchor in protected Brundige Inlet on the north end of Dundas Island and remain in Canadian waters. If conditions allow a crossing of Dixon Entrance late in the day you can proceed to Foggy Bay for the night. The next day go from Foggy Bay to Ketchikan.

For planning purposes, it's about 26 miles from Metlakatla, BC to Brundige Inlet. It's an additional 22 miles from Brundige Inlet to Foggy Bay through mainly open water. Foggy Bay to Ketchikan is 32 miles. The total distance from Prince Rupert to Ketchikan is 82 miles—a long day for a displacement-speed cruising boat.

② **Moffatt Islands.** For an interesting and scenic passage, depart Metlakatla Bay and head west to Melville Island. Carefully pick your way through the channel between Dunira Island and the Moffatt Islands. Cross to Dundas Island and Holliday Passage and proceed to the north end of Dundas Island. Several small anchorages are along the way in the Moffatt Islands. Sailing Directions cautions against this route without local knowledge. We found it easy enough to follow with good charts.

③ **Brundige Inlet.** Brundige Inlet extends for about 2.5 miles. Enter at Prospector Point. The inlet is well protected, though windblown and barren in areas. You have a couple of anchoring options in Brundige Inlet; one is in the inlet south of Fitch Island in 30 to 40 feet of water, another is at the southwest end of Brundige Inlet in 35 to 45 feet of water, where there is room for many boats. Some have advised of vicious black flies on the island. Not the prettiest anchorage, but a good protected departure point to cross Dixon Entrance.

LOCAL KNOWLEDGE

Fishing Nets: Cape Fox to Tree Point, you may encounter many gillnet fish boats. Gillnets can extend up to 1800 feet from the boat (mostly from the stern, but sometimes from the bow) and show hard-to-see small white floats along the top of the net. The end is marked by an orange float, which is often difficult to see in choppy seas. They sometimes monitor VHF 16 when their nets are set.

Portland Inlet & Tongass Passage Route. This route is preferred when northern outflow winds from Portland Inlet create a sharp chop in Chatham Sound. It reduces the open water across Portland Inlet to less than 5 miles. The total distance from Metlakatla Bay to Foggy Bay is about 50 miles.

If planning to overnight in Foggy Bay, the skipper must call U.S. Customs and Border Protection (907) 225-2254 in Ketchikan and inform them.

⑤ **Port Simpson.** (250) 625-3293; adminassist@laxband.com or cao@laxband.com. North of Metlakatla Bay, Port Simpson can be used as a jumping-off point for crossing Portland Inlet. Port Simpson is a tribal village protected behind Rose Island. There are several floats, they're often filled with fish boats, requiring rafting. Call ahead for available space, 60-foot limit; 20 amp power. No showers. Fuel dock has gas and diesel.

⑥ **Lincoln Channel.** Lincoln Channel, between Tongass Island and Kanagunut Island on the west and Sitklan Island and the mainland on the east, provides an interesting stop with easy access for boats coming from either Ketchikan, or Nichols Bay on Prince of Wales Island. The south end of Lincoln Channel is only two miles from the Canadian border and 38 miles from Prince Rupert, making it a good departure point for vessels heading south.

This is a popular anchorage for fish boats during the gillnet season. Several fishermen keep float houses here. Tongass Island was the site of Fort Tongass, the first U.S. Customs office in Alaska, and a major Tlingit village. The rocky shores of Kanagunut Island contain interesting rock formations. You may even find garnets near Garnet Point on the south tip of the island.

Enter at either the north or south end of the channel, or between Tongass Island on the north and Kanagunut Island on the south. If entering between Tongass and Kanagunut, follow Chart 17437 or your chartplotter carefully and watch for rocks. The best anchorage is north of a small unnamed island in 80-100 feet. Anchorage can also be found off Tongass Island or, in northerly winds, south of the unnamed island.

Crossing Dixon Entrance: Heading South. Southbound vessels coming from Southeast Alaska must clear Canadian Customs in Prince Rupert before stopping or anchoring in British Columbia. There is no designated process for obtaining permission to anchor prior to checking in with customs agents in Prince Rupert.

Approach Prince Rupert through Metlakatla Bay and Venn Passage, or continue down the west side of Digby Island and enter through Prince Rupert Harbour.

Once in the harbor, proceed to one of the four marinas where customs reporting is allowed by telephone: Fairview Terminal, the Cow Bay Marina at Atlin Terminal, Prince Rupert Rowing & Yacht Club, or Rushbrooke Floats. Call Canadian Customs and Border Services Telephone Reporting Center by cell phone at (888) 226-7277.

Until cleared, all crew must remain on the boat. Canadian Customs may send agents to your boat for an inspection. Once cleared, you will be given a clearance number to post on the dockside window of your vessel and record in the ship's log.

See the *Canadian Customs Information* section of the *Compendium* chapter at the front of the book for more about clearing customs.

If the weather deteriorates and you must anchor in Canadian waters before clearing customs in Prince Rupert, call Canadian Customs by phone, or notify the Canadian Coast Guard on VHF 16.

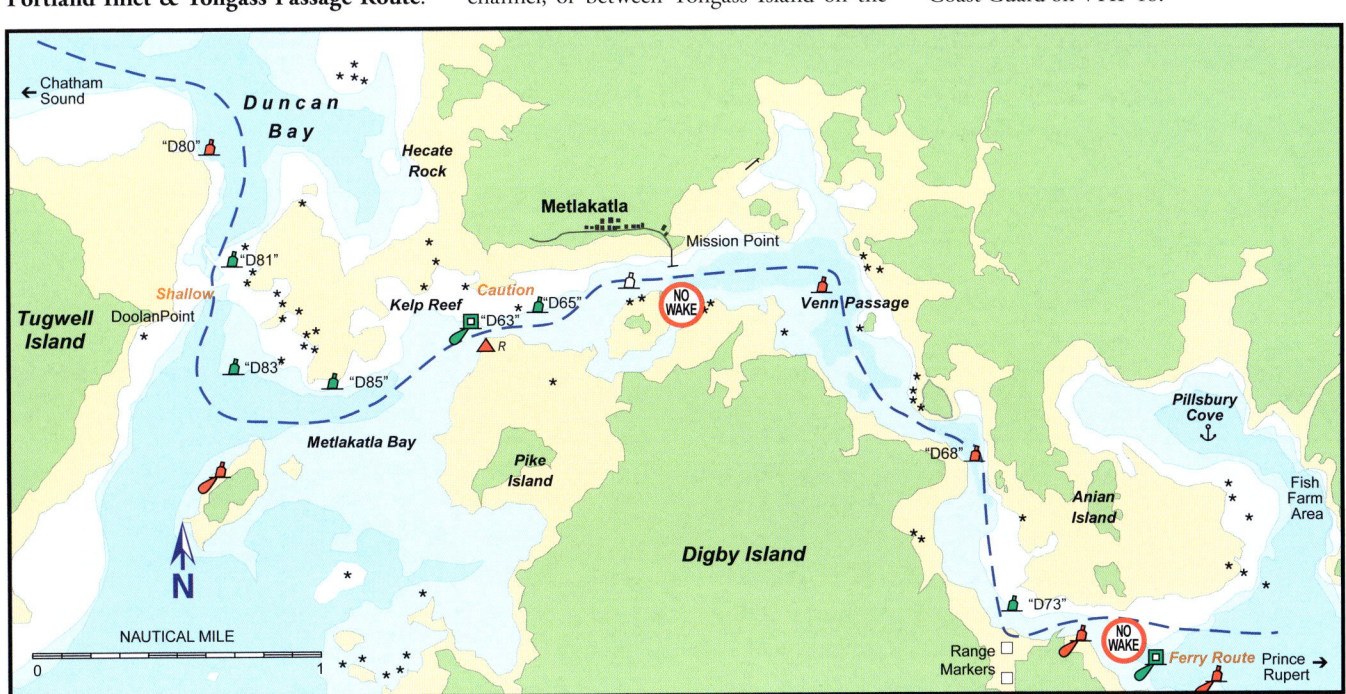

Venn Passage

Southeast Alaska

GLACIERS & PASSAGES
Le Conte • Tracy Arm • Dawes • Marjorie • Grand Pacific
Wrangell Narrows • Rocky Pass • Fords Terror

CLARENCE STRAIT & BEHM CANAL
Ketchikan • Metlakatla • Meyers Chuck • Thorne Bay

JUNEAU, PETERSBURG & WRANGELL
Douglas • Auke Bay • Wrangell Narrows • Anan Bay

LYNN CANAL & ICY STRAIT
Haines • Skagway • Hoonah • Elfin Cove
Glacier Bay National Park • Bartlett Cove

CHATHAM STRAIT & SITKA SOUND
Tenakee Springs • Warm Springs Bay • Red Bluff Bay
Sitka • Peril Strait • Goddard Hot Springs

PRINCE OF WALES ISLAND
Craig • Point Baker • Hydaburg • Port Protection

Scan the Latest Southeast Alaska Information

tinyurl.com/WG22xCh19

*Eldred Rock Lighthouse
Lynn Canal*

Cruising Southeast Alaska. Boaters visit Southeast Alaska each year for the unsurpassed scenery and wildlife. Southeast Alaska offers some of the best opportunities to see black bears and brown bears. Bear observatories, managed by State Parks and the Forest Department, are located at Anan Bay and Pack Creek. It would be unusual not to see bears at these locations during salmon migrations (generally July and August). Bears are often seen at Misty Fjords National Monument, and along the shore in anchorages such as Hanus Bay, Red Bluff Bay, and Sandborn Canal off Stephens Passage, to name a few. Throughout Southeast Alaska, watch for bears foraging along the shoreline and grassy lowlands, turning over rocks looking for their next meal. You're almost assured to see Humpback whales off Point Baker, and will occasionally see whales in other main passages.

Witnessing calving glaciers either from your own boat, or with a local tour operator is a special treat. Tour operators out of Petersburg take visitors to nearby Le Conte Glacier, and tour operators that leave from Juneau provide day trips to Dawes Glacier in Endicott Arm, or to the glaciers in Tracy Arm. The North and South Sawyer Glaciers in Tracy Arm have a limited amount of ice flow, allowing most recreational boaters to get within a reasonable distance to see the calving and deep blue colors of the glacier face. Glacier Bay National Park, located northwest of Juneau off Icy Strait, is considered a highlight of Southeast Alaska and encompasses the Grand Pacific and Margerie Glaciers. Watching and listening to the calving glaciers from the serenity of your own boat is a very special experience. Whether you take your own boat or go with a tour operator, Glacier Bay National Park has much to offer.

Mining played a large part in Southeast Alaska's history and contributed to its growth. Mining sites, ruins, museums and mine tours can be found in Juneau, and visitors will find a rich history of gold prospecting in Haines and Skagway. The fishing industry produced the proliferation of canneries; now fish processing plants dominate the fishing industry, with Petersburg being one of the major commercial fishing communities. Cannery ruins from an earlier time can be found in Taku Harbor, Red Bluff Bay, and elsewhere in Southeast Alaska.

Alaska was occupied by various indigenous peoples thousands of years before the arrival of Europeans. Native culture is evident in all of the Native villages of Southeast Alaska including Hoonah, Kasaan, and Metlakatla. Native culture and historic sites have been preserved in the larger towns as well, such as Ketchikan, Wrangell, Juneau, Haines, and Sitka.

Reference Materials. In addition to having the latest edition of the *Waggoner Cruising Guide*, reference material should include U.S. Coast Pilot 8, published by NOS and NOAA, downloadable from nauticalcharts.noaa.gov. The current edition of Ports and Passes, by Chyna Sea Ventures Ltd., is an important reference for tides and currents, needed to safely transit rapids and narrow passages at times of slack water. *Exploring Southeast Alaska*, Third Edition, by Don Douglass & Reanne Hemingway-Douglass, has detailed descriptions of all the possible anchorages in Southeast Alaska and includes tips for crossing Dixon Entrance. Their "Inside Passage Route Planning Map, North Portion" serves as a convenient reference. Dale Philman's book, *Alaska's Inside Passage – Nature, History, Native Culture and Industries*, is an excellent read.

Time and Distances. The distances in Southeast Alaska are so vast that most pleasure boaters will want to make multiple trips in order to see the many unique sights, towns and villages. Allow enough travel time, with weather contingencies, in addition to time needed to enjoy each destination. The following tables serve as a general guideline for distances and time needed for some of the most popular destinations.

Time Zone Change. Don't forget to set your clocks to Alaska Time, which is one hour earlier than Washington State and British Columbia. Set clocks back one hour when you arrive in Alaska.

Communications. Cell service can be found throughout Southeast Alaska from U.S./Canada border in Dixon Entrance to the northern most towns of Haines, Skagway, and Hoonah. Coverage is not continuous and you will find much of the unpopulated areas without any service. Cell service can be found near and around most towns, both big and small. AT&T, Verizon, T-Mobile, and Sprint have voice, data, and messaging service. Cell phone amplifiers help boost your phone's signal and increase the available service area.

VHF radio service is available through most of Southeast Alaska waters. VHF weather channels can be heard in most areas. However, there are locations in the shadow of transmitters where you will lose VHF signal. The Coast Guard may not always be accessible on Channel 16. Most areas have VHF repeaters to carry VHF signals; however, in recent years, some of the repeaters were in need of maintenance and the Coast Guard reported that they may not be able to establish VHF Channel 16 communication in all locations.

Satellite communication is a good addition when cruising in Southeast Alaska. If you need uninterrupted communication and you plan to cruise in more remote areas, satellite phone, satellite messaging, or satellite internet access should be part of your onboard communications plan. If you don't mind being without messaging capability for a day or two, then you will be fine with cellular communication.

Insurance. Watercraft insurance policies traditionally have a "Navigation Limits" clause on the policy's Declaration Page. Check this clause to ensure that the waters you plan to cruise are covered. It may be necessary to contact your insurance agent to request broader coverage. Cape Caution or 51° North, Dixon Entrance, and Cape Spencer are some common geographic limits found in most policy "Navigation Limits." Also check for calendar date restrictions. Some policies limit coverage north of Cape Caution or 51°North, with specific spring or summer months and dates (for example between May 15th and September 15th). Some policies require a specified number of qualified crew onboard when the vessel is north of Cape Caution or 51° North.

Alaska Pilotage Requirements. Non-U.S. flagged vessels longer than 65 feet must employ an Alaska Marine Pilot when operating in Alaskan waters or apply for and receive an exemption. The State of Alaska offers a downloadable Yacht Navigation Package with useful information; visit www.commerce.alaska.gov.

Fuel. Diesel and gasoline are available at nearly all towns and populated areas. However, the distances between towns requires a boat with longer range capabilities. Ample supply and quality of fuel in SE Alaska has not been a problem. Petro Marine and Delta Western are the two major suppliers/retailers with stations in major towns. Fueling stations are often located in small villages, but it is best to phone ahead to check on availability. A few outlying fueling stations may only carry diesel.

Weather. Southeast Alaska's proximity to the Pacific Ocean waters gives it cool summers and mild winters. Its proximity to the ocean also means plenty of moisture which in the summer, falls as rain. Precipitation amounts vary noticeably with wetter to the south and dryer to the north. Earlier in the summer is better than later. August is the wettest month of the year. Driest months are April, May, and June. May, June, and July are the best months for cruising Southeast Alaska.

Ketchikan gets more than 150 inches of rain each year. Its driest month (July) is wetter than Seattle's wettest month (November). Juneau gets less than half the rainfall as Ketchikan.

Daytime summer temperatures typically range from the high 40s to the mid 60s, but occasionally reach into the 80s. Rain boots, better known as "Alaska Sneakers," are readily available in local stores. Locals swear by the brown XtraTuf brand. However, other boots will do the job.

Charts and Chart Plotters. Survey information used to prepare nautical charts for SE Alaska is often based on old data. Charts therefore may lack detail and are usually small scale. Some of the older survey information may not be GPS accurate. Shoreline contours may be representative but not in the correct

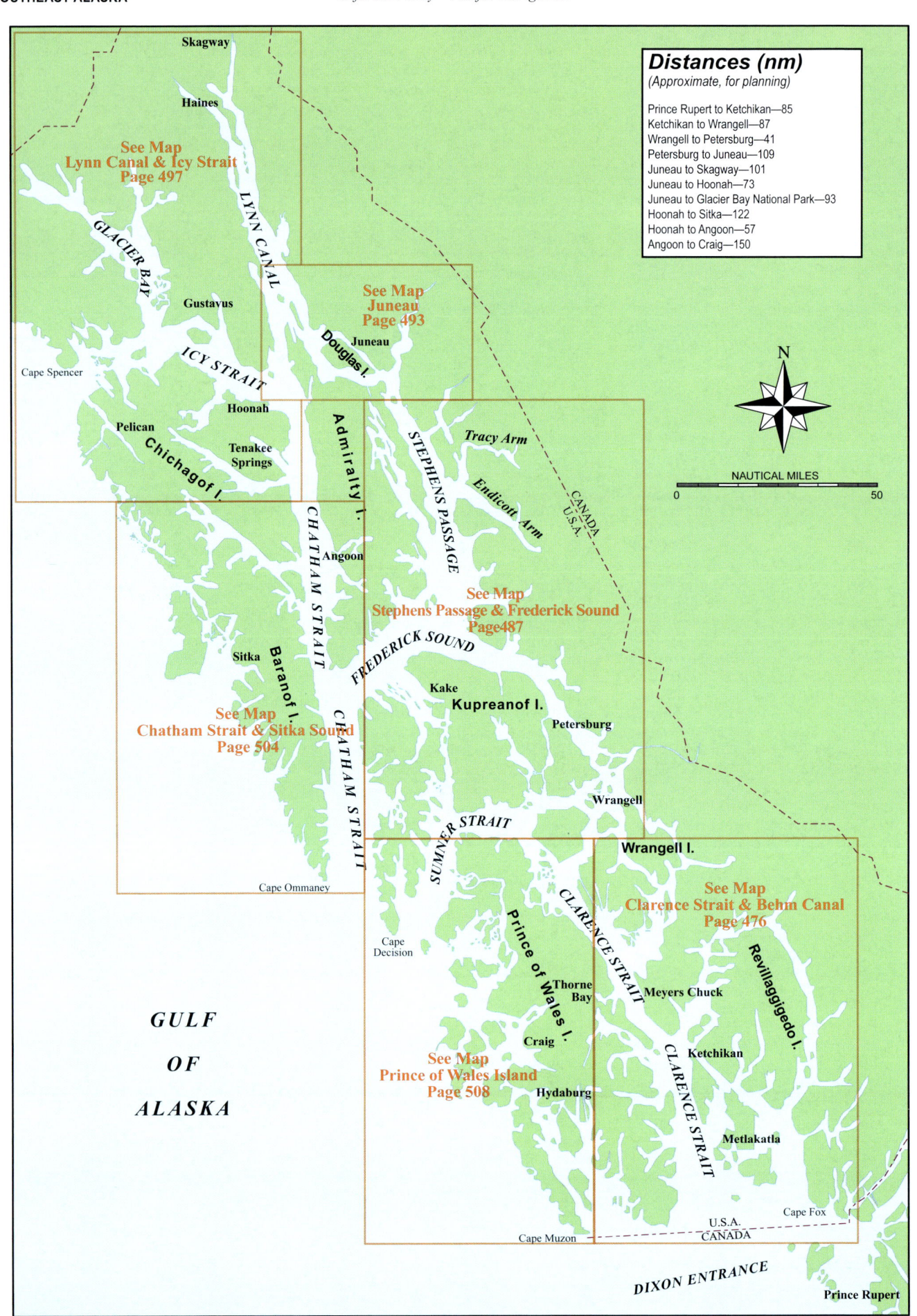

SOUTHEAST ALASKA

Reference Only – Not for Navigation

Distances (nm)
(Approximate, for planning)

Prince Rupert to Ketchikan—85
Ketchikan to Wrangell—87
Wrangell to Petersburg—41
Petersburg to Juneau—109
Juneau to Skagway—101
Juneau to Hoonah—73
Juneau to Glacier Bay National Park—93
Hoonah to Sitka—122
Hoonah to Angoon—57
Angoon to Craig—150

Southeast Alaska

SOUTHEAST ALASKA

See Area Map Page 474 - Maps Not for Navigation

location. As a result, your chartplotter may show your vessel on land instead of in water.

Due to high mountains surrounding waterways, GPS receivers may be receiving GPS signal from fewer satellites than normal, diminishing position accuracy.

Trapline Loop. The waterways of Southeast Alaska form a natural loop, starting in Ketchikan and returning back to Ketchikan, which can be done in either direction. The loop takes you through the main destinations of Wrangell, Petersburg, and Juneau with optional destinations like Haines, Skagway, and Glacier National Park. Side trips include Hoonah, Sitka, and Thorne Bay. We coined the term "trapline" after realizing we saw the same boats and reconnected with friends at each stop along the main route during the summer seasons. The route also affords many opportunities to meet new friends and share cruising adventures. Relatively few pleasure boats cruise Southeast Alaska, with only about 500 to 600 boats each season.

Outfitting for Alaska. While you will most likely have rain on occasion in Southeast Alaska, very warm conditions can occur in June and July; we suggest dressing in layers. Don't forget your raingear and high-topped rubber boots for hiking the trails and for stepping out of the dinghy when going ashore. Be bear aware when hiking – use an airhorn or make noise as you walk; talking loudly is a good thing, and helps scare away any bears that might be in the area. It's a good idea to bring hand-held radios when going ashore for communication; a portable VHF radio for the dinghy; and a SPOT or Garmin InReach device for emergencies. Life jackets and survival gear should always be on the list of needed supplies. When cruising Southeast Alaska, you'll want to have a good pair of binoculars and a camera to capture the fabulous scenery and diverse wildlife.

Experiencing wildlife in the natural setting of Southeast Alaska is truly inspiring.

Cruise Ship Ports. While cruise ships are good for the local economy, the character of these remote destinations temporarily changes when the cruise ships are in town. Thousands of passengers aboard these vessels can affect the local cell system, slowing data rates and sometimes affecting voice calls. Cruise ships usually depart by 4:30 p.m., a good time for recreational boaters to make calls and check weather conditions. Ports visited by cruise ships include: Glacier Bay (2 per day); Juneau (5-6 per day); Skagway (4 per day); Haines (1-2 per day); Ketchikan (4-6 per day); Wrangell (1 per day); Hoonah (2 per week); and Sitka (2 per day).

Alaska's Rich History. Alaska was granted U.S. Statehood in January 1959. In the 1890s gold rushes in Alaska and the nearby Yukon Territory brought thousands of miners and settlers into Alaska. The fishing industry established villages and canneries and then later fish-processing plants. WWII saw the construction of military bases and airports. In the 1960's oil was discovered bringing more jobs and income to Alaskan residents.

It was 1795 when Alexander Baranov, who had been hired to manage Shelikhov's fur enterprise, sailed into Sitka Sound and claimed the area for Russia. Sitka, then called

---

SOUTHEAST ALASKA'S TRAPLINE LOOP

When we were planning our first cruise through Southeast Alaska, we noted that the geography of SE Alaska invited a loop route, beginning and ending in Ketchikan. The major waterways of Clarence Strait, Wrangell Narrows, Frederick Sound, and Stephens Passage take the cruising traveler to Juneau. Lynn Canal, with Haines and Skagway, is the northern-most leg of the loop before turning south back down Lynn Canal to Glacier Bay National Park, another main destination on the loop. From Glacier Bay and Icy Strait the 130 nautical mile long Chatham Strait takes you southbound. Sumner Strait takes the boater around the top of Prince of Wales Island and connects you back to Clarence Strait for the home-stretch back to Ketchikan.

We titled this loop the "Trapline Loop" since we encountered many of the same boaters along the way, traversing the same loop and making the same stops. The loop was a natural progression of stops, and we found ourselves establishing new contacts with fellow adventuresome boaters.

SE Alaska is huge with a world of boating destinations. On our subsequent trips to SE Alaska, we discovered a number of side-trips off this Trapline Loop. After additional cruising seasons in SE Alaska, we ventured beyond the Trapline Loop. Yakutat is technially part of SE Alaska, but a destination very seldom visited by recreational cruisers. As part of an attempt to reach Prince William Sound, we had the opportunity to discover the remoteness and beauty of Yakutat. 130 nautical miles northwest of Glacier Bay, Yakutat is the definition of one of those Beyond the Trapline Loop destinations.

Take time to enjoy the many sights, sounds, and wonders of Southeast Alaska's Trapline Loop and its side-trips that offer years of discovery and adventures that will last a lifetime.

[Lorena and Leonard Landon]

2023 Waggoner Cruising Guide

SOUTHEAST ALASKA

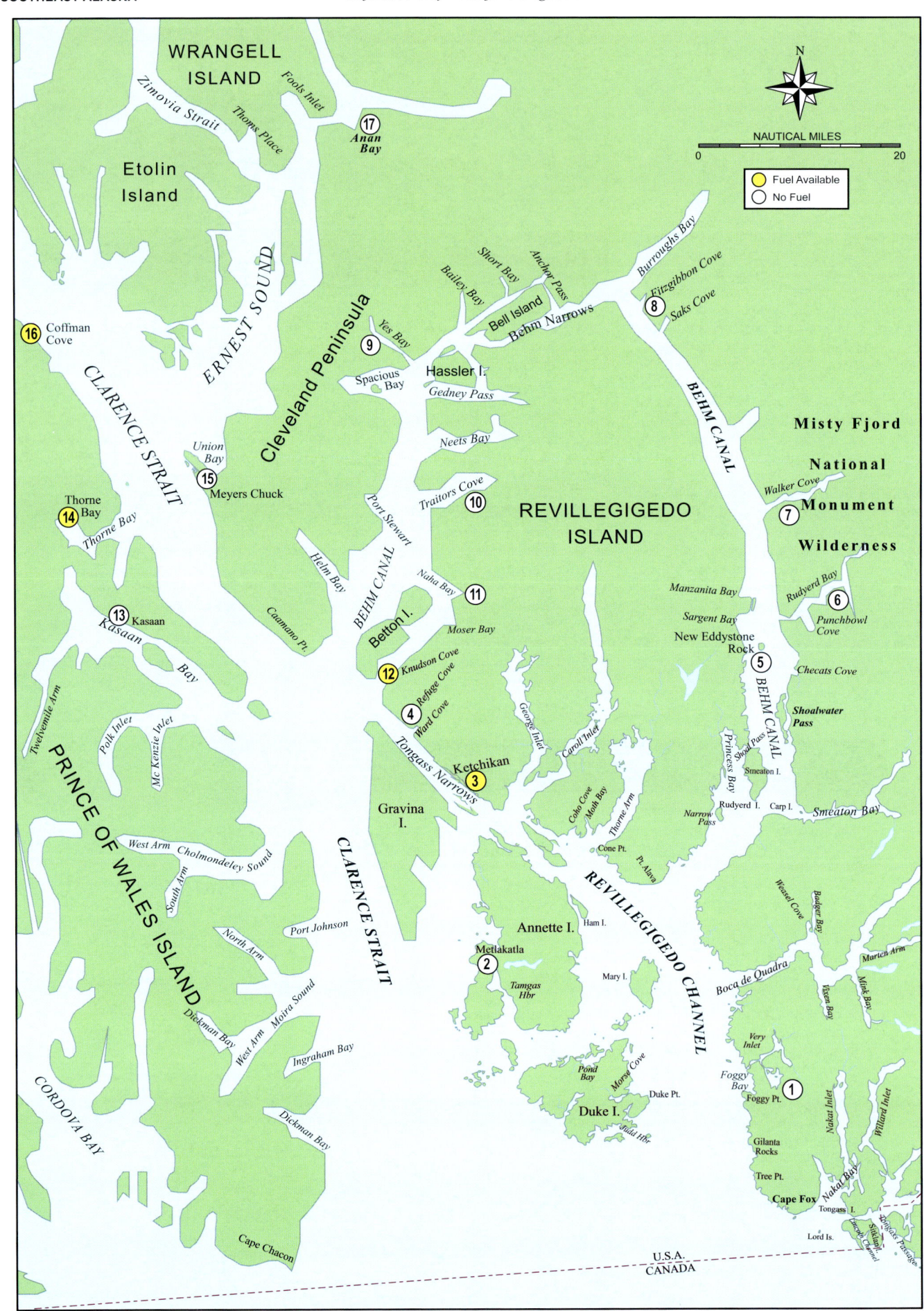

Reference Only – Not for Navigation

Clarence Strait & Behm Canal

Native villages welcome visitors to experience their art and culture.

Native art can be found in many museums.

New Archangel, became the colonial capital of Russia-America. The Russian Orthodox Church was introduced in 1794 and is an enduring legacy in modern-day Alaska. Due to the decline of the sea otter fur trade and Russia's defeat in the Crimean War, Russia offered to sell Alaska to the U.S. in 1859, the U.S. response came later in 1867. When Secretary of State William Seward took up the offer from Russia to purchase Alaska, U.S. citizens called the 7.2 million-dollar purchase "Seward's Folly," but the future proved to be anything but foolish.

Customs Clearance. Vessels entering Alaska from B.C. are required to clear customs in Ketchikan. There are three methods to report arrival to U.S. Customs and Border Protection (CBP). Boaters may use the CBP ROAM App on their Android or iOS mobile phone or tablet to report their arrival. Cellular phone service, which usually begins near Cape Fox, is required in order to use this option. The ROAM App satisfies U.S. CBP requirements to report your arrival. See *U.S. and Canadian Customs Information* for more about CBP ROAM. If all aboard are enrolled in a Trusted Traveler Program such as Nexus, Global Entry, or I-68, then you can report arrival by calling the CBP Small Boat Reporting Office (800) 562-5943 by cellular or satellite phone upon entering U.S. waters in Dixon Entrance. The third option remains, reporting in-person to a CBP Officer upon arrival in Ketchikan by calling Ketchikan CBP at (907) 225-2254.

Vessels are not allowed to drop anchor or land in Alaska until they have reported their arrival and obtained a CBP clearance. With prior approval, Ketchikan CBP typically allows vessels that need more than one day to arrive in Ketchikan for in-person customs clearance to stay one night in Foggy Bay before proceeding to Ketchikan for customs clearance.

The procedure is to call (907) 225-2254 and advise CBP of your plans. It is best to call CBP before departing Prince Rupert. A CBP agent will take all of the necessary information about your vessel and crew. Be ready with your information when you call. The next day when you arrive in Ketchikan, the agent will have this information when he or she comes to your boat. At this point, all they need to do is verify ID. If weather or other unforeseen circumstances cause you to anchor in U.S. territory before reporting to CBP and you can't make telephone contact, hail U.S. Coast Guard on VHF and report your circumstance.

If you will be reporting arrival in-person in Ketchikan and you will be arriving after normal office hours, call ahead. CBP officers do check the marinas to confirm that all vessels have checked in.

You'll pass a fuel dock as you approach Ketchikan. Upon request, and if workload allows, CBP may meet you at the fuel dock for clearance, allowing you to refuel and clear customs at the same time. Call first to see if this is possible.

In our experience, we have found that CBP agents often take a common sense approach to bringing fruits and vegetables into Alaska. They may request that you commit to consuming the items. Declare all items.

Non-U.S. flagged vessels that don't already have a Cruising License (including Canadian vessels), may request a Cruising License upon clearing customs; a Cruising License reduces the cost and complexity for foreign-flagged vessels. See the *Cruising License* topic in the *U.S. and Canadian Customs Information* in the Compendium chapter. Cruising Licenses do not affect customs reporting requirements.

Note: U.S. flagged vessels that have departed from a U.S. port without stopping or clearing Canada customs do not need to clear customs in Ketchikan.

Hot-Berth Moorage. Marinas throughout Southeast Alaska use a system of hot berthing moorage slips to accommodate guest boats. Permanently assigned slips are temporarily assigned to visiting boats when the permanent tenant is away from their slip. The marina's harbormaster coordinates all hot berthing activity.

Permanent slip tenants notify the Harbormaster of dates when their slip will be unused. The Harbormaster then matches these unused dates with guest boater requests.

Visiting boats are hot-berthed into one of these slips when the local boat is gone. Most marinas do not take advance reservations. Things change by the hour; the office will work with you to find moorage. For many first-time visitors, especially with larger boats, not having a reservation is disconcerting. The staff works hard to fit everyone in.

For a slip assignment, harbor staffers are often on the docks checking the status of slips matching visiting boaters' planned stays with permanent tenant vacancies. Sometimes, though, a permanent tenant returns to their slip sooner than planned. If this happens, the office will re-assign the visiting boat to a new slip and you must be available to move your boat. The Harbormaster's office will contact you with instructions to move to another slip, sometimes between marinas.

When your crew goes out touring or shopping, they could come back to find the boat has moved to a new moorage. It helps to have a communication plan in case things change.

Shore power may not be available at all hot-berthed slips. Specify your power requirements when requesting a slip. Most shore power hookups, whether locked or not, are privately owned by the permanent tenant; do not plug into power without permission from the Harbormaster. There is a separate charge for shore power.

① **Foggy Bay.** Foggy Bay is a well-protected stopping place between Prince Rupert and Ketchikan. For those headed north, it can provide an escape from rough conditions in Dixon Entrance. Headed south, it is a good overnight anchorage to shorten the leg to Prince Rupert and allows for an early morning departure to cross Dixon Entrance. Most boats anchor in the "inner cove," which provides a view of the conditions in Foggy Bay and Dixon Entrance. Uncharted rock awash reported at 54º 57.518'N, 130º 57.280' W. If you want privacy in a remote environment, cruise deep into Very Inlet to the "north basin." Use the Douglass' *Exploring Southeast Alaska* for detailed information on the anchorage in Foggy Bay and other interesting anchorages in the area.

Foggy Bay or Mary Island to Ketchikan. This route appears to be a straight shot up Revillagigedo Channel to Ketchikan, although weather conditions can vary from one side of the channel to the other. You might also encounter changing conditions as you pass Behm Canal, Thorne Arm or other inlets, depending on the wind direction and speed. Expect to see more recreational vessels, fish boats, tugs with tows and even large cruise ships maneuvering in Tongass Narrows as you approach Ketchikan.

Note the location of Behm Canal as you pass. Later in the trip you might want to visit some of the majestic cruising areas in Misty Fjords.

Danger Pass. At the south end of Mary Island and off Edge Point, this narrow passage will allow you to move out of the main channel and along the back side of Mary Island. Depending on the wind direction, this route allows you to travel in the lee of Mary Island.

② **Metlakatla.** The city of Metlakatla is located on the west side of Annette Island off Nichols Passage. The community is primarily of Tsimshian lineage and is governed by the Metlakatla Tribal Council. Metlakatla, meaning saltwater passage, takes its name from another village of the same name in British Columbia on Metlakatla Passage near Prince Rupert. In 1886, Anglican Missionary William Duncan had a doctrinal difference of opinion with the church authorities in Metlakatla, BC. He and a devoted group of 823 Tsimshian followers departed in canoes for Annette Island to establish a new Metlakatla. U.S. President Cleveland had granted them rights to Annette Island. The book, *Challenge the Wilderness*, by George Tomlinson (a descendent of Robert Tomlinson who worked with Duncan), includes first-hand accounts of missionary work of the time, travels in the rugged Northwest, relationships with the natives, and the history of the two Metlakatla villages. The book is an insight to the challenges of the time and includes historic photos.

Today, Metlakatla remains the only Indian Reserve in Alaska. The community is friendly and welcoming. Visit the Duncan Cottage Museum located at 501 Tait Street, open 8:30 a.m. to 12:30 p.m., Monday through Friday during the summer months. Private showings available by calling the museum at (907) 886-3637. Naomi Leask is the Museum Curator. Duncan Cottage is listed on the National Register of Historic Places. The Longhouse, located upland from the harbor docks, is the place where dances, potlatches, and other events are held. Boaters can join the scheduled In-Town Tours by calling Raena Janes at (907) 886-8687; a nominal fee is charged for the tour.

② **Metlakatla Harbor.** (907) 886-4441 or (907) 886-4646 Harbormaster; info@visitmetlakatla.com; www.visitmetlakatla.com. Upon arrival, check-in with the Harbormaster (Carleto) at the red shack above the docks (open 8:00 a.m. to 4:00 p.m., Monday-Friday); space is limited. He will take your information and provide the cost for moorage. Moorage fees are paid at the Council Chamber. All visitors to Annette Islands Reserve must report in person at the Council Chamber within 2 hours of arrival (907-886-4441) to receive a Visitor's Permit and to pay moorage. The Office is located at Upper Milton & 8th Avenue, open 8:00 a.m. to 4:30 p.m., Monday through Friday. 20, 30, and 50 amp power available at the docks; no water. Transient side-tie space and slip moorage on a first-come, first-serve basis; possible to call ahead regarding available space.

③ **Ketchikan.** Tongass Narrows is the transition from crossing Dixon Entrance to arrival in a bustling maritime city. The transition begins at Mountain Point, and the closer you get to the city, the more signs of humanity you see. Overhead, floatplanes take summer tourists to Misty Fjords and other sites. The shoreline changes from remote and pristine to a few homes, then a few more, and eventually a developed roadway. Soon, cars are whizzing by. Off in the distance, up Tongass Narrows, the shapes of what seems to be a major city appear. In reality, they are the profiles of cruise ships lined up at the docks, towering 10 stories high, dwarfing the buildings below.

We enjoy visiting Ketchikan. Shopping is good. Several restaurants serve excellent food. The airport is convenient for exchanging crew or flying home. Boat repairs can be arranged, although the local mechanics cater mostly to the fishing fleet. The Fourth of July parade and fireworks are a favorite.

Cruise ships frequent Ketchikan. Three to five cruise ships are typically moored in Ketchikan during the day, with passengers touring the city, shopping, or just hanging out and absorbing their first (or last) stop in Alaska. You may encounter one of the cruise ships headed towards you, an imposing sight. Remember that federal law requires boats stay at least 100 yards from cruise ships. Occasionally the Coast Guard will escort cruise ships in and out of town and require 200 yards of separation. Listen to VHF channel 16 or 13 for Securité calls from cruise ships (and other commercial ships) as they prepare to get underway, and be prepared to alter course to maintain adequate separation.

Ketchikan calls itself "Alaska's First City"—the first city visitors see when they arrive in Southeast Alaska by boat. The cruise ships typically arrive early in the morning and depart by mid-afternoon or early evening. During the day the town can be bursting with 10,000 visitors if several cruise ships are docked. When the ships leave, usually in late afternoon or early evening, the tourist shops close and Ketchikan returns to a sleepy little Alaskan town.

Ketchikan has three public marinas and three private marinas for transient moorage, each with its own advantages, disadvantages, and personality.

A Walmart north of town runs a free shuttle between their store and the cruise ship docks. Ketchikan has several options for provisioning and picking up parts and marine hardware.

Ketchikan also has a number of local attractions and museums, including the Totem Heritage Center, the Southeast Alaska Discovery Center, and the Tongass Historical Museum. All are within walking distance of the marinas. Totem Bight State Park and Saxman Native Village are accessible by bus. The buses run every 30-45 minutes. The Gateway Aquatic Center at 601 Schoenbar Road has a nice pool, lap pool, water slides and fountains.

Ketchikan has a good public bus system, the Ketchikan Gateway Borough Bus, that shuttles passengers to the main attractions, or from the airport ferry to downtown. Individual rides are $2; a day pass is $5, please have exact change. The bus also runs to several places you may want to visit, such as Totem Bight State Park, Saxman Native Village, and additional shopping farther from the waterfront. Taxis are also available, though they seem to use "cruise ship flat rate pricing" to some destinations. The bus is convenient and low cost, with stops near the three marinas. Schedules are posted at bus stops.

Ketchikan Airport. The Ketchikan Airport is convenient for visitors and crew. Alaska Airlines and Delta Airlines each have several daily flights to Seattle. The airport is located across Tongass Narrows on Gravina Island, and connects with Ketchikan by a ferry that departs and arrives just north of Bar Harbor Marina. The ferry leaves the airport terminal on the hour and half-hour,

Metlakatla, Alaska is home to an active tribal village on Annette Island.

See Area Map Page 476 - Maps Not for Navigation

SOUTHEAST ALASKA

daily. The ferry leaves the Ketchikan side on the quarter hours. Crossing time is approximately 10 minutes. If flying out, allow time for the ferry schedule and walk to the airport.

Stairs and ramps connect the airport terminal with the ferry. If you have considerable luggage, it's best to take an airport shuttle van that will deliver you and your luggage door-to-door. On the airport side of the narrows and north of the ferry terminal, a small public float located below the covered stairway, is available for short-term stays. Dinghies and boats under 40 feet can tie-up to drop off or pick up guests and luggage. The modest short-term moorage fee is paid in an honor box on the dock. Do not tie to the floatplane dock immediately north.

Mail and Shipments: Marinas normally will not accept mail or packages for guest or transient boaters. If you need to have mail or packages shipped to you, Ketchikan's Frontier Shipping & Copyworks (907-247-2705) will accept and hold your mail and packages for a nominal fee. Your items will be waiting for you at their store location in the Ketchikan Plaza mall next to the Safeway near Bar Harbor. It's best to call ahead and make arrangements.

Fuel: Diesel, gasoline, and propane are available at two Petro Marine locations - one located south of town near the Coast Guard Station and the other north of town near the airport ferry landing.

Moorage: City of Ketchikan manages three marinas in Ketchikan, Thomas Basin, Bar Harbor, and Casey Moran. Harbormaster assigned hot-berth slips are located in Thomas Basin and Bar Harbor Basins.

Refuge Cove Marina, near Ward Cove, north of town has guest moorage and accepts advance reservations. Two more private marinas, Doyon's Landing and Ketchikan Moorage (Ellis Floats), cater primarily to larger yachts with limited moorage for other boats.

Ketchikan Yacht Club is on float 2 in City of Ketchikan's Thomas Basin and has some transient (no reciprocal) moorage available. The members are friendly, helpful, and a good source of local knowledge.

Provisions: Safeway is located south of Bar Harbor South, A&P Market is located north of Bar Harbor North; liquor stores are near both grocery stores; A&P Market has a large Costco Kirkland brands section, and a Walmart is located 2 miles north of town.

Speed Limit: A 7-knot speed limit for vessels over 23 feet extends from Buoy 9 in the north to the East and West Channel regulatory markers on Tongass Narrows.

③ **City of Ketchikan Harbors.** The city's Port & Harbors department manages five marinas in and around Ketchikan. Thomas Basin, Bar Harbor, and Casey Moran are along the Ketchikan waterfront. Knudson Cove is about 12 miles north of town, and Hole-In-The-Wall is about 8 miles south. Thomas Basin and Bar Harbor basins have permanently assigned slips where visiting boats are hot-berthed into one of these permanently assigned slips when the local boat is gone. First-come, first-served open moorage can be found at Casey Moran, and in designated areas of Thomas Basin, Bar Harbor Basins, Knudson Cove, and Hole-In-The-Wall.

The City Port & Harbors office does not take reservations. Things change by the hour; the office works to find a hot-berthing moorage. For some visitors, especially with larger boats, not having a reservation is disconcerting. The harbor staff is good at fitting everyone in. For a slip assignment, call "Ketchikan Harbormaster" on VHF 73 (preferred), or phone (907) 228-5632. Harbormasters are on duty 7-days a week 6:00 a.m. to 10:00 p.m. May through September, and 8:00 a.m. to 5:00 p.m. October through April. The office is open 8:00 a.m. to 5:00 p.m. 7-days a week during summer months and Monday through Friday during winter. For moorage at one of the first-come, first-served areas, take an unoccupied space and then register and pay at the office. See maps in this section or www.ktn-ak.us/harbors for designated open moorage. There are limited options for unattended long-term moorage in Ketchikan.

All vessels must register with the

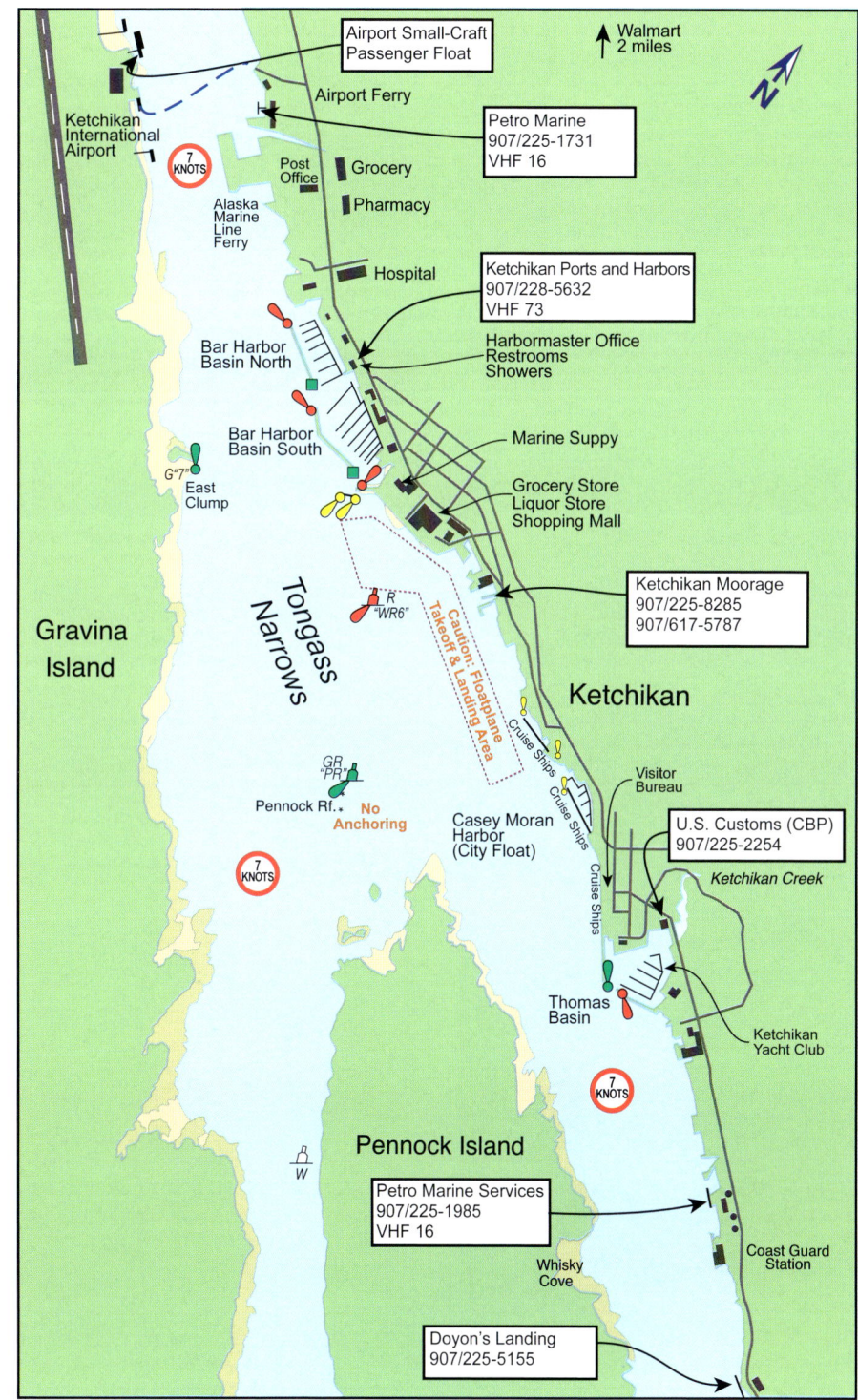

Tongass Narrows

2023 Waggoner Cruising Guide 479

SOUTHEAST ALASKA

See Area Map Page 476 - Maps Not for Navigation

A view of Ketchikan's waterfront when cruiseships are gone

Thomas Basin is within walking distance of Creek Street.

Harbormaster's office at Bar Harbor North (2933 Tongass Ave) by visiting the office or by phone; or by emailing an electronically completed registration form to the email address indicated on the form which can be downloaded from the City website at www.ktn-ak.us/harbors. It is recommended that you pre-register your information on the Harbor's website in advance of your arrival, which helps facilitate a quicker check-in. Moorage fees are paid by calling the harbor office with credit card information, or in person at the harbor office with credit card, cash, or check.

Shore power may not be available at all hot-berthed slips. Specify your power requirements when requesting a slip at Thomas Basin or Bar Harbor basins. Most shore power hookups, whether locked or not, are privately owned by the permanent tenant; do not plug into power without permission from the Harbormaster. At Casey Moran, all shore power hookups are available for use. In Thomas Basin and Bar Harbor basins, power hookups marked with a red "HP" (Harbor Power) sticker near the electric meter face are available for use. There is a separate charge for shore power. Shore power has been upgraded to ELCI-protected circuits at Thomas Basin and floats 8, 9, 10, and 11 at Bar Harbor.

Thomas Basin, the first major marina you'll see when approaching from the south, is at the foot of Creek Street in the heart of the tourist district. It's an easy walk to local shops and attractions.

Casey Moran Harbor, formerly known as (and still often called) "City Floats," is next. It's small and in the middle of downtown, right in the shadow of the cruise ships. Moorage is first-come, first-served anywhere with unpainted bull rails.

Bar Harbor North and South are about a mile north of the center of Ketchikan. A Safeway, shopping mall, and chandlery are a short walk away.

LOCAL KNOWLEDGE

TONGASS NARROWS. A large volume of traffic comes in and out of Ketchikan and transits through the quarter-mile wide Tongass Narrows. At its narrowest point, less than a 1,000 feet wide, watch for traffic that's everything from dinghies and recreational vessels, to ferries, tugs with barges, and mega-cruise ships transiting north and south.

Up to 7 cruise ships arrive and depart Ketchikan on a daily basis and pass through Tongass Narrows. Cruise ships routinely announce their arrival and departure on VHF 16 and 13.

There are two designated cruise ship anchorages located on the Tongass Narrows north of Pennock Island. Also take note of the floatplane landing area off downtown Ketchikan and another off the airport floatplane dock.

③ **Thomas Basin - Ketchikan Harbors.** (907) 228-5632; www.city.ketchikan.ak.us. Monitors VHF 73. Located at the foot of Creek Street, with moorage for boats to 60 feet, call ahead for a slip assignment, or find an unoccupied space in first-come, first-served areas. Water, pumpout, garbage and waste oil disposal, tidal grid to 100 tons (reservations required for grid). Power varies from slip to slip, check with the harbor office and inform them of power requirements when requesting a slip. All power is ELCI-protected. A hot berth system is maintained. You may be asked to move if the owner of a slip returns sooner than scheduled. Restaurants, shops, and bars nearby. Many attractions within walking distance. Local bus and taxi available on nearby Steadman Street. This area was called Indian Town in earlier times.

③ **Casey Moran - Ketchikan Harbors.** (907) 228-5632; www.city.ketchikan.ak.us. Monitors VHF 73. First-come, first-served moorage for boats to 90 feet, 30 & 50 amp power, water, garbage drop, pumpout, and waste oil disposal. White bull rails designate loading, blue designates handicap access. Unpainted bull rails show open moorage area, rafting is allowed. Close to all downtown attractions and in the shadow of cruise ships during the day. Restaurants, bars, and marine supplies nearby. Bus and taxi service are on the busy street above the marina.

③ **Bar Harbor North and South - Ketchikan Harbors.** (907) 228-5632; www.city.ketchikan.ak.us. Monitors VHF 73A. First-come, first-served moorage available on the ends of floats 3 - 5; 9 - 15; and the north side of float 7. All other slips reserved. Do not moor in a slip without

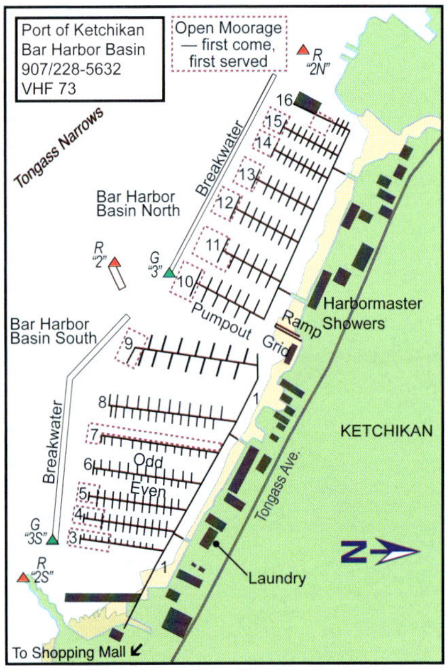

Port of Ketchikan, Bar Harbor Basin

Port of Ketchikan, Thomas Basin

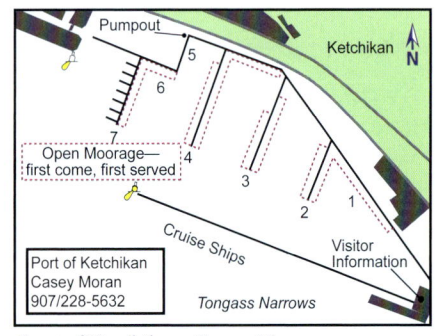

Port of Ketchikan, Casey Moran

authorization from Harbormaster. Limited power (some of the docks are old). Power on docks 8 through 11 have been upgraded to ELCI-protected. Pumpout, water, restrooms, coin operated showers, garbage and waste oil disposal at the head of the dock. Tidal grid available by reservation. Restaurants, groceries, laundry, chandlery and shopping mall nearby. The marina is walking distance to the Alaska Marine Highway ferry terminal and the local ferry to the airport. The downtown area is about a 1.5 mile walk. Bus and taxi service available. The harbor office, with restrooms and showers, is in the green building between the north and south areas of the harbor.

③ **Ketchikan Yacht Club.** Clubhouse phone (907) 225-3262 relays the Port Captain's number; info@ketchikanyachtclub.com; ketchikanyachtclub.org/blog. On float 2 in Thomas Basin, with guest moorage when a member's slip is not being used. Pick an empty slip that fits your boat and check the whiteboard at the head of the slip for the return date of the slip holder. South side: boats 36-45 feet. North side: boats 24-39 feet. Slips cannot be reserved. Moorage is paid in the honor box at the clubhouse. Power is 30 & limited 50 amp. A keycode to the clubhouse is available for guest boats. The clubhouse has Wi-Fi, restrooms, showers, laundry, kitchen, barbecue and social area. Guests are welcome to use the facility.

③ **Doyon's Landing.** 1716 South Tongass Highway, Ketchikan, AK 99901; (907) 225-5155; moorage@mistyfjords.com; www.doyonslanding.com. No VHF. Open May through September. 50 and 100 amp power, water, 24-hour security, internet; no showers or laundry. Call for reservations. This marina caters to large yachts. Located south of town near the Coast Guard station.

③ **Petro Marine Services.** 1100 Stedman St., P.O. Box 7398, Ketchikan, 99901; (800) 478-7277; (907) 225-2106; www.petromarineservices.com. Monitors VHF 16. Located on Tongass Narrows next to the U.S. Coast Guard station (buildings with red roofs). In summer, open 7 days a week from 7:00 a.m. to 7:00 p.m. In winter, Monday through Saturday, 8:00 a.m. to 5:00 p.m. and Sunday 9:00 a.m. to 5:00 p.m. Gasoline, diesel, propane, lubricants, and waste oil disposal. Restrooms, showers, and garbage.

③ **Ketchikan Moorage** (Ellis Floats). (907) 225-8285, or (907) 617-5787; info@ketchikanmoorage.com; www.ketchikanmoorage.com. No VHF. Open May through September. Moorage for boats to 170 feet, 30, 50 & 100 amp (single and 3-phase) power, water, garbage drop, free Wi-Fi and secure gate; no showers or laundry. Reservations encouraged. This marina caters to larger yachts with a limited number of slips. Located north of Casey Moran and south of Bar Harbor.

③ **Petro Marine Services.** 4161 Tongass Avenue, Ketchikan, AK 99901; (907) 225-1731. Located on Tongass Narrows just south of the airport ferry. Gasoline, diesel, and lubricants. In summer, staffed 7 days a week, 7:00 a.m. to 7:00 p.m. In winter, Monday through Friday, 8:00 a.m. to 5:00 p.m.

③ **Airport Small-Craft Passenger Float.** An 80-foot-long float located north of the Ketchikan airport terminal is available for boats up to 40 feet for stays of up to 4 hours to drop-off and pick-up flight passengers. The float is attached to the southwest end of the large floatplane dock. A self-payment box is located at the end of the float where a ramp and short pathway lead to the terminal building. Do not tie to the floatplane dock.

④ **Refuge Cove Marina.** 8119 N Tongass Hwy Ketchikan, AK 99901; (907) 225-1958 or (907) 617-2829 cell; ntms@kpunet.net. A small private marina located 8 miles north of Ketchikan. Ample side-tie transient moorage (140-foot dock and a 210-foot dock); 30-amp power; water-rain catch. No showers, no laundry. Trails and bus stop nearby. Call or email for reservations. Sabrina (Brea) Macauley is the manager. Ask about the complimentary use of a vehicle. It may be a U-Haul truck since they also operate a U-Haul rental business. Air Marine Harbor, a do-it-yourself boatyard with marine service vendors, is located next door (907-225-2282); outdoor and covered storage. Beautiful Totem Bight State Park is a mile to the north.

Doyon's Landing has moorage for large vessels.

THINGS TO DO

- **Totem Heritage Center.** Located Northeast of Thomas Basin and within walking distance. Museum displays of historic totems from the 1800's of the Tlingit, Tsimshian, and Haida.
- **Saxman Native Village and Totem Bight State Park.** A glimpse into the traditions of the Tlingit culture. Both locations can be reached by bus. Saxman has tours and ceremonial dances; Totem Bight Park has 14 poles and a Longhouse, no charge.
- **Southeast Alaska Discovery Center.** Located just above Thomas Basin. This National Park Service museum includes exhibits and interactive displays about the land, people, and culture of Southeast Alaska.
- **Creek Street.** Just above Thomas Basin. Specialty shops and galleries; boardwalk over the creek with a sordid past.
- **Tongass Historical Museum.** Located at the top of Creek Street. This is the town museum; small and well done, covering the history of Ketchikan.
- **Cannery Tour.** Contact Allen Marine Tours (907-225-8100) for a seafood tasting tour and visit to Historic Libby Cannery on George Inlet. Tours not available by private boat.
- **Floatplane to Misty Fjords.** A number of operators along the waterfront offer breathtaking tours of Behm Canal and Misty Fjords. Tip: Ask for the "local rate."
- **Tongass Trading Company.** Above the Casey Moran Floats, this large store has souvenirs and gifts. The second floor has a good selection of outdoor clothing and boots.
- **Local Area Trails.** Pick up a trail map at the Ketchikan Ranger Station.
- **Aquatic Center.** Take a swim at the Gateway Recreation Center about 1/2 mile from downtown with its indoor swimming pool.

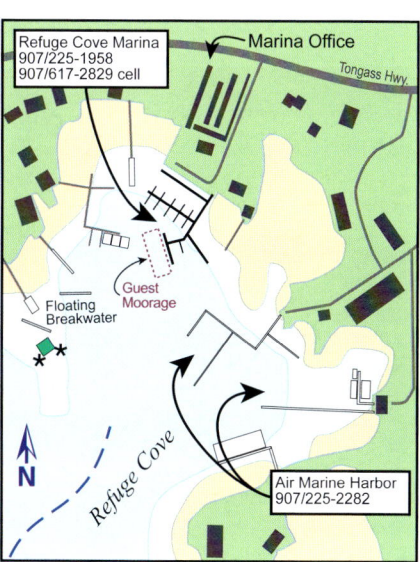

Refuge Cove

SOUTHEAST ALASKA

NATURE'S CATHEDRAL - MISTY FJORDS

Visiting Walker Cove, Rudyerd Bay, and Punchbowl Cove, located on the eastern side of Behm Canal, is like stepping into a grand cathedral of nature's making. Intricate waterways lead through steep-sided granite walls with cirques, bowls, and spires. Waterfalls roll down vertical faces from snow fields high above, and rich estuaries deposited by rivers provide grasslands for bears and other wildlife. Passing through this incredible place is like a religious experience; one feels small and insignificant, yet a sense of belonging feeds the soul, as if part of the grandeur of nature's creation. Photos cannot capture the scale and grandeur of the fjords.

The Misty Fjords area is part of an immense National Monument administered by the U.S. Forest Service, and is the largest wilderness in Alaska's national forest. This National Monument includes both sides of the eastern arm of Behm Canal, from Revillagigedo Channel to Behm Narrows. While mist hangs around the mountain tops and through the valleys, it usually clears later in the day – always misty, always impressive.

Steep mountain faces and deep water means limited opportunities for anchorage. There is one mooring buoy in Punchbowl Cove and one mooring buoy in Walker Cove, along with a couple spots to anchor, best done with a stern-tie. We have named the anchorage bight in Walker Cove, Champagne Bight, for the unusual phenomenon seen at high tide levels, when a field of tiny bubbles rise from fissures in the shallow seabed. Look for the field of air bubbles a few yards from the creek entrance. You are likely to see bears foraging in the grasslands in the early evenings at both Walker Cove and Punchbowl Cove. While exploring inside the fjord area, keep in mind that VHF reception is very limited, including continuous broadcast weather.

Some thoughtful planning is required when making the 100-mile circuit around Behm Canal from Ketchikan. Most boats go counterclockwise when cruising the Behm Canal loop. Shoalwater Pass is a logical stop and offers anchorage for a number of boats, is well protected, and has good holding. A buoy close to shore is usable for smaller boats. Beautiful Manzanita Bay, with a large delta area, has appropriate anchoring depths in a couple of spots. Continuing around the loop, anchorage for several boats can be found in lovely Fitzgibbon Cove, offering nooks and beaches to explore by dinghy. Farther west is a mooring buoy just inside Anchor Pass. Next is Yes Bay, with several cozy anchorage locations in a pretty setting on the northwest side of Behm Canal.

Visiting Misty Fjords National Monument is very doable with a little advance planning. Behm Canal itself may seem rather average with no hint of what lies inside the fjords. Once you enter nature's hidden cathedral off the main Behm Canal loop, be prepared to be inspired and awe struck.

[Lorena Landon]

LOCAL KNOWLEDGE

RESTRICTED AREA: Caution for the restricted area (334.1275) on the west side of Behm Canal; see Coast Pilot 8.

Behm Canal. Pronounced "beam canal," this side loop is an excellent one-week trip for guests flying in or out of Ketchikan. The canal circles around Revillagigedo Island and can be taken in either direction from Ketchikan. Anchorages along the 130 nautical-mile loop include Shoalwater Pass, Yes Bay, and Naha Bay, with a trail at Roosevelt Lagoon. Don't miss visiting Misty Fjords, an inlet along the east side of Behm Canal, offering scenic, towering granite cliffs, waterfalls, and cirques.

New Eddystone Rock is a dramatic 230-foot high feature in Misty Fjords near the entrance to Rudyerd Bay. Rudyerd Bay, with Punchbowl Cove, is one of the main scenic attractions of Misty Fjords.

Misty Fjords National Monument. Misty Fjords is part of an immense National Monument administered by the U.S. Forest Service, lying 22 miles east of Ketchikan. The Misty Fjords National Monument Wilderness is the largest wilderness in Alaska's national forest, encompassing 2.3 million acres across Tongass National Forest, of which Misty Fjords is one piece set aside for visitors. The Monument encompasses all of the uplands on both sides of the eastern arm of the Behm Canal, from Revillagigedo Channel to Behm Narrows. The preserve's most picturesque areas include Walker Cove, Rudyerd Bay and Punchbowl Cove, which offer dramatic waterfalls, granite bowls, and sheer vertical cliffs that rise 3,000 feet above the sea. A permit is not required for recreational boating or land activities in Misty Fjords National Monument. The 100-mile Behm Canal that cuts into the Monument and circles Revillagigedo Island, offers the perfect side trip for boaters based out of Ketchikan.

Misty Fjords is aptly named due to the constant precipitation causing a mist that evokes an eerie, mystical aura. You will likely see brown bear, black bear, and a variety of birds in addition to whales and other sea life. The deep-water depths of the Behm Canal make anchoring a challenge. Shoalwater Pass is one area that provides protection and offers good anchorage just south of the Forest Service cabin. Checats Cove, located farther north, offers good holding and protection in southerly winds behind Checats Point.

www.WaggonerGuide.com

See Area Map Page 476 - Maps Not for Navigation

SOUTHEAST ALASKA

Views of the iconic New Eddystone Rock, the 230-foot landmark jutting up from the sea bottom, can be seen from Checats Cove. If you go ashore from any anchorage, no more than 12 persons are permitted at a time in one location within the Misty Fjords National Monument Wilderness.

The U.S. Forest Service has a number of cabins for rent. Some of these cabins include mooring buoys for permitted cabin renters. Other mooring buoys near cabins are available on a first-come, first-serve basis, including the one in Alava Bay (western shore), the one in Anchor Pass east of Bell Island, and two in Shoalwater Pass. Mooring buoys without cabins that are open to the public are found at the head of Punchbowl Cove, and in Walker Cove midway along the south shore.

Shoalwater Pass. Nearly 4 miles long, located behind Winstanley Island on the east shore of Behm Canal. A scenic restful setting. The pass has three narrow and shallow necks that are passable at high water. The south neck is deeper than charted, favor the east shore where you should find least depths of 40 feet. Favor the west shore along Winstanley Island at the middle neck where depths are as charted. At the north entrance, depths at the shallow part are less than charted, pass on mid to high tide.

There are two mooring buoys on Shoalwater Pass. One charted mooring buoy is located off a grassy flat on the east shore at the south entrance, open to southerly winds. The other mooring buoy is located on Winstanley Island near the north entrance. A Forest Service rental cabin is just upland from the buoy. Well-protected anchorage at the north entrance can be found in 40 to 50 feet near the islet; holding is good over a mud bottom. Crabbing is excellent. Grassy flats are found throughout Shoalwater Pass where bears are often seen foraging.

⑤ **New Eddystone Rock.** Located southeast of Revillegigedo Island in the eastern arm of Behm Canal is the much-photographed New Eddystone Rock landmark. This rock is actually the neck of an undersea volcano that erupted about 15,000 years ago. The dense, spire-shaped volcanic plug, eroded by time, stands 237 feet above the sea. Captain George Vancouver documented seeing this amazing pillar of basalt in his journal notes of 1793, and named the rock after a lighthouse near Plymouth, England. When approaching this unusual landmark, take note of the charted rocks and shoals surrounding New Eddystone Rock.

⑥ **Rudyerd Bay and Punchbowl Cove.** The sculptured fjord inlet of Rudyerd Bay, which includes Punchbowl Cove, is considered the highlight of the Misty Fjords National Monument. Rudyerd Bay stretches eastward for 11 miles, with a north and south arm, sporting steep granite walls, bowls, waterfalls, and estuaries. Grizzly bears are often seen in the upper arm of Rudyerd Bay. The waters of Rudyerd are too deep for convenient overnight anchorage, except for Punchbowl Cove near the entrance of Rudyerd Bay.

The majestic granite wall at Punchbowl Cove is one of the most dramatic sights of Misty Fjords. The 3,000-foot granite face is located on the east side of the cove. A mooring buoy is located at the south end, where a trail leads from the southeast corner to Punchbowl Lake.

Anchorage is possible near the mooring buoy. The one-mile trail begins on an easy-grade boardwalk, then becomes quite steep with many switchbacks. About half-way along, the trail branches to an overlook with views of a beautiful waterfall. A three-sided shelter and an outhouse are located at the Lake.

Manzanita Bay. Located north of New Eddystone Rock on the eastern shore of Revillegigedo Island. Manzanita Bay is home to an extensive river delta, where eagles hunt for prey, and grizzlies may be seen on occasion. It's possible to take a kayak and walk on the delta, but be bear aware. Anchorage can be taken in about 70 feet near the center of the bay, or in the notch to the south in 60 feet or less. Manzanita Bay provides an overnight option before or after visiting Rudyerd Bay.

⑦ **Walker Cove.** Located along the east arm of Behm Canal, Walker Cove is part of the Misty Fjord National Monument and rivals Punchbowl Cove for beauty and rugged wilderness. Anchorage can be taken in the unnamed bight on the south shore of Walker Cove, where a creek flows into the cove. We have named it for the unusual phenomenon seen at high tides, when a field of tiny bubbles rise from fissures in the shallow seabed. Look for the streams of air near the mouth of the creek. The creek can be explored a short distance by dinghy at high tide.

Upslope and downslope winds are possible through the valley to the south. Steep granite faces rise abruptly displaying cascading waterfalls from snow fields high above. Watch for bears foraging in the grassy flats on nearby shores.

One substantial mooring buoy is found in Walker Cove's Champagne Bight. Anchoring depths of 40 to 60 feet for a couple of boats can be found in the bight, a stern-tie may be best.

New Eddystone Rock is one of the prominent features along the Behm Canal.

⑧ **Fitzgibbon Cove.** Located on the north end of east Behm Canal near the juncture with Burroughs Bay, Fitzgibbon Cove has ample anchorage and is sheltered from all winds. The cove is larger than it looks on the charts, with plenty of convenient anchoring depths in the center. The attractive cove is conducive for exploration by dinghy or kayak, and has several meadows where you might see bears.

⑨ **Yes Bay.** Five-mile long Yes Bay inlet is located at the north end of the west arm of Behm Canal. Intriguing Yes Bay is home to Yes Bay Lodge, which accepts dinner reservations with 2-day advance notice. No fuel. The bay becomes quite narrow at one spot half way along the channel in front of a prominent fishing lodge; watch for traffic and note the charted rocks. At the head Yes Bay is a scenic, well protected anchorage with room for a dozen or more boats.

⑩ **Traitors Cove (Marguerite Bay).** Located on the west side of Revillegigedo Island along the west arm of Behm Canal, 26 miles north of Ketchikan. Marguerite Bay is a U.S. Forest Service wildlife observation site. A bear viewing platform over a creek is accessed by a 1.25-mile trail; be sure to make noise as you walk so as not to startle a bear that may be nearby. Rangers are in the area, but may not always be at the platform or on the trail. Black bears feed on spawning salmon in August and September. A permit is not needed to visit the area. Anchorage in Marguerite Bay is available near the dock, or near the center of the bay in 40-50 feet of water; 6 to 9 foot depths at zero tide. Moorage is available at the 100-foot dock; a portion is set aside for floatplanes. A public mooring buoy is in the bay.

⑪ **Loring and Naha Public Docks.** Ample guest side-tie moorage is available on the outside (deep water side) of the Loring Public Dock in Naha Bay. Best used in settled weather as the dock is exposed. Rafting two-deep allowed. No charge for overnight stays.

Located south past Dogfish Island, and near the rapids to Roosevelt Lagoon, is the Naha State of Alaska public dock with guest moorage for about three medium-sized boats. No charge for overnight stays. Anchoring near the dock is a challenge but doable. A trail from the Naha dock leads past the rapids to the lagoon.

2023 Waggoner Cruising Guide

SOUTHEAST ALASKA

See Area Map Page 476 - Maps Not for Navigation

⑫ **Knudson Cove.** City of Ketchikan facility, located 16 miles north of Ketchikan at 407 Knudson Cove Road, Ketchikan, AK 99901; 907-228-5632; guest moorage located on Float 7 (110-foot dock) for boats up to 40 feet; first-come, first-served. Download registration form at ktn-ak.us/harbors and make payment by phone after submitting registration. Payment box for launch ramp only. Vault toilet; no water, no power. Fuel dock (gas and diesel) at the adjacent, private Knudson Cove Marina, open to the public for fueling (907-247-8500) year-round; limited hours in the off-season. Seasonal outdoor restaurant at the marina and cafes nearby

⑬ **Kasaan.** (907) 542-2230 Tribe, or (907) 542-2212 City; ovk@kasaan.org; www.kasaan.org. This Native village is located on the east side of Prince of Wales Island on Kasaan Bay. Kasaan is one of two Haida villages in Alaska and has a population of about 50 people, with a quiet, peaceful appeal. Transient moorage is available at the State of Alaska dock on a first-come, first-serve basis at no charge. Potable water at the docks available seasonally. No power, no launch ramp. Propane and jerry can gas and diesel. The inside of the floating dock breakwater is the most protected. Within walking distance is the Kasaan Tribal Hall, which includes a gift shop and the Totem Trail Café, open on weekends during the summer months. Don't miss the Kasaan Arts & Museum located on the northwest end of town (907-723-1426). A fee is charged to tour the museum and carving facility. Carver Stormy Hamar has revived the ancestral canoe. Native canoes are traditionally carved from a single cedar log, then steamed with hot rocks and water. The heat and pressure from the steam widens the canoe and makes it seaworthy.

Guest moorage at Kasaan is located on the inside.

A two-third mile walk on a forest trail west of the village leads past old totems and to the refurbished "Whale House." It feels magical visiting this special site, which is considered sacred. Access to the Kasaan Totem Park and the Sonihat Whale House is by tour only, contact Michael Jones at (907) 401-1731 to arrange for a tour.

Haida people migrated north from Haida Gwaii (Queen Charlotte Islands) in the early 1700's to Prince of Wales Island and established a village in Skowl Arm, located south of present-day Kasaan. In 1892 the Copper Queen Mine built a sawmill, camp, and store on Kasaan Bay, and the Haida relocated to this new village. Chief Sonihat built the Whale House, which became the focus of the new Kasaan Totem Park, established during the 1930's. Many of the totems left from the old village site were moved to the park in 1938.

⑭ **Thorne Bay Harbor.** Situated northwest of Ketchikan and southwest of Meyers Chuck on the east side of Prince of Wales Island – Thorne Bay is a logical destination when completing or starting the Southeast Alaska circle route, which we have coined "the Trapline." Thorne Harbor encompasses several bays, nooks, and crannies. Entrance into the harbor is narrow, and current can be strong. Transit the entrance at slack water – see Ports and Passes for tides and currents. Many anchoring options can be found throughout the harbor.

The community of Thorne Bay is located at the far north end of the harbor on the eastern shore and offers transient moorage. A café, hardware store, liquor store, and a well-stocked grocery are within easy walking distance. Thorne Bay is a prime location if you're planning to leave your boat in Alaska over the winter; be sure to reserve space ahead of time. There is an added fee for regular boat monitoring. Thorne Bay is serviced by floatplane to and from Ketchikan. The Inter-Island Ferry at Hollis, or the Airport at Hollis are other transportation options.

Thorne Bay started as a logging camp for the Ketchikan Pulp Co. and was one of the world's largest logging camps operating from the late 1960's into the early 1980's. As logging operations shifted, Thorne Bay became the hub for transporting logs. A huge grapple, that hoisted bundles of logs weighing up to 200,000 pounds, can be seen along the road just outside of town – the grapple is known as "The Claw." Guests off a small pocket cruiser are given a tour of the town by the local library staff; if you happen to be in town when the small tour boat is in, you're welcome to join the walking tour.

Car/Truck rentals are available at the Adventure Alaska Lodge (907-828-3907) located a 206 Hemlock Loop in Thorne Bay,

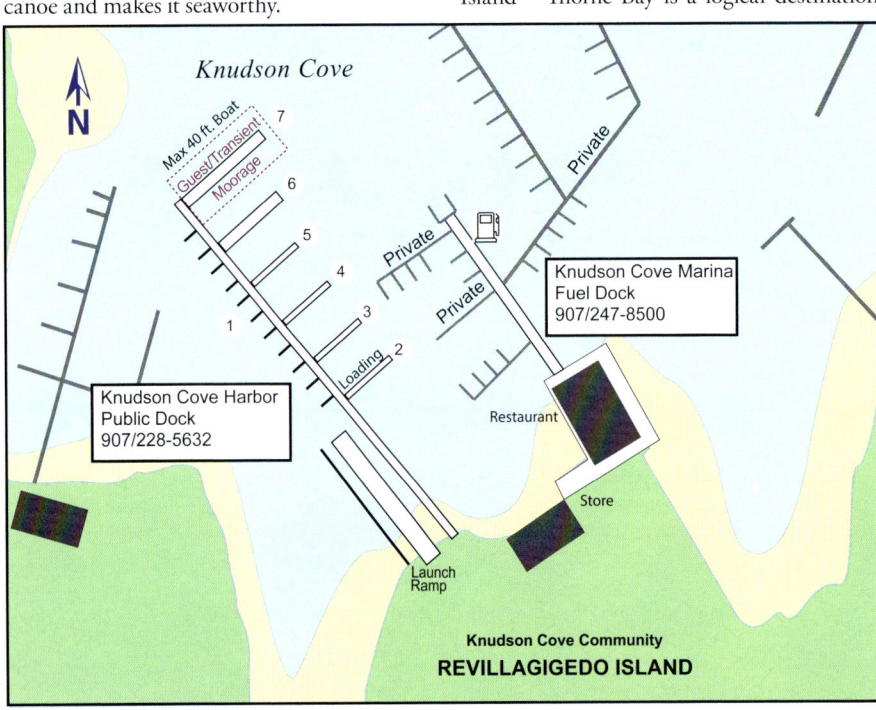

Port of Ketchikan, Knudson Cove

Kasaan

Side-tie guest moorage at Thorne Bay is on the south side of the marina.

and at the Welcome Inn Bed and Breakfast (907-828-3950). Renting a vehicle is an easy way to visit Klawock and Craig on the other side of the island, or a visit to the native village of Kasaan to the south. Perhaps the most unique site on Prince of Wales Island is El Capitan Cave, the largest known cave in Alaska (northwest of Thorne Bay). Fossil bones dating back 12,000 years have been found in this cave system. To arrange for a tour inside the cave, contact the Thorne Bay Ranger District (907) 828-3304. They can coordinate a day and time to meet you at the designated parking lot near the boat launch at El Capitan Passage; be prepared to hike some steep stairs with switchbacks up the mountain to the head of the cave. For a list of towns and marinas on Prince of Wales Island, go to visitpow.com.

LOCAL KNOWLEDGE

CURRENT: Watch for current flowing perpendicular to the side-tie guest moorage at Thorne Bay. It ebbs to the north and floods to the south. It is stronger at the deep-water end of the float.

⑭ **Thorne Bay Marina.** 120 Freeman Dr. Thorne Bay, AK 99919; (907) 204-0815 Harbormaster Ron Wendel, or (907) 828-3380 City Hall; thornebay-ak.gov. Located on the far northwest end of the harbor. Monitors VHF Ch 16. 300 feet of transient side-tie moorage on the south side of the south float. Slips are assigned for extended stays as available. Call ahead to check on availability. Potable water, 30 and 50 amp power, restroom and showers. Tidal grid and launch ramp. Marina office hours are Monday-Friday, 8:00 a.m. to 4:00 p.m. There are many anchoring options that can be found throughout the harbor. The fuel dock is located north of the marina.

⑭ **Port Thorne Bay Fuel.** (907) 828-3995; www.thornebayport.com; info@thornebayport.com; 1212 Shoreline Dr, Thorne Bay, Alaska 99919. Fuel dock with gas, diesel, and propane is located north of Thorne Bay Marina along the eastern shore, immediately in front of a convenience store that houses the Thorne Bay post office.

Davidson Landing. (907) 204-0815 Harbormaster, or (907) 828-3380 City. A city of Thorne Bay facility located on the southeast shore, part of the Southside subdivision. 200 feet of transient moorage along the front face; first-come, first-served; space is usually available. No power or water on the transient dock. Restroom upland, no showers. Covered picnic area. Launch ramp. No services on shore. Pay moorage at the harbormaster's office at Thorne Bay Marina, or call the Harbormaster, who can come over by skiff.

LOCAL KNOWLEDGE

ROCK AWASH: When entering Meyers Chuck, favor the left side of the channel until passing the green can buoy, then favor the right side of the channel. There is reportedly a rock awash east and north of the green can buoy. Start the turn to starboard at the red day mark to avoid the rock.

ANCHORING: Locals prefer that boats use the dock instead of anchoring. Both sides of the dock are available for moorage.
When anchoring in Meyers Chuck, do not anchor in the floatplane operations area along the east side of Meyers Island.

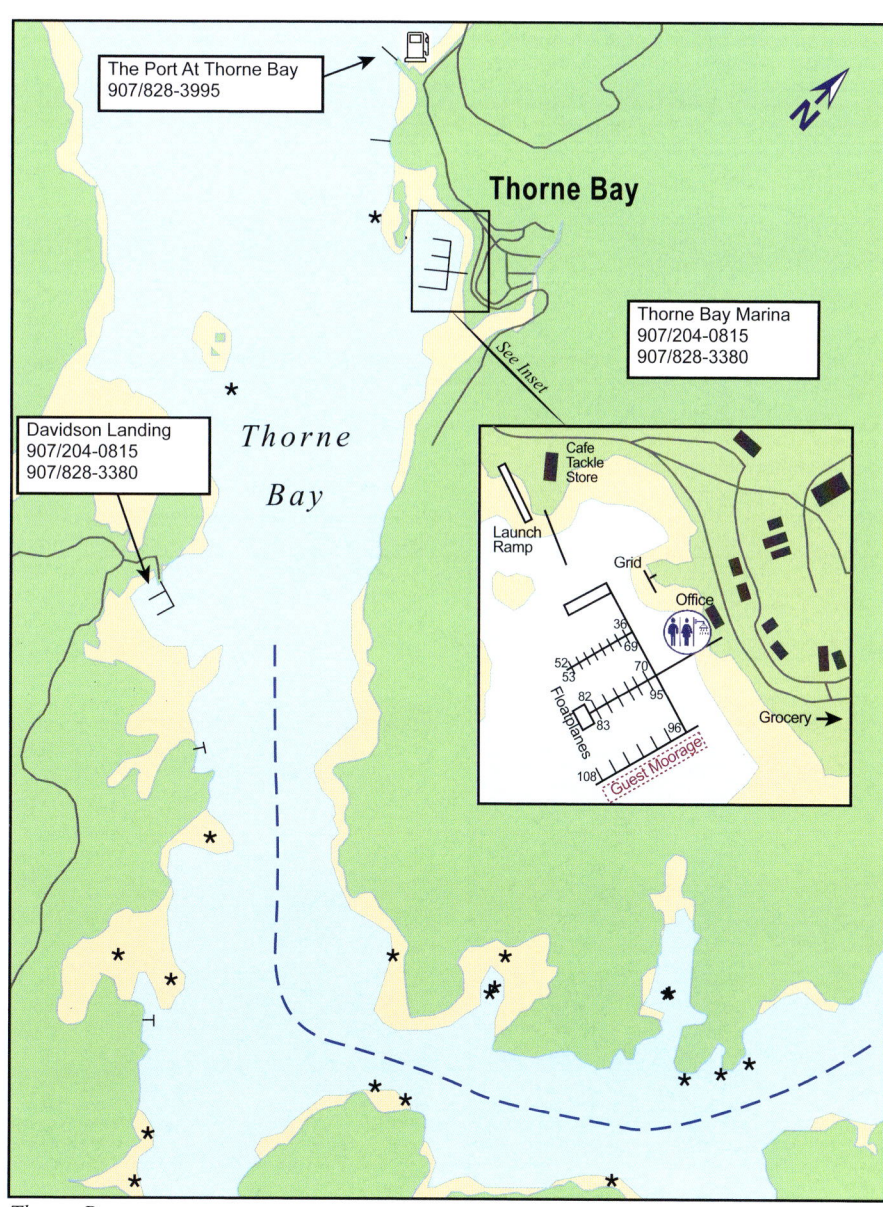

Thorne Bay

2023 Waggoner Cruising Guide 485

SOUTHEAST ALASKA

⑮ **Meyers Chuck.** A tiny village of about 20 people, tucked inside a well-protected harbor. Verne Meyers settled here in the late 1800's and lived along the shore of the back chuck (small body of water). The harbor and back chuck are ideal for exploring by dinghy. Moorage is available at the 325-foot public float (operated by the City of Wrangell) on a first-come, first-serve basis. No power or facilities ashore; locally produced water available at the float. Rafting is encouraged during the busy summer season. Both sides of the float are available for moorage. Anchorage is available in the harbor near the float; avoid the floatplane operations area near Meyers Island. A tidal grid, suitable for medium-sized boats, is nearby.

Charming Meyers Chuck, with its small post office, community workshops, forest trails, and friendly locals, is an authentic Alaskan destination. When moored at the dock, a local may ask if you want to place an order for cinnamon rolls to be delivered the next morning. Be sure to walk the gravel pathways that meander along the shore, around the homesteads, and through the forest. Interesting sculptures and art work can be found along the trail. Tucked among the trees is an art gallery/gift shop open to the public; the shop keeper's phone number is posted on the door.

⑯ **Coffman Cove.** Located on the northeastern shore of Prince of Wales Island, off Clarence Strait behind Coffman Island. This village of approximately 170 people offers a small marina with transient moorage and fuel (gas, with diesel by delivery truck). The adorable Riggin Shack has groceries and general merchandise; the Bait Box offers take-out hamburgers and sandwiches. The Doghouse Saloon and liquor store are nearby.

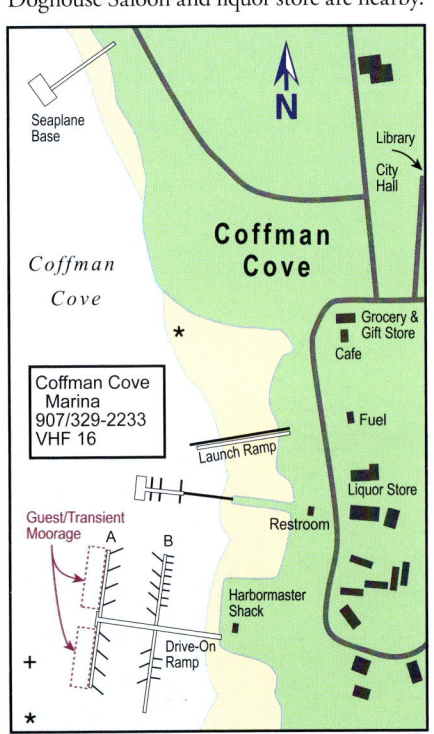

Coffman Cove

Moorage is available on both sides of the Meyers Chuck dock.

Enjoy a picnic lunch under the covered picnic tables at the community Seaside Park.

Fishing lodges and bed-and-breakfast accommodations draw in the sport fishing crowd. Guided fishing charters are available. Nearby trails lead to fishing streams and cabins. Annual fishing derbies are held during the summer months. Fish-cleaning stations are at the marina.

Coffman Cove is also a popular destination for paddlers, taking up the challenge of traversing the Honker Divide Canoe Route. The Route is a challenging 33-mile paddle on rivers and lakes through the heart of the island (Hatchery Creek/Thorne River System). It takes an average of 3-5 days to complete the journey. The Route is accessed at Honker Canoe Launch, 10 miles south of Coffman Cove. The first seven miles are against the current; portages can be muddy. Renting the Honker Lake Cabin for an overnight stay is recommended – see recreation.gov.

⑯ **Coffman Cove Marina.** 102 Denali Coffman Cove, AK 99918; (907) 329-2233 City Hall; ccalaska.com. The marina offers 180 feet of transient side-tie moorage on a first-come, first-serve basis located on the outer rail of the main dock. Boaters can call ahead regarding available space. Seasonal potable water at the docks, restrooms located upland.

Limited 30 amp power. Showers are available at the local RV park, open seasonally. A for-fee Wi-Fi service is available at the kiosk building near the docks. The fuel dock has propane and gas; diesel can be delivered by truck. Boat launch on site. Groceries and eateries within walking distance of the docks.

Kindergarten Bay. Located on the NW side of Etolin Island, where Stikine Strait meets Clarence Strait, a protected anchorage with good depths and room for several boats with swing room. Whales frequent the waters just off of Steamer Point near Kindergarten Bay.

⑰ **Anan Bear & Wildlife Observatory.** Located 35 nm south of Wrangell at Anan Bay off Bradfield Canal, this bear viewing facility is accessible only by boat or floatplane. Black and brown bears are seen feeding on migrating salmon at an observation platform above the falls on Anan Creek. Best viewing is in July and August. Permits are required to go ashore from July 5th through August 25th. Twelve permits are issued each day for individuals arriving by private boat. There is a nominal fee for permits. For more information and to obtain a permit online, go to www.recreation.gov and search on "Anan Wildlife Observatory Permits." In the town of Wrangell, four daily permits are available

Coffman Cove is a popular sport fishing destination.

Reference Only – Not for Navigation

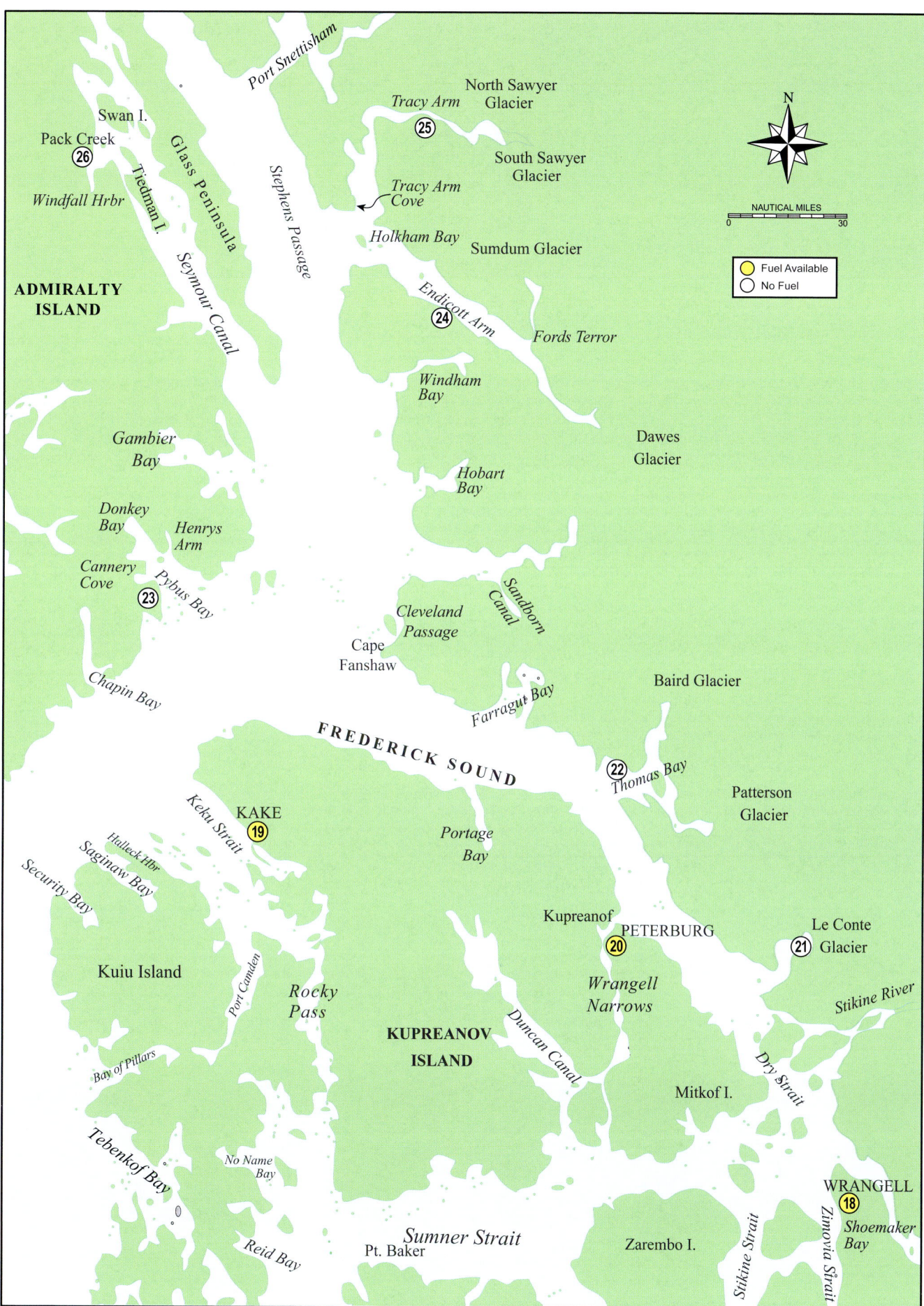

SOUTHEAST ALASKA

Stephens Passage & Frederick Sound

SOUTHEAST ALASKA

See Area Map Page 487 - Maps Not for Navigation

Anan provides opportunities for unique bear viewing that is safe for bears and people.

in person through a weekly lottery at the Wrangell Forest Service Office (907-874-2323) on Bennett Street.

Anchorage in Bradfield Canal is limited; holding is marginal, current runs through the channel and a large charted cable area includes all of Anan Bay. It's not recommended to leave the boat unattended, so it is best to leave someone onboard and take turns going ashore. Do not tie to the Ranger's Cabin float. Boats 36 feet and under with a shallow draft, may tie-up at the Forest Service Anan Bay rental cabin float when space is available; the 40-foot float is located in front of the cabin and is first-come, first-served for shallow draft boats.

Call the Anan Observatory Ranger on VHF Ch 16 for permission to come ashore; don't forget to bring an image of your permit. The dinghy landing area is south, southeast of the anchorage area. Visiting hours are 8:00 a.m. to 6:00 p.m. A one-mile trail leads from the dinghy landing area to the viewing platform which was reconstructed in 2022. Pets are not allowed on shore at any time. There is no dinghy dock or moorage system for dinghies. You may want to shuttle your guests to shore and return to your boat with the dinghy; kayaks and light dinghies can be hauled-up on shore.

While not the most convenient destination to visit by private boat, the Anan Bear Observatory is not to be missed. Bears often climb up the hillside to the platform within a few feet of human observers. Bears also crawl under the flooring of the platform to enjoy their catch-of-the-day. It's truly an incredible experience. This is a popular destination, plan ahead to secure permits. Commercial tours operating out of Wrangell provide floatplane transportation to Anan, along with the required permits.

Shoemaker Bay Harbor – Wrangell. Located five-miles south of Wrangell; (907) 874-3736; This is a 250-slip facility for permanent moorage. Transient boaters may request space and are occasionally assigned to vacated slips (hot berthing). Potable water at the docks; 30 and 50 amp power. Restrooms, no showers, no laundry. Tidal grid and boat launch. A bike path, separate from the highway, leads into town. A 0.6 mile well-maintained boardwalk trail leads to a viewing platform of Rainbow Falls. Nearby park with tennis courts, playground, camping, and trails.

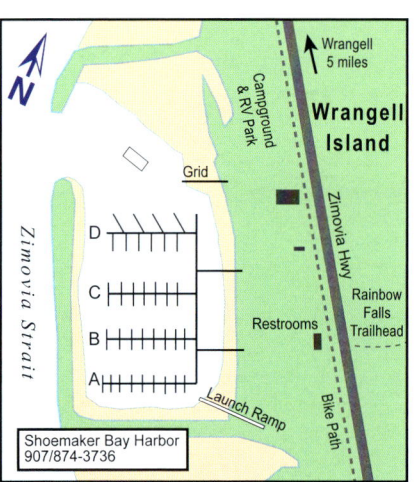

⑱ **Wrangell.** Wrangell is a delight and has that Alaskan western charm with false-front buildings, offering a selection of good restaurants, shops, and grocery stores for provisioning. A community market is held on the first Saturday of the month, May through September. Local tour operators offer excursions up the Stikine River to Shakes Glacier and/or the village of Telegraph Creek in B.C.; or you can opt for a tour to the Anan Bay Bear & Wildlife Observatory located 35 nm southeast of Wrangell, or to Le Conte Glacier near Petersburg. The Wrangell Bearfest is held during the last week and weekend of July. A parade, prop-boat races, and fireworks are held on July 4th.

Wrangell was founded by the Russians, who began trading furs here with the Natives in 1811. Baron Ferdinand Petrovich Wrangel was put in charge of government affairs. Around 1840, the Hudson Bay Co. leased land from the Russians. The Tlingits resided here thousands of years before the arrival of Europeans, as evidenced by the petroglyphs found along Petroglyph Beach located on the

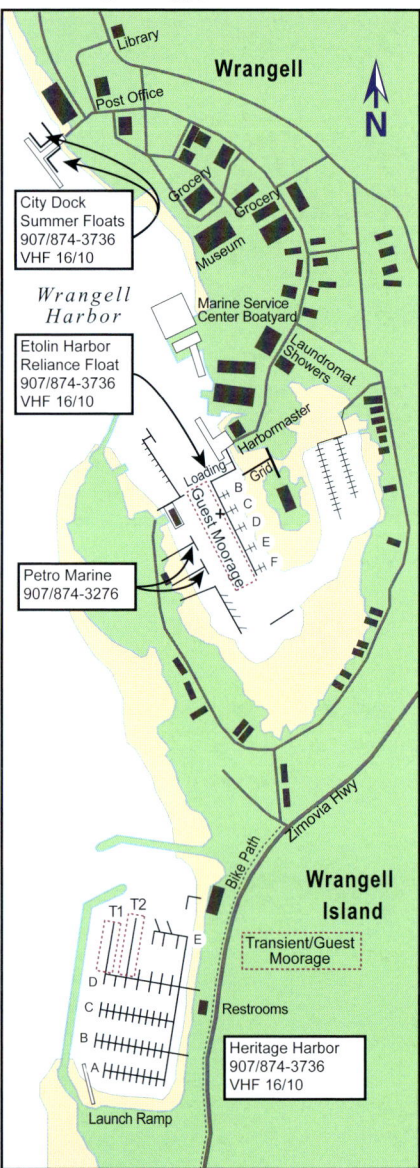

Anan Bay

Shoemaker Bay Harbor

Wrangell Harbor

488   www.WaggonerGuide.com

Chief Shakes Tribal House near Etolin Harbor in Wrangell

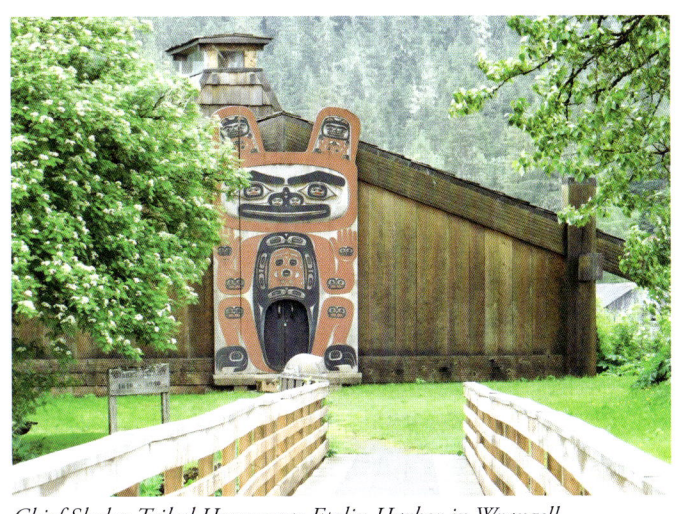

Main Street Wrangell has fully-stocked stores, shops, and eateries.

edge of town, accessible by taxi or bicycle; visit at low tide to see the petroglyphs along the rocky shore. Don't miss visiting Chief Shakes Tribal House, a reproduction of the 1775 original tribal house. The Wrangell Museum in town is excellent and shouldn't be missed for a look into Wrangell's past.

The Wrangell Airport serves regularly scheduled airline flights, convenient for picking-up guests and crew. The Alaska Marine Highway facility and seaplane float provide other transportation options.

Fuel: Marine fuel is available at two floats in Etolin Harbor from Petro Marine (907) 874-3276, adjacent to the Reliance guest float.

⑱ **City and Borough of Wrangell.** The city of Wrangell manages three marinas: Etolin Harbor (Reliance Guest Float), Heritage Harbor docks, and Shoemaker Bay Harbor. Moorage is first-come, first-served at the Reliance Guest Float and Heritage Harbor. Contact the Harbormaster at (907) 874-3736 or on VHF Ch 16; the office is located at Reliance Harbor. Vessels over 100 feet should provide 8-hours advance notice for moorage instructions. The City also manages the Summer Floats at the City Dock which are used for load/unload. For haulout and repairs, contact Wrangell Marine Service Center (907-874-3736), offering 150- ton and 300-ton haulout, self-work areas, contractor services, and on-the-hard long-term storage for boats up to 42 feet. The Harbormaster's office maintains a contact list of trades people and service providers in the area.

LOCAL KNOWLEDGE

ROCK - A rock and shallow area on Reliance Transient Float is marked by a yellow painted bull rail.

⑱ **Etolin Harbor (Reliance Guest Float) – Wrangell.** Shakes Street; Shakes Street; (907) 874-3736; Monitors VHF Ch 16. Close to the downtown area and the Harbormaster's office. The west side of Reliance Float has 600 feet of first-come, first-served side-tie moorage. Boats 50 feet and larger on the north one-third and boats under 50 feet on the south two-thirds. The east side finger floats and slips are permanent moorage. Potable water at the docks, mostly 20 amp power with a few 30 amp and one 50 amp. Garbage drop and waste oil collection. 165 feet of 4-hour load/unload side-tie is located below the Harbormaster's office. Two tidal grids. A floatplane dock is located at this facility.

⑱ **Heritage Harbor – Wrangell.** Located one-mile from downtown Wrangell; (907) 874-3736; Monitors VHF Ch 16. First-come, first-served for transient side-tie space on T1 and T2 docks; 30 and 50 amp power. Potable water at the docks. Restrooms and boat launch. No showers, no laundry. Boaters must report to the Harbormaster's office at Reliance Harbor within 2 hours of arrival. Contact the Harbormaster for access to the locked shore power. Walk to town and harbormaster's office or take the dingy to Reliance Harbor.

⑱ **City Dock – Wrangell.** Located on the north end of town is the cruise ship and super yachts terminal. Inside the cruise ship pier are two areas of floats for boat moorage. The U-shaped set of floats on the north has 300 feet of side-tie space; the L-shaped two floats on the south has 275 feet of space. Water but no power. Contact the Harbormaster, call (907) 874-3736. The shoreside of the inside float in the north has space for dinghies, with convenient access to downtown.

Wrangell Narrows. The primary inside passage that connects Sumner Strait with Frederick Sound, heavily used by commercial and recreational vessels. Large cruise ships do not use this passage; however, commercial vessels including barges and the Alaska Marine Ferries, transit the Narrows. Running north/south, the waterway is 21 nm long and well-marked with 60 plus channel markers and 5 ranges. Plan ahead and study the charts. Enter Wrangell Narrows in either direction at the end of a flood tide in order to be at mid-point (South Flat) at slack – see Ports & Passes for tidal current predictions. Current in the Narrows runs to just over 4 knots. The tidal flow meets between channel markers R44 and R48. Sections of the Narrows are dredged channels that are 300 feet wide; seemingly wide until encountering a 100-foot-wide barge in tow. Some areas of the channel are quite narrow, leave room for passing traffic; pull over at wider areas for passing barges. Keep watch ahead and behind.

At the south end of Wrangell Narrows, an unnamed cove northwest of Deception Pt., offers good anchorage before entering and after exiting the Narrows. Petersburg is the logical stopping point northbound.

⑲ **Kake.** On the way to or from Rocky Pass is the Tlingit community of Kake. Just off Keku Strait is Kake Harbor with shallow water approaches to several mooring locations. Temporary anchoring is possible in the harbor. The city pier and float are located near the center of the village with limited small craft mooring. The Portage Bay floats, about 2 miles south of town, have limited guest moorage with water and power.

The grocery store is located in town above the city pier and float. Fuel can be delivered by truck by contacting tribal fuel for an appointment (907) 785-3601.

Rocky Pass. A passage that runs between Kuiu Island and Kupreanof Island. This route requires navigating a challenging 20 nm narrow pass with very shallow areas. This is the shortest route but requires honed navigational skills. The passage is very narrow in places including what's known as The Summit. The passage is also very shallow in a number of places. It is best to transit the passage at or near high-water slack – see Ports and Passes for tides and currents. The key is to be in the right sections of the passage at the right times. Devil's Elbow is the most challenging spot, requiring nearly 90 degree turns. This route is not for the faint of heart or inexperienced. Plan ahead and study the charts carefully. See the Douglass' book, *Exploring Southeast Alaska*, for a detailed description of Rocky Pass.

SOUTHEAST ALASKA

LOCAL KNOWLEDGE

SPEED LIMITS - Speed is limited to 7 knots in Wrangell Narrows off Petersburg Harbor. Speed is restricted to a 4 mph No Wake limit within the harbors.

[20] **Petersburg.** Velkommen (welcome) to Petersburg. Located at the north end of Wrangell Narrows, Petersburg is a favorite destination in Southeast Alaska, offering stunning scenery and three marina facilities managed by the Borough of Petersburg. The harbormaster office, showers and restrooms are located in the North Harbor. CAUTION, strong current runs through all the harbor slips and fairways, especially the outer most slips.

Regular scheduled airline service and the Alaska Marine Ferry Terminal are convenient options for meeting guests or crew. A seaplane float is also located at Petersburg. Provisioning available at the downtown grocery, or at the Hammer & Wilken grocery near the airport, which makes deliveries. Shops, eateries, hardware and marine supplies can be found in town. A list of service providers is available through the Borough of Petersburg website at www.ci.petersburg.ak.us. This commercial fishing community is the real Alaska; you won't find any cruise ships here.

Norwegian immigrant Peter Buschmann built a cannery, sawmill, and dock in the late 1800's. Ice from nearby Le Conte Glacier was used to preserve fish. Today, Petersburg remains one of Alaska's major commercial fishing communities, with three fish processing companies. Petersburg's Norwegian heritage is celebrated on the third weekend in May, Norwegian Constitution Day – this "Little Norway Festival" is a popular celebration for locals and visitors alike. For some local history, visit the Clausen Museum at 203 Fram Street.

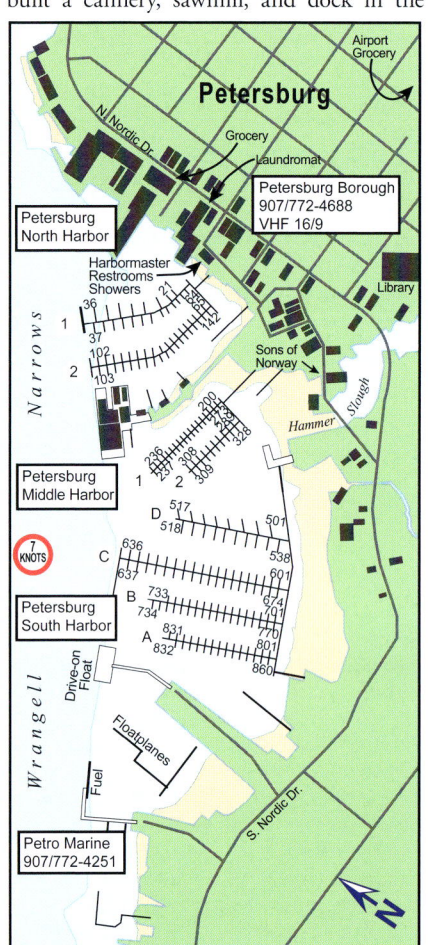

Be sure to visit Sing Lee Alley and Hammer Slough, the commercial and residential beginnings of Petersburg. Period homes line the boardwalk along Hammer Slough, very picturesque at high tide. A visit to nearby Le Conte Glacier is a must – local tour operators can take you there, or you can take your own boat on the 22-mile passage for a convenient day trip. Petersburg offers several hiking trails; stop by the Visitor Center for a map. Take the dinghy across the channel from the South Harbor docks and tie-up at the Kupreanof public dock and hike the boardwalk trail through the muskeg; be bear aware. Another lovely hike with views can be found at Sandy Beach, northeast of downtown Petersburg.

Fuel: Petro Marine fuel is located south of South Harbor; contact (907) 772-4251. For propane, contact Piston & Rudder at (907) 772-4240.

[20] **Petersburg Borough - Port & Harbor.** 223 Harbor Way, Petersburg, AK 99833; (907) 772-4688. Petersburg Borough operates three marina harbors in Petersburg. Guest moorage is assigned by the harbormaster's office in unoccupied slips in one of the three harbors. Harbormaster's office is located at the head of ramp to the docks in North Harbor. Guest washrooms and showers are located adjacent to the harbormaster's office. Contact the harbormaster on VHF Ch 16, switch to Ch 9, no advance reservations taken, but boaters may call ahead regarding availability.

[20] **North Harbor – Petersburg.** 223 Harbor Way, Petersburg, AK 99833; (907) 772-4688. Contact the harbormaster on VHF Ch 16/9, no reservations taken, but boaters may call ahead regarding availability. Docks are located close to town and services. Docks are in good condition with ELCI-protected shore power; 30, 50, and 100 amp; potable water. Garbage and waste oil disposal.

[20] **Middle Harbor – Petersburg.** Mostly permanent moorage, with limited transient moorage as available. Contact the harbormaster on VHF Ch 16/9. Garbage and waste oil disposal.

[20] **South Harbor – Petersburg.** South Nordic Drive, Petersburg, AK 99833; (907) 772-4688. Contact the harbormaster on VHF Ch 16/9; call ahead regarding availability. Located a half-mile from the harbormaster's office, showers and restrooms, but noticeably situated farther from the fish processing plants and the smell of money. Potable water at the docks; 30, 50, and 100 amp power. No ELCI/GFI power stations at this time. Garbage and waste oil disposal.

Kupreanof Dock. Across Wrangell Narrows from Petersburg's South Harbor is a State of Alaska public pier and float providing access to several hiking trailheads. The dock is convenient for tying the dinghy, while exploring the City of Kupreanof site. The town today consists of a few homes and trails. Trailhead signs greet you at the top of the dock. The Petersburg Creek Trail is an easy 45-minute boardwalk hike that takes you through a muskeg ridge with lovely views, and on to the creek about ¾ of a mile from the dock. An unmaintained Kupreanof Loop trail takes about 45-minutes round trip. The Petersburg Mountain trail takes you 2,700 feet up and requires about 6 hours. The 50-foot float has no power or water.

Ideal Cove. Located off Frederick Sound on Mitkof Island behind Cosmos Point north of Dry Strait. Correspondents Steve and Toni Jefferies report that Ideal Cove is well protected, with room for several boats. Numerous crab pots stored along the shore indicate that the cove may be littered with pots from time to time. Anchor in 40 feet of water, holding is good on a mud bottom. Take care to avoid the mud flats when entering the

Petersburg's Nordic heritage can be found throughout the town.

Petersburg Harbor

Bergy bits throughout Le Conte bay provide shelter for seals and pups.

Le Conte glacier is known for its above and below water calving.

cove. A nearby 6.2-mile loop trail can be accessed via dinghy or kayak; the trailhead is located outside Ideal Cove in a bight to the northwest of Ideal Cove near a creek. The trail starts west of the creek and may be difficult to locate by dinghy per Steve and Toni Jefferies. The boardwalk trail passes by two lakes, with a spur trail to a third lake. Dogs allowed on leash. Ideal Cove is a convenient jumping off point for an excursion to Le Conte Glacier.

㉑ **Le Conte Bay Glacier.** The southernmost tidewater glacier in Southeast Alaska and one of the most interesting. Located 22 nm northeast of Petersburg at the head of Le Conte Bay. The glacier dumps ice that stretches 9 miles from its face. Icebergs are often seen in Frederick Sound near Petersburg. Some vessels may not be able to venture to the face of the glacier due to the ice floes; we recommend booking a tour with one of the small aluminum tour boat operators based in Petersburg for a day's excursion to this calving glacier, with its unique underwater "shooters," huge icebergs that rise-up from the ocean floor and roll over like sea monsters. Should you chose to take your own boat, be prepared to negotiate tidal glacier ice floes and icebergs on the way to the glacier face. You can find a list of local tour operators at the Petersburg Visitor Information Office (907) 772-4636.

㉒ **Thomas Bay.** Big, beautiful, and popular best describes this area 11 miles north of Petersburg. Creeks from impressive mountains empty into this large bay with several coves and bights for exploring and anchoring. Entry to the bay is marked with lateral buoys. The cove at the southeast end of Ruth Island at the river delta from Patterson Glacier is the most popular anchorage; you will find favorable anchoring depths and room for a number of boats. The area east of Spray Island and south of Cascade Creek has some favorable anchoring depths in a small cove, where a charted mooring buoy no longer exists. Glimpses of Baird Glacier can be found on the northeast end of Thomas Bay, along with stunning Scenery Cove, which has steep canyon walls rising on both sides from a deep, flat bottom of 90 to 100 feet; however, just inside the entrance to the cove is an area with depths of 50 to 90 feet.

Portage Bay. Located on the south shore of Frederick Sound on Kupreanof Island, Portage Bay offers well-protected anchorage for many boats. Anchor in 30 to 48 feet over a good holding mud bottom. Anchor throughout the bay. The S-shaped entry channel is marked and is best transited on high-water slack, but the current that can run to nearly 3 knots can be challenged. Listen for a VHF securité call from the tug that tows a supply barge in and out of the bay routinely. Marginal cell service can be found deeper into the bay.

㉓ **Pybus Bay.** This is a popular stop for boaters transiting Frederick Sound and Stephens Passage. Deep valleys cut into the mountains rising to the west on Admiralty Island. **Cannery Cove** is the most popular anchoring spot with room for about half-a-dozen boats in 5 to 8 fathoms and space for a few more boats in much deeper water. A series of beautiful waterfalls cut through a mountain valley. **Henrys Arm** has well-protected anchorage for several boats in 8 to 10 fathoms with room to swing and a view window to the mountains and valleys to the southwest. **Donkey Bay** has a couple of anchoring spots along the south shore. Similar to Cannery Cove, Donkey Bay has a series of waterfalls cascading from snow fields high above. Anchoring depths of 6 to 9 fathoms can be found in the bay between the **San Juan Islands** in Pybus Bay; a nice pebble beach with a scenic mountain backdrop makes for a lovely anchorage, but the cove is open and exposed to east through northeast.

Cannery Cove is home to the extensive full-service **Pybus Point Lodge** fishing resort. Their well-maintained buildings and docks are on the south shore as you enter Cannery Cove. When space is available, visiting boaters may be able to join one of their dinner meals. Contact Pybus Point Lodge on VHF 16 or 72 to inquire about availability. Dinner service is between 6:30pm and 8:30pm. Guest boaters may also purchase items at the resort liquor store. Cash or credit cards are accepted. Please ask about dinner space well ahead of time and ask where to tie your dinghy at their docks.

Savor the views along muskeg trail at Kupreanof.

Good anchorage is in the cove southeast of Ruth Island in Thomas Bay.

The viewing platform at Pack Creek gives you a close but safe perspective

Stephens Passage. A 105-mile long passage that separates Admiralty Island on the west and the Alaska mainland to the east. The city of Juneau lies near the north end of the Passage. There are no towns and no services along the length of Stephens Passage. There are many good anchorages along the passage, most are on the Admiralty Island side. Icebergs are often seen farther north in Holkham Bay, the entrance to Tracy Arm and Endicott Arm, with impressive glaciers at their head.

Entrance Island (Hobart Bay). A state maintained public float not connected to land is located in the small bay on the southeast side of Entrance Island. Offering both side-tie moorage and anchorage, the bay is well protected and is only a short distance off of Stephens Passage in the outer area of Hobart Bay.

Holkham Bay. A wide bay that serves as the entrance to Endicott Arm and Tracy Arm, and their respective tidal glaciers. Icebergs are often seen adrift in the Bay and along Stephens Passage, originating from the glaciers. Use caution when transiting.

Tracy Arm Cove. Douglass' given name for this unnamed cove on the southeastern tip of Snettisham Peninsula at the entrance to Tracy Arm. With anchoring depths from 3 to 10 fathoms, this cove serves well as staging before or after venturing up Tracy Arm or Endicott Arm. Holding varies from fair to good. It may take several tries to get a set. Open to the southeast. This popular anchorage has room for a number of boats. Grizzly bears are frequently seen foraging along the shore near the creek.

㉔ **Endicott Arm.** A 30 nautical mile arm, accessed via Holkham Bay, terminating at Dawes Glacier. There are no convenient anchorages in Endicott Arm. Dawes Glacier is a popular tidal glacier viewing location with glacier calving activity. Calving and ice floes can keep boats at least a couple of miles from the face of the glacier. Half-way along Endicott Arm on the north side is a 5-mile inlet known as Fords Terror, seldom visited by pleasure boaters. Fords Terror is a remote area that is poorly charted, with an outer and inner basin connected by a set of rapids. Correspondent Stephen Jefferies says Fords Terror is spectacular and a must see; despite the name, it's no problem if you follow the tide guidelines.

㉕ **Tracy Arm.** The charted and marked bar entrance to Tracy Arm is via Holkham Bay. Pocket cruise ships, high speed tour boats from Juneau, large cruise ships, and private power and sailboats all venture up Tracy Arm to view the spectacular 4,000-foot-high granite walls, deep valleys, waterfalls, and the two glaciers, **North Sawyer** and **South Sawyer**. South Sawyer, with its calving glacier face is the favorite. North Sawyer has receded and the newly formed terminal moraine means that most of the glacier face is no longer a tidal glacier. Plan a full day for the trip up to view both glaciers, and for the trip back down. Leave time for stops along the way to view the awesome granite faces, waterfalls, eagles, and seals with pups on the ice floes at South Sawyer.

Once clogged with ice, pleasure boats can now travel 22 miles up scenic Tracy Arm, which splits to North Sawyer Glacier and South Sawyer Glacier. Currents at the entrance bar can run to just over 4 knots, check Ports & Passes for tidal current predictions. Due to river and glacier outflow, there is a ½ knot or better outflow in Tracy Arm. The only good overnight anchorage in the Arm is found in the unnamed cove (see Waggoner-named Tracy Arm Cove) about 1.5 miles north of Tracy Arm entrance. Monitor VHF 16 and 13 for larger vessel position reports inbound and outbound at "The Great Bend" – mile 8 and "The S-Turns" – mile 17.

Seymour Canal. A 35-mile long inlet that cuts northwest into Admiralty Island. The upper reaches, beyond Tiedman Island, have numerous rocks, reefs, and islands. According to Coast Pilot 8, survey information for the Canal is old and incomplete, and that dangers exist beyond those shown on charts. Anchorage can be found in Short Finger Bay, Pleasant Bay, Windfall Harbor and at the Pack Creek Bear Viewing Area.

At the head of Seymour Canal is Fool Inlet with rocks, reefs, and current. The area is poorly charted. Coast Pilot 8 recommends local knowledge to navigate the Canal above Tiedman Island. A 1/2 mile canoe and kayak portage with a hand-operated tram separates Fool Inlet and Oliver Cove.

㉖ **Pack Creek Bear Viewing Area.** Located 24 nm up Seymour Canal, Pack Creek on Admiralty Island provides the opportunity to view brown bears (grizzlies) in the wild, best seen during July and August during the salmon migration. Access is by boat or floatplane only (tour operators fly guests in from Juneau). The Area is managed by Alaska Fish & Wildlife Rangers and Forest Service personnel. Access is by permit from June 1st through September 10th; fees vary. For more information and to obtain a permit online, go to www.recreation.gov and search on "Pack Creek Bear Viewing Area." There is a limit of 24 visitors per day during the peak season.

Contact the Ranger on VHF Ch 16 prior to coming ashore, be sure to bring an image of your permit (one per person). Guests are greeted by a Ranger and accompanied to the estuary, where bears are often seen foraging. Visitors may walk the one-mile trail to an observation tower overlooking the Creek; best to walk in groups and make noise as you go. Pets are not allowed on shore at any time.

CAUTION, as you enter the bay, do not motor between the two orange buoys, which mark a dinghy clothesline system. Dinghies are to be tied off to this clothesline and pulled out to sea, out of reach from bears. Day anchor the mother ship south or east of the dinghy clothesline; overnight stays in calm weather only. Overnight anchorage is also available in Windfall Harbor.

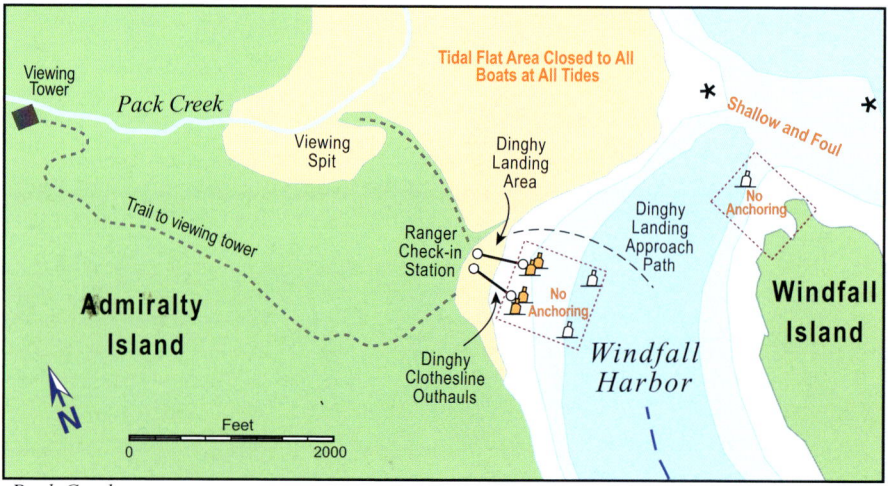

Pack Creek

㉗ **Taku Harbor.** The well-protected harbor of Taku, located off Stephens Passage, serves as a convenient overnight stop on the way to or from Juneau, 20 nm away. The public dock has ample side-tie moorage at no charge. Anchorage is possible in Taku Harbor, with the best protected spot at the south end of the bay in 40-50 feet of water at zero tide. An Alaska State Parks cabin (Tiger Olsen Cabin) near the head of the dock is available for rent – contact Southeast Area Parks at dnr.pkssoutheast@alaska.gov or call (907) 465-4563. The remains of a 1904 salmon cannery lie upland; be bear aware. Taku was once the site of Fort Durham, a Hudson's Bay Co. trading post in 1848.

㉘ **Juneau.** Located in Gastineau Channel at the north end of Stephens Passage. Beware of the 5-knot speed limit in Gastineau Channel. Coast Guard boardings and inspections are common practice in the area. The Borough of Juneau manages three marina facilities near Juneau: Harris Harbor and Aurora Harbor on the north end of Gastineau Channel, and Douglas Harbor southwest of Juneau on Douglas Island. The harbormaster's office is located upland between Aurora and Harris harbors and is open Monday through Friday from 8:00 a.m. to 4:30 p.m. Vessels bound for Harris and Aurora Harbors must pass under the Douglas Bridge (clearance 51 feet at Mean High Water) in order to access these marinas north of the bridge. Douglas Harbor is located south of the bridge.

Due to the rugged, mountainous terrain surrounding Juneau, there are no roads connecting Juneau to the rest of Alaska. Access is by plane, floatplane, or boat. The Juneau Airport is located north of town near Auke Bay.

If you need to have packages sent to Juneau, contact Eagle Raven Global at (907) 957-4733; they can hold your packages for pick-up. With a population of 32,000, Juneau offers a variety of gift shops, restaurants, and grocery stores for provisioning. Big box stores like Costco, Fred Meyer, and Home Depot are located north of town. A visit to the Alaskan Brewing Co. (907-780-5866), at 5429 Shaune Dr., is another point of interest.

The city is named after Joe Juneau, a gold prospector, who along with his partner Richard Harris, found a large gold deposit in the late 1800's. Juneau became the state capital in 1906, when what used to be the District of Alaska moved from Sitka. Today, Juneau is a major cruise ship destination for its outstanding scenery and recreational activities. A variety of tour operators are available in Juneau.

The visitor center is located near the cruise ship terminal. Visit Mendenhall Glacier located along Glacier Highway, accessible by taxi, rental car, or tours. Reminisce about gold mining days at the Last Chance Mining Museum & Historic Park, or take a tour inside the A-J Mine; both sites are located above present-day downtown Juneau. The Mount Roberts Tramway that runs up the mountainside from downtown is a must-do. The views from the top are spectacular, have

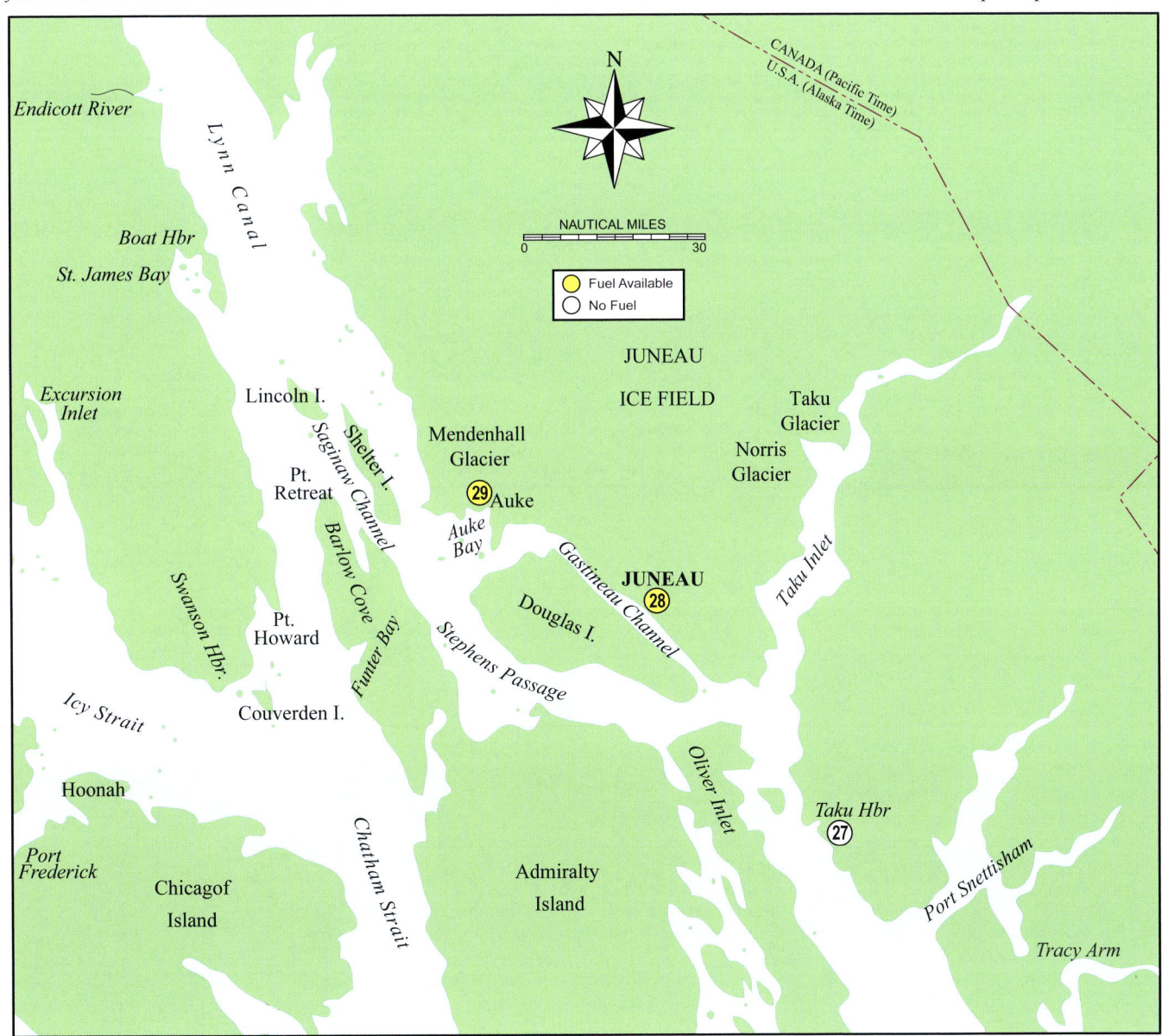

Juneau Area

The Whale Project located at the Juneau end of the Douglas Bridge is a most impressive park and fountain - definitely worth a visit.

lunch and hike the mountain trails. The tram operates May through September. Don't miss the ruins of the Treadwell Mine on Douglas Island, just inside the forest adjacent to the beach and harbor docks. This is a local's best kept secret, with miles of trails and reader-boards explaining the history of this company town that once housed and employed 2,000 people.

Fuel Docks: Petro Marine has two fuel docks in Juneau, one located across the channel from Harris Harbor (907-586-4400) with gas, diesel, and propane; the other is located south of downtown (907-586-1276) with diesel.

LOCAL KNOWLEDGE

TOW SERVICE - Boat Tow service is available through Melino's Marine Services (808) 754-2602.

US COAST GUARD - Juneau's Coast Guard station is on the north shore of Juneau Harbor. It's not uncommon for boats to be safety inspected by USCG when transiting Juneau Harbor.

㉘ **Harris Harbor.** 1600 Harbor Way; (907) 586-5255; (907) 321-1115 harbormaster cell; juneau.org/harbors. Vessels must pass under the Douglas Bridge (51-foot clearance at Mean High Water). Transient moorage is first-come, first-served; boats are assigned to vacated slips (hot berthing). Most slips have water and power – 20, 30, and 50 amp available in this 204-slip facility. Hail on VHF Ch 73 for slip assignment when entering Gastineau Channel. Garbage, launch ramp and grid. Pumpout station located on the southeast corner of Harris Harbor. Tidal grid, register with the office before use. Harris is located within walking distance of downtown. Shower and self-service laundry facility on Egan Drive across from Harris.

㉘ **Aurora Harbor.** 1600 Harbor Way; (907) 586-5255; (907) 321-1115 harbormaster cell; juneau.org/harbors. Vessels must pass under the Douglas Bridge (51-foot clearance at Mean High Water). Transient moorage is first-come, first served; boats are assigned to vacated slips (hot berthing). Most slips have water and ELCI-protected 20, 30, and 50 amp power in this 449-slip facility. Hail on VHF Ch 73 for slip assignment when entering Gastineau Channel. Garbage and used oil disposal. Showers and self-service laundry located on Egan Drive. The Juneau Yacht Club is located north of Aurora Harbor, no reciprocal docks but they do have event space for rent.

㉘ **Seadrome Dock.** 76 Egan Drive Juneau, AK 99801; (907) 586-0292 for reservations. This is a private marina located in downtown Juneau offering 560 feet of moorage, primarily for pocket cruise ships and large yachts from 50-250 feet in length. Water, garbage; 30, 50, and 100 amp power included with moorage. Fuel and shoreside services available for hire upon request.

㉘ **Intermediate Dock.** 1600 Harbor Way; (907) 586-0292 for reservations; juneau.org/harbors. Located between the cruise ship berths near the base of Mt. Roberts tram, this City of Juneau 375-foot float has side-tie space by reservation only for large vessels 65 feet and over. Garbage; water at the docks; 30, 50, and 100 amp power. A lovely boardwalk above the docks provides great views and a pleasant, short walk into town.

㉘ **Mike Pusich Douglas Harbor.** Savikko Road; (907) 586-5255; juneau.org/harbors. Three miles south of Juneau on Douglas Island, west side of Gastineau Channel. Water and garbage; 20, 30, and 50 amp power. Transient side-tie moorage is available on a first-come, first-serve basis on south side of C-dock. Hot berth slips are assigned on request to the harbor office in Juneau, phone or hail on VHF Ch 73 for slip assignment. Douglas Harbor is the best option for vessels with a vertical clearance greater than 51 feet; the harbor lies south of the Douglas Bridge. Shallow off D-dock during minus tides. Pumpout station (by appointment) and launch ramp located at the north end.

Two pubs and a cafe are in Douglas. A bus stop near the harbor serves downtown Juneau. Savikko Park and Sandy Beach are located at the south end of the harbor – hike the trails through the woods to see ruins of the once world-famous Treadwell Mine.

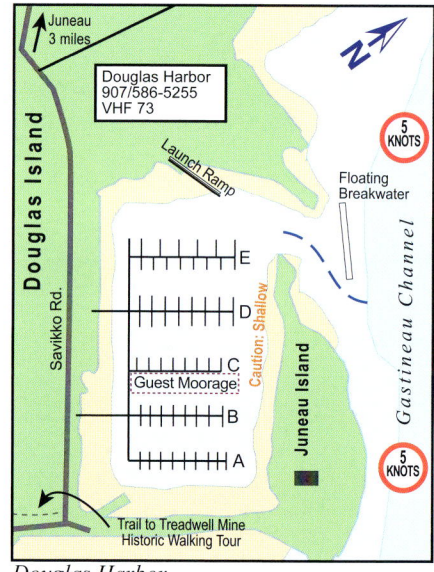

Douglas Harbor

See Area Map Page 493 - Maps Not for Navigation

SOUTHEAST ALASKA

Aurora Harbor in the foreground and Harris Harbor beyond, require passing under the fixed Juneau-Douglas bridge.

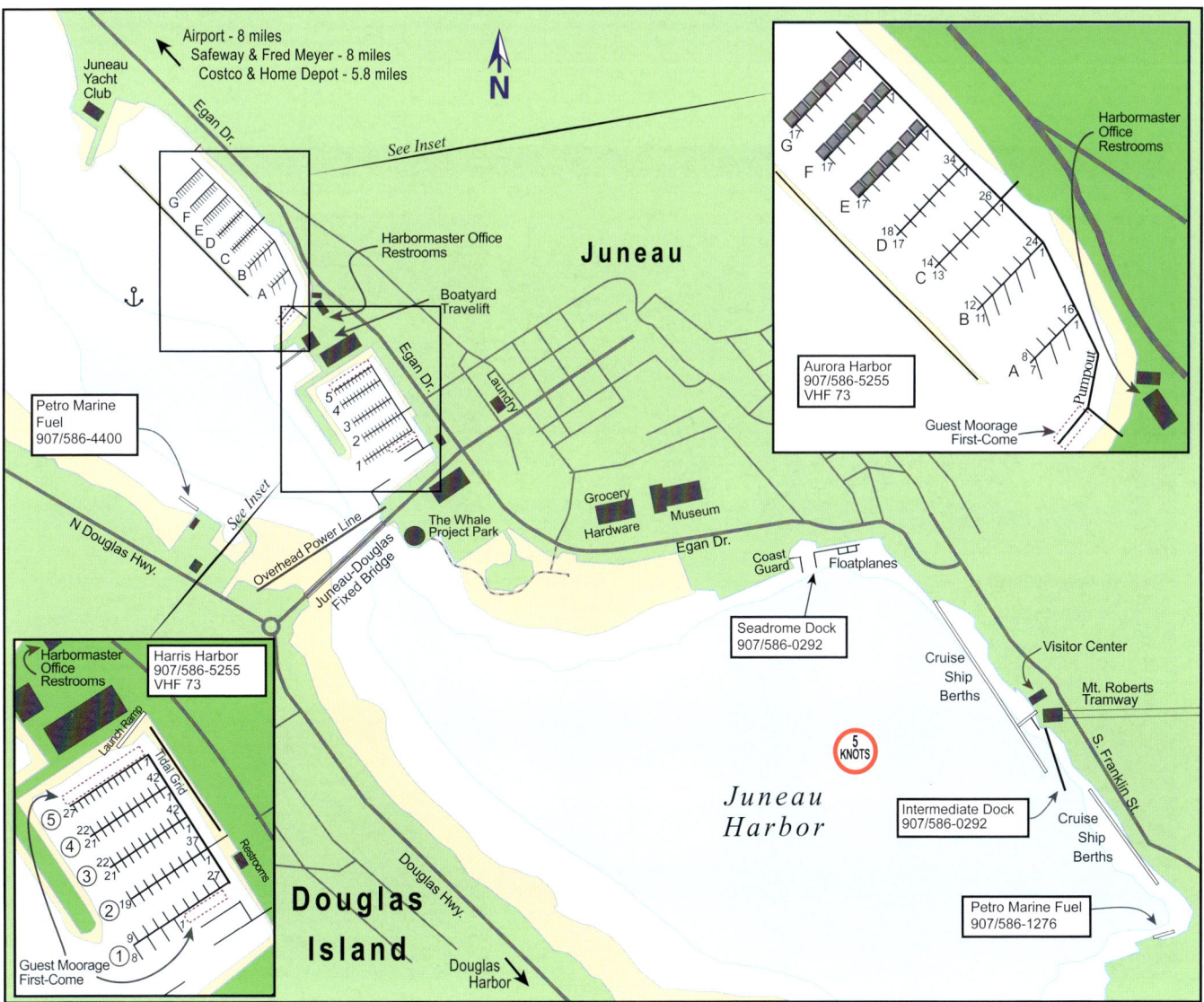

Juneau Harbor

㉙ **Auke Bay.** Located north of Juneau on mainland Alaska, off the north end of Douglas Island. Auke Bay is home to Statter Harbor docks, managed by the Borough of Juneau. Car rental agencies and the Juneau Airport are nearby. The Alaska Marine Ferry Terminal is adjacent to the Statter Harbor docks, with scheduled runs to Haines, Skagway, Hoonah, Angoon, and many other locations throughout Alaska.

㉙ **Statter Harbor.** 11497 Auke Bay Harbor Road; (907) 789-0819; juneau.org/harbors. Marina facilities located in Auke Bay offer side-tie transient guest moorage on a first-come, first-serve basis on docks C, D, and the inside of the floating breakwater. Reservations taken only for vessels over 65 feet for space on the outside of the breakwater; which can be very rough. This is a busy harbor with a 10-day movement rule for transient boaters from May 1st to October 1st. Phone the Statter Harbor Office or hail on VHF Ch 74 for instructions. Water available at the docks during the summer months; 20, 30, and 50 amp power. No power on the breakwater. Restrooms and shower facilities on-site. A pumpout is located on the main spine dock below the office. Laundromat, small grocery, and eateries nearby. Garbage, used oil disposal, and pumpout station.

This active harbor includes sport fishing boats, charter boats, whale watching vessels, and visiting pleasure boats. This Borough of Juneau managed marina is closest to the airport and shopping mall. A bus line runs into downtown Juneau.

Fuel: Petro Marine fuel dock located in Statter Harbor on the south side of B Dock; contact (907) 790-3030.

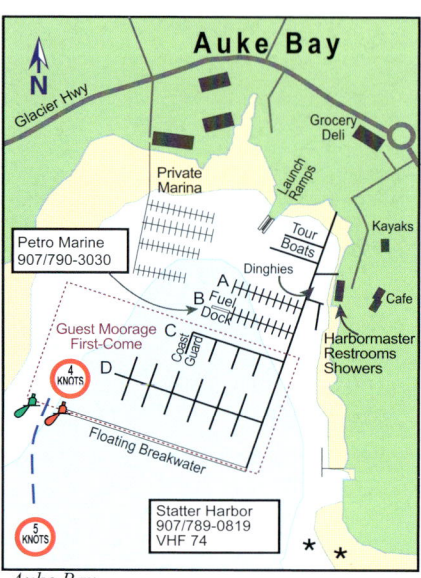

Auke Bay

THINGS TO DO

- **Glacier Viewing**. Take a taxi, or tour to Mendenhall Glacier, walk the trails with up-close views of the glacier.
- **Pan for Gold**. Visit the Last Chance Mining Museum (907-586-5338); see historic mining equipment and pan for gold in the creek.
- **Shops on Franklin Street**. Tour the many specialty gift shops and stores along Franklin Street in downtown Juneau.
- **Go Inside A Mine**. Take a tour inside the A-J Mine, a Gastineau Mill Tour (907-463-5017) with demonstrations of hard-rock mining.
- **Tram Ride**. Ride the Mt. Roberts Tramway up the steep mountainside for tremendous views of Gastineau Channel and Juneau; hike the mountain trails (907-463-3412).
- **Treadwell Mine Trails**. Hike the trails and discover ruins from the once famous Treadwell Mines found in the forest near Douglas Harbor.
- **Alaska State Museum**. Visit the State museum at 395 Whittier St. (907-465-2901); learn the State's history and see the large etched floor map of Alaska.

ALASKA STATE MUSEUM - JUNEAU

The Alaska State Museum, located at 395 Whittier Street (907-465-2901), has one of the most outstanding collections of Alaska Native artifacts and Russian colonial era artifacts. Commerce and transportation are also highlighted. The impressive displays cover the life, culture, and history of the diverse peoples of northern, eastern, southern, and western Alaska.

The impressive modern building sports a large Alaska State Map, including the Aleutian Chain extending to Kamchatka Peninsula, etched in the polished granite floor of the foyer.

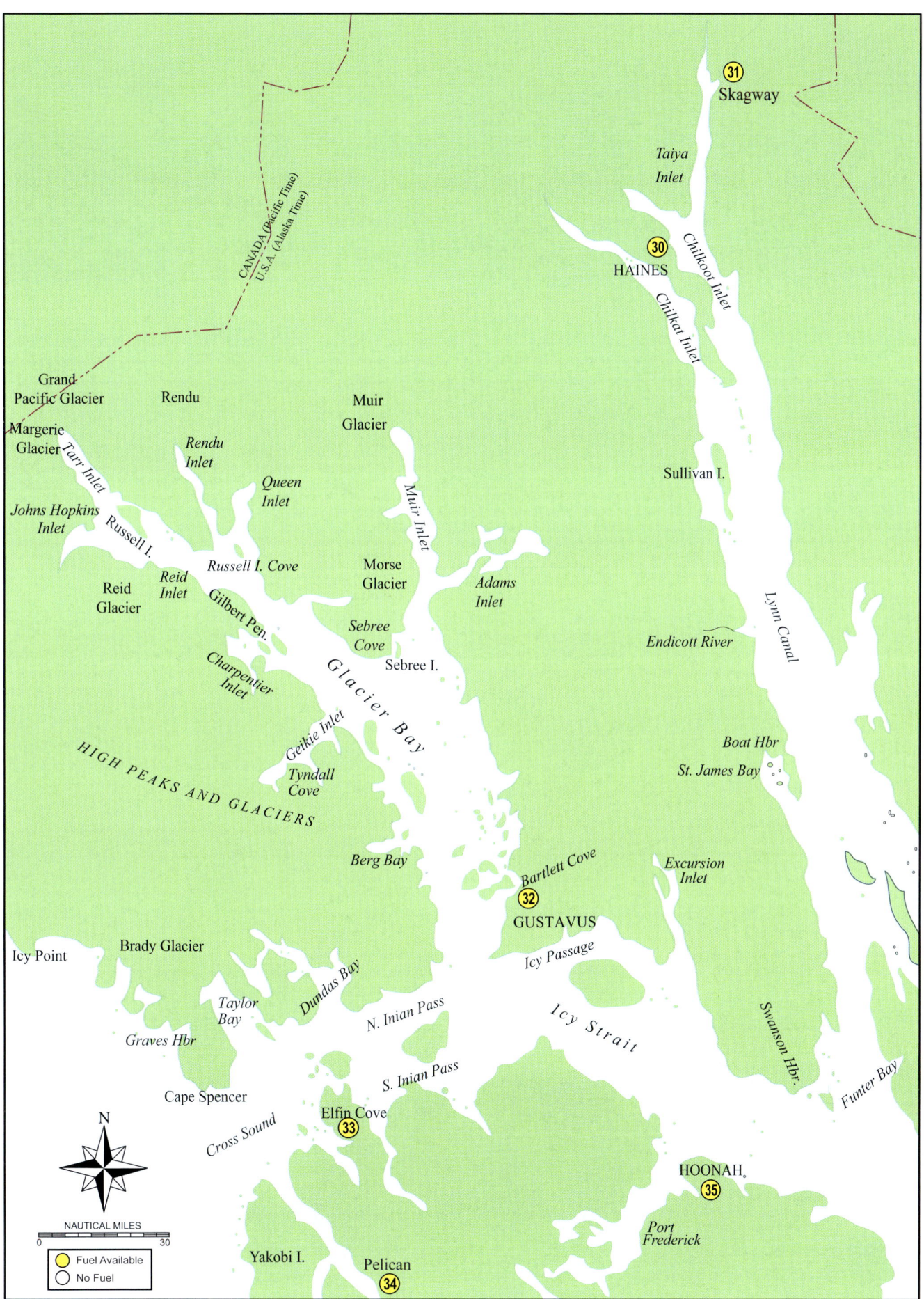

Lynn Canal, Icy Strait & Glacier Bay

SOUTHEAST ALASKA

See Area Map Page 497 - Maps Not for Navigation

The breakwater protected harbor at Haines is close to town with grocery, restaurants, and museums.

Lynn Canal. A 90-mile fiord inlet that runs north from the confluence of Chatham Strait and Stephens Passage. Majestic Eldred Rock Lighthouse backed by hanging glaciers and snow-capped mountains create a stunning scene. Haines is located at the north end of Lynn Canal, where Taiya Inlet continues to Skagway. It's a 14-mile journey by boat between Haines and Skagway, compared to 350 miles overland by car. During the Klondike Gold Rush, Lynn Canal was a major route to Skagway and Dyea for prospectors heading into the Klondike gold fields.

Due to the long fetch on Lynn Canal, seas can build quickly when the winds are up. Watch for wind against current. Study the charts and beware of Vanderbilt Reef. The *SS Princess Sophia* struck the reef in 1918, with the loss of all 343 passengers, the worst maritime disaster of the Inside Passage. The book, *The Final Voyage of the Princess Sophia – Did they all have to die?* By Betty O'Keefe and Ian Macdonald, tells the story of her final hours.

Anchorages can be found along Lynn Canal, but you may need to compete for space with fish boats during the fishing season, coming in to anchor for the evening. Bridget Cove, 22 nm north of Auke Bay, is protected from all but westerlies. On the west side of the canal is St. James Bay (protected from all but southeast winds); William Henry (open to the northwest); and Sullivan West Bight (open to northeast winds). Beware of numerous fish nets in Lynn Canal during fishing season.

㉚ **Haines.** One of the most iconic and authentic towns in Southeast Alaska; located at the north end of Lynn Canal with views of the Coast Range. Two well-stocked grocery stores, gift shops, a bakery, and good restaurants. Small cruise ships stop occasionally at Haines. The well-maintained Haines Boat Basin offers transient moorage, but space may be limited. If you plan to leave your boat at the docks to tour the area, inquire about boat-watch service. Anchoring is possible in Portage Bay.

Howsers IGA grocery is located between Second and Third Avenue within easy walking distance of the docks. Olerud's Market Center is located at 420 Main Street. Haines Brewing Company is located on Main Street, and several good restaurants are in town. Car rentals available to explore Central Alaska. The Alaska Marine Highway ferry terminal is located approximately 4 1/2 miles north of town.

Haines had its boom period during the Klondike Gold Rush of 1898; the Dalton Trail, today's Haines Highway, was one of the paths to the gold fields. Be sure to visit Fort Seward, the last of a series of eleven military posts established in Alaska during the gold rush era. The Fort was also Alaska's only military facility between 1925 and 1940. During WWII, the fort barracks became an induction center and rest camp for military personnel. Today, the buildings house shops, a hotel, cafe, a distillery, and art galleries. Located just upland from the harbor docks is the fascinating Hammer Museum, with 1700 different hammers, each one unique. Haines Sheldon Museum, with interesting exhibits, is across the street. The Bald Eagle Foundation, located in town on Haines Highway, is also of interest. Children like visiting the fair grounds on the edge of town, with the White Fang movie set.

LOCAL KNOWLEDGE

BLIND CORNER: The tall wave attenuator breakwater has a blind corner at the entrance to Haines Boat Basin, sound a horn or swing wide.

㉚ **Haines Boat Basin.** 32 S Front Street Haines, AK 99827; (907) 766-6450 or (907) 314-0173 cell. Harbormaster Tracy Harmon. VHF Ch 12 and 16. Transient moorage in slips and side-tie space in breakwater protected marina. First-come, first-served; call ahead regarding available space. Limited space with a maximum boat size of 100 feet. Water at the docks is seasonal; 30 and 50 amp power. No showers or laundry at the marina. Garbage, recycle, and used oil disposal; launch ramp.

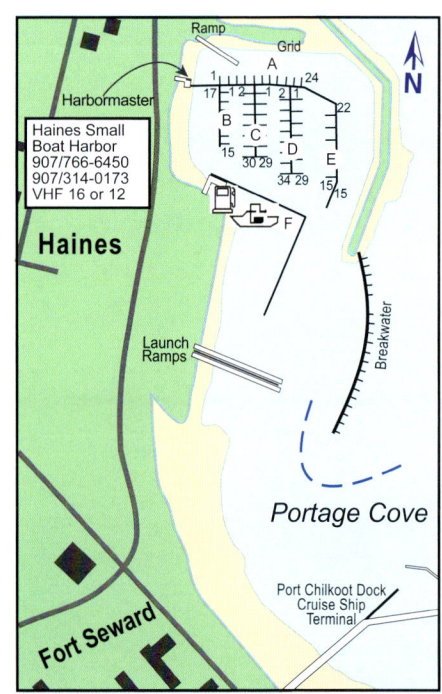

Haines

498 www.WaggonerGuide.com

It's a short walk to Skagway from the Harbor

Harbormaster's office located upland; office hours are Monday-Saturday 8:00 a.m. to 5:00 p.m., Sundays till 2:00 p.m. Future plans include adding additional moorage behind the new wave attenuator.

Fuel: Delta Western fuel dock with gas and diesel is to port as you enter the basin. The fuel dock closes at 4:30 p.m. Monday-Saturday and at 2:00 p.m. on Sundays. Contact the harbor office for fuel.

Letnikof Cove. Borough of Haines, (907) 766-6450. Located four miles south of Haines along the northeastern shore of Chilkat Inlet; protected anchorage from southeast winds; anchor near the head of the cove in depths ranging from 26-60 feet. Public seasonal (April through September) moorage docks in the cove are available for overnight stays. The docks are used by local boats. Make payment at the self-registration payment box at the head of the docks. Each leg of the u-shaped facility is approximately 200 feet in length.

The south portion of the Chilkat Peninsula is the site of Chilkat State Park with the 5.8-mile Seduction Point Trail. Along the south shore of Letnikof Cove is a fish packing plant that sells products at their retail store in Haines.

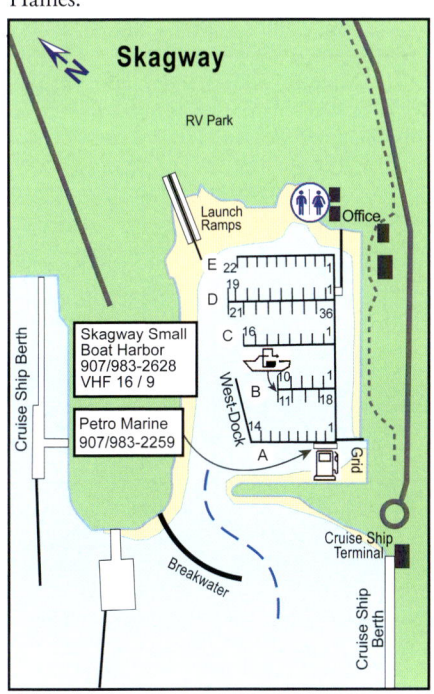

Skagway

㉛ **Skagway.** Located northeast of Haines at the head of Taiya Inlet. Visiting Skagway is like stepping back in time, gold-rush era buildings have been preserved as part of the Klondike Gold Rush National Historic Park. Shopkeepers dress in period costume adding to the atmosphere of the wild west. At one time 20,000 people lived in Skagway, about 900 people live here today; cruise ships deposit thousands of visitors to Skagway during the summer months. Visitors arriving with their own vessels can find fuel and transient moorage at Skagway Harbor. Grocery, gift shops, cafes, and museums are in town. The Fairway Market grocery is located at 377 State Street.

Visit the Skagway Cemetery (Boot Hill), where the infamous con-artist Soapy Smith is buried and Frank Reid, the wharf guard, who also died during this historic duel. A short, easy trail from the cemetery leads to Lower Reid Falls. The cemetery is just over 2 miles from town, best done with bicycles. Head northeast on Alaska Street, then cross the railroad yard; the cemetery is in the forest across the railroad tracks.

Don't miss taking the very scenic journey by rail over the Chilkoot Pass. Built in 1898, the White Pass & Yukon Railroad (narrow gauge) runs vintage locomotives to the summit of White Pass, which parallels the Chilkoot Trail. If you purchase tickets to Bennett Lake/Carcross Station in the Yukon Territory, don't forget to bring your passport. If planning to hike the Chilkoot Pass, one-way tickets from Bennett back to Skagway can be booked.

Each year thousands of hikers complete the 33-mile recreational Chilkoot Trail from Dyea to Lake Bennett. Hundreds of artifacts can be seen along the trail left by early gold seekers. Nine campgrounds are available by permit along the trail. A permit is required to hike the Chilkoot Trail from June 1st through the first week in September, plus a camping permit listing your chosen campgrounds. Call (907) 983-9200 for more information or search on Chilkoot Trail for the appropriate website.

㉛ **Skagway Small Boat Harbor.** 295 Congress Way; (907) 983-2628; m.oboyle@skagway.org (Matt O'Boyle); skagway.org/harbor. Monitors VHF Ch 16 (switch to 09) in the summers during business hours. Breakwater-protected marina for commercial and pleasure vessels up to 150 feet. Transient moorage is first-come, first-served; however, calling or emailing 2-days in advance is recommended for moorage assignment. Potable water, 20 and 50 amp power, garbage receptacles, and pumpout. Seasonal restrooms and showers. Launch ramp, tidal-grid, harbor crane, and haulout for shallow draft vessels up to 20 tons.

Fuel: Petro Marine fuel dock located on the south side of Float A inside the breakwater at Small Boat Harbor (907) 983-2259.

Skagway mixes mountain and town views

Funter Bay. Located mid-way on the west shore of Mansfield Peninsula on Admiralty Island, Funter Bay offers good protection when transiting between Lynn Canal, Icy Strait, and Chatham Strait. Several anchorages such as Coot Cove and Crab Cove, along with a State float are found in Funter Bay. The State public float is located on the southeast side of the bay and has side-tie space for several boats; no charge. The float is not connected to land. The nearby buildings were once part of a cannery.

Caution: check the depths inside the bay and along the inside of the float.

Crab Cove has a few vacation homes at the head of the cove. A private float and a couple of private moorings are near the head of the cove. Fair to good holding on a mud, shell and gravel bottom can be found in 7 to 10 fathoms. Signage at the entry gate to an historic cemetery can be seen on the point of land to starboard when entering the cove.

Coot Cove offers private anchorage with good wind protection. Anchor in 5 to 8 fathoms.

Swanson Harbor. Swanson Harbor is located at the south end of Lynn Canal at the intersection with Chatham Sound and Icy Strait. Two public floats are located on the east side of the bay. Anchorage can be taken in the northeast bight on the northeast end of Ansley Island. Consult charts to avoid submerged rocks at Sharp Ledge and No Use Ledge. The Douglass' book, *Exploring Southeast Alaska*, describes these anchorages in detail.

Checkout the many hikes around Skagway

SOUTHEAST ALASKA

499

2023 Waggoner Cruising Guide

Short stays are allowed at Bartlett Cove dock.

Glacier Bay is best experienced in good weather.

㉜ **Glacier Bay National Park.** PO Box 140, Gustavus, AK 99826; glba_vis@nps.gov; nps.gov/glba; Visitor Information Station at Bartlett Cove (907) 697-2627. Visitor Station open May 1st through September 30th; 8:00 a.m. to 5:00 p.m. Vessels are to contact "KWM20 Bartlett Cove" on VHF Ch 16 or 12 when entering the Park Boundary. Boaters need to stop at Bartlett Cove for an orientation. See additional information under Bartlett Cove.

Consisting of 3.3 million acres of mountains, glaciers, fiords, and wild coastline, Glacier Bay National Park is a portion of the much larger 25-million-acre World Heritage Site. This National Park, with its spectacular scenery, glaciers, and wildlife is considered a highlight of Southeast Alaska.

Permits. A permit is needed (per boat) from June 1st to August 31st in order to enter the Park Boundary, which includes Bartlett Cove. Permits are issued to the vessel operator, who may hold up to 2 permits at any given time; each permit may be issued up to 7 days and 6 nights for a maximum of 14 days. Applications for permits are processed in the order in which they were received. A limited number of boats (25) are allowed in the Park per permit period – maximum 7-day stay per permit. There is no charge for the permit(s). 60-day Advance Notice Permit requests are strongly advised for the prime season of June 20th through July 20th. Permits must be confirmed within 48 hours of the start of the permitted day or the permit will be cancelled. Tenders must have their own permit if being operated at the same time as the mothership. If you are denied an Advance Notice Permit, you may try for a Short Notice Permit, issued to boaters 48 hours in advance of the requested entry date. Applications are accepted no sooner than 7:00 a.m. Alaska Time on the day the application may be submitted. See the Park's website for details regarding the permitting process.

When visiting Glacier Bay National Park outside the required permitting season, vessels still need to initiate radio contact with Bartlett Cove when entering and exiting the Park boundary. Vessels over 18 feet must remain one nautical mile from shore in designated "whale waters." In narrow areas where this is not possible, navigate a mid-channel course.

Glacier Bay is the spiritual homeland of the Huna Tlingit, who were forced to leave by an advancing glacier over 250 years ago. Today, the Huna Tlingit live across Icy Strait in the village of Hoonah. The tribal house in Bartlett Cove (Huna Ancestors' House) was dedicated in August 2016, and is used as a gathering place for tribal members to hold ceremonies, workshops, and programs for visitors. Park visitors are invited to learn about Tlingit history and culture. You can hike the Forest Loop Trail as you recount the ancient clan stories. Guided hikes are offered by Park Service rangers

The Margerie and Grand Pacific Glaciers are favorite destinations within the Park. Due to icebergs and ice floes, most boats will not be able to make it to the face of the glaciers. Visitors may want to book the daily tour boat that departs Bartlett Cove each morning, contact Glacier Bay Lodge & Tours at (888) 229-8687; the tour boat can drop off campers and kayakers at designated camper locations. For tour operators based in Gustavus, go to gustavusak.com or call (907) 500-5143.

㉜ **Bartlett Cove.** Boaters can anchor in Bartlett Cove (site of the Visitor Station) overnight; anchor 300 feet off the dock beyond the white buoys. Bartlett Cove is a no "black water" discharge zone. A fee-based Wi-Fi service from Gustavus is marginal. Temporary tie-up for dinghies and pleasure boats is permitted at the Bartlett Cove dock while attending the required orientation; 3-hour maximum stay. Pumpout station, and water available; gas and diesel are available at the adjacent fuel dock if needed. Boaters

---

GLACIER BAY NATIONAL PARK - REGULATIONS & TIPS

- Radio KWM20 Bartlett Cove on VHF Ch 16 or Ch 12 when entering and exiting the Park Boundary and when entering and exiting Bartlett Cove.
- All boat operators need to complete an annual Orientation, either in-person at Bartlett Cove Ranger Station or evidence of completion of the online orientation.
- Maintain 1 nm from shore or mid-channel in the Lower Bay Whale Waters.
- Anchor in Bartlett Cove at least 300 feet away from the dock.
- Park Weather Broadcasts are given on VHF Ch 9 at 8:45 a.m. and 4:45 p.m.
- Pets must remain aboard vessels; however, pets on leash are allowed on the roads in Bartlett Cove.
- Be aware of extreme tidal range (up to 25 feet) and strong currents. Be aware of winds coming off glaciers and large waves caused by calving.
- Stay 100 yards from nesting seabirds and Stellar Sea Lions hauled out on rock/land. Stay 1/4 mile (400 yards) from Harbor Seals hauled out on ice/land.
- Stay at least 1/4 mile from the face of glaciers and give icebergs a wide berth.
- Vessels are not to operate within 400 yards of a whale.
- Fishing within the Park requires an Alaska State Fishing License; all fishing rules and regulations apply.
- Be aware of non-motorized boat areas within the Park, protected islands with 100-yard approach limits, and closed areas such as Johns Hopkins Inlet.
- Don't run generators between 10:00 p.m. and 6:00 a.m. in noise restriction areas.
- Drones and Personal Watercraft are prohibited.
- No collection of seashells or plants.

See Area Map Page 497 - Maps Not for Navigation

SOUTHEAST ALASKA

are reminded that Bartlett Cove is within the Glacier Bay National Park boundary; therefore a permit is needed from June 1st to August 31st before entering the cove. Orientations for Park visitors are held at the Bartlett Ranger Station building. Orientations include information about areas that may be closed for seal pupping or other wildlife concerns. While ashore for the orientation, be sure to visit the Glacier Bay Lodge, and the adjacent Huna Tlingit Ancestors' Tribal House. The Lodge has showers, laundry, and a restaurant.

Gustavus. The small town of Gustavus is located about 1.5 miles from the State Dock on Icy Passage. The town has a small grocery store, two cafes, gift shops and a small airport. The State Dock on Icy Passage has an Alaska Marine Highway ferry terminal, with 300 feet of side-tie moorage inside of the ferry landing, with a maximum stay of 2 hours. About 100 feet of the side-tie space is marked as load/unload only. No overnight stays allowed at the dock except in the case of an emergency, call the posted phone number to report your stay. All of the floating dock area is exposed to Icy Passage, with strong wind and current at times. The floats can be busy with everything from a water taxi to small charter fish boats and tour boats. Be prepared with lots of fenders and lines.

Good anchoring depths with good holding can be found on Icy Passage behind Pleasant Island. Check the winds and choose the best protected area. Wind and current can run through the passage, so check the weather carefully. Icy Passage is one of the closer anchorages for a planned trip to Glacier Bay National Park. Good cell coverage in the anchorage.

Berg Bay. Two good anchoring areas are in scenic Berg Bay with suitable anchoring depths. Entrance is south of Netland Island where rocks that dry at zero tide obstruct the middle of the channel. A shallow bar extends to either side of the rocks, with the shallower area to the south of the rocks. When entering north of the rock, steer toward the middle of the channel once past the mid-channel rock.

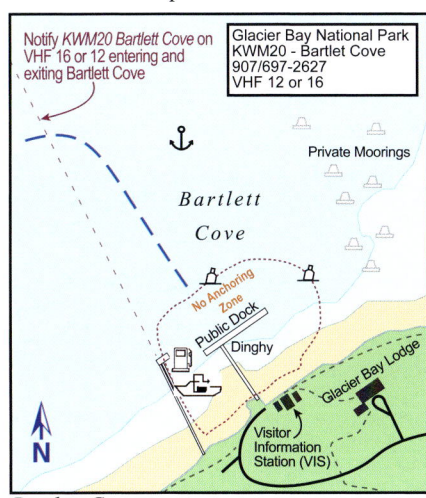

Glacier Bay is an immense cruising area with unparalleled scenic vistas.

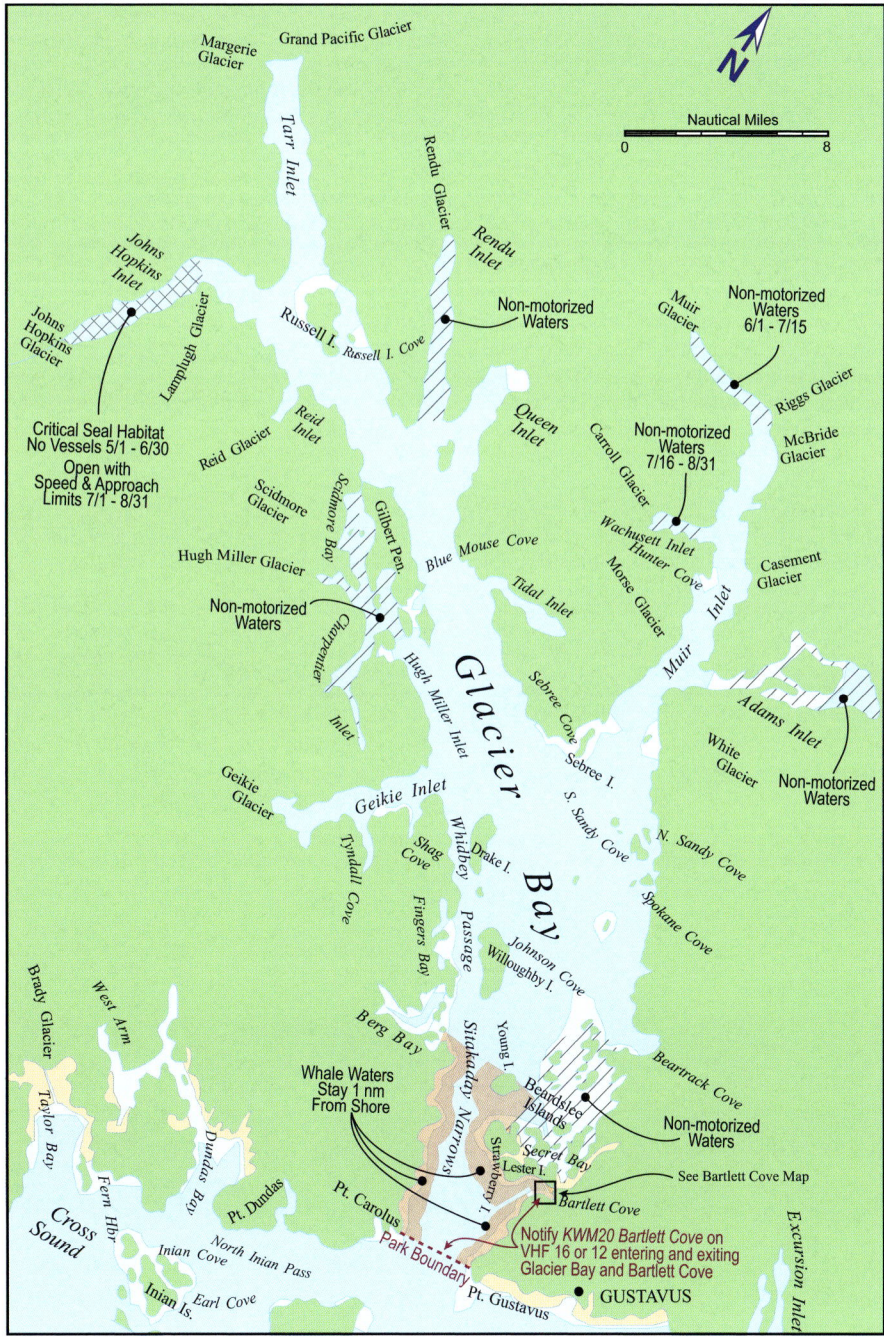

Bartlett Cove

Glacier Bay

2023 Waggoner Cruising Guide

SOUTHEAST ALASKA

Fingers Bay. The south bay has two good anchoring areas and a third for smaller boats. The north bay has good anchoring in the southwest cove. Mountains rise to the west; bay openings to the east afford good views of Whidbey Passage.

Blue Mouse Cove. The cove has room for a number of boats with good anchoring depths around the cove. Choose your location based upon forecast winds as wind waves from Glacier Bay can work their way into the large opening to the Cove. Low terrain to the south offers minimal wind protection from southerly winds. This is a convenient anchoring location for taking kayak tours of the large non-motorized boat area in Hugh Miller Inlet.

North Sandy Cove. Good anchoring depths are in the channel south of Puffin Island, or in the cove at the southeast end of Puffin Island.

South Sandy Cove. Anchor in 5 to 8 fathoms with good protection from all except westerly winds. A small floating ranger's cabin is in the eastern basin of this large cove, do not tie to the ranger cabin float.

Dundas Bay and Taylor Bay. These two bays, located west of Gustavus Point, are within the boundary of Glacier Bay National Park but do not require a permit to visit or enter the bays. Both bays offer wildlife viewing and wonderful scenery. Check the tides and currents when visiting; strong current can be present in the outer bay of Dundas. Anchorage can be found inside the southwest arm and near the head of the northwest arm of Dundas Bay. Taylor Bay is open to the south and subject to shoaling; day anchoring is possible during settled weather while exploring the area. Taylor Bay lies at the base of Brady Glacier and is the setting for John Muir's true story, Stickeen, an adventure with a dog and a glacier.

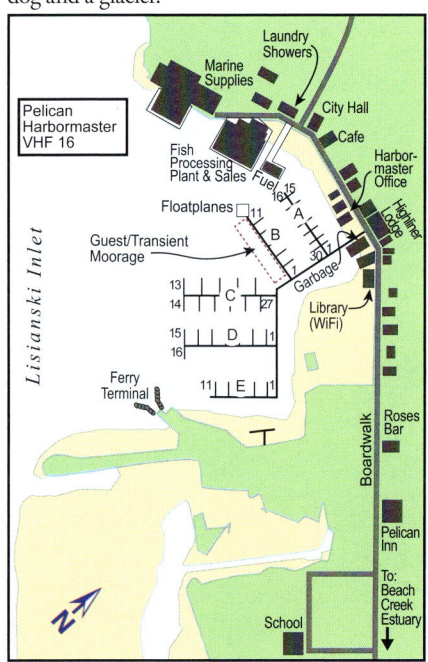

Pelican

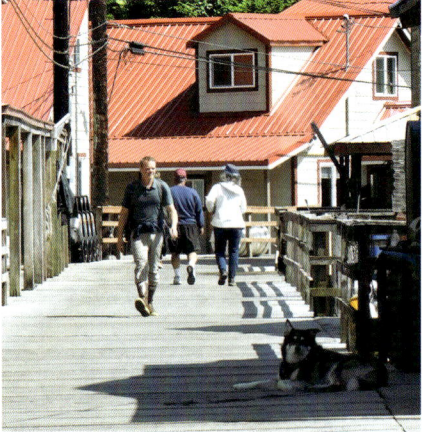

Mainstreet in Pelican is a boardwalk.

㉝ **Elfin Cove.** This quaint boardwalk village with a grocery store, café, and several thriving sport fishing lodges is located on the edge of Cross Sound. A boardwalk circles the central village and leads to the inner harbor. The outer harbor has a fuel dock and a complimentary guest dock with side-tie moorage; no power or water. The inner harbor offers protected anchorage and docks for permanent moorage and additional guest moorage, with a few water spigots and a few power stanchions. The State docks are managed by the Elfin Cove community and are first-come, first-served.

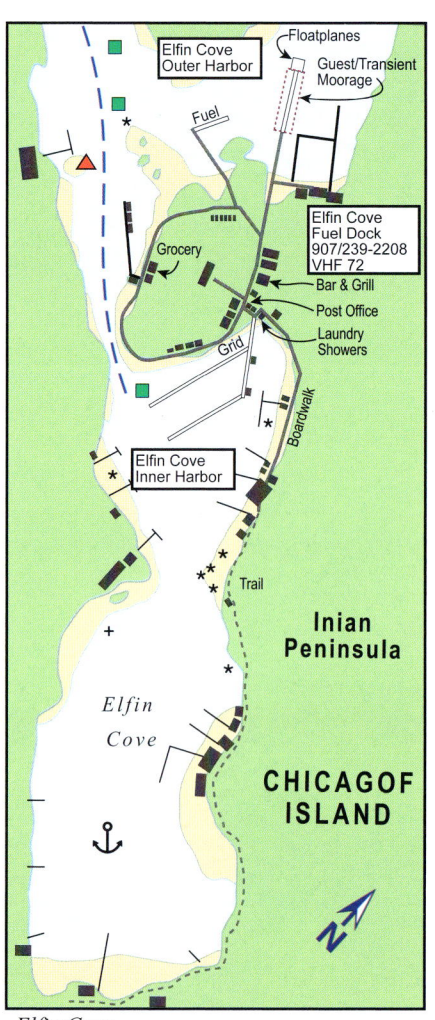

Elfin Cove

Elfin Cove's guest moorage float

No charge for moorage in the inner harbor; for power access and payment for electrical service, contact the general store. A 1/3-mile partial boardwalk and trail is found behind the community's laundry/showers building, which leads along the shoreline of the inner harbor. Fringe area cell service may be available in Elfin Cove, with a stronger signal found in Cross Sound farther from shore. Elfin Cove has six year-round residents, with a population that swells to over 40 during the summer season for a party-like, friendly atmosphere; a home-away-from-home.

Elfin Cove was established in the 1930's when Ernie Swanson moved his collection of docks, cabins, and a restaurant into the harbor, which served as a safe haven for fishermen. One of the float houses was used to salt and package fish for shipping to Juneau. A plaque in his memory is found at the beach above the community picnic firepit.

Fuel: Hours vary by season; contact on VHF 72 or (907) 239-2208.

㉞ **Pelican.** This charming village, fronting the eastern shore of Lisianski Inlet, has a mile-long boardwalk connecting village homes and town buildings that are on pilings, including the Post Office, City Hall, sport fishing lodges, a liquor store, the Lisianski Inlet Café, and Rose's Bar. At the north end of the boardwalk is a marine supply & hardware store, where you will also find the Yakobi Fisheries (907) 209-1053 selling a variety of frozen and fresh locally caught fish in season; look for the buzzer to ring for service. The Pelican Inn offers pizza and a small selection of convenience groceries. The all-inclusive Highliner Lodge offers meals to the public on a space available basis, call (877) 386-0397 to inquire. For tours to nearby White Sulphur Hot Springs, contact Terry Wirta of Chicobi Charters (907) 735-2233 or 957-3228.

Guest moorage is located along the south side of B-dock with 300 feet of first-come, first-serve, side-tie space; water and one 30-amp power stanchion. Slips may also be available for guest moorage, contact the harbormaster on VHF 16. Self-register and make payment at the harbormaster's office located upland on the boardwalk, or pay at City Hall (907) 735-2202. Garbage drop is located above the ramp behind a fenced area. Public showers and a laundromat are located just north of City Hall. No cell service, but free Wi-Fi is available at the village Library – the password is posted on the door. Fuel and propane available at the north pier with limited hours; contact on VHF 16.

The village is active in the summer months with ATVs, bicyclists, and residents strolling along the boardwalk. Views of the 2,000 to 3,000-foot mountains to the west inspire the soul in this off-the-grid village with floatplane service. Pelican was founded in 1938 by Finnlander Raatikaine, who named the site after his vessel, the Pelican. Folklore has it that in earlier times the site served as a Russian camp set up by survivors of a Russian shipwreck. Recent diggings have uncovered iron and copper pieces from the Russian America period.

㉟ **Hoonah.** Hoonah lies off Icy Strait on the north end of Chichagof Island in Port Frederick. Primarily a Tlingit community of 700 people. The ferry terminal at Hoonah is serviced by the Alaska Marine Highway System. In times past, the Hoonah Tlingits inhabited nearby Glacier Bay but were forced to leave as the glaciers advanced several hundred years ago. The panels and posts completed for the Longhouse in nearby Glacier Bay were carved in Hoonah.

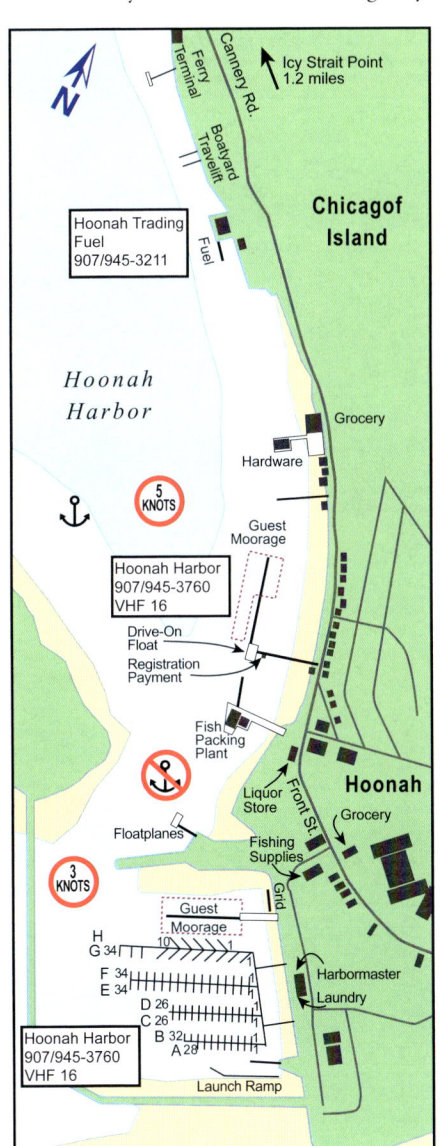

Groceries are available at the well-stocked Hoonah Trading Company grocery; and a selection of Costco Kirkland Brand items, along with a limited selection of groceries, can be found at Colette's Cupboard. Hardware, a tackle shop, gift shops, and restaurants in town, including the Icy Strait Brewing Pub.

Xunna (Hoonah) means protected from the North Wind in the Tlingit language. The breakwater protected inner harbor offers transient moorage, and the outer harbor has fuel and a temporary side-tie dock. The harbor is within easy walking distance to town. Fish can be purchased at the adjacent Hoonah Packing Company.

Kayak rentals are available through Fairweather Kayak Tours (907-957-6452). Not to be missed is a visit to "Icy Strait Point," a refurbished cannery from 1912, that houses shops and historic cannery equipment. The cannery buildings serve as a tourist site and museum, with outdoor seasonal food vendors and waterfront restaurants. The facility is open when the cruise ships are in town. Ask for the cruise schedule at the harbormaster's office. It's a pleasant 2-mile walk from town to Icy Strait Point. There are two cruise landing terminals at Icy Point, with a half-mile long gondola that runs between them.

The cannery is also the site of the world's largest ZipRider zipline – mile-long lines run from atop the 1,550-foot high Hoonah Mountain across the valley floor, terminating at the base near the cannery. ZipRider tickets are sold at the cannery. A gondola, that replaced the bus ride to the top of the mountain allows visitors the option to see the grand views without having to ride the zipline.

In addition to the two gondolas added in 2021, visitors can enjoy the Adventure Park in the forest, with tree-top rope courses, including nets and bridges, ranging from easy to challenging.

㉟ **Hoonah Harbor.** PO Box 260, Hoonah, AK 99829; (907) 945-3670; (907) 203-1317 cell; cityofhoonah.org. Water and garbage; 30 & 50 amp power; laundry at the harbormaster office. Transient/guest moorage available in the breakwater-protected inner harbor in unoccupied slips, as assigned. First-come, first-served side-tie moorage is on the first float to the left entering; no power and one water spigot at the bottom of the ramp. Reservations accepted online via Dockwa.

First-come, first-served side-tie transient moorage is also available in the outer harbor; self-registration and payment at the top of the ramp. Docks are within easy walking distance of town. Tidal-grid, 220-ton travel lift, dockside hoist, 35-ton hydraulic trailer, and launch ramp. Boat storage available in a secured, fenced yard.

Fuel: Hoonah Trading Co. fuel dock in the outer harbor has gas and diesel (907) 945-3211 Ext 105.

There is guest moorage at both inner and outer Hoonah harbors.

Hoonah Harbor

Icy Strait Point at Hoonah is a destination full of adventure and history.

SOUTHEAST ALASKA

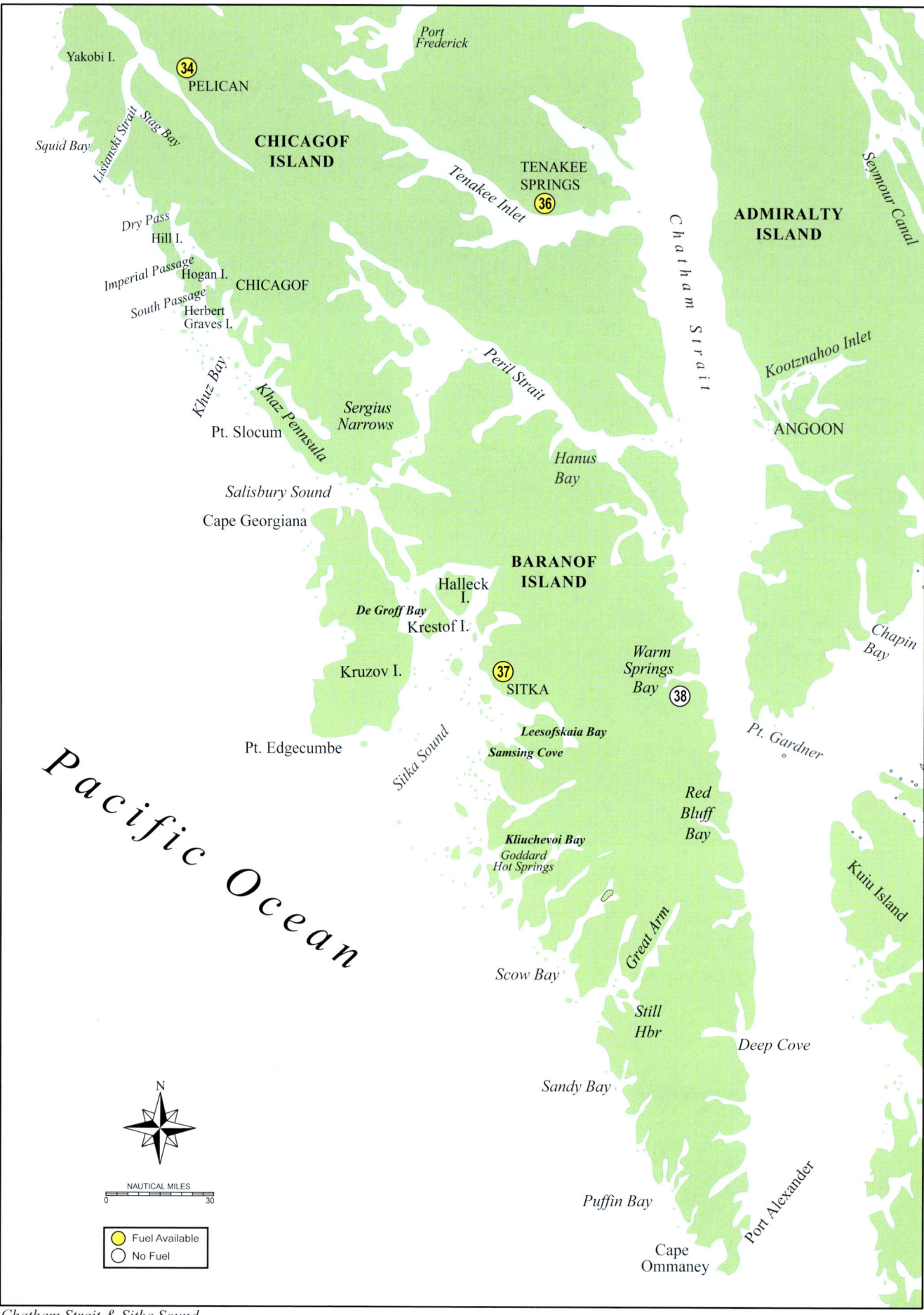

Reference Only – Not for Navigation

Chatham Strait & Sitka Sound

㊱ Tenakee Springs. Located near the entrance to Tenakee Inlet off Chatham Strait on Chichagof Island, Tenakee Springs is a tiny village of about 130 people. Houses overlook the shoreline, connected by a gravel pathway adorned with wildflowers. The local grocery store (907-736-2288) is well-stocked and housed in an historic building from the 1800's, with a modern refurbished interior. The Moon Cafe opened in 2021 and is located near the grocery store. The town has a very rustic bathhouse with a 106-degree sulfur hot mineral spring; hours are posted for gender-based usage. The bathhouse is posted as a no-swimsuit facility. Tenakee is a destination for kayakers coming from Hoonah, having paddled the 32 nautical mile Tenakee Inlet. Breakwater-protected-docks, with transient side-tie moorage, are within a half-mile walk of town.

㊱ Tenakee Springs Harbor. The harbor is protected by two floating breakwaters. Transient side-tie moorage is available along both sides of the western float. First-come, first-served. Moorage is limited to boats 65 feet and under. Docks are unattended with a phone number posted at the head of the dock, along with a self-registration station.

Fuel and untreated water at the pier located at the center of the village. Call the fuel dock (907-736-2288) for hours.

Hanus Bay. Located in Peril Strait off Chatham Strait on the northwest side of Catherine Island. Hanus Bay is a convenient stop when transiting Peril Strait to or from Sitka. Anchorage can be had in the cove behind Dead Tree Island; CAUTION for submerged pilings and logs lying southwest of Dead Tree Island. Anchorage can also be taken in the cove behind Point Moses. A trail head at 57.24.655 N and 135.03.767 W leads to Lake Eva; be bear aware. It's a short, easy hike along the river to the lake.

Peril Strait. A channel that connects Chatham Strait with Salisbury Sound, cutting between Baranof and Chichagof Islands. Peril Strait is used by commercial boats and pleasure boaters heading to and from Sitka. You will most likely feel some ocean swell in Salisbury Sound for about 2 miles before heading into the protected straits of Neva and Olga north of Sitka. Anchorages along Peril Strait include Hanus Bay, Appleton Cove, Rodman Bay, Deep Bay, Baby Bear Bay, Schulze Cove (west of Sergius Narrows), and St. John Baptist Bay in Neva Strait. A detailed description of these anchorages can be found in Douglass' guidebook, *Exploring Southeast Alaska*.

Boaters will need to plan ahead for transiting Sergius Narrows, located between Sergius Point and Rapids Island in Peril Strait; strong current and tide rips, especially on an ebb tide, are dangerous. Transit Sergius Narrows at slack water only; see Ports and Passes for tides and currents. You may wish to make a securite' call when transiting the narrows in limited visibility or heavy traffic.

Goddard Hot Springs awaits visitors from nearby Sitka and Sitka Sound.

Sitka Sound. The body of water near Sitka that encompasses the area from Cape Edgecumbe to Aspid Cape. Numerous islands and inlets afford many anchoring opportunities. Anchorages near Sitka include Leesoffskaia and Samsing Cove. De Groff Bay north of Sitka on Krestof Island has room for many boats if you don't mind the tricky entrance.

De Groff Bay. Located 9 nautical miles northwest of Sitka on Krestof Island; excellent protection in this nearly landlocked anchorage with ample swinging room for many boats. Flat, soft-mud bottom. Correspondent Chuck Wengenroth reports that some wind makes its way into the bay. The first narrows is deep and straight forward; the second entrance is narrow with rocks on the south side and a rock on the north side in the neck of the entrance, requiring a nearly 90-degree turn; check the charts carefully. A fun place to explore by dinghy or kayak.

Leesoffskaia Bay. Located southeast of Sitka across Eastern Channel. This is an intimate anchorage tucked behind a group of islands. Well-protected anchorage is found near the end of the bay with good holding. Entrance to the bay is narrow, with a drying mud flat on the south shore.

Samsing Cove. Located south of Sitka near Cape Burunof; offers protection from all winds on a mostly flat bottom with good holding. A mooring buoy and Forest Service rental cabin are in the cove.

Kliuchevoi Bay. Located just northeast of Goddard Hot Springs; a convenient anchorage while visiting the springs. The small bay is protected by rock islets. Entering from Hot Springs Bay, pass south of the charted rock mid-channel, then turn to port to avoid the rock and shoal charted along the south shore of the entrance.

Goddard Hot Springs. Located 16 miles southwest of Sitka off Sitka Sound near Hot Springs Bay. The natural hot springs water is available for visitors in two cedar shelters for about 4+ people in each pool. The Springs are a favorite with the locals from Sitka. Take temporary anchorage near the springs, or arrive by dinghy from the mothership anchored in nearby Kliuchevoi Bay, or Herring Bay on Elovoi Island.

Kliuchevoi Bay at Goddard has room for several boats at anchor; steer clear of the entry rocks.

SOUTHEAST ALASKA

See Area Map Page 504 - Maps Not for Navigation

㊲ **Sitka.** The town of Sitka is located on the west side of Baranof Island tucked inside Sitka Sound and protected by a series of islands facing the Gulf of Alaska. Sitka was the headquarters of Russia America until 1867, when the United States purchased Alaska. Sitka then became Alaska's first capital city. There are 22 buildings in Sitka on the National Register of Historic Places. Sitka is accessible only by air or sea and offers a diverse history, culture, and natural beauty. Mt. Edgecumbe and Mt. Verstovia are seen towering over Sitka, along with other impressive mountain peaks. Visitors will find grocery stores, gift shops, good restaurants, and several museums and historic points of interest. Moorage for transient boaters can be found at Eliason Harbor and ANB Harbor inside the Sitka Harbor Channel, with a 5 mph no-wake zone. Anchorage is available northwest of the Eliason Harbor docks behind the channel entrance breakwater. A laundromat is located across the street from McDonalds at 906 Halibut Pt. Road; call (907) 747-7284 for hours of operation. If you need packages sent to Sitka, you can have them mailed to the harbormaster's office at 617 Katlian Street Sitka, AK 99835 marked with your boat name on the package.

The annual Sitka Summer Music Festival is a month-long festival held in June, showcasing world-class musicians performing beautiful chamber music. Events are held at the Harrigan Centennial Hall, Stevenson Hall, and the Odess and Naa Kahidi theaters. For more information and tickets, see sitkamusicfestival.org or call (907-747-6774).

There are several museums and historic sites that shouldn't be missed. The Sitka History Museum (907-738-3766) covers the Tlingit, Russian, and American history of Sitka; The Sheldon Jackson Museum (907-747-8981) has a fine collection of Native art and artifacts; this small museum was founded in 1887 by Presbyterian Missionary Dr. Jackson to retain his collection of Native artifacts. St. Michael's Cathedral, the Russian Orthodox Parish of Sitka, houses rare religious art dating back to the 17th Century; the church is an iconic feature in downtown Sitka. For a beautiful walk through the forest, visit the Sitka National Historical Park. This National Monument Park is located at the mouth of Indian River, which is where a battle between the Russians and the Tlingits took place in 1804; historic totems stand among the tall trees in the Park. Traditional Native dances are performed in town at the Sheet'ka Kwaan Naa Kahidi Theater (907-747-7290), see sitkatours.com.

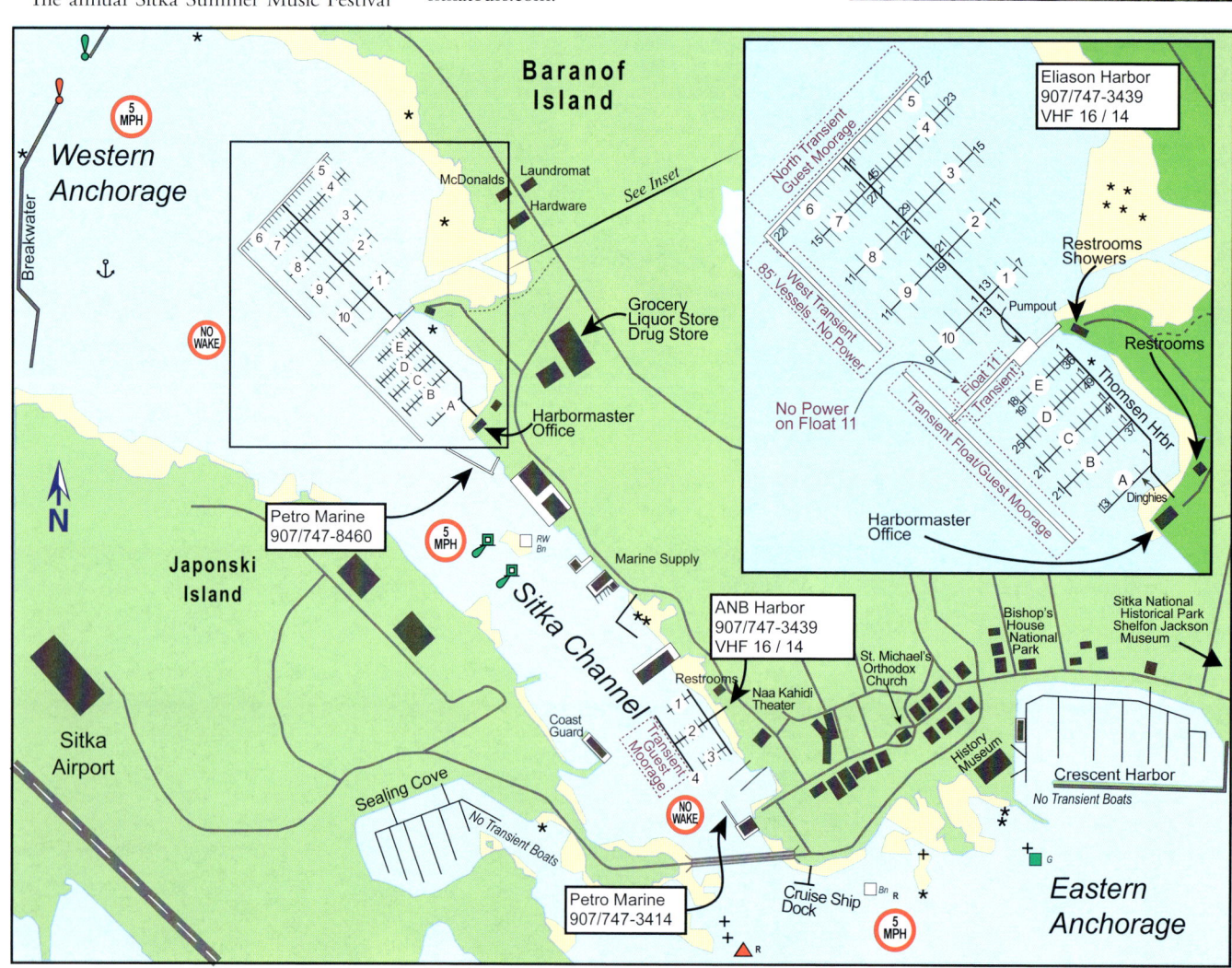

Sitka Harbor

See Area Map Page 504 - Maps Not for Navigation   SOUTHEAST ALASKA

Sitka has stunning scenery and numerous historical sites.

Russian blockhouses once guarded Novo-Archangelsk (Sitka).

A must see in Sitka is the Bishop's House, constructed in 1842 by the Russian-American Co. as the residence for the Bishop of the Orthodox Church. This large two-story house was purchased in 1972 by the National Park Service and was included as part of the Sitka National Historical Park. The building was refurbished, retaining its original floor and wall construction done by Finish Shipwrights of the time. The lower floor contains artifacts from the Russian-American period, including an original Russian Land Marker, declaring Russian occupation. The lower floor was used by Bishop Ivan Veniaminov as classrooms for the indigenous people. The Bishop's quarters and Chapel of the Annunciation is located on the upper floor and available by tour from a Park Ranger every 30 minutes.

Fort Rousseau Causeway State Historic Site, accessible only by dinghy or kayak, is another point of interest. Located just west of Sitka Airport on several interconnected islands is a 60-acre park with ruins left over from WWII, including lookouts, gun emplacements, ammunition magazines, and a command center. For a map and more information, go to sitkatrailworks.org/fort-rousseau.

㊲ **Eliason Harbor.** 617 Katlian Street Sitka, AK 99835; (907) 747-3439; (907) 738-0835 harbormaster; stan.eliason@cityofsitka.org. VHF Ch 16. Transient moorage is first-come, first-served; call ahead regarding available space. Transient moorage is located in three different docks at Eliason: North Transient side-tie dock (outside only); the West Transient side-tie dock (both sides); and the Breakwater side-tie dock (outside only). Restrooms and showers located upland near the harbormaster's office. 30 and 50 amp power; no power on the West Transient dock. Potable water on all docks. Pumpout at the drive-on loading area. The AC Lakeside Grocery is up the hill at 705 Halibut Point Road. White painted lines on docks are for 1-2 hour stays.

㊲ **ANB Harbor.** (907) 747-3439; stan.eliason@cityofsitka.org (harbormaster). VHF Ch 16. Transient side-tie moorage located on the outside of the breakwater; 30 and 50 amp power, potable water. First-come, first-served. Contact the harbormaster. This facility is nearest to downtown Sitka but is more exposed to boat wakes than Eliason Harbor. White painted lines on docks are for 1-2 hour stays.

㊲ **Petro Marine Sitka.** Two Petro fuel docks located in Sitka: an L-shaped float southeast of the Eliason Breakwater guest dock (907-747-8460); and the other float near the east end of the O'Connell Bridge (907-747-3414).

THINGS TO DO

- **Music Festival.** Enjoy classical music performed by world-class musicians at the month-long Sitka Music Festival in June; concerts held at Stevenson Hall.
- **Russian History.** Visit the Sitka History Museum at 330 Harbor Drive, showing Russian, Tlingit, and American history and artifacts (907-738-3766).
- **Native Artifacts.** The Sheldon Jackson Museum at 104 College Drive has a fine collection of Native art and artifacts.
- **Totems Walk.** Walk the beautiful trails at Sitka National Historic Park located near Indian River east of town, the site of a battle between Russian traders and the Tlingits.
- **Russian Orthodox Cathedral.** See religious art and artifacts dating back to the 17th century at St. Michael's Cathedral, the Russian Orthodox Parish in downtown Sitka.
- **Bishop's House National Park Site.** The Bishop's House, constructed in 1842 by the Russian-American Company, is a main attraction in Sitka. Both the House and the items inside serve as a museum maintained by the National Park Service. Located at 501 Lincoln St. (907-747-0110).

Sitka has stunning scenery and numerous historical sites.

The hazard of locking your bike at high tide

2023 Waggoner Cruising Guide

SOUTHEAST ALASKA

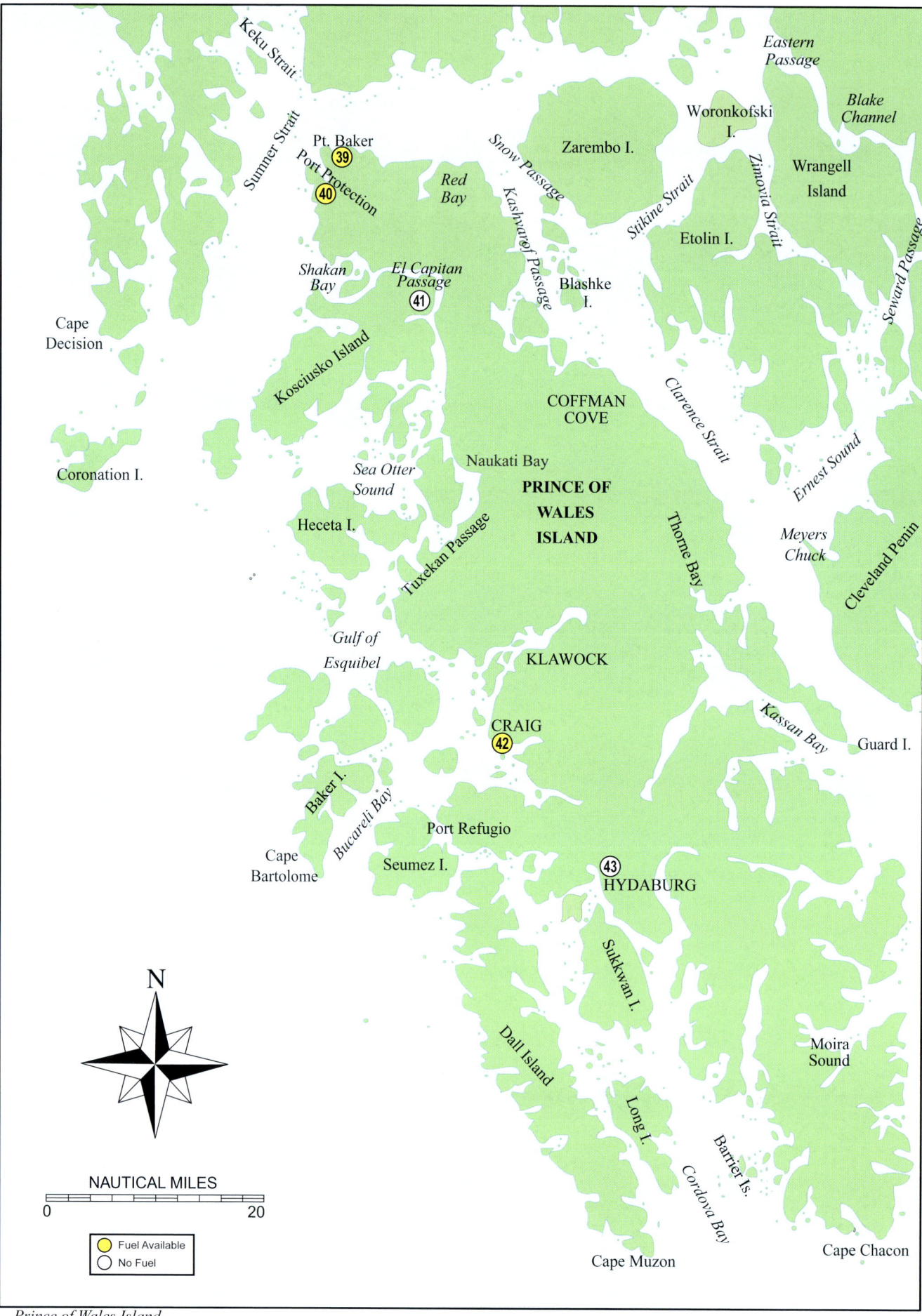

Reference Only – Not for Navigation

Prince of Wales Island

㊳ **Warm Springs Bay.** City & Borough of Sitka; (907) 747-3439; stan.eliason@cityofsitka.org. A 250-foot long public dock with no water or power is located at the head of the bay near a waterfall; the dock fills quickly at this popular destination. First-come side-tie moorage with self-registration and payment box located upland; payment required April 15 - September 15; cash, visa, or check accepted. Limited to boats 65 feet and under and rafting to 2 deep is encouraged. The western end of the dock is reserved for floatplanes. If the dock is full, anchorage can be found in the cove tucked behind the prominent peninsula in the bay, or in the unnamed inlet to the south. Lake outflow pushes northeast upon approach; a rock shoal blocks most of the flow.

This is a well-protected bay located along the eastern shore of Baranof Island, with a beautiful 100-foot waterfall at the head of the bay. The waterfall once provided hydropower for the tiny community of Baranof. A half-mile boardwalk leads to the natural hot springs, where visitors can soak in the pools that overlook the lower portion of the falls. Some boaters opt for soaking in the comfortable bathhouse tubs near the dock, with views of the bay – hot, spring water is piped to three tubs in the bathhouse.

Red Bluff Bay. This beautiful bay is located approximately mid-way along the east side of Baranof Island off Chatham Strait. Aptly named, one can't help but notice the warm-red colored bluff on the north side of the entrance to the bay. Several small islands sit at the entrance, consult nautical charts for safe passage. Cannery ruins are found a short distance inside the bay on the north shore; anchorage is possible in the bight off the cannery ruins, with views of a large waterfall across the bay. Anchorage can also be found near the head of the inner basin on the north shore. Bears are often seen at the river estuary at the head of the inner bay.

Return Routes South. There are three routes or choices when heading back south after visiting stops on Chatham Strait: 1) Cape Decision Route; 2) Rocky Pass Route; and 3) the Petersburg/Wrangell Narrows Route.

Cape Decision Option. This route requires exiting the south end of Chatham Strait then rounding Cape Decision, which is open and exposed to ocean swell. A good weather window is required. After rounding the Cape, this route takes you back north up Sumner Strait. Point Baker on the tip of Prince of Wales Island is a logical overnight stop. From Point Baker it's a familiar trip back down Clarence Strait to Ketchikan.

Rocky Pass Option. A 20 nm narrow passage that runs between Kuiu Island and Kupreanof Island between the village of Kake on the north and Point Baker on the south. The Pass may not accommodate deep draft vessels. See Rocky Pass earlier in this chapter for a complete description of the Pass.

The Warm Springs Bathhouse has three tubs for soaking and views of the bay, waterfall, and boardwalk. Hike the trail to the natural hot springs pools.

Petersburg/Wrangell Narrows Option. The longer route when returning from southern Chatham Strait but the most straightforward. This route takes you through Frederick Sound and back to Petersburg, then south through Wrangell Narrows. This is the most familiar route for many boaters.

㊴ **Point Baker.** (907) 559-2204 Community Association. Located on the northwest point of Prince of Wales Island off Sumner Strait, with a year-round population of 15 residents. The community is tucked inside the bay behind the Point, with community buildings on floats. Free transient moorage, first-come, first-served. A 440-foot State of Alaska float is in front of the "community center," convenience store, pub, and seasonal café. While the pub looks rustic from the outside, it's surprisingly nice on the inside; you can even purchase a T-shirt; and don't forget to tack a dollar bill to the pub wall with your boat name written on the bill.

There are three fishing lodges in the bay, offering opportunities to take advantage of the fish runs heading for the Stikine River. Whales too, take advantage of the volume of water and salmon moving through Sumner Strait; you are almost guaranteed to see whales off the Point.

Fuel: Gas and diesel at Point Baker; call ahead regarding availability.

㊵ **Port Protection.** (907) 489-2222. Located on the northwest end of Prince of Wales Island. A rustic, tiny village of about 40 people is tucked behind Jackson Island in Port Protection. The area was aptly named by Captain George Vancouver for its sheltered spaces. A State float is located in the bay but is usually occupied by local fish boats. Anchorage opportunities can be found in Port Protection in several nooks and crannies.

"Wooden Wheel" Johnson settled here in the early 1900's, establishing a store, fuel dock, and fish-buying scow. In 1946, Buckshot Woolery opened the B.S. Trading Post to replace the scow. A warehouse was built in the 1950's in hopes of establishing a shrimp cannery. The trading post closed in 1973, but Woolery's buildings still remain.

Fuel: Boats in need of fuel can tie-up in front of the community store, which sits above the shore on pilings. A hose is sent down to the dock and fuel is pumped from above; call ahead regarding availability.

㊶ **El Capitan Passage.** This approximately 18-mile-long passage extends from Shakan Strait in the north, to Sea Otter Sound at the south end, and runs between Prince of Wales Island and Kosciusko Island. While the passage is well marked, one should pay close attention to the charts. The passage is narrow, winding, and mostly shallow throughout, offering numerous anchoring options.

El Capitan Cave is one of the interesting stops along the passage. Tongass Forest Service conducts no charge guided tours of the cave during the summer months. A dinghy dock is located on the north shore of the passage at 56°09.65'N/133°19.33'W. It's a short walk to the parking lot, where you can meet the Thorne Bay District Ranger for a tour of the El Cap Cave; call the District Office at (907) 828-3304 to schedule a date and time. The tour begins with a steep hike up a 250-foot stairway to the cave entrance. Visitors are taken 500 feet into the cave; the tour lasts about 2 hours. For more information go to www.fs.usda.gov and then search on El Cap Cave. Anchorage is in the basin to the west.

Continuing south about 4.5 miles, Devilfish Bay on the western shore offers well-protected anchorage and is nearly landlocked. Anchorages farther south on the eastern shore include the small bight of Sarheen Cove and the larger Sarkar Cove. Sarkar Cove is home to El Capitan Lodge, a high-end sport fishing facility; keep a watch for floatplanes arriving and departing.

Naukati Bay, located on the south end of Tuxekan Narrows near Tahka Point, has a public dock with limited transient moorage. The small community about a mile away has limited groceries. There are several routes that lead to Sea Otter Sound, with additional anchorages along the way – see the Douglass' *Exploring Southeast Alaska* guidebook for more anchorages.

SOUTHEAST ALASKA

㊷ **Craig.** The town of Craig is located on the east side of Prince of Wales Island at the south end of Klawock Inlet, sheltered by Fish Egg Island to the northwest. Craig is an active commercial fishing port and has recently become popular for sport fishing, with the addition of several sport fishing lodges. Prince of Wales Island has one of the most extensive road systems in SE Alaska. You can rent a vehicle from Rainforest Auto Rentals (907-826-CARS) or Wilderness Car Rental (907-826-5200) to visit other communities on Prince of Wales Island, or visit nearby Klawock with its interesting totem park. Family members may enjoy a swim in the pool at Craig's Aquatic Center, call (907) 826-2794 for hours and location.

Craig is divided by a small neck of land, creating West Craig and East Craig. In West Craig, also called Downtown Craig, you will find the popular JT Browns General Store, which carries marine supplies, the Dockside Café, the Hill Bar & Liquor store, and T.K.'s Café in the historic Grain Inn. The Craig Public Library in West Craig has internet. East Craig is where you'll find the well-stocked ACO Thomson House Grocery, the West Wind Plaza Mall with several gift shops, a clothing store, a pharmacy, and Papa's Pizza. Annie Betties Bakery is located just east of the grocery. East Craig has a small industrial area with a NAPA store, Klein Marine Diesel, and outboard engine services. Boat Haulouts for vessels up to 52 feet, weighing up to 50 tons are available by appointment through the Harbor Office, call (907) 826-3404 to schedule.

The small neck of land is also the dividing point between Craig's two boat harbors, North Cove Harbor and South Cove Harbor, both of which have guest moorage. The North Cove Harbor docks are for larger vessels, while the South Cove Harbor docks are mainly for smaller to medium-size boats. There is ample anchorage in the bay west of the North Cove Harbor docks, with a small City Dock along the waterfront available for guest moorage. The Harbor Office is conveniently located on the neck of land between the two main harbors. Nice restrooms and showers are located in the Harbor Office building on the first floor. The Harbor Office also manages transient moorage at the City Dock located in West Craig. The Petro Marine Fuel Dock (907-826-3296) is located a short distance north of the North Cove Harbor docks. A laundromat is located in East Craig, north of the Plaza Mall at 330 Cold Storage Road.

When in Craig, don't miss walking around the remains of the historic cannery buildings and boardwalk in West Craig. The City of Craig is in the process of developing a 2-5-year plan for constructing a new marina and breakwater to be located in front of the old cannery site. It has not yet been determined if the historic cannery buildings will be preserved.

See Area Map Page 508 - Maps Not for Navigation

West side downtown Craig waterfront with eateries and marine supply

LOCAL KNOWLEDGE

PRIVATE: Waterfall Resort on the eastern shore of Ulloa Channel near Point San Antonio is a private sport fishing lodge and the site of an historic cannery. Both the property and cannery site are private, and the lodge actively discourages boaters from landing.

㊷ **North Harbor - Craig.** 410 Hamilton Dr. Craig, AK 99921; (907) 826-3404; harbormaster@craigak.com; www.craigak.com; VHF 16. Transient moorage is first-come, first-served; call ahead regarding available space. Side-tie transient moorage is located on the T-shaped dock at the north end of the North Harbor marina docks, with 30- and 50-amp power; potable water; restrooms and showers upland at the Harbor Office. Laundry located in town. Permanent slips (hot berthing) are also used for guest moorage as assigned; power not available for guests in permanent slips. Garbage bins located upland from the docks. Register and pay moorage at the Harbor Office located upland between North Harbor and South Harbor; the office is open Monday-Friday; self-registration and payment at the office; off-hours try VHF 16. Diesel and gas available at the Petro Marine fuel dock (907-826-3296) located north of North Harbor.

㊷ **South Harbor - Craig.** 410 Hamilton Dr. Craig, AK 99921; (907) 826-3404; harbormaster@craigak.com; www.craigak.com; VHF 16. Transient moorage is first-come, first-served; call ahead regarding available space. Side-tie transient moorage is

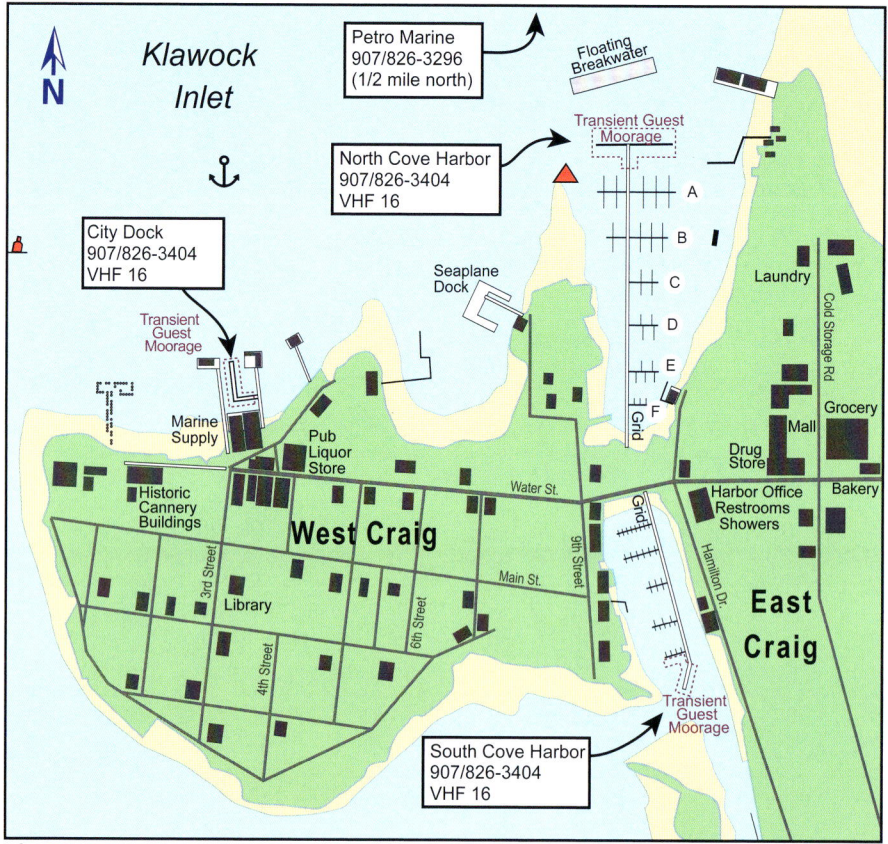

Craig

located on the south end of the South Cove Harbor docks, with 30- and 50-amp power; potable water; restrooms and showers upland at the Harbor Office. Laundry located in town. Garbage bins located upland from the docks. Register and pay moorage at the Harbor Office located between North Harbor and South Harbor on Hamilton Drive; the office is open Monday-Friday; off-hours try VHF 16.

㊷ **City Dock - Craig.** 1 Front St. Craig, AK 99921; (907) 826-3404; harbormaster@craigak.com; www.craigak.com; VHF 16. Located on the north shore in West Craig adjacent to a fish-processing business; 250 feet of side-tie space for guest moorage; first-come, first-served. Seasonal water, no power. Register and pay moorage at the Harbor Office located on Hamilton Dr. between the North and South Harbor docks.

㊸ **Hydaburg.** Hydaburg, located on the southwest coast of Prince of Wales Island, was founded in 1912. The Haida people migrated from Haida Gwaii beginning in the early 1700's and established several villages on Prince of Wales Island. In 1911, these villages consolidated to become Hydaburg, which is the most populous community of Haidas in the U.S. There is a small grocery with limited supplies located about one-half mile from the harbor on the south end of town. No bank or laundromat in town.

A totem park was created in the 1930's and new poles have recently been added to the park. Visitors can often watch carvers working in the carving shed, which is located along the waterfront next to the community Longhouse. A highlight for visitors is attending the annual Hydaburg Culture Camp & Haida Festival held during the last week in July, when the community celebrates with song, dance, carving, weaving, beading, and traditional food gathering. You can contact the Haida Cooperative Association at (907) 285-3666 for more information. From the bridge in town overlooking Hydaburg River, you can watch swarms of salmon during the spawning season.

㊸ **Hydaburg Harbor Docks.** PO Box 49, Hydaburg, AK 99222; (907) 285-3761 City Hall; (907) 401-1742 Harbormaster; VHF Ch 16. Contact City Hall upon arrival. Ample side-tie transient moorage located on an L-shaped dock on the southwest end of the marina; docks in good condition. Additional daily charge for 30-amp power. Potable water at the docks. Payment and boat information can be taken over the phone or in person at City Hall located a half-mile into town at 101 8th Street (cross the bridge and turn left up the hill). There is no self-registration-payment box at the docks. Grid and boat launch at the harbor. Waste oil-drop located upland from the docks, contact the Harbormaster for instructions.

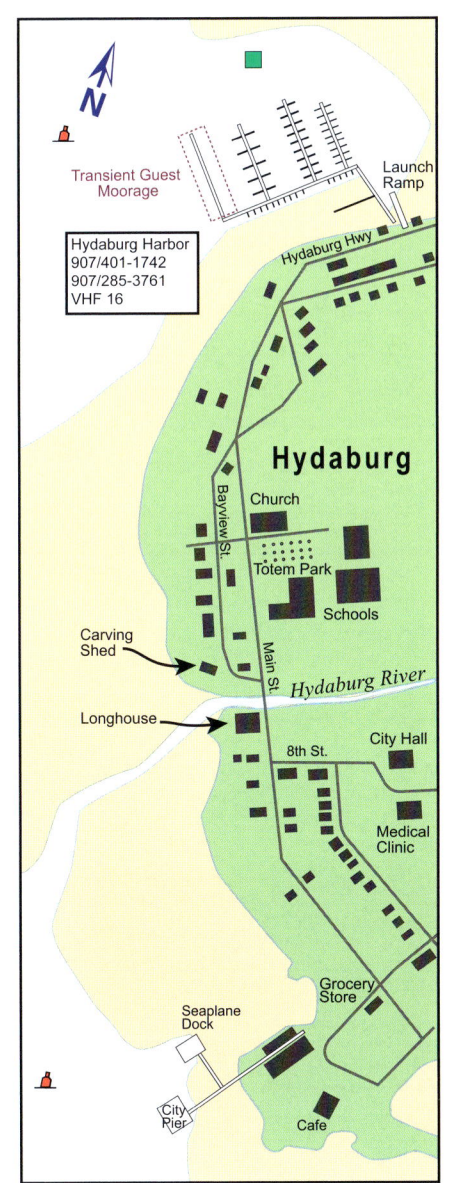

Totem Park and school at Hydaburg

Hydaburg

Visitors are welcome at the Carving Shed in Hydaburg

CONTACT PHONE NUMBERS & WEB ADDRESSES

U.S. COAST GUARD
U.S. Coast Guard Emergencies	VHF CH 16 or call 911
	(206) 217-6001 or (206) 220-7001
U.S. Coast Guard Emergency Juneau	911 or (907)463-2000
Cellular Phones Only	**911**
U.S. Coast Guard District Office: Seattle	(206) 220-7000
U.S. Coast Guard Spill Line	(206) 217-6230
U.S. Coast Guard Smart phone App	

U.S. TOWING
Fremont Tugboat Co.	(206) 632-0151
TowBoatUS all locations 24-hour dispatch	(800) 888-4869
TowBoatUS Anacortes	(360) 675-7900
TowBoatUS Everett	(425) 344-3056
TowBoatUS San Juan (Friday Harbor & Roche Harbor)	(360) 378-1111
TowBoatUS Lake Washington	(206) 793-7375
TowBoatUS Oak Harbor	(360) 675-7900
TowBoatUS Olympia	(360) 790-9008
TowBoatUS Port Townsend	(360) 531-4837 or (360) 301-9764
TowBoatUS Port Hadlock	(360) 301-9764
TowBoatUS Seattle	(253) 312-2927
TowBoatUS Tacoma	(253) 312-2927
Marine Services Whidbey (Deception Pass)	(360) 675-7900

U.S. WEATHER INFORMATION NUMBERS
Seattle	(206) 526-6087
Dial-A-Buoy	(888) 701-8992
	(301) 713-9620

U.S. CUSTOMS CLEARANCE NUMBERS
For customs entry call:	(800) 562-5943
Anacortes	(360) 293-2331
Friday Harbor/Roche Harbor	(360) 378-2080
Point Roberts	(360) 945-5211 or (360) 945-2314
Port Angeles	(360) 457-4311
By Appointment Only:	
Bellingham	(360) 734-5463
Blaine	(360) 332-8511
Everett	(425) 259-0246
Port Townsend	(360) 385-3777
Seattle	(206) 553-0770
Tacoma/Olympia	(253) 593-6338
Ketchikan	(907) 225-2254

WA PARKS INFORMATION NUMBERS
WA State Parks Launch & Moorage Permit Program	(360) 902-8500
San Juan County Parks	(360) 378-8420
WA Department of Natural Resources	(360) 708-1692

CANADIAN COAST GUARD
Canadian Coast Guard Emergency Numbers	VHF CH 16
Cellphone	*16
Search and Rescue: Vancouver	VHF CH 16 or (800) 567-5111
Search and Rescue: Victoria	(250) 413-8933 or (800) 567-5111
Search and Rescue: Other areas	(800) 567-5111
Canadian Coast Guard District Office: Victoria	(250) 480-2800

B.C. TOWING
Vessel Assist Gulf Islands	(800) 413-8222
C-Tow	VHF CH. 07A or (888) 419-2869

Covers Victoria to the north end of Vancouver Island & the Tofino area

Port McNeil	(250) 974-5305

CANADIAN WEATHER INFORMATION NUMBERS
Campbell River	(250) 286-3575
Nanaimo	(250) 245-8899
Port Hardy	(250) 949-7147
Prince Rupert	(250) 627-1155
Ucluelet	(250) 726-4648
Vancouver	(604) 666-3655
Victoria	(250) 363-6717

CANADIAN BORDER SERVICES CLEARANCE NUMBER
All locations & CANPASS
contact Canada Border Services Agency toll-free:	(888) 226-7277

CANADIAN PARKS INFORMATION NUMBERS
B. C. Parks General Information	(604) 582-5200
Gwaii Haanas National Park Reserve	(250) 559-8818
Gulf Islands National Park Reserve	(250) 654-4000 or (866) 944-1744

MARINE MAMMAL RESOURCES
San Juan County Marine Mammal Stranding Network is a collaborative program of the Whale Museum (Friday Harbor) and the National Marine Fisheries.
To Report a Stranding in San Juan County
Call 1-800-562-8832 or email hotline@whalemuseum.org
This hotline is a voicemail system that is checked frequently throughout the day. Leave your name and phone number.

NOAA Marine Mammal Disentanglement Network is a program for boaters to help entangled marine mammals in U.S. waters.
To report entangled whales call NOAA Fisheries hotline at (877) 767-9425.
NOAA 24/7 Hotline - To report injured or stranded whales, dolphins, porpoises, seals and sea lions, or to report incidents of marine mammal harassment:
Call NOAA's 24/7 hotline at (800) 853-1964.

BC Marine Mammal Response Network – handles marine mammal matters in B.C. waters; they ask that boaters report all injured, distressed and dead marine mammals and sea turtles.
Call their 24/7 hotline (800) 465-4336

FISHERIES & FISHERIES MANAGEMENT

Paralytic Shellfish Poisoning PSP shellfish closures can be expected without warning at any time during the season.
For PSP closures in Washington, phone (800) 562-5632. Washington State Dept. of Health Paralytic Shellfish Poisoning page: www.doh.wa.gov and search PSP. The website has a PSP fact sheet and links to PSP toxin closed areas of Puget Sound and San Juan Islands.

Washington State Dept. Fish and Wildlife information fishing and shellfishing: wdfw.wa.gov/fishing/

U.S. Fish and Wildlife Service Fisheries and Habitat Conservation: www.fws.gov/fisheries/

For PSP closures in B.C., phone the Openings and Closures Toll Free Line: (866) 431-3474 or (604) 666-2828 in the Lower Mainland, or go to: www.pac.dfo-mpo.gc.ca/fm-gp/contamination/biotox/index-eng.htm

Fisheries Management Areas. Download map of Fisheries Management Areas to enable you to decipher closure areas at: www.pac.dfo-mpo.gc.ca

Rockfish Conservation Areas booklet contains chartlets of all conservation areas. Many people do not realize that RCA's prohibit ALL hook and line fishing, not just fishing for rockfish. To view or download a copy of the booklet, go to: www.pac.dfo-mpo.gc.ca

VHF RADIO CHANNELS

Channel Number	WASHINGTON	BRITISH COLUMBIA	SOUTHEAST ALASKA
05A / 1005	VESSEL TRAFFIC SERVICE SEATTLE Northern Puget Sound and Strait of Juan de Fuca. Vessels not required to participate are encouraged to maintain a listening watch. .	VESSEL TRAFFIC SERVICE SEATTLE Strait of Juan de Fuca west of Victoria.	Port Operations
06	INTERSHIP SAFETY. For Search and Rescue (SAR) liaison with Coast Guard vessels and aircraft.	INTERSHIP SAFETY. For Search and Rescue (SAR) liaison with Coast Guard vessels and aircraft.	INTERSHIP SAFETY. Only for ship-to-ship use for safety communications.
09	INTERSHIP AND CALLING ALL VESSELS	VESSEL TRAFFIC SYSTEM AND INTERSHIP	INTERSHIP AND CALLING ALL VESSELS
11	VESSEL TRAFFIC SERVICE VICTORIA Strait of Juan de Fuca east of Victoria; Haro Strait; Boundary Passage	VESSEL TRAFFIC SERVICE VICTORIA Strait of Juan de Fuca east of Victoria; Haro Strait; Boundary Passage; Gulf Islands; Southern Strait of Georgia.	Commercial
12		VESSEL TRAFFIC SERVICE VICTORIA Vancouver and Howe Sound.	Commercial
13	Vessel BRIDGE to Vessel BRIDGE, large vessels. Low power only. Ships greater than 20 meters maintain a listening watch on 13. May also be used to contact locks and bridges BUT use sound signals in the Seattle Call.	Vessel BRIDGE to Vessel BRIDGE, large vessels. Low power only. Ships greater than 20 meters maintain a listening watch on 13.	Vessel BRIDGE to Vessel BRIDGE, large vessels. Low power only. Ships greater than 20 meters maintain a listening watch on 13.
16	INTERNATIONAL DISTRESS AND CALLING. Calling channel. Used only for distress and urgent traffic, for safety calls and contacting other stations. Listen first to make sure no distress traffic is in progress; do not transmit if a SEELONCE MAYDAY is declared. Keep all communications to a minimum. Do not repeat a call to the same station more than **once every two** minutes. After three attempts, wait 15 minutes before calling the same station. Pleasure vessels in US waters may also use Channel 09 for calling.		
22A / 1022	U.S. COAST GUARD. Safety and Liason communications with the Coast Guard. Coast Guard does not normally monitor 22A so first establish communications on Channel 16.		U.S. COAST GUARD. Safety and Liason communications with the Coast Guard. Coast Guard does not normally monitor 22A so first establish communications on Channel 16.
66A / 1066	PORT OPERATIONS - Most Marinas use this Channel	PORT OPERATIONS - Most Marinas use this Channel	PORT OPERATIONS - Most Marinas use this Channel
67	INTERSHIP ONLY FOR ALL VESSELS Working channel.	INTERSHIP AND SHIP-SHORE Working Channel	INTERSHIP ONLY FOR ALL VESSELS Working channel.
68	INTERSHIP and SHIP-SHORE VESSELS ONLY. Working channel.	INTERSHIP and SHIP-SHORE VESSELS ONLY. Working channel.	INTERSHIP and SHIP-SHORE VESSELS ONLY. Working channel.
69	INTERSHIP and SHIP-SHORE FOR PLEASURE VESSELS. Working channel.	INTERSHIP and SHIP-SHORE FOR PLEASURE VESSELS. Working channel.	INTERSHIP and SHIP-SHORE PLEASURE VESSELS. Working channel.
70	Digital Selective Calling (Voice Communications Not Allowed)		
71		VESSEL TRAFFIC SERVICE VICTORIA Northern Strait of Georgia to Cape Caution. Prince Rupert, Dixon Entrance and Chatham Sound.	
72	INTERSHIP FOR PLEASURE VESSELS. Working channel.	INTERSHIP. All vessels. Working channel	INTERSHIP FOR PLEASURE VESSELS. Working channel.
74		VESSEL TRAFFIC SERVICE VICTORIA Fraser River, West of Vancouver Island	
78A / 1078	INTERSHIP and SHIP-SHORE FOR PLEASURE VESSELS. Working channel.		INTERSHIP and SHIP-SHORE PLEASURE VESSELS. Working channel.
83A / 1083		COAST GUARD LIAISON. Primary Canadian Coast Guard Safety and Communications Channel. Also known as Channel 83 U.S. mode.	

REFERENCE PAGES

2023 WAGGONER CRUISING GUIDE

SPEED LIMIT AND NO WAKE ZONES

Speed limit and boat wake control zones exist throughout our boating region. Few if any are depicted on our nautical charts. Often, but not always, the speed zones are marked by on-water buoys or signage along the shore. Signage for No Wake zones is often private to protect nearby docks or marinas. Speed limits and no wake rules are imposed by a variety of different jurisdictions, including federal government, state/provincial government, port authorities, county government, and local/city government. Some are suggested or requested speed and wake control areas. Various controlling authorities, including police, enforce speed limit and no wake zones for the safety of people, boats, marinas, and shorelines. Boaters are expected to operate their vessels in compliance with these regulations.

NOTE: This is not a complete list but does include many of the commonly visited locations.

In general:
- Speed should be reduced and wake minimized when within 100 yards/meters of shore.
- Reduce speed and minimize wake when near beaches, swimmers, kayaks, canoes, and divers.
- A "No Wake 5-knot speed zone" requires a speed that produces a minimized wake which may be less than the 5-knot maximum.
- Kill your transom wake by briefly halting outside a marina entrance.
- Big fast boats should be especially careful with their powerful large wakes.
- Speed limit laws in BC are often legislated in km/hour and have been converted and rounded.

Puget Sound	Budd Inlet, Olympia	7-knot speed limit from Olympia Shoal to an East/West line at the North tip of Port of Olympia peninsula, where a 5-knot limit begins and extends south in both the east and west channels. No Wake speed limit in all City of Olympia waters.
Puget Sound	Amsterdam Bay, Anderson Island	5-mph No Wake speed is requested to protect shoreline.
Puget Sound	Foss Waterway, Tacoma	A No Wake speed limit exists throughout the Thea Foss Waterway.
Puget Sound	Commencement Bay Waterways	5-mph speed limit in the Hylebos, Blair, St. Paul, Milwaukee, Sitcum, and Middle waterways off of Commencement Bay.
Puget Sound	Gig Harbor	5-mph No-Wake speed limit is enforced in Gig Harbor and 200 feet outside the entrance.
Puget Sound	Salmon Bay, Ship Canal, and LakeUnion	7-knot No Wake speed limit is enforced from Hiram M. Chittenden Locks to Webster Point.
Puget Sound	Washington Narrows between Sinclair Inlet and Dyes Inlet	A Minimum Wake speed is requested to protect shoreline and boats moored at the marina.
Puget Sound	Liberty Bay, Poulsbo	5-knot speed limit on the north half of the bay; a marked buoy signals the south end of the speed limit zone.
Puget Sound	Keyport	An on-shore sign at the Keyport Naval Research facility marks a No Wake speed limit zone in front of the Naval facility docks.
Puget Sound	Eagle Harbor	5-knot speed limit begins at buoy.
Puget Sound	Port Ludlow	5-mph No Wake speed limit is in effect throughout Port Ludlow and applies to all vessels, including dinghies.
Swinomish Channel	La Conner	A No-Wake Zone extends from Hole-In-The-Wall on the south end to the railroad swing bridge on the north end.
Puget Sound & San Juan Islands	Orca Whales	A 7-knot No Wake speed limit is required and enforced within one-half nautical mile of Southern Resident Orca Whales within inland Washington waters.
San Juan Islands	Pole Pass	7-mph speed and low-wake zone marked by white cylindrical buoys extends 1/3 mile northwest of Pole Pass then eastward and southward to Bell Island; enforced by the County Sheriff.
San Juan Islands	Mosquito Pass	7-mph speed and low-wake zone extends throughout Mosquito Pass; enforced by County Sheriff.
San Juan Islands	Fisher Bay Channel	5-mph speed limit zone extends through the entrance channel.
Gulf Islands, Strait of Juan de Fuca, Fraser River Outlets	Killer (Orca) Whales	7-knot or slower speed is requested of all vessels when within 1 km (1/2 mile) of Killer (Orca) Whales.
Gulf Islands	Victoria Harbour	7-knot speed limit begins at Ogden Point and extends to Shoal Point, where a 5-knot speed limit begins and extends throughout the inner harbour.
Gulf Islands	Oak Bay, near Victoria	4-knot speed limit is in effect throughout the harbour area north of the breakwater and west of Mary Tod Island.
Gulf Islands	Brentwood Bay Tod Inlet	4-knot speed limit exists from a line between the Brentwood Ferry Terminal to the northeast boundary of Gowlland Tod Provincial Park (approximately the unnamed point on the peninsula west of Daphine Islet.)

SPEED LIMIT AND NO WAKE ZONES

Gulf Islands	Pender Canal, between North Pender and South Pender Islands	5-knot speed limit exists from Ainslie Point to Mortimer Spit.
Gulf Islands	Ganges Harbour	5-knot speed limit zone throughout the harbour begins at a mid-channel buoy near Rock Point.
Gulf Islands	Tsehum Harbour, Sidney	A No Wake, speed limit of 4-knots is in force in Tsehum Harbour.
Gulf Islands	Birds Eye Cove/Maple Bay	A white buoy entering Birds Eye Cove from Maple Bay marks a 5-knot No Wake speed limit zone.
Gulf Islands	Nanaimo, Newcastle Channel	5-knot speed limit zone protects marinas along Newcastle Channel from Bate Pt. to Shaft Pt.
Gulf Islands	Nanaimo Harbour	5-knot speed limit is in effect within 150 meters of shore and when near or around anchored vessels, floatplanes, and beach areas.
Vancouver	False Creek	5-knot No Wake speed limit extends throughout False Creek Inlet and begins off Sunset Beach.
Vancouver	Vancouver Harbour, First Narrows	A 15-knot speed limit in the waters around First Narrows, Lions Gate Bridge.
Vancouver	Coal Harbour	5-knot speed limit is enforced in Coal Harbour.
Vancouver	Indian Arm North	5-knot speed limit begins at Croker Island and extends to the north end of Indian Arm
Vancouver	Indian Arm South	5-knot speed limit begins at Boulder Island and extends north to Jug Island.
Vancouver	Indian Arm, Bedwell Bay	5-knot speed limit is enforced in Bedwell Bay.
Sunshine Coast	Princess Louisa Inlet	A no-wake speed limit is in effect throughout the inlet.
Desolation Sound	Pendrell Sound, East Redonda Island	3-knot speed limit is in effect throughout the north half of Pendrell Sound to protect seed oyster growing operations.
Desolation Sound	Gorge Harbour	A No Wake speed limit is in effect throughout the harbour.
Johnstone Strait	Cordero Channel, Cordero Lodge	A No Wake speed is requested when passing Cordero Lodge.
North Vancouver Island	Port Hardy	3-knot speed limit exists in the Inner Harbour.
West Coast Vancouver Island	Bull Harbour	3-knot speed limit is requested inside the harbour.
Northern B.C. Coast	Prince Rupert	5-knot speed zone is enforced within 600 yards of the harbour's south shore from Fairview Container Terminal to Ritchie Point. No buoys mark the zone.
Northern B.C. Coast	Porpoise Harbour, Prince Rupert	5-knot speed limit exists throughout the harbour.
Northern B.C. Coast	Venn Passage, Prince Rupert area	Two 5-knot speed limit zones in Venn Passage: off the airport dock on Digby Island, and off the village of Metlakatla.
Southeast Alaska	Tongass Narrows, Ketchikan	7-knot speed limit for vessels over 23 feet extends from Buoy 9 in the north to the East West Channel regulatory markers to the south.
Southeast Alaska	Gastineau Channel, Juneau Harbor	5-knot speed limit within Juneau Harbor; 7-knot speed limit in Gastineau Channel from Juneau Island and Douglas Harbor north to Juneau Harbor.
Southeast Alaska	Auke Bay, Juneau	5-knot speed limit within 1,000 feet of the harbor breakwater and entrance 4-knot speed limit within the breakwater.
Southeast Alaska	Sitka Harbor	5-mph speed limit throughout the harbor; and No Wake within the marinas.

SYMBOLS

1st Avenue South Bridge 117
24th Avenue Landing 120
52 Steps Dock 403

A

Acland Islands 240
Actaeon Sound 355
Active Cove 214
Active Pass 235
Active Pass Auto & Marine 236
Actress Passage 355
Admiralty Inlet 146
Adventure Cove 397
Agamemnon Channel 293
Agate Passage 130
Ahclakerho Channel 420
Ahousat 396
Alderbrook Resort & Spa 140
Aleck Bay 192
Alert Bay 363
Alert Bay Boat Harbour 365
Alexander Inlet 445
Alice Bight 170
Allan Island 170
Allcroft Point 449
Allies Island 310
Alliford Bay Ferry 464
Allison Harbour 418
Allyn Waterfront Park Marina 101
Alston Cove 447
American Camp 195
Amos Island 383
Amphitrite Point 400
Amsterdam Bay 102
Anacortes 165
Anan Bear & Wildlife Observatory 486
ANB Harbor 507
Anchoring 40
Anderson Bay 271
Anderson Passage 448
Andrews Bay 125
Anglers Anchorage Marina 242
Anna Inlet 465
Annette Inlet 240
Anthony Island 466
April Point Marina 321
April Point Resort & Spa 321
Arabella's Landing 108
Arran Rapids 333
Arthur Island 441
Arthur Passage 455
Atkins Cove 378
Atkinson Island 353
Auke Bay 496
Aurora Harbor 494
Azimuth Island 449

B

Bacchante Bay 395
Backeddy Resort & Marina 294
Bag Harbour 466

Bainbridge Island 130
Baker Inlet 454
Ballard Locks 117
Ballard Mill Marina 120
Ballard Oil Co. 120
Ballet Bay 296
Bamfield 407
Bamfield Inlet 407
Bamfield Lodge 408
Bargain Bay 290
Bar Harbor North & South 480
Barkley Sound 401
Barnard Harbour 448
Barnes Bay 319
Barnes Island 211
Barnet Marine Park 282
Barter Cove 383
Bartlett Cove 500
Bathgate Store, Resort & Marina 294
Battle Bay 382
Bauza Cove 362
Baynes Sound 266
Bay of Plenty 447
Bayshore West Marina 281
Bazett Island 403
B.C. Points of Entry 21
B.C. Towing Phone Numbers 512
Beach Gardens Resort & Marina 299
Beales Bay 434
Beaumont Marine Park 231
Beaver Cove 362
Beaver Harbour 369
Beaver Inlet 336
Beazley Passage 318
Becher Bay Marina & Campground 410
Bedwell Bay 283
Bedwell Harbour 230
Behm Canal 482
Belcarra 283
Belfair State Park 141
Bella Bella 433
Bella Coola 436
Bella Coola Harbour Authority 437
Belleisle Sound 352
Bellevue Marina 125
Bell Harbor Marina 116
Bellingham 173
Bend Island 345
Bennett Bay 236
Benson Island 406
Berg Bay 501
Bessborough Bay 336
Beware Passage 360
Bickley Bay 334
Big Bay 330
Big Frypan Bay 424
Big Salmon Resort 185
Billy Proctor's Museum 349
Birch Bay 175
Bird Cove 316
Birds Eye Cove Marina 246
Bishop Bay Hot Springs 452
Blackfish Archipelago 358

Blackfish Marine 280
Blaine 176
Blaine Harbor 176
Blake Island Marine State Park 114
Blakely Harbor 133
Blakely Island 193
Blakely Island Store & Marina 193
Blenkinsop Bay 338
Blind Bay 296
Blind Bay (San Juan Islands) 194
Blind Channel Resort 335
Blind Island Marine State Park 194
Bliss Landing Estates 303
Blubber Bay 271
Blue Mouse Cove 502
Bluenose Marina 244
Blunden Harbour 417
Boat Basin 392
Boat Bay 338
Boat Harbour Marina 255
Boat Haven 149
Boat Inlet 441
Boat Pass 234
Bockett Islets 343
Bodega Cove 390
Bold Island Anchorage 317
Bolin Bay 443
Bond Sound 347
Bones Bay 345
Booker Lagoon 356
Booker Passage 356
Boot Cove 234
Bootleg Bay 357
Boston Harbor 99
Boston Harbor Marina 99
Bottleneck Bay 395
Bottleneck Inlet 450
Boughey Bay 343
Boukind Bay 439
Boundary Bay 274
Bowen Island 285
Bowen Island Marina 285
Bowman Bay 161
Brandt's Landing 215
Breaker Pass 424
Breakwater Marina 109
Breezy Bay 234
Breezy Bay Vineyards 234
Bremerton Marina 127
Brentwood Bay 242
Brentwood Bay Resort & Marina 242
Bridgeview Marina 128
Bridgeview Marine 464
Brigade Bay 286
Brigantine Bay 189
Briggs Inlet 439
Broad Spit Park 137
Broken Group 406
Brooks Bay 380
Brooks Peninsula 380
Broughton Archipelago 356
Broughton Lagoon 352
Broughton Street Pier 223

Browning Harbour Public Wharf 232
Browning Inlet 378
Browning Passage 398
Brown's Bay Marina & RV Park 326
Browns Point Park 112
Brownsville 128
Brundige Inlet 471
Brydon Anchorage 428
Brydon Channel 428
Buccaneer Bay 288
Buccaneer Marina & Resort Ltd. 290
Budd Inlet 95
Buie Creek 447
Bull Harbour 375
Bullock Channel 440
Bullock Spit Cove 440
Bull Passage 271
Bunsby Islands 382
Burdwood Bay 316
Burdwood Group 350
Burfoot County Park 99
Burgoyne Bay 245
Burial Cove 343
Burke Channel 435
Burly Bay 354
Burnaby Strait 466
Burrard Civic Marina 279
Burrows Island State Park 170
Butchart Cove 243
Butchart Gardens 243
Butedale 451
Bute Inlet 317
Bywater Bay 135

C

Cabbage Island 235
Cachalot 385
Cadboro Bay 224
Call Inlet 343
Calm Channel 317
Calmus Passage 397
Cama Beach State Park 156
Camano Island State Park 156
Cameleon Harbour 334
Cameron Island Marina 260
Campania Island 448
Campbell Bay 236
Campbell River 322
Canadian Customs Information 20
Cannery Cove 491
Canoe Bay 229
Canoe Cove Marina 229
Canoe Passage 274, 360
Cape Beale 408
Cape Caution 412
Cape Cockburn 296
Cape Cook 380
Cape Lazo 270
Cape Scott 376
Cape Sutil 376
Cap Sante Marina 167
Captain Coupe Park 157
Captain's Cove Marina 275

Carillon Point Marina 125
Carriden Bay 353
Carrie Bay 358
Carrington Bay 316
Carr Inlet 103
Carter Bay 450
Carter Passage 355
Cartwright Bay 352
Casey Moran 480
Castle Island 192
Cates Park 282
Cathedral Point 436
Cattle Pass 195
Caulfeild Cove 284
Causeway Marina 223
Caution Cove 360
CBP One App 18
CBP ROAM App 18
Centennial Wharf 239
Centre Bay 286
Chained Islands 326
Chambers Creek Bridge 105
Chapple Inlet 448
Charles Bay 334
Chartering 44
Charts 55
Chatham Channel 343
Chatham Islands 224
Chatham Sound 455
Checleset Bay 381
Chemainus 247
Chemainus Municipal Wharf 247
Chettleburgh Point 448
Chiefs Bathtub 359
China Creek Marina & Campground 405
Chinook Landing Marina 112
Chonat Bay 319
Choquer & Sons Ltd. 295
Chuckanut Bay 172
Church House 317
Cigarette Cove 403
City Dock - Craig 511
City of Des Moines Marina 113
City of Richmond Imperial Landing 275
City of White Rock Pier 274
Clallam Bay 184
Clam Bay 253
Clam Cove 375
Clarke Island 406
Clark Island Marine State Park 211
Clatse Bay 439
Claydon Bay 353
Clayoquot Sound 395
Clear Passage 385
Clerke Point 381
Cliffside at Echo Bay 349
Clio Channel 345
Clothes Bay 445
Clutesi Haven 406
Coal Harbour 379
Coal Harbour Chevron 280
Coal Harbour Marina 280
Coastal Mountain Fuels 260, 370

Coast Marina 323
Coast Victoria Harbourside Marina 223
Cochrane Bay 307
Cockburn Bay 296
Cockle Bay 441
Codville Lagoon 431
Coffman Cove 486
Coffman Cove Marina 486
Coghlan Anchorage 452
Coho Marina and RV Resort 293
Colby Bay 449
Coles Bay 242
Collison Bay 466
Columbia Cove 381
Columbia Fuels Fuel Dock 437
Colvos Passage 112
Commencement Bay 109
Comox 268
Comox Bar 268
Comox Harbour 269
Comox Municipal Marina 269
Comox Valley Harbour Authority 269
Comox Valley Marina 269
Conover Cove 254
Coot Cove 499
Copeland Islands 303
Cordero Islands Anchorage 336
Cordero Lodge 334
Cornet Bay 160
Corney Cove 446
Cortes Bay 314
Cortes Island 312
Cougar Annie's Garden 392
Coulter Bay 316
Coupeville 157
Coupeville Wharf 157
Courtenay 269
Cousins Inlet 431
Covich-Williams Chevron 120
Coward's Cove 446
Cow Bay Marina 457
Cowichan Bay 244
Cowichan Bay Fishermen's Wharf 244
Cow Island Group 421
Cowlitz Bay 215
Coyote Cove 395
Cozy Cove and Fairweather Bay 125
Crab Cove 430, 499
Cracroft Inlet 345
Craig 510
Crawford Anchorage 334
Crescent Bay 184
Crescent Beach 274
Crescent Beach Marina Ltd. 274
Crescent Harbor 159
Crescent Inlet 465
Critter Cove 391
Critter Cove Marina 391
Crofton Public Wharf 246
Cufra Inlet 253
Cullen Harbour 356
Culpepper Lagoon. 443
Curlew Bay 453

Curley's Resort 185
Curme Islands 308
Currents and Tides 36
Customs Information 18, 19
Cutter Cove 343
Cutts Island Marine State Park 104
Cypress Harbour 352
Cypress Head 171
Cypress Island 170

D

Daajing Giids (Queen Charlotte) 463
Dabob Bay 137
Dana Passage 465
Danger Pass 478
Darby Channel 424
D'Arcy Island 224
Dark Cove 298
Dash Point State Park 112
Davidson Landing 485
Davis Bay 355
Dawsons Landing 423
Days Island 106
Dead Point 361
Dean Channel 437
Deas Slough 275
Decatur Island 189
Deception Pass 161
Deception Pass Marina 160
Deception Pass Marine State Park 160
De Courcy Group 254
Deep Bay 267
Deep Bay Harbour Authority 267
Deep Cove 242, 283
Deep Cove DAA Anchorage 283
Deep Cove North Shore Marina 283
Deep Cove Public Wharf 283
Deep Harbour 356
Deepwater Bay 171, 326
Deer Harbor 206
Deer Harbor Marina 206
Degnen Bay 256
Degnen Bay Public Wharf 256
De Groff Bay 505
De la Beche Inlet 465
Delin Docks 111
Delkatla Slough Harbour Authority 462
Denham Bay 333
Denman Island 267
Denman Island Community Dock 267
Dent Island Lodge 332
Dent Rapids 333
Departure Bay Gas N Go 261
Des Moines 113
Desolation Sound 305
Dickson Island 356
Dinner Bay 235
Dinner Rock 301
Dionisio Point Park 254
Discovery Bay 182
Discovery Cove 438
Discovery Harbour Fuels 325
Discovery Harbour Marina 325

Discovery Hrbr. Small Craft Harbours 325
Discovery Island Marine Park 224
Discovery Passage 321
Dixie Cove 385
Dixon Entrance Heading North 469
Dixon Entrance Heading South 471
Dock Street Marina 111
Dock Street North Pier 111
Dockton Park 112
Doctor Bay 310
Dodd Narrows 258
Dodger Channel 408
Doe Bay Resort 210
Doe Island Marine State Park 210
Dogfish Bay 256
Doig Anchorage 448
Dolomite Narrows 466
Donkey Bay 491
Dosewallips State Park 138
Douglas Harbor 494
Dowager Island 441
Doyon's Landing 481
Draney Narrows & Draney Inlet 423
Drew Harbour 319
Drumbeg Provincial Park 256
Dsulish Bay 421
Duck Bay 246
Duncanby Lodge 421
Dundas Bay 502
Dundas Island Route 470
Dundivan Inlet 440
Dungeness Spit 183
Dunn Passage 448
Duwamish Bridge 117
Dyes Inlet 128

E

Eagle Harbor (Bainbridge Island) 132
Eagle Harbor (Cypress Island) 171
Eagle Harbor Marina 133
Eagle Harbor Waterfront Park 133
Eagle Harbour 284
Eagle Island Marine State Park 102
Eagle Marine, Ltd./Columbia Fuels 403
Eagle Nook Resort 404
East Bamfield Public Dock 408
East Channel Bridge 125
East Cove 378
East of Eden 357
East Passage 112
Eastsound 208
East Sound 208
Eastsound County Dock 208
East Waterway 116
Echo Bay 213, 348
Echo Bay Marina & Lodge 349
Echo Harbour 465
Edmonds 153
Edward Channel 427
Effingham Bay 406
Effingham Inlet 404
Egmont 294
Egmont Public Wharf 294

El Capitan Passage 509
Elcho Harbour 437
Eld Inlet 99
Elfin Cove 502
Elger Bay 156
Eliason Harbor 507
Eliza Island 172
Ellerslie Lagoon 440
Elliott Bay 114
Elliott Bay Marina 115
Elworthy Island 310
Embley Lagoon 353
Emergencies & Contingencies 76
Emily Bay 439
Emily Carr Inlet 448
Endicott Arm 492
End Of The Road Parking 302
English Camp National Park 204
Entrance Inlet 403
Entrance Island (Hobart Bay) 492
Esperanza 388
Esperanza Inlet 386
Espinosa Inlet 386
Esquimalt Harbour 221
Estero Basin 333
Estevan Point 392
Ethel Cove 421
Etolin Harbor 489
Eucott Bay 438
Europa Hot Springs 452
Evans Bay 316
Eveleigh Island 309
Evening Cove 248
Everett 154
Ewing Cove 214
Ewin Inlet 391

F

Fair Harbor Marina 101
Fair Harbour 385
Fair Harbour Marina & Campground 385
Fairhaven Moorage 172
Fairview Small Craft Harbour 457
Fairwinds Marina 265
False Bay 270
False Creek 279
False Creek Fuels 279
False Creek Harbour Authority 279
False Creek Yacht Club 279
False Narrows 258
Fancy Cove 432
Fannie Cove 432
Fanny Bay 267, 334
Fanny Island 337
Farewell Harbour 359
Fast Fuel LP 463
Fay Bainbridge Park 131
Fernwood Public Wharf 241
Fidalgo Marina 169
Field Correspondents 6
Fifer Bay 425
Fife Sound 356
Filucy Bay 102

Fingers Bay 502
Fin Island 453
Finis Nook 421
Finlayson Arm 243
Finlayson Channel 445
Finn Bay 424
Finn Cove 301, 302
Fiordland Conservancy 443
Fish Creek 195
Fisher Channel 430
Fisheries 512
Fisherman Bay 191
Fisherman Harbor 137
Fishermans Cove Marine Fuels 284
Fisherman's Landing & Lodge 331
Fisherman's Wharf 370
Fisherman's Wharf (Campbell River) 323
Fisherman's Wharf/Victoria 223
Fishermen's Harbour 405
Fishermen's Terminal/Port of Seattle 120
Fishermen's Wharf 279
Fishing Bay & Judd Bay 208
Fishing & Shellfish Collecting 72
Fish Trap Bay 425
Fitzgibbon Cove 483
Flat Top Islands 256
Fleming Beach 221
Fleming Island 407
Fletcher Bay 129
Flotilla Cruising 47
Flounder Bay 170
Fly Basin 420
Foggy Bay 477
Ford Cove 266
Ford Cove Harbour Authority 266
Fords Terror 492
Forit Bay 435
Fort Ebey State Park 152
Fort Flagler Marine State Park 148
Fort Rupert 369
Fort Townsend Marine State Park 147
Fortune Channel 397
Fort Ward Park 126
Fort Worden Marine State Park 151
Forward Bay 338
Forward Harbour 336
Foss Harbor Marina 111
Fossil Bay 213
Foss Waterway Seaport 111
Fougner Bay 435
Fox Cove 213
Fox Island 104
Frances Bay 317
Fraser Reach 451
Frederick Arm 333
Freeman Island 215
French Creek Harbour Authority 266
Freshwater Marina and Boatyard 325
Friday Harbor 197
Friendly Cove 392
Friendly Dolphin Cove 396
Frye Cove County Park 99
Frypan Bay 424

Fulford Harbour 236
Fulford Inner Harbour 237
Fulford Outer Harbour 236
Funter Bay 499
Fury Cove 424

G

Gabriola Passage 256
Gabriola Sands Park 258
Galiano Oceanfront Inn & Spa 236
Galley Bay 308
Galley Restaurant 192
Gambier Island 286
Ganges 238
Ganges Breakwater Float 239
Ganges Centennial Wharf 239
Ganges Kanaka Wharf 239
Ganges Marina 239
Garden Bay 291
Garden Bay Marina 292
Garrison Bay 204
Gas N Go Marine Ltd. 269
Gedney Island 153
Gene Coulon Memorial Beach Park 125
Genoa Bay 244
Genoa Bay Marina 244
Georgeson Passage 234
Gerrans Bay 293
Gibson Cove 397
Gibson Marine Park 396
Gibsons 287
Gibsons Landing Harbour Authority 287
Gibsons Marina and Fuel Dock 288
Gig Harbor 106
Gig Harbor Marina and Boatyard 108
Gillam Channel 386
Gillard Passage 331
Glacier Bay National Park 500
Glen Ayr Resort 138
Glen Cove 104
Glendale Cove 346
Glenthorne Passage 240
Goat Cove 450
Goat Island Anchorage 358
Goddard Hot Springs 505
God's Pocket 375
Gods Pocket 397
God's Pocket Resort 375
Goldstream Boathouse 243
Goldstream Harbour 427
Goldsworthy Pier 281
Goletas Channel 374
Good Hope Cannery 423
Goose Bay 421
Goose Bay Cannery 421
Gordon Cove 464
Gorge Harbour 315
Gorge Harbour Marina Resort 315
Gorge Harbour Public Dock 316
Gosse Bay 435
Gossip Island. 217
Gowlland Harbour 321
Grace Harbour 307

Graham Island 462
Graham Preserve 194
Graham Reach 451
Granite Bay 326
Granite Bay Park Dock 327
Granite Falls 283
Granite Point 327
Grant Anchorage 446
Granville Island 279
Granville Island Boat Yard 280
Granville Island Public Market Dock 280
Grappler Sound 353
Grasshopper Pub 293
Grays Cove 466
Greater Victoria Harbour Authority 223
Grebe Cove 358
Green Bay 293
Green Cove 405
Greene Point Rapids 336
Green Island Anchorage 425
Grenville Channel 453
Grief Point 300
Griffin Bay 195
Griffin Bay Park 195
Grindstone Harbor 208
Growler Cove 361
Guemes Channel 169
Guise Bay 377
Gulf Islands 219
Gulf Islands National Park Reserve 219
Gulf Islands No-Go Zones 230
Gunboat Bay 292
Gunboat Passage 434
Gunner Inlet 398
Gustavus 501
Guthrie Bay 208
Gwaii Haanas National Park Reserve 460

H

Hadlock Public Dock 147
Haida Gwaii 460
Haida Heritage Centre 460
Haines 498
Haines Boat Basin 498
Hakai Beach Institute 426
Hakai Luxvbalis Conservancy 426
Hakai Passage 427
Hale Passage 104
Halfmoon Bay 288
Halkett Bay 286
Halkett Bay Fircom Dock 286
Hammersley Inlet 100
Handfield Bay 334
Hankin Cove 385
Hansen Bay 377
Hanson Island 361
Hanus Bay 505
Harbor Island Marina 117
Harbor Marine Fuel 174
Harbour Authority of Salt Spring Island 239
Harbour Green 280
Harbour Marina 133
Harbour Quay 405

Harbourside Lodge 408
Harbour Village Marina 124
Hardy Bay 374
Hardy Island Marine Park 296
Harmony Islands Marine Park 297
Haro Strait 181
Harper State Park 112
Harris Harbor 494
Harstine Island 100
Harstine Island State Park 102
Hartley Bay 452
Harwood Point Regional Park 271
HASSI 239
Háthayim Provincial Marine Park 316
Havannah Channel 343
Hawk Bay 453
Hayden Passage 395
Hayle Bay 350
Health Bay 358
Heater Harbour 466
Heather Civic Marina 280
Heelboom Bay 398
Helen Bay 354
Helmcken Island 337
Hemasila Inlet 421
Hemming Bay 334
Henderson Inlet 105
Henry Island 204
Henry Island Preserve 204
Henrys Arm 491
Herb Beck Marina 138
Herbert Inlet 397
Heriot Bay 320
Heriot Bay Inn & Marina 320
Heriot Bay Public Wharf 320
Heritage Harbor 489
Hernando Island 301
Herring Bay 255
Herron Island 102
Hesquiat Harbour 392
Hevenor Inlet 449
Heynen Channel 397
Hicks Bay 194
Hidden Basin 296
Hiekish Narrows 451
Higgins Passage 446
Hill Island 316
Hilton Harbor Marina 174
Hiram M. Chittenden Locks 118
Hisnit Inlet 391
Hjorth Bay 317
Hobart Bay 492
Hoeya Sound 346
Holberg Inlet 380
Holkham Bay 492
Holmes Harbor 157
Holmes Inlet Nook 395
Home Bay 421
Homfray Channel 309
Honeymoon Bay 157
Hood Canal 135
Hood Canal Floating Bridge 135
Hood Canal Marina 140

Hood Head 135
Hoodsport 140
Hook Bay 405
Hoonah 503
Hoonah Harbor 503
Hootla-Kootla Bay 395
Hope Bay Public Wharf 234
Hope Island 160
Hope Island Marine State Park 99
Hopetown Passage 353
Hornby Island 266
Horsefly Cove 451
Horsehead Bay 104
Horseshoe Bay 284
Horseshoe Bay Public Wharf 285
Horton Bay 234, 236
Hoskyn Channel 316
Hospital Bay 291
Hospital Bay Public Wharf 291
Hotel Bellwether 174
Hotham Sound 297
Hotspring Island 466
Hot Springs Cove 393
Howe Sound 284
Howling Wolf Farm Float 252
Hoya Bay 465
Hoya Passage 465
Hoy Bay 353
Huckleberry Island 164
Hughes Bay 192
Humchitt Island 430
Hunter Bay 190
Hurricane Anchorage 429
Hyack Terminal 223
Hydaburg 511
Hydaburg Harbor Docks 511
Hylebos Waterway 112

I

Iceberg Island 192
Ideal Cove 490
Ikeda Cove 466
Illahee Marine State Park 128
Illahie Inlet 425
Inati Bay 175
Indian Arm 282
Indian Arm Marine Park 283
Indian Cove 194
Indianola 131
Inner Boat Basin 260
Inner Port Madison 131
Intermediate Dock 494
Ire Inlet 449
Irish Bay 234
Irondale 147
Iroquois Passage 229
Irvines Landing 291
Isabella Island 237
Island Cove 398
Islands Marine Center 191
Island West Resort 403
Isle-de-Lis at Rum Island 225

J

Jack's Boatyard 302
Jackson Cove 138
Jackson Passage 441
James Bay 240, 441
James Island Marine State Park 189
Jamieson Point Anchorage 446
Jane Bay/Franks Bay 404
Jane Cove 433
Jarrell Cove 100
Jarrell Cove Marine State Park 101
Jarrell's Cove Marina 101
Jedediah Island 271
Jennis Bay 355
Jennis Bay Floats 355
Jenny Inlet 437
Jerisich Dock 108
Jervis Inlet 297
Jetty Island 155
Jock's Dock 410
Joe Cove 357
Joemma Beach State Park 102
Joe's Bay 425
John Henry's Resort & Marina 291
John Passage 229
Johnson Street Marina 223
Johns Pass 217
Johnston Bay 423
Johnstone Strait 337
John Wayne Marina 183
Jones Island Marine State Park 205
Joseph Whidbey State Park 153
Juanita Bay 124
Judd Bay 208
Julian Cove 378
Juneau 493

K

Kake 489
Kakushdish Harbour 434
Kamils Anchorage 383
Kanaka Wharf 239
Kanish Bay 326
Kasaan 484
Kayak Point County Park 156
Kelp Passage 455
Kelsey Bay 337
Kenary Cove 255
Kenmore 124
Kennedy Cove 398
Kenneth Passage 354
Kent Inlet 447
Ketchikan 478
Ketchikan Airport Small-Craft Float 481
Ketchikan Moorage 481
Ketchikan Yacht Club 481
Ketron Island 105
Keyport 129
KHFN Echo Bay 349
Khutze Inlet 451
Kiixin Tour 408
Kiket Island 160

Kildidt Narrows 428
Kildidt Sound 428
Kilisut Harbor 148
Kiln Bay 448
Kiltik Cove 430
Kimball Preserve 189
Kindergarten Bay 486
Kingcome Inlet 351
Kingfisher Marina 408
Kingston 145
Kinnaird Island 353
Kirkland 124
Kisameet Bay 430
Kitasu Bay 446
Kitimat 452
Kitkatla 450
Kitsap Memorial Marine State Park 135
Klahoose Wilderness Resort 310
Klaoitsis Island 345
Klaskino Inlet 380
Klaskish Inlet 380
Klekane Hot Springs 451
Klemtu 445
Klewnuggit Inlet 454
Kliktsoatli Harbour 434
Kliuchevoi Bay 505
Knight Inlet 345
Knox Bay 337
Knudson Cove 484
Koeye River 430
Kohl Island Anchorage 447
Kooryet Bay 449
Kopachuck Marine State Park 104
Koprino Harbour 378
Koskimo Bay 378
Koskimo Islands 378
Kukutali Preserve 160
Kumealon Island 454
Kumlah Island Anchorage 347
Kupreanof Dock 490
K'uuna Llnagaay 465
Kwakshua Channel 426
Kwakume Inlet 430
Kwatna Inlet 435
Kwatsi Bay 347
Kwatsi Bay Floats 347
Kxngeal Inlet 454
Kynoch Inlet 443
Kynumpt Harbour 440
Kyuquot Sound 382

L

Labouchere Channel 437
La Conner 161
La Conner Landing Fuel Dock 164
La Conner Marina 161
Lacy Falls 347
Ladner 275
Ladner Yacht Club 275
Lady Boot Cove 357
Lady Douglas Island 441
Ladysmith Community Marina 250
Ladysmith Fisherman's Wharf 249

Ladysmith Harbour 248
Ladysmith Marina 249
Lagoon Cove 344
Lagoon Cove Marina 344
Lakebay Marina & Resort 104
Lake Union 121
Lake Union Piers 122
Lake Washington 124
Lakewood Moorage 125
Lama Passage 432
Lancelot Inlet 307
Langara Island 462
Langley Boat Harbor 156
Langus Waterfront Park 156
Laredo Channel 446
Laredo Inlet 446
Larrabee State Park 172
Larsen Harbour 450
Lasqueti Island 270
Laura Bay 350
Laura Cove 309, 350
Lawson Harbour 455
Le Conte Bay Glacier 491
Leesoffskaia Bay 505
Lemmens Inlet 397
Lemmens Northwest Cove 397
Leone Island 359
Letnikof Cove 499
Lewis Channel 311
Liberty Bay 130
Lieber Haven Resort 210
Lighthouse Bay 254
Lighthouse Marine County Park 178
Lighthouse Pub & Marina 295
Lime Kiln Point 204
Lime Point Cove 450
Lincoln Channel 471
Lions Bay Marine Ltd. 286
Little Bull Passage 271
Little Nimmo Bay 354
Little River 270
Lizzie Cove 432
Logboom Park 124
Lohbrunner Island 446
Lonesome Cove Resort 199
Longbranch Improvement Club Marina 103
Long Harbour 239
Long Point Cove 431
Lopez Island 189
Lopez Islander Resort & Marina 192
Lopez Pass 189
Lopez Sound 189
Loring Public Dock 483
Louise Narrows 464
Louscoone Inlet 466
Lowe Inlet 454
Lower Rapids 319
Lucky Creek 403
Lummi Island 175
Lummi Island Recreation Site 175
Lund 301
Lund Automotive & Outboard Ltd. 302
Lund Resort 302
Lund Small Craft Harbour 302

Lund Water Taxi 302
Lyall Harbour 234
Lyall Harbour Public Wharf 234
Lynn Canal 498
Lynnwood Marina 282

M

Macaulay Park 221
Mackaye Harbor 192
Mackenzie Sound 354
Madeira Marina 293
Madeira Park Public Wharf 293
Madiera Park 292
Mahatta Creek 378
Makah Marina 185
Malaspina Inlet 307
Malaspina Strait 299
Malcolm Island Lions Harbour 366
Malibu Rapids 298
Manchester State Park 126
Mannion Bay 285
Mansons Landing 314
Mansons Landing Marine Park 314
Mansons Landing Public Dock 314
Mantrap Inlet 425
Manzanita Bay 129, 483
Maple Bay 245
Maple Bay Marina 246
Maple Bay Public Wharf 246
Maquinna Marine Provincial Park 393
Marble Cove 407
Margaret Bay 421
Marguerite Bay 483
Marina Mart 122
Marina Park 124
Marine Mammal Disentanglement 512
Mariners Rest 284
Marine Weather 24
Maritime Pier 109
Marktosis 396
Marvin Islands 446
Mary Cove 450
Mason's Olson Resort 185
Massacre Bay 207
Masset 462
Masset Sound 463
Mathieson Narrows 443
Matia Island Marine State Park 211
Matilda Inlet 396
Matilpi 343
Matlset Narrows 397
Mats Mats Bay 147
Mattson's Bay Marine 131
Maury Island Marine Park 113
Mayne Passage 334
Mayo Cove 104
McArdle Bay 192
McBride Bay 420
McIntosh Bay 350
McKay Bay Lodge 408
McLane Cove 101
McMicken Island Marine State Park 102
McMicking Inlet 448

McNeil Island 103
McRae Cove 297
Meay Inlet 427
Melanie Cove 309
Menzies Bay 326
Mermaid Bay 333
Mesachie Nose 437
Metcalf Island 319
Method Marine Supply 400
Metlakatla 478
Metlakatla Bay 470
Metlakatla Harbor 478
Meydenbauer Bay 125
Meyers Chuck 486
Meyers Passage 446
Meyers Passage Anchorage 446
Middle Arm Fraser River 276
Middle Harbor, Petersburg 490
Mike Pusich Douglas Harbor 494
Milbanke Sound 440
Miles Inlet 418
Mill Bay 243
Mill Bay Community Wharf 243
Mill Bay Marina 243
Millbrook Cove 421
Miller Bay 131
Milltown Marina 277
Miners Bay 235
Mink Island 308
Minstrel Island Harbour 343
Mistaken Island 265
Misty Fjords National Monument 482
Mitchell Bay 204, 366
Mitlenatch Island 301
MK Bay Marina 452
Moffatt Islands 471
MOHAI Docks 122
Monckton Inlet 449
Monday Anchorage 357
Monks' Wall 361
Montague Harbour 240
Montague Harbour Marina 241
Montague Harbour Marine Park 240
Montague Harbour Public Wharf 241
Montlake Cut 122
Morehouse Bay 439
Moresby Camp 464
Morrison's North Star Marine 121
Mosquito Creek Marina 281
Mosquito Harbour 398
Mosquito Pass 203
Mound Island 359
Mount Gardner Park Public Dock 286
Moutcha Bay Resort 391
Mowgli Island 254
Mud Bay 190
Muirhead Islands 355
Mukilteo 153
Murden Cove 132
Murray Labyrinth 418
Musgrave Landing 245
Mussel Inlet 443
Mystery Bay Marine State Park 148

N

Naha Public Dock 483
Nahwitti Bar 375
Nahwitti Bar Inner Route 375
Nakwakto Rapids 418
Namu 430
Nanaimo 258
Nanaimo Port Authority 260
Nanoose Harbour 265
Nan Sdins Village Site 466
Narrows Inlet 296
Narrows Marina 106
Narvaez Bay 235
Nascall Bay 438
Nash Narrows Cove 440
Nash Passage 440
Native Anchorage 360
Nautical Landing Marina 121
Naval Base Kitsap (Bangor) 137
Neah Bay 185
Neekas Cove 440
Nepah Lagoon 354
Neroutsos Inlet 378
Nettle Island 406
Newcastle Island Marine Park 261
Newcombe Harbour 449
New Eddystone Rock 483
Newport Shores 125
Newton Cove Resort 386
New Vancouver 359
Nimmo Bay Wilderness Resort 354
Nisqually Reach 105
Nitinat Narrows 409
Nodales Channel 333
No Discharge Zones-B.C. Waters 39
No-Go Zones 230
Nootka Light Station 392
Nootka Mission 388
Nootka Sound 391
North Arm Fraser River 276
North Arm Transportation 462
North Bay Anchorage 196
North Bentinck Arm 436
North Cove 253
Northern Gulf Islands 247
North Galiano 254
North Harbor-Craig 510
North Harbor, Petersburg 490
North Harbour 378
North Island Marina 366
North Lake Marina 124
North Pacific Cannery 455
NorthPoint Landing 98
North Saanich Marina 228
North Sandy Cove 502
North Sawyer 492
North Shore Dock 141
Northumberland Channel 258
Northwest Bay 265
Northwest Fuels Ltd. 458
Northwest McConnell Rock 205
Nowish Cove 445
Nuchatlitz Inlet 386
Nuchatlitz Provincial Park 386
Nuttal Bay 265
Nuyumbalees Cultural Centre 321

O

Oak Bay 147, 224
Oak Bay County Park 147
Oak Bay Marina 224
Oak Harbor 158
Oak Harbor Marina 158
Oakland Bay Marina 100
Oatwish Bay 443
O'Brien Bay 350
Obstruction Pass 193
Obstruction Pass State Park 210
Ocean Falls 431
Ocean Falls Lodge 432
Ocean Falls Small Craft Harbour 431
Oceanfront Suites at Cowichan Bay 244
Octopus Islands Marine Park 318
Odlin San Juan Co. Park 190
Okeover Harbour Authority 307
Okisollo Channel 318
Old Bank Inn 432
Old Bella Bella 433
Old Town Dock 109
Olga 210
Olympia 96
Oona River 455
Open Bay 204
Open Bight 421
Orcas Island 206
Orcas Landing 208
Oro Bay 102
Oscar Passage 441
Osment Inlet 446
Ostrich Bay 128
Otter Bay Marina 233
Otter Channel 448
Otter Cove 327
Otter Island 308
Outer Islands 406
Outpost at Winter Harbour 377
Owen Bay 318, 319
Oyster Bay (Northern BC) 425
Oyster Bay (Puget Sound) 128

P

Pacific Boulevard Marina 279
Pacific Gateway Marina 409
Pacific Playgrounds Resort & Marina 270
Pack Creek Bear Viewing 492
Padilla Bay 164
Page Passage 229
Page's Inn on Silva Bay 257
Page's Resort & Marina 257
Painted Boat Resort Spa & Marina 293
Palmer Anchorage 447
Pamphlet Cove 378
Panther Point 254
Parks Bay 194
Parksville 265

Parson's Anchorage 446
Patos Island Marine State Park 214
Patricia Bay 242
Peale Passage 100
Pearse Islands 363
Peavine Pass 193
Pedder Bay 410
Pedder Bay Marina 410
Pelican 502
Pelican Bay Marina 280
Pelican Beach 171
Pender Canal 231
Pender Harbour 291
Pender Harbour Hotel 293
Pender Harbour Resort and Marina 291
Pendrell Sound 310
Penelakut Island 252
Peninsula Yacht Basin 109
Penn Cove 157
Penn Harbour 448
Penrose Bay 307
Penrose Island Marine Park 424
Penrose Point Marine State Park 104
Perceval Narrows 441
Percival Landing 97
Peril Strait 505
Peter Cove 230
Petersburg 490
Petrel Channel 449
Petroglyph Cove 385
Petro Marine Services 481
Petro Marine Sitka 507
Philip Inlet 424
Phillips Arm 334
Phinney Bay 128
Phone Numbers 512
Pickering Passage 100
Picnic Cove 195
Pier 65 (Dungeness Marina) 244
Pier 73 Marina & Yacht Club 276
Pierce Bay 424
Piers Island Public Wharf 230
Pillar Point 184
Pillsbury Cove 458
Pilot Bay 258
Pinkerton Islands 403
Pipestem Inlet 403
Pirates Cove Marine Park 255
Pitt Island 446, 448
Pitt Passage 103
Pleasant Harbor 138
Pleasant Harbor Marina 138
Pleasant Harbor Marine State Park 138
Plumper Bay 326
Plumper Cove Marine Park 286
Plumper Sound Area 230
Poets Cove Marina 230
Poett Nook 406
Poett Nook Marina & Campground 407
Point Atkinson 284
Point Baker 509
Point Defiance 109
Point Defiance Marina 109
Point Doughty 215

Point Grey 277
Point Hudson Marina 151
Point No Point 146
Point Roberts 178
Point Roberts Marina Resort 178
Point Robinson 113
Point Wilson 152
Point Wilson Tide-Rip 181
Poise Cove Marina 295
Poison Cove 443
Pole Pass 206
Polkinghorne Islands 356
Porlier Pass 254
Porpoise Bay Government Wharf 296
Porpoise Harbour 455
Portage Bay 122, 491
Port Alberni 404
Port Alberni Marine Fuels & Services 406
Port Alberni Yacht Club 407
Port Alexander 375
Port Alice 378
Port Alice Yacht Club 378
Port Angeles Boat Haven 184
Port Angeles City Pier 184
Port Blackney 441
Port Browning 232
Port Browning Marina 232
Port Clements 463
Port Clements Small Craft Harbour 463
Porteau Cove 286
Port Elizabeth 346
Port Gamble 135
Port Graves 286
Port Hadlock 147
Port Hadlock Marina 147
Port Hardy 369
Port Harvey 343
Port Harvey Marine Resort 343
Portland Inlet 471
Portland Island 230
Port Ludlow 146
Port Ludlow Resort and Marina 146
Port Madison 130
Port McNeill 366
Port McNeill Federal Docks 368
Port McNeill Harbour 368
Port Moody 282
Port Moody DAA Anchorage 282
Port Neville 338
Port of Allyn 101
Port of Allyn North Shore Dock 141
Port of Anacortes 167
Port of Bellingham 174, 176
Port of Brownsville 128
Port of Edmonds 153
Port of Everett Marina 154
Port of Friday Harbor 198
Port of Friday Harbor Fuel Pier 199
Port of Hoodsport 140
Port of Keyport Marina 129
Port of Kingston 145
Port of Manchester 126
Port of Port Townsend Boat Haven 149
Port of South Whidbey 156

Port Orchard 126
Port Orchard Marina 126
Port Plaza Dock 98
Port Protection 509
Port Renfrew Community Dock 409
Port San Juan 409
Portside Marina 242
Port Sidney Marina 226
Port Simpson 471
Port Susan 156
Port Thorne Bay Fuel 485
Port Townsend 148
Port Townsend Boat Haven 149
Port Townsend Canal 147
Port Washington Public Wharf 233
Posey Island Marine State Park 203
Possession Sound 153
Potlatch Marine State Park 140
Potts Lagoon 345
Poulsbo 130
Poulsbo Marina / Port of Poulsbo 130
Powell River 300
Preedy Harbour 252
Prevost Harbor 216
Prevost Island 240
Prideaux Haven 309
Prince Rupert 456
Prince Rupert Rowing and Yacht Club 457
Princesa Channel 390
Princess Cove 254
Princess Louisa Inlet 298
Princess Louisa Society 299
Princess Royal Island 446
Pritchard Park 132
Pruth Bay 426
Punchbowl Cove 483
Pybus Bay 491
Pybus Point Lodge 491
Pylades Island 255

Q

Qlawdzeet Anchorage 455
Quadra Island 319
Quait Bay 397
Quarry Bay 296
Quartcha Bay 439
Quarterdeck Inn & Marina Resort 370
Quartermaster Harbor 112
Quartermaster Marina 112
Quartz Bay 316
Quathiaski Cove 321
Quathiaski Cove Public Wharf 321
Quatsino First Nations Dock 379
Quatsino Narrows 379
Quatsino Sound 377
Quatsino Village 380
Quayside Marina 279
Queen Charlotte (Daajing Giids) 463
Queen Charlotte Harbour Authority 463
Queen Charlotte Strait 362
Queen Cove. 386
Quigley Creek Cove 447
Quilcene Bay 137

R

Racoon Island 283
Rae Basin 392
Rafting Protocol 43
Rainier Beach 125
Rainy Bay Cove 404
Ramsay Hot Springs 393
Ramsay Passage Cove 466
Raven Point Marina 251
Raymond Passage 440
Raymur Point Customs Dock 223
Reach Island 101
Read Island 316
Reads Bay 189
Rebecca Spit Marine Park 319
Red Bluff Bay 509
Redonda Bay 317
Redondo 113
Reed Point Marina 282
Reef Harbour 235
Refuge Cove 312
Refuge Cove General Store 312
Refuge Cove (Haida Gwaii) 462
Refuge Cove Marina 481
Refuge Island 403
Reid Bay 351
Reid Harbor 217
Reid Passage 441
Reliance Guest Float 489
Rendezvous Islands 317
Rescue Bay 441
Resolution Cove 392
Retreat Cove 254
Retreat Passage 357
Richards Channel 413
Richmond Bay 355
Richmond Chevron 276
Rich Passage 126
Right Smart Cove 138
Riley Cove 395
Ripley Bay 439
Rivers Inlet 421
ROAM App 18
Robbers Passage 407
Roberts Bay 225
Robson Bight 338
Roche Harbor 201
Roche Harbor Marina 202
Rock Bay Marine Park 327
Rock Inlet 430
Rocky Bay 102, 199
Rocky Pass 489
Rocky Point 159
Roesland/Roe Lake 233
Roffey Island 309
Rolfe Cove 211
Rolling Roadstead 386
Rosario Resort & Spa 209
Rosario Strait 170
Roscoe Bay/Roscoe Bay Marine Park 310
Roscoe Inlet 439
Rosedale 104
Rose Harbour 466

Rose Inlet 466
Royal Reach Marina & Hotel 296
Ruckle Park 237
Rudyerd Bay 483
Rugged Point Marine Park 385
Rumble Beach Marina 378
Rupert Inlet 379
Rushbrook Small Craft Harbour 458
Russell Island 236
Ruston 109
Ruxton Island 255

S

Saanich Inlet 242
Saanichton Bay 225
Sac Bay 466
Saddlebag Island Marine State Park 164
Safety Cove 426
Saint Edward State Park 124
Salmon Bay 120, 441
Salmon Bay Marina/Port of Seattle 120
Salmon Bay Marine Center 120
Salmon Inlet 296
Salmon Point Resort 270
Salsbury Point County Park 135
Saltery Bay 297
Saltery Bay Harbour 297
Saltery Bay Provincial Park 297
Salt Spring Marina 239
Saltwater State Park 113
Samsing Cove 505
Sand Heads 274
Sand Point 124
Sandspit 464
Sandspit Harbour 464
Sandspit Harbour Fuel Dock 464
Sandwell Park 258
Sandy Island Marine Provincial Park 268
Sandy Point 175
San Josef Bay 377
San Juan County Park 204
San Juan Island 195
San Juan Islands 187
San Juan Islands (Alaska) 491
San Mateo Bay 405
Sansum Narrows 245
Santa Gertrudis Cove 392
Sarah Point 307
Saratoga Passage 156
Sargeaunt Passage 346
Satellite Island 216
Savary Island 301
Scenic Beach State Park 137
Schooner Channel 418
Schooner Cove 265
Schooner Reef 265
Scott Cove 348
Seabeck Bay 137
Seabreeze Cove 357
Seadrome Dock 494
Seaforth Channel 438
Seagate T-Floats 370
Sea Otter Cove 377

Sea Otter Inlet 430
Seascape Waterfront Resort 322
Seattle 114
Sechelt Inlet 294, 295
Sechelt Rapids 295
Second Narrow 282
Secretary Islands 254
Secret Cove 290
Secret Cove Marina 290
Secret Cove Public Wharf 290
Secret Harbor 171
Selby Cove 240
Selma Park 288
Semiahmoo Marina 177
Sequim Bay 182
Sequim Bay Marine State Park 183
Serpent Group 428
Sewell's Marina Ltd. 285
Seymour Canal 492
Seymour Narrows 325
SGang Gwaay 466
Shack Bay 439
Shallow Ba 212
Shark Creek Falls 396
Sharpe Cove 161
Sharpe's Landing 303
Shaw General Store 194
Shaw Island 194
Shawl Bay Marina 351
Shawl Bay & Moore Bay 351
Shearwater Hot Springs 452
Shearwater Resort & Marina 434
Shelter Bay Marina 161
Shelter Island Marina Inc. 276
Shelter Sheds 381
Shelton 100
Shilshole Bay Fuel Dock 119
Shilshole Bay Marina 119
Shine Tidelands State Park 135
Shingle Bay 232
Ship Canal Bridge 119
Ship Point Marina 223
Shoal Bay 190, 334
Shoal Bay Cottages 334
Shoal Channel 287
Shoal Harbour 349
Shoalwater Pass 483
Shoemaker Bay Harbor 488
Shushartie Bay 375
Sidney 225
Sidney Bay 336
Sidney Beacon Ave 226
Sidney Spit 225
Silva Bay 256
Silverdale Marina 128
Similk Bay 160
Simoom Sound 350
Sinclair Island 172
Sir Alexander Mackenzie Rock 437
Sir Edmund Bay 350
Sitka 506
Sitka Sound 505
Skagit Bay 159
Skagit Island 160

Skagway 499
Skagway Small Boat Harbor 499
Skedans Bay 465
Skidegate 463
Skidegate Channel 463
Skidegate Ferry 464
Skookum Inlet 99
Skull Cove 418
Skull Island 207
Skyline Marina 170, 276
Slingsby Channel 413, 418
Small Inlet Marine Park 327
Smelt Bay Provincial Park 314
Smith Cove 378
Smith Sound 420
Smuggler Cove 288
Smuggler's Villa Resort 215
Snohomish River Delta 155
Snoring Bay 213
Snug Basin 405
Snug Cove 285
Snug Cove Public Wharf 285
Snug Harbor Resort 204
Sointula 365
Solander Island 380
Sooke Harbour 409
Sooke Harbour Authority 410
Sooke Harbour Resort & Marina 410
South Arm Fraser River 274
South Bentinck Arm 436
Southeast Alaska 473
Southeast Cove 403
Southey Bay 254
Southgate Group 417
South Harbor-Craig 510
South Harbor, Petersburg 490
South Park Marina 117
South Puget Sound 95
South Sandy Cove 502
South Sawyer 492
South Whidbey State Park 152
Souvenir Passage 425
Spanish Bank 277
Speed Limit and No Wake Zones 514, 515
Spencer Spit Marine State Park 190
Spicer Islands 450
Spider Anchorage 429
Spider Island area 429
Spiller Channel 439
Spiller Inlet 440
Spitfire Channel 429
Spitfire North Anchorage 429
Squalicum Harbor 174
Squamish 286
Squamish Boat Harbour 287
Squamish Harbor 137
Squamish Yacht Club 287
Squirrel Cove 313
Squirrel Cove Public Dock 313
Squirrel Cove Trading Co. Ltd. 313
Squitty Bay 270
Stag Bay 301
Stan Sayers Memorial Park 125
State and Provincial Parks 39

Statter Harbor 496
Steamer Cove 395
Steep Island Lodge 321
Steilacoom 105
Stephens Passage 492
Stern-tie 41
Steveston 274
Steveston Chevron 275
Steveston Harbour Authority Wharf 274
Still Harbor 103
St. John Harbour 440
Stones Marina 260
Stopper Islands 403
Strait of Georgia 263
Strait of Juan de Fuca 181, 372
Strathcona 283
Strawberry Island - Cypress Island 171
Strawberry Island - Deception Pass 160
Stretch Island 101
Stretch Point Marine State Park 101
St. Roch Dock 281
Stuart Channel 247
Stuart Island Community Dock 330
Stuart Island (Johnstone Strait) 330
Stuart Island Marine State Park 216
Stuart Narrows 354
Sturdies Bay 236
Sturt Bay 271
St. Vincent Bay 297
Subtle Islands 316
Sucia Island Marine State Park 212
Sullivan Bay Marina Resort 352
Sulphur Passage 395
Summertide Resort & Marina 140
Sunday Harbour 357
Sunderland Channel 336
Sunny Shores Resort & Marina 410
Sunrise Motel & Resort 140
Sunset Marina Ltd. 285
Sunshine Bay 424
Sunshine Coast Resort & Marina 292
Suquamish 131
Surf Inlet 448
Surge Narrows 318
Surge Narrows Settlement 317
Surprise Island 385
Sutil Point 314
Sutlej Channel 352
Swanson Bay 451
Swanson Harbor 499
Swantown Marina 98
Swartz Bay Public Wharf 230
Swifts Bay 190
Swindle Island 446
Swinomish Channel 162
Sydney Inlet 395
Sydney Inlet Unnamed Cove 395
Sylvan Cove 189

T

Table Island 420
Tacoma 109
Tacoma Fuel Dock 112

Tacoma Narrows 106
Tahsis 390
Tahsis Narrows 390
Taku Harbor 493
Taku Resort & Marina 320
Talbot Cove 312
Tallheo Hot Springs 436
Tangent Island 449
Tanu Island 465
Tatchu Point 385
Taylor Bay 102, 421, 502
Teakerne Arm 312
Telegraph Cove 362
Telegraph Cove Marina 362
Telegraph Cove Resort 362
Telegraph Harbour 252
Telegraph Harbour Marina 252
Telescope Passage 296
Tenakee Springs 505
Tenedos Bay 308
Tent Island 251
Texada Boat Club 271
Texada Island 271
Thatcher Pass 189
Thea Foss Waterway 110
The Blow Hole 344
The Creek Marina 281
The Cut 253
The Fish 'N' Hole 149
The Gap 287
Theodosia Inlet 307
Thetis Island Resort 252
The Trap 431
Thomas Basin 480
Thomas Bay 491
Thompson Bay 440
Thompson Sound 347
Thornbrough Bay 286
Thorne Bay 484
Thorne Bay Marina 485
Thrashers Cove 409
Thunder Bay 297
Thunderbird Marina 284
Thurston Bay Marine Park 333
Thurston Harbour 465
Tides and Currents 36
Tides Tavern 106
Titlow Park 106
Toba Inlet 311
Toba Wilderness Marina 311
Tod Inlet 243
Tofino 398
Tofino 4th Street Public Dock 399
Tofino Harbour Authority Crab Dock 400
Tofino Resort & Marina 400
Tolmie Marine State Park 105
Tom Bay 441
Topaze Harbour 336
Toquaht Bay Marina 403
Totten Inlet 99
Town of La Conner Public Floats 164
Tracey Harbour 355
Tracy Arm 492

Tracy Arm Cove 492
Trail Bay 288
Traitors Cove 483
Tramp Harbor 113
Tranquilito Cove 398
Trevenen Bay 307
Tribune Bay 266
Tribune Channel 346
Triton Cove State Park 138
Triton Head 138
Troup Narrows 439
Troup Passage 438
Tsakonu Cove 345
Tsapee Narrows 398
Tsehum Harbour 226
Tsehum Harbour Public Wharf 228
Tsowwin Narrows 390
Tugboat Passage 333
Tulalip Bay 153
Tumbo Island 235
Tuno Creek Anchorage 441
Turnbull Cove 354
Turn Island 337
Turn Island State Park 196
Turret Island 406
Turtle Bay 406
Twanoh Marine State Park 141
Twin Islands 314
Twin Rocks 210
Tyee Landing 405
Tyee Marina 112
Tzartus Cove 407
Tzoonie Narrows Park 296

U

Uchucklesit Inlet 405
Ucluelet 401
Ucluelet Small Craft Harbour 403
Uganda Passage 316
U'mista 363
U'mista Cultural Centre 365
Union Bay 122
Union Passage 454
Union Steamship Co. Marina 285
Upper Barkley Sound 404
Upper Rapids 319
Upright Channel Park 190
U.S. Coast Guard 512
U.S. Customs Clearance Numbers 512
U.S. Customs Information 22
Useless Inlet 404
U.S. Points of Entry 23
U.S. Towing 512

V

Vananda 271
Van Anda 271
Vancouver Harbour (North) 281
Vancouver Harbour (South) 280
Vancouver Marina 276
Van Isle Marina 228
Van Riper's Resort 185

Varney Bay 379
Vaughn Bay 102
Vendovi Island 172
Venn Passage 470
Verney Falls 454
Verney Passage 452
Vernon Bay 404
Vessel Traffic Service 64, 65
Vesuvius 246
VHF Channels 35, 65
VHF Radio Channels 513
Victim Island 207
Victoria 221
Victoria Area 221
Victoria Harbour Authority 223
Victoria International Marina 223
Victoria Mandatory Traffic Lanes 223
Victoria Marine Fuels Ltd 223
Village Bay 235
Village Island 359
Viner Sound 348
Volcanic Cove 385
Von Donop Inlet 316
Von Geldern Cove 104
VTS 64

W

Waddington Bay 357
Waddington Channel 310
Waddington Harbour 317
Waggoner Guide 9
Wahkana Bay 347
Wahshihlas Bay 346
Waiatt Bay 318
Wakeman Sound 352
Wakes Cove 256
Waldron Island 215
Walker Cove 483
Walker Group 412
Walker Hook 241
Walker Island Group 411
Wallace Island Marine Park 254
Walsh Cove Marine Park 310
Walters Cove 382
Walters Cove Public Wharf 383
Walters Cove Resort 383
Warm Springs Bay 509
Warren Islands 343
Warrior Cove 430
Washington Park 169
Wasp Islands 204
Waterfall Inlet 425
Waterfront Suites & Marina 260
Watmough Bay 192
Watson Cove 347
Watts Narrows 454
Weinburg Inlet 448
Welcome Harbour 450
Welcome Passage 288
Wellbore Channel 336
Wells Passage 355
W.E. Mills Landing & Marina 260
West Bamfield Public Dock 408

West Bay 286
West Bay Marina 98
West Beach Resort 215
West Coast Wilderness Lodge 294
Westcott Bay 204
Westcott Bay Shellfish Co 204
Westport Marina 228
West Sound 207
West Sound Marina 207
Westview Harbour 300
Westview Marina & Lodge 390
Westview/Powell River 300
West Waterway 116
West Whitepine Cove 397
Whaleboat Island Marine Park 255
Whaler Bay 236
Whaler Bay Public Wharf 236
Whaletown 316
Wharf Street Floats 223
Whirlpool Rapids 336
Whiskey Golf 264
Whiskey Landing 403
Whiskey Slough Public Wharf 293
White Rock 274
Whiterock Passage 317
Wigham Cove 439
Wigwam Inn 283
Wild Side Trail 396
Windy Bay 398, 443, 466
Winslow Wharf Marina 133
Winter Cove 234
Winter Harbour 377
Winter Harbour Authority 378
Wollochet Bay 105
Woods Bay 353
Woods Nose 409
Wootton Bay 307
Work Bay 450
Wouwer Island 406
Wrangell 488, 489
Wrangell Narrows 489
Wright Sound 452

Y

Yaculta 321
Yaculta Public Dock 321
Yarrow Bay Marina 125
Yellow Island 205
Yes Bay 483
Yorke Island 337
Young Bay 395
Yuculta Rapids 330
Yukon Harbor 114

Z

Zeballos 386
Zeballos Fuel Dock Inc. 388
Zeballos Municipal Wharf 388
Zeballos Small Craft Harbour 388
Zittel's Marina Inc. 105

Symbols
#MindTheZone 122

A
Alderbrook Resort 140
Alert Bay Visitor Centre 364
Altra Marine West 121
Anacortes Chamber of Commerce 56
Anthony's Restaurants 12, 98, 106, 108, 109, 113, 116, 120, 124, 128, 153, 154, 167, 174
Aspen Power Catamarans - 156, Inside Front Cover

B
Beach Gardens Resort & Marina 299
Blaine Harbor Marina 176
Blind Channel Resort 335
Boat Haven 150
Boats Afloat Show 69
Bremerton Marina 127
Butchart Gardens 54

C
Campbell River Harbour Authority 326
Cap Sante Marina 166
Comox Marine & Woodworking 268
Cow Bay Marina 457
Cowichan Bay Fishermen's Wharf 244
Cruisers College 61
Cutwater Boats 528

D
Dawsons Landing General Store 423
Deer Harbor Marina 206
Delta Marine Service 229
Dent Island 332
Desolation Sound Yacht Charters 45, 269, 307
Devlin Boat 31, 63
Discovery Harbour Fuels 324
Discovery Harbour Marina 324

E
Echo Bay Marina & Lodge 348
Elliott Bay Marina 115
Everett Yacht Service 155

F
Fisheries Supply 32, 38, 67, 70
Fisherman's Wharf, Campbell River 326
Flagship Maritime 16
Fluid Motion Inside Back Cover, 528
Fusion Apollo 38
Friday Harbor Marina 198
Friday Harbor Seaplanes 75

G - H
Garmin 70
Go2marine 78, 172
Gorge Harbour Resort Marina 315
Guzzle H2O 121
Haines Borough, Alaska 498
Hampton Yachts 1
Hide-A-Davit 37

I
Irwin Yacht Sales 52
Islands Marine Center 191

J - K
Jarrell's Cove Marina 101
Kachemak Gear Shed 78
Kings Marine Center 197

L
La Conner Marina 163
La Conner Maritime Service 37, 163
Ladysmith Community Marina 250
Lagoon Cove Marina 344
LFS Marine Supplies 78, 172
Lopez Islander Resort 192

M
Martin Marine 276
Monkey Fist Marine 121
Montague Harbour Marina 241

N
Nordhavn Yachts Northwest 58
North Harbor Diesel & Yacht Service 168
North Island Marina 367
Northwest Center for Excellence 61
Northwest Maritime Center 148
Northwest Rigging 25, 167
Northwest Seaplanes 75
Northwest Yacht Brokers 69

O
Ocean Falls 431
Ocean Pacific Marine Store & Boatyard 323
Ocens 33
Onboard Wireless 50
Otter Bay Marina 233
Outer Reef Yachts 52

P
Pacific Fiberglass 122
Page's Resort & Marina 257
Page's Inn 257
Peoples Bank 14
Philbrook's Marine & Boatyard 226
Pleasant Harbor Marina Resort 139
Point Hudson Marina and RV Park 150
Point Roberts Marina Resort 178
Port Ludlow Resort & Marina 146
Port McNeill Harbour Authority 368
Port of Anacortes 166
Port of Bellingham- Blaine Harbor 176
Port of Bellingham-Squalicum Hrb. 174
Port of Bremerton-Bremerton Marina 127
Port of Bremerton-Port Orchard 126
Port of Everett 154
Port of Friday Harbor 198
Port of Kingston 145
Port of Olympia-Swantown Marina 98
Port of Port Townsend-Boat Haven 150
Port of Port Townsend-Point Hudson 150
Port of Seattle-Bell Harbor 116
Port of Seattle-Shilshole Marina 119
Port of Skagit-La Conner Marina 163
Port Orchard Marina 126

R
RBAW-#MindTheZone 122
Ranger Tugs Inside Back Cover
Refuge Cove 312
Roche Harbor Marine Services 201
Roche Harbor Resort & Marina 202

S
Sea Grant 46
Sea Sport Marine & Clothing 456
Seattle Yachts Sales & Service 48
Secret Cove Marina 290
Shaw General Store 194
Shearwater Marina 435
Shearwater University 47
Skyline Marine Center 170
Spencers Marine Supply & Consignment 226
Squalicum Harbor 174
Steveston Marine & Hardware 274
Sullivan Bay Marina Resort 352
Swantown Marina & Boatworks 98

T
Thetis Island Resort 253
Toba Wilderness Marina 311

U
Union Steamship Back Cover
Union Steamship Marina & Resort 285

V
Van Isle Marina 228
Vesper Cortex 32
Vetus Maxwell 67
Victron Energy 121

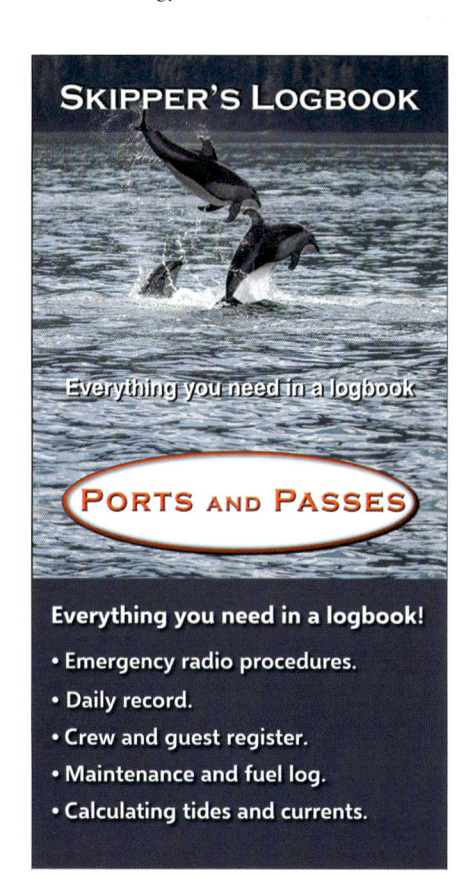

DO IT ALL

CutwaterBoats.com

CUTWATER

FISH, CRUISE, EXPLORE & MORE